Physiological Psychology
A Neuroscience Approach

Physiological Psychology
A Neuroscience Approach

Timothy K. Smock

University of Colorado, Boulder

PRENTICE HALL, Upper Saddle River, New Jersey 07458

Library of Congress Cataloging-in-Publication Data

Smock, Timothy K.
    Physiological psychology: a neuroscience approach /
Timothy K. Smock
        p.   cm.
    Includes bibliographical references and index.
    ISBN 0-13-673112-0
    1. Psychophysiology.   2. Neurosciences.   I. Title.
QP360.S58   1999   98-26733
612.8–dc21   CIP

Editorial Director: Charlyce Jones Owen
Editor in Chief: Nancy Roberts
Executive Editor: Bill Webber
Acquisitions Editor: Jennifer Gilliland
Assistant Editor: Anita Castro
AVP and Director of Manufacturing and Production: Barbara Kittle
Senior Managing Editor: Bonnie Biller
Assistant Managing Editor/Project Manager: Mary Rottino
Director of Development: Susanna Lesan
Development Editor: Karen Trost
Director of Marketing: Gina Sluss
Senior Marketing Manager: Michael Alread
Manufacturing Manager: Nick Sklitsis
Prepress and Manufacturing Buyer: Tricia Kenny
Creative Design Director: Leslie Osher

Interior and Cover Designer: Tom Nery
Illustrations: Medical Scientific Illustrators (William Ober, M.D. and Claire Garrison, R.N.), Academy Art Studio, Karen Noferi, Scott Garrison
Line Art Coordinators: Guy Ruggiero & Meg Van Arsdale
Formatting Manager: John Jordan
Formatter: R. Ross
Editorial Assistant: Kate Ramunda
Director, Image Research Center: Lori Morris-Nantz
Photo Research Supervisor: Melinda Reo
Image Permission Supervisor: Kay Dellosa
Photo Research: Stuart Kenter Associates
Copyeditor: Lynn Buckingham

Acknowledgments for copyrighted material may be found beginning on p. 489 which constitutes an extension of this copyright page.

This book was set in 10/12.5 Clearface Regular by Prentice Hall Production Services and was printed and bound by RR Donnelley & Sons Company-Roanoke. The cover was printed by The Lehigh Press, Inc.

Printed in the United States of America
10 9 8 7 6 5 4 3

ISBN   0-13-673112-0

Prentice-Hall International (UK) Limited, *London*
Prentice-Hall of Australia Pty. Limited, *Sydney*
Prentice-Hall Canada Inc., *Toronto*
Prentice-Hall Hispanoamericana, S.A., *Mexico*
Prentice-Hall of India Private Limited, *New Delhi*
Prentice-Hall of Japan, Inc., *Tokyo*
Pearson Education Asia Pte. Ltd., *Singapore*
Editora Prentice-Hall do Brasil, Ltda., *Rio de Janiero*

For Sam and Jesse

BRIEF CONTENTS

Contents

CHAPTER 4

*COMMUNICATION AMONG
NEURONS: THE ACTION
POTENTIAL   64*

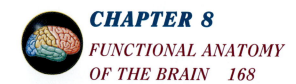

CHAPTER 9

SENSORY SYSTEMS 192

CHAPTER 10

MOTOR SYSTEMS 229

CHAPTER 15
DEVELOPMENT AND LEARNING   355

CHAPTER 18

*THE BIOLOGY OF MENTAL
ILLNESS   436*

APPENDIX

*FURTHER TOPICS
IN BIOLOGY
AND CHEMISTRY   455*

PREFACE

The field of psychology is changing rapidly. Every aspect of the discipline has been influenced by advances in other disciplines, such as biology, and the boundaries between psychology and these other disciplines have become obscured as a consequence. Particularly in neuroscience dramatic new developments are changing current thinking in the traditional disciplines of psychology. An appreciation of the impact of neuroscience depends on a certain degree of understanding of the biology, chemistry, anatomy, and physiology of the brain that may not be available to students in psychology departments. As the title implies, **Physiological Psychology: A Neuroscience Approach** is intended to provide such understanding to readers who, while they may or may not be students of neuroscience, require an accessible review of modern developments in this field to flourish in their own psychological specialties.

Two events in particular inspired the writing of this book. First, a series of reports by the Carnegie Commission on Higher Education outline a crisis in the teaching of scientific subjects at the college level. The reports describe how scientific training of variable quality is available to science majors but is often of poor quality or lacking altogether for students not majoring in the sciences. According to the Carnegie Commission, this creates the danger of segregation and isolation of certain disciplines, including the natural sciences themselves, together with the attendant hazards of scientific illiteracy and loss of competitive advantage in a progressively more technical society. Second, an initiative by the Howard Hughes Medical Institute calls attention to the fact that the inaccessibility of science is especially problematic for those students traditionally underrepresented in the scientific fields. In other words, shortcomings in the presentation of scientific material to students not majoring in the sciences selectively hurts those individuals who are in most need of access to scientific education; individuals who have for one reason or another turned away from the scientific approach. The intent of this text is to make modern neuroscience available and accessible to students who otherwise might not be tempted to investigate the field.

In my fifteen years of teaching this subject at the college level, I have discovered that the best method for introducing scientific concepts is to use the humanities to attract attention to the scientific issues at hand, many of which are themselves the product of humanistic concerns. Thus, I have drawn heavily on material from the arts, literature, and philosophy to focus attention on scientific issues that might otherwise tempt the student to daydream.

Features

Adding the natural science and humanistic themes (actually, I should say *re-emphasizing* these themes, since they have always been there) required some reorganization of the material typically found in physiological psychology texts. The explanation of behavior, the universal goal of psychology, is approached in a step-wise manner. First, questions are posed to orient the student to the purpose of the investigation—what behavior are we trying to explain? Second, explanations are offered involving the consideration of pertinent neuroanatomy, neurophysiology, and neurochemistry. Clinical examples are presented to illuminate the importance and relevance of the answer(s). Expanded examples in selected topic areas are provided periodically in the form of illustrated boxes. Finally, compelling questions are posed in the text to encourage further study on the part of the student. Further encouragement is provided in the "Thought Questions" at the end of each chapter, which consist of additional critical thinking questions designed to make the student want to go further and learn more. Another pedagogical tool found at the end of the chapter is the section of "Review Questions," a set of objective questions that tests the student's knowledge of the chapter. An Appendix provides a ready avenue for the student or instructor to expand his or her understanding of the more important scientific concepts. At the end of the book, in addition to the standard reference section, I have gathered pertinent resources in a section entitled "Further Readings." Many of these are articles submitted by my colleagues who intended to inspire readers in the selection of research topics.

Perhaps the most powerful pedagogical tool in the book is the art program. The best scientific illustrators have been used to produce the finest and most accessible illustrations available. Together with the invaluable advice of consultants with extensive experience in teaching the material, the art has been carefully coordinated with the text to guide the student step-by-step through the most difficult concepts.

Organization

The text begins with a presentation of philosophical issues in Chapter 1. However, consideration of philosophical issues is not limited to a single chapter; rather, important concepts, such as the mind-body problem, are introduced in Chapter 1 and brought up again and again throughout the text.

Chapters 2-10 cover the scientific basis of neuroscience from the micro (cell) to the macro (system) level in a straightforward, approachable style appropriate for a student with little exposure to science at the college level. Chapter 2 presents the cellular basis of behavior, the nuts and bolts of the anatomy of a neuron, along with brief coverage of genetics and of the chemistry necessary to understand subsequent chapters. Chapters 3-5 deal with communication among neurons in the form of membrane potentials, action potentials, and synaptic potentials. Chapters 6-10 proceed to the system level, with coverage of the autonomic nervous system, the spinal cord, and the brain, with separate chapters on sensory systems (Chapter 9) and motor systems (Chapter 10).

With this biological background, students can better understand the behaviors covered in Chapters 11-16: pleasure and pain (Chapter 11), sex and reproduction (Chapter 12), sleep and dreaming (Chapter 13), eating and drinking (Chapter 14), learning and development (Chapter 15), and language and higher cognitive function (Chapter 16). These chapters, along with Chapters 17 and 18, emphasize current experimentation and research in physiological psychology. Chapter 17, "Psychopharmacology," covers all of the major categories of drugs, including both short-term and long-term physiological and psychological effects. Chapter 18, "The Biology of Mental Illness" discusses what we know about the physiological causes of mental illness, and what remains to be discovered, hopefully by the readers of this text and others, who may be part of the next generation of neuroscientists. These chapters have been written to supplement, rather than supplant, the exposure to these topics the typical undergraduate will have acquired elsewhere in the psychology curriculum. For example, learning theory is not emphasized in Chapter 15; instead, learning is presented in the broader general context of neural plasticity and development to emphasize the contribution of advances in neuroscience to this exciting and rapidly growing field.

Ancillaries

Physiological Psychology: A Neuroscience Approach is accompanied by a superb set of ancillary teaching materials. They include the following:

Instructor Supplements

Instructor's Resource Manual, by Francis X. Brennan of Wilkes University. This thorough manual contains a wealth of useful and practical teaching ideas. Contents for each chapter include features such as a one-page chapter organizer; detailed lecture outlines; additional Lecture and Discussion Topics; suggested Classroom Demonstrations and Student Activities; and a complete listing of Prentice Hall and other video resources.

Teaching Transparencies for Physiological Psychology. A full set of color transparencies add visual impact to the study of physiological psychology. Designed in large format for use in lecture hall settings, many of these high quality images are not found in the text.

Test Item File. This comprehensive manual contains multiple choice, short answer, and essay questions.

Prentice Hall Custom Tests for Windows, Macintosh, and DOS. A computerized version of the Test Item File, Prentice Hall's exclusive testing software supports a full range of editing and graphics options, network test administration capabilities, and greater ease-of-use than ever before. If offers two-track design for constructing tests: "Easytest" for novice users and "Fulltest" for more advanced users. The Custom Testing also offers features such as OnLine Testing and Electronic Gradebook.

"800-Number" Telephone Test Preparation Service. A toll-free test preparation service is also available. Instructors may call an 800-number and select up to 200 questions from the Test Item File available with the text. Prentice Hall will format the test and provide an alternate version (if requested) and answer key(s), then mail it back within 48 hours, ready for duplication.

Student Supplements

Study Guide, by Francis X. Brennan of Wilkes University. The Study Guide is designed with an attractive visual format that incorporates line drawings and illustrations from the textbook. Each chapter includes unique features such as an outline; thought-provoking chapter-opening questions; learning objectives; detailed guided reviews; flash cards to reinforce concepts; and multiple-choice tests with explanations of correct answers.

Web Site

In keeping with recent advances in technology, Prentice Hall has established a web site for psychology. Please visit this site at: http://www.prenhall.com/psychmap

In addition, there is a web site specifically for this book. You may access it at: http://www.prenhall.com/smock

Acknowledgments

The writing of the book itself has benefited immensely from the attention and input of my undergraduate and graduate students, many of whom have since adopted careers in neuroscience or medicine. In particular, the production of portions of the text was aided by the efforts of four students each of whom deserves much gratitude. The author would like to thank Lorien Batt for extensive collaboration on Chapter 13, "Sleep and Dreaming"; Frank Brennan for extensive collaboration on Chapter 17, "Psychopharmacology"; Judy Grisel for extensive collaboration on Chapter 14, "Eating, Drinking, and Homeostasis"; and Gail Perez for extensive collaboration on Chapter 15, "Development and Learning." Each of these chapters is the product of a joint effort and I am most fortunate to have had the assistance of such talented individuals.

Revisions of the text and innumerable details of figures and citations also required the help of capable student assistants. In particular, the author would like to thank Cari Worley and Chris Seitz for extensive collaboration on revisions, figure captions, and bibliography. Christina Adams, Brett Davis, Dina Khaled, Troy Knapp, Amber Pollock, and Cory Rabiner also collaborated extensively in these areas and each deserves my heartfelt thanks. The patience and good humor of Kathi Hoskins and Beth Smith in typing the manuscript is gratefully acknowledged. David Albeck, Herbert Alpern, Daniel Barth, Eva Fifkova, Jon Hammack, John Johnson, Michael Jones, Kurt McDonald, Ken Short, Robert Spencer, and Patrick Stark all assisted with particular subjects outside the author's expertise. Finally, the assistance of innumerable individuals for confirmation of fact and for "field testing" of various parts of the manuscript must be acknowledged. That I fail to mention each by name is not to imply that the work has not been improved by their contributions.

Many a student and instructor will decide that the illustrations are the most valuable feature of this text. For these, I am most grateful to Bill Ober, M.D., and Claire Garrison, R.N., at Medical Scientific Illustrators for the superb line drawings and to Stuart Kenter and Tom McCarthy for the outstanding photo research. These, together with talented individuals at Prentice Hall and elsewhere, made my clumsy and primitive models into first-class scientific figures.

Anyone with experience in publishing knows how little the manuscript that leaves the office of the writer resembles the final product. Large numbers of people go to work on the manuscript after its arrival at the publisher. Prentice Hall is fortunate to have the best editorial staff and consultants in the business of scholarly publishing. I would like to acknowledge in particular the unflagging good efforts of Jennifer Gilliland, Acquisitions Editor, and Bill Webber, Executive Editor, at Prentice Hall. Without their encouragement and guidance the book could not have been written. The revisions benefited greatly by the patience and insight of the Development Editor, Karen Trost, who turned a first effort into a presentable work. The publishing of this work could not have been accomplished without the professionalism and experience of Mary Rottino, Assistant Managing Editor and Project Manager. Finally, the author is grateful to the rest of the Prentice Hall team for their invaluable efforts.

The manuscript has been improved by the contribution of a large number of referees and reviewers, notable among them Gerry Sanders whose experience in textbook writing was of immense aid to the author. Others include: Jeffrey R. Alberts, Indiana University; Daniel S. Barth, University of Colorado at Boulder; Terry D. Blumenthal, Wake Forest University; Francis X. Brennan, Wilkes University; John P. Bruno, Ohio State University; Rebecca A. Chesire, University of Hawaii; Andrea D. Clements, East Tennessee State University; James V. Corvin, Northern Illinois University; Kenneth F. Green, California State University; Carl J. Erickson, Duke University; Douglas L. Grimsley, University of North Carolina, Charlotte; Andrew Harver, University of North Carolina, Charlotte; Shelton Hendricks, University of Nebraska, Omaha; K.W. Jacobs, Loyola University of New Orleans; Cheryl L. Kirstein, University of South Florida; Richard Marracco, University of Oregon; Robert R. Mowrer, Angelo State University; Antonio Nunez, Michigan State University; Matthew Olson, Hamline University; Peter H. Platenius, Queen's University; Michael J. Renner, West Chester University; Neil Rowland, University of Florida; David J. Sanders, Oregon State University; Robert J. Schneider, Metropolitan State College of Denver; Susan Travers, Ohio State University; Charlene Wages, Francis Marion College; and Douglas A. Weldon, Hamilton College.

Timothy K. Smock

ABOUT THE AUTHOR

Tim Smock is associate professor of psychology at the University of Colorado at Boulder. He received his B.A. in history from Reed College in Portland, Oregon, and his Ph.D. in neuroscience from the Department of Physiology, University of California at San Francisco. After a post-doctoral fellowship in pharmacology at the University of London in Great Britain, he began teaching courses in physiological psychology, neuropharmacology, neurochemistry, and behavioral endocrinology. He has received several student-initiated awards for his teaching.

Smock publishes regularly in the field of neuroscience and is author of nearly 70 research reports, reviews, and presentations. Most of his research activity has been directed toward the understanding of reproductive behavior in a variety of animal species.

Outside of the classroom and laboratory, he has an interest in field biology, archaeology, and anthropology, subjects that he pursues with world travel and writing for the popular press. He lives in Boulder with his two sons Jesse, 13, and Sam, 8.

Physiological Psychology
A Neuroscience Approach

The unexamined life is not worth living.

Socrates (469–399 B.C.)
Plato's Apology

Philosophical Issues in Neuroscience

When embarking on a new subject of study it is common to wonder about why the new subject is important and to ask, "Why should I, the reader, use my valuable time to learn this material?" To this question I can answer that, in contrast to most academic subjects with specific or delineated boundaries, neuroscience is literally limitless, pertinent to all other subjects, and central to the most perplexing and profound questions in life. There is, quite literally, a neuroscience of everything.

Socrates makes the point that, because each of us inhabits the earth for a limited period, from all of the alternatives we must choose the most *enjoyable,* most *productive*, and most *elevating* pursuits to make the most of our lives. But how do we go about selecting those activities that give us the greatest enjoyment, make the best use of our productivity, and are the most rewarding or elevating?

Most people claim that they have little trouble in choosing the most enjoyable activities and need little advice on how to proceed. By the time you are old enough to read this book you have already identified certain activities that are more pleasurable than others and, were it not for concerns other than pure entertainment, you might simply spend the rest of your life in pursuit of these enjoyments alone. Nevertheless, such choices are by no means as simple as they seem. If you have not tried the entire range of human experience on an experimental basis, then how do you know that your choices are indeed the most enjoyable? What *is* enjoyment, anyway? As Louis Armstrong responded to a question about the definition of jazz, "If you don't know already, I can't possibly explain it to you"; however, in this book I will try to convince you that the actual nature of enjoyment is quite a bit more complex than you might think. We are fortunate to share this planet with a number of other animals that are capable of having fun; study of these animals shows that pleasure and sorrow are not opposite poles of a continuum, but rather processes and emotions that can be associated simultaneously with a single activity.

While the concept of enjoyment may be a bit fuzzy, productivity seems, at least on the surface, to be more straightforward. By the time you reach college, you have probably set some sort of general personal goals. Presumably, these vary considerably, but they might include graduation, lucrative employment, marriage, procreation, prosperity, and comfortable retirement. But what is necessary to achieve these goals? Why do some people succeed and others fail? Qualities like hard work, perseverance, creativity, intelligence, motivation, and drive undoubtedly play a part (not to mention charm and sex appeal), but how do you know if you have each quality? For example how do you recognize intelligence? What makes one person motivated and another self-indulgent and indolent? For that matter, what makes a single person driven one day and lazy the next? When is the proper time to start a family, the best method to foster development of happy children, the best way to cope with life's disappointments, and the best age for retirement? What is the nature of sexual attraction and emotional attachment, and how can we make these processes best work to our advantage? Here too it seems that if the general concept of productivity seems easy to understand, understanding of its specific aspects is by no means straightforward. Again, study of the behavior of other organisms, as described in this book, gives us much insight into the answers to specific questions. Furthermore, study of human beings from a scientific perspective, described throughout the book, gives us insight into the processes that inspire productivity and, if this insight is properly applied, may help us in better understanding and thereby achieving our own goals and ambitions.

The answer to the question, "What pursuits are the most elevating?" seems to be the most fateful, the most difficult, and the most intricate of all. Most of us have, at least momentarily, wondered what purpose our lives might have beyond the (relatively!) simple issues of enjoyment and productivity. Is there some grand plan for our presence on earth? Does an individual behave better if he or she progresses beyond what has been achieved by others? It seems to most of us that it is a worthwhile goal to set a new record, for example, or to develop a new understanding or knowledge about the world or, by some act of selflessness, to improve the human condition or the condition of other sentient creatures. In endeavors of this kind we are pursuing a purpose that as far as we can tell is uniquely human. While other animals pursue the goals of individual enjoyment and productivity, in a manner very similar to us, our close physiological and genetic relationship with other organisms does not help us explain our desire to progress *as a species*. No dog reads a book about dog-nature, or even thinks about the meaning of dog-life or wonders what it would be like to be a different type of animal. Capacity for self-reflection, as well as the capacity for studying and empathizing with the lives of other species, is ours alone; when we exercise this capacity we are exercising the most human of our faculties. Some theorists believe these faculties are correlated to the enlarged surface of the cerebral cortex, which is disproportionately large for our body size. (Figure 1–1).

The purpose of this book is to act as a guide to those who wish to explore self-reflection to discover the nature of awareness. In it we will evaluate those aspects of our nature that we share with related animals and those structural and functional characteristics that are unique to our species. In the process we will develop a better understanding of and empathy for all species, human and nonhuman. For these reasons, I believe that the study of neuroscience and physiological psychology is intrinsically the most elevating and the most noble of all human endeavors. It will most certainly be a very worthwhile use of your time.

Studying the Brain

A mind reflecting on itself is a singular phenomenon that raises a number of philosophical issues. How can one mind, the subject's, have enough intellectual machinery to comprehend an equally complicated mind, the object? How do concepts of subject and object apply when the subject and the object are the same thing? It seems that ultimate understanding, that is, simultaneous and complete self-awareness, is an unattainable goal (at least one that will elude us in this book!). However, comprehension is not necessary to say that "we understand" something. For example, it is safe to say that the workings of a very elaborate computer are "understood," even though no one person can conceive, let alone be expert in, each of its processes all at once. It is adequate to say that, at *one point* and by *somebody* each element has been understood and that this understanding has been reduced to some archival form (i.e., written down so that we can each refer to it when necessary.) While it is obviously available for computers (they *do* work, at least most of the time!), this level of understanding is not presently available for the human mind. In the pages that follow I will divide study of the mind into separate categories and fill each with as much understanding as is available, like filling glasses with water, to give you, the reader, an impression of how much progress has been made and which areas of mystery remain.

Practical Concerns

A traditional approach to self-awareness predates the scientific study of mind but still may be of great use to us. Intro-

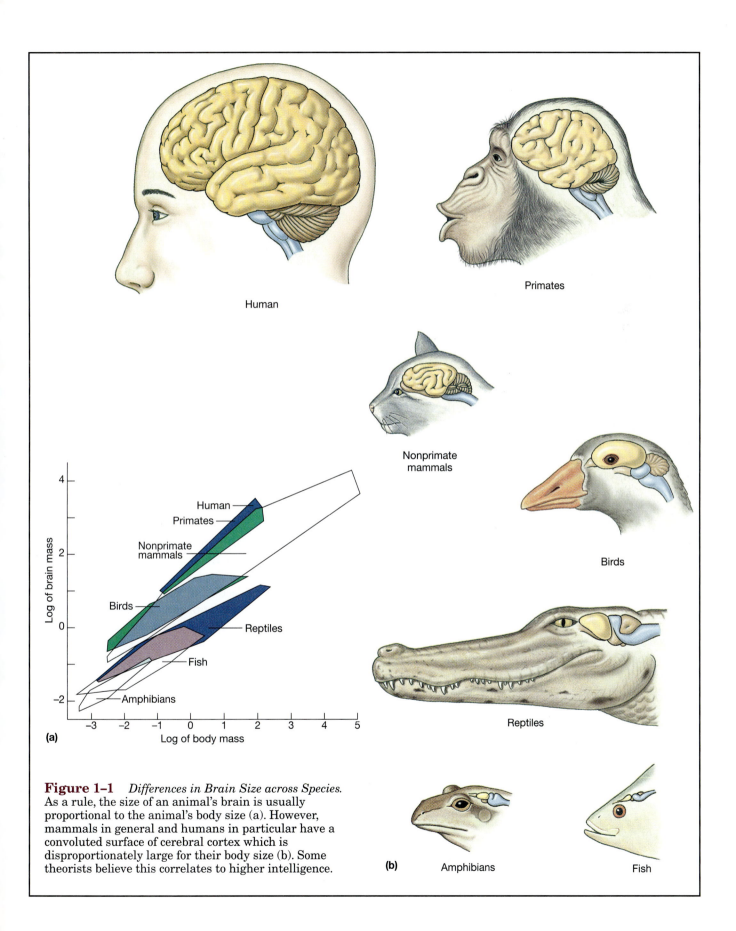

Figure 1–1 *Differences in Brain Size across Species.* As a rule, the size of an animal's brain is usually proportional to the animal's body size (a). However, mammals in general and humans in particular have a convoluted surface of cerebral cortex which is disproportionately large for their body size (b). Some theorists believe this correlates to higher intelligence.

spection, as practiced in philosophy, some religion, and many aspects of psychology, involves the contemplation of internal thought processes and arrival at truths through direct apprehension (thinking about thought). An example of introspection at work is the insight of the Enlightenment philosopher, René Descartes, that certain truths were not open to challenge. His dictum "I think, therefore I am" *(cogito, ergo sum)*, was the product of his effort to establish an element of knowledge (the *a priori*) that did not require any verification from the senses to be certain. Introspection provided, and continues to provide, two types of insight that will be of value to us here. First, Descartes and subsequent practitioners of introspection have discovered that certainty acquired from introspection is very limited. Paradoxically, the identification of some statements that are self-evident and true without question illustrated that most do *not* fall into this category. A second insight from introspection, and one that has gained support in recent years, is **heuristic imagery**. A heuristic image is one that, while not immediately apprehended, suggests the ultimate possibility of sensory confirmation (i.e., can be tested by experiment).

Another form of direct apprehension of truth is **received knowledge**. For example, in some religious doctrines a sacred text is considered true without the necessity of independent verification. In pure mathematics, assumptions in the form of **axioms** are the basis for an internally consistent body of corollaries and subordinate conclusions that are accepted as fact.

Truth derived from introspection or received knowledge is the first step in **deductive reasoning** (a general statement leading to specific findings). The a priori, the text, or the axiom is the general principle; every consequence tested follows the general principle logically and with absolute certainty. The problem with deductive reasoning, as the reader has no doubt already anticipated, is that there is little agreement among thinkers on a priori truths, religions, doctrines, or universal axioms.

The foundations of scientific understanding take a different form. Scientific knowledge is developed from specific observations that lead to general truths. This type of understanding is called **inductive reasoning**. An example of inductive reasoning that will be encountered throughout this book is the **scientific method**. The scientific method arrives at its truths through the use of the following steps:

1.   **Observation:** A scientific observer perceives regularities in nature, leading to curiosity about the underlying principle for the regularity.

2.   **Hypothesis:** A possible underlying principle is described in the form of a statement, or postulate. It is not necessary that the truth of hypothesis be evident or even likely, only that the hypothesis be *falsifiable* by further observations if it isn't true.

3.   **Experiment:** One (rarely) to several (more often) attempts by a scientist to find observations that would disprove the hypothesis.

4.   **Conclusion:** Rejection of the hypothesis if experimental observations contradict it, or provisional acceptance of the hypothesis, in the form of a **theory**, if experiments provide consistent evidence. Acceptance of a theory is always contingent on further experimentation and observation.

As previously stated, inductive truth is always contingent, as is deductive truth; the difference is that the contingency for induction lies in consistency of observation while the contingency for deduction lies in the veracity of the axiom, doctrine, or introspective insight. Either method can lead to conclusions that are intrinsically quite secure or intrinsically insecure.

Although much of what we will cover in this book is the product of the scientific method, and hence is inductive, other forms of understanding also play a role, especially in the form of heuristic imaging explained above.

The Disciplines of Neuroscience

The history of the scientific study of mental processes has been characterized by false starts, ideological battles, and disputes between disciplines. It is important to discuss these events in order to provide historical context, but equally important not to confuse these outdated beliefs with current knowledge of the field. Early investigators held that insights derived from introspection or received doctrine were wholly unreliable and insisted that the science of mind, which could not be examined directly, should solely be conducted in the area of behavior, which could be observed. These **behaviorists** discovered regularities that led to principles governing animal behavior, especially in the field of learning and memory; we will consider these principles at several relevant points in the text. Some behaviorists believed that the connections between the brain and behavior were unsuitable for scientific investigation. However, the majority of scientists, and historically the triumphant faction, believed that behavior could be reduced or broken down into intangible mental processes, physical brain processes, or both, a concept called **reductionism**. Reductionism has taken two historically important forms. The first, **physiological (or biological) psychology** was derived from the academic discipline of psychology. Defined as the study of the biological basis of behavior, physiological psychology started with observed behavior and attempted to break it down into underlying mechanisms. This field gave rise to investigation in a number of subareas (see Table 1–1), most notably *psychophysiology* (the study of the relationship between the autonomic nervous system and behavior, Chapter 6) and *psychophysics* (the study of sensory stimuli and behavior, Chapter 9). The other major school of reductionistic thought, **neurobiology**, arose largely from the academic disciplines of biology and medicine. Neurobiology incorporates several scientific and medical specialties such as *biophysics* (physical chemistry as applied to ion channels and receptors), *neuroanatomy* (anatomy of the brain), *neurochemistry* (chemistry of the brain), *neurophysiology* (function of the brain), and *neuropharmacology* (effect of drugs on the brain).

Physiological psychology can be thought of as a "top-down" approach to mind, in that the strategy takes a large, ultimate phenomenon (behavior) and seeks to identify its smaller components. In this analogy neurobiology is a "bottom-up" approach, starting with smaller brain processes and assembling them to see if an explanation of mind emerges from the conglomerate.

At one point physiological psychology and neurobiology were parallel and independent approaches. In the 1970s an amalgam of the two was created, called *neuroscience*; its practitioners sought to harmonize results and advances of the two reductionistic disciplines. Specialists in computer science, in the clinical practice of *neurology* (brain disease), *neurosurgery* (brain surgery), *neuroradiology* (imaging of the living brain), and *psychiatry* (treatment of mental disease) found a common academic purpose. Finally, the discipline of neuroscience also incorporates the field of *neuropsychology*, the noninvasive study and treatment of brain damage in people.

It should be obvious to the reader that, without a program, it would be hard to distinguish among the players in neuroscience since the names of disciplines do not always directly describe the pertinent activity. Fortunately, the modern tendency is to collapse disciplinary distinctions, though it is my experience that earnest and ambitious students in neuroscience often unwittingly choose courses and even graduate programs based on a misunderstood name for a discipline that is quite different from their actual interests. My own academic background is a quite thorough mixture of neuroscientific

Table 1–1	THE DISCIPLINES OF NEUROSCIENCE
Biophysics	The study of physical chemistry as applied to ion channels and receptors
Neuroanatomy	The study of the anatomy of the brain
Neurochemistry	The study of the chemistry of the brain
Neurology	The study of brain disease
Neuropharmacology	The study of the effects of drugs on the brain
Neurophysiology	The study of the function of the brain
Neuropsychology	The study and treatment of brain damage in people
Neuroradiology	Imaging of the living brain
Neurosurgery	Brain surgery
Psychiatry	The treatment of mental disease
Psychophysics	The study of sensory stimuli and behavior
Psychophysiology	The study of the relationship between the ANS and behavior
Physiological Psychology	The study of the biological basis of behavior

specialties (neurobiology in college, neurophysiology and neurochemistry in graduate school, neuropharmacology in postdoctoral work, and at the time of writing, thirteen years as a professor of psychology).

The plan of this book assumes the hybrid nature of neuroscience. In this chapter and the final two the "top-down" approach is emphasized. Throughout, the reader will find discussion, in boxes, that attempts to relate material at one level of analysis to understanding at other levels. Questions are posed in the text to lead the reader to consider issues from an interdisciplinary perspective. Answers to the questions, when provided, may be idiosyncratic to the author and, when not, may be considered a challenge to the reader to develop interdisciplinary research independently. Reference citations are used customarily in the text, but more resources are gathered by subject in the section entitled "Further Readings" at the end of the book. This section contains the most accessible sources for information on the subjects treated in the text, and these are probably the best places to begin your own inquiries into the particular aspects of neuroscience that interest you.

The Mind/Body Problem

Almost as far back as it is possible to go, using historical, archaeological, and anthropological investigation, it seems that humankind has engaged in a search for the location of the soul, debated whether it was spiritual or physical, and wondered which organ of the body was most imbued with it. It has not always been the case, nor is it everywhere the case now, that the stuff inside the cranium is identified as especially important in personhood, internal experience, or even behavior as a whole. Variously in history other organs of the body, such as the liver, the blood, or the heart, were thought to be the seat of these essential qualities; alternatively these qualities have been thought of not as physical, but as spiritual in nature. The brain, in its raw and coarse aspect, does not inspire a lot of respect. Roughly the consistency of stiff yogurt, it has nothing of the dynamic quality of, say, the heart and hence our language refers often to "heartfelt emotions," taking things "to heart," "heartbreak," and so forth but rarely, at least in original usage, does it incorporate reference to the brain in such manner. Indeed, damage can be sustained to much of the brain (see Box 1–1 and Chapter 16) without jeopardizing life, whereas early observers must have noticed that injury elsewhere, such as to the heart, invariably ended it. The quest for the location of the soul takes many forms, incorporating religion, cosmology, and art as well as science. In philosophy, the issue is called the **mind/body problem**.

Hippocrates and Aristotle

In Western history, the Greek physician Hippocrates (c. 460– c. 377 B.C.) (Figure 1–2) was the first to record an opinion connecting mental events with the brain. Known as the first physician, he observed individuals with brain injury and concluded from his observations that mental function was somehow a property of brain function, that is, that all mental processes are brain processes. Because this would mean that the mind and brain were essentially identical, the followers of this school of thought are called **monists** (mono = one). Almost as soon as his theory was announced, it ran into trouble from his contemporaries. Aristotle (384–322 B.C.) (Figure 1–3), in his treatise *De Anima*, said of the association of the brain with the mind:

> There is, however, a peculiar inconsistency which we may note as marking this and many other psychological theories. They

Figure 1–2 *Hippocrates (c. 460– c. 377 B.C.).* Contributing to monistic thought, Hippocrates believed the mind was a function of the brain's physiological processes.

Figure 1–3 *Aristotle (384–322 B.C.).* Contributing to dualistic thought, Aristotle believed the brain was separate from, although somehow connected to the mind.

> place the soul in the body and attach it to the body without trying in addition to determine the reason why, or the condition of the body under which such attachment is produced.
>
> De Anima *(1.3.22–23)*

Aristotle, the Greek naturalist/philosopher, presumed that there was another entity, entirely nonphysical, that existed in parallel with the brain and worked jointly with the brain to determine behavior. Those, like Aristotle, who believed mind was separate from brain (however they may be connected) are called **dualists** (duo = two).

Descartes

It should be apparent that the issue debated by Hippocrates and Aristotle involved more than the brain and the mind. It really concerns the nature of reality itself, since its resolution depends on belief in a spiritual world. (In fact, the issue is sometimes called the mind/brain problem, but since parts of the body sometimes seem to have "a mind of their own" and since the spirit world, if accepted, may extend far beyond the body, the best overall term for the issue is mind/body problem).

Most Western thinking since Aristotle, and all of Christianity, is overwhelmingly dualistic. A spiritual plane has been assumed to coexist with the material world; the issue is how and to what extent the two planes of reality are associated. The

Box 1–1

Trephining

In a lecture in medical school, I was once shown a film of brain surgery conducted by a tribal physician in a non-Western culture. The patient, who had complained of headaches, was seated in a tent and the scalp was opened without anesthetic. Then, the skull was perforated with a stone awl, the scalp wound closed, and the surgery terminated with attendant ritual. Some days later the patient was interviewed, seeming no worse for the procedure, and was asked if the headaches had returned. He said they had not and claimed to be content with the treatment he had received. The film was shown to the class to illustrate evidence for the instructor's assertion that the three most important words in medicine are "Thank you, doctor." Patients tend to place great faith in their physicians, often will feel better when told that they ought to (see discussion of "placebo analgesia" in Chapter 11), and will often submit gratefully to medical procedures of dubious value.

Brain surgery performed ritualistically and with simple implements is called **trephining**. This phenomenon captures the ambiguity inherent in any mechanistic explanation of behavior. At one level, trephining might be experienced as beneficial by the patient merely because it is more painful than the initial complaint. Relief that the ordeal was over might eclipse all other concerns. On the other hand, perhaps the patient's positive report was merely an attempt to placate the doctor. After all, if he had reported that the procedure was ineffective, perhaps the doctor would try it again, determined to do it right this time. Finally, we should give greater respect to the

straightforward interpretation: that in a certain cultural environment trephining may be a valid and beneficial medical procedure. Though I suspect that not many of you will seek trephining in relief of aches and pains, I wonder about how many current medical procedures will one day be viewed as equally clumsy or unscientific. All science, and medicine, is accomplished in a particular social and cultural context; when removed from that context it acquires a peculiar or ridiculous quality.

The ambiguity attached to the understanding of trephining is a good model for many issues we shall consider in this book. The interface between the brain and behavior is innately one of the most perplexing subjects for research, and the reader should always be alert for the too-facile interpretation, the hidden assumptions, and the cultural bias that may accompany the science we will discuss. When aware of them, I will point them out myself.

French philosopher René Descartes (1596–1650) (Figure 1–4) favored a rather extreme form of dualism in which the two worlds were mostly separate (he thought they communicated through the pineal gland, buried deep within the brain, which he called "the seat of the soul"). An oversimplification of Descartes' belief, in the years after his death, was that there was no communication whatsoever between the spiritual world and the material one. This belief came to be called *Cartesian dualism*, an unfortunate description since Descartes didn't really believe it. A better term for it is **absolute dualism**. There are not very many absolute dualists around, since the posi-

tion is open to logical challenge. (If there is no connection between the spirit world and the material one of speech and writing, how did we come to suspect its existence?) Most dualists (Descartes included) propose instead that there is some avenue between the worlds whereby spirit can influence matter and material events can have spiritual consequence. Such a belief is called **interactionist dualism**.

Berkeley and La Mettrie

Contemporaries of Descartes espoused monism; within monism there were two schools of thought. One school had a

Figure 1–4 *René Descartes (1596–1650).* Maintaining an extreme version of dualism, Descartes believed the mind and brain communicated through the pineal gland or what he called "the seat of the soul." (Frans Hals "Portrait of René Descartes" (1596–1650). Louvre, Paris, France. Giraudon/Art Resource, NY)

major proponent in George Berkeley (1685–1753) (pronounced "Barklay"), who was a bishop in the Anglican Church. Somewhat paradoxically (as most Christians are dualists) Berkeley proposed that there was but one form of reality. However, he postulated that this reality was *purely spiritual*. **Spiritual monism** denies the existence of the material world, holding that it is an illusion in the mind of humans or imagination in the mind of God. When first encountered, spiritual monism may seem, like absolute dualism, to be somewhat counterintuitive. However, there is considerable logical security in the position, and the problems with all other alternatives (discussed later) have caused several prominent thinkers to take refuge in the doctrine (see Box 1–2).

Also in the eighteenth century, a French *philosophe* named Julien Offray de La Mettrie ("la metree") (1709–1751) best articulated the complementary position to spiritual monism. Writing at the beginning of the Industrial Revolution, La Mettrie proposed that all mental events were mechanical, obeying laws of physical nature. This **material monism** in essence denied the existence of the spiritual world. Material monists believe that mental events are brain events, obeying laws that may be unperceived but nevertheless are consistent with the laws governing all physical processes. In

the words of La Mettrie, "Man is a machine and . . . in the whole universe there is but a single substance variously modified" (La Mettrie, 1748).

Do You Have to Choose?

When I entered the field of neuroscience I had assumed that most of its practitioners would be material monists. After all, wouldn't it be more attractive to believe that the object of our endeavors, understanding the brain, explained *all* of internal experience instead of just a part of it? It came as somewhat of a surprise to me to discover that, apart from some scattered solipsists (one who believes he or she is the only person in the universe) and relativists (one who believes the only reality is cultural; see Box 1–2), that most neuroscientists were interactionist dualists. To understand the reason for this, consider the opinion of one of the founders of neuroscience, Sir Charles Sherrington (1857–1952), about monism:

> I should myself have supposed that the (monist) view would impair the "zest" of the waking day, nor can I imagine the achievements of (for example) ancient Rome emerging from such a doctrine (Sherrington, 1947).

To Sherrington monism was a sterile, desiccated belief, one that deprived the human experience of meaning. An empiricist, defined by his or her devotion to the scientific method or to what can be measured and perceived directly by the senses, might well be depressed by spiritual monism. On the other hand, anyone who felt that he or she had a choice in how to behave might be put off by material monism.

If behavior is like all other physical processes, the choice is an illusion. Material monism is inconsistent with the notion of **free will** because, according to the law of cause and effect (one of the laws of the physical universe that all events must obey), every outcome is solely dependent on the physical circumstances that preceded it. The problem is that most of us are very attached to the concept of free will. (One philosopher has said, "If we didn't have free will we would have to invent it.") Because much Western language is predicated on the concept of free will, a purely monistic position is often hard even to articulate.

Sherrington and his followers, while pursuing reductionistic science, continued to hold to the dualistic position even as they discovered the mechanistic basis for the behaviors that are described in the chapters that follow. Being reductionists, however, many of them tried to identify the means whereby nondeterministic free will could fit into an otherwise deterministic universe.

The effort has occupied such an important part of our intellectual history that it is only possible to give a cursory treatment of it here. One approach to neuroscientific dualism,

Box 1–2

Solipsism and Social Relativism

If you are looking for a simple answer to the mind/body problem here, you will be disappointed. The intellectual burdens of straightforward monism or dualism are such that many very capable thinkers have proposed solutions to the problem that may seem outlandish to the uninitiated. One such solution, called **solipsism**, has attracted a number of adherents over the years. Basically an extreme form of spiritual monism, a solipsist believes that he or she is the only person in the universe. To a solipsist, all other personalities are in the same category as the rest of the material world, simply an illusion. Before dismissing solipsism as the recourse of a very lonely and perhaps sociopathic individual, consider the following: You cannot argue with a solipsist. In response to whatever reasoned case is presented from dualism or some more moderate form of monism, a solipsist can simply reply (if so motivated) that the arguments are just as illusory as the person who is making them. This intellectual security has been too tempting to resist for some very determined logicians. The British empiricist Bertrand Russell (1872–1970) migrated toward solipsism in his philosophical work but maintained a remarkably social sense of humor. In one otherwise dry treatment of the subject, he quoted from a letter written by an admirer who gushed, "Dear Dr. Russell, I am pleased to find that you are also a solipsist. I only wonder why there aren't more of us."

A strange complement to solipsism is to be found in a philosophical tendency quite common on college campuses in the 1960s and 1970s: **social relativism**. A social relativist believes that the only reality is cultural. While a proponent of this school of thought may or may not accept the existence of the physical world (and hence may be either a monist or a dualist), he or she denies the existence of objective knowledge. Citing well-established beliefs (often in Western culture) that subsequently proved to be wrong, the relativist proceeds to the conclusion that all truth is an illusion. As with the solipsist, argument with a relativist is somewhat futile since, from this perspective, all ideas have an equal claim to respect merely because somebody has thought them. Apart from offering a convenient excuse to skip class, social relativism has little practical value since universal adherence to the doctrine would have prevented the development of science, mathematics, technology, medicine, law, and so forth (since people couldn't agree on a single set of terms, premises, and rules). Ironically, the strongest argument against social relativism is a social one: Society cannot possibly flourish and progress if truth is held to have no shared meaning. In this connection, the reader may be entertained by one of the great academic hoaxes of recent years in which a physicist wrote an analysis of Einstein's theory of relativity from a perspective of social relativism, intending the result to be satire. The result is hilarious to the initiated, but was taken at face value by the editors of an academic journal and published as a serious inquiry by mistake (see Sokal, 1996).

Solipsism and social relativism provide ready escapes from the dilemma of the mind/body problem. You readers who find either to be attractive should by all means pursue the belief, provided, of course, that you are prepared to live with the consequences. As for the rest of you, read on.

---

emergent property dualism, holds that the mind may be a function of the physical brain, but the whole is more than the sum of its parts. Each brain function may be wholly deterministic, but added together the parts may acquire a new ("emergent") meaning. The problem with this view becomes evident when it is applied to "wholes" other than the brain. Is a bicycle, for example, more than the sum of its parts?

Another avenue for free will to create a nondeterministic mind was sought in a famous result in physics called the **Heisenberg uncertainty principle**. This dictum, soundly based in empirical result, holds that the behavior of certain sub-atomic particles is innately unknowable. Some famous neuroscientists, notably Sir John Eccles (1903–), a follower of Sherrington, proposed that this ineffable *uncertainty* led to *indeterminacy* in the behavior of microscopic brain function and hence allowed free will to overcome the law of cause and effect. An argument against this (in addition to the previous one that it would have to apply to nonsentient systems as well) is that the uncertainty principle is the result of a limitation in knowledge, not a limitation in possibility. As one prominent physicist has said, in a somewhat ineffectual attempt to clarify the situation, "There is nothing in quantum mechanics that violates the law of cause and effect. However, in the behavior of subatomic particles, sometimes the effect happens first and the cause happens later."

A final source of argument for interactionist dualism deserves mention because it has attracted a great deal of current support. It is a robust finding in nature, also well supported by quantum mechanics, that certain processes are random and some random processes are so sensitive to perturbation that seemingly minor differences in initial conditions can yield wildly unpredictable consequences, or **chaos**. Some writers have found in chaotic systems hopes for indeterminacy in mental processes and hence grounds for belief in free will.

I encourage you to consult more extensive treatments of the mind/body problem listed as "Further Readings" at the end of this book, to help you make up your mind (or is that your body?). For the moment, consider my argument that you must eventually make a choice. Logically, monism and dualism are mutually exclusive: The mind and the brain are either the same, or they're not. Material monists have the burden of accounting for free will if they are to effectively defend their position, while dualists must find an avenue for free will to enter into physical brain processes to effectively defend theirs. We will revisit the mind/body problem throughout the book, to help you refine your position.

Teleology versus Deontology

In the Middle Ages or medieval period all Western philosophy was dualistic. In Europe, Catholicism dominated academic debate, which was for the most part carried out among clerics. These were anointed priests of the church, who believed in a distinction between the material and the spiritual domain. Though there was agreement on this aspect of the mind/body problem, many lively debates occurred throughout the medieval period regarding the precise relationship between the two planes of reality. Conducted when the modern university system was being developed, this debate had lasting influences, both positive and negative, on the development of skeptical inquiry. During the ensuing Renaissance, scholars emphasized the negative features of medieval discussion. Medieval "scholastic" debate sometimes dwelled on trivial, or ridiculous, aspects of how spirituality and carnality were related. The caricature of an argument over "how many angels can dance on the head of a pin," resolved by solemn referral to apostolic authority and citation of scripture, was used to illustrate the pedantic nature of scholarly work of the medieval time. In reality, scholastic debate often had considerable substance and provided the structure for much of our scientific thinking today.

Natural philosophy (now called natural history) was a major component of scholastic inquiry (or medieval thought).

Figure 1–5 *Questions of Teleology.* The teleological school of thought sought a purpose for all creations. In observing the above phenomena, a teleological thinker might ask: (a) Why do male elk spar? (b) What advantage does the lion fish have in being able to camouflage itself? (c) What function does coiling serve for the snake? or (d) What is the purpose of the beautiful colors found in seashells?

One school of scholastic thought regarded nature, the object of divine creation, as marvelously complex. According to this view, any purpose in the mind of God in making animals and plants in the way they are is so remote from the mind of man that human intellect has no hope of ever grasping it. Indeed, according to this school of thought, there may have been no purpose at all in making things the way they are. God may have created parts of the universe simply by whim; and humans, infinitely less knowing, would never be able to sort out which aspects were placed there with some godly purpose and which were capricious. This system of belief became known as **deontology**.

Another school of thought, equally vigorous and pious, was called **teleology** (Figure 1–5). Teleological thinkers believed that since the mind of God was perfectly rational (as well as all-powerful and all-knowing) then the manifestation of this mind in creation would also be perfectly rational. The mind of man, though weaker and less powerful than God's, was created to be rational as well and could understand, in favorable circumstances, the rational purpose behind creation. Thus, unlike deontologists, teleologists sought order and purpose in each element of the natural world, especially in the structure and function of living creatures.

Does Life Have a Purpose?

According to teleologists, each animal and plant has a divine purpose. Often this purpose was taken to be to serve man by providing food, labor, shelter, and so forth. This tenet of teleology has been used as justification for exploitation of natural resources and mistreatment of animals, one of our unfortunate legacies from the middle ages. However, teleology viewed creation as being much more purposeful than just for human utility. Animals and plants were equipped to procreate their species, to acquire a livelihood, to provide for safety, and for all other purposes that benefited the organism itself. Life had purpose on two levels: a divine purpose during creation (to enable God's creations to live) but also a continuing purpose, one in which all observed behavior and all parts of the body worked together to further the interests of the species or individual.

Darwin's Theory

The theory of evolution by natural selection rejected the notion of divine creation but otherwise borrowed the notion of teleology to a remarkable degree. In Darwin's theory, species change over time because fortuitous mutations in individuals allow them to reproduce more efficiently than others. Evolutionary forces were seen as so strong that no useless structure or behavior could have survived generations of selective pressure for only the fittest and most efficient. Anything that emerged from an evolving system must therefore have utility, even if that utility is not immediately obvious.

Like monists and dualists, theistic and atheistic scientists collaborate with one another and understand each other to a remarkable degree. In biology, this consensus comes largely from the fact that all act as teleologists in their work. Controversy may exist regarding the *level* at which teleology is to be applied (for example in the ongoing and robust debate as to whether it is genes, organisms, broods, or species that exhibit self-interest). There may even be a large chunk of biology in which there is indeed purposeless tissue, organs, or information (as in the bulk of DNA which appears to code for no protein and is merely passed on from generation to generation without genetic significance). Nevertheless, it is a biologist's first impulse when confronted with a new act or observation, to ask "*Why* is it there?" "*What* is its purpose?" "*What* advantage does it supply to the organism?"

Teleological Reasoning

It is my habit to ask teleological questions in this text. When studying the action potential (Chapter 4) you will be asked "*Why* is myelin there?" and "*Why* is the squid giant axon so giant?" In the study of sensory and motor systems (Chapters 9 and 10) you may be asked "What is the *purpose* of surround inhibition?" or "*Why* do sensory neurons display adaptation?" or "*What* is the function of the cerebellum?" Some of these questions have fairly plausible answers. These I will provide for you in the text. Other teleological questions are open to debate, and if no answer or several are provided you may view this as an invitation to investigate the matter on your own. Finally, there is no guarantee that all biological systems will be sensible and rational; some may be accidental, or even whimsical depending on your point of view.

The Whole and the Parts

The medieval debates between monism and dualism and between teleology and deontology were never purely speculative nor were they purely derived from citation of scriptural authority. Rather, there was ongoing empirical investigation in natural science to discover the physical influence on behavior, limited of course by the techniques and knowledge available at the time. It could be observed that the brain and spinal cord were different than many organs in that they were connected, by fibers, with all the other parts of the body. Today, we recognize all of the fibers as nerves and call them the **peripheral nervous system (PNS)**, in distinction to the brain and cord, which is called the **central nervous system (CNS)** (see Figure 1–6). Of the other organs, only the heart and all the blood vessels were similarly distributed throughout the body in a manner that could coordinate movements of the body and create behavior. Which system was closest to the soul?

"Neurohumors"

Many medieval and Renaissance scholars chose the cardiovascular system, and the fluid-filled chambers of the body, as the likely source of the tangible aspects of mental processes. Differences in external aspect (or mood) were thought to reflect the presence of different substances in the general circulation (bile, blood, phlegm, and so forth). Collectively, these substances were called *humors*. (Obviously the etymology of the phrase "sense of humor" is medieval).

The medieval notion, like so many others, has current application. There are indeed substances that have general influence on the body and on demeanor. Specialists call these *global* influences. The agents that create global influences are called *humoral agents* (or sometimes *neurohumors*) after the original concept. However, humoral agents are not fluids themselves, as the medievals imagined, but chemical constituents (**hormones** and **transmitters**) of fluids that act on diverse targets in the body.

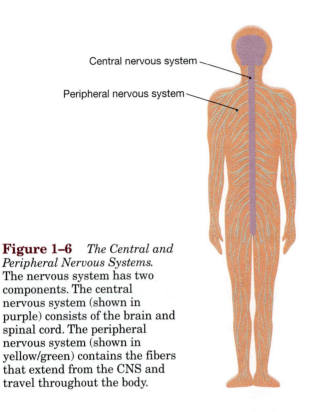

Central nervous system

Peripheral nervous system

Figure 1–6 *The Central and Peripheral Nervous Systems.* The nervous system has two components. The central nervous system (shown in purple) consists of the brain and spinal cord. The peripheral nervous system (shown in yellow/green) contains the fibers that extend from the CNS and travel throughout the body.

Renaissance investigations of the nervous system largely followed medieval lines. Leonardo da Vinci (1452–1519), among his many and various activities, examined human autopsy specimens in the course of inquiry into the basis of behavior. He noticed that the central nervous system could be divided into regions of brain surrounding fluid-filled chambers (now called **ventricles**). Leonardo proposed, following classical beliefs of Galen and Hippocrates, that the vital aspects of mind were properties of the ventricles and the liquid circulating within them. The concept that emerged from these early investigations was that the physical substance(s) that influenced behavior suffused the entire body all at once, governing the body by taking control of all its processes simultaneously.

The Patients, and Patience, of Paul Broca

The idea that the brain, as opposed to the circulation, governed specific behaviors gained support after the Middle Ages since people began to live longer and were able to survive strokes and other damage to the brain and become the object of medical investigations. Franz Joseph Gall (1758–1828) pioneered the method of examining living patients with behavioral abnormalities, waiting for them to die (usually from other causes), exhuming the corpses, and dissecting the brains. On the basis of this research, Gall developed a theory that specific personality traits were located in specific brain regions and that greater expression of

these traits created larger specific brain regions in certain individuals. This difference in size was assumed to be so large that it could be palpated across the skull of a living individual, giving as it were a personality profile derived from bumps on the head. This theory became known as **phrenology**. As is often the case with new scientific theories, phrenology represented a genuine advance in understanding combined with a sincere misinterpretation of the data; this ambiguous quality had a long-lasting impact that was both good and bad. The insight that behavior was a product of the brain, and that particular brain regions might have specific contributions to behavior, was essentially correct and gave rise to the science of *diagnostic neurology*. The assumption, quite plausible at the time, that expression of better behavior necessitated a larger brain region, turned out to be substantially wrong. In the chapters that follow we will see evidence that the brain is not like a muscle. It does not grow with exercise, or even consume more energy when engaged in intellectual activity, and most certainly is not larger in smart people and smaller in stupid ones. The more extreme aspects of phrenology were quickly dismissed as unscientific and are often held up to ridicule as an example of *pseudoscience*, a superstition made to look scientific by borrowing jargon and style from contemporary scientific disciplines. If you are interested in more detailed treatment of phrenology, you can consult the work by S. J. Gould listed in the References.

One follower of Gall was a French physician named Paul Broca (1824–1880) (Figure 1–7). Broca adopted Gall's methodology without falling into the trap of overinterpretation of the results. Interested in the particular form of brain damage that yielded inability to communicate (called **aphasia**), Broca likewise patiently waited for aphasic patients to die, collected the cadavers, and cut up the brains. Broca noticed that aphasics, as opposed to people with different behavioral deficits, had signs of damage only on the *left* side. In particular, patients with inability to speak, but in whom comprehension of speech was intact (latter called **Broca's aphasics**) had dam-

Figure 1–7 *Paul Broca (1824–1880).* By studying the corpses of aphasics, Paul Broca was able to identify an area in the brain responsible for the ability to speak.

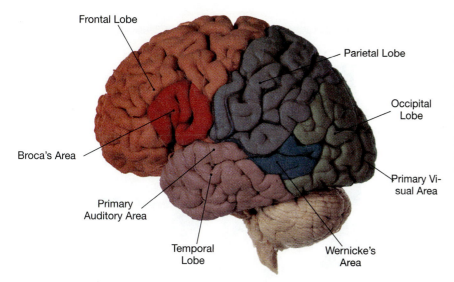

Frontal Lobe

Parietal Lobe

Occipital Lobe

Broca's Area

Primary Visual Area

Primary Auditory Area

Temporal Lobe

Wernicke's Area

Figure 1–8 *The Lobes of the Brain.* There are four major lobes of the brain: the frontal lobes, the parietal lobes, the occipital lobes, and the temporal lobes. *Broca's Area.* Broca's area, the region of the brain responsible for the ability to speak, although not the comprehension of speech, is found on the left side of the frontal lobe. *The Neural Circuitry of Language.* On the left side of the brain, the comprehension area (Wernicke's) in the temporal lobe relays information to the speech area (Broca's) in the frontal lobe.

age only to a portion of the frontal lobe on the left side (Figure 1–8). Broca's statement *"nous parlons avec le hémisphere gauche"* ("we speak with the left hemisphere") became a founding principle in neurology and was quickly taken up by other investigators. In Germany, Carl Wernicke (1848–1905) identified another brain region, again only on the left side, associated with aphasics, but this time in patients with intact vocalization of speech but deficit in comprehension (**Wernicke's aphasics**). We know today that language arises from a circuit in which a comprehension area next to the primary auditory cortex in the temporal lobe relays information to a speech area adjacent to primary motor cortex for the mouth, pharynx, and larynx in the frontal lobe, in each case usually on the *left* side of the brain, not the right (see Figure 1–8).

The successes of Broca and Wernicke inspired similar approaches to observation of other behavioral deficits and examination of other brain regions among professional neurologists. Among the public the advances inspired fascination as well as horror and fear. Exhuming the remains of patients was sometimes done without permission from the relatives, and the work was thus somewhat dangerous to the researchers. Caricatured as mad scientists ("Igor, get me a brain"), researchers were forced to work surreptitiously, since laws were passed providing the death penalty for desecrating a grave for scientific purposes. Mary Shelley's novel *Frankenstein* was written at the time of Broca and Wernicke and provides an excellent historical introduction to the mixture of awe and fear created in the popular imagination by the great advances in neuroscience that occurred at the end of the nineteenth century. Though the scientific circumstances may be different today, the interplay between scientific advance and popular response is a theme of continuing rele-

vance and one that we will explore throughout this book (see Box 1–3).

"The Law of Equipotentiality"

The findings of diagnostic neurology contradicted the medieval and Renaissance idea that the physical basis of behavior was evenly distributed through the body. Indeed, even within the brain there seemed to be powerful evidence for regional specialization. However, experimental evidence also mounted to suggest that some functions *were* distributed widely in the brain, not confined to specific regions. In the 1930s, an American psychologist named Karl Lashley was particularly interested in where memories were stored in the brain. He made a monistic assumption that each memory would have a physical basis in brain changes, the so-called **engram**, but was uncertain where in the brain the engram was stored. He conducted an experiment by training rats to run a maze for a food reward and then removing, or **lesioning**, parts of the brain to see if the memory could be erased. To his surprise, there was no single part of the cortex that disrupted maze-running performance. Rather, it seemed necessary to remove many different parts of the cortex before the memory could be eliminated. Lashley concluded that the engram for maze-running was not localized at all but spread diffusely throughout the cortex, probably overlapping with other engrams. Because each part of the cortex had an equal probability of containing part of the engram, Lashley called his discovery the **law of equipotentiality**. Lashley's "law" was soon challenged. Subsequent investigators concluded that Lashley's rats were forming numerous strategies for maze-running (based on vision, touch, odor, and so forth) and hence were storing many engrams, not just one. Nevertheless, the location of specific engrams still escapes investigators (see

Box 1–3

Split Brains

Events in the central nervous system can be divided into two categories, **excitation** (to enhance a subsequent action or event) and **inhibition** (to prevent a subsequent action or event). Usually, inhibition overwhelmingly dominates excitation; for this reason inhibitory processes use up most of the brain's energy, which is taken from glucose (sugar) and oxygen in the blood. On occasion, some trauma interrupts the supply of glucose and oxygen to the brain (difficult delivery in childbirth, asphyxiation, drug overdose, and so forth). When this happens the lack of energy causes processes normally inhibited to be turned on (or excited), possibly to the extent of pathological results. When this situation is chronic, a clinical condition known as epilepsy results (see Chapter 16). If epilepsy is confined to a small part of the brain, the ensuing seizures are mild. However, if the epilepsy spreads so that unbounded excitation occurs throughout the brain, the seizures can be life-threatening, since proper activity of the CNS is necessary to breathe.

Severe epilepsy of this form is currently treatable with drugs, but in the past it has led to drastic surgical intervention to save the patient's life. In the 1960s, in about twenty-five patients, neurosurgeons Joseph Bogen and Peter Vogel severed the fiber bundle, called the **corpus callosum**, that connectes the two halves of the brain to confine the epilepsy to only one half of the brain. The surgery proved successful and a group of neuroscientists including Roger Sperry, Michael Gazzaniga, and others decided to study these individuals to determine what their internal experience was like in the absence of direct communication between the two halves of the cortex (Sperry, 1982).

Sperry made use of the fact that people (and all animals as far as we can tell) have an organizational principle in the nervous system called **decussation**. Decussation means, in simple terms, "everything crosses." Motor function for the left side of the body is a function of the right hemisphere of

Chapter 15), and the extent to which higher function, such as memory, is restricted to a brain region or shared among brain regions is still very much open to debate (Chapter 16).

Aggregate field theory describes processes such as neurohumors and Lashley's engram that appear to arise everywhere at once or to be distributed evenly across brain regions. Cellular **connectionism** refers to processes that, like Broca's and Wernicke's localization of language, appear confined to discrete brain regions. Unlike the mind/body problem, there is considerable intermediate ground in the issue of aggregate field theory versus cellular connectionism. As we shall see, there is not really much doubt that some central functions are accurately described as obeying cellular connectionism, and virtually all neuroscientists would agree that some processes probably are organized around the lines of aggregate field theory. The dispute, such as it exists, involves *how much* cen-

the brain and motor function on the right is a function of the left hemisphere. Sensory function is similarly crossed; sensation from the right side goes to the left side of the brain and sensation from the left side goes to the right. In humans, because the eyes point in the same direction, the *visual world* is divided by the segregation of the fibers from each eye.

I have never encountered a good teleological explanation for why decussation exists so universally; perhaps you can provide one. We shall return to the concept periodically as we consider motor systems and vision in more detail. For the moment, understand that the crossing sensory and motor fibers were spared in the split-brain surgery; only the fibers that coordinated cortical function between the halves were cut. Sperry and Gazzaniga made use of decussation to address sensory input to the two hemispheres independently. By presenting hybrid, or chimeric, images of people, they could cause the severed hemispheres to have separate experiences.

Let's say the hybrid image as shown in the upper left part of figure is of two people known to the split-brain patient, Mary on the right and Jane on the left. Now let's say the image is flashed up so quickly that the subject could not move his eyes (in other words, so that each image occupies only one half of the visual world). The subject is asked who he saw. What do you think he would say?

Recall that the visual world is crossed, so that the left half (Jane) goes to the right hemisphere and the right half (Mary) goes to the left. You will remember from Broca's investigation that "we speak with the left brain," so the subject will say "Mary" when asked who he saw. Mutely, however, the right half experiences a different stimulus, Jane, and many indicate its preference by pointing to her (with the *left hand*, of course).

With this powerful method of independently communicating with the hemispheres, Sperry and Gazzaniga discovered that the personalities and experiences of the two halves of the brain were quite different, *for split-brain patients*. The left half seemed to specialize not only in language but also in mathematical reasoning and cognition, while the right side appeared more devoted to spatial reasoning and spatial relationships.

From this important scientific breakthrough a growth industry developed, but much of this expansion was based on popular overinterpretation of the results, as with phrenology. Some psychologists and educators quickly seized on the split-brain results to categorize normal people as either "right-brained" or "left-brained," schools of education rapidly developed new curricula designed to instruct either one half or the other, and for awhile, an entire field of scientific research was devoted to *hemispheric lateralization* studies in normal people.

The thoughtful reader will have no doubt realized the nature of the overinterpretation; normal people have intact corpus callosums and hence hemispheres that work together as a unit. Sperry and co-workers discovered an important *latent* feature of the two sides that becomes expressed upon brain damage ("latent" means present but not seen until a change occurs). We shall return to this latent function when we consider brain damage in Chapter 16. Sperry, who won the Nobel Prize for this work, was careful to emphasize the limits of the results to the proper scientific domain. If you would like to learn more about the phenomenon of the popularization of science, and the other philosophical subjects discussed in this chapter, you can begin with Sperry's (1980, 1982) articles on split-brain surgery and the mind/body problem.

---

tral function belongs in each category, with some very important results (such as Sperry's, 1980, 1982; see Box 1–3) appearing to favor both possibilities.

Parallel versus Serial Processing

We will return to cellular connectionism and aggregate field theory throughout the book. For the moment, since neuroscience is an amalgam of other disciplines, it is necessary to describe some overlapping nomenclature. Computer scientists and cognitive psychologists developed many ideas about sophisticated mental processes independently from the biological findings that have just been described. Now, as they coalesce with the biologists in the new field of *cognitive neuroscience* (the collaboration of neuroscientists and cognitive psychologists), it has been discovered that data processing algorithms similar to those discovered in nervous systems also emerged from modeling studies of human cognition and computer function. Depending on the source being consulted, the term **serial processing**, as for many conventional analog and digital computers, may be used in place of *cellular connectionism*, and the term **parallel processing**, as for some supercomputers, may be used in place of *aggregate field theory*.

SUMMARY

Inquiry proceeds by many methods including introspection, deduction, heuristic imagery, and received knowledge. Scientific inquiry proceeds by induction and the use of observation, hypothesis, experiment, and conclusion. Neuroscience is the scientific study of the brain and is a reductionist composite of psychology, biophysics, anatomy, chemistry, physiology, pharmacology, neurology, neurosurgery, neuroradiology, psychiatry, and computer science.

Three philosophical issues permeate neuroscience. The first, the mind/body problem, concerns the nature of reality. Material monists believe that all mental events are also physical events in the brain. Spiritual monists deny the existence of the physical world; and dualists propose that there are two planes of reality, material and spiritual, usually positing an interaction between the two. Second, teleologists believe that aspects of life can be explained by reference to the concept of utility, whereas deontologists believe that life may have properties that cannot be assigned values based on utility. Third, cellular connectionism holds that specific behavioral functions are properties of individual brain regions while aggregate field theorists believe that important function is distributed across neural tissue. Unlike the mind/body problem, which logically compels belief in one of two possibilities, the teleology/deontology and cellular connectionism/aggregate field theory issues have elements of truth on both sides and involve varying degrees of adherence.

REVIEW QUESTIONS

1. How did Berkeley and La Mettrie differ on the mind/body problem?
2. How did Hippocrates and Aristotle differ on the mind/body problem?
3. Give an example of teleological reasoning.
4. What is the difference between aggregate field theory and cellular connectionism?
5. What is the "law of equipotentiality"?
6. How did Paul Broca contribute to diagnostic neurology?
7. What is trephining?
8. What is solipsism?

THOUGHT QUESTIONS

1. Are you a monist or a dualist? Why?
2. Do you think phrenology is completely bogus? Why or why not?
3. Does animal behavior accurately model human behavior? If not, is it interesting in its own right?

KEY CONCEPTS

absolute dualism (p. 7)
aggregate field theory (p. 14)
aphasia (p. 12)
axioms (p. 4)
behaviorists (p. 4)
Broca's aphasics (p. 12)
cellular connectionism (p. 14)
central nervous system (CNS)
    (p. 11)
chaos (p. 10)
conclusion (p. 4)
corpus callosum (p. 14)
decussation (p. 15)
deductive reasoning (p. 14)
deontology (p. 10)

dualists (p. 6)
emergent property dualism
    (p. 9)
engram (p. 13)
epilepsy (p. 14)
excitation (p. 14)
experiment (p. 14)
free will (p. 8)
Heisenberg uncertainty
    principle (p. 9)
heuristic imagery (p. 4)
hormones (p. 11)
hypothesis (p. 4)
inductive reasoning (p. 4)
inhibition (p. 14)

interactionist dualism (p. 7)
introspection (p. 2)
law of equipotentiality (p. 13)
lesioning (p. 13)
material monism (p. 8)
mind/body problem (p. 6)
monists (p. 6)
neurobiology (p. 5)
observation(p. 4)
parallel processing (p. 16)
peripheral nervous system
    (PNS) (p. 11)
phrenology (p. 12)
physiological psychology
    (p. 4)

received knowledge (p. 4)
reductionism (p. 4)
scientific method (p. 4)
serial processing (p. 16)
social relativism (p. 9)
solipsism (p. 9)
spiritual monism (p. 8)
teleology (p. 10)
theory (p. 4)
transmitters (p. 11)
trephining (p. 7)
ventricles (p. 12)
Wernicke's aphasics (p. 13)

In historical events great men—so called—are but the labels that serve to give a name to an event, and like labels, they have the least possible connection with the event itself. Every action of theirs, that seems to them an act of their own free will, is in an historical sense not free at all, but in bondage to the whole course of previous history, and predestined from all eternity.

Count Leo Nikolayevich Tolstoy (1828–1910)

2

The Cellular Basis of Behavior

No science is conducted in a social vacuum. All of it takes place in a context of other social, scientific, artistic, literary, and political events. In this book we shall highlight the influences of such contemporary forces on advances in neurobiology where appropriate. First, let's see how the birth of neurobiology itself was influenced by the simultaneous development of *cell theory* in biology (this Chapter) and *electrical theory* in physics (Chapters 3 and 4) and use this background to introduce our modern understanding of these topics.

Neuron Doctrine versus Reticular Theory

Fresh brain tissue is soft and mushy, kind of like yogurt in consistency (the solid kind, not the runny kind). It was very difficult for early anatomists to discern any structure at all within samples of brain. If placed on glass and held up to the light, slabs of brain could be seen to consist of opaque as well as translucent regions. Opaque regions appear white when illuminated, and hence were referred to as **white matter,** and the translucent ones are darker and were called **gray matter.** White matter, it was discovered, makes quite acceptable glue when dried, prompting the name for the predominant material in white matter, **glia,** or "nerve glue." Apart from a "black region," the *substantia nigra*, and a "blue spot," the *locus coeruleus* of which we will hear more presently, nothing but gray matter and white matter could be found.

After the invention of the microscope, technology was borrowed from the clothing industry to visualize more structure in biological tissue. From the tanning industry, the idea of "pickling" material in *formaldehyde* ("formalin") to make it stiffer was used to toughen brain so it could be sliced thinner and its form preserved. From the textile industry, dyes used in coloring cloth were used to stain the thin "fixed" tissue so the minute structure could be visualized.

18

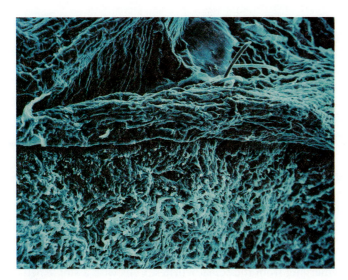

Figure 2–1 *Nonneural Cells.* An electron micrograph of epithelial cells (those that form linings and skin).

When slides were prepared in this fashion and placed in the microscope, they had the appearance of a dense web of fibers, so much like cloth itself that anatomists called it a "reticulum" (or "net") that was interrupted by blobs of *protoplasm* (fluidlike tissue). While these methods led to greater understanding than the simple distinction between white matter and gray matter, there was still little clue as to how the tangled, fibrous web might produce mental properties (or their physical correlates).

Elsewhere in the body (and in tissue from plants) (Figure 2–1) the material seemed to be composed of spheres or cubes, each with a central, heavily stained blob in the middle. **Cell theory** arose from study of such specimens, stating that the unit of life was a seed, or **nucleus**, surrounded by a fluid called **perikaryon** (literally "surrounding the seed," pl. "perikarya") and separated from other units by a **cell membrane** and often a small amount of outside space. The perikaryon was given other names as knowledge was gained of its nature: **cytosol** (*cyto* = cell, *sol* = liquid) when conceived as mostly fluid, and **cytoplasm** when both liquid and structural elements were included. Later a supporting network of fibers, the **cytoskeleton**, was discovered and named.

Cell theory was accepted so completely by biologists that many naturally sought to apply it to the nervous tissue. However, no clear boundary could be seen between perikarya in the brain, the fibers being so dense and long that no one could tell where, or even if, they ended. As the telegraph and telephone were being invented at the time and the marvelous complexity of telephone exchanges and networks was appreciated, it was natural to imagine that the communicative properties of nervous systems might also be mediated by

"nerve wires." (Indeed as we shall see, there is a great deal of truth to this simplistic view.) **Reticular theory**, the notion that perikarya are *directly* connected to one another by nerve wires, proposed that brain was a dense fibrous mat of continuous nerve wires (Figure 2–2a). Reticular theory was inconsistent with cell theory, since it posited that no membrane or extracellular space separated perikarya. In essence, it held that there *were no cells in brain*, that it was a *syncitium* (or continuous cytosol). Those unwilling to abandon cell theory for the brain held that, despite appearances, the nerve wires were not continuous but rather were separated from one another by a small outside space called a **synapse**. The postulated nerve cells were called **neurons** and the theory of their existence became known as the **neuron doctrine** (Figure 2–2b). As no synapses had ever been seen in the microscope, it was not possible to determine directly which theory was correct, and debate between proponents of each became quite protracted and acrimonious.

Golgi's Stain

One particularly devoted disciple of reticular theory was an Italian physician named Camillo Golgi (Figure 2–3). Golgi made a number of fundamental discoveries in biology and a number of structures bear his name including the *Golgi apparatus* (this Chapter) and the *Golgi cell* (Chapter 10). He experimented with a number of methods for discerning structure within the nervous reticulum and finally discov-

Figure 2–2 *Reticular Theory and Neuron Doctrine.* (a) Reticular theorists imagined the brain to be one continuously connected cytosol. (b) Conversely, the neuron doctrine holds that the brain is made up of individual cells that are divided by a tiny space called the synapse.

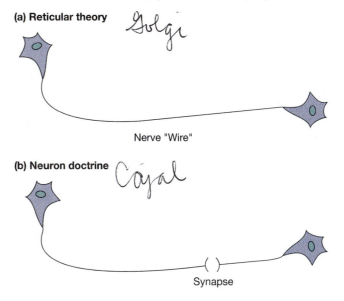

(a) Reticular theory

Nerve "Wire"

(b) Neuron doctrine

Synapse

Figure 2–3 *Camillo Golgi (1844–1926).* Although a devout reticular theorist, Golgi invented the silver impregnation technique, which showed the neuron doctrine to be more accurate.

ered one (called, of course, the *Golgi stain*) that allowed individual perikarya to be visualized. The technique involved making a black oxide of silver, which is taken up by some perikarya and not others; hence, it is also called the **silver impregnation technique**. (There is some irony here. Golgi had managed, perhaps by forsaking his practice for research, to impoverish himself. Even in this state, however, he found the money to buy silver for his work). Figure 2–4 shows the appearance of central nervous system tissue stained by the Golgi method.

As its efficacy became known, use of Golgi's technique spread rapidly. The most famous person to adopt it was Santiago Ramón y Cajal (Box 2–1). He used the stain to produce voluminous and detailed descriptions of the microscopic structure of brain tissue (called *cytoarchitechture*) that remain today the best source of information on the neuroanatomy of some brain regions. Based on the appearance of Golgi-stained sections, Ramón y Cajal became a proponent

Figure 2–4 *Golgi-Stained Sections.* The appearance of the central nervous system tissue as seen by the Golgi method.

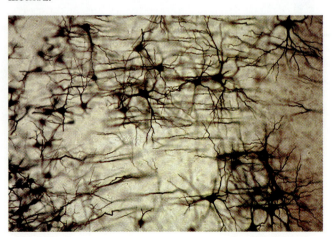

of the neuron doctrine (in fact, it's commonly perceived to have originated with him). Though synapses were still invisible to him, Ramón y Cajal found it impossible to reconcile the selective staining of perikarya with the notion of a continuous fiber network. Thus, he proposed that the nervous system was *not* an exception to the cell theory, and that nerve cells were the basis of nervous system function. They were, he thought, the units of **integration** (the assembly of sensory input into a decision to act) much like atoms had been discovered to be the units of matter.

Parts of the Neuron

Ramón y Cajal noticed that neurons varied in structure from one part of the brain to another. Each had a perikaryon, which he called the **soma** (pl. **somata**). He called the nerve fibers emerging from the soma **neurites**. Cells with a single neurite coming from the soma came to be called *monopolar cells* (Figure 2–5a), those with two neurites, *bipolar cells* (Figure 2–5b), and those with several, *multipolar cells* (Figure 2–5c). Some neurons lack neurites altogether. These tend to be found in sensory systems (Figure 2–5d).

Ramón y Cajal also found similarities among neurons. Bipolar and multipolar cells predominate in the brain. Among these cells the neurites appeared to have two different morphologies. One kind was densely branched in the vicinity of

Figure 2–5 *Types of Neurons.* (a) A monolpolar neuron has a single neurite extending from the soma; (b) a bipolar neuron has two neurites; (c) multipolar neurons have many neurites.

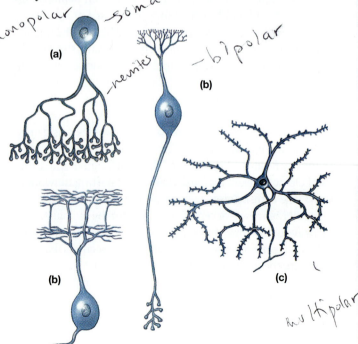

Box 2–1

Santiago Ramón y Cajal

Ramón y Cajal's photograph is suggestive of a man who did not suffer fools gladly, and in fact his biography indicates that he took himself very, very seriously. In particular, he was preoccupied in his early life with the mind/body problem. After years of attacking the issues of free will, causality, and the nature of spirit and matter from a philosophical perspective (and without success), Ramón y Cajal gave up this endeavor as he saw it unworkable. (You will have this experience also, if you engage in any serious discussions of the subject. Western language is dualistic by nature of its Judeo-Christian, Greek, and Latin origins, and since much of ideation is determined by language our thoughts on the mind/body problem are constrained in the dualistic direction. Commentators on Western understanding of monistic thought, such as D. T. Suzuki who first introduced Zen Buddhism to American audiences, have identified this linguistic heritage as a barrier to enlightenment.)

Ramón y Cajal instead decided to break the problem up and solve it piecemeal (a practical strategy, well understood by anyone who has solved complex, but much less daunt-

ing, problems). In essence, his thinking was to understand each element of the brain, add them together to form ensembles of elements, then systems of ensembles, and finally entire circuits, fully understanding the function of each until the brain was understood. If, at the end, he came up with the equivalent of mind then monism was the answer; if not, dualism was true. Ramón y Cajal said, "In the seamless warp of the brain, we can only proceed step by step," and thus the discipline of neuroscience born.

While we are still waiting to see the outcome of this process, the issue of reticular theory versus the neuron doctrine has been more or less decided. As you have gathered from the text, neuron doctrine prevailed. However, there are some aspects of reticular theory that hold true in some systems, electrotonic synapses being the best example (Chapter 5). Camillo Golgi, whose technical breakthrough enabled Ramón y Cajal to provide the best evidence for the neuron doctrine, never abandoned his initial opposition to the doctrine. Golgi and Ramón y Cajal battled rancorously all their lives, even refusing to share the stage when the Nobel Prize was awarded to them jointly in 1906.

---

the soma (Figure 2–6) and each of these branches had twiglike extensions. These were called **dendrites** (from the Latin word for "branches"). The twigs became known as **dendritic spines**. Another type of neurite was fine in caliber, emerged directly from the soma, and traveled far through brain tissue before ramifying. This Ramón y Cajal called the **axon**; the region of soma that gave rise to the axon became known as the **axon hillock**. At the end of the axon (which may split up into branches as well) were found enlargements that had a "buttonlike" appearance and hence became known by the French word for button, **bouton**.

Finally, the neurons had structures in common with all cells, neural and nonneural (see Figure 2–6). Within the soma were found, in addition to the nucleus and the **chromosomes** containing genetic material, **ribosomes** and **endoplasmic**

reticulum, now known to be the sites for protein synthesis, and the **Golgi apparatus**, now known to be the machinery for packaging protein destined for transport to various parts of the cell. The neurons were also found to contain **mitochondria**, known to supply the cell's energy needs; **microtubules**, which are hollow rods of **tubulin** protein found in the cytoplasm of all eukaryotic cells; **microfilaments**, which are solid rods of actin protein in the cytoplasm that make up part of the cytoskeleton; and **myelin**, an insulating coat of the cell membrane. Surrounding everything, as for all cells, is a membrane called the **plasma membrane**.

"The Law of Dynamic Polarization"

Since Ramón y Cajal thought that he had found the *unit of integration*, he surmised the function of the various parts of

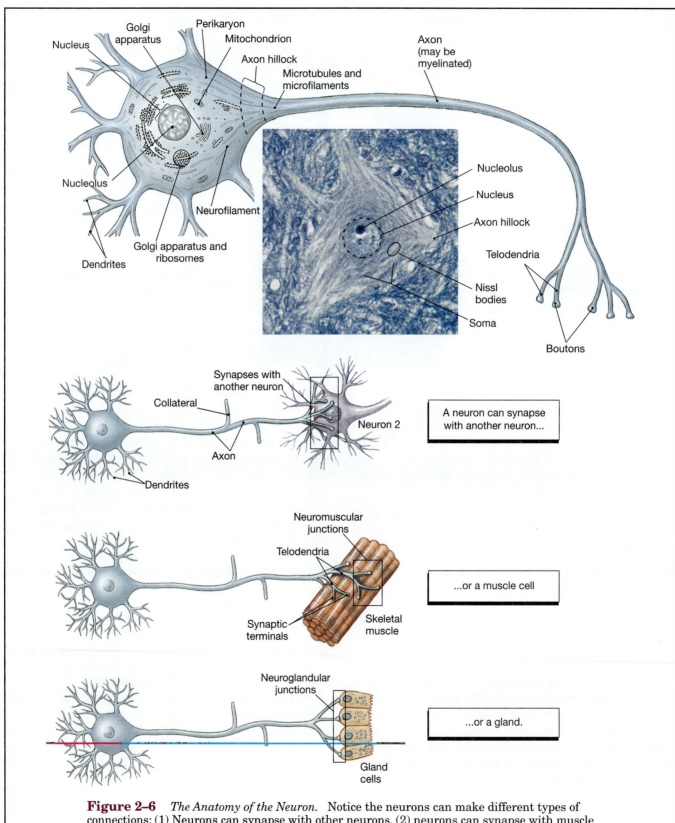

Figure 2–6 *The Anatomy of the Neuron.* Notice the neurons can make different types of connections: (1) Neurons can synapse with other neurons, (2) neurons can synapse with muscle tissue, (3) neurons can synapse with gland cells.

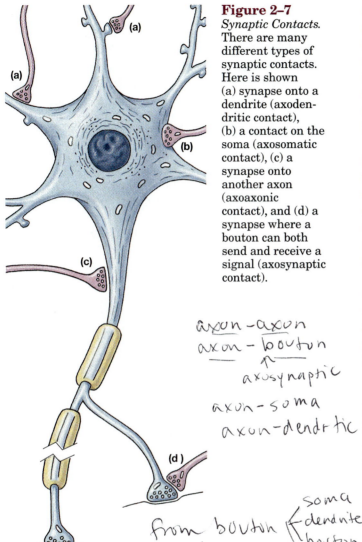

Figure 2–7
Synaptic Contacts.
There are many
different types of
synaptic contacts.
Here is shown
(a) synapse onto a
dendrite (axoden-
dritic contact),
(b) a contact on the
soma (axosomatic
contact), (c) a
synapse onto
another axon
(axoaxonic
contact), and (d) a
synapse where a
bouton can both
send and receive a
signal (axosynaptic
contact).

ure 2–7, many synapses are made on dendrites (*axodendrit-ic* contacts) (Figure 2–7a), but some are made directly onto the soma (*axosomatic* contacts) (Figure 2–7b), thus apparently bypassing the dendrites in the flow of information. Indeed, there are *axoaxonic* contacts (Figure 2–7c) that bypass the soma and (quite a large number) of *axosynaptic* contacts (Figure 2–7d) in which, in direct contradiction to the law, the bouton of a cell receives as well as makes a synaptic contact.

It might be best, therefore, to revise the law to state that for *each synapse information flows in only one direction,* from the **presynaptic side** (bouton) to the **postsynaptic side** (dendrite, soma, axon, or bouton). In this form the law is generally quite reliable and, for the purposes of this text, may be committed to memory. Minor exceptions that occur, such as *electrotonic synapses* (Chapter 5), will be discussed as they arise in particular contexts.

In sum, the neuron doctrine is more accurate than reticular theory and the law of dynamic polarization governs transmission of information across synapses, which is most always in one direction only. The concepts of presynaptic and postsynaptic apply to specified synapses. As can be seen in Figure 2–8, **sensory cells** bring information *into* the CNS

Figure 2–8   *Presynaptic and Postsynaptic.* The interneuron can be seen as presynaptic or postsynaptic. When compared to the sensory neuron it is postsynaptic. However, it is presynaptic to the motor neuron. (Note to reader: Dendrites are not shown for simplicity.)

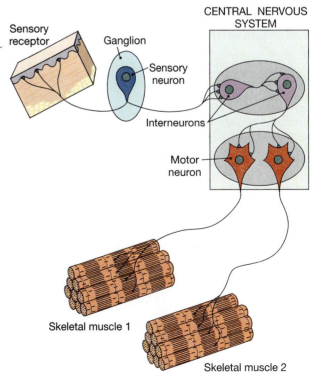

the nerve cell based on their likely role in integration. For the most part his conjectures were correct. If a nerve cell takes *diverse input* and converts it into a *single output* then the dendrites would seem suited, by their anatomy, to specialize in receiving input and the axon would seem suited to specialize in creating output. Well before the advent of direct physiological recording procedures (the subject of the next chapters), Ramón y Cajal visualized the direction of information flow through cells and articulated this theory as the "law of **dynamic polarization.**" Briefly stated, the law of dynamic polarization holds that information normally flows *from dendrite to soma to axon and thence across the synapse to the dendrites of another cell,* never the other way around (i.e., axon to soma to dendrite).

As for many theories that are stated as "laws," the law of dynamic polarization is not always correct. As shown in Fig-

and **motor cells** transmit information *out* to the muscles, but all the other neurons in the brain, and the vastest number by far, are **interneurons** that lie between sensory input and motor output. Such cells, of course, are *presynaptic* to some neurons and *postsynaptic* to others. The concepts of presynaptic and postsynaptic, as they embody the law of dynamic polarization, are very important in the study of neuroscience. When they are used properly, the referent synapse is always specified, as *postsynaptic to the sensory cell* (Figure 2–8). You should pause here and make sure you understand these essential concepts before you proceed to the next section.

The Plasma Membrane

If you are like me, if given a *list of things* to remember you can do quite well, but if given *two* things to remember, you'll get them switched. This can be especially troublesome in beginning the study of neuroscience because there are several such dichotomous concepts that must be grasped before the interesting stuff will make sense. As you have probably guessed from the foregoing discussion, the synapse is the site of many important events in brain function. The plasma membrane is another site of many important brain events. Fundamental to an understanding of the chemical basis of nerve signaling is the knowledge that the inside of cells has a different chemical composition than the outside. The term **intracellular environment** is used to describe chemical events, structures, and processes on the *inside of cells* and **extracellular environment** to describe things and processes on the *outside of cells*, with the plasma membrane defining the boundary between the two environments.

Hydrophilicity and Hydrophobicity

You have been informed, I am sure, that more than two-thirds of the body is made up of water. Both the intracellular environment and the extracellular environment are composed predominantly of water; cells are much like bags of water floating in water. Such bags can be formed experimentally in the absence of life, and undoubtedly were formed before life evolved. They were, in fact, a prerequisite for life. It is easy, given an understanding of some basic chemical concepts, to see how this happened. Water (H_2O) is bent around the oxygen atom (Figure 2–9). Because oxygen "likes" (attracts) electrons more than hydrogen does, the water molecule acquires a "polar" character, with a slight negative electrical charge on one side and a slight positive charge on the other. Some water molecules "fall apart" altogether into more highly charged particles called **ions**, which then interact with one another and with the larger water molecules so that the positive and negative charges align with one another (Chapter 3).

Certain organic (carbon-containing) molecules lack charge. (Although the term *organic* implies association with life, there was ample carbon around before life evolved.) This is true, for example, for *fat* (grease, oil, and so forth), much of which is made up chiefly of chains of carbon atoms (C) with hydrogens (H) attached, like this:

$$\begin{array}{ccccccccc}
H & H & H & H & H & H & H & H & H - \to \\
| & | & | & | & | & | & | & | & | \\
H-C & -C & -C & -C & -C & -C & -C & -C & -C - \to \\
| & | & | & | & | & | & | & | & | \\
H & H & H & H & H & H & H & H & H - \to
\end{array}$$

Figure 2–9 *The Polarity of Water.* (a) Because oxygen attracts electrons from hydrogen, the negatively charged particle is "pulled" towards it, leaving a slight positive charge on the hydrogen and a slight negative charge on the oxygen. The result is a polarized molecule that will interact with other polarized molecules. (b) This interaction forms a free sliding lattice-like structure in liquid water.

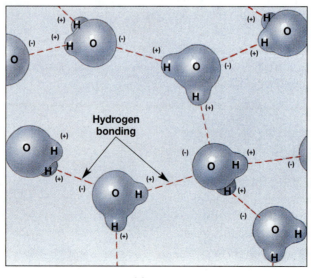

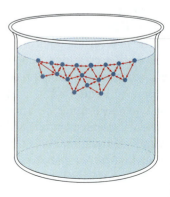

(a)

(b)

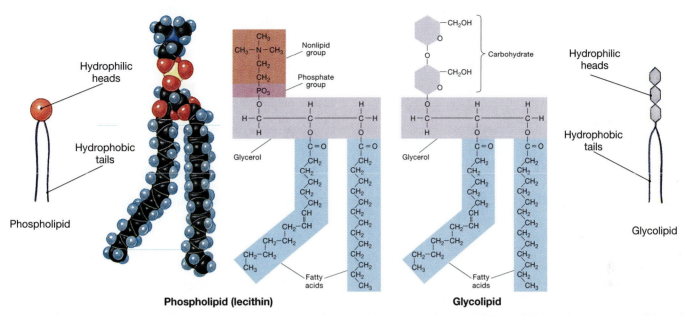

Figure 2–10   *A Phospholipid Molecule.* A phospholipid molecule is amphipathic; it has a hydrophobic tail region and a hydrophilic head.

Hydrocarbon bonds (like those above between hydrogen and carbon), unlike those between hydrogen and oxygen in water, are not bent in such a way as to develop polarity, and as a consequence they cannot interact with water molecules as other water molecules are able to do ("oil and water don't mix"). This is because too many water interactions would need to be broken to admit the uncharged oil molecule. Sometimes fat molecules acquire a charged phosphorus-containing group at one end (Figure 2–10), in which case they are called **phospholipids**. Phospholipids have a restricted region, just around the charged portion, where they are able to interact with water, and extended regions, the hydrocarbon "tails," where they are unable to do so.

Those charged structures that can interact with water we call **hydrophilic** ("water loving"), those uncharged structures that are unable to interact with water we call **hydrophobic** ("water fearing"), and those molecules, like phospholipids, that have both a hydrophilic and a hydrophobic region we call **amphipathic** ("likes both"). Now when amphipathic molecules like phospholipids are exposed to water, they orient themselves so the charged hydrophilic regions interact with water and the uncharged, hydrophobic regions do not. For *phospholipid*, the major constituent of plasma membranes, this means forming a double sheet, or **bilayer**, in which the hydrophobic tails of the two sheets associate with one another on the inside and the charged hydrophilic phosphate heads point outwards where they associate with the water (see Figure 2–11). Even these sheets cannot last, however, for what about the loose hydrophobic regions at the edges? Ultimately (in fact, quite quickly), these curl under, drawing together, until a *sphere* is formed with water outside and inside but with the hydrophobic regions wholly isolated from it. (It is very useful to visualize why lipid behaves in this way. Study Figure 2–11 until you can see how.) These processes, which will take place any time a phospholipid is exposed to water, cause the formation of lipid water-bags. As they undoubtedly existed before life, you can think of these water-bags as being **protocells** (cell-like structures that preceded cells in evolution and, conceptually, help us to understand why cells have the properties that they have.)

A "Fluid Mosaic"

In the protocell the hydrophobic interior of the membrane *poses a barrier to any charged particle crossing* since such a particle would have to cross a "hostile" environment. Ramón y Cajal, of course, could not see the plasma membrane itself as he had access only to a **light microscope**, an instrument that uses lenses to focus light on the specimen. The thickness of the membrane (about 7 *nanometers*, or 10^{-9} meters) is smaller than the wavelength of visible light, rendering it invisible even with a theoretically perfect light microscope. Seeing the structure itself required the advent of the **electron microscope** in the early 1930s. In the electron microscope a focused beam of *electrons*, with much smaller wavelength, is used to visualize structures made opaque to electrons by some very dense stain. "Heavy metal" ions are used for this purpose, and since they are charged they do not interact with

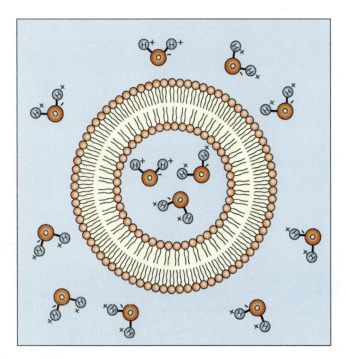

Figure 2–11 *The Phospholipid Bilayer.* The hydrophobic tails of the phospholipid molecules must orient themselves away from the polarized water molecules. The most efficient means by which this is achieved is to orient the polar heads toward the water and hide the tails within the bilayer sphere.

the membrane interior. Thus, the lipid bilayer appears in the electron microscope as two dark layers, where the stain has associated with the charged phosphates, separated by the unstained hydrophobic layer (Figure 2–12). Initially microscopists saw the structure of the membrane and thought they were actually stiff leaflets of lipid, like a cellular "skin." Later, it became apparent that in living cells the lipid is fluid, like the soap swirling on the surface of a bubble.

But living cells continuously exchange *nutrients* and *metabolites* (breakdown products) with their environment. Since most of these are charged particles, how do they get across the membrane? **Protein** exists in the membrane of real cells, comprising about 60 percent of the total for some cells or as little as 25 percent for others, such as *glia*, that have very fatty membranes. These protein molecules are themselves amphipathic (they have to be to exist in the membrane) and many span the membrane entirely, forming hydrophilic **channels** and **pumps** for the exchange of waterborne substances. Many of these proteins float freely in the lipid like ships on the sea, while others are *anchored* to a particular portion of membrane like ships in a harbor. Because so many proteins in various cells are free-floating, the membrane is commonly referred to as a **fluid mosaic** of protein and lipid. However, as we shall see shortly, a critical feature of neurons not displayed by all cells is *membrane specialization*, regions of membrane with *fixed proteins* that enable, for example, presynaptic membrane processes to be restricted to bouton membrane and postsynaptic membrane processes to be restricted to dendrite membrane.

Genetics in a Nutshell

We have seen how the protocell must have adopted the shape and structure it has. How does a *real* cell (in essence a protocell with protein and reproductive capability) acquire its

Figure 2–12 *The Electron Micrograph of Adjacent Cell Membranes.* Each membrane consists of two very distinct dark lines (the phospholipid heads) and a lighter area between (fatty acid tails). Between the two membranes is a granular intercellular space. Note the double nuclear membrane in the cell above.

Phospholipid bilayer

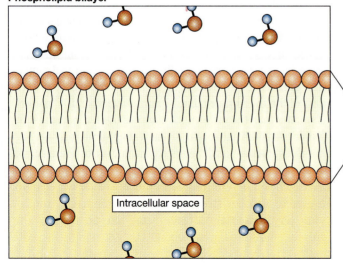

Intracellular space

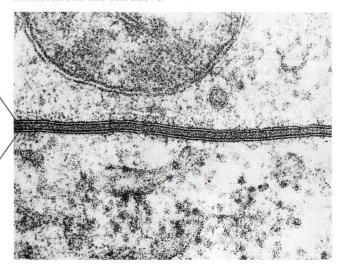

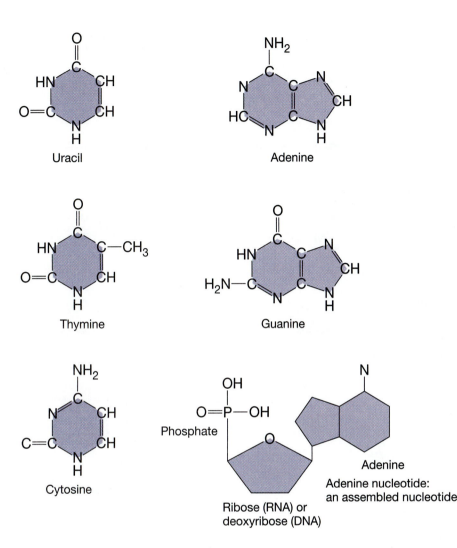

Figure 2–13 *The Structure of the Bases.* The bases found in nucleic acid are adenine, cytosine, guanine, uracil, and thymine. Uracil occurs only in RNA with thymine found in its place in DNA. The bases are rings of nitrogen and carbon with hydrogen and oxygen side groups. Once assembled into nucleotides (base, sugar, phosphate) they can be linked together to form RNA or DNA.

Uracil

Adenine

Thymine

Guanine

Cytosine

Phosphate

Ribose (RNA) or deoxyribose (DNA)

Adenine

Adenine nucleotide: an assembled nucleotide

properties? The answer will require some basic knowledge of *genetics*, the study of heredity. You may be frustrated at having to learn basic principles from yet another discipline, but allow me to stress its importance. Not only is genetics critical to the concept of evolution, but the precise functioning of our genetic machinery is essential for our day to day growth and survival. Genetic instructions determine the characteristics of the aforementioned nutshell, from the ridges on a walnut to the funny shape of a peanut shell. Even more striking is what happens when genetics goes awry. Down's syndrome (Chapter 16) is a genetic disorder that causes abnormal formation of brain structures resulting in developmental disability among many other problems. Without properly functioning genes, the nervous system is incapable of supporting normal neuronal growth. Now that you can appreciate the importance of this field, let's consider how proteins were (probably) assembled in evolution and how they (most certainly) became the essential mediators of all membrane processes in real cells today.

Let's begin with the basic structure of genetic material, RNA and DNA. Simple organic molecules, such as those shown in Figure 2–13, can join together chemically into lengthy strands known as **polymers**. One such complex molecule, a polymer of the sugar *ribose* phosphate (a small ion containing phosphates, oxygen, and hydrogen) and one of the bases **adenine, guanine, cytosine,** and **uracil** is known as *ribonucleic acid*, or RNA (Figure 2–14a). Recent research by Thomas Cech (1989) has determined that RNA is a remarkable molecule that probably played a role in the transformation of protocells into cells at the origins of life. While all of the marvelous properties of living things, including the function of complex nervous systems, are the product of organic polymers, RNA is perhaps the most amazing of these since it has the ability to *self-replicate*, which is one of the characteristics of a living organism. In other words, in the absence of any other chemical besides water and free *ribonucleotides* (ribose plus the bases), an RNA strand can assemble a molecular strand similar to itself, acting as both template for the

Figure 2–14   *RNA and DNA.*
(a) RNA has ribose as a sugar and uracil as a nucleotide. Additionally, RNA is found single-stranded in cells. (b) The DNA nucleotide contains a deoxyribose sugar, phosphate, and one of the bases guanine, adenine, thymine, or cytosine. In cells, DNA is found double-stranded. (Lehninger, 1993)

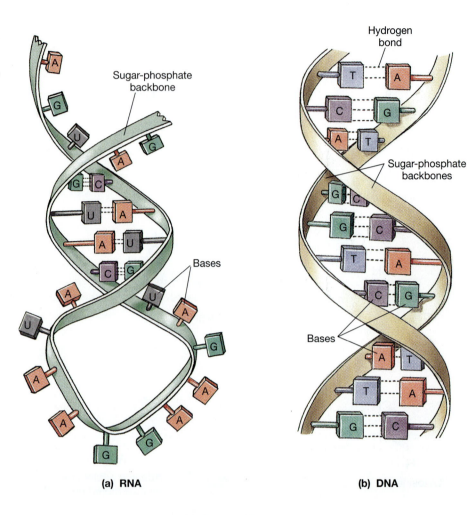

(a) RNA   (b) DNA

sequence of ribonucleotides and *catalyst* for its formation. Heterogeneous RNA (different forms of RNA, trapped inside a protocell) can direct the synthesis of different polymers altogether; protein, which is a polymer of simple organic molecules called **amino acids**, and *deoxyribonucleic acid* (**DNA**), which is a polymer of the sugar *deoxyribose* and the bases listed above for RNA with **thymine** replacing *uracil* (Figure 2–14b). In all cells today, DNA replaces RNA as the template for the genetic sequence, but the principle remains the same: *storage of vital information in the sequence of simple molecules within complex polymers.* As these self-replicating mechanisms extended themselves to the formation of new spheres, protocells became cells and the story of life began. (For more on how scientists are able to distinguish one complex polymer from the next, see "Methods of Chemical Identification" in the Appendix.)

A Four-Letter Code

The four bases of DNA, adenine, guanine, cytosine, and thymine, are assembled into the DNA polymer in a sequence specific to one's hereditary information, forming a different code for every organism. Two DNA strands (polymers) bond chemically in such a way that each base binds to a complementary base on the other strand. They are called complementary because adenine binds only to thymine and guanine binds only to cytosine thus forming long sequences of ATs, TAs, GCs, and CGs, each of which is called a *base pair*. The end product, a structure called a **double helix**, resembles a twisted ladder (see Figure 2–14b); the chain of sugar and phosphate forms the sides while the base pairs connect to form the rungs. (Recall from your high school biology course that these ladders are twisted and scrunched up into chromosomes, the macrostructures of genetic material present in the nucleus of every cell in your body).

A fraction of the DNA is associated with regions called **promoters** that are sites for regulation of nucleic acid synthesis and are associated with particular **genes**, the units of hereditary information (one strand of DNA will contain many gene sequences). Depending on whether the promoters are repressed or activated, an enzyme called *RNA polymerase* interacts with the DNA and makes an RNA copy of the gene in this region by again matching complementary base pairs along the DNA sequence. This process is called **transcription** (Figure 2–15) and produces a single strand of nucleic acid called *messenger RNA (mRNA)* because it bears the message of the same sequence of base pairs in a single gene of DNA. This is the initial step in the activation and expression of any gene. The mRNA exits through pores in the nuclear membrane and interacts with ribosomes, which are subcellular particles that form the site for protein synthesis. There may be either free ribosomes floating in the cytoplasm or ribosomes bound to the endoplasmic reticulum, which is a set of membranes within the cell that is used for making the finishing touches to proteins, including those amphipathic proteins destined for the plasma membrane. So gene expression begins with the formation of a certain protein.

A Twenty-Letter Alphabet

At the ribosomes the mRNA is "read" by a second kind of RNA called *transfer RNA* (**tRNA**). Again by matching base pairs, tRNA binds to mRNA within the ribosome, three bases or one triplet at a time. Each small tRNA molecule carries with it one of about twenty different amino acids. (The structures of the common amino acids, i.e., the ones that are used in protein synthesis, are shown in Figure 2–16.) Each set of three bases determines which tRNA will bind and hence which amino acid will be carried into the ribosome. This insures that each amino acid will be placed in its proper position in the growing protein. It is the number, kind, and position of each amino acid in the chain that determines which specific protein (there are thousands) is being assembled. The three-base sequence representing an animo acid is the **codon**. The complete list of codons for the 20 amino acids of protein is called the **genetic code** (Figure 2–17). As each amino acid is borne in, it forms a **peptide bond** with the previous one, eliminating a water molecule (Figure 2–18). This process, called **translation** (so-called because the nucleic acid sequence of mRNA is *translated* through the genetic code into the sequence of much different molecules), forms proteins that can be analogous to a "word" made up of the amino acid "letters." As successive amino acids are added during translation, the newly synthesized protein is extruded from the ribosome (Figure 2–19).

Figure 2–15 *Transcription.* In the process of transcription, the DNA double stand opens, and RNA polymerase, a giant enzyme complex, transcribes the base sequence of DNA into a single-stranded mRNA molecule. This is achieved by base pairing; guanine pairs with cytosine, adenine pairs with uracil, the RNA base. The mRNA strand leaves the nucleus, entering the cytoplasm where its work begins. At the end of translation, the DNA returns to its inactive coiled double helix form.

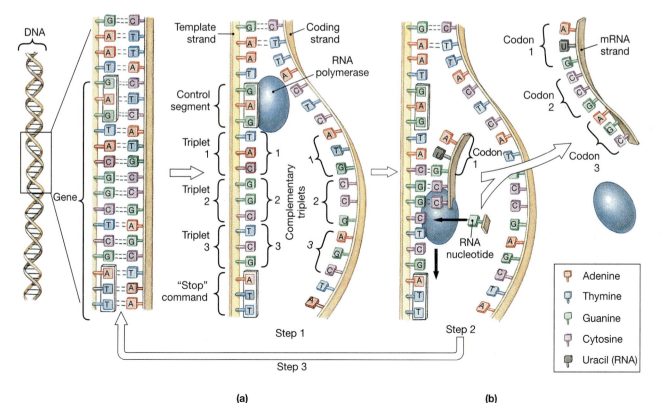

(a)   (b)

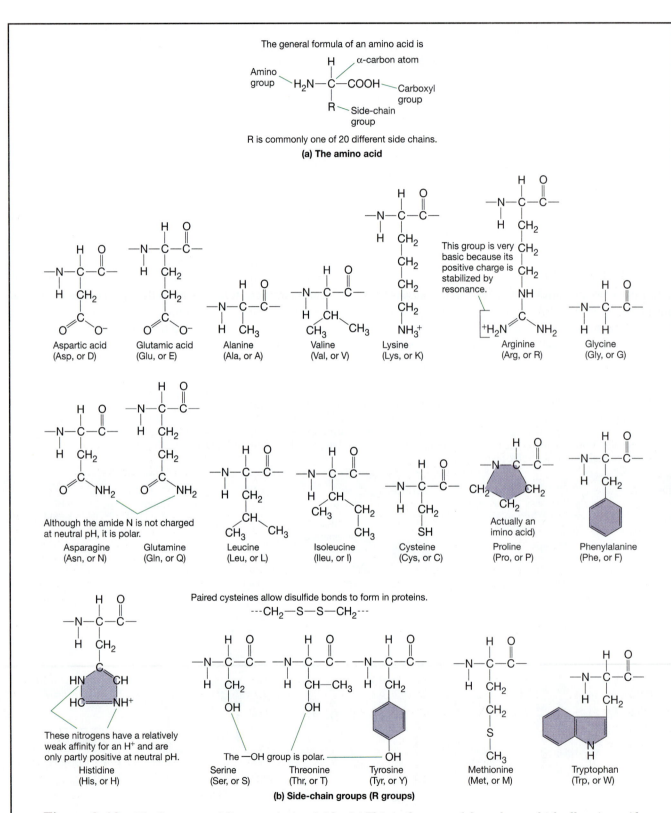

Figure 2–16 *The Structure of Common Amino Acids.* (a) This is the general formula on which all amino acids are based. R is commonly one of 20 different side chains. (b) These are several common amino acids; notice the general structure pointed out in (a); further, notice that only the side groups are different.

1st position	2nd position				3rd position
	U	**C**	**A**	**G**	
U	Phe	Ser	Tyr	Cys	U
	Phe	Ser	Tyr	Cys	C
	Leu	Ser	STOP	STOP	A
	Leu	Ser	STOP	Trp	G
C	Leu	Pro	His	Arg	U
	Leu	Pro	His	Arg	C
	Leu	Pro	Gln	Arg	A
	Leu	Pro	Gln	Arg	G
A	Ile	Thr	Asn	Ser	U
	Ile	Thr	Asn	Ser	C
	Ile	Thr	Lys	Arg	A
	Met	Thr	Lys	Arg	G
G	Val	Ala	Asp	Gly	U
	Val	Ala	Asp	Gly	C
	Val	Ala	Glu	Gly	A
	Val	Ala	Glu	Gly	G

Phe: Phenylalanine	Ser: Serine	His: Histidine
Leu: Leucine	Pro: Proline	Gln: Glycine
Ile: Isolucine	Thr: Threonine	Asn: Asparagine
Met: Methionine	Ala: Alanine	Lys: Lysine
Val: Valine	Tyr: Tyrosine	Asp: Aspartic acid
Glu: Glutamic acid	Cys: Cysteine	Trp: Tryptophan
Arg: Arginine	Gly: Glycine	

Figure 2–17   *The Genetic Code.* In the genetic code, three-letter (base) codons represent the 20 amino acids used in protein. Actually, some of the bases signal START (AUG) and STOP (UAA, UAG, UGA), serving as punctuation in the message. During translation, sets of three bases (codons) on the mRNA bind with complementary bases on a tRNA molecule/amino acid complex. Since each codon has a particular amino acid/tRNA complex to which it will bind (for example CCC and CGG correspond to proline and arginine, respectively), the sequence of the mRNA can be translated into a specific sequence of amino acids. (Note that most amino acids are represented by more than one codon. All organisms from bacteria to blue whales use this code.)

Amino acids have other roles besides making up protein. Some have special functions of their own, especially in the nervous system. Glutamate and aspartate are thought to produce *excitation* at some synapses, glycine is thought to produce *inhibition*, at others and tyrosine, tryptophan, and histidine are precursors for substances thought to mediate central states such as mood, arousal, and consciousness. We will consider these functions of amino acids more fully in Chapter 5.

Some Proteins Important to Cell Function

Why all the fuss over transcription and translation, codons and base pairs? This seemingly endless parade of polymers marches in formation to compose the building blocks of life

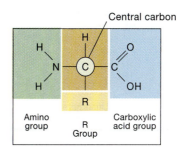

Structure of an amino acid
"R" is different for each amino acid

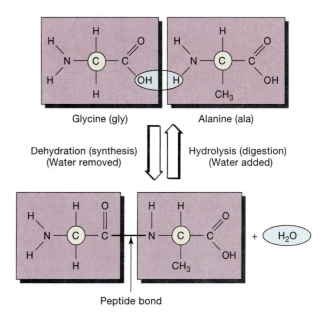

Figure 2–18   *The Peptide Bond.* When two amino acids are joined together, a peptide bond occurs. A chain of amino acids is called a polypeptide. When the peptide bond forms, a hydroxyl (OH) group is removed from the carboxyl (COOH) group of one amino acid and a hydrogen (H) is removed from the amino group (NH_2) of another amino acid to form a bond between the nitrogen (N) of one and the carbon (C) of the other. A water molecule is formed each time. (Note that the process of synthesis is reversible—commonly called digestion.)

as we know it. Some of these building blocks of particular import to the cellular basis of behavior are described in the following sections.

Structural Proteins

Ribosomes bound to the endoplasmic reticulum produce proteins (such as transporters and some **receptors**) that are bound to the plasma membrane or others (such as **peptide hormones** and **enzymes**) that are destined to be released from the cell entirely. Free ribosomes produce proteins (like other **enzymes**) that float freely in the cytoplasm, as well as structural proteins that give shape to the cell. Such proteins give structure to the

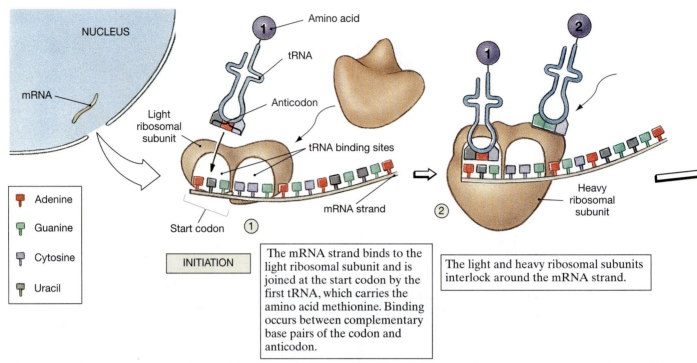

Figure 2–19 *Translation.* Cells are able to express their genetic code in the form of proteins by first transcribing mRNA from DNA and then translating the mRNA into an amino acid chain or protein. Note the three parts: *initiation* (bringing the mRNA, a tRNA, and the two subunits of a ribosome together), *elongation* (binding of the ribosome to the next mRNA codon), and *termination* (when elongation reaches a stop codon, "derailing" the ribosome and releasing the completed protein).

cytoskeleton. **Actin** and **tubulin** form latticelike structures that help determine cell shape and certain movement in the cell. Hence cells often adopt morphologies more intricate than the spherical protocell; neurons for example, send out axons and dendrites. As we shall see in the section "Axoplasmic Transport," the structural proteins form the avenues for other protein to be transported to particular locations and to be anchored there to serve specialized cellular functions.

Enzymes

Most chemical reactions that drive cell functions happen spontaneously. [Chemists say that they are *thermodynamically favored* (see Appendix)]. However, some of these spontaneous reactions happen so slowly that, unassisted, they could *never* mediate something so fast as the speed of thought or conversation. Many of these chemical reactions are accelerated by *catalysts* that cause them to pursue their natural tendency to create **products** from the initial reactant, called **substrates**. When these catalysts are proteins, they are called enzymes. Other, nonprotein molecules are called **coenzymes**, which sometimes work with enzymes, hence the name (*co* = with).

Receptors and Channels

Amphipathic proteins (protein with strands of *uncharged* amino acids alternating with strands of *charged* amino acids)

become embedded in the membrane of the endoplasmic reticulum as they are synthesized. Some of these then become incorporated into the plasma membrane (see if you can guess how before it is explained later in the section "Exocytosis and Endocytosis"). There they become oriented so their charged strands are either inside or outside the cell and their uncharged strands lie in the membrane interior. Some of these form the channels and pumps discussed earlier and allow passage of metabolites and other charged particles across the cell membrane. Others form channels but, in addition, have recognition sites for particular extracellular signals such as synaptic **transmitters**. These **binding sites** recognize the transmitter, much like a lock accepts only a particular key, in a process of geometric and electrical mating known as **stereochemical attraction**. The degree of attraction between a small molecule that binds to a protein, called a **ligand**, and its much larger membrane-bound protein receptor, is called **affinity**. Affinity is described further in the Appendix.

Many receptors (and some other proteins) contain complex, branched *sugars* in addition to a single, always unbranched, chain of amino acids. These are called **glycoproteins** and usually exist with the sugars oriented outside the cell as shown in Figure 2–20. Glycoproteins serve many functions; *mucins*, in particular, coat and protect the mucous membranes in the respiratory and gastrointestinal tracts. Some

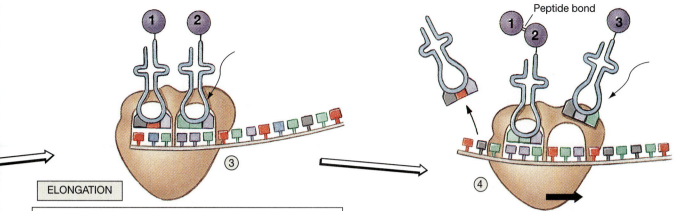

ELONGATION

A second tRNA arrives at the adjacent site of the ribosome. The anticodon of the second tRNA binds to the next mRNA codon.

The first amino acid is detached from its tRNA and is joined to the second amino acid by a peptide bond. The ribosome moves one codon farther along the mRNA strand; the first tRNA detaches as another tRNA arrives.

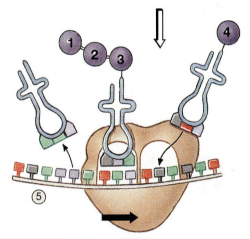

This cycle is repeated as the ribosome moves along the length of the mRNA strand, binds new tRNAs, and incorporates their amino acids into the polypeptide chain.

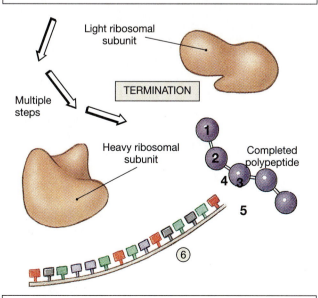

TERMINATION

Elongation continues until the stop codon is reached; the components then separate.

complex channels and receptors are made up of several different glycoproteins in association (literally a *polymer of polymers*). Figure 2–21 illustrates that a single protein of such an aggregate is called a *monomer,* two a *dimer*, three a *trimer*, four a *tetramer*, and so forth.

The Active Neuron

Proteins provide the avenue for the inside of the cell to exchange molecules needed for cell function, or **metabolites**, with the outside. For single-celled organisms the outside might be a pond or the ocean itself, but for eukaryotes, at least those with complex nervous systems, the outside is tissue fluids or blood or, within the central nervous system, the **cerebrospinal fluid (CSF)**. The outside fluid contains nutrients absorbed from the gut, such as certain essential amino acids, that cannot be synthesized by the cell. Most importantly for neurons, the outside fluid contains glucose and oxygen, which together form virtually the only source of energy used by the central nervous system.

Figure 2–22 shows a general scheme for how the energy provided by food consumption is made available for body functions. In the brain, glucose (purple box in Figure 2–22) enters a *three-step metabolic scheme* in which it is broken down into CO_2 (carbon dioxide) and water, producing much energy in the process. The first step is called **glycolysis** (meaning "breakdown of glucose," red arrow in Figure 2–22) and consumes no oxygen, hence it is called *anaerobic* (*an* = without, *aerobic* = oxygen) *metabolism*. The details of glycolysis are given in Figure 2–23. The energy produced by glycolysis is in the form of a chemical compound called *adenosine triphosphate*, or ATP (Figure 2–24a). ATP serves all sorts of cell functions, some of which will be described in Chapter 3 and Chapter 12. Anaerobic glycolysis is not terribly efficient, producing four molecules of ATP directly (and some indirectly) but *consuming* two molecules of ATP in the process.

Figure 2–20
*The Plasma
Membrane.*
(a) The structure
of a glycoprotein.
(b) The plasma
membrane.
(Alberts et al.,
1994)

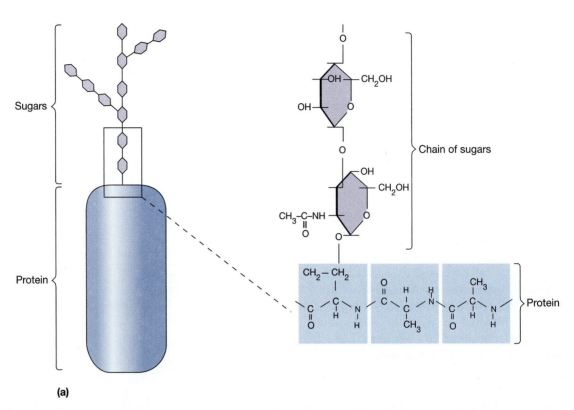

(a)

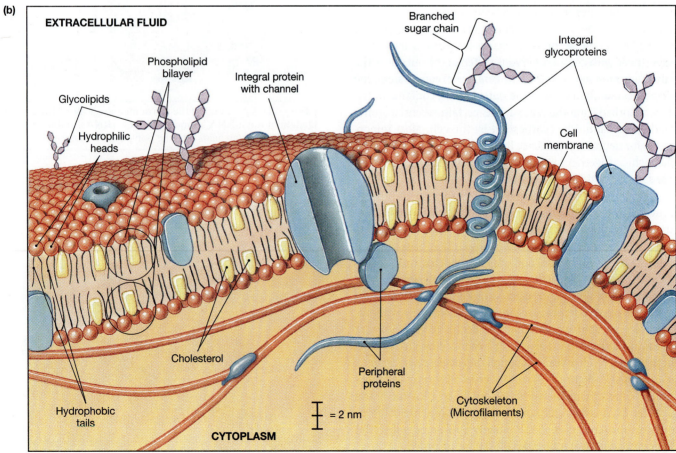

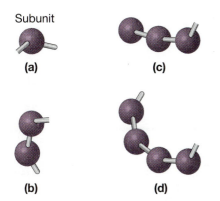

(a)

(b)

(c)

(d)

Figure 2–21 *Protein Structures.*
(a) Protein subunits, called monomers, can form in aggregate to create (b) dimers, (c) trimers, (d) tetramers, and so forth. These subunits are capable for forming extremely long chains or rings.

However, **pyruvate**, the end product of glycolysis, enters a much more fruitful metabolic scheme, **aerobic metabolism** (also know as the *citric acid cycle* or the *Krebs cycle* after its discoverer, Charles Krebs) (see Figure 2–22). As the name implies, aerobic metabolism consumes oxygen and is the primary reason the brain has such a great demand for oxygenated blood (Chapter 12). Aerobic metabolism generates *another* high-energy version of adenosine, **acetyl-CoA** (Figure 2–24b). Acetyl-CoA transfers an acetyl group (CH$_3$-COOH) from pyruvate to an intermediate, creating *citrate*. The metabolism of citrate during the citric acid cycle creates many molecules of yet another high-energy form of adenosine, **NADH**, together with some other high-energy products (GTP, FADH$_2$). NADH is the major source of energy used by cells in aerobic metabolism. Each molecule of NADH sends electrons and protons it picks up in the citric acid cycle through an electron transport system wherein a number of protons are transferred across the inner membrane of an important *organelle* (microscopic cell structure) called the mitochondrion. In the process the protons create an energy gradient for the ultimate generation of much more ATP. Thus, the three stages of glucose metabolism (glycolysis, citric acid cycle, and proton transfer) ultimately increases cellular levels of the primary energy source for most cell functions, ATP.

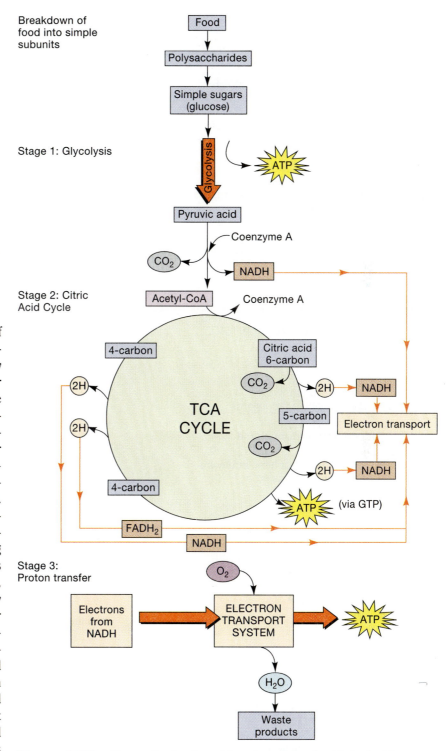

Figure 2–22 *Energy Production.* After the polysaccharide in food is broken down into glucose by digestion, glucose enters three stages in order to produce energy. The first stage takes glucose and converts it to pyruvate by a process known as glycolysis. Pyruvate is then converted to acetyl-CoA which enters the second (citric acid cycle) and third (proton transfer) stages of energy production. Here, acetyl-CoA is oxidized to H$_2$O and CO$_2$ while simultaneously producing energy in the form of ATP.

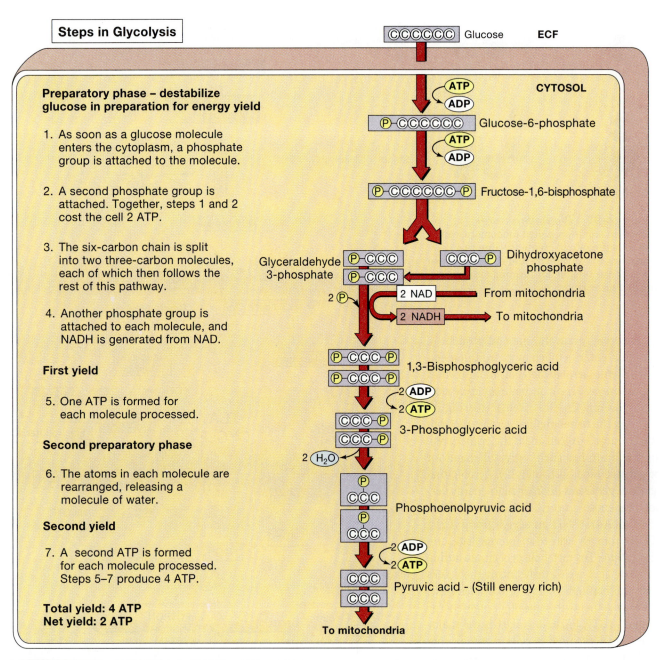

Figure 2–23. *Glycolysis.* At the first stage of energy production, glycolysis converts glucose into pyruvate. Four molecules of ATP are produced during glycolysis. However, two molecules are necessary to initiate the reaction.

The mitochondria are concentrated in those structures, such as the boutons, where energy consumption is high (Figure 2–25). Mitochondria bear many resemblances to bacteria in structure and have many independent functions similar to those of tiny, single-celled (*prokaryotic*) organisms. This fact has led some to speculate that the ancient protocell trapped some bacteria within it leading to a cooperative, or *symbiotic*, relationship between prokaryotes and

eukaryotes and that the symbiotic prokaryotes developed into mitochondria.

Axoplasmic Transport

Among the active processes driven by ATP in the neuron is the trafficking of newly synthesized protein to distant locations in the neurites. This process has acquired the rather unfortunate name of **axoplasmic transport**, inaccurate since such

Figure 2–24 *The Structures of ATP, Acetyl-CoA.* (a) A molecule of ATP consists of an adenine nucleoside to which three phosphate groups have been joined. Cells most often store energy by attaching a third phosphate group to ADP. Removing the phosphate group releases the energy for cellular work, including the synthesis of other molecules. (b) Note the strong similarity in ATP and acetyl-CoA. The difference is where the third phosphate exists in ATP; acetyl-CoA has a carbon-nitrogen chain.

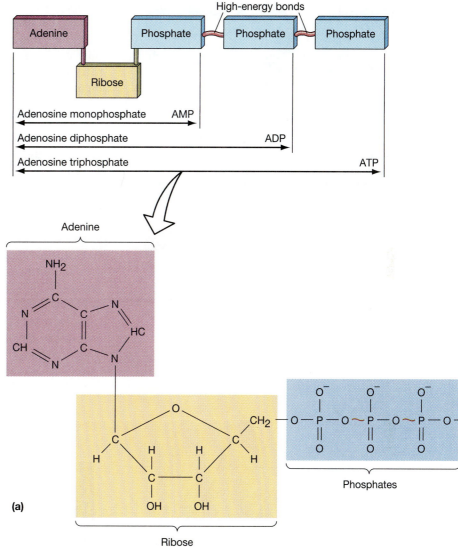

(a)

(b) Acetyl CoA

transport takes place in the dendrites as well as in the axon. This traffic goes in both directions, away from the soma (in which case it is called **orthograde transport** or *anterograde transport*) and toward the soma (in which case it is called **retrograde transport**). Further, axonal transport can occur at different rates. In **slow transport**, involved in the transfer of structural proteins, materials move at the rate of around 1 mm each day. Protein destined for the cell membrane and protein for release into the outside environment are moved by **fast transport** at about 400 mm/day.

Structural proteins themselves provide the basis for axonal transport. **Microtubules**, **neurofilaments**, and **actin filaments** make up a cytoskeletal network in the axons and dendrites that has the appearance of railroad tracks (Figure 2–26). Indeed, large particles in transport appear to be bump-

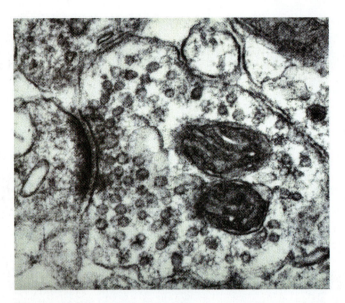

Figure 2–25 *An Electron Micrograph of Mitochondria.* The mitochondrion is the site of aerobic metabolism. The high energy consumption used in synaptic events explains the presence of many mitochondria in the boutons, as shown in the micrograph.

ing along the tracks much like train cars in line. Among the particles that move are small membranous spheres that *pinch off* from the rough endoplasmic reticulum and move to the Golgi apparatus. These are essentially bags of water and other materials within the plasma membrane and are called **vesicles** (Figure 2–27).

Exocytosis and Endocytosis

As vesicles in orthograde transport approach the plasma membrane they can become coated with a protein called **clathrin**. Normally, the two membranes would repel one another, since the phosphate groups on the lipid molecules in each are negatively charged (recall from your high-school physics course, "like charges repel"; see Chapter 3). However, with clathrin, calcium, and the consumption of ATP, the vesicle membrane and the plasma membrane can draw quite close and ultimately *fuse*. This process is called **exocytosis** (*exo* = outside, *cyto* = cell) since, as a moment's reflection on Figure 2–28 will reveal, *the fluid contents of the vesicle will be released into the extracellular fluid.* Also, during exocytosis any membrane-bound protein in the vesicle mem-

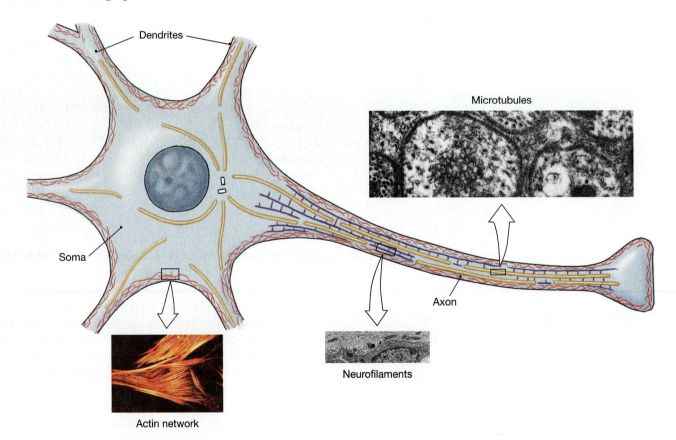

Figure 2–26 *Axonal Cytoskeleton.* The cytoskeleton of the neuron is of special significance in both support and transport. The neurofilaments help maintain cell shape and integrity, whereas the microtubules and certain associated proteins (RR tracks and ties shown in cross section) are important in the transport of materials to and from the soma. Cell strengthening actin filaments are concentrated just under the plasma membrane around the cell perimeter. (Hall, 1992)

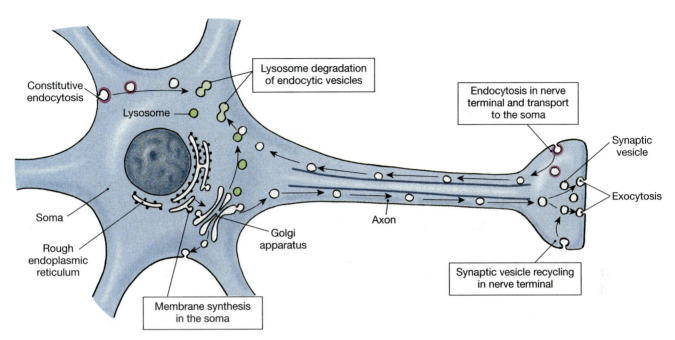

Figure 2–27 *The Movement of Vesicles in an Axon.* Newly synthesized membrane and membrane proteins travel from the Golgi apparatus to the cell membrane in the form of a vesicle where exocytosis takes place. Axonal transport, occurring in all neurites, aids in neurite growth and maintenance. Proteins are transported along the cytoskeletal structure to reach distant locations. If the proteins are moving away from the soma it is called orthograde transport. Conversely, retrograde transport occurs when the protein is moving toward the soma.

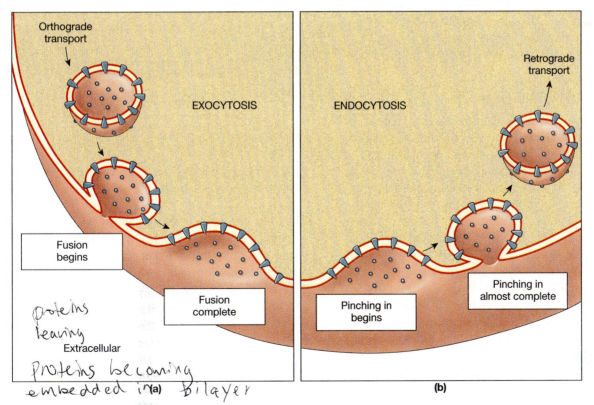

Figure 2–28 *Exocytosis and Endocytosis.* During exocytosis (a), contents from the intracellular medium are released into the extracellular medium. During endocytosis (b), contents from the extracellular medium are brought into the cell.

Figure 2–29 *The Neuron in Development.*
(a) During axon growth, exocytosis exceeds endocytosis. (b) When an axon makes contact with an inappropriate target, the axon must withdraw, causing endocytosis to exceed exocytosis. (c) When an axon reaches its destination, the membrane specialization is maintained as exocytosis is balanced with endocytosis.

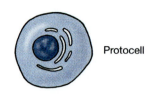

Protocell

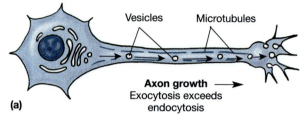

Vesicles   Microtubules

(a) **Axon growth** →
Exocytosis exceeds
endocytosis

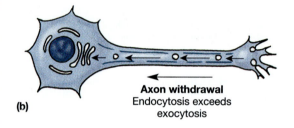

(b) **Axon withdrawal**
Endocytosis exceeds
exocytosis

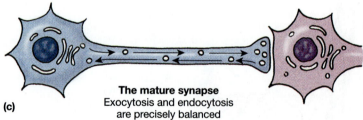

(c) **The mature synapse**
Exocytosis and endocytosis
are precisely balanced

brane will become embedded in the plasma membrane because of fusion of the two membranes. The orientation of such protein will be such that the end that points in to the vesicle interior will point *out* of the cell after exocytosis takes place. (Now you know how receptors arise in the plasma membrane after synthesis in the endoplasmic reticulum). Contents within the vesicle fluid, such as some *hormones* synthesized by neuron cell bodies, are also released into the exterior by a consequence of exocytosis called **secretion**, defined as the liberation of the vesicle contents into the outside water environment.

The opposite of exocytosis (and the opposite of secretion) also occurs. This is called **endocytosis** (see Figure 2–28) and entails a piece of the plasma membrane pinching back to form a new vesicle (and taking a bit of the outside material back into the inside of the cell). Both endocytosis and exocytosis are very important in the function of the synapse. They are also very important in synapse *formation*, or the normal *development* of nerve cells and their connections, as we shall see in the next section.

The Neuron in Development

Embryonic nerve cells begin life having a visual appearance very much like the ancient protocell. They are spherical or cube-shaped and lack axons, dendrites, and synapses. Very early in embryonic development, however, they begin to send out neuritic processes, transiently encountering other cells, and extending the fibers throughout neural as well as nonneural tissue. As elongation occurs, structural protein making up the neurofilaments and neurotubules must be added to the end and new membrane must be inserted into the growing tip. Thus in axon growth, (Figure 2–29), *exocytosis exceeds endocytosis*. From time to time the axon encounters an inappropriate target or region of neural tissue and withdraws back to the cell body. In such case *endocytosis will exceed exocytosis* at the tip until withdrawal is complete. Finally, for many but not all cells, contact with the proper partner or **target cell** occurs and a mature synapse is formed. For this mature synapse, and for the lifetime of the organism as long as the synapse exists, *exocytosis and endocytosis are precisely balanced*. Each act of exocytosis must be accompanied by an equal act of endo-

cytosis or else the bouton at the tip would blow up like a balloon or shrivel like a raisin.

The Chemoaffinity Hypothesis. What causes an axon (or dendrite) to elongate in a particular direction, to withdraw, or to maintain a synaptic contact throughout life? Recall that *exocytosis* releases a bit of the cell interior to the outside and *endocytosis* takes a little sample of the outside in. One mechanism that has been proposed for guidance of axon elongation and synapse formation is called the **chemoaffinity hypothesis**, since it proposes that chemical signals are exchanged between potential synaptic partners, perhaps by endocytosis and exocytosis, and that these signals determine attraction. The affinity of cells for one another, both as they are being drawn together and as they maintain their association, is called a *trophic interaction* and hence the postulated chemical signals are called **trophic factors**. Such

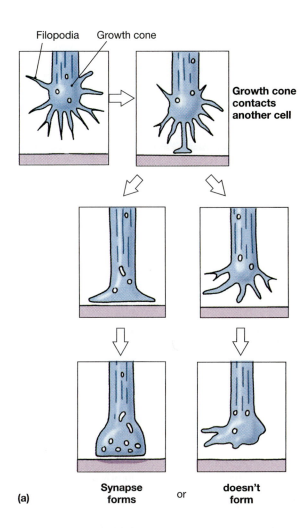

(a)

Filopodia   Growth cone

Growth cone contacts another cell

Synapse forms   or   doesn't form

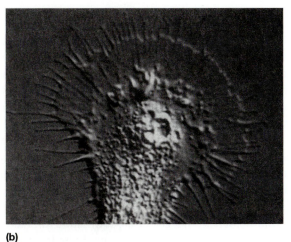

(b)

Figure 2–30 *The Growth Cone.* (a) During neuron development and growth, the tip of an axon or the growth cone sends out little extensions called filopodia, which, through trophic interactions, determine the path the axon should follow. Either a synapse will form or fail to form. (b) Micrograph of a growth cone in cell culture.

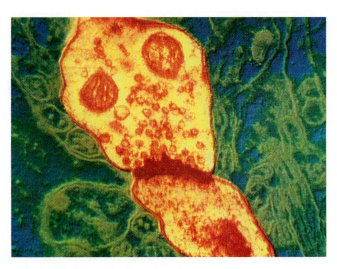

Figure 2–31 *The Presynaptic and Postsynaptic Densities.* This electron micrograph of a synapse shows the abundance of protein found in the presynaptic and postsynaptic regions of the neuron.

interactions have been likened to the role of cologne or perfume in the initiation and continuance of human romance.

The chemoaffinity hypothesis explains a great deal of what goes on during neural development and has some compelling experimental support. For example, for axon elongation in the autonomic nervous system a protein trophic factor called **nerve growth factor** is secreted by potential postsynaptic cells and draws forth innervation from potential presynaptic partners (see Box 15–1). Axon growth of this type can actually be visualized in living cells in the light microscope (Figure 2–30). The tip of the growing axon, called a **growth cone**, sends out little extensions in various directions (called **filopodia** or "finger feet") that seem, anthropomorphically, to be "sniffing" gradients of potential trophic attractants. From time to time tiny fibrils called *microspikes* are sent forth, much like a grappling hook, to draw the axon tip toward a potential mate. The advancing growth cone withdraws from some cells and is drawn towards others in the target cells. Finally, when the appropriate contact is made, the filopodia withdraw. Exocytosis on each side of the emerging synapse then fills a second type of trophic function. Protein is inserted into the plasma membrane on both sides. We know this because the inside and outside parts of membrane-bound protein are charged, and the protein takes up electron-dense metal stains. The region of increased protein concentration appears in the electron microscope as darker or more dense and hence when these dense areas are found in the presynaptic or postsynaptic domains, the regions are called the **presynaptic density** and the **postsynaptic density**, respectively (Figure 2–31). The presynaptic density probably is made up largely of proteins, such as calcium channels, that prepare the bouton for synaptic transmission (Chapter 5). The postsynaptic density is probably made up of proteins, like receptors, that prepare the dendrite for arrival of the synaptic signal.

Up-Regulation and Down-Regulation.   Even after the mature synapse is formed, the trophic influence is maintained between the cells. When death or disease of one cell or the other disrupts the trophic influence, the intact partner is also disrupted. When, for example, the presynaptic cell puts out less trophic influence one consequence is expression of *more* receptor in the postsynaptic cell in a process known as **up-regulation.** Up-regulation allows the postsynaptic cell to be more sensitive to declining quantities of synaptic transmitter. Up-regulation can produce a state of *denervation supersensitivity*, since the postsynaptic membrane becomes so sensitive to any transmitter present. **Down-regulation** also occurs, as when there is an excess of trophic influence that produces a reduction in postsynaptic receptor numbers. In a mechanism similar to up-regulation, down-regulation allows the postsynaptic cell to become less sensitive to increased quantities of synaptic transmitter. These trophic influences have numerous clinical correlates; denervation supersensitivity has been proposed as a potential mechanism for *phantom-limb pain* (pain felt as arising from a limb that has been amputated). Down-regulation has been suggested to be a potential mechanism for *drug addiction* (more and more drug is needed to achieve the same effect because of the decrease in sensitivity of the postsynaptic cell which has been bombarded) and *withdrawal* (failure of native transmitter to activate a reduced population of receptors after down-regulation has occurred in response to excess stimulation by the drug).

Testing the Chemoaffinity Hypothesis.   The chemoaffinity hypothesis can also be used to explain trophic interactions in simple developing systems involving only a few different candidates for the presynaptic and postsynaptic cells. Postsynaptic structures are exposed to a number of incoming axons; the potential presynaptic partners appear to "compete" for postsynaptic trophic factor. In the synapses made by motor neurons on muscle cells, for example, a large number of synaptic contacts are made at first, with each postsynaptic muscle fiber innervated by several presynaptic motor neurons. Later, as competition among the presynaptic elements for (presumably) limited supply of postsynaptic trophic factor intensifies, extraneous motor neuron contacts are withdrawn

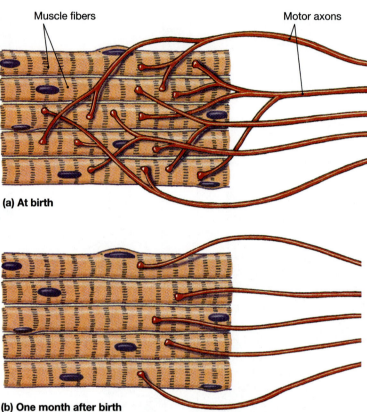

(a) At birth

(b) One month after birth

Figure 2–32   *Competition for Trophic Factors.* (a) At birth, each muscle fiber is innervated by several presynaptic motor neurons. (b) One month following birth, trophic factor competition causes all extraneous contacts to withdraw. (Hall, 1992)

leaving each muscle cell innervated by a single axon, which is the situation that endures throughout the adult life of all vertebrates (Figure 2–32). Similarly, ingrowing sensory cell axons appear to innervate many postsynaptic cells in the spinal cord at first, but subsequently withdraw extra contacts until only a few postsynaptic cells are innervated by each sensory cell.

In the central nervous system, however, the burden of chemoaffinity becomes much more complex. Millions of axons in, say, the optic nerve all have to find their appropriate targets and these are all jammed together into a tiny piece of brain. Can there really be such a great variety of central "colognes" that each unique synaptic interaction is mediated by one of them? Experiments by Roger Sperry (same Sperry as for the split-brain studies in Chapter 1) are indicative that, at least in some cases, chemoaffinity also seems to explain central nervous system development. Sperry made use of the fact that salamanders and other amphibians have brains that can regenerate new connections

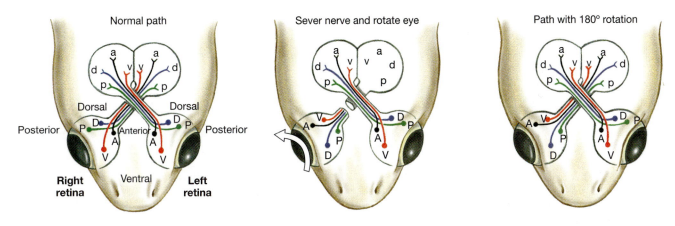

Figure 2–33   *Chemoaffinity on the CNS.* In the salamander, different regions of the eye (A, P, V, and D) innervate different regions in the brain (a, p, v, and d, respectively). When Roger Sperry extracted, rotated 180°, and reinserted the salamander eye, the fibers that were generated formed contacts with their original, correct brain regions, demonstrating the presence of trophic interactions.

throughout life (Sperry, 1963). (Other vertebrate brains, including ours, are unable to do so for reasons I will explain shortly). Normally, different regions of the salamander eye (labeled A, P, V, and D in Figure 2–33) innervate corresponding regions of a brain region called the tectum (labeled a, p, v, and d). Sperry extracted one eye from an adult salamander, rotated it 180°, and reinserted it, allowing the fibers to grow back towards the tectum. He reasoned that if the fibers were merely following some sort of mechanical program ("go in 3mm, turn left, go 1mm, and make a synapse") then the fibers of the rotated eye would make reversed contacts in the tectum (i.e., A with p, P with a, and so forth). If, on the other hand, the ingrowing axons followed some trophic cologne to find their partners then the *same* connections would be made as if the eye had not been rotated (A with a, P with p, etc.) even though the route taken by the axons would be different ("right" instead of "left"). In fact, the fibers found their proper, original targets, just as if they recognized them chemically by detecting a gradient of diffuse trophic factor. (Quick, figure out what the world looks like to a salamander with *both* eyes rotated, before the answer is provided at the end of this paragraph). Subsequent experiments showed that the trophic influence on incoming optic nerve fibers is so intense that they can be induced to grow through central tissue in a completely absurd direction (e.g., up to the tectum from the spinal cord) if guided by appropriated trophic influences. The trophic factors, if present, must be in very small quantities and have yet to be chemically identified for brain synapses. (Answer: The world looks upside down and backward to a salamander with both eyes rotated. Such salamanders will always orient away from food and must be force-fed. Ironically, people with inverted

visual worlds [this is accomplished with goggles, not by inverting the eye!] are able to adapt by mentally rotating the appearance of the outside world until it looks normal. It seem paradoxical that salamanders, which *can* make new connections throughout life, *cannot* rotate the visual world, whereas people, who are *unable* to make new connections in adulthood, *can* rotate the world. Think about this conundrum before we revisit it in Box 15–2.)

The search for trophic factors within the central nervous system, not only for axon elongation and *synaptogenesis* (synapse formation) but also for other developmental events, is a very exciting area of current research. Progress is hampered, however, by several factors. First, cells in the brain of vertebrates other than amphibia do not regenerate in adulthood. Damage to the brain, therefore, is *structurally* irreversible. The reasons for this are obscure, but appear to involve the *glial cells* that support central neurons. In the PNS, nerve coating or **myelin** is provided by glial cells called **Schwann cells**, each separated by a patch of unmyelinated membrane called a **node of Ranvier** (Figure 2–34). Each Schwann cell is associated with a single axon; when that axon is severed it reacts promptly to form a tube to guide the regenerating axon to its target. However, myelin in the CNS is provided by different glial cells, **oligodendrites**, each of which supplies *several* axons, not just one. This additional duty was made necessary by the need, in evolution, to compress more neural structures into the skull as lifestyles became more complex. Perhaps because the myelin of oligodendrites cannot distinguish among axons, it fails to respond when one axon is injured, merely collapsing about the remains and forming a tough, leathery barrier to any attempt at regeneration. This problem with the CNS of most vertebrates both

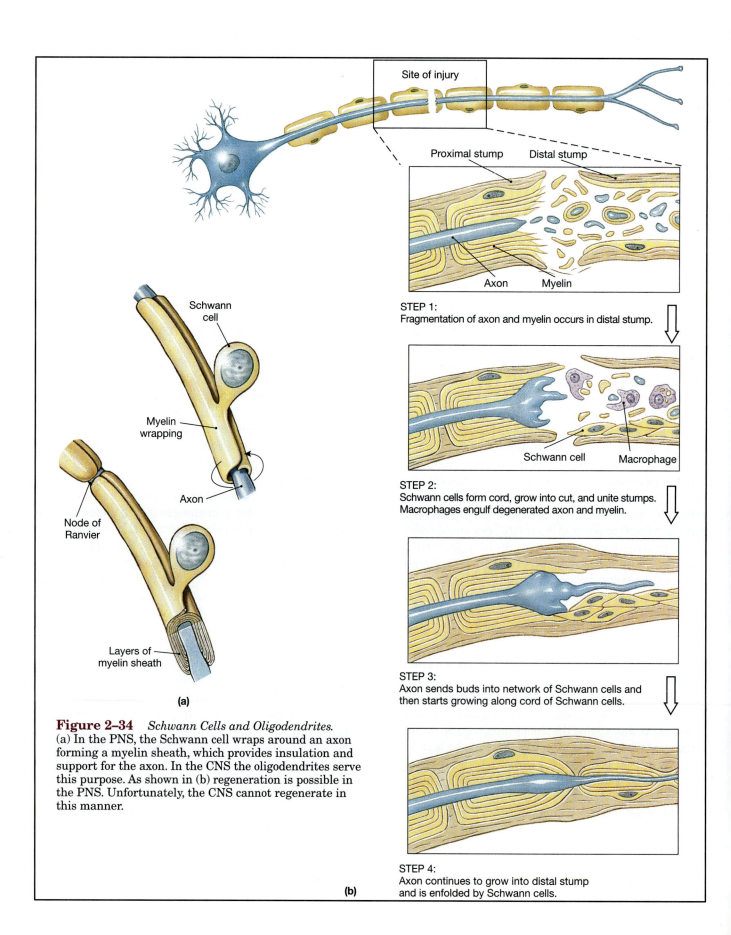

Site of injury

Proximal stump   Distal stump

Axon   Myelin

STEP 1:
Fragmentation of axon and myelin occurs in distal stump.

Schwann cell   Macrophage

STEP 2:
Schwann cells form cord, grow into cut, and unite stumps.
Macrophages engulf degenerated axon and myelin.

STEP 3:
Axon sends buds into network of Schwann cells and
then starts growing along cord of Schwann cells.

STEP 4:
Axon continues to grow into distal stump
and is enfolded by Schwann cells.

Schwann
cell

Myelin
wrapping

Axon

Node of
Ranvier

Layers of
myelin sheath

(a)

(b)

Figure 2–34 *Schwann Cells and Oligodendrites.*
(a) In the PNS, the Schwann cell wraps around an axon
forming a myelin sheath, which provides insulation and
support for the axon. In the CNS the oligodendrites serve
this purpose. As shown in (b) regeneration is possible in
the PNS. Unfortunately, the CNS cannot regenerate in
this manner.

poses an obstacle to further investigation of trophic interactions (e.g., making Sperry's experiment impossible to perform on mammals in most cases) and makes the case for pursuing such investigation very compelling, since if the barrier to reinnervation could be overcome effective cures for brain damage might be envisioned.

A second barrier to the application of the chemoaffinity hypothesis to the brain lies in the results of the most recent developmental work. This research indicates that trophic effects are intimately associated with the *electrical activity* of neuron membranes and may even be mediated by such activity. In order to better understand modern theories of development we must consider the nerve cell in its *working environment*; one with synaptic signals arriving and departing and carrying information from one part of the brain to another. Let's now turn to the basis for communications among nerve cells, that is, the electrical signals involved in the *membrane potential* (Chapter 3), the *action potential* (Chapter 4), and the *synaptic potential* (Chapter 5), before returning with greater understanding to development in Chapter 15.

SUMMARY

Major developments in the history of neuroscience were accompanied by parallel contemporary accomplishments in other fields of endeavor. Light microscopy produced a theory that the brain was made up of continuous filaments. This theory became known as reticular theory. Application of the Golgi impregnation technique led to a compelling theory, the neuron doctrine, which held that the brain was, like other tissue, made up of discrete cells called neurons. Ramón y Cajal made a thorough study of neuron structure and named parts of the cell based on their postulated function: dendrite for receiving information, soma for metabolic support, axon and bouton for transmission of information. His theory, the law of dynamic polarization, and the neuron doctrine became widely accepted and are known today to be generally correct. The plasma membrane is the boundary between neurons and the extracellular environment. It is made up of amphipathic phospholipids that create a hydrophobic barrier that prevents passage of most ions and other charged substances. Passage of ions, nutrients, and other metabolites requires carrier proteins known as channels and pumps. These become inserted into the membrane after synthesis in the rough endoplasmic reticulum. On the ribosomes, mRNA, transcribed from the DNA template in the genome, directs translation of the genetic code into the sequence of amino acids in proteins. Among the proteins are structural proteins that give shape to the cell, enzymes that catalyze chemical reactions, and receptors that receive chemical signals outside the cell. The neuron continuously engages in axoplasmic transport of vesicles to and from the soma. Vesicles also participate in exocytosis, releasing their contents into the outside space, and are formed by the process of endocytosis which draws a small amount of extracellular fluid into the cell. These processes are immensely important in development as well as in synaptic transmission, as trophic signals are exchanged between potential synaptic partners. Nonneural cells, such as Schwann cells and oligodendrites, also have a major trophic role in regeneration in the PNS and normal development. Chemoaffinity describes many developmental events, but others are related intimately to the electrical activity of the neuron membrane, as we shall see in subsequent chapters.

REVIEW QUESTIONS

1. Describe the difference between the neuron doctrine and the reticular theory.

2. What is the silver impregnation technique?

3. Which way did Ramón y Cajal imagine information flows across the neuron?

4. How does the synapse relate to the law of dynamic polarization?

5. Which part of the cell membrane is hydrophilic? hydrophobic?

6. Describe the structure of DNA.

7. Describe the structure of protein.

8. How do enzymes differ from receptors? How are they similar?

9. Contrast exocytosis and endocytosis.

10. What is a trophic factor?

THOUGHT QUESTIONS

1. What is the main structural difference between neurons and other cells?

2. Of the amino acids shown on page 30, five appear to be especially important in communication between neurons. Guess which ones and provide your reasoning.

KEY CONCEPTS

acetyl-CoA (p. 35)
actin (p. 32)
actin filaments (p. 37)
adenine (p. 27)
aerobic metabolism (p. 35)
affinity (p. 32)
amino acids (p. 28)
amphipathic (p. 25)
ATP (p. 33)
axon (p. 21)
axon hillock (p. 21)
axoplasmic transport (p. 36)
bilayer (p. 25)
binding sites (p. 32)
bouton (p. 21)
cell membrane (p. 19)
cell theory (p. 19)
cerebrospinal fluid (CSF) (p. 33)
channels (p. 26)
chemoaffinity hypothesis (p. 40)
chromosomes (p. 21)
clathrin (p. 38)
codon (p. 29)
co-enzymes (p. 32)
cytoplasm (p. 19)
cytosine (p. 27)
cytoskeleton (p. 19)
cytosol (p. 19)
dendrites (p. 21)
dendritic spines (p. 21)
DNA (p. 28)

double helix (p. 28)
down-regulation (p. 42)
electron microscope (p. 25)
endocytosis (p. 23)
endoplasmic reticulum (p. 21)
enzymes (p. 31)
exocytosis (p. 38)
extracellular environment
    (p. 24)
fast transport (p. 37)
filopodia (p. 41)
fluid mosaic (p. 26)
genes (p. 28)
genetic code (p. 29)
glia (p. 18)
glycolysis (p. 33)
glycoproteins (p. 32)
Golgi apparatus (p. 21)
gray matter (p. 18)
growth cone (p. 41)
guanine (p. 27)
hydrophilic (p. 25)
hydrophobic (p. 25)
integration (p. 20)
interneurons (p. 24)
intracellular environment
    (p. 24)
ions (p. 24)
law of dynamic polarization
    (p. 23)
ligand (p. 32)

light microscope (p. 25)
metabolites (p. 33)
microfilaments (p. 21)
microtubules (p. 21)
mitochondria (p. 21)
motor cells (p. 24)
mRNA (p. 29)
myelin (p. 43)
NADH (p. 35)
nerve growth factor (p. 41)
neurites (p. 20)
neurofilaments (p. 37)
neuron doctrine (p. 19)
neurons (p. 19)
node of Ranvier (p. 43)
nucleus (p. 19)
oligodendrites (p. 43)
orthograde transport (p. 37)
peptide bond (p. 29)
peptide hormones (p. 31)
perikaryon (p. 19)
phospholipids (p. 25)
plasma membrane (p. 21)
polymers (p. 27)
postsynaptic density (p. 41)
postsynaptic side (p. 23)
presynaptic density (p. 41)
presynaptic side (p. 23)
products (p. 32)
promoters (p. 28)
protein (p. 26)

protocells (p. 25)
pumps (p. 26)
pyruvate (p. 35)
receptors (p. 31)
reticular theory (p. 19)
retrograde transport (p. 37)
ribosomes (p. 21)
RNA (p. 27)
Schwann cells (p. 43)
secretion (p. 40)
sensory cells (p. 23)
silver impregnation technique
    (p. 20)
slow transport (p. 37)
soma (pl. somata) (p. 20)
stereochemical attraction
    (p. 32)
substrates (p. 32)
synapse (p. 19)
target cell (p. 40)
thymine (p. 28)
transcription (p. 29)
translation (p. 29)
transmitters (p. 32)
tRNA (p. 29)
trophic factors (p. 40)
tubulin (p. 32)
up-regulation (p. 42)
uracil (p. 27)
vesicles (p. 38)
white matter (p. 18)

In all things in nature there is something marvelous.

Aristotle (384–322 B.C.) Parts of Animals, book 1

3

Communication Among Neurons: The Membrane Potential

By now, you have undoubtedly concluded that the nervous system is quite complex. Perhaps, like some early anatomists, you feel that unraveling the "seamless warp" is so daunting a task as to be hopeless. Identifying the function of but a single synapse among the billions in the brain is a task not unlike finding a needle in the proverbial haystack.

Fortunately, there are approaches to the analysis of the nervous system other than Ramón y Cajal's "step-by-step" strategy, and many of these provide an understanding of the brain that is very much simpler than the actual connectivity patterns of neurons. In this chapter we begin to explore the manner in which neurons communicate with one another. In contrast to the almost unfathomable intricacy of cell networks, we shall see that almost all of brain function can be explained by reference to three fundamental forces. These forces, the potassium battery, the sodium battery, and the chloride battery, never change in our bodies from birth to death. Indeed, we shall see how these forces, or some version of them, must be the same for all nervous systems everywhere, even on other planets.

At the end of this chapter and in the next two chapters, we shall investigate the circumstances in which these forces are allowed to exert their influence. Each force has a gate. When the gate is open the force is at work, and when it is closed the force is at rest. Although there are a number of signals that can cause the gates to open and shut, an initial understanding of just three forces and three types of gates will bring us far toward an understanding of how the brain controls behavior.

The Basics of Chemistry

To explain the forces the following section gives a brief review of the necessary background, much of which you may remember from your

47

Figure 3–1 *Molecules and Ions.* (a) The water molecule has an overall neutral charge. However, due to the electrophilic (electron-loving) nature of oxygen, a water molecule may separate itself to form two ions: the hydroxide ion (⁻OH) with a negative charge and a hydrogen ion (H+) with a positive charge. (b) A similar phenomenon occurs with molecular salt. In an aqueous environment the molecular form of salt dissociates into two ions: the positively charged sodium cation and the negatively charged chloride anion. It is this characteristic that is responsible for salt's ability to dissolve in liquid.

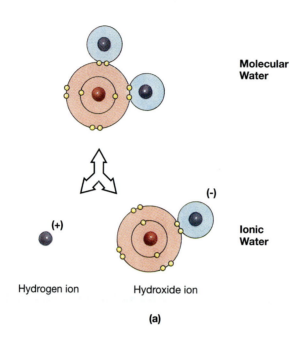

Molecular Water

(-)

Ionic Water

Hydrogen ion   Hydroxide ion

(a)

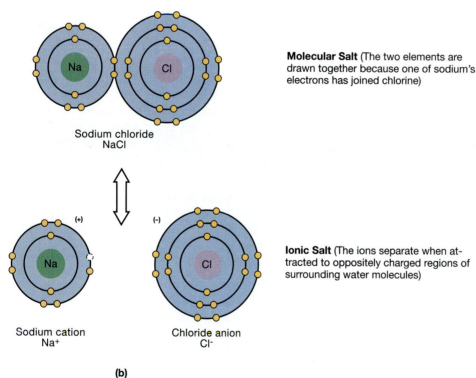

Sodium chloride
NaCl

Molecular Salt (The two elements are drawn together because one of sodium's electrons has joined chlorine)

Ionic Salt (The ions separate when attracted to oppositely charged regions of surrounding water molecules)

Sodium cation
Na⁺

Chloride anion
Cl⁻

(b)

atoms to form aggregates called molecules.

Much life exists in the ocean, which is an enormous reservoir of water, and the rest of the living things on this planet that have left the ocean for life on land appear to have carried off their own stores of water which make up the majority of the body size and weight for each organism. For the very tiny processes we are about to consider, even the smallest gnat should be considered, like the ocean, to be a vast reservoir of water. The water molecule (Figure 3–1a) is made up of a single atom of oxygen and two atoms of hydrogen held (because of the orbital structure of the oxygen atom) at an angle. But water is a substance of variable characteristics, and it is partly this variability that makes life possible in aqueous, or watery, environments. For example, sometimes a hydrogen molecule pulls away from the oxygen leaving an electron behind (as it happens, for hydrogen this abandoned electron is the only one it possessed). Because electrons have a single unit of negative electrical charge, the oxygen and hydrogen left behind acquire a net negative charge and the free hydrogen (less the negative charge) has a positive charge. These atoms and molecules that have lost or gained an electron (or electrons) are called **ions**.

Those that have lost electrons (and hence are positively charged) are called **cations** (pronounced cat-ion) and those that have gained electrons are called **anions** (pronounced an-ion). Only a portion of the water in each vast reservoir undergoes this transformation, and for various reasons the amount of hydrogen cation can exceed the amount of oxygen/hydrogen anion (or "hydroxide") left behind. The amount of hydrogen ion in a given reservoir of water is expressed on a logarithmic scale called the **pH scale**. Low values of pH correspond to a large proportion of hydrogen cations relative to hydroxide anions and are considered acidic. High values cor-

high-school chemistry class. All matter is formed of atoms, and each atom belongs to a family of identical particles called elements. Each element is distinguished from the others by the structure of its positively charged nucleus and by the number of negatively charged particles, or electrons, that orbit the nucleus. Atoms of most elements have a vacancy in one or more electron orbitals and this creates a tendency for atoms of this type to bond together with other

respond to a smaller proportion of hydrogen cations and are considered basic. The ocean and the water in our bodies tend to be neutral in pH. In other words, there is about the same amount of hydrogen cations and hydroxide anions, with the great bulk of the water in the intact or molecular form.

What else is in the ocean besides water? One thinks of "fish" or, unfortunately for these times, "garbage," but in fact the largest component of sea water, besides water itself, is salt. Table salt exists in the molecular form of a bond between two elements, but this only happens after all the water has been evaporated away. In the ocean (and the body) it adopts ionic characteristics just like water itself except that *virtually all of the salt falls apart*. When salt is in the molecular form, we write it "NaCl" for "sodium chloride," but in water all of the sodium exists as free cation separate from chloride, and all of chloride exists as free anion (Figure 3–1b). A note on nomenclature: Most of the elements that will concern us have sensible abbreviations; O for oxygen, H for Hydrogen, C for Carbon, Ca for Calcium, S for Sulfur, P for Phosphorus, and so forth. Unfortunately, the abbreviations for sodium, Na, and potassium, K, come from the Latin names for these substances, which most of us have forgotten if we ever knew them in the first place. So you will need to exercise your synapses to memorize them, hopefully tucking them away in long term memory.

Opposite Charges Attract

Just as there is a force that drives particles apart (as when salt dissolves in water) so there is a force that brings them together (as when salt forms in crystals after sea water evaporates). Particles never coalesce randomly, however. A principle of nature determines that a sodium cation will coalesce with a chloride anion but never, for example, with another sodium cation. This principle, simply stated, is that *opposite charges attract and like charges repel*. This is true both for individual charges on ions and for substantial charges on larger structures. When a substantial charge accumulates on a structure, we name that structure according to which ions it attracts. A negatively charged surface attracts positive ions (cations); hence we call such a surface a **cathode**. A positively charged surface attracts negative ions (anions) and hence is termed an **anode** (Figure 3–2).

Quantity and Concentration

What if we wished to describe the *amount* of salt in the sea? This would be a very large number, so we might want to sample a volume of sea water, determine the amount, and then multiply for larger volumes. Even so, we would have a choice between counting the number of particles (mass) or, since salt is exclusively ionic in the ocean, the amount of charge.

Let's begin with number of particles. By convention, the unit for quantities of gas, liquid, and solid are expressed as **moles** (not to be confused with gophers). In terms of actual numbers, a mole is quite large, around 6×10^{23} actual particles of the substance being measured. However with salts and, as it turns out, just about everything else we will consider in this text, actual amounts are not nearly as important as *concentrations*. This is because we are dealing with events that take place in living organisms that involve interactions between dissolved solids in a liquid environment. So, we define a certain concentration of solid dissolved in liquid as "one mole per liter" and call such a solution a **molar** solution. In actual practice, the biological events we will be discussing tend to involve quantities a thousandfold less than the unit in question, so we give these quantities the prefix *milli-* (hence *millimolar* for concentration, millivolts for charge, milliseconds for time, and so forth). Table 3–1 gives a summary of this and other forms of shorthand scientific notation. For our purposes we will rarely have need for these units, quantities, and abbreviations below the 10^{-6} level, but it is obvious that should the occasion arise we could be quite impressive as we describe quantities that are infinitesimally small. At a party you could ask your friends, "How many particles are in a femtomole?" and amaze them with the answer, if they stick around that long.

A Semipermeable Membrane

You will recall from Chapter 2 that each cell (including the neuron) is enveloped by a lipid membrane (mainly phospholipids) that forms the boundary between the cell and its environment, whether this environment is sea water, blood, or whatever. Because the membrane has a *hydrophobic* region

Table 3–1	**Common Scientific Units**		
Prefix	Concentration Molar (M)	Time Second (s)	Charge Volt (V)
milli- (10^{-3})	mM	msec	mV
micro- (10^{-6})	μM	μsec	μV
nano- (10^{-9})	nM	nsec	nV
pico- (10^{-12})	pM	psec	pV
femto- (10^{-15})	fM	fsec	fV

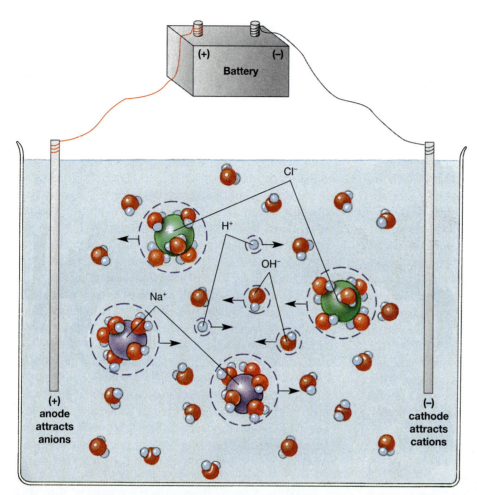

Table 3–2 provides actual quantities for the pertinent ion types for the intracellular region and the extracellular region of a model neuron. For comparison, the composition of blood is also shown. Sea water *itself* is the extracellular medium for many single-celled animals that live in the ocean (Figure 3–3).

One thing that is immediately apparent from Table 3–2 is the similarity between the two types of extracellular environments, sea water and blood. Biologists explain this similarity by reminding us that early evolution took place within the ocean, and that land-dwelling animals carry with them sufficient "sea water" (blood) outside of cells to provide an extracellular environment consistent with their origins.

Secondly, note that the relative concentration of the two major cations, potassium and sodium, are quite different on the inside of the cell and on the outside. The intracellular environment is rich in potassium, whereas the extracellular environment is proportionally richer in sodium ion. Perhaps this came about because early cells (protocells) formed their cell membranes in a restricted, potassium-rich reservoir of water, such as a lake or tide pool, and were subsequently washed out to sea. We are not sure how this happened since nobody was there to observe it; but some terrestrial environments are potassium rich and all the ocean is sodium-rich, so it is likely that the protocell formed in a body of fresh water. At any rate, this pattern is found in all animals. Though the data in Table 3–2 happens to be taken from a squid, similar values are observed in the cells of any organism.

Left out of Table 3–2 is the concentration of organic ions (proteins, amino acids, and nucleic acids among them) on the inside of cells, many of which are anions and take the place of chloride in balancing the charge of the cationic species. The contribution of these organic anions yields perfectly equal amounts of total dissolved particles on both sides, and virtually complete charge balance between anions and cations.

Figure 3–2 *Anode and Cathode.* In a water molecule, oxygen forms polar covalent bonds with two hydrogen atoms. Because the hydrogen atoms are positioned toward one end of the molecule, the molecule has an uneven distribution of charges. This creates a slight positive charge at one end and a slight negative charge at the other. The anode attracts negatively charged ions (anions) causing the hydroxide ion ($^-$OH) from the water molecule and the chloride ion (Cl^-) from the salt to migrate toward the electrode on the left. The cathode attracts cations (positively charged ions) causing the hydrogen ion (H^+) from water and the sodium (Na^+) from salt to migrate toward the electrode on the right. The ions serve to close a circuit so current can flow. In the cell, the two sides of the membrane serve the function of the electrodes with the inside being the cathode and the outside being the anode.

that separates the inside from the outside, no water can enter the membrane or cross it freely and *no ions of either charge can cross*. Only if there was a pore, or channel, across the hydrophobic membrane could such charged particles pass. Because of this barrier, it is possible for the chemical composition of the aqueous environment on the inside to become different from that on the outside and remain that way for a long time, and indeed it does. Hence when speaking of concentration, charge, or any other quantity or process we must be very careful to segregate the intracellular from the extracellular regions.

[handwritten: K + Na are cations — neg charged]

[handwritten: polymers = channel]

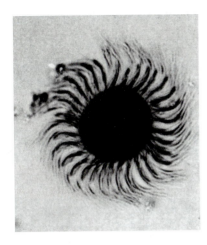

Figure 3–3
L. spiralis. The single
celled organism,
L. spiralis, has the
ocean as its
extracellular
environment.

Entropy and Enthalpy

Now imagine the primordial cell, rich in potassium, floating in an ocean of sea water, poised on the threshold of the
evolution of life on earth. Up to now little mystery is associated with the development of the protocell, since phospholipid can only associate in bilayers and these must form small
spheres in aqueous solution (Chapter 2). Scientists are just
beginning to get a glimmer of an idea of what happened next.
Very likely, one or more such membranous balls of saltwater
formed around molecules of ribonucleic acid (RNA), which
catalyzed enough chemical reactions with other organic *[handwritten: polymer]*
compounds to self-replicate and aid in the replication of the *[handwritten: allow]*
protocell (Cech, 1989). Among the molecules assembled in *[handwritten: only]*
this way were proteins, which are made of chains of amino *[handwritten: though]*
acids believed to have formed spontaneously in the primal sea
(Chapter 2), and among these proteins were some that inserted into the cell membrane, actually spanning the distance from the intracellular water to the extracellular water.

Figure 3–4a shows one such protein we believe might
have arisen early in the history of life. The ends of the chain
of amino acids lie within the intracellular region, but between
the ends there are six transmembrane strands that together
allow the protein to reach the outside. Obviously, the amino

acids in the transmembrane region must be hydrophobic (uncharged), and the amino acids on the inside and the outside
must be hydrophilic (charged) in nature. (Find examples of
uncharged and charged amino acids in Figure 2–16.) Proteins of the type shown in Figure 3–4 have the additional
property of being able to aggregate or combine. When alone,
the proteins are called **monomers**, and when they collect, the
aggregate is called a **polymer**. In the case of the protein shown
in Figure 3–4, four monomers join together to form a polymer, which then has no fewer than twenty-four transmembrane regions. (Please see Figure 2–21 for an explanation of
protein folding.)

The center of the polymer forms a hole that also spans
the membrane completely. Let us say that this hole is big
enough to allow the potassium cation through from one side
to the other but is not big enough to allow any of the other
charged or uncharged particles through. In other words, imagine that water, sodium ion, calcium ion, chloride ion, and so
forth are all too large to fit through the hole. (The actual principle of ion selectivity is quite a bit more complicated than
this, as we shall see, but for now imagine that the selectivity
is based on size). The protein would provide a passageway, or
channel, for the passage of potassium ions across the membrane. For this reason the polymeric protein is dubbed the
potassium channel. It exists not only in our imaginary protocell, but (in one form or another) in all cells everywhere.

Let us consider what consequence an open potassium
channel may have for the cell. Intuition tells us that potassium will pass through the potassium channel, but how much
potassium and in which direction, in or out? Here we must
make use of some laws of nature, known as the laws of thermodynamics. Explanations of these very fundamental laws
have a tendency to sound both grandiose and arcane, but appreciation of them can provide great insight into the ways of
the natural world. We encounter a manifestation of the laws
when we consider the very formation of ions. A force exists
that pulls apart molecular salt into separate ions, and there
is another opposite force that draws them back together ("opposite charges attract"). Every sin-
gle particle is subject, all the time,
to the pressure of both forces.

The first force, called **entropy**
is the measured degree of disorder
or chaos of a system. It is this force
that dissolves salt in water, sugar
in coffee, or *makes any system less
organized*. Although coffee that is
uniformly sweet may seem highly
organized to the drinker, in fact it
is more chaotic than a segregated

Table 3–2	CONCENTRATION IN mM		
Ion	Intracellular	Extracellular (Sea water)	Blood
potassium (K⁺)	400	10	20
sodium (Na⁺)	50	460	440
chloride (Cl⁺)	40	540	560
calcium (Ca⁺⁺)	0.1	10	10

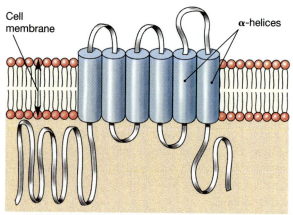

(a) **Components of one subunit**

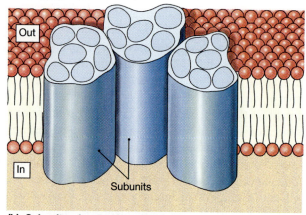

(b) **Subunits of potassium channel**

(c) **Four subunits aggregate to form potassium channel**

Figure 3–4   *The Potassium Channel.* (a) Note the six characteristic localized regions of alpha-helices in the secondary structure of the potassium channel. (b) The potassium channel embeds itself into the lipid bilayer. (c) The quaternary structure of the potassium channel as seen from the top shows a polymer consisting of four subunits. The subunits aggregate in such a way that a hole or pore remains which allows only potassium ions to pass. (Hille, 1992)

system with sugar on the bottom and unsweetened coffee above. A sugar crystal is more orderly than dispersed ions of sugar, and hence we describe the force that diffuses these ions as an "entropic" force. A colloquial version can be found in the saying "nature abhors a vacuum." A vacuum sucks air, fluid, and so forth into itself to fill the void, but it is equally accurate to think that *pressure* on the outside (entropy) forces it in. Entropy is precisely quantifiable (the units need not concern us here) and has the chemical effect of tending to even out differing concentration gradients. Thus particles (including charged ions) tend to flow from regions of high concentration to regions of low concentration in order to achieve the same concentration everywhere (like our uniformly sweetened coffee) by a process called **diffusion** (Figure 3–5).

What effect does entropy have on a membrane permeable to potassium ions alone (the semipermeable membrane)?

Entropy will push potassium ions *out* (down the concentration gradient), and the amount of "pushing" (precise quantity of entropy) will be determined by the difference in concentration outside and inside the membrane (Figure 3–6). Other factors may, in theory, enter into the force that pushes potassium out (e.g., temperature, as in our sweetened coffee example; sugar dissolves more readily in hot coffee than cold), but in actual systems these factors tend to be constant.

How far can this entropic force carry the potassium? Is it possible for the force of entropy to achieve equal potassium concentrations everywhere? This could be possible if potassium was uncharged, like sugar, or if no barrier existed to the passage of other ions, but in the protocell membrane potassium is the *only* particle that can pass, and each particle carries a positive charge. As entropy "pushes" ("pulls" is equally accurate) progressively more potassium cation out of the cell,

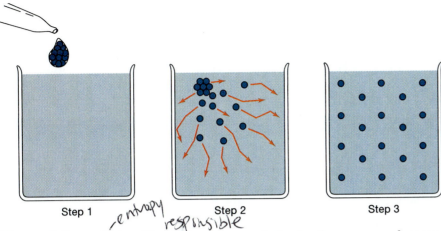

-entropy responsible

Figure 3–5 *Diffusion.* The random movement of molecules causes a substance to move further into areas where there are fewer molecules of its kind or from an area where it is in high concentration to an area where it is in low concentration. This process, called diffusion, ends with a uniform concentration throughout the available medium (water, air, coffee, etc.).

of the cell becomes negative and this pulls the positively charged potassium ions back in. This "electrostatic" force is a manifestation of the general thermodynamic force of enthalpy. Obviously, there will be a point at which the entropy and the force of enthalpy precisely balance each other, a process known as **equilibrium**. In fact, this happens for most cells after the passage of only a few thousand individual potassium ions. Given that there are vast numbers of potassium ions on both sides of the membrane (10^{21}/liter or more), the amount that cross before the balance is reached should be considered negligible. For more on entropy and enthalpy, see "Einstein and Thermodynamics" in the Appendix.

the inside of the cell becomes more negative (and the outside becomes more positive because of the addition of positively charged particles) (see Figure 3–6).

Now enthalpy comes into play (the aforementioned principle that "opposite charges attract"). The growing separation of charge across the membrane creates a charge gradient that tends to have an effect opposite to entropy. The inside

An "Equilibrium Potential" for Potassium

How can we quantify the point at which balance between entropic and electrostatic forces is achieved? Intuitively, we might expect that there would be two ways of specifying the point of balance. The precise amount of entropic force at the point of balance is primarily a function of the ratio of the con-

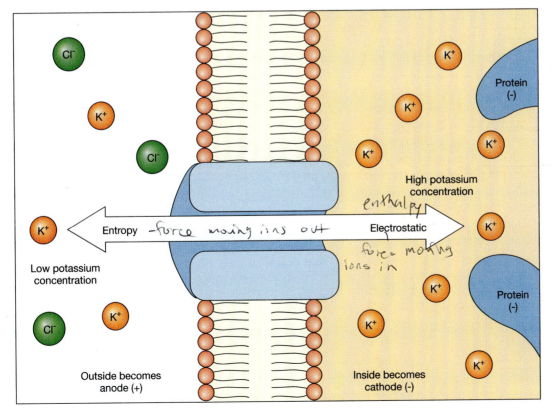

Figure 3–6 *Entropy and Electrostatic Forces Balance.* Because the inside of the cell is negative relative to the outside of the cell, the inside pulls positive ions (K^+) in. However, at the same time, the process of diffusion desires the outward movement of potassium in order to equalize the concentration differences of K^+ across the membrane. There exists a point where the force moving ions out (entropy) and the force moving ions in (electrostatic) balance each other and no net movement of K^+ will occur.

Box 3–1

The Nernst Equation and the Goldman Equation

Let's express concentrations for the various ions in brackets and, for shorthand, let's drop the plus and minus signs usually associated with positive and negative ions so they won't be confused with arithmetic procedures. Thus "the concentration of potassium cation on the outside of the cell" becomes expressed as $[K]_o$, the intracellular concentration of potassium becomes $[K]_i$, and the ratio we need for the *entropic force* becomes

$$\frac{[K]_o}{[K]_i}$$

We define a term E for the potential (electrical charge measured in millivolts) developed by a cell at the point of balance between entropy and enthalpy, or the point of "equilibrium." For the potential developed by a membrane permeable to potassium alone, let's use the notation E_K. Adding the constants and converting to a logarithmic scale, the potential can be related to the entropic force as follows:

$$E_K = \frac{RT}{zF} \ln \frac{[K]_o}{[K]_i}$$

where ln is the natural logarithm, R is the ideal gas constant, T is the absolute temperature (in degrees Kelvin), F is the faraday constant (the quantity of charge in a mole of ion), and z is the charge on each ion, which for potassium is one. Taken together, the expression relates the diffusion tendency (entropy) of a charged ion to the voltage (enthalpy) that develops as a consequence of its diffusion. This is called the Nernst equation after its creator (who developed it in ignorance of nerve cell physiology, by the way). Based only on the laws of thermodynamics, it applies with equal force to any semipermeable membrane, whether or not part of a living cell, and for any ion on this planet or any other one. Since the difference in absolute temperature between a warm body and a cold one (let's say a human and a squid) is negligible, and since R and F are constants, it is possible to create a simpler version of the Nernst equation by condensing these quantities. Converting to the more familiar base 10 logarithms in the process, we obtain

$$E_K = 58 \log \frac{[K]_o}{[K]_i}$$

Solving for the specific case of a known concentration gradient is easy (you will need a calculator with a log button or a set of log tables). Using values from Table 3–2:

$$E_K = 58 \log \frac{10}{400}$$

$$= -93 \text{ mV}$$

Thus, the inside of the cell must be 93 mV *more negative* than the outside for the electrostatic force to balance the diffusion force provided by the difference in concentration of potassium inside and outside the cell.

As indicated in the text, the Nernst equation applies to the calculation of the potential of any ion, not just potassium. In order to calculate the membrane potential, the contributions of potassium, sodium, and chloride must all be considered. This can be accomplished by applying the **Goldman equation:**

$$E_m = \frac{RT}{zF} \ln \frac{P_K[K]_o + P_{Na}[Na]_o + P_{Cl}[Cl]_i}{P_K[K]_i + P_{Na}[Na]_i + P_{Cl}[Cl]_o}$$

where P_K, P_{Na}, and P_{Cl} are the relative permeabilities for potassium, sodium, and chloride, respectively, in the ratio of 1 : 0.04 : 0.45. There is ambiguity in the z-value, which for sodium, and potassium is 1 and for chloride –1, but we dispense with this nuisance by inverting the ratio for chloride concentration in the final term (the logarithm of a ratio is equal to the negative logarithm of the reciprocal ratio). Therefore, the outside chloride concentration is in the denominator while the outside sodium and potassium concentrations are found in the numerator. Condensing the constants and converting to base 10 logarithms:

$$E_m = 58 \log \frac{P_K[K]_o + P_{Na}[Na]_o + P_{Cl}[Cl]_i}{P_K[K]_i + P_{Na}[Na]_i + P_{Cl}[Cl]_o}$$

Substituting the concentration values from Table 3–2 and the permeability ratios

$$E_m = 58 \log \frac{1[10] + 0.04[460] + 0.45[40]}{1[400] + 0.04[50] + 0.45[540]}$$

$$= -67 \text{mV}$$

centrations of potassium ion inside and outside the cell (plus terms for more-or-less invariant quantities like temperature and a constant that governs diffusion pressure). The precise amount of electrostatic force, or enthalpy, can be expressed as an electrical potential (the net difference in positive and negative charges) in volts (mV actually) that exists across the cell membrane at the point of balance. A formula expressing the balance would hence have a voltage term on one side of the equal sign and a concentration ratio (and constants) on the other side. The details of this formula, the Nernst Equation, are outlined in Box 3–1.

Measuring the Membrane Potential

In Box 3–1 we determined the *difference* in charge between the outside of the cell and the inside. If we measure the concentrations of potassium inside and outside the cell using the Nernst equation we can also calculate the theoretical *amount* of negative charge inside the cell caused by the exit of potassium. We could also use the equation to accomplish the *reverse process*, that is, to measure the potential and calculate the concentration gradient. In order for us to begin to understand how the cell uses simple natural laws to produce behavior, let's consider how these quantities can be measured directly.

Polarity and Ground

An **electrode** is inserted through the cell membrane and into the intracellular fluid in order to detect the charge on the inside of the cell. The inside of the electrode is made of material that conducts electricity easily but the outside of the electrode is made of material that will seal tightly to the cell membrane and not allow any leakage of potassium around the electrode itself. Often the electrode for intracellular recording is a very fine tube of glass filled with electrically conducting salt solution. The inside of the electrode is connected to one terminal of a device called an **electrometer**. For more on the workings of the electrometer and its components, see "The Electrometer" in the Appendix.

Charge gradients are relative. In other words, when we say a region (such as the inside of a cell) is "negative," we imply that this negativity is in relation to another region (such as the outside of the cell) that is more positive. The region of relative negativity could appear positive if compared to another reference point of even greater negativity. Thus physiologists (and everyone who deals with electricity) are careful to identify an external referent that is invariant to make the comparisons meaningful. This reference is called *ground* (or *earth* in Great Britain) and is quite literally a large metal rod driven down into the soil in the vicinity of your local power plant. In the laboratory and at home, we find ground as the bottom prong in the electrical outlet, which is

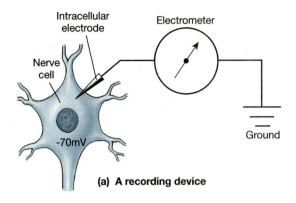

(a) A recording device

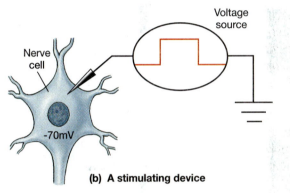

(b) A stimulating device

Figure 3–7   *Instrument Symbols.* (a) If one wanted to record the activity of a cell, one might use a recording device consisting of an electrometer connected to ground at one end and to a recording electrode at the other. (b) To stimulate a cell, one would use a voltage source connected to both ground and a stimulating electrode.

connected ultimately to the other terminal of the electrometer. Figure 3–7 shows the symbols for ground, an electrode, the electrometer, and another device used for *introducing* an electrical signal called the stimulator.

Certain aspects of the description of electrical circuits are arbitrary. This is not to say that the gradients and the forces that give rise to them are arbitrary or subject in the slightest to change by human convention. Merely the *language* we use to describe the circuit is arbitrary. For example, nothing forbids the experimenter from switching the terminals on the electrometer between ground and the electrode on the inside of the cell. In this configuration the electrometer would measure the charge of the outside world with reference to the inside of the cell, which is an equally accurate, if somewhat cumbersome, means of measuring the transmembrane electrical gradient. The alert reader will have noticed that one aspect of the Nernst equation is equally arbitrary, namely the choice of the outside concentration of potassium as the numerator and the inside as the denominator in the concentration ratio. Why not have it the other way around, that is, the inside over the out? This is perfectly valid as well, and solving the Nernst equation in this configuration would yield the potential of the outside world with reference to the inside of a cell that is semipermeable to potassium (i.e., +93 mV instead of –93 mV). With a number of different cells and ions it becomes difficult to discuss all these different influences on the potential of the world, so when we discuss intracellular potentials we will always discuss the inside with reference to ground. (Later in the context of extracellular potentials we will discuss forms of recording called "differential" recording where the referent is independent of ground).

Depolarization and Hyperpolarization

Another aspect of cell electricity that is subject to convention is the manner in which information about electrical events is displayed. The symbol for the electrometer (see Figure 3–7) implies that this information might simply be read from the face of a dial, but this would not be adequate to represent complex or fast events. In practice, data regarding events at the cell membrane are displayed as traces from an oscilloscope screen, which are *plots of voltage versus time* (Figure 3–8 and Appendix). We know that the membrane is usually "polarized" (one side is negative, the inside, and one side is positive, the outside), and we represent this negativity as a *downward* deflection of the oscilloscope trace. When an electrode is outside the cell, it only detects ground and thus the electrical difference is zero. Upon entry into the intracellular environment the new position of the trace represents the negative membrane polarity. We call this new

position the resting "membrane potential" since it has the potential to do electrical work in the form of generating currents. We can now define terms to describe changes in the membrane potential. Since the cell is polarized at rest any movement that decreases the difference in charge across the membrane is called **depolarization**. Movement of the membrane potential toward zero (any change that makes the inside of the cell more positive and hence decreases the charge difference between the inside and out) would be *depolarizing*. Any movement that increases the polarity (makes the inside of the cell more negative and hence increases the charge difference between the inside and out) we will call **hyperpolarization**. Depolarization is always represented as "up" on the oscilloscope screen and hyperpolarization is always represented as "down." However, because of the possible confusion with "positive" and "negative," it is unwise to describe the membrane potential as going "up" or "down." Instead, in this book we will always use the more precise terms *depolarization* and *hyperpolarization*. What if the membrane potential were to depolarize *past zero* (i.e., reverse in sign)? Entering a period of inside positivity, the membrane potential is once again becoming more polar as one side (now the inside) is still positive while the other is negative. Always in science there is some such detail to distract us from our real purpose. Let's agree to call these large upward deflections depolarization as well, so that any movement upward, no matter the magnitude, is always depolarization.

Three Forces and Three Gates

It is apparent that the potential created by potassium (E_K) is one force involved in generating the membrane potential. However, is it the only one? Let us abbreviate the actual membrane potential as measured by the electrometer V_m, to distinguish it from the potassium potential calculated using the Nernst equation. After all, we *think* our theory of a membrane semipermeable to potassium may account for the resting potential but we do not know how complete our theory is until we match predictions with reality. Indeed, inspection of Figure 3–8 reveals that V_m is close to E_K but not identical to it. A measured resting membrane potential for a typical nerve cell or muscle is about –70 mV, or 23 mV depolarized from E_K. Obviously, there are forces other than the potassium potential that contribute to the membrane potential. We can predict a little about what the forces other than E_K must be like. They must have a depolarizing tendency with reference to E_K, since E_K is more hyperpolarized than V_m. Because the potassium channel is selective for potassium, there must be other channel types able to transport other types of charged particles; this ability to pass charged particles must be greater or lesser, in some propor-

Figure 3–8 *Oscilloscope Traces.* When a recording electrode enters a cell, the oscilloscope shows the inside of the cell is –70 mV (the resting membrane potential) relative to the outside of the cell. When the electrode leaves the cell, the potential is no longer being recorded, hence the oscilloscope shows a measure of 0 mV.

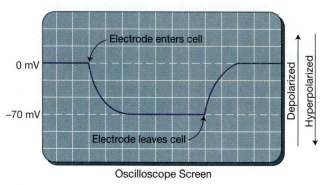

Oscilloscope Screen

[handwritten margin notes: Nernst — EK / Gol — Cl- depolariz / Na+ depolarizes / K+ hyper / 3 forces combine form membrane potential]

tion, than the ability of the potassium channel to let potassium through.

Nernst Values for Sodium and Chloride

Reference to Table 3–2 provides excellent candidates for the other forces: sodium and chloride. Sodium in particular has a concentration gradient opposite to that of potassium (outside sodium rich, inside sodium poor) so it may very well be the depolarizing influence we are looking for. As stated in Box 3–1, the Nernst equation holds for all ions and all membranes. When it is used to calculate E_{Na}, the equilibrium potential for sodium, the value arrived at is +56 mV. As we suspected, a reversed concentration gradient yields an equilibrium potential of the opposite polarity. Sodium passage does indeed have a depolarizing influence on the membrane potential.

What about chloride? The computation is only slightly more complicated due to the fact that chloride is an anion. The z-value is thus –1 (see Box 3–1 if you've forgotten what this is already), and this must be included in the simplified Nernst equation for a calculated value of –66 mV.

Although E_{Cl} is negative, it is less negative than E_K. Hence, chloride also will have a depolarizing effect relative to potassium. It should be apparent from the calculated values for the sodium potential and the chloride potential that the charge on the ion alone cannot be used to predict its impact on the membrane potential. Sodium and potassium are both cations, but their influence on the membrane potential is of different polarity. The magnitude and the polarity of the equilibrium potential is a function of the charge on the ion *and* the concentration gradient.

E_K, E_{Na}, and E_{Cl} (which we'll now call the three forces) combine together in some manner to determine the membrane potential. E_K and E_{Na} are also very important quantities in determining the behavior of the action potential (Chapter 4), and E_{Cl} becomes very important in the understanding of synaptic potentials (Chapter 5) and psychopharmacology (Chapter 17).

The equilibrium potential for calcium, E_{Ca}, plays no role in the cell membrane potential or in the action potential in the axon, but it will appear as an important contributor to synaptic processes. For this reason, using Table 3–2, the more adventurous among you might wish to calculate its value as an exercise. (Hint: Don't forget that the charge, or z-value, on each calcium cation is +2).

Permeability Ratios

The actual resting membrane potential is close to E_K and E_{Cl} but far from E_{Na}. The relatively small contribution made by sodium to the resting potential is due to the fact that the sodium channel has less of a tendency to let sodium through than

[handwritten margin notes: Na-doesn't get through it's channel as easily]

the other two channel types have for their respective ions. In other words, it has a smaller permeability ratio. If an experimental value could be assigned to the readiness, or alacrity, with which each channel passed its ion, one could conceivably account for the membrane potential quantitatively and completely. Such was the reasoning of Alan Hodgkin, Andrew Huxley, and Bernard Katz when they incorporated these measurements into a complete model for the electrical properties of the cell membrane (Hodgkin, 1976).

The actual task of measuring and understanding the permeability of each channel was quite daunting, however. The first problem was a theoretical one that bedevils channel researchers even today. If, as we simplistically argued earlier, the potassium channel has the property of ion selectivity because it is *too small* for sodium to pass through, how can there be a sodium channel large enough for sodium cation yet unable to allow the presumably smaller potassium ion through? The answer, still imperfectly understood, probably involves the way individual ions become coated, or "hydrated," with water molecules and ions in solution. It is these more complicated structures that pass, not the ions alone. Another difficulty, this one a technical impediment, arose in the process of measuring the permeability of the membrane to the various ions. The only strategy available was to use **isotopes**, or radioactive versions of sodium, potassium, and chloride, loading either the inside or the outside with these labeled ions and then measuring the amount that crossed (for a given patch of membrane in a given time) using a device that could detect the decay of each isotope, that is, the emissions it created. These experiments were quite dangerous, for some of the isotopes produced deadly radiation and the early history of these experiments is rife with reports of researchers suffering the ill effects of radiation exposure. Furthermore, the work needed a large amount of cell membrane and a cell big enough to provide experimental access to the inside as well as the outside. The giant axon of the squid, introduced to Hodgkin and Huxley by J. Z. Young, provided the solution to this latter technical problem (Hodgkin, 1976).

The actual permeability values need not concern us here since we need only the *relative* contribution made by the flux of each ion to the membrane potential. As they suspected, potassium permeability was the highest, followed distantly by sodium (about 0.04 times the permeability of potassium).

The Goldman Equation

How then to use the relative values calculated via the Nernst equation to "weigh" the contribution of each equilibrium potential? What would an equation with such a proportionality factor for each species look like? The constants of nature would be the same as for the Nernst equation, but the concentration

[handwritten note: NaK Pump / 3 Na out / 2 K in]

gradient terms would look rather elaborate, since both values for all three ions (potassium, sodium, and chloride) would have to be taken into account. The Goldman equation provides the solution for E_m, the theoretical membrane potential, and looks like three Nernst equations lumped together, with the proportional permeability values thrown in. The details of this rather ungainly equation are shown in Box 3–1.

Using the Goldman equation, Hodgkin, Huxley, and Katz arrived at a value of –67 mV for E_m (the theoretical potential) that approached within 3 mV of V_m (the observed quantity of –70 mV described earlier).

The Sodium/Potassium Pump

If I had arrived at the Goldman result of E_m = –67 mV, I would have been quite proud of myself. In fact, I would have been so happy to have come so close to the experimental value that I would have dismissed the pesky 3 mV difference as experimental error. After all, what's a few millivolts between friends? But Hodgkin et al. persevered in their pursuit of a complete explanation of the membrane potential, even to an intent examination of the 3 mV that cannot be accounted for by E_K, E_{Na}, or E_{Cl} (see account in Hodgkin, 1976).

They first observed that nerve cell preparations (they were working on a squid giant axon for the technical reasons mentioned earlier) slowly depolarized in the hours after removal from the organism so that eventually the theoretical value of –67 mV was approached. Next they observed that if cell metabolism was disrupted, such as with the plant-derived poison *ouabain*, the membrane potential would promptly assume the theoretical value. Ouabain is a specific blocker of certain cell processes that use ATP as an energy source, but it does not interfere with ATP production from glucose (see "The Concept of Affinity" in the Appendix to understand how ouabain can block the binding of ATP). They then reasoned that there must be some energy-consuming process that gives rise to the 3 mV hyperpolarizing influence. Perhaps the concentration gradients decay over a long period of time or under the influence of toxins. In other words, perhaps the nerve cell requires some mechanism to replenish the gradients as (like the batteries in a flashlight) they slowly weaken over time.

Such a process would involve pushing potassium ions *against* their concentration gradient (i.e., to put back in any that had leaked out through the potassium channel). Sodium ions would need to be forced against both the concentration gradient *and* the electrostatic gradient as they were pumped from the inside to the outside. Obviously these processes would require help in the form of energy to overcome these obstacles. The protein that accomplishes this could not be a channel, for channels allow passage *down* electrical and concentration gradients. Instead, it is an enzyme known as Na/K ATPase or, more functionally, by the name of the **sodium/**

potassium pump. Were the pump mechanism simply reciprocal, with movement of one sodium cation out for each potassium cation in, there would have been little evidence of its existence in the squid giant axon; no current would be created and there would be no electrical consequence for V_m. Curiously, however, the pump for most nerve cells is not strictly reciprocal. Typically, *three* sodiums are moved out for *two* potassiums moved in (Figure 3–9). This asymmetry means the pump is **electrogenic** (defined as the active transport of ions across a cell membrane that results in a net transfer of charge) and it is responsible for creating the potential difference of 3 mV.

Two points must be emphasized concerning the sodium/potassium pump. First, it makes a negligible contribution to the processes that interest us the most (i.e., resting potentials, action potentials, synaptic potentials, and, for the monists among you, the effects of these on religion, love and free will). Students have a tendency to find explanations for all sorts of phenomena in the pump (such as action potentials and synaptic potentials), but it merely *maintains the gradients and contributes 3 mV to the resting potential*. It has no more relevance to momentary brain function than visiting a gas station (necessary as it is from time to time) has to do with the process of driving a car. The second point, to be appreciated in the context of the first, is that the pump is overwhelmingly the predominant energy-consuming process of the brain (Chapter 14). When consciousness is maintained by breathing, eating, and so forth, the pump is continuously maintaining the concentration gradients at *precisely the same value throughout life*. This fact enables us to reduce what we have learned about the membrane potential to a few simple concepts: There are three main gates (**sodium conductance, potassium conductance,** and **chloride conductance,** i.e., the conductance of these ions across the membrane) and three main forces (E_K, E_{Na}, and E_{Cl}) that contribute to the membrane potential of a cell.

The "Equivalent Circuit"

The analogy between the three forces comprising the membrane potential and the batteries of a flashlight is quite apt, and indeed the cartoon representation of an idea as a glowing light bulb also has merit as a metaphor (see Box 14–1). In fact in a very real sense the equilibrium potentials *are* batteries. Batteries (rated in voltage) that are used in cars, boats, calculators, radios, and flashlights are "electrochemical cells" that have stored chemical gradients composed of charged particles (not necessarily sodium, potassium, and chloride, but similar ions) and make use of these to create a potential difference between the poles. When the device is switched off, the batteries do nothing but maintain this "potential" to do work, but when the device is switched on by a switch that

Goldman —
theoretical
membrane
potential

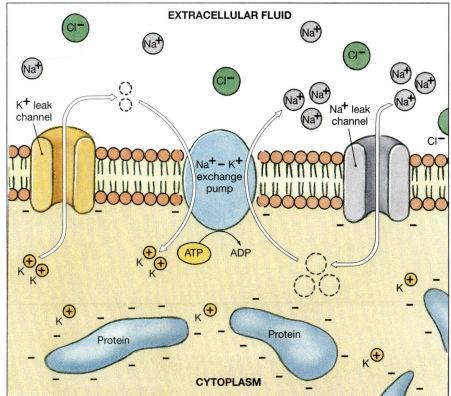

Figure 3–9   *The Sodium / Potassium Pump.* The sodium/potassium pump transports three sodium ions out of the cell in exchange for two potassium ions into the cell. Since this transport moves ions against their respective concentration gradients, it is an example of active transport, ATP is consumed, and an electrical current is produced.

closes the circuit between the poles, current flows from one to the other and work is performed in terms of turning a crank, playing music, shining a light, and so forth. Everything that we have discussed can be understood in precisely these terms, and thus an alternative description of the membrane potential (together with action potentials and synaptic potentials) is a model called the **equivalent circuit**. The equivalent circuit model is preferable to the model based on thermodynamics (once the thermodynamics are understood), since it permits us to dispense with consideration of charged particles, gradients, attraction, repulsion, and so forth and merely concentrate on **batteries** (the forces) and **conductors** (the gates).

Batteries and Conductors

Electrical processes (and chemical processes that have an electrical "equivalent") are governed by a simple relation among **potential, current,** and **resistance** known as **Ohm's law** (see Box 3–2). The relation can be expressed as

$$V = IR$$

where V is potential (in volts), I is current (in amps), and R is resistance (in ohms). For a given potential, current is high when resistance is low and current is low when resistance is high. In biological terms it is convenient to think of the reciprocal of resistance, which we define as **conductance:**

$$g = 1/R$$

where g stands for this new quantity, measured in "mhos" (don't say Ohm didn't have a sense of humor, however dry). Substituting for this new term Ohm's law becomes

$$V = I/g$$

For a given voltage, when conductance is high, current flows readily. Low conductance means low current.

Batteries (a source of energy or voltage) and conductors (devices capable of conveying current) can be represented symbolically, with their connections represented by a "circuit diagram." Figure 3–10a shows the symbols for batteries and conductors (a conductor has the same symbol as a resistor, a device that has the ability to resist the flow of charge). Also shown is a symbol for a **capacitor.** A capacitor lessens the effect of any sudden change in potential (in our case, membrane potential) by collecting charge and releasing it over a period of time. It need not concern us much here, save to remind us that there is a limit to how fast membrane potential can change.

Imagine a tiny patch of membrane, a minute fraction of the whole cell membrane. All that we know to exist in each tiny patch is illustrated symbolically in Figure 3–10b. The batteries of the membrane are the membrane potentials E_K, E_{Na} and E_{Cl} (with E_K and E_{Cl} oriented to make the inside negative and E_{Na} oriented to make the inside positive). The potassium channels, the sodium channels, and the chloride channels, which regulate permeability to their respective ions, are represented as conductances. We have given abbreviations g_K, g_{Na}, g_{Cl} as shorthand for these conductances when we wish to refer to them in the text. Add the membrane capacitor and our equivalent circuit is complete. Sometimes it helps to think of the equivalent circuit as "a flashlight with three batteries, one reversed," but if you use this analogy you must

Box 3–2

Ohm's Law Simplified

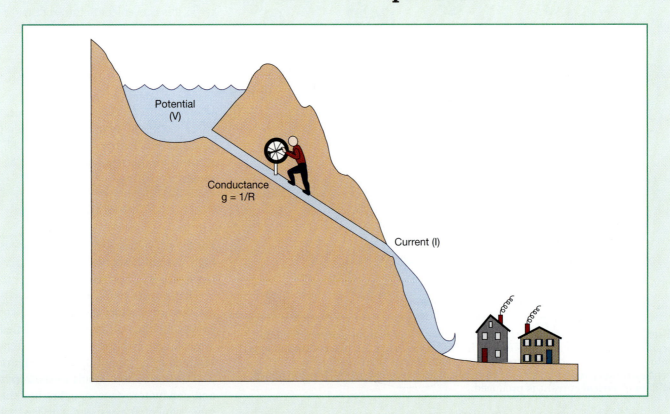

A simple analogy will help you understand the concepts of potential, current, and conductance and visualize the application of Ohm's law (V = I/g).

Imagine a manmade lake or reservoir high in the mountains and a city down below. (In Boulder, the lake is called Barker Reservoir and the mountains are very beautiful slabs of rock called the Flatirons. You should visit sometime). The city engineer controls the floodgate at the dam and regulates how much water flows down to water lawns, fill bathtubs, and so forth (see diagram).

The pressure of the water in the reservoir (or the entropy and enthalpy forces when considering the membrane potential) is analogous to potential (V in Ohm's law) as it has the potential to do work. The flow of the water downhill is analogous to current (I in Ohm's law), and when the floodgate (ion channel) is open, conductance (g in Ohm's law) is high and current flows readily; when the floodgate is shut conductance is low and little current flows.

remember that a flashlight has a single on/off switch for all three batteries, while each battery of the equivalent circuit has its own on/off switch.

The entire cell membrane (e.g., the squid giant axon) can now be visualized as a vast mosaic of these tiny equivalent circuits, joined on the inside and outside by resistors representing the electrical conductance of the saltwater on the inside and the outside of the cell.

Constancy of the Batteries

Each ion will move across the membrane so as to make the membrane potential equal to its own equilibrium potential,

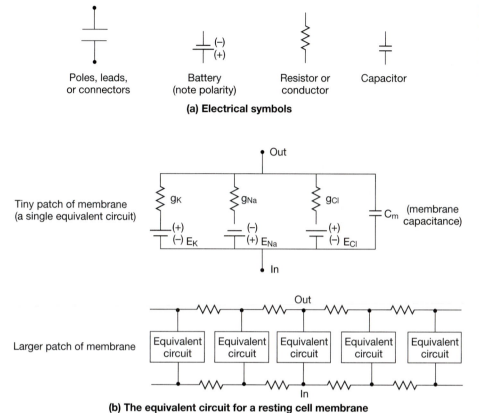

Figure 3–10 *The Equivalent Circuit.* (a) The electrical symbols defined. (b) Two views of the excitable membrane: a small bit (top) and a larger patch (bottom) (Nicholls et al., 1991).

Poles, leads, or connectors

Battery (note polarity)

Resistor or conductor

Capacitor

(a) Electrical symbols

Tiny patch of membrane (a single equivalent circuit)

Out

g_K g_{Na} g_{Cl}

C_m (membrane capacitance)

$(+)$ $(-)$ $(+)$
$(-) E_K$ $(+) E_{Na}$ $(-) E_{Cl}$

In

Larger patch of membrane

Out

Equivalent circuit Equivalent circuit Equivalent circuit Equivalent circuit Equivalent circuit

In

(b) The equivalent circuit for a resting cell membrane

at which point the "driving force" on the ion will vanish. Hence, at the resting potential of –70 mV, sodium moves *in* (so as to bring the membrane potential closer to +56 mV), potassium will move *out* (a positive ion must leave if the membrane potential is to approach the potassium equilibrium potential of –93 mV), and chloride is more-or-less at rest (since V_m is quite close to E_{Cl}). If we were to hyperpolarize the membrane, let's say to –120 mV, chloride would acquire a driving force, leaving the cell (–66 mV is less negative than –120 mV, so an anion must leave to depolarize the cell). Which way would potassium move if V_m were –120 mV? (Answer: It would move *into* the cell, as its driving force reversed direction when the membrane potential passed –93 mV, or E_K). At "rest" (–70 mV) the net ion flux is zero, but since various forces are working in different directions it is not quite proper to call this "resting state" an "equilibrium." A compulsive electrochemist would call it a "steady state" meaning there is no net movement of the systems' overall charge or ion concentration.

Obviously, if the membrane potential were to change in a complex fashion it would get cumbersome to sort out what is happening to each ion type. Thinking of the *electrical equivalent* of the driving forces, or batteries in the equivalent circuit, will help eliminate this difficulty.

The concentrations of various ion species on the inside and the outside may vary slightly from species to species, and so the values of the batteries may differ very slightly, but within a healthy organism the pump will keep the concentration gradients *exactly as they are*. Passage of ions across the membrane, such as during the action potential (Chapter 4) and synaptic potentials (Chapter 5) may add or subtract minute quantities to either side, but considering the vast reservoir of particles on each side (literally an ocean for the outside of some animals) this passage during the action potential and the synaptic potential should be thought of as trivial. Since the equilibrium potential values depend *only* on constants and the concentration gradients, this means that the values are also invariant. Hence a sound (and useful) appreciation of the equivalent circuit in Figure 3–9 can be obtained if you remember the simple dictum *"the batteries don't change."* They are always the same as long as life endures (Box 3–3).

Variability of the Conductances

I promised you at the beginning of this chapter that the immense complexity of brain function could be reduced to a few simple principles, and indeed they can. The simplification requires you to appreciate that the values of the batteries in the

Box 3–3

A Biologist's Definition of Life and Death

I once asked a biology professor of mine to define *death*. He said, "Death is when an organism becomes indistinguishable from its environment." Though his answer may have been somewhat facetious, I have often thought about his definition and what it implies for the definition of life.

Life really concerns the boundary, rather than the substance of things. I mean this not just in the sense of territorial boundaries or the slim margin of adaptation that separates the successes from the failures in evolution. These things certainly are part of what we mean when we say "life." But it is at the more concrete borders between self and the outside world where so much that we call life transpires. For sentient beings virtually all momentary experience and awareness comes about because of events of the cell membrane. Sensation, perception, recall, speaking, and listening are all products of electrical changes at the cell membrane. This thin film of lipid and protein creates the membrane potential, as we have seen, and the membrane potential is the driving force for all the electrical

events we are about to consider. In a practical sense neurophysiologists define a healthy cell by the presence of a full membrane potential and occasionally have the macabre experience of rupturing a cell membrane and hearing, through an audioamplifier, a neuron "scream" or "sigh" as the membrane potential dissipates.

At the level of thermodynamics, we can think of the forces of entropy as trying to create chaos out of our bodies and fuse them with the environment; on the cellular level entropy tries to diffuse the potassium gradient and eliminate the basis for the membrane potential itself. A workable definition of life—albeit one that would cause anyone who has not studied thermodynamics to go "Huh?"—could be "a system that resists entropy by maintaining and replicating a chemical and electrical boundary." However, since most of us think of life as in "our lives," in dynamic terms ("what happened"), a more accessible definition might be "life is a product of three stored forces that together create the potential for *action*."

equivalent circuit *summarize* all the discussion of ions, gradients, and so forth that preceded them. Although the understanding of these systems is essential, concentrate on the summaries (i.e., E_K, E_{Na}, and E_{Cl}). The values of the conductances change in response to voltage signals (for the action potential) and chemical signals (for the synaptic potential) and when this happens the membrane potential (V_m) will

change from the resting value and go towards the value of the battery that corresponds to that conductance. A slightly (but permissibly) anthropomorphic conception of this can be found in the rule "*each ion wants the membrane potential to be equal to its own equilibrium potential. The degree to which it can accomplish its desire is determined by its relative conductance.*"

SUMMARY

The cells of all animals are bathed in saltwater that is very similar in composition to sea water. The inside of cells is also composed of saltwater, but the predominant positive ion type on the inside is potassium cation, whereas on the outside the predominant cation is sodium. Nerve cells at rest are permeable mostly to potassium, and diffusion forces a small amount of potassium out of the cell through the potassium channel. Since potassium is positively charged, this diffusion creates a membrane potential, which begins to pull the potassium ions

back in. The point at which the diffusion force and the electrostatic attraction balance is described by the Nernst equation. Solving the equation for potassium yields a constant equilibrium potential of –93 mV for this ion. Solving the Nernst equation for the other major ion species, sodium and chloride, yields values of +56 mV and –66 mV, respectively. Combining these values with estimates of the relative permeabilities for potassium, sodium, and chloride at rest results in a mathematic expression called the Goldman equation. Solving this equation leads to a theoretical value for the membrane potential of –67 mV. The 3 mV difference between the theoretical value and measured value (–70 mV) is entirely accounted for by a small electrogenic contribution from the sodium/potassium pump. Each equilibrium potential can be thought of as a battery and each permeability can be thought of as a conductance. All electrical signaling, and hence all brain processes (action potentials and synaptic potentials), are powered by the three batteries, which never change. When the relative conductance for (permeability toward) a given battery (ion) is high, the membrane potential will move towards the potential of that battery. When the relative conductance for a given battery is low, the membrane potential will move toward the potentials of the other batteries.

REVIEW QUESTIONS

1. How does a cation differ from an anion?
2. How does entropy differ from enthalpy?
3. How does depolarization differ from hyperpolarization?
4. Name the three Nernst batteries.
5. Name the three variable conductances.
6. What is the role of the sodium/potassium pump?
7. Why are the batteries always the same?
8. How is membrane potential measured?
9. What is the equivalent circuit?

THOUGHT QUESTIONS

1. What would the nervous system of an alien being look like if the alien evolved on a planet that had an abundance of a single cation (let's say sodium) but a variety of anions (let's say chloride and fluoride)?
2. Why is a mixture of potassium and chloride used as a means of execution by lethal injection?

KEY CONCEPTS

anode (p. 49)
anions (p. 48)
batteries (p. 59)
capacitor (p. 59)
cathode (p. 49)
cations (p. 48)
chloride battery (p. 47)
chloride conductance (p. 58)
conductance (p. 59)
conductors (p. 59)
current (p. 59)
depolarization (p. 56)
diffusion (p. 52)
electrode (p. 54)
electrogenic (p. 58)
electrometer (p. 54)
enthalpy (p. 53)
entropy (p. 51)
equilibrium (p. 53)
equivalent circuit (p. 59)
Goldman equation (p. 55)
hyperpolarization (p. 56)
ions (p. 48)
isotopes (p. 57)
molar (p. 49)
moles (p. 49)
molecules (p. 48)
monomers (p. 51)
Nernst equation (p. 55)
Ohm's law (p. 59)
pH scale (p. 48)
polymer (p. 51)
potassium battery (p. 47)
potassium channel (p. 51)
potassium conductance (p. 58)
potential (p. 59)
resistance (p. 59)
salt (p. 49)
sodium battery (p. 47)
sodium conductance (p. 58)
sodium/potassium pump (p. 58)
stimulator (p. 54)

All is flux, nothing stays still. . . . When is death not within ourselves? . . .
Living and dead are the same, and so are awake and asleep, young and old.

Heraclitus (c. 540–c. 480 B.C.)

4

Communication Among Neurons: The Action Potential

If the resting membrane potential is the very essence of life itself, what are we to make of those events, the action potential and synaptic potential, that alter the membrane potential from its resting value? As we learn more about the fundamental nature of experience in the ensuing chapters, we will find, even as our knowledge grows, the essence of life and death (and for that matter, wakefulness and sleep, youth and old age) will become elusive and hard to specify.

Recall that Ramón y Cajal's "law of dynamic polarization" states that electrical information flows in only one direction across the synapse (Chapter 2). The axon of one cell has electrical properties that specialize it for transmitting a signal and the dendrites of another cell have electrical properties that specialize them for receiving a signal. The three forces described in Chapter 3 are always the same everywhere (i.e., for axon, soma, and dendrite), but the properties of the three gates differ. In fact, we can divide the neuron into two parts, or domains, depending on the properties that cause the gates to open and close. The dendrites and soma make up the **chemically excitable domain**, which is sensitive to the presence of the neurotransmitter chemical and hence suited for signal reception across the synapse. The axon and bouton comprise the **electrically excitable domain**, which is sensitive to small electrical changes at the axon hillock; the axon hillock amplifies and conducts these changes very quickly down the axon to the bouton. Thus this domain is suited for signal transmission across the synapse to the chemically excitable domain of another cell.

We learned that the three forces are chemical in origin with an electrical "equivalent" (Chapter 3). Please do not be confused, therefore, by our discussion of chemical vs. electrical domains. Since the forces are at work equally in both domains, everything we have to discuss will be both electrical and chemical. In making the distinction between the electrically excitable domain and the chemically excitable domain we are discussing merely *the signal that causes* the gates to open and close. It is easiest to think of events

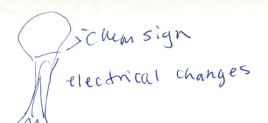

in the soma and dendrites as electrical changes initiated by a *chemical signal* and to think of changes in the axon and bouton as electrical changes initiated by an *electrical signal*. Let us begin by considering how a small electrical stimulus to the axon gives rise to another, quite different electrical response.

The Electrically Excitable Domain

When small amounts of negative current are injected into a cell, small hyperpolarizations occur. These hyperpolarizations increase proportionately to progressively larger current stimuli, indicating that the total conductance of the cell membrane does not vary when the membrane potential becomes more negative (Figure 4–1a). In other words, when conductance is constant, voltage is linearly related to current, since according to Ohm's law

$$V = I/g$$

(Recall that V = potential (voltage), I = current, and g = conductance.) Similarly, depolarizing the cell by injecting positive current yields proportional adjustment to the voltage, also indicating no conductance change in this region of the current/voltage reaction (known in neurophysiology lingo as an "I/V curve"). Larger steps in the depolarizing direction, however, produce a region of instability in the current/voltage relation, as shown in Figure 4–1b.

Now at first the task of determining the physical basis for the unstable region seems quite daunting. Since the voltage curve is changing in the region of instability (with at least three phases in the space of a few milliseconds), which value of voltage should we use to plug into Ohm's law? Furthermore, depending on which value we choose, the I/V curve for this unstable region could indicate either a region of *negative resistance* or one of *positive resistance*. While this notion might appeal to a student with a fondness for conundrums, I rather prefer my explanations simple, straightforward and to-the-point.

Fortunately, a solution to this problem becomes available if we consider this waveform, the **action potential**, in terms of its stimulus-response properties and its component parts.

An All-or-None Event

Action potentials are abrupt depolarizations that are the basis for neural signaling in the electrically excitable domain. Action potentials are very predictable. The first phase is always a rapid depolarization (less than a millisecond) that takes the membrane potential *past zero*. This deflection approaches, but never quite reaches, the sodium equilibrium potential (+56 mV). Then a hyperpolarizing phase takes over, bringing

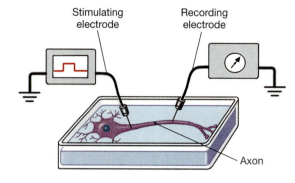

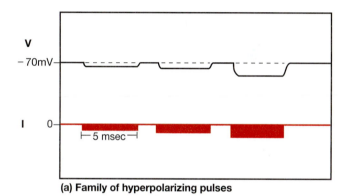

(a) Family of hyperpolarizing pulses

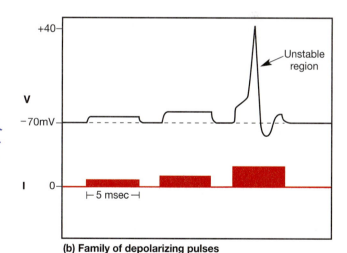

(b) Family of depolarizing pulses

Figure 4–1 *Current/Voltage Relations.* When injected with small amounts of negative current (a), the cell experiences small hyperpolarizations from the resting potential (–70 mV). This change in voltage is proportional to the amount of negative current added to the cell. According to Ohm's law (V = I/g), the conductance must remain constant to account for this phenomenon. When a cell is injected with small amounts of positive current (b), the cell is depolarized from the resting potential and the voltage change is proportional to the amount of positive current. However, as the cell is further depolarized there is a region of instability. According to Ohm's law, there must be a change in conductance to account for this region.

the membrane potential down past the resting value and momentarily close to the potassium equilibrium potential (–93 mV). Finally, a third depolarizing phase returns the membrane potential to the resting value (–70 mV). We can say that the action potential is characterized by an overshoot (transiently depolarized past zero) and an undershoot (transiently hyperpolarized past the resting value).

Significantly, all the overshoots and undershoots are the same. Each action resembles every other action potential. We say that the action potential is all-or-none, in that electrical stimuli either elicit the full, self-propelling event or else have negligible impact. No intermediate responses are encountered. This property of action potentials is illustrated in Figure 4–2, where four stimuli are given (each a brief electrical shock to a piece of axon membrane). Three of these stimuli yield perfect, nearly identical action potentials, while the

fourth has only a minor effect on membrane voltage. In experiment after experiment, it can be shown that these are the only two outcomes possible in the electrically excitable domain of the cell. But what determines which outcome will be displayed? To find out, please read on.

Threshold and Refractoriness

In a sequence of many such experiments, you would see that small shocks (stimulus 4 in Figure 4–2) rarely elicit an action potential while larger ones (stimuli 1, 2, and 3 in Figure 4–2) almost always do so. The value of a just-barely effective stimulus (measured in mV of depolarization) is called the threshold (Figure 4–3) for the action potential. This value is very important for the function of the neuron and varies somewhat from cell to cell, usually in the range of 0 to 10 mV above the resting membrane potential. Figure 4–4a shows action potentials in a neuron that have a threshold a few mV depolarized from rest. The neuron is "silent" or inactive until a depolarizing stimulus raises V_m past this value, whereupon the cell fires a series of action potentials. What role do you think a "silent" cell might have in behavior? Also shown (Figure 4–4b) is a neuron with a threshold very close to the resting potential, rendering the cell spontaneously active. These cells, called bursting cells or pacemakers, appear to have "free will" since no stimulus is required to get them going. Do you think spontaneous actions are the result of activity in such cells?

Another interesting property of the electrically excitable domain is found when superthreshold stimuli are presented in rapid succession. Normally, each would produce an action potential, but if they are very close together in time the second stimulus sometimes fails to elicit an action potential, even when it moves the membrane potential past threshold. This state of inexcitability is called refractoriness. Like threshold, refractoriness plays a very important role in the life of a neuron. The occurrence and duration of refractoriness vary somewhat from cell to cell, though every cell displays the phenomenon to some degree. What do you think the function of refractoriness is for the electrically excitable domain of a cell?

Potential, current, and conductance are all changing at once during the action potential waveform. For more on what *fundamental* processes are at work, see the application of an experimental trick called the "voltage clamp" accomplished with a little help from a squid (See Box 4–1 on page 68).

The Real Basis of the Action Potential

Since "the batteries don't change" (Chapter 3), the membrane potential must be fluctuating during the action potential because the *relative contributions* of the batteries are changing. The contribution of each battery is determined

Figure 4–2 *Superimposed Action Potentials.* When a cell is stimulated, there are two possible outcomes. The first outcome (seen in 1, 2, and 3) results in an action potential which is characterized by an overshoot (transiently depolarized past zero) followed by an undershoot (transiently hyperpolarized past the resting potential). In the second outcome (4) there is only a minor effect on the resting potential. This all-or-none event is characteristic of all cells when determining if an action potential will be fired.

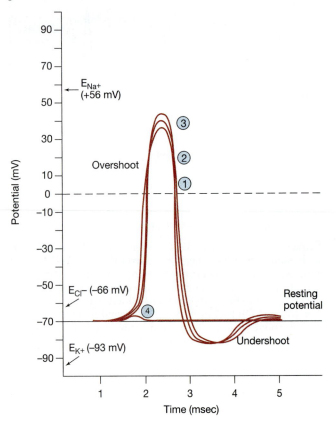

Figure 4–3 *The Concept of Threshold.*
The threshold value of a cell is similar to a
dam protecting a town from a water source.
When the water level is below the height of
the dam (a), no water will flow over. As soon
as the water reaches the top (b), water will
flow over the dam into the town.

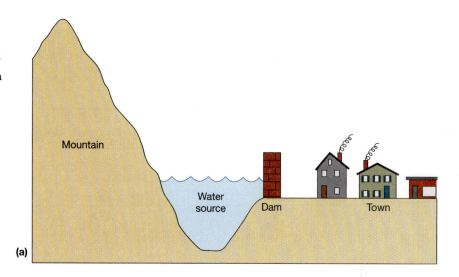

(a)

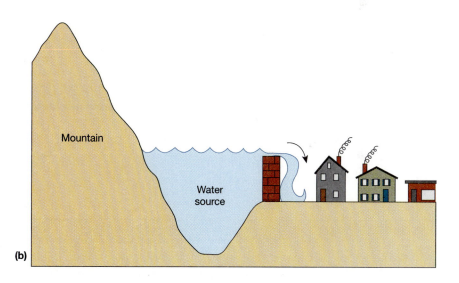

(b)

by its *relative conductance* (Chapter 3). Therefore the real
basis for the action potential is to be found in the individual conductance values, preferably studied in isolation from
other variables. We can begin this process of isolation by
manipulating Ohm's law so that the other terms (for voltage and current) are grouped together on the other side of
the equation:

$$I/V = g$$

With this version of Ohm's law it can be seen that conductance would be directly proportional to current if voltage
were held constant. This is accomplished by the **voltage clamp**
which does just what the name implies: It holds the voltage
steady, or it clamps it, at a particular value. Voltage clamp
records are essentially reflections of membrane conductance.
Since membrane conductance is the sum of the individual

conductances of sodium, potassium, and chloride, it is merely a matter of eliminating the other conductances, one by
one, until the behavior of each can be studied in isolation
from other variables.

The Action Potential Explained

As explained previously, by holding voltage constant with the
voltage clamp we can measure current and calculate conductance, according to Ohm's law. If the value for voltage we
choose is *below* threshold for an action potential, little current flows (at –70 mV for example, *no* net current flows).
However, if the voltage we choose is *above* threshold then
the cell will *try* to generate an action potential. Since it is
"clamped" no actual change in membrane potential will
occur, but the membrane currents will flow in an attempt to
change the potential.

Box 4–1

The Squid Giant Axon and the Voltage Clamp

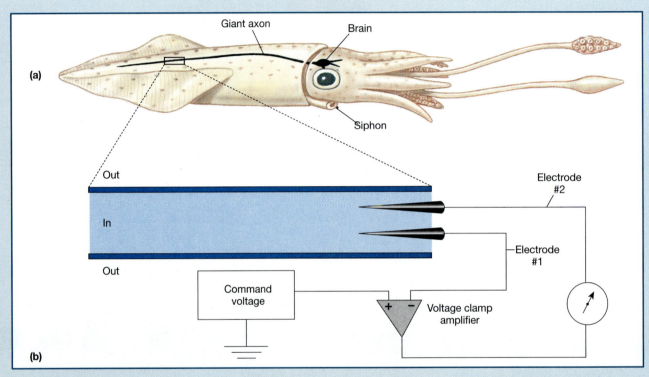

A famous actress currently very popular in movies was asked during an interview how she came to be in show business. She replied that she originally had an interest in psychology and majored in it for awhile. However, in her early coursework her professor seemed unable to talk about anything but *squids*, and so she decided that her interests could be best served by pursuit of another career.

The world of film is richer because of her decision, but squids (and frogs, insects, and various other crunchy and squishy critters) have enormously enriched our understanding of the brain and behavior. How such simple organisms came to contribute so greatly to our understanding of complex systems such as the human brain is a fascinating story.

The principles of electrical signaling (the resting potential and the action potential) were developed by Hodgkin, Huxley, and their colleagues using scientific insights that you have already learned by reading this text and may learn more about by reading historical accounts (Hodgkin, 1976; Katz, 1966). However, experimental veri-

fication of the ideas was made possible, to a substantial degree, by accident. Hodgkin and Huxley's genius and greatest intellectual contribution was the integration of these accidentally discovered specifics with general principles, the combination of experiment and theory. The final understanding of the conductance changes that create the action potential was obtained using a device called a voltage clamp.

The first series of observations came from biologists such as Cornelius Wiersma, Ted Bullock, and Graham Hoyle who were working on the nervous systems of diverse, nonvertebrate species in the 1930s, '40s, and '50s. Comparison of their results made clear a general feature of nervous systems, namely that *they all behave the same way at the cellular level*. Though the mechanisms of electrical signaling were still poorly understood, it was apparent that they were conserved in evolution so that organisms with very different body plans (a crayfish, say, and a human being) had quite similar membrane potentials, action potentials, and synaptic potentials.

The next development came from an English biologist, J. Z. Young, who happened upon the Mediterranean squid while conducting comparative studies of invertebrate nervous system anatomy. He came across a structure in the mantle (the muscular organ responsible for breathing and jet propulsion, see part (a) of figure) that he first took to be a blood vessel. Large (almost a millimeter in diameter) and long, it spanned the entire mantle wall. Further investigation revealed it to be a giant axon, larger than any known before or since. So large was the axon (*why* so large?) that Hodgkin and Huxley, after they learned of it, found that they could squeeze out the fluid from the inside, like a tube of toothpaste, and replace it with a fluid of their own choosing. In this manner they could, for example, determine the role played by internal potassium in the action potential, simply by eliminating it and seeing what had changed.

The size of the axon was such that it was possible to insert *two* electrodes, instead of just one, and to thread these electrodes down the entire length of the axon cylinder.

Meanwhile the American scientists H. J. Curtis and K. S. Cole had developed a device for exerting rapid and automatic control over voltage fluctuations. This circuit, derived from technology having no connection with neurophysiology, was called the "voltage clamp" to signify its ability to maintain voltage in a system at any value desired by the experimenter. A simplified version is shown in part (b) of figure.

Two electrodes are used in a voltage clamp, one to detect membrane potential (Electrode 1) and one to inject current (Electrode 2). With both electrodes placed inside the axon, the signal detected by the first electrode is compared to the desired voltage, switched in sign, amplified many times very quickly, and pumped back into the cell through the second electrode. The effect is the cell membrane potential goes to the desired value and stays there as long as the clamp is maintained. For example, let's imagine an actual voltage clamp experiment. The desired voltage is the normal resting value of –70 mV. A potential of this size is inserted between the ground pole and the amplifier ("command voltage"). The other pole of the amplifier detects –70 mV from Electrode 1 inside the cell. The differential amplifier compares –70 mV from the command voltage to –70 mV from Electrode 1, the result being 0 mV, the circuit passes no current. In other words, the clamp needs to do no work to keep the cell where it wants to be anyway.

But now imagine that the command voltage is made some nonresting value, say –50 mV, that is above threshold for firing an action potential. The circuit detects a difference of –20 mV, amplifies it many times very quickly and sends it back to the axon, depolarizing the cell until the membrane potential and the command voltage are identical (i.e., –50 mV). The positive current necessary to do this is measured. If the axon tries to fire an action potential in response to the nonresting voltage value, the clamp circuit will take any current generated by the cell and cancel it perfectly and quickly by generating a current of equal value but opposite sign. Membrane currents (what the axon is trying to do) can be measured precisely (they are the exact opposite of the voltage clamp output). Since the device has eliminated variance in the voltage, these currents are directly proportional to conductance (g in Ohm's law). Since conductance is the electrical equivalent of the permeability of the ion channels, the behavior of these channels can now be studied in isolation from other influences.

I have chosen to write the text of this book so as to emphasize the theory of nervous system function and to subordinate the experimental details by presenting them outside the text flow. After all, the membrane potential and the action potential are universals while the squid giant axon and the voltage clamp are not. However, this should not be taken to reflect the relative importance of theory as opposed to experiment. The tension between theory and practice imbues all of science, and each individual scientist has his own, often fervently held, views on the subject. Theory has the grand egalitarian quality that, with proper preparation, it is accessible to anyone. No special equipment or personal standing is required to engage in it. On the other hand, theory without the steady and immediate infusion of practical experience tends to become effete and focused on progressively greater abstractions until, in extreme cases, a trivial quality develops. We say in common language that it "becomes removed from reality."

The principles of neurophysiology have very little meaning until the student can see them at work, at all times, in everyday life. By a similar token the most important function of this book, an appreciation of the scientific method as an organizing approach to reality, cannot be accomplished without a consideration of the actual experimental steps in the creation of the understanding of the brain, minute as they may be. As a famous novelist and a literary critic said, in a context not so very different from this one, "God dwells in the details."

[handwritten annotations in margins: "Na+", "Na+", "TTX", "K K K", "TEA", "Potassium Channel", "Na Channel"]

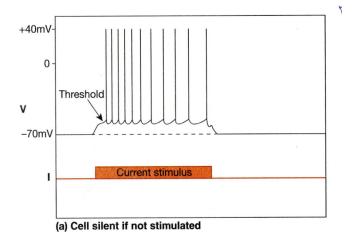

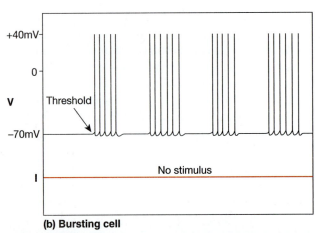

(a) Cell silent if not stimulated

(b) Bursting cell

Figure 4–4 *Threshold in Neurons.* In neurons, when the threshold value is reached, an action potential will be fired. This threshold value varies from cell to cell. In a silent cell (a), the threshold is a few mV above the resting potential. In a bursting cell (b), the threshold is very close to the resting potential. Under these circumstances, no stimulus is needed to bring the membrane to threshold. The cell will spontaneously fire on its own.

Two Currents Drive the Action Potential

Shortly after the cell is clamped above threshold an inward current begins (i.e., positive charges move *in*, which *would* be depolarizing were the cell not clamped). It peaks in about half a millisecond and declines to nothing in about 3 milliseconds. About a millisecond *after* the clamp is turned on, an outward current begins (i.e., positive charges move *out*, which *would* be hyperpolarizing). This current never shuts off as long as the clamp is maintained. Since no other currents are seen, these two currents are all that drive the action potential. But how are the currents carried in and out of the cell?

The Effects of Toxins on Current

Hodgkin and Huxley suspected that the depolarizing current was carried into the cell by sodium; when they re-

moved sodium from the surroundings, this current disappeared.

A toxin new to science but available in nature for millions of years provided another means to evaluate the ionic basis for the inward current. The Pacific puffer fish defends itself from attack by inflating its body and presenting the predator with poisonous spines radiating outward. The poison is made by a visceral gland and is one of the deadliest known to man. Named after the scientific name for the puffer fish (*tetraodontidae*), it is called tetrodotoxin and abbreviated TTX. Hodgkin and Huxley found that TTX also eliminated the inward current. It became apparent that TTX binds to a site on the inside of the sodium channel and blocks the channel so that sodium ion can no longer pass through. Thus TTX is very useful as a probe for processes mediated by sodium currents. Curiously, puffer fish is used to prepare a form of sushi that is considered a great delicacy. Part of the art of making puffer fish sushi is the skill of leaving just enough of the TTX gland in the fish so that the diner experiences a faint tingling sensation in the mouth. From time to time the gland is removed improperly and a customer is poisoned, sometimes fatally.

The delayed outward current could be mediated by either potassium or chloride flux. Chloride removal from either side of the membrane had no effect on this current. In fact, chloride plays no role in action potential conduction, though it is very important in establishing the resting potential and in synaptic inhibition, as we shall see in Chapter 5. Removal of potassium from the inside of the cell obliterated the delayed outward current, indicating this current must be carried by potassium. Tetraethylammonium, or TEA, is a toxin that blocks the potassium channel in the same way that TTX blocks the sodium channel. TEA also eliminated the delayed outward current, affirming that the outward current is carried by potassium efflux, which we shall discuss in more detail later.

Thus the results of the voltage clamp experiments indicate that two currents produce the action potential. First there is a quick sodium current that peaks and declines quickly. After a delay there is a long potassium current that endures as long as the cell is depolarized. By looking at the behavior of these currents at a range of (clamped) voltage values, conductances at the various points of the action potential can be calculated, once again using our old friend Ohm's law.

How Conductances Create the Waveform

Figure 4–5 shows the voltage of an action potential (in mV, left scale) superimposed on the conductance curves for sodium and potassium (in mmhos, right scale). No curve is shown for chloride conductance since, as we have discussed, it doesn't change during the action potential. An *electrical signal*

[handwritten annotation at bottom: "Cl conductance doesn't change during act. potential"]

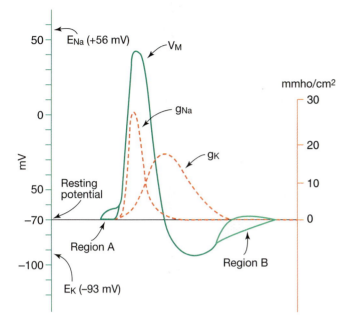

Figure 4–5 *Conductances Create the Action Potential.* There are two conductances that are responsible for the action potential: sodium conductance and potassium conductance. Sodium conductance (g_{Na}) is responsible for depolarizing the cell from threshold to a value close to E_{Na}. The potassium conductance (g_K) is responsible for then hyperpolarizing the cell to a value close to E_K. In the figure, Region A, caused by the synaptic potential, is the depolarization that brings the membrane potential from its resting value to threshold. Region B, responsible for restoring the membrane resting potential, is caused by the sodium/potassium pump. (Nicholls, et al., 1991)

(threshold) causes the sodium conductance to increase from its low resting value to a substantially higher one. Thus, we say that the sodium conductance is **voltage dependent** and, as a consequence, the axon is electrically excitable. Because *each ion wants the membrane potential to be equal to its own equilibrium potential* (Chapter 3), the increased sodium conductance causes the membrane voltage to soar momentarily close to the sodium equilibrium potential. The membrane voltage never quite reaches this value, however, because the sodium conductance only lasts for a millisecond or so. We say the sodium conductance is also **time dependent** because it shuts itself off.

Because the sodium conductance is falling, the membrane voltage starts to return to the resting state away from its peak near the sodium equilibrium potential. However, there is another cellular process that accelerates the descent of the curve. The potassium conductance is also voltage dependent and it increases just as the sodium conductance is declining. Because the equilibrium potential for potassium is below the resting potential, the membrane voltage briefly un-

dershoots the resting value. At this point the potassium conductance declines because it too is voltage dependent and the membrane voltage falls below the activation threshold. The potassium conductance is delayed to avoid competing with the sodium conductance for control over the membrane voltage. (The figure shows potassium conductance returning to zero, but there is always a small "leak" of potassium conductance that maintains the resting potential).

We have now explained everything in the action potential quantitatively, except for the two areas shown in Figure 4–5 labeled Region A and Region B. Region A is a bit of depolarization at the beginning of the action potential that cannot be due to the voltage-dependent sodium conductance since this has yet to begin. This region is the depolarization that brings the electrically excitable domain to threshold in the first place. We have described this stimulus as an electrical shock delivered by the experimenter, but of course this never takes place in the normal function of the nervous system. Normally, Region A arises from electrical activity in the *chemically excitable domain*. It is a *synaptic potential* of the kind we will consider in Chapter 5.

Region B is a bit of hyperpolarization that cannot be due to the voltage-dependent potassium conductance since g_K has already declined to its resting value. During the action potential, a tiny bit of sodium enters the cell during the action potential and a tiny bit of potassium leaves. The sodium/potassium pump (Chapter 3) detects these tiny quantities and works more energetically than at rest to pump the sodium back out and the potassium back in. Since the pump is "electrogenic," this results in a small current and the resting potential is maintained. As stated earlier, you should not imagine that a large number of ions cross the membrane during the action potential (only about 10,000 do) or that the pump makes a substantial impact on the membrane voltage. The pump affects only this little tag end of the action potential.

Functions of the Sodium Channel

Let us now consider the physical correlate of the voltage- and time- dependent sodium conductance, the sodium channel protein itself.

The channel is made up of four monomers, each of which spans the membrane six times (Figure 4–6). Each monomer is a chain of about 2,000 amino acids, for a total of about 8,000 amino acids. (There is some uncertainty regarding the complete channel structure since there may be uncharacterized subunits responsible for full channel function and other complex molecules, like carbohydrates, that attach to the monomers.)

The amino acids have structural properties that enable the channel to cross the membrane. Hence transmembrane chunks of hydrophobic amino acids are separated by hy-

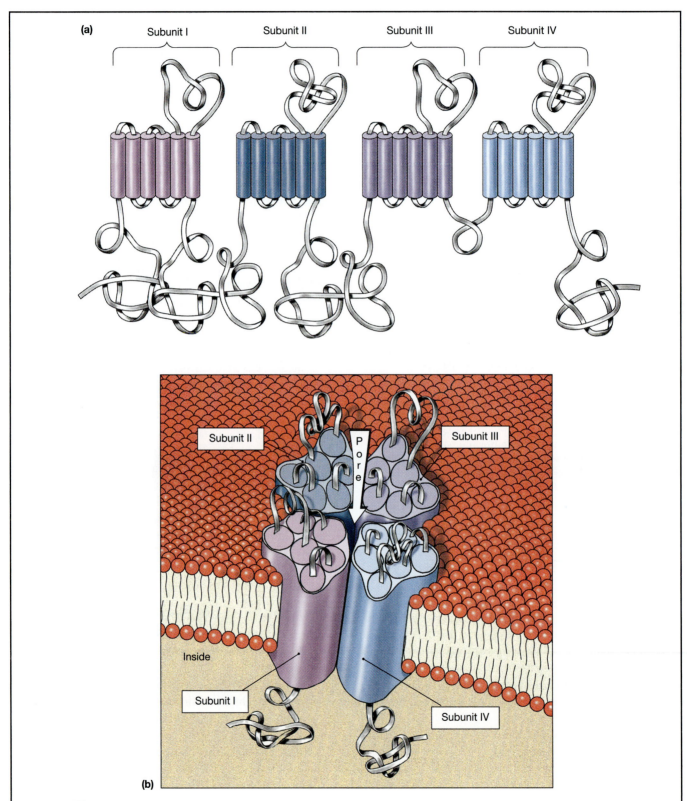

(a) Subunit I   Subunit II   Subunit III   Subunit IV

Subunit II   Pore   Subunit III

Inside

Subunit I   Subunit IV

(b)

Figure 4–6   *The Structure of the Sodium Channel.* The sodium channel consists of four monomers each with six transmembrane regions (a). When the four monomers aggregate in the lipid bilayer, a pore or channel is formed which allows the passage of sodium ions (b).

drophilic regions that interact with the fluid on the inside and the outside (Figure 4–6a). But in addition to the channel function certain parts of the amino acid chain lend the protein dynamic properties, such as ion selectivity, voltage dependence, and time dependence.

The Sodium Channel as a Selectivity Filter

At first blush the statement that the sodium channel is selective for sodium (see Figure 4–7) does not seem to be a very extravagant claim. However, if you consider that other channel proteins, such as the potassium channel, are also selective for particular ions, you will discover that the selectivity property is perhaps the most remarkable accomplishment of channel evolution. The selectivity cannot be based on atomic size, because any channel that is large

enough to pass a large ion would necessarily have to pass all smaller species the way a sieve that passed sand would also pass water. Nor can ion charge account for selectivity since both sodium and potassium have identical charge. The exact mechanism of how a few amino acids at the outside lip of the sodium channel determines ion selectivity remains an enduring challenge for channel biophysicists; we will explain the process in a general sense in the following sections.

The Sodium Channel as a Voltage Sensor

Embedded somewhere within the interior of the channel is a strip of a few positively charged amino acids that have freedom to rotate into the hole and block it. Normally the negative membrane potential draws this sequence inward and keeps this little gate closed, preventing the passage of sodium ion. However, when the membrane potential becomes less negative (Region A in Figure 4–5) mechanical tension on this strip somehow causes it to reorient in the membrane and unblock it. In this open position the sodium ions flow freely through. Since the gate itself is charged it generates a tiny current when it rotates in the membrane. Under proper conditions, it is possible to measure these **gating currents** that are too small to be visible in Figure 4–5.

The Sodium Channel as a Time Sensor

Many sodium ions can go through the open channel (about 10 million per second), but in fact far fewer pass, because the same gate that is voltage-sensitive is also connected to a little molecular timer. This timer, also made of a strand of amino acids, allows the channel to stay open only about a millisecond, and hence only a few ions cross each time an individual channel is open. This is a negligible amount considering the total quantity of sodium on each side of the membrane (Chapter 3). The sodium battery (E_{Na}), the voltage sensor, and the timer work together to ensure that the sodium current is very fast, very large, and very brief, and also to ensure that the ion concentration on each side does not change significantly. No more efficient system could be devised to drive the first phase of the action potential.

Figure 4–7 *A Selectivity Filter.* The sodium channel is a selectivity filter that is voltage- and time-dependent. There are two gates that, when closed (a), allow no sodium ions to pass. When they are open (b), sodium ions will enter the cell. The first gate is the voltage-sensor and the second is the inactivation gate. The inactivation gate remains closed longer than the first gate, rendering the sodium channel inactive and the axon refractory to another action potential.

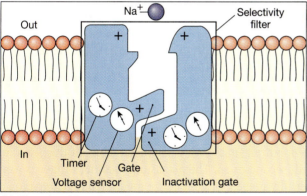

(a) Closed and inactivated

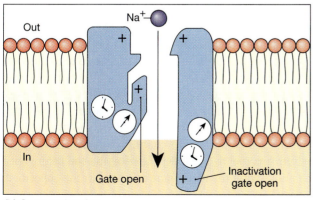

(b) Open and active

The Sodium Channel as an Inactivation Mechanism

Finally, on the cytoplasmic face of the sodium channel there is yet another gate that can block the passageway, connected to still another voltage sensor and timer. This voltage sensor is less sensitive than the first one we discussed, responding only when the membrane is considerably depolarized (as during the action potential). With large or lengthy depolarizations, this sensor closes the second gate. Likewise, the timer associated with this gate is slower than the first. It may render the channel unable to open for milliseconds, seconds, or even longer depending on the circumstances and hence is called the **inactivation gate** (Figure 4–7b). An inactivated sodium channel will not pass current regardless of the state of the first gate sensor and timer and renders the axon refractory to another action potential until the gate is removed.

Functions of the Potassium Channel

Only about twenty amino acids are used in making protein, but somehow they become assembled in such a way as to endow electrically excitable channels with ion selectivity, voltage-measuring, and time-keeping functions that are as elaborate and accurate, in a way, as any equipment humans can assemble. Equally remarkable is the manner is which the potassium channel's properties provide a perfect functional harmony with those of the sodium channel.

The Potassium Channel as a Selectivity Filter

The atomic radius of potassium is larger than that of sodium, so the potassium channel's ability to exclude sodium is obviously not based on size. In fact a little sodium does leak through an open potassium channel (see Figure 3–4 and Figure 4–8) but the channel overwhelmingly favors potassium as the "charge carrier." How did evolution solve this problem using only the four-letter genetic code and the twenty-letter amino acid alphabet? (Some theoretical questions in this book are ultimately answered and some are not. This question is one that cannot be answered at this time and is currently under research).

The Potassium Channel as a Voltage Sensor

Like the voltage sensor of the sodium channel, the potassium channel's sensor causes the gate to open only when the membrane is depolarized. There is, however, no inactivation mechanism for the potassium channel. Once open, the channel will remain so only until the membrane potential hyperpolarizes below the voltage sensor's threshold. This is accomplished, in part, by the passage of potassium, which has a hyperpolarizing effect.

The Potassium Channel as a Delay Mechanism

Since the potassium channel closes when the voltage sensor detects hyperpolarization below its threshold and not after a certain amount of time has passed, we do not say it is "time dependent" like the sodium channel. However, there is a timing mechanism in the potassium channel. It starts timing as soon as the membrane becomes depolar-

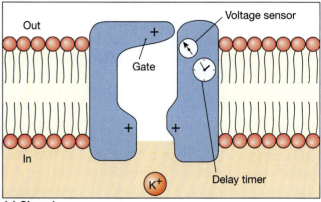

(a) Closed

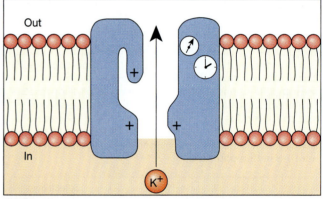

(b) Open

Figure 4–8   *Two Views of the Potassium Channel.*
(a) The voltage-dependent potassium channel is delayed in opening until the cell is depolarized. (b) When the channel opens, potassium exits the cell.

ized, but its effect is to delay the opening of the gate for a millisecond or so. The potassium channel's timer is wonderfully prepared *to allow the sodium conductance to depolarize the cell* before initiating the hyperpolarizing potassium current that drives the falling phase and undershoot of the action potential.

Thus two channels, the sodium channel and the potassium channel, their proteins arising from the action of different genes and possibly those on separate chromosomes, exquisitely complement one another in function. The sodium channel is suited for quick depolarization in response to a stimulus, but also to close quickly in order for the potassium channel to do its work without competition for control of V_m. The potassium channel, in turn *waits* for the sodium channel to finish depolarizing the cell before opening and driving the membrane potential in the opposite direction.

Heterogeneity and Homology

Recent insight into channel structure (Box 4–2) has revealed that some channels are quite a bit more complex than previously believed. The good news is that some are quite a bit simpler.

Most channel types come in more than one version. **Heterogeneity** allows some proteins to do more or less the same thing although they differ in amino acid sequence and hence come from different genes. Sodium channels do not seem cursed with this complexity, but potassium channels appear quite heterogeneous. We have represented a type of potassium channel earlier (see Figure 3–4 and Figure 4–8), which is called the "delayed rectifier" to indicate that it waits after the overshoot to restore, or *rectify*, the resting membrane potential; but there are many more than just this one type. Claims of seven and more different potassium channels appear in the literature of "channelology." Several types of potassium channels are also voltage-dependent like the delayed rectifier, but differ from the delayed rectifier in threshold and time-dependency. Others, such as the **calcium-dependent potassium channel**, are activated by the presence of another ion (calcium in this case). Though the delayed rectifier has ubiquitous importance in nerve cells, the others should not be assumed to be unimportant. The calcium-dependent potassium channel in particular seems to turn up in many neurons in many different organisms.

The phenomenon of heterogeneity in protein structure is not restricted to channels. Enzymes, receptors, and hormones all display this property. Although heterogeneity of functionally similar proteins may seem redundant, this most likely reflects our naiveté regarding the biological importance of each mediated process. Restoring the membrane potential by hyperpolarization may seem a suitable task for a single potassium channel, but the genome that devotes so much space to several such channels may be more concerned with *how much* hyperpolarization, *where* to hyperpolarize, and *when* to hyperpolarize.

Lest you despair of ever keeping up with the seemingly endless number of heterogeneous channels, enzymes, and receptors, it turns out that there is also substantial *similarity* among related (and even unrelated) proteins. Voltage-gated channels, for example, all appear to have a monomeric structure consisting of six transmembrane domains (compare Figure 4–8, the potassium channel, with Figure 4–6, the sodium channel). We have not included examples of the actual decoded amino acid sequences of various channels (which are quite lengthy and make dull reading except to geneticists), but inspection of these would reveal *long segments with identical sequences* of amino acids (Figure 4–9). These shared sequences cannot be due to

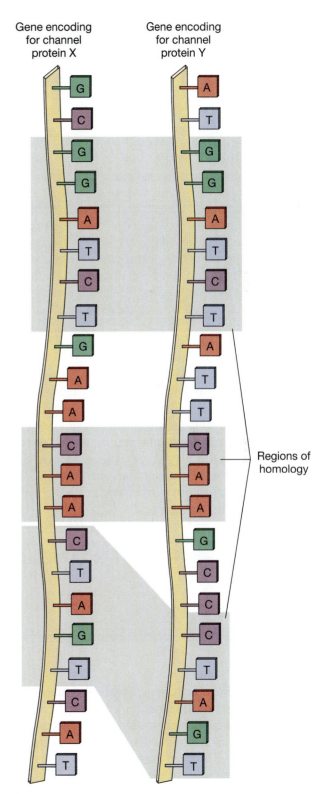

Figure 4–9 *Homology of Proteins.* Although the proteins that compose the different channels are all encoded by different genes, there are regions of identical sequences or homology.

Box 4–2

Discovering Channel Structure

Buried within any electrical record of activity at the cell membrane is a constant hum and flutter known to instrumentation engineers as "noise." But in biology is *noise* really just tiny events that the physiologist is unable to analyze and hence tends to dismiss? Within the noise produced by the excitable membrane are the minute currents generated by *individual channels opening and closing*. Using a very fine pipette with a smooth tip, it is possible to draw up a tiny bit of plasma membrane and tear it away from the cell altogether. With luck, the tiny *patch* will have only a few individual channels in it (perhaps only one) and if the experimenter were to increase the amplification of the signal greatly he or she might see revealed electrical activity of a single channel protein. Such a technique eliminates any contribution by the ion "batteries" since the membrane potential and salt gradients are obliterated when the patch is removed from the cell. The experimenter must *introduce* an arbitrary transmembrane potential; hence the technique is called **patch clamping** (essentially a voltage clamp of a single channel). It is possible to obtain patches with the outside face pointing out as well (so as to be able to study receptor-activated channels, for example).

Voltage-activated channels in patch clamp recording behave in a *probabilistic* manner, which is to say the chances that an individual channel will open increase as the membrane potential passes threshold for that channel type. It is the behavior of many individual channels, each acting probabilistically, that yields such clear-cut changes in the behavior of the membrane voltage during the action potential in an intact cell and causes all of the noise.

Sometimes it is difficult (as in the vertebrate brain) to find a naked patch of membrane to clamp. Also, sometimes a piece of membrane is so rich with channels of various types that it is not possible to just find one of the desired type in a patch. It has recently become quite popular to overcome this difficulty by culturing the channels in the laboratory. Messenger RNA from brain tissue is separated and screened for regions that code for the channel of interest. Once located, the channel RNA is injected into a cell that possesses protein synthesis machinery but lacks transmembrane channels. Typically the frog oocyte (fertilized egg) is used for this purpose, since its membrane does not have many of the channels normally expressed by the brain. The host cell translates channel protein from the injected RNA and the channels eventually appear in the membrane. (For a review of transcription and translation see Chapter 2.) Then patch clamping can be performed just as if the channel was in brain. For more on the use of RNA as a template in research see the section "Genetic Engineering" in the Appendix.

a shared gene, since they are punctuated by stretches of nonsimilar sequence (all sequences would be the same if the channels were coded for by the same gene). Rather, they come from different genes in which long sequences of base pairs are *identical*. This phenomenon of *similarity* in structure (also seen in enzymes, receptors, and hormones) is called homology (*homo* = same). The similarity in sequence is so striking in many cases that it is statistically unlikely that the two (or more) proteins *evolved independently*. Rather, it is thought that they must have had a *common evolutionary ancestor* (in our case a primordial potassium channel in the good old days when only one type of hyperpolarization was required). The existence of homologous structures implies that *a useful sequence of amino acids was duplicated and the products were applied to different purposes* by evolution.

Homology is quite striking especially in the nervous system, but is less apparent in gross features of the body or in the body plan itself. The squid and I bear very little physical resemblance to each other (or at least I did not notice the similarity this morning when I looked in the mirror). Nevertheless, our potassium channels (and sodium channels, chlo-

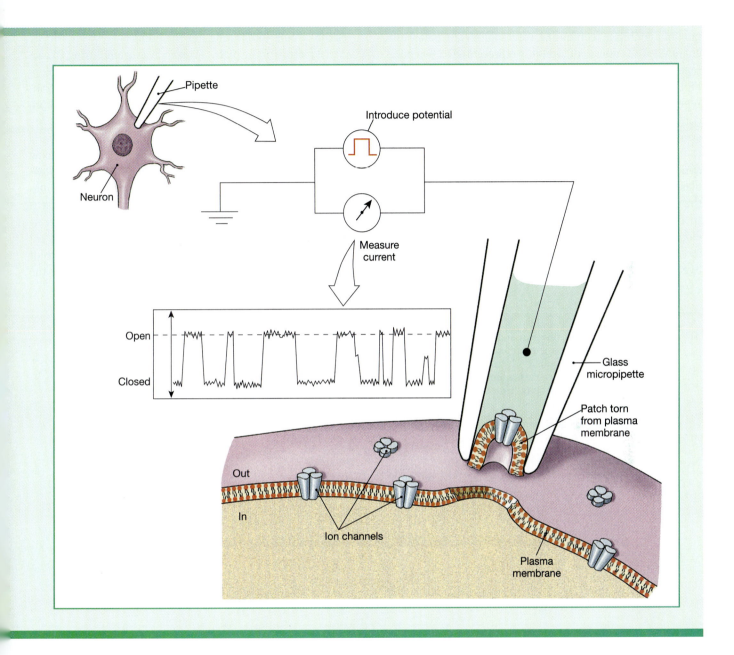

ride channels, calcium channels, and so forth) are substantially the same. Almost certainly a common evolutionary ancestor of people and squids had already evolved the basics of channel structure.

The phenomenon of homology in the nervous system has two corollaries of note. One is that nervous systems are *conserved in evolution* (meaning that they change very slowly). As you read Chapter 5 (synaptic potentials) try to determine why this is so. Another is that *study of simpler organisms can tell us a great deal about ourselves* because of the homology at the molecular and cellular level. Thus the **simple**

systems approach (like Hodgkin and Huxley's study of the squid giant axon) has been one of the more fruitful fields in neuroscience.

The "Equivalent Circuit" Revisited

So far what we've had to discuss involved only a very small patch of excitable membrane, ultimately one so small that it contained only a single channel protein. But how do these processes combine to create the function of a larger patch, say a node of Ranvier, an internodal region, or the entire axon? To answer this we must recall that everything we have described has a pure electrical equivalent. For a small region of membrane (containing a few sodium and potassium channels) the equivalent circuit is represented as two poles separated by the conductors and batteries (see Chapter 3, Figure 3–10b, top). In this configuration the membrane is represented as an **open circuit**. As shown, the circuit cannot conduct electricity because the system is interrupted. However, in a larger section of membrane (Figure 3–10b, bottom) the individual circuits are joined together by conductors on the inside (representing the ability of cytoplasm to conduct electricity) and the outside (representing the ability of the extracellular fluid to conduct electricity). In this configuration the membrane is represented as a **closed circuit**. *Electricity cannot flow through an open circuit.* When the light switch on the wall is "off" the circuit between the positive and negative poles of the line is interrupted (an open circuit). Turning the switch "on" closes the circuit and illuminates the bulbs.

A picture of the pathway taken by current during the action potential is shown in Figure 4–10a. During the peak of the action potential (when the inside of the cell becomes transiently positive) current flows in through the active sodium conductances, through the inside conductors, and then back to the source through the outside conductors. To understand this we must wholly adopt the *electrical equivalent* model for the cell membrane. *Kindly do not think of individual sodium ions jumping into the cell, running down the axon, jumping back out, and running back.* This image is erroneous as well as fatefully confusing. *Abandon* the concern of what carries the charge. Just as the ionic source of electric current becomes irrelevant to a consideration of the flow of current through lights, a microwave, a TV, and so forth, so does the

Figure 4–10 *The Active Equivalent Circuit.* During an action potential (a), the current flows in a circuit by going first through the sodium conductances, then through the inside conductors and finally back to the source. When the axon is myelinated (b), this equivalent circuit is larger because the current must travel all the way to the next node before it can leave the cell. Teleologically, this is important for the cell because the speed of propagation is increased.

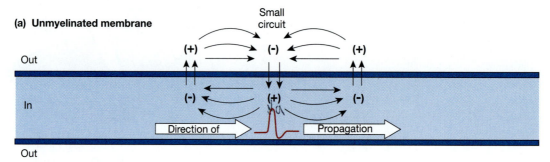

(a) Unmyelinated membrane

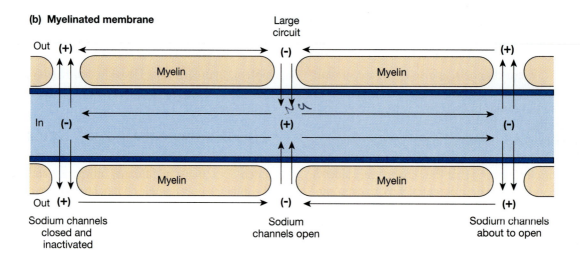

(b) Myelinated membrane

ionic source of membrane current become irrelevant to the consideration of the active equivalent circuit.

The active equivalent circuit is symmetrical because the conductivity of cytoplasm and extracellular fluid is the same regardless of the location of the action potential. Picture the entire equivalent circuit moving down the axon in the direction of action potential propagation, leading with a wave of depolarization and trailing a wave of depolarization behind it. The circuit is "passive" in the sense that no additional channels need to open or close in order for it to be conducted. It is *created* by active channel opening, but *propagated* by purely electrical means.

The Teleology of Refractoriness and Myelin

What prevents an action potential from going all the way down an axon and then turning around and going back up? Theoretically this is a possibility since the membrane is entirely electrically excitable and the equivalent circuit leaves an area of depolarization behind it as it passes. The reason why the action potential doesn't reverberate endlessly in the electrically excitable domain lies in sodium channel inactivation. Though the equivalent circuit is symmetrical, the trailing end of the action potential is passing through a region of sodium channels that have recently experienced opening and are now refractory. The inactivation gate of the sodium channel is in essence the molecular basis of Ramón y Cajal's law of dynamic polarization (Chapter 2). Action potentials begin at one end of the axon and conduct down to the bouton, where they are extinguished so that the axon can prepare for another transmission. Conduction in this fashion is called **orthodromic** flow of information. The opposite, **antidromic** flow, generally occurs experimentally, not in nature.

Let's ask a teleological question about the squid introduced to us in Box 4–1. Why is the squid giant axon so big? Certainly not for the convenience of the curious researchers. You can think of the neuron as a cable (see Box 4–3 on page 80); increased conductance means a given amount of current (such as the inward current of invariant size produced by the action potential) will travel *further* down the axon before leaking out of the membrane and returning to the source. A large diameter cable (i.e., a large diameter axon) will have proportionally greater conductance than a small diameter one. Because passive electrical conduction is much quicker than active channel opening, a larger diameter axon also conducts more quickly than a small one. The squid giant axon innervates the mantle muscle, which constricts to shoot the squid backward by jet propulsion. Squids that do this quickly gain an evolutionary advantage over squids that are a few milliseconds slower ("the quick and the dead"). Hence a teleological explanation of the size of the squid giant axon might be that it is *large* so as to produce a *faster* escape response.

Escape systems in all organisms tend to be characterized by large diameter (fast conducting) fibers. These are found in annelids (worms), crayfish, and vertebrates as well. For example the two giant escape cells in fish (one on each side) are called the **Mauthner cells.** They employ the speed of passive electrical conduction through large diameter fibers to create the darting evasion response any angler is familiar with. Mauthner cells are the only neurons in the vertebrate CNS that are readily identifiable (unique and distinguishable from all others), and they are the closest we get in our phylum to a "giant axon."

Teleologically, why does myelin exist? Recall from Chapter 2 that myelin wraps around and coats an axon. If we look at a membrane model (Figure 4–10b) or consider the cable properties of cells (Box 4–3) we can see that nature holds another solution to the problem of creating speedy responses. The speed of passive propagation can be increased by increasing the conductance of the core (increasing axon diameter) *or* by *decreasing the conductance of the resting membrane*. If the resting membrane resistance (in the "return" portions of the equivalent circuit) is increased by the myelin then the depolarizing current produced by the action potential will travel farther before completing the circuit. As before, this means the equivalent circuit will be *larger*; and since passive electrical conduction is quicker than channel-mediated processes, *larger* means *faster*.

Saltatory Conduction

In practice, the presence of myelin increases the size of the equivalent circuit so that it occupies *three nodes of Ranvier* and *two myelinated regions* (Figure 4–10b). Put in other words, *when inward current predominates at a node, the current must travel all the way to the next node before escaping*. Nothing of interest happens between the nodes except passive electrical conduction. In fact, recent studies suggest that the internodal region lacks electrically excitable sodium channels altogether. Instead, these sodium channels of the fluid mosaic (see Chapter 2) are anchored in the nodal regions of the membrane and do not drift into myelinated axon.

Thus when an action potential occurs, it sets up an equivalent circuit in which the leading edge of the equivalent circuit depolarizes the next node to threshold. Sodium conductance in that region sets up another equivalent circuit. The trailing edge of the new equivalent circuit depolarizes the first node, which is refractory, and the leading edge depolarizes the next one to threshold, and so forth. For a typical cell (Figure 4–11), this process begins with depolarization of the first node of Ranvier (the "axon hillock," labeled 1) and proceeds to each next node in a *leaping* or *stepwise* fashion called **saltatory conduction** (Latin *saltare*, to leap). All the action potentials are identical, except for the

Box 4–3

Cable Properties of Neurons

Since electrical signaling is a common feature of the nervous system and most modern instruments, there is a rich history of "cross-pollination" between neurophysiology and electrical engineering. Ideas have been traded in both directions between the disciplines and, in this book, we will describe several of these exchanges.

One of the earliest examples was the engineering challenge posed by the attempt to lay a transatlantic telephone cable across the ocean floor. It was discovered that much of the signal tended to diffuse off into the ocean unless steps were made to contain it within the cable. Two approaches to this containment are possible: The signal could be confined to the cable by *increasing the core conductance* or by *increasing the resistance between the cable and the sea*. Practically, the core conductance could be enhanced by using a highly conducting material (copper was used) and by increasing the cable diameter. Stout rubber insulation was used to increase the resistance of the boundary between the cable and the sea water. Fifty years later is was discovered that the same equations ("cable equations") that applied to electrical cables in sea water also applied to axons in sea water. Though the core conductor of an axon is salt and not copper, the same principles apply.

Two quantities describe the *passive* conductance of a signal in a cable, the **time constant** and the **space constant**. The space constant is defined by the *length* of cable in which a signal of given magnitude falls to a fixed fraction of its initial value. The size of the space constant increases with cable radius. The time constant is defined by the *rate of rise and fall* of a current signal in a cable or axon. It is directly proportional to the resistance and capacitance of the axon membrane. Thus, increasing diameter increases the space constant and improves transmission, whereas increasing insulation increases the time constant and improves transmission. Both solutions were adopted by the telephone engineers and by the squid (and most organisms) in evolution.

The figure shows a myelinated axon in the body. The resemblance to an insulated wire is quite apparent. The influence of cable properties can be conveniently recalled by reference to the following rules. All things being equal *a large diameter axon conducts more quickly and faithfully than a small one* and a *myelinated axon conducts more quickly and faithfully than an unmyelinated one*.

In the axon, cable properties are combined with *active properties* (i.e., channels opening and shutting). In the dendrites and soma, however, there are fewer regenerative (electrically excitable) channels, so cable properties (i.e., dendrite caliber, resistance, and capacitance) become the major determinant of the effectiveness of electrical transmission. The combined space constants and time constants of many passively conducting dendrites determine *how* convergent synaptic input will be encoded in action potential frequency. This process is called **integration** and is thought (by proponents of Ramón y Cajal's neuron doctrine) to be the cellular basis of thought. This topic will be explored more thoroughly in Chapter 5.

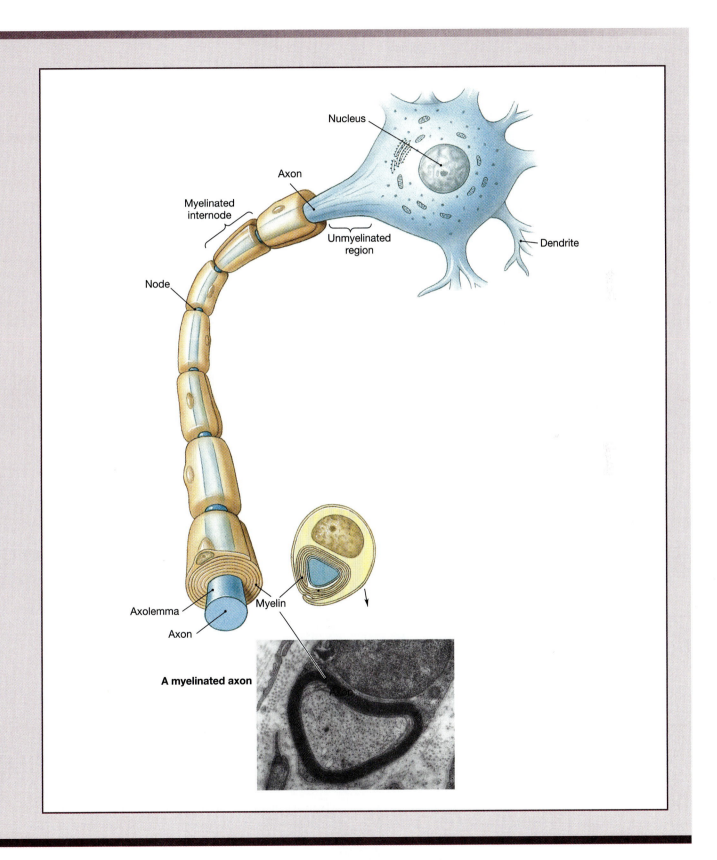

A myelinated axon

Figure 4–11 *Saltatory Conduction.* Saltatory conduction increases the speed of an action potential by enabling the depolarizations to leap from one node of Ranvier to the next. As the current is propagated along the axon, the action potential at each node is exactly the same, with two exceptions: The action potential at the first node (1) has a synaptic potential influence (Region A in Figure 4–5) and the action potential at the last node (15) is longer in duration.

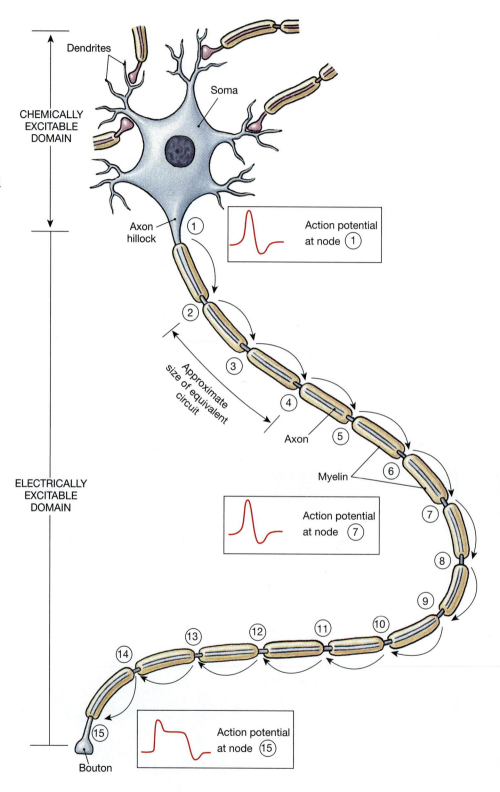

very first (remember it has a little bit of synaptic potential in it, Region A in Figure 4–5) and the last (which has a special current unique to boutons that facilitates exocytosis of vesicles). The neuron depicted in Figure 4–11 has 15 nodes, but a typical cell might have many more, perhaps hundreds. According to the law of dynamic polarization, the process always starts at the first node, always goes to the last, never changes from action potential to action potential and only varies in the frequency with which the electrically excitable domain is activated.

Extracellular Records of Neural Activity

We are very close to understanding one-half of the neuron, namely, the electrically excitable domain. From the perspective of the *inside* of the cell we now know the reason for the waveform appearance of each action potential. In actual practice, however, we will rarely be able to adopt the point of view of the inside of the cell. This is because the tiny neurons inside the brain are very difficult to impale with an intracellular electrode without damaging them in the process. Most of our information about their behavior comes from records *outside* the cell, using an **extracellular electrode**. Fortunately the appearance of these extracellular records is a mere reflection of what is happening intracellularly and therefore they can be interpreted with ease.

As we saw in Figure 4–10 the equivalent circuit has three phases (outward, inward, and outward currents). If you imagine a *stationary* extracellular electrode with the equivalent circuit *passing by*, you can see that the extracellular manifestation of the action potential will be a *triphasic* waveform reflecting first extracellular positivity (leading edge), then extracellular negatively (peak of action potential), and finally extracellular positivity again (trailing edge) (Figure 4–12a). With an intracellular record the membrane resistance forces a large part of the signal through the amplifier to ground and hence the record is faithful to the actual size of the event (about 100 mV). However, only a small portion of extracellular current passes through the instrumentation so the signal is only a small sample of the total extracellular current that is flowing (reflected as a voltage signal about 100 µV in size). Note that extracellular recording is not referred to ground but rather to a distant "indifferent" electrode (in a manner called "differential recording"). Since there is no membrane to introduce a voltage drop, extracellular records are direct reflections of membrane *currents*. (Why doesn't the *intracellular* action potential also have a triphasic appearance? Outward currents do indeed exist at the leading and trailing edges on the inside, but these are tiny compared to the voltage change [depolarizing] introduced by the cable properties of the membrane.)

Depending on extracellular electrode location, one phase or another of the triphasic action potential may be exaggerated in the record (usually the *last* phase; can you think why?). Generally, however, the extracellular record is *condensed* by the experimenter so as to collapse the phases into a single, abrupt deflection. To make it sound more dramatic to outsiders, electrophysiologists call these extracellular action potentials **spikes**, as in "the neuron is firing more *spikes* than it was a moment ago" (see Figure 4–12b).

Frequently, the record is fed into a speaker called an "audio monitor" which produces pops and crackling sounds corresponding to the action potentials as they occur. (This is done because the human ear has finer discriminative powers than the human eye; see Chapter 9). Since the action potentials of a given cell are always the same, the cells that generate them are called **units**. Extracellular recording from a single cell is called **single unit recording** and a recording in which there are several cells that can be distinguished based on the shape of their respective spikes is called **multiunit recording**.

In one form of *multiunit recording* it is possible to record the activity of many hundreds of cells, but it is not possible to resolve individual units. This form is called **field potential recording** because the activity of an entire *field* of cells generates the current. In the example shown in Figure 4–12c the spike is negative for the reasons we have described, but other currents (arising largely from remoter synaptic processes) distort and exaggerate the positive aspects of the waveform.

Ultimately, it is possible to perform field potential recording with electrodes that are *outside the skull entirely*, as for an awake human volunteer. In such cases it is likely that neurons in many fields contribute to the record (perhaps the entire brain contributes). Here, *even though the waveform is all due to the good old-fashioned equivalent circuit*, it is sometimes difficult to separate the various phases of synaptic and action potentials. Nevertheless, this type of recording can be very revealing regarding central processes. It is called **electroencephalography**, or **EEG** (Figure 4–12d). **Biofeedback research** (in which the subject uses his or her own EEG, converted to an auditory signal, to relax or concentrate) is one area that employs the EEG technique. We shall consider some of the many other uses of biofeedback elsewhere in the book.

Special Channels for Calcium

The function of the electrically excitable domain is not just to get information from the soma to the axon tip. To fulfill its purpose it must also *transmit that information across the synapse*. This is done by the third class of electrically excitable channels, calcium channels. (Do you remember what the first two were?) Be certain, in what is to follow, to separate **presynaptic** ("before the synapse") processes (calcium influx, vesicle fusion) from **postsynaptic** ("after the synapse") ones (synaptic potentials); we will consider the latter in detail in the next chapter.

Presynaptic Calcium Channels

The action potential changes its shape when it invades the bouton after the last node of Ranvier. It becomes longer in

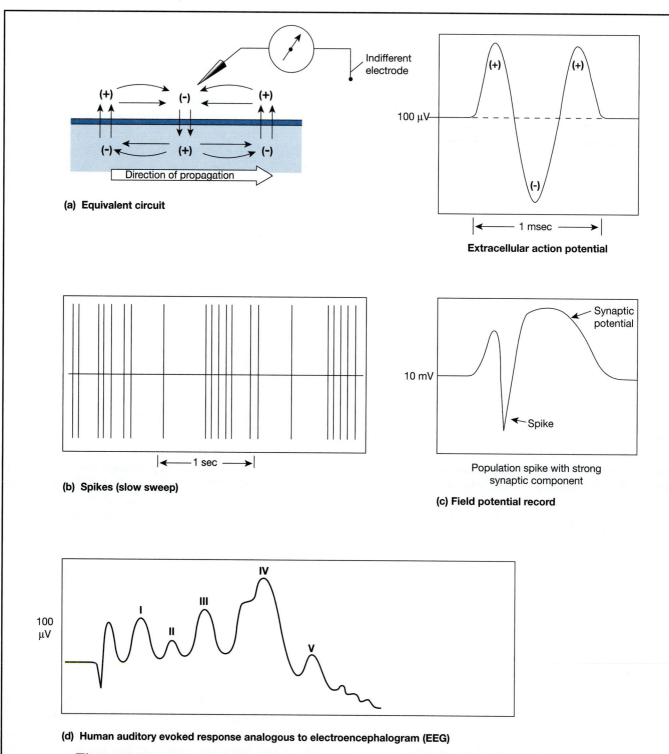

(a) **Equivalent circuit**

Extracellular action potential

(b) **Spikes (slow sweep)**

Population spike with strong synaptic component

(c) **Field potential record**

(d) **Human auditory evoked response analogous to electroencephalogram (EEG)**

Figure 4–12   *Extracellular Records.* (a) When measuring a single cell, the nature of the equivalent circuit produces a triphasic waveform on an extracellular record. (b) Usually the waveform or spike is condensed by the experimenter so the three waves collapse into one. (c) When many cells are simultaneously being recorded by the method of field potential recording, the entire population of cells contribute to the spike. (d) When the entire brain is being measured, different regions of neurons (for instance regions I, II, III, IV, or V) elicit their own spike. The various phases of the spike's action and synaptic potentials are difficult to distinguish.

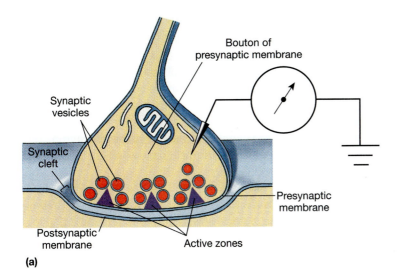

(a)

Figure 4–13 *Presynaptic Calcium Current.* (a) When recording the potential at the bouton of the presynaptic cell, the action potential (b) at the last node is seen to be of a longer duration than for previous nodes. (c) In an experiment performed to isolate the conductance responsible for this effect, the sodium currents (dashed lines) are blocked with TTX and the bouton of the presynaptic cell is stimulated. The results indicate that calcium current is responsible. The influx of Ca^{++} causes vesicles containing synaptic transmitter to fuse with the plasma membrane by exocytosis (d) releasing transmitter into the synaptic cleft.

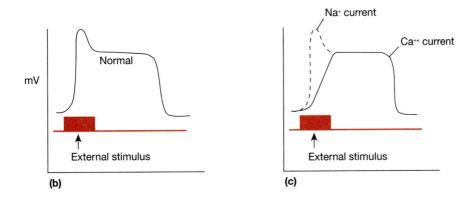

(b) **(c)**

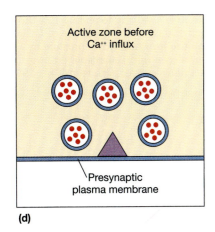
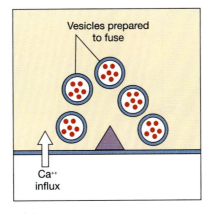
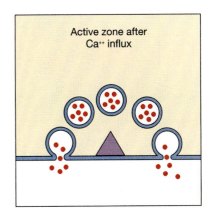

(d)

duration, resembling a "fat" action potential (Figure 4–13). Under special circumstances it is possible to analyze the ionic mechanisms for this last action potential of the presynaptic neuron, termed the bouton action potential because it ends at the bouton of the presynaptic neuron. (Which circumstances? Why, through the use of the squid giant *synapse* of course.) If we stimulate the bouton directly (Figure 4–13a) and then block the voltage-dependent sodium currents with TTX, only *part* of the bouton action potential is affected (Figure 4–13b). Removal of sodium eliminates only the *first part* of the bouton action potential, leaving the "hump" unaltered. Obviously some other ion mediates the late portion. Since potassium and chloride can be eliminated (because as we saw in Chapter 3 their equilibrium potentials do not permit depolarization), calcium cation is the most likely candidate. In fact, the Nernst potential for calcium (Chapter 3) indicates that there is a strong driving force for calcium to *enter* the cell.

Thus there are voltage-dependent calcium channels, analogous to those sodium channels we are familiar with, but they are located only in the bouton. When the incoming action potential signals these channels to open, calcium flows into the cell (since it "wants" the membrane potential to be equal to its own equilibrium potential). This **calcium current** depolarizes the bouton. (I got a value for E_{Ca}^{++} of +58 mV using the Nernst equation, with $z = 2$; see Box 3–1 if you'd like to try it.)

Vesicle Fusion and Exocytosis

What happens next is a subject of considerable scrutiny. Within the boutons are vesicles that contain synaptic transmitters. Calcium, being a divalent cation (having two positive

charges), may interact with the *inside face* of the plasma membrane and the *outside face* of vesicle membranes to allow the two to approach each other. (Recall that each is coated with the negatively charged phosphate groups and hence repel each other.) Processes involving a calcium-binding enzyme known as **calmodulin** and other intracellular energy-consuming (ATP-consuming) enzymes further promote *fusion of the vesicle membrane and the plasma membrane* (Figure 4–13c). The place in the membrane where this occurs is called the **active zone**.

The fusion takes place so quickly that it is rarely captured in an electron micrograph. However, if the presynaptic membrane is quickly frozen *just at the moment* that the calcium channels open, say by launching the synapse into a vat of liquid helium, then vesicles can be observed in the act of exocytosis (so called because it involves the transfer of cell contents to the outside of the cell). Figure 4–14 is a famous example of one such experiment. Figure 4–14b shows *a face view* of the presynaptic plasma membrane moments before the calcium-dependent action potential arrives. The observ-

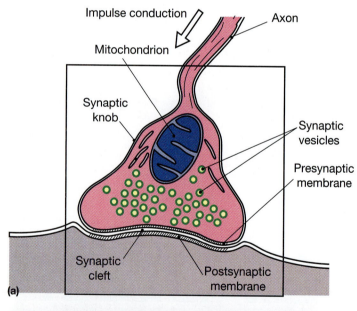

(a)

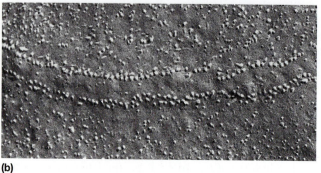

(b)

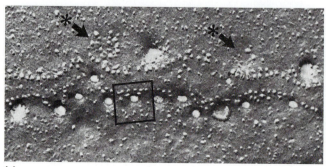

(c)

Figure 4–14 *Calcium-Mediated Exocytosis.* The freeze-fracture technique involves the freezing of the membrane followed by fracturing the frozen cell through the hydrophobic region of the lipid bilayer. When the resulting faces are shadowed with platinum, proteins will appear as bumps and a model of the membrane can be made and viewed under an electron microscope. In the experiment below, (b) the presynaptic membrane was frozen and fractured before the calcium-dependent action potential arrives and (c) immediately after. The ridge in (b) is made up of the calcium channels waiting to open. After the channels are open and calcium enters the cell, the vesicles fuse with the presynaptic membrane by exocytosis. The pits seen in (b) correspond to the vesicles in the act of exocytosis. (Heuser et al., 1979)

er thus adopts the perspective of the postsynaptic cell. The narrow rows of particles are thought to be the calcium channels themselves, just opening or preparing to open. Figure 4–14c, taken from the presynaptic plasma membrane just a millisecond later, shows pits corresponding to vesicles fusing with the membrane in the process of exocytosis and hence releasing synaptic transmitter into the extracellular space. Of course, when the cell is not growing or retracting, each act of exocytosis must be accompanied by an act of endocytosis (Chapter 2). This endocytosis and recycling of vesicle membrane also happens very fast, so that a photograph a few milliseconds later would resemble the adjacent panel. No vesicle "pits" would be apparent.

Thus the action potential involves transfer of electrical information from the axon hillock to the bouton. It begins with a *postsynaptic* event (depolarization of the cell membrane at the axon hillock) and ends with a *presynaptic* event (vesicle exocytosis and release of synaptic transmitter at the bouton. Now that you thoroughly understand everything in the electrically excitable domain of the cell, we can consider the processes in between the bouton and the axon hillock, i.e., the physiology of the *chemically excitable domain*.

SUMMARY

The neuron can be divided into two parts: the electrically excitable domain and the chemically excitable domain. The axon and bouton constitute the electrically excitable domain, in which transmission of information takes the form of action potentials. The action potential is an abrupt, all-or-none depolarization of the cell membrane. It arises in the first node of Ranvier next to the soma and is conducted stepwise without decrement from node to node until the bouton is reached. In the axon, the action potential is created by two conductances, the sodium conductance and the potassium conductance. The sodium conductance is voltage-dependent since it requires a small depolarization past threshold to take place. It is time-dependent since it shuts itself off after a brief period. The potassium conductance is also voltage-dependent, since it is activated only at depolarized membrane potentials. However, it is delayed so as to allow the sodium conductance to depolarize the cell before repolarization towards E_K begins. The conductances are the property of two transmembrane pro-

teins: the sodium channel and the potassium channel. The sequence of amino acids in these channels contains the voltage sensors and timing devices necessary for the action potential to occur. The sodium channel has an inactivation mechanism that, by creating refractoriness, ensures that the action potential is conducted only in the orthodromic direction.

Consideration of the action potential in terms of its electrical equivalent is much easier than consideration of the behavior of individual ions. Use of the "equivalent circuit" model explains much about the importance of myelin, the significance of axon diameter, the basis of integration, and the waveforms displayed by extracellular records.

At the bouton the mechanisms present in the axon are supplemented by a new voltage-dependent conductance mediated by the calcium channel. Calcium influx catalyzes vesicle fusion and exocytosis which leads to transmitter release. The presynaptic membrane and the active zone of exocytosis both belong to the electrically excitable domain.

REVIEW QUESTIONS

1. Why is an action potential "all-or-none"?
2. What does "threshold" refer to in the neuron membrane?
3. What is a "voltage clamp" and why is it needed?
4. What toxins were used to block active currents in the squid giant axon?
5. Name the properties of the sodium channel.
6. Name the properties of the potassium channel.
7. How do the two channels complement each other?
8. What is "saltatory conduction"?
9. What is the molecular basis for the "law of dynamic polarization"?
10. How does an intracellular record of the action potential differ from an extracellular record, and why?

THOUGHT QUESTIONS

1. Speaking of patch clamping, a famous neuroscientist was heard to remark, "One man's signal is another man's noise." Comment on this observation discussing its relevance to the scientific endeavor, life in general, and gender politics.

2. Some action potentials require stimulation to occur, but others are spontaneous. Comment on the relevance of spontaneous bursters to the mind/body problem.

KEY CONCEPTS

action potential (p. 65)
active zone (p. 86)
all-or-none (p. 66)
antidromic (p. 79)
biofeedback research (p. 83)
bursting cell (p. 66)
calcium current (p. 86)
calcium-dependent potassium channel (p. 75)
calmodulin (p. 86)
chemically excitable domain (p. 64)
closed circuit (p. 78)

electrically excitable domain (p. 64)
electroencephalography (EEG) (p. 83)
extracellular electrode (p. 83)
field potential recording (p. 83)
gating currents (p. 73)
heterogeneity (p. 75)
homology (p. 76)
inactivation gate (p. 74)
integration (p. 80)
Mauthner cells (p. 79)

multiunit recording (p. 83)
open circuit (p. 78)
orthodromic (p. 79)
overshoot (p. 66)
pacemakers (p. 66)
patch clamping (p. 76)
postsynaptic (p. 83)
presynaptic (p. 83)
refractoriness (p. 66)
saltatory conduction (p. 79)
simple systems approach (p. 77)
single unit recording (p. 83)

space constant (p. 80)
spikes (p. 83)
tetraethylammonium (TEA) (p. 70)
tetrodotoxin (TTX) (p. 70)
threshold (p. 66)
time constant (p. 80)
time dependent (p. 71)
undershoot (p. 66)
units (p. 83)
voltage clamp (p. 67)
voltage dependent (p. 71)

Synapses are protoplasmic kisses . . . the final ecstasy of an epic love story.

Santiago Ramón y Cajal (1852–1934)

Communication Among Neurons: The Synaptic Potential

The **synapse**, the junction between two neurons, is the primary venue for neurons to communicate with one another. All multicelled organisms above the level of sponges are seen to have synapses (and sponges may have synapselike structures that serve some of the same purposes). Thus we could say with some hope of accuracy that synaptic communication and its product, neural integration, defines the boundary between simple and complex organisms. It takes two cells to make a synapse. The presynaptic bouton is the end point of the *electrically excitable domain* of one cell and the *postsynaptic* dendrite is where the *chemically excitable domain* of the other cell begins.

The Chemically Excitable Domain

In concept, everything that happens in the chemically excitable domain is the same as for the electrically excitable domain *except for the signal that opens the gate in the various ion channels*. Everything that we have learned about batteries, cable properties, and so forth holds with equal force for the chemically excitable domain *except that the conductances are regulated by the presence of the synaptic transmitter*. This does not mean that there are no voltage-dependent processes in the soma and dendrites, but the voltage-dependent sodium channel and the voltage-dependent potassium channel (the "delayed rectifier") appear to be wholly missing from this part of the neuron.

No action potentials of the kind we have considered (Chapter 4) can take place in the chemically excitable domain. Instead of large all-or-nothing signals, the chemically excitable region experiences smaller, longer, and *continuously variable* changes in membrane potential induced by transmitter-activated sodium, potassium, and chloride conductance. These **postsynaptic potentials** are incremental, that is, they can be found in a range of sizes in the depolarizing and hyperpolarizing directions.

For each cell in the brain there are typically hundreds of synaptic contacts but often only a single axon, and hence only a single axon hillock. Since the axon hillock is the first piece of excitable membrane (see Figure 4–11), the decision to fire or not fire an action potential depends on whether the axon hillock reaches threshold or not. Thus, *synaptic potentials are classified according to their*

(a)

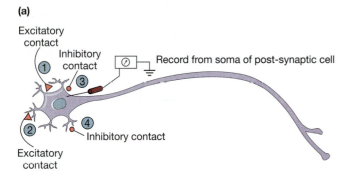

(b) EPSPs mediated by increase in g_{Na}

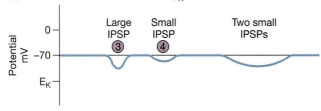

(c) IPSPs mediated by increase in g_K

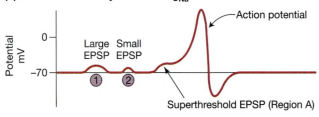

Figure 5–1 *Depolarizing and Hyperpolarizing Postsynaptic Potentials.* **(a)** The chemically excitable domain experiences changes in membrane potential of varying amplitudes in the depolarizing (excitatory contact) or in the hyperpolarizing (inhibitory contact) direction. **(b)** Cells 1 and 2 produce an EPSP mediated by an increase in g_{Na}. If the EPSP is large enough to reach threshold, an action potential will result. **(c)** Cells 3 and 4 produce an IPSP by increasing g_K.

influence on the axon hillock. Synaptic potentials that are conducive to action potential generation (usually because they depolarize the dendrites and soma) are called *excitatory* postsynaptic potentials (universally referred to as EPSPs). Synaptic potentials that tend to prevent the axon hillock from reaching threshold (by hyperpolarizing or by *blocking depolarization* in the dendrites and soma) are called *inhibitory* postsynaptic potentials (universally known as IPSPs). Figure 5–1 illustrates EPSPs and IPSPs.

Excitatory Postsynaptic Potentials

EPSPs may come about in any of three ways. In fact, only three are *possible,* given what we have learned about electrical signaling. It is not surprising that all three are employed by nature, which has a way of leaving no opportunity

unexploited. Pause here and see if you can guess the three mechanisms.

The first (and perhaps most prevalent) mechanism for the generation of EPSPs is a postsynaptic increase in sodium conductance (g_{Na}). Since the sodium equilibrium potential (E_{Na}) is depolarized from rest, this increase in g_{Na} leads to depolarization just as for the rising phase of the action potential, except that the sodium-mediated EPSP is neither as large nor as fast.

The only other ion species with an equilibrium potential depolarized from rest is calcium. One transmitter-gated ion channel known at present admits calcium (probably activated by glutamate or aspartate, discussed later in this chapter), and there are several other transmitters thought to activate a calcium conductance by indirect means (i.e., by second or third messengers, see Chapter 6).

If only sodium conductance and calcium conductance can depolarize the cell, what could the third EPSP mechanism involve? The membrane is negative in the first place because of high *resting* potassium conductance. What if this conductance were *decreased* or attenuated by transmitter action? In fact a growing number of synapses have been found to act by this means, essentially by activating a *resistance* to potassium flux. At first regarded as exotic, attenuation of potassium conductance as a means of promoting excitation now appears to be a major synaptic mechanism in the brain. Not only the resting potassium conductance but also voltage-dependent and novel *calcium-dependent potassium conductances* are involved in this type of EPSP. Figure 5–1b also illustrates the result when the EPSP is large enough to cause an action potential.

Inhibitory Postsynaptic Potentials

Of the large variety of possible IPSP mechanisms (how many can you think of?) only two seem to be widely employed by synapses in the brain. Figure 5–1c illustrates IPSPs that act by *directly hyperpolarizing* the postsynaptic cell membrane. Since there is only one ion species with an equilibrium potential more negative than the resting potential, these IPSPs must be mediated by potassium efflux. (Recall that the resting sodium conductance is very small, so reduction of this value would not yield much hyperpolarization). In fact, it is possible to demonstrate directly that the IPSP is potassium-mediated, by employing the concept of **reversal potential** (Figure 5–2). When the neuron membrane potential (V_m) is at rest (–70 mV) activation of an inhibitory contact will cause the membrane to fluctuate momentarily in the hyperpolarizing direction. But what if the synapse is activated when the membrane potential is at some other value? This could be done by "clamping" the membrane at some other value of potential and measuring current (see Box 4–1). Or this could be

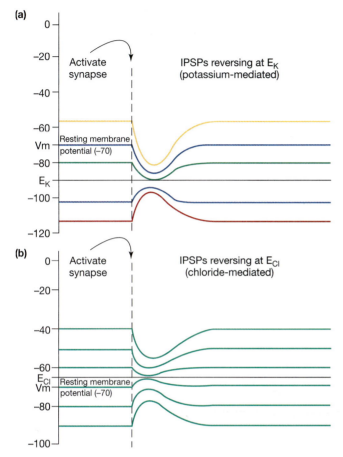

(a)

Activate synapse

IPSPs reversing at E_K (potassium-mediated)

Resting membrane potential (–70)

Vm

E_K

(b)

Activate synapse

IPSPs reversing at E_{Cl} (chloride-mediated)

E_{Cl}
Vm

Resting membrane potential (–70)

Figure 5–2 *Reversal Potentials for IPSPs.* Two conductances may be responsible for IPSPs: g_K and g_{Cl}. Because each ion wants the membrane potential to equal its own equilibrium potential, the potassium battery (a) hyperpolarizes the cell, drawing the potential in the opposite direction of threshold. The chloride battery (b) produces an IPSP by maintaining the resting potential and therefore counteracting any effect produced by a depolarizing ion conductance. The reversal potentials for these conductances is the best means of demonstrating their role in the production of IPSPs.

achieved by simply injecting current to hyperpolarize or depolarize the cell with a device called a **bridge circuit** which also permits voltage measurements to be acquired at the same time. A family of such bridge circuit records for a potassium-mediated IPSP is shown in Figure 5–2a. When a hyperpolarizing inhibitory synapse is activated at membrane potentials that are *depolarized* from rest, the IPSP seems *larger* (yellow line) because it has farther to go to reach the potassium potential (E_K). This is because the driving force on potassium is greater the farther the membrane voltage (V_m) is from E_K. On the other hand, as V_m *approaches* E_K (values for V_m hyperpolarized from rest) the size of the IPSP *diminishes* because the driving force is weaker (green line). Finally, if V_m

passes E_K in the hyperpolarizing direction, the appearance of the IPSP *reverses* (red line). Each ion wants the membrane potential to be equal to its own equilibrium potential *and will move in whatever direction is needed to accomplish this*. Reversal at E_K is the best evidence for mediation by potassium efflux. To date all hyperpolarizing IPSPs reverse at E_K, indicating that they are all mediated by a synaptic transmitter that opens a chemically sensitive potassium channel.

However, it is a startling revelation for students new to neuroscience that many, if not most, IPSPs are not hyperpolarizing at all. Recall that IPSPs are defined by their tendency to prevent the axon hillock from reaching threshold. This can be accomplished by hyperpolarization to be sure, *but also by any process that tends to keep the neuron at rest*. The value of the chloride potential, E_{Cl}, (–66 mV) is very close to the resting membrane potential (–70 mV). Thus activation of a chloride conductance by a synaptic transmitter would have very little impact on V_m. In fact, as seen in Figure 5–2b, a chloride-mediated synaptic potential might actually have a very small *depolarizing* effect when activated. However, the increased chloride conductance would have the effect of *counteracting any other depolarizing or hyperpolarizing synaptic potential*, since it will simultaneously draw the membrane potential back toward the equilibrium potential for chloride. The chloride conductance acts as a *shunt* (or short-circuit) for any other active currents flowing across the dendrite membrane. This **chloride shunt**, by decreasing total membrane resistance, changes the cable properties of the dendrites, effectively *reducing* the size of the equivalent circuit. As we learned in the last chapter, small equivalent circuits conduct more *slowly* and with more *attenuation* of the signal. The net result is that all other EPSPs and IPSPs in the vicinity will have diminished impact on the axon hillock. The hillock will be less likely to reach threshold and hence chloride-mediated synaptic events are all IPSPs. The synaptically mediated chloride shunt is very important in neuroscience. We shall have occasion to discuss it in many contexts, such as our consideration of tranquilizers and sedatives (Chapter 17) and in the section on mental illness (Chapter 18).

Summation and Integration

Picture the dendritic arbor as having hundreds of synaptic contacts and continuously experiencing IPSPs and EPSPs. The reduction of this synaptic input to action potentials is called **integration**. For simplicity, Figure 5–3 shows a cell that receives only five contacts, but keep in mind that a single neuron can receive hundreds of contacts. Excitatory contacts are colored magenta, and inhibitory contacts are colored blue. Recall that these boutons have vesicles that contain transmitters (Chapter 4) that activate *postsynaptic* sodium, potassium, or chloride conductances (g_{Na}, g_K, or g_{Cl}). We have left

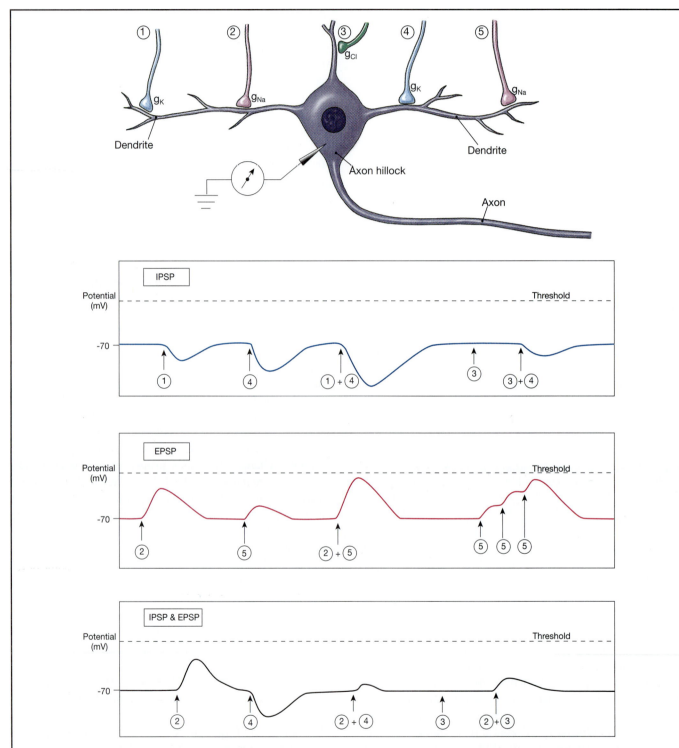

Figure 5–3   *Summation and Integration.* Each cell may receive many signals from various cells. This information must be combined or integrated into one response. Contacts farther away from the soma (1 and 5) will have less of an effect compared to closer contacts (2 and 4). Due to spatial summation, when two potassium-mediated IPSPs or two EPSPs are added, the result is a larger effect than with one alone (1 + 4 and 2 + 5). Temporal summation occurs when a potassium-mediated IPSP or an EPSP is activated in quick succession and the responses pile on top of one another (5 + 5 + 5). Finally, when an IPSP (potassium- or chloride-mediated) and an EPSP combine, they counteract each other (2 + 4 and 2 + 3).

out the synapses that act by other mechanisms, and have presented all the synaptic events as subthreshold for action potential generation (threshold indicated by dashed line).

Two synapses that activate a postsynaptic potassium conductance are shown, labeled 1 and 4. Synapse 1 contacts its dendrite at a position far from the soma, and hence it has less impact on the membrane potential than 4, with a contact closer to the cell body. When 1 and 4 are simultaneously active, the IPSP is larger than for each alone (Figure 5–3). Their impact on the membrane voltage has been added together, a process known as **spatial summation**. The combined IPSP is close to being the arithmetic sum of the two individual IPSPs, but not quite. This is because the driving force on potassium ion changes as the membrane potential approaches the potassium equilibrium potential.

Synapse 3 is chloride-mediated. When active alone, little or no change in postsynaptic membrane potential is seen (see Figure 5–3). This is because increased chloride flux merely forces the membrane potential close to the chloride potential, which is close to the value of the membrane voltage at rest. However, should there be a simultaneous activation of another conductance (such as the potassium conductance of synapse 4), the IPSP is much smaller than usual. The potassium conductance must compete with the chloride conductance of synapse 3 for control of the membrane voltage.

Interaction among EPSPs is very similar (Figure 5–3). An excitatory contact close to the soma (2) has a greater impact than one that is farther away (5). The equivalent circuit for each may be the same size (i.e., the synapses may be equally strong), but the cable properties of dendrites are such that significant attenuation of the distal (or more removed) EPSP occurs before it reaches the soma. The circuits are small and passively conducted. No regeneration or propagation of sodium, potassium, or chloride currents occurs because there are no voltage-dependent channels for these ions in the chemically excitable domain.

EPSPs display spatial summation just like IPSPs (2 and 5 combine to form a much larger potential than either alone, see Figure 5–3). Another common feature of synaptic potentials, both excitatory and inhibitory, is **temporal summation**. This is illustrated by the combined impact that a weak synapse (5) has if it is activated repetitively in quick succession (see Figure 5–3). EPSPs and IPSPs last longer than action potentials since they are not time-dependent and can actually pile on top of one another. In this manner even a distant, relatively ineffective synapse can have a major impact on whether an action potential occurs.

Summation works in the negative direction also (I suppose we should call this "subtraction," but we don't). A strong EPSP (2) and IPSP (4) will cancel each other out when they occur simultaneously (Figure 5–3). The chloride conductance activated by a synapse like 3 is so strong that it is almost as effective as the other IPSP mechanism (4) in blocking the EPSP (2).

You might surmise that an IPSP has little purpose without an EPSP to block. Indeed, you might suspect that IPSPs are saved by the brain and used only when blockade of an EPSP is necessary. After all, the only thing that counts is whether the axon hillock reaches threshold or not. An IPSP that prevents an EPSP from creating an action potential has a purpose in life, and one that does not is the ultimate in lost information, as useless as a nut without a bolt or a phone call when nobody's home. However, this is one occasion in which teleology fails us, for in fact IPSPs occur often in the absence of excitation. Central neurons are typically bombarded with a barrage of IPSPs all day, all night, and throughout life. Qualitatively, inhibition is a much more abundant process than excitation, with IPSPs outnumbering EPSPs by a large factor. Qualitatively, we might even be able to say that inhibition is *more important* than excitation, for behavior is sometimes better characterized not by the description of which neural circuits are active, but by a description of which ones are *not*. This last point is a significant one that deserves a bit of reflection.

Think of all the things you could be doing right now. Let's not just think of preferences ("I'd rather be sailing, golfing, whitewater rafting, etc.") but think also of *possibilities*. Think of all the things you *have* done, all the things you *can* do and all the things you *will* do someday. Think of the things you might do but hopefully won't. Think of everything, in short, that the neural circuits in your brain *enable* you to do.

Now, for contrast, think of what you are actually doing. You are sitting (or perhaps lying down) and reading Smock's book. While this may involve more excitation for some of you than for others, it is safe to say that for each of you the overwhelming process is inhibition. All the things you could be doing, but aren't, are behaviors that are being inhibited by the brain. They are the products of latent neural circuits, restrained by the barrage of IPSPs and waiting for their moment of expression. Furthermore, even in a lifetime rich with experience only a fraction of the circuits will *ever* find expression; the rest will be suppressed forever by inhibition. Some suppressed circuits deserve to be that way; the well-being of the organism would be jeopardized by display of certain behaviors at the wrong place or time such as tap-dancing while on a tightrope without a net. Some deserve expression, as pundits of the "human potential" movement are fond of pointing out, but will never be expressed simply because life is too short for everything.

Do not mourn the fate of latent circuits however, for mankind has long been aware of the vast reservoirs of experience that must forever lie only in the world of possibility. In the words of the poet Thomas Gray (1716–1771):

> Full many a gem of purest ray serene
> The dark unfathomed caves of ocean bear:
> Full many a flower is born to blush unseen
> And waste its sweetness on the desert air.
>
> *(Elegy Written in a Country Churchyard)*

Special Channels for Calcium

We know about the special voltage-dependent channels for calcium in the *presynaptic* half of the synapse. (These admit calcium ions that facilitate exocytosis, Chapter 4.) There are also voltage-dependent calcium channels on the *postsynaptic* (dendritic) membrane. These present something of a wrinkle in our model, which so far has segregated the electrically excitable domain from the chemically excitable domain, since voltage-dependent calcium channels sometimes lead to action potentials in the dendrites.

Postsynaptic Calcium Channels

It is not clear how common regenerative calcium currents (see Figure 4–13) are in dendrites, since it is only in favorable preparations (i.e., accessible to the experimenters) that recordings of them can be obtained. Figure 5–4 shows some records from one such preparation in which the experimenter was able to extract intracellular records from dendrites (Llinás & Sugimori, 1980). Recordings from distal dendrites (those far from the soma) have long-duration **calcium spikes** similar to those found in the bouton (Figure 5–4a). Recordings of more proximal dendrites (close to the soma) have fewer (Figure 5–4b, c), presumably because some calcium spikes fail to propagate from very tiny to large diameter dendrites. Finally, when recording from the soma, only a small residue of the calcium current in the dendrites is apparent. This is because the soma lacks electrically excitable calcium channels and so the calcium spikes don't invade at all. We say that they are **electrotonically remote** to indicate that their equivalent circuit does not extend as far as the electrode. Also, sodium spikes from the axon hillock (much larger and electrotonically closer) tend to swamp the calcium spikes (Figure 5–4d). It is possible that these dendritic calcium spikes are quite common in central neurons but have been overlooked because recording is commonly only possible in the soma. Other, nonelectrical ways of looking for calcium spikes indicate they may often arise in dendritic membrane. Most of our theories of integration employ the cable properties of dendrites as a model of how sodium-, potassium-, and chloride-dependent EPSPs and IPSPs add and subtract. The presence of voltage-

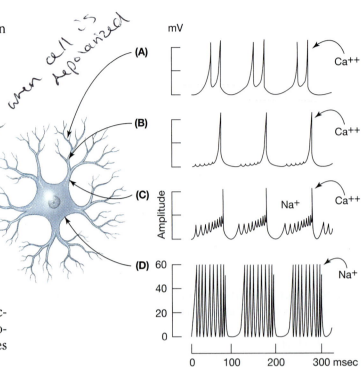

activate when cell is depolarized

Figure 5–4 *Postsynaptic Calcium Currents.* Intracellular records of calcium currents show that when the recording electrode is in a dendrite far from the soma (a), depolarization produces calcium spikes long in duration. When recorded from dendrites close to the soma (b, c), there are fewer calcium spikes. (d) In the soma of the cell, few calcium spikes are apparent and the majority of the spikes are sodium-mediated. (Adapted from Llinás and Sugimori, 1980)

dependent calcium channels in dendrites and thus the presence of regenerative events in addition to cable properties poses a challenge to a simple computational model of neuron function. Though the calcium spikes may not directly affect the axon hillock, they may cause an otherwise faint signal to propagate closer to the soma, increasing its efficacy.

The Quantal Nature of Synaptic Transmission

We have now described the electrical activity of a single neuron completely. It is composed of an *electrically excitable domain* (axon and bouton), in which signaling takes the form of the presence or absence of an all-or-none action potential, and a *chemically excitable domain* (dendrites and soma), in which signaling takes the form of synaptic potentials that are continuously variable in amplitude both in the positive and negative direction (along with some calcium spikes). Those with an affinity for computers might wish to think of the neuron as a chip that contains an analog-to-digital converter. The neuron is the unit of integration in an elaborate computer (the brain) that acquires many analog signals (synaptic potentials) and converts them into a digital output (the decision to fire or not to fire an action potential).

Much of what we have learned comes from *first principles*. A student with a thorough grasp of the physical basis for the resting potential (Chapter 3) might have been able to deduce the mechanisms employed for electrical signaling in the brain. But now we are about to enter into an area of neuroscience that is conceptually different from what we've been through. We must now investigate the means used by neurons to communicate with one another and the pattern of their connections that permits behavior to emerge from their combined synaptic potential and action potential activity. Here we will find that first principles are of little use to us. How could anybody predict the diversity of individual transmitter compounds, their structures and receptor types, their synthesis and breakdown schemes using only "first principles"? Furthermore our convenient (and, within a single cell, perfectly accurate) analogy between the neuron and a computer chip will also break down when ensembles of neurons are considered. No electrical equivalent exists for the variety of chemical transmitters; each one possesses not only the ability to manipulate postsynaptic membrane potential but also possesses *specificity, connotation,* and even *nuance* of meaning for the chemically excitable domain of another cell since only cells that express the right *receptor* can respond to the transmitter in question. In short, mechanisms of communication *between* cells more closely resembles a *language* than electrical signals in a computer chip. Analogies with computer languages and algorithms will again be useful to us when we discuss higher functions (Chapters 9, 10, and 16), but study of the next few chapters will be much like learning a human language. There will be general principles to guide us (like the rules of grammar and syntax) but many features will be specific and unique (like vocabulary and spelling).

Let us begin by examining what happens at the microscopic level in an individual synaptic contact between two neurons.

Theories of Quantal Transmission

Examined carefully, postsynaptic potentials are not actually smoothly graded in size as shown in Figure 5–5. Rather, they are made up of units of postsynaptic charge, each one so small that it is not commonly observed in isolation from the rest, giving the impression that the postsynaptic potentials are continuously variable. One way to observe these units of synaptic transmission (called quanta; sing., **quantum**) is to obtain a preparation in which presynaptic action potential activity can be eliminated. The contact between the motor neuron and the skeletal muscle of a frog was used first, because it could be removed intact from the frog. Spontaneous

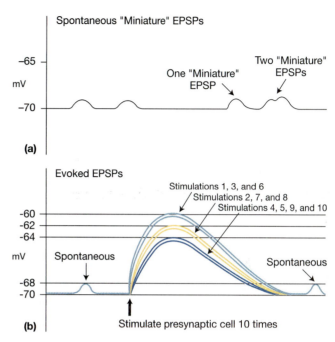

Figure 5–5   *Quantal Transmission.* (a) In the absence of an action potential, a spontaneous EPSP occurs in the postsynaptic cell. For each cell, these EPSPs are all the same size and are considered equal to one quantum. (b) If the presynaptic cell fires an action potential, the postsynaptic cell experiences an evoked EPSP. The size of the evoked EPSP is always a multiple of the size of the spontaneous event and the quantal content of the evoked EPSP is equal to a multiple of the spontaneous EPSP size. Above, one quantum is equal to 2 mV. Evoked EPSPs equal to 6 mV (4, 5, 9, and 10) have a quantal content of 3 (6 mV/2 mV = 3), evoked EPSPs equal to 8 mV (2, 7, and 8) have a quantal content of 4 (8 mV/2 mV = 4), and evoked EPSPs equal to 10 mV (1, 3, and 6) have a quantal content of 5 (10 mV/2 mV = 5).

action potentials in the presynaptic cell were automatically eliminated since only the axon of the motor neuron was removed after the soma and dendrites were left in the spinal cord. Then, the amplification, or "gain" of the amplifier (see "The Electrometer" in the Appendix), was turned up very high (so as to see very small events) and *spontaneous, miniature* EPSPs were observed. These are bits of synaptic transmission that occur in the absence of action potentials in the bouton and hence, presumably, in the absence of calcium influx. *They are all the same size* ("size" being defined here in terms of magnitude of postsynaptic depolarization, Figure 5–5a). Of course, if the presynaptic cell is activated electronically, an action potential ensues, calcium enters the bouton, vesicles fuse with the plasma membrane, transmitter is released, and much more substantial EPSP results (Figure 5–5b). This is called an evoked event (to differentiate it from a spontaneous EPSP). If this activation is repeated (let's say ten times) a very interesting result is obtained. *Even though every presynaptic action potential is identical, the evoked EPSPs fluctuate around a mean (average) value in increments equal to the size of the spontaneous events*. Since nothing smaller than the spontaneous EPSP is observed at this level of resolution, the spontaneous events can be assumed to be equal to one quantum. For example, the spontaneous events in Figure 5–5b depolarize 2mV; stimulations 4, 5, 9, and 10 depolarize on average 6mV, stimulations 2, 7, and 8, 8mV; and stimulations 1, 3, and 6, 10mV. If the 2mV depolarization of the spontaneous event is considered one quantum, stimulations 4, 5, 9, and 10 can be said to contain, on average, 3 quanta; this is said to be their **quantal content**. A typical evoked event, as in Figure 5–5, might have *four* quanta in it, but others might have *three* or *five*. With many stimuli, some EPSPs would deviate more greatly with *two* or *six* quanta of postsynaptic charge involved.

What do you think the physical basis for the quantum is? Possibilities include the number of receptors activated by a single molecule of transmitter, the current through a single chemically activated channel, or the current through a fixed number of chemically activated channels available for binding to transmitter. However, these possibilities can be eliminated by investigations that show the number of transmitter molecules necessary to elicit a quantum-sized event is actually very high (around 10,000) as is the number of channels that need to open. Thus fluctuations in transmitters or receptor number would be smaller than a quantum. The clue to the identity of the quantum came when the number of transmitter molecules in a single *vesicle* became known. For the neuromuscular junction of the frog the number of transmitter molecules in a single vesicle is around 10,000. Thus an individual act of exocytosis (one vesicle fusing with the presynaptic bouton membrane) liberates about the same amount of transmitter needed to create a quantum. In a powerful experiment, John Heuser et al. (1979) showed that for evoked potentials the number of vesicles that fused with the presynaptic membrane was precisely the same as the number of quanta experienced by the postsynaptic side. Hence synaptic transmission is quantal because of variability in the number of vesicles that undergo exocytosis with each incoming action potential.

Though the mean quantal content of a synapse is not random, the quantal content of a single postsynaptic potential is random within a certain range. For example, it is not possible to predict whether the next EPSP in a synapse with a mean quantal content of *seven* will contain *five, six, seven, eight*, or *nine* quanta.

Much has been made of the random nature of synaptic transmission. *Interactionist dualists* must identify a pathway for the spirit world to enter into and influence the physical world (Chapter 1). Sir John Eccles (of whom we shall hear more in Chapter 7) is an interactionist dualist who has proposed that the number of quanta in an individual EPSP, while confined to the normal range by the physical principles we have described, is nevertheless determined by factors that have *no physical correlate or cause*. Hence the apparently random fluctuation of synaptic potential amplitude can provide an avenue for *free will* to enter the brain and determine behavior. Monists would argue that random processes (which also occur in systems that have no "will" at all, "free" or otherwise) are *unpredictable* but nevertheless *constrained* by the law of cause and effect (i.e., "determined"). You may now wish to review the discussion of the mind/body problem in Chapter 1 in light of the random nature of synaptic transmission. Either as the origin or the vehicle for the impulse to act the synapse is very important to behavior. Let us consider, therefore, the chemical basis for synaptic transmission in more detail.

Receptor Theory

Figure 5–6 shows an electron micrograph of a synapse in the brain. Presynaptic structures (boutons) are readily identifiable by the presence of synaptic vesicles. Mitochondria are somewhat more prevalent in presynaptic structures because exocytosis is an energy-consuming process. (Mitochondria are the energy producers of the cell.) Also apparent is the *presynaptic density* (Chapter 2), a region of membrane that takes up the heavy stain in greater quantities than nonsynaptic membrane, indicating that transmembrane protein is concentrated in this region. Very likely, the calcium channels that facilitate exocytosis make up much of the protein in the presynaptic density (also known as the active zone; see Figure 4–13 and Figure 4–14).

The membrane of dendrites on the postsynaptic side also displays specialization. At regions of synaptic contact there is a *postsynaptic density,* which indicates a region of high transmembrane protein concentration in the dendrites. These transmembrane proteins are anchored to the cytoskeleton, much in the way calcium channels are anchored to the presynaptic membrane, to keep them from diffusing away into nonsynaptic membrane. Most of these proteins are *receptors* for the synaptic transmitter that is liberated by exocytosis on the other side of the synapse. The term *ligand* (Chapter 2) is used to describe any substance, such as the aforementioned transmitters, that binds to the receptors.

Individual receptor proteins are similar in many ways to the voltage-gated channel proteins we have considered (see Figure 4–7 and Figure 4–8). They are made up of monomeric subunits, each one with several hydrophobic segments that span the membrane separated by hydrophilic regions located inside and outside of the cell. Together these components form a pore that is selective for a particular type of ion. Like voltage-gated channels they display *heterogeneity* (several

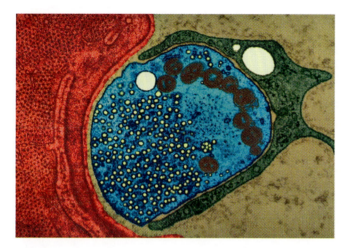

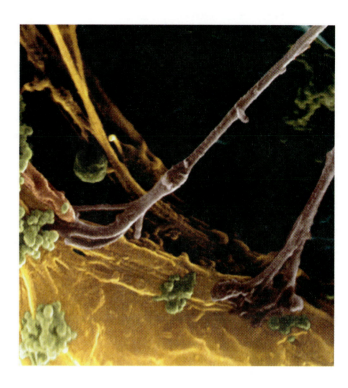

Figure 5–6 *Structure of the Synapse.* The synapse above has many specialized characteristics. The electron micrograph shows the vesicles containing the synaptic transmitter, the abundance of mitochondria necessary for energy production and the abundance of protein in the presynaptic and postsynaptic densities. At the right are incoming axons (purple) contacting dendrites (yellow) with non-neural cells nearby (green).

receptor types *with distinct properties* exist for each transmitter at various synapses) and *homology* (even functionally discrete receptors may have structural similarity in the sequence of their amino acids, see Chapter 4). A feature that distinguishes receptor proteins from voltage-gated channels is the presence of a **binding site** for the ligand and a gate that opens or closes when the binding site is occupied. For now, it is easy to think of receptors being restricted to the chemically excitable domain. Later, in Box 5–3 and in Chapter 6 (autoreceptors), we shall consider receptor mechanisms that occur in the electrically excitable domain as well.

Figure 5–7 shows a typical receptor protein. (Compare to the voltage-gated potassium channel in Figure 4–8.) It happens to be one of the receptor types for the transmitter acetylcholine (ACh), but because of homology it can be taken to represent a family of receptor proteins for various transmitters including gamma-aminobutyric acid and glycine. A single monomer spans the membrane *four times* (with the amino- and carboxy-terminals outside the cell; Figure 5–7a). The entire receptor is a polymer made up of five monomers. Two monomers (the "alpha subunits," labeled α in Figure 5–7b) are identical and each contains a binding site for the transmitter. The other subunits ("beta, gamma, and delta," labeled β, γ, and δ) share sequence homology with alpha subunits but lack binding sites. Together they cluster around a membrane-free region that forms the ion channel. Figure 5–8 shows a schematic cross section of the receptor taken just through the alpha subunits. There is no voltage-sensor or timer mecha-

nism as in the potassium channel, only a transmitter-activated gate (represented as a doorknob and keyhole). The receptor is shown in the unoccupied and closed position (Figure 5–8a). Were one or both of the binding sites to be occupied by transmitter (generically represented as a hatched diamond) the gate would open and ions would flow across the membrane to create (depending on ion selectivity) an IPSP or an EPSP. For example, the **nicotinic acetylcholine receptor** is largely (but not exclusively) selective for sodium, so an EPSP results when it is activated (Figure 5–8b). However, the same general structures are used for homologous receptors that are specific for chloride and hence produce IPSPs when occupied and active. Indeed, recent research indicates that during the manufacture of receptors, subunits can be exchanged among receptor populations, a "mix-and-match" process that greatly increases receptor heterogeneity.

A more schematic diagram, generic for all transmitter-gated ion channels, is shown in Figure 5–9. This figure shows transmitter molecules binding to an excitatory receptor after release by exocytosis. While this model accounts for most of the synaptic events in the brain, there are others that are very important that are not adequately described by the model. For instance, in some cases the receptor protein and the ion channel are actually *different polymers* that communicate through the use of *intracellular enzymes* and other small intracellular molecules. These other transmitter receptor mechanisms are conceptually the same as the ones shown in Figure 5–8 except for the mechanism of channel activation (the sig-

Figure 5–7   *The Structure of the Nicotinic Acetylcholine Receptor.* (a) A single monomer spans the membrane four times. (b) The nicotinic acetylcholine receptor consists of five subunits that form a pore by orienting themselves in a particular way in the lipid bilayer. The alpha subunits contain the binding site for the transmitter.

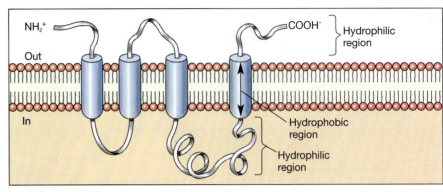

(a) Subunit structure

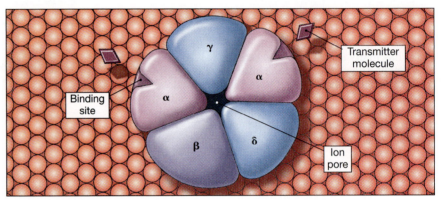

(b) Top view of polymer

nal transduction mechanism) and will be discussed more fully in the next chapter.

Each vesicle represented in Figure 5–9 contains a few transmitter molecules, but the actual value is closer to 10,000 per vesicle as we have discussed. Just as each symbol represents thousands of transmitters, each receptor symbol on the postsynaptic side actually represents thousands of receptors. When a transmitter binds to a receptor a process ensues that is very much like what happens when a key fits into a lock, turning a latch and opening the door. In this case the key is the transmitter, the lock is the binding site, the latch is the transmitter-activated channel gate, and the door is the pore that, when open, allows the passage of ions across the membrane. A channel with ion selectivity for sodium is illustrated (EPSP arises from inward current) but the same principles hold for IPSP mechanisms. *The transmitter molecule never passes through the postsynaptic membrane.* It merely acts as the signal to open the ion channel.

Two Types of Ligands

At one point the lock-and-key analogy breaks down. The transmitter molecules are actually bouncing on and off the receptors rapidly in a manner very much unlike a key fitting into a keyhole. While a key either works in a lock or doesn't,

the action of transmitters (and hormones, enzyme substrates, and all other ligands) is better thought of as a *continuum* of efficacy. There is a range of values that describe the speed with which a ligand binds a receptor, a concept called affinity (see "The Concept of Affinity" in the Appendix). In short, a compound with high affinity need not be present in very high concentrations to fill a large number of binding sites.

The concept of affinity has a precise, but limited definition. It says nothing about what the ligand does once bound. The act of *binding* is separate from the act of *turning the key and opening the gate.* Ligands that bind the receptor tightly may be weak at opening the gate and vice versa. To describe the *biological efficacy* of a compound we need a new value, one that describes its **potency.** Compounds that are highly effective once bound (those with high potency) need not be present in very high concentrations to produce the intended biological response. The literature of neuroscience may seem very confusing to a novice unaware of the definitions of affinity and potency and of the distinction between the concepts. *The understanding of these terms is very important in pharmacy, medicine, clinical psychology, and psychopharmacology.*

We can subdivide ligands into two categories. **Agonists** bind to the receptor *and* activate it biologically. *Weak agonists* have either low affinity or low potency, or both, and *strong ag-*

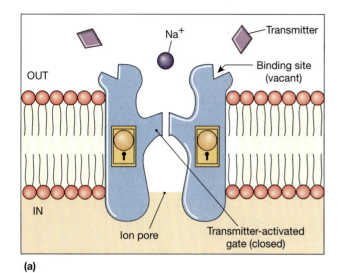

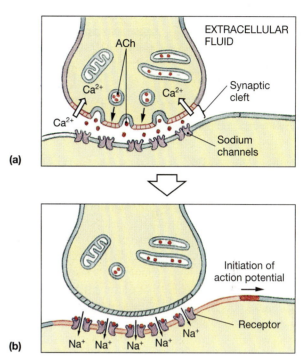

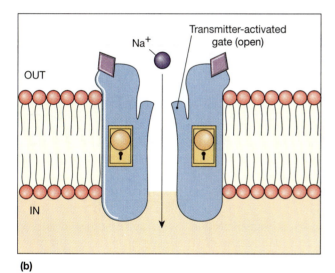

Figure 5–8 *The Nicotinic Acetylcholine Receptor.* When no transmitter is bound to the binding site (a), the gate is closed and no sodium will enter the cell. When transmitter is bound (b), the gate opens and sodium rushes in.

Figure 5–9 *Receptor Function.* (a) Within the active zone of the presynaptic cell, there are vesicles containing the transmitter ACh. When calcium enters the cell, the vesicles fuse with the membrane by exocytosis, releasing transmitter into the synaptic cleft. (b) The transmitter then binds to the receptors located on the postsynaptic membrane. The activated receptor opens the channel, permitting the influx of Na+.

onists have either high affinity or high potency, or both. Antagonists bind to the receptor but have *no potency* (i.e., nothing happens once the ligand is bound to the receptor). Generally, the affinity of an antagonist is high (in other words it binds tightly) but it causes no biological response at the receptor on its own. Once an antagonist occupies the receptors, agonists can no longer bind. Hence the biological response to an antagonist arises because of receptor *blockade* (Figure 5–10).

To return to our lock-and-key analogy, I have many keys on my key ring that all look more or less the same. However, *only one will open my office*; the others will fit into the keyhole (because all keys at the University of Colorado have the same general shape), but they will not turn the latch. Coming in one morning in a greater fog than usual I might jam the wrong key into the keyhole. *As long as the wrong key is in the hole, the correct key cannot be used.* If I were to wrestle with the wrong key and snap it off in the keyhole (this has never happened, thankfully), I would experience a more or less permanent inability to get into my office. In our analogy the correct key (the one that opens the lock) is an *agonist* and the incorrect key (the one that simply occupies the lock) is an *antagonist*.

Again the lock-and-key metaphor is useful, but limited. The body may produce several agonists for a given receptor *but never produces an antagonist for its own receptors* (see Figure 5–10b). The term **endogenous** is used to describe substances that the body manufactures, and **exogenous** to describe foreign substances, that is, substances manufactured outside the body. Antagonists are found in nature as *drugs* or *poisons* that are absorbed by the body and act upon it, but never arise in the body itself (unless made by one animal to be used externally, i.e., to poison another animal). In other words, antagonists are always exogenous. Some agonists are

Box 5–1

The Importance of Poisons and Toxins

In general, all drugs and all poisons work because they are either agonists or antagonists at a particular transmitter or hormone receptor. Whether the nature of the effect is desirable or undesirable depends on the function of the receptor. As a consequence the field of neuroscience is rife with exotic poisons and drugs of all kinds.

We have already encountered two of these. Ouabain is a plant-derived toxin that poisons the ATP-consuming sodium/potassium pump. It was used to demonstrate the contribution of this pump to the membrane potential (Chapter 3). Tetrodotoxin, or TTX, is a poison derived from the puffer fish that blocks the voltage-dependent sodium channel (Chapter 4). In fact, there are poisons derived in nature that block many of the voltage-dependent channels we have considered. One of the most deadly animals in the sea is the cone snail (actually a genus of several species); paradoxically, the cone snails' shells are among the most beautiful seashells and are the most highly prized by collectors, selling today for many thousands of dollars. Historically they were even more valuable. In Holland at around the time of the "Tulip Craze" in the eighteenth century cone shells sold for exorbitant amounts of money. At one auction paintings by the Dutch master Vermeer were also offered for sale, but individual cone shells drew higher bids! It is one of

life's delicious ironies that these shells should be so dangerous to gather when occupied by the original inhabitant. The cone snail is carnivorous and normally eats small fish, but it is very slow moving (as snails tend to be). The poisons (called "conotoxins") are delivered by a dart, connected like a harpoon to the poison gland by a hollow cord. When an unsuspecting fish (or collector!) comes close enough, the snail launches the dart and injects the poison into the victim. Paralysis occurs within seconds and death shortly thereafter.

Think for a moment about the evolutionary obstacle a snail must overcome in order to eat a fish. The poison must act so quickly that the fish cannot escape before the slow-moving snail can find it; to accomplish this the poison must act on the nervous system.

Baldomero Olivera et al. (1985) have investigated the cone snail venom to discover how it acts. It is comprised of a variety of small peptide toxins, mostly acting on voltage-dependent channels. There is a toxin for the presynaptic calcium channel (to block synaptic transmission) and several for potassium channels. Toxins for receptor-activated channels are also found. Thus the cone snail has adopted the same strategy as the puffer fish, but for different purposes. The puffer fish makes TTX for defensive purposes (i.e., to poison a predator), and the cone snail makes its venom for acquiring food (i.e., to poison its prey).

A rule of thumb is that naturally occurring poisons and, to a lesser extent, psychoactive drugs are *made by*

exogenous as well. Indeed, drugs and toxins are almost universally either agonists or antagonists for some receptor system (see Box 5–1). (A recent description exists of an endogenous antagonist for the "interleukin II receptor," but for now let's view this as an anomaly). Receptors are generally named for the antagonists that bind to them. Here, the reader might ask, "Why should we name receptors for antagonists? Why not name them for the endogenous agonist, the transmitter itself?" Recall that receptors like many biochemical structures tend to be heterogeneous. The nicotinic acetylcholine receptor, which dominates in the peripheral nervous system and is the *sole* receptor at the vertebrate neu-

predators to kill prey or by prey to kill predators. Furthermore, the most effective means of poisoning an animal is to attack its nervous system. Since the poky predator must catch up to its poisoned prey in order to eat it, it is desirable to have paralysis precede death.

Another especially instructive example of this feature of poisons is to be found in the category of naturally occurring antagonists for the acetylcholine receptor. The nicotinic receptor for acetylcholine (the one shown in Figure 5–7 and the one used at the neuromuscular junction of vertebrates) is blocked by poison made by a South American tree. The tree makes a poison, called curare, to kill its predators (animals that feed on its bark). Native South Americans have used extracts from the bark and from the skin of frogs that contain a curarelike substance to poison the tip of blowgun darts. Curare enters the bloodstream of the quarry (often a monkey or another tree-dwelling mammal) and the animal becomes paralyzed because of blockade at each of its neuromuscular junctions. The paralyzed quarry may remain inaccessible in the tree for some time, testing the patience of the hunter, but eventually paralysis gives way to asphyxiation and death since the diaphragm of vertebrates, necessary for inspiration, is also paralyzed. The dead prey then usually rewards the patient hunter by falling out of the tree.

A complement to curare is another toxin that binds to the nicotinic acetylcholine receptor, alpha-bungarotoxin. Bungarotoxin is taken from the venom of *Bungarus bungarus* (a snake commonly known as the banded krait). Like the conotoxins, bungarotoxin is exceptionally potent, producing paralysis and death in seconds. Though faster than a cone snail, the krait nevertheless has an interest in not allowing its target (a small or medium-sized rodent) to run too far before collapsing. Antagonists of natural origin thus tend to have higher *affinity* for the receptor than agonists, or even including the transmitter itself.

Receptors and transmitters sometimes tend to be named by historical accidents. An example is the *nicotinic acetylcholine receptor*, so named upon the discovery that **nicotine** (the psychoactive ingredient in tobacco) has a weak affinity for it. At low con-

centrations nicotine has an agonistic effect on this receptor, which probably gives rise to its mild stimulating properties as well as some of its (debilitating) side effects. At higher concentrations nicotine has an antagonistic effect (a weak agonist nevertheless occupies the receptors and blocks transmission). This effect was thought to be very dangerous and nicotine was regarded as a poison for some time. There is a story, perhaps apocryphal, that Hitler's deputies carried cigars to be consumed orally as a means of suicide should they fall into enemy hands. Albert Speer (the minister of science and technology in the Third Reich) was supposed to have attempted suicide in this way. Of course, the attempt failed and he spent his life in Spandau Prison having been convicted of war crimes. Today we regard nicotine as dangerous for another reason. It is an addictive drug that leads to smoking behavior and ingestion of carcinogens (cancer-causing compounds, see Chapter 17).

romuscular junction, is only one of two general classes of acetylcholine receptors. The other (and the one that is most prevalent in the brain) is the **muscarinic acetylcholine receptor**. This is also named after a weak agonist of minor importance and historical accident. The mushroom *Amanita muscaria* contains mood-altering substances ingested by members of certain cultures (Scandinavian and Siberian natives among them) as part of religious ceremonies. The compounds *muscimol* and *muscarine* act at the brain receptors for acetylcholine to produce some of the effects.

Amanita muscaria is also known as "fly agaric" since its poisons induce a stupor in flies, which are one of its preda-

Figure 5–10 *Ligands: Agonists and Antagonists.* Agonists and antagonists bind to the same binding site as transmitter. An agonist has potency so it activates the cell biologically (a). Antagonists bind and have no potency (b). An antagonist produces its effect by blocking the binding site, preventing a transmitter from binding and producing its biological effect.

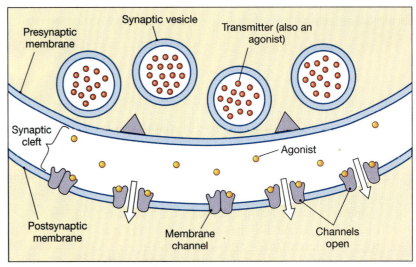

(a) Strong agonist activates receptors without transmission

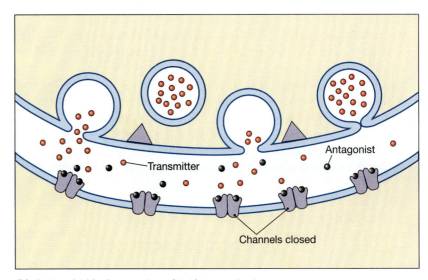

(b) Antagonist blocks receptors. Agonist cannot act.

tors. However, the toxins do not kill the flies, nor are humans killed by eating the mushroom. This gives rise to the speculation that some poisons evolved not really to *kill* predators but rather to render them helpless and subject to *their* predators in turn. Many recreational drugs such as cocaine, opium, heroin, and marijuana (not to mention nicotine) arise from plant sources but do not immediately kill the consumer (Chapter 17). One theory is that these confer evolutionary advantage on the plant by debilitating predators instead of killing them. Another evolutionary theory holds that perhaps the drugs have evolved positive or rewarding qualities so they would be consumed and the seeds dispersed. While controversy and debate may attend the investigation of a plant's evolutionary strategy for synthesizing a psychogenic

compound, almost invariably the compounds produced obey the law that poisons and drugs have effect because they act as agonists or antagonists at some receptor system in the body. A rich line of research uses these poisons and drugs of abuse as probes for hitherto undiscovered transmitters. Of this we shall hear more as we explore the function of specific receptor systems.

Figure 5–11 shows the numerous ligands that bind to receptors. The group of agonists include the endogenous transmitters and hormones and the exogenous drugs. Antagonists include drugs and poisons of exogenous origin only. **Allosteric modifiers** are substances that bind to a receptor, but to a binding site (an "allosteric" site, see Figure 5–12) different from the one occupied by agonists and antagonists.

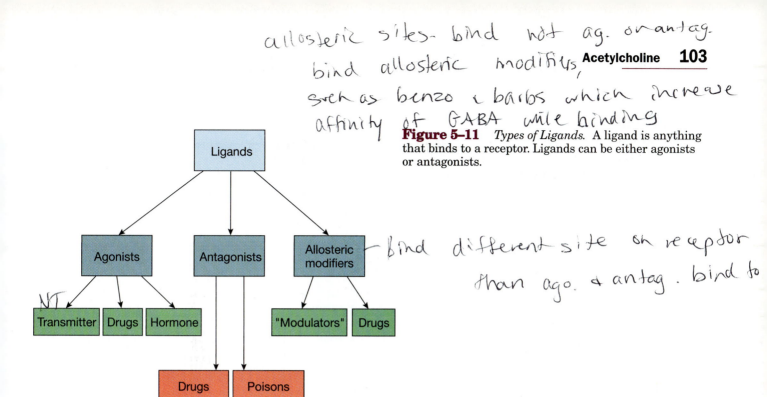

*allosteric sites- bind not ag. or antag.
bind allosteric modifiers,
such as benzo & barbs which increase
affinity of GABA while binding*

*bind different site on receptor
than ago. & antag. bind to*

Figure 5–11 *Types of Ligands.* A ligand is anything that binds to a receptor. Ligands can be either agonists or antagonists.

This class includes a few endogenous compounds (modulators) and a great many drugs.

Agonists, antagonists, and allosteric modifiers aside, there are a great number of things that can influence neurotransmission. As we shall see, anything that impacts the manufacture of transmitters (**synthesis**), the release of transmitters by exocytosis (**secretion**), the removal of transmitters from the synaptic cleft (**breakdown**), or the recycling of the molecular constituents or, in some cases, the whole transmitter (**re-up-**

take) will also influence the EPSPs and IPSPs that the transmitters produce. In this context the words *agonist* and *antagonist* are often used to mean "anything that does something" and "anything that does the opposite." But imprecise language often leads to imprecise thinking and nowhere does imprecise thinking presents greater hazards to comprehension than in the fields of neuroscience and psychology.

Acetylcholine

Synthesis and Breakdown

Acetylcholine (ACh) was the first transmitter to be described (Box 5–2) and to this date is the best understood of the synaptic transmitters. It is synthesized in the bouton by the fusion of **acetate**, a simple organic molecule, and **choline**, a molecule containing a nitrogen atom. The acetate arrives in the terminal as a starting product of the citric acid cycle in the mitochondria (see Box 2–2). Because transmitter synthesis and exocytosis require both energy from glucose, mitochondria tend to concentrate in the presynaptic region. Choline is derived from phospholipid (the membrane constituent) and is pumped into the bouton of cells that use ACh as a transmitter. The genome of cells destined to use ACh makes **cholineacetyltransferase** (**CAT**) and sends it down the axon where it accumulates in the terminals. Often enzymes are named in an attempt to describe their function. CAT, as the name implies, *transfers the choline to the acetate* to make ACh. A helper enzyme called coenzyme A is involved and a water molecule is liberated by forming the bond between the acetate and choline. The resulting compound is called an **ester** in organic chemistry lingo to refer to a carbon bound to two oxygen atoms in a larger molecule (Figure 5–13a).

Figure 5–12 *Allosteric Site.* An allosteric site is a binding site on a receptor different from the agonist and antagonist binding site. An allosteric modifier binds to the allosteric site. Notice that when the allosteric modifier is bound to the allosteric site, the conformation of the binding site is changed making it bind tighter to a transmitter, agonist, or antagonist.

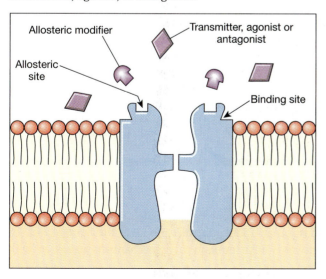

Box 5–2

Otto Loewi and the Frog Heart

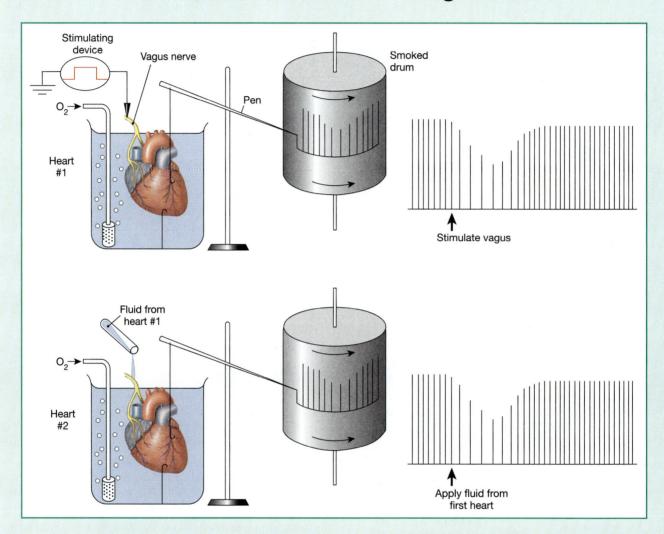

The heart muscle of vertebrates has it own collection of sodium, calcium, and potassium channels, each different in some respects from the voltage-dependent neural channels we have considered. These channels render the heart muscle *spontaneously excitable*, like the pacemakers mentioned in Chapter 4. The rhythm of the heartbeat is thus endogenous to the muscle itself. We say that the heartbeat is *myogenic* to indicate that no input from the central nervous system is needed to keep it going. (In this respect the heartbeat is quite different from that other rhythmic activity,

You may have wondered what terminates a synaptic potential. As we saw in Chapter 4, the action potential is brought to an end by the *time-dependency* and *inactivation* of the channel protein, but the **acetylcholine receptor (AChR)** and most other transmitter receptors lack these properties. The answer is to be found in three mechanisms possessed by the

breathing, which requires continuous input of motor commands from the spinal nerves to the diaphragm muscles).

This is not to say the heart receives no innervation. In fact, it receives two types (Chapter 6). One is a set of nerves from a chain of ganglia next to the spinal cord and another is a pair of nerves from the brainstem called the **vagus nerves**. It was discovered early on that even though the beat itself was myogenic, the first nerves caused the heart to beat *stronger* and *faster* and the second set (the vagus nerves) caused it to beat *slower* and *more softly*.

The fact that the heartbeat is intrinsic to the heart itself was exploited in the 1920s to gain information about synaptic transmission even before the microelectrode had been invented. A German scientist, Otto Loewi, began to study the effects of stimulating the vagus nerve on a frog heart maintained in vitro.

The myogenic frog heart beat on its own when the proper amount of oxygen and glucose was supplied and the salt concentration of the bathing medium was adjusted to match that of frog blood (almost exactly the concentrations we have cited for "extracellular" saline; see Chapter 3). Loewi found that when the heartbeat was recorded by a pen scratching on a drum covered with soot so as to make a trace, the heartbeat amplitude and rate were very consistent. (Students: Please do not complain about the conditions in your laboratory for this course. When I studied this subject in college we were required to smoke our own drums by setting fire to benzene, now known to be a very carcinogenic procedure.)

Loewi also found that stimulation of the vagus nerve produced the same effect as in the whole animal, namely that it caused the heart to beat slower and more softly (heart 1 in the figure). Most significantly, when Loewi transferred a sample of the bathing medium from one heart to another (heart 2 in the diagram), *he found that the second heart also beat more softly and more slowly*. This transference of the inhibitory influence could only

happen if the sample was withdrawn quickly after an electrical stimulus was delivered to the vagus nerve of the first heart. (Note that heart 2 had a vagus nerve that received no electrical stimulus). Samples before stimulation or a few moments after were ineffective. He concluded that there was some diffusable substance contained within the vagus nerve, and liberated from it by electrical stimuli, that inhibited the heart. He called the substance *vagusstoff*, which is German for "the stuff that's in the vagus."

It was obvious from the experiment that a chemical was the signal from the vagus to the heart. It was also obvious from the results that the chemical was very unstable (*volatile* is the chemical term). In the presence of water the chemical *hydrolyzed* easily into simpler breakdown products. A Swedish scientist named U. von Euler took up the search for *vagusstoff* by making extracts of hundreds of frog vagus nerves in *nonaqueous* solvents (to prevent hydrolysis into the breakdown products). He was frustrated by the discovery that the vagus nerves contained not one but *several* compounds that affected the heart. One complex and stable molecule could be collected in the form of a white powder. Since von Euler could not characterize it using the techniques available to him at the time, he set it aside with the label Substance P (for "powder"). The vial of Substance P sat unnoticed for many years until a later discovery revealed the importance of this compound. (Should you be the type of reader that turns to the end of a mystery novel to discover the killer, you may wish to leap ahead to Chapter 11 to discover what became of Substance P.)

In separate fractions *vagusstoff* became concentrated enough and stable enough to evaluate using the spectroscopic and other analytical methods of the time. Its volatility was discovered to be due to an easily hydrolyzable ester linkage; *vagusstoff* was ultimately found to be an ester of acetate and choline, or acetylcholine (see Becq, 1995, for a historical review of his process of discovery).

synapse. One is **desensitization**. Transmitter receptors, the AChR included, respond to the continuous presence of agonist by slowly losing responsiveness to the agonist. Desensitization is analogous to refractoriness except that it takes a while to develop and lasts a long time. Indeed, it is unclear whether desensitization ever plays a role in the normal life of

Figure 5–13   *Synthesis and Breakdown of Acetylcholine.* Cholineacetyltransferase transfers choline to the acetate of an acetyl CoA molecule to produce acetylcholine (a). Water and CoA are also produced in the process. Acetylcholine is broken down by the addition of water and the enzyme acetylcholinesterase. The products are choline and acetic acid (b). (Siegel et al., 1989)

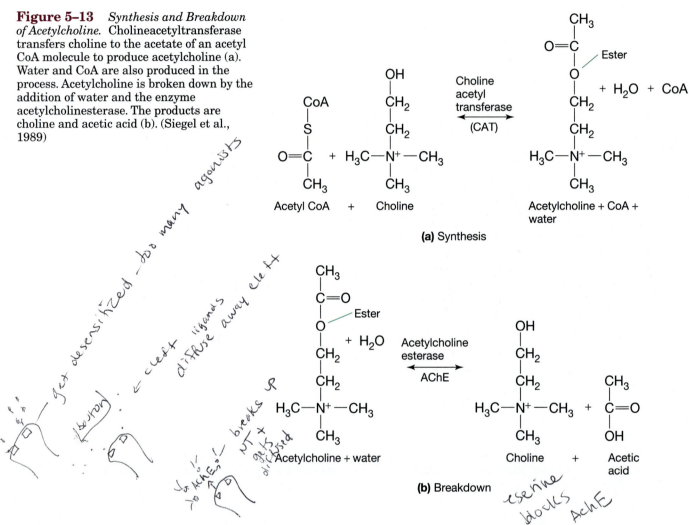

(a) Synthesis

(b) Breakdown

a synapse, though it can be very important when the action of drugs on transmitter receptors is considered.

The second mechanism, only known for a few peptide transmitters, is termination by simple diffusion away from the synaptic cleft.

The third mechanism for terminating the postsynaptic potential is very common, if not quite ubiquitous, and is probably the most significant physiologically. Breakdown enzymes, often produced by the postsynaptic cell, become embedded in the extracellular environment of the synapse (a network of collagen in the cleft called the **extracellular matrix**), where they destroy the transmitter quickly. For synapses employing acetylcholine this enzyme is called **acetylcholinesterase (AChE)**. As the name implies, AChE *breaks the ester linkage between acetate and choline*, consuming water in the process (Figure 5–13b). The free acetate diffuses away in the form of acetic acid, but the choline is rapidly taken up again by the presynaptic side for resynthesis as ACh (Figure 5–14).

Given the propinquity of certain animals and plants to make poisons that are agonists and antagonists for receptor

proteins (see Box 5–1), it is hardly surprising that there are natural toxins directed against *enzymes*. One such is eserine (also called physostigmine), which blocks AChE. This plant-derived toxin acts on the nervous system to *exaggerate* ACh-mediated transmission, through interference with the mechanism for terminating the action of ACh. However, it is more common in pharmacology to find enzyme blockers of human origin (i.e., synthesized in chemistry labs). In this category are insecticides (of the "organophosphate" variety like Malathion) and nerve gases (like Sarin). These compounds are also AChE blockers (more potent than eserine). They have their deadly effects because they exaggerate and prolong ACh-mediated transmission. In mammals, this AChE blockade produces spastic paralysis of the neuromuscular junctions and suffocation because the synapses of the diaphragm are unable to operate. Neurotransmission can thus be rendered ineffective either by blockade of the receptor (such as with the plant deritive curare) or by overstimulation of the receptor (such as with an AChE inhibitor).

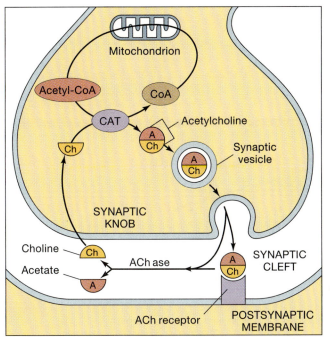

Figure 5–14 *The Cholinergic Synapse.* Vesicles in the presynaptic cell contain ACh and release it into the synaptic cleft by exocytosis. The free ACh will then bind to the ACh receptor on the postsynaptic cell. Milliseconds later, ACh separates from the receptor and is broken down by AChE to choline and acetic acid. The choline uptake pump brings choline back into the presynaptic cell where it is converted into ACh by the action of CAT. The finished product is stored in the vesicles ready to again be released.

Synapses that employ acetylcholine as a transmitter are called **cholinergic** synapses. (We shall use similar terminology for the other transmitters: "GABAergic" for GABA, "adrenergic" for the catecholamines and indolamines collectively, or "dopaminergic," "noradrenergic," and "serotonergic" for each individually, and so forth.) A cell's choice of transmitter is called its transmitter **phenotype**. Each stage in the existence of a single molecule of ACh is labeled in Figure 5–14. The molecules lie dormant for an indeterminate period of time awaiting secretion by exocytosis, whereupon they exist briefly as unbound ACh in the extracellular space. A *fraction* of the free ACh binds to the receptor. Receptor theory (see Appendix) calls for continuous exchange between bound and free pools of ACh, so that a balance or equilibrium exists that is determined by the *affinity* of the ligand/receptor interaction. This balance does not endure long, however, for AChE consumes the free ACh and eventually the bound ACh as well since the bound ACh eventually comes off the receptor. Acetic acid from hydrolyzed ACh diffuses from the synapse to be metabolized elsewhere, but the choline is quickly taken back up

by the presynaptic cell using a pump unique to cholinergic neurons. Inside cholinergic cells an enzyme, CAT, reassembles ACh from the recycled choline and the acetate produced by the citric acid cycle. Empty vesicles have been formed by endocytosis (which must match exocytosis step for step; Chapter 2). These empty vesicles are then filled with newly synthesized ACh and prepared for rerelease.

The process shown in Figure 5–14 and described above is *fast*, the entire cycle taking only a few milliseconds to complete. Similar mechanisms are at work in all synapses of the body, both cholinergic or noncholinergic.

The Neuromuscular Junction

In addition to the cholinergic inhibition of the heart that is mediated by the muscarinic receptor for this transmitter (see Box 5–2 about the discovery of this mechanism), acetylcholine has an important (in fact, the *only*) role to play in transmission of information from the motor neuron to the skeletal muscle fiber. The contact between the motor neuron and the skeletal muscle fiber is different from other synapses in the body because it is larger and has a more specialized structure (Figure 5–15). For this reason, specialists call it a **neuromuscular junction** instead of a synapse. The postsynaptic part is called an **end plate** to indicate that the postsynaptic structure is not a dendrite of another neuron, but rather a specialized invagination of the skeletal muscle membrane. Unlike smooth muscle (viscera) and cardiac muscle (heart), skeletal muscle only has *one type* of innervation, and this is *cholinergic and excitatory*. Obviously, the transmission cannot be mediated by a muscarinic receptor such as the one that appears in the heart, since the muscarinic receptors are inhibitory. Indeed all neuromuscular junctions in all vertebrates employ the *nicotinic cholinergic receptor* (see Figure 5–7). This active receptor preferentially (but not exclusively) admits sodium ions and hence mediates excitation. How the cholinergic, nicotinic EPSP (called an **end plate potential**) is transduced into a muscle twitch will be discussed more thoroughly in Chapter 7.

Consideration of the cholinergic (*muscarinic*) transmission of the vagus nerve to the heart and the cholinergic (*nicotinic*) transmission of the motor neuron to the skeletal muscle illustrates a major point in neurobiology (to be committed to memory and cherished forever). The same transmitter, acetylcholine, mediates inhibition in one part of the body and excitation in another. *Excitation and inhibition are not properties of the transmitter molecule, but properties of the receptor protein. The nature of a synaptic potential is determined by the postsynaptic cell, not by the cell that secretes the transmitter.* Although a few exceptions exist, in general a postsynaptic cell will make only a single receptor type for a given transmitter at a particular synapse, and hence

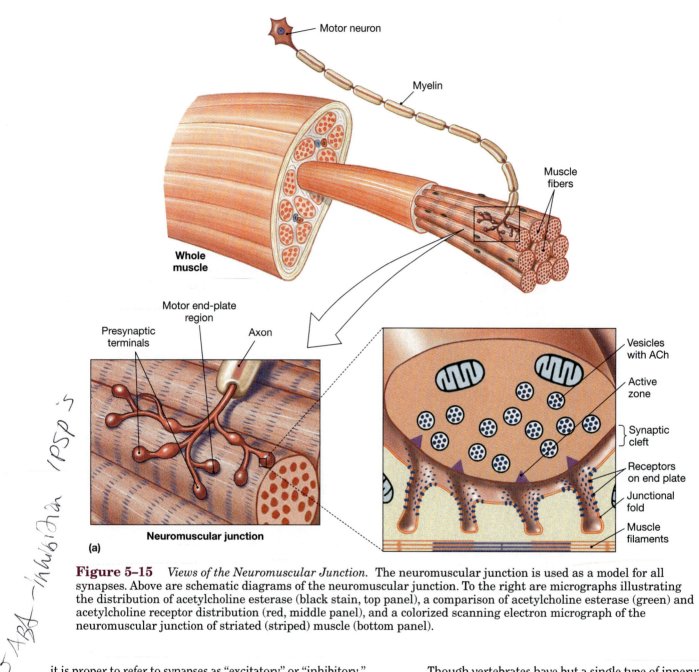

Figure 5–15 *Views of the Neuromuscular Junction.* The neuromuscular junction is used as a model for all synapses. Above are schematic diagrams of the neuromuscular junction. To the right are micrographs illustrating the distribution of acetylcholine esterase (black stain, top panel), a comparison of acetylcholine esterase (green) and acetylcholine receptor distribution (red, middle panel), and a colorized scanning electron micrograph of the neuromuscular junction of striated (striped) muscle (bottom panel).

it is proper to refer to synapses as "excitatory" or "inhibitory." Transmitters should never be referred to as "excitatory" or "inhibitory," however great the temptation.

Gamma-Aminobutyric Acid (GABA)

Almost everywhere it is encountered, the transmitter **gamma-aminobutyric acid** (or GABA) evokes inhibition. However, the *nature* of the inhibition varies from cell to cell and, of course, is determined by the receptor type expressed by the postsynaptic cell. Some GABA receptors activate a potassium conductance and others, better understood and perhaps more prevalent, activate a chloride conductance.

Though vertebrates have but a single type of innervation of the skeletal musculature, many invertebrates (e.g., lobsters, crayfish, and all insects) have *two* types of innervation, excitatory and inhibitory. Applying the "simple systems" approach that was so successful in elucidating the action potential, E. Kravitz, S. Kuffler, L. Iverson, Z. Hall, and others at the Department of Neurobiology at Harvard determined that GABA was the transmitter employed by the inhibitory half of the arthropod neuromuscular system (Nicholls et al., 1991; Hall, 1992). We now know that GABA is prevalent in inhibitory systems everywhere and, given the importance of inhibition that we have discussed, may be

acids). However, GABA is *made* from one of the 20 amino acids that makes proteins, **glutamic acid**. The action of a descriptively named enzyme **glutamic acid decarboxylase (GAD)** removes a carboxyl group (COOH) to produce GABA in cells that express it (called GABAergic cells). Figure 5–17 shows a GABAergic synapse. Another enzyme, **GABA transaminase** recycles GABA into glutamine for re-uptake and resynthesis.

Allosteric Sites

The GABA receptor type that possesses a chloride channel is well understood and belongs to the same receptor family as other transmitter-activated ion channels (i.e., it has *sequence homology* with the nicotinic ACh receptor and others like it, see Figure 5–7). However, there are also nonhomologous regions of the GABA receptor that lend it special properties. In addition to the binding site for agonists and antagonists, there are at least two other binding sites of the *allosteric* variety (i.e., sites that bind other ligands). We know of the other sites because one is the site of action of benzodiazepines (tranquilizers, see Chapter 17) and the other is the site of action of barbiturates (downers and sleeping pills, see Chapter 17). These compounds by themselves neither open nor close the chloride channel (and hence they cannot be called agonists) but they *increase the affinity of the GABA binding site for GABA.* Thus if there is any GABA around, it binds more tightly in the presence of benzodiazepines or barbiturates resulting in greater inhibition (Figure 5–18). As with most drugs, it seems likely that the drugs act in place of native, or endogenous, ligand for these allosteric sites.

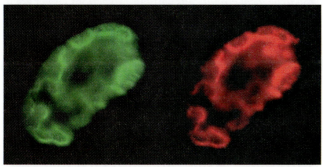

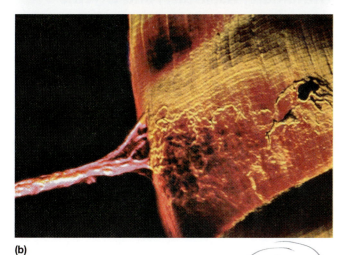

(b)

Brain
IPSP → GABA

quantitatively the most commonly employed neurotransmitter in biology.

Synthesis and Breakdown

As the name implies, GABA itself is an amino acid. However, it is not one of the amino acids that can make peptide bonds in proteins. As shown in Figure 5–16, GABA is a simple molecule with three carbons separating the amino groups from the carboxylic acid (instead of one in the common amino

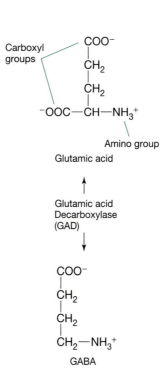

Figure 5–16 *Synthesis of GABA.* Glutamic acid decarboxylase converts glutamic acid into GABA. Do you think it is interesting that the major transmitter mediating inhibition in the brain is so closely related chemically to the major transmitter for mediating excitation? Teleologically, why do you think this relationship exists?

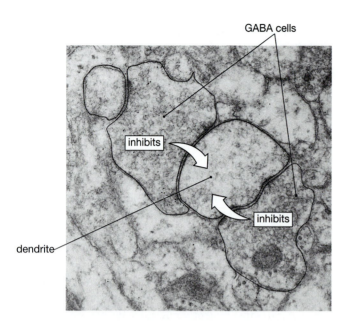

GABA cells

inhibits

inhibits

dendrite

Figure 5–17   *A GABAergic Synapse.* Most synapses in the brain employ GABA as a transmitter and produce inhibition of the postsynaptic cell. (Courtesy of Eva Fifkova)

Importance in the Brain

The bulk of the synapses in the brain are inhibitory; in turn, the bulk of inhibitory synapses are GABAergic. A large number of these employ the special GABAergic, chloride-mediat-

ed mechanism of **presynaptic inhibition** in which GABA blocks the invasion of the bouton by the incoming action potential (Box 5–3 on page 112). We know of this not only because of histochemical probes for GABAergic phenotype but also by use of GABA antagonists to test for GABA-mediated processes. For example, the GABA antagonist bicuculline can be used to block many GABAergic synaptic processes throughout the brain. In a tiny chunk of cortex bicuculline produces unrestrained excitation which gives the electrical appearance of an epileptic discharge. In a behaving animal bicuculline produces seizures similar to epilepsy. Obviously GABAergic inhibition plays a large role in restraining excitatory circuits, and as we have seen this inhibition is the most prominent activity of the brain. Indeed, it seems that GABAergic inhibitory cells (which tend to be *local circuit* cells without projections elsewhere in the brain) are more metabolically active than the other systems that use different transmitters. As a result, trauma to the brain (such as lack of oxygen) is likely to affect the GABAergic inhibitory cells first. One theory of how epilepsy occurs is that lack of oxygen (due, say, to damage to an infant in the birth canal) causes a *focus* of excitation to emerge where the GABAergic inhibitory cells have dropped out. Epilepsy is often treated with drugs that enhance the action of GABA.

Glutamate, Aspartate, and Glycine

Many likely transmitters are common amino acid themselves. It is curious that a transmitter that mediates most *excitation* in the brain is closely related to GABA. In fact, it is glutamic

Figure 5–18   *The GABA Receptor (Chloride-Conducting).* The GABA receptor binds GABA, opening the gate and allowing chloride ions through the pore. The GABA receptor also has two allosteric sites, which bind benzodiazepines and barbiturates.

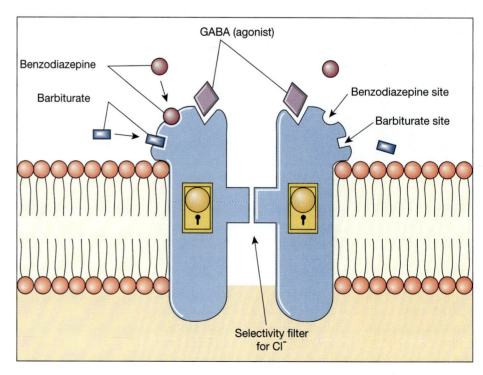

GABA (agonist)

Benzodiazepine

Barbiturate

Benzodiazepine site

Barbiturate site

Selectivity filter for Cl⁻

acid, the chemical precursor of GABA (see Figure 5–16). The identity of amino acid transmitters is not known for sure. *This is because all cells must contain every common amino acid since they use all twenty to make essential proteins.* We can use the presence of a substance like GABA or ACh as a good indicator that a cell uses the compound as a transmitter. Alternatively, we can use the presence of the enzyme used to synthesize the substance, such as GAD or CAT, as another reliable sign. However, for cells that may use an amino acid like glutamic acid these criteria are useless to us. In fact, it is unclear whether glutamic acid or a very similar amino acid, **aspartic acid**, is the transmitter at excitatory contacts in brain. Researchers have claimed that both are involved, or that neither are. Even in simple systems (such as the excitatory fibers in arthropods) good evidence exists for both glutamic acid and aspartic acid, and it is unclear which plays the larger role. At least three different receptors have been described for the excitatory amino acids (for a review, see Hall, 1992).

There is a common amino acid important in inhibition as well. **Glycine** appears to mediate inhibition particularly in the spinal cord, at least partly taking the place of GABA in

that area of the CNS. The glycine antagonist *strychnine* is a dangerous poison that produces spinal seizures, indicating the importance of inhibition in spinal circuits (Chapter 7).

Catecholamines, Indolamine, and Histamine

Another family of transmitters is derived from the common amino acid **tyrosine** (Figure 5–19). All cells contain tyrosine, since, like glutamic acid and aspartic acid, this amino acid is necessary to make virtually any protein. Only *some* cells contain the enzyme **tyrosine hydroxylase (TOH)**, which converts tyrosine to an amino acid that is not used in making protein. Though there is an attempt to make enzyme nomenclature rational, sometimes the system breaks down a bit. The name *tyrosine hydroxylase* suggests that a hydroxyl group is *either* removed from or added to tyrosine. In this case, a hydroxyl group is added to tyrosine's ring structure to produce the intermediate L-dopa. The next enzyme, aromatic amino acid (AAA) decarboxylase is aptly named, for it removes the carboxyl group from L-dopa *as well as from other aromatic*

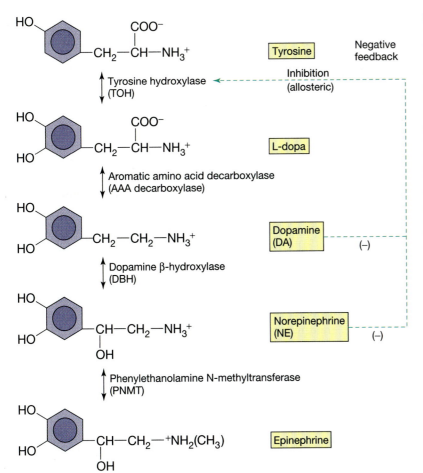

Figure 5–19 *Synthesis of Catecholamines.* The synthesis of catecholamines is a cascade of reactions involving many enzymes and intermediates. Two of the intermediates (dopamine and norepinephrine) and the final product (epinephrine) are important in transmission. The system has the ability to regulate the amount of intermediates and products synthesized. When too much dopamine and norepinephrine are produced, they bind to an allosteric site on TOH, rendering it unable to perform its action on tyrosine. With inactive TOH, the cascade cannot progress and no more of the catecholamines will be produced. This property is called negative feedback. When product levels are low, they do not bind to TOH, allowing it to begin the cascade and produce more catecholamine.

Box 5–3

How GABA Blocks the Action Potential

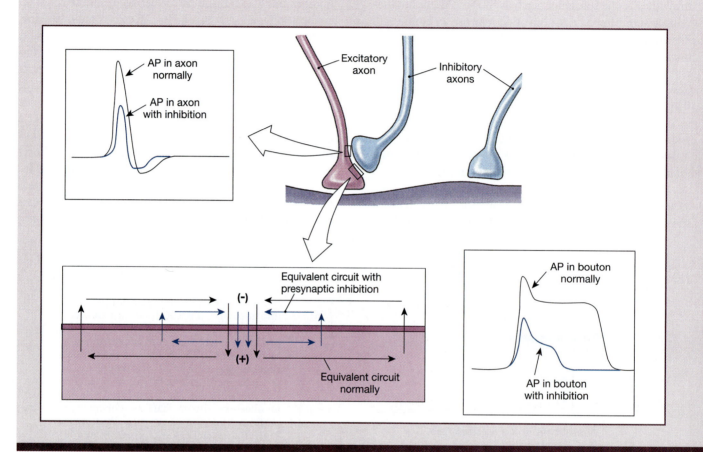

amino acids (those that have their hydrogens and carbon groups arranged in rings; an aromatic ring with two hydroxyl groups is called a catechol ring). In this case the enzyme produces the compound **dopamine (DA)** from L-dopa. Lacking an acid group but retaining the catechol ring and the nitrogen, or amino group (NH_3), dopamine is referred to as a **catecholamine**. As we shall see, dopamine plays a profound role in central nervous system function.

Some cells contain TOH and AAA decarboxylase only, and in these the synthesis scheme stops at dopamine. These cells are called dopaminergic neurons. However, some cells that contain these two enzymes also contain a third enzyme, dopamine β-hydroxylase (DBH). This enzyme adds another hydroxyl group, this time to an area called the β-position on dopamine, which yields the transmitter substance **norepi-**

nephrine (NE). This compound is also called *noradrenaline* and cells that employ it as a transmitter are called *noradrenergic* cells. Because dopamine is a precursor to norepinephrine, *all cells that have norepinephrine in them also contain dopamine.* As for the amino acid transmitters considered above (glutamate and aspartate), this leads to some overlap in transmitter action and in transmitter phenotype within the catecholamines.

Finally, some cells contain TOH, AAA decarboxylase, DBH, and a fourth enzyme. This enzyme glories in the name phenylethanolamine N-methyltransferase (PNMT) and transfers a methyl group (CH_3) to the nitrogen-containing amine at the end of NE. The product of this reaction is **epinephrine**, which is also known as **adrenaline**. There are a few cells in the brain that employ epinephrine as a transmitter, but the bulk of

The GABA receptor is probably the most prevalent receptor in the brain and much of the receptors appear to be found on *presynaptic* structures. The GABA-mediated chloride shunt will resist *any* deviation of membrane potential from the chloride potential. Hyperpolarizing as well as depolarizing postsynaptic potentials are diminished by GABA action, and *even the action potential* can be reduced by the chloride shunt. In the previous chapter we learned that the action potential is an all-or-none event, and indeed it is, but propagation between excitable regions (at the nodes of Ranvier) is *passive* and governed by the *cable properties* of the axon and myelin. *Increase* in membrane resistance introduced by myelin makes the equivalent circuit large and conduction fast and faithful, but a *decrease* in membrane resistance brought about by an increase in chloride conductance would have the *opposite effect*. The equivalent circuit would be small and the action potential would be "shunted away" through the active chloride conductance. (Remember to think of this in purely electrical terms. Don't bother with what happens to individual ions during the action potential).

This is precisely what is accomplished by a special form of synaptic transmission called *presynaptic inhibition*. In presynaptic inhibition the synaptic contact is made not on a dendrite but on another axon (an "axoaxonic" contact). When the presynaptic contact is active, GABA is released, a chloride conductance is opened in the *bouton* of the follower cell, and all invading action potentials are smaller in the axon terminal because of the diminished equivalent circuit. Less depolarization means that fewer voltage-dependent calcium channels open with each incoming impulse, less transmitter is released, and a smaller synaptic potential is encountered in the third or final postsynaptic cell.

Here the words *presynaptic* and *postsynaptic* must be used with caution since the bouton in the middle is *both* presynaptic and postsynaptic. In fact, you may think that presynaptic inhibition violates the law of dynamic polarization, since the mechanism bypasses the chemically excitable domain of the soma and dendrites. In fact the violation is more apparent than real, since the *polarity of each synapse is preserved*. Information travels in only one direction across the synapse, from pre- to postsynaptic membrane. The only wrinkle in what we have come to believe so far is that the bouton (part of the electrically excitable domain) actually may contain some transmitter receptors also (and hence may be part of the chemically excitable domain as well).

Historically the mechanism of presynaptic inhibition has been subject to some controversy. The version presented here was developed by Stephen Kuffler (Dudel and Kuffler, 1961) but another, competing, explanation for presynaptic inhibition in the cat spinal cord (possibly mediated by glycine) was put forth by Sir John Eccles. In recent years it has become apparent that presynaptic inhibition is quite common and is probably evoked by a number of transmitters utilizing a number of ionic mechanisms. We will encounter a particularly interesting example in Chapter 11, when we discuss the action of *endorphins*.

the body's epinephrine is used in the peripheral nervous system where it is produced by the adrenal gland (along with dopamine and a rather large amount of norepinephrine, Chapter 6).

The most important point to be gained from Figure 5–19 is indicated by the arrows pointing *back to TOH* from the end products DA and NE. TOH is a *rate-limiting* enzyme, meaning that not all tyrosine goes down the synthetic path to L-dopa. TOH controls the amount of catecholamine produced because it is the *bottleneck* in the synthesis scheme, the "traffic jam" for tyrosine on its way to L-dopa. Further, and most importantly, TOH contains an *allosteric* site that receives the ultimate products DA and NE; like those of protein receptors, an enzyme's allosteric sites neither bind substrate nor generate product. In this particular case the end products (DA and NE) *inhibit* the action of the enzyme (TOH) used to create them. Let's consider for a moment how such **negative feedback** inhibition would work. When product (DA or NE) builds up in a cell, the product binds to the allosteric site on TOH, causing it to cease acting (and to cease forming more product). When the concentration of DA or NE declines (after its secretion from the cell) the product is released from the allosteric site; TOH resumes its job and the necessary levels of NE and DA are restored. Such a negative feedback scheme, therefore tends to *even out* changes in transmitter level. *When there is more secretion from the cell there is more synthesis; when there is less secretion from the cell there is less synthesis. The net result is that transmitter concentrations stay the same.* A corollary, very important for what is to come, is that *the brain will resist any attempt to change transmitter concentration* (Box 5–4).

Box 5–4

Parkinson's Disease and Homeostasis

In 1817 a British physician named James Parkinson described a "shaking palsy" that he had encountered in a number of his neurological patients. The disease that later became associated with his name, *Parkinson's disease*, is a progressive and irreversible movement disorder. At first patients have little difficulty except in tasks, such as writing, in which fine voluntary motor control is necessary.

> As the disease proceeds similar employments are accomplished with great difficulty, the hand failing to answer with exactness to the dictates of the will. Walking becomes a task which cannot be performed without considerable attention. The legs are not raised to that height, or with that promptitude which the will directs, so that the utmost care is necessary to prevent frequent falls. (Parkinson, 1817)

Later in the course of the disease a characteristic "pill-rolling" tremor of the hands develops (as if the patient is rolling invisible balls between the thumb and fingers). A shuffling "Parkinson's gait" characterizes efforts at walking.

> The patient seldom experiences a suspension of the agitation of the limbs. Commencing for instance in one arm, the wearisome agitation is borne until beyond sufferance, when by suddenly changing the posture it is for a time stopped in that limb, to commence, generally in less than a minute in one of the legs, or in the arm of the other side. (Parkinson, 1817)

The vehemence of the agitation grows over years until extreme exhaustion presages the arrival of death, which Parkinson described as a "wished-for release" (Parkinson, 1817).

At around the time Paul Broca was cutting up the brains of his aphasic patients after death (Chapter 1), like-minded scientists began to examine posthumous speci-

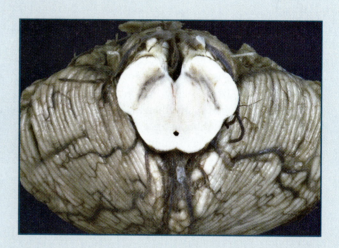

mens of the brains of Parkinson's victims. Lacking the sophisticated histochemical techniques available today, these early pathologists could only evaluate the appearance of fresh brain tissue. They discovered that a part of the brainstem called the **substantia nigra** (which is Latin for "black substance") was noticeably atrophied (less dense) in the brains of Parkinson's patients compared to specimens taken from individuals who died of other causes (compare top figure, a normal brain, to the figure on the right, the brain of a Parkinson's victim). Today we know that the substantia nigra is an important source of the transmitter *dopamine*. It appears black in fresh tissue because it contains high concentrations of *tyrosine hydroxylase* (TOH), which normally exists in a complex with ionic *zinc*. The metal gives the substantia nigra the opaque or dark appearance.

It thus became apparent that Parkinson's disease was due to a *lack of dopaminergic transmission in the brain*. Specifically, a lack of dopamine disrupted the function of part of the motor system called the basal ganglia (Chapter 10) that is especially important in voluntary muscle movement. At this point you are probably saying to yourself, well, if a lack of dopamine is the problem, then why not give the patient extra dopamine to compensate? The brain is insulated from the body by a membrane that is impermeable to most chemicals (the blood-brain barrier, Chapter 8) presenting an obstacle to this obvious therapy for Parkinson's disease. Direct dopamine supplements (in the diet or by injection) are ineffective because the extra dopamine is excluded by the blood-brain barrier.

The brain cannot exclude *all* compounds, however, since it requires nutrients from the blood in order to function. In addition to glucose (its sole source of energy), vitamins, and minerals (like the zinc complexed with TOH), the brain requires *amino acids* for use in synthesizing proteins and transmitters. *Pumps* that span the blood/brain barrier recognize and actively take up amino acids. *Tyrosine*, for example, is readily taken up, as is L-dopa, which is also an amino acid (having yet to experience decarboxylation, it resembles tyrosine enough to "fool" the pump in the blood-brain barrier; see Figure 5–19). Though tyrosine itself is an ineffective therapy for Parkinson's disease, L-dopa, which is after the regulating step in the cascade, will enter the brain and then cascade into dopamine by the activity of the nonspecific decarboxylation enzyme AAA decarboxylase. It is for this reason that L-dopa therapy has proved to be a very useful treatment of Parkinson's disease.

The success of this breakthrough can hardly be overemphasized. Symptoms can be alleviated in a large percentage of sufferers by L-dopa treatment. However, L-dopa does not cure Parkinson's. As a consequence, much recent research is devoted to understanding the causes of the condition and to developing an eventual cure (reviewed in Chapter 10).

As so often happens in science, the tremendous success story of L-dopa therapy has spawned a host of other "therapies" for various maladies that are commonly based on the notion of *precursor loading* to enhance brain transmitter levels. Often, these involve diet supplements of precursor compounds (tyrosine for catecholamines, tryptophan for serotonin, choline for ACh, and so forth). These new-age dietary supplements are pervasive enough that we shall have occasion to discuss them at greater length elsewhere (Chapters 17 and 18). For the moment, however, consider the synthesis scheme for the catecholamines that is presented in Figure 5–19. Negative feedback inhibition regulates the amount of transmitter present in the terminals. Precursor loading may lead (by the "law of mass action") to an increase in the amount of amino acid that goes down the synthetic pathway, *but as soon as this yields a change in transmitter level, the negative feedback will kick in and slow the synthesis back down.* Similar feedback regulatory schemes exist for the other transmitters and, indeed, for all biological systems. The tendency to maintain a *constant internal environment* is called homeostasis. In the L-dopa treatment of Parkinson's disease, homeostasis is circumvented by bypassing the rate-limiting step and by the fact that homeostasis has already been disrupted by the disease process itself (i.e., the level of dopamine is already below the "set-point" for homeostatic regulation of TOH). However, in *normal* conditions homeostasis will resist any attempt to perturb brain chemistry. Thus, whatever the efficacy of diet supplements of transmitter precursors might be (and here you should judge for yourself after reading Chapters 17 and 18), there is a strong *biochemical* reason for skepticism.

AAA decarboxylase (the same enzyme discussed earlier) is also involved in generating **serotonin** and **histamine**, two other important transmitter substances from the common aromatic amino acids **tryptophan** and **histidine**, respectively. Collectively, the transmitters are called (especially in the older literature) **biogenic amines** and hence transmission mediated by any of them has come to be called **aminergic transmission**.

We will have many occasions in this book to consider the biogenic amines since brain scientists tend to have an aminergic theory for almost everything. Those of you that have a taste for impersonation can do a very credible imitation of a psychiatrist, neuroscientist, or physiological psychologist, while a gathering of these is discussing any pertinent subject, by merely remarking, "Do you think that _____ [mention your favorite amine] is involved? I am quite certain that it must be." You can be quite confident, if you use this gambit, that a lively discussion will ensue and you will be taken for a very thoughtful and up-to-date member of the profession.

Peptide Synthesis

The transmitters we have considered up to now have been simple molecules, either amino acids or products of enzyme action on amino acids. A large and very diverse group of transmitters consists of *complex* molecules made of *chains* of amino acids. When a chain of amino acids is long, it is called a *protein*; if it is short, it is called a **peptide**.

Special Properties

With minor exception, amino acids cannot be chained together into peptides at the terminals of **peptidergic** cells (cells that use peptides as transmitters). The exact sequence of amino acids in a peptide, like that in a protein, is determined by the sequence of base pairs in messenger RNA and ultimately by instructions from nucleic DNA (Chapter 2). Since the axon tip lacks the equipment to store all this information (no chromosomes, ribosomes, Golgi apparatus, etc.) *peptides must be synthesized in the soma and sent down the axon to the site of release by orthograde axoplasmic transport.* Invariably, synthesis of peptides at the soma first takes the form of a large **protein precursor**, which is cleaved into the smaller active peptides on the way to the terminals. As a consequence, peptides are not recycled at a peptidergic contact since synthesis can only transpire elsewhere. Rather, they have action that is terminated by *diffusion* of the peptides away from the junction or by enzymatic breakdown (called **proteolysis** for peptides) and subsequent diffusion of the breakdown products. As you can see, peptidergic transmission is *metabolically expensive* compared to that using simpler transmitters. As a consequence, peptide transmitters tend to act at *low concentrations* and to evoke responses that last a *long time*.

Simple Systems

As for the other transmitters, an understanding of peptidergic transmission was first achieved by investigation of simple systems such as the nervous system of invertebrates and the peripheral ganglia in the vertebrate body.

In a way, the first peptide transmitter to be described was **Substance P** (see Box 5–2). Known to be present in peripheral nerves (like the vagus) and to play a role in inflammation in the periphery (Chapter 11), it was reasonably surmised that the central projections of neurons containing Substance P would use it as a transmitter substance. The venerable English physiologist Henry Dale speculated on this point, leading to a great deal of confusion later on when his "principle" was erroneously taken to apply to all transmitters and all neurons. Though it is virtually certain that Substance P has an important role to play in the spinal cord and brain, its action in the peripheral nervous system remains much better understood than its effects on the CNS.

In the 1970s, an elegant demonstration that a peptide hormone known as luteinizing hormone releasing hormone (LHRH) acts as a transmitter in the autonomic nervous system of frogs emerged from Stephen Kuffler's laboratory at Harvard (Jan et al., 1979). Peptides that act as transmitters in the simple brains of invertebrates (such as egg-laying hormone, or ELH, in the brain of the sea slug *Aplysia*) were also reported in the literature (Branton et al., 1978).

Endorphins

In the brain the complexity of neural circuits is such that it is rarely possible to record directly from the presynaptic as well as the postsynaptic elements of a synapse. As such, synaptic potentials mediated by peptides are difficult to evaluate. The best understood central peptides are those for which there are specific *antagonists* for use as probes. A family of peptide transmitters called, collectively, **endorphins** (see Chapter 11) have such an antagonist. Developed by the pharmaceutical industry to treat drug overdoses, *naloxone* blocks central endorphin-mediated processes. Use of naloxone has identified one endorphin, methionine enkephalin, as a transmitter in some parts of the brain.

Vasopressin and Oxytocin

Two other peptides known to act as hormones in the body appear to be transmitters in the brain as well, **vasopressin** and **oxytocin**. As before, this discovery depended on the availability of a specific antagonist (this one made to prevent premature delivery in women). Like any other transmitter, the

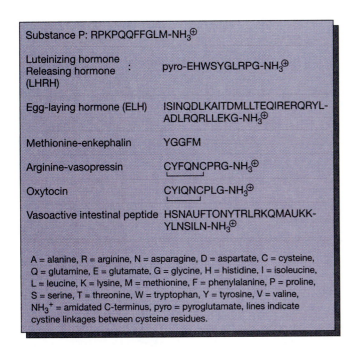

Substance P: RPKPQQFFGLM-NH$_3^\oplus$

Luteinizing hormone
Releasing hormone : pyro-EHWSYGLRPG-NH$_3^\oplus$
(LHRH)

Egg-laying hormone (ELH) ISINQDLKAITDMLLTEQIRERQRYL-
ADLRQRLLEKG-NH$_3^\oplus$

Methionine-enkephalin YGGFM

Arginine-vasopressin CYFQNCPRG-NH$_3^\oplus$

Oxytocin CYIQNCPLG-NH$_3^\oplus$

Vasoactive intestinal peptide HSNAUFTONYTRLRKQMAUKK-
YLNSILN-NH$_3^\oplus$

A = alanine, R = arginine, N = asparagine, D = aspartate, C = cysteine,
Q = glutamine, E = glutamate, G = glycine, H = histidine, I = isoleucine,
L = leucine, K = lysine, M = methionine, F = phenylalanine, P = proline,
S = serine, T = threonine, W = tryptophan, Y = tyrosine, V = valine,
NH$_3^+$ = amidated C-terminus, pyro = pyroglutamate, lines indicate
cystine linkages between cysteine residues.

Figure 5–20 *Amino Acid Sequence of Some Peptide Transmitter Candidates.* Each amino acid is represented by a code (see Chapter 2).

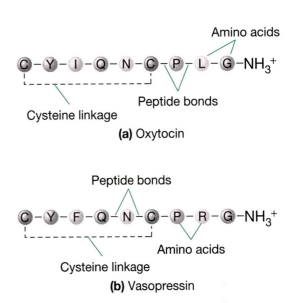

(a) Oxytocin

(b) Vasopressin

Figure 5–21 *Oxytocin and Vasopressin.* The structures of the two peptides show homology.

action of these peptides is not intrinsic to the cells that secrete them but is instead determined by the receptor within the postsynaptic cell. Vasopressin and oxytocin (and the endorphins also) have multiple receptor types that mediate different actions. The role of oxytocin and vasopressin in behavior (which we will discuss in the chapters that follow) is a property of the various receptor systems.

Again, peptides (like other proteins) display *homology* and *heterogeneity* (Figure 5–20). Oxytocin and vasopressin are closely related structurally, and hence are thought to be homologous (Figure 5–21). The endorphins also share sequence homology, as does Substance P and a family of peptides called **bradykinins**, a group of gut-derived peptides including gastrin and cholecystokinin, and a family of peptides similar to adrenocorticotrophic hormone (ACTH), known as melanocyte-stimulating hormones (Table 5–1). Current estimates of the number of probable peptide transmitters are very high (possibly as many as 300 in the human brain). We shall discuss individual peptides throughout the text in the context of systems in which they appear to play a role.

The Concept of Neuromodulation

The large number of transmitters likely to exist in the brain (especially peptide transmitters) presents the possibility for great complexity in chemical signaling. If inhibition and excitation were the only functions of a synaptic relationship,

then you might surmise that only *two* transmitters would be necessary. (Or, even more parsimoniously, *one* transmitter with two receptor types). The fact that there are more indicates that something a great deal more elaborate than simple IPSPs and EPSPs must be involved in integration. We are only now beginning to get an inkling of what this level of complexity might entail.

For example, after a false start in the direction of a doctrine that held that each neuron contains and secretes but a single transmitter, we now know that there are cells that contain two and possibly more transmitter substances. Peptides especially tend to be **cotransmitters** with other transmitters like NE, DA, and serotonin; and recent evidence indicates that ubiquitous compounds like *adenosine, AMP,* and *ATP* (together called *purines*) may participate in transmission at some synapses as well.

A temptation has been to derive a new category for cotransmitters (as distinguished from transmitters). The term **neuromodulator** (Figure 5–22) has been proposed for substances that act only by influencing the action of another transmitter and not by acting alone. However, since all transmitter systems influence the action of other systems (because the neurons of the brain are connected together synaptically) this definition seems somewhat imprecise. In this book we shall use a more restricted definition of "neuromodulator": *a transmitter or cotransmitter without intrinsic effect that acts by allosterically modifying the affinity of a receptor for another transmitter.* A good example of a neuromodulator is the peptide vasoactive intestinal peptide (VIP), which acts by increasing the affinity of the muscarinic receptor for

Table 5–1	PARTIAL LIST OF KNOWN NEUROPEPTIDES
Peptide Hormones	Adrenocorticotrophic Hormone (ACTH) Melanocyte-Stimulating Hormone (MSH) Somatostatin (SS) Thyrotropin-Releasing Hormone (TRH) Renin Angiotensin Cholecystokinin (CCK) Gastrin Prolactin Calcitonin Corticotropin-Releasing Factor (CRF) Insulin Growth Hormone (GH) Nerve Growth Factor (NGF) Glucagon Secretin
Other Peptides	Lipotropin Hormone (LPH) β-endorphin Neurotensin Cerulein Neuropeptide Y (NPY) Avian Pancreatic Polypeptide (APP) Bombesin Bradykinin Proctolin FMRF-amide Dynorphin Calcitonin-gene-related Peptide (CGRP) Substance P Eledoisin Sauvagine Small cardioactive peptide (SCP) N-aspartylglutamate

ACh. It seems likely that the GABA receptor, among others, is the site of action of a number of *neuromodulators* since its allosteric sites accept a number of these compounds.

Criteria for Transmitter Identification

Back when it was assumed (wrongly) that each synapse employed but a single transmitter, criteria were established and universally recognized for identification of the substance acting as a transmitter. More recently, with the discovery that synaptic transmission was considerably more complicated, involving numerous transmitters and receptors, there has been a tendency to overlook these criteria and to accept many compounds as transmitters based on the *likelihood* that they

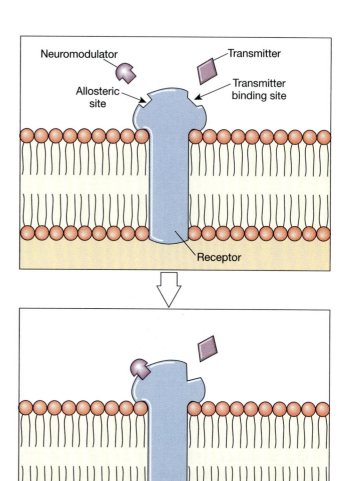

Presence of the neuromodulator alters the transmitter binding site, increasing its affinity for the neurotransmitter.

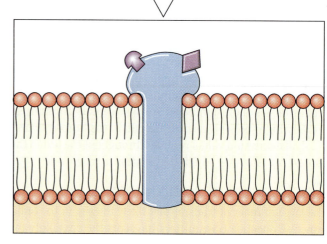

Figure 5–22 *Neuromodulators.* Neuromodulators act by influencing the affinity of a receptor for another transmitter. (Cooper et al., 1991)

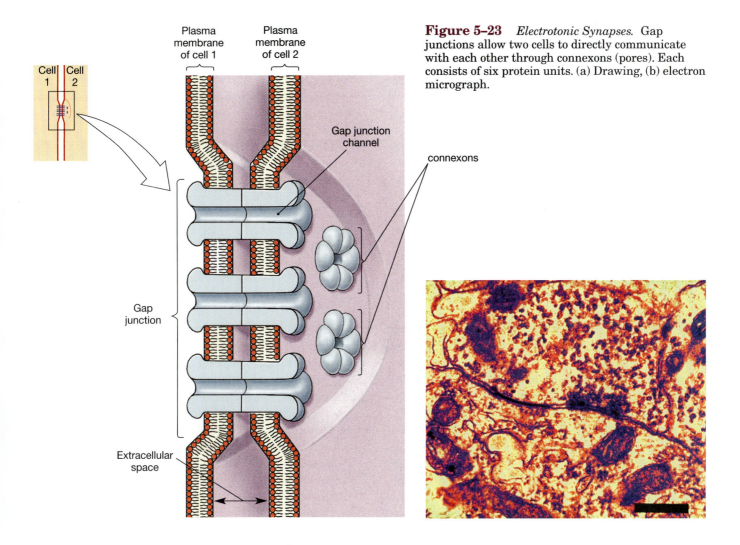

Plasma membrane of cell 1

Plasma membrane of cell 2

Cell 1 | Cell 2

Gap junction channel

connexons

Gap junction

Extracellular space

Figure 5–23 *Electrotonic Synapses.* Gap junctions allow two cells to directly communicate with each other through connexons (pores). Each consists of six protein units. (a) Drawing, (b) electron micrograph.

somehow play a role. However, the challenge of complexity calls for more *strict* rather than looser application of rigorous standards of proof. The following are the classic criteria for identification of transmitters, updated to incorporate our new knowledge of cotransmission and neuromodulation:

1. A proposed transmitter substance must be *synthesized* or *stored* by the presynaptic cell.

2. The substance must be *secreted* by the presynaptic cell (i.e., released in the presence of calcium).

3. The substance must have *postsynaptic effect* that duplicates in mechanism the effect of activating the synapse.

4. The *amount* released must be adequate to account for the entire postsynaptic effect (for cotransmitters, the amount is the total of all substances involved).

5. An antagonist that *blocks the action* of the substance must also *block* the postsynaptic potential (or

that portion of it proposed to be due to its action as a cotransmitter).

The history of neuroscience is rife with compounds that, by satisfying *some* of these criteria, appeared to be transmitters but were subsequently found not to be (*taurine* is a historical example, present and effective postsynaptically but not secreted). *Because of homology in mechanisms that are applied to diverse purposes in the body, many substances may appear to be transmitters but are not.* A full understanding of the brain requires that the mechanisms of chemical transmission be established with confidence. Hence, for substances that satisfy some but not all of the criteria listed above, it is most proper to use the description "transmitter candidate," a convention that we will follow in this text.

Electrotonic Synapses

Synapses that employ a simple transmitter candidate like ACh or GABA tend to have a **synaptic delay** on the order of *one mil-*

lisecond or so, an interval that is almost completely due to the time necessary for vesicles to fuse with the presynaptic membrane. Amines and peptides tend to have action at the longer latencies, several milliseconds or even longer. These longer intervals are probably due to the time taken to diffuse to a target from a remote site of release (Chapter 6). In a few systems that require *very fast* transmission (escape systems especially), synaptic communication may *bypass exocytosis and chemical transmission altogether*. In these synapses a *direct contact* is made between the presynaptic cell and the postsynaptic one. There is, in other words, *no synaptic cleft*. The electrically excitable domain of one cell directly impacts the (otherwise) chemically excitable domain of the other using cable properties alone. As we have seen, passive propagation

is much *faster* than other mechanisms. Such synapses without transmitters are called **electrotonic synapses** or **gap junctions**, and the channels that mediate the transmission are called *connexins* (Figure 5–23). Electrotonic synapses have been shown to play an important role in neural mechanisms for escape behavior in crayfish. Obviously, evolution has favored such a quick mechanism for transmission, saving the millisecond needed for chemical transmission, so as to save the lives of crayfish. Recent results show that vertebrates also use electrotonic synapses in escape behavior. The *Mauthner cells* in fish are the only neurons in vertebrates large enough to be readily identifiable in each specimen; they produce the darting escape behavior familiar to anyone who goes fishing and appear to be activated by electrotonic synapses.

SUMMARY

The chemically excitable domain experiences depolarizing events called excitatory postsynaptic potentials (EPSPs) and events that counteract depolarization known as inhibitory postsynaptic potentials (IPSPs). Impinging EPSPs and IPSPs are integrated at the axon hillock where the sum of their effects determines whether an action potential will be fired. EPSPs and IPSPs arise because a chemical transmitter secreted by the presynaptic cell binds to a receptor on the postsynaptic cell. Transmitters and other agonists activate the receptor, which in turn induces a conductance change. In contrast, antagonists such as some drugs and poisons occupy the receptor without having influence. These compounds have effect only by blocking the action of an agonist. The first synaptic transmitter to be described was acetylcholine. Acetylcholine can be excitatory (as at the neuromuscular junction) or inhibitory (as at the vertebrate heart) depending on the receptor expressed by the postsynaptic cell. Gamma-aminobutyric

acid (GABA) usually activates a chloride conductance in the follower cell and evokes an IPSP. Sometimes this IPSP can occur in the bouton of a cell, which has the effect of producing presynaptic inhibition of transmission through a second synapse. Many transmitters are amino acids (glutamic acid, aspartic acid, and glycine) or derivatives of amino acids (catecholamines, serotonin, and histamine). Because of similarity in structure, common mechanisms are employed by diverse transmitters and there is overlapping specificity of action. The largest group of transmitters appears to be peptide transmitters. Here too homology provides overlapping structures and overlapping specificity. Some transmitters act together at a single synapse. When this occurs they are called cotransmitters. Some transmitters act on receptors for another transmitter. When this occurs they are called neuromodulators. Gap junctions provide for direct communication between neurons, without the participation of a chemical transmitter.

REVIEW QUESTIONS

1. How does an EPSP differ from an IPSP?
2. How does the chemically excitable domain differ from the electrically excitable domain? How is it similar?
3. How does an agonist differ from an antagonist?
4. What is integration?
5. Describe a transmitter receptor protein. Is it hydrophilic or hydrophobic?

6. How was acetylcholine discovered?
7. What is the action of GABA in the brain?
8. What is an allosteric site?
9. Which are the amino acid transmitters?
10. What is an electrotonic synapse?

THOUGHT QUESTIONS

1. Tranquilizers, sleeping pills (downers), and alcohol all appear to act by increasing GABA action in the brain. How does this relate to "shunting" inhibition?

2. How does the existence of the electrotonic synapse speak to the issue of reticular theory versus neuron doctrine?

KEY CONCEPTS

acetate (p. 103)
acetylcholine (ACh) (p. 97)
acetylcholine receptor (AChR) (p. 104)
acetylcholinesterase (AChE) (p. 106)
adrenaline (p. 112)
agonist (p. 98)
allosteric modifier (p. 102)
aminergic (p. 116)
antagonist (p. 99)
aspartic acid (p. 111)
binding site (p. 97)
biogenic amines (p. 116)
bradykinins (p. 117)
breakdown (p. 103)
bridge circuit (p. 91)
calcium spikes (p. 94)
catecholamine (p. 112)
chloride shunt (p. 91)
choline (p. 103)
cholineacetyltransferase (CAT) (p. 103)

cholinergic (p. 107)
cotransmitters (p. 117)
desensitization (p. 105)
dopamine (DA) (p. 112)
electrotonic synapses (p. 120)
electrotonically remote (p. 94)
endogenous (p. 99)
endorphins (p. 116)
end plate (p. 107)
end plate potential (p. 107)
epinephrine (p. 112)
EPSPs (p. 90)
ester (p. 103)
exogenous (p. 99)
extracellular matrix (p. 106)
GABA transaminase (p. 109)
gamma-aminobutyric acid (GABA) (p. 108)
gap junctions (p. 120)
glutamic acid (p. 109)
glutamic acid decarboxylase (GAD) (p. 109)

glycine (p. 111)
histamine (p. 116)
histidine (p. 116)
homeostasis (p. 115)
integration (p. 91)
IPSPs (p. 90)
muscarinic acetylcholine receptor (p. 101)
negative feedback (p. 113)
neuromodulator (p. 117)
neuromuscular junction (p. 107)
nicotine (p. 101)
nicotinic acetylcholine receptor (p. 97)
norepinephrine (NE) (p. 112)
oxytocin (p. 116)
peptide (p. 116)
peptidergic (p. 116)
phenotype (p. 107)
postsynaptic potentials (p. 89)
potency (p. 98)
presynaptic inhibition (p. 110)

protein precursor (p. 116)
proteolysis (p. 116)
quantal content (p. 96)
quantum (p. 95)
re-uptake (p. 103)
reversal potential (p. 90)
secretion (p. 103)
serotonin (p. 116)
spatial summation (p. 93)
Substance P (p. 116)
substantia nigra (p. 114)
synapse (p. 89)
synaptic delay (p. 119)
synthesis (p. 103)
temporal summation (p. 93)
tryptophan (p. 116)
tyrosine (p. 111)
tyrosine hydroxylase (TOH) (p. 111)
vagus nerves (p. 105)
vasopressin (p. 116)

6

The Autonomic Nervous System

In this chapter we will begin examination of transmitters in their functional context, that is, transmitter *physiology*. We will start with the innervation of the viscera, for this study illuminates many processes mediated by the same transmitter candidates in the brain and is very useful in the study of medicine and the mechanism of drug action. Then, in Chapter 7, we will begin the study of the physiological control of the rest of the body.

The entire nervous system of vertebrates can be divided into the **peripheral nervous system (PNS)** and the **central nervous system (CNS)**. Historically, the boundary between the PNS and CNS was taken to be an intricate membranous network that partly isolates brain and spinal cord tissue from the blood (the **blood-brain barrier** or **BBB**). In practice the separation is not this straightforward. For now, let's consider the brain and spinal cord as the CNS and all other neural tissue in the body as the PNS. We will emphasize the exceptions to this rule as they arise in this and the next two chapters. The organization of these various elements of the nervous system is shown in Figure 6–1.

The PNS in turn can be divided into systems with distinct anatomy and physiology. The **somatic nervous system** consists of the nerves that carry the axons of motor neurons to innervate muscles that attach to the skeleton and that carry sensory fibers from the muscles, skeleton, and body surface (*soma* = body). In other words, the somatic system emits motor commands that cause the body to move and relays sensory information regarding joint position and cutaneous sensation (touch) into the spinal cord.

The **autonomic nervous system (ANS)** comprises the second half of the PNS. The autonomic system consists of motor and sensory nerves that innervate the internal organs of the body (heart, viscera, lungs, bladder) and also glands and nonskeletal muscle throughout the body (sweat glands, tear- and saliva-producing glands, muscles for genitalia, blood vessels and body hair, sphincter muscles in the eye and digestive system). The motor component of the autonomic nervous system includes the control of heart rate and blood pressure. The sensory component includes sensations of satiety and illness. Since the ANS involves a number of different transmitters, it is the

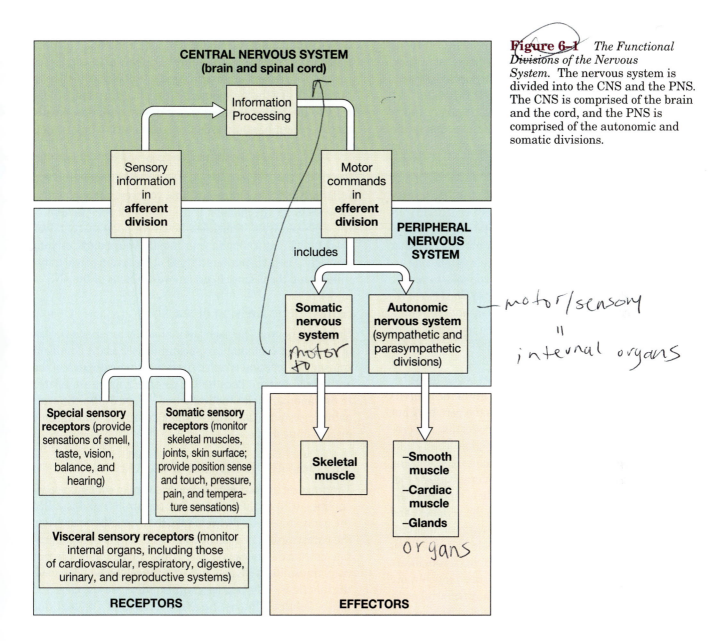

Figure 6–1 *The Functional Divisions of the Nervous System.* The nervous system is divided into the CNS and the PNS. The CNS is comprised of the brain and the cord, and the PNS is comprised of the autonomic and somatic divisions.

perfect place to apply what we learned about synaptic potentials in the last chapter.

Though few students enter the study of neuroscience with a burning desire to understand the physiology of the viscera, study of the autonomic nervous system can be rewarding. Recall the mind/body problem discussed in the first chapter. The word *autonomic* was chosen to describe functions independent of conscious control (or "autonomous" functions). This is certainly a feature of some functions of the autonomic nervous system (e.g., the constriction of the pupil in response to light), and we are all familiar with the feeling that parts of the body sometimes act as if they have "minds of their own." Indeed, much of the function of the PNS and CNS involves processes that do not impinge on our conscious awareness. However, there are other functions, such as urination, sexual function, and hunger that we are very much aware of. To a neurophysiologist, "mind" would appear to be only a small part of "brain" and an even smaller part of "body," since so many mental events and bodily functions are not "mental" in the sense of "conscious." How then can there be identity between mind and body as the doctrine of monism requires (Chapter 1)? The answer, for some monists, lies in an expanded definition of *mind*. As we shall see, this definition will have to be quite different from the colloquial one if it is to encompass the function of the autonomic nervous system.

On a practical level, study of the autonomic nervous system is a very large part of internal medicine. Activation of the sensory component of the autonomic nervous system (sensations of satiety, illness, and pain) is often the first symptom of disease of the internal organs. Similarly, much of drug therapy involves manipulation of the action of the various autonomic transmitters. Many prescription and over-the-counter drugs (e.g., cold medication, antihypertension drugs, and drugs for both staying awake and going to sleep) act on autonomic targets. Since each transmitter system has more than one receptor type associated with different postsynaptic responses (e.g., excitation and inhibition, Chapter 5), it is difficult to design or obtain drugs that have *only* the desired action without undesirable side effects. How often does the antihistamine you take to relieve cold symptoms put you to sleep, for example? Thus much research in medicinal chemistry requires an understanding of the transmitters and receptors involved in various autonomic functions. This understanding is also valuable to the educated consumer.

Finally, the autonomic nervous system is of interest because of its extraordinary *accessibility*. Many of the neurons involved have their axons and neurites in the periphery but also have their somata located there. A collection of nerve cell bodies outside the CNS is called a **ganglion**. The ganglia of the autonomic nervous system communicate at one end with the CNS and at the other with the internal organs that are innervated using terminal junctions. These junctions (two for most autonomic ganglia) lie wholly in the periphery and are amenable to experimental investigation in a way that central synapses are not; there is no blood-brain barrier to contend with, and a large number of these peripheral ganglia are packed into a small space. Because they are so much more accessible we know quite a bit more about peripheral cells, axons, neurites, and synapses than about central ones. We humans share many autonomic functions with simpler organisms, such as invertebrates, some of which have little else to their behavioral repertoire other than functions we would describe as "autonomic." Because evolution of these functions apparently occurred early on, before a great deal of speciation had occurred, we can use these "simple systems" (Chapter 5) as a basis for understanding our own autonomic functions.

Dual Innervation

Ignoring the sensory component and considering for the moment only the *motor* component of the autonomic nervous system, we find that there are a few principles which can organize our thinking about this portion of the system. The first of these is the principle of **dual innervation**. Each target organ has contact with, or is innervated by, two types of neu-

rons with different, generally opposing, action and distinct transmitter chemistry. The entire periphery of invertebrates such as insects and other arthropods displays dual innervation much like the autonomic system of vertebrates. In contrast to the motor autonomic nervous system, the somatic motor system has only excitatory, cholinergic innervation (Chapter 5).

Try to recall the last time you met somebody of the opposite sex that interested you. Or the last time you took a roller coaster ride. Or the last time you went for a job interview. Defer for the moment consideration of your *feelings* of the time and try to remember how your *body* reacted. Was there a different feeling in your mouth, your palms, or your stomach? These changes are a result of the action of two transmitters and the balance between two divisions of the ANS.

Sympathetic Division of the ANS

One set of neurons for each autonomically innervated organ of vertebrates contains norepinephrine (NE) as the dominant transmitter type and is called the **sympathetic division** of the autonomic system. Because the catecholamines are related to one another biosynthetically (see Figure 5–19), the sympathetic system also contains some dopamine, and in some places, epinephrine.

Parasympathetic Division of the ANS

The other set of fibers innervating each organ contains acetylcholine (ACh) as the predominant transmitter and is called the **parasympathetic division**. Like the sympathetic division, the parasympathetic system contains a variety of neuropeptide cotransmitter candidates. While the action of the primary transmitters NE and ACh are relatively well understood, the functions of the peptide cotransmitters are less clear and are the subject of intense current investigation. Our best clue to their role comes from study of vasoactive intestinal peptide (VIP) which may be a cotransmitter with ACh in a particular subset of parasympathetic neurons (see Chapter 5). Here VIP acts synergistically with ACh at the cholinergic receptor, increasing the affinity of the receptor for ACh, causing more saliva to form in the mouth (Figure 6–2).

Anatomy

The sympathetic and parasympathetic divisions also can be distinguished on the basis of anatomy. Both the sympathetic and the parasympathetic neurons that innervate each target organ arise from ganglia that lie wholly outside the CNS, *but the relative location of the ganglia differs in the two systems.* The sympathetic ganglia lie adjacent to the spinal column (but outside the cord) in a network called the **paravertebral chain**. There is one paravertebral chain of sympathetic ganglia on

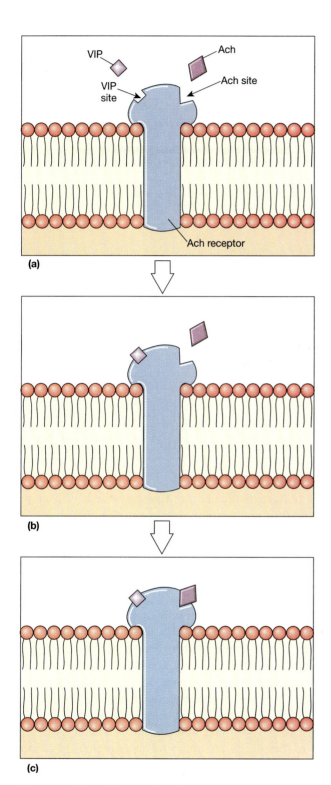

Figure 6–2 *VIP as a Peptide Cotransmitter.* In some parasympathetic neurons, VIP acts synergistically with ACh by increasing the affinity of ACh to the cholinergic receptor. When VIP is not bound to the receptor, ACh is less likely to bind (a). When VIP binds to the receptor, the ACh binding site is made more accessible (b) and ACh will more readily bind (c).

each side of the spinal cord. The parasympathetic ganglia lie in locations that are remote from the CNS. Generally the parasympathetic ganglia are located *in or near the target organs themselves.* These relations are summarized in schematic form in Figure 6–3.

Preganglionic Fibers

Another way of considering the distinction between the sympathetic and parasympathetic divisions of the ANS involves the anatomy of the individual axons. Each ganglion is associated with two axon types. The **preganglionic fibers** (*pre* = before) emerge from the CNS to convey motor commands to the nerve cells in the ganglia. In Figure 6–3 the ganglia are represented as single cell bodies receiving single preganglionic contacts, but in fact there are roughly a hundred cells in each ganglion and hence about a hundred preganglionic fibers. Also, the contacts are shown to be axosomatic (i.e., there are no dendrites shown). This convention will be used to simplify synaptic relations elsewhere in the book, and here it is close to accurate. Many autonomic neurons lack dendrites and receive preganglionic contacts directly at the cell body.

In the sympathetic system the preganglionic fibers are short, since they arise in the spinal cord and connect to the paravertebral chain that lies adjacent to the cord. In the parasympathetic system the preganglionic fibers are long, since they must reach from the cells of origin in the CNS all the way to the target organ where the parasympathetic ganglia are located.

Postganglionic Fibers

The fibers that emerge from autonomic ganglia (i.e., the axons of the ganglionic cell bodies) are called **postganglionic fibers** (*post* = after). This is a source of confusion for some students who feel that since the fibers belong to the cells of the ganglion they should more properly be called ganglionic fibers. Nevertheless, generations of medical education and usage insist on the term *postganglionic* for these axons.

Sympathetic postganglionics are long as they must extend all the way from the paravertebral chain to the target organ. Parasympathetic postganglionic fibers are short as the ganglia are generally located in the vicinity of the target organ.

The anatomy of the human autonomic nervous system is shown in Figure 6–4. Here the fibers are shown *in situ* (meaning "as they are in the intact body"). You will easily see the long preganglionics of the parasympathetic system (solid green fibers). It will be harder to find the short sympathetic preganglionics (solid yellow) and short parasympathetic postganglionics (dashed green). Figure 6–5 is a schematic representation of the anatomy of the two systems in the body (lacking the coding system used in the previous figure). Note that the preganglionics for the sympathetic system all arise

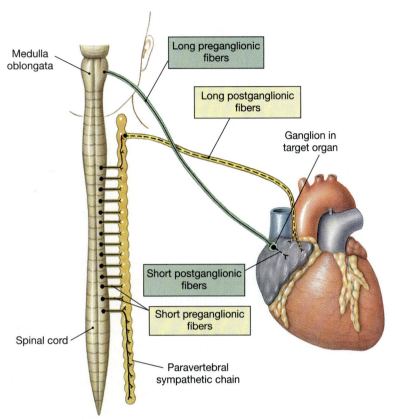

Medulla oblongata

Long preganglionic fibers

Long postganglionic fibers

Ganglion in target organ

Short postganglionic fibers

Short preganglionic fibers

Spinal cord

Paravertebral sympathetic chain

Figure 6–3 *Parasympathetic and Sympathetic Ganglia.* The sympathetic ganglia (yellow) are located in the paravertebral chain adjacent to the spinal cord. The preganglionic fibers (solid) are therefore short and the postganglionic fibers (dashed), extending all the way to the target organ, are long. In contrast, the parasympathetic ganglia (green) are located in the target organs. The preganglionic fibers (solid) are therefore long and the postganglionic fibers short (dashed).

from the middle part of the spinal cord. When we consider the cord in the next chapter we shall locate the cell bodies for these preganglionic fibers. Note that the preganglionics for the parasympathetics have two sources: the base of the brain and the base of the spine ("sacral" spinal cord).

Receptors

For each cell in the autonomic ganglia we have two synapses to consider: the synapse made by the preganglionic fiber onto the cell body in the ganglion and the one made by the postganglionic fiber onto the target organ. Consult Table 6–1 (see page 130) for an overview of the characteristics of the synapses of the autonomic nervous system.

Preganglionic Synapses

In the contacts of the preganglionic fibers with both the sympathetic and parasympathetic ganglia, the transmitter employed is acetylcholine (ACh); recall that such synapses are called cholinergic synapses. The postsynaptic response is excitatory, mediated by the *nicotinic* ACh receptor type. Since transmission at the somatic neuromuscular junction is also cholinergic and nicotinic, we might say that this transmission mechanism is the sole medium by which the CNS exerts control over the body.

Postganglionic Synapses

The postganglionic fibers of the sympathetic division predominantly contain norepinephrine (NE) and those of the parasympathetic division contain predominantly ACh, but this permits no conclusion regarding the nature of the response of the target organ. As stated earlier, *the action of a transmitter is determined by the receptor expressed by the postsynaptic cell*. NE receptors, for example, can be divided into **alpha-adrenergic receptors** (α) and **beta-adrenergic receptors** (β), each with distinct modes of action on the postsynaptic cell. Thus it is impossible to generalize about the nature of sympathetic transmission to target organs, since this is a function of the receptor type that appears in the organ. The heart, for example, expresses beta-adrenergic receptors and is *excited* by sympathetic activation. (This is why some people take antagonists for the beta-adrenergic receptor, or "beta-blockers," to control hypertension). In contrast, sympathetic innervation of other organs, such as the gut, is mediated by a different receptor and the receptor is inhibitory in nature. Cholinergic transmission from parasympathetic postganglionics is predominantly muscarinic, but this knowledge doesn't allow prediction of the effect either. Muscarinic receptors for ACh in the heart cause inhibition (see Box 5–2), but elsewhere (such as the intestines) excitation is

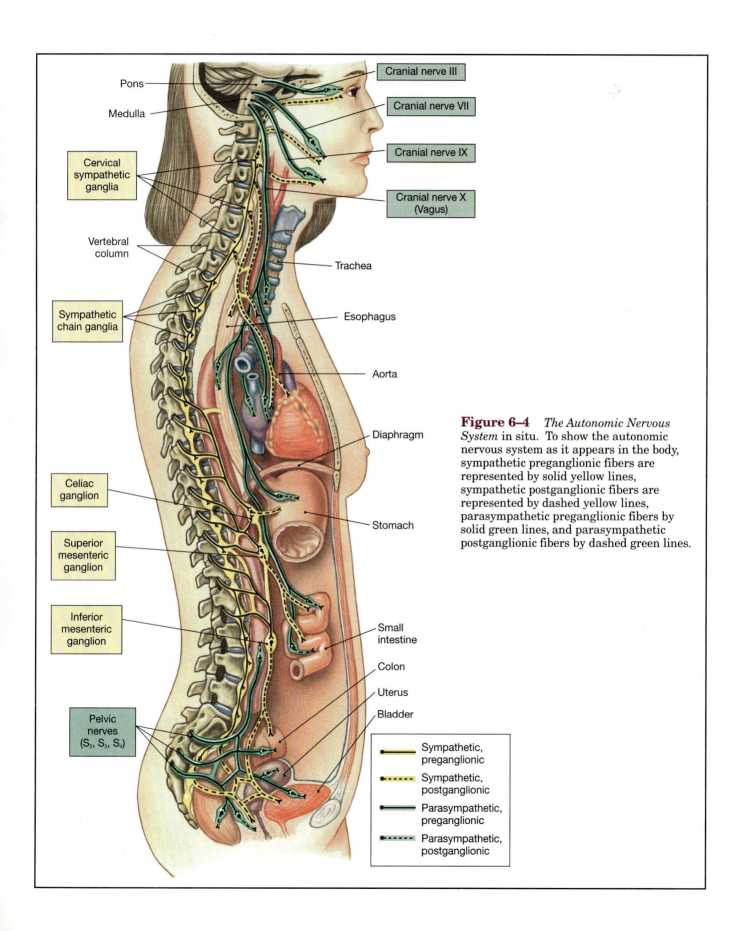

Figure 6–4 *The Autonomic Nervous System* in situ. To show the autonomic nervous system as it appears in the body, sympathetic preganglionic fibers are represented by solid yellow lines, sympathetic postganglionic fibers are represented by dashed yellow lines, parasympathetic preganglionic fibers by solid green lines, and parasympathetic postganglionic fibers by dashed green lines.

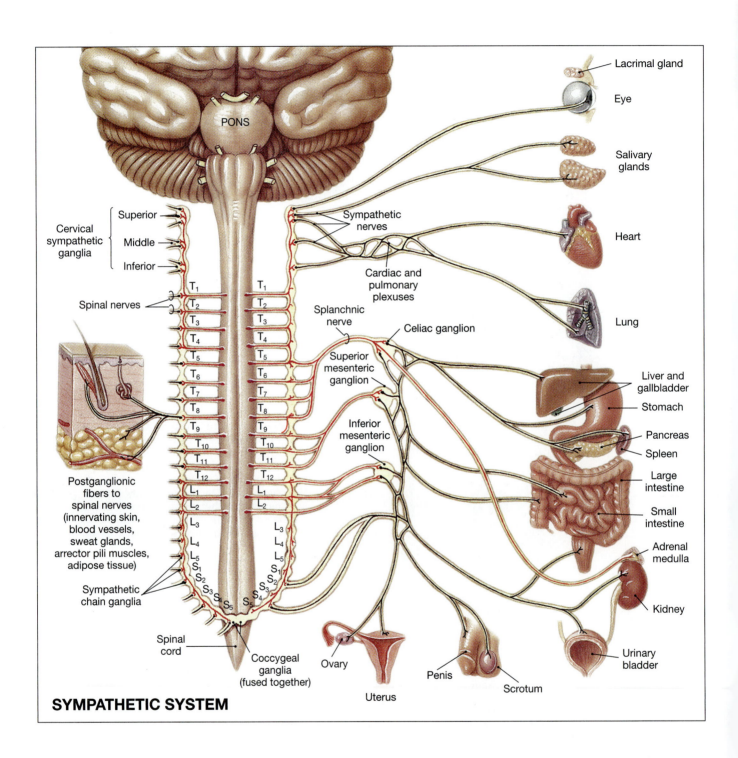

SYMPATHETIC SYSTEM

mediated by the muscarinic receptors of the parasympathetic system.

Still, it is possible to gain a general appreciation of the relationship between the two divisions because in most target organs the sympathetic and parasympathetic postganglionic fibers have antagonistic effects. In other words, if the sympathetic receptor is excitatory, the tissue will tend to express

an inhibitory parasympathetic receptor, and *vice versa*. The state of the target organ depends, therefore, on the relative amount of sympathetic and parasympathetic activity (or **tone**). Much of the time there is a balance between sympathetic tone and parasympathetic tone. Sometimes one or the other will dominate. Furthermore, the balance between sympathetic tone and parasympathetic tone tends to shift everywhere in

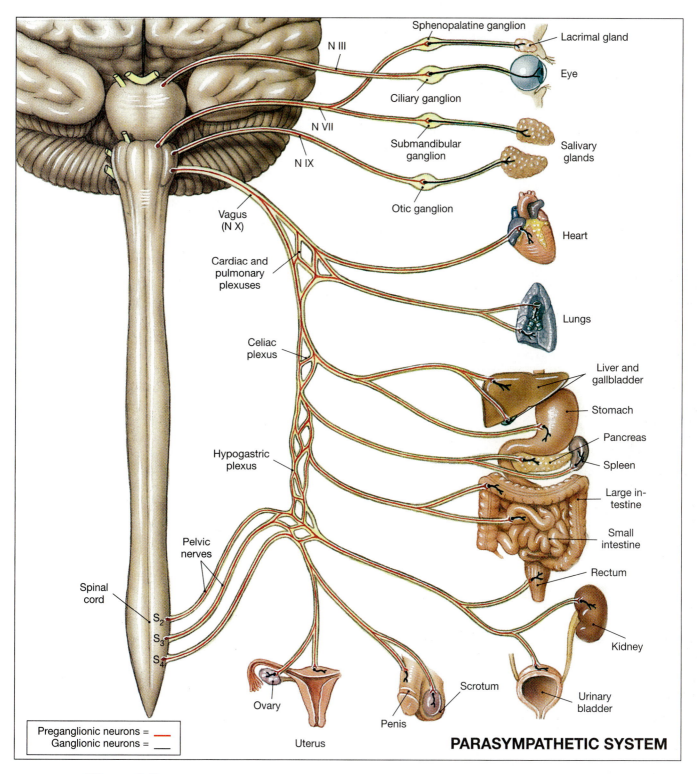

Sphenopalatine ganglion

Lacrimal gland

N III

Eye

Ciliary ganglion

N VII

Submandibular
ganglion

Salivary
glands

N IX

Otic ganglion

Vagus
(N X)

Heart

Cardiac and
pulmonary
plexuses

Lungs

Celiac
plexus

Liver and
gallbladder

Stomach

Pancreas

Hypogastric
plexus

Spleen

Large in-
testine

Small
intestine

Pelvic
nerves

Rectum

Spinal
cord

Kidney

S₂
S₃
S₄

Scrotum

Urinary
bladder

Ovary

Penis

Uterus

Preganglionic neurons = ___
Ganglionic neurons = ___

PARASYMPATHETIC SYSTEM

Figure 6–5   *A Schematic View of the Autonomic Nervous System.* Each organ is innervated by both a parasympathetic and sympathetic fiber. The different fibers often have antagonistic effects.

Table 6–1	THE SYNAPSES OF THE AUTONOMIC NERVOUS SYSTEM		
	Preganglionic Fibers	Postganglionic Fibers	Transmitter at Target Organ
Sympathetic Division	short; cholinergic, nicotinic receptors	long; aminergic, α and β receptors	norepinephrine
Parasympathetic Division	long; cholinergic, nicotinic receptors	short; cholinergic, muscarinic receptors	acetylcholine

the body all at once, so that the entire organism can be said to come under the influence of one division or the other. How the two halves of the autonomic nervous system can bring about such diffuse and general changes can best be appreciated by a consideration of the mode of transmission at the postganglionic contacts with the innervated organs.

Nonsynaptic Release

In some cases the autonomic postganglionic contact is a true synapse. However, in many cases the transmission from the postganglionic fibers to the target organ is not mediated by conventional synapse with bouton, narrow synaptic cleft, and postsynaptic specialization. Often, autonomic contacts are looser networks of terminals in which considerable extracellular space (micrometers instead of nanometers) separates the site of release (postganglionic fiber) from the site of action (target organ). Such a network, is called a **plexus** and the site of release is called a **varicosity**. Compare Figure 6–6, which illustrates a catecholamine-containing peripheral nerve plexus, with the conventional synapse shown in Figure 4–14. Varicosities are sometimes called *"en passant* synapses" to indicate that the fibers continue on to other parts of the target organ to create other varicosities and sites of release (*en passant* is French for "in passing"). Each varicosity contains (for the sympathetic plexus) **electron-dense vesicles** that contain the catecholamine transmitter, together with some other substances, such as dopamine-beta-hydroxylase (DBH), which

is also secreted. Curiously, such varicosities also often contain larger **dense-cored vesicles** (Figure 6–7). The function of these larger vesicles is the subject of considerable debate and speculation. Perhaps they have no role in exocytosis but merely function as an intracellular organelle to sustain the metabolism of the varicosity. Alternatively, they may be reservoirs of peptide cotransmitters or trophic factors that are destined for release at an appropriate time.

Fibers that participate in the formation of a nerve plexus in the periphery tend to have very fine diameter and lack a myelin sheath. Recall from Chapter 4 that such axons conduct *slowly* in comparison to stouter, myelinated fibers. This property of slow conduction due to *small, unmyelinated axons* is shared with part of the pain transmission system (Chapter 11) and with the aminergic innervation of the brain and spinal cord. You may be surprised to discover that systems associated with alarm, distress, and response to emergency are slow conducting rather than fast conducting. Teleologically, it seems that these systems should conduct quickly instead of slowly. An answer to this apparent paradox will be provided in Chapter 11. See if you can guess why before you get to the coverage of pleasure and pain.

Second and Third Messengers

We have considered the physiology of fast-conducting (large myelinated) axons and the actions of the transmitters secreted by such cells, which often also act very quickly by directly

Figure 6–6 *Sympathetic Nerve Plexus and Varicosities.* In the autonomic nervous system, some postganglionic fibers form a loose network of fibers called a plexus that allows contact to the target organ through a varicosity instead of the conventional synapse.

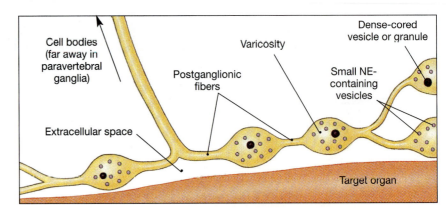

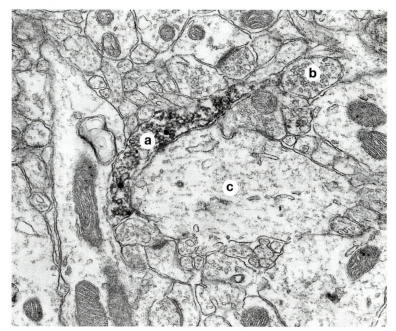

About That Enough

Figure 6–7 *Electron Micrograph of Catecholamine-Containing Terminal.* The micrograph shows the catecholamine terminal (a) as distinguished from a regular synaptic bouton (b) and the postsynaptic dendrite (c).

opening ion channels in the receptor proteins (Chapters 4 and 5). Yet here in our consideration of the autonomic nervous system (and later when we discuss the aminergic system of the brain and the action of hormones) we have cells that conduct slowly, because of their small size and unmyelinated nature, and transmitters that arrive slowly at their targets, because of the time necessary for the transmitter to diffuse to the receptors from a remote site of release. The action of many of these transmitters of the ANS is also slower than action of transmitters like GABA and glutamate. This is because there are several steps between the binding of the ligand to the receptor and the subsequent biological effect. Though slower, the more intricate mechanism of action of these substances allows for a more diverse, and in many ways more profound, impact on the state of the postsynaptic cells.

As a first step in comprehending the very challenging subject of intracellular (*intra* = within) signaling (or the cytoplasmic consequences of ligand/receptor interaction, currently the area of most explosive growth in the neurosciences), recall that *the channel property of transmembrane proteins is distinct from the gating property.* For example, many depolarizing channels in the axon and the dendrite are similar in their selectivity properties: They both admit sodium. They *differ*, however, in that axon channels are *gated by voltage* whereas the dendritic channels are *gated by the synaptic transmitter*.

The mode of action of the autonomic transmitters (and for the same transmitters, generally, when they act in the CNS) takes this distinction one step further. The receptors for the transmitters (actually a family of homologous receptors) *lack channels altogether*. The channel that is ultimate-

ly activated or inhibited lies elsewhere in the membrane (see Figure 6–8). A complex chain of enzymatically catalyzed reactions, taking place on or near the *inside* of the plasma membrane, intervenes between the binding of the transmitter to the receptor and the ultimate effect on membrane potential. In other words, the receptors are enzymes instead of channels.

The events catalyzed by an enzyme-linked receptor can be extremely intricate and it is beyond the scope of this book to describe them all in detail. We will discuss just one well-worked out-mechanism, but keep in mind that a similarly elaborate story could be told for each of four or five such mechanisms that are presently under investigation.

In the postganglionic fibers of the autonomic nervous system and, for the most part, in the CNS, ACh acts on a type of muscarinic receptor subtype. This receptor, when occupied by ACh, binds to an enzyme closely associated with the phospholipid on the inside of the cell membrane. The enzyme is called a **G protein**, since it derives energy for its work by binding *guanine triphosphate* (GTP). In the bound state the G protein activates another enzyme, **phospholipase C**, which acts to break up the phospholipid of the cell membrane itself. It is selective in its action, however, ignoring most of the phospholipid that is necessary for membrane integrity and cleaving only one type, *phosphatidylinositol biphosphate* (or PIP_2). The products of this action are two important signaling molecules, *inositol triphosphate* (IP_3), which is the charged head of the lipid that comes free into the cytoplasm, and *diacylglycerol* (DAG), the hydrophobic tail, which remains embedded in the membrane. Both IP_3 and DAG have action on a wide range of cellular processes and they are called second messengers, since they are much like the first messenger (ACh) except they find receptors that are *wholly intracellular*. For example, IP_3 binds to a receptor on the endoplasmic reticulum of cells. This receptor spans the membrane of this organelle and contains an ion channel, just like the receptors we encountered in Chapter 5 except both sides of this membrane are intracellular. Activation of this receptor by IP_3 causes redistribution of ions *within* the cell, specifically the release of stored calcium from the interior of the endoplasmic reticulum to the cell cytoplasm. The ensuing increase in calcium has numerous consequences, one being to interact with DAG (the other, membrane-bound portion of PIP_2) to activate another enzyme called C kinase, which could be considered the "third messenger." The name *kinase* is the chemical term for "enzyme that adds a phosphate to things." C kinase, in particular, phosphorylates the channel protein that is ultimately affected by ACh.

The action of ACh can be excitatory or inhibitory, depending both on the receptor type *and the identity of the G protein associated with it.* More significantly, the complexity of second messenger signaling mechanisms allows neurotransmitters to have effects that *transcend simple excitation and inhibition,* providing more subtle modification of the electrical activity of the cell.

For example, a classic effect of parasympathetic tone is *dilation* of blood vessels in some parts of the body, meaning the blood vessels get bigger and allow more blood to flow to a particular area. (When's the last time someone made you blush?) But the mechanism of the cholinergic effect must involve more than one cell, since the ACh receptors are on endothelial cells that surround each blood vessel and the cells that control vessel diameter are smooth muscle cells that lack

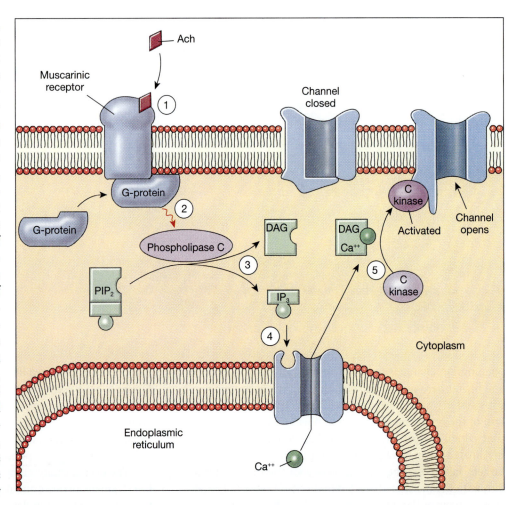

Figure 6–8   *Second and Third Messengers.* In the autonomic system, some receptors for transmitters do not have channels. Instead the receptors activate messengers within the cell that will then activate the channel. When ACh binds to the muscarinic receptor (1), the receptor binds to an enzyme located on the inner surface of the lipid bilayer called a G protein (2). When bound, this complex activates phospholipase C (3). Activated phospholipase C cleaves PIP_2 into IP_3 and DAG, which act as second messengers. IP_3 binds to a receptor on the membrane of the endoplasmic reticulum, causing the release of Ca++ from the endoplasmic reticulum to the cell cytoplasm (4). The released Ca++ will bind to DAG, which together will activate C kinase, a third messenger, which acts upon the channel (5). (Hall, 1992)

ACh receptors. How do the muscles respond to the transmitter? Here's how it appears to work. ACh binds to the muscarinic receptor on the endothelial cell and causes all changes we have outlined here. The calcium that is freed up intracellularly binds to another intracellular regulator called calmodulin. (Is it a third messenger? a fourth messenger?) Calmodulin (see Chapter 4), when activated by bound calcium, in turn activates an enzyme, *nitric oxide synthetase,* which forms a gas, **nitric oxide,** from amino acids inside the cell. Of course, the gas is *dissolved* in the saltwater environment of the cytoplasm (don't think of little bubbles of gas forming), but it is also *freely diffusable across membranes*

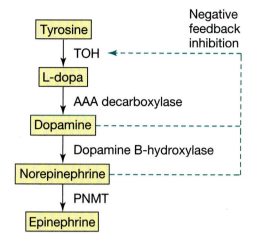

Negative feedback inhibition

Figure 6–9 *The Synthesis of Catecholamine.* The synthesis of the catecholamines is a cascade of reactions involving many enzymes and intermediates. The presence of particular enzymes in a cell determines which intermediates will be produced. Some cells in the sympathetic ganglia have only TOH and AAA decarboxylase. In these cells, only dopamine is produced. Some cells also have dopamine β-hydroxylase and both norepinephrine and dopamine are synthesized. Cells in the adrenal gland have a fourth enzyme, PNMT, producing dopamine, norepinephrine, and epinephrine.

amine N-methyltransferase (PNMT) is found, which makes epinephrine from NE. However, PNMT levels and activity vary among adrenal cells, so that a mixture of catecholamines are released (a little DA, with about 20 percent NE and 80 pecent epinephrine, see Figure 6–9).

The adrenal gland receives cholinergic, nicotinic innervation from the spinal cord, much like the sympathetic ganglia. However, instead of sending out postganglionic fibers, the adrenal gland secretes its contents directly into the blood. The adrenal gland can be thought of as an unusual, large sympathetic ganglion, lacking axons altogether and accessing its targets through the bloodstream.

Since most of the targets of the adrenal gland also receive direct sympathetic innervation and since most of their receptors have *overlapping affinity* for both NE and epinephrine, each target organ gets a "double dose" of adrenergic activation: one from the sympathetic nerve plexus and another from the blood. It's as if evolution has placed a high priority on the signals supplied to the body by the sympathetic nervous system and has developed duplicate sources to ensure that the signal gets through when needed. Read on for an explanation of one reason why this sympathetic signal has such significance for the survival of the organism.

(much like its cousin, nitrous oxide, or "laughing gas"). Indeed, it diffuses out of the endothelial cell entirely, entering the smooth muscle cell where it activates an enzyme (guanylylcyclase) that creates the second (third? fourth? fifth? most scientists have decided not to keep track since the intracellular processes are so elaborate) messenger cGMP (cyclic guanosine monophosphate). Finally, this signal acts on channels in the smooth muscle cell membrane to cause the muscles to relax and the vessel to dilate.

Obviously, you should not be expected to commit all this to memory. Point this out, if necessary, to any overzealous teaching assistant who may be carried away by the beauty of intracellular signaling systems. But note also, that signaling systems such as the one described here are soon to be shown to control the most important and mysterious of brain and body functions. In particular, we shall have cause to consider IP₃, calmodulin, and nitric oxide mechanism in the fields of vision, learning, cell development, and synaptogenesis and in diverse areas of medicine such as cancer and hypertension, depression and schizophrenia. Though the number of transmitter substances may be large, the number of biological responses is even larger. Much of the intervening complexity is provided by intracellular signaling systems.

The Adrenal Gland

Recall that norepinephrine (NE) is the immediate precursor of epinephrine, or **adrenaline**. Adrenaline is so named because it is found in the **adrenal glands**, two organs that lie on top of the kidney on each side of the body. Some cells of the sympathetic ganglia contain the enzymes necessary to make dopamine (DA) from tyrosine, and the synthesis stops there. Most sympathetic ganglia also have the enzyme necessary to make norepinephrine (NE) from DA so NE prevails at the site of release. In the adrenal gland the enzyme *phenylethanol-*

The Fight-or-Flight Response

You knew you shouldn't have stayed at the club so late. It's a weeknight, you have a 9:00 class tomorrow and, besides, how are you going to get home? The band was great, but your friends had the good sense to leave after the second set, and they took the car with them. They urged you to come along, pointing out that the neighborhood was tough and a cab ride across town would be expensive, more than you could afford. But you stayed on. The band never played your favorite tunes until the last set and, besides, you thought, there might be other, well, "possibilities."

Now it's 1:30 in the morning and you are alone and hiking briskly to where you hope the subway station is located. At last you see the little light marking the stair and you dart down the stairs just in time to make the train. Your luck is holding, you think, when the doors to the nearest car swing open to reveal no one inside. You ride alone until the transfer station, where the others get on. Three of them, not your favorite type, you notice as they walk down the aisle. Why did they sit right in back of you when they had the whole car to choose from? One of them asks you the time. "Two o'clock," you say, glancing at your watch. This still might not be too

Figure 6–10 *The Fight-or-Flight Response.* The state of arousal in response to danger is called the fight-or-flight response. It is characterized by an increase in heartbeat, dilation of airways in the lungs, dilation of the pupils, and the release of glucose from the liver into the blood. In order to reserve energy, systems such as digestion that are not needed in a physical emergency will slow down.

bad, you think. Then another asks about your jacket. Where did you get it? How much did it cost? Then they ask if you have any money on you.

At this point you will be experiencing a coordinated activation of the sympathetic division of the autonomic nervous system and discharge of the adrenal gland together with *reduced* parasympathetic tone. I cannot claim that your knowledge of G proteins and second messenger systems will be of much use to you in situations like this, but I *can* use the occasion to illustrate an important principle regarding the organization of the autonomic nervous system. The state of arousal in response to danger is called the **fight-or-flight response** (Figure 6–10) because it prepares the body for *physical* emergencies. The heart beats strong and fast to circulate the blood more quickly. Airways in the lung dilate so that the extra blood becomes oxygenated. Glucose is released into the blood by the liver, and blood vessels in the muscles dilate to permit this oxygen- and energy-rich blood to get to where it is needed most in the event of a struggle. Pupils of the eye di-

late (get large) so that more light gets through and vision is more acute. Not all autonomic targets are activated during the fight-or-flight response, however. For example, peristalsis in the gut and other digestive functions are inhibited during the response, presumably to make the energy they consume available for other purposes. NE-containing cells in the CNS are probably also active, preparing the brain and spinal cord for fight-or-flight.

Other features of the fight-or-flight response cannot be as easily incorporated into an explanation of the body's response to emergency. Perspiration might help cool the body during prolonged exertion, but dry mouth and piloerection (hair standing up) are parts of the fight-or-flight response that are probably holdovers from an earlier time in the history of our species. Furry animals, for example, use piloerection to appear larger and more dangerous during the response (think of a cat arching its back and hissing).

This last point brings up an issue that is very important in the field of *health psychology*. The fight-or-flight response, which we share with many organisms, *evolved at a time when most if not all emergencies were physical ones*. It is safe to surmise that most of its features had an adaptive advantage for such circumstances. However, as a species our lifestyle has changed to the point that only *some* of our emergencies are physical ones, the others being stressful circumstances of an intellectual, social, or professional nature. Though we have evolved other, appropriate mechanisms for dealing with stress of this kind, the fight-or-flight response frequently crops up during these times even when no physical danger is present. For example, you might experience a pounding heart, sweaty palms, or a dry mouth at an examination, while talking to the boss, while witnessing a sports event, or even, on occasion, for no apparent reason at all. At these times we might say that the entire *peripheral autonomic* portion of the fight-or-flight response (piloerection, dry mouth, pounding heart, visceral and vascular effects, and so forth) has lost its adaptive significance.

Indeed, according to many specialists in *behavioral medicine*, the fight-or-flight response might be *maladaptive*. One theory, which has yet to be thoroughly supported by the evidence, holds that some forms of **hypertension** (high blood pressure) are caused or made worse by chronic activation of the heart due to either an excessive *amount* of stress or an excessive *response* to stress. It has been claimed that other disease processes such as coronary heart disease and disorders of immune function are stress-related as well. Competing with this view is the opinion that hypertension, heart disease, and so forth are more closely tied to variables such as diet, obesity, exercise, and heredity that are only indirectly connected with the psychological concept of stress and the physical experience of the fight-or-flight response. If this debate sounds familiar, don't be alarmed. We again return to the old mind/body problem. You should carefully consider your position on the mind/body problem and then consult the suggested readings in the back of this text before forming an opinion on this very timely and urgent issue in clinical psychology and medicine. Most practitioners of rehabilitative medicine incorporate at least some psychological theories of stress into their practice. Recent studies, for example, have identified certain personality traits as being predisposing for an additional heart attack: repressed or expressed hostility and a domineering or competitive attitude.

Transmitters, Hormones, and Everything in Between

In time we discuss **endocrinology** (the study of hormones released by glands and of neurohormones released by neurons), but from the foregoing discussion it is obvious that the difference between classic neurotransmitters (which act synaptically) and hormones (which are distributed through the blood to their targets) is a matter of degree rather than a concrete distinction. In fact, the body possesses a *continuum* of chemical signaling systems. They stretch from transient chemical changes in a tiny patch of excitable membrane and molecules that act wholly *intracellularly* (second and third messengers) to synaptic transmitters that act by exocytosis, *neurohormones*, released from axon tips into the blood and destined for specific targets, to *hormones*, such as epinephrine, which is released from the adrenal gland to circulate freely and act throughout the body. As an extension of this continuum we might include *pheromones*, chemicals that mediate communication *between organisms* (Chapter 12).

It might be desirable to set aside the categories "transmitter," "neurohormone," and "hormone" momentarily and consider instead how *specificity* is conferred in the responses to chemical signals (in other words, the means by which responses are confined to some cells but not others). Synaptic transmission can be thought of as analogous to telephone communication. It is essentially a *private* communication between neurons, mediated by electrical signals traveling down wires (the electrically excitable domain) and sound that is produced and absorbed by the handset (the chemically excitable domain). In contrast, the chemical signals we have encountered in this chapter are more analogous to a local radio broadcast (autonomic transmitters) or network TV communication (hormones) in the sense that the signal is broadcast regionally or globally to be received by any radio or TV tuned to the right frequency. In contrast, specificity is conferred on some systems by *anatomy* (i.e., the exact location of a sodium channel in a cell membrane or the exact location of the synapse). Specificity is conferred on more widely dispersed signals (like hormones and some transmitters) by the type of receptor expressed.

We would anticipate that the complexity of membrane proteins would reflect the degree of specificity demanded of them. In fact this is the case, as shown in Figure 6–11. Voltage-gated channels tend to share sequence homology (i.e., resemble one another) and are composed of a single strand of protein that crosses the membrane many times. Ligand-gated channels (recall that a ligand is any compound that binds to a receptor) also display sequence homology (implying common evolutionary origin). Greater discrimination is required of ligand-gated channels since they exhibit *transmitter selectivity* as well as ion selectivity that all channels display. Ligand-gated channels tend to be made up of *polymers* of five separate proteins; each polymer spans the membrane many times.

Receptors expressed by autonomic targets are made up of a different family of homologous proteins. Typically, they are single strands that span the membrane *seven times*, which would make them simpler than voltage-gated and ligand-gated channels. However, the receptors for the autonomic transmitters (ACh, NE, epinephrine, and many peptides) *do not themselves possess ion pores or capacity for biological response*. These functions are mediated by other, more complex proteins that lie elsewhere in the membrane and cytoplasm. These other proteins function as a highly complex response system, as would be expected of a cell that is exposed simultaneously to many different chemical signals and generates specific and intricate responses to only some of the signals.

The autonomic target receptors in this last family are called **G protein–coupled receptors**; the *effector*, or substance that causes the change in the target cell, is the protein bound to the inside face of the plasma membrane, called a G protein, discussed earlier. Because the ion pore or channel is yet another protein, it is called a **G protein–linked channel**. A sequence of events (which can be quite complicated) conveys the signal from the bound receptor to the G protein, then to enzymes that create various intracellular second messengers and finally to the channel itself, which may in turn be a voltage-gated or ligand-gated channel and which may be activated or inhibited by the second messenger system.

Examples of receptors in this family are *muscarinic acetylcholine receptors*; *dopamine, serotonin*, and *histamine receptors*; receptors for numerous *peptides*; *alpha-* and *beta-adrenoreceptors*; and other hormones. With the exception of the preganglionic contacts, which are ligand-gated nicotinic acetylcholine receptors, virtually all the transmitter actions in the autonomic nervous system proceed by this mechanism. The action of the same transmitters in the brain also appears to be G protein-mediated, though these systems are only now

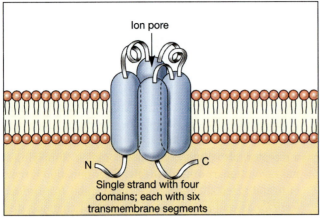

(a) Voltage-gated channel

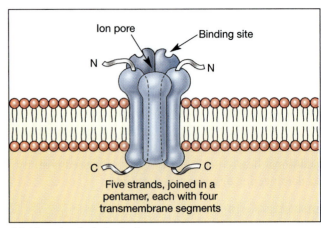

(b) Ligand-gated channel

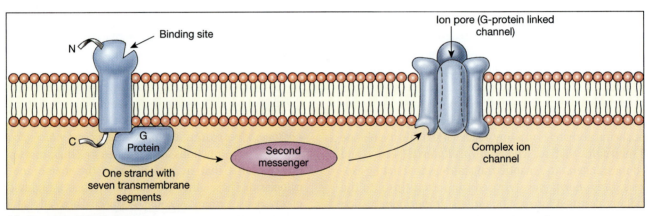

(c) G-protein-linked channel

Figure 6-11 *Families of Ion Channels.* As the specificity of a membrane protein increases, so does the complexity. (a) A voltage-gated channel that is selective only to the ion type is the simplest with a single strand of four domains each with six transmembrane segments. (b) A ligand-gated channel is selective for a specific ligand and the ion. The complexity increases with five strands joining together to form the ion pore. (c) The G-protein-linked channel is more complex, involving second and third messengers.

becoming fully understood. (Recall the difficulty in studying the CNS because of the blood-brain barrier.)

Finally, many *hormones* have G-protein-coupled receptors. Let us consider the details of one such system to gain insight into the power and utility of this signaling mechanism.

Glucose Mobilization

Not all biological responses are mediated by ion flux across the cell membrane. Recall that during the fight-or-flight response, glucose is mobilized from energy stores in the liver and released into the bloodstream so that the organism has ample energy to respond to an emergency. This response is initiated by the brain, which perceives the emergency and uses the sympathetic division of the autonomic nervous sys-

tem, specifically *epinephrine* from the *adrenal gland*, which has as one of its effects an action on *hepatocytes* (or liver cells) (Figure 6–12).

Each hepatocyte expresses *beta-adrenergic* receptors (which bind both epinephrine and norepinephrine). A beta-adrenergic receptor bound by epinephrine acts on several G proteins, by allowing GTP to bind to each G protein and activate it. Already a seemingly minor event, a single ligand (epinephrine) binding to a single receptor (beta-adrenergic receptor), creates a larger response (activation of several G proteins). Each G protein activates an enzyme called **adenylate cyclase**. Adenylate cyclase then catalyzes the production of *cyclic adenosine monophosphate* (**cAMP**) from ATP.

It seems somewhat of a paradox that one of the early steps in energy *production* involves *consumption* of cellular ener-

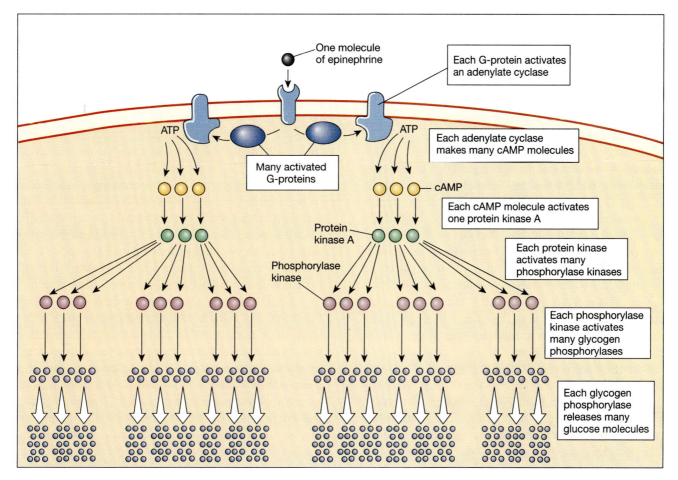

One molecule
of epinephrine

Each G-protein activates
an adenylate cyclase

ATP

ATP

Many activated
G-proteins

Each adenylate cyclase
makes many cAMP molecules

cAMP

Each cAMP molecule activates
one protein kinase A

Protein
kinase A

Each protein kinase
activates many
phosphorylase kinases

Phosphorylase
kinase

Each phosphorylase
kinase activates
many glycogen
phosphorylases

Each glycogen
phosphorylase
releases many
glucose molecules

Figure 6–12 *Glucose Mobilization by Epinephrine.* During the fight-or-flight response, large amounts of glucose are needed in order to prepare the body for an emergency. The G protein/second messenger system amplifies one molecule of transmitter into an enormous response. One ligand/receptor complex activates many G proteins, which will all eventually activate many second and third messengers. The result is maximum production of glucose.

gy in the form of ATP. Recall that *glycolysis*, or the breakdown of glucose, also consumes ATP (Chapter 2). The paradox is resolved when it is realized that only a little ATP is used in glucose production and utilization in return for a *large* amount of ATP at the end.

Each cAMP molecule acts as a second messenger and a catalyst, by removing an inhibiting factor from another enzyme called protein kinase. Each molecule of protein kinase adds phosphate groups to *many* molecules of its substrate, *phosphorylase kinase*, activating each one. Each phosphorylase kinase adds a phosphate to *many* of *its* substrate, *glycogen phosphorylase*. Each of these activated enzymes is capable of acting on stored glucose. Glucose is stored in the liver in the form of **glycogen**, a large molecule almost like crystalline sugar. The glycogen phosphorylase adds a phosphate group to each glucose molecule, which then be-

comes free from the larger glycogen molecule, and upon removal of phosphate, becomes free glucose, which can then be transported out of the cell to used by the muscles and the brain.

This mechanism, first elucidated by Earl Sutherland in 1957 (well before the discovery of G proteins) is a very important one in biology (Alberts et al., 1994). After the discovery of the importance of cAMP and phosphorylation in glucose production, cyclic nucleotides (usually cAMP but also cGMP, cyclic guanosine monophosphate) were discovered to be involved in many processes ranging from vision to elemental forms of learning. For now, we should concentrate on its general features in the context of the demands made on the autonomic nervous system. First, chemical messages are often called upon to accomplish tasks more complicated than opening or closing a channel. Such tasks require the diversity of

G proteins to mediate the various effects. The G proteins are related to one another (like the other families of signaling proteins, they are *homologous*), but they mediate different, even opposing actions. For example, another type of G protein *depresses* cAMP levels and ultimately *removes* glucose from the blood. To refine our earlier analogy, the function of *turning the receiver to a desired station* is accomplished by the G proteins and their coupled receptors.

A second major feature also recalls our analogy of a radio broadcast. A low *concentration* of ligand due to dispersal throughout the body via the blood is analogous to a faint radio signal that requires amplification to be heard. Clearly, the cAMP/protein kinase cascade accomplishes this bountifully, since at almost every step many products are made by each activated enzyme (see Figure 6–12). From a single molecule of epinephrine millions of glucose molecules are produced, an act of amplification that rivals the performance of the most sensitive radio receiver. Amplification and tuning mechanisms are essential features of the autonomic nervous system, in which specificity is provided by receptors on a target distant from the site of release.

Shortly before reading this section many of you performed an experiment using the beta-adrenergic/cAMP signaling system and probably didn't know it. Normally, elimination of cAMP from the interior of cells (and subsequent removal of glucose from the blood) is accomplished by another enzyme, **phosphodiesterase**, which converts cAMP to plain old AMP, which has no signaling role. In the body, phosphodiesterase activity is regulated by another G protein and receptor complex, but it is possible to circumvent this and act on the enzyme directly by consuming certain drugs. **Caffeine**, found abundantly in regular coffee but also in "decaffeinated" coffee, tea, and many soft drinks, binds to phosphodiesterase and *inhibits* its action. This causes cAMP accumulation just as if catecholamines had bound to beta-receptors throughout the body. One consequence is glucose production, as above, but the fact that caffeine has other "psychogenic" and "arousing" effects should act as a clue to the function of beta-adrenergic transmission in the brain. (In other words, an autonomic transmitter that turns up in the brain might also have some similarity in function between its central and peripheral actions.)

How "Autonomic" Is It?

We can think of the body as constantly experiencing a tension, or balance, between sympathetic and parasympathetic tone. At times one system dominates and at times the other prevails. Occasions of sympathetic dominance are associated with arousal, with very high levels of sympathetic tone experienced during the body's response to physical emergency. During this state some organs (e.g., the heart) are ex-

cited and some organs (e.g., the gut) inhibited. Contrasting effects are obtained when the parasympathetic system is dominant. The heartbeat slows (because of the action of *vagusstoff*, see Box 5–2) and peristalsis in the gut increases so as to favor digestion. If you use the fight-or-flight response to organize your thinking about the sympathetic system then you might imagine watching TV after a large dinner as an occasion of parasympathetic dominance. The parasympathetic system mediates body functions we might describe as "vegetative."

Apart from genuine physical emergencies, in which sympathetic discharge can truly be described as involuntary, most occasions of sympathetic or parasympathetic dominance have at least some volitional component. The adrenaline rush experienced with, say, bungee jumping might be uncontrollable but the jumping itself *is* controllable. Likewise, it is possible to induce parasympathetic outflow more or less at will.

Use of the adjective *autonomic* to describe the system is thus somewhat inappropriate (though we are stuck with the term) since much of its function is not truly independent of volition and control. Rather more important is the concept of *awareness*. Autonomic functions can proceed without our *consciousness* of them, and without awareness the capacity for control is not exercised by the mind. The issue of how increased *awareness* can lead to increased *control* of autonomic function (e.g., whether meditation can help control hypertension) is a very important and controversial one in psychology and in biology. If your curriculum for this course includes a laboratory, it is possible that you could conduct experiments yourself on indices of autonomic function such a "vagal tone" (electrocardiogram) or the "galvanic skin response" measured by a lie detector test (See Box 6–1 on page 140). This will help you develop an informed opinion on the subject of whether awareness can substantially alter autonomic function. (Or you could just concentrate really hard and see if you can speed digestion of that pizza you consumed during your all-nighter.)

The Special Case of Sex

Be reminded that the organizing principles we have cited (that systems are *opposed*, sympathetic equals *response to physical emergency*, parasympathetic equals *vegetative*) are only generalities. Examples abound of the two systems working in concert, which is an exception to these organizing principles. A classic example involves male reproductive function (it was researched at a time when most medical students were men). Erections are produced by parasympathetic activity yet ejaculation is a product of sympathetic activity. Thus the two divisions of the autonomic nervous system appear to act in concert to produce a behavior that is neither a response to physical emergency nor strictly vegetative. Furthermore, the

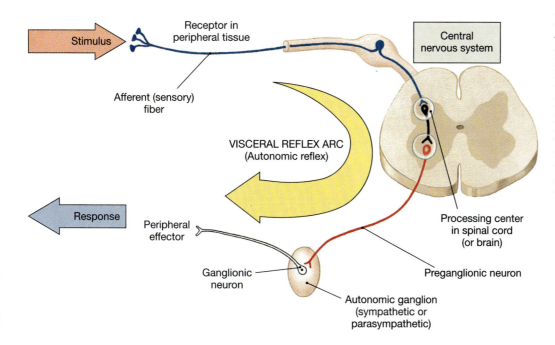

Figure 6–13 *The Autonomic Sensory Modality.* In the sensory modality of the ANS, the fibers do not remain within the parasympathetic and sympathetic ganglia. Instead, the fibers travel toward the CNS with these ganglia, but then they join the nerves of the somatic system where they enter the spinal cord.

sympathetic innervation of the genitalia in males as well as females does not follow the pattern established for the sympathetic innervation of other organs. The genitalia (as well as the bladder, the ileum, and other organs near the bottom of the abdominal cavity) are innervated by tiny sympathetic ganglia that lie in the organ that is innervated instead of being located in the paravertebral chain, the usual position of the sympathetic ganglia.

The Sensory Component

For many autonomic nerves the bulk of the fibers are not motor but sensory. However, the anatomy and physiology of these fibers is not organized in such a way as to permit easy categorization. First, sensation from the viscera is limited in nature, largely but not completely confined to the modality of pain or "nociception" (Chapter 11); pain is generally limited to discomfort caused by swelling or distention of the innervated organ. The transmitter chemistry is complex, with various neuropeptides thought to play a major role in visceral pain transmission.

"Referred Pain"

Another complicating feature of the autonomic sensory modality (and one that is very important clinically) is that the fibers are only partly associated with the nerves and ganglia of the sympathetic and parasympathetic nervous systems. After traveling *toward* the CNS through these nerves and ganglia, the fibers of the sensory cells join the *other half* of the peripheral nervous system, the *somatic* system (see Figure 6–13). These then pass through *somatic* ganglia and enter

the spinal cord where they innervate structures primarily devoted to sensation from the body surface.

This fusion of autonomic and somatic sensory fibers leads to a phenomenon in which visceral and somatic sensation are confused within the CNS. In other words, visceral feelings (usually painful) are perceived by the organism as arising from the body surface instead of from within. A well-known example of such **referred pain** is **angina pectoris**. In angina, painful sensation arises from the heart as a consequence of coronary artery disease (lack of oxygen) and is conveyed *through* autonomic fibers into the cord through structures that also convey sensation from the left chest, shoulder, and arm (Figure 6–14a, page 142). A person suffering from this condition experiences the pain *as if it had originated in the left arm.* Heart patients and their friends and relatives soon learn to look for pain in the left arm as a possible sign of impending heart attack.

Other examples of referred pain include that which may arise from liver disease or disease of the bile duct or gallbladder. Here the pain is referred to the *right* side of the body (Figure 6–14b), since autonomic fibers from these organs fuse with somatic fibers from the *right* shoulder and midabdominal region on the right. Other examples are less well understood. It is possible that aspects of *migraine* may be due to referred pain from blood vessels in the head. In contrast, other sensations that arise from the viscera (e.g., a full bladder) are almost never referred to the body surface.

Here and elsewhere in the book I shall cite examples drawn from the medical literature *only to illustrate general physiological principles*, not to educate the reader about med-

Box 6–1

Psychophysiology and the "Lie Detector" Test

Often things find their way into textbooks not because they are true but because they have such great and enduring historical significance that they cannot be ignored. One of these is a prominent theory of emotions called the **James-Lange theory**. Promulgated by a prominent psychologist (William James) and a Swedish physician (C. G. Lange) towards the end of the nineteenth century, the theory held that the *autonomic and somatic manifestations of an emotion* (anger, say, or embarrassment) *were themselves the cause of the emotion*. In other words, we get embarrassed *because* our face turns red, we feel fear *because* our heart is beating faster and our palms are sweaty, and so forth.

The theory became discredited when it was shown to be inconsistent with experimental observations. For example, individuals with damaged autonomic nervous systems (e.g., ganglia severed from the CNS) report a normal range of human emotions even though their autonomic expression is lacking.

While the James-Lange theory has a few proponents today, an important field of research called **psychophysiology** is devoted to the study of the relationship between psychological states and the activity of the autonomic nervous system. The central premise of psychophysiology is that autonomic changes *reflect* central emotional processes and the dispute, to the extent that there is one, is only over the *degree* to which the peripheral changes are faith-

ful to the central condition. For example, proponents of psychophysiology might claim that changes in heart rate ("vagal tone") are "windows into the mind," perfect indicators of a subject's internal experience. Others not so enamored with psychophysiology might claim that peripheral changes are trivial consequences of brain events or totally unreliable indicators of what is happening centrally.

Whatever your perspective, the study of psychophysiology is very valuable since it is one of only a few methods available for the study of nervous systems in conscious and (hopefully) cooperative human beings. Strategic and

icine. In the absence of real medical training a little bit of knowledge can be worse than none at all since it may lead to erroneous self-diagnosis. The only disease the reader should be concerned with here is the **Medical Student Syndrome**, which can also apply to students of physiological psychology. This is the well-known condition in which a new student encounters descriptions of various diseases for the first time and then begins to perceive every little twinge or jitter as an early symptom of one or more life-threatening conditions. Remind yourself that it is highly unlikely that you will develop a disease shortly after reading about it for the first time. For every-

thing except the Medical Student Syndrome, which you can self-treat by getting a grip on your imagination, see a doctor.

The Enteric Nervous System and Other Simple Systems

Some portions of the autonomic nervous system are sufficiently different from the rest so that they merit separate consideration. The gut (as well as the gallbladder and a few other organs) has *intrinsic* networks of sensory and motor fibers that function independently of the CNS as well as sympathetic

painless attachment of a few electrodes to parts of the skin allows use of the electrocardiogram as a quantitative measurement of sympathetic tone in the heart. The conductance between two electrodes on the skin (the "galvanic skin response") is a sign of sweating. The electrical signal from these simple electrodes is conveyed to a multichannel amplifier and chart recorder (**polygraph**) where a continuous record is made as the subject is exposed to various conditions intended to modify his or her affective state.

Early on it was discovered that this psychophysiological measure (the "polygraph test") could be used to detect the subtle autonomic correlate of fear and guilt that most people experience when they aren't telling the truth. Objections to these applications of psychophysiology (e.g., lie detector tests as used for pre-employment screening) also developed early on. Accomplished liars, it was suggested, could beat the test by "keeping cool." Likewise, psychopaths who are, by definition, unable to distinguish fantasy from reality, should be able to beat the exam.

Conversely, there are people who behave guiltily whether or not they really are. Recall the scene in the Woody Allen movie in which the hero and his girlfriend are having breakfast together at home. She is reading the paper and casually remarks, "Oh, did you see that a woman was assaulted in the park on the corner last night?" After a moment, Woody Allen blurts, "I was nowhere *near* the park last night!" Some people experience arousal, which

may be interpreted as a guilty response, regardless of truth.

Polygraph administrators employ a battery of procedures designed to identify the cool liar and the overreactor. For example, at the beginning of the test a subject is often asked simple questions such as name, address, and so forth, and physiological response is recorded as a baseline against which responses to later questions are measured. In other words, each person's physiological measures are compared only to his or her *own range* of affective responses. When these precautions are taken, psychophysiologists claim that there is a high degree of reliability for the test, citing studies in controlled environments (volunteers telling programmed "lies") that show very few "false positives" (innocent people wrongly accused) and only slightly more "false negatives" (guilty people exonerated), even when criminal psychotics are used as test subjects. However, polygraph advocates are careful to point out that the "lie detector" test detects only *arousal*, not lies per se.

Controversy regarding the lie detector test tends to wax and wane according to the frequency of its use. Some generations seem to favor it and some do not, but even when it is used perennial challenges are made to its interpretation. At some point in your life the test may be in use for employment interviews as well as for criminal and civil proceedings.

and parasympathetic innervation. This intrinsic network contains interneurons as well and is capable of organizing simple reflexes without additional input from the CNS. Also, the sympathetic ganglia that innervate the gut are remote from the paravertebral chain and can be thought of as part of the **enteric nervous system** (*enteric* = relating to the intestine).

Simple ganglia that produce simple behaviors are properties that the enteric system shares with the entire nervous system of simpler animals, and the entire behavioral repertoire of some organisms appears to be "visceral." Though the synaptic relations that mediate autonomic reflexes are not

completely understood, the equivalent reflexes in lobsters (and somewhat different ones in mollusks, crabs, and insects) are well understood at the cellular level. This is because invertebrates often display the property of **eutely**, meaning that the number, location, and synaptic connections of neurons is precisely the same from specimen to specimen. This, coupled with the large size of the cells, means that each individual cell is *identifiable* (i.e., can be named and its unique pattern of electrical activity determined). In a few cases (as in the lobster stomach) a wiring diagram of **identifiable neurons** can be established that *explains the behavior entirely*. Similar wiring

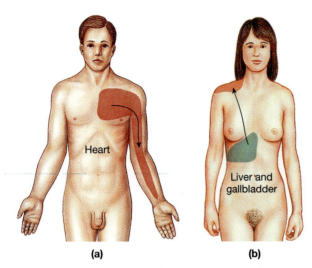

(a)   **(b)**

Figure 6–14   *Referred Pain.* Visceral and somatic sensations are indistinguishable in the CNS due to the fusion of the autonomic and somatic sensory fibers. An organism sometimes perceives sensations arising in the viscera to be coming from the body surface. In angina pectoris, pain due to coronary heart disease is experienced in the left arm (a). In hepatic biliary disease, the sensations felt from liver, bile duct, or gallbladder disease are perceived to be coming from the right side of the body (b).

diagrams can be constructed for swimming in the leech, egg-laying in sea slugs, and escape systems in mollusks and crayfish. We will examine them from time to time as models for what we would hope to accomplish one day for complex behavior mediated by more elaborate networks, such as neural mechanisms for vocalization and cognition.

Transmitters Common to the ANS and CNS

The principal autonomic transmitters, acetylcholine (ACh) and norepinephrine (NE), turn up also in the central nervous system together with their major receptor types and some of the same second and third messenger mechanisms.

Modes of Action

Since brain circuits are so much more complicated than the peripheral nervous system and are less accessible, we know less about how the transmitters ACh and NE help organize brain function than about how they act in the autonomic nervous system. Each has been implicated in a number of behaviors that we shall study in ensuing chapters. However, *direct* comparison in terms of mechanism of action has been accomplished for one brain target: cells of the rat hippocampus maintained alive in vitro in the form of a brain slice prepa-

Figure 6–15   *A Living Slice of the Rat Hippocampus.* Portions of the brain can be maintained alive in culture.

ration (Figure 6–15). In this technique, parts of the brain that have all axons and dendrites oriented in a particular direction are *sliced* so that the axons and dendrites remain intact. The slices are maintained in an oxygen-rich warm saline environment, supplemented with glucose. In this way it is sometimes possible to approximate the "simple systems" condition of eutely and defined synaptology that has enabled us to understand the autonomic nervous system and the brains of invertebrates so thoroughly. In the hippocampal slice preparation, ACh appears to act on muscarinic receptors (just as it does in parasympathetic targets) and NE appears to act on beta-adrenergic receptors (just as it does in sympathetic targets). ACh action is mediated by the G protein that initiates phosphatidylinositol production and NE action is mediated by the G protein that creates cAMP as a second messenger, in both cases just as in the periphery. *However*, the ultimate action on the hippocampal neurons in the CNS *appears to be the same* for both ACh and NE, in stark contrast to their opposing effects in the periphery. Each appears to *shut down* a calcium-activated potassium channel that is responsible for *accommodation* to prolonged depolarization. The net consequence is to allow hippocampal cells to *fire more action potentials in response to each incoming stimulus*. Whether this pattern is repeated elsewhere is still a matter of active research, but recent results with slices of the cerebellum and other brain structures appear to indicate that the mechanisms are general in the brain.

Autoreceptors

For norepinephrine, dopamine, and serotonin, transmission is complicated by the fact that the *presynaptic* structure (the varicosity) also expresses receptors for the transmitter. In general, these **autoreceptors** are of a different type than the receptors expressed by the *postsynaptic* cell. For example (Figure 6–16), if the *postsynaptic* cell has excitatory beta-adrenergic receptors it is common for the *presynaptic* cell to express inhibitory alpha-adrenergic receptors. The function of such receptors, in this example, would be *homeostatic*. Upon transmission across the junction, electrical activity in the *presynaptic* varicosity would be reduced by the alpha-adrenergic inhibition, returning the plexus to the resting or inactive condition. Autoreceptor mechanisms are very important in higher function and we will return to them again in future chapters.

Turnover and Breakdown

Turnover and breakdown of neurotransmitters are the sources of yet more differences among the various transmitters. For example, while ACh (at CNS as well as at postganglionic parasympathetic contacts) is broken down by enzymes in the cleft and the parts *recycled* for rerelease, NE is sometimes taken up *intact* by the *presynaptic* cell and packaged into vesicles for rerelease without enzymatic breakdown. The presence of so many bonding sites for each transmitter (receptors, re-uptake pumps, allosteric sites, breakdown enzymes) leads to problems in specificity for drugs (See Box 6–2 on page 144).

Many drugs that act upon the autonomic nervous system do so by interfering with turnover or breakdown of the transmitters involved or of their respective second and third messengers. An example of a drug that acts on turnover mechanisms is cocaine. Cocaine blocks the re-uptake mechanism for dopamine and norepinephrine, leaving these around for a longer period of time in the extracellular space (see Chapter 17). An example of a drug that acts on breakdown mechanisms is Viagra (seldenafil). Viagra acts on the specific form of phosphodiesterase that breaks down the third messenger cGMP in the penis. Normally, acetycholine released by the parasympathetic system acts on vascular cells to release the second messenger NO (nitric oxide) which then brings about the creation of the third messenger cGMP. The

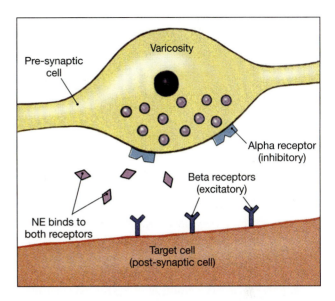

Figure 6–16 *Autoreceptors.* Characteristic of some synapses is the presynaptic expression of receptors for the transmitters the presynaptic cell releases. These autoreceptors usually have a different effect on the presynaptic cell than those receptors that bind the transmitter on the postsynaptic cell.

third messenger then permits the penis to become engorged with blood and become erect. Viagra, by blocking the breakdown of the third messenger, makes these erections longer and more complete than they would be if the cGMP were destroyed by the phosphodiesterase. The discovery of Viagra thus provides a promising therapy for male sexual dysfunction. A new, if somewhat controversial, line of investigation is whether the use of Viagra can improve the sex lives of those that are not experiencing sexual dysfunction. One opinion holds that men and women may find that Viagra, by its action on the breakdown of cGMP, can be used as a means to improve sexual function. This belief has yet to be confirmed scientifically, however.

Peptide Action in Gut and Brain

Recall from Chapter 5 that peptides are another type of transmitter. Like the transmitters norepinephrine and acetylcholine, each peptide discovered in the sympathetic and parasympathetic systems has generally been shown to occur in the brain as well, either in identical form or in a slightly modified form. Examples include vasoactive intestinal peptide (VIP), gastrin, insulin, and glucagon. Speculation abounds regarding the correlation of the central action of these peptides with their peripheral effects (see the story of cholecystokinin, or CCK, in Box 14–3). We will take up the consideration of these peptides in the context of specific systems where they are thought to play a role (e.g., feeding, drinking, and sexual behavior).

Box 6–2

Difficulties in Drug Design

Let us pause a minute to consider all of the substances that bind NE and all the processes mediated by the substances. Since NE is released nonsynaptically, it interacts with *various kinds* of beta-receptors (excitatory and inhibitory), *various kinds* of alpha-receptors (some of them autoreceptors), proteins for *re-uptake*, enzymes for *breakdown*, and even enzymes for *synthesis* (recall the negative feedback inhibition of TOHase from Chapter 5). The array of receptors and regulatory processes that confronts the pharmaceutical chemist who wishes to design drugs to act on only *specific symptoms* of disease is bewildering. Remember that *each binding site for NE must resemble every other binding site to some degree, since the native agonist for each NE biding site is the same*. It is one of the great challenges of modern medicine to acquire specific antagonists and exogenous agonists for each binding site.

Consider just one example, one to which we shall return again in the future chapters. The mental illness known as *depression* (Chapter 18) is thought to involve a *deficit* in transmission at central catecholamine nerve plexuses (possibly a deficit of NE). Therapy has focused on supplying *agonists* for NE to balance the deficit. However, knowing about the role of NE in the autonomic nervous system, you can imagine what problems might exist for such a strategy. Some people who suffer from depression are overweight or elderly, and hence are at risk of *hypertension*. Using an agonist of NE to activate beta-receptors in the CNS to alleviate depression is likely to exacerbate hypertension by activating beta-receptors in the *heart*. Thus an important pharmaceutical advance in the treatment of depression was the introduction of families of drugs that have fewer side effects on the heart but still work well centrally.

These new drugs provide only a partial solution. It has probably occurred to you while reading this chapter that drugs that act on autonomic receptors could have *deadly* effects, considering the regulatory role these receptors play in regulating vital bodily functions. For example, overstimulation of beta-receptors can *stop the heart*. Since a diagnostic feature of depression is *thoughts of suicide* (Chapter 18) it seems unwise to place an effective means of suicide into the hands of a depressed patient. Even if small doses might alleviate the condition the possibility of overdose may outweigh the benefit.

For this reason, much work has been devoted to finding an effective antidepressant that had no lethal dose (or very high lethal dose). One such compound seemed very promising until it was found to cause *priapism* (continuous erection) in male patients. In addition to the desired sites in the CNS, adrenergic receptors in the penis were preferentially accessed by the new drug. While this side effect is indeed preferable to hypertension and suicide, priapism is a painful condition that must be surgically corrected, further adding to the troubles of an already depressed individual.

Tremendous advances are being made in the design of antidepressant medication. We shall have occasion to discuss these, together with other modern developments in the understanding of noradrenergic, dopaminergic, and serotonergic transmission in future chapters (especially Chapters 8, 11, 12, 13, 15, 17, and 18). However, always bear in mind the complications introduced by the fact that the body expresses *multiple binding sites for each agonist and that these have overlapping specificity*.

SUMMARY

The peripheral component of the nervous system may be divided into the somatic nervous system and autonomic nervous system. The autonomic nervous system in turn is comprised of the sympathetic and the parasympathetic divisions which together innervate the internal organs of the body. The sympathetic division consists of short preganglionic fibers that emerge from the spinal cord and contact ganglia of the paravertebral chain. Transmission at this contact is cholinergic and nicotinic. The postganglionic fibers are long, noradrenergic, and innervate the target organs; their effects on these visceral organs are mediated by alpha- and beta-adrenergic receptors. The parasympathetic division consists of long preganglionic fibers from the brainstem and the bottom of the spinal cord, which contact remoter ganglia that lie in the target organs. Parasympathetic transmission to the ganglia is cholinergic and nicotinic just as for the sympathetic preganglionic fibers. However, the short postganglionic fibers are cholinergic and have muscarinic action on the organs that are innervated. Autonomic ligands (hormones and transmitters), some of which are also located in the CNS, have complex action mediated by G proteins and second and third messengers in the intracellular region of target cells. Often they are released nonsynaptically to act on distant targets. The adrenal gland is an extreme example of nonsynaptic ligand release. The adrenal gland acts like a large sympathetic ganglion and releases epinephrine through the bloodstream to act throughout the body.

The motor functions of the two divisions of the autonomic nervous system tend to oppose each other. The sympathetic division is generally associated with physical arousal while the parasympathetic half is associated with vegetative functions or relaxation. Each division also has a sensory component, though this system is poorly organized and thus pain from the viscera is often referred by the brain to part of the body surface. The degree of awareness of sympathetic and parasympathetic tone that can be developed is an area of great medical and social importance. The function of the autonomic system is paralleled in the brains of simpler animals, where it is well understood, and in the brains of complex animals, where it is poorly understood. Many aspects of physiological psychology, the neuroscience of learning, psychopharmacology, and the study of mental illness depend on knowledge of the central action of norepinephrine, acetylcholine, and the other autonomic transmitters, the biologically active peptides.

REVIEW QUESTIONS

1. How does the transmitter chemistry differ between the two halves of the autonomic nervous system?

2. How does the anatomy differ between the two halves of the autonomic nervous system?

3. Describe the difference between "preganglionic" and "postganglionic."

4. What is a second messenger? a third messenger?

5. What does the adrenal gland do?

6. What is "referred pain"?

7. What are "autoreceptors"?

8. What is a "peptide" transmitter and how does it differ from other types of neurotransmitter?

THOUGHT QUESTIONS

1. What drugs might enable an unscrupulous person to "beat the lie detector test"? Comment on the legal, ethical, and societal dimensions of this problem.

2. Based on the effect of caffeine in tea, coffee, or soda pop, propose a theory for the function of norepinephrine in the brain.

KEY CONCEPTS

adenylate cyclase (p. 136)
adrenal glands (p. 133)
adrenaline (p. 133)
alpha-adrenergic receptors
 (p. 126)
angina pectoris (p. 139)
antagonistic effects (p. 128)
autonomic nervous system
 (p. 122)
autoreceptors (p.143)
beta-adrenergic receptors
 (p. 126)
blood-brain barrier (BBB)
 (p. 122)
caffeine (p. 138)
cAMP (p. 136)

central nervous system (CNS)
 (p. 122)
C kinase (p. 132)
dense-cored vesicles (p. 130)
dual innervation (p. 124)
endocrinology (p. 135)
electron-dense vesicles
 (p. 130)
enteric nervous system
 (p. 141)
eutely (p. 141)
fight-or-flight response
 (p. 134)
ganglion (p. 124)
glycogen (p. 137)
G protein (p. 131)

G protein–coupled receptor
 (p. 135)
G protein–linked channel
 (p. 135)
GTP (p. 131)
hypertension (p. 134)
identifiable neurons (p. 142)
James-Lange theory (p. 140)
Medical Student Syndrome
 (p. 140)
nitric oxide (p. 132)
parasympathetic division
 (p. 124)
paravertebral chain (p. 124)
peripheral nervous system
 (PNS) (p. 122)

phosphodiesterase (p. 138)
phospholipase C (p. 131)
plexus (p. 130)
polygraph (p. 141)
postganglionic fibers (p. 125)
preganglionic fibers (p. 125)
protein kinase (p. 131)
psychophysiology (p. 140)
referred pain (p. 139)
second messenger (p. 132)
somatic nervous system
 (p. 122)
sympathetic division (p. 124)
tone (p. 128)
varicosity (p. 130)

To describe the action of nerve as integrative is, although true, hardly sufficient for a definition. If the nature of an animal be accepted as being that of a whole presupposed by all its parts, then each and every part of the animal is integrative. This is illustrated strikingly by cancer, the growth of which being outside the integrative plan of the body is destructive both to the normal body and to itself. Our search for a more satisfying definition of nerve has then to ask what is the specific contribution which nerve makes to animal integration. Finger-pointings toward an answer are that nerve in any strict sense of the term is not an element of the plant-world. Nor is it found in unicellular animals, although it is practically universal in the multicellular. In these latter, similarly universal, is an organ of mechanical work, muscle, executant of movements and attitudes, the animal's motor behaviour. This behaviour falls into two divisions. One digestive, excretory, in short visceral; the other inclusive of all which is not merely visceral. This latter behaviour is that of external relation, so called. In it, motor behaviour reaches its highest speeds and precision, nerve attains its greatest and supreme developments.

Sir Charles Sherrington
The Integrative Action of the Nervous System *(1947)*

7

The Spinal Cord

As we continue to embark on the study of central **neuroanatomy** it is normal to experience some trepidation. After all, if such "simple systems" as the autonomic nervous system present challenges to understanding, how much more difficulty will we experience in dealing with the somatic half of the PNS and the entire CNS in this and the following chapter? Since these together organize all sensation, conscious awareness, and every behavior except for the few visceral reflexes we have already discussed, we can expect the mechanisms to be quite complex.

Fortunately, there are nodes of simplicity that await us in this study, anatomical regions in which input from diverse sources *coalesces* or *focuses* on discrete structures. At these nodes we find that there is *order* and *structure* that can be reduced to organizing principles beginning with where the nerves enter and leave the CNS.

All sensation and all behaviors in people are a property of activity in a fixed and relatively small number of *nerves*, or bundles of neurites. These nerves are the thirty-one **spinal nerves** on each side of the body (62 total) and twelve **cranial nerves** on each side of the body (24 total). Thus 86 nerves constitute a node of simplicity between the body and the brain, since they convey all sensory stimuli from the *outside* of the brain to the *inside* (including autonomic sensory fibers) and convey all motor commands from the *inside out* (including the preganglionic sympathetics and parasympathetics). The cranial nerves will be discussed in the next chapter. For now, let's concentrate on the organizing principles governing transmission through the 31 spinal nerves.

A Functional Segregation

Let's begin with the definition of terms. We use the CNS as a referent to describe where nerve fibers originate and terminate. Sensory fibers conveying action potentials towards the CNS are called **afferent fibers**, and motor fibers conveying motor commands in the form of action potentials from the CNS to the muscles are called *efferent* fibers. Why, you may ask, don't we simply call them "sensory" and "motor" and dispense with these additional terms? The reason is that we shall use "afferent" and "efferent" to describe other projections that are not clearly either sensory or motor, such as projections *to* (afferent) and *from* (efferent) various brain nuclei.

Orientation

Anatomy involves many axes of orientation and requires a fair amount of spatial reasoning to understand well. Considering a quadruped (let's say a salamander, Figure 7–1) we see that the body is divided into two parts horizontally and two parts vertically, each divided by a structurally imaginary yet functionally real midline. The direction towards the tip of the head is called **rostral** and the direction towards the tip of the tail is called **caudal**. The upper surface of the body is called **dorsal** and the bottom surface **ventral**.

For bipeds, like us, the situation is complicated a bit since the head is swiveled on top of the spinal cord so it faces forward. Yet we still use the term *dorsal* to refer to structures, such as our backs, that *would* face upwards if we were quadrupeds. *Ventral* is used to describe structures, such as our stomachs, that would face downwards if we were salamanders. For people, the term **anterior** is sometimes used in place of *rostral* and the term **posterior** is sometimes used in place of *caudal*.

Other relative terms useful in anatomy are **medial** (close to the midline) and **lateral** (farther from it), **proximal** (close to a given structure such as the spinal cord) and **distal** (farther from it). In this book we will use two planes of section to display anatomical structures; **transverse** or **cross sections** (in the plane of the dorsal/ventral axis) and **sagittal sections** (in the plane of the medial/lateral axis). These terms are illustrated in Figure 7–1.

The thirty-one spinal nerves split into **dorsal roots** and **ventral roots** at the boundary between the PNS and the CNS. This boundary consists of *dura mater* (see Chapter 8), a tough but thin layer of connective tissue that covers and protects the entire CNS (Figure 7–3). It is a source of great convenience for neuroscientists (and for students trying to learn all of this!) that the dorsal roots are composed primarily of *sensory* fibers and the ventral roots primarily of *motor* fibers. This functional segregation endures in the CNS, where the **dorsal horn** contains sensory cells and the **ventral horn** motor cells (Figure 7–4a). Indeed we will be able to follow the segregation up into the brain, where it will eventually disappear as sensory and motor pathways merge. For now, recite and remember the simple mnemonics: *"dorsal, sensory, afferent"* and *"ventral, motor, efferent."*

Cell bodies for all sensory cells entering the cord lie outside the CNS in a chain of ganglia called the **dorsal root ganglia (DRGs)**. These are not to be confused with sympathetic ganglia of the paravertebral chain, which are not part of the somatic system. The two chains lie side by side in the middle (thoracic) section of the spinal cord, but the DRGs extend all the way from the rostral pole to the caudal pole whereas the paravertebral chain is just in the middle.

Note, however, that the spinal cord *itself* does not fill the spinal column (Figure 7–2). Long spinal nerves from the caudal segments dangle down to innervate the legs and lower abdomen and also carry afferent fibers from these regions. The long dangly spinal nerves are securely ensheathed by the bony vertebrae and resemble a horse's tail. Hence it is not surprising to find that it is called the **cauda equina**, which is Latin for "horse's tail."

The fact that the caudal portion of the spinal column has only nerves and not gray matter has been exploited by modern medicine to benefit women and their offspring during childbirth. During the "baby boom" of the 1950s and 1960s many women were under general anesthesia during childbirth (i.e., unconscious). General anesthesia affects not only the mother but the infant as well, since mother and fetus share a common blood supply. Because it was felt better for the newborn to come into the world in an undrugged condition, there has been a return to natural childbirth. However, as the moment grows near and the pain of childbirth increases, mothers sometimes opt for the "subdural" procedure in which *local* anesthetic is injected directly into the cauda equina. The needle passes between vertebrae and causes no damage since there is no spinal cord in this region. The nerves that bring sensation from the legs and lower torso are merely pushed aside by the needle tip. Local anesthetic at the spinal level anesthetizes the mother below the waist but allows her to remain fully conscious and leaves the neonate unexposed to drugs, since the anesthetic does not enter the bloodstream. An "epidural" anesthetic is one that accomplishes the same purpose without going all the way into the cauda equina.

Gray Matter and White Matter

Early anatomists cut up fresh tissue from brain and spinal cord because they lacked a suitable method for preserving ("fixing") biological specimens. Fresh CNS tissue has the consistency of gelatin and has a pale color. Upon close examination, some regions are translucent to light and thus appear *gray* and other areas are opaque to light and thus appear *white*. We know today that axons are usually enveloped by glial cells, which supply them with myelin, a dense and opaque coat of "nerve glue" (see Chapter 2). Hence **white matter** in the CNS is a region in which axons prevail over other neural structures. A bundle of axons in the CNS is often called a **tract**, a fas-

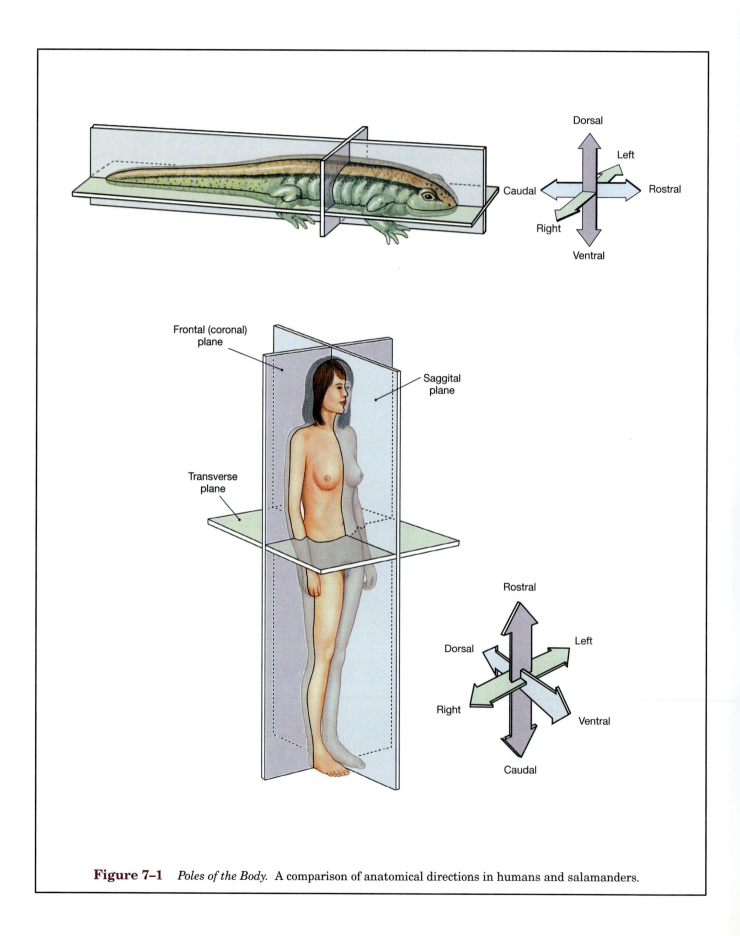

Figure 7–1 *Poles of the Body.* A comparison of anatomical directions in humans and salamanders.

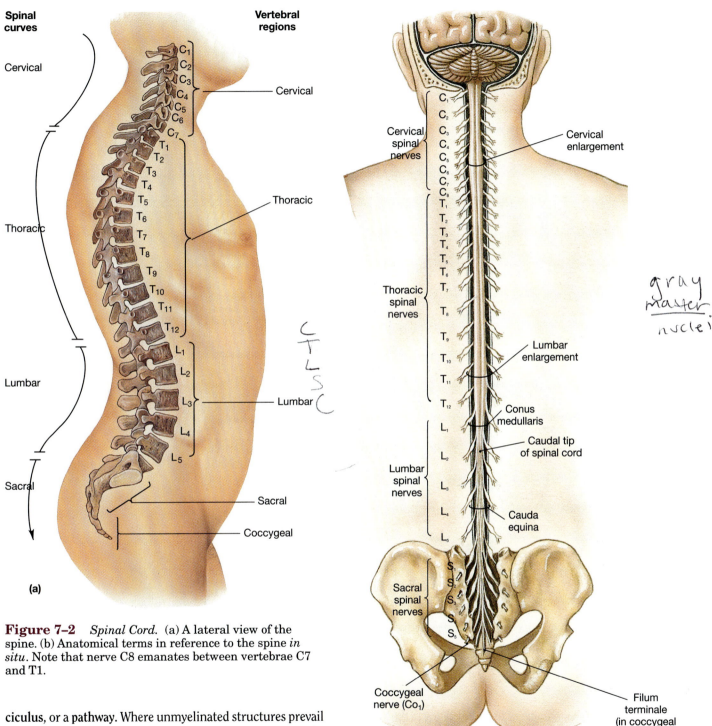

Figure 7–2 *Spinal Cord.* (a) A lateral view of the spine. (b) Anatomical terms in reference to the spine *in situ*. Note that nerve C8 emanates between vertebrae C7 and T1.

ciculus, or a **pathway**. Where unmyelinated structures prevail (such as cell bodies) the tissue is **gray matter**, since it substantially lacks myelin. Examples of gray matter are nuclei (a collection of cell bodies in the CNS) and layers of cell bodies in various parts of the brain. Unfortunately, the word "nucleus" is used to describe both the organelle in the soma (Chapter 2) as well as the collection of cell bodies in the CNS.

In the spinal cord, gray matter occupies the central region, around the **central canal**, which is essentially a spinal exten-

sion of the ventricles of the brain. In the central canal the gray matter forms a four-lobed structure where the *cell bodies* for the spinal sensory function (dorsal) and motor function (ventral) are located (see Figure 7–4). The white matter of the spinal cord

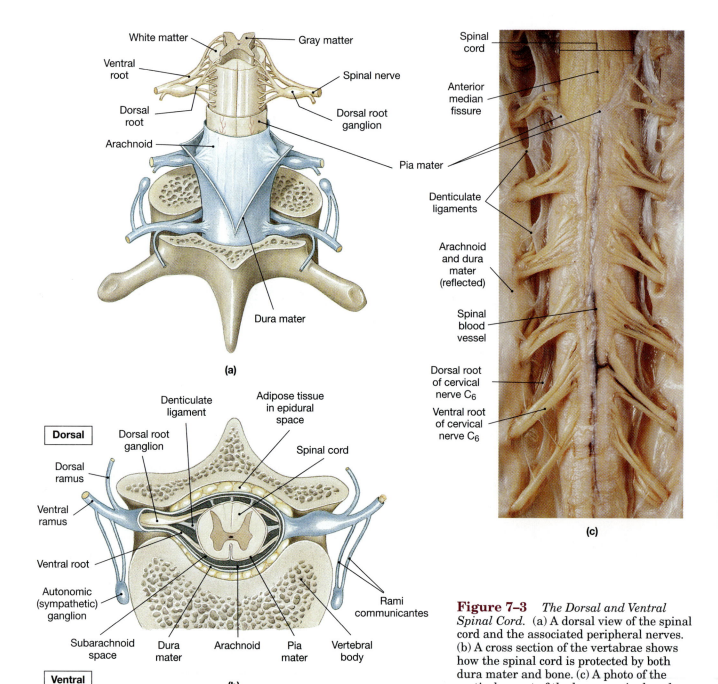

White matter

Gray matter

Ventral root

Spinal nerve

Dorsal root

Dorsal root ganglion

Arachnoid

Pia mater

Dura mater

(a)

Denticulate ligament

Adipose tissue in epidural space

Dorsal

Dorsal root ganglion

Spinal cord

Dorsal ramus

Ventral ramus

Ventral root

Autonomic (sympathetic) ganglion

Rami communicantes

Subarachnoid space

Dura mater

Arachnoid

Pia mater

Vertebral body

Ventral

(b)

Spinal cord

Anterior median fissure

Denticulate ligaments

Arachnoid and dura mater (reflected)

Spinal blood vessel

Dorsal root of cervical nerve C_6

Ventral root of cervical nerve C_6

(c)

Figure 7–3 *The Dorsal and Ventral Spinal Cord.* (a) A dorsal view of the spinal cord and the associated peripheral nerves. (b) A cross section of the vertabrae shows how the spinal cord is protected by both dura mater and bone. (c) A photo of the vertical aspect of the human spinal cord.

consists of all the sensory, *afferent* fibers ascending to the brain (color-coded blue in Figure 7–4) and all the motor, *efferent* fibers descending down from the brain (color-coded red in Figure 7–4). These groups of myelinated axons form a white boundary around the gray matter core.

Dermatomes

It is common knowledge that insects, earthworms and so forth are *segmented* organisms, but it is less well known that vertebrates, including people, are segmented as well. Figure 7–5 shows the portions of the body, called **dermatomes**, that are innervated by each spinal segment. The thirty-one dermatomes correspond to the thirty-one spinal nerves (the face is composed of *brachial* segments derived from gill slits in evolution and is innervated by *cranial nerves*, not spinal nerves). *Each dermatome corresponds to that portion of the body innervated by one set of spinal nerves, a sensory root and a motor root on each side.* We are not often made aware of our dermatomes. One not-so-uncommon occasion is during a minor yet frightening disease known as **shingles**. Shingles is caused by a virus (related to the *herpes* virus) that infects the terminals of spinal nerves, migrates up the processes to the spinal cord, and dwells there in the gray matter harmlessly for extended periods. Then, for unknown reasons, the virus erupts, travels back down the axon and causes the inflammation of the dermatome for that segment. A red stripe appears across the body surface corresponding to one of the stripes in Figure 7–5. The condition, though striking, disappears after a few weeks and never recurs. No one who has experienced it will doubt that we, like the earthworms, are segmented organisms.

Note that the dermatomes can be grouped into categories corresponding to discrete regions of the spinal column and respective spinal cord. Beginning at the *rostral* end of the spinal cord there are eight **cervical** segments, followed by twelve **thoracic** segments, followed by five **lumbar** segments and, most caudally, five **sacral** segments. The single **coccygeal** segment innervates only the fused vertebrae that are remnants of the prehensile tail possessed by our ancestors and does not appear as a dermatome. Look at the sample cross sections of cord at the various regions in Figure 7–4B. Proceeding rostrally to caudally, there is a general tendency for gray matter to occupy more and more of the spinal cord, that is, there is more *white matter*, proportionally, in

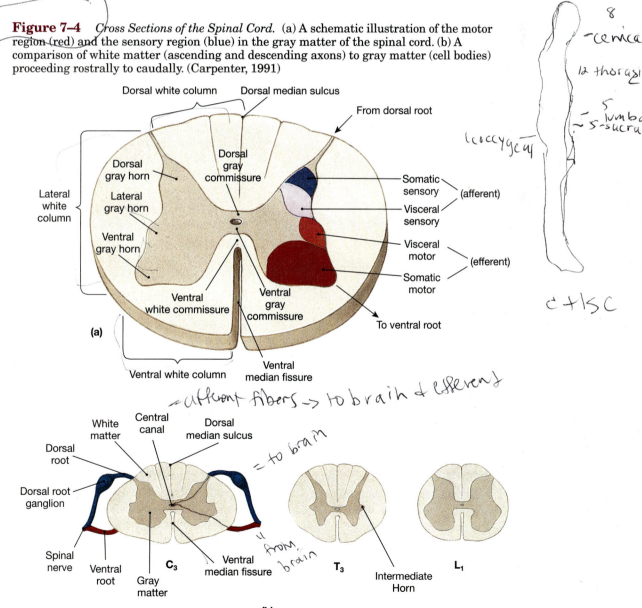

Figure 7–4 *Cross Sections of the Spinal Cord.* (a) A schematic illustration of the motor region (red) and the sensory region (blue) in the gray matter of the spinal cord. (b) A comparison of white matter (ascending and descending axons) to gray matter (cell bodies) proceeding rostrally to caudally. (Carpenter, 1991)

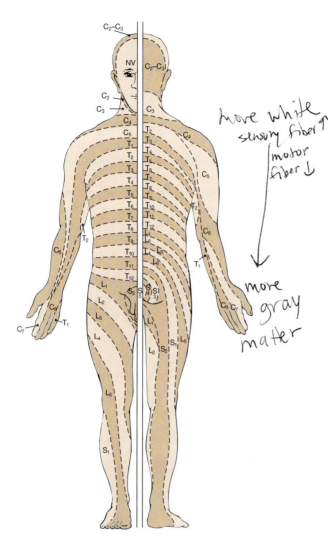

[handwritten annotations: "more white sensory fiber ↑", "motor fiber ↓", "more gray matter"]

Figure 7–5 *Dermatomes.* The human body segmented by the dermatomes that correspond to the thirty-one spinal nerves.

cervical cord than in *sacral* cord. Why do you think this is? There is, however, an irregularity in this sequence. Notice the *thoracic* cord has little gray matter compared to adjacent *cervical* and *lumbar* cord.

Recall the function of the white matter tracts: to convey sensory fibers *up* and motor fibers *down*. High cervical cord must contain all the fibers for the cervical dermatomes (arms and hands) as well as those *for every section caudal to the cervical dermatomes*, since the fibers must pass *through* cervical cord to reach thoracic, lumbar, and sacral dermatomes. In contrast, sacral cord needs only white matter for its tracts, motor fibers for other segments having already terminated in more rostral regions and sensory fibers having not yet inserted as they will in more rostral regions.

The sparse gray matter of thoracic cord is in contrast to the *swelling* of gray matter in cervical and lumbar cord. The cervical enlargement exists because there are *more muscles to innervate* in the arms and hands than there are in the abdomen. Also, somatic sensation in the hands is more acute than in the torso. This can be shown by a quick laboratory exercise. Have a friend take a drawing compass and press the two tips, separated by a fairly large distance, into your back. See if you can feel one point or two. If you can feel two points pressing into your back, have her decrease the distance between the two tips until only one point is felt, then note the actual distance between two tips. Now, repeat the exercise on your hand while your eyes are closed. You will notice that the distance between the two tips is much smaller when the experiment is performed on your hand as compared to your back, demonstrating more acute somatic sensation. For this reason, more *sensory structure* is required (larger dorsal horns) for innervation of the hands. The lumbar enlargement provides greater neural space for the legs and feet than the abdomen receives. If you look carefully, you will see a slight swelling between the dorsal and ventral horns in thoracic cord. What do you think this "intermediate" horn is for?

We shall not see another figure like Figure 7–5, which is a map of the body surface in terms of neural equivalents. Instead, we will see many maps of *neural space* in terms of the *body surface equivalents* (see, e.g., Figure 9–2). We will see that all neural structures, both sensory and motor, are organized to correspond to the body plan. We find these maps of the body surface (and of the other "spaces"; visual space and auditory space) at many levels of the neuraxis. A useful guide to the challenging maze of neuroanatomy can be found in the following statement: *The CNS is largely a collection of maps of the body and maps of the outside world, each topographically faithful but distorted by being jammed and packed into the cranium and spinal column.* Much of what is to come in this and the next three chapters involves following these maps from synapse to synapse and understanding their construction.

Decussation

There is another, more mysterious, property that our nervous system shares with earthworms, insects, and most other animals. The phenomenon of **decussation** is displayed when nerve fibers *cross the midline* to innervate structures on the other side of the body. Thus, for motor systems, the left brain controls the right side of the body and the right brain controls the left side of the body. For sensory systems, sensation due to stimuli on the right side is a property of the left brain and sensation due to stimuli on the left side is a property of the right brain. Many, but not all, nerve tracts decussate *at some point*. When a particular projection crosses, it is called contralateral (*contra* = against); and when it does not cross, it is called ipsilateral (*ipsa* = same). Several synaptic links of, say, a sensory system may project ipsilaterally. Then a single contralateral projection completes the decussation. I have never encountered a satisfactory teleological theory of why decussation occurs, nor can I think of one. If you can, I would love to hear from you. Such an explanation would go far toward making sense of hemispheric specialization (see Box 1–3).

Sensory Pathways

To understand how somatic sensation occurs we must follow the fiber bundles as they insert into the spinal cord from the dorsal roots, make synapses, decussate, and form maps. But first we need a method of identifying individual neurons in the circuit. For the first stages of processing, the synaptic connections are *systematic* and *hierarchical* (i.e., there is "serial processing" instead of "parallel processing," Chapter 1). In this sense hierarchy means that neurons synapse in layers like a triangle. Thus we can assign a number to each level of the hierarchy to identify it (we would like to assign a number to each *cell*, but for the vertebrate CNS this is not possible because there are too many). At the first level in the sensory system, the signal is received by a neurite out in the peripheral nervous system. The neurite is the part of the nerve cell that we have been referring to as a dendrite, but the first cell in a sensory system is not postsynaptic to anything, hence, the fiber is not accurately called a dendrite in this particular case. Let us call this cell the **first-order neuron** (Figure 7–6). *The soma of the first-order cell for all somatosensory systems in vertebrates lies outside the CNS in the dorsal root ganglia (DRGs).* As you already know from our description of the neurite, the first-order somatosensory cell has a structure that is different from most neurons. It is monopolar, meaning it has a single process extending from the cell body. This process splits into the aforementioned neurite (with terminal out in the skin, muscle, or internal organ) and into the axon which enters the CNS and makes a synapse. The cell (in the CNS for somatosensory systems) that receives a synapse from the first-order neuron is the second-order neuron. The cell that receives a contact from the *second-order neuron* is the **third-order neuron** and so forth for *fourth-order, fifth-order,* and *higher-order neurons* (Figure 7–6). Though the numerical identity of very high order cells (and, indeed, their very existence) is in dispute, the sequence of synaptic relations through the fourth or fifth level of the triangle is pretty well known for most sensory systems (Chapter 9). Note that we describe the neurons at each level as single cells and show them as such in pictures like Figure 7–6, but this is just for

simplicity. In fact we are referring to *levels of processing*, each of which involves hundreds of cells.

Projection of Large Mechanoreceptors

Sensation from the body surface is of several types. Some are easily recognized: pain in response to burn or abrasion, pressure, the feeling upon deflection of body hair. Others are less obvious. For example, you have knowledge of the position of your limbs in space without looking at them. This is so much a part of everyday experience that it surprises some people to learn that special sensory fibers (**proprioceptors**) are devoted just to this sensory function.

A cross section of a dorsal root ganglion would reveal two general populations of fibers: large myelinated fibers and small unmyelinated fibers. Electrical stimulation of the ganglion causes two types of action potentials; one quickly conducting (due to the large, myelinated fibers) and one slowly conducting (due to the small unmyelinated fibers). Numerous experiments have shown that the slowly conducting fibers are preferentially activated by noxious stimuli (burns, cuts, and abrasions). Therefore, the large, quickly conducting fibers must be responsible for all the other somatosensory systems.

Once inside the spinal cord the projection of the large fibers (which we will lump together for the moment and call **mechanoreceptors**) differs from the small fiber projection. The first-order mechanoreceptor cell enters the cord by the dorsal root and then ascends ipsilaterally in dorsal white matter *without synapsing* (Figure 7–7). Two stout bundles arise on each side of the body, one from the legs called the **fasciculus gracilis** (think of walking *gracefully*) and one from the arms called the **fasciculus cuneatus**. Together, these fiber tracts are called the **dorsal columns**. Then in the brainstem the cells contact the *second-order neuron* for the mechanoreceptor system in the *nucleus gracilis* and the *nucleus cuneatus*. The second-order cell's axons then decussate and ascend contralaterally to the thalamus where the third-order neuron is found. The fasciculus gracilis is lateral in the dorsal, or sensory, white matter, and within it the fibers from the toes are most lateral, followed by the shins, knees, thighs, and so forth medially. A tiny bundle of fibers from the abdomen add to the medial side as the fasciculus passes to thoracic cord and then, in order, fibers from fingers, hand, wrist, forearm, and so on add from cervical segments.

Projection of Small Nociceptors

The small diameter, unmyelinated fibers (together with some small diameter *myelinated* fibers that are also nociceptors) convey information regarding *tissue damage* into the cord.

Pain is a sensory system quite different from all the others (Chapter 11). *Its experience is not a direct property of*

Figure 7–6 *The First-Order Somatosensory Cell.* (a) The first-order neuron soma is located outside the CNS in the dorsal root ganglion. (b) The hierarchical organization of synaptic connections for a somatosensory pathway. Motor pathways are separated into upper motor neurons and lower motor neurons.

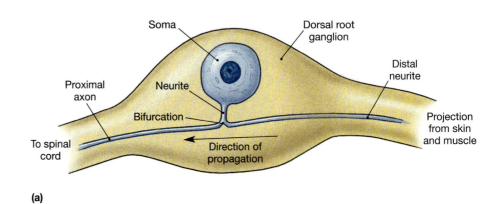

(a)

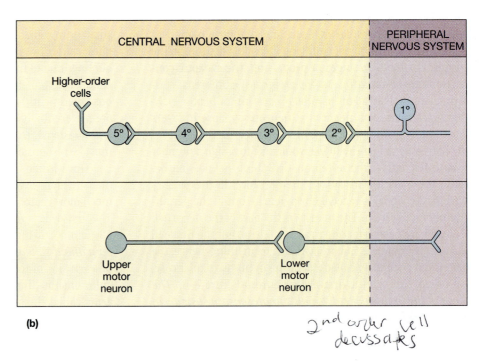

(b)

discharge in these tiny fibers, and as a consequence we avoid calling them "pain fibers." Instead they are called **nociceptors** to convey the fact that they respond preferentially to stimuli usually found to be noxious.

The likely transmitter in first-order nociceptors is Substance P, the byproduct of the original purification of *vagusstoff* (see Box 5–2). As for all somatosensory systems, the first-order cell body is in the DRGs.

The projection of the fibers upon entry into the spinal cord is quite different from that of the large mechanoreceptors. The nociceptors synapse *immediately* onto the second-order cell. The second-order cell is located in the gray matter dorsal horn of the segment of entry (in fact in the most superficial layers of the dorsal horn, the **marginal zone**). The axon of the second-order cell then decussates (again at the segment of entry) and ascends to the brainstem in the **lateral spinothalamic tract** (the tract from the spinal cord to the thalamus).

The third-order cells are located in the contralateral thalamus and in the reticular formation (Ramón y Cajal's "seamless warp") where the meshwork of fibers and cell bodies is so dense that it is difficult to locate them precisely.

Notice that the mechanoreceptor system (see Figure 7–7) and the nociceptor system (Figure 7–8) are similar in that the second-order cell in each is the one that decussates. The difference is in the location of the second-order cell body and the level of the decussation. Box 7–1 presents a clinical example to help you better understand this central neuroanatomy.

Motor Pathways

To a *certain extent* there is a hierarchy of sensory processing with the first-order cells on the bottom of the triangle and the highest-order cells at the very top. We might reasonably expect a hierarchy similar to that of the sensory

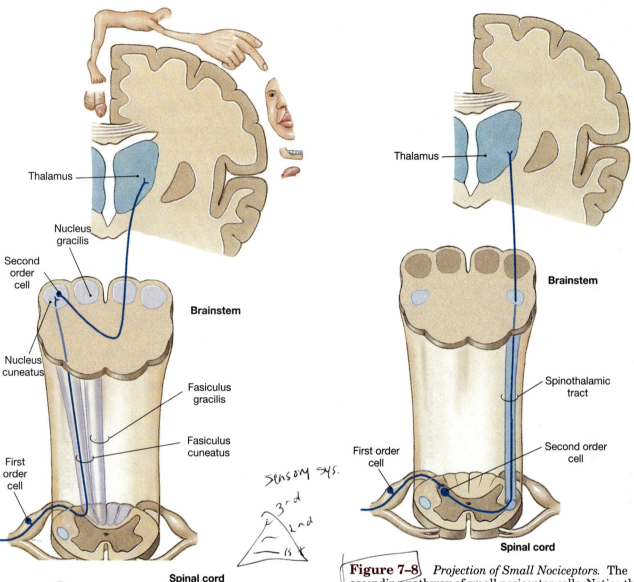

Figure 7–7 *Projections of Large Mechanoreceptors.* The pathway of a large mechanoreceptor as it ascends the dorsal column ipsilaterally before synapsing on the second-order cell in the brainstem. It then decussates before ascending to the third order cell (not shown) in the thalamus.

Figure 7–8 *Projection of Small Nociceptors.* The ascending pathway of small nociceptor cells. Notice that the first-order cell synapses with the second-order cell in the dorsal horn before it decussates and ascends up the spinothalamic tract.

system to exist in motor systems as well. A problem arises with the realization that the triangle for the motor hierarchy is *inverted*. The origin for motor commands lies mysteriously in the cerebral cortex (if you are a monist), and the apex of the triangle is down in the cord where the *final common path* for motor commands to the body is found in the ventral roots outside the spinal cord. The present point of this discussion is that the terminology *first-order, second-order, third-order,* and so forth is inappropriate for

motor systems since the presumed first-order cell at the base of the motor triangle (the mystery cell in the cerebral cortex) is the *least understood, least accessible to experimental analysis, and most remote from the simple segregation of function at the level of the spinal cord.* Thus a different convention must be adopted. The lower motor neuron is the neuron that exits the CNS to innervate the skeletal muscles of the body and is the *final common path* for the brain to exert its will on the body. The cell that contacts the lower motor neuron, whose dendrites, soma, and axon lie wholly within the CNS, we will call the upper motor neuron (see Figure 7–6). Many cells of different origin contact the

Box 7–1

Brown-Séquard Syndrome

We owe the discovery and first description of the **Brown-Séquard Syndrome** to one of the last truly colorful figures in the origins of modern medicine. A French physiologist and neurologist, Charles E. Brown-Séquard ran a traveling medicine show in the western United States near the turn of the twentieth century, visiting little cow towns, performing a mixture of vaudeville and public lectures on medicine, and selling his "elixir" as a **panacea**, or cure-all. The elixir, the active ingredient of which was testosterone derived from the gonads of bulls, was sold to treat a variety of internal ailments (rheumatism, heart conditions, and miscellaneous complaints). Since the small communities he visited seldom had medical help of any kind, accident victims were often presented when the medicine show came to town. Given the rough-and-tumble nature of life on the Western frontier, these injuries included gunshot wounds, knife wounds, arrow wounds, and injuries to cowboys kicked by cows, stomped by horses, and so forth, many of whom suffered permanent neurological deficits as a result of the damage. It was uncertain what the "doctor" could do for these individuals (except, of course, to prescribe his elixir), but over the years he noticed a pattern to some of the injuries when the wound occurred in the back.

In addition to partial **hemiplegia** (paralysis on one side) the victims in this category had segregated sensory deficits. Always caudal to the level of the injury, the patients reported loss of mechanoreceptor sensation (pro-

prioception, deep pressure sensation, or light touch perception) on one half of the body and complete lack of nociception (and temperature pain perception) *on the opposite side* (see figure).

Let's reflect on what we have learned about the anatomy of the spinal cord to discover the nature of the **lesion** (central damage) in Brown-Séquard Syndrome. The bony spine on the medial dorsal face (middle back) of each vertebra tends to deflect an incoming object (let's say, a knife) to one side or other. This deflection creates a tendency for spinal injuries to be *partial*, on *one side only*. The hemiplegia confirms this; the nature of the sensory deficits in the example shown in the figure suggests hemisection of the cord at the *midthoracic* level. Of course, only sensory and motor function distal to the lesion are affected, since dermatomes proximal to the brain do not send fibers through more caudal cord. But *which* side of the cord was damaged? In the example shown, mechanoreception on the *right* side is lacking and nociception is lacking from the *left*. This indicates the lesion is on the *right* side since the mechanoreceptor projection is *ipsilateral* to the level of the brainstem. Since the nociceptor projection is *contralateral*, an injury to the *right* cord produces a deficit on the *left* side.

"Where is the lesion?" is the central question of **diagnostic neurology**, in which measurements of *behavioral deficits* are taken and the nature of the central damage *deduced* from knowledge of neuroanatomy. When confirma-

---

upper motor neuron in turn. We will discuss their origins separately and also call them, collectively, *upper motor neurons*.

Lower Motor Neurons — in gray matter ventral horn

The cell bodies for all of the lower motor neurons lie in the gray matter of the ventral horn of the spinal cord (and a few cranial nerve nuclei that are essentially continuation of the ventral horn). Their axons exit the CNS exclusively through the ventral roots and, outside the cord, make contacts only on skeletal muscle. These are exclusively cholinergic, nicotinic, and excitatory in nature. In the mature condition, each muscle fiber receives a contact from only one lower motor neu-

ron (though one lower motor neuron may contact many muscle fibers). A motor neuron and the cells it contacts are collectively called a **motor unit** (Figure 7–9). All motor commands of the brain to the body and all behavior (except for the very simple behavior due to autonomic action on viscera) are a property of the motor units. However, sometimes this system breaks down, motor function making it impossible (see Box 7–2).

Postsynaptic potentials in the dendrites of the lower motor neuron summate at the axon hillock and lead to the "decision" to fire or not to fire an action potential. The action potential is conducted across myelinated segments in saltatory fashion down to the end plate located on the mus-

tion by post-mortem examination is possible, the practice of diagnostic neurology can provide powerful insights into the structure and function of the human brain, and indeed lies at the origin of the field we call neuroscience (recall Broca's brain from Chapter 1). To this day some of our best insights into *human* neuroanatomy come from diagnostic neurology done with large populations of brain-injured patients (e.g., gunshot victims from the Civil War).

Nowadays the practice of diagnostic neurology is receding in favor of noninvasive imaging procedures such as CAT scans and PET scans (Chapter 16). These new procedures allow visualization of the lesion directly (obviating the need for diagnostic neurological examination), provide the most dramatic pictures of the living brain available, and have tremendous potential for teaching us more about human neurophysiology.

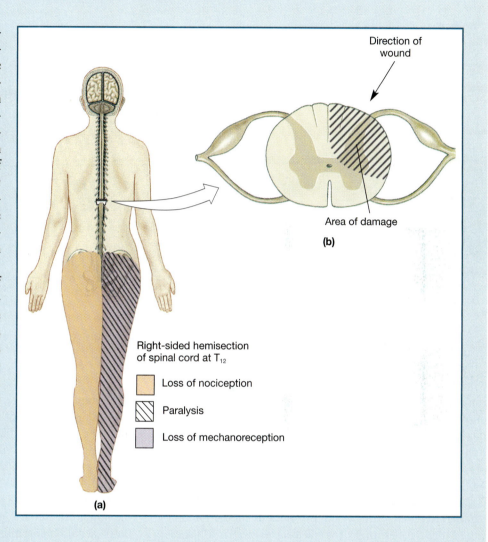

Direction of wound

Area of damage

(b)

Right-sided hemisection of spinal cord at T_{12}

☐ Loss of nociception

▨ Paralysis

▨ Loss of mechanoreception

(a)

cle fiber (see Figure 7–9, see also Figure 5–15). Upon ACh release by exocytosis and ACh binding to excitatory nicotinic acetylcholine receptors, an *excitatory end plate potential* results. A consequence is a regenerative action potential in the *muscle* membrane. The plasma membrane of muscle contains pits and crevasses. Among these are elaborate networks of hollow plasma membrane called **T-tubules**. These thread deeply into the interior of each muscle fiber and *carry the regenerating action potential into the cell*. Here depolarization acts to liberate stored Ca^{++} from the **sarcoplasmic reticulum** (an organelle similar in structure to the smooth endoplasmic reticulum [see Chapter 2] which sequesters Ca^{++} from the cytosol). The increase in $[Ca^{++}]_i$ catalyzes a muscle

filament called **myosin** to consume ATP. The energy provided by ATP causes thick myosin filaments to pull on thin filaments made of a protein called **actin**. The sliding of actin filaments into myosin is simultaneous throughout the fiber because of the conduction of the action potential, and this sliding is what causes the muscle to twitch.

Though all behavior is expressed through the lower motor neuron, not all behavior requires the constriction of skeletal muscle. For example, the electric fish is capable of producing a jolt of electricity so intense as to stun prey. Electric fish also use electrical pulses to communicate with one another in their environment (muddy freshwater) where visual contact is impossible. This behavior is generated by a

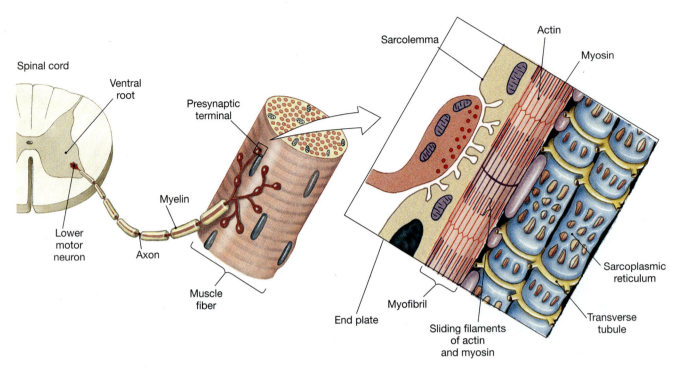

Figure 7–9 *The Motor Unit.* The cholinergic synapse of the lower motor neuron onto the end plate of a muscle fiber.

spinal motor neuron pool that makes dense synaptic contacts onto specialized **electric organs**. The contact is cholinergic, nicotinic, and excitatory just as for the neuromuscular junction, except that the follower cells lack the actin and myosin of muscle cells. Instead, they have sufficient stored ionic potential (good old E_{Na} and E_{Ca}) that the postsynaptic response is *itself* the behavior, an EPSP so strong that it is conducted through water and can give quite a shock to another organism nearby. Needless to say, the end plate for electric fish does not resemble your normal end plate. Its great size and density provides a richer source of *cholinergic vesicles* and *cholinergic receptors* than anywhere else in the animal kingdom. Scientists have exploited this fact to deduce the structure of cholinergic vesicles and receptor proteins. Much of the information presented on cholinergic transmission in Chapter 5 was acquired using the electric eel and the electric ray as experimental animals.

Upper Motor Neurons

The brain uses two stout fiber bundles (on each side) to activate the lower motor neurons. These bundles, the **pyramidal tracts** and the **extrapyramidal tracts** (not to be confused with the triangular hierarchies we have described for the sensory and motor pathways!) contain the *upper motor neurons* whose cell bodies lie *in the brain* and whose efferent axons descend to contact the lower motor neurons in the ventral horn

of the spinal cord. Lower motor neurons receive both excitatory and inhibitory contacts from the upper motor neurons. Since the synapses of the spinal cord are so small and densely packed (no electric organs here, or even large contacts such as the neuromuscular junction), the transmitter chemistry is less well known. It is likely that the excitatory contacts employ *glutamate* or some similar compound such as *aspartate*; the inhibitory contacts probably employ *glycine* and *GABA*. Both excitation and inhibition of lower motor neurons can occur in the cord itself, as we shall see shortly (in the section: "Inhibition of Antagonist Muscles").

Pyramidal System. The pyramidal system made up of the two pyramidal tracts on each side is the simpler of the two upper motor neuron pools. Only two cells are involved in each pathway of the pyramidal system; the lower motor neuron with cell body in the spinal cord and the upper motor neuron with cell body in the frontal lobe of the brain. The cell body of the upper motor neuron is very large (the largest in the mammalian brain because it must support axons that may extend all the way to the sacral spinal cord). The upper motor neurons are called pyramidal cells because they have a vaguely pyramidal shape, but curiously this is not the origin for the name pyramidal tract. The name comes from the fact that the stout fiber bundles (one on each side of the midline) get squeezed as they leave the skull through the hole

Box 7–2

Diseases of the Upper
and Lower Motor Neuron

A variety of paralyzing diseases afflicts the upper and lower motor neurons. Knowledge of the *trophic* relations between cells (Chapter 2) and the relative anatomy of the two stages of neuromuscular control allow the physician to discriminate among the diseases.

The muscle depends on the lower motor neuron for trophic support. When the lower motor neuron is diseased or absent the muscle lacks its only excitatory input. The result is **paralysis**. Subsequently, the muscle fibers begin to express more acetylcholine receptors and these receptors spread to parts of the muscle cell other than the end plate. A consequence of excess receptors is *hyperexcitability*, the neurological expression of which is **fasciculation** (uncontrollable twitching of small muscle fiber bundles). Finally, after long-term removal of trophic support, the muscle shows a degeneration of muscle tone, known as *wastage* or **atrophy**, in which the size of the limb actually declines. Examples of lower motor neuron disease of this kind (called *peripheral neuropathies*) are poliomyelitis (polio) and muscular dystrophy.

When the upper motor neuron is attacked, muscle appearance and bulk is normal, because the trophic input from the *lower* motor neuron to the muscle is intact. The problem here is the receipt of incorrect instructions by the lower motor neuron from the upper motor neuron. The lack of trophic support from the upper motor neuron to the lower motor neuron causes the lower motor neuron to become hyperexcitable. This results in **spasticity** of limbs, in which muscle power is normal but control is erratic. Amyotrophic ("not affecting muscle") lateral sclerosis, or ALS, is an example of upper motor neuron disease. It is also known as "Lou Gehrig's disease" after the famous baseball player who was afflicted with the disorder but is now more famous as the disorder affecting the cosmologist Stephen Hawking, whose book *A Brief History of Time* presents our best understanding of the origin of the universe.

Disorders that affect only the pyramidal system or only the extrapyramidal system have characteristic symptoms as well. An example of the expression of an extrapyramidal disorder would be the *tremors* and deficit in the *voluntary initiation of gait* seen in Parkinson's disease (see Box 5–4), and another would be the sudden involuntary movements known as *hemiballismus* seen in Huntington's disease (Chapter 10).

(*foramen*) at the base. This happens just as they are crossing the midline in what is known as the "decussation of the pyramids" because, in cross section, the tracts appear triangular at this level.

The pyramidal tracts in the spinal cord are thus *contralateral*, originating from one side of the brain and crossing to the *opposite* side of the body. They descend in lateral white matter to insert into the ventral horn in each segment and innervate the lower motor neurons. Though many lower motor neurons receive innervation from the pyramidal system, few are *exclusively* innervated from this source, each cell typically receiving both pyramidal and extrapyramidal contacts. Curiously, an exception to this rule are the fingers of the human hand, which are overwhelmingly controlled by the pyramidal system. Thus when we write, for example, we do so under the direct control of the frontal lobes of the brain.

The Extrapyramidal System. The extrapyramidal system has not one source but many and not one location in the white matter of the cord but several. A number of extrapyramidal systems cluster in the medial ventral part of the white matter. Though the pyramidal projections are *contralateral*, some extrapyramidal projections are *ipsilateral*, arising from subcortical and brainstem nuclei to innervate lower motor neurons on the same side of the body. The functional anatomy of the extrapyramidal system is diverse and quite complex. Chapter 10 discusses the extrapyramidal system in detail in connection with volitional movement, ballistic movement, and upper motor neuron disease.

The "Intermediate" Horn

As we have seen that the somatic sensory and motor functions of the body are neatly distributed between the dorsal horn and its white matter and the ventral horn and its white matter. But the spinal cord does have additional functions. Among them are the *sympathetic* functions such as the fight-or-flight response. Recall that the sympathetic ganglia lie alongside the cord in the paravertebral chain of ganglia (Chapter 6). In the thoracic section of the spinal cord, these ganglia lie adjacent to the DRGs. In the gray matter of only the thoracic spinal cord a small enlargement can be seen *between* the smallish dorsal horn and ventral horn (see Figure 7–4). This **intermediate horn** is where the cell bodies for the preganglionic sympathetic cells are located.

Integrative Circuits in the Cord

The sensory afferent function, the motor efferent function, and the autonomic sympathetic function of the cord account for many important functions of the CNS. Oh, but the spinal cord does much more! So much that the circuits of the cord can almost be thought of as a minibrain, capable of reflex action, maintenance of posture, organization of gait, reaction to noxious stimuli, and a portion of the sexual behavior of both genders. The spinal cord is not simply a relay between the brain and the body, but has its own capacity to *integrate* afferent input into appropriate output.

In one view the behavior of organisms is believed to occur predominantly as *a response to stimuli*, either external (as in the fight-or-flight response) or internal (as in hunger or thirst). Proponents of this view would assert that the sole function of the CNS is *integration* of these stimuli and responses. Whether or not you subscribe to this belief, it is instructive to discover how much integration is purely spinal, not involving the brain. An understanding of these spinal circuits leads to a better appreciation of brain functions, the subject of the following chapter (and, indeed, of much of the rest of this text).

Spinal Behaviors

Not all sensory fibers ascend to the brain in the dorsal columns and the lateral spinothalamic tract. Some synapse onto other spinal neurons, cells whose axons lie wholly in the cord. Similarly, not all contacts received by lower motor neurons come from the pyramidal and extrapyramidal systems. Some arise from the aforementioned local spinal neurons or from first-order sensory cells. (Technically, this would make these first-order sensory cells "upper motor neurons" also, but let's not quibble. Things are going to get a little complicated here in the CNS).

Some behaviors that the spinal cord can organize *on its own*, without input from brain, are certain sexual behaviors. Animals that have had complete spinal transections (surgical isolation of the cord from brain) will show erection and ejaculation in response to genital stimulation, a fact well-documented for humans as well in the clinical literature of spinal cord injury and in popular accounts of death by hanging. In rodent models this has been shown to be a property of afferent input to the spinal nucleus of the bulbocavernosus, a region of ventral sacral cord that projects motor fibers to the muscles of the genitalia (Chapter 12). Female reproductive reflexes, too, are spinally organized. *Lordosis*, the stereotypic response to mounting in female rodents, can be obtained in spinally isolated animals. None of this is to say that reproductive activity *as a whole* is spinal. Aspects such as attraction, courtship, and orgasm are organized by brain structures.

A large component of locomotion is also purely spinal. Quadrupeds with high cervical cord transections fail to *initiate* movement (this is a function of brain motor centers such as the basal ganglia, Chapter 10). However, if *pushed forward*, as on a treadmill, such animals can generate a coordinated sequence of limb movements, alternating one limb with another much as in normal walking. Bipeds (such as the proverbial "chicken with its head cut off") can perform this also using purely spinal circuits, but organs of balance (which use brain mechanisms) are required to remain upright. The neural basis for this reciprocal limb movement probably involves contralateral inhibition of certain limbs simultaneous with initiation of stepping in others. In other words, activation of one motor neuron pool initiates stepping in some limbs but also activates spinal interneurons that momentarily *inhibit* the equivalent pool for other limbs. While such locomotor circuits are now being elucidated in simple systems (e.g., systems that coordinate the alternating movement of the six legs of insects and other forms of locomotion discussed in Chapter 10), the network that organizes this complex behavior in vertebrates is still under investigation.

To understand how the spinal cord might organize a significant component of behavior such as walking, we must examine what is known about integrative circuits in the spinal cord. In the sections that follow, I will present *four spinal circuits* known to exist in vertebrates: the monosynaptic reflex, the inhibition of antagonist muscles, alpha- and gamma-activation and the Renshaw cell. Each one, by itself, is not too complicated. Your task, once each circuit is understood individually, is to *try to imagine all four at work together*. This will provide a background for further inquiry into the spinal basis for movement and the neural language that the brain uses to address the spinal cord.

The Monosynaptic Reflex

Each muscle of the body has sensory structures in it and is innervated by the lower motor neurons we have just discussed. Thus the distinction between the sensory and motor modality is not nearly as clean in the muscle as it is in the

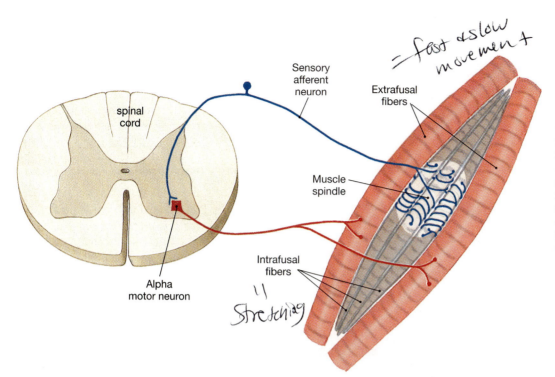

— fast & slow movement

Stretching "

Figure 7–10 *Spinal Circuit #1: The Monosynaptic Reflex.* A tap on the tendon stretches the intrafusal fibers of the muscle. This stretch is detected by the muscle spindle sensory afferent, which then signals the alpha motor neuron in the spine to send a message to the extrafusal muscle fibers, causing them to contract.

spinal cord. One such sensory structure is the **muscle spindle organ**. Skeletal muscle actually has several kinds of fibers in it. **Extrafusal fibers** (comprising the fibers used for fast jerks and slow prolonged contractions) make up the bulk of the muscle and do all the work. **Intrafusal fibers** make up a much smaller proportion of the total and contain a **stretch receptor** (a receptor sensitive to stretching motion). When the fibers are stretched (for example, with muscle elongation caused by movement of the limb or digit), the sensory ending in the muscle spindle organ depolarizes. This sets up an action potential in the sensory afferent fiber which is then conducted up the nerve, through the DRG, and into the spinal cord. Some of the fibers ascend to the brain to provide proprioception, but others insert directly into the gray matter of the cord and make synaptic contacts with spinal neurons. In the simplest case (indeed, the simplest neural circuit in the body) this excitatory contact is onto a lower motor neuron *that innervates the extrafusal fibers of that same muscle.* Only two cells are involved (the sensory afferent fiber and the lower motor neuron) and, in the CNS, only one synapse. Hence the circuit is called the **monosynaptic reflex** (*mono* = one) (Figure 7–10).

The monosynaptic reflex was described thoroughly by one of the progenitors of neuroscience, Sir Charles Sherrington (who is quoted at the beginning of this chapter). Sherrington called the phenomenon the "reflex arc" and devoted much effort to trying to explain it, while maintaining a firmly dualistic attitude towards the higher functions of the brain. Actual demonstration that the circuit existed fell to Sherrington's pupil, Sir John Eccles. Eccles carefully measured

the *conduction velocity* (the speed of propagation) of the afferent fiber and of the lower motor neuron. Then measuring the length of each fiber, he found that the latency of the reflex arc was exactly the time of conduction in the sensory cell plus the time of conduction in the motor cell plus *one millisecond.* Since the *synaptic delay* (Chapter 5) had been shown for many synapses to be about a millisecond, Eccles concluded that there was no room for any additional cells in the circuit and that it was a direct influence of a sensory cell on the lower motor neuron. Having explained the simplest of vertebrate behaviors in this way, Eccles remained, like Sherrington, a dualist, skeptical that all of higher function could be explained in terms of neural mechanisms.

What is the function of the monosynaptic reflex? The reflex can be readily demonstrated in class by sharply tapping the tendon of the knee with a rubber hammer. This stretches the intrafusal fibers passively and causes the "knee-jerk" motion of the extensor muscle. The net consequence of the circuit's existence is to *counter any stretch of a muscle with a constriction of that muscle.*

It was once very common for a physician to test the "knee-jerk" monosynaptic reflex of the patient in a routine medical exam. Doctors subsequently became less likely to routinely perform this procedure since, as we shall see, it would be impossible for the patient to walk into the examination room and sit down if the reflex were not intact. Still, the classic tendon-tap exam is an important part of neurological assessment as it can be of assistance in diagnoses. For example, defects in calcium metabolism may render spinal reflexes hyperexcitable.

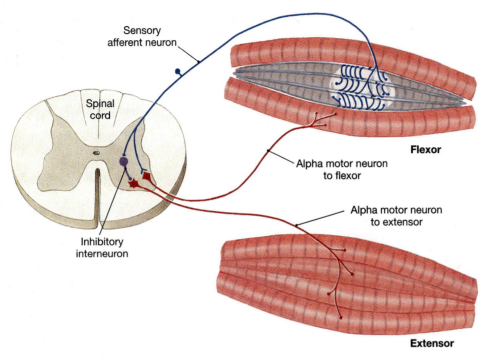

Figure 7–11 *Spinal Circuit #2: The Inhibition of the Antagonist Muscle.* The spindle sensory afferents from the flexor muscle activate both the alpha motor neuron for that muscle and an inhibitory interneuron, which then inhibits the excitation of the extensor motor neuron.

Inhibition of Antagonist Muscles

Be reminded that every muscle of the body has a monosynaptic reflex. If we adopt the simplified view that each limb and digit has a **flexor** muscle and an **extensor** muscle, we see that limb position is a consequence of two muscles that work against one another in *antagonistic relation*. Constriction of one causes the stretch of the other's stretch receptor, which, according to our model, should activate the monosynaptic reflex. What prevents monosynaptic reflexes of antagonist muscles from fighting each other, causing the limb to bounce from position to position or freeze up from the tension?

There is another circuit (Figure 7–11) that *blocks the antagonist monosynaptic reflex* by inhibiting the motor neurons. Imagine that the *flexor* is stretched. Imagine that the monosynaptic reflex *for the flexor* is active. To prevent the *extensor* from constricting, the *flexor* spindle afferents activate an inhibitory interneuron (color-coded black), which blocks excitation in the extensor motor neurons.

For voluntary movement to come about, one circuit must dominate the other: excitation of the constricting muscle and inhibition of the antagonist. Descending input from the brain determines this balance. In fact, when the descending influ-

ence is interrupted by injury to the spinal cord the situation described above is precisely what comes about. The monosynaptic reflexes struggle with each other and as a consequence the limbs are stiff, a condition known as **spinal rigidity**. In this condition, the body is stiff, like a board, though the patient still lives (and thus is not to be confused with *rigor mortis*).

Thus the descending influence of the brain on the spinal cord is not only excitatory. Some circuits are activated and *some inhibited* by the upper motor neuron pool. A compelling example of the specificity of the signals from the brain to the spinal cord is a neurological sign shown upon damage to the pyramidal system. Babies respond to a scratch down the sole of the foot by raising the foot and fanning the toes (try it on a baby you know). However, adults respond to this stimulus in the opposite way, moving the foot down and curling the toes (this is called the **plantar reflex** and it is thought to be part of the reflexive behavior needed for walking). During development the infant response is inhibited by the plantar reflex. However, upon spinal injury to the pyramidal system, the adult reflex resembles the infant's. This is known as the **Babinski sign** and is widely used in emergency rooms to assess the severity of spinal cord damage. For our purposes it is useful as an example of *latent spinal circuits* that are normally inhibited by the brain.

Alpha- and Gamma-Activation

We have established, then, that the brain communicates with the spinal cord by encouraging some reflexes (excitation) and discouraging others (inhibition). But how do the upper motor neurons of the brain activate the lower motor neurons?

Just as muscle fibers can be divided into two types (extrafusal and intrafusal), the lower motor neuron pool on the ventral horn has two types of cells. **Alpha motor neurons** contact the *extrafusal* muscle directly and **gamma motor neurons** contact the *intrafusal* muscle directly. The gamma motor neuron contact is quite the same as the alpha (cholinergic, nicotinic, and excitatory); the difference is that, as we have seen, *the intrafusal fiber contains a sensory organ*. Con-

Box 7–3

Animal Welfare and Animal Rights

The number of animals used in research is small compared to the number used for other purposes (e.g., for food, clothing, and testing, etc.). Their use in neuroscience research is an even smaller fraction of the total. Nevertheless, in recent years there has been a growing concern over the treatment of research animals. As a result, scientists have been forced into a dialogue (in my opinion a very healthy one) in which they must explain the importance of what they do in language intelligible to the layperson and appeal to the public's values to justify their work.

Public concern over laboratory animal care springs not from one movement, but from two. The first I call the **animal welfare movement**, which includes organizations such as the Humane Society. Proponents of this movement maintain that every effort should be made to eliminate unnecessary suffering in laboratory animals and that the minimum number should be used that is consonant with the goals of furthering medical and veterinary research. This movement is very broadly based and very widely supported.

Members of the animal welfare movement tend to be realists. They know that death is a necessary consequence of birth, that pain, thirst, and hunger are a part of the life of wild animals, but that the better part of human nature moves us to try to eliminate these discomforts from the lives of animals in our care.

Animal welfare groups are quite active in pursuit of their goals. They visit university laboratories, inspect animal care procedures, and place representatives on animal use review committees. In my experience, which includes personal contact with one of the most vocal animal welfare groups, these interactions are very positive experiences. The activists emerge, by and large, with their fears allayed because most researchers share their values. Most of us chose a career in animal research because of a fondness for animals and their behavior. Of all the people I have met in my field, I know of no one who took joy in the discomfort of animals and only a very few who were unconcerned about their welfare.

The Society for Neuroscience has explicit guidelines for the protection of laboratory animals. They state "the fundamental principle of ethical animal research is that experimental animals must not be subjected to avoidable

distress or discomfort." All invasive procedures (surgery) must be done under anesthesia and postoperative care must be provided to prevent discomfort or infection. Papers are rejected and participation in meetings refused when individuals are found to have disobeyed these rules.

At American universities, all proposed research must be reviewed and approved in advance by federally mandated "Institutional Animal Care and Use Committees" (IACUC). These committees contain representatives from the non-university community and can and sometimes do reject proposed research procedures.

The **animal rights movement** has a radically different agenda from the animal welfare movement. According to adherents of the animal rights movement, no use of animals is ethical, unless it would also be ethical if humans were used. Since animals are incapable of giving "informed consent" to medical procedures as human patients do, this group's position is that the use of animals for research is immoral. Organizations such as People for the Ethical Treatment of Animals (PETA) want to end all use of animals for any research purpose, despite the benefits such research has provided for animals as well as people. Ingrid Newkirk, cofounder of PETA, has stated that

> [Medical research is] . . . immoral even if it's essential (*Washington Post*, May 30, 1989)

and

> If my father had a heart attack, it would give me no solace at all to know his treatment was first tried on a dog. (Horner, 1991)

Most people find the logical and practical consequences of equating people with animals to be too extreme to endorse. As Constance Horner, Undersecretary for Health and Human Services, has said:

> The idea of animal rights may set out to ensure that animals are treated as human beings, but by blurring the essential distinction between the two, it lends itself just as readily to the suggestion that human beings may be treated as animals. Thus, the doctrine that purports to elevate the status of all living things is, in the end, a doctrine that debases the status of mankind.

(*Neuroscience Newsletter*, March/April 1991)

it is an excellent example of **surround inhibition** (see Chapter 9). Almost ubiquitous in the brain, surround inhibition creates contrast in time and space, allowing only a *discrete* signal to emerge from a network that experiences *diffuse* activation. Surround inhibition is especially important in understanding *sensory physiology*, and we shall return to it many times. For now, remember the following general principle: *The CNS is a contrast detector and a contrast creator. It uses surround inhibition and efference copy to create distinctions in sensation, perception, ideation, cognition, and ultimately, action.*

Experimental Research

Most of the research we have discussed up to this point was conducted on rats, mice, or "lower" organisms such as squids or frogs. The historical importance of clinical neurology (i.e.,

work done on people with neurological damage) has been noted where appropriate. Currently, people, rodents, chickens, amphibians, fish, and invertebrates are the experimental subjects of choice in neuroscience research, with the occasional bat, owl, or songbird being used as a subject for specialized areas of investigation. It becomes more difficult to read about experiments performed on the "higher" mammals, which are more "like us" and some of which we may even keep as pets.

Cats are in use for some areas of spinal cord physiology (discussed here) and for study of the visual system (Chapter 9), and monkeys are occasionally used for investigation of motor physiology in the brain (Chapter 10). When these experiments are considered, you may find that you have questions regarding the nature of laboratory animal treatment. This is a concern shared by scientists throughout the discipline, and it is discussed in Box 7–3.

SUMMARY

The spinal cord is the avenue for sensory signals from the body to reach the brain and for motor commands from the brain to affect the body. It also has behavioral capacities that arise from intrinsic spinal circuits. The cord can be divided into gray matter (cell bodies) and white matter (axons). The gray matter and white matter of the dorsal cord are generally devoted to sensory function and the gray matter and white matter of the ventral cord are generally devoted to motor functions.

The first neuron cell body for all somatosensory systems lies outside the CNS in the dorsal root ganglia. For the mechanoreceptor systems this first-order cell sends an axon into the cord, which ascends ipsilaterally and without synapse in the dorsal columns. The second-order cell body is found in the brainstem and sends an axon across the midline (decussates) to synapse in the contralateral thalamus.

The central projection of the first-order nociceptor is different in that it synapses immediately in the spinal cord segment of entry. The second-order nociceptor axon then decussates and ascends contralaterally to the brainstem.

Efferent motor pathways consist of two cell types: the upper motor neuron and the lower motor neuron. The lower motor neuron and the muscles it innervates are called the "motor unit." The motor unit is the final common pathway

for all motor commands to the body musculature. Upper motor neurons are found in two tracts, the contralaterally projecting pyramidal system and the ipsilaterally projecting extrapyramidal system. Observation of the sensory and motor deficits seen upon spinal injury and knowledge of the projection schemes of the various tracts can be used to identify the site of damage.

Intrinsic circuits in the spinal cord maintain posture without input from the brain and refine the motor commands of the brain. The monosynaptic reflex is the source of resistance to movement of the limbs; inhibition of the reflex promotes limb movement.

Each muscle contains intrafusal fibers with stretch receptors (muscle spindle organs) in addition to extrafusal fibers that do the bulk of the work. Alpha motor neurons cause extrafusal muscle to constrict directly. Gamma motor neurons cause intrafusal muscle to constrict, which activates the muscle spindle organ. The ensuing monosynaptic reflex activates alpha motor neurons to stimulate extrafusal fibers. The brain uses both alpha- and gamma-activation to create voluntary movements. Efference copy and surround inhibition are mechanisms that the cord uses, in common with the rest of the CNS, to refine the nature of its output.

REVIEW QUESTIONS

1. What is the functional difference between the rostral and the caudal spinal cord?

2. What is the functional difference between the dorsal and the ventral spinal cord?

3. What is "decussation"?

4. Describe the difference between the central projection of primary nociceptors and primary mechanoreceptors.

5. Where are primary sensory cell bodies located?

6. How do upper motor neurons differ from lower motor neurons?

7. Draw a picture of the "monosynaptic reflex" and explain its function.

8. What is the difference between the alpha motor neuron and the gamma motor neuron?

THOUGHT QUESTIONS

1. What would life be like without proprioception? Without nociception?

2. Teleologically, why do we have *two* mechanisms for voluntary movement (*alpha-activation* and *gamma-activation*) when only one should suffice?

KEY CONCEPTS

actin (p. 157)
afferent (p. 146)
alpha motor neurons (p. 162)
animal rights movement (p. 165)
animal welfare movement (p. 165)
anterior (p. 147)
atrophy (p. 159)
axon collateral (p. 163)
Babinski sign (p. 162)
Brown-Séquard Syndrome (p. 156)
cauda equina (p. 147)
caudal (p. 147)
central canal (p. 149)
cervical (p. 151)
coccygeal (p. 151)
contralateral (p. 153)
cranial nerves (p. 146)
cross sections (p. 147)
decussation (p. 152)
dermatomes (p. 150)
diagnostic neurology (p. 156)

distal (p. 147)
dorsal (p. 147)
dorsal columns (p. 153)
dorsal horn (p. 147)
dorsal root ganglia (DRGs) (p. 147)
dorsal roots (p. 147)
efference copy (p. 164)
efferent (p. 146)
electric organs (p. 158)
extensor (p. 162)
extrafusal fibers (p. 161)
extrapyramidal tracts (p. 158)
fasciculation (p. 159)
fasciculus (p. 147)
fasciculus cuneatus (p. 153)
fasciculus gracilis (p. 153)
first-order neuron (p. 153)
flexor (p. 162)
gamma motor neurons (p. 162)
gray matter (p. 149)
hemiplegia (p. 156)
intermediate horn (p. 160)

intrafusal fibers (p. 161)
ipsilateral (p. 153)
lateral (p. 147)
lateral spinothalamic tract (p. 154)
lesion (p. 156)
lower motor neuron (p. 155)
lumbar (p. 151)
marginal zone (p. 154)
mechanoreceptors (p. 153)
medial (p. 147)
monosynaptic reflex (p. 161)
motor unit (p. 156)
muscle spindle organ (p. 161)
myosin (p. 157)
neuroanatomy (p. 146)
nociceptors (p. 154)
panacea (p. 156)
paralysis (p. 159)
pathway (p. 149)
plantar reflex (p. 162)
posterior (p. 147)
proprioceptors (p. 153)
proximal (p. 147)

pyramidal tracts (p. 158)
Renshaw cell (p. 163)
rostral (p. 147)
sacral (p. 151)
sagittal sections (p. 147)
sarcoplasmic reticulum (p. 157)
second-order neuron (p. 153)
shingles (p. 150)
spasticity (p. 159)
spinal nerves (p. 146)
spinal rigidity (p. 162)
stretch receptor (p. 161)
surround inhibition (p. 166)
third-order neuron (p. 153)
thoracic (p. 151)
tract (p. 147)
transverse (p. 147)
T-tubules (p. 157)
upper motor neuron (p. 155)
ventral (p. 147)
ventral horn (p. 147)
ventral roots (p. 147)
white matter (p. 147)

8

Functional Anatomy of the Brain

The study of anatomy has many features in common with learning a foreign language. At first there is a lot of rote memorization, in order to acquire vocabulary and learn the rules of grammar. Then there is the need for *practice*, as there sometimes seems to be little logic to the names of central structures, or foreign terms as it may be. Rehearsal is the only way to keep them straight.

The names sometimes seem illogical because early anatomists would use references to classical Greek or Latin literature to describe what they saw, or choose a name based on some fanciful resemblance to other objects. Protuberances on the surface of some brain region might be called the Mounds of Venus or the mammillary bodies, for example, reflecting the active imagination of the original investigators. Unfortunately, many structures were first described by two or more individuals, who gave them different names. It is not uncommon to find that both or all of the original names endure to some extent, yielding even more confusion.

Subsequent generations of medical students, frustrated by the bewildering array of neuroanatomical terms, formulated mnemonic devices to keep them straight. Almost invariably, these take the form of limericks or poems that are either sexist, obscene, or both, and hence are unsuitable for reproduction in a textbook.

So how are you to find your way through this confusion? In this book I will select one term for brain structures and use it uniformly throughout. When introduced, the term will appear in **boldface**. For those terms with widely accepted alternatives, the alternative terms will be listed also, but will appear only once and in *italic* type. When a particular term is in general use throughout the field, I will not even mention alternative descriptions.

This chapter is intended to give an *overview* of brain structures. In subsequent chapters the same structures will be *grouped by function* (visual system, pain system, language, and so forth). An understanding of both the *spatial relations* between structures and the *synaptic*, or *functional, relations* between structures is essential to an appreciation of central neuroanatomy.

Orientation

Recall that the CNS of quadripeds is organized with the brain and the spinal cord in the same plane (see Figure 7–1). Thus we can think of structures as lying on an imaginary line, called the **neuraxis**, with the caudal tip of the sacral cord at one end and the tip of the nose at the other. In bipeds such as humans, the neuraxis is bent 90° just at the point where the spinal cord leaves the brain. The conventions that apply to quadripeds are used for bipeds as well, as if the human neuraxis was straightened out into a straight line (as it is when you adopt the quadruped posture of all fours with the head pointing forward). Thus, a *cross section* of human brain is parallel to a *cross section* of human cord, the frontal lobes are more *rostral* (forward) than the parietal lobes (Figure 8–1), and the nose (not the top of the head) is once again the most rostral structure.

Gross Subdivisions of the Brain

The most caudal portion of brain, that which is contiguous with the spinal cord, is called the **brainstem** (Figure 8–2). The brainstem is relatively small in human brains and contains structures that we share with other vertebrates. The principal structures of the brainstem, proceeding caudal to rostral, are the **medulla** (*myelencephalon*), the **pons** and **cerebellum** (*metencephalon*, or together with the medulla, the *rhombencephalon*), the **tectum** and the **tegmentum** (together called the *mesencephalon*, or *midbrain*).

The forebrain, which includes the two **cerebral hemispheres**, makes up the bulk of our brains and the brains of so-called higher vertebrates. This is divided into **cortex** (the highly convoluted matter on the outside) and **subcortical structures** (buried within). At the core of the subcortical structures is the **thalamus**, which can be thought of as an extension of the brainstem. The **hypothalamus** lies ventral to the thalamus (and together with the thalamus makes up the *diencephalon*). The remainder of forebrain (*telencephalon*) is made up of the subcortical structures called the **basal ganglia** and the four major cortical subdivisions of the cortex, the **frontal lobes**, the **parietal lobes**, the **temporal lobes**, and the **occipital lobes**. These four major lobes appear in pairs, one on each side of the corpus callosum, which, as you recall, splits the brain into functional as well as structural halves. Together, these lobes make up *neocortex* (*neo* = new). There are other cortical structures somewhat different in organization that are thought to be "older" in evolution than neocortex because they appear, like brainstem structures, in most vertebrates. These I will call (as did Paul Broca), the **limbic lobes**, which include the **olfactory bulbs** and **olfactory cortex**, the **cingulate gyrus** (*gyrus* = a bulge in the cortex) and **subiculum** on the deep medial surface of each cerebral

hemisphere, as well as the **hippocampus** and the **amygdala** on each side of the brain (Figure 8–7).

Attempting to group brain regions into larger categories with terms such as telencephalon or rhombencephalon, leads to confusion, even among professionals. Concentrate on *individual brain regions*, and ignore all categories except for *brainstem* and *forebrain*. Later, we will try to group various regions by *function*.

Cranial Nerves

Embryologically, the body segments corresponding to the face and neck arise from structures that look like gill slits on a fish and are related to the gills of our ocean-dwelling ancestors. These portions of the body surface and skeletal muscle are called **brachial segments** (from the Latin word for "gill"). They are much like the somatic dermatomes we have considered so far, but they are innervated by twelve *cranial nerves* on each side, instead of spinal nerves. The cranial nerves mediate somatosensory function of the face and neck and also control the motor functions of this region. In addition, they provide the preganglionic *parasympathetic* fibers to the entire body (except for those emanating from the base of the spinal cord) and mediate the sensory input from the *visual, auditory, olfactory*, and *gustation* modalities. In short, everything not performed by the dorsal and ventral spinal nerves is done by the cranial nerves. Figure 8–3 provides an outline of the cranial nerves and their function.

It is common practice to use Roman numerals to describe the cranial nerves. The **olfactory nerve (I)** projects ipsilaterally from the olfactory bulbs in the nose to olfactory cortex in the limbic lobes and brings information regarding smells and odors into the brain. It is considered to be a very primitive structure, since simpler organisms such as sharks have a very large portion of the entire brain devoted to the olfactory bulbs and associated structures (see Box 8–2). In our brains, however, these structures are comparatively small.

The **optic nerve (II)** is also purely sensory. In most vertebrates, the optic nerve projects contralaterally to the thalamus and brainstem (thus following the general principle of *decussation*). In animals with both eyes in front (binocular organisms like owls, cats, monkeys, and people) the nerve only partially decussates, resulting in a crossing of the visual world rather than of the projections of each eye (see Figure 9–21).

Cranial nerves III, IV, and VI are grouped together since they have similar function (skipping V for the moment). These are responsible for moving the eyes in the orbit and are collectively called the *oculomotor nerves*, specifically **oculomotor nerve (III)**, **trochlear nerve (IV)**, and **abducens nerve (VI)**. The oculomotor nerve (III) is a hybrid in the sense that it has the *somatic motor* role of moving the eye up, down, and inward but also has the *parasympathetic* function of

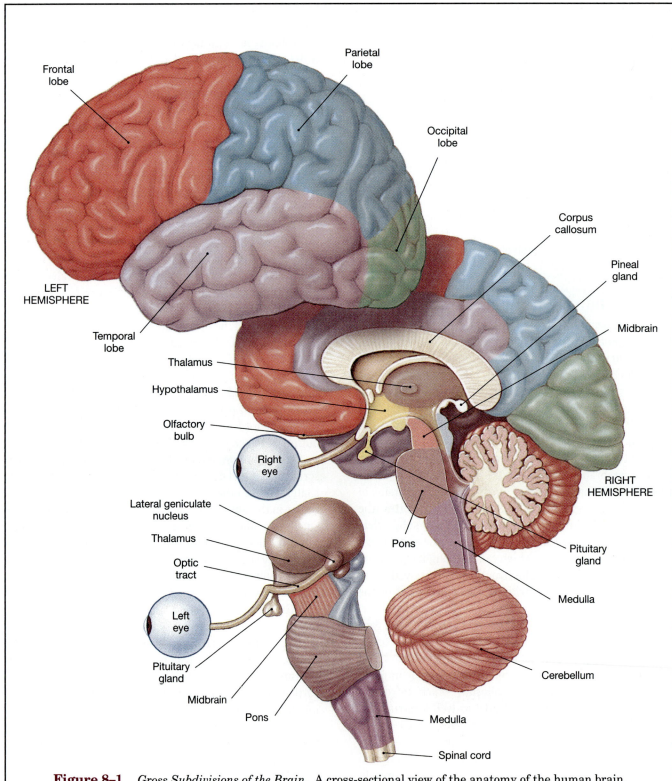

Figure 8–1 *Gross Subdivisions of the Brain.* A cross-sectional view of the anatomy of the human brain.

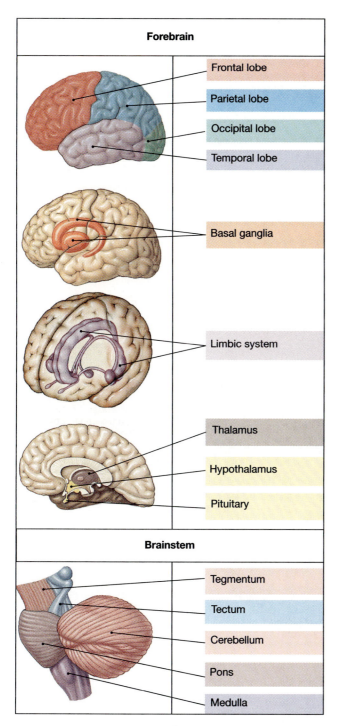

Forebrain	
	Frontal lobe
	Parietal lobe
	Occipital lobe
	Temporal lobe
	Basal ganglia
	Limbic system
	Thalamus
	Hypothalamus
	Pituitary
Brainstem	
	Tegmentum
	Tectum
	Cerebellum
	Pons
	Medulla

Figure 8–2   *Table of Brain Structures.* Each region is given a color code for use throughout the book.

constricting the pupil (recall the *sympathetic* influence is the opposite: dilation of the pupil). Each trochlear nerve projects to the *contralateral* eye (the only cranial motor projection that is contralateral) and causes it to move down and outward. The abducens nerve causes the eye to move outward as well.

The **trigeminal nerve (V)** also has mixed function. Mostly sensory, it relays *mechanoreceptor* and *nociceptor* sensation from the mouth and face to the thalamus and then on to the somatosensory cortex. Like all other somatosensory pathways, the first-order trigeminal cells lie *outside the CNS* in the **trigeminal ganglion**. The trigeminal ganglion, located just outside the medulla, is just like a large DRG for the brachial segments. Spinal nerves exit the CNS between the bony vertebrae of the spinal column. When the cartilage between the vertebrae is damaged (a "slipped disk") the nerves can get pinched, resulting in uncomfortable *neuralgias* and *parasthesias*. Such phenomena can occur for the trigeminal ganglion and nerve as well. One example is **temporal-mandibular joint (TMJ) pain**, which arises from irritation of the trigeminal nerve. In addition to its primary sensory function, the trigeminal nerve carries axons of motor neurons that supply the muscles of mastication (chewing).

Most of the motor innervation of the face comes from the **facial nerve (VII)**. The facial nerve controls muscles starting at the top of the forehead and continuing down to the neck. While spinal nerves enter and exit the CNS between bones, cranial nerves must pass through holes in the skull called **foramena**. The location and size of fossa is very indicative of individual species and is used in vertebrate paleontology and zoology to classify specimens. For humans, it happens that the fossa for the facial nerve is quite small in diameter, a fact that leads to susceptibility to peripheral nerve damage (Box 8–1).

The **acoustic nerve (VIII)** (*cochlear, vestibulocochlear*) is purely sensory, but of two different modalities. It relays afferent fibers from both the peripheral ganglia in the *cochlea*, involved in hearing, and from the *vestibular* apparatus, involved in sensing balance. Both the cochlea and the vestibular apparatus are organs of the ear. In the next chapter we shall discuss these ganglia and their central projections through the acoustic nerve in more detail.

The motor component of the **glossopharyngeal nerve (IX)** controls the muscles in the pharynx important for swallowing and vocalization. Its sensory component relays *gustation* from the posterior third of the tongue, the remainder of gustation being a sensory function of the *facial nerve*.

The **vagus nerve (X)** is already familiar as the source of "vagusstoff" (Chapter 5). Its function is purely parasympathetic (preganglionic motor and sensory) for most of the internal organs of the body.

The **accessory nerve (XI)** controls muscles of the neck and is purely motor. Also purely motor is the **hypoglossal nerve (XII)**, which innervates muscles in the tongue. A common por-

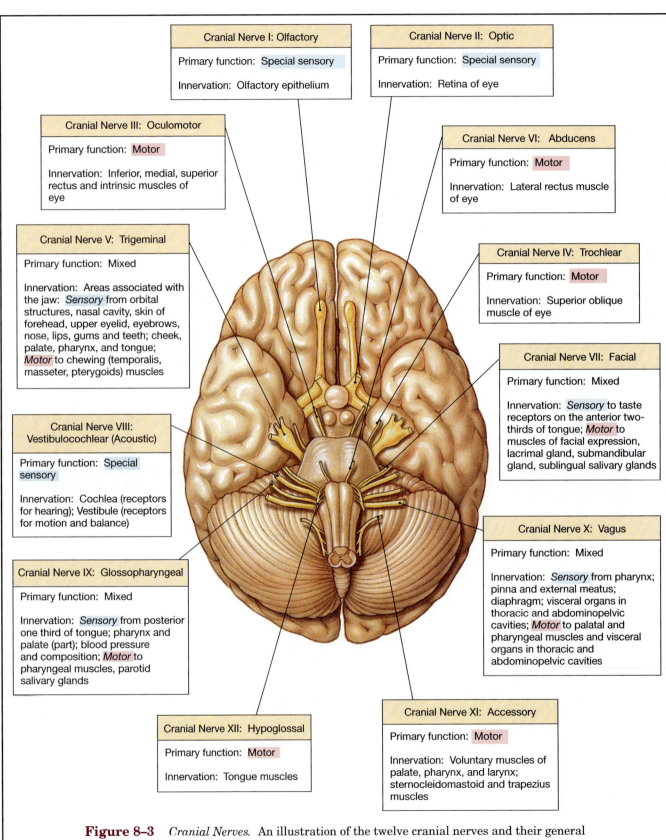

Figure 8–3 *Cranial Nerves.* An illustration of the twelve cranial nerves and their general destinations and functions.

Box 8–1

Bell's Palsy
and Carpal Tunnel Syndrome

You wake from a particularly sound and heavy sleep, gaze at your groggy image in the mirror and realize that half your face is paralyzed. Worse, it is sagging limply around the eyes and mouth, resembling the appearance of a person who has suffered from a stroke.

In distress, you head for the doctor's office. The doctor first performs a general neurological exam. Then she asks you to wrinkle the top of your forehead, noting that the scalp moves on the side of the paralysis. Then she asks you to clench your teeth, feeling the masticator muscles on the side of the deficit and determining that they are strong.

Then she tells you not to worry, you don't have a stroke. Your face will return to normal after a few weeks. She has made a diagnosis of **Bell's palsy**, a peripheral nerve lesion of the facial nerve. A stroke that affected the pyramidal system in motor cortex or the somewhat more common stroke that affects the extrapyramidal system in the basal ganglia would have affected motor function in more than one nearby motor root. The ability to move the scalp on the side of the lesion rules out involvement of the first cervical motor root and the ability to clench the teeth on the side of the lesion rules out trigeminal nerve involvement. Since the deficit is restricted to the motor field of the facial nerve, it is this nerve and not some central structure that is damaged. This is very good news since, as you will recall from Chapter 2, peripheral nerves, including cranial nerves, are supported by Schwann cells and have the capacity to regenerate after damage, but central fibers supported by oligodendrocytes do not have this capacity. Therefore, while prognosis for stroke is prolonged recovery associated with lasting deficit, prognosis for Bell's palsy is for a relatively rapid and total recovery upon peripheral nerve regeneration.

Bell's palsy, which is rather more common than you might think, is one of a number of unfortunate aspects of the human condition that is inflicted upon us by our evolutionary history. The emergence of our species was characterized by three changes in lifestyle that had profound effects on the nervous system. The organs of expression and vocalization, such as the muscles innervated by the facial nerve, became elaborate with the onset of language and complex society. The motor innervation of the hand became greater and more finely developed, especially in the pre-

hensile thumb required to grip tools. Finally, the nervous system evolved the more elaborate mechanisms for balance, posture, and gait that were required for walking upright.

As these changes in the nervous system were taking place, the skeleton was also evolving to accommodate the new lifestyle, *but the skeleton could not keep up with these rapidly changing functions*. The facial nerve increased in diameter because of the larger number of motor neuron axons needed for facial expression, but the foramena in the skull for this nerve did not expand proportionally. In consequence, the nerve is a little too large for the hole and tends to get compressed, squeezed, or even pinched from time to time. A severe case of such compression results in Bell's palsy.

Motor nerves for the hand leave through cervical roots, not cranial nerves, and hence have no foramena to squeeze through. However, there is a passageway in the wrist bone that the nerves must pass through to innervate the digits. These nerves, like the facial nerve, have increased in size over time because of all of the additional motor units required for manipulation of objects, yet the skeletal passageway has not kept pace. The consequence is **carpal tunnel syndrome**, a disorder characterized by weakness in the hand that seems to be more common with people whose jobs require repetitive movement of the hands and fingers, such as computer operators, mechanics, craftsmen, and musicians. Carpal tunnel syndrome is sometimes so severe that surgical intervention to widen the tunnel is necessary.

Only some of us will ever suffer from Bell's palsy or carpal tunnel syndrome, but many of us who live a long life will suffer from the final legacy of our evolutionary past. Walking upright freed our hands to use tools and, in a sense, permitted us to be human. However, cartilage between the spinal vertebrae and especially in the knees has yet to evolve the ability carry the full weight of the body for an entire lifetime. One way to think of it might be to consider that the knee joints can sustain half the body weight of a four-legged animal for a full life, but for two-legged animals they begin to deteriorate about halfway through. As many would testify, this deterioration of cartilage begins

tion of a neurological exam for disorders such as Bell's palsy is to examine the lateral mobility of the tongue. Paralysis of the face but ability to move the tongue is indicative that there is no central or peripheral hypoglossal nerve involvement.

The hypoglossal nerve and its central motor nuclei are essentially extensions of the ventral motor structures of the spinal cord. Note in Figure 8–3 how fine the rootlets of the accessory nerve are before they fuse into a ventral root. This is also a feature of all spinal rootlets, which tend to coalesce into a stouter nerve just at the point where they leave the CNS. This has profound consequence in the lower cranial nerves and the high cervical nerves right around the hole in the skull where the spinal cord exits (the **foramen magnum**). Here the cord experiences great *movement* as the head turns on the neck. You may do an experiment to determine the consequence of *physical distortion* on axon physiology by merely moving your head (lack of peripheral motor or sensory phenomena with this movement indicates that there isn't much).

However, when the head moves *too much* with reference to cord, the very fine sensory and motor rootlets in the region of the foramen magnum are susceptible to *tearing* and *breaking*. A colloquial name for this condition among emergency room personnel is the "motorcycle syndrome," since it is frequently seen in motorcycle accidents when the driver is wearing a helmet. Abrupt forward, backward, or lateral movement of the head upon striking the curb rips the rootlets either from the spinal cord or from the nerve, leading to partial paralysis. (Riders who don't wear helmets are generally referred to as organ donors.)

Prognosis for motorcycle syndrome is very difficult, since the damage occurs *just at the margin between the PNS and the CNS*. If the damage is peripheral, recovery of function may ensue because of Schwann cell involvement in the repair of damaged nerves; whereas if it is more central, the prospects are worse. It is very often hard to tell with either radiology or other neurological exams exactly where the lesion is. Stories of accident victims who were told they would never recover but who, with physical therapy, made "miraculous" comebacks are quite likely due to the highly ambiguous nature of damage to dorsal and ventral rootlets of the spinal cord or the hypoglossal nerve.

Brainstem

Figure 8–4 shows the nuclei that carry out cranial nerve function. At the caudal end of the medulla, motor structures

Figure 8–4   *Cranial Nerve Nuclei.* The cranial nerves as they emanate from the brainstem. (a) A dorsal view. (b) A lateral view of the brainstem. This figure shows the position of the cranial nerve nuclei, but does not distinguish between sensory and motor nerves.

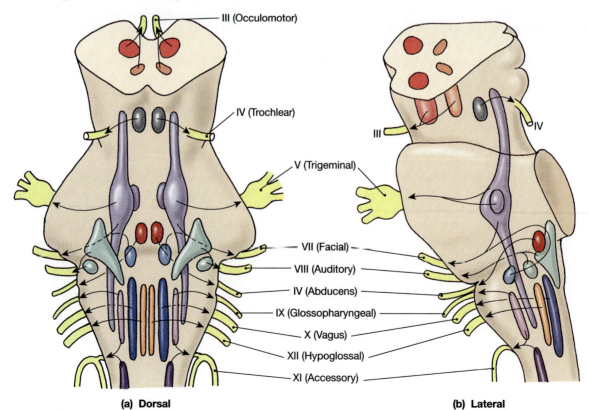

III (Occulomotor)
IV (Trochlear)
V (Trigeminal)
VII (Facial)
VIII (Auditory)
IV (Abducens)
IX (Glossopharyngeal)
X (Vagus)
XII (Hypoglossal)
XI (Accessory)
III
IV

(a) Dorsal   **(b) Lateral**

such as the accessory nerve nuclei form a continuum with the ventral horn of the spinal cord; sensory nuclei such as the sensory nucleus of the trigeminal nerve form a continuum with the dorsal horn. More rostrally, there is a *general* tendency for dorsal structures to remain sensory and ventral structures motor, but in the pons this tends to break down. The pons is really composed of two regions. The **pontine nuclei** are related to cranial nerve function and to other primitive brainstem functions. The **cerebellar peduncles** are composed of nuclei and fiber tracts in the ventral, bulb-shaped portion of the pons and arose somewhat later in evolution; as its name implies, this region is associated with the cerebellum. These two regions both project fibers into the cerebellum and are part of the extrapyramidal motor system. From its present-day appearance, it seems as though the later evolution of the pons has squished the ventral motor structures dorsally, so that the anatomical segregation of sensory and motor systems is no longer complete. For example, look at the *abducens nucleus* in Figure 8–4. Its position is dorsal, though its function is oculomotor. It appears to have *dragged the central portion of the facial nerve dorsally as it migrated*, since the facial nerve is *draped over* the abducens nucleus in the brainstem.

More rostrally, past the bulging pons and cerebellum, the functional segregation of sensory and motor structures seems to be restored. Dorsal structures of the tectum are sensory in nature, *visual* for the two rostral bumps called the **superior colliculi** and *auditory* for the two caudal bumps called the **inferior colliculi**. A Latin name for the tectum is *corpora quadrigemina*, which means "four bumps." Ventral to the tectum is the tegmentum, which contains the **substantia nigra**, an important brainstem projection to the forebrain involved in the extrapyramidal motor system (see later section).

The cranial nerve nuclei are intimately associated with one another in the small space of the brainstem, and their synaptic interactions subserve some of the fastest, most robust, and most primitive reflexes that our nervous system is capable of producing. An example is the *vestibulo-ocular reflex*, or doll's head reflex, so named for the tendency for the eyes to rotate in the orbits so as to maintain a fixed point of gaze as the head is turning. This reflex is such an important part of behavior that doll makers have exploited it to create more lifelike dolls. But a very few synapses between the vestibular projections of the *acoustic nerve* and the *oculomotor nuclei* mediate this response. As a consequence it is very robust, enduring after unconsciousness. It is one of the last brainstem reflexes to be lost during coma or deep anesthesia. Also, because the reflex is *plastic* or flexible (the *amount* of movement can be changed by glasses that change the magnification of the visual field), it is one of the best models for study of learning in simple systems (i.e., systems involving only a few synapses; see Chapter 15).

The oculomotor nuclei are also in very close contact with one another, so that the eyes in binocular organisms move *in concert* with one another. A special example of this is to be found in the regulation of pupil diameter. The parasympathetic, preganglionic portion of the central oculomotor nuclei (known to cognoscenti as the *Edinger-Westphal* nuclei) are in close excitatory synaptic relationship with one another, and with information about the visual world that is relayed from the retina to the superior colliculus. In consequence, when light illuminates the retina, the pupil of that eye *constricts*. Importantly, if the light falls on only one eye, the *pupil of the other eye* will also constrict, because of the synaptic interaction between the oculomotor nuclei on either side of the brainstem. This is called the consensual pupillary light reflex, and it is commonly checked after trauma to test the integrity of the brainstem as part of *triage*, or the initial assessment of the severity of a patient's injury and chances of survival. You can try this as an experiment in the lab if you wish. Use a penlight in a darkened room. Once your partner's eyes have adjusted to the darkness, carefully shine the penlight on one of your partner's eyes while focusing on the pupil of the other. Be careful not to use a very bright light for this; it may cause damage to the retina.

Brainstem Projections to the Forebrain

The brainstem is densely packed with all the nuclei and fiber tracts that make up the central portion of cranial nerve function and the structures of the pons and cerebellum. But don't forget the stout fiber bundles and brainstem nuclei that are devoted to sensory function from cord to brainstem (the dorsal column nuclei and the spinothalamic tract) as well as those motor tracts and nuclei for the pyramidal and extrapyramidal systems going from brain to cord (see Chapter 7). These structures interweave to some extent in the brainstem, especially in the pons where neural "traffic" is very heavy. Early anatomists noted this and gave the name **reticular system** to this portion of the brainstem (*reticulum* meaning a "netlike structure"). It was this portion of the brain that Ramón y Cajal called a "seamless warp" since the task of unraveling its synaptic relations appeared to be so daunting to him (see Chapter 3).

Yet the reticular system contains still more nuclei and fiber tracts in addition to the ones devoted to cranial nerve and spinal sensory, motor, and autonomic functions. Among these are three groups of cells that are the focus of great interest among physiological psychologists, psychopharmacologists, and biological psychiatrists. They are the **raphé nuclei**, the **locus coeruleus**, and the substantia nigra (shown for the rat brain in Figure 8–5).

Raphé Nuclei

A strand of nuclei straddle the midsagittal line of the neuraxis in the pons and medulla. Collectively they are called the *raphé nuclei* (*raphé* pronounced "raffay" and meaning "seam" or "midline").

In 1965 the Swedish scientists Dählstrom and Fuxe made use of the fact that the monoamine transmitters serotonin (5-HT), norepinephrine (NE), and dopamine (DA) react with formaldehyde to form fluorescent compounds, each with a characteristic wavelength. They used this *fluorescence histochemistry* technique to map the CNS systems that contained these compounds. The raphé nuclei and the tiny fibers they projected throughout the brain reacted positively for 5-HT; and we now recognize the raphé nuclei as the primary source for this transmitter in the brain and the spinal cord (Figure 8–5A). There are probably peptide cotransmitters in at least some of the serotonergic neurons of the raphé.

Some raphé nuclei project caudally to the spinal cord where they terminate in the gray matter of the dorsal horn. There they appear to play a role in regulating nociception, a feature we will consider in detail later on (Chapter 11). In the brain, 5-HT has been implicated in a wide variety of systems. We will have opportunity to discuss some of these when we consider sleep in Chapter 13 and psychopharmacology in Chapter 17.

The raphé terminals in brain are very diffuse, similar to the varicosities found in adrenergic nerve plexuses. Like that of NE, the action and release of 5-HT is nonsynaptic and many cells respond to the transmitter; almost every cell in cortex can be thought to have connections with raphé neurons.

Locus Coeruleus

Early anatomists found more than gray matter and white matter when they inspected fresh tissue. Looking carefully, it is possible to find a tiny blue spot on either side of the dorsal pons. They called this structure the locus coeruleus, which is Latin for "blue spot" (see Figure 8–5B). Today we know the reason for the faint bluish cast to this structure. Dopamine-β-hydroxylase (DBH, Chapter 5), which converts DA to NE, is associated with oxidized copper, which has a blue color. The locus coeruleus, which contains about 5,000 cells on each side, including a small nucleus known as the *subcoeruleus* that projects noradrenergic fibers down to the spinal cord, is the brain's primary source of NE. The adrenergic cells project to cortex and subcortical structures in such a way that it is impossible to topographically map its projections. Each cell contributes to the meshwork of the nerve plexus, and the nerve plexus envelops each cortical cell in a loose, nonsynaptic network of varicosities. Hence, as for the serotonin system, it appears that the entire cortex, in some way, receives infor-

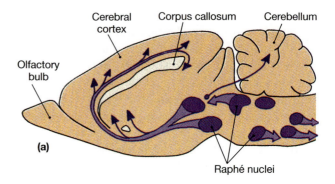

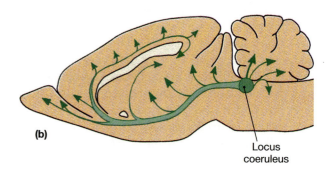

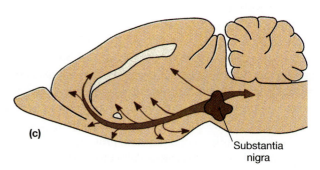

Figure 8–5 *Monoamine Projections from Brainstem.* (a) Projections of serotonin-containing neurons from the raphé nuclei throughout the rat brain. (b) Norepinephrine-containing neurons as they originate in the locus coeruleus and project throughout the rat brain. (c) Projections of dopamine-containing neurons that originate in the substantia nigra. (Cooper, Bloom & Roth, 1996)

mation from the NE-containing cells of the locus coeruleus. Even more so than for serotonin, the holistic and nonsynaptic nature of the NE projection has led to widespread curiosity about the role of the locus coeruleus in behavior. We shall have occasion to consider it again in Chapter 11 (Pleasure and Pain), Chapter 12 (Hormones, Sex, and Reproduction), Chapter 13 (Sleep and Dreaming), Chapter 15 (Development and Learning), Chapter 17 (Psychopharmacology), and Chapter 18 (The Biology of Mental Illness). As you can see from the number of cross-references for the NE projection of the locus coeruleus, it can truly be said that there is a noradren-ergic theory for everything.

Substantia Nigra

Finally, in the tegmentum of the ventral brainstem, early observers found tissue that appeared darker than sur-rounding gray matter; they called this area the substan-tia nigra, which is Latin for "black substance." This is a major source of DA for brain, but not the only one. It projects to subcortical structures such as the basal gan-glia (the *nigrostriatal* projection) where dopamine plays a major role in the organization of extrapyramidal motor behavior (see Box 5–4). Other DA projections from the tegmentum terminate in regions of the limbic system via a fiber tract known as the **medial forebrain bundle (MFB)** (also called the *mesocortical* and the *mesolimbic* projections) where it seems to play a role in reward sys-tems (Chapter 11) and the action of abused drugs (Chap-ter 17). The DA neurons, like the 5-HT and NE cells, terminate not in individual synapses but in varicosities within a nerve plexus.

Basal Ganglia

Though *ganglion* is a term normally reserved for neu-ron cell bodies in the PNS, several masses of gray matter in the center of each cerebral hemisphere have also ac-quired the name basal ganglia. The specific structures that make up the basal ganglia are the **caudate nucleus**, the **putamen** (these two together are called the *lentiform* nucleus), and the **globus pallidus**. Associated with the basal ganglia are the *amygdala* and the *pulvinar* nucle-us of the thalamus.

Seen in cross section (Figure 8–6) the basal ganglia appear as three layers of gray matter, separated by thin sheets of white matter called the *internal* and *external capsules*. Despite the appearance of separation, these three nuclei are, in fact, connected to one another be-cause they are contiguous and because the capsules are interrupted by strands of caudate, putamen, and globus pallidus. This admixture of gray and white matter give this brain region another name that is in wide use: *cor-pus striatum* (striped body).

The strands of the basal ganglia are very delicate and it happens, in humans, that the blood vessels that invest this region are also of very fine caliber. Being small, they are especially susceptible to *occlusion* (blockage) or rup-ture. An occlusion or rupture would produce a local in-terruption of blood supply known as an *infarction*, and this may lead to local tissue damage and the clinical condition known as **stroke**. Since strokes are especially common in this area of the *extrapyramidal motor system*, a typical symptom

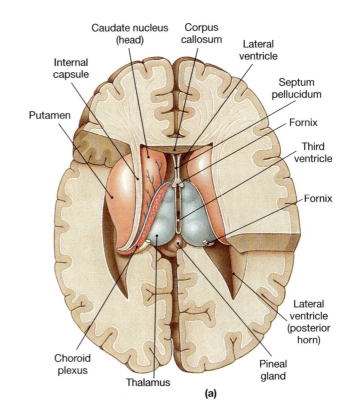

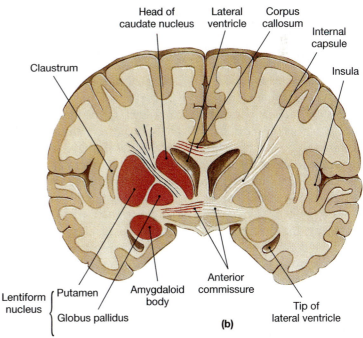

Figure 8–6 *Two Views of the Basal Ganglia.* (a) A view from the top, with cerebral hemispheres removed. (b) A cross section of the brain with the position of the basal ganglia indicated in red.

of stroke would be hemiplegia (partial paralysis on one side of the body). Since the *optic radiations* (Chapter 9) pass through this region as well, another, somewhat less common, symptom of stroke is a visual field deficit. Strokes elsewhere in the brain yield symptoms appropriate to the function of the particular brain regions. Some may seem quite exotic as a consequence of the relative rarity of vascular accidents in particular brain regions (Chapter 16).

Limbic System

Though they are all part of the forebrain, the basal ganglia, thalamus, hypothalamus, and limbic structures are similar among vertebrates in ways that the cortex is not. Like the brainstem, they may be thought to carry out primitive functions that are sometimes referred to as "old brain" behaviors. Since all living animals have had equal time to evolve, it is erroneous to think of these brain regions as "old," and anticipated similarity between the structures in our brains and those in, say, a reptilian brain can lead to mistakes regarding their role in behavior (see Box 8–2). Nevertheless, discernible function of structures in the brainstem and forebrain core appear to be *basic* in the sense of universality or near universality, at least among mammals.

An example is the **limbic system**, which is really an amalgam of structures that can be assigned to other systems as well (Figure 8–7). Early investigators discovered that damage to portions of the limbic system produced animals that were normal in at least the superficial aspects of sensory, motor, and autonomic function, but appeared to react to situations with abnormal *affect* (emotion).

As commonly perceived today, the limbic system is composed of the amygdala (also associated with the basal ganglia), the **mammillary bodies** (also part of the hypothalamus), the olfactory bulbs and **olfactory nuclei** (primary sensory structures responsible for smell), together with the **septum** and hippocampus (made up of *dentate gyrus, hippocampus*, and *fimbria*) and the **habenula**. This network of structures, some incorporated in other systems, is bound together in synaptic interaction mediated by bundles of axons in white matter tracts such as the *stria terminalis*, the *fornix*, the *stria medullaris*, and the *medial forebrain bundle*. If the complexity of the limbic system seems daunting, be consoled by the fact that professionals are also confused as to its nature. The hippocampus, in particular, is the subject of much controversy regarding potential function. However, since much of the neuroscience we shall consider involves these structures (e.g., in chapters on pleasure, pain, aggression, and sex), it is wise to gain some appreciation for their nomenclature and position in the neuraxis.

Hypothalamus and Pituitary

On the ventral surface of the forebrain is a midline cluster of nuclei and a gland that looks like a ball hanging from a pendulum (Figure 8–8). The nuclei of the hypothalamus receive

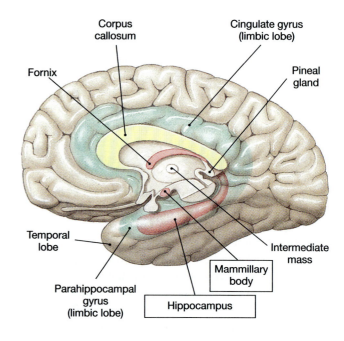

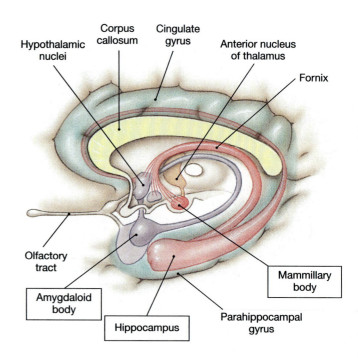

Figure 8–7 *The Limbic System.* An illustration showing the relationship of the structures of the limbic system.

diverse input from limbic and brainstem sources and send fibers down the **infundibulum** (Latin for "funnel") into the **pituitary gland**. The pituitary gland secretes peptide hormones with functions too diverse to discuss here. Some of the

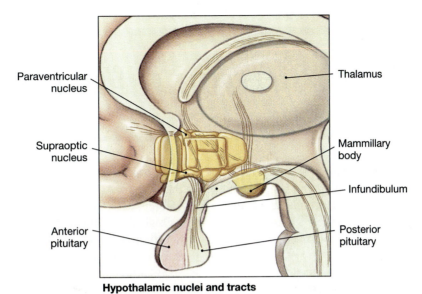

Paraventricular nucleus

Supraoptic nucleus

Anterior pituitary

Thalamus

Mammillary body

Infundibulum

Posterior pituitary

Hypothalamic nuclei and tracts

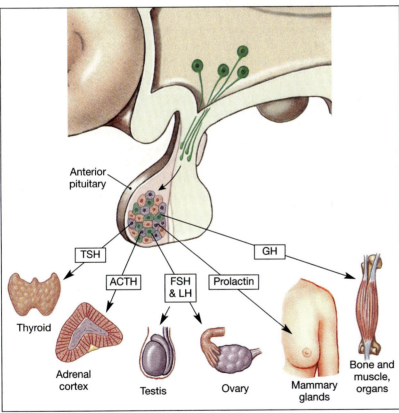

Anterior pituitary

TSH

ACTH

FSH & LH

Prolactin

GH

Thyroid

Adrenal cortex

Testis

Ovary

Mammary glands

Bone and muscle, organs

Anterior pituitary hormones

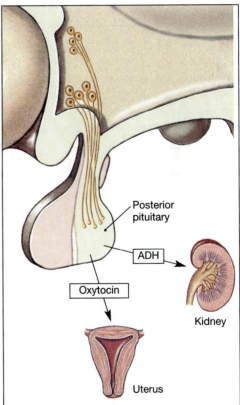

Posterior pituitary

ADH

Oxytocin

Kidney

Uterus

Posterior pituitary hormones

Figure 8–8 *Hypothalamus and Pituitary.* The anterior and posterior lobes of the pituitary in relation to the hypothalamus. Functions of these hormones will be described in Chapter 12.

peptides are released into the blood from axon tips in the **posterior lobe**. These cells have their cell bodies in the hypothalamus itself. Other peptide hormones are released into the blood by glandular cells that have a morphology different

from that of neurons. These cells in the **anterior lobe** of the pituitary are controlled by neural input from hypothalamic nuclei via the infundibular stalk. Together the hypothalamus and pituitary constitute a third (not somatic, not autonom-

Box 8–2

The "Hierarchy of Being"

In the discipline of **comparative anatomy** scientists examine the structures of related species to derive insights into evolutionary relationships and to better understand *function* by looking at the ways in which those structures have adapted to different biological demands such as lifestyle and environment.

In comparative *neuroanatomy* brain structures and features of the skull and jawbone are compared. As I have emphasized earlier, the nervous system has not changed much in the process of evolution. The major structures and principles of operation of our brains resemble those of a shark much more than our bodies resemble shark bodies (arms and legs instead of fins, lungs instead of gills, kidneys where sharks have none). As a consequence, comparative anatomists favor brain and skull resemblances as an indicator of evolutionary relations more than body plan similarities, making comparative neuroanatomy an important part of comparative anatomy.

When the neuroanatomy of vertebrates is compared, it is noted that while brainstem and subcortical structures resemble one another (for example, there are 12 cranial nerves throughout, though the locations of the fossae in the skulls vary) there is variation in the size and shape of the cerebellum and neocortex. The temptation is overwhelming to organize vertebrate brains, each with similar subcortical structures, into a linear series based on the relative size of the cerebellar and cerebral hemispheres (see Figure B8–2).

Aspects of this series are useful to an extent. The similarity of our subcortex to that of a frog suggests that its function is to enable behaviors that we *share with frogs* (orientation, locomotion, eating, drinking, breathing). By implication the elaborate human cerebral hemispheres must serve other functions. Since our common ancestry with frogs presumably occurred long ago, it is with some justification that we call the subcortical structures the **"old brain"** and the behaviors they mediate "old brain" behaviors, in contrast to the **"new brain"** structures and functions of neocortex.

One aspect of vertebrate evolution is redundancy of neural systems. As we shall see, invertebrates have only a few neurons devoted to single functions, but vertebrates (at levels higher than the motor unit) appear to have many cells with similar functions. Whether cells in the brain can have *identical* functions is a matter of some debate (see *serial vs. parallel processing* in Chapter 1), and until the debate is resolved *we are unable to assert that increased brain size necessarily means increased neural complexity*. However, the volume of the cerebral hemispheres increases along the continuum shown in the figure. Even if body weight is taken into account, the *relative* brain volume increases *somewhat* across the species in the order shown. More significant is cerebral *surface area*, which increases dramatically among mammals, becoming quite large with reference to body size among quadriped predators and primates. If you adopt the common (and probably correct) assumption that the behavioral repertoire of the animals with large brains is more complex than that of animals with small brains, you can surmise that the neural structures are also more complex. A human bias in favor of complexity over simplicity leads us to call the animals at one end of the series *higher* vertebrates and the ones at the other end *lower* vertebrates, a usage I don't particularly care for but that is universal and so it can't be ignored.

However, remember that *we* assembled the brains of different species in the order shown, not nature. Nature has no particular bias in favor of complexity, as shown by the fact that it tolerates simple organisms such as cockroaches and nematodes in greater abundance than complex ones, such as ourselves. With equal validity we could display the brains in reverse order or in some order based on some other favored feature of organization, such as smell (the olfactory lobes are much more highly developed in rats than they are in humans). Nature would have them in no order at all.

All living beings have had an equally long period of time in which to evolve. In consequence, no organism can

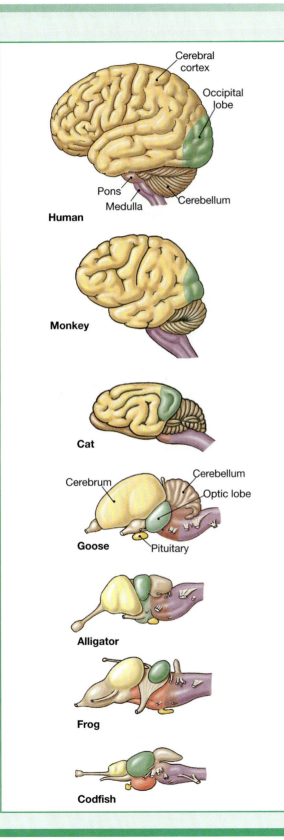

Cerebral cortex

Occipital lobe

Pons

Medulla

Cerebellum

Human

Monkey

Cat

Cerebrum

Cerebellum

Optic lobe

Goose Pituitary

Alligator

Frog

Codfish

be considered the epitome, or culmination of creation and no brain can be viewed as a superior instrument to any other. It should be said that *existence is the sole indicator of nervous system quality*, for a frog's brain is as excellent, for a frog, as ours is for us.

In fact, evolution has caused not refinement but *redistribution* of function among brain regions. Thus we may expect the old brain functions of feeding and sex, for example, to have become redistributed between cortical and subcortical regions in higher vertebrates. In all, it is wise not to make too many assumptions regarding the function of brain regions based solely on supposed evolutionary relationships. Comparative anatomy can be used as a complement, but not a guide, to the investigation of the working of the brain.

An example of the heuristic (hypothesis-generating) use of comparative neuroanatomy is to be found in consideration of the pineal gland. The structure synthesizes melatonin, an indolomine similar to serotonin in structure (see Figure 17–13.)

It seems that a common feature of midline structures is secretion of indolomines, in distinction to other transmitter systems and structures that are bilaterally symmetrical (one on each side). When the anatomy of the pineal gland is traced throughout the vertebrates, it is seen to lie more superficially in animals such as birds and reptiles that do not have large or thick neocortex.

Indeed, in some species the pineal body is so superficial that it appears on the surface of the head and appears to be light sensitive. It is possible, for example, that birds use the pineal body and its secretion, melatonin, to regulate light/dark cycles and organize migration. What does this comparative approach suggest about the functions(s) of melatonin and serotonin in humans?

Consider this question before we return to it again in Chapter 13.

ic) pathway for the brain to regulate body functions. This **endocrine** pathway plays a major role in growth and development (Chapter 15), sexual function (Chapter 12), and feeding and drinking (Chapter 14).

Thalamus

The most central structure of forebrain is the thalamus, an "old brain" region that communicates with the brainstem. Though we share the thalamus with "lower" vertebrates, the thalamus has acquired *new functions* as a consequence of the greater development of the cerebral hemispheres in humans. In a loose sense you can think of the thalamus as the location for the cortex to communicate with the brainstem, where the "new brain" meets the "old brain." In a stricter sense, we can *define* thalamic nuclei in terms of the following specific projections between brainstem and cortex (Figure 8–9).

Relay Nuclei

Some thalamic nuclei receive projections from specific brainstem systems and project in turn to discrete regions of cortex. When these can be associated with a specific *sensory modality*, they are called **relay nuclei** to indicate that infor-

mation is thought to be passed essentially unaltered through the thalamus into the cerebrum. Examples are the **lateral geniculate nuclei (LGNs)**, so-called because they resemble knees on the surface of the thalamus (*genu* being Latin for "knee"). The LGNs on each side relay visual information from the retina to visual cortex. Similarly, the **medial geniculate nuclei (MGNs)** relay auditory information from brainstem to auditory cortex, and the **ventral posterior lateral nuclei** and **ventralposterior medial nuclei (VPLs and VPMs)** relay somatosensory information into cortex. Motor commands, emitted by motor cortex, also pass through the thalamus in some cases. The **ventrolateral nuclei (VLs)** may be thought of as relay nuclei for efferent motor signals to reach extrapyramidal structures in the brainstem.

Association Nuclei

Other thalamic structures may have very specific cortical and subcortical connections, but because they cannot be assigned a simple sensory or motor modality, they are not considered relay nuclei. It is common to call them **association nuclei** to indicate that they are thought to occupy an intermediate position between sensory and motor modalities. Examples would be the

Figure 8–9 *The Relationship Between the Thalamus and the Neocortex.* (Left top) the thalamus in situ. (Left bottom) schematic diagram of the thalamus. (Right) two views of the neocortex connected to the thalamus. (Top) right medial view; (bottom) left lateral view.

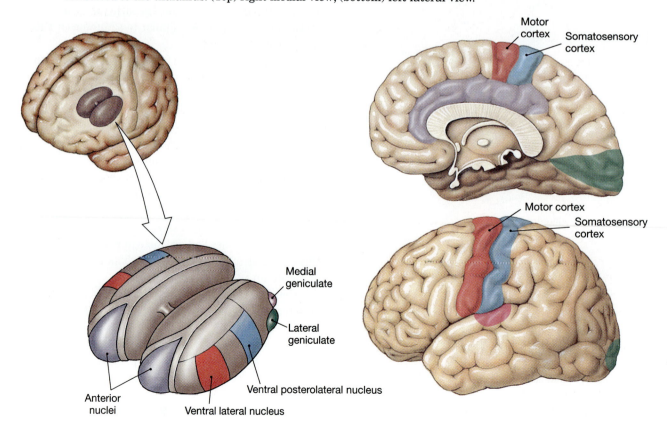

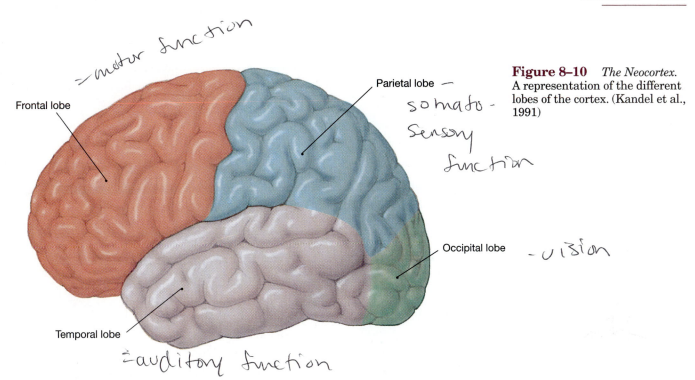

— motor function

Frontal lobe

Parietal lobe —

somato-sensory function

Figure 8–10 *The Neocortex.* A representation of the different lobes of the cortex. (Kandel et al., 1991)

Occipital lobe

— vision

Temporal lobe

= auditory function

anterior nucleus with direct connections to the cingulate gyrus in the limbic lobes, the pulvinar with connection to occipital lobes and basal ganglia, and the medial dorsal nucleus with extensive connection to the rostral frontal lobe region.

The distinction between the relay function and the association function of thalamus is a practical one based on our knowledge, or rather lack of knowledge, of brain function. Primary sensory and motor functions are close to our "nodes of simplicity" in the cord and cranial nerves, so we tend to emphasize these. However, the association nuclei undoubtedly have important relay functions as well. Exploring these relay functions and assigning particular roles to various association nuclei is an exciting avenue for future research. In addition, the relay nuclei probably have integrative functions other than mere passage of information from one place to another. Collectively the thalamic relay and association functions are among the most essential brain functions. Thalamic lesions of any size almost always lead to coma or death.

Neocortex

The bulk of the human brain consists of two heavily convoluted hemispheres, collectively called the **neocortex**. At a very coarse level of analysis, the neocortex can be divided into *lobes*. Proceeding clockwise from top left in the diagram shown in Figure 8–10 are the frontal lobes, the parietal lobes, the occipital lobes, and the temporal lobes (one of each type in each hemisphere). Each of these lobes can be thought to mediate a particular general function. For example, the frontal lobes contain cortex devoted to motor function (color-coded red in Figure 8–10). The other lobes are generally connected to sensory functions as follows: parietal for

somatosensory function, occipital for vision, and temporal for audition. However, as we shall see, only a *portion* of these lobes are genuinely restricted to these functions. The remaining cortex of each lobe is devoted to various aspects of *sensorimotor integration*.

The cerebral hemispheres are actually a mosaic of discrete units. Depending on the species, these units are 0.5 to 2.0 mm square and perhaps 1 mm deep and vary in structure and function so that they might almost be thought of as nuclei. Each of the units (or **columns**) has **intrinsic circuitry** (cells whose axons and dendrites lie wholly within the unit) and **projection fibers** that provide input (e.g., from a thalamic relay nucleus) or output (e.g., to an upper motor neuron). The columns also have discrete layers, which in vertebrate neocortex are *six* in number (Figure 8–11). Afferent projection fibers tend to terminate in layer IV and efferent projection fibers tend to originate from cell bodies in layers V and VI, though there are exceptions to this rule. Layer I consists largely of white matter and layers II and III of intrinsic circuits or **local circuit cells**.

Primary Cortex

Though all neocortex is made up of six layers, pronounced differences are found from region to region. Using stains such as the Golgi technique (Chapter 2), detailed maps of the cytoarchitecture or cellular appearance of each cortical region were assembled earlier in this century.

Now we know that the cytoarchitecture of specific regions corresponds to functional properties. Primary cortex, or cortex that receives a direct projection from thalamic relay nuclei such as the LGN, MGN, or VPL, has a pronounced, large layer IV to accommodate all the afferents. Motor cortex

Figure 8–11 *Microstructure of Neocortex.* The cortex as it divides into separate layers (I–VI) with layer I being the most superficial. Notice the difference in the thickness of each layer between the primary sensory, association, and primary motor cortex. Also notice the different types of cells that are found in each layer.

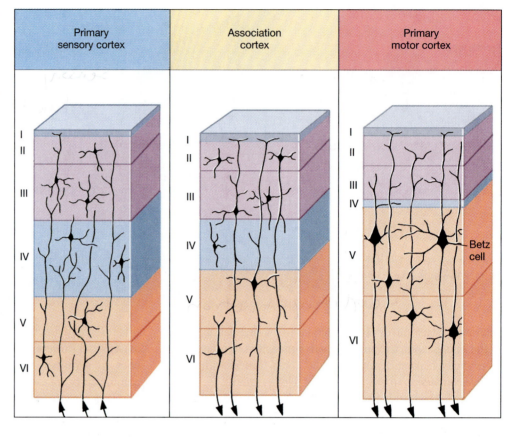

such as that containing upper motor neuron cell bodies for the pyramidal system, has a pronounced, expanded layer V and layer VI to accommodate all the motor neuron cell bodies. These can be quite large as in the case of Betz cells for the pyramidal system which are almost 0.1 mm in diameter (see Figure 8–11).

Association Cortex

Between the two extremes of motor and sensory cortex lies cortex of intermediate structure (see Figure 8–11) which tends to communicate with the association nuclei of the thalamus or, more frequently, with other cortical regions. Consistent with the nomenclature for the thalamus, we will call this intermediate cortex **association cortex**. Although the vast majority of cortex is association cortex, the primary cortex is the best understood of the cortical regions. This may be because as one progresses away from primary cortex in all brain regions, assignments of modality become less secure.

Temporal Lobes

On the side of the brain, next to the temples of the head, lie the temporal lobes of neocortex. The temporal lobes are separated from the other lobes of cortex by the **lateral sulcus** (*Sylvian sulcus*, sulcus meaning *fissure* or *cleft*) and, caudally, are contiguous with the occipital lobes (see Figure 8–1). Tucked into the sulcus, with only a bit appearing on the lateral aspect, is the primary auditory cortex, which receives projection from the MGN.

Beneath the temporal lobe, not apparent on the surface, is the **insula**, a region of cortex sometimes considered a lobe of its own.

Occipital Lobes

The caudal tip of the skull is called the *occiput* and the lobes underneath are called the occipital lobes. Larger than they appear on the lateral aspect, the occipital lobes tuck into the longitudinal fissure that separates the hemispheres. On this medial surface of the occipital lobe lies the *calcarine sulcus* around which lies the primary visual cortex with input from the LGN.

Parietal Lobes

Along the surface of the cerebral hemispheres runs the **central sulcus** (easier to see on a sheep or human brain than in rats or lower vertebrates). Caudal to the central sulcus are

Box 8–3

Frontal Lobotomy

The practice of lobotomy stems from experiments performed by Egas Moniz on mental patients in the 1930s. Moniz found that some obstreperous and intractable inmates could be rendered more manageable by ablation of portions of the frontal lobes. The technique was "perfected" by his followers, who devised the method of inserting a spatula into the frontal lobes through the orbit of the eye and mushing that portion of the brain by moving the spatula around, a procedure that was often performed in the doctor's office instead of the operating room. During the heyday of *psychosurgery* in the 1940s and 1950s, tens of thousands of helpless individuals were subjected to the operation. Only slowly did it become apparent that the surgery had no therapeutic value and was done primarily for the benefit of the hospital staff.

In retrospect the psychosurgery movement seems like an example of a particularly destructive fad. It was not grounded in animal research and hence had no controlled scientific basis. Ethical objections were swept away by the power of a new and vastly oversimplified view of frontal lobe function. While it is true that frontal lobotomy does not interrupt primary motor function, illustrating that association cortex need not have intimate relation with nearby primary cortex, the notion that the frontal lobes were the specific location of disease

and that a patient could benefit from their removal turned out to be almost wholly wishful thinking. In fact, Moniz himself was shot and paralyzed by one of his patients that had survived the surgery, ironically demonstrating that the procedure did not always render its victims more passive.

But it is not right to view psychosurgery as an isolated and curious episode in the history of science, for many others like it can be identified. Science, like all human endeavors, is subject to crowd psychology, universal error, and even mass idiocy. For his "contribution" Moniz was awarded the Nobel Prize in Medicine and Physiology in 1949. While the highest accolade of scientific research was also bestowed for some fine and enduring contributions, the prize to Moniz in 1949 illustrates that the contemporary judgment of the scientific community is no valid indicator of good science. A corollary to the observation that good science often goes unrecognized is the observation that bad science is often recognized in its place. It would be arrogant to believe that this generation or any future generation of scientists would be immune to folly, so in science (as in so many aspects of the human condition), "let the buyer beware."

---

the parietal lobes. The **postcentral gyrus** (the first ridge caudal to the central sulcus) is the primary somatosensory cortex with input from the VPL nucleus in the thalamus.

Frontal Lobes

All cortex rostral to the central sulcus is considered part of the frontal lobes. The **precentral gyrus**, immediately rostral to the the central sulcus, constitutes the primary motor cortex in which upper motor neurons for the pyramidal tract are located and where extrapyramidal efferents that project to, among other places, the VL nucleus of the thalamus and the basal ganglia arise. As with the other lobes of cortex, the frontal lobes also contain association cortex adjacent to its primary cortex that does not necessarily have a motor modality. For example, the rostral pole of the frontal lobes cannot

be assigned a purely motor function but probably plays a role in ideation and cognition. This is the region separated from the rest of the brain in the surgery known as *frontal lobotomy* or *prefrontal lobotomy* (easy to recall using Jack Nicholson's line in the film *One Flew Over the Cuckoo's Nest*, "I'd rather have a free bottle in front of me than a prefrontal lobotomy") (see Box 8–3).

The frontal lobes are also important because they seem more elaborate and proportionally larger in humans than in other primates. The evolutionary distinction does not indicate that people are more advanced than our nearest relatives in biological terms, merely that our lifestyles call for more frontal lobe functions that does that of, say, a chimpanzee, which has proportionally greater elaboration of other brain structures. Nevertheless, the large size of the human frontal

Box 8–4

Pseudoscience

One of the most powerful ideas in neuroscience, and indeed all of psychology, is the belief that differences in gross brain structure that undeniably separate species can also be used to discriminate among individuals within a species. Once Broca and his contemporaries promulgated the idea that certain functions could be localized to certain regions of cortex (Chapter 1), it became popular to imagine that *all* functions, especially personality traits, could also be localized, and that individuals with a given trait would have a *larger* cortical region devoted to that trait ("bigger is better"). A final plausible assumption was made, that bulges in cortical regions would give rise to detectable bumps on the surface of the skull, and the discipline known as **phrenology** was born.

The practice of phrenology involved feeling the heads of subjects and developing a personality profile based on the contours of the skull. Serious practitioners pursued it in academic settings, but it was also immensely popular in the nineteenth century as a parlor game or a carnival sideshow.

Phrenology has no scientific validity. It is easy to make fun of it today, but it is more instructive to consider it in its historical context. Phrenology is only one example of **pseudoscience**, in which a major valid scientific advance captures the imagination of individuals, fre-

quently scientists themselves, who then make *plausible* assumptions and extensions from these observations, which do not hold up under further scientific investigation. The important point here is that the methods of pseudoscience are all *plausible* in historical context. You need not be a fool to get caught up in them.

But real science does not proceed by plausible assumptions; each extension of the original observation

---

lobes has inspired generations of scientists to make comparisons between species (see Box 8–2) and even within species (see Box 8–4).

Other Neocortex

Not all cortex can be neatly categorized as a portion of one of the four major lobes of neocortex. Some structures in the limbic system, such as the hippocampus and the olfactory bulbs, give the appearance of cortex but have fewer than six layers. Other cortex, such as the gyri on the medial surface, has synaptic affinity with the limbic system and has been evolutionally associated with the primitive olfactory system. We will group these cortical regions, mostly association cortex, under the rubric limbic lobes.

Finally, several stout medial pathways, called **commissures**, form a type of neural bridge that permits *communi-*

cation between the hemispheres. These cannot be assigned to a particular lobe since they vary in location and all lobes take part. The largest of these covers much of the midline and is called the **corpus callosum**.

Ventricles

In the center of the brain and down through the core of the spinal cord are contiguous fluid-filled chambers called the **ventricles** and the **central canal** (Figure 8–12). There are two large ventricles on either side of the cerebral hemispheres called the *lateral ventricles* (also apparent in Figure 8–12), a smaller one in the center called the *third ventricle*, and, more caudally in the brainstem, a *fourth ventricle* that communicates with the central canal.

The fluid in the ventricles is called **cerebrospinal fluid** (**CSF**), which has a very similar composition to blood plas-

must be investigated under controlled circumstances before it is accepted scientifically. When this is done, the plausible assumptions of phrenology prove to be false. For example we shall see that personality traits are probably *not* well localized in cortex (Chapter 16).

The notion that "bigger is better" also has a choppy history when examined scientifically. Large "cranial capacities" have often been thought to correlate with high intelligence. In the nineteenth century it was common to measure skull volume of famous people after death to acquire evidence for this assumption (one of the largest measured was that of the great philosopher Immanuel Kant, but the prize winner was the skull of a hydrocephalic idiot). The practice of measuring the size of skulls in scientific manner is called **craniometry**. As it acquired greater scientific respectability, craniometry led to profound, and in some cases disastrous, social consequences. Women's skulls are smaller than men's (though not out of proportion to body weight), and this was accepted as evidence of the intellectual inferiority of the female gender. The cranial capacities of different races were compared, with measurements made to support the *assumed* superiority of Northern Europeans. (For a fascinating account of how these measurements were unconsciously biased to favor the desired conclusion, read *Mismeasure of Man* by Stephen Jay Gould).

The "bigger is better" notion has thorough foundation in comparative anatomy, where increased cranial capacity does appear to be associated with greater neural complexity in different species. Even in human origins there is evidence that a region of the left temporal lobes increased in volume at a point in the evolutionary process thought to correspond with the development of language (Chapter 16). However, the assumption that "bigger is better" as it applies to individuals of the same species has not survived the test of scientific examination. The study of cranial capacity is still part of current scientific inquiry (well-known post-mortem examinations of Einstein's and Lenin's brains, for example), and it is always possible that some careful and well-replicated observation will change what we believe to be true today. However, it seems more likely that traits such as individual personality are the product of some much more subtle physical property, such as the *pattern* of individual synaptic connections (where, as we shall see in Chapter 15, it may even be the case that, paradoxically, "less is better"). In general, *the brain is not a muscle. It is neither large in smart people, nor small in stupid people; and exercise in the form of study and thought will not cause it to expand in volume.*

ma. However, it lacks the blood cells and much of the protein found in regular blood and, therefore, appears more clear or pinkish instead of red. CSF circulates slowly through the brain and cord, ensuring a constant extracellular environment. It is manufactured in the heavily vascularized **choroid plexus**, found in the lateral ventricles, where fluid and salt is taken from the blood and converted into CSF.

Meninges and the Blood-Brain Barrier

The entire brain and cord are enveloped by membranes that, together with the skull and vertebrae, insulate the CNS from mechanical disturbance, such as a mild bump to the head (Figure 8–13). Close to the CNS is the **pia mater** (Latin for "gentle mother") and **arachnoid** (derived from the Greek word for "spider") **membranes**, which are delicate and separated by blood vessels and CSF. On the outside, beneath the bone, is a tough, leathery membrane called the **dura mater** (Latin for "tough mother").

Blood and oxygen is supplied to the brain by arteries that generally run deep within the brain tissue, while the veins, which carry blood away from the brain, generally lie more superficially. Some of the veins merge together to form much larger veins, which, because of their size, can become a source of uncontrollable bleeding (*hematoma*) if injured. The vessels are also insulated from brain tissue by an elaborate membrane called the **blood-brain barrier (BBB)**. The BBB is a *hydrophobic* barrier that passes only fat-soluble, nonpolar molecules. In addition the BBB has special pumps to take up needed polar molecules such as amino acids and glucose. As you might expect, the BBB *isolates the brain from perturbations in blood chemistry* so, with a few exceptions, the brain

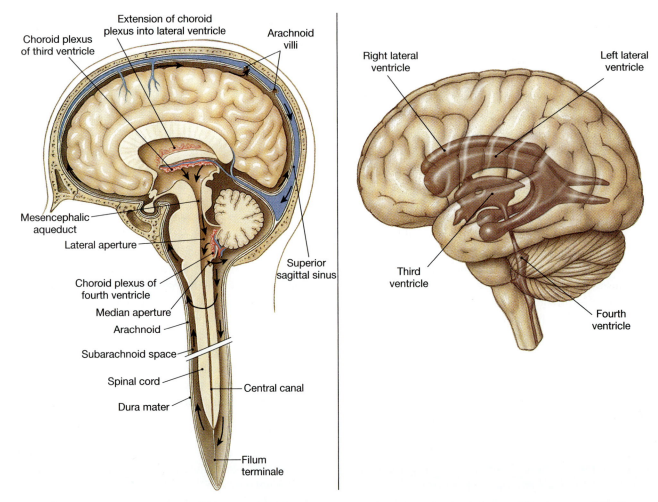

Figure 8–12 *Ventricles of the Brain.* The ventricles of the brain and the circulation of cerebrospinal fluid. CSF is formed in the choroid plexus, circulates through the third, fourth, and lateral ventricles and enters the central canal of the spinal cord.

is not affected directly by large or polar molecules, such as many hormones or drugs, that cannot pass through the BBB. In research, drugs that cannot permeate directly into the brain from the blood are injected into the ventricles experimentally (intracerebroventricular, or ICV, injections).

Tract-Tracing Techniques and Stereotaxy

How do we acquire knowledge of brain connections? Two general approaches have permitted the synaptic relations outlined in this chapter to be understood.

Much of our knowledge comes from the fact that central tissue, once damaged, does not readily repair itself. Thus a lesion that destroys a cluster of neurons also leads to degeneration of the distal structures connected to the cell bodies within the lesion, such as axons and boutons. This is known

as **orthograde degeneration**. Since cell bodies are also unable to regenerate axons, any axon destroyed within a lesion would lead to pathological changes within the connected cell bodies. This pathway of degeneration moving from the axon back to the cell body is known as **retrograde degeneration** (also called *chromatolysis* because the cell bodies of damaged cells tend to take up more of a particular stain). Separate histochemical reactions for either degenerating *cell bodies* or *axons* reveal which nuclei projected fibers in the lesioned tract and where the tract projects.

Refinements of these techniques allow the origin and destination of fiber tracts to be determined without lesions. The fact that all active cells undergo *endocytosis* and *retrograde axonal transport* (Chapter 2) can be exploited to make a retrograde label of the cell bodies that project to a particular brain region. In one major method, *horseradish peroxidase* (HRP) is injected into a specific area in some brain

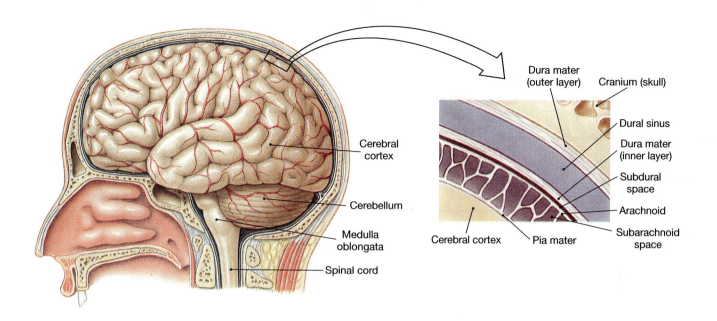

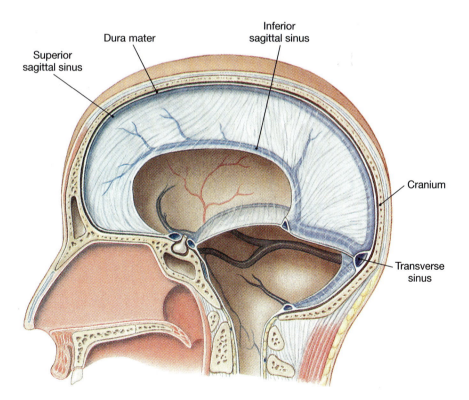

Figure 8–13 *Meninges.* The three layers of meninges and their relation to one another and to the brain.

nucleus. The enzyme (native to the horseradish but not to the brain) is then taken up by endocytosis and sent back to the cell bodies. There it is found in tissue sections by developing the HRP with special chemicals to produce a visible reaction. For example, HRP injected into primary visual cortex would be found in the LGN of the thalamus.

The opposite can be accomplished by applying amino acids to the nucleus of neurons to make an **orthograde label** of where the nucleus projects. The amino acid is made radioactive (^{3}H-proline, which is proline with one atom of the isotope *tritium* replacing a hydrogen, is often used for this purpose). Since the cell body uses the amino acid to make protein (such as a transmitter synthesis enzyme) and sends the protein down the axon to the terminal, sections of the brain can be examined for radioactivity to determine the locations of the terminals. This is done by coating the sections with a thin film of photographic emulsion and allowing the radioactive decay to develop the film (a process known as **autoradiography**). For example, amino acids injected into the MGN of the thalamus would appear as radioactive protein in the primary auditory cortex of the temporal lobe.

Projection pathways elucidated in this fashion can be explored physiologically using microelectrodes to stimulate cell bodies or axons and activate postsynaptic cells, whose responses are recorded electrically. Placement of the electrodes is done by consulting a map, or atlas, of the brain and locating the desired structures by measuring their distance, in three dimensions, from landmarks on the surface of the skull. Typically, for rats and for humans, these landmarks are located where plates of bone meet one another, also known as **sutures**. The atlas is then used to find the *anterior-posterior coordinates* (generally a page with distance from the suture noted on the bottom). Once the proper section of brain is located, the *medial-lateral* position of the desired nucleus is measured and the *depth* coordinates are determined (using the surface of the *brain*, not the skull surface, as a reference). Then, with an anesthetized and immobilized animal, electrode holders with millimeter scales are used to drop the electrodes into the right places. This process is called **stereotaxy** and is usually coupled with post-mortem examination of the brain to ensure that the measurements were right and the electrode was placed correctly.

SUMMARY

The brain consists of two major subdivisions, the brainstem and the forebrain. Moving caudal to rostral, the brainstem contains the medulla, pons and cerebellum, the tectum and the tegmentum. Contiguous with the brainstem in the forebrain are the thalamus and hypothalamus, which lie medially in the cerebral hemispheres. Around the core of the thalamus are found the subcortical structures of the basal ganglia and limbic system and cortical structures of the limbic lobes. Most superficially lie the neocortical areas, which are the temporal lobes, the occipital lobes, the parietal lobes, and the frontal lobes. Cortex can be divided based on its relationship with thalamus. Cortical areas with direct relation to relay nuclei of the thalamus are associated with primary sensory and motor modalities as follows: temporal lobes and medial geniculate nuclei, audition; occipital lobes and lateral geniculate nuclei, vision; parietal lobes and ventral-posterior lateral nuclei, somatosensation; frontal lobes and ventrolateral nuclei, extrapyramidal motor. Other cortical areas surrounding primary cortex are called association cortex, and nonrelay nuclei of thalamus are called association nuclei. Surrounding the brain and cord are membranes known as meninges, and at the center of brain and cord are cerebrospinal fluid-filled chambers called ventricles. Oxygen, glucose, and vital nutrients are allowed to pass from the blood to the cerebrospinal fluid, but otherwise the brain is insulated from changes in blood chemistry by a membranous network called the blood-brain barrier.

REVIEW QUESTIONS

1. List the cranial nerves and their functions.
2. Where are the brain's dopamine cells located?
3. Where are the brain's serotonin cells located?
4. Where are the brain's norepinephrine cells located?
5. List the relay nuclei of the thalamus, their corresponding cortical regions, and their functions.
6. List the meninges.
7. What are ventricles?
8. How do the basal ganglia differ from the limbic system? How are they similar?

THOUGHT QUESTIONS

1. What do you think our brains would look like if we had evolved to be born earlier in life, like kangaroos and opossums, so that most CNS development occurred outside the womb?

2. What function would you expect "relay nuclei" of thalamus to have for an animal, let's say a frog, that had very little neocortex?

KEY CONCEPTS

abducens nerve (VI) (p. 169)
accessory nerve (XI) (p. 171)
acoustic nerve (VIII) (p. 171)
amygdala (p. 169)
anterior lobe (of the pituitary) (p. 179)
arachnoid membranes (p. 187)
association cortex (p. 184)
association nuclei (p. 182)
autoradiography (p. 190)
basal ganglia (p. 169)
Bell's Palsy (p. 173)
blood-brain barrier (BBB) (p. 187)
brachial segments (p. 169)
brainstem (p. 169)
carpal tunnel syndrome (p. 173)
caudate nucleus (p. 177)
central canal (p. 186)
central sulcus (p. 185)
cerebellar peduncles (p. 175)
cerebellum (p. 169)
cerebral hemispheres (p. 169)
cerebrospinal fluid (CSF) (p. 186)
choroid plexus (p. 187)
cingulate gyrus (p. 169)
columns (p. 183)
commissures (p. 186)
comparative anatomy (p. 180)
corpus callosum (p. 186)

cortex (p. 169)
craniometry (p. 187)
cytoarchitecture (p. 183)
dura mater (p. 187)
endocrine (p. 179)
facial nerve (VII) (p. 171)
foramen magnum (p. 174)
forebrain (p. 169)
foramena (p. 171)
frontal lobes (p. 169)
globus pallidus (p. 177)
glossopharyngeal nerve (IX) (p. 171)
habenula (p. 178)
hippocampus (p. 169)
hypoglossal nerve (XII) (p. 171)
hypothalamus (p. 169)
inferior colliculi (p. 175)
infundibulum (p. 178)
insula (p. 184)
intrinsic circuitry (p. 183)
lateral geniculate nuclei (LGNs) (p. 182)
lateral sulcus (p. 184)
lesion (p. 188)
limbic lobes (p. 169)
limbic system (p. 178)
local circuit cells (p. 183)
locus coeruleus (p. 175)
mammillary bodies (p. 178)
medial forebrain bundle (MFB) (p. 177)

medial geniculate nuclei (MGNs) (p. 182)
medulla (p. 169)
neocortex (p. 183)
neuraxis (p. 169)
"new brain" (p. 180)
occipital lobes (p. 169)
oculomotor nerve III (p. 169)
"old brain" (p. 180)
olfactory bulbs (p. 169)
olfactory cortex (p. 169)
olfactory nerve (I) (p. 169)
olfactory nuclei (p. 178)
optic nerve (III) (p. 169)
orthograde degeneration (p. 189)
orthograde label (p. 189)
parietal lobes (p. 169)
phrenology (p. 187)
pia mater (p. 187)
pituitary gland (p. 178)
pons (p. 169)
pontine nuclei (p. 175)
postcentral gyrus (p. 185)
posterior lobe (of the pituitary) (p. 178)
precentral gyrus (p. 185)
prefrontal lobotomy (p. 185)
primary cortex (p. 183)
projection fibers (p. 183)
pseudoscience (p. 186)
putamen (p. 177)

raphé nuclei (p. 175)
relay nuclei (p. 182)
reticular system (p. 175)
retrograde degeneration (p. 188)
septum (p. 178)
stereotaxy (p. 190)
stroke (p. 177)
subcortical structures (p. 169)
subiculum (p. 169)
substantia nigra (p. 175)
superior colliculi (p. 175)
sutures (p. 190)
tectum (p. 169)
tegmentum (p. 169)
temporal lobes (p. 169)
temporal-mandibular joint (TMJ) pain (p. 171)
thalamus (p. 169)
trigeminal ganglion (p. 171)
trigeminal nerve (V) (p. 171)
trochlear nerve (IV) (p. 169)
vagus nerve (X) (p. 171)
ventral posterior lateral nuclei (VPLs) (p. 182)
ventral posterior medial nuclei (VPMs) (p. 182)
ventricles (p. 186)
ventrolateral nuclei (VLs) (p. 182)

9

Sensory Systems

The senses are theoreticians in practice.

Karl Marx

Do the senses instruct the mind or does the mind instruct the senses? Historically, resolution of this question occupied the efforts of philosophers, scientists, and poets and, in fact, gave rise to the discipline of psychology itself in the early part of the nineteenth century. Today, the question can be resolved in favor of both alternatives. The intense interest in sensation that created psychology and its progeny, neuroscience, provoked research that provides us with a better understanding of sensory processes than of any of the other CNS functions. The research tells us that consciousness and internal awareness is the sole property of sensory experience, but also that these states are *plastic*, malleable by development in childhood, by learning later in life, and even by "receptivity" or "state of mind" in daily experiences. With much truth we can say that *we see what we wish to see, hear what we wish to hear*, and, most of all, *feel what we wish to feel*. In this and the next chapter we will explore how sensation creates, and is created by, the mind.

As we develop our understanding of sensory physiology, it will become apparent that there are some general principles that apply to most forms of sensation. One such principle is that sensory systems must have a means to "filter out" stimuli that are continuously present, so as to concentrate on novel stimuli. This is known as *adaptation* and will be described more fully when we discuss somatosensory systems. Another principle is that the intensity of a stimulus is represented by action potential *frequency*, a necessity since action potentials are "all-or-none" and hence cannot vary in size for a large or a small stimulus. Third, each sensory system has subcortical and cortical structures that are devoted only to that sensory function, or *modality*. Within these structures the neural machinery is organized so as to make a *central map* of the sensory surface. Within these maps, local circuit *inhibition* creates *contrast* between adjacent responses, as we will see when we discuss vision. Finally, sensory systems are not one-way projections from the outside in. Rather, there are also *efferent* projections

that control the intensity of the percept, a feature particularly well illustrated in the auditory systems. Thus, as we review the somatosensory, auditory, and visual systems, we shall develop the evidence for each of these principles of sensory physiology. Then, they will be revisited for review in the last section of this chapter.

Somatosensory Systems

Feelings from the body come from not one, but many sensory systems. We have already discussed visceral sensation, and pain will be a topic for Chapter 11, but even the sensation of touch and bodily awareness from the skin and joints; that is, *somatic sensation*, arises from several individual afferent fiber groups and several distinct populations of sensory receptors. Pressure on the body surface, vibration of the skin, and deflection of hair on the body surface all contribute to bodily awareness, and each of these sensations arises from specialized end organs at the tip of large diameter myelinated fibers of first-order sensory cells. Cold and warmth also are properties of fiber systems devoted to these sensory modalities. There are even fiber systems that carry afferent information to the brain and cord that rarely, if ever, penetrates consciousness, raising the question of whether discharge in these systems can properly be called "sensory" at all. Elements of the proprioceptor system, for example, activate spinal reflexes that are continuously working and essential for behavior but are wholly independent of mental control or awareness (Chapter 7). Let us consider each somatosensory system (mechanoreception, proprioception and nociception) in turn, starting with the specialized end organs and then following the projections into the cord and brain to see how they combine to create the conscious and unconscious aspects of somatosensation.

Organs of Touch

Some peripheral terminals of dorsal root ganglion (DRG) cells are very simple. These naked or **free nerve endings** belong to small myelinated and unmyelinated fibers, known as nociceptors (Chapter 7), that transport information regarding noxious stimuli to the CNS. Tissue damage, such as that arising from bruises, abrasions, or burns, causes depolarization of free nerve endings of these nociceptors directly (perhaps you can think of some mechanisms; we'll review them in Chapter 11).

Sensory terminals for the other DRG neurons do not respond to stimuli directly but have associated sensory organs that change physical energy in the form of pressure, stretch, or vibration into neural energy in the form of alteration of membrane potential. This process is known as **transduction** and the sensory organs that accomplish this for the nerve endings are known as **end organs**.

The end organs vary in structure for various sensations and for various parts of the body. We have encountered one end organ, the muscle spindle organ, which is the stretch receptor for proprioception (Chapter 7). Others are *hair receptors* (for the sensation that arises from deflection of body hair) and receptors for the sensation of pressure in *glabrous* (hairless) skin as well as hairy skin.

Adaptation and Generator Potentials

Since primary sensory neurons are not followers of any other cell (i.e., they are "postsynaptic to nothing"), the nerve processes peripheral to the DRGs are not dendrites, but rather are neurites that conduct action potentials in much the same way that axons do. For an action potential to occur, transduction of physical energy (pressure, stretch, or vibration) first gives rise to depolarization at the most peripheral patch of excitable membrane. This is in a manner analogous to summation of postsynaptic potentials at the axon hillock of other cells (Figure 9–1). The depolarization at this region is called a **generator potential** (to distinguish it from true synaptic potentials, which occur when a presynaptic cell stimulates the postsynaptic cell through the synapse) and is graded in **amplitude** according to the strength of the physical stimulus. In sensory cells, this *generator potential amplitude is then converted (encoded) into action potential frequency*. A small generator potential arises from a mild stimulus (let's say pressure from one particular type of mechanoreceptor), and this small depolarization gives rise to a few action potentials at the first electrically excitable patch of membrane (the first node). An increase in pressure produces an increase in the amount of depolarization and many more action potentials are conducted up the sensory nerve end into the central nervous system. *Since action potentials cannot vary in amplitude (they are "all-or-none"), the universal code for representing intensity is increased frequency of firing.* Sensory systems use this code, as do motor systems and, very likely, association systems. Are there cells in your brain that fire a few action potentials when you see somebody you find a little attractive and fire many action potentials when you see somebody you find very attractive? As we shall see in Chapter 12, the answer is probably "yes."

Another interesting insight into somatosensory physiology can be obtained by taking another look at Figure 9–1. Generator potentials are *self-terminating*; they do not endure throughout the presence of the stimulus. In the example, pressure is applied for a period of time to the nerve ending, but depolarization is not found throughout the duration of the pressure. Rather, there is a brief generator potential at the time of application and another at the time of removal. This property of sensory systems is called **adaptation**. The importance of adaptation to internal experience can perhaps

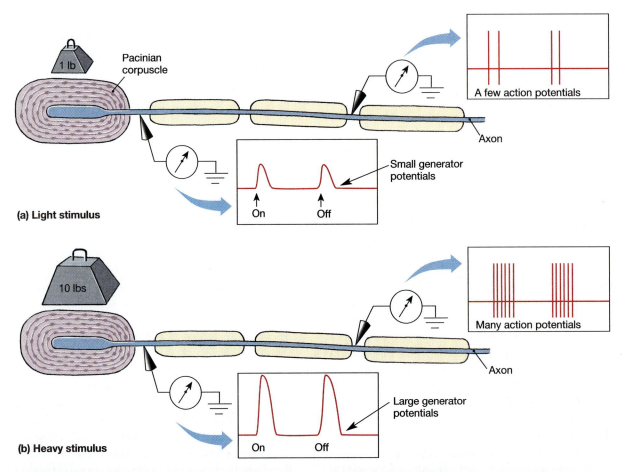

(a) Light stimulus

(b) Heavy stimulus

Figure 9–1   *Transduction in Mechanoreceptors.* (a) A mild stimulus produces a generator potential of low amplitude, which is then transduced into action potentials of a proportionate frequency. (b) A stronger stimulus will result in a higher amplitude for the generator potential and, consequently, action potentials of a higher frequency.

best be illustrated by reflecting on the fact that, until this moment, few of you are aware that you are sitting on your butts. (My apologies to those readers who are lying down or perhaps even standing up.) You became aware of pressure on your nether region when you sat down and you will be aware of it again momentarily when you stand up, but normally continuous input from mechanoreceptors does not impinge into consciousness, unless you are sitting on a very uncomfortable chair! What chaos our lives would be if it did! Constant input from every part of the body exposed to pressure would compete with unadapted input from hair cells and cutaneous receptors for central awareness. To appreciate the importance of adaptation in these systems, recall your awareness of your clothes when you put them on this morning, anticipate your awareness of them again when you take them off tonight, and be thankful that you can conduct your daily life with the quiet knowledge that you are dressed but not the continuous sensory experience informing you of that fact.

Add to the somatosensory stimulation the unadapted input from the visual, auditory, olfactory, and gustatory modalities and you can imagine what a cacophonous and intense life we would lead without adaptation. Indeed, we would be unable to attend to anything else but the unabated stimulation of all our sensory systems. Adaptation occurs at higher levels of sensory processing as well as in the first-order cells, further filtering out undesirable sensory experience. Failure of adaptation is thought to account for certain pathological conditions in infancy and adulthood, such as attention deficit disorder (see Chapter 15) and schizophrenia (see Chapter 18).

If adaptation is so powerful in determining which stimuli enter our awareness, how is it possible to overcome it, as when our attention is focused on the adapted stimulus to the seated butt? Novel stimuli can overcome adaptation. Though cutaneous receptors are continuously adapted to the presence of cloth when we wear pants, nevertheless they can respond vigorously to an unusual stimulus, such as the presence of a crawling insect. The remarkable *plasticity* of adapted somatosensory systems is still incompletely understood, but by analogy with audition (Box 9–2) and nociception (Chapter 11) we surmise that *efferent control over the percept* (i.e., descending influence on sensory systems) probably plays a role.

Adaptation is not a property of the nerve ending itself, which does indeed respond continuously to deformation if stimulated alone. Rather, adaptation is conferred on nerve endings by the specialized end organs (the **pacinian corpuscle** for the rapidly adapting deep pressure cell, as seen in Figure 9–1, and *Meissner's, Merkel's,* and *Ruffini's* corpuscles for rapidly and slowly adapting cutaneous sensations of light touch and for slowly adapting pressure sensation, respectively). The end organs themselves are not neural structures but rather elaborations of myelin or, in some cases, unusual modifications of epithelial or skin cells. In sensitive skin, like the human fingertips, there are 2,500 such end organs in each square centimeter of surface (about 1,600 rapidly adapting and about 900 slowly adapting). Each is connected to more than one afferent fiber and each fiber innervates more than one corpuscle, so that about 300 primary afferents carry information into the cord from the 2,500 corpuscles (Kandel, Schwartz, & Jessell, 1991).

Central Projections

The neurites bearing the action potentials that arise from somatosensory stimulation lead to the dorsal root ganglia, where the bifurcation of the monopolar primary sensory fiber is located. Then the action potentials enter the CNS through the axon, which terminates either in the cord or brainstem, depending on the modality and the portion of the body surface represented. The central projections of mechanoreceptors are remarkably orderly (Figure 9–2). When the projection fibers insert into the cord they add on to the *lateral* surface of the dorsal columns in order from caudal to rostral. In other words, the lumbar cord fibers from the feet form the most medial aspect of the fasciculus gracilis on that side, then fibers from shins add on laterally, then fibers from thighs add on laterally, and so forth all the way to the brainstem where fibers from the head and face (Quick—which cranial nerve innervates the face?) are added on laterally until an entire map of the ipsilateral half of the body is found. A synapse is made and then the little half-figure "stands up" and crosses the midline to innervate the contralateral VPL. From there, after a synapse, the half-figure is found draped across the postcentral gyrus of the parietal lobe.

This half-figure is known as the primary sensory **homunculus** (literally "little man") in the brains of both men and women (Box 9–1). Though not as commonly illustrated, there are several *other* cortical sensory homunculi in prima-

ry and nearby association cortex (at least a total of five in humans). Together, these homunculi are the central structures responsible for the sensation from the body surface that comes from each of the submodalities of mechanoreceptor (i.e., slowly and rapidly adapting receptors) and for *refinements* of this sensation at progressively higher levels of abstraction and cognition. For example, a brain lesion (such as from a stroke or trauma) to the area of the primary cortex corresponding to the right big toe might produce lack of conscious awareness of stimuli presented to this toe. Meanwhile the *reflexive* aspects of sensation are left intact since these are mediated by the spinal cord and brainstem. However, lesions to homunculi in *association* sensory cortex in the parietal lobe may produce more exotic symptoms such as apparent intact sensation *but denial that the limb or portion of the body belongs to the self* (see "Unilateral Neglect" Box 16–4).

Proprioceptors and Their Projections

Some proprioceptors terminate in the cord and participate in circuits that are purely spinal (recall the "monosynaptic reflex" from Chapter 7). Others project rostrally to the brain, primarily to brainstem structures. The cerebellum in particular is a major destination for these afferents. Each proprioceptor has specialized end organs (the muscle spindle organ is one we have already considered). The proprioceptors differ, however, from the mechanoreceptors in that adaptation and conscious awareness of proprioceptive input are not always displayed.

What do you think life would be like without this ever-present but largely subconscious sensory process? Maintenance of posture and locomotion would be difficult, to be sure. However, there seems to be an intimate association between proprioception and the sense of *possession of the body*. The weird feeling you had the last time your leg went to sleep came not so much from the numbness but from the experience that your *leg was not there*. To imagine what this might be like if felt all over the body, read "The Disembodied Lady," in *The Man Who Mistook His Wife For a Hat*, by Oliver Sacks.

Auditory System

In the consideration of the somatosensory system we analyzed how the two dimensions of the skin surface are mapped onto two dimensions in neural structures in the cord, brainstem, and cortex. In our consideration of the auditory system we shall also find maps, **tonotopic maps**, that represent the range of *frequency* of sounds that penetrate the ears. However, pitch or tone is *unidimensional*, as is the sensory surface that detects it. Thus, for each of the many relay nuclei for audition, a single dimension of sensory input is mapped onto two dimensions of neural surface, when only one would logically seem to be required. What do you think the extra di-

[handwritten margin note: homunculi - little man if damaged may not recognize arm as your own]

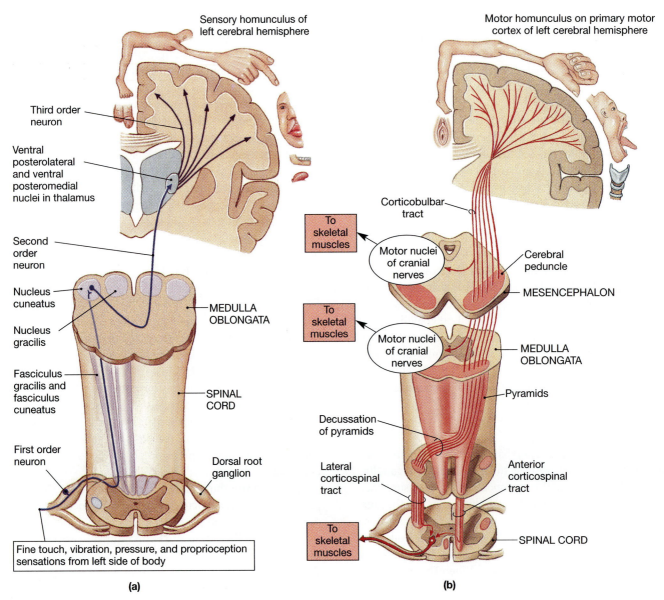

Figure 9–2 *Topographic Organization.* An illustration of how the somatotopic maps (homunculi) of both (a) sensory and (b) motor pathways are organized in the spinal cord.

mension is used for in the auditory brain? In the discussion that follows, try to guess the answer before it is provided for you. (Hint: It's not amplitude or loudness. Intensity in the auditory system is encoded by action potential frequency just as it is for the other sensory modalities.)

Organs of Hearing

The ear in mammals consists of three parts. The visible portion is primarily the **pinna**, which are flaps of skin and cartilage that focus sound waves on the sensitive portions of the middle and inner ear (Figure 9–3). The astounding variation among species in the shape of the pinna reflects the different

levels of sensitivity needed during the evolutionary process for each species. For example, the pinna for many animals is movable to permit active or directed listening for particular sounds. In humans the pinna is somewhat less malleable, but still participates in active listening, hence the phrase "to prick up the ears."

Separating the outer from the middle ear is the eardrum, or **tympanic membrane**. Vibrations in the air (really alternating waves of low and high air pressure) cause compression of the tympanic membrane, which in turn moves the first of three tiny bones of the middle ear, the **malleus** ("mallet"). The malleus hammers upon the **incus** ("anvil"), which

[Handwritten notes at top of page:]
pinna
tympanic membrane - separates outer + ~~inner~~ middle ear
malleus - incus - ~~stapes~~ stapes
oval window separates middle & inner ear   air   fluid
round window

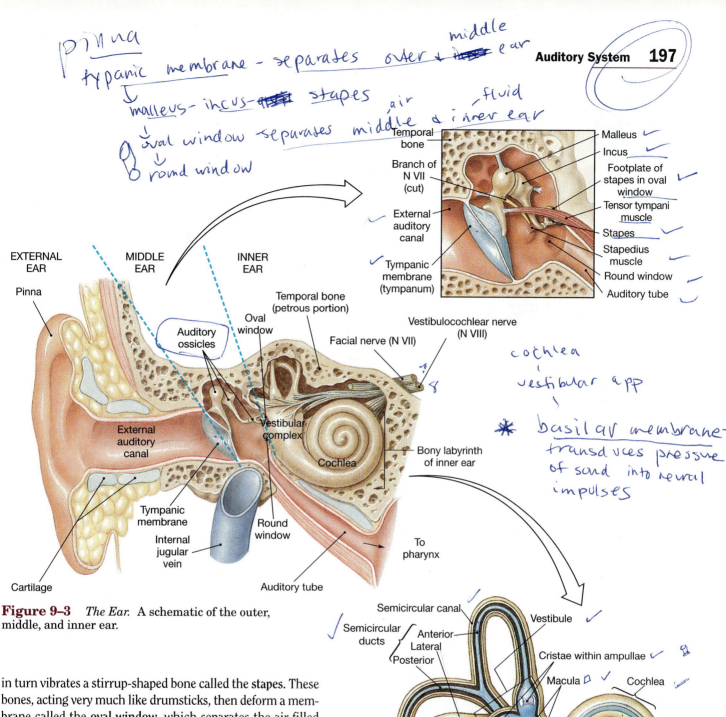

Figure 9–3   *The Ear.* A schematic of the outer, middle, and inner ear.

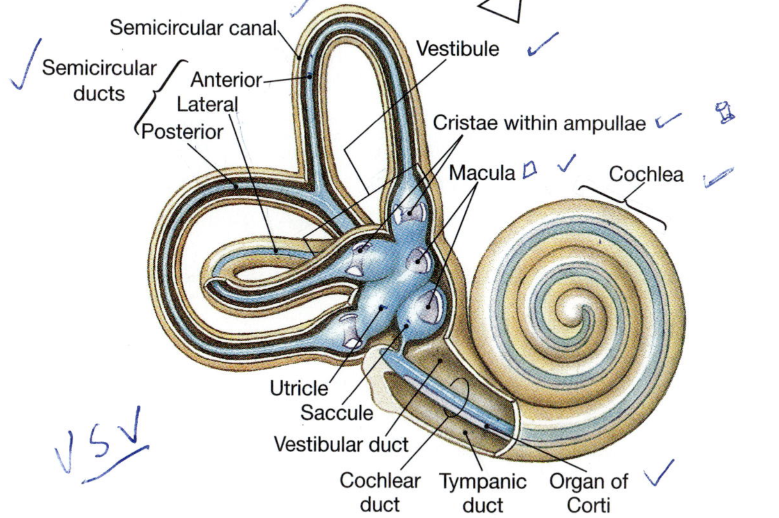

[Handwritten notes right side:]
cochlea
vestibular app
✱ basilar membrane - transduces pressure of sound into neural impulses

[Labels on main figure:]
EXTERNAL EAR — Pinna, External auditory canal, Tympanic membrane, Internal jugular vein, Cartilage
MIDDLE EAR — Auditory ossicles, Oval window
INNER EAR — Temporal bone (petrous portion), Facial nerve (N VII), Vestibular complex, Vestibulocochlear nerve (N VIII), Cochlea, Bony labyrinth of inner ear, Round window, Auditory tube, To pharynx

[Labels on inset figure:]
Temporal bone, Branch of N VII (cut), External auditory canal, Tympanic membrane (tympanum), Malleus, Incus, Footplate of stapes in oval window, Tensor tympani muscle, Stapes, Stapedius muscle, Round window, Auditory tube

[Labels on lower right figure:]
Semicircular canal, Semicircular ducts, Anterior, Lateral, Posterior, Vestibule, Cristae within ampullae, Macula, Cochlea, Utricle, Saccule, Vestibular duct, Cochlear duct, Tympanic duct, Organ of Corti

in turn vibrates a stirrup-shaped bone called the **stapes**. These bones, acting very much like drumsticks, then deform a membrane called the **oval window**, which separates the air-filled middle ear from the fluid-filled inner ear. Liquid, you will recall, is not mechanically compressible, and hence movements of the sound window are conducted with high fidelity throughout the chambers of the inner ear, yielding reciprocal deformations of a membrane at the other end, the **round window**. The inner ear is made up of the **cochlea** (Latin for "snail," since in humans it is coiled up like a snail) and the **vestibular apparatus**.

Figure 9–4 shows a cross section of the cochlea. The *scala media* is a second fluid-filled chamber in the middle of the cochlea (recall that the other two chambers, the *scala vestibuli* and *scala tympani*, are actually a single fluid-filled space). Within the scala media is a stiff, resonant structure called the **basilar membrane**, in which the actual neurons that transduce sound into neural impulses are located. The basilar

membrane actually consists of two plates with the motion-sensitive neurons between them.

The best way to appreciate how the basilar membrane transduces sound into neural impulses is to hold the palms of your hands pressed together as in prayer. Now move the fin-

Box 9–1

Homunculi

I am occasionally asked by a student (usually shortly before a major exam) if I couldn't please "sum it up"; kindly provide a general overview of the important points of, say, neuroanatomy or neurophysiology. The best short description of human neuroanatomy that I can think of is that *the brain is a collection of little half-men and half-women, together with maps of the outside world, all mashed and squished together so as to fit inside a skull that has not kept pace with the brain's growth in evolution*. I must confess that rather than evoking the calm, soft glow of understanding in my listener it more frequently produces the uncomprehending stare that suggests doubt as to my sanity.

The somatotopic map or homunculus is a neural representation of the body surface. It is superimposed on top of pictures of the corresponding neural structures of the brain based on electrical recordings of individual brain cells in response to stimuli applied to the body surface. Thus, neurons that *respond* to stimuli to the feet are adjacent to neurons that respond to stimuli applied to the lower legs. Neurons that respond to the touch of one finger are adjacent to those that respond to an adjacent finger, and so forth.

The homunculi are "topographically faithful" representations of the body surface; geometric relations are preserved. However, there are distortions in size that reflect the fact that some portions of the skin are more sensitive to touch than others and hence must have proportionally more space devoted to them. In particular, for people, the hands, face, and tongue have exaggerated neural repre-

sentation. (Which features would be exaggerated in the somatotopic map of the rabbit?) As we have learned, the somatosensory system is not just one sensory modality, but several. In addition to the various end organ types in skin, each with its own map in the CNS, there are also proprioceptive afferents; these also receive somatotopic representation in the cord and the brain, particularly in the cerebellum. There are homunculi for *motor* systems as well (shown in red in the figure), which turn up in the primary motor cortex. Finally, there are somatotopic maps, not directly sensory or motor precisely, that lie in regions of association cortex. When the sensory and motor *relay nuclei* in thalamus (VPL and VL) and the hindbrain nuclei for sensory and motor structures (e.g., the dorsal column nuclei and the *red nucleus*) are taken into account, it can be appreciated that a great deal of central gray matter is made up of these little men (for a man) and little women (for a woman). If you keep in mind that white matter (also topographically organized into homunculi) connects the maps to one another (see Figure 9–2), it is obvious that a tremendous amount of central tissue is devoted to these structures.

It has been proposed that maps of the *outside world* also exist in the brain, constructed of the modalities that project their sensibilities inward from the body surface (e.g., a *retinotopic* map for vision, a *cochleotopic* or *tonotopic* map for audition). These would also have multiple representations in thalamic and cortical neural space, occupying what neural space is not already devoted to the

gers first to one side, then the other, bending your hands in the process. You should feel a *shearing force* as your hands move against one another. This is precisely what happens when sound impinges on the cochlea. Sound causes a wave of motion (your moving fingers) that penetrates down the basilar membrane to varying degrees depending on the frequency of the sound. As the basilar membrane is deformed by the wave, shearing force between the plates (between your hands) bend the motion-sensitive vibrissae attached to the neurons located between the plates. The scientific name for the motion detectors is **stereocilia**, which bear a resemblance

to tiny hairs when viewed with the electron microscope (Figure 9–5). For this reason the primary sensory cells for audition (the neurons and their attached stereocilia) are called hair cells. When the wave shears the stereocilia in one direction, the hair cells depolarize (due to the influx of Ca++), and when the stereocilia bend in the other direction the hair cells hyperpolarize (due to the efflux of K+). *Thus, the membrane potential oscillates at precisely the frequency of the sound that comes in.*

Part of this specificity is a mechanical property of the basilar membrane. It is narrow and short next to the stapes,

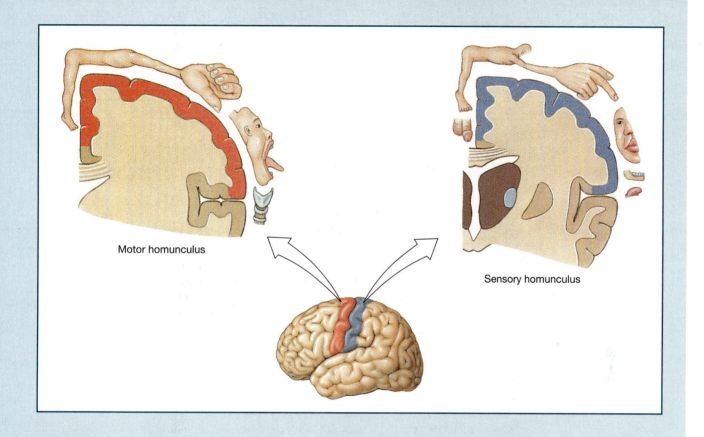

Motor homunculus

Sensory homunculus

sensory and motor homunculi. Supporters of this theory expect to find maps of all other sorts of organized experience, from familiar territory (your favorite pizza parlor) to the passage of time. The attempt to discover the locations and function of these abstract maps is a very exciting and lively area of contemporary research.

and this region vibrates preferentially to tones of high pitch (Figure 9–6). Further from the stapes the basilar membrane becomes broader and more flexible and hence responds preferentially to tones of low pitch.

Miraculously, this tuning specificity is complemented by a gradient of *electrical responsiveness*. Hair cells at the base of the basilar membrane have K^+ channels and Ca^{++} channels that oscillate at high frequencies, and the channels at the apex have oscillatory properties at low frequencies. As they oscillate, the hair cells *themselves* can deform the basilar membrane, actually *producing* sounds at their optimal frequency. These sounds that the ear actually *produces* are called "cochlear microphonics" and are the subject of intense research.

Hindbrain Projections

The hair cells lack axons and fire no action potentials. Instead the second-order cells of the auditory system, located outside the CNS in the **spiral ganglion** (see Figure 9–4), send forth a dendrite to receive the oscillating synaptic transmission from the hair cells. For the human cochlea, about 33,000 spiral ganglion cells receive input from 3,000 hair cells, so each

hair cells - auditory waves move stereocilia depolarize + hyperpolarize

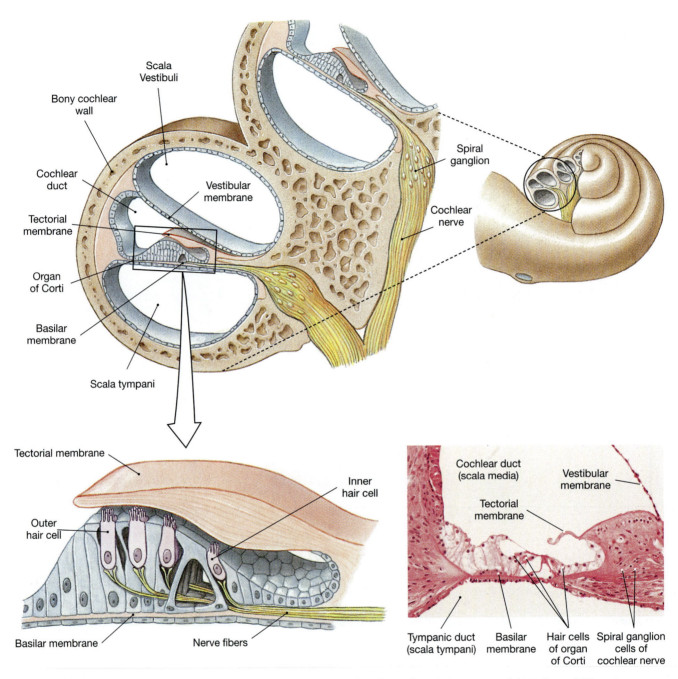

Figure 9–4 *The Cochlea.* A cross section of the cochlea shows how it is separated into three different fluid-filled chambers. Below it are two views of the basilar membrane.

hair cell drives approximately ten spiral ganglion cells. These second-order neurons have axons and fire action potentials. For low frequency spiral ganglion cells at the apex of the cochlea, the action potentials follow the depolarizing oscillations of the hair cells, similarly representing sound *frequency* as neural activity of the same frequency. However, the range of frequency responses of the human ear is from low tones of around 20 Hz (the unit "Hz" stands for "hertz"

and means "cycles per second") to very high frequencies of around 20,000 Hz. Although action potentials can keep up with stimuli at 20 Hz (20 action potentials per second), they cannot keep pace at frequencies higher than about 5,000 Hz because the refractory period will not allow action potentials to follow so quickly upon one another. At high frequencies some other strategy must be employed. It is thought that, because one hair cell may be innervated by multiple spiral

Figure 9–5 *Hair Cells.* An electron microscope image of hair cells and their attached stereocilia.

ganglion cells, high frequencies may cause the associated ganglion cells to fire at different points in the cycle of hair cell transmission and encode frequency in this fashion. Hence both the representation of the hair cell oscillation (known in audition as the *volley principle*) and the location of the spinal ganglion cell within the cochlea (known as the *place principle*) serve to confer **tuning selectivity**, the ability to detect specific frequencies, on higher-order cells in the auditory system.

Sound has two dimensions that must be translated into action potentials for effective hearing: frequency and amplitude. We would expect, given the function of the somatosensory system, that volume, or intensity (measured in dB, or **decibels**) would be encoded in action potential frequency, but action potential frequency already responds to pitch, or tone. How can action potential frequency encode both pitch and amplitude?

Here's how: Each higher-order cell has an *optimal* frequency at which it will respond to a faint tone. However, its preference is not absolute. As tones of similar frequencies are encountered, the higher-order cell will also respond, but the tone must be louder. The relation between amplitude or *loudness* (in dB) and pitch or *frequency* (in Hz) for an auditory cell is called a **tuning curve** (Figure 9–7). Every higher-order auditory cell has such a tuning curve, each one with different frequency/amplitude relations based on the cell's place in the tonotopic map.

Thus at each relay nucleus for audition (and there are *many*, not just one as for the other modalities), there is a one-dimensional map made up of progressive tuning curves ranging from low-frequency preference at one end to high-frequency preference at the other end.

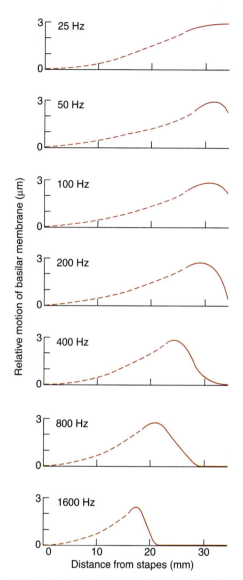

Figure 9–6 *Tuning Properties of the Basilar Membrane.* A graphic illustration of the relative motion of the basilar membrane. The peak of each graph represents the maximum amount of motion for the basilar membrane at each Hz level. Notice as the Hz increases, the distance from the stapes decreases. (Adapted from Von Békésy et al., 1960)

The second-order auditory neuron of the spiral ganglion projects through the eighth cranial nerve (acoustic nerve) to the dorsal and ventral **cochlear nucleus**, where the third-order cells are found in topographic array. From there, there is a *divergence* of projections to higher-order cells. A substantial bundle of third-order fibers crosses the midline to innervate the contralateral **superior olive** (so named because in cross section it resembles a cocktail olive. Yes, really.). The fourth-order cells of the superior olive project to higher-order cells of additional relay nuclei, the **nucleus of the lateral lemnisci**

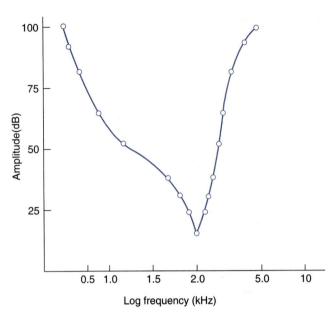

Figure 9–7 *Tuning Curve in Higher-Order Auditory Neuron.* A graph illustrating the tuning curve of a higher-order auditory neuron. This particular neuron responds optimally to a frequency of 2.0 kHz, needing only 25 dB to respond. As the frequency deviates from the optimal tone, the number of decibels must increase in order to make the cell respond.

and the **inferior colliculus**. It is impossible to specify the order of these relay auditory cells because of *convergent input from lower orders* (both third- and fourth-order cells project to the inferior colliculus, for example) and because of *substantial contralateral, or binaural, projections at each level.*

Thalamic and Cortical Projections

From the inferior colliculus, auditory fibers project to the **medial geniculate nucleus (MGN)** of the thalamus, and from there to the *primary auditory cortex* in the temporal lobe, partly obscured because it is tucked into the **lateral sulcus** (or *Sylvan sulcus*, Figure 9–8). Have you guessed the function of the second dimension of neural surface in all these auditory projections? The extensive contralateral projection in the brainstem provides a clue. At the very earliest levels of integration in the auditory system, in the superior olive, *binaural comparisons* are made of sound stimuli. Less than 50 μs (microseconds) separate the time of arrival of sound at the two ears, yet the binaural projections can detect the smallest of differences in arrival time in this range and use the difference to compute the *location of the sound source*. Auditory acuity is enhanced by having the comparisons made by *short fibers* crossing within the hindbrain rather than fibers from the hindbrain to the thalamus or to the cortex, which would

be longer and hence would take longer to conduct the information. The auditory system has, in fact, greater acuity for isolating the *time* of a stimulus than any of the other sensory modalities. Electrophysiologists are quite familiar with this feature of audition. Experimentally, electrical activity of cells is fed into an *audio monitor* (really just a stereo amplifier and speaker) in addition to the oscilloscope so that the slightest changes in activity can be detected, usually more easily by ear than by eye. Individual neurons in such experiments can be described as having a unique "voice." "Dying" neurons, such as those whose membranes have been damaged by the electrode, emit a little "scream" that diminishes in amplitude as the salt gradients on either side of the membrane dissipate and the action potentials cease.

Teleologically, we might account for the remarkable binaural acuity of the auditory system by reference to the obvious need to place accurately a faint sound *from behind*. The vertebrate ancestor that was stalked, say, by a meat-eating dinosaur would need to know which way to run without taking time to turn its head.

Efferent Projections

As shown in the previous section, sensory afferents hook up to one another in systematic fashion. However, there are also **efferent projections** from each higher-order structure back down to lower-order structures. Hence the auditory cortex sends fibers to the MGN, the MGN to the inferior colliculus, and so forth. Ultimately, efferent fibers arrive *in the cochlea itself* where they synapse upon spiral ganglion afferents and even upon hair cells themselves.

Much of what we know of these efferent projections comes from studying bats, which as you can imagine are very auditory animals. With its echolocating ability, a bat uses infinitesimal binaural differences to detect the locations of its prey based only on the sound reflection of the cry the bat emitted a short time before. Since the cry and the echo are at the same frequency and the cry is much louder than the echo, how does the bat avoid interference between the cry and the echo (i.e., how does it avoid momentarily deafening itself from the sound)? It seems that the *efferent projections* to the bat's cochlea are inhibitory and *flatten the tuning curves* at the appropriate frequency, rendering the afferents momentarily insensitive to the sound of the cry. Then, sensitivity is restored just in time to respond to the echo.

Studies on other organisms also show inhibitory sensory efferents, unlike the motor efferents which, as you will recall for the lower motor neuron, are excitatory. However, it does appear that they employ *acetylcholine* as the transmitter just as the motor efferents do. In various species the cochlear efferents appear to effect plasticity in the tuning

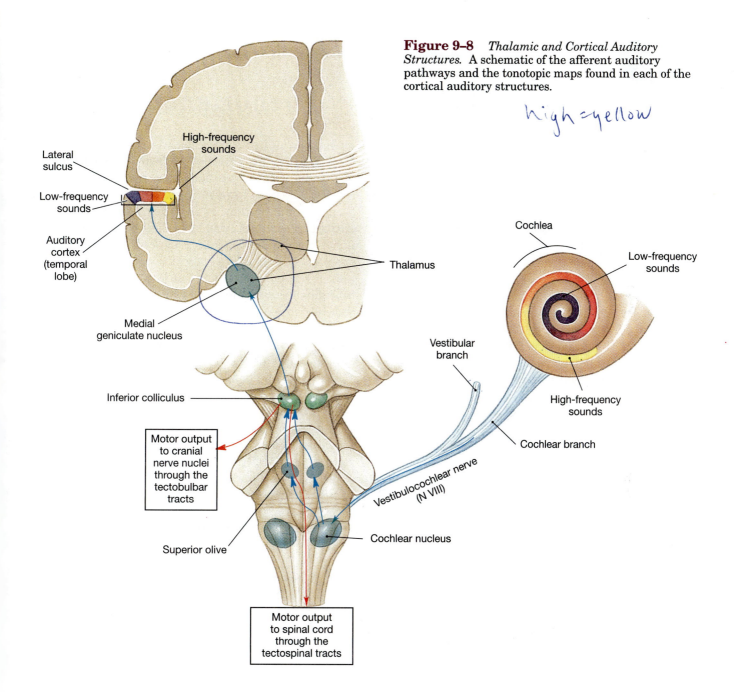

Figure 9–8 *Thalamic and Cortical Auditory Structures.* A schematic of the afferent auditory pathways and the tonotopic maps found in each of the cortical auditory structures.

high = yellow

Lateral sulcus

High-frequency sounds

Low-frequency sounds

Auditory cortex (temporal lobe)

Medial geniculate nucleus

Thalamus

Cochlea

Low-frequency sounds

Vestibular branch

High-frequency sounds

Cochlear branch

Inferior colliculus

Motor output to cranial nerve nuclei through the tectobulbar tracts

Vestibulocochlear nerve (N VIII)

Superior olive

Cochlear nucleus

Motor output to spinal cord through the tectospinal tracts

curves, in essence providing a mechanism for *active listening* for sounds of particular frequencies. Since efferent projections abound at all levels of processing of auditory information, it is thought that the central nervous system continuously filters and processes auditory input, *eliminating signals of undesirable location and frequency and enhancing those of important, or attended, source and frequency*, in each case by flattening (attenuating) or sharpening (focusing) the pertinent tuning curves. It is possible that even very high order auditory phenomena may be ex-

plained in this way (Box 9–2). Efferent projections occur in the visual system and somatosensory system too. What role do you think they play there?

Vestibular System and Its Projections

It should be plain by now that *sensation* and *awareness* are entirely different things. Many sensory afferents give rise to proprioceptive reflexes, such as the monosynaptic reflex in the spinal cord, that produce a result without a sensation entering conscious awareness. Furthermore, awareness is an

Box 9–2

"The Cocktail Party Phenomenon"

Many of us recall lectures from primary school on the important difference between merely hearing and actively listening and can now marvel at the insight into physiology possessed by our elementary school teachers. Mrs. Jones was well aware of the importance of *efferent control over the percept* in the auditory system. Listening is indeed an active process, and one that is mediated by efferent, cholinergic projections very much like those of the motor system.

There are many layers of processing of auditory information in the brainstem and cortex, and at each level, including the very first level among the hair cells, there are efferent projections that create active listening. At the cochlear and hindbrain levels this active listening appears to take the form of selective enhancement and/or suppression of particular frequencies or tones. At higher levels the active listening processes suggested by the efferent projections undoubtedly modify perception of sound in more abstract ways.

Perhaps you have had the experience of suddenly hearing your name mentioned in a conversation across a room crowded with people. Suddenly, your attention focuses on the voice that said your name. The other voices in the room, including that of the person who is speaking to you at the time, are suppressed so that you may pursue the natural human tendency to find out what people are saying about you. Everyone has experienced this very well-known phenomenon at one time or another. In psychophysics it is in fact called "the Cocktail Party Phenomenon" because it is so common on that occasion. Little scientific evidence exists that directly links the Cocktail Party Phenomenon with efferent projections in the auditory system, primarily because the neural mechanisms involved in the comprehension of speech are themselves so poorly understood. However the existence of efferent projections to higher auditory centers provides an excellent theoretical mechanism to explain the phenomenon.

Efferent projections abound in high order processing of other sensory modalities as well. If, with great truth, it can be said that we "hear what we wish to hear," with much truth it can also be said that we "see what we wish to see" and "feel what we wish to feel," statements limited in their application only by our failure to understand the function of efferent projections elsewhere to the degree we understand them in the auditory system.

active process in which the brain selects, by means of adaptation and efferent projections, which subset of afferent, sensory signals to attend to (recall the cocktail party phenomenon). Here in our consideration of the **vestibular system** we find yet more evidence for the distinction between sensation and awareness, because the senses of balance and of angular movements of the head are often wholly subconscious. Indeed, it might be said that they enter consciousness most acutely when they are missing or abnormal, as in the experience of dizziness or the disorienting feeling experienced on rides at an amusement park. Like familiar sights on the way to work, the vestibular senses are part of everyday subconscious experience and generally are made conspicuous only by their absence or by unexpected changes.

Consider for a moment what information the brain must receive to construct a stable image of the body in relation to the outside world. First, there must be a sense of *position* with regard to some external referent. Most animals use gravity, or the earth, as that referent. Then, the brain must acquire continuing sense of motion in regards to the outside world. The static sense of position with regard to gravity is provided by two sensory structures in each inner ear, the **utricle** and the **saccule** (Figures 9–3 and 9–9). Within each chamber is a sensory surface comprised of hair cells much like the primary sensory cells of the cochlea. Like the primary sensory cells of the cochlea, those of the utricle and saccule lack axons and fire no action potentials. Rather, their "hairs" (*stereocilia* and *kinocilia*) extend into a gelatinous matrix made denser than surrounding tissue by the presence of calcium carbonate crystals (**otoliths**). When you bend your head to one side or the other, this matrix sags as a consequence of its weight and bends the hairs of the hair cells (Figure 9–10).

The generator potential that ensues in hair cells is somewhat unusual for primary sensory cells. The extracellular fluid on one side of the cells has unusual salt composition (high in K^+ and low in Na^+). This sets up extraordinary Nernst relations across the hair cell membrane and enables the hair cells to respond with a generator potential to deflection of the hairs

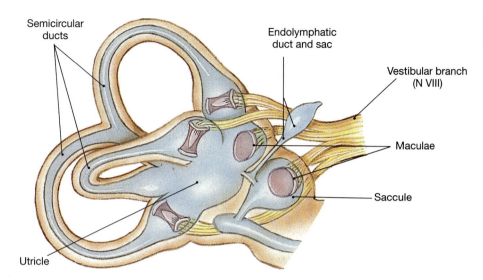

Semicircular ducts

Endolymphatic duct and sac

Vestibular branch (N VIII)

Maculae

Saccule

Utricle

in either direction. *Movement in one direction along the hair cell axis yields depolarization, and movement in the other cause hyperpolarization.* This is transduced into more or fewer action potentials, respectively, in the second-order cells

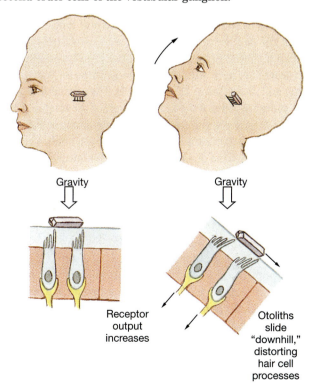

Figure 9–10 *Mechanics of Vestibular Hair Cells.* Any movement of the head results in a bending of the stereocilia and kinocilia of the vestibular organ. The hyperpolarization or depolarization that ensues in these cells (depending on the direction) is transduced into action potentials by the second-order cells of the vestibular ganglion.

Gravity

Gravity

Receptor output increases

Otoliths slide "downhill," distorting hair cell processes

of the vestibular ganglion. Across the surface of the utricle the axis of the hair cells changes in an orderly fashion so that static head position *of any angle* can be represented neurally by maximal depolarization of specifically oriented hair cells of one ear and hyperpolarization of the complementary cells of the other ear. Thus, sense of head position with respect to gravity comes from *bilateral integration* of the input from the two vestibular organs. For this reason damage to *only one* vestibular organ can be profoundly disorienting, since the input from the undamaged side is not balanced (literally) by the other side. This can be demonstrated experimentally by cooling or heating one vestibular organ by irrigating one ear with cold or hot water, altering the sensitivity of one vestibular organ versus the other and producing a momentary shift in the perception of which way is up. You are not advised to try this without expert assistance, however.

The dynamic sense of movement of the head is provided by the **semicircular canals** on either side of the head. These are three fluid-filled tubes on each side oriented approximately in the three axes of importance. Here movement of the fluid through the ducts causes deflection of hair cells at a sensory surface called the **ampulla** in a manner analogous to the mechanics of hair cells in the saccule and utricle. Bilateral comparisons in the vestibular nuclei of the brainstem then provide a representation of the angular position of the head. The organs responsible for static sense, the utricle and the saccule, obviously also experience changes with head movement and contribute to dynamic sensation as well.

Olfaction and Gustation

Taste and smell are very closely related sensory modalities. Like proprioception and somatosensation, they are not commonly separated in everyday experience. Odors, especially strong ones, can be experienced as tastes, and the taste of food

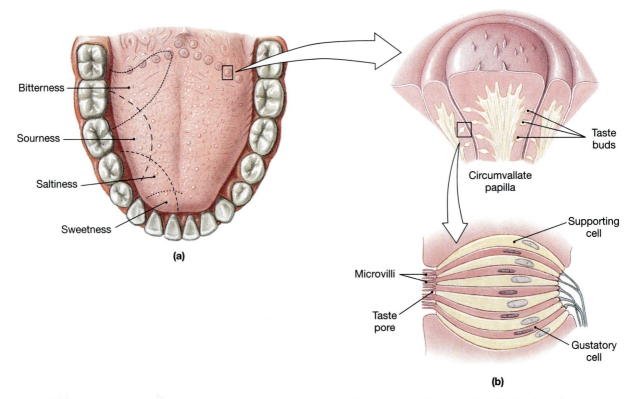

Figure 9–11 *The Tongue and Gustation.* (a) A map of the tongue showing the relative locations sensitive to each of the four basic tastes. (b) A cross-sectional view of an individual taste bud.

or drink often has an olfactory component. Thus, lack of smell, or **anosmia**, diminishes the savory quality of food, an experience that you probably had the last time you had a head cold. Even with a cold, however, there is not complete anosmia, hence few of us can appreciate what gustatory experience would be like in the complete absence of olfaction. The sensory surfaces for taste and smell are so different from the other sensory surfaces, being comprised of **chemoreceptors**, or cells that respond to chemical stimuli, that it was long thought that the neural organization of taste and smell would differ dramatically from that of the other sensory modalities. Indeed, as we shall see in the sections that follow, there are features unique to olfaction and gustation. However, the lessons of the most recent research on the chemical senses seem to indicate that smell and taste display the same properties and obey the same laws of organization as the other senses.

Organs of Taste

The first-order cells for taste in the **taste buds** lie in between bulges on the tongue, in the throat, and in part of the esophagus. These bulges are called **papillae**. Like some other primary sensory cells, taste buds lack axons and fire no action potentials. Rather, they produce generator potentials in response to specific chemical stimuli. It is unclear how many

of the thousands of possible taste experiences are mediated by specific receptors. It seems that to a certain degree taste is assembled from *combinations* of taste bud types. In other words, the number of specific receptors is considerably smaller than the range of tastable substances. Four types of specific receptors have been studied extensively, those for *bitter, sour, salty*, and *sweet* flavors (Figure 9–11). The perception of bitter flavors arises from the rearmost part of the tongue. These taste buds have receptor proteins in the membrane that bind the bitter substances much like a receptor binds a neurotransmitter. Instead of directly opening or shutting channels, the activated receptor produces a generator potential by second messenger means, possibly involving inositol triphosphate mechanisms (Chapter 5). Sweet flavors are perceived by the anterior or tip of the tongue. These receptors also act by second messenger means, possibly employing cAMP to produce the generator potential.

Apprehension of sour or salty stimuli seems to employ mechanisms unique to gustation. Sour, or acid, flavors come from liquid with high H^+ content (hydrogen cation, actually just a proton). These ions pass through ion channels (for protons) and affect membrane potential directly. Salty flavor arises from salty liquid, often salty because it contains the same salts that make up the extracellular environment of cells, Na^+,

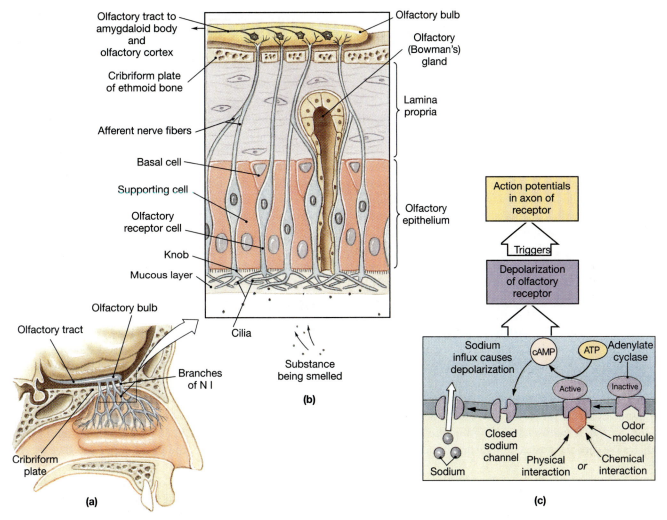

Figure 9–12 *Organs of Smell.* (a) The olfactory epithelium, located at the apex of the nasal passage, passes through the cribriform plate to converge and synapse with the second-order neurons in the olfactory bulb. (b) A close up of a primary olfactory bipolar cell responsible for detecting odorants. (c) Second messengers transduce olfactory signals.

K^+, and Ca^{++}. These salts also pass directly through ion channels, in essence altering the Nernst batteries to produce generator potentials. Cells that respond to sour stimuli lie in the middle of the tongue, as do cells that respond to salty stimuli.

Organs of Smell

Primary olfactory cells are neurons called bipolar cells because in addition to their sensory surfaces, which are embedded in the mucus-covered *olfactory epithelium*, they have axons that extend into the brain throughout apertures in the base of the skull, or *cribriform plate* (Figure 9–12). First-order olfactory cells *are* capable of firing action potentials. They are unusual among vertebrate neurons (but not quite unique, see Chapter 12) in that they are produced anew by mitosis throughout life. The knoblike end of the cells in the

mucosal lining of the nose has fingerlike extensions or *cilia* that are rich in transmembrane receptor proteins for specific odorants. Again, it is not clear whether each of the wide range of possible smells has a unique receptor type. Instead, it seems more probable that combinations of a smaller set of specific receptors form the complex chemical response to most odors. The receptor proteins have in some cases been isolated and characterized. They appear to be homologous to transduction proteins in other sensory systems (e.g., the retina) and are homologous to the family of G-protein-binding receptors for neurotransmission. This second-messenger association allows for great neural amplification of very faint odors (a few parts per trillion of some odorants can be detected in vertebrate noses; even tinier concentrations of some *pheromones* can be detected by insects, Chapter 12). Though there is some variation in the distribution of specific receptor types across the olfactory epithelium, in general the neural representation of smell does not have the topographic organization displayed by other sensory systems.

Central Projections

Gustation.   Cranial nerves VII (facial), IX (glossopharyngeal), and X (vagus) bear gustatory signals from the taste buds into the brainstem. The fact that the vagus nerve has a parasympathetic afferent and efferent role as well (Chapter 6) indicates that aspects of taste coalesce with visceral sensations, as would be expected from a sensory modality so closely associated with food intake. This association has novel consequences for higher functions of the brain, such as those involved in forming preferences for or aversions to certain flavors. This form of learning involves associations between gustatory and visceral experiences and its mechanism is different from other forms of learning in rather striking ways (Chapter 15). Upon arrival in the brainstem the gustatory afferents terminate in the **gustatory nucleus** (*nucleus of the solitary tract*). Ultimately, taste projections from this region activate brainstem structures that mediate the reflexive, subconscious aspects of eating and drinking (swallowing, chewing, and so forth). A cortical projection to the thalamus and association parietal cortex (in a region adjacent to the tongue in the somatosensory homunculus) very likely mediates the conscious aspects of gustation such as pleasure or its opposite.

Gustation may involve much more than the sense of taste. Gustation is used by many animals, along with the sense of smell, for determination of the identity of conspecifics, territorial boundaries, and the location of fodder or prey. For example, have you ever paused to consider how a snake finds its prey after envenomating it? Most snake venom does not act so quickly that the prey, say a rodent, cannot run off some distance into a den before expiring. Prairie rattlesnakes have shown that they can identify a rodent that they have struck even apart from other rodents struck by other snakes. It seems that it is the taste of each rodent's blood that enables this sophisticated discrimination to occur (Chiszar *et al.*, 1993).

Olfaction.   Central olfactory projections go (via the olfactory nerve [I]) directly to cortical structures, bypassing the brainstem relay nuclei seen in other systems. However the cortex that receives these projections is different in structure and possibly in origin from other sensory cortex. It has *three cell layers* instead of the six of other cortical regions, and it is called **paleocortex**, as distinct from neocortex, to indicate that its structure is thought to have changed little from primitive vertebrates to advanced ones. Of course, these are misnomers to a certain degree, since all brain structures in a given organism have had an equal time in which to evolve (see Box 8–2). The projections go, with little obvious topography, from the second-order cells in the olfactory bulbs on the base of the brain to diverse destinations including the *anterior olfactory nuclei*, the *olfactory tubercle*, the *pyriform cortex* and to regions of the *limbic system* including the *central amygdaloid nucleus* and the *entorhinal area*, which project to the *hippocampus* and other structures associated with *affect* and *emotion*. This connection between olfactory and limbic structures undoubtedly helps explain the redolent, evocative, and emotional qualities of most strong smells. (Do an experiment in your class: Record how often strong odors result in a change of facial expression, in a group of unwitting subjects, in comparison to strong stimuli of other senses.) Ultimately, as for gustation, there are thalamic and neocortical olfactory projections that likely lead to the conscious perception of smell.

Vision

El Greco is the colloquial name of a great Spanish painter of the sixteenth century. His style was very distinctive, featuring vertically elongated scenes and impossibly thin and gaunt figures (Figure 9–13). In the 1970s an optometrist published an interesting paper in which he claimed insight into El Greco's unique style. Because El Greco painted before the advent of eyeglasses and since his style involved distortion in one dimension (the vertical), the paper suggested that this style came about because the painter had a distortion in the curvature of the lenses in each eye (or **astigmatism**) that made everything appear elongated. What do you think of this theory? Think about it as you read the section that follows on the subject of vision, artistic and otherwise. If you are unable to form an opinion don't worry—the issue is discussed further at the end of this chapter.

The subject of vision is one of the most fascinating and intricate subjects in neurobiology. Because visual experience is such a large part of our lives, it seems that we have accumulated a far better understanding of vision than of the other senses. A detailed understanding of vision provides a model for all other sensory systems as well as for every other brain function.

However, because research is so extensive, the study of vision is daunting to the neophyte. Invertebrate eyes, such as those of the well-studied horseshoe crab, *Limulus*, are set up much in the way you or I would probably organize them. (The significance of "design" in the visual system is a point we shall consider later). The vertebrate visual system on the other hand, is organized in a counterintuitive way. Vertebrate eyes and vertebrate visual brains, including our own, tend to have things "backward," "reversed," "inside out," and "upside down." This is true at the molecular, cellular, and systems

[handwritten notes at top: fovea cones; fovea = more loves than rods; project 2nd order cells = bipolar cells; rods = black & white; cones = color → = 3 primary colors]

Figure 9–13 *A Painting by El Greco.* Did astigmatism influence the depiction of figures in this piece? (El Greco, 1541–1614, "Vision of St. John" [Opening of Fifth Seal] ca. 1608. The Metropolitan Museum of Art, Rogers Fund, 1956. (56.48) Photograph © 1979 The Metropolitan Museum of Art.)

levels. Recollection of this theme will assist you in evaluating what is to follow.

Anatomy and Circuitry of the Retina

The anatomy of the eye is shown in Figure 9–14. Let us examine how light penetrating the retina is transduced and transmitted neurally.

It is a well-known fact that the image of the outside world is inverted and upside down on the retina. The lens of the eye inverts the image much like the lens of a slide projector inverts a slide, which must be inserted in a carousel backward and upside down in order to appear correctly on the screen. The visual cortex, the ultimate "seeing" brain, is located at the occipital pole on the back of the brain, so you can visualize the lens of the eye projecting the image *all the way through the brain* to a screen where "viewing" occurs. Of course light energy is *transduced* into neural energy in the process, so even though you may feel that way, you do not really have an image of this page imprinted on your brain.

The transduction occurs in two populations of **photoreceptors** (cells that respond to light), known as **rods** and **cones** (Figure 9–15). The rods, which respond to light of a broad range of wavelengths, are responsible for black-and-white vision. Cones, which respond to specific bands of wavelength, are responsible for color vision; there is a specific type of cone for each of the three primary colors. The visual field is organized so that the center is focused on a spot in each retina called the **fovea** (see Figure 9–15). The fovea is a place where cones far outnumber rods. Cones in the fovea project to second-order cells (called **bipolar cells**, but different from the bipolar cells used in olfaction) in such a manner that each bipolar cell receives only a few cone synapses. Rods, in contrast, *converge* onto bipolar cells, so that each bipolar cell receives many rod synapses. Since adjacent photoreceptors respond to light arising from adjacent parts of the visual world, the convergent property of rods means that they have *low spatial resolution* (or an inferior ability to distinguish details) in contrast to cones, which have *high spatial resolution*. It follows that greatest visual *acuity* is to be found in the center of the visual field, for the fovea has the most cones. Further, cones have generator potentials that arise and subside quickly, in contrast to rods, whose generator potentials subside more slowly. This means that cones also have more *temporal resolution* (as for the detection of *flicker* or *motion*) than rods. Rods and cones both have a region of elaborate membranous folds called the **outer segment** (because it lies toward the back of the retina), distinct from the **inner segment** (toward the front of the retina), which contains the nucleus and the synaptic terminal. The folds are wholly intracellular in rod cells and are called **discs** because they resemble stacked poker chips. In the cones the folds are invaginations of the plasma membrane (see Figure 9–16). The fold of the outer segment contains the photoreceptor proteins, or **photopigment**. There are more folds in rods than in cones, and more photopigment, and hence rods are more *light sensitive* than cones. In sum, rods have high light sensitivity, but low spatial and temporal resolution, and are responsible primarily for night vision and peripheral vision where black-and-white sensation prevails. (Avert your eyes from a colorful object and sense its color disappear—you're using your peripheral rods!) Cones are less sensitive to light than rods, with high spatial and temporal resolution, and are responsible for the perception of color.

In addition to synapsing with bipolar cells, rods and cones synapse with **horizontal cells** (Figure 9–16), so named because they are oriented in the same plane as the surface of the retina, perpendicular to the photoreceptors and bipolar cells in the *outer plexiform layer*. Bipolar cells synapse with **ganglion cells** in the *inner plexiform layer*. Ganglion cells are the first cells in the visual system with the ability to fire action potentials, and it is the ganglion cells that send the information about visual stimuli up the optic nerve and into the brain. In the inner plexiform layer, besides ganglion cell bodies, lie a fifth type of retinal cell, the **amacrine cells**, which

[handwritten notes in right margin: brain; a-p; ganglion cell]

[handwritten note at bottom: image seen on occipital pole → bipolar]

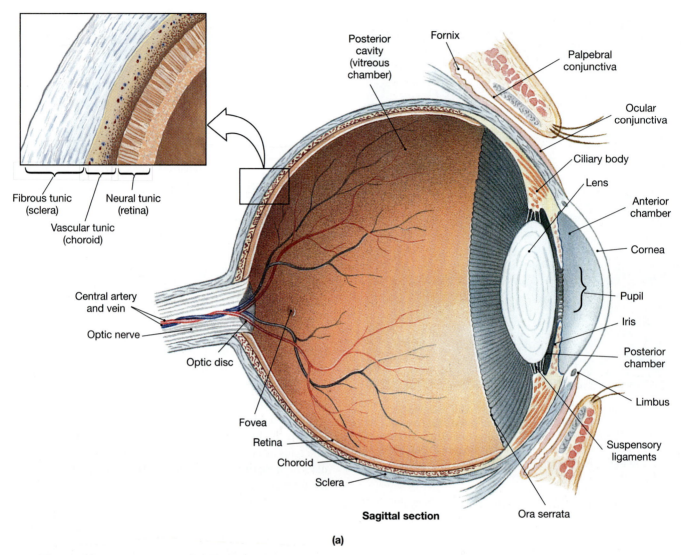

Fibrous tunic (sclera)

Vascular tunic (choroid)

Neural tunic (retina)

Posterior cavity (vitreous chamber)

Fornix

Palpebral conjunctiva

Ocular conjunctiva

Ciliary body

Lens

Anterior chamber

Cornea

Pupil

Iris

Posterior chamber

Limbus

Central artery and vein

Optic nerve

Optic disc

Fovea

Retina

Choroid

Sclera

Suspensory ligaments

Ora serrata

Sagittal section

(a)

Figure 9–14 *The Eye.* (a) A sagittal section of the eye and an enlarged look at the fovea. (b) A section of the retina showing the layers of neurons within. (c) A cross section of the optic disc. (d) A photograph of the retina as seen through the pupil.

also lie in the flat dimension of the retina, perpendicular to the rods and cones and to the bipolar cells.

Light must pass not only through the lens of the eye and its fluid-filled center (the *vitreous humor*) before it reaches the outer segments of the photoreceptors, but also all the way through the four other cell types in the inner and outer plexiform layers before it is detected by the rods and cones. In the fovea there is a dimple to reduce the light-scattering properties of all the retinal circuitry, but still it is remarkable that nature has designed vertebrate eyes in such an apparent "inside out" fashion, in which the photopigment is almost the last structure to be contacted by light in the eye.

At the back of the outer segments lies a nonreflective surface called the *pigment epithelium*. Its purpose is to absorb

light not already absorbed by discs, to synthesize the photopigments themselves, and to provide metabolic support for the photoreceptors, which are continually and rapidly shedding discs and outer segments and making new ones.

Transduction of the Light Stimulus

Did you ever wonder why your mother or father urged you to eat carrots to improve your night vision? Well you are about to discover the answer.

Embedded densely in the membrane of the discs of rods is a photopigment called **rhodopsin**. (Similar pigments exist in each of the three types of cones. Since there is only one type of rod and hence only one type of pigment to describe, the following discussion will focus on the rod system for simplicity.)

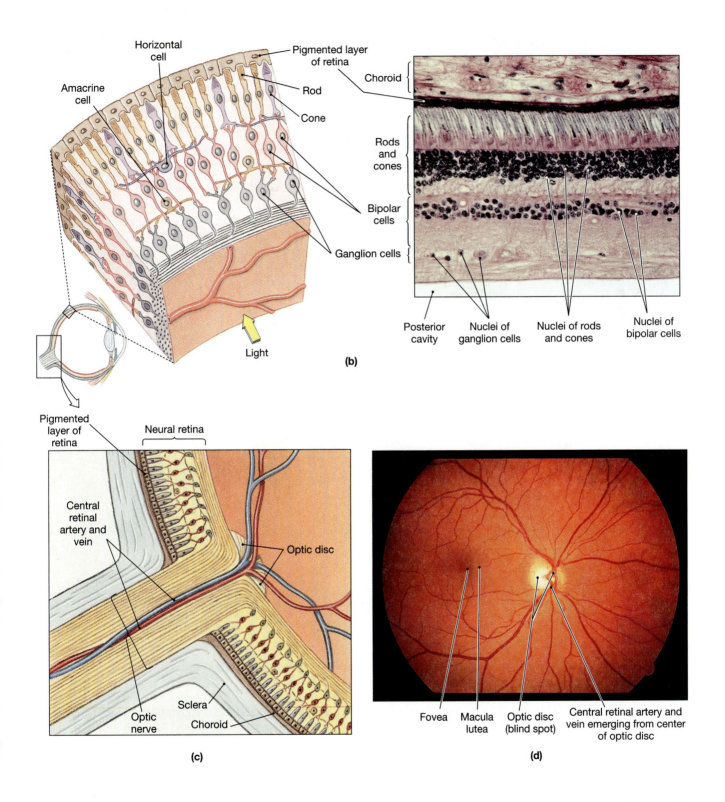

Horizontal cell

Amacrine cell

Pigmented layer of retina

Choroid

Rod

Cone

Rods and cones

Bipolar cells

Ganglion cells

Light

(b)

Posterior cavity

Nuclei of ganglion cells

Nuclei of rods and cones

Nuclei of bipolar cells

Pigmented layer of retina

Neural retina

Central retinal artery and vein

Optic disc

Sclera

Optic nerve

Choroid

(c)

Fovea   **Macula lutea**   **Optic disc (blind spot)**   **Central retinal artery and vein emerging from center of optic disc**

(d)

Rhodopsin is very much like the ligand-activated receptors associated with some receptors for transmitters linked to second-messenger systems (it is in fact structurally *homologous* to them) but is present in much greater quantity, so that the discs can be thought of as fairly well packed with rhodopsin.

Both sides of the rhodopsin molecule are wholly intracellular, since the discs themselves are wholly intracellular; thus rhodopsin differs from conventional ligand-activated receptors in which the binding site is extracellular. Furthermore, the ligand that activates the rhodopsin, **retinal**, has the prop-

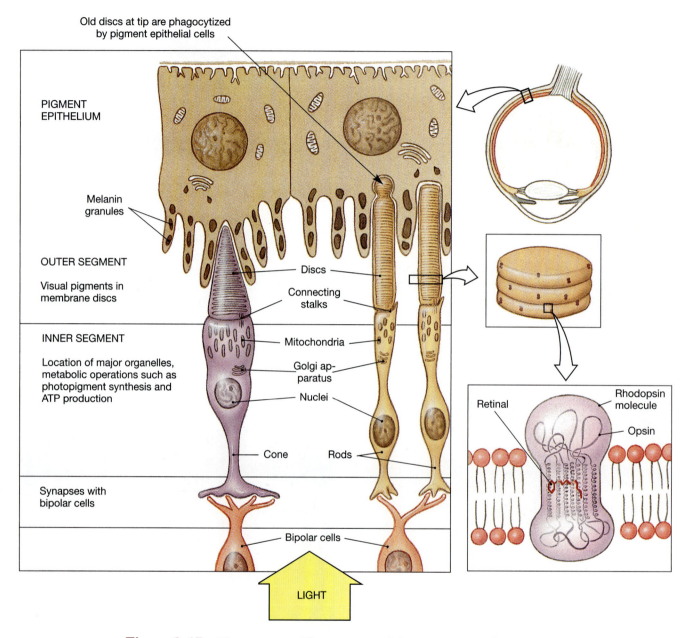

Figure 9–15   *Photoreceptors.*   The two types of photoreceptors: rods and cones.

erty of being normally bound to the receptor. In other words, the prevailing state of rhodopsin is *bound and activated*, the condition that exists in the dark. When a photon of light strikes bound retinal, its energy is absorbed by the retinal's chemical ring structure and the molecule undergoes a structural change to an unstable (thermodynamically unfavorable) state. This does not change the chemical makeup of retinal at all, merely the angle of rotation around a single carbon bond. The *cis*-isomer of retinal springs momentarily to the *trans*-isomer (*isomer* meaning "structural form") and hence the process is

called **photoisomerization** (Figure 9–17). Since the *trans*-isomer is geometrically (*stereochemically*) different, it is no longer recognized by the binding site of rhodopsin and is momentarily released. The unbound photopigment (now called merely *opsin*) enters the inactive phase, but only for about 100 msec, since the unstable *trans*-isomer snaps back to the stable *cis*-form and quickly binds opsin to make rhodopsin again. In contrast to intuition, the first step in visual transduction is the *unbinding* of a ligand to its receptor and the *inactivation* of a receptor-linked second-messenger system that

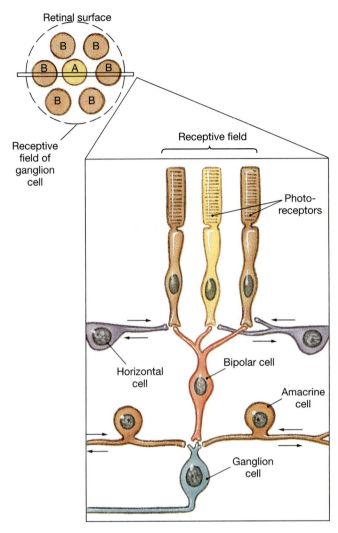

Retinal surface

Receptive field of ganglion cell

Receptive field

Photo-receptors

Horizontal cell

Bipolar cell

Amacrine cell

Ganglion cell

Figure 9–16 *Circuitry of the Retina.* The five major types of neurons, arranged in layers, found in the retina of the eye.

is active all the time in the dark. Retinal, the photopigment for rods, is structurally similar to vitamin A, from which it is derived biosynthetically. Hence your parents, who may have been ignorant of the molecular processes you have just learned, were nevertheless quite right to tell you to eat carrots, a rich source of vitamin A, to improve your night vision.

The second-messenger produced by active rhodopsin in the absence of a visual stimulus such as light is cGMP (*cyclic guanosine monophosphate*). This protein accumulates in the outer segment and acts *directly* on sodium channels in the plasma membrane of the rod cell. Sodium ion channels are present in such density that E_{Na} makes a greater contribution to V_m than in other cells. Because resting sodium conductance (g_{Na}) is high, V_m for rods is *intermediate* between E_K

and E_{Na}, in fact around –40mV. Thus rods (and, for that matter, cones) are depolarized in the absence of visual stimuli (in the dark). The light stimulus to rhodopsin causes a drop in the level of cGMP, which closes the sodium channels, causing *hyperpolarization* as E_K prevails on V_m. *Counterintuitively, for all photoreceptors in all vertebrates, the first step in visual sensation is inhibitory.* The eye, which is considered wholly within the CNS, provides a striking demonstration of the importance of inhibition in the CNS. In each step of photo-transduction in rods and cones, from *unbinding* of rhodopsin to *inactivation* of rhodopsin to *hyperpolarization* of the photoreceptor and, ultimately, release of *less* transmitter by the photoreceptor to its followers (the bipolar and horizontal cells), we see that neural signals can be as equally well expressed by inhibition as by excitation.

Surround Inhibition

Early investigators lacked the technology to record the generator potentials of rods and cones. Indeed, all the cell types of the retina (bipolar, horizontal, amacrine, and ganglion) are too small to study with conventional intracellular microelectrodes. Special whole-cell recording methods were needed to acquire the knowledge we have just presented. As the ganglion cell is the only retinal cell type that fires action potentials, it was also impossible to gain insight into their response properties with extracellular, or "single unit," recording, at least within the retina. The best available

Figure 9–17 *Photoisomerization.* A comparison of the molecular formations of the *cis*-retinal molecule and the *trans*-retinal molecule.

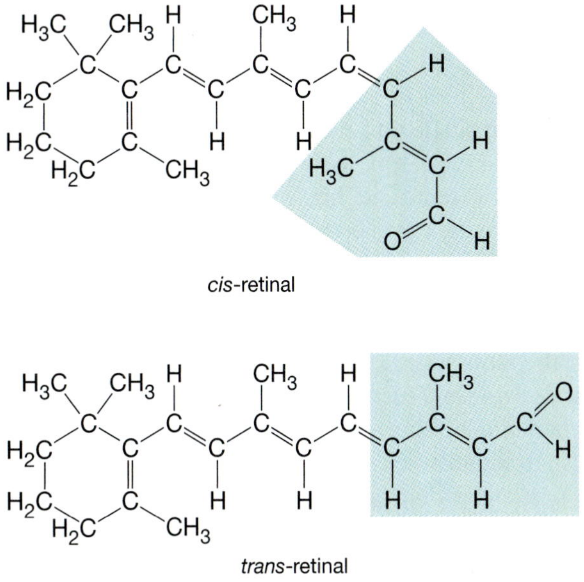

cis-retinal

trans-retinal

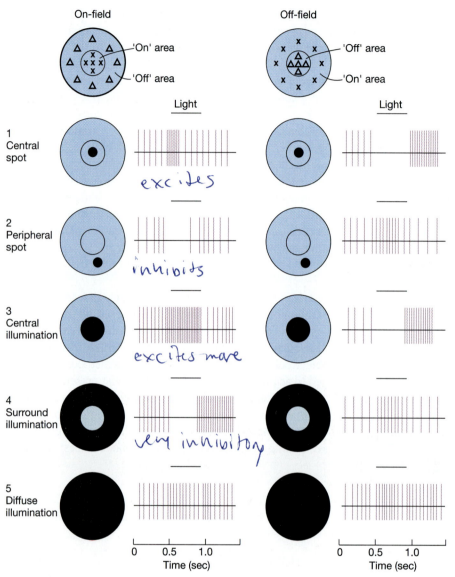

Figure 9–18 *Retinal Receptive Fields.* The receptive field characteristics of an on-center cell and an off-center cell and their respective action potential patterns. Shown are two columns of visual fields (on-center on the left and off-center on the right), each represented as a blue circle. Each column illustrates the response of a single ganglion cell (action potentials in purple) to illumination of various parts of the visual field (shown as black). The period of illumination is shown by the black horizontal line above each action potential record. (Adapted from Kuffler, 1953)

method was single unit recording of action potential activity in ganglion cell axons in the optic nerve, or from relay cells in the lateral geniculate nucleus (LGN), or in higher-order cells in occipital visual cortex.

A very surprising result was obtained from these recordings. Diffuse illumination of the retina was ineffective or at best weakly effective in eliciting action potentials. Knowing that the retina's surface was in essence a neural map of the outside world and surmising that the LGN and cortex would contain similar neural or **retinotopic maps**, the scientists began to stimulate *specific regions* of visual space by projecting light and dark images onto a screen in front of the anesthetized subject, usually a cat, since cats share with people the property of having the eyes in front of the head to acquire *binocular* information and *depth perception*. (Frogs and other

experimental subjects were also used.) It was thus discovered that, depending on the probe's position in the retinotopic map, only light stimuli in a *particular part* of the screen, corresponding to the **receptive field** in the subject, would evoke action potential activity. Even within the receptive field, response properties were complex. Diffuse illumination of the receptive field alone was also weakly effective. Rather, it was found that *each receptive field had two parts*, one part excitatory and one part inhibitory. Illumination of both parts of the field has the effect of canceling, and thus little net excitation ensued. The parts invariably consisted of a circle, or spot, surrounded by a ring, or *annulus*. In some cells the spot was excitatory and the ring inhibitory. Cells of this type were dubbed **on-cells**. These receptive field characteristics are shown in Figure 9–18. The boundaries of the receptive field are shown in conventional form as black lines against a white background. To represent light itself impinging on the receptive field, it would be proper to show white against an all-black background, but this poses problems for the illustrator since this would obscure the boundaries and all other information in the diagram. *Hence in Figure 9–18 and for subsequent figures showing receptive fields, light is represented as solid black against a blue background*, making the illustrator's life easy and, unfortunately, your life more difficult. Look at the column on the left, illustrating the receptive field of an *on-cell*. The single unit record of action potential activity is next to the receptive field pictures, with the period of the light stimulus, preceded and followed by total darkness, indicated by the bar labeled "light." A tiny dot of light in the middle of the receptive field is mildly effective in eliciting action potentials in an on-cell (#1 left), whereas a larger spot that completely occupies the center is maximally excitatory (#3 left). A tiny dot of light on the edge of the receptive field of an on-cell is mildly inhibitory (#2 left), whereas complete illumination of the ring (and not the center) is maximally inhibitory (#4 left). The opposite relations for the off-cell are shown in the column on the right. After you have carefully studied and understood Figure 9–18, go back and examine Figure 9–16. How do you think these circular receptive fields with antagonistic surrounds are constructed in the retina?

The receptive fields are not all the same size. Those for ganglion cells receiving projections from cones in the center of gaze are small, and those for ganglion cells receiving projections from rods in the periphery are larger. Furthermore, within each cell type there are both large and small receptive fields that convey to the brain different aspects of the percept. Small fields convey information about edges and detail, whereas the larger fields add information about texture, color (in cones), depth, and so forth.

Obviously the ultimate contribution of receptive fields with antagonistic surround is to convey, indeed *create*, information about *contrast*. The *boundaries* between light and dark regions are emphasized by these cells and conveyed deeper into the CNS. Indeed, aspects of the light that comes into the eye other than boundaries are discarded at the level of the ganglion cell. The receptive field structure also emphasizes contrast in *time*. Examine the records in Figure 9–18 in which profound inhibition occurred (# 4 left, for example). Note that upon *removal* of the inhibitory stimulus there is a burst of action potential activity. This is known as **postinhibitory rebound**. It may occur because sodium inactivation is removed after a period of hyperpolarization, allowing more action potentials to fire in the absence of stimulation. Teleologically, its function in the retina is to enhance perception of the *moment* that a stimulus ceases. The brain uses this to construct a dynamic image of moving objects, since the re-

bound exaggerates the moment the stimulus moves out of the receptive field.

In addition to being of various sizes, the receptive fields are plastic, or malleable. A well-understood example is found in the phenomenon of adaptation in rods. Rods are capable of producing meaningful generator potentials in the range of -40 to -70 mV over a range of ambient illumination that varies more than a thousandfold from low light (as in a darkened room) to high light (as outside on a sunny day). The sensitivity of rods to light is adjusted by intracellular Ca^{++} levels. In the light-adapted eye, $[Ca^{++}]_i$ in rods decreases. Because of a reciprocal molecular relation between $[Ca^{++}]_i$ and $[cGMP]_i$ this yields an increase in $[cGMP]$ and a *depolarization* of rods. The depolarization renders the photoreceptor less capable of producing a hyperpolarizing generator potential and hence makes it less sensitive. In the dark-adapted eye the opposite occurs, making the rod ultimately capable of responding to a single photon of light captured by the discs. In this case the receptive field characteristics change in such a manner that the surround is no longer antagonistic to the center of the ganglion cell's receptive field; the entire receptive field is now excitatory in response to a light stimulus. In other words, ganglion cells are truly light detectors in the extremely dark-adapted eye, but in other circumstances they are contrast detectors.

How do you think the receptive field characteristics of contrast detectors are created? The fundamental nature of visual receptive fields is that light in one part of the retina has the opposite effect in immediately adjacent parts of the retina. Such opposite responses would create perception of contrast at the boundary between the two regions of the receptive field. Inspection of Figure 9–16 suggests that *horizontal cells*, by virtue of their anatomy that places them in the flat dimension of retinal surface, are likely candidates for accomplishing this information transfer. Indeed it is the horizontal cells that take inhibition and turn it into excitation to create the antagonistic "off" surround of an on-cell and take excitation and turn it into inhibition to create the antagonistic "on" surround of an off-cell.

Comprehending the circuits that perform these transformations is a challenging but rewarding task. Consider Figure 9–18. (It's best to do this when you have a moment to reflect, not while on the bus or watching TV). A complete cellular explanation of retinal receptive fields for ganglion cells has four components:

1. The on-center of an on-cell
2. The off-center of an off-cell
3. The on-surround of an off-cell
4. The off-surround of an on-cell

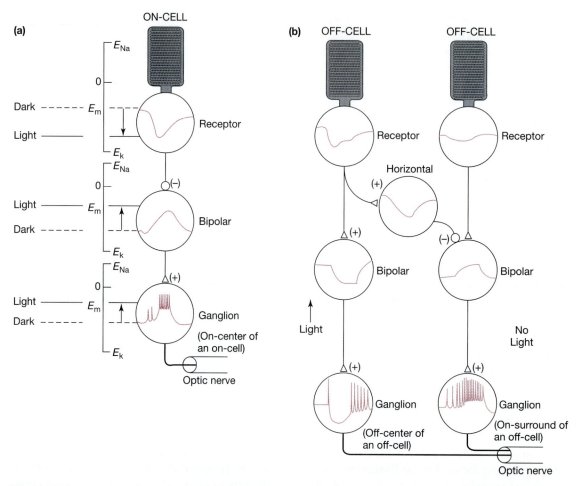

Figure 9–19 *Cellular Basis for Receptive Field Organization.* (a) Light causes the photoreceptors in the on-center of an on-cell to hyperpolarize, thus decreasing its inhibitory effect on the bipolar cell. The bipolar cell depolarizes as a consequence and increases the release of excitatory neurotransmitters at its synapse with the ganglion cell. (b) An illustration of the surround inhibition that occurs between the off-center of an off-cell and the on-surround of an off-cell. (Adapted from Dowling, 1979)

We will take these in turn and describe the cellular mechanism for each, always remembering that *only the ganglion cell has receptive field properties.* The other cells of the visual system have no action potentials and merely contribute to the ganglion cell's response properties.

Recall that *disinhibition yields excitation* and *disexcitation yields inhibition* (Chapter 5).

On-center of an on-cell. In this circuit the rod continuously inhibits its follower, the bipolar cell, in the dark (see Figure 9–19). A light stimulus in the center of the receptive field produces a hyperpolarizing generator potential and disinhibition, or excitation, of the bipolar cell. The bipolar cell makes an excitatory contact onto the ganglion cell, and the excitatory response to light causes

the ganglion cell to fire an action potential and conduct it up the optic nerve into the brain.

Off-center of an off-cell. In this circuit the rod makes an excitatory contact onto the bipolar cell exciting it in the dark. Light yields disexcitation, or inhibition, and this is what the ganglion cell experiences (Figure 9–19).

On-surround of an off-cell. A horizontal cell accepts excitatory synapse from a photoreceptor, meaning that it is continuously excited in the dark and transiently inhibited by light (Figure 9–19). Its orientation in the plane of the retina means that it can convey this transient hyperpolarization to an adjacent region that does not experience light where it converts it (by disinhibition) into excitation of a neighboring bipolar and ganglion cell circuit.

Off-surround of an on-cell.   Inhibition of the surround is produced by horizontal cell disexcitation. In other words, the synapses of the horizontal cell shown in Figure 9–19 are reversed, the one from the photoreceptor being inhibitory and the one made upon the bipolar cell being excitatory.

Though other information leaves the retina via the optic nerve (e.g., regarding ambient illumination to control the diameter of the pupils) the vast majority of the information that leaves consists of these dots and circles: on-cells with off-surrounds and off-cells with on-surrounds. These function to select information about the border between minute regions of light and dark and to discard other forms of information about light. In other words, *the eye is a contrast detector, a contrast enhancer, and ultimately, a contrast creator*, emphasizing stimulus differences instead of information about the stimuli themselves.

Profound understanding of the brain can be acquired by appreciating the fact that locally antagonistic influences are very common if not ubiquitous in the CNS. *Lateral inhibition* is similar to a feature we have described before as surround inhibition (Chapter 7). As we shall see, at the level of the visual cortex, more elaborate receptive fields, also with antagonistic surrounds, will emerge from neural processing of the dots and circles. From these, progressively more abstract receptive fields arise, but these circuits also have inhibitory interactions mediated by "local circuit interneurons" that create mutual inhibition of efferent, or output, cells. In somatosensory thalamus and cortex, surround inhibition produces more complex geometrical receptive fields with antagonistic surrounds, each serving to enhance the *contrast* in afferent activity. In motor systems, too, we find surround inhibition in abundance, such as for the Renshaw circuit in the spinal cord (Chapter 7), which serves to *create* precise boundaries in time and space for descending motor commands. Finally, for cortical regions with obscure function, such as association neocortex or hippocampus, projection cells generally produce self-inhibition and surround inhibition of other projection cells by axon collateral activation (Chapter 7) of local circuit interneurons (Figure 9–20). As our knowledge of the function of association cortex grows more obscure the farther it lies from primary sensory or motor cortical regions, so does our understanding of the role of surround inhibition in these areas. However, based on the function of surround inhibition elsewhere, it is reasonable to surmise that it serves to detect, enhance, and ultimately create *contrast* in time and space in the association cortex as

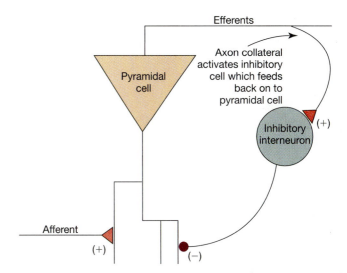

Figure 9–20   *A Cross Section of Hippocampus.* A schematic of local circuit inhibition in the hippocampus.

well. This contrast, of course, will not be of simple sensory or motor modality, but rather contrast in higher function. Those students of the human condition who hope to understand language, love, religion, or politics would do well to ponder what surround inhibition, contrast detection, and contrast creation would entail if encountered in the central structures that produce these phenomena.

Thalamic and Brainstem Projections

Lizards (Hawaiian geckos in the author's experience) have the odd habit of "bobbing" up and down on the front legs, alternating between a prone and upright posture. Teleologically, why do you think they do this?

A predator has both eyes pointing in the same direction (**binocular** vision, in which the visual fields of the two eyes overlap) so as to compare the angle of incidence of light emanating from its prey to each eye and thereby gain information regarding the distance to dinner (the farther away, the smaller the angle of incidence of light). As you may already have guessed, depth perception for a predator is important since the organism must know how far to spring to catch its prey. Dogs, cats, owls, and hawks, to name a few common predators, all have eyes in front of the head.

Prey animals, often herbivores, have eyes on the side of the head. Forming an estimate of distance and depth is less important than having a wide range of vision so as to detect, for example, something that is creeping up behind them. Rabbits, mice, cows, and horses are animals you might think of that show this **monocular** organization of the visual system in which the visual fields of the two eyes do not overlap. Rab-

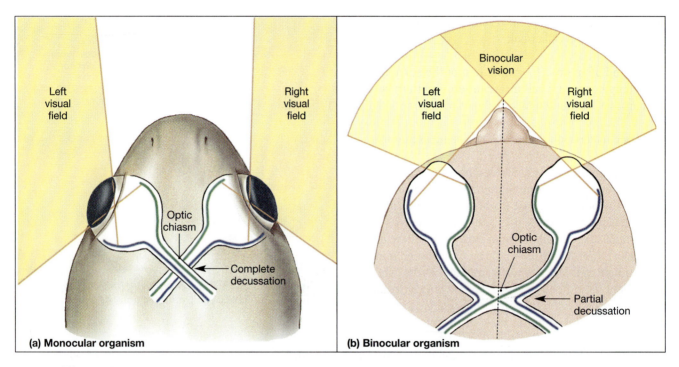

(a) Monocular organism

(b) Binocular organism

Figure 9–21 *Projection of the Visual World.* Projections of the visual world in a monocular organism and in a binocular organism.

bits in particular have eyes so far lateralized that they are virtually able to see directly behind them.

Some animals are both predator and prey. Lizards tend to have eyes on the side of the head (monocular vision) so as to avoid predation by birds and weasels. Nevertheless, for capturing prey and for social purposes, lizards must still form an impression of depth and distance. It is possible for such a monocular organism to create binocular comparisons in *time* by bobbing the head. Instead of comparing the angle of incidence of light of each eye at a single moment in time, the angles of incidence from an object coming into a single eye are compared at two moments in time. Test this theory by measuring the accuracy of a person's depth perception under two circumstances: with a patch over one eye and the head motionless and with one eye patched and the head allowed to "bob" like a lizard's.

People and their evolutionary relatives, monkeys and apes, have eyes in front of the head and binocular vision. Presumably this reflects common carnivorous ancestry, though vegetarians would cite this fact as an example of biology *not* being destiny. Since we are naturally more interested in the human visual system than that of lizards, scientists have sought an experimental animal that is, like us, binocular. Cats predominate as an experimental organism for vision research but monkeys are also used. In the experiments the subjects are completely anesthetized and unconscious, yet enough activity remains in the

ganglion cells and their followers to construct a theory of what would be happening in a conscious animal.

More than a million fibers leave from the ganglion cells in each eye, the total for both eyes being more than all the other sensory afferents in the body. The fibers obey the principle of *decussation* ("everything crosses," Chapter 7), but the nature of the crossing depends on the species. Monocular visual systems (Figure 9–21) decussate completely. The left eye projects to the right brain and the right eye projects to the left brain. Binocular organisms display *partial decussation*. Since the image of the outside world is inverted on the retina, the half of the retina next to the nose (the *nasal hemiretina*) sees the lateral part of the field of view, and the half of the retina next to the temples (the *temporal hemiretina*) sees the medial part of the field of view. Only the fibers from the nasal hemiretina cross, hence the term *partial* decussation. At a central location called the **optic chiasm** the fibers of the optic nerve segregate themselves into an ipsilateral projection (temporal) and a contralateral projection (nasal). Once the fibers have segregated at the chiasm and regrouped with the fibers from the temporal hemiretina that are projecting ipsilaterally, the fiber bundle is called the **optic tract**. The consequence of the crossing of the nasal fibers and the ipsilateral projection of the temporal fibers is that the *visual world* is decussated completely (see Figure 9–21), with the left brain receiving the right visual field representation

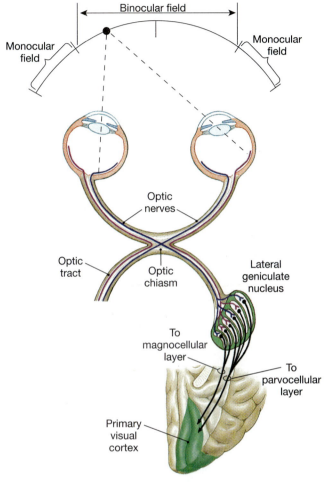

Figure 9–22 *The Lateral Geniculate Nucleus.* The LGN of the thalamus receives information about the contralateral visual field and separates it into layers.

from both eyes and the right brain receiving the left visual field representation *from both eyes.*

Most of the optic nerve fibers in amphibians and reptiles wind up in a part of the dorsal brainstem called the **optic tectum**. In mammals this projection exists also, much of it terminating in a part of the tectum called the **superior colliculus.** The colliculus in turn projects to oculomotor nuclei and cerebellum to coordinate tracking movements of the eyes and orienting movement of the head and reflexes such as the pupillary constriction to light. In a loose sense, the midbrain projections in humans can be thought of as mediating those aspects of vision that we share with amphibians and reptiles.

Mammals have another projection, not found to the same degree in amphibians and reptiles, that contains a much larger share of the optic nerve fibers. This is the one to the lateral geniculate nucleus (LGN), the thalamic relay for vision. There is one LGN on each side of the thalamus. Here the contralateral visual world is mapped in alternating bands (Figure

9–22). Within the map created by the LGNs are two different cell types, the *magnocellular layers* concerned primarily with detection of movement and *parvocellular layers* concerned with analysis of detail and color. In each, the circular receptive field structure found in retina is preserved and projected onto the primary visual cortex unaltered (Figure 9–23). However, the LGN receives many other projections besides ganglion cell axons, including some efferent projections from visual cortex similar to the efferent projections in the auditory system (described in Box 9–2). Since the receptive field structure of the retina appears to remain unaltered by the LGN, the function of these other projections is obscure. Their existence indicates we have much to learn about the "relay" role of the thalamus.

Studies of the LGN have provided insight into central processes that have general significance for the understanding of brain function. For example, loss of visual acuity during aging is well documented in people, but where and how do these deficits develop? Animal studies show that there is no substantial loss of neurons of the LGN during aging and

Figure 9–23 *Projections from LGN to Visual Cortex.* Optic radiations from the LGN to the primary visual cortex (a) whole brain; (b) expanded view of visual cortex.

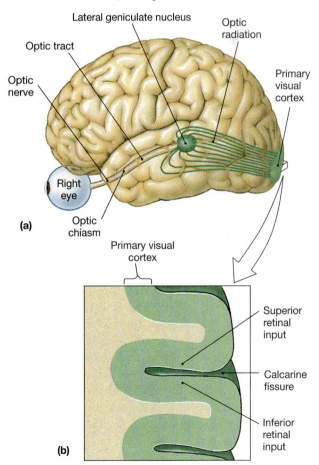

no alteration of their physiological properties (Spear, 1993). Hence those who study aging, like those who study learning (Chapter 15) have discovered that more sophisticated hypotheses involving patterns of connectivity and multiple brain regions are needed to replace the notion that plasticity of the CNS can be accounted for by simple changes of neuron numbers or size of responses.

Cortical Circuits and Columns

The LGN afferents terminate in the primary visual cortex at the occipital pole of the brain (also known as *striate cortex* or *Brodmann's area 17*). The cells that receive the afferents lie in layer IV (neocortex has six layers, see Chapter 8) and have response properties that also consist of circular receptive fields with antagonistic surrounds. Needless to say, these receptive fields form yet another *retinotopic map*, so that the visual cortex in layer IV can be thought of as a mosaic of dots and circles that represent the visual world (although upside down and backward). The map is topographically faithful in that adjacent regions of cortex represent adjacent areas of the retina and adjacent portions of the image. However, there is quantitative distortion in that the projections from the small receptive fields in the fovea, or center of gaze, take up a disproportionately large share of cortex. As a result, the retinotopic map is larger for the center of gaze than for the periphery.

Outside of layer IV, in the other five layers of cortex the circular and annular receptive fields are not to be found. This fact confounded early vision researchers who discovered that neither diffuse nor punctuated illumination would drive higher-order cells even though these cells (in layers I, II, III, V, and VI) received a direct or indirect projection from layer IV. A chance discovery by vision researchers David Hubel and Torsten Wiesel at Harvard Medical School in the early 1960s resolved the paradox (Hubel & Wiesel, 1979). Most cells in visual cortex respond to *edges* or *bars* of light or dark and then only of particular *orientation* in respect to the retina. Since these cells had the simplest cortical response property they could find, Hubel and Wiesel called them **simple cells**. In the example shown in Figure 9–24, the cell in question responded preferentially to the vertical bar of light shown in 1e, with decreasing responses to bars that deviated in either diagonal direction from vertical (1a–d, f–g). Horizontal bars and diagonal bars that deviated from the horizontal were without significant effect, as were spots (2a, b) and diffuse light (2c). Adjacent regions of cortex contained cells with different orientation preferences, but this variation was found to be systematic. In other words, as cells were encountered by an electrode moving across cortex, the preferred orientation selectively passed sequentially through the 180 degrees of possible orienta-

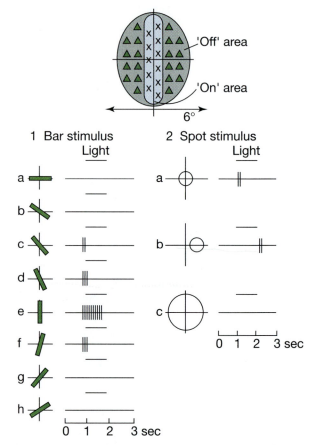

Figure 9–24 *Simple Cells in the Cortex.* A simple cell in the visual cortex. Notice the receptive field for these cells is linear. (Adapted from Hubel & Wiesel, 1959)

tions and then began again for a different part of the visual field. Thus each half of the visual cortex can be thought of as consisting of bands of cells of particular orientation selectivity (with soft edges like a sine wave rather than sharply defined ones) that cover all possible lines and edges for one half of the visual field. Indeed, psychologist Russel DeValois has found that the response properties of the simple cells could be described equally well by the *texture* of a visual stimulus (DeValois and DeValois, 1989). These bands of orientation (or "spatial frequency") can be visualized by exposing experimental animals to lines of a given orientation and then examining the cortex with a histological technique that reveals which cells are metabolically most active (presumably reflecting greater action potential activity). The result of such an experiment is illustrated in Figure 9–25. The orientation bands swirl over the cortical surface much like the lines of a thumb print.

As the eyes of binocular organisms project to their respective areas of visual cortex, there are also alternating bands for each eye's input. These too resemble the bands of a thumb

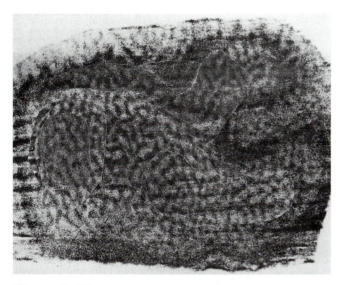

Figure 9–25 *Orientation Bands.* A visualization of the orientation bands in the visual cortex of a monkey.

print. The orientation bands and the bands for each eye's input intersect one another at right angles, so that for a given portion of cortex (and a given portion of the visual world) there are *columns* of simple cells that respond to stimulation of one eye in a particular orientation. Thus, when *both* orientation and ocular input is considered, the cortex is best thought of as consisting of **orientation columns** and **ocular dominance columns**. The points of intersection appear as swellings in Figure 9–25.

A complete cortical representation of a piece of the visual world would be *two* ocular dominance columns (one for each eye) and 180 degrees of orientation columns that intersect the ocular dominance columns. This structure is called a **hypercolumn** (Figure 9–26). The hypercolumn is the unit of integration at the simple cell level, and the primary visual cortex can be thought of as a mosaic of hypercolumns (each about 1mm^3 in dimension). Embedded within each hypercolumn are regions specialized to add the element of color to a world made up, at this level of abstraction, of lines and edges. These regions of projection by the cone system (via the LGN) have the rather inelegant name of **blobs** as a consequence of their appearance in histological section (see Figure 9–26).

Of course, vision consists of more than static lines and color. Elements of depth perception, angle, and motion are also encoded at the level of the primary visual cortex. In their pioneering work, Hubel and Wiesel used the terms **complex cell** and **hypercomplex cell** to describe cells that failed to respond to diffuse light, spots of light, or static edges of any orientation or either ocular origin. Such cells require more elaborate stimuli such as *moving edges or cor-*

ners to reach threshold and fire action potentials. Current work has found cells in primary visual cortex that assemble even more intricate stimuli to create their receptive field properties.

How do you think a simple cell of the primary visual cortex acquires its response property? Recall that convergence of photoreceptor input to individual ganglion cells, with the mediation of bipolar horizontal and amacrine cells, created the circular receptive fields with antagonistic surrounds that come into cortex. Hubel and Wiesel (1979) postulated, and subsequently showed experimentally, that it is convergence of these circular receptive fields that drives a simple cell of the primary visual cortex (Figure 9–27). *Adjacent* circular receptive fields, all on-cells in this case, represent a *line of stimuli* from the retina and visual world, surrounded on each side by an off region assembled from the antagonistic surrounds.

Figure 9–26 *The Hypercolumn.* A hypercolumn includes a set (one from each eye) of ocular dominance columns, blobs, and orientation columns. All this information is integrated in order to analyze a discrete region of the visual field. (Adapted from Kandel et al., 1991)

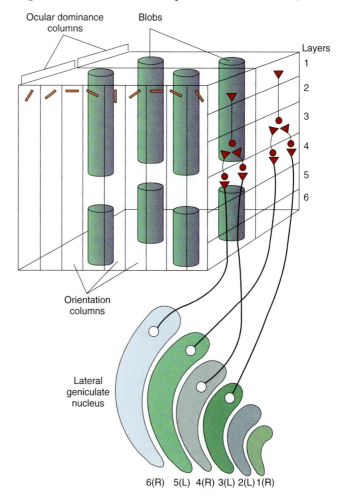

Ocular dominance columns

Blobs

Layers
1
2
3
4
5
6

Orientation columns

Lateral geniculate nucleus

6(R) 5(L) 4(R) 3(L) 2(L) 1(R)

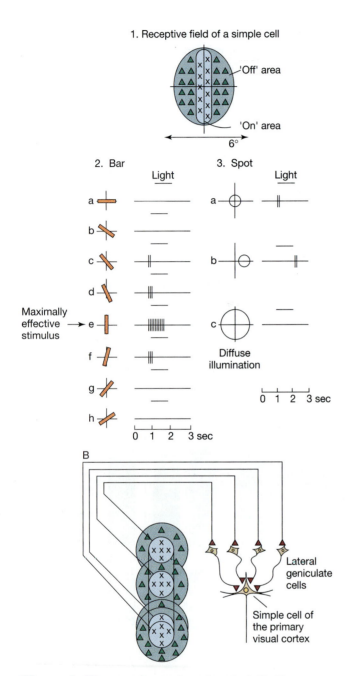

Figure 9–27 *The Circuit for a Simple Cell.* The rectangular receptive field of a simple cell represents several adjacent circular receptive fields of a particular orientation. (Adapted from Hubel & Wiesel, 1962)

Imagine now that a single synaptic input to the simple cell was inadequate to bring it to threshold, that two were inadequate, but that three or more synaptic inputs *were* adequate. The cell would then fire only to a line of light occupying *all the adjacent centers* of the ganglion cell receptive fields and would be maximally inhibited by lines occupying the sur-

rounds. Obviously, a line of different orientation would occupy only some ganglion cell centers and some ganglion cell surrounds and would only poorly drive the cell, which is precisely how simple cells behave (see Figure 9–27). A great deal of physiological and anatomical evidence supports the circuit shown in Figure 9–27. How do you think the more elaborate receptive fields are assembled, that is, for the complex and hypercomplex cell or for some higher-order cell in some association visual cortex whose response properties are so elaborate that they respond only to a *very* specific stimulus, such as the face of your grandmother? Think about this issue and then read Box 9–3.

Association Visual Cortex

As we have discussed, parallel projections from the LGN (the magnocellular and parvocellular) carry information about depth, color, and motion to the simple cells of the primary visual cortex. There, at least *three* parallel pathways arise to convey processed information to association visual cortex (*Brodmann's areas 18 and 19*) and association cortex in other lobes (parietal and inferotemporal), where sensory information is integrated for use in either motor output programs or complex cognitive activities. One pathway is primarily occupied with color vision; another with depth, form, and color; and the third with motion, depth, and form of stimuli arising in the rod (black-and-white) system. These projections have been well studied experimentally, but there are probably many other parallel projections. For example, at least twenty separate retinotopic maps can be found in areas 18 and 19 (sometimes called *extrastriate* cortex). While some of these are serial representations of lower-level maps, there are probably parallel representations in these brain regions as well. Furthermore, the striate and extrastriate cortices engage in reciprocal connections with the contralateral cortices and with subcortical visual structures. There is an *efferent* projection from cortex to the LGN, for example, which contributes to the substantial nonretinal input to this nucleus. The superior colliculus projects to the cortex and this projection, together with one of the parallel cortical pathways, is thought to organize the perception of moving objects either by motion of the image across the retina or by movement of the eyes as they track an object (due to "efference copy" to the colliculus, see Box 10–3).

These retinotopic maps are created by the physical connections we have described and involve orderly topological representations of the retina's surface, but ultimately these maps give way to feature detectors that respond to complex stimuli *anywhere* in the visual world. Because so much of these projections are parallel, it is most accurate to think of the neural correlate of perception of, say, a human face as

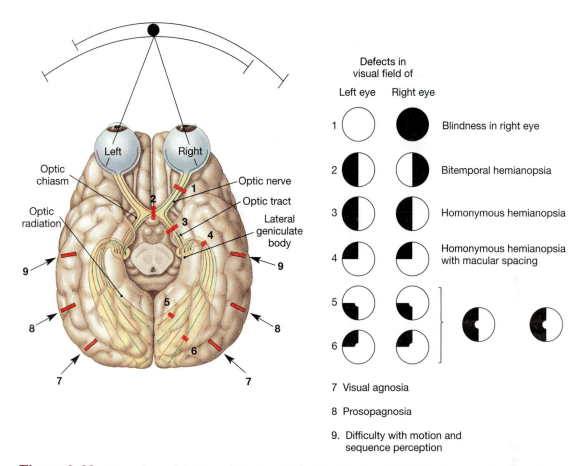

Figure 9–28 *Neurology of the Visual System.* Defects in the visual field (dark areas) that result from the corresponding lesions (1–9) along the visual pathway. Lesions to the visual cortex result in very different visual deficits. (Adapted from Kandel et al., 1991)

being a pattern of activity in the striate, extrastriate, parietal, and inferotemporal regions of cortex.

Diagnostic Neurology of the Visual System

Because of the complexity of parallel processing and lack of retinotopic organization, the function of very high order visual cortex is hard to evaluate experimentally. Some of our best information about high order cortex comes from people who have suffered selective damage to portions of the visual system. The testable visual field deficits in such patients can be used to explain the underlying anatomy (Figure 9–28).

Lesions before the simple cell level merely confirm the experimental observations on the spatial organization of the visual system. Complete damage to one of the optic nerves renders the subject unable to see in that eye (Figure 9–28, #1). However, damage to the optic nerves as they enter the optic chiasm produces a distinctively different visual field deficit (Figure 9–28, #2). Rather more common than you might imagine as a consequence of pituitary tumors pushing up against the chiasm from the infundibulum (Chapter 12), lesions here damage *just the fibers from each nasal hemiretina* that are crossing through the chiasm. The result is blindness in both *temporal* visual fields, since the image of the outside world is reversed on the retina (*bitemporal hemianopsia*). Recall that once the fibers have segregated at the chiasm and regrouped with the fibers from the temporal hemiretina that are projecting ipsilaterally, the fiber bundle is called the optic tract. The optic tract is small in diameter since its destination is a small target (the LGN). As a consequence brain damage to the optic tract is uncommon. Since the *visual field* decussates in humans, lesions to the optic tract produce blindness in the same half of the visual world in each eye (*homonymous hemianopsia*) (Figure 9–28, #3). After the LGN, fibers in the visual system form a fan-shaped structure called the **optic radiation** since it spreads from a small source (the LGN) to innervate a large target (the striate cortex). Because of the structure's size brain damage usually does not affect *all* of the optic radiation, but it is not rare

Box 9–3

Serial or Parallel Processing?

The visual system consists of a series of filters that screen out much of the light stimulus and allow only aspects of the percept to pass to higher levels. Thus, light-adapted retinal ganglion cells respond to only a tiny fraction of the photoreceptor generator potentials in their receptive fields since only illumination that fits the center-surround structure is effective. All the rest is discarded as if it never entered the eye. Likewise, simple cells in cortex discard many of the dots and circles that come in from the LGN, only allowing those that form lines and edges to cause action potentials.

Very likely there are filters at the complex and hypercomplex cell levels that discard many of the static lines and edges to form ever more abstract images, and perhaps there are very sophisticated filters that, at some level of conscious awareness, eliminate all but a holistic image. This image, or **gestalt**, appears to be a single entity, not a collection of minute, separate stimuli. After all, when you gaze at the face of a loved one, say your grandmother, you see just her face, not a collection of dots or circles, lines or edges, moving edges, corners, texture, or color. Generally only the complete image penetrates consciousness, giving support to the notion that converging input to ever higher-order feature detectors screens out most complex and hypercomplex receptive field activity, just as we know to be the case for photoreceptor, ganglion cell, and LGN input.

This formulation depends on a hierarchical organization of the visual system in which photoreceptors form a (very broad) base of a pyramid of connections. In such a hierarchy, what would be expected to occupy the apex of the pyramid? Using the not-quite-capricious example above, vision researchers have called this theoretical apex the **grandmother cell**, to indicate that the peak of the pyramid would probably consist of a very, very high order feature detector, perhaps a single cell or small group of cells for *each familiar percept*. This theory incorporates the notion of serial processing of visual information (Chapter 1) as the percept passes upward through the pyramid.

There is, indeed, solid experimental evidence for serial processing in the visual system. The circuits that hierarchically form circular receptive fields and antagonistic surrounds in the retina are well documented experimentally by the work of Stephen Kuffler, John Dowling, and others (Kuffler, 1953; Dowling & Werblin, 1971), just as there is little question that converging input of LGN neurons to simple cells form the linear receptive fields in Hubel and Wiesel's scheme (see Figure 9–28). At higher levels things become a bit more obscure, mostly because of the lack of anatomical support for very sound physiological data that seem to support serial processing. High order visual processing takes place in adjacent regions of the occipital lobe as well as, ultimately, portions of the temporal lobe and other cortex. In the temporal lobes of monkeys, Charles Gross (1973) and others have shown that there are single cells that fire not in response to dots, circles, line, edges, corners, or moving structures of any orientation, either eye, or any part of the visual world, but rather fire only in response to a complex stimulus such as the picture of an *individual monkey's face or the back of a monkey's hand*. Furthermore, the firing occurs equally well in *either* eye or *anywhere* in the visual field.

Objections to the notion of serial processing all the way to the grandmother cell are theoretical as well as experimental, and perhaps you have thought of some of them yourself. The visual cortex occupies an enormous portion of the brain (up to one-half of all cortex in primates) and much of this is occupied with the (relatively) simple task of constructing lines, edges, moving images, and texture out of the dots and circles that come in. Is there enough room in adjacent cortex to hold all the pyramids leading to each specific image? How would new images form in the brain? Certainly not by assembly of a new hierarchy, but rather by reapplication of a pre-existing hierarchy to the new percept. Indeed, different high order percepts clearly must involve activation of some of the same ganglion cell receptive fields and simple cell receptive fields since they share some of the same dots and lines.

It is clear that some other integrating scheme must take over from serial processing at some level of analysis and that this must entail divergent connections from lower levels to higher levels in addition to the convergent projection that make up serial processing networks. This combination of divergence and convergence gives rise to the concept that information flows from lower levels to higher ones by activation of many pathways side by side, hence the name parallel processing (sometimes "parallel distributed processing") that is applied to this algorithm.

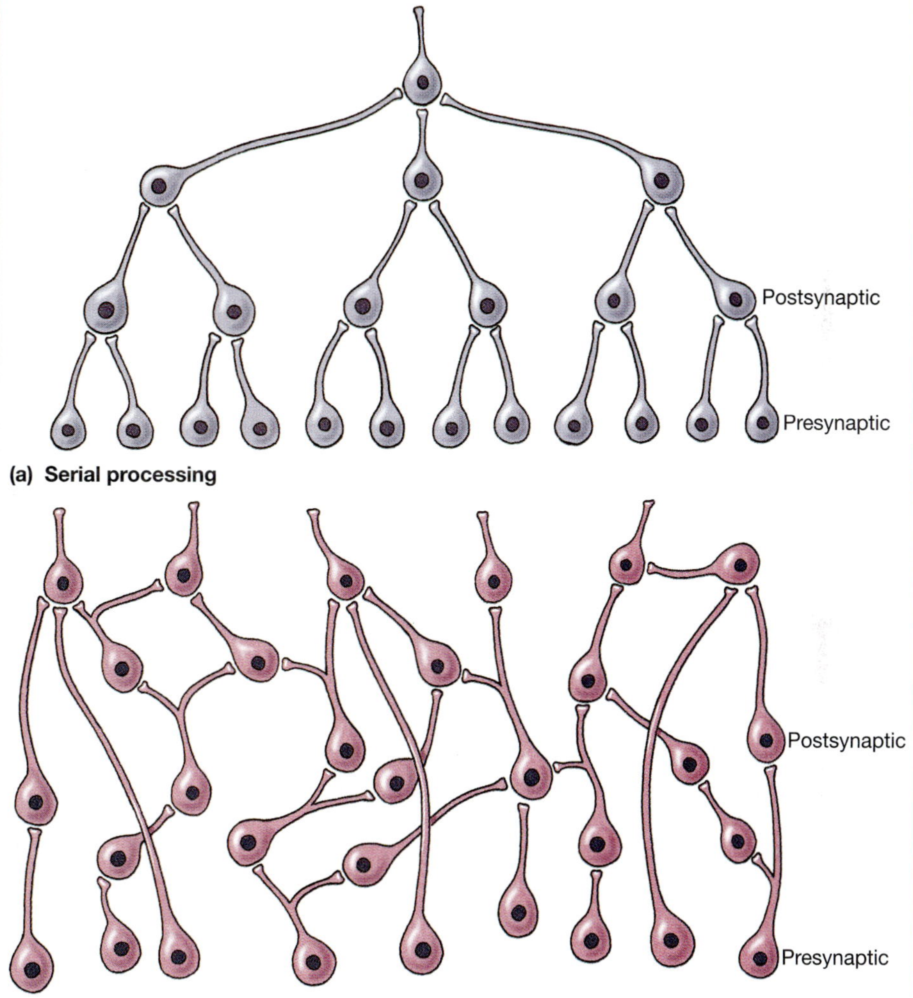

Parallel processing almost certainly takes over from serial processing in the visual system after the level of the simple cell. For example, complex and hypercomplex cells receive direct thalamic projections at a density equal to or greater than they receive projections from simple cells. Hence it is not possible to construct the same type of "wiring diagram" for the complex cell's receptive field that we have described for the simple cell (see Figure 9–28). The higher you go in the visual system the more experimental evidence for parallel processing accumulates, so that cortical regions can be described that appear to be activated not only by visual stimuli but by stimuli in other sensory modalities as well. As research on the visual system provides our best understanding of cortical organization to date, we find support for the "aggregate field theory" (Chapter 1) that was developed to account for other results. In essence, serial processing (or "cellular connectionism") appears to prevail throughout the nervous system at levels immediately responsible for behavior; whereas in brain regions ultimately responsible for behavior (i.e., association cor-

(a) Serial processing

Postsynaptic

Presynaptic

(b) Parallel processing

Postsynaptic

Presynaptic

tex), parallel processing (or "aggregate field theory") seems to prevail. As simple nervous systems, like those of invertebrates, provide some excellent examples of serial processing, it is tempting to think that simple *functions* require nothing more than this type of processing and that complex functions such as learning and cognition require organization by parallel processing. We will consider this issue more fully in Chapter 15.

to find damage to part of the radiation since it lies in a brain region that is invested with very tiny blood vessels. As an unfortunate consequence of their small diameters, these vessels are vulnerable to strokes (Chapter 8). While a stroke can occur anywhere in the CNS, in the region of the optic radiations it often damages part of the extrapyramidal motor system called the *internal capsule*, producing partial paralysis on the opposite side of the body. The associated visual field deficit is *incomplete hemianopsia* in the contralateral visual field (Figure 9–28, #4). If the lesion occurs in the wide fan region of the radiation where much of the neural space is occupied by fibers from the fovea, it is unlikely that it would be large enough to damage all of the fibers for the center of gaze. This produces a condition known as **macular sparing** in which only peripheral vision is affected (Figure 9–28, #5 and #6). Occasionally, patients with a stroke producing homonymous hemianopsia with macular sparing are unaware that there is anything wrong with their vision, since as soon as gaze is directed at an object it is seen perfectly clearly. Evidence of damage to the visual system is, in these cases, only made apparent upon neurological exam.

What about damage to association visual cortex? As you would expect after reading the previous section, such lesions do not produce complete blindness in one part of the visual world but rather partial blindness in the entire visual world. Thus, damage to area 18 might produce **agnosia** (sight but not recognition of objects) or perception of form and pattern but not color (Figure 9–28, #7). Lesions of nearby parietal lobes might produce more elaborate agnosias, such as accurate perception of all but a special class of objects (*prosopagnosia*, for example, is a lack of ability to perceive faces; Figure 9–28, #8; see also Box 16–2). Lesions to inferotemporal cortex may result in lack of motion perception and/or a difficulty in distinguishing the proper sequence of visual events in time (Figure 9–28, #9). The clinical literature abounds with reports of special agnosias arising from tumor, stroke, or brain damage in the various association cortical regions that are part of the visual system, but since no two lesions are precisely alike it is difficult to provide a systematic explanation of cortical function in these areas based on diagnostic neurology alone. Experiments with noninvasive imaging techniques on conscious human volunteers (Chapter 16) complement clinical data to provide our best current understanding of higher cortical function.

It is difficult to imagine what internal experience must be like for an individual with very high order vision deficits and much easier to relate to the effect of a lower-order vision defect, such as astigmatism. Yet even here the experts can be fooled. The proposal that El Greco was astigmatic has appeal since we all know what distorted lenses can do to the appearance of reality. However, the act of painting involves *creating* a visual image, not merely seeing it. This creation must be expressed through the same lenses and filters, distorted or otherwise, through which perception occurs. If an astigmatic person attempted to accurately reflect reality in a painting, it would come out much the same as everyone else's since the eyes he or she would use to check the quality of the work would be the same as those used to perceive the model. Thus it is not possible to tell whether El Greco was astigmatic or not based solely on the appearance of his work. The difference between the paintings of El Greco and those of his contemporaries is more likely due to a very high order aspect of his visual system, *artistic vision*, not a distortion of the lenses in his eyes.

Six Principles of Sensory Physiology

Our curiosity about sensation is boundless and our knowledge of sensory systems, by comparison to other central processes, is vast. In a single chapter it is not possible to do justice to this curiosity and this knowledge, and so I have adopted the strategy of dispersing some topics in sensation throughout the book in chapters where they are relevant to behavior. You may look back at this chapter and wonder how to organize all the details into a coherent theme that incorporates common laws or rules of sensation. It happens that for sensory systems in general (pain is an exception, see Chapter 11) there *are* such rules. This chapter has been written to emphasize especially good examples of the rules and, for summary, I will list them here.

1. *Sensory systems display adaptation.* Tranquil internal experience requires that much sensory stimuli be "filtered out." Similarly, during periods of low sensory stimuli, mechanisms must exist to enhance sensation over a wide range of physical intensity. Such mechanisms often exist in the very first sensory cell at the level of the generator potential. An especially clear example is to be found in the pacinian corpuscle of the somatosensory system, which is prevented by adaptation from sending continuous information about pressure on the body surface to the brain and spinal cord.

2. *Stimulus intensity is encoded by action potential frequency.* The generator potential is analogous to a postsynaptic potential in that it continuously varies in amplitude. However, such signals decay in time and space and cannot be conducted centrally without being altered. Hence, at some point the system must introduce electrically excitable membrane to propagate this information in the form of all-or-none action potentials. This transformation may occur at the level of the first-order cell (somatosensation and olfaction),

the second-order cell (audition and vestibular sense), or the third-order cell (vision); but ultimately the brain will accept sensory information only as it is *encoded* in action potentials with *frequency* representing the strength of the stimulus.

more frequent stronger stimuli

5.

3. *There is much modality segregation in sensory systems.* For the first few synapses information that arises in one sensory modality remains uncontaminated by stimuli in other modalities. However, for each modality this segregation ultimately breaks down. This breakdown can occur subcortically, for example at the level of the colliculus and LGN in vision, which receive substantial somatosensory, auditory, vestibular, and efferent input, or at cortical levels in association cortex for each system.

4. *The sensory surface is topographically organized subcortically and cortically.* The topographic organization of olfactory and gustatory experience is vague and has only recently become apparent experimentally. For the other modalities and for most levels of processing, *maps* of the sensory surface are found (*retinotopic* maps for vision, *tonotopic* maps for audition, and *somatotopic* maps for touch). These maps prevail as the

physical basis of sensory processing, at least to the level where modality segregation breaks down.

5. *Receptive fields have antagonistic surrounds.* A manifestation of an even more general principle of neural organization known as surround inhibition since it often is mediated by inhibitory interneurons, this principle is exemplified by circular receptive fields in the retina and simple cell receptive fields in visual cortex. It can also be seen in all the other systems, where it helps to create the perception of contrast in space and time.

6. *Sensation is characterized by efferent control over the percept.* Only now becoming recognized as true of all the modalities, it is clear that the brain sends projections *to* sensory structures in addition to receiving a projection *from* them. Certainly in the case of the cochlea, these efferent projections modify the sensory input even at the level of the first-order cell but in the other systems efferent control may be stronger at higher-order cells. Thus, as educators, artists, and philosophers have known for years, sensory experience is an active process and one in which our nervous system creates as abundantly as it experiences.

SUMMARY

Sensation is a creative process. Some aspects of sensory physiology, such as features of proprioception, never enter awareness; others only occasionally enter consciousness. Adaptation to stimuli regulates the amount of physical energy that is transduced into neural energy in the form of generator potentials in all systems. The adapted signal then enters the CNS as all-or-none action potentials. Generally, for systems other than nociception (pain perception), the strength of a stimulus is represented by action potential frequency. In the somatosensory system these processes take place in the first-order neuron and its associated end organ, the pacinian corpuscle. In the auditory, vestibular, olfactory, gustation, and visual systems the first-order cell is unable to fire action potentials, instead producing generator potentials. Higher-order cells effect the conversion from generator potential to action potentials. In audition, the basilar membrane of the cochlea forms a one-dimensional surface that transduces vibration into neural energy by bending cilia of hair cells, the first-order neurons. This response is represented in the spiral ganglion, cochlear nucleus, superior olive, nucleus of the lateral lemnisci, inferior colliculus, and ultimately, in the MGN and auditory cortex by tonotopic maps. Substantial binaural comparisons take place at each level of processing. The vestibular system encodes information about the position and angular velocity of the head using similar mechanisms. Olfaction and gustation are highly related modalities; chemoreceptors use direct or second-messenger mechanisms to create responses to odorants and flavors, and these are conveyed to subcortical or paleocortical destinations. Visual transduction is inhibitory at the level of photoreceptors. Photoreceptors and bipolar cells make up the center of retinal ganglion cell receptive fields, and horizontal and amacrine cells construct antagonistic surrounds. This receptive field structure is preserved in the LGN and part of visual cortex, but is supplanted in another part by simple cell receptive fields composed of edges and lines of static orientation and ocular dominance. Complex receptive fields are created to respond to moving edges, corners, textures, and ultimately, forms, depth, color, and intricate features. Serial processing of information dominates up to the simple cell level but then parallel processing appears to take over. At all levels of vision and other forms of sensation, contrast is emphasized and efferent projections modify the nature of incoming information. Six rules of sensory physiology emerge from current research: adaptation, frequency encoding of intensity, modality segregation, topographic organization, surround inhibition, and efferent control over the percept.

REVIEW QUESTIONS

1. What is adaptation? Why is it needed?

2. What is proprioception?

3. List the specialized end organs for touch.

4. What is efferent control of the percept?

5. What parts of the brain are associated most closely with olfaction and gustation?

6. How does the retina create and enhance contrast?

7. Which retinal cell type is the first to fire action potentials?

8. What is a grandmother cell?

9. What is a hypercolumn?

THOUGHT QUESTIONS

1. Some psychologists say that Hubel and Wiesel's results on the visual cortex can be accounted for by *textures* instead of lines and edges. What do you think of this theory?

2. Do you think high order feature detectors in the visual system, (e.g., for individual faces) are active when we *dream* of the faces in addition to when we perceive them directly?

3. We commonly hear the phrase "the five senses," but in fact there are probably many more than five. For example, do you think the detection of the passage of time is a sensation? What would the "relay nucleus" for this sensation be like and what properties would you expect to find in primary "time cortex"? How would you recognize time cortex if you found it?

KEY CONCEPTS

adaptation (p. 193)
agnosia (p. 226)
amacrine cells (p. 209)
amplitude (p. 193)
ampulla (p. 205)
anosmia (p. 206)
astigmatism (p. 209)
basilar membrane (p. 197)
binocular (p. 218)
bipolar cells (p. 209)
blobs (p. 221)
chemoreceptors (p. 206)
cochlea (p. 197)
cochlear nucleus (p. 201)
complex cell (p. 221)
cones (p. 209)
decibels (p. 201)
discs (p. 209)
efferent projections
    (p. 202)
end organs (p. 193)
fovea (p. 209)

free nerve endings (p. 193)
ganglion cells (p. 209)
generator potential (p. 193)
gestalt (p. 224)
grandmother cell (p. 224)
gustatory nucleus (p. 208)
hair cells (p. 198)
homunculus (p. 195)
horizontal cells (p. 209)
hypercolumn (p. 221)
hypercomplex cell (p. 221)
incus (p. 196)
inferior colliculus (p. 202)
inner segment (p. 209)
lateral sulcus (p. 202)
macular sparing (p. 226)
malleus (p. 196)
medial geniculate nucleus
    (MGN) (p. 202)
monocular (p. 218)
nucleus of the lateral lemnisci
    (p. 201)

ocular dominance columns
    (p. 221)
off-cells (p. 215)
on-cells (p. 214)
optic chiasm (p. 218)
optic radiation (p. 223)
optic tectum (p. 219)
optic tract (p. 218)
orientation columns (p. 221)
otoliths (p. 204)
outer segment (p. 209)
oval window (p. 197)
pacinian corpuscle (p. 195)
paleocortex (p. 208)
papillae (p. 206)
photoisomerization (p. 212)
photopigment (p. 209)
photoreceptors (p. 209)
pinna (p. 196)
postinhibitory rebound (p. 215)
receptive field (p. 214)
retinal (p. 211)

retinotopic (p. 214)
rhodopsin (p. 210)
rods (p. 209)
round window (p. 197)
saccule (p. 204)
semicircular canals (p. 205)
simple cells (p. 220)
spiral ganglion (p. 199)
stapes (p. 197)
stereocilia (p. 198)
superior colliculus (p. 219)
superior olive (p. 201)
taste buds (p. 208)
tonotopic maps (p. 195)
transduction (p. 193)
tuning curve (p. 201)
tuning selectivity (p. 201)
tympanic membrane (p. 195)
utricle (p. 204)
vestibular apparatus (p. 197)
vestibular system (p. 204)

This is the gift that I have . . . a foolish extravagant spirit, full of forms, figures, shapes, objects, ideas, apprehensions, motions, revolutions. These are begot in the ventricle of memory, nourished in the womb of the pia mater, and delivered upon the mellowing of occasion.

William Shakespeare (1564–1616)
Love's Labour's Lost

10

Motor Systems

But for the Renaissance notion that mental processes are more closely associated with the *ventricles* of the brain than the brain itself (Chapter 1), Shakespeare's understanding of the origin of action is quite consistent with modern research on motor systems of the brain. The "spirit" that inspires action actually contains a number of discrete elements such as forms of the body, the central representation of shapes and objects in the outside world, the motivation to act in the nature of ideas and apprehensions, and finally the neural mechanism for action itself, which is supplied by the motor neurons.

Remember that the hypothetical destination of hierarchical sensory systems is called the grandmother cell. We saw in Box 9–3 that, for complex nervous systems at least, the grandmother cell probably doesn't exist. Rather, the central representation of "grandmother" probably entails a pattern of activity in a regional network of cells each contributing some aspect of the image.

Try to imagine what the equivalent to the grandmother cell would be for motor systems. If *serial processing* of motor impulses is presumed, then this cell would also occupy the apex of a pyramid, but instead of being the result it would be the *origin* of action potential activity that spreads downward through the pyramidal and extrapyramidal systems, the upper motor neurons and, finally, the lower motor neurons and muscles at the base of the pyramid. For a given behavior (in its way as specific as the perception of grandmother) this cell's activity would be *necessary* as well as *sufficient* for its display. It would in effect "command" the behavior, and, in fact, this hypothetical cell is called the **command neuron**. However, as Shakespeare anticipated, the source of action is probably more diffuse and complex than the concept of command neuron would imply.

229

Consider the experimental and theoretical reasons to doubt the existence of the grandmother cell; are there similar doubts about the command neuron? As you read the section that follows, reflect on this issue. You will appreciate, of course, that it is a philosophical as well as a neurobiological question. What cells drive the command neuron? Does the command neuron have its own intrinsic activity, independent of synaptic input? What motor behavior would we display without external stimuli? If such a cell existed, where would we find it and how would we recognize it? What neural events occur when we make *a decision to act*?

The Frontal and Parietal Lobes

The frontal lobes are associated primarily with motor function, and the parietal lobes are associated primarily with sensory function. *However, at all levels in both systems there is substantial overlap between sensory and motor function.* We have seen one example of such overlap outside the CNS in the muscle spindle organ, which is essentially a sensory structure interposed between two lower motor neurons, the gamma motor neuron and the alpha motor neuron (Chapter 7). In the cortex there are extensive interconnections between the parietal and frontal lobes because of their overlapping functions.

"Psychomotor" Cortex

In a loose sense we can dissect the impetus for behavior into four stages: motivation, readiness, plan for action, and execution. The *motivation* to act is combined with information about the body's *readiness* to act, and this produces a *plan for action*. This plan, once formed, is brought to *execution* by activation of descending motor pathways. This formulation is intuitive (e.g., it corresponds to general notions of how decisions are made in organizations), but it also corresponds well with known structural relations in a part of the brain known unfortunately as **psychomotor cortex** (*psychology* is the study of behavior, and all parts of the brain contribute equally to behavior; hence no part of the brain can be accurately considered more "psycho" than the rest).

The *motivation* for action arises in the limbic system. Information about the body's *readiness* to act most likely arrives in portions of the frontal lobes known as the **premotor cortex** and the **supplementary motor area (SMA)** through a projection from the **posterior parietal cortex** (Figure 10–1). Part of *association somatosensory* cortex, the posterior parietal cortex contains somatotopic maps of the body, but these are more abstract than those found in primary sensory or motor cortex. Neurological literature of brain damage to this region indicates that it is not some straightforward feature of the location, quality, or intensity of touch that is encod-

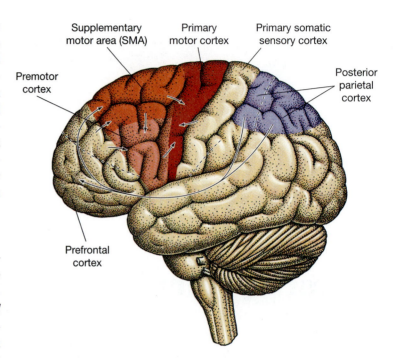

Figure 10–1 *Psychomotor Cortex.* A plausible hypothesis of the impetus for behavior follows a path through several regions of psychomotor cortex. From the cingulate gyrus in the limbic system, the *motivation* to act travels both to the premotor cortex and SMA and to the posterior parietal cortex, which assesses body awareness. With this information, the premotor cortex and SMA can determine the body's *readiness* to act, and conceive a *plan for action* that is brought to *execution* by primary motor cortex. (Roland et al., 1980)

ed by the posterior parietal cortex, but rather the *awareness* that a limb, digit, or muscle belongs to the body and may be used by it. For example, posterior parietal lesions can produce the phenomenon of **unilateral neglect**, in which the patient denies ownership of a portion of the body (see Box 16–4). The parietal lobes also contain circuitry that allows recognition of familiar objects such as utensils or faces (see Box 16–2). The *plan for action* appears to arise in the premotor cortex and the SMA. The motivation for action very possibly influences the plan for action by a projection to the premotor cortex and the SMA from the **cingulate gyrus**, a part of the limbic system, and the most medial bulge of cortex deep within the midsagittal fissure.

The *plan for action* is conveyed from the premotor cortex and SMA to the **primary motor cortex** for *execution*. To use an everyday example, I am thirsty (cingulate gyrus), I see a glass of water and know I have an arm to grasp it (posterior parietal cortex). I conceive of a plan to drink the water (premotor cortex and SMA), and I direct my arm, mouth, tongue, and throat to do so (primary motor cortex). The example used is of a very simple act, and much of our behavior is substantially more complex. A more demanding solution to the same problem might involve recollection of the location of a soda machine, ascertaining the possession of correct change, planning a route to the machine, and so forth. The neural basis for such a program would involve all the brain regions and projections alluded to above, together with many other convergent projections to the premotor cortex and SMA. Frequently, the **prefrontal cortex** is cited as one source for this more "intellectual" influence on the premotor areas.

The foregoing discussion is more *plausible* than scientifically secure. This is partly because of philosophical uncertainty regarding the ultimate cause of behavior (see Boxes 10–1 and 11–1) but also because of a very concrete and practical difficulty in the execution of experiments on the motor system. Experiments on simple systems (such as autonomic ganglia, the neuromuscular junction, or the brains of invertebrates) can proceed with isolated preparations of nervous tissue (such in vitro experiments provide much if not most of the knowledge developed in previous chapters). Experiments in sensory physiology can be done on intact organisms exposed to *stimuli systematically determined by the experimenter*. Because of the greater degree of *control* the researcher has over the experimental circumstances, we know more about sensation than any other higher function. Experiments on the higher aspects of motor physiology require, by definition, an animal that is conscious and able to formulate a plan of action, and in most cases these plans depart significantly from the desires of the scientist studying motor systems.

Only when the research subject is trainable, cooperative, and, ultimately, "friendly" with the experimenter can data be obtained on the function of "psychomotor" cortex, since the subject must agree to follow the research plan. For this reason, much of our current understanding of motor physiology has been obtained using people as research subjects, some of them normal volunteers and others patients with neurological deficits as a result of exposure to radiological or neurosurgical procedures. Most of the present discussion and that in the next section is based, for example, on experiments done by Wilder Penfield (1958) with conscious neurosurgery patients in which he discovered that stimulation of parietal cortex produced sensation or awareness of particular contralateral body parts, stimulation of prefrontal cortex produced complex ideation, stimulation of primary motor cortex produced discrete contralateral movements of muscles, and stimulation of premotor areas produced coordinated movements of limbs and digits involving groups of contralateral muscles. (These data will be discussed more thoroughly in Chapter 16.) Experimental confirmation of Penfield's observations required an organism with sufficient intellectual prowess to understand the experimental procedures at some level and cooperate with them.

For this reason monkeys predominate as the experimental subject for research on premotor cortex. E. V. Evarts, Vernon Mountcastle, and others found that single cells in cortical areas associated with the motor system fired in anticipation of muscle movements, as would be expected (Evarts & Tanji, 1976; Mountcastle, 1978). However, they only fired in anticipation of *certain types* of muscle movement. Neurons in the posterior parietal region became active only before *purposeful* movements, such as those performed for a food reward. Similar movements done reflexively or without identifiable purpose were not preceded by unit discharge. Trained jaw clenching would elicit a unit discharge in the appropriate premotor area, but chewing might not, even though identical muscles and movements are involved. For this reason the anticipatory firing of "psychomotor" neurons was thought to signify a "state of readiness" to act. With electroencephalography it is possible to record a **readiness potential** in premotor areas that precedes volitional movements by almost a second. Lesions of premotor areas do not yield muscle weakness or influence reflexive motions, but they do interfere with the ability to execute planned movements. For example, people with lesions to the SMA may be able to reflexively avoid a ball that is thrown at them, but they would be unable to coordinate the postural balancing and arm motion necessary to throw the ball back.

If there is a central location for the neural structure that makes (or receives) "free will" or the "decision to act," it is most likely to be found somewhere within psychomotor cortex, a fact that has not escaped the attention of motor system physiologists (see Box 10–1).

The Motor Homunculus

In the **precentral gyrus**, the first fold rostral to the central sulcus, lies a map of the body analogous to the somatotopic map in the *postcentral gyrus* caudal to the central sulcus (see Chapter 9). This **motor homunculus** is oriented across the surface of the brain in a manner just like the somatosensory homunculus: feet medially in the crevice between the hemispheres and exaggerated face and hands laterally (Figure 10–2). The symmetry of sensory and motor structures across the central sulcus is probably not an accident of evolution. We have seen in Chapter 7 that motor function at the level of the cord involves intimate feedback from sensory systems. Activation of alpha motor neurons causes extrafusal muscle to contract as desired by the brain, but adjustments are made if resistance to limb movement is encountered. These adjustments involve the muscle spindle organ and the monosynaptic reflex, which are part of the sensory system. Resistance stretches the spindle organ and recruits more motor units, thus evoking greater muscular effort. On a higher level there are analogous mechanisms to

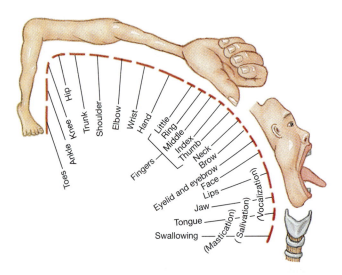

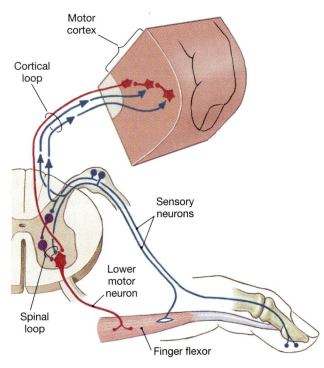

Figure 10–2 *The Motor Homunculus.* Analogous to the sensory homunculus encountered in Chapter 9, a motor homunculus exists as a somatotopic map of motor function in primary motor cortex in the precentral gyrus. The disproportionate allocation of cortex to the control of fine muscle movements in the hands and face allows us our many facial expressions and enables concert pianists to perform Beethoven. Are the magnitudes of the rest of the representations consistent with your experience?

Figure 10–3 *Spinal and Cortical Feedback Circuits.* Movement is a product of two-way communication between cortex, cord and muscle.

Figure 10–4 *Upper Motor Neuron Terminals in Cord.* One corticospinal axon may innervate several levels and, in each level, several motor neurons in the gray matter of the spinal cord. (a) Along the axis of the spinal cord, axon collaterals branch from white to gray matter at several cervical and thoracic levels. (b) At one particular level of the cord, an axon branches again to synapse on lower motor neurons. (Adapted from Shinoda et al., 1981)

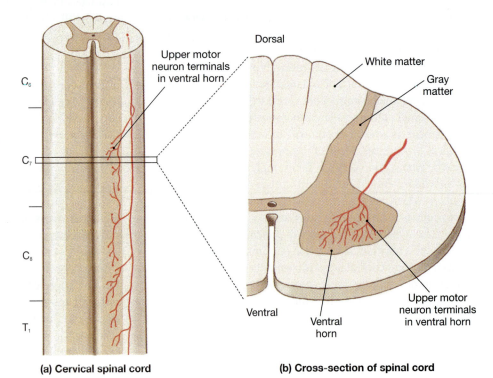

(a) Cervical spinal cord

(b) Cross-section of spinal cord

counteract unexpected resistance, as when an object to be lifted is heavier than imagined. These entail proprioceptive feedback to upper motor neurons in cortex (Figure 10–3). When the cortical sensorimotor circuit is activated the frequency of upper motor neuron commands is increased, causing muscles to constrict with more force.

Primary Motor Cortex

Commands emerging from psychomotor cortex are continually refined as they pass caudally toward the lower motor neuron pools. Direct stimulation of premotor cortex evokes general movements, sometimes bilateral, that involve many muscles and rotation of several joints. Direct stimulation of primary motor cortex elicits more localized contralateral movements, mostly involving a single joint and a few muscles. This is consistent with the anatomy of cortical upper motor neurons, each of which sends off axon collaterals in

cord to innervate several lower motor neuron pools (Figure 10–4). Brainstem and spinal circuits then fine-tune the command from the psychomotor cortex to produce the desired movement.

Recordings taken from upper motor neurons in primary motor cortex appear to confirm that their activity reflects a more general, or less precise, indication of the desire of the premotor cortex's plan to move the body. Figure 10–5 shows a number of recordings of the activity of a single cell in primary cortex. Each mark represents a single action potential that occurred before or after the movement at time zero. Several movements were made in each of several directions (arrows in the figure) and multiple action potential records for each position are stacked for comparison (several sweeps gathered around the initiation of movement at time zero). Experiments such as this one, conducted by Apostolos Georgopoulos and colleagues (1982), reveal that cortical cells fire

Figure 10–5 *Direction Selectivity in Primary Motor Cortex.* A monkey was trained to move a handle in eight different directions around a circle. The frequency of action potentials for one neuron with multiple trials in each direction are shown in raster plots. A single neuron in primary motor cortex shows increased responsiveness to movement in a particular range of the circle, in this case, between 90° and 225°. Other neurons would be direction selective to other ranges, and movement in a specific direction can be accomplished by a summation of inputs from multiple overlapping ranges. This result of this computation is a *population vector*. (Georgopoulos et al., 1982)

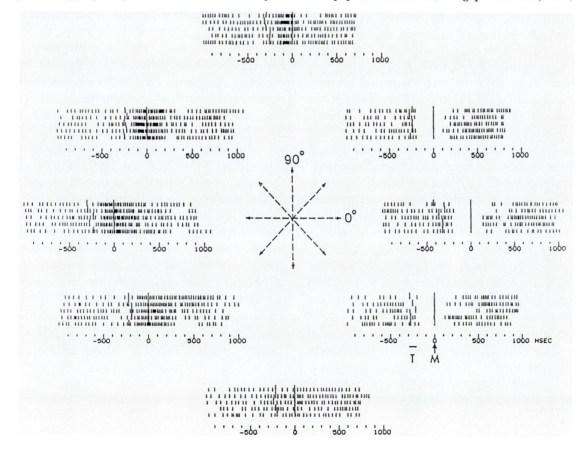

Box 10–1

Intention, Volition, and "Free Will"

This "I" which when I move my hand I experience as "I doing," how do I perceive it? I do not perceive it. If perception means awareness through sense I do not perceive the "I." My awareness and my self are one, I experience it. The "I doing" is my awareness of myself in the motor act. This "I" belongs more immediately to our awareness than does even the spatial world about us, for it is directly experienced. It is the "self." • Sir Charles Sherrington

René Descartes, whose name is associated with a particular type of dualism (Chapter 1) believed that the brain contained a portal, or *nexus*, that allowed the spiritual world to express an influence on material, or behavioral, processes. In particular, he felt that the **pineal body**, a medial bulge on the dorsal brainstem, was the "seat of the soul" or in more modern terms the pathway for "free will" to regulate brain processes (Chapter 1).

Evolutionarily and embryologically, the pineal body is related to an actual functioning "third eye," a fact which may have suggested mystical significance to early anatomists. Among animals, only the tuataran (*Sphenodon punctatus*), a monitor lizard, has a homologous (structurally equivalent) "third eye" on the surface of the head that is capable of focusing an image; but other reptiles, amphibians, and possibly some birds have thin enough skulls and dorsal enough pineal bodies that some light may actually penetrate far enough to illuminate them. A glandular structure, the pineal is light-sensitive and secretes a substance, melatonin, that may be involved in regulating sleep and waking cycles (Chapter 13). Though its function is obscure in mammals, it is highly unlikely, given its cell structure and projection fields, to be the medium for free will to influence the body. Where would a modern dualist search for a nexus between the mind and body? Remarkably, it is probably just where a monist would search for a command neuron or neurons, namely, somewhere in psychomotor cortex.

Apart from the fact that the pyramidal cell bodies in primary motor cortex are somewhat larger than other cells

in the brain, a fact that is usually explained by the need to metabolically support the very long axons of the corticospinal tract, nothing in the neural anatomy or physiology of any of the areas of the psychomotor cortex suggests that any one of them would be a special receptacle for the influence of nonmaterial forces.

The actual location of the decision to act can be estimated with some precision by use of modern, noninvasive imaging techniques of the functioning human brain. These make use of the fact that brain regions that are more electrically active are also more metabolically active, enabling a range of measurements involving cerebral blood flow and glucose utilization to be made (Chapters 14 and 16). The figure shows metabolic measurements done with an awake human volunteer in a variety of circumstances. Areas of increased metabolic activity are represented by the small black dots. When the subject is asked to flex a finger, an increase in metabolism is found in the contralateral primary motor cortex in the region where the hand is represented (a). Since motor control entails continuous somatosensory input (in our example this input is updated information about the position of the finger, the degree of flexion, and so forth), the corresponding region in the primary somatosensory cortex is also activated. When a more complex movement of the fingers of the contralateral hand is requested, such as playing the piano, increased metabolism in the SMA is also found, because of the role of this region in orchestrating coordinated motor activity (b). Finally, when the subject is asked to mentally rehearse the performance,

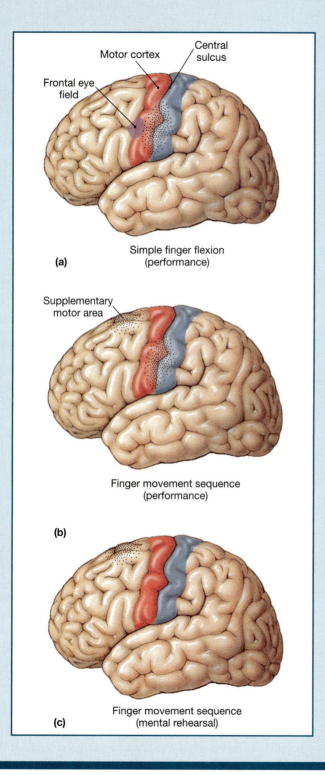

(a) Simple finger flexion
(performance)

Frontal eye field

Motor cortex

Central sulcus

(b) Finger movement sequence
(performance)

Supplementary motor area

(c) Finger movement sequence
(mental rehearsal)

without actually moving the hand, the SMA *alone* shows a metabolic increase (c).

It seems apparent from these data that the *decision to act*, at least in this case, occurs somewhere between the SMA and the primary motor cortex. It is in these SMA synapses, dendrites, somata, axons, or boutons, or in post-synaptic specializations in primary cortex, or within cortical interneurons, or initial segments of axons, or in the *pattern* of connectivity among any or all of these elements that the dualist must find an avenue for free will to enter the body. The monist, on the other hand, must find a command neuron or some suitable substitute from among these elements. Which do you think is more likely?

The "I" which performs the act initiated by the SMA actually appears to reside elsewhere in the brain. The posterior parietal cortex has been found (since Sherrington's time) to contain neural structures necessary for recognition, or "ownership," of a particular body part such as an arm or leg. Because the posterior parietal region is connected to the SMA, it is reasonable that actions normally require a prior awareness of the body's capacity to act. However, "awareness" seems to imply "consciousness" and consciousness seems to require understanding of "the self." It is this last bit that has flummoxed so many thinkers on the subject of volition. If, as Sherrington suggests, the self is not perceived but instead is "experienced," then what brain region is responsible for it? As we shall see in Chapter 16, the search for consciousness and the self is by no means a trivial undertaking.

in anticipation of movement (as they must if they are the cause of it) and their discharge is direction-selective (dependent on the direction of motion). The cell shown in the figure fired in anticipation of arm movements between 90° and 225°, but did not fire at all or actually showed a decrease in firing rate in anticipation of movements in other directions.

How can direction-selective cells in primary cortex dictate movement if their range of selectivity is so broad? Undoubtedly the motor cortex intended a more precise movement of the arm than "somewhere between 90° and 225°." The resolution may be found when the activity of many upper motor neurons is taken into account. Georgopoulos (and colleagues (1982) found that when a **population vector** (an expression of the tendency to fire with movement in a particular direction) of a large number of cortical unit records, with movements in various directions, was computed mathematically, it corresponded closely to the actual direction of limb movement. These results suggest that a similar mathematical computation is performed by some subcortical structure and is used by the brain to reduce the vague directions (plan for action) from the cortex into precise vectoral limb movements (execution).

In people and other primates, only the lower motor neurons controlling the digits of the hand are under the direct control of primary motor cortex. In the human brain there are some 30,000 giant pyramidal cells, called **Betz cells**, in each primary motor cortex. These combine with equal numbers of fibers that originate in premotor and somatosensory cortex to form the **pyramidal tracts** (or *corticospinal tracts*) that descend directly to innervate lower motor neurons in cervical cord.

Most of the fibers of the pyramidal tracts decussate in the brainstem to form the *lateral corticospinal tracts* in cord, but a few project ipsilaterally in the *ventral corticospinal tracts*. All other motor function in primates, and most motor function in quadrupeds, is provided by another network, the **extrapyramidal system**, in which the outflow of motor cortex is subjected to computations and refinements by the subcortical basal ganglia, the thalamus, and the cerebellum.

The Basal Ganglia

After a decision to act has been made, movement still requires the participation of a group of nuclei in the center of the cerebrum collectively known as the **basal ganglia** (Figure 10–6). The afferent and efferent projections of the basal ganglia are widespread in thalamus and neocortex, a fact that has made physiological investigation of their function difficult. As a consequence we know much less about the basal ganglia than about other brain regions. However, the basal ganglia in humans seem to be especially prone to a variety of diseases. The treatment and clinical investigation of these disorders con-

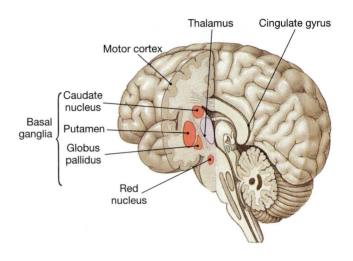

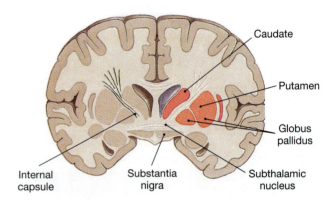

Figure 10–6   *Elements of the Basal Ganglia.* The extrapyramidal motor system originates in the basal ganglia.

tributes insight into the purpose of the basal ganglia in the human brain. Diseases of the basal ganglia may produce cognitive or emotional deficits and may or may not be fatal. A feature common to all basal ganglia disorders is *inhibition of voluntary movements and initiation of involuntary movements.* Thus it is widely believed that the intricate intracortical connections made by the basal ganglia are essential to the volitional aspects of motor performance.

Caudate, Putamen, and Globus Pallidus

Innervation of the basal ganglia arises from all cortical areas including primary motor cortex, premotor areas, and frontal association cortex as well as limbic structures. Much of this input arrives in two nuclei, the **caudate nucleus** (so named because of its taillike appearance) and the **putamen**. Together, the caudate and putamen are called the **striatum** because the structures interdigitate with white matter in the **internal cap-**

sule, giving the appearance of alternating gray and white stripes in fresh tissue. In general, the *corticostriate* ("from cortex to striatum") projections to putamen are associated with descending motor commands, though projections to the caudate and ventral striatum appear to add cognitive and affective input from the frontal lobes and limbic system, respectively.

The striatum projects within the basal ganglia to the **globus pallidus**, a spherical structure at the end of the caudate's "tail" (see Figure 10–6). Two other structures are associated with the output of the basal ganglia, the **subthalamic nucleus** and the dopaminergic projection from the tegmentum that originates in the **substantia nigra** (see Box 5–4). The output is predominantly back to cortex via thalamic *motor relays* in the **ventrolateral nucleus (VL)** and two other thalamic nuclei, the *ventral anterior* and *mediodorsal*, all of which project substantially and diffusely back to the frontal lobes of the brain. Hence the connections of the basal ganglia suggest an organizing and integrating function with regard to motor, premotor and psychomotor cortex.

The Pathobiology of Stroke and Diseases of the Basal Ganglia

The vascular supply of the internal capsule and striatum consists of a very fine mesh work of *arterioles* (fine arteries) and *venules* (fine veins). These are more susceptible, in humans, than other cerebral vessels to suffer rupture or blockage by a blood clot or other object, an event called a stroke. The consequence is local **ischemia** (loss of blood flow), **infarct** (tissue damage due to coagulation), and **hypoxia** (inadequate oxygen) or **anoxia** (absence of oxygen). As oxidative glucose utilization ("respiration") is the sole source of cerebral energy consumption (Chapter 14), these pathological consequences of stroke lead to nerve cell death. This produces, in some cases, **hemiplegia** (partial paralysis on the side of the body opposite the lesion, or stroke damage). Since sensory structures of the internal capsule interdigitate with the basal ganglia in the striatum, there is usually attendant loss of contralateral sensory function as well, such as numbness or paresthesia (Chapter 9). Treatments for stroke include attempts to dissolve blood clots, surgical intervention to excise or widen blood vessels, and attempts to lower acutely the metabolic rate of the affected area.

Parkinson's disease and Huntington's disease are two other disorders of the basal ganglia. The symptoms of these diseases are instructive because they reflect different cellular deficits among the nuclei. Parkinson's disease is a deficit in the amount of dopamine secreted by cells of the substantia nigra, and Huntington's disease (sometimes called "Huntington's chorea") is a defect in cells that secrete acetylcholine and GABA within the basal ganglia.

Parkinson's disease is a disorder characterized by an inability to initiate movement, or **akinesia**, especially walking, and by a "pill-rolling" **tremor** in which the patient appears to be rolling objects between the fingers and thumb of each hand. The *palsy*, or motor defect, in Parkinson's disease seems to be specifically associated with voluntary movements. A Parkinson's patient may have normal reflexes and may be able to perform complex and sequential behaviors, such as walking, but may appear to be unable to initiate a motor sequence. Spouses of Parkinson's patients tell of husbands or wives that pause in doorways or at curbs, unable to begin to walk across but who are able to do so when given a little push by their partners. Indeed, a novel and experimental treatment for Parkinson's disease entails an electrical *pacemaker* placed in the globus pallidus so as to provide the periodic impulse to act that Parkinson's patients lack (see Siegfried & Lippitz, 1994).

Although L-dopa administration is also an effective therapy for Parkinson's disease (see Box 5–4) it is not a cure. Since the therapy requires *some* intact dopaminergic cells, it can become ineffective as the disease proceeds, and long-term use can become complicated by side effects. Current strategies for effecting a cure involve two approaches. First, in an attempt to replace the damaged dopaminergic fibers, surgeons have made use of the fact that the CNS is "immunologically privileged" in that the blood-brain barrier isolates it from bloodborne antibodies. Hence there is little danger of rejection of transplanted tissue. Since aminergic fibers typically lack myelin investment altogether (Chapter 5), scientists reasoned that the usual barriers to regeneration that the CNS puts up might not apply with equal force to the dopaminergic innervation of the basal ganglia. Dopaminergic cells from two sources, pig adrenal glands and aborted human fetuses, have been surgically transplanted into the region of the internal capsule on both sides of the brain of Parkinson's patients. While there is convincing evidence of transplant *viability* (in other words, the transplanted cells survived) and even some evidence of axon extension and apparent reinnervation, there is considerable controversy over whether the implants are clinically effective. For this reason, some prominent researchers have called for a halt to these experimental surgeries until more animal research on the method is complete, whereas others have questioned the ethical implications of using human fetal tissue.

The second approach to a cure is to identify Parkinson's disease early in its progress and intervene in the disease process. This entails understanding of the **etiology**, or underlying cause, of the disorder and so far this understanding has been elusive. An unexpected step forward was taken when a batch of illegally synthesized heroin became contaminated by a byproduct of the synthesis: 1-methyl–4-phenyl–1,2,3,6 tetrahydropyridine, or MPTP. This compound was absorbed by accident by seven drug users and each developed striking symptoms of Parkinson's disease. Subsequent animal trials showed that MPTP destroyed cells of the substantia nigra, by a yet unknown mechanism, and produced degeneration of dopaminergic fibers in the basal ganglia just as is found upon autopsy of Parkinson's victims. This research had two impacts on the search for the cure. First, it led some investigators to posit that the etiology of Parkinson's disease normally involved an as yet undetected environmental toxin similar to MPTP. This new theory competes with other models, such as viral or genetic etiology, that are currently under investigation. Perhaps more importantly, a second outcome of the discovery is the development of a useful animal model for Parkinson's disease. By determining how MPTP damages dopaminergic cells in rats or mice, scientists may be able to discover what processes are at work in the substantia nigra of people who are suffering from the condition.

The symptoms of Huntington's disease present an interesting contrast to those of Parkinson's disease. In place of the inability to initiate movement and the rigidity of Parkinson's disease, there is excess of undesired movement and lack of muscle tone in Huntington's disease. The movements consist of **chorea** (sudden movements of the limbs), which are sometimes violent and dramatic, in which case they are called **hemiballismus.** *Athetosis* and *dystonia* (writhing movements and grotesque posture, respectively) are also symptoms of some basal ganglia disorders.

Theories of the etiology of Huntington's disease focus most intently on probable genetic causes. All Huntington's patients appear to be descended from two individuals from Suffolk County in England who emigrated to New England with the pilgrims in the seventeenth century. The disease appears to be due to a dominant gene, and hence transfers to offspring a 50 percent chance of inheriting the disorder. Efforts to eliminate Huntington's focus on testing for a **genetic marker** for the disorder, in this case an abnormally large number of repeated nucleotide sequences in a gene on the short arm of chromosome 4, so that carriers of the gene can be identified before the disease commences and counseled about the chances of passing it on to their children. Unfortunately, for those genetically programmed to develop the condition there is currently no effective therapy. Researchers seeking to understand the disease are studying the interactions between the abnormal proteins produced by this gene and proteins vital to brain function (see Burke et al., 1996, and Kalchman et al., 1997).

The Cerebellum

Whereas the basal ganglia appear to exert a diffuse influence over the output of the motor cortex and hence appear to influence the "volitional" aspects of motor function, the con-

nections and anatomy of the cerebellum are suggestive of a more precise, limited influence over the activity of the extrapyramidal system, specifically in the area of refinement of *execution*.

As we have seen, execution of behavior itself is no trivial matter, as it is composed of many different elements. Which part of execution is particularly cerebellar? Think of this question as we consider the input to the cerebellum, its output, and its intrinsic circuitry.

Afferents

The cerebellum in people is a cauliflower-shaped structure, about the size of a clenched fist (OK, maybe the clenched fist of a child), located dorsal to the pons and the fourth ventricle (Figure 10–7). It is commonly divided into *lobes* based on anatomy, but it is more convenient to consider functional regions based upon input from evolutionary history. The phylogenetically "oldest" part of the cerebellum receives input directly from the vestibular organs and hence is called the **vestibulocerebellum**. It lies most caudally in a lobe called the *flocculonodular lobe* (also *archicerebellum*). It is the smallest of cerebellar regions in many animals, and the only cerebellar region in fish and sharks.

Running medially across both the *anterior* and *posterior* lobes that make up the bulk of the human cerebellum is the **spinocerebellum** (or *paleocerebellum*). Its principal input is from proprioceptors in the spinal cord, together with various sensory afferents from the cranial nerves. Also spanning the anterior and posterior lobes, surrounding the spinocerebellum laterally and dorsally, is the **corticocerebellum.** As the name implies, it's principal input is from cortex, *extrapyramidal motor cortex* in particular. It is the most recently evolved part of the cerebellum (not found in animals that lack cerebral cortex, for example); hence it is also known by the name *neocerebellum.* Both the spinal and the cortical inputs to the cerebellum are somatotopically organized, as we have come to expect.

Efferents

As there are three principal *inputs* to the cerebellum, (vestibular, proprioceptive, and extrapyramidal motor), so there are three principal *outputs.* The vestibulocerebellum projects back to vestibular structures directly, but all the output of the other two divisions flows through intermediary structures known as the **deep cerebellar nuclei** (Figure 10–8). The spinocerebellum projects inward to the **fastigial nucleus** and the **interposed nucleus** (otherwise known as the *globose* and *emboliform nuclei*) and from there to descending extrapyramidal structures including the **red nucleus** in the hindbrain, which leads, ultimately, back to the spinal cord. The outflow of the corticocerebellum is through both sides of the bilateral **dentate**

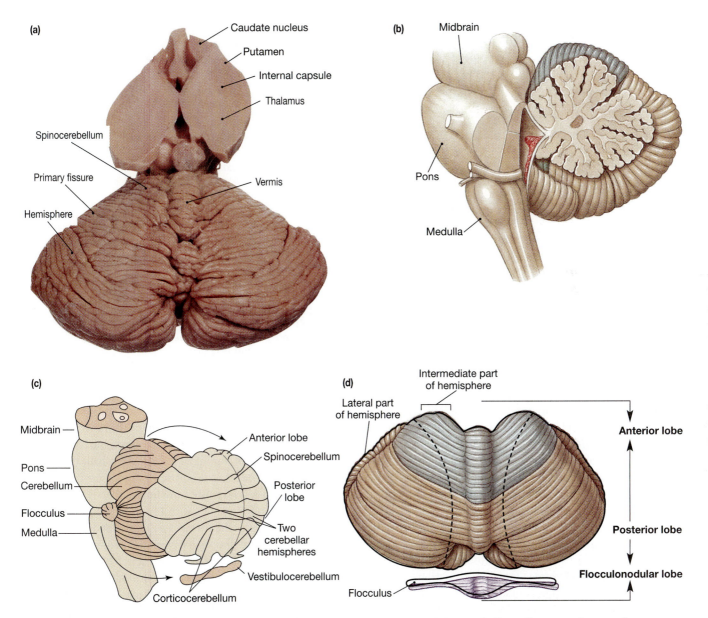

Figure 10–7 *Divisions of the Cerebellum.* Four different renderings of the cerebellum illustrate the complex geometry of this structure. (a) Dorsal view shows the relation to the basal ganglia. (b) Midsagittal view through the brainstem. (c) Perspective view of the hindbrain shows the location of the three phylogenetically distinct regions of the cerebellum: vestibulocerebellum, spinocerebellum, and corticocerebellum. (d) Dorsal view of the cerebellum divided by fissures and regions. The anterior and posterior lobes are divided by the primary fissure. Laterally, the cerebellum is divided into intermediate and lateral portions, which correspond roughly with the spinocerebellum and corticocerebellum, respectively. The flocculus roughly corresponds with the vestibulocerebellum. (Adapted from Nieuwenhuys, Voogd, & van Huijzen, 1988)

nucleus, which also projects to the red nucleus, and ultimately back to cortex. The output to cortex arrives in the SMA and premotor areas where it is thought to organize, among other things, the postural adjustments that are necessary to maintain the body in upright position during execution of limb movements (see Box 10–2). Output to spinal cord is *ipsilateral* and output to cortex is *contralateral* (reversing the crossing of the pyramidal tracts). As a consequence the cerebellum is unusual among brain regions in that damage to the structure results in behavioral deficit *on the same side as the lesion*.

Intrinsic Circuitry

Within the cerebellar cortex, in each of the three divisions, lies a deceptively simple synaptic circuit that is well understood

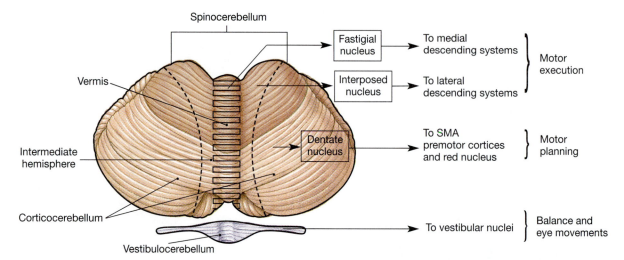

Figure 10–8 *Output of the Cerebellum.* Each of the three regions of the cerebellum sends motor information to a group of nuclei. The vestibulocerebellum projects through the vestibular nuclei, while the spinocerebellum and corticocerebellum project through the deep cerebellar nuclei. In particular, the spinocerebellum sends muscle commands to the body through the fastigial and interposed nuclei, while the corticocerebellum sends balance and planning information through the dentate nucleus to the SMA and premotor cortex where a plan for action is conceived.

because it is very attractive to neurophysiologists and those that fund their work, in part because of its potential application to physical science. In controlling the *execution* of movements, the cerebellum must be very adept at manipulating directions in space. Many physical quantities, such as velocity and momentum (velocity multiplied by mass), have a direction associated with them, because in order to be able to compute how an object will move in space, we need to know which direction the object is traveling. In physics, these directional computations are known as **vector analysis**. The vector analysis involved in moving a missile or an airplane requires computers of tremendous sophistication, and the refinement of such computers (including "supercomputers" that attack problems with parallel processing strategies) is a subject of much interest to the military. Even the best of these computers fail in comparison to the human cerebellum, which has a capacity for vector analysis that vastly surpasses manufactured machines in both data quantity and efficiency. This explains the sizable military support of research on cerebellar circuitry. The cerebellar circuit, with a latticelike organization that has been compared to a crystalline array, probably also uses parallel processing strategies (see Box 9–3) to solve the enormously complicated problems of human motion. Consider, for example, a task as seemingly simple as throwing a baseball at a target. The weight of the ball (proprioceptive input) and the distance and direction to the target must be assessed, and then the necessary velocity and acceleration of the hand and arm through space must be calculated (vestibular) and continuously readjusted (vestibular

and extrapyramidal motor) in less than one second. The force of gravity on the ball both held and aloft must be computed and all the other limbs of the body must move in harmony with the throwing arm to maintain balance and continuity. To the motor cortex's command to "throw the ball" the cerebellum adds a *rehearsed program of execution* to make the throw. The task is far more complicated than it seems at first glance, but in individuals with talent, practice, and a functional cerebellum, the throw is a graceful and accurate one.

The specific inputs (vestibular, proprioceptive, and motor) arrive in the cerebellar cortex in a type of axon called a **mossy fiber** because instead of terminating in numerous discrete boutons it terminates in a single large ending that attracts numerous dendrites, yielding a "mossy" appearance (Figure 10–9).

Like other "old" cortex (see Chapter 8), the cerebellum has not six layers, but three. The layer of mossy fiber terminals is the deepest of these, called the **granular layer** because **granule cells** are the predominant cell type. Granule cells receive the mossy fiber input, which is excitatory. The excitation is modified by a local inhibitory cell, the **Golgi cell**, which creates inhibitory surrounds from the incoming excitation. The middle layer is made up of the followers of the granule cells, the **Purkinje cells**, and thus it is called the *Purkinje cell layer*. The dendrites of Purkinje cells extend into the most superficial layer, the **molecular layer**, where they branch extensively *in one dimension only*, adopting a flat fanlike morphology. The axons of granule cells also extend to the molecular layer where they bifurcate and synapse onto the

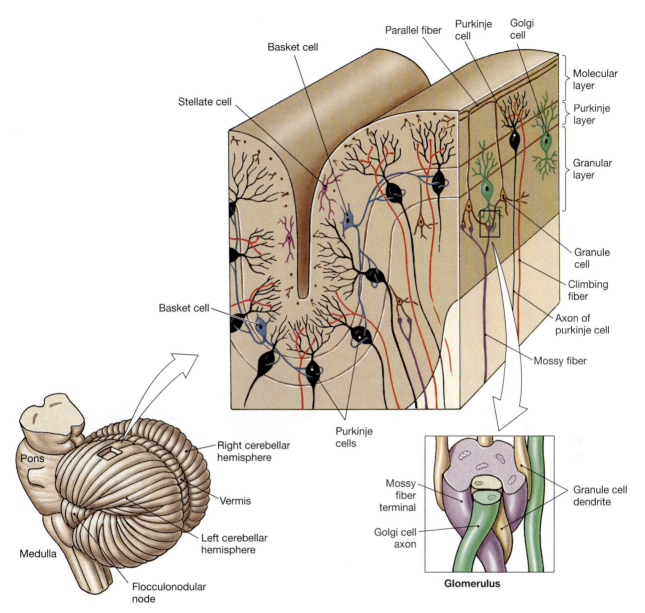

Figure 10–9 *Circuitry of the Cerebellum.* The cerebellar cortex, like other "old" brain structures, has just three layers, each containing different cell types. The innermost granular layer houses the excitatory termination of mossy fibers onto granule cells, which in turn have an inhibitory input from Golgi cells. In the Purkinje cell layer, the Purkinje cell bodies extend their axons inward to the granular layer and dendrites outward into the molecular layer, where they receive excitation from both parallel fibers (groups of granule cell axons) and climbing fibers. Also in the molecular layer, basket cells and stellate cells function to inhibit the Purkinje cell firing rate. A glomerulus (from the root Latin word for "ball of yarn") is where multiple Golgi cell axons and granule cell dendrites form synapses with the large bouton of a mossy fiber.

Purkinje cell dendrites. These rays of granule cell axons are called **parallel fibers** as a consequence of their orientation parallel to one another. Two cell types, the **stellate cell** and the **basket cell** (so named because of their appearance in stained sections of cerebellum), focus excitatory activity within a beam of parallel fibers by creating local circuit inhibition in the molecular layer.

The Purkinje cell dendrites are stacked upon one another like poker chips or wafers and the parallel fibers synapse upon them with great density, as many as 200,000 parallel fiber contacts for each Purkinje cell. This barrage of excitation (modified, of course, by the three inhibitory cell types: Golgi, stellate, and basket) drives the Purkinje cells to fire at great frequency (50 to 100 spikes per second) approaching

Box 10–2

The Cerebellum as a Vector Analyzer

The cerebellum was a puzzle to neurobiologists for many years. The efferent projections to motor structures suggested involvement in the extrapyramidal system, and the combined vestibular, proprioceptive, and extrapyramidal afferents suggested an integrative function in coordinating large movements involving adjustments throughout the body. Ablation experiments, however, provided inconclusive results. After animals with cerebellar lesions awake from surgery their condition is such that for a period of time they must be hand-fed to survive. Slowly, ability to move about is restored and the basic features of their motor behavior appear normal. Human autopsy results also proved confusing, as individuals with grossly normal motor capacities while alive were found to have cerebellar damage or atrophy. (Apocryphal reports exist that Louis Pasteur was one of these, though he managed sufficient motor ability to conduct experiments proving the germ theory of life.) So confounding were the original observations of cerebellar function that one neurophysiologist was heard to remark in mock frustration that perhaps the function of the cerebellum is merely to act as padding or stuffing, just to keep the brainstem from flopping about as we move.

Real understanding of cerebellar function awaited investigation of the cellular circuitry of the structure. The

the theoretical limit imposed by the refractory period. In addition to the thousands of parallel fibers that synapse on it, each Purkinje cell receives input from exactly one of another type of cerebellar afferent fiber, the **climbing fiber**. All climbing fibers arise from a single source in the brainstem, the **inferior olive**.

Each parallel fiber is effective in driving the Purkinje cell to fire a single action potential (Figure 10–10), and the vast majority of Purkinje cell activity is from this type of excitation. Although each Purkinje cell receives input from only one climbing fiber, this fiber diverges and makes numerous contacts on the soma and proximal dendrites of the Purkinje cell and thus it is also very powerful in evoking excitation. Spikes due to climbing fiber excitation are dense and multiple and are called complex spikes. The excitation due to the climbing fibers also appears to have a condition-

ing effect on Purkinje cell excitability that endures beyond the complex spike. For example, the firing pattern of specific Purkinje cells changes if a movement encounters unexpected resistance. During a "training period" when the subject is learning to apply more force to complete a movement, complex spikes (reflecting climbing fiber input) increase in frequency. After learning is complete, complex spike activity ceases, *but the Purkinje cell's response to parallel fiber excitation is altered to accommodate the new demand on the motor system*. Scientists believe that an interaction between the synaptic inputs from parallel fibers and climbing fibers (called heterosynaptic facilitation, Chapter 15) is the actual basis for motor learning in simple tasks. The cerebellar cortex and deep nuclei have been implicated in more intricate forms of learning as well, as for classical conditioning of the eyeblink response to novel stimuli and for

cerebellum is very densely packed with cells (as many, by some counts, as the rest of the brain combined). The principal cell type, the Purkinje cell, is among the most electrically active in the brain; as a consequence the cerebellum is metabolically very active. This high rate of metabolism renders the cerebellum more susceptible than other brain regions to physiological stress (metabolic *insult* is the term that is used). For example, the blows to the head experienced by boxers result in mechanical stress to the cerebellum, which lies at the back of the skull and is bashed against it with each blow to the face. Short- and long- term stress of this kind produces a "punch drunk" condition in which gait is impaired ("drunken sailor's gait") and speech is slurred. This condition is an example of **cerebellar ataxia**, or a loss of muscle coordination characteristic of cerebellar damage. Short- and long-term exposure to physiological stressors such as alcohol can produce cerebellar ataxia as well, either acute or chronic.

In fact, getting drunk is essentially an experiment in cerebellar physiology, though it is not one recommended by the author nor one that is likely to get you any extra credit from your instructor. All the motor functions possessed by an individual while sober, minus the ones retained when drunk, are probably as close to being a description of human cerebellar function as any other. The **roadside sobriety test**, developed by police over years of experience, is a systematic examination of these functions. A sober person can usually tilt the head backward with the eyes closed and maintain balance and posture while standing, but a drunk person may be unable to do so, a test of the integrity of *vestibulocerebellar* function (balance). "Walking the line" with the eyes either open or closed tests vestibulocerebellar function as well as the *corticocerebellar* capacity to coordinate balance with the graceful movement of all four limbs. A test in which the subject is asked to alternately touch his or her own nose and the police officer's moving finger tests *spinocerebellar* function, as proprioceptive feedback is necessary to smoothly track a moving object through space with the arms. Inability to perform this task is known to specialists by the hideous name *dysdiadochokinesia*, which is a symptom of cerebellar ataxia. Cortical pyramidal circuits and other extrapyramidal circuits are able to compensate for this somewhat in ataxic individuals, but continuous adjustments in space are needed to seek the object, and as a result the tracing movements appear jerky and uncertain. Smooth, skilled coordination of limb movement in space requires continuous feedback regarding limb position, accuracy of motion, the force and direction of gravity, resistance to motion, and above all, calculations of *likely trajectory* (the direction in which the officer is likely to move his or her finger). These functions, which can loosely be described as *ballistic computations*, are the motor functions contributed by the cerebellum.

changes in the vestibulo-ocular reflex (see below and Chapter 15). Thus it seems likely that the climbing fibers from the inferior olive that project to the cerebellum have a major role to play in behavioral plasticity.

There is yet another projection received by cerebellar cortex that is only recently becoming understood. The locus coeruleus and raphé nuclei of the brainstem (see Figure 8–5) project noradrenergic and serotonergic fibers, respectively, to cerebellum just as they project such fibers to the cerebral hemispheres and other cortex. The work of Floyd Bloom, Barry Hoffer, and Roger Nicoll, among others, indicates that these diffuse projections have the effect of *increasing the membrane resistance* of primary cells such as Purkinje cells, probably by inhibiting a calcium-dependent potassium conductance (Chapter 5). This renders the primary cells *more responsive to other synaptic input*, both excitatory and inhibitory, yet *less active in the absence of such input*. This is because with higher resistance each synaptic current is less able to leak out of the cell before it can alter transmembrane voltage. The behavioral consequences of this "modulatory" effect is unclear, but it appears that the monoaminergic influence induces a state of "quiet readiness" for action in the primary cells of cerebellum, cerebrum, and hippocampus that may be the neural basis of attention and arousal (Nicoll et al., 1990).

The Purkinje cell is the *only* cell that projects axons out of cerebellar cortex, and these projections are *exclusively inhibitory*. GABA is the likely transmitter of Purkinje cell impulses to the deep cerebellar nuclei. The high rate of Purkinje cell firing means that the deep cerebellar nuclei are subjected to intense, continuous inhibition, or **tonic inhibition**, and that the cerebellar influence on the extrapyramidal motor

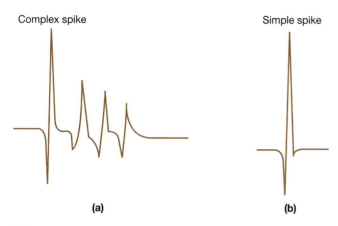

Complex spike   Simple spike

(a)   (b)

Figure 10–10 *Purkinje Cell Action Potential.* A Purkinje cell's response to excitatory input depends on the type of cell exciting it: (a) the response to a climbing fiber; (b) the response to a parallel fiber. (Llinás & Sotelo, 1992)

system and the planning and execution of behavior is expressed exclusively by inhibition and disinhibition.

The Importance of Inhibition

No more dramatic demonstration of the importance of inhibition in the brain can be found than in the output of the cerebellar cortex. Dense with inhibitory Purkinje cells, each firing at 50 to 100 Hz, the cerebellum can be imagined to bombard brainstem motor structures with inhibition all the time, day and night, pausing only to coordinate (by disinhibition) some general movement of the body such as walking, running, or throwing a ball.

Dramatic examples abound elsewhere in motor systems as well. We have already considered the Renshaw circuit in the spinal cord in which collateral excitation is converted, by activation of an inhibitory interneuron, into self-inhibition and surround inhibition as a mechanism for making motor commands more discrete at the level of the lower motor neuron (Chapter 7). Now let's consider two other examples, one in the brainstem and another in cortex, showing the importance of inhibition in all levels of motor function.

Efference Copy in the Oculomotor System

The control of the movement of the eyes in the orbits of the skull has many features in common with other motor systems but a few that are unique. For example, oculomotor neurons lack the monosynaptic reflex of spinal motor neurons. The feedback regarding muscle stretch is not necessary because the load on the eye muscles (the mass of the eye) is always the same (as opposed to the arms or legs, whose muscles bear different masses at different times). The eyes have no need to adjust for unexpected resistance as spinal motor units do. Furthermore, they lack the Renshaw circuit, its

function being replaced by oculomotor circuitry intrinsic to the brainstem.

Six separate brainstem systems influence the movements of the eyes. The first, the **vestibulo-ocular reflex**, is also called the doll's head reflex (Chapter 8) since its purpose is to keep the eyes stable in space as the head moves, a universal feature of visual systems that toy makers have exploited to make dolls more unnervingly lifelike. Indeed, this and the other five oculomotor systems may be the *most* lifelike behaviors we display, for the eyes are called "windows to the soul" not only because of the importance of what goes through the eyes to the brain but also because their movements and those of the facial muscles surrounding them are so expressive of interest, mood, attentiveness, and so forth.

The simplest circuit for the vestibulo-ocular reflex is quite simple indeed, involving only three cells and thus three synapses: vestibular neurons, interneurons of the vestibular nucleus, and oculomotor neurons. Vestibular neurons drive interneurons of the vestibular nucleus. The interneurons inhibit oculomotor neurons driving *ipsilateral* movement of the eyes and excite oculomotor neurons driving *contralateral* movements of the eyes (Figure 10–11).

The vestibulo-ocular reflex can be modified under a number of circumstances. Eyeglasses, for example, either expand or reduce the size of the visual image, which therefore requires an adjustment in the magnitude of the compensatory reflex. Experimentally, human subjects have worn glasses that expand or reduce this magnitude by as much as a factor of two, and even have *reversed direction* of the reflex using spectacles that invert the image on the retina. This last experiment is considerably disorienting during the period of adjustment and a similar period of disorientation occurs again when the spectacles are removed at the end of the experiment. However, after this initial period of disorientation, the cerebellum compensates for the artificial distortion and the subjects see normally. Steven Lisberger and his colleagues have shown that this plasticity of the reflex involves participation of the vestibulocerebellum in modifying the reflex magnitude of the circuit shown in Figure 10–11 (Lisberger et al., 1987).

Finally, the entire vestibulo-ocular reflex can be inhibited when it is undesirable. For example, when both the head and an object of interest are moving, the vestibulo-ocular reflex would normally draw gaze away from the object of interest. In this circumstance a second reflex takes over, the **optokinetic reflex**, which integrates vestibular input and visual input to hold the image stable.

Three forms of eye movement track objects when the head is still. **Saccades** are small darting movements of the eyes (easily detected while reading). **Smooth pursuit** involves a different set of signals from oculomotor nuclei to maintain gaze on a moving object. In the case of saccades, smooth pur-

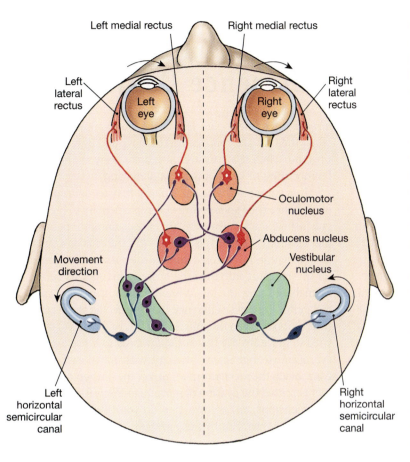

Left medial rectus   Right medial rectus

Left lateral rectus   Right lateral rectus

Left eye   Right eye

Oculomotor nucleus

Abducens nucleus

Movement direction

Vestibular nucleus

Left horizontal semicircular canal

Right horizontal semicircular canal

Figure 10–11   *Vestibulo-ocular Reflex.* The "Doll's Head Reflex" is a very basic indicator of life and is used in triage.

suit, and the oculomotor reflexes, the eyes move in the *same direction*. A separate system is required to organize movements of the eyes in opposite directions, as when they follow an object growing closer or going away. These movements are called **vergence** movements. They are organized by the oculomotor nuclei and higher structures such as the *pontine* and *mesencephalic reticular formations*, the superior colliculus and a region of the frontal lobes called the **frontal eye fields** (see figure in Box 10–1). Several of these areas contain maps of the visual world and, when stimulated electrically, cause the eyes to move to a spot in the visual world corresponding to the site of the electrode within the map.

All of these movements create demands on the visual system that are greater than you might expect. In order to make sense of the visual world, it is essential that the CNS keep track of which visual stimuli arise from eye movements themselves. The mechanism that is used is efference copy, the subject of Box 10–3. (Also see Chapter 7.)

Finally, a sixth projection to the eyes from the third cranial nerve and from the sympathetic ganglia of the paraver-

tebral chain regulates the diameter of the pupil. Part of this is reflexive in that the pupil constricts upon high levels of ambient illumination and dilates in low light without input from the brain. However, there is a nonreflexive aspect to the central control of pupil diameter as well. Large, dilated pupils are considered a sign of interest and alertness and at various times throughout history have been considered to be a very attractive female feature. Dilation is a sympathetic function mediated by norepinephrine; "sympathomimetics" (substances that mimic sympathetic activity) such as the plant alkaloid **belladonna** have been used to dilate the pupils cosmetically. Indeed, the word *belladonna*, literally translated, is "beautiful woman." In larger doses, however, the alkaloid can cause psychosis, paralysis, coma, or death, and therefore is also known as "deadly nightshade."

Epilepsy and Seizures

The transmitter *GABA* is likely to be the mediator of most inhibitory synapses in the brain, and the transmitter candidate *glycine* likely mediates most inhibition in the cord. GABA antagonists such as *bicuculline* and glycine antagonists such as *strychnine* (rat poison) produce **seizures**, or convulsive, unrestrained motor excitation involving part or all of the body. Knowledge of the mechanism of action of these poisons supports the idea that all motor circuits are poised for expression all the time and are restrained at most times by tonic inhibition. Disinhibition, in this model, would be the central signal for occasional, or *phasic*, expression of appropriate motor programs.

Clinical conditions that have seizures as one of their manifestations are collectively called **epilepsy**. Epilepsy is probably not a single disorder with one etiology but several. Partial or *focal epilepsy* entails seizures in only part of the body and arises from unbounded excitation in a restricted brain region (usually contralateral to the seizure). At times the excitation will spread from the focus to adjacent regions of brain, producing spreading partial seizures known as **Jacksonian March** after the early neurologist John Hughlings Jackson who described seizures that started in the fingers and spread proximally to include one-half of the body musculature.

The causes of epilepsy are many, with the common feature of damage to inhibitory systems. As we have seen, continuously active inhibitory cells are more metabolically demanding than their normally silent excitatory counterparts and hence more susceptible to metabolic stress. Trauma in the birth canal, for example, can render an infant's inhibitory sys-

Box 10–3

An Experiment in Efference Copy

Why doesn't the world appear to move when you move your eyes? This is another deceptively simple question in neurobiology, since most of you probably have never been aware that the world *ought* to appear to move when the eyes do.

Convince yourself that the world *ought* to move by doing the following experiment: Stare straight ahead with both eyes open and (gently!) push one eyelid inward, moving the eye. The world as seen through that eye will appear to move with reference to the world as seen through the other, stationary eye. Now try it with the other eye closed, pushing only the open eye. Notice the world move. Finally, with one eye closed, use the oculomotor muscles of the open eye to shift your gaze by an equivalent amount. The world will appear stationary. Why?

Though the oculomotor neurons lack Renshaw circuits, they nevertheless have axon collaterals that feed back into the CNS from the fibers that exit to innervate the oculomotor muscles. The efference copy borne in by these axon collaterals is directed to the superior colliculus and other centers that organize gaze, informing them that the appearance that the world is moving is merely a consequence of eye movement. *Neurally, the image of the stationary world is moved an equal amount in the same*

direction. The net result is that the world appears stable when the eyes are commanded to move and only appears unstable when the eyes are moved passively, without efference copy, or when it is actually moving.

It is rumored that a particularly zealous neurophysiologist once tried an experiment complementary to the one you just conducted. Knowing that the oculomotor neuron, like all motor neurons, is cholinergic and acts at a nicotinic receptor, he injected curare, the specific antagonist for this receptor, into the orbit of one of his eyes. As curare is unable to pass the blood-brain barrier, it left the axon collaterals that cause efference copy unaffected at the same time as it paralyzed the muscles of the eye. Then, when he tried to move his eye the *world appeared to move* but the eye, of course, remained stationary. With only the efference copy intact, the mechanism to *correct* the illusion of movement *created* the illusion of movement. Now, for the insatiably curious, which direction do you think the world appeared to move in this experiment, in the same direction as the intended movement, or the opposite? A little rehearsal with the much less drastic experiment outlined above will spare you the trouble of injecting curare into your eye. (You will discover, I think, that the world moves in the opposite direction of the intended eye movement.)

tem so hypoxic (lacking oxygen) that the inhibitory cells are permanently damaged, producing epilepsy. Drug abuse, failed suicide attempts, and cerebrovascular accidents can have similar consequences later in life. In addition, there are sufficient other occasions for seizures, such as alcohol withdrawal and febrile convulsions (produced by fever), to suggest that seizures have multiple etiologies.

Generalized epilepsy entails seizures involving the entire body. **Petit mal seizures** are sometimes called *absence seizures* since the convulsions are not dramatic or life threatening but nevertheless correspond to a period of unconsciousness. Unconsciousness also occurs with **grand mal seizures**, but these also involve forceful muscle constriction producing rigidity (**tonus**) followed by dramatic jerking movements of the limbs (**clonus**). The patient suffering grand mal seizures falls to the ground and, because the diaphragm is

involved, may stop breathing and die. Generalized epilepsy may also involve a focus of activity in one part of the brain that then spreads to the entire brain. Clinical evidence for this includes the fact that patients sometimes experience a foreboding of seizures, or **aura**, which varies according to location of the likely focus of activity as detected by **electroencephalography (EEG)**, a procedure wherein conductors attached to the scalp measure electrical potentials in the brain. Epileptics with focuses of activity in the temporal lobes, for example, might experience auditory hallucinations as an aura of an impending seizure. The temporal lobes seem to be more susceptible than other brain regions to the damage that creates an epileptic focus. Auras of temporal lobe epilepsy often have an emotional component, as was the case for Russian author Fyodor Dostoyevsky who experienced intense spiritual feelings as an aura of epileptic episodes.

Seizures can be induced experimentally in animals to investigate the likely cause of epilepsy in people. In these animal models seizure activity in the EEG corresponds to a sudden wave of depolarization inside the cell called the **paroxysmal depolarization shift** (Figure 10–12). This depolarization may reflect a transient failure of first local and then general inhibition. Following or concurrent with this initial intracellular spike, the cell may fire numerous action potentials, and the surface recording may show a spike called an *interictal EEG paroxysm*. After the paroxysmal depolarization shift, the cortical neurons are hyperpolarized and go through a "silent period." Further interictal paroxysms occur in greater frequency until commencement of the tonic seizure. The research into the causes of the paroxysmal depolarization shift has led to the most effective current drug treatments for epilepsy, many of which involve compounds that enhance the action of inhibitory transmitters.

Epilepsy is effectively treated by drugs that enhance inhibition, generally by increasing the affinity of GABA for its receptors (Chapter 17). On occasion, surgery is also employed to break epilepsy. Recent work indicates that seizure activity following brain injury may not always be best treated with anticonvulsant drugs (Hernandez et al., 1997).

Command Neurons and Motor Tapes

Much of this chapter has been devoted to the vertebrate motor system. However, study of simple nervous systems can also be very illuminating in understanding how action comes about.

Invertebrate nervous systems often display the property of **eutely**, the exact same number of neurons in the brain of each member of a particular species. For example, the nematode *C. elegans* has exactly 302 neurons in its brain, each of which can be assigned an identity based on its position in the *cell lineage* of mitotic events leading back to the zygote, or fertilized eggs (Figure 10–13). Figure 10–13a shows two cells that can be identified in specimen after specimen since they are always found in the same place. These are known as HSNL and HSNR and function for the worm as lower motor neurons would in a vertebrate. In Figure 10–13c a portion of the cell lineage is shown, illustrating that portions of the nervous system arise from several specific cells in the early embryo. Only one of these produces HSNL and HSNR, the more specific lineage shown in Figure 10–13b. An equally elaborate and specific lineage can be provided for all the neurons in the nematode. The behavioral repertoire of the nematode is not very elaborate (302 cells cannot organize more than a few stereotypic behaviors), but animals with more elaborate capacity for behavior also display eutely. Insects, crustaceans, and mollusks have all provided examples of "hard-wired," eutelous nervous systems in which **identified neurons** make

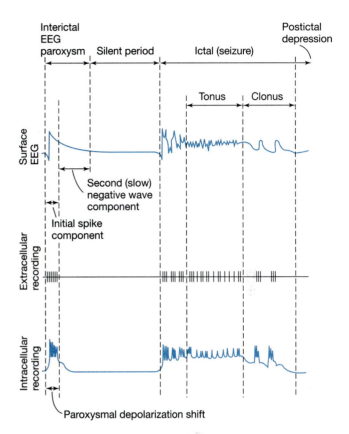

Figure 10–12   *Seizure Activity in the Brain.* Focused cortical seizures induced in a laboratory animal show that prior to the development of a prolonged seizure (tonus and clonus periods), there are EEG *paroxysms* (spasms), the first of which is linked to a rapid intracellular depolarization of the cortical neurons (paroxysmal depolarization shift). After the cortical neurons recover from hyperpolarization, the frequency of the EEG paroxysms increases, and the seizure becomes imminent. (Alaya et al., 1973)

synaptic connections in a genetically programmed and very stereotypic manner (Chapter 15).

Some of the best understood of these motor networks organize locomotion in general and escape behavior in particular. Locomotion entails alternate movements of muscle groups on each side of the body. Rhythmic behaviors such as locomotion appear to arise by activation of **central pattern generators** (Figure 10–14). These are networks of *mutually inhibiting* interneurons that produce oscillating (alternating) outputs. Inhibitory synapses are shown as solid circles in Figure 10–14. The inhibitory contacts transiently suppress the motor circuit for one side while the other side is constricting. These outputs can easily be modeled by computers and model electrical circuits. The oscillations drive the reciprocal movements in leech swimming (see Figure

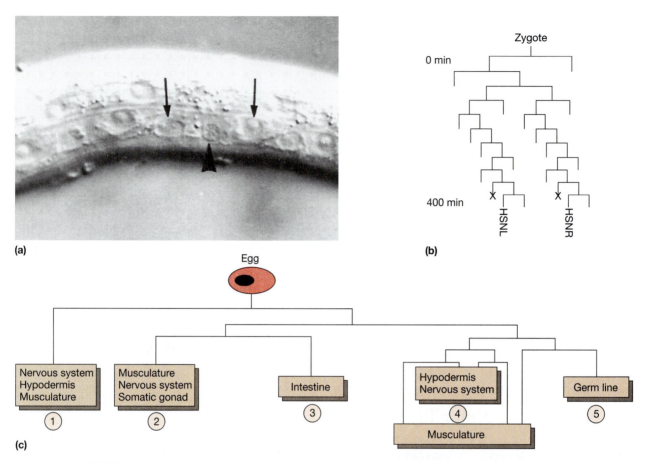

Figure 10–13 *Eutely in Nematodes.* Each nematode *Caenorhabditis elegans* develops exactly 302 distinct neurons, each following a specific genesis. The relative simplicity (in contrast to vertebrates) and invariance of their neural development makes nematodes ideal for motor function study. (a) Markers identify the HSNL and HSNR neurons of a nematode under a microscope. The developmental lineage is understood both for specific cells (b), as well as general structures (c). (Sulston & Horvitz, 1977; Desai et al., 1988)

10–14) and the alternating movements of the limbs in cockroach walking and other simple systems. Figure 10–15 shows a simplified version of a well-worked-out circuit for escape behavior in crayfish. "Giant fibers" (which are large, teleologically, so as to be able to conduct action potentials quickly) collect sensory information regarding tactile stimuli, using both chemical excitation (triangles) and electrical excitation (resistor signs), and activate a motor neuron pool that generates the tail-flip escape response. Vertebrates do not possess many identifiable neurons and almost certainly are not eutelous, but in fish and amphibians there are a pair of giant fibers, the **Mauthner cells** that similarly organize escape behavior by rapidly conducting action potentials and electrotonically activating tail movement motor neuron pools (Figure 10–16). The Mauthner cells are the only identified vertebrate neurons. All others appear to be part of functionally related pools, with a certain degree of redundancy and overlap of function.

The types of behaviors organized by these eutelous and hard-wired nervous systems fall into the general category of fixed **action patterns** (more accurately called *modal action patterns* by those in the know). Fixed action patterns, as the name implies, are behaviors often "released" by a momentary sensory stimulus that play themselves out in very stereotypic or fixed form. Such patterns of activity seem to scientists that study them to arise from a **motor tape** or program of motor activity that is stored in the circuits that are activated by *command neurons*. Vertebrate fixed action patterns (yawning and sneezing are frequently cited, but see discussion of sexual behavior in Chapter 12) may also arise from motor tapes and command neurons, but two factors complicate attempts to apply these concepts to behaviors beyond those simple systems discussed here. First, true examples of command neurons (single cells both necessary and sufficient for eliciting the behavior) are rare even in eutelous nervous systems. De-

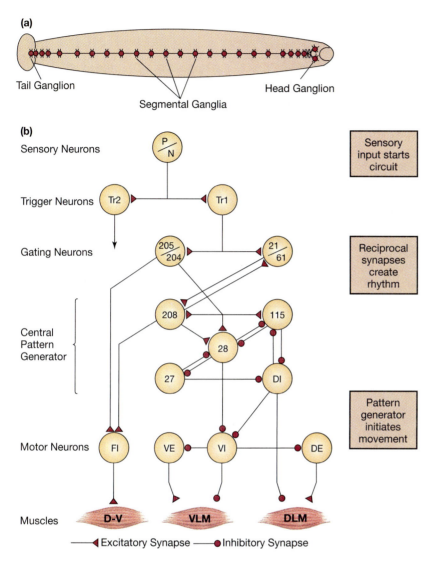

(a)

Tail Ganglion

Segmental Ganglia

Head Ganglion

(b)

Sensory Neurons

Trigger Neurons

Gating Neurons

Central Pattern Generator

Motor Neurons

Muscles

◄ Excitatory Synapse ● Inhibitory Synapse

Sensory input starts circuit

Reciprocal synapses create rhythm

Pattern generator initiates movement

Figure 10–14 *Central Pattern Generators.* In another example of a well-understood motor system, the leech coordinates swimming movements with the aid of central pattern generators. (a) Segmental ganglia along the longitudinal axis are responsible for managing muscle contraction along the body. These contractions must follow a precise alternation to be effective in swimming. (b) Central pattern generators, consisting of a network of mutually inhibitory neurons, help regulate the alternation of muscle contractions along the body. (Adapted from Friesen, 1989)

tailed investigations of simple systems often reveal that "command" decisions are the property of "committees" of cells and that even eutelous neurons can be redundant, rendering them, in the strict sense, "unnecessary." Second, it is unclear how applicable fixed action patterns are to complex behaviors. Konrad Lorenz and Niko Tinbergen, the concept's inventors, found numerous examples throughout the animal kingdom (see Lorenz, 1970), but modern ethologists (students of behavior in its natural context) find that few complex behaviors, however uniform in appearance, are truly *fixed* as they would have to be if they were a product of such motor tapes.

The development of eutelous circuits in many cases involves the process of neuron elimination known as *apoptosis* or *programmed cell death*. The cross marks in Figure 10–13b indicate the position of such cell deaths in the developmen-

tal lineage of the nematode nervous system. Such orderly suicide of neurons also occurs in non-eutelous organisms. What role do you think this mechanism has in behavior? Very likely, the acquisition of skills and cognitive abilities involve the *elimination* of synapses and even neurons in growth and adulthood. It seems that in development, just as in learning (Chapter 15) *less is more in the brain*.

As we have seen in the last two chapters, complex behaviors seem to arise from *parallel processing in non-eutelous systems*, rendering the search for the vertebrate "command neuron" as elusive as the search for the grandmother cell, and for much the same reasons. Still unaccounted for in our discussion of motor systems is the central basis of motivation. This subject, however, moves us closer to the desire of organisms to seek pleasure and avoid pain, the topic of our next chapter.

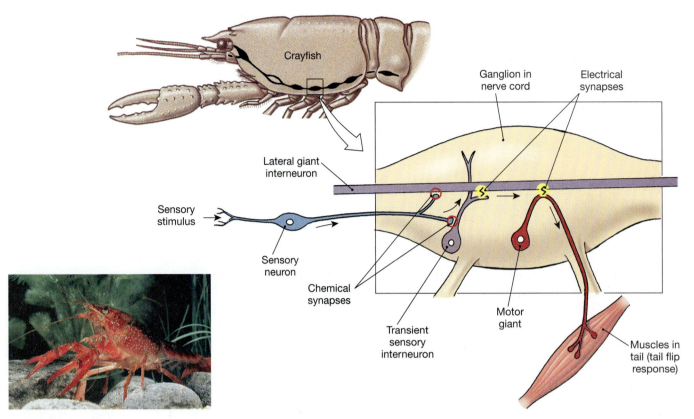

Figure 10–15. *Escape Circuit in Crayfish.* The crayfish's tail-flip response is mediated by both chemical and electrical means. (Adapted from Wine and Krasne, 1982)

Figure 10–16. *Escape Circuit in Fish.* The Mauthner cells in fish and amphibians are the only identified neurons in vertebrates. This circuit creates the escape response of a fish, which, when startled, will turn 90° in a fixed action pattern resulting from a motor tape.

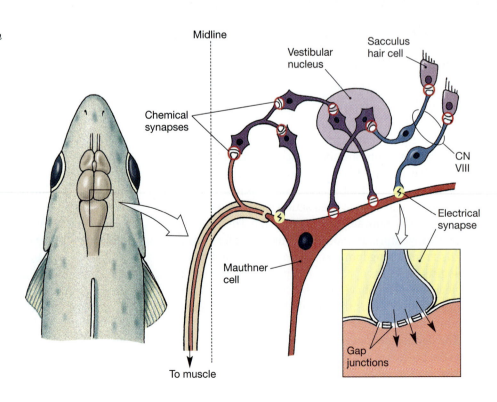

SUMMARY

The decision to act is made somewhere between sensory structures in the parietal lobe (where the readiness to act is determined) and primary motor cortex in the frontal lobe (where execution begins), in a network of associated cortical regions called psychomotor cortex. These associate motor areas include the premotor cortex, the supplementary motor area, the cingulate gyrus, and the prefrontal cortex (which together are responsible for organizing the plan for action). Primary motor cortex in the precentral gyrus contains one of many motor homunculi for the opposite side of the body. Betz cells in this region form the origin of part of the pyramidal tracts, which directly control the movements of the fingers in primates. Many of the other motor functions of the body are controlled by the extrapyramidal system, which includes the basal ganglia, cerebellum, parts of the thalamus, and the red nucleus in the hindbrain. The basal ganglia (which are involved with motivation to act) are the caudate nucleus, the putamen, and the globus pallidus, plus associated substantia nigra and subthalamic nuclei. Stroke, Huntington's disease and Parkinson's disease are among the disorders of the basal ganglia, which appear to organize the volitional aspects of movement.

The cerebellum refines a decision to act after it has been made. It integrates vestibular, proprioceptive, and extrapyramidal motor afferents into a single type of inhibitory output to the deep cerebellar nuclei and the extrapyramidal system. Its high cell density and high rate of metabolism render the cerebellum highly susceptible to physical or chemical stress; its crystalline circuitry renders it a model for complex vector analysis in other systems. The vestibulo-ocular reflex and other oculomotor systems govern the movement of the eyes. Eye movements are made compatible with sense of stability with reference to the outside world by efference copy and inhibitory circuits. Studies of epilepsy also illustrate the importance of inhibition in motor control. While simple nervous systems display the properties of eutely, hierarchy, serial processing of information, fixed action patterns, and motor tapes, complex nervous systems display the properties of parallel processing, redundancy of cell circuits, and distribution of function.

REVIEW QUESTIONS

1. How do the motor functions of the frontal and parietal lobes relate?

2. Where does volitional movement begin?

3. What is a command neuron?

4. List the basal ganglia and describe their function.

5. What does the cerebellum contribute to motor function?

6. What is efference copy? Why is it important?

7. Where does stroke occur most often in people? What are the symptoms?

8. How does epilepsy occur?

THOUGHT QUESTIONS

1. You already know that it is dangerous to drink and drive. Now describe *why* it is dangerous to drink and drive.

2. How would one go about designing an effective therapy for Huntington's disease?

3. Fixed action patterns in invertebrates can be elicited by brief electrical stimuli, a feature that has recently been applied to the field of *robotics*. Can you think of any engineering applications for fixed action patterns?

KEY CONCEPTS

akinesia (p. 237)
anoxia (p. 237)
aura (p. 246)
basal ganglia (p. 236)
basket cell (p. 241)
belladonna (p. 245)
Betz cells (p. 236)
caudate nucleus (p. 236)
central pattern generators (p. 247)
cerebellar ataxia (p. 243)
chorea (p. 238)
cingulate gyrus (p. 230)
climbing fiber (p. 242)
clonus (p. 246)
corticocerebellum (p. 238)
deep cerebellar nuclei (p. 238)
dentate nucleus (p. 238)
electroencephalography (EEG) (p. 246)
epilepsy (p. 245)
ethologists (p. 249)

etiology (p. 237)
eutely (p. 247)
extrapyramidal system (p. 236)
fastigial nucleus (p. 238)
fixed action patterns (p. 248)
frontal eye fields (p. 245)
genetic marker (p. 238)
globus pallidus (p. 237)
Golgi cell (p. 240)
grand mal seizures (p. 246)
granular layer (p. 240)
granule cells (p. 240)
hemiballismus (p. 238)
hemiplegia (p. 237)
hypoxia (p. 237)
identified neurons (p. 247)
infarct (p. 237)
inferior olive (p. 242)
internal capsule (p. 237)
interposed nucleus (p. 238)
ischemia (p. 237)
Jacksonian March (p. 245)

Mauthner cells (p. 248)
molecular layer (p. 240)
mossy fiber (p. 240)
motor homunculus (p. 231)
motor tape (p. 248)
optokinetic reflex (p. 244)
parallel fibers (p. 241)
paroxysmal depolarization shift (p. 247)
petit mal seizures (p. 246)
pineal body (p. 234)
population vector (p. 236)
posterior parietal cortex (p. 230)
precentral gyrus (p. 231)
prefrontal cortex (p. 231)
premotor cortex (p. 230)
primary motor cortex (p. 230)
psychomotor cortex (p. 230)
Purkinje cells (p. 240)
putamen (p. 236)
pyramidal tracts (p. 236)
readiness potential (p. 231)

red nucleus (p. 238)
roadside sobriety test (p. 293)
saccades (p. 244)
seizures (p. 245)
smooth pursuit (p. 244)
spinocerebellum (p. 238)
stellate cell (p. 241)
striatum (p. 236)
substantia nigra (p. 237)
subthalamic nucleus (p. 237)
supplementary motor area (SMA) (p. 230)
tonic inhibition (p. 243)
tonus (p. 246)
tremor (p. 237)
unilateral neglect (p. 230)
vector analysis (p. 240)
ventrolateral nucleus (VL) (p. 237)
vergence (p. 245)
vestibulo-ocular reflex (p. 244)
vestibulocerebellum (p. 238)

11

Pleasure and Pain

Is joy the absence of sorrow? Is sorrow the absence of joy? Are "feeling good" and "feeling bad" two extremes of a single dimension, differences in activity in some brain circuit that governs feelings? Or are there separate brain structures responsible for each, a *pleasure circuit* and a *pain circuit*? Is it possible to simultaneously experience both pleasure *and* pain?

We know that each category has numerous *nuances*. "Joy" is not exactly the same as "pleasure," for example, nor is "sorrow" the same thing as "pain." Indeed, it is the effort to capture the nuance of emotion that inspires much of our art and literature. It seems that this rich contribution to our culture reflects astounding diversity in our experience of feelings. In other words, perhaps there are *multiple* circuits for pleasure and pain. Analogy with the sensory systems and motor systems we have just considered suggests that this might be the case, for there are numerous maps of the body surface in the somatosensory system, each contributing a different nuance to the experience of bodily awareness. Likewise there are multiple motor homunculi, each with a slightly different role to play, and numerous retinotopic maps and cochleotopic maps, each providing a different aspect of vision and audition. As rich as these systems are in neural representation, our language to describe these experiences is impoverished in comparison to the language used to describe the subtle varieties of pain and pleasure (Table 11–1) and the other affectively laden senses, olfaction and gustation. If language reflects the complexity of central structures, we should expect to find many circuits mediating positive and negative feelings.

Anyone who has watched the evening news lately knows that there are many more words to describe pain than pleasure. Why? Based on the reasoning used earlier, perhaps there are a smaller num-

Table 11–1				EXPRESSING PAIN AND PLEASURE
Pleasure	amusement appreciation beatitude bliss care charm cheer comfort coziness	delectation delight ease ecstasy enchantment enjoyment euphoria felicity gaiety	gladness glee gratification gusto happiness harmony heaven joy luxury	paradise rapture relish satiety satisfaction sweetness thrill titillation zest
Pain	ache affliction aggravation agony ailment angst anguish annoyance bedevilment bite bitterness bother burning pain chafe chagrin desolation discomfort disconcertion displeasure dissatisfaction distress dolor	exasperation excruciating pain fretfulness gnawing pain grief gripe harassment headache heartache hell horror hurt infelicity injury irritation malaise misery molestation mortification nausea nightmare nip	nuisance ordeal pang peeve persecution perturbation piercing pain pinch pique plague provocation rankling rawness sadness sharp pain shock shooting pain sickness soreness sorrow splitting pain stabbing pain	stomach ache stretch suffering throbbing pain throe toothache torment torture trial tribulation trouble tweak twinge uneasiness vexation worry wound wrench wretchedness

ber of pleasure mechanisms than pain mechanisms in the brain, and this is reflected in our language. As we shall see in the sections that follow, one major pathway from brainstem to forebrain appears to mediate much of pleasurable experience. On the other hand, it appears that there are numerous pain systems with different projection schemes and transmitter mechanisms rather than a single central "pain nucleus" or fiber tract.

The Problem of Definitions

Sensory systems *create* as actively as they *experience* stimuli; similarly, the experiences of pleasure and pain appear to be created centrally. It is not as if external stimuli do not contribute to pleasurable or painful sensations, but the internal experience produced by a given stimulus is so varied (among individuals as well as within a single individual at different times) that the stimulus can be accurately described as ancillary to the central event. The central experience of pleasure or pain is like eating a meal, and the stimuli that make the experience pleasant or unpleasant are the condiments, music, company, and appetite. Condiments, music, and company that are pleasant on one occasion can have the opposite effect on another occasion; *they are not in themselves inherently pleasant or unpleasant.* At an elegant dinner in a French restaurant, loud heavy-metal music probably would be considered unpleasant by most people. The same music played at a wild party might seem appropriate and even pleasurable. Similarly, you might like gravy on your potatoes at dinner, but not on your pancakes at breakfast. Your like or dislike of gravy depends on the context of its use.

The transitory and contingent quality of pleasure and pain is compounded by the fact that experimental animals are unable to indicate directly the degree of each experience that is taking place at a given moment. Indeed, much of the time this can be very difficult for people as well (quick—on a scale of 1 [sad] to 10 [happy], rate your present condition). Because of these difficulties researchers in this area tend to adopt technical definitions (*operative* or *working definitions*) for stimuli that are considered conducive to pleasure or pain.

Working definitions of **pleasure** usually include the concept of **reward**. A reward, in this context, is a stimulus that an organism such as a rat or a person will work to obtain. Ordinarily, a model is introduced based on anthropomorphic common sense ("If I were a rat, I'd like this") and subjects are tested to see if they will pursue the stimulus. Sometimes, however, stimuli unrelated to anthropomorphism or common sense are used (see next section). In this case the reward is still defined as the stimulus pursued by the subject.

Operative definitions of **pain** fall into two categories. Stimuli are defined as *noxious* if they produce *tissue damage*, covering cuts, bruises, burns, scrapes, and so forth. Some of these, as you know, may be painful, some innocuous, and some even pleasurable (such as eating very spicy foods) but all are, by definition, noxious stimuli. Neurons that respond uniquely, preferentially, or partly to noxious stimuli are called nociceptors and the central response to such stimuli is called nociception (see Chapter 7).

The second category of pain, or at least unpleasantness, mirrors the working definition of pleasure. Again using common sense, experimenters assume that an animal (rats prevail in pain research) will object to the same type of stimuli people find objectionable. This is defined as painful and quantified according to how much, or how quickly, an animal will work to avoid it. For example, the **tail-flick test** is a common procedure in pain research. A radiant heat source of fixed intensity is administered to the tail of a rat and the time taken to flick the tail away is measured. The stimulus does not damage the tissue of the tail, and hence is not noxious according to the strict definition of pain above, since the animal removes its tail before it gets burned. Interestingly, the latency to the tail flick under a variety of conditions is the same as the time taken for a human volunteer to remove a finger from the same heat source. Furthermore, results of the tail-flick test on rodents closely correspond to subjective human reports of pain and pain relief when drugs that alleviate pain, **analgesics** (from the Greek *an* = without, and *al-*

gesia = pain), are administered or when other pain-alleviating conditions are evaluated.

Is There a "Pleasure Circuit" in the Brain?

There are probably several pleasure circuits in the brain. However, we shall consider only two here, since they are better understood than the others. One employs the catecholamine transmitter candidate, **dopamine**, and the other employs a class of peptide transmitters collectively called the **endogenous opiates**. The fact that both transmitter systems have important roles in other central processes (dopamine in motor systems and perception, endogenous opiates in pain modulation) underscores the difficulty of defining the central correlate of pleasurable experience.

Self-Stimulation Studies

In the 1950s James Olds and Peter Milner made a discovery that had a profound effect on the development of physiological psychology (Olds & Milner, 1954). As is rather often the case on such occasions, they were pursuing a research purpose unrelated to the direct investigation of pleasure or pain but chanced on an observation critical to such investigation. They had implanted indwelling electrodes into the skull of rats, securing them with tiny screws and dental cement, and then they had allowed the rats to recover from the surgery. After recovery was complete they allowed the rats to move freely about an observation chamber, a procedure now known as a *chronic physiological paradigm* or model. At intervals, they applied electrical stimuli, activating the brain structures in the vicinity of the tips of the electrodes. The researchers noticed that the rats tended to favor a location in the observation chamber where they had previously received stimulation. Reasoning that animals avoid circumstances of unpleasant association and seek circumstances with pleasant association, they surmised that the brain stimulation that the rats received had some positive association like that of reinforcement in learning theory (Chapter 15).

Interested in this result, the researchers provided a lever for rats to initiate the electrical stimulation themselves. Rats explored the chamber and, upon pressing the lever, were apparently reinforced for the behavior much in the same manner as food or water might reinforce a behavior in a conventional learning experiment (Figure 11–1). The rats frequently also displayed various **appetitive behaviors** (motivated by a biological or psychological need), such as eating, drinking, and copulation if suitable opportunities were available. Such appetitive behaviors display **satiety** or diminished frequency upon satisfaction of an appetite. However, self-administered

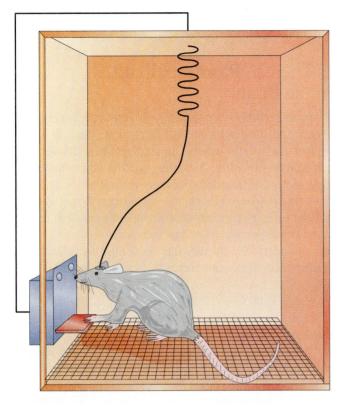

Figure 11–1   *Self-stimulation Studies.* By means of a lever, rats with electrodes in the medial forebrain bundle will continuously self-administer electric shocks. Stimulation in this region does not result in satiety.

electrical stimulation appeared to accelerate, not decrease, the rat's appetite for stimulation. Indeed, in the absence of opportunity for other appetitive behaviors, the rats would continuously administer the electrical stimuli, pressing the lever until exhausted. The failure of *central* reinforcement to display satiety challenged accepted notions of motivation and led to a rethinking of the underlying mechanisms for the generation of behavior (Box 11–1).

The Medial Forebrain Bundle

Olds and Milner (1954) carefully reconstructed the positions of the electrode tips by performing histology on the rat brains after sacrifice. They found many locations within the CNS that could produce self-stimulation. Sensory structures, motor structures, and limbic structures such as portions of the amygdala all contained sites where electrical stimulation appeared to be rewarding based on the rats' self-stimulation behavior. However, one region seemed to produce self-stimulation more reliably than others and at lower electrical intensities. This region was not a nucleus of cell bodies but rather a fiber tract, the **medial forebrain bundle**, a collection of axons projecting from the hindbrain to forebrain and cor-

tex. The terminal fields, or areas of innervation, of the medial forebrain bundle include portions of the limbic system, such as the *cingulate gyrus* ("limbic cortex") and the *septum* and *amygdala* (logical targets for a system involved in reward), but also olfactory and frontal neocortex and parts of the basal ganglia. In particular, a structure known as the **nucleus accumbens** receives terminals of fibers in the medial forebrain bundle and has been the focus of investigations into the mechanism for the rewarding quality of medial forebrain bundle stimulation. The projections of the medial forebrain bundle are shown in Figure 11–2.

Dopamine and Reward Systems

The cells of origin for some of the fibers in the medial forebrain bundle are found in the *substantia nigra* and *ventral tegmentum,* two regions of dopamine-containing cell bodies in the brainstem (see Figure 11–2). The projection from the substantia nigra is called the **nigrostriatal pathway** as it terminates in the *striatum* (the caudate nucleus and putamen of the basal ganglia). The connection of this dopaminergic projection to reward is unclear since its primary function is to expedite the volitional aspects of motor function (Chapter 10). However, as sensations can be pleasurable, so can movement, and perhaps the nigrostriatal portion of the medial forebrain bundle contributes to the positive affective quality of stimulation by encouraging movement, much like pulling a lever on a slot machine is rewarding to compulsive gamblers.

The projection from the ventral tegmentum is called the **mesocortical and mesolimbic projection,** since it projects medially to both the neocortex and the limbic system. More attention has focused on this complement of dopaminergic fibers in medial forebrain bundle, and there is more direct evidence for involvement of these fibers in reward mechanisms. Electrical stimulation of the ventral tegmentum alone is reinforcing. Figure 11–3 (see page 260) illustrates the results of an experiment by Fibiger et al. (1987) in which the number of times a rat pressed a lever to self-administer electrical stimulation of the ventral tegmentum is shown on the vertical axis and the electrical intensity of the stimuli is shown on the horizontal axis. As can be seen, the rats will work very hard to obtain maximal stimulation of this area, up to 1,200 lever presses in just five minutes (open circles).

Electrical stimulation of the ventral tegmentum is mediated by the dopaminergic mesocortical and mesolimbic projections. In one experiment, researchers used a specific poison, 6-hydroxydopamine (6-OH-DA), to destroy dopaminergic fibers on one side of the brain. This toxin is a synthetic (not naturally occurring) derivative of dopamine, that apparently is taken up by dopaminergic cells in the place of dopamine, but jams up dopamine packaging systems in the

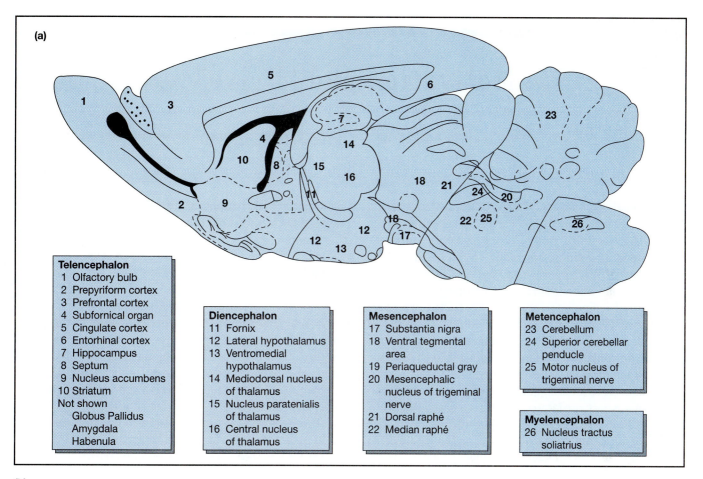

Telencephalon
1 Olfactory bulb
2 Prepyriform cortex
3 Prefrontal cortex
4 Subfornical organ
5 Cingulate cortex
6 Entorhinal cortex
7 Hippocampus
8 Septum
9 Nucleus accumbens
10 Striatum
Not shown
  Globus Pallidus
  Amygdala
  Habenula

Diencephalon
11 Fornix
12 Lateral hypothalamus
13 Ventromedial
  hypothalamus
14 Mediodorsal nucleus
  of thalamus
15 Nucleus paratenialis
  of thalamus
16 Central nucleus
  of thalamus

Mesencephalon
17 Substantia nigra
18 Ventral tegmental
  area
19 Periaqueductal gray
20 Mesencephalic
  nucleus of trigeminal
  nerve
21 Dorsal raphé
22 Median raphé

Metencephalon
23 Cerebellum
24 Superior cerebellar
  penducle
25 Motor nucleus of
  trigeminal nerve

Myelencephalon
26 Nucleus tractus
  soliatrius

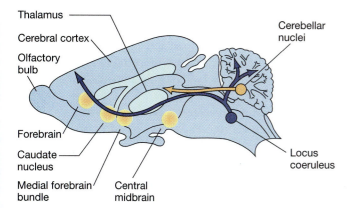

Figure 11–2 *Self-stimulation Sites in the Brain.* The medial forebrain bundle is one of the many sites in the brain where electrical stimuli are rewarding: (a) a section of the rat brain listing some of the sites for self-stimulation; (b) a rat brain section showing the medial forebrain bundle and other self-stimulation sites in the same pathway (yellow circles).

vesicles sufficiently to actually destroy them. When the fibers are destroyed on one side of the brain, electrical activation of the tegmentum on that same side (ipsilateral) is no longer rewarding (solid symbols), though the tegmentum on the contralateral side, with fibers in the intact medial forebrain bundle, can still produce reward.

The tegmental projection terminates widely in forebrain (including the olfactory tubercle, entorhinal cortex, septum,

amygdala, and pyriform cortex). Which target in particular is the site of dopaminergic reward? An experiment by Stellar, Kelley, and Corbett (1983) indicates that it is the *nucleus accumbens* in particular that is involved. Injections of spiroperidol, a dopamine antagonist, into the nucleus accumbens eliminates the rewarding quality of medial forebrain bundle activation. Other investigators have shown that microinjections of dopamine into this region are rewarding,

Box 11–1

Motivation and "Drive"

I want to say, in all seriousness, that a great deal of harm is being done in the modern world by belief in the virtuousness of work, and that the road to happiness and prosperity lies in an organized diminution of work. • *Lord Bertrand Russell,* In Praise of Idleness *(1935).*

Bird-watching is a hobby of mine. Unfortunately, sleeping late is also one of my hobbies and a consistent feature of bird behavior is that most of it happens early in the morning (or early evening, depending on the species). Song erupts shortly before dawn and continues through sunrise as mates are relocated and territories reestablished. Later in the morning song gives way to "notes," which are chirps and whistles of a sociable nature often emitted as warnings to other birds of potential dangers encountered while foraging for food. Finally, around 9:00 or 10:00A.M. in the summer (about the time my coffee is made, breakfast done and cleared away, lunch packed, books, bags, bottles and binoculars located, driving done, and I'm finally in the field) bird activity ceases altogether. Birds are then hard to locate and hard to identify because they are *doing nothing.* They are not sleeping, as might commonly be believed, for diurnal birds (the opposite of nocturnal) sleep at night. Nor does the heat of the day (at nine or ten o'-clock) keep them inactive. Rather, it is the common opinion of bird-watchers that they are inactive, merely sitting around in bushes and trees, *because their basic daily needs for food, drink, and social contact have already been met.* Further activity is an expenditure of energy that adds nothing to, and probably detracts from, their reproductive viability and evolutionary success.

Of course, this observation is not unique to birds and those who would watch them. Hunters and fishermen, for example, will immediately recall similar observations acquired in pursuit of their quarry. Domestic animals also

often appear to do nothing, an exception being those, like horses and cows, that basically eat all the time.

Commonplace observations such as these led to the notion of **drive** as a primary explanation of behavior. The incentive to behave in certain ways in animals was thought to consist of several basic urges or drives (food, drink, thermoregulation, and reproduction being the primary ones). Brain mechanisms existed to detect when the urges were not fulfilled and to produce satiety when they were fulfilled. Reward consisted of the satisfaction of these urges, or satiety. Thus drive is a concept that depends on another, satiety; while motivation is a concept that is independent of satiety.

Problems with the commonplace notion of drive arose when the search began for its correlate in the central nervous system. In the last chapter we encountered the notion of a command neuron and considered networks of neurons, called *pattern generators,* that act together to produce discrete behaviors called *fixed action patterns.* Aspects of eating, drinking, and sexual behavior in vertebrates very much resemble fixed action patterns in simple systems where the activity of command neurons and pattern generators may very well be the impetus that produces the behavior.

But what drives the command neuron? Some well-known command neuron candidates lie at the apex of ascending sensory cells and appear to integrate sensory stimuli into a "decision" to respond. Escape circuits in particular appear to work in this fashion (Chapter 10). A very

even in the absence of electrical stimulation. Much attention has focused on the nucleus accumbens as the site of action of the drugs cocaine and amphetamine, which are thought to act by depressing dopamine re-uptake and thus leaving more dopamine available to bind to postsynaptic receptors and resulting in a prolonged dopaminergic response (Chapter 17).

Experimental work has shown that cocaine injections increase extracellular dopamine concentrations in the nucleus accumbens while increasing the rewarding quality of tegmental stimulation (Phillips, Blaha, & Fibiger, 1989). Research in this area is very lively as a consequence of the general effort to understand and treat drug abuse (Chapter 17).

like the type it displays while still within the slug. Indeed, in isolation it displays a *circadian pattern* of activity, bursting more intensely at some times of the day than others. Could it be this single cell, or another like it, that inspires the sea slug to become active? Could there be analogous cells in our brains that lend "zest" to "the waking day" (in Sherrington's phrase, Chapter 1) and motivate us to work, play, create, tease, flirt, and engage in acts of kindness and generosity that cannot be explained away as mere responses to stimuli?

As we shall see in the next two chapters, there are very likely candidates for spontaneously active brain regions that impel us to such acts and thus appear to be the central correlates of motivation. The search for the central correlate of *drive* has been so elusive, however, that the very concept has come into disrepute. In our present discussion of brain reward mechanisms we discover that dopaminergic fibers in the medial forebrain bundle may mediate much of the pleasurable sensation we feel upon completion of appetitive behaviors. However, the activity of this system in no way resembles drive as commonly conceived. Drive displays satiety after it is exercised, so that we are no longer thirsty after drinking or hungry after eating. Activation of the medial forebrain bundle does not show this property, since it seems only to create more drive instead of dissipating it. Chemical mimicry of the system, as with drugs of abuse, creates the desire to take more drugs in the process of addiction rather than eliminating such desire as would be the case if drive were the dominant central mechanism.

Science proceeds as often by discarding concepts as by creating new ones. Although I cannot tell you why birds appear to do nothing after ten o'clock any more than I can explain why some people appear to do more than others (Bertrand Russell was the most prolific British philosopher of his time), I can counsel you that drive, as commonly understood, probably has little to do with it.

simple model (*much too simple*) views escape circuits as merely responses to *external* stimuli, and views appetitive behaviors as responses to *internal* stimuli (hunger, thirst, and so forth). The internal stimuli might themselves be sensory in a way, since *osmoreceptors* are thought to detect rising blood salinity to trigger thirst and *glucose receptors* may be involved in detecting low blood sugar to trigger hunger (Chapter 14).

More intricate appetitive behaviors (such as those that arise from the desire for exercises, sex, and fun) are harder to explain by reference to sensory stimuli, either internal or external, and seem to suggest the existence of some *spontaneously active command structure* in the brain.

Here too research on simple systems has provided insight into the cellular basis of motivation (as distinct from drive, which depends on satiety). Felix Strumwasser (1974) has described single neurons isolated from the sea slug *Aplysia californica* that exhibit spontaneous action potential bursting activity. The neuron R15, for example, can be surgically removed from the organism, upon which it resumes action potential activity of a variety very much

Reward should not be associated with dopamine in particular, since as for every other transmitter the action of dopamine is a function of the postsynaptic cell that expresses the receptor(s). In addition to their locations in the projections of the medial forebrain bundle, dopamine cells are also found in the retina, olfactory bulb, and hypothalamus, where they mediate sensory and endocrine functions unrelated to reward.

Ascending Nociceptor Systems

Primary nociceptors are cells with neurites in the periphery, cell bodies in the dorsal root ganglia, and axons inserting into

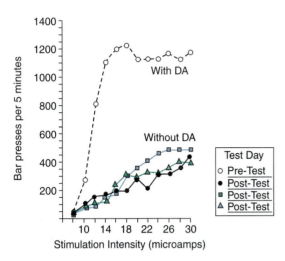

Figure 11–3 *Stimulation of the Ventral Tegmentum and Dopaminergic Reward.* Rats will work very hard pressing a bar which adminsters electric impulses to continuously stimulate the ventral tegmentum, enabling a form of nonsatiating dopaminergic reward. Rats with lesions to this area are not as driven to the lever-pressing behavior. (Adapted from Fibiger et al., 1987)

the spinal cord. They tend to be of small diameter, and the neurites in the skin are not associated with specialized nerve endings. Figure 11–4 shows a schematic of the tiny naked nerve endings (of course there are similar endings in bone, muscle, and viscera). Transduction of a noxious stimulus by nociceptors occurs by means different from all other sensory fibers with their specialized nerve endings. Innocuous stimuli have little effect on these cells, which respond primarily to tissue damage. Mechanical damage can influence the membrane potential of nociceptors by several means. Rupture of cells releases the intracellular fluid, which of course is rich in potassium ion. Elevation of the concentration of K^+ outside the cell, as we have seen in Chapter 3, can depolarize cells by changing E_k and raising V_m. Other local consequences of tissue damage are release of **histamine** from specialized cells very much like neurons but for lack of an axon (called **mast cells**) and from the damaged cells, a peptide, **bradykinin**. Both substances depolarize the nociceptor terminals and have other actions, such as dilation of nearby blood vessels, producing inflammation. (Now you know why you take *antihistamines* to control irritation of the nose and eyes from colds and hayfever.) Other local messengers including **prostaglandin** and **serotonin**, released from the damaged or nearby cells, spread the inflammation and nociceptor discharge to local regions, producing tenderness, known to specialists as **hyperalgesia**, in adjacent, undamaged tissue. Thus the first events in nociception are more diffuse, and in many ways more complex, than those in the first-order cells at other sensory systems.

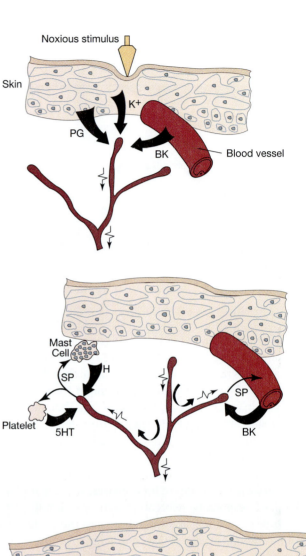

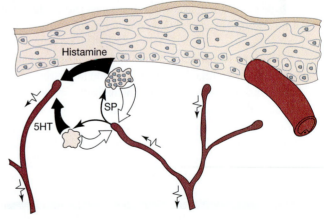

Figure 11–4 *Free Nerve Endings of Nociceptors.* A noxious (damaging) stimulus triggers a response in first-order nociceptive cells. Potassium and bradykinin (BK) released from the intracellular fluid of damaged cells depolarize the free nerve endings. Serotonin (5HT) and prostaglandin (PG) released from this fluid diffuse to nearby regions and spread the signal. Histamine (H), released from mast cells, depolarizes the free nerve endings as well and causes dilation of the blood vessels (inflammation). (Fields, 1987)

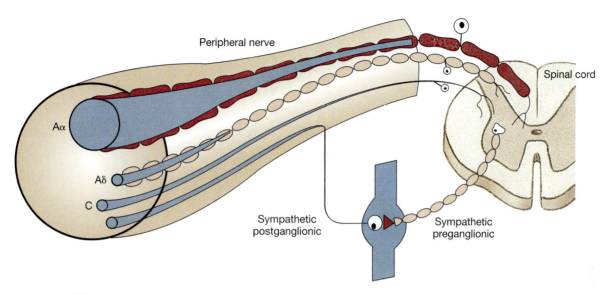

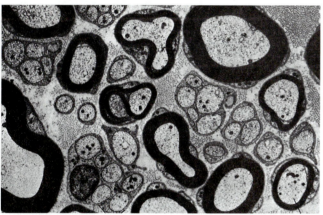

Figure 11–5 *Small Diameter Nociceptors.* Primary nociception (resulting from tissue damage) is conveyed to the CNS via two small peripheral nerve afferents shown in (a): myelinated Aδ-fibers with cell bodies in the dorsal horn, and unmyelinated C-fibers. The larger Aα-fibers carry mechanoreception information. (b) The electron micrograph shows a cross section of a peripheral nerve including all three fiber types. The dark black rings are myelin. (Dyck et al., 1975)

The volley of nociception is carried centrally by small *unmyelinated* fibers called **C-fibers** and by small *myelinated* fibers called **Aδ-fibers** (A-delta fibers) (Figure 11–5). The larger, myelinated fibers (Aα) (A-alpha) are for mechanoreception and conduct more rapidly. Activation of all the fibers at once, as in electrical stimulation of an afferent nerve, reveals the distinct electrical volleys (or synchronous cell firings) created by each fiber population (Figure 11–6).

Upon arrival in the cord, the Aδ- and C-fibers bifurcate, with the C-fibers terminating in superficial areas of the dorsal horn (the **substantia gelatinosa**) and the Aδ-fibers terminating superficially as well as deeply. Both terminal fields are diffuse in comparison to mechanoreceptor terminals (Figure 11–7).

You may be puzzled to learn that "pain fibers" conduct slowly and project diffusely. After all, internal experience suggests that a painful stimulus, such as touching a hot stove, evokes sharp, well-localized sensation and immediate response. The resolution of this apparent paradox is to be found in the fact, already emphasized in Chapter 7, that *nociception and pain are not the same thing.* As we shall see in the following sections, nociceptor discharge can be innocuous and even pleasurable and is essential to well-being. Pain, in contrast, can arise in the absence of nociception (see Box 11–3) and carries a component of fast-conducting mechanoreceptor activity so that it may be well localized and rapidly attended to. In the example mentioned, it may be that we *first* remove our hand from the hot stove (nociception), *then* feel the pain for having touched it. Let's consider what happens to the nociceptor information after it enters the cord to see how this might be true.

Substance P

Recall from Chapter 5 the story of Otto Loewi's isolation of *vagusstoff. Vagusstoff,* of course, turned out to be acetylcholine, the parasympathetic vagus nerve being rich in this autonomic transmitter. Recall also that a technical barrier to the identification of *vagusstoff* was the fact that the vagus

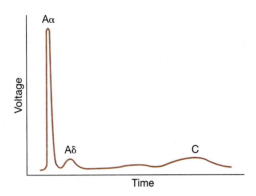

Figure 11–6 *Afferent Fiber Volleys.* The electrical pattern of a peripheral nerve event shows that the myelinated fibers (Aα, Aδ) conduct more rapidly than the unmyelinated C-fibers.

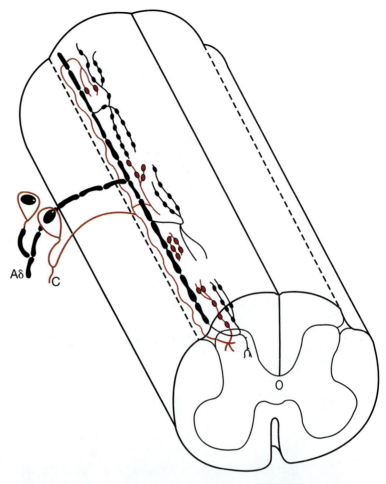

Figure 11–7 *Nociceptor Terminals in Cord.* Each Aδ- and C-fiber bifurcates and terminates at many places along the spinal cord; Aδ fibers also reach both an inner and an outer layer of the dorsal horn gray matter, while the C-fibers terminate mostly in the outer layer.

nerve contained several cardioactive substances, with acetylcholine being the predominant one. One of the others was found by Von Euler, a follower of Loewi, to be a complex molecule, and was not amenable to chemical characterization by the methods available in his day. It was, however, stable in powder form. This he called Substance P ("P" standing for "powder" as I recall) and left it alone for future analysis. There it sat for some fifty years until Susan Leeman, then at Harvard University, who was working on the *sialogogic* (saliva-producing) transmitter in another autonomically innervated structure, the cat salivary gland, determined that her transmitter was a peptide (chain of amino acids) similar in size and molecular weight to Von Euler's Substance P. Indeed, upon **sequence analysis** (removing each amino acid in turn and determining its identity by comparing its migration to a standard in **thin-layer chromatography**) it was determined that they were the same peptide.

The remarkable story of scientific serendipity behind the discovery of Substance P and the unraveling of its identity (shown in Figure 11–8) had an enormous (and also serendipitous) impact on pain research. An "undecapeptide" (peptide with eleven amino acids, Figure 11–8), Substance P was shortly located in other neurons besides the parasympathetics (like all other transmitter candidates, peptides do not have intrinsic functional properties but rather have different functions determined by the receptors on the cells in the specific circuit that employs them). As shown in Figure 11–9a, the marginal layers of the dorsal horn (the very region where the nociceptors terminate, see Figure 11–9) are rich in Substance P, and it is in this very region where receptors for Substance P are found most abundantly. Peptide is found in tissue sections by the process of **immunocytochemistry** (Figure 11–9a);

receptors are found in tissue sections by the process of **autoradiography** (Figure 11–9b).

As you well know from Chapter 5, much information is needed before a transmitter can be identified; enough has been gathered to confirm Substance P as the transmitter for at least some primary nociceptors. Upon electrical activation of nociceptors, Substance P is released into the extracellular space of the spinal cord (detected by yet another biochemical technique called **radioimmunoassay**, a technique wherein radioactive peptides are used to determine the presence and amount of other peptides, discussed in the Appendix). Application of synthetic Substance P to nociceptors mimics the synaptic effect of afferent activation. Synthesis and transport of the peptide in the dorsal root ganglia can be demonstrated easily by labeling newly synthesized peptides with radioactive amino acids and tracking them after synthesis.

The stumbling block to showing that Substance P is *the* (or at least *a*) transmitter for primary nociceptors came, as is often the case, in finding an antagonist for the receptor and in using this antagonist to block the action of both the endogenous transmitter and the action of the exogenous (applied) peptide, proving that they are the same. For reasons that we will discuss shortly, the medical community views pain or at least nociception as being a very good thing, and hence there has been comparatively little effort directed towards synthesis of a Substance P antagonist. (In apparent irony, there is an abundance of very fine antagonists for transmitters that *inhibit* pain, the product of many years of dedicated effort by pharmaceutical chemists. Try to guess the motive for this before reading it in Chapter 17).

While there has been some success in partly blocking nociceptor transmission to cord with weakly effective Substance

Figure 11–8 *The Sequencing of Substance P.* (a) The amino acid composition of Substance P was elucidated by fixing one end of the molecule and cutting one amino acid at a time from the other end, determining its identity with thin-layer chromatography (TLC) and repeating the process for each amino acid of the chain. (b) The results of this investigation showed Substance P to be composed of eleven amino acids.

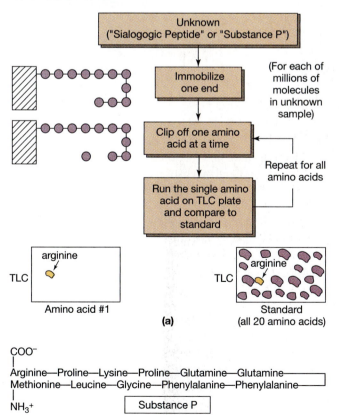

(a)

```
COO⁻
|
Arginine—Proline—Lysine—Proline—Glutamine—Glutamine
Methionine—Leucine—Glycine—Phenylalanine—Phenylalanine
|
NH₃⁺          Substance P
```

(b)

P antagonists (Konishi & Otsuka, 1985), the best evidence for Substance P as the endogenous transmitter comes from yet another serendipitous set of discoveries. A group of Hungarian scientists set out to find the active ingredient in paprika, the hot spice used in goulash and other regional delicacies. It turned out to be the same as the active ingredient in many hot spices of other national origin such as chili peppers of various kinds. The compound, **capsaicin**, has the property of depolarizing primary nociceptors and thus releasing Substance P. Indeed, it is the release of this nociceptor peptide that lends *pleasurable* quality to well-spiced hot food. Ethnographic data from many cultures shows that affinity for hot food is *acquired,* in the sense that small children the world over prefer their food more bland. While this may reflect the fact that *learning* can change an aversive stimulus into a pleasurable one (everything from tickling to playing football shows this to be true of children, since both are acquired tastes), there is another explanation for this phenomenon. It seems that developing nervous systems are more susceptible to the effects of capsaicin than mature ones, so much so that the depolarizing effects of capsaicin can actually destroy nociceptors in babies.

This was exploited experimentally in an attempt to deplete Substance P content in the spinal cord of newborn rats (Nagy et al., 1983). Substance P levels in the spinal cord were reduced to undetectable levels in the rats exposed to capsaicin. Importantly, they lost nociception as well, displaying little or no response to noxious stimuli. These results go far toward establishing Substance P as the transmitter for at least some of the nociceptors, or perhaps at least some of each nociceptor (Box 11–2)

From time to time people suffer depletion of spinal Substance P as a consequence of damage to small diameter afferents (not as a consequence of eating spicy foods, though). Such unfortunate individuals suffer from **pain insensitivity syndrome**. When this happens in childhood, most times as a congenital defect, debilitating effects accumulate and early death occurs, usually in adolescence (due to abnormal skeletal development). When it happens in adulthood, for example as a consequence of *syphilis, osteoporosis* is a debilitating consequence. Continuous postural adjustments are normally made as a consequence of subconscious (and hence, *not painful*) nociceptor discharge. When this doesn't occur, weight on the skeleton is not redistributed normally and the bones deteriorate.

Because pleasure often entails nociceptor input (such as in the effect of spicy food) and because such input is necessary to maintain good health, we can agree with specialists in this area that nociception is a good thing. But what about pain? Is it a good thing, too? Further, if pain is not a direct

Figure 11–9 *Substance P and Substance P Receptors in the Spinal Cord.* (a) In the photo on the left, we see that antibodies to Substance P react in the marginal layers of the dorsal horn (dark area), indicating the neurotransmitter is concentrated in this area. In the photo on the right, binding sites of Substance P are illuminated in roughly the same region. (b) The process of immunocytochemistry was used to obtain the photo on the left illustrating the presence of Substance P. Immunocytochemistry is a process wherein radioactive or dye-encoded antibodies label peptides of interest, thus illuminating the locations of these peptides. (c) The process of autoradiography was used to detect Substance P receptors in the photo on the right. In autoradiography, the peptides themselves, rather than the antibodies to them, are made radioactive and sections of a thinly sliced tissue sample are exposed to photography film.

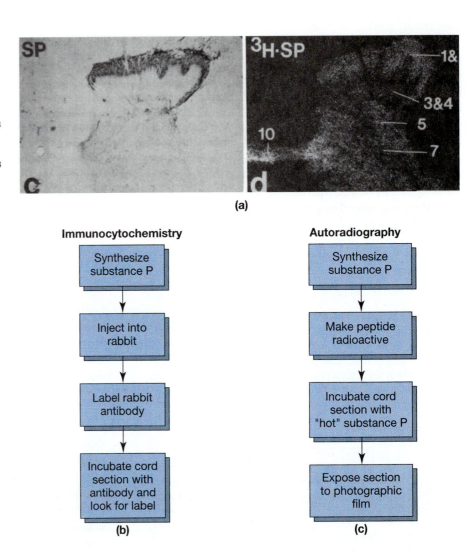

(a)

Immunocytochemistry

Synthesize substance P

↓

Inject into rabbit

↓

Label rabbit antibody

↓

Incubate cord section with antibody and look for label

(b)

Autoradiography

Synthesize substance P

↓

Make peptide radioactive

↓

Incubate cord section with "hot" substance P

↓

Expose section to photographic film

(c)

property of nociceptor input, then where does it come from? Let's examine what happens to the nociceptor input after it enters the cord (and brainstem for facial afferents) in an attempt to answer these questions.

The Spinothalamic Tract

The second-order nociceptors in the cord also are of two varieties. In the superficial layers there are cells that receive contacts from both Aδ- and C-fibers and have response properties only to noxious stimuli. They are called **nociceptive specific cells**. Deeper in the dorsal horn are found second-order cells that receive projections from Aα mechanoreceptors in addition to those from Aδ nociceptors. They have hybrid response properties to innocuous as well as noxious stimuli and for this reason they are called **wide dynamic range cells** and **polymodal nociceptors**. These cells have larger receptive fields than nociceptive specific cells. Still deeper in cord are high-order cells, called *complex cells,* that have loosely organized response properties that may include

noxious stimuli in many parts of the body. Hence, right at the level of the cord we find that there is substantial overlap between nociceptor and mechanoreceptor modalities and, to a certain degree, loss of topographic organization in the pain transmission system.

Second-order nociceptors immediately send their axons across the midline and ascend to the brainstem in the **lateral spinothalamic tract** (also called the *contralateral anterolateral quadrant* because some of the fibers in it actually project to areas besides the thalamus).

As shown in Figure 11–10, the spinothalamic tract interacts with two different regions of thalamus, a fact that is important because the two areas are thought to mediate different aspects of the pain percept. One area, the *medial thalamus*, receives a projection that is partly provided by third- and higher-order cells in the *reticular formation* and is known as the *paramedian* portion of the spinothalamic tract. The medial thalamic projection is thought to organize the negative affective (or emotional) quality of pain, as opposed to the

Box 11–2

"Dale's Law"

We have already noted some unusual features of the free nerve endings that mediate nociception. Another unusual feature of the endings is that they *secrete* in the periphery as well as *conduct* centrally (see Figure 11–4). As sensory fibers, their ability to "transmit at the receiving end" appears to violate the law of dynamic polarization (Chapter 2), which states that neurons normally conduct information in only one direction.

Peripheral release of Substance P causes vasodilation (and inflammation), edema (swelling), and the further release of bradykinin, histamine, and serotonin in part of the characteristic (and universally understood) response to a burn, bruise, scrape, or cut. The distinguished British neuroscientist Henry Dale, in noting this remarkable efferent property of these afferents, went on to speculate that their central processes would also secrete Substance P, a surmise that we have seen was substantially correct. After Dale's death, his followers took his insight and, much as gossip is changed as it passes from person to person, modified its meaning to the point that a generation of young scientists were taught **Dale's law:** that each neuron contained but a single transmitter and used that transmitter at all of its synapses. The "one cell, one transmitter" notion is now known to be false. Cells may switch from one transmitter to another in development, transiently expressing both (Chapter 15), and even in the mature condition may express as many as three or more transmitters. The figure shows typical data that supports this finding. A single cell can be sliced into very thin sections, and these sections mounted on slides. Then, immunocytochemistry for different transmitters can be done in consecutive sections, to show which cells contain multiple transmitter types. Alternatively, consecutive rounds of immunocytochemistry can be done on a single section to show how many transmitters exist in that section, or, as in the figure, antibodies for different transmitters labeled with *different colors* can show the presence of multiple transmitters simultaneously. In this case the yellow stain on the left shows cells that contain GABA and the red stain on the right shows that some of the same cells contain the peptide transmitter candidate CCK. Since there are so many different transmitter candidates, it is hard to test for all of them and as a consequence we are as yet unsure whether **colocalization** of transmitters is a general fea-

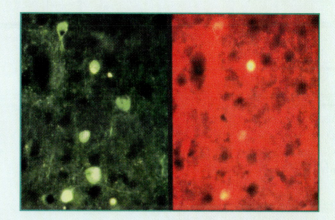

ture of all cells. However, as recent evidence accumulates, more and more systems have been shown to employ multiple transmitters in each cell. Indeed, it now appears that "Dale's law" is not even true of the primary nociceptor, which is now thought to contain additional transmitters and to depend on them for part of its action.

Though "Dale's law" was found to be incorrect, Dale's observations were not, and much can be learned from study of the small diameter nociceptor. Consider the phenomenon of **stigmata**, in which lesions *spontaneously* appear on the body surface without identifiable cause. Often-cited examples (which are so rare that they may be untrue) are welts that arise in hypnosis when a subject is convinced that an ice cube in the hand is a hot coal, or the injuries that appear in appropriate places on the bodies of religious ascetics in contemplating the wounds of Christ. Often the appearance of stigmata is assigned a supernatural explanation, but see if you can come up with a physical one based on the neurophysiology of the pain system. Generally the questions I pose in this book are securely answered elsewhere in the text. However, stigmata are so rare that they are not amenable to scientific investigation under controlled circumstances. (I cannot even confirm or deny their *existence*.) Therefore, the only explanation I can offer you, should you fail to come up with one on your own, is merely a *plausible* one based on the evidence. This explanation is included at the end of this chapter, after an explanation of the mechanism of pain transmission, which is necessary background to understanding the possible physiological basis of stigmata.

Figure 11–10 *The Spinothalamic Tracts.* Two distinct pathways of the nervous system regulate different aspects of pain perception.

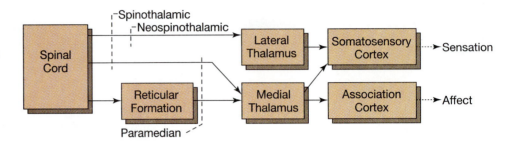

localization of pain to a portion of the body. Electrical stimulation of the spinothalamic tract as a whole produces painful sensations in parts of the contralateral body surface, but stimulation of the medial thalamus produces only **angst**, a vague feeling of discomfort not referred to a particular part of the body. The localization of pain to a portion of the body is thought to be mediated by the phylogenetically newer *neospinothalamic* projection to the *lateral thalamus* and, afterwards, to somatosensory cortex.

Thus pain as commonly experienced involves the activation of *two physiologically and anatomically distinct pathways,* both in spinal cord and brainstem, and can be thought to arise from *two sensory modalities.* One, involving the mechanoreceptor modality at the level of the second-order and higher-order transmission cell, is responsible for *location;* the other, associated with phylogenetically older brainstem relays, is responsible for the *unpleasant* quality of some nociceptor activation.

Pain and the "Six Principles" of Sensory Physiology

In Chapter 9 we summarized the organization of sensory systems with "six principles" that are displayed, in some measure, by vision, audition, vestibular sense, olfaction, gustation, and somatosensation. The first, *adaptation,* may be found for some painful experiences, as when a wound hurts more sharply right after it is acquired than it does somewhat later. However, pain systems also display the opposite of adaptation, **summation**, in which continuous noxious stimuli of *constant physical magnitude* are experienced as pain of *increasing,* not decreasing, intensity. As in the other sensory systems, action potential frequency encodes stimulus intensity for pure nociceptors. Recall, however, that the discomfort and unpleasantness of pain, or **dysphoria**, arise from activity of more than one cell type in the cord and more than one projection system from cord to thalamus. The magnitude of pain perception is not a direct function of action potential frequency in either projection system (in fact, as we shall see later, action potentials in some projection cells may actually *inhibit* pain perception). Modality segregation is not displayed by the pain system. The pain

system integrates Aα-mechanoreceptor input with the activity of Aδ- and C-fibers at the level of a cell called the polymodal nociceptor. Unlike the other sensory systems, which have detailed somatotopic organization with precise receptive fields, the pain system is poorly organized topographically, with very large and overlapping receptive fields. Surround inhibition occurs in the pain system, but as we shall see shortly, this too entails cross-modal interactions. Only in the final principle, efferent control over the percept, do we find consistency between the organization of the pain system and that of the other sensory modalities. Just as the brain "sees what it wishes to see" and "hears what it wishes to hear" it (usually) "feels the pain it wishes to feel." Students usually find the evidence for this, the topic of the next section, to be one of the most fascinating subjects in a course on neuroscience.

Descending Analgesia Systems

In 1976, Huda Akil, John Mayer, and John Liebeskind made an observation regarding the nociceptive threshold of rats receiving electrical stimulation of various brain regions. They found that electrical stimuli applied to various brainstem sites would render an animal analgesic, or unresponsive to noxious stimuli (the word *analgesic* refers to the state of pain insensitivity as well as to those drugs and procedures that produce the state). Soon after, Howard Fields, Alan Basbaum, and others (1981) showed that the brainstem structures involved (which included the *periaqueductal gray region* and the *raphé nucleus,* discussed in later sections) influenced pain transmission neurons in the cord by a descending pathway called the **dorsolateral funiculus** (Figure 11–11). The analgesia produced by electrically activating the descending, or efferent, projection was as profound as that produced by naturally occurring analgesic drugs, such as morphine (Figure 11–12). The next step in the understanding came from the use of drugs to study the experimental analgesia. Chemists in the pharmaceutical industry had discovered that the addition of carbon and hydrogen atoms to one portion of analgesic drugs ("agonists" for pain relief) converted them to antagonists, enabling them to block the action of analgesics such as morphine and other analgesic

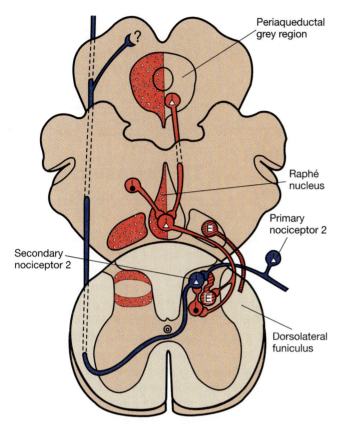

Figure 11–11 *Descending Analgesia Systems.* The descending pathway known as the dorsolateral funiculus has potent analgesic effects (E = enkephalin-containing interneuron).

opiates. In fact, they were peptides of various sizes (Table 11–2). One type that was found primarily in pituitary and in brain was called **endorphin** (a conjunction of the terms *endogenous* and *morphine)*. Beta-endorphin is a molecule composed of thirty one amino acids. Other, smaller peptides prevailed in the adrenal gland and in the spinal cord and were collectively called **enkephalins**. The enkephalins are *pentapeptides* (five amino acids long; *penta* = five) and differ from one another by only one amino acid (compare *methionine-enkephalin* with *leucine-enkephalin* in Table 11–2. Remarkably, the endorphins and enkephalins share sequence homology, with the initial sequence Tyr-Gly-Gly-Phe (tyrosine, glycine, glycine, phenylalanine). In fact, it is this sequence that contains the **active site** of the molecule, that portion that binds to the opiate receptors and activates them. To distinguish the endorphins and enkephalins from the *exogenous* ligands, the *opiates,* these *endogenous* peptides are collectively called **opioids.**

Like all peptides, the opioids are synthesized first in large protein precursors that are packaged into vesicles, transported axoplasmically, and then cut up into the mature peptides (Figure 11–13). Each molecule of enkephalin precursor contains many enkephalin sequences and produces both leucine-enkephalin and (in greater quantity) methionine-enkephalin. The precursor for endorphin contains the hormone ACTH (*adrenocorticotropin*) and the biologically active peptide MSH (*melanocyte-stimulating hormone*) as well as beta-endorphin and hence the precursor is given a name that incorpo-

drugs such as their former, carbon-poor selves (providing a useful therapy for narcotic overdose, Chapter 17). These antialgesics *also blocked the analgesic effects of electrical stimulation.*

Nearly simultaneous discoveries elsewhere provided the missing insight needed to complete one of the most dramatic breakthroughs in the history of neuroscience. Scottish scientists Hughes, Smith, and Kosterlitz (1975), found that extracts of brain, spinal cord, adrenal gland, and pituitary contained material that had the same effect as morphine on several bioassays. These compounds are called **opiates**, since they are derived from alkaloids found in the opium poppy. Further, the synthetic opiate antagonist **naloxone** would block the action of the endogenous substances taken from the body, indicating that they were acting at the same receptors as the analgesic drugs.

Enkephalins and Endorphins

The extracts were subjected to chromatography (see Appendix) to characterize the active molecules, which turned out to be larger in molecular weight than morphine or the other

Figure 11–12 *Analgesics and Analgesic Antagonists.* Two common analgesics and their antagonists show structural similarity.

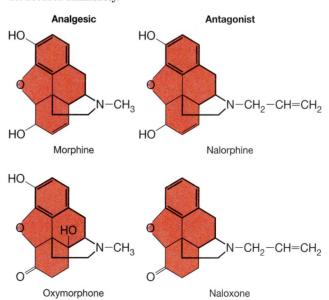

Table 11–2	ENDORPHINS AND ENKEPHALINS
Name	**Amino acid sequence**
Leucine-enkephalin	Tyr-Gly-Gly-Phe-Leu-OH
Methionine-enkephalin	Tyr-Gly-Gly-Phe-Met-OH
β-Endorphin	*Tyr-Gly-Gly-Phe-Met*-Thr-Ser-Glu-Lys-Ser-Gin-Thr-Pro-Leu-Val-Thr-Leu-Phe-Lys-Asn-Ala-Ile-Val-Lys-Asn-Ala-His-Lys-Gly-Gin-OH
Dynorphin	*Tyr-Gly-Gly-Phe-Leu*-Arg-Arg-Ile-Arg-Pro-Lys-Leu-Lys-Try-Asp-Asn-Gln-OH
α-Neoendorphin	*Tyr-Gly-Gly-Phe-Leu*-Arg-Lys-Tyr-Pro-Lys

Source: Fields (1981).

rates reference to the active fragments, *pro-opiomelanocortin* (**POMC**). The enkephalin precursor (*pro-enkephalin*) is designed to produce large quantities of opioid signal exclusively with minimal biosynthetic expense. POMC, on the other hand, produces equal quantities of each of the different products (endorphin, ACTH, and MSH). Neither ACTH nor MSH has opiate action and both are thought to organize aspects of the organismic response to stress other than analgesia. Endorphin's and enkephalin's role in analgesia mechanisms is still very much in debate among peptide neurobiologists. Scientists have speculated (myself among them) that posttranslational modifications of either ACTH or beta-endorphin might actually change the *quality* of the peptidergic signal in POMC-containing cells (changing excitation, for example, into inhibition, or vice versa) and thus might be an important mechanism for behavioral plasticity (Smock & Fields, 1981). Evidence has accumulated that **acetylation** (addition of a car-

boxyl group to the amino terminus) of POMC products may be the post-translational mechanism that activates some products and inactivates others, providing a moment-to-moment alteration in the nature of the signal. This issue will be discussed in more detail in Chapter 12.

The Mechanism of Opioid Peptide Action

Enkephalin immunoreactivity (i.e., the stain for enkephalin in immunocytochemistry) is found throughout the central nervous system, with concentrations in the basal ganglia and in the spinal cord. Within the cord, enkephalin is especially predominant in the marginal layers of the dorsal horn, precisely the region where the small diameter nociceptors insert and make their synapses (compare Figure 11–14, for enkephalin, with Figure 11–9, for Substance P). Thus the anatomy of this opioid peptide class suggests that it has a role in mediating stimulation-produced analgesia, which, being blocked by naloxone, is known to be opiate receptor–mediated. Indeed, as shown in Figure 11–15, the dorsal horn of the spinal cord is rich in opiate receptor.

Somewhere in the dorsal horn the opioids are blocking transmission from the primary nociceptor to the higher-order cells. But how? Hughes et al. (1975) in their original studies showed that morphine acted on autonomically innervated targets (such as the guinea pig *ileum* and the mouse *vas deferens*) by depressing the amount of norepinephrine released

Figure 11–13 *Opioid Precursors.* The three precursors shown are cleaved by enzymes to yield the endogenous opioid peptides. At top, pro-opiomelanocortin yields one copy of beta-endorphin, while pro-enkephalin (middle) yields leucine-enkephalin and several copies of methionine-enkephalin. At bottom, cleavage of pro-dynorphin results in the production of another endorphin, dynorphin (ME = methionine-enkephalin, LE = leucine-enkephalin, β-endo = beta-endorphin, dyno = dynorphin).

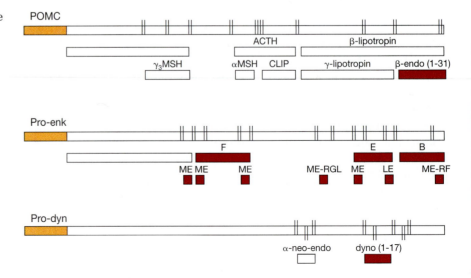

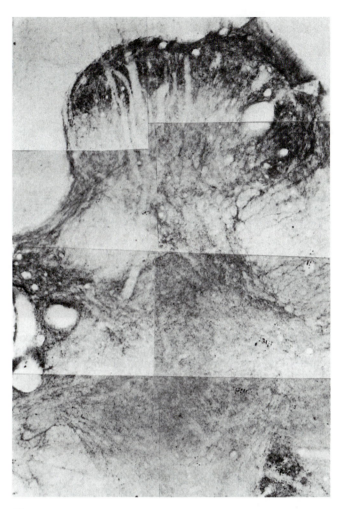

Figure 11–14   *Enkephalin in the Dorsal Horn.* In the same way that immunocytochemistry demonstrated the presence of Substance P in Figure 11–9, it has also demonstrated the presence of leucine-enkephalin in the dorsal horn of the spinal cord, strongly suggesting a role in pain mediation or modification.

with each incoming postganglionic action potential. Jessell, Iverson, and others (1977) showed that depolarization of brain tissue (say by increasing $[K^+]_o$) in the presence of enkephalin would release less central Substance P and that this effect was blocked by naloxone.

These observations connecting enkephalin action to less Substance P release were extended to the spinal cord by Fields et al. (1980), who showed that section of the dorsal roots ("dorsal rhizotomy") depleted the dorsal horn not only of Substance P but of opiate receptor as well. Finally, Mudge, Leeman, and Fischbach (1979) managed to directly visualize opioid action in the cord using a developmental trick. Normally it is possible to record from dorsal root ganglion cell bodies with intracellular electrodes but not from the

tiny afferent terminals in the spinal cord. However, in spinal cord *culture* the axons are not as long, the terminals are close to the cell bodies, and electrical events at the terminal can be recorded by an electrode in the cell body (Figure 11–16). While normally only a Na^+-mediated action potential can be recorded, in the *in vitro* cord a Ca^{++}-mediated spike is found (Figure 11–16). This reflects the Ca^{++} entry necessary for exocytosis and transmitter release (Chapter 5), in this case release of Substance P from primary nociceptors onto the secondary nociceptors. When enkephalin is added the Ca^{++}-mediated part of the action potential of the primary afferent synapse is diminished, an effect (like all the others up to now) that is reversed by naloxone blockade of opiate receptors. Thus, the experiment by Mudge et al. showed that the method of opioid action in the cord was *presynaptic,* since it involved transmitter release, not transmitter action. Less Ca^{++} entry with enkephalin meant less exocytosis, less Substance P release, and less depolarization of second-order nociceptors with each incoming stimulus.

Figure 11–15   *Opioid Receptors in the Spinal Cord.* In addition to the proof of enkephalins in the dorsal horn, there is also evidence of enkephalin receptors in the spinal cord and brain (PAG = periaquaductal gray, NRM = nucleus raphé nucleus, DLF = dorsolateral funiculus).

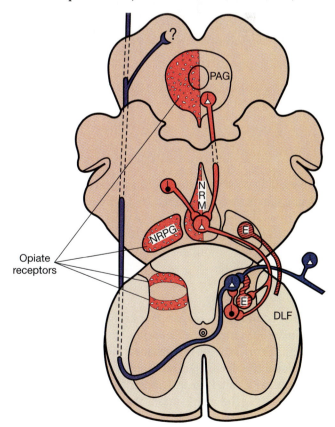

Figure 11–16 *Opioid Action in the Spinal Cord.* (a) Normally, only sodium-mediated action potentials can be recorded in the dorsal root ganglion cells. (b) By recording the cells' electrical potentials in a lab dish, where the axon terminals are closer to the cell bodies, the calcium contribution to the action potential can be observed. In nociception systems, it is this calcium potential that triggers the release of Substance P. Application of enkephalin reduces the calcium potential, and therefore reduces the amount of Substance P released and the strength of the nociceptive signal to the brain. Adding naloxone, an enkephalin antagonist, restores the calcium potential to near its normal level.

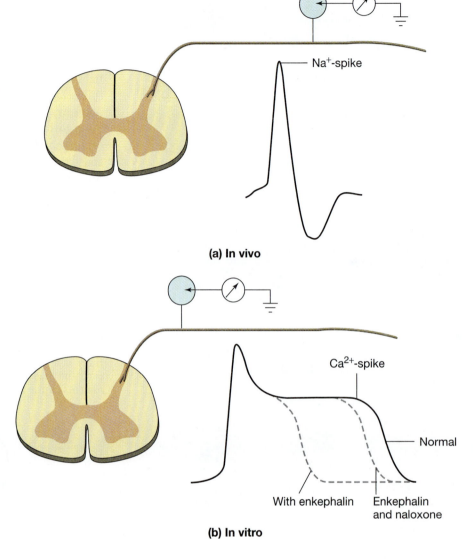

(a) In vivo

(b) In vitro

The prevailing visualization of analgesic intervention in pain transmission is shown in Figure 11–17. Now we know that there are also postsynaptic actions of opiates (also inhibitory by activation of a K⁺-channel). However, a substantial amount of opioid action and of spinal analgesia is due to presynaptic inhibition.

The Raphé Nuclei

But what activates the release of enkephalin to shut down the primary afferent synapse? Evidence has accumulated that aminergic neurons of the **rostroventral medulla (RVM)** send fibers down the dorsolateral funiculus to synapse on the enkephalinergic cell. Principal among these fibers are *serotonergic* cells of the raphé nuclei, the **nucleus raphé magnus** among them. Also, there are noradrenergic cells of the *nucleus subcoeruleus* and synapses that directly modulate

spinal nociception without the medium of the enkephalinergic cell.

The Periaqueductal Gray

The raphé nuclei in turn receive a projection from cells in the ventral portion of the midbrain next to the fluid-filled passageway that links the third and the fourth ventricles (called the *Sylvian aqueduct*). This region of cell bodies is called the **periaqueductal gray (PAG)** and has an excitatory effect on the descending analgesia system. The PAG, like the RVM and the dorsal horn, is a region of high opiate receptor density (shown as stippled regions on the left of Figure 11–15), and microinjections of morphine in any of these regions (presumably mimicking the action of the native opioid transmitter) will produce analgesia. However, if opiates act by presynaptic inhibition, how can injections into regions

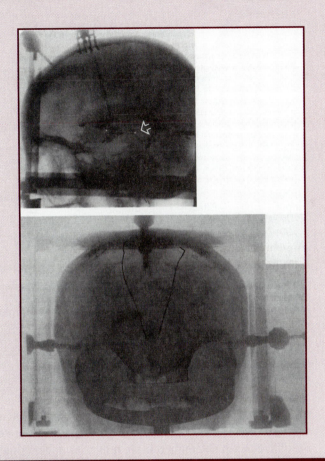

stored her life to normal, reunited her family, and enabled her to go back to work. The only problem reported at that time was a slow reduction in the efficacy of the stimulation, which Hosobuchi successfully reversed with dietary *tryptophan* supplements. See if you can guess Hosobuchi's reasoning for this before it is provided at the end of this box.

More recently, stimulation therapy for relief of chronic pain has employed electrodes in the PAG (see figure). Though such implants may seem extreme, the fact that patients and their doctors are willing to accept such surgery is testimony to the harsh reality of chronic pain experienced by many individuals.

(Hosobuchi's reasoning: The raphé nuclei are a critical link in the descending analgesia system. Since these nuclei are serotonergic, perhaps there is depletion of serotonin in the cord with chronic activation of the raphé. Tryptophan, the amino acid precursor of serotonin, might drive synthesis metabolically much as L-dopa administration can favor dopamine synthesis in Parkinson's patients. While precursor loading cannot drive synthesis and increase transmitter levels in normal people, and in the case of L-tryptophan can actually cause serious problems [see Hertzman et al., 1990] those with abnormally low levels, such as Hosobuchi's patient, *can* benefit from consuming precursor amino acids.)

tively, perhaps the two are aspects of a single continuum of activity in a central circuit, comprised of dopaminergic and peptidergic cells, that determines the balance between the two states. Determination of the answer to this issue (one pathway or two) will require understanding of the mechanism(s) for PAG and forebrain bundle activation. At present, we have only vague and uncertain insights into the circumstances under which the system(s) is/are influenced behaviorally. This is the subject of the next two sections and of Box 11–4.

Acupuncture

Wounded animals lick an injured region, possibly because natural antibiotics exist in saliva, but probably also because it makes them feel better. Similarly, people will often rub an affected part of the body and obtain some relief from pain in doing so. Wouldn't it feel great right now for someone to rub your shoulders, cramped from hunching over this book? In 1965, Melzack and Wall produced a novel theory to account for these and other phenomena such as the pain that some-

times occurs when large myelinated fibers are stimulated individually. They postulated correctly that there was a "pain gate" in the spinal cord that allowed nociception to pass rostrally when opened but blocked nociception when shut. They further postulated, again correctly, that activity of large diameter mechanoreceptors could somehow close the gate on some occasions. Finally, they produced a mechanism for their gate control theory, a modified version of which is shown in Figure 11–19. As we have discussed earlier, some polymodal and wide dynamic range nociceptors (T) receive a projection from large myelinated Aα afferents (M) as well as from small fibers (U). Melzack and Wall proposed that these cells also received input from an inhibitory interneuron (I). Furthermore, they speculated that nociceptors inhibited the interneuron and mechanoreceptors excited it. Thus primary nociceptors only excite the pain transmission cell, directly and by disinhibition, whereas mechanoreceptors both excite and inhibit the pain transmission cell, modifying its output and partly alleviating pain.

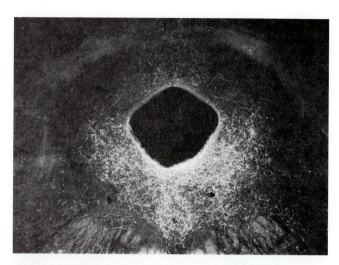

Figure 11–18 *The Periaqueductal Gray and Beta-Endorphin.* Immunocytochemistry illustrates the presence (bright regions) of beta-endorphin in the PAG.

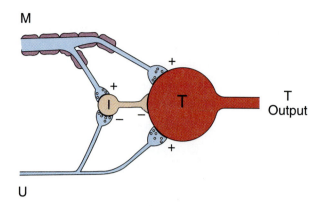

Afferent Input	I Cell Effect	T Cell Effect	T Cell Output (T-I)
M	+	+	0
U	−	+	+ +
M + U	0	+	+

Figure 11–19 *Gate Control Theory.* Proposed by Melzack and Wall (1965) to account for the palliative effect of mechanoreceptor input on pain, Gate Control Theory posits convergence between myelinated mechanoreceptors (M) and unmyelinated nociceptors (U) onto transmission cells (T) and inhibitory interneurons (I). Simultaneous activity in M and U has less impact on T excitability than U input alone.

Gate control theory is useful clinically, but so far the search for the postulated inhibitory circuit (I) shown in Figure 11–19 has been futile. There is almost certainly some form of correlate in the pain system to the antagonistic surrounds formed in other sensory systems, but to date the actual cellular circuitry that constructs the antagonistic surround has not been elucidated, even though other "pain gates" have been found, such as the ones already described. This is partly because pain receptive fields are large, loosely organized, and multimodal in nature. In **acupuncture** (analgesia obtained with the insertion of needles) and **acupressure** (analgesia obtained by application of pressure) pain relief and perhaps other therapeutic benefits can be obtained by stimulation of parts of the body quite remote from the painful skin area or internal organ. Very likely this is because of surround inhibition of some form or gate control circuitry as shown in Figure 11–20. However, until the circuitry is understood, some clinicians and pain scientists are reluctant to accept the efficacy of these procedures.

Stress-Induced Analgesia

Everyone has had the experience of engaging in sports or some other form of strenuous activity and unconsciously acquiring an injury. Only later, after the excitement has dissipated, does the injury become painful. Of course, there are many more examples in common experience in which injuries are obtained that *immediately* become painful, a fact that nicely illustrates some of the difficulties encountered in doing pain research at the behavioral level. Pain and analgesia thresholds vary so much from person to person (and animal

to animal) that it is hard to get sufficiently reliable responses to perform carefully controlled experiments. Because of the difficulties in obtaining reliable responses, subjects such as *meditation for the relief of pain, hypnosis for pain relief, "runner's high,"* and *dietary remedies* are not yet thoroughly understood and therefore will not be examined in this text. Like *stigmata,* these phenomena probably do occur, but at such low frequency and in so few individuals that we can only speculate about their probable biological basis. (Speaking of stigmata, here's that explanation I promised you back in Box 11–2. A popular topic of conversation among pain scientists is the notion that stigmata occur by central *activation* of primary nociceptors and antidromic [reverse nerve conduction] activation of small diameter fibers leading to the peripheral release of Substance P. If there is efferent *inhibition* of primary nociceptors, why not efferent *excitation?*)

This is not to say that we have no understanding of the behavioral circumstances that activate the descending analgesia systems. In particular, **stress-induced analgesia** is a robust form of behavioral analgesia in people and experimental animals. It has been confirmed experimentally that *fear* in people has an analgesic quality and *electric shock, cold water swims,* and *restraint* produce analgesia in experimental animals. Current results indicate that only *part* of stress-induced analgesia

Box 11–4

Placebo and Opioid Peptides

Pure and complete sorrow is as impossible as pure and complete joy. • *Leo Tolstoy* War and Peace *(Book IV, Chapter 1)*

We have seen how the body contains mechanisms to allow pain to execute its biological function, to alert the organism to potentially harmful circumstances. We have also seen how the body contains corrective mechanisms to alleviate pain when its biological function is no longer needed, or when the pain itself threatens the well-being of the organism. Such attenuation of pain, and its "psychological" manipulation, is one of the most practical aspects of modern neuroscience, as understanding of it has immediate clinical application.

Another of Tolstoy's messages in *War and Peace* is the accidental nature of much of human affairs. While human affairs are determined by historical antecedents (he was a monist, I believe), these antecedents are invisible to us much of the time, so much so that we stumble into, or away from, many of the events that shape our lives. I often think of the formative years of my scientific career (the first years of graduate school, for example) and of the many important scientific discoveries that were being made at that time. Some of them are described in this book and I even had the occasional opportunity (not always taken) to participate in some of the research. One project that I particularly regret not working on led to one of the most dramatic and powerful results in the field of pain research and a development with wide-ranging implications including, I think, some insight into the mind/body problem.

In 1979 Levine, Gordon, and Fields contacted a group of medical students who had just had their wisdom teeth extracted. There is, as some of you know, postoperative pain following this procedure, pain that is normally treated with codeine. These students were divided into two groups and treated with other substances. Instead of codeine, those in the first group were treated with **placebo**, while those in the second were given a pill containing the opiate antagonist *naloxone* in addition to the placebo. Placebo is a psychological manipulation in which the doctor gives the patient a sugar pill or something to swallow that has *no active ingredient*. In a "double blind" study such as this one, the subjects were not aware that their medication did not contain analgesics, and the doctor did not know which type of pill he or she was issuing. Among the students in the first group, a full one-third reported pain relief from placebo alone. The belief that one will be cured or relieved of discomfort is known as the *placebo effect*. Of the students in the second group, who, in addition to the placebo unknowingly received the antianalgesic naloxone, none reported pain relief! In other words naloxone blocked the placebo analgesia, a purely "psychological" form of pain relief.

Obviously, placebo, like many of the other forms of analgesia we have considered, is mediated by endogenous opioids. The "psychological" nature of placebo is a dualistic concept, one that presumes a distinction between the mind and the brain. Monists can take comfort in the fact that psychological processes at work in placebo are also brain processes, processes mediated by endogenous opioid peptides.

is opioid-mediated (i.e., can be blocked by naloxone). Part, therefore, must be produced by other transmitter systems.

The mechanism for stress-induced analgesia and the chemical mechanisms that may be involved are a very exciting area of current research. Among the prominent models for this phenomenon in humans is **learned helplessness**. In this model rats are subjected to stress in the form of electrical shocks to the tail. Each rat is paired with another, but only one has the ability to manipulate the shock by pressing a lever. The other is passively exposed to the shocks received by the first and lacks control over the stressor. Use of this model has elucidated the component of the stress response that is mediated by opioids and the part that is mediated by other compounds and has provided one of our best models for reactive depression and coping mechanisms in people (for review, see Peterson, Maier, & Seligman, 1993). Among the candidates for non-opioid control of analgesia and nociception are ACTH (Smock & Fields, 1981; Belcher, Smock, & Fields,

1982) and cholecystokinin (CCK) (Wiertelak, Maier, & Watkins, 1992), but there are many other candidate neuromodulators for alteration of pain perception as well. In the next chapter and Chapter 14 we will review the function of some of these peptide transmitters and hormones in the context of other regulatory processes.

SUMMARY

Pleasure and pain are universally experienced but hard to describe. For example, in answer to the question "what is pain?" the best an instructor can do is to say "come here and I'll show you." Pain sensitivity varies remarkably from individual to individual (in comparison to other sensory acuities) and pleasurable experience is even more subjective. Some pleasures, such as those experienced upon satisfying an appetite, appear to be mediated by dopaminergic cells with fibers in the medial forebrain bundle. These fibers arise from cells in the ventral tegmentum and project to cortical and subcortical structures, including the nucleus accumbens. Rats permitted to self-stimulate in the medial forebrain bundle will do so to exhaustion, presenting an apparent paradox in that the system thought to be involved in the satisfaction of appetite also appears to be involved in the creation of appetite. It is not always possible to distinguish pain from pleasure mechanistically. Pain is not a property of nociception alone but is created centrally from a mixture of nociceptor and mechanoreceptor projections and poorly understood limbic influences. Nociceptors are small diameter myelinated (Aδ-fiber) and unmyelinated (C-fiber) systems containing, among other substances, Substance P as a primary neurotransmitter candidate. Second-order cells are either pure nociceptors or polymodal, wide dynamic range, and complex nociceptors. Many of these send axons across the midline to project rostrally in the lateral spinothalamic tract. Some terminate upon cells in the hindbrain reticular formation that then project to thalamus. Of the six principles of sensory physiology, pain obeys most fully the rule of efferent control over the percept. Descending analgesia systems from periaqueductal gray to raphé nuclei to peptidergic cells in the dorsal horn modulate the transmission from the primary to the secondary nociceptors. Endorphin appears to play this role in the brain, and enkephalin in the cord, but there are other opioid peptides that may play a role in pleasure and analgesia, or pain relief. A major mechanism for opioid peptide action but perhaps not the only one is attenuation of a presynaptic Ca^{++}-current and consequent depression of exocytosis. Analgesia produced by electrical stimulation, acupuncture/acupressure, and placebo, as well as mimicry of opioid mechanisms by opiate analgesics are all clinical procedures for the relief of pain. Gate control theory is a useful model for understanding pain relief in people, and stress-induced analgesia is a useful research tool for the investigation of endogenous analgesia in experimental animals. Much remains to be learned regarding the modulation of pain and its possible correlate, the production of pleasure.

REVIEW QUESTIONS

1. What transmitter is associated with the medial forebrain bundle? What is it's function in the brain?

2. Draw the ascending nociception system and describe it's function.

3. Draw the descending analgesia system and describe it's function.

4. Which "Laws of Sensory Physiology" are obeyed by the pain system and which are violated?

5. How do enkephalins act in the CNS?

6. How was Substance P discovered?

7. What is capsaicin and how is it significant?

8. What is naloxone and how is it significant?

9. How are pain and pleasure related?

THOUGHT QUESTIONS

1. If scientists produced a drug that created pure pleasure, all the time, with no addiction, side effects, or health hazards, would you take it? Why or why not?

2. Do you think scientists are looking for such a drug? Why or why not?

3. Which do you think evolved first, pleasure or pain? List the organisms that experience each of these, in your opinion.

KEY CONCEPTS

acetylation (p. 268)
active site (p. 267)
acupressure (p. 274)
acupuncture (p. 274)
Aδ-fibers (p. 261)
analgesics (p. 255)
angst (p. 266)
appetitive behaviors (p. 255)
arcuate nucleus (p. 272)
autoradiography (p. 262)
bradykinin (p. 260)
C-fibers (p. 261)
capsaicin (p. 263)
chronic pain (p. 272)
colocalization (p. 265)
Dale's law (p. 265)
dopamine (p. 255)

dorsolateral funiculus (p. 266)
drive (p. 258)
dysphoria (p. 266)
endogenous opiates (p. 255)
endorphin (p. 267)
enkephalins (p. 267)
gate control theory (p. 273)
histamine (p. 260)
hyperalgesia (p. 260)
immunocytochemistry (p. 262)
lateral spinothalamic tract
   (p. 264)
learned helplessness (p. 275)
medial forebrain bundle (p. 256)
mast cells (p. 260)
mesocortical and mesolimbic
   projection (p. 256)

naloxone (p. 267)
nigrostriatal pathway (p. 256)
nociceptive specific cells (p. 269)
nucleus accumbens (p. 256)
nucleus raphé magnus (p. 270)
opiates (p. 267)
opioids (p. 267)
pain (p. 255)
pain insensitivity syndrome
   (p. 263)
periaqueductal gray (PAG)
   (p. 279)
placebo (p. 275)
pleasure (p. 255)
polymodal nociceptors (p. 264)
POMC (p. 268)
prostaglandin (p. 260)

reward (p. 255)
radioimmunoassay (p. 262)
rostroventral medulla (RVM)
   (p. 270)
satiety (p. 255)
sequence analysis (p. 262)
serotonin (p. 260)
stigmata (p. 265)
stress-induced analgesia
   (p. 274)
substantia gelatinosa (p. 261)
summation (p. 266)
tail-flick test (p. 255)
thin-layer chromatography
   (p. 262)
wide dynamic range cells
   (p. 264)

12

Hormones, Sex, and Reproduction

Sex occurs in most animals for a reason (apart from giving us something to do between birth and death). It is not strictly necessary for propagation of all species, since many plants and some animals reproduce *asexually.* Such organisms produce offspring that are genetically identical to their parent by budding, dividing, or producing spores and in the process conserving much of the energy other organisms spend on mating. However, because of the uniformity of their genomes, asexually reproducing organisms evolve slowly and may adapt poorly to rapidly changing environmental conditions, such as those that require new diet or body temperature. *Sexual* reproduction confers the following advantages: (1) reconstituted genomes can be created by reassortment of chromosomes; (2) new chromosomes can be created by crossing over of genetic material; and (3) deleterious (harmful) recessive mutations can be masked in a majority of the offspring of a diploid organism by preservation of a normal unmutated gene (Chapter 2).

The hereditary or genetic code of organisms is contained within chromosomes. Different species may have different numbers of chromosomes, as well as single or multiple copies of each. Most cells of sexually reproducing organisms are **diploid** (from the Greek words for "double appearance"), meaning that they contain two copies of each of a fixed number of chromosomes. In humans, there are twenty three such pairs in each cell of the body, with the exception of the reproductive cells, which are called gametes (more commonly know as sperm and eggs). Gametes are **haploid** (from the Greek for "single appearance"), meaning that they have only one chromosome from each pair (try to figure out why the gametes could not be diploid). As the haploid gametes from the two parents fuse in the process of fertilization, they produce a new diploid cell, the zygote, which is the only cell within a sexually reproducing species capable of forming a new organism. Thus, reproduction in sexual organisms involves alternating phases of haploidy and diploidy.

Sexual reproduction in complex lifeforms requires *gender,* but determination of gender involves much more than the influence of chromosomes. *Hormones* of two varieties (peptide and steroid) act in combination upon the body to produce gender. Hence, the sections that follow will describe the production and activity of these two types of hormones.

Hormones and "The Master Gland"

Peptide Hormones

Communication between glands in the body and the central nervous system requires molecules that can cross the blood-brain barrier by virtue of their hydrophobic nature. Communication between organs in the periphery is not restricted by a hydrophobic barrier such as the blood-brain barrier and is often mediated by hydrophilic compounds. Often these hydrophilic compounds are derivatives of single amino acids. Examples are epinephrine, or *adrenaline* (a derivative of tyrosine that mediates part of the "fight-or-flight" response, Chapter 6), and thyroxine. Thyroxine, as the name implies, is produced by the thyroid glands on either side of the throat and is also a derivative of tyrosine. Thyroxine regulates metabolism in the body as well as growth and reproduction and is produced by addition of *iodine* groups to the ring structure of the amino acid. Lack of iodine in the diet (most often seen among people who live far from the ocean) produces hypertrophy (enlargement) of the thyroid glands as they struggle to make more hormone. This condition, known as **goiter**, is associated with other problems of metabolism, growth, and development and is, fortunately, becoming quite rare because iodine is now routinely added to commercial preparations of table salt (i.e., a small amount of sodium iodide [NaI] is added to the sodium chloride [NaCl]).

Many more endocrine actions among organs of the body are mediated by groups, or chains, of amino acids called *peptides*. We have encountered peptides in our consideration of trophic factors (Chapter 2), transmitters (Chapter 5), the autonomic nervous system (Chapter 6), and pain (Chapter 11) and will visit them again in Chapter 14. Here they concern us because, apart from the neural output of the spinal and cranial nerves, peptide hormones constitute the *only* vehicle whereby the brain can communicate with the other organs. Endocrine communication, in other words, is primarily accomplished on the brain by steroid action, and on the other organ systems by either steroid, amino acid, or peptide action. The brain influences other endocrine organs by peptide action only.

Peptide Synthesis

All cells synthesize protein, of course, and it is probably the case that every cell contains and uses small proteins, or peptides, for communication with other cells. What is certain, based on every peptide studied so far, is that they are all de-

rived from larger proteins by proteolytic cleavage (sequential hydrolysis of bonds). Particularly well understood is the biosynthesis of *insulin*, a peptide, or small protein, hormone involved in blood glucose regulation. As shown in Figure 12–1, insulin is embedded in a larger structure called *proinsulin*, which is synthesized on ribosomes in the endoplasmic reticulum (Chapter 2). Then vesicles bud off of the endoplasmic reticulum and fuse with the Golgi apparatus. The pro-hormone then is inserted into the lumen of the Golgi apparatus. Then, vesicles containing the proinsulin and a proteolytic enzyme are formed, and *en route* to exocytosis, the mature, active form of insulin is produced by specific cuts between basic pairs of amino acids.

Also well-understood is the synthesis of *adrenocorticotropic hormone* (ACTH). This peptide, important in the body's response to stress, is initially part of a protein precursor called *pro-opiomelanocortin* (POMC). This precursor is shown in Figure 12–2 and is of particular interest because other fragments of POMC may have biological action as well. Alpha-, beta-, and gamma-melanocyte-stimulating hormone (αMSH, βMSH, and γMSH), beta-endorphin, met-enkephalin, and gamma-lipotropin, all fragments of POMC, have become the focus of interest because of their association with a known hormone (ACTH), and though the scientific community is still arguing about this issue, it appears that these other peptides may also play a role in the POMC-mediated stress response (Chapter 11). Of particular interest is the fact that protein precursors of peptide hormones have such an apparently vast array of signaling capabilities for targets throughout the body. Seen throughout the animal kingdom, plasticity in the production of peptides from common precursors suggests intriguing mechanisms for behavioral plasticity (Arch et al., 1986).

Not all fragments of hormone precursors have biological activity, however. **Oxytocin** and **vasopressin** are very small peptides (each only nine amino acids long) and are made from precursors almost entirely composed of inactive sequences called *neurophysins*. The fact that the neurophysins are not biologically active does not mean that they have no function, however. They appear to act as "counter-ions" enabling storage of large amounts of positively charged oxytocin and vasopressin in small granules prior to release. Some of the smallest peptides are the **hypothalamic releasing factors**, peptides with the sole function of causing other peptides to be secreted. Some of these are but *three* amino acids long, and scientists suspected at first that they might be assembled from free amino acids by enzyme action. However, further investigation revealed that these too were made at first as part of a large precursor and severed from it by proteolytic processes before exocytosis.

The fact that all peptides are made from protein precursors has special intrigue for neuroscientists because it

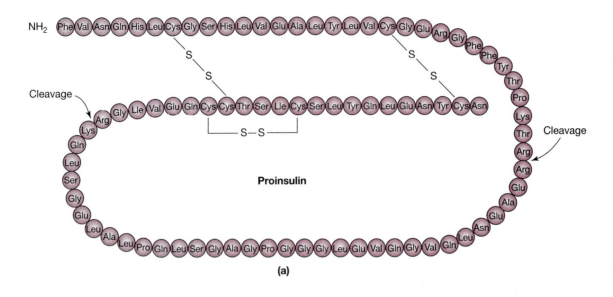

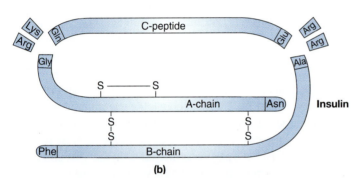

Figure 12–1 *Precursor of Insulin.* The proinsulin molecule is converted to insulin through proteolytic cleavage of specific bonds between amino acids. The resulting insulin peptide consists of two short amino acid chains bound together by two disulfide bridges. (a) Proinsulin; (b) Insulin created by cleavage

Figure 12–2 *Pro-opiomelanocortin (POMC).* In an elegant biological mechanism possibly enhancing the plasticity of peptide communication, many different peptide hormones can arise from a single precursor by varying the site of cleavage. In this case, pro-opiomelanocortin serves as the precursor for several peptides, including ACTH, thought to mediate the body's response to stress. (Nakanishi et al., 1995)

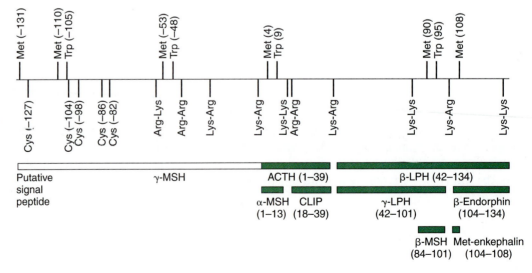

Pro-opiomelanocortin

provides many more opportunities for plasticity in the nature of the final signal that is expressed than would be the case for simpler transmitters or hormones. For example, changes in the proteolysis of POMC, described earlier, could dramatically alter the nature of a stress response from one dominated by ACTH action to another type of response, perhaps mediated mostly by beta-endorphin or some other POMC product (Smock & Fields, 1981). One response might be characterized by enhanced pain perception and arousal and the other by analgesia and withdrawal. In this manner healthy, or "adaptive," responses to stress may be distinguished from less fortunate responses that could lead to pathology; knowledge of such plasticity in proteolysis might even lead to the prospect of clinical manipulation of the POMC system to avoid a pathological response to stress.

The Plan of the Pituitary

The brain's production of peptide hormones is substantially the function of a single structure, the **pituitary gland,** and for this reason the pituitary is sometimes called "the master gland." The pituitary hangs from the ventral surface of the brain like a pendulum (Figure 12–3). Indeed, the stalk suspending the gland is called the "infundibulum" (Latin for "pendulum"). The pituitary has its own supply of blood vessels called the **portal system** to distinguish them from regular arteries and veins. The purpose of the portal system is to collect the peptide products of the pituitary for distribution throughout the body. There is a cavity in the cranium that holds the infundibulum and pituitary and connects the portal system to the rest of the body. In humans, this cavity is right above the soft palate in the mouth, so it is possible to actually feel the pituitary gland by pressing on the roof of the mouth gently with a finger. In preserved specimens (such as sheep brains that you may be lucky enough to dissect in your lab) the cavity usually grips the pituitary as the brain is removed from the skull, so that your specimen will lack the pituitary in most cases.

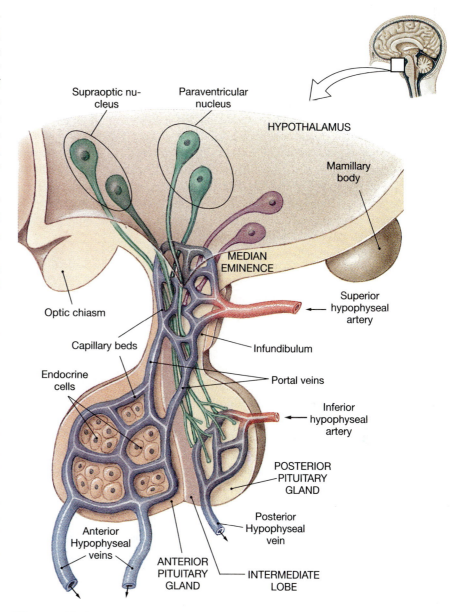

Figure 12–3 *The Pituitary Gland.* Also known as "the master gland," the pituitary gland has anterior and posterior portions and is connected to the hypothalamus *via* the infundibulum. Hormones released into the bloodstream from the pituitary gland exert their effects on remote glands throughout the body. A network of veins known as the portal system transports releasing hormones from the hypothalamus to the anterior pituitary, which stimulate the production of other hormones in the anterior lobe. The anterior pituitary is thus both a neural structure and an endocrine gland. Neural projections from the hypothalamus to the posterior and intermediate pituitary lobes deliver the other hormones (primarily vasopressin and oxytocin).

In mammals, the pituitary gland has two parts (see Figure 12–3), the **anterior lobe,** and the **posterior lobe.** The posterior lobe (pars nervosa) is a neural structure. Both of the cell bodies of these neurons lie outside of the pituitary in the hypothalamus, where the peptides oxytocin and vasopressin are manufactured (in the *supraoptic nucleus* and the *paraventricular nucleus*) and are transported down axons into the infundibulum. The blood vessels of the posterior pituitary are innervated by the axon terminals and disperse oxytocin and vasopressin into the blood. Electrical recordings from the supraoptic and paraventricular nuclei reveal that the peptide-containing cells (called **neuroendocrine cells** because they are neurons but secrete hormones instead of transmitters) are active at different times. Vasopressin-containing cells are tonically active, meaning that they are often firing action potentials. Assays of the blood for vasopressin reveal, as expected, that there is usually some vasopressin around. The circulating peptide has one known function and one postulated function. The vasopressin-containing cells are known to be osmotically sensitive (i.e., they fire in response to increased salinity of the blood). When vasopressin is released from these cells it acts on the kidney to increase water retention by the blood. (Actually, it *restores* water to the blood from the urine and hence another name for vasopressin is *antidiuretic hormone,* or ADH.) At high concentrations, vasopressin causes constriction of peripheral and central blood vessels and original theories of its function postulated some role in controlling blood pressure. However, circulating levels of vasopressin never seem to rise high enough to cause this action and this function for vasopressin remains uncertain. Ironically, the pressor (constricting) effect was the first to be described and thus the name of the peptide reflects the original postulated effect rather than the well-established one.

Oxytocin also has two functions in the blood, but both of these are documented and accepted. The oxytocin-containing cell bodies fire phasically, meaning that they are usually inactive, with rare bursts of activity. These bursts (and oxytocin release) occur at two points in the life of female mammals. One occasion is after parturition (birth) when oxytocin acts on the smooth muscles of the uterus to cause constriction and expulsion of the placenta. The pulsatile (or abrupt) release of oxytocin may not follow birth immediately, and for humans oxytocin is sometimes administered directly in the hospital to facilitate placenta expulsion after birth. The other function of oxytocin is also part of reproductive physiology. After lactation has begun (this is caused by another peptide hormone, **prolactin**), oxytocin

causes the reflex action of milk letdown. Often this reflex can be produced in the absence of infants by particular sensory cues (such as in a cow by the sound of a bleating calf or a human mother when her new-born baby cries) and thus the evolutionary necessity for a neuroendocrine mechanism is apparent (as opposed to slower mediation by a regular gland). The posterior pituitary of male mammals contains oxytocin as well, but the role in males has yet to be elucidated. What function would you guess oxytocin has in the male body?

Vasopressin and oxytocin are very similar in structure, with only two amino acids different between them (the structure of several pituitary peptides is shown in Figure 12–4). Almost certainly this reflects **homology**, or correspondence in

Figure 12–4 *Structures of Peptide Hormones.* Structure of peptides is a reflection of amino acid sequence.

Structures of peptide hormones

Vasopressin

Cys-Tyr-Phe-Glu(NH$_2$)-Asp(NH$_2$)-Cys-Pro-Arg-Gly(NH$_2$)

Oxytocin

Cys-Tyr-Ileu-Glu(NH$_2$)-Asp(NH$_2$)-Cys-Pro-Leu-Gly(NH$_2$)

GH

H-Phe-Pro-Thr-Ile-Pro-Leu-Ser-Arg-Leu-Phe-Asp-Asn-Ala-Met-Leu-Arg-Ile-Leu-Ser-
1   10
Leu-Glu-Leu-Ile-Ser-Try-Leu-Glu-Pro-Val-Glu-Phe-Ala-His-Arg-Leu-His-Gln-Leu-Ala-
20   30
Phe-Asp-Thr-Tyr-Glu-Glu-Phe-Glu-Glu-Ala-Tyr-Ile-Pro-Lys-Glu-Gln-Lys-Tyr-Ser-Phe-
40   50
Leu-Gln-Asp-Pro-Glu-Thr-Ser-Leu-CyS-Phe-Ser-Ser-Ile-Glu-Ser-(Asp,Pro,Pro,Thr)-Arg-
60   70
Glu-Glu-Thr-Gln-Lys-Ser-Asp-Leu-Glu-Leu-Leu-Arg-Ser-Val-Phe-Ala-Asn-Ser-Leu-Val-
80   90
Tyr-Gly-Ala-Ser-Asn-Ser-Asp-Val-Tyr-Asp-Leu-Leu-Lys-Asp-Leu-Glu-Glu-Gly-Ile-Glu-
100   110
Thr-Leu-Met-Gly-Arg-Leu-Glu-Asp-Pro-Ser-Gly-Arg-Thr-Gly-Gln-Ile-Phe-Lys-Glu-Thr-
120   130
Tyr-Ser-Lys-Phe-Asp-Thr-Asn-Ser-His-Asn-Asp-Asp-Ala-Leu-Leu-Lys-Asp-Tyr-Gly-Leu-
140   150
Leu-Tyr-Cys-Phe-Arg-Lys-Asp-Met-Asp-Lys-Val-Glu-Thr-Phe-Leu-Arg-Ile-Val-Gln-Cys-
160   170
Arg-Ser-Val-Glu-Gly-Ser-Cys-Gly-Phe-OH
180   188

TRH

pGlu-His-Pro-NH$_2$

GnRH

1   3   10
pGlu-His-Trp-Ser-Tyr-Gly-Leu-Arg-Pro-Gly-NH$_2$

Somatostatin

1   14
Ala-Gly-Cys-Lys-Asn-Phe-Phe-Trp-Lys-Thr-Phe-Thr-Ser-Cys

GHRH

1   10   20
Try-Ala-Asp-Ala-Ile-Phe-Thr-Asn-Ser-Tyr-Arg-Lys-Val-Leu-Gly-Gln-Leu-Ser-Ala-Arg-
                          30
Lys-Leu-Leu-Gln-Asp-Ile-Met-Ser-Arg-Gln-Gln-Gly-Glu-Ser-Asn-Gln-Glu-Arg-Gly-
40   44
Ala-Arg-Ala-Arg-Leu-NH$_2$

structure, meaning that they are derivations of a common ancestor (from a phylogenically older organism with simpler endocrine relationships).

In contrast to the purely neural structure of the posterior lobe, the anterior lobe of the pituitary contains both neuroendocrine (brain) structures and regular endocrine cells; that is, it functions both as part of the brain and as a gland, controlled by the hypothalamus through the neurohormones secreted into the portal system but also synthesizing its own hormones locally. Furthermore, it contains and secretes a larger variety of peptides than the posterior lobe (see Figure 12–4). The bulk of the anterior lobe comprises cells that lack axons and dendrites but fire action potentials and secrete by exocytosis just like nerve cells. They are not derived from neurectoderm, however, and hence are officially nonneural. The nonneural cells come in a number of varieties and are named according to which peptide(s) they secrete. *Corticotrophs* produce POMC (mentioned earlier) and secrete ACTH (mentioned earlier). Gonadotrophs secrete **follicle-stimulating hormone (FSH)**, which fosters the growth of the follicle of cells surrounding the ovum, and **luteinizing hormone (LH)**, which helps cause this follicle to break apart, resulting in *ovulation*. Other products of the anterior pituitary include **growth hormone (GH)** and thyrotropin, or **thyroid-stimulating hormone (TSH)**, which regulate body metabolism by stimulating the release of *somatomedins* and *thyroxines* from other endocrine glands. The neural portion of the anterior lobe consists of peptidergic cells in the hypothalamus that send axons down the infundibulum just as for the posterior lobe hormones. Here, however, their contents are released into the portal system act locally to regulate the secretion of the endocrine cells of the anterior lobe. Thus **thyrotropin-releasing hormone (TRH)** causes the release of TSH, **gonadotropin-releasing hormone (GnRH)** regulates LH and FSH release, and **growth-hormone-releasing hormone (GHRH)** regulates GH release. Hypothalamic neurohormones also inhibit anterior lobe cells. **Somatostatin** inhibits GH secretion, and **dopamine** (not a peptide) inhibits the release of prolactin.

It should be apparent that another reason for the pituitary to be called "the master gland" is that so many of its peptides act on other glands. All of the hypothalamic releasing factors act primarily on the anterior pituitary but TSH, GH, FSH, LH, and ACTH have targets in other endocrine structures as well. These other structures produce hormones that act on final targets in tissues such as bone, muscle, and skin, but also provide feedback to the brain to regulate the release of the initial neuropeptides. As discussed later, this feedback usually requires a molecule like a *steroid hormone* that can cross the blood-brain barrier (exceptions will be discussed later). Most often, the feedback results in hormonal equilibrium, or *homeostasis,* since the final product acts to

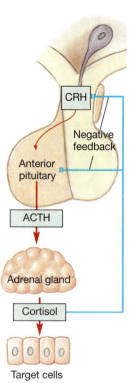

Figure 12–5 *The HPA Axis.* Endocrine systems are feedback regulated, meaning that existing endocrine products stimulate or inhibit further production of themselves. In one example of a negative feedback system, the hypothalamo-pituitary adrenal (HPA) axis, the adrenal steroid cortisol inhibits further production of itself by crossing the blood-brain barrier and shutting off the first step of its production cycle.

inhibit further release of the pituitary hormone. This type of **negative feedback** is very common in homeostatic mechanisms since it functions to dampen the signal once it is expressed (see discussion of negative feedback in transmitter synthesis in Chapter 5). An especially good example of negative feedback is the *hypothalamo-pituitary adrenal axis* (HPA axis), a feedback loop that incorporates corticotrophin-releasing hormone (CRH), ACTH, and an adrenal cortical steroid (Figure 12–5). Upon stressful stimuli, nerve signals activate CRH-containing cells in the hypothalamus, which discharge CRH into the anterior lobe, depolarizing the corticotrophs. ACTH is then liberated into the blood where it circulates throughout the body, acting ultimately upon the outside layer (or *cortex*) of the adrenal glands on top of each kidney. (We have considered another adrenal hormone, *epinephrine* or *adrenaline,* that is released by the interior, or *medulla,* of each adrenal gland during stress, Chapter 6). The adrenal cortex in turn releases a steroid (*corticosterone* in rats) into the blood where it acts on many tissues in various ways to prepare the body for injury or to promote recovery. Collectively these adrenal steroids are called *glutocorticoids* (you may have received an injection of **cortisol**, the human equivalent of corticosterone, into a joint to reduce swelling and inflammation). In addition to these peripheral actions, however, corticosterone feeds back onto the brain and pituitary where it acts to inhibit both the synthesis and the further release of CRH, shutting off the HPA axis.

There are signs that other brain receptors for corticosterone/cortisol may be involved with other behavioral responses to stress (Sapolsky, Krey, & McEwen, 1986; Young, Spencer, & McEwen, 1990). Some central actions of the steroids may be deleterious and there is even evidence that in humans clinical depression in response to stress may involve a disorder in the regulation of the HPA axis. Injection of a nonnative steroid, *dexamethasone,* will suppress the operation of the HPA axis in normal people but, for unknown reasons, fails to do so in a fraction of seriously depressed patients. Thus, the **dexamethasone-suppression test** is a significant, if somewhat unreliable, tool in the diagnosis, treatment, and clinical investigation of depression (see Chapter 18).

The Determination of Gender

In humans and other mammals, females carry two copies of a chromosome, called the **X chromosome,** in each diploid cell. In the ovaries, diploid cells divide to produce female gametes, called *ova,* each of which carries a single X chromosome. Each diploid cell of males contains one X chromosome and a different chromosome, called the **Y chromosome.** Thus, two types of haploid gametes are formed in males, some carrying the Y chromosome and some carrying the X chromosome. Upon union of male and female gametes the type of sex chromosome carried by the penetrating sperm determines whether the fertilized egg will contain two X chromosomes, producing a female offspring, or an X chromosome and a Y chromosome, producing a male (Figure 12–6).

The Y chromosome, but not the X chromosome, contains genetic material coding for a protein called the **H-Y antigen.** Production of this protein may be the major function of the Y chromosome, which is the smallest of human chromosomes. The H-Y antigen, if present, may work with a *testes determination factor* to influence the *primordial gonads* in the embryo to embark on a developmental program that elaborates the inner core (medulla) into **testes** (the word medulla applies to many different structures) and may influence the production of sperm by the structure later in development. In the absence of the influence, the outer layers elaborate to become **ovaries** (Figure 12–7). Strangely enough, from this moment forward genes are uninvolved in determination of gender; the differentiated gonadal tissue takes over and expresses chemical signals that determine sexual characteristics. These chemical signals have action and structure different from any others that we have considered so far. Collectively they are called **sex steroids.**

Steroid Hormones

Steroid hormones are unlike some transmitters in that they open or shut no membrane channel and they are associated with no second- or third-messenger systems. Rather, *they dif-*

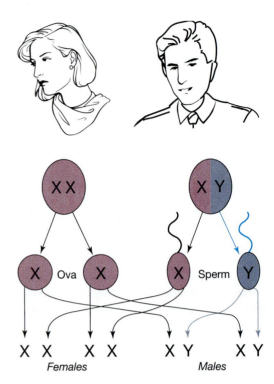

Figure 12–6 *Chromosome Arrangement in Fertilization.* When fertilization occurs, an X chromosome from the mother's ovum is united with either an X- or Y chromosome (they are equally likely) from the father's sperm. Of the resulting zygote, an XX genotype will be female, an XY genotype male.

fuse directly across cell membranes to interact with target cells and influence their developmental fate. Strictly speaking, the X and Y chromosomes, in collusion with the H-Y antigen and TDF, determine *gender.* However, everything that we associate with gender in people is a property of steroid action. This action falls into two generally recognized categories. **Organizational effects** of steroids cause the physical changes that separate the genders, such as development of genitalia and musculoskeletal differences, and create central nervous system circuits that program reproductive behaviors. For example, a target cell of the primordial genital tubercle will develop into the penis if it comes in contact with testosterone; the same target cell will develop into the vagina if it does not. **Activational effects** are those seen throughout life in which the continued presence of the steroids acts on the structures that were organized in embryonic development, infancy, childhood, and adolescence to permit continued expression of sexual physiology, such as production of gametes and sexual behavior. For example, males who become unable to produce testosterone cannot then produce sperm, and will eventually lose sexual function. To understand how these two types of effects take place, it is essential that the molecular and cellular aspects

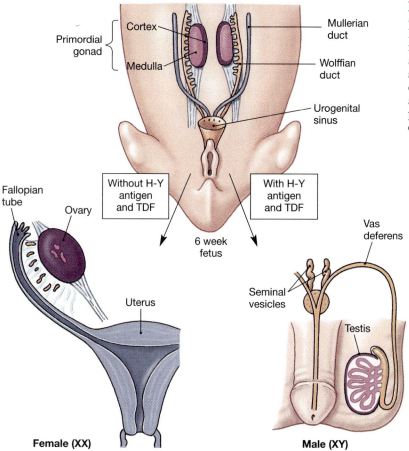

Cortex

Primordial gonad

Medulla

Mullerian duct

Wolffian duct

Urogenital sinus

Without H-Y antigen and TDF

With H-Y antigen and TDF

6 week fetus

Fallopian tube

Ovary

Uterus

Vas deferens

Seminal vesicles

Testis

Female (XX)

Male (XY)

Figure 12–7   *Embryonic Development of Gonads.* In the early developmental stages of life, male and female gonadal tissue is identically organized. The presence of the H-Y antigen and the TDF gene product, whose synthesis is directed by the male Y chromosome only, influences the development of testes. In the absence of the H-Y antigen and the TDF gene product, this primordial tissue develops into ovaries.

of steroid *endocrinology* (the study of hormones and their effects) are understood. Let's begin by examining the chemical structures of steroids.

Mechanisms of Steroid Synthesis

You have undoubtedly been told of the health risks associated with excess dietary **cholesterol**. It may come as a surprise to you, therefore, to discover that cholesterol serves several very useful functions in the body. As shown in Figure 12–8, cholesterol is the biosynthetic precursor for all the steroid hormones. As a consequence, the steroids are structurally very similar. Cholesterol consists of four hydrocarbon rings, a single hydroxyl (OH) group, and a hydrocarbon chain. The chain is removed, an oxygen added and the hydroxyl group modified to produce **progesterone**. Progesterone is one of two hormones that regulate female reproductive physiology in vertebrates. Addition of a hydroxyl group in place of the original hydrocarbon chain produces **testosterone**, called an **androgen** by virtue of its organizational and activational role in *male* reproductive physiology (testosterone comes from the Latin root for male gonad, *testis*). The second major female steroid, **estradiol**, is produced by adding simple hydrogen to

testosterone in a process known as **aromatization** since the ring structure produced resembles the structure of many volatile, or "aromatic," hydrocarbons.

Progesterone, testosterone, estradiol, and the intermediates are found in abundance in the blood of both genders. It is not the mere presence of androgen or **estrogen** (progesterone and estradiol) that controls reproductive physiology and secondary sexual characteristics, but rather the relative quantities of each at various points in development, at different sites in the body, and at different times in reproductive cycles. Table 12–1 shows the ambient blood levels of the various sex steroids in adult humans. Note the overlapping concentration ranges of estrogens between men and women during the "follicular phase" of the menstrual cycle and that normal levels of testosterone can differ by as little as twofold between the genders. Not only are the structures of androgens and estrogens very similar and their concentrations in the blood of males and females only slightly different but, as we shall see in the next section, testosterone is actually converted back to estradiol in men before it acts at its final molecular target. What then accounts for the differences between the sexes that seem so profound to us? The answer is to be

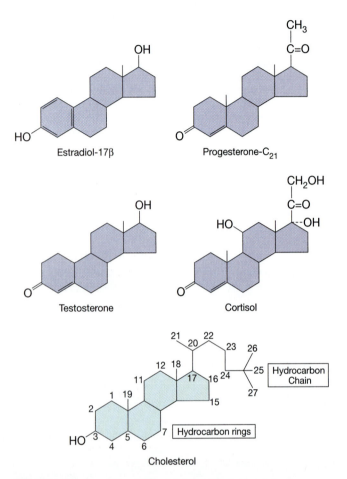

Figure 12–8   *Steroid Synthesis.* Cholesterol is the building block for all steroid hormones.

found in the receptor protein expressed by the target cells (sound familiar?). In other words, the gender differences that are apparent to us arise from the differential expression of binding substances in the cytosol of steroid targets in males and females.

Mechanisms of Steroid Action

Up to now we have dealt with chemical signals that carry a net positive charge (acetylcholine, the catecholamines, and serotonin) or have multiple charged structures within them (GABA, glutamate, and the peptides). Recall that such charges make these compounds *hydrophilic* (water-loving), giving them the ability to diffuse from the site of release through the aqueous extracellular environment to the site of action. To act upon the target cell, these hydrophilic signals must have amphipathic (polar) receptors that span the hydrophobic part of the cell membrane in order to conduct the signal from the outside to the inside of the cell in the process

of transduction (Chapter 2). A moment's inspection of the structures shown in Figure 12–8 will reveal that signal transduction for these steroid messengers must be quite different. The steroids are all *uncharged, nonpolar* structures and are hence *hydrophobic* (water-hating). They can diffuse freely across the interior of the cell membrane and thus require no membrane-bound receptor. However, they require amphipathic proteins to carry them through the extracellular space (and, it happens, the intracellular space as well). These proteins are essentially waterborne receptors for steroids. Since they float freely through the blood plasma, cytosol of some cells, and cerebrospinal fluid, they are called **carrier proteins**. These are globular proteins with a hydrophobic binding site for the steroid in the middle and a hydrophilic exterior to enable the bound protein to mix with water. Because of the similarity of steroid structures, bloodborne carrier proteins are relatively nonspecific, each binding estradiol, testosterone, and progesterone to some degree. As they approach the plasma membrane they discharge the steroid into the lipid bilayer (Figure 12–9). The membranes of all cells throughout the body are in contact with the same concentration of steroids at any moment in time. However, only certain cells have a suitable carrier protein waiting inside. All cells contain intracellular cortisol receptors (regulating general metabolism), but only some cells contain intracellular receptors for estrogen and testosterone. During development and throughout life, they move the bound steroid into the nucleus where the steroid interacts with regions of DNA that promote or repress particular genes, regulating the transcription of those genes into mRNA and their translation into protein (Chapter 2). Receptors for estrogen, for example, are concentrated in human breasts, vagina, uterus, and a few brain regions where they regulate the expression of proteins that develop these female structures. Testosterone receptors are concentrated in genitalia, hair follicles, certain muscle groups, and a few brain regions, and they regulate male development.

Primary and Secondary Sexual Characteristics

On the surface of the embryonic kidney there is a bulge called the *germinal ridge.* If unaffected by an external signal, the germinal ridge will develop into an ovary (mammalian development initially follows a female program for both genders, this program being modified by testosterone for males, Box 12–1). On the Y chromosome that genetic males receive, there is a gene for a trophic factor (or developmental signal, Chapter 2) known as **testis determination factor (TDF)**, which alters the fate of the germinal ridge by causing it to form a testis instead of an ovary. The developmental state of the gonad is referred to as the **primary sex-**

Table 12–1		STEROID HORMONE LEVELS IN THE BLOOD		
Steroid		CR (L/day)	PR (mg/day)	SR (mg/day)
Men				
Androstenedione		2200	2.8	1.6
Testosterone		950	6.5	6.2
Estrone		2050	0.15	0.11
Women				
Androstenedione		2000	3.2	2.8
Testosterone		500	0.19	0.06
Estrone	F	2200	0.11	0.08
	L	2200	0.26	0.15
Estradiol	F	1200	0.09	0.08
	L	1200	0.25	0.24
Progesterone	F	2100	2.0	1.7
	L	2100	25.0	24.0

PR, production rate; CR, clearance rate; SR, secretion rate; F, follicular phase of menstrual cycle; L, luteal phase of menstrual cycle.
Source: Yen and Jaffe (1991).

ual characteristic of the organism; other, more visible features of gender such as body type and facial hair are considered **secondary sexual characteristics**. As the primordial gonad is *indifferent* (in that it has the potential to be either female or male dependent on the presence of TDF), so are the secondary sexual characteristics initially bipotential. For example, the internal genitalia originally come in two forms in each organism, one male and one female. The male system is called the **Wolffian duct** and the female is called the **Müllerian duct**. Here again the "default" setting on the mammalian development program is female; in the absence of other signals the Wolf-

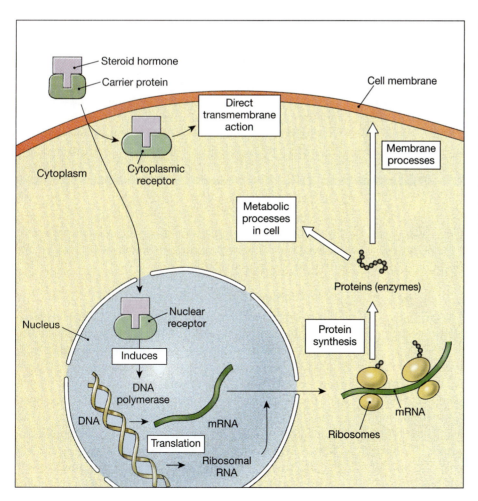

Figure 12–9 *Steroid Action.* Upon arriving at the cell attached to extracellular carrier proteins, steroids diffuse directly across the membrane due to their nonpolar (hydrophobic) nature. Inside the cell, however, they again require carrier proteins for transport. The presence or absence of appropriate intracellular carrier proteins depends on the gender of the organism and the location of the cell. If these carrier proteins are present, the hormones will now interact with DNA and mRNA to effect protein synthesis, directing myriad cellular processes.

Box 12–1

Mammals are Basically Female with Male Characteristics Added

The organizing effects of testosterone and its more potent relative, DHT, are illustrated by the unusual situations in which these compounds fail to act normally. A defect in the X chromosome causes an anomaly called **testicular feminization mutation (TFM)**. Cells in these individuals have one X chromosome and one Y chromosome and hence are genetic males, but have a single amino acid switched in the androgen receptor, causing it to lose its affinity for testosterone and DHT (Imperato-McGinley et al., 1974; Yarbrough et al., 1990). Though hormone levels are normal, the hormone cannot enter the cells, thus, as shown in the photo at the right, people with TFM develop as females in most respects, including behaviorally. They exhibit feminine interests in childhood and heterosexual orientation in puberty, often marrying and attempting to start a family. It is only at this point that the abnormality becomes apparent, since conception between two genetic males is not possible. Most individuals with TFM, after learning this surprising news in midlife, continue well-adjusted lives as women.

Less complete developmental anomalies do occur, with more confusing results for gender identity. Recall that testosterone mediates many of the organizational and activational aspects of gender determination, but not all. Some, such as the development of male external genitalia, require the more potent form of testosterone, DHT. On rare occasion, an individual is born lacking the enzyme activity needed to convert testosterone to DHT during the period in fetal development in which the male genitalia take form. **5α-reductase deficiency** produces a clinical condition in which the male genitalia are rudimentary, having only testosterone's influence on their development. These individuals are usually reared as female and are considered as such until puberty, at which point testosterone causes other male developments, such as growth of body hair and deepening of the voice. The condition has a hereditary component and hence turns up in some populations more than others. A particularly well-known example of 5α-reductase deficiency is the *guevedoces* of the Dominican Republic, who experience

fian duct degenerates and the Müllerian duct grows to form the *fallopian tube, uterus,* and *vagina*. In the presence of testosterone from the testes and another peptide trophic factor called **Müllerian regression hormone**, the Müllerian duct degenerates and the Wolffian duct forms the *vas deferens, seminal vesicle,* and *prostate gland*. The remainder of the secondary sexual characteristics are determined by the action of gonadal steroids.

For example, the *external genitalia* (clitoris and labia or penis and scrotum) are formed from indifferent primordial structures as well, but their appearance is mainly dependent on the absence or presence of testosterone early in development. For this determination to occur, there is a need for an especially potent metabolite of testosterone, 5α-dihydrotestosterone (DHT) to form during embryonic life. All other secondary characteristics such as body hair, breasts, pattern of fat deposition, structure of the larynx and phar-

ynx, and production pattern of peptide *gonadotropic hormones* (see later section) are the function of estrogen and testosterone action later in life.

A Critical Period of Development

Since time immemorial it has been known to keepers of livestock that castration of males has feminizing effects. For example, removal of the gonads (castration) of male chicks (done to produce a more tender bird, or "capon") prevents development of physical characteristics and behavior typical of adult roosters, such as wiry and tough muscles for fighting. Arnold Adolph Berthold, in 1849, showed that this *caponization* could be reversed by transplantation of testicles from a normal chick to a capon, yielding a rooster-like adult. This experiment, really the first in the field of endocrinology, demonstrated that a diffusible substance secreted by the gonads determined sexual differentiation.

sufficient testosterone in puberty to develop a scrotum and descended testes (hence the name, which means "balls at twelve").

Genetic and metabolic abnormalities can also affect female development. For example, absence of one of the X chromosomes in **Turner's syndrome** results in lack of substantial estrogen needed for puberty. Though clearly female, people with Turner's syndrome require hormonal supplements to initiate puberty and sometimes suffer from other developmental problems, including mental retardation, before the condition is recognized.

The three clinical examples cited here clearly establish that female development will occur in the absence of testosterone or DHT, but that estrogen is required for full development of female function. There are examples of masculinization of genetically female individuals as well. In **congenital adrenal hyperplasia (CAH)**, an overabundance of androstenedione (a normal product of the adrenal gland in both genders) produces an artificially

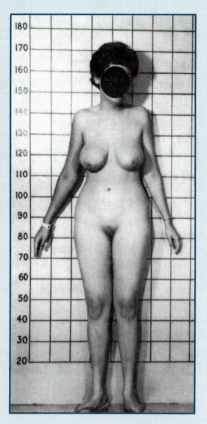

high level of its biosynthetic product, testosterone (see Figure 12–8). When this happens in females there is partial masculinization of the genitalia. Such partial masculinization can also occur with artificial exposure of a fetus to steroids such as *diethylstilbestrol* (DES) upon medical treatments of the mother during pregnancy. Finally, it has long been known that females of rodent species born adjacent to fetal male siblings appear to be affected by the nearby source of androgen and may be sterile (a *freemartin*). A growing body of research is suggestive of a birth-order influence of prenatal androgen exposure in females of species that have large litters, such that females born next to males may display more masculine characteristics.

In sum, development in mammals will spontaneously proceed in the female direction in the absence of sex hormones. Estrogen is required for puberty in girls, and all gender development in boys is dependent on testosterone and DHT action during critical periods of sexual differentiation.

It had also been known for some time that the gentling and feminizing effects of castration were most readily obtained if the procedure was performed early in life, well before the adult body form began to appear. Thus, folk wisdom and animal husbandry anticipated scientific investigation of the organizational and activational effects of the sex steroids considerably, in that there has long been cultural awareness of a **critical period** of sexual development in which the gonads have a more profound effect on the body than at other times of life.

Unfortunately, this cultural awareness derived from animal husbandry also led to some inaccurate assumptions about the influence of gonadal secretions. For example, it has been widely believed, even among scientists, that human homosexuality could be explained by some postulated perturbation in the steroid environment of the fetus or infant during the critical period. In spite of this assumption, scientific investi-

gation has found no evidence correlating childhood endocrine abnormalities and homosexuality, nor do adult homosexuals of either gender display any difference in hormone levels with age-matched heterosexual controls (Bancroft, 1984). Indeed the experience of the *guevedoces* (Box 12–1) would seem to reject endocrine theories of homosexuality, as well as other facile theories involving childhood environment, since these individuals lack normal hormonal signals during the critical period, are raised as girls, and yet develop as males at puberty and appear to acquire heterosexual orientation at that time. Much controversy surrounds interpretation of the *guevedoces* phenomenon (for example, societal pressures in the Dominican Republic may be such that homosexual impulses may be suppressed at puberty in favor of more highly rewarded heterosexual male behavior). Nevertheless, the example illustrates an important point about the neurobiology of sexual behavior. To a degree much greater than for the other features of neuroscience we have discussed, research on animals in this area does not appear to have direct translation into an understanding of human behavior.

Sexuality in Humans and Other Animals

Homosexuality as we understand it in society may have no natural equivalent elsewhere in the animal kingdom. While there are numerous reports of homosexual activity in animals (operationally defined as sexual activity within the same gender), a literature search reveals no account of *preferential* or *exclusive* homosexual behavior in animals. Thus the same-sex activity (which seems to be particularly abundant among domesticated species) is really a better model for *bisexuality* in people. Homosexuality in people may be a phenomenon exclusive to our species and more complicated than a simple hormonal or environmental explanation will allow. This has led to some rather extreme attempts to explain homosexuality by other means, such as recent claims of evidence for a genetic basis. Such proposals overlook the common-sense objection that there would be no evolutionary, or selective, pressure for an orientation not conducive to reproductive success and also ignore the well-established fact that monozygotic, or genetically identical, twins are known to develop disparate sexual preferences much of the time (Bailey & Pillard, 1991; Buhrich, Bailey, & Martin, 1991). One highly publicized study claims to have found a size difference in one hypothalamic nucleus between deceased homosexual and heterosexual human subjects, suggesting a possible biological basis of homosexuality (LeVay, 1991). Some other scientists have challenged this implication, saying the study used statistically insignificant sample sizes and that many of the subjects with abnormal size nuclei died from a disease which may have influenced the size of the neuroanatomy at issue independently of sexual orientation. Homosexuality is not well explained by any of the theories put forth so far, and since it seems to be exclusively human, it is unlikely to yield soon to any scientific explanation based on animal research.

Animal husbandry, the observation of wildlife, and common belief have given us other assumptions about human sexuality that deserve reconsideration in light of scientific fact. Who has not encountered the notion that men who display particularly vigorous male-typical behaviors must have an abundance of testosterone in the blood, or the idea that a man with lost or damaged testicles would suddenly develop a high-pitched voice (see Box 12–2)? Here too we will find a paucity of answers in animal experimentation since human sexuality appears to have unique aspects. The few available answers tend to have an anecdotal quality, such as the well-known but anonymous report from a lighthouse keeper who weighed his whiskers after shaving every morning. According to the keeper's data, his beard growth increased just prior to his trips to shore to visit his girlfriend. Since beard growth is related to testosterone level, the results presumably reflected a testosterone surge in anticipation of sexual activity. Rather more complete and systematic studies on this subject have also been done. Blood levels of testosterone appear to increase in male graduate students upon winning in competitive sports, winning an experimental lottery, or receiving a doctorate degree (Booth et al., 1989; Mazur & Lamb, 1980; Tegelman, Carlström, & Pousette, 1988). However, the results seem better correlated with the overall state of emotional satisfaction or contentment rather than any male-specific behavior per se. Correlative studies on women and estrogen levels in similar circumstances are sadly lacking.

Better understood (primarily because the data have clinical utility and hence have been gathered more assiduously) is the overall correlation between blood testosterone, aging, and sexual activity in men. Figure 12–10a shows the distribution of blood testosterone concentrations in men of various ages. The average level increases from low concentrations at puberty to a plateau in the mid–20s that lasts until the age of 60, at which levels begin to decline. Studies of human sexual behavior are sparse, perhaps due to modesty on the part of researchers and subjects, but more likely due to reluctance on the part of funding agencies to support potentially "scandalous" research. Our best data on human sexual behavior is relatively old and has been subject to much methodological criticism. The product of the famous Kinsey research team in the 1940s, the data was greeted with skepticism immediately and little has transpired in the intervening years to improve this negative image. Some of these data are shown in Figure 12–10b. Sexual activity in men shows a plateau roughly comparable to the testosterone increase, declining with the steroid concentration to very low levels after the age of 70. However, more remarkable than this rough correlation is the broad range of normal testosterone values from Figure 12–10a; healthy individuals in midlife can have anywhere from 400 to 1000 ng/100 ml. As shown in Figure 12–11, there is broad variation in the frequency of male sexual activity as well (defined as heterosexual, homosexual, or autoerotic activities). Normal men can engage in a level of sexual activity ranging from once a week to more than twelve times a week. Confirmation of our notion that virility correlates with testosterone level would entail examination of the sexual activity of individuals with correlative testosterone measurements. These data are not available, except in anecdotal form. Though the sexual activity of hypogonadal men (with pathologically low testosterone) clearly benefits from testosterone supplements, the sexual activity of men with normal testosterone levels is reported to have little direct dependence on blood testosterone. Surgical removal of one testicle, for example, is thought to have little negative impact on sexual behavior.

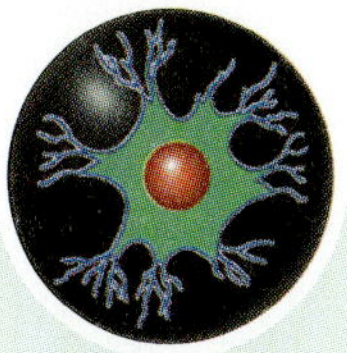

Box 12–2

Feminizing Effects of Pollution?

Some men seem to develop a particular terror of losing their masculine traits and becoming feminized. Adding to this, the scientific community has from time to time created alarm that borders on mass hysteria by announcing preliminary findings that some current practice might lead men to develop female characteristics. A prominent example occurred in the 1970s when a claim was made that marijuana use led to shrinking of testicles and eventual impotence (later shown to have no scientific validity).

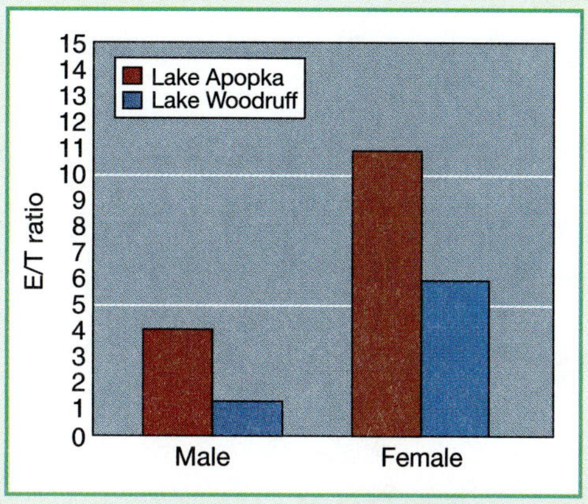

Recently, similar claims have been made regarding possible feminizing effects of the environmental toxins DDT and PCBs (polychlorinated biphenyls). In contrast to the isolated studies on marijuana, these newer concerns seem to be based on more substantial evidence and converging support from independent and reliable sources. For example, alligators in a polluted lake in Florida have lower reproductive rates and show greater expression of feminine traits in both genders than alligators in a nearby, ecologically similar but clean lake (Guillette et al., 1994). The figure shows that this can possibly be explained by greater ratios of estrogen to testosterone in both genders. (Lake Woodruff is the clean lake and Lake Apopka is the polluted one.) Since other studies have shown that PCBs that pollute the lake can act like estrogen in animals (Raloff, 1994), it is unclear whether the feminizing effect is a direct one of the toxin or whether it is an indirect effect mediated by an increase in estrogen itself.

Similar findings have been reported for seagulls exposed to DDT and, in a less documented but more widely publicized case, for the endangered Florida panther, whose numbers have declined in part due to *cryptorchidism,* or undescended testes. Cryptorchidism is on the rise in humans, too, as are other reproductive disorders, such as testicular cancer, that may be attributed to endocrine imbalances. Some studies have shown that in certain countries sperm counts have declined in men by as much as 50 percent (Carlsen, et al., 1992), lending support to the fear that environmental toxins affect our species as well.

Valid or not, these scientific studies serve the purpose of raising awareness of social problems such as drug abuse and pollution. Regrettably, it is often the case that such problems are generally ignored until they become frightening. With regard to pollution, perhaps these latest studies will motivate the analysis and avoidance of further problems that probably should have occurred before these potentially dramatic results.

Indeed, in adulthood, complete castration has no clear impact, with some studies reporting no loss of sexual capacity and others showing decline in only a portion of the subjects (Heim & Hursch, 1979; Money, 1961). Such variability casts doubt on the effectiveness of the use of castration, physical or chemical, as a treatment of last resort for rapists and child molesters (see Box 12–3).

What about the idea that damage to the testes can cause a change in physical properties, such as voice? Here too historical experiment provides more answers than modern scientific investigation. Castrated men, or **eunuchs,** were used to guard harems in imperial courts as late as the twentieth century, and the historical record does indicate that the procedure rendered them "safe" for association with women since they were incapable of sexual activity. More pertinent is the example of **castrati** sopranos used in nineteenth-century opera. It was found that if boys were castrated early enough, before puberty, the voice in adulthood had the range of a woman but the timbre and resonance of a man, creating an especially powerful dramatic presence. As such they were highly sought after and well rewarded, and families would volunteer male offspring for the procedure. The historical accounts of eunuchs and castrati dispel the notion that a man's voice, once established, can be altered by castration in adulthood.

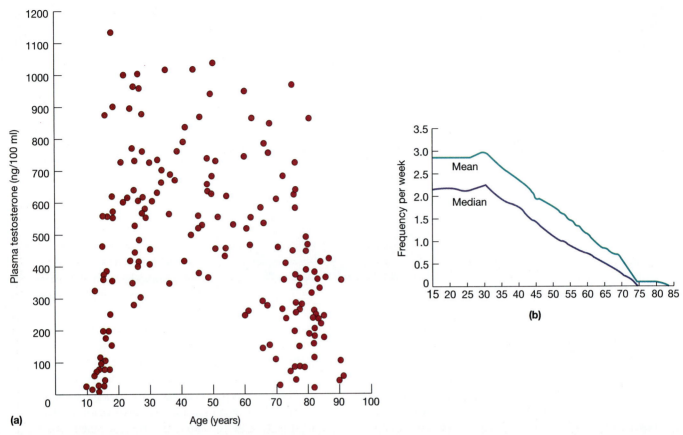

Figure 12–10 *Male Testosterone Levels and Age, Frequency of Male Sexual Episodes and Age.* (a) Each dot on this figure represents a male subject whose blood testosterone and age were recorded. Blood testosterone increases dramatically through puberty, levels off through most of adulthood, and declines in later years. Notice also, however, that this is only the trend—individual levels may vary widely such that a very old man may have the same level as a man in his 20s. (b) Between the ages of 15 and 30, the average number of sexual episodes (heterosexual, homosexual, or autoerotic) per week for the human male stays roughly constant. Though there is a decline in sexual activity after age thirty, this is probably not correlated with a change in blood testosterone content, since these levels stay the same until the age of seventy or so. (Vermuelan, 1972; Kinsey, 1948)

The evidence presented in this section and the previous establishes that there is a *critical period* for development of gender-specific form and function in humans just as for other mammals. However, humans seem to be more malleable than our vertebrate relatives in some respects, less malleable in others, and in many respects unique in displaying gender-specific and sexual behaviors that have no animal model and may be independent of steroid influence.

Sexual Dimorphism in the Brain

Since steroid hormones circulate everywhere in the body and permeate all cell membranes, every central neuron is exposed to the compounds (they also freely diffuse across the blood-brain barrier). However, as previously stated, not every cell has cytoplasmic receptors waiting on the inside to convey the hormonal signal into the nucleus to affect gene expression.

Those cells with appropriate receptors and the accompanying intracellular responses change their *differentiated state* during development, sending out more or fewer dendrites; expressing more, less, or a different transmitter; making more or fewer synaptic contacts; or, as we shall see, undergoing even greater dramatic changes in morphology. A small portion of the neurons in the brain have receptors for the sex steroids and when they respond in this fashion some of them become **sexually dimorphic nuclei**, parts of the brain that differ in structure and appearance between the two genders.

One of the most fascinating and best understood of these nuclei exists in the brain of passerine songbirds. These birds (canaries, finches, and the like) sing to advertise sexual availability and to defend breeding territory. Normally, only the males sing and then only during the breeding season. Researchers were eager to find if there was a seasonal change in a sexually

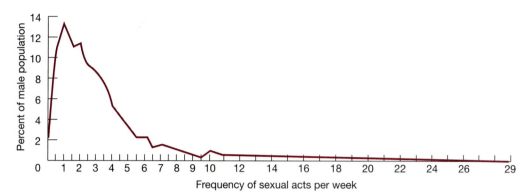

Figure 12–11 *Variability of Male Sexual Episode Frequency.* In this plot of the average number of sexual episodes (heterosexual, homosexual, or autoerotic) performed by men per week, we see a wide distribution, between 0 and 12 episodes, although a small percentage exceed the latter as well. (Kinsey, 1948)

dimorphic region of the brain that could account for the gender differences in behavior. Two locations were found that, in particular, varied between males and females in numbers of neurons, in the size of the cell bodies, and in the elaboration of dendrites. Figure 12–12 shows a nerve fiber stain of a sagittal section of a male brain (left) and a female brain (right), with the sexually dimorphic nuclei indicated by the arrows. Using radiolabeled steroids, it was shown that these areas did indeed have steroid receptors, suggesting that the substances either had a positive trophic effect in males and no effect in females or a negative trophic effect in females and no effect in males. Most surprising of all was the finding that emerged when radioactive nucleotides, the building blocks of genetic material, were used as a probe to determine whether cell division was occurring. In canaries it was found that new neurons were generated by mitosis of stem cells throughout adult life! This was hard to believe at first since it went against the established doctrine (Chapter 2) that vertebrate neurons are fixed in number at birth and only decline in number afterward. While this genesis of new neurons is not confined to the dimorphic nuclei responsible for birdsong, some of the birdsong structures do undergo mitosis throughout adulthood.

For other vertebrates including mammals, there is no neuronal mitosis in adulthood. Furthermore, the sexual dimorphisms that exist in mammals are not nearly as dramatic as those shown in Figure 12–12. Indeed, the extent of such dimorphisms in humans, and the postulated behaviors that can be considered gender-specific, are the source of much controversy. (Box 12–4 later in this chapter).

Steroids and Aggression

The effect of steroids on the organization of secondary sexual characteristics is enhanced, after the critical period, by activational effects which maintain and develop sexually dimorphic features. Such activational effects have been exploited by some athletes who use *anabolic steroids,* which are steroids like androgens that favor building, or anabolism,

of body mass. There is little evidence that such use really enhances athletic competitiveness. Rather, it is change in body image, subjective or objective, that the steroid users are typically seeking. The adverse health consequences of anabolic steroid use include liver, kidney, and cardiovascular problems; and these dangers, combined with the notion that the steroids may create unfair advantage in competition, have led all major athletic associations to ban their use. Less well known and less well documented are the psychological dangers of steroid use. One such danger is known from anecdote in the body-building community as 'roid rage—elevated tendencies towards aggressive behavior, including crimes of violence. A study of forty one individuals using steroids found that twenty eight had experienced psychiatric disturbances such as aggression as probable side effects of drug use (Pope & Katz, 1989). Note that, as for many such studies, psychiatric problems could have been what caused the drug use rather than being the effect of the drug use.

What basis for a connection between sex steroids and aggression can be found in experimental studies? The males of most species are clearly more aggressive than females (except in the case of females with young). In laboratory animals this can clearly be associated with testosterone levels but, as discussed previously, only early in life during the critical period. In castrated mice, androgen replacement must begin immediately after castration and continue throughout life to promote aggressiveness. Androgen administration to either sex in adulthood produces little effect on aggression (Edwards, 1969, 1970). Other studies show that there is no correlation between aggressiveness in adult male mice and levels of blood testosterone (Barkley & Goldman, 1977; McKinney & Desjardins, 1973). Many features of social dominance and intermale aggression in fact appear to be independent of gonadal steroids, as shown by studies that reveal that castration affects only specific aspects of aggression in *particular* individuals (Haug, Brain, & Kamis, 1986; Johnson & Whalen, 1988) and studies that indicate that social position of dogs

Box 12–3

The Future of Chemical Castration

It may not be nice to be good, little 6655321! It may be horrible to be good. And when I say this to you I realize how self-contradictory that sounds. I know I shall have many sleepless nights about this. What does God want? Does God want goodness or the choice of goodness? Is a man who chooses the bad perhaps in some way better than the man who has the good imposed upon him? Deep and hard questions, . . . • A Clockwork Orange, *Anthony Burgess, 1962*

In *A Clockwork Orange* (a novel by Anthony Burgess later made into a Stanley Kubrick film of the same name) a morally ambiguous protagonist is brought to justice for a series of violent crimes by being forced to take a drug that suppressed violent tendencies. A major theme of the book, apart from the relationship between the individual and the modern state, is the tension between good and evil in each person, the fact that the good is often intertwined inseparably with the evil. The drug given by the prison wardens, for example, blocked the subject from acting on violent fantasies but also destroyed many of the positive features of his character.

Much has been made about new technology for treatment of criminal sex offenders that stems from chemical modification of the sex steroids or their receptors. One modified compound, **Depo-provera** (MPA, medroxy-progesterone acetate) was synthesized for use as a contraceptive but was later found to have extensive properties as an *androgen antagonist,* reducing testosterone levels in males and effecting a state that is the same as reversible chemical castration (Gordon et al., 1970; Meyer et al., 1985).

Though physical castration of rapists has been advocated as an appropriate sentence by some, constitutional prohibitions against mutilation as punishment have made sentences of this kind rare and isolated in our criminal justice system. However, with the advent of "chemical castration," a number of legal venues in Texas, South Carolina, and Michigan, have explored the use of Depo-provera as an alternative to incarceration for sex offenders. Though there is psychiatric literature suggesting that Depo-provera is somewhat effective in medical treatment of **paraphilia** (a mental disorder of sexual deviation), the nature of the effect appears not to involve a reduction in physical arousal to paraphilic stimuli but rather to render the patient more responsive to psychotherapy (Cooper, 1986; Langevin et al., 1979; Money & Bennett, 1981). Use of the drug to treat rapists, other than paraphiliacs, is not supported by psychiatric studies and would appear to be a medical experiment conducted by judges outside of the medical or research establishments.

As you might imagine, chemical castration is controversial. Studies have shown that male rapists and normal men do not differ in the nature of the stimuli that lead to sexual arousal but rather in their hostility towards women (Abel et al., 1977, Malamuth, Heim, & Feshbach, 1980). Thus the decision whether to use Depo-provera as treatment for rapists would depend on whether the crime is perceived as sexual deviance or as a hate crime against a woman. Feminist groups are at odds among themselves over this issue, with some leading the charge to chemically "disarm rapists" and others holding that such attitudes misconstrue the nature of the crime. For example, the president of one chapter of the National Organization for Women called a case of chemical castration in her region "barbaric" since it "reinforces the notion that rape is a sexual act and not an act of violence" ("Rapists sentenced to choice between prison and castration" Associated Press, Nov. 19, 1983).

What is your opinion of the judicial use of chemical castration? The sections in this chapter on the *critical period of development, sexual dimorphism in the brain,* and *steroids and aggression* should help you develop a well-informed scientific opinion. If your instructor has solicited term papers for your course perhaps this would be a suitable topic.

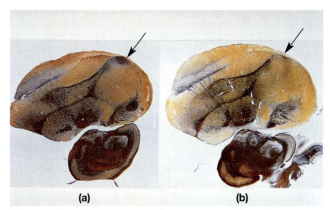

Figure 12–12 *Sexual Dimorphism in the Songbird Brain.* Comparison of male (a) and female (b) zebra finch brains stained to show areas of high neural activity. A nucleus in particular known to control birdsong (arrows) shows dense neural activity in the male, who must learn and sing specific patterns. The females, who do not sing these same songs, do not show the same activity in these regions.

and monkeys in their hierarchies is stable after castration (Dixson, 1980).

Human and animal studies seem to support the idea that levels of aggressiveness, like other behaviors that differ between the genders, seem to be dependent on steroids early in life but less so and to a much more variable degree in adulthood.

Conception, Pregnancy, and Birth

In mammals, most of the factors that determine whether sexual behavior will lead to conception are under the control of the female. This extends to whether sexual behavior will occur at all. Historically, female sexual behavior has been characterized by the notion of **receptivity** (or occasional passive acceptance of male advances, as opposed to the usual active resistance). Male mammals were seen as always available and motivated for copulation and females generally reluctant, with periodic episodes in which the reluctance was abandoned and mating occurred. More recent laboratory studies and, to a lesser degree, field studies have led to a modification of this concept in favor of a model in which females are seen as more the instigators of sexual contact rather than passive objects of male attention.

Along with the notion that females are passive sexual participants is the equally outmoded idea that females are always more invested in rearing and caring for the offspring than males. Reproduction strategies among vertebrates vary widely, from species like many fish that multiply by spawning and invest little energy in rearing of young, to birds, such as most songbirds, where both parents participate fully in raising chicks. Though physiological investment in reproduction is

generally greater in the female that must produce the egg or fetus, there are examples (such as the spotted sandpiper) in which parental duties such as incubation of eggs and feeding of chicks are assumed by the male. The female spotted sandpiper displays and defends breeding territory, duties assumed by the male in most bird species. Mammals likewise display a range of parenting strategies from male roles limited to conception alone (some large felines) to communal parenting (lions, some primates, and herding animals), and partnership characterized by pair-bonding and mutual assistance in caring for young (humans and some rodents). In animals that form partnerships it is sometimes difficult to determine which parent makes the greater physiological investment in procreation. Though female mammals support the fetus, nurture their young through lactation after birth, males may play a bigger role in foraging, hunting, or defending the brood and its territory. An impromptu classroom debate will reveal no simple answer to the question of which parent assumes the most demanding duties in the human species! Nevertheless, when all mammals are taken into account, including social species in which a single dominant male fertilizes all reproductively active females, there is a justifiable tendency to view male investment in each individual conception as being smaller than that of females. From this perspective, the favored (dominant) male can be perceived as relatively indiscriminate in mating. In such species the females appear more discriminate, accepting advances only from the dominant male. Thus for animals that breed seasonally, in which both genders undergo physical changes to prepare for procreation, the female might be seen as more *selective* than males; selectivity, rather than *receptivity*, might be a better description of the role played by the female in determining when and with whom mating will occur.

Even the notion of selectivity has its problems. Females that "select" only the dominant male may in fact merely be obeying a selection made among the males themselves after contests for dominance have been resolved, and in species other than herding animals the indiscriminate role of the male has been grossly exaggerated. For example, the oft-cited fact that one volume of human ejaculate contains enough semen to impregnate every fertile woman in North America, while true in a technical sense, is completely misleading in terms of human biology. Apart from artificial insemination, it would be biologically impossible for a single man to father more than a few hundred children. In reality, cultural limitations created, implemented, and enforced in many cases by men themselves, restrict the number of children fathered by a single man to a much lower number; and it may be that laws and moral suasion are not even necessary to accomplish this restriction. An anonymous survey of the men in your class, in which each is asked how many children he would choose to

Box 12–4

Neurobiology and the "Battle of the Sexes"

Given the substantial sexual dimorphism in the body and gender differences in behavior seen in most vertebrates, the overall impression obtained by reviewing the literature on mammals is that there is a surprising paucity of evidence for correlative dimorphism in the brain. Moreover, review of the data obtained from humans reveals even fewer concrete gender differences; those that exist are relatively minor, and there is no consensus on their significance. Apart from some fairly robust findings of a general nature, such as the fact that men's brains are slightly larger than those of women and that women consistently perform slightly better than men on most tests of sensory acuity (reviewed in Becker, Breedlove, & Crews, 1992; Nelson, 1995), the search for specific dimorphisms between men and women in the CNS has been plagued by ideological preferences and irreproducibility (see Gould, 1981; Tavris, 1992). Studies giving an advantage to one sex are contradicted by other studies, raising suspicion that the results may sometimes be affected by the desire for a particular finding. Sometimes not even basic findings can be agreed upon. In one study of human cadavers, a female researcher found that women have a larger corpus callosum than men (and hence, one might surmise, were capable of greater "integration" between hemispheres). Subsequently, male researchers using noninvasive imaging of the living human brain were unable to confirm this finding. In cases such as these it is difficult to judge who may be correct since each may have a motivation to come to one conclusion or the other.

Rather paradoxically, much research on gender differences (as well as any other "hot" topic) could escape some controversy and acquire more scientific certainty by use of a simple device employed widely in less politically charged areas. It is common for scientists to use a **double-blind paradigm** when evaluating hypotheses in which the experimenter has even a mild personal interest. In this paradigm, the data is gathered and interpreted by different individuals. The first is ignorant ("blind") as to the hypothesis being tested and the second ("double-blind") is ignorant as to the identity of the samples. Only after the experiment is completed and the samples analyzed is the code broken and the results exposed to view. While a double-blind approach to research on living subjects is sometimes impossible since gender is usually an obvious quality, double-blind research on preserved specimens such as anatomical sections or biochemical assays is almost always possible. Alas, until such methods are universally in place among gender researchers we shall have to wait, and speculate, about what neurobiology has to tell us about relations between men and women.

sire if no responsibility was attached to his actions, might be instructive. It may turn out that most men, just like most women, would prefer to have just a few offspring, to know them well, and to take an active part in their upbringing.

Moreover, the notions of receptivity and selectivity fail to recognize the proactive, or motivated, behavior of female mammals in seeking copulation. The word **estrus** (which means "in a frenzy") is the name of the sexual stage of a female physiologically driven to seek copulation. Colloquially, such animals are said to be "in heat" and many people can testify to the highly driven search for males by female cats or dogs in this condition. Animals in heat cannot easily be contained indoors or in yards and vocalize constantly to attract potential mates. Indeed, laboratory studies have shown that estrous females will risk punishment to achieve contact with a sexually active male, to a degree even greater than that punishment a male will endure to gain access to a female. Field studies of primates also show that females are highly motivated to seek copulation and will risk bodily injury, injury to offspring, or even death to achieve contact with a sexually active male (see Nelson, 1995, for a discussion of these studies). Rodent sexual behavior is also characterized by proactive behavior on the part of the female. Called **proceptivity** by researchers, this activity entails overt seeking of sexual contact and is proportionally greater in magnitude than the relatively passive role played by males. The estrous female rat, for example, will dart in front of the seemingly indifferent male and solicit contact by hopping about and wiggling her ears (Figure 12–13). Extensive investigations in my own laboratory have shown that virtually all estrous females will engage in such solicitation, whereas only a portion of the males will respond by following the female, investigating her flanks, grooming her, and finally mounting. Female rodents in natural environments also seem to control the timing of mating, but seem to copulate relatively indiscriminately with all males that respond. Living in colonies called *demes,* females come into estrus synchronously and pace contact with males so as to maximize the likelihood of reproductive success. While males sometimes appear to initiate sexual contact as well, only 3 percent of male-initiated contacts led to intromission whereas 90 percent of female-initiated contacts were successful in this way (McClintock, 1987). Thus proceptivity appears to be a better concept than either receptivity or selectivity in describing female rodent sexual behavior.

In sum, the early study of reproductive behavior, and consequently much popular thinking on the subject, appears to be confounded by archaic concepts involving a sexually active role for males and a passive one for females and the notion that females are more "invested" than males in the welfare of offspring. Modern research and field studies provide a more accurate picture of reproductive behavior, one in which both genders are equally motivated to procreate and, when given the opportunity, similarly selective in choosing the proper mate. Distribution of parenting responsibilities ranges from sharing in many animals to exclusively female in a few and may be difficult to assess accurately in social animals.

Regulation of the Estrus and Menstrual Cycles

Most feedback systems utilize negative, or inhibitory, control, like the HPA axis. A few employ **positive feedback:** Rather than inhibiting further production, the presence of a hormone stimulates further production of itself. A good example in biology is the endocrine regulation of the estrus cycle in animals and the menstrual cycle in people (Figure 12–14). In males and females a mechanism in the hypothalamus induces releasing hormone secretion in a *pulsatile* manner, meaning that there are periodic fluctuations in the amount of hormone released. For example, GHRH, and hence GH, is released primarily at night. Also pulsatile in nature is GnRH secretion from the anterior hypothalamus and the subsequent appearance of LH and FSH in the blood within a few hours. Since LH and FSH in turn regulate the production of other sex steroids, the concentrations of these other

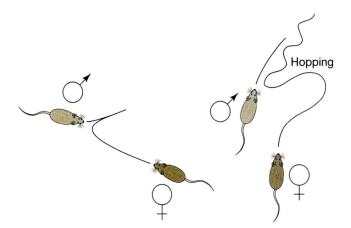

Figure 12–13 *Female Proceptivity.* More than just receptive or selective for mating partners, female rats in estrus will actively seek sexual relations with males by darting in front of them or hopping up and down and wiggling the ears. (Nelson, 1995)

steroids are dependent on GnRH levels as well. In males, high concentrations of these other sex steroids result in negative feedback for GnRH production, thus keeping the sex steroid levels nearly constant. In females, however, there is a "surge" mechanism in the GnRH release center, wherein rising levels of the sex steroid estradiol trigger a positive feedback mechanism, resulting in the release of *more* GnRH rather than less, and therefore ultimately more estradiol as well. The peak of this blood peptide along with LH initiates ovulation, in which the mature egg follicle from the **follicular phase** ruptures and the released ovum proceeds through the fallopian tubes to await fertilization. After ovulation, the follicle remnant forms a glandular structure called the **corpus luteum** which secretes progesterone into the blood during the **luteal phase** of the cycle. Here the normal negative feedback loop involving GnRH is restored; LH, FSH, and estrogen levels fall towards non-estrus amounts; and the increased progesterone prepares the uterus for possible pregnancy. The peptide hormone *inhibin* also creates an inhibitory, or negative feedback loop to the pituitary. For some animals, such as those with sporadic or seasonal cycles, the late luteal phase is associated with behaviors similar to pregnancy even if no fertilization occurs (hence called **pseudopregnancy**). In other, more regularly cycling species the sequence resumes if no pregnancy occurs and is associated with periodic (estrogen-induced) episodes of *periovulatory* (around the ovum) sexual interest.

As you may have come to expect from reading this chapter, primates and humans differ somewhat from the estrus physiology and behavior of other vertebrates. Though estro-

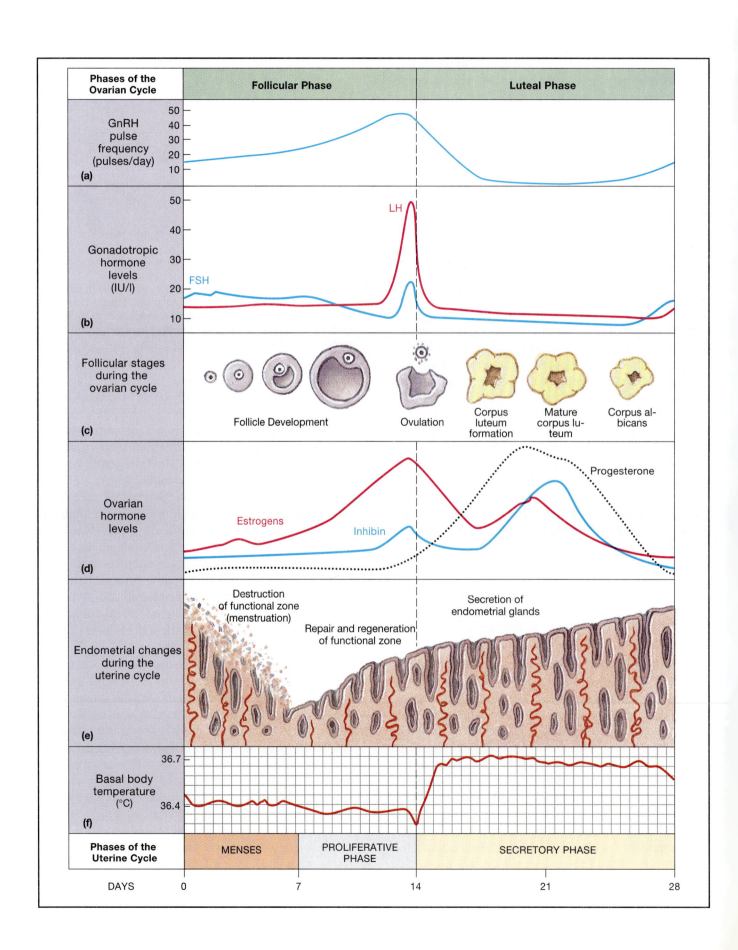

Phases of the Ovarian Cycle		Follicular Phase	Luteal Phase

(a) GnRH pulse frequency (pulses/day) — 50 40 30 20 10

(b) Gonadotropic hormone levels (IU/l) — 50 40 30 20 10 — LH, FSH

(c) Follicular stages during the ovarian cycle — Follicle Development — Ovulation — Corpus luteum formation — Mature corpus luteum — Corpus albicans

(d) Ovarian hormone levels — Estrogens, Inhibin, Progesterone

(e) Endometrial changes during the uterine cycle — Destruction of functional zone (menstruation) — Repair and regeneration of functional zone — Secretion of endometrial glands

(f) Basal body temperature (°C) — 36.7 36.4

Phases of the Uterine Cycle	MENSES	PROLIFERATIVE PHASE	SECRETORY PHASE

DAYS   0   7   14   21   28

Figure 12–14   *Events of the Human Menstrual Cycle.* Pulsatile secretions of GnRH from the anterior hypothalamus result in elevated LH and FSH levels. These hormones aid in the development of the the follicle and trigger the release of estrogen from the follicle and ovaries. Rising estrogen levels during this follicular phase have a positive feedback effect on the hypothalamic release of GnRH, resulting in more production of LH, FSH, and estrogen. Ultimately, these peak levels cause the follicle to rupture and release the ovum (ovulation). In the presence of LH, the ovum develops into a *corpus luteum* (yellow body), beginning the luteal phase. At this point estradiol no longer has positive feedback effects on the hypothalamus, and LH, FSH, and estradiol levels drop, while progesterone produced by the corpus luteum builds up the uterine lining, in anticipation of pregnancy. If no fertilization occurs, progesterone levels drop, and the uterline lining is sloughed off in the process of *menstruation* or *menses.*

gen levels regulate peptide production as described earlier, they do not appear to control sexual activity in the same way as in rodents, cats, dogs, and other mammals. Estrogen and progesterone supplements (e.g., by use of birth control pills) do indeed appear to increase libido in women, but some studies suggest that sexual interest is more clearly related to blood androgen levels in women than to blood estrogen levels (Sherwin & Suranyi-Codotte, 1990). Early experiments with female animal models clearly showed that estrogen alone could induce sexual behavior in a majority of cases, but that progesterone was needed as well to induce sexual behavior in the remaining cases. Furthermore, studies have shown that sexual activities in nonhuman primates can occur throughout the cycle in artificial environments, though there is a suggestion that in natural environments sexual activity is more often confined to the periovulatory peak in blood estrogen concentration (Figure 12–15, Wallen, 1990).

The fact that some cycles of ovulation are not always closely associated with cycles of sexual interest in females has led to the use of the term **menstrual cycle** (instead of estrus cycle) to describe the physiological cycle of organisms that do not display estrus behavior (in other words, organisms with sexual interest throughout the cycle). The mechanism for the menstrual cycle is otherwise the same as for estrus cycles; events of the human menstrual cycle are shown in Figure 12–14.

The transition from estrus to menstrual behavior may have played an important role in the origins of civilization. The data shown in Figure 12–15 indicate that social forces can cause a switch from one to the other in nonhuman primates, and it is reasonable to assume that our primate ancestors also experienced this plasticity at some point. Estrus behavior, as we have seen, commands the attention of males only at certain intervals, leaving the majority of their time free for foraging and roaming. The switch to menstrual behavior would compel more constant attendance by males, both to reap the satisfaction of more frequent intercourse and to guard proceptive females from interlopers. This need for constant attendance would work against a hunter/gatherer lifestyle and would instead favor tribal relations, fire building, tool manufacture, and agriculture, a lifestyle in which

more consistently intimate relations between the genders could be maintained. (Remember, you read it here first.)

Peptide Hormones and Sexual Behavior

Some peptide hormones that regulate reproductive physiology are thought to generate sexual behavior as well. GnRH (also called luteinizing-hormone releasing hormone, **LHRH**) may produce sexual behavior in female mammals (Moss & McCann, 1973). Oxytocin and vasopressin appear to do the same thing in males (Argiolas et al., 1988; Winslow et al., 1993) as well as generating maternal behavior in females, including in some that had never been pregnant (Pedersen et al., 1982).

How could a peptide that regulates reproductive physiology also affect behavior? One possibility is that the peptide gets into the brain from the blood to activate neural receptors. Since peptides cannot cross the blood-brain barrier, one of the "windows in the brain" (Chapter 14) would have to be involved. A somewhat more likely mechanism involves the si-

Figure 12–15   *Female Periovulatory Sexual Interest.* A female monkey placed in a group environment (with other male and female monkeys) shows a distinct preference for complete sexual intercourse (with ejaculation) in the days near her peak estrogen level. When isolated with just one male monkey, however, the correlation is less strong. This indicates that social forces, as well as intrinsic ones, play a role in sexual behavior. (Wallen, 1990)

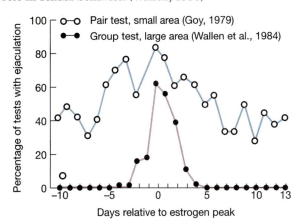

multaneous appearance of peptides in more than one place with compatible functions (see Chapter 5). For example, **egg-laying hormone (ELH),** which produces egg deposition in *Aplysia,* a marine mollusk, also has action on the mollusk brain where it alters the output of specific neurons in the central circuit for reproductive activity (Arch & Smock, 1977; Branton et al., 1978). At the end of this chapter we shall consider the intriguing possibility that peptides such as oxytocin and vasopressin might similarly act as central transmitters in circuits for reproductive behavior.

Endocrine Control of Pregnancy and Parturition

Progesterone levels remain high throughout pregnancy, slightly rising over time in rats and steadily rising in humans, until parturition (giving birth) occurs. Estradiol levels start low and steadily increase until the time of birth (Rosenblatt, Mayer, & Giordano, 1988). After birth, progesterone levels drop dramatically but estradiol levels remain high. The high level of this hormone accounts for the breast enlargement seen in infants of both genders immediately after birth. In humans, this enlargement disappears in the first few weeks of life. In the mother, two peptide hormones increase in level right after birth. First, oxytocin, from the posterior pituitary, surges briefly to expel the placenta and contract the uterus to control bleeding. Second, prolactin, from the anterior pituitary, rises to increase milk production. Milk release during suckling is a reflex that is also mediated by pituitary oxytocin pulses.

Pheromones

As the impetus to sexual behavior, we have thus far considered mainly the self-initiated hormonal signals circulating within an organism. Another chemical signal type, called **pheromones,** can act from one organism (vertebrate or invertebrate) to another, having sexually attracting or repulsing effects, or communicating information about sexual condition. Different types of pheromones accommodate animals with different living environments, as well. For instance, terrestrial organisms have volatile pheromones (easily evaporated into the air), aqueous organisms have hydrophilic pheromones, and those animals that communicate by contact often store pheromones in body secretions. When organisms are separated by considerable distances the pertinent pheromones can act at extremely low concentrations. An oft-cited example is the pheromonal communication between certain moths (Figure 12–16) in which only a few hundred molecules of airborne attractants released by a female can cause many male moths, equipped with sophisticated, pheromonally sensitive antennae, to change direction.

Visual and auditory cues seem more important than chemical signals in the social life of birds and fish, though some aspects of fear and territoriality may be pheromonally

Figure 12–16 *The Luna Moth.* The male's sophisticated antennae are capable of sensing molecular pheromones released by females. In the extreme case but a single molecule of pheromone can ellict a neural response.

mediated in fish. Among vertebrates, mammals appear to use pheromones quite copiously in exchanging information about reproductive condition. In rodents, many of these pheromones are found in feces and urine and, at least for males, may involve derivatives of sex hormones.

In addition to determination of estrus, reproductive physiology that may be pheromonally mediated include several phenomena, each named for the discoverer(s), in which social influences on female physiology are observed. The **Lee-Boot effect** is seen when female mice are housed independently of males. In the absence of the male cues, the estrus cycles, normally four to five days long, are interrupted by long phases of pseudopregnancy, or lapses in ovulation. This may work to conserve energy when ovulation is not likely to lead to pregnancy. When a male is introduced, the **Whitten effect** is observed; females synchronize their estrus cycles and go into estrus more frequently (on the third night after the male arrives).

Two other effects show that social influences can impact more than just the estrus cycles. In the **Bruce effect,** the presence of a unfamiliar male mouse can terminate pregnancy. On the surface, this might not appear to be advantageous to the propagation of the species. However, if this new mouse has managed to displace the mouse which impregnated the female, this suggests that the new mouse is stronger and probably genetically superior. The termination of the pregnancy allows the female to mate with the stronger mouse and propagate better genes. In the **Vandenbergh effect,** the presence of males can accelerate puberty in female mice.

The extent to which pheromones influence sexual behavior in people is a matter of great interest but also considerable controversy. Human equivalents for the Whitten effect have been proposed to account for data, such as in Mc-Clintock (1971, 1978), showing that college women living together tend to synchronize menstruation after seven to eight months. Rodent pheromonal communication is thought to be mediated by a structure called the **vomeronasal organ,** which projects to the accessory olfactory bulbs. Historically, primates, including humans, were thought to lack vomeronasal organs and hence were thought to be relatively unresponsive to pheromonal signals or to miss them altogether. The recent discovery of a rudimentary vomeronasal organ in humans has caused rethinking of this assumption. It is quite certain that this new development has not escaped the attention of the research departments of cosmetics and perfume companies.

Neural Circuits for Mating and Reproduction

The neural basis for mating is intricate because, perhaps more than for any other behavior, mating consists of discrete stages, or "fixed action patterns" (Chapter 10) such as those associated with copulation (mediated in vertebrates largely by brain-

stem and spinal circuits and *proximate* to copulation in the sense that they are the immediate cause) and ultimate fixed action patterns associated with attraction and arousal (mediated by forebrain circuits and *ultimate* to copulation in the sense that they are responsible for starting copulation in the first place).

Spinal and Brainstem Circuits

The proximate fixed action pattern in the females of most quadruped species is called **lordosis.** In lordosis the female adopts a posture that makes intromission by the male easily accomplished. For mammals such as rodents this involves flexion (arching) of the back, elevation of the hindquarters, and deflection of the tail (Figure 12–17). The neural circuitry for lordosis has been thoroughly researched and consists of a sensory projection from cord to brainstem and an efferent projection from brainstem to cord resulting in activation of motor programs (Pfaff & Schwartz-Giblin, 1988; see Figure 12–17). Estrogen receptors at two levels activate the circuit during estrus. First, spinal estrogen receptors expand the sensitivity of sensory cells with receptive fields in the flank region where the male is performing mounting behavior. This

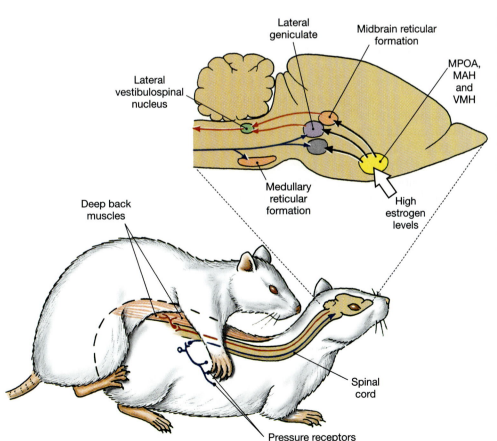

Figure 12–17 *The Lordosis Response.* Sensory receptors in the females' flanks, made more sensitive by increased estrogen levels, convey information to the reticular formation in the midbrain. This information is integrated with forebrain structures suffused with estrogen: the medial preoptic area (MPOA), medial anterior hypothalamus (MAH), and ventromedial hypothalamus (VMH). A projection to the spinal cord through the lateral vestibulospinal nucleus activates the lordosis flexion response circuitry.

Lateral geniculate

Midbrain reticular formation

MPOA, MAH and VMH

Lateral vestibulospinal nucleus

Medullary reticular formation

High estrogen levels

Deep back muscles

Spinal cord

Pressure receptors in flank

increased neural discharge to stimuli from the male is conveyed to the midbrain, where neurons of the reticular formation integrate this input with descending influences from the **medial preoptic area (MPOA)** and other hypothalamic nuclei including the *medial anterior hypothalamus* and *ventromedial hypothalamus*. These forebrain structures also concentrate estrogen; and when suitably primed by steroids, the two inputs to the midbrain activate a descending influence, conveyed in part by the **lateral vestibulospinal nucleus**, which then activates the spinal motor neuron pool for lordosis (see Figure 12–17).

Proximate fixed action patterns for male mammals include erection, intromission, and ejaculation. Brainstem circuits for these are not as elaborate as for lordosis but this probably reflects the fact that the circuits are mostly confined to the spinal cord. Several of the proximate male sexual behaviors can be seen, for example, in decerebrate animals in which the cord is isolated from the brain (see Chapter 7). Substantial sexual dimorphism in genitalia creates substantial dimorphism among the motor neurons controlling muscles in the genitalia. One such dimorphic nucleus, larger in males than females, is called the **spinal nucleus of the bulbocavernosus** (*Onuf's nucleus* in humans). This nucleus concentrates androgens and requires perinatal androgen to develop (Breedlove, 1984). Very likely there are other sexually dimorphic structures in the cord, yet to be described, that connect with the bulbocavernosus to integrate proximate spinal reflexes for male sexual behavior.

Forebrain Circuits

Birds and amphibians have substantial sexually dimorphic and steroid-concentrating regions in forebrain that are thought to organize vocalization for attraction of males by females and defense of territory (Kelley, 1986), which are considered ultimate fixed action patterns. In amphibians, there appears to be a special interplay between the action of steroids on these structures and the release of a peptide transmitter, **arginine vasotocin (AVT)** (Moore, 1992). AVT then acts on limbic structures to produce courtship and copulation.

In mammals the homologs of AVT are oxytocin and vasopressin. Though there are fewer, and smaller, sexually dimorphic and steroid-concentrating nuclei in the mammalian brain (see Box 12–4), one such nucleus appears to synthesize a vasopressinlike peptide in response to steroid priming and may play a role in male sexual behavior (DeVries et al., 1985). The nucleus is part of the limbic system and is called the **medial amygdaloid nucleus (AME)**. The AME in the rat receives projections from the genitalia and from olfactory structures thought to play a role in pheromonal communication (Figure 12–18). The nucleus in turn communicates with other limbic structures, such as the medial preoptic area, that are

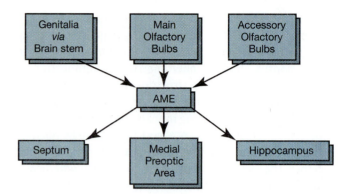

Figure 12–18   *The Medial Amygdaloid Nucleus.* Some inputs and outputs of the medial amygdaloid nucleus (AME).

thought to instigate the proximate phases of sexual behavior. This communication is almost certainly mediated by the vasopressinlike peptide contained within the AME since the limbic influence can be duplicated when vasopressin is applied and the influence can be blocked when a vasopressin antagonist is applied (Albeck et al., 1990; Smock et al., 1990). Injected vasopressin induces sexual behavior in males, as does electrical stimulation of the AME, and the vasopressin antagonist used to block the limbic action also blocks sexual behavior (Albeck et al., 1991; Argiolas et al., 1988; Stark et al., 1998).

Recording from the peptidergic cell bodies in the AME shows that they become active well before the proximate aspects of sexual behavior. Figure 12–19 shows a rate meter record of one such single cell recording. The single action potential is shown in the inset bar, and the main bar graph shows how fast the unit was firing in the brain of a male rat before, during, and after exposure to a receptive female (indicated by the arrows). The symbol "C" stands for individual episodes of copulation, revealing that the AME is activated well before this proximate behavior and probably mediates some ultimate feature of male sexual behavior involving attraction and arousal (Minerbo et al., 1994). Recording from the limbic targets of the peptide shows that they experience the action of the peptide well before copulation (Garritano et al., 1996). Stimulation of the AME elicits sexual behavior in male rats, even in conditions when it would not otherwise occur such as in the presence of a non-proceptive female or another male (Stark et al., 1998). Indeed, there is reason to believe that central processes mediated by AVP may be very numerous and far-ranging in significance, possibly even including the social forces that created the human family structure in the evolution from ape origins (Smock et al., 1998).

Thus it seems that, for males, limbic vasopressin, oxytocin, or a similar peptide produces the ultimate aspects of re-

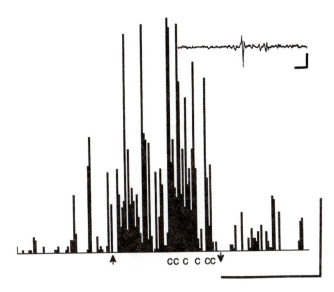

Figure 12–19 *AME Activity.* The response of one cell in the male rat AME shows a markedly heightened firing rate in the presence of a receptive female.

productive behavior responsible for attraction and arousal. There is also evidence that the peptide may be involved in such social events as pair-bond formation (Carter, DeVries, & Getz, 1995), nest-building behavior (Bult et al., 1992) and other social behaviors (Whitman and Albers, 1995). Further, this peptide action may be the same for humans as it is in other animals (Murphy et al., 1987).

How does sexual attraction in females come about? We have seen that the ultimate features of female sexual behavior are as recognizable as those for males (proceptive behavior of females "in heat," for example), and indeed there is evidence that the same limbic peptide organizes these as well (Smock et al., 1992). However, ultimate sexual behavior in female rodents is complicated by the estrus cycle, and as a consequence research in the neural mechanisms of females has proceeded more slowly. Current investigation of this subject is certainly one of the most exciting and interesting areas of research in the study of sexual behavior and in neuroscience as a whole.

SUMMARY

Sexual reproduction confers evolutionary advantages on organisms that adopt it. Haploid gametes combine to form diploid organisms in which, for mammals, the Y chromosome confers male genetic identity. Morphological gender identity is controlled by other factors, such as the H-Y antigen and sex steroids, which create male genitalia; in their absence, female phenotype develops. Organizational and activational effects of the sex steroids, acting via carrier proteins in blood and cytosol and influencing gene expression, determine all other secondary sexual characteristics.

The effect of steroids later in life is complicated and varies by species. In many animals, including humans, a critical period of developments restricts plasticity later in life. Sexual dimorphism in the brain mediates gender-specific behaviors and may account for aggressive behavior in some organisms. In most vertebrate species, both genders are highly motivated to mate and raise young.

Peptide hormones mediate most of brain endocrine influences on the body. These control growth, development, and metabolism as well as reproductive function. Peptides are always synthesized from larger protein precursors and are released from neuroendocrine and endocrine structures in the hypothalamus, the anterior pituitary, and the posterior pituitary. The peptides tend to display sequence homology with other peptide hormones and transmitters and participate in negative (and sometimes positive) feedback relationships to create stable or oscillating systems. The estrus cycle, in which sexual interest is restricted to the periovulatory period, and the menstrual cycle, in which sexual interest is displayed continuously, are examples of such peptide-mediated feedback circuits.

Pheromones have a large influence on reproduction in many mammals, possibly including humans. Peptide hormones that regulate reproduction in the periphery also seem to act as transmitters in the brain. The central regulation of sexual behavior can be divided into behaviors proximate to copulation, which seem to be mediated by steroid-dependent nuclei in the spinal cord and brainstem, and ultimate behaviors, which appear to be produced by steroid-dependent action of peptides in the forebrain. For much of male reproductive behavior in experimental animals, and possibly female reproductive behavior, these central peptides are vasotocin, vasopressin, and oxytocin. The extent to which human sex, love, and attachment can be explained by similar mechanisms is a point that awaits future research.

REVIEW QUESTIONS

1. What determines whether a fetus is male or female?

2. Contrast the anterior pituitary with the posterior pituitary.

3. Contrast steroid hormone action and peptide hormone action.

4. What is a pheromone?

5. How is testosterone chemically different from estrogen? How is it similar?

6. What CNS circuits are responsible for the consummatory aspects of mating?

7. What CNS circuits are responsible for the appetitive aspects of mating?

8. What is the "critical period" for gender development?

9. How does sexual behavior relate to aggression?

THOUGHT QUESTIONS

1. You are hired by a major cosmetics company to isolate and identify the human sex pheromone. How do you proceed?

2. What impact would the marketing of the human sex pheromone (if one exists) have on society?

3. Though by most objective measures people are largely the same, some people seem strikingly more attractive than others. Review the section on surround inhibition in Chapter 9 and the material on sexual behavior in this chapter before proposing an explanation for this phenomenon.

KEY CONCEPTS

activational effects (p. 284)
ADH (p. 282)
androgen (p. 285)
anterior lobe (p. 281)
arginine vasotocin (AVT) (p. 302)
aromatization (p. 285)
Bruce effect (p. 300)
carrier proteins (p. 286)
castrati (p. 291)
cholesterol (p. 285)
congenital adrenal hyperplasia (CAH) (p. 289)
corpus luteum (p. 297)
cortisol (p. 283)
critical period (p. 289)
Depo-provera (p. 294)
dexamethasone-suppression test (p. 284)
diploid (p. 278)
dopamine (p. 283)
double-blind paradigm (p. 296)
egg-laying hormone (ELH) (p. 300)
estradiol (p. 285)
estrogen (p. 285)
estrus (p. 296)

5α-reductase deficiency (p. 288)
eunuchs (p. 291)
follicle-stimulating hormone (FSH) (p. 283)
follicular phase (p. 297)
goiter (p. 278)
gonadotropin-releasing hormone (GnRH) (p. 283)
growth hormone (GH) (p. 283)
growth-hormone-releasing hormone (GHRH) (p. 283)
haploid (p. 278)
homology (p. 282)
HPA axis (p. 283)
H-Y antigen (p. 284)
hypothalamic releasing factors (p. 279)
lateral vestibulospinal nucleus (p. 302)
Lee-Boot effect (p. 300)
LHRH (p. 299)
lordosis (p. 301)
luteal phase (p. 297)
luteinizing hormone (LH) (p. 283)
medial amygdaloid nucleus (AME) (p. 302)

medial preoptic area (MPOA) (p. 302)
menstrual cycle (p. 299)
Müllerian duct (p. 287)
Müllerian regression hormone (p. 288)
negative feedback (p. 283)
neuroendocrine cells (p. 282)
organizational effects (p. 284)
ovaries (p. 284)
oxytocin (p. 279)
paraphilia (p. 294)
pheromones (p. 300)
pituitary gland (p. 281)
portal system (p. 281)
positive feedback (p. 297)
posterior lobe (p. 281)
primary sexual characteristic (p. 286)
proceptivity (p. 296)
progesterone (p. 285)
prolactin (p. 282)
pseudopregnancy (p. 297)
receptivity (p. 295)
'roid rage (p. 293)
secondary sexual characteristics (p. 287)

selectivity (p. 295)
sex steroids (p. 284)
sexually dimorphic nuclei (p. 292)
somatostatin (p. 283)
spinal nucleus of the bulbocavernosus (p. 302)
testes (p. 284)
testicular feminization mutation (TFM) (p. 288)
testis determination factor (TDF) (p. 286)
testosterone (p. 285)
thyroid-stimulating hormone (TSH) (p. 283)
thyrotropin-releasing hormone (TRH) (p. 283)
thyroxine (p. 279)
Turner's syndrome (p. 289)
Vandenbergh effect (p. 300)
vasopressin (p. 279)
vomeronasal organ (p. 301)
Whitten effect (p. 300)
Wolffian duct (p. 287)
X chromosome (p. 284)
Y chromosome (p. 284)

Dreams are necessary to life.

Anaïs Nin (1903–1977)

13

Sleep and Dreaming

One of the most common behaviors exhibited by animals of all types is also one of the least understood. Though you may not consider it as such, sleep is a behavior. Like all behaviors, it is governed by the complex interactions of a number of various physiological processes. As we examine the neural mechanisms underlying the sleep cycle, you will see how little we really know about this behavior. Obviously, we have some need for sleep, or the drive with which we are all quite familiar would not be so intense. However, the exact nature of this need is still unclear. Throughout the chapter, keep in mind that much of what we discuss is still under study, and further research is necessary before any definite conclusions can be drawn. We will begin our study of sleep by examining the nature of circadian rhythms and the neural mechanisms that govern them.

Circadian Rhythms

The daily lives of all living things are filled with various changes that take place cyclically throughout the day and night. The term **circadian rhythm** (*circa* = around, *dies* = a day) refers to an endogenous (intrinsic) daily cycle that controls these various behavioral and physiological changes in plants and animals. The sleep-wake cycle is one such intrinsic rhythm. But how do we know the cycle is not simply a response to environmental factors? You have probably experienced the proof of this yourself while studying late for an exam. Regardless of whether you know the actual time, you probably find yourself growing tired around 11 P.M. as your body tells you it's time to go to sleep. If completely isolated from environmental and social cues, as in experiments in which human subjects stay in a cavern with no sunlight or contact with the outside world, individuals adopt a sleep-wake cycle approximately twenty five hours in duration (though most circadian rhythms are twenty four hours, the human sleep-wake cycle runs slightly longer). The emergence of this twenty five-hour cycle *while isolated from external stimuli* shows that the human sleep-wake cycle is indeed endogenous in nature.

How then is this internal, free-running "clock" set? The term used to describe an environmental time cue that maintains an endogenous cycle is the German word **zeitgeber** ("time giver"). The primary zeitgeber is the *day-night cycle* of the sun. However, research has indicated that there are other ways of manipulating circadian rhythms unrelated to light. For example, food availability determines the daily rhythm of many foraging animals (Hau & Gwinner, 1997).

Where Is the Clock?

The primary site responsible for generating endogenous rhythms is believed to be the **suprachiasmatic nucleus (SCN)**. The SCN is a group of cells located at the bottom of the third ventricle in the hypothalamus. It was first noted that lesions in the SCN resulted in a disruption of the sleep-wake cycle. These observations led to the theory that the SCN functioned as an internal pacemaker.

Single neurons in eutelous organisms have been shown to contain their own endogenous pacemaker activity and this activity can be enhanced by light to vary on a circadian fashion (Chapters 4 and 10). This property also appears to apply to individual cells of the SCN of non-eutelous animals (Liu et al., 1997). Thus, each individual neuron of the SCN may be an independent clock that reports time to the rest of the brain by giving action potentials.

Strong evidence that the SCN functions as an internal pacemaker comes from an experiment involving the transplantation of mutated SCN tissue in hamsters (Menaker et al., 1990). The mutation used in this experiment resulted in a significantly shorter sleep-wake period. The SCN from the mutant hamster was transplanted into a hamster whose normal SCN had been removed. It was proposed that if the SCN is responsible for regulating the sleep-wake cycle, a hamster with the transplanted tissue would exhibit the shorter sleep-wake cycle. And, indeed, this is precisely what happened. The results of this experiment decisively proved that the SCN functions as a biological clock.

Now that we have established that the SCN functions as the circadian pacemaker, you may wonder by what mechanisms it "keeps time." Because light is the primary zeitgeber, it seems obvious that the SCN must receive some input from retinal projections. However, it has been shown that severing both the primary optic tracts and the accessory optic system caudal to the optic chiasm has no effect on the sleep-wake cycle. Instead, information about light is conveyed by a separate and unique projection, the **retinohypothalamic tract**, which exits the optic chiasm and projects to the SCN of the hypothalamus (Moore & Lenn, 1972). Recent evidence indi-

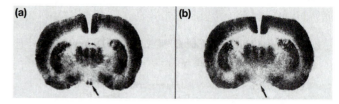

Figure 13–1 *Evidence of SCN Regulation of Circadian Rhythms.* The shaded areas of these autoradiographs indicate the presence of radioactive sugars injected in the rat's brain during both the light and dark phases of the circadian cycle to illustrate regions of activity. Dark areas show regions of greater metabolic activity. The arrow at bottom points to the suprachiasmatic nucleus. (a) During the light phase of the test, the suprachiasmatic nucleus is active. (b) Activity disappears during the dark phase of the test. See Figure 14–7 for an explanation of this technique.

cates that glulamate is the transmitter of this pathway and that a peptide called "Neuropeptide Y" interacts with glulamate to set the clock (Biello et al., 1997).

Figure 13–1 shows the metabolic activity in the SCN during light and dark phases. In this experiment, 2-deoxyglucose, a radioactive, synthetic glucose analog, was used to identify brain regions with high metabolic needs, presumably reflecting an increase in action potentials and hence greater sodium/potassium ATP-ase activity. The SCN is visible when the glucose consumption is measured in the light (Figure 13–1a) but not when measured in the dark phase of the animal's circadian cycle (Figure 13–1b).

In the last chapter we encountered arginine-vasopressin (AVP) as a potential organizer of reproductive behavior (Chapter 12). However, as for all transmitters, the addition of AVP is varied in the body and is determined in each case by the postsynaptic cell and the receptor it expresses. AVP is found in the SCN and there is evidence in mice that it organizes circadian rhythms in the projection fields of the SCN (Bult et al., 1993).

A number of studies have proposed that other transmitters are involved in regulating SCN activity. One study has implicated GABA and the GABA$_A$ and GABA$_B$ receptors in the modulation of the rhythms (Menaker & Ralph, 1989). In another study, Turek and Wee (1989) showed that carbachol, an ACh agonist, mimics some of the effects of light on the internal clock, indicating that ACh may play some role in the circadian system.

Just as there may be more than one zeitgebers, more then one brain region may be responsible for each. Some experiments have studied the effects of *ambient temperature* on the circadian cycles of various rodents (Coleman & Francis, 1987). The researchers concluded that temperature is only a mild zeitgeber for rats but a strong zeitgeber for another mammal, the stripe-faced dunnart (Figure 13–2)

Figure 13–2   *The Stripe-Faced Dunnart.* Circadian rhythms can be regulated to a small degree by factors other than light. In the case of the stripe-faced dunnart, environmental temperature helps to set the biological clock. Threshold temperatures in the morning and evening help the animal know when to wake and when to sleep.

(though still weak compared to light). In addition to circadian rhythms, there are also *seasonal rhythms,* such as those that inspire mating and hibernation. Control of seasonal rhythms appears to be located in the **pineal gland** (just rostral to the cerebellum) (Figure 13–3), which secretes **melatonin,** named for its ability in some animals to turn the skin dark (*melas* = black). The pineal gland secretes melatonin in response to input from the SCN (Thorpy & Yager, 1991). The melatonin then influences hormone secretion and other physiological factors. Melatonin is secreted during the night; thus, when nights are long in the winter a large amount of melatonin is secreted; less melatonin is secreted during the shorter summer nights. The involvement of melatonin in regulating sleep cycles is controversial. Some studies find involvement of the pineal gland in some rhythms (e.g., body temperature) but not others (such as locomotion; Tosini & Menaker, 1998).

Melatonin is synthesized from tryptophan in a manner very similar to the synthesis of serotonin. In fact, melatonin is an indolamine with structure almost the same as serotonin (see Figure 17–13). Like serotonin, melatonin is thought to play a role in affect and emotion in addition to its possible role in sleep and dreaming, an aspect of its physiology addressed in Chapter 10. For the moment, reflect on the fact the only two midline structures in the brain (cell groups that we have once in the middle rather than twice, once for each side) are the raphé nuclei and the pineal gland and each of these cell groups secrete indolamines. Perhaps Descartes was right in assigning special teleological importance to these regions.

As you have seen, research on circadian rhythms and their mechanisms is incomplete. We now turn to the most

mysterious and fascinating portion of one of the circadian cycles, about which we understand even less—sleep.

Stages of Sleep

Sleep is not the same thing as unconsciousness. Genuine unconsciousness such as in coma or anesthesia differs from sleep in many respects. Most importantly, sleep has discrete stages and elements and thus reflects a number of active and restorative processes.

As noted earlier, if you are isolated from external stimuli, an endogenous sleep-wake cycle of approximately twenty five hours will emerge. Curiously, the metabolic activity of the brain, reflective of it's electrical activity, does not change significantly across the phases of wakefulness and sleep (Braun, et al., 1997). But what of the cycles seen during sleep itself? Through numerous studies, researchers have identified two different divisions of sleep in the normal, functioning adult human. These two divisions exhibit different physiological mechanisms as well as different behavioral and physiological traits. The first, **non-REM (NREM) sleep,** is itself divided into four stages, each with its own distinguishing physiological

Figure 13–3   *The Pineal Gland.* Seasonal rhythms (such as hibernation) may be regulated by the pineal gland, which is surrounded by the thalamus and the superior colliculi. The pineal gland secretes melatonin, which has been implicated in both types of biological rhythms (seasonal and circadian), and is currently a subject of the investigation into the causes of aging.

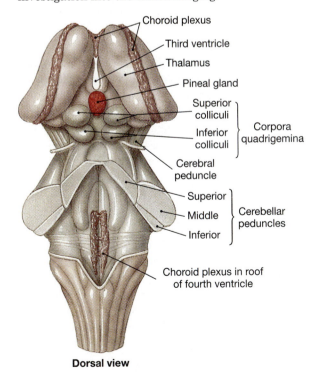

Choroid plexus
Third ventricle
Thalamus
Pineal gland
Superior colliculi
Inferior colliculi
Corpora quadrigemina
Cerebral peduncle
Superior
Middle
Inferior
Cerebellar peduncles
Choroid plexus in roof of fourth ventricle

Dorsal view

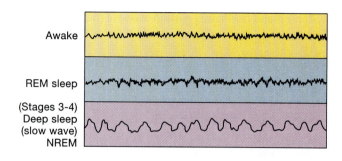

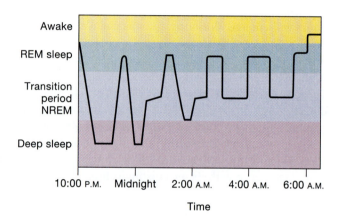

Figure 13–4 *Cycles of Sleep.* During sleep, we move in cycles among several stages of NREM sleep, ranging from light (Stages 1 & 2) to deep sleep (Stages 3 and 4). Approximately every ninety minutes, we move from NREM to REM sleep for a short time. REM sleep is also known as paradoxical sleep because the brain wave patterns resemble those of a wakeful or drowsy state.

characteristics. As the body enters sleep, it adopts a pattern in which these fours stages of NREM sleep are interrupted by the second main division of sleep, **REM sleep** (rapid eye movement), also known as *paradoxical sleep.* Studies have shown that a normal sleep pattern consists of alternations between REM and NREM sleep in about a ninety-minute cycle (Figure 13–4). In addition, Stages 3 and 4 of the NREM division, also known as **slow-wave sleep**, are more prevalent in the beginning of the night, tapering off later to allow longer periods of REM sleep.

The EEG and EMG

The primary tool used by researchers to identify the various sleep stages is the **electroencephalogram (EEG)**, a recording of electrical activity in the brain that also has broad applications in other areas of neurophysiology (Chapter 4). Electrodes applied to various regions of the scalp are used to measure the flow of extracellular current from the brain cells. The EEG activity is characterized by the *frequency* (how many per second) and *amplitude* (how big) of the elec-

trical potentials recorded. The frequencies of the potentials range approximately from 1 to 30 hertz (1 hertz [Hz] = 1 cycle per second) and have been divided into four main groups: *delta* (0.5–4 Hz), *theta* (4–7 Hz), *alpha* (8–13 Hz), and *beta* (13–30 Hz). Each of these groups possesses characteristic amplitudes, ranging from 10 to 100 microvolts (μV). Alpha activity is low in amplitude, usually 10 to 20 μV. Beta waves are also low, up to 30 μV. Theta waves have amplitudes as high as 50 μV, and delta waves are the highest, up to 100 μV. The frequencies and amplitudes of these groups are indicative of various states of sleep and wakefulness. Alpha activity is typical of a drowsy, but awake, state as well as REM sleep. Theta and delta waves are observed in NREM sleep, with the stages of deepest sleep showing mostly delta range activity (hence the term slow wave sleep). Examples of EEG measurements in various waking and sleep states are shown in Figure 13–5.

A second tool used by researchers to record sleep and wakefulness is the **electromyogram (EMG)**. The EMG is a recording of the electrical potentials of muscles and represents the level of muscle activity. In sleep research, electrodes are placed over the tip of the jaw to record activity in the mentalis muscle, which is taken to be representative of somatic muscle activity in general. EMG activity is typically highest during wakefulness, and decreases progressively through the sleep stages until REM sleep, where it ceases altogether. This paradoxical lack of muscle activity will be discussed in the later section on REM sleep. The electromyogram was used to ascertain that the monomine transmitter, serotonin, may be the signal that suppresses REM sleep in favor of non-REM sleep (Horner et al., 1997).

Non-REM (NREM) Sleep

Non-REM sleep, sometimes referred to as quiet sleep, is primarily characterized by low-frequency, synchronous brain activity and relaxed, but not completely flaccid, muscle tone. The four stages of NREM sleep, each defined primarily by characteristic EEG readings, are shown in Figure 13–6: drowsy, Stage 1, Stage 2, and delta sleep. Upon closing his or her eyes, a subject shows an alpha rhythm indicative of the **drowsy state**. As the subject falls into **Stage 1 sleep**, the alpha pattern is slowly replaced by a pattern of mixed frequency (mostly theta waves) and lower amplitudes. Because a person in Stage 1 sleep is quite easily woken, this stage is said to have a *low arousal threshold*. Stage 1 generally persists for about one to seven minutes at the onset of sleep and comprises about 4 to 5 percent of the total sleep time.

Following the brief period of Stage 1 sleep is **Stage 2 sleep**, which initially lasts for ten to twenty five minutes and comprises the greatest amount of total sleep time, about 45 to 55 percent. Stage 2 sleep is characterized by two distinct EEG

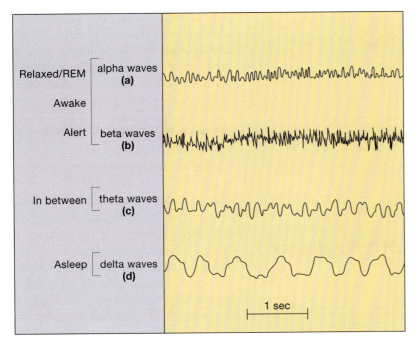

Figure 13–5 *EEG Patterns.* The four types of brain waves are distinguished by their frequencies and amplitudes. As you might expect, high-frequency waves indicate asynchronous activity, while high-amplitude waves indicate neuron firing synchronicity. (a) Alpha waves are of moderate frequency (8–13 Hz) and low amplitude (10–20 µV). Alpha waves are observed during the awake but drowsy or relaxed state, often when the eyes are closed, and similar waves are observed during REM sleep. (b) Beta waves, characteristic of wakefulness and alertness (with the eyes open, or when concentrating or thinking intently) have the highest frequencies (13–30 Hz) but low amplitudes. These waves are also similar to those observed in REM sleep. (c) Theta waves can be observed as a subject falls asleep, in the lighter stages of NREM sleep such as Stage 1 sleep. Theta waves are lower in frequency (slower firing) at only 4–7 Hz, but are more synchronous, having amplitudes up to 50 µV. (d) Delta waves are the slowest to occur (having frequencies of only 0.5–4 Hz) but have the highest amplitudes (up to 100 µV). They occur during the deepest part (highest arousal threshold) of the sleep cycle, Stages 3 and 4 sleep (slow wave sleep).

patterns, sleep spindles and K complexes. A **sleep spindle** (Figure 13–6) is a burst of 11 to 15 Hz waves which last for 0.5 to 1.5 seconds and are an example of several low-frequency components to the EEG in sleep (Achermann & Borbely, 1997). A decrease in spindle activity may be seen in the elderly; increases can be a result of medications, such as benzodiazepines, often prescribed as sleep medications or antianxiety drugs. **K complexes** (see Figure 13–6) are high-voltage EEG waves that have a sharp negative component followed by a slower, positive wave. It is theorized that K complexes are the result of specific sensory activity in the central nervous system, since they can be evoked by external stimuli such as loud noises and also accompany slow rhythms in the sleep EEG (Amzica & Steriade, 1997).

Stage 3 (not shown in Figure 13–6), comprises 4 to 6 percent of the total sleep time and is characterized by theta waves as well as some delta activity. This stage is often combined with Stage 4 and termed *slow wave sleep* or delta sleep due to the low frequency EEG activity. Stage 4 is the deepest stage of sleep and usually comprises 12 to 15 percent of the total sleep time. It is during Stage 4 that **sleep terrors** (not to be confused with nightmares) may occur. Sleep terrors are episodes in which the individual wakes suddenly in terror, usually screaming. They are common in childhood and are usually not treated medically and less common in adulthood but when seen can be treated with tranquilizers (Schenk & Mahowald, 1996). Often sleep terrors are associated with feelings of falling or being chased. Upon awakening, a confused, agitated state follows during which the person remains terrified, often trying to flee the room. The episode can last up to fifteen minutes, after which the person falls rapidly back into sleep. Unlike nightmares, the episode is rarely remembered after the person awakens. Sleep terrors are often associated with another sleep arousal disorder, *sleepwalking,* which also occurs during Stage 4 sleep. Sleepwalking, also known as **somnambulism** (from the Latin *somnos,* to sleep, and *ambulare,* to walk), is an event characterized by movement while the individual is still in the sleep state. Like sleep terrors, the sleepwalking episode is usually forgotten after awakening and occurs most frequently in childhood.

Stages 3 and 4 are also characterized by a decrease in sympathetic nervous system activity (heart rate and blood pressure) and an increase in parasympathetic activity (gastrointestinal activity). Slow wave sleep predominates early in the sleep pattern, replaced by longer periods of REM sleep later in the cycle.

Rapid Eye Movement (REM) Sleep

Often termed the fifth stage of sleep, REM sleep is defined by a desynchronized (low-voltage/mixed-frequency) EEG recording, loss of muscle tone in the skeletal muscles (atonia), and periodic bursts of rapid eye movements together with characteristic waves of electrical activity proceeding from the pons rostrally to the visual system. Despite muscular flaccidity, the brain activity of REM sleep most closely resembles that of the waking state; indeed, it is in REM sleep that almost all dreaming takes place. Teleologically, one might suspect that the atonia, especially that of the torso and postural muscles, exists to prevent potential injuries resulting from acting out one's dreams. Consider an active, dreaming mind in an inert

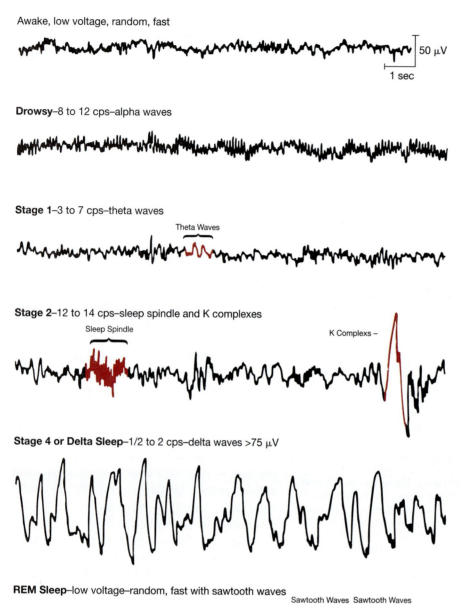

Awake, low voltage, random, fast

50 μV

1 sec

Drowsy–8 to 12 cps–alpha waves

Stage 1–3 to 7 cps–theta waves

Theta Waves

Stage 2–12 to 14 cps–sleep spindle and K complexes

Sleep Spindle

K Complexs –

Stage 4 or Delta Sleep–1/2 to 2 cps–delta waves >75 μV

REM Sleep–low voltage–random, fast with sawtooth waves

Sawtooth Waves   Sawtooth Waves

Figure 13–6 *Stages of Sleep.* Alpha, theta, and delta waves comprise the waves seen during the various stages of sleep and wakefulness. Also shown are sleep spindles and K. complexes (see text). (Arkin, Antrobus, & Ellman, 1978)

body and you will understand why REM sleep is also called *paradoxical sleep.*

As mentioned, the first indicator of REM sleep, the desynchronized EEG, closely resembles the pattern of the waking state (see Figure 13–6). The EEG may also contain *sawtooth waves* prior to and during a REM period. Another subcortical pattern seen in mammals is the ponto-geniculo-occipital spike, or **PGO spike.** These waves, generated in the

pons, propagate through the lateral geniculate and other thalamic nuclei to the occipital cortex. The PGO spikes are thought to be regulators of certain phasic activities during REM sleep, such as eye movements and changes in respiration and heart rate.

The second property of REM sleep, **muscle atonia,** is detected by a lack of EMG activity and is unique to this state of sleep. The loss of muscle tone is due to inhibitory hyperpolarization of the alpha motor neuron. However, as you may have realized, though most skeletal muscles become flaccid, there are necessary exceptions. Although immobility is necessary to prevent injury during dreaming, complete muscular atonia would not be beneficial; it would be devastating (survival would be difficult if you couldn't breathe during sleep!). In order to eliminate this potential problem, the diaphragm and the muscles controlling the eyes retain muscle tone. In addition, muscular paralysis may be interrupted by brief muscle twitches, which often accompany PGO spikes and rapid eye movements.

Another interesting exception to muscle atonia during REM sleep is the sexual arousal in both males and females that occurs during REM sleep. Males usually experience partial or complete penile erection and females show an increase in vaginal secretions. Studies have found that these changes do not necessarily indicate a dream with sexual content, though some dreams can culminate in orgasm for both males and females (so-called wet dreams).

Another distinguishing characteristic of REM sleep is **rapid eye movements,** similar to the rapid eye movements observed in the awake state. These movements occur in bursts, rather than continually, throughout the REM stage. Once thought to be the visual scanning of dreams, these movements have been shown to bear no relation to dream content; their exact purpose remains unknown.

Neural Mechanisms for Sleep and Waking

As we begin our study of the neural mechanisms involved in sleep and waking, you should keep in mind that most of the areas that will be discussed are still under research, and there are currently a number of lively debates on the subject of neural mechanisms. It is becoming increasingly clear that there is no simple system that maintains the sleep-wake cycle. Instead, the cycle is regulated through the complex interactions of a number of different neural and humoral factors.

Since the beginning of sleep research, scientists have repeatedly proposed the hypothesis that wakefulness leads to the accumulation of a sleep-inducing substance in the brain and, likewise, the subsequent sleep period leads to the accumulation of a wake-inducing substance. This simple but logical theory has been gradually revised to include a more complex description of the variables regulating sleep. Periodic reports of sleep- or wake-inducing substances are followed by claims for different candidates. Most researchers now deem it extremely unlikely that there is a single hormone or transmitter that regulates sleep and waking. Nevertheless, the system can be organized into neural and humoral factors that tend to induce sleep and those that induce wakefulness. These factors are shown in Table 13–1.

The Search for the "Sleep Transmitter"

There are a number of natural factors that are thought to have the effect of inducing sleep. Due to the difficulty in unambiguously establishing an endogenous sleep substance (since all transmitters contribute to sleep), these factors are defined rather vaguely as **sleep-inducing factors.** They were first suggested by Henri Pieron in 1913 when he found that sleep was induced in a dog after it was injected with cerebrospinal fluid from a sleep-deprived dog (Cooper, 1994). Since then, these factors have been found to include some of the neurotransmitters that you studied in earlier chapters as well as a group of substances termed sleep peptides.

One of the primary neurotransmitters implicated in sleep maintenance (particularly slow wave sleep) is **serotonin** (Vodelholzer et al., 1998). You will recall that serotonin is a monoamine derivative of tryptophan (Chapter 5). The **raphé nuclei** of the brainstem are the main sites of serotonergic neurons involved in sleep regulation. Lesions of the raphé nuclei of cats or administration of a tryptophan hydroxylase inhibitor (which inhibits serotonin synthesis) both lead to insomnia though this insomnia is not permanent or irreversible. Recall that tryptophan hydroxylase allows the serotonin precursor tryptophan to be converted to serotonin. In addition, administration of a serotonin precursor, 5-hydroxytryptophan (5-HTP), enhances slow wave sleep (but suppresses REM sleep) in cats and rabbits (Koella et al. 1968). Figure 13–7 illustrates the effects of a serotonin uptake inhibitor, fluoxetine, on the

Table 13–1	FACTORS INVOLVED IN SLEEP AND WAKEFULNESS	
Sleep-inducing substances		**Arousal-inducing substances**
serotonin		acetylcholine (ACh)
muramyl peptides (MP) (Factor S)		norepinephrine (NE)
delta sleep-inducing peptides (DSIP)		dopamine (DA)
adenosine		histamine

sleep pattern. It is apparent that this drug and antidepressant drugs of the same family (Chapter 18) do not enhance REM sleep but in fact disrupt it.

Other experiments have shown that an increase in central serotonin levels caused by administration of the MAO inhibitor *nialamide* leads to an increase in slow wave sleep and nearly complete suppression of REM sleep in cats (Jouvet, Vimont, & Delorme, 1965). The tricyclic antidepressants, which may function by inhibiting the re-uptake of serotonin, also decrease REM sleep. Paradoxically, some antidepressants are also prescribed as sleep aids. It has been hypothesized that the therapeutic effect is due to the suppression of REM sleep, but this is still uncertain. Although the mechanism for REM suppression is not known, it has been noted that drugs that increase serotonin levels (MAO inhibitors, 5-HTP, clomipramine) all tend to reduce or suppress the PGO waves indicative of REM sleep. When drugs that decrease serotonin concentration are given, PGO spikes (or REM-like activity) appear in NREM sleep and waking (Dement et al., 1969). However, the role of the PGO waves is still unclear.

Much remains to be learned about serotonin and the mechanisms by which it affects the sleep system. A theory by Jouvet et al. (1986) proposes that serotonin may act as a neurohormone, causing the synthesis or release of other sleep-inducing factors. Let us now consider one class of these, the rather vaguely defined **sleep peptides.**

In the 1960s and 1970s, Pappenheimer, Miller, and Goodrich (1967) found that an injection of cerebrospinal fluid from a sleep-deprived goat induced sleep in rats, cats, and other animals. The active substance was subsequently isolated from large amounts of human urine (certainly a bizarre place to look for it, but see Box 18–2) and named *Factor S*. Factor S enhances slow wave sleep and increases body temperature when administered to rabbits and other animals. This small glycoprotein has since been identified as a **muramyl peptide (MP)**, a compound found mostly in the cell walls of bacteria (Imeri et al., 1997). While injections of MPs always increase the amount of slow wave sleep, their effect on REM sleep is dependent on species, dosage, and type of MP. One fascinating feature of these peptides still under study is their *interaction with the immune system.* Research has

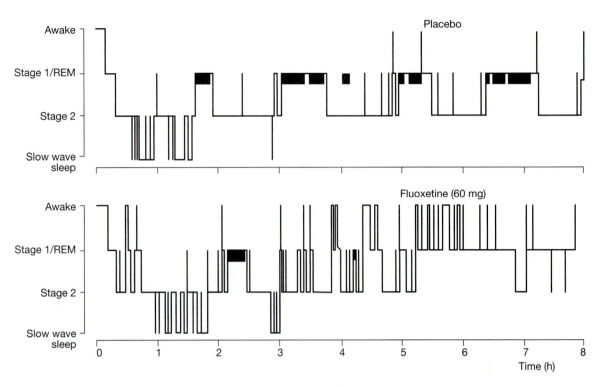

Figure 13–7 *Antidepressant Drugs Can Alter Sleep Patterns.* A control (placebo) and antidepressant (fluoxetine, long-term administration) are compared.

shown that MPs increase antibody release and alter the activity of macrophages (Chedid, 1983). Such immunological effects suggest sleep may have a restorative function, but the full purpose of MPs and the mechanisms of their actions are still far from clear.

A second peptide, **delta sleep–inducing peptide (DSIP)**, has also been identified. When administered to a rabbit, this substance induces (you guessed it!) a delta EEG pattern. While some studies report an increase in total sleep time in humans and an increase in slow wave sleep in mice as a result of DSIP administration, other experiments have failed to confirm this. DSIP may be associated with various psychiatric disturbances that disrupt sleep (Soyka & Rothenhaeusler, 1997).

The last sleep factor we will examine is the nucleotide **adenosine**, a sugar attached to a purine base (Chapter 6). Adenosine's sleep-inducing effect may be due to its inhibition of various neurotransmitters such as acetylcholine and norepinephrine, two transmitters involved in arousal. Interestingly, it has been found that the excitatory effect of caffeine may be due to its antagonistic effects at adenosine receptors (Figure 13–8). In the figure we see the effects of caffeine on the sleep cycle. The sleep stage transitions for four different levels of caffeine consumption are shown, starting with zero (normal) at the top. At the higher levels of caffeine (200 and 300 mg) we see decreases in REM sleep, and the

highest level (300 mg) the subject's sleep duration is drastically reduced. Keep these results in mind next time you indulge in a Mountain Dew!

It is clear that there is much we do not know regarding the sleep-inducing substances. The information here is but a brief introduction to a complex array of substances still under study. The same ambiguity awaits us in the next section, as we examine the "wake" part of the sleep-wake cycle.

Transmitter Systems and "Arousal"

The arousal system is a hypothetical construct thought to produce both the waking state and increased awareness during waking. The search for this system in the brain has led to a number of false starts and much controversy (see Box 13–1). The main substances thought to be involved in the arousal system are also neurotransmitters. Though their functions are better established than the "sleep peptides," there is still much uncertainty regarding their mechanisms of action in the sleep-wake cycle. In particular, you should note the paradoxical way in which many of these transmitters affect REM sleep.

The first neurotransmitter is one with which you should be quite familiar already. **Acetylcholine** (ACh, Chapter 5) seems to regulate circadian rhythms by interaction with the SCN (Liu et al., 1997). This implies that ACh plays a central

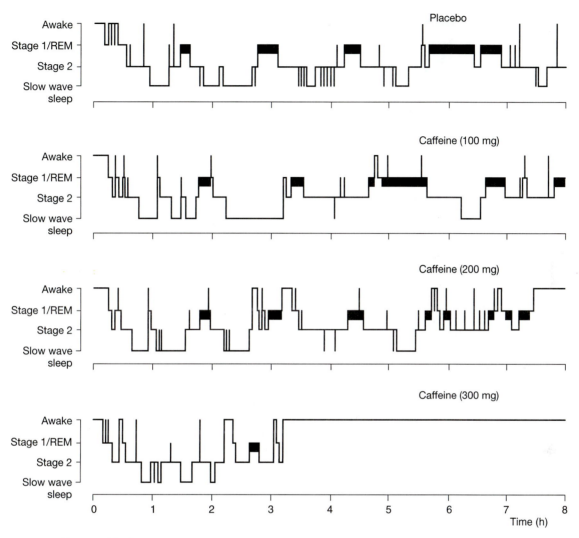

Figure 13–8 *Caffeine and the Sleep Cycle.* The sleep-inducing effects of adenosine are interfered with by caffeine, which acts as an antagonist at adenosine receptors. The four plots show sleep cycles observed in a normal subject after ingestion of various levels of caffeine. Notice the decreased time spent in REM sleep at 200 and 300 mg, and the dramatic reduction in overall sleep time at 300 mg.

role in the sleep-wake cycle. This cholinergic theory of waking has been supported by studies that alter the level of ACh activity. Administration of substances that lead to an accumulation of ACh, such as acetylcholinsterase inhibitors (physostigmine), induces REM sleep in humans (Gillin et al., 1991). In addition, administration of ACh antagonists, such as atropine, induces and prolongs slow wave sleep while suppressing REM sleep.

ACh also appears to regulate another feature of REM sleep, muscle atonia. Muscarinic ACh blockers, such as atropine, decrease the muscle atonia of REM sleep and reduce **cataplexy,** a sudden loss of muscle tone similar to the atonia observed in REM sleep. Administration of physostigmine (in-

creasing the levels of ACh in blockers AChE, Chapter 5)) increases cataplexy in dogs (Delashaw et al., 1978). Cataplexy will be discussed in greater detail when we examine narcolepsy later in the chapter.

The mechanism by which ACh functions is not clear. There is an increase in pontine neuronal activity during REM sleep and injections of ACh agonists into the pontine reticular formation lead to an increase in REM sleep (Shiromani & McGinty, 1986). These findings support the theory that the *pontine reticular formation cholinergic neurons* regulate REM sleep, but their exact role is still unclear.

A second major neurotransmitter involved in arousal is **norepinephrine (NE)** (Chapter 8). The **locus coeruleus** (Chap-

Box 13–1

The "Reticular Activating System"

Some of the pioneering work on the neural mechanisms of sleep and waking was done by Frederick Bremer in 1935. Bremer was interested in determining which part of the brain was responsible for regulating the sleep-wake cycle. He experimented on cats, making various cuts through their brains and observing how their sleep-wake cycle was affected. The first cut he made just caudal to the forebrain and termed it *cerveau isolé* (French for "isolated brain," refer to the figure). He found that this cut prevented the cat from waking; it slept constantly. He then made a second cut caudal to the first, closer to the brainstem. He termed this cut *encephalé isolé,* for "isolated head." After this cut, the cat still exhibited a normal sleep-wake pattern. From these results Bremer proposed that there was a reticular activating system, located between the two cuts, which was responsible for arousal (Bremer, 1935). When the first cut was made, this system was isolated from the forebrain, preventing arousal. The second cut, further from the brain, did not affect the sleep-wake cycle because it did not interfere with the communication between the brain and this arousal system. Later experiments by Moruzzi and Magoun (1949) found that electrical stimulation of the midbrain reticular formation led to cortical arousal. This discovery lent credence to the theory of a reticular activating system.

Since then, researchers have clearly established the existence of an **ascending reticular activating system**

(ARAS), a long pathway that projects dorsally to thalamic nuclei and ventrally to the hypothalamus, subthalamus, and ventral thalamus through to the basal forebrain (Steriade, 1996). The ARAS comprises the brainstem reticular formation, including the medulla, pons, and midbrain. The area contains the noradrenergic cells of the locus coeruleus as well as cholinergic cell bodies of the pontine tegmentum such as the pedunculopontine tegmental and lateral dorsal tegmental nuclei (Chapter 5). Destruction of the ARAS leads to a severe decrease in arousal, and electrical stimulation results in increased arousal, further implicating ACh and NE in behavioral and cortical arousal.

Moruzzi and Magoun (1949) expanded upon Bremer's original work, making a third transsection between the first two (see figure). Although lacking an interesting French name (can you think of one?) this third cut prevented the cat from sleeping. From this result, the researchers proposed that there was a *reticular inactivating system* located in the lower brainstem. As you can see from the diagram, the third cut lies caudal to the locus coeruleus and rostral to the raphé nuclei. The results of their experiment corroborate the theory that the serotonergic neurons of the raphé nuclei may be responsible for generating sleep and the noradrenergic neurons in the locus coeruleus may control arousal. Other studies have shown that stimulation of the dorsal reticular formation

ter 8), a region of cells extending from the pons to the midbrain, is thought to be the primary site for NE regulation of wakefulness and REM sleep (Berridge, 1998). All central NE activity is mediated by two receptor types, alpha and beta (Chapters 5 and 6). One subtype of the alpha receptor, the alpha–2 adrenoreceptor, is thought to be the primary NE regulator of sleep and wakefulness.

Though NE appears to produce wakefulness, experimental results are conflicting. Researchers have hypothesized that noradrenergic input from the locus coeruleus and serotonergic input from the raphé nuclei inhibit the REM sleep–inducing cholinergic neurons (Sakai, 1980). This would indicate that REM sleep is due to a decrease in inhibitory input from these two centers. However, the mechanism of

norepinephrine and serotonin activity is still unknown. The difficulty in defining the exact role of NE (and other transmitters) stems in part from the fact that NE is used in several transmitter systems, each with distinct receptor populations. As stressed throughout this text, *neurotransmitter effects are a function of the receptor, not the transmitter*. We will not be able to clearly define the role of NE in the sleep-wake cycle until we know more about its function in each of the systems that utilize it.

Another neurotransmitter involved in the sleep-wake cycle is the metabolic precursor to NE, **dopamine (DA)** (see Chapter 5). Studies show that DA concentrations are high during waking and decrease with the onset of sleep. This would seem to indicate DA plays a role in wakefulness. However,

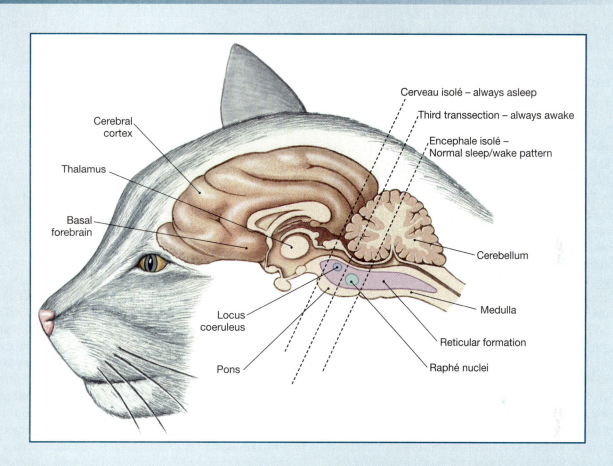

Cerebral cortex

Thalamus

Basal forebrain

Locus coeruleus

Pons

Cerveau isolé – always asleep

Third transsection – always awake

Encephale isolé – Normal sleep/wake pattern

Cerebellum

Medulla

Reticular formation

Raphé nuclei

and the solitary tract nucleus produce EEG synchronization indicative of slow wave sleep. Lesions of these areas cause a sleeping animal to exhibit the EEG patterns of a waking state. These findings indicate that the function of the dorsal reticular formation and the solitary tract nucleus is to generate sleep. The mechanism is thought to involve the inhibition of the ARAS but direct influence upon the forebrain may also occur.

recordings from single cells in the *substantia nigra* (which you will recall contains dopaminergic neurons) show little change throughout the sleep-wake cycle (Cooper, 1994). This ambiguity is also observed in studies involving the DA agonist apomorphine. In low doses, apomorphine increases total sleep time and reduces wakefulness, while at higher doses, it increases wakefulness, delays sleep onset, and reduces REM sleep (Gessa et al., 1985; Mereu et al., 1979). DA receptor antagonists tend to increase slow wave sleep and reduce wakefulness. Amphetamines, which release DA and inhibit NE re-uptake, lead to marked wakefulness. These observations imply that DA somehow functions to regulate wakefulness, though, like many of the other substances, its exact role in the cycle is still unclear. Curiously, there may be a closer as-

sociation between dopamine and a common sleep disorder **restless legs syndrome**. Between one and five percent of the population experience difficulty in going to sleep because of a nagging desire to move the legs. This disorder is sometimes treated using dopamine agonists (Wetter & Pollmacher, 1997).

Another arousal candidate is **histamine**, a substance usually released in response to tissue damage (Vizuete et al., 1997, Chapter 11). Histamine acts on two different receptors, the H_1 and H_2 receptors. It was found that H_1 antagonists impaired wakefulness but did not affect sleep, and H_1 agonists increased wakefulness, suggesting that the H_1 system aids alertness. H_2 antagonists did not affect wakefulness but did cause an increase in slow wave sleep. Interestingly, it has been found that histamine levels fluctuate with circadian rhythms. In rats, histamine synthesis is increased during darkness so that histaminergic neurons may be fully active during the day (Orr & Quay, 1975). Experimental inhibition of histamine synthesis leads to decreased wakefulness and increased NREM sleep. Through various other studies, researchers have confirmed that histamine influences alertness during the waking portion of the sleep-wake cycle more than the progression through the various stages of the cycle.

When confronted with a parade of substances all claimed to accomplish the same thing, the student should be reminded of the principle established in Chapter 5, and reiterated throughout this book, that no behavior is the consequence of the action of a single molecule, but rather all behaviors are the product of every transmitter system acting simultaneously. Perturbation of one system, for instance with an agonist or antagonist, may have some influence on a single, narrowly defined behavior (such as "sleep" vs. "wakefulness"), but confusion will certainly result when attempting to broadly apply such simple models to complex systems. Hence, we have a large number of "arousal transmitters." It might be more accurate, although less enlightening, to say that "all transmitters are involved in arousal."

Neural Mechanisms of Dreaming

We will now examine the neural mechanisms of one of the most enigmatic aspects of sleep, dreaming. As we have already discussed, most dreams occur during REM sleep. On average, six to nine people out of ten will report a dream if woken during REM sleep, while only one out of ten people report dreams if woken during NREM sleep. In addition, dreams reported during REM sleep often include substantial plots as well as visual and auditory experiences, contrasting the muddled, fragmented dreams reported during NREM sleep. A breakdown of the various sensations experienced while dreaming and their frequencies is provided in Figure 13–9.

The identity of the neural mechanisms underlying the dreaming process are unclear and speculative at best. In 1977, Hobson and McCarley proposed an **activation-synthesis theory** of dreaming. This theory states that dreaming is due to an activation of forebrain cognitive structures, which are also active during the day but are quiescent during NREM. This is consistent with the presence of PGO waves during sleep. Our brains use information stored in memory combined with signals generated by various brain circuits to create a dream. For instance, auditory experiences are due to an activation of the auditory circuit, which the auditory cortex perceives as a signal coming from the external world.

Suppressors of REM sleep and dreaming include the tricyclic antidepressants. This fact calls into question the use of

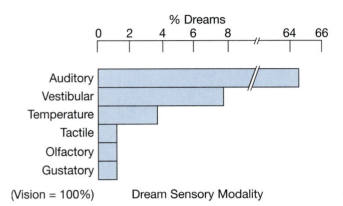

Figure 13–9 *Sensory Experiences during Dreaming.* Almost 65 percent of subjects reported experiencing auditory sensations in addition to visual sensations during dreaming. Other sensations occurred less often. (McCarley et al., 1981)

these drugs as sleeping medications. It is speculated that these drugs act by increasing NE and serotonin levels, indicating these compounds play a role in dreaming in addition to their respective roles in arousal and sleep maintenance that we have already discussed. Serotonin in particular is thought to act as a "dream suppressor," though clear evidence has not been found. Interestingly, the hallucinogenic drug lysergic acid diethylamide (LSD) may provide some insight into the relationship between serotonin and dreaming. LSD acts as a serotonin agonist at an autoreceptor, stimulating the autoreceptor and thereby inhibiting serotonin release normally inhibited by serotonin itself in a negative feedback mechanism. Recall that homeostasis controls the level of transmitter released (Chapter 5). Though it is chemically an agonist, LSD has the effect of reducing the amount of serotonin secreted. It has been hypothesized that the hallucinogenic effects of LSD are, in effect, "waking dreams" resulting from the inhibition of serotonin release. As serotonin levels drop, so does dream inhibition, allowing dreams to enter the waking state.

As of yet, we have found no clear mechanisms to explain the enigmatic process of dreaming. We will continue our discussion of dreams later in the chapter when we examine psychological theories of sleep.

Why Do We Sleep?

Now that we have examined the nature of sleep and the neural mechanisms underlying it, we must address another key question regarding sleep: What is its function? A process which occupies roughly one-third of our lives must have some purpose. Any of you who have tried to deprive yourselves of sleep (ever pull an all-nighter?) know how difficult it is to resist. As demonstrated in Box 13–2, sleep deprivation experiments clearly indicate a need for sleep. Although the question has been around for centuries, researchers have yet to find a definitive answer except for the teleological one that "we sleep because we're sleepy." The uncertainties surrounding various aspects of sleep, some of which we have already discussed, will cause the debate on the function of sleep to continue well into the future. This section will discuss some of the major hypotheses regarding the purpose of sleep.

Sleep in Evolutionary Perspective

A logical way to begin our examination of the function of sleep is to trace the development of sleep along the evolutionary tree. As far as we know, sleep occurs in all vertebrates, though only warmblooded animals exhibit signs of REM sleep. A list of the total sleep and REM sleep times of various animals is provided in Table 13–2. One way to regard the question of sleep is to look at its teleological roots. If the theory of evolution holds, sleep must be a useful behavior that was inherited from our ancestors. However, it is not clear that our ancestors always slept, since some animals alive today rarely or never do. Webb (1974) suggested the **immobilization theory**, which regards sleep

Table 13–2 SLEEP DURATIONS OF VARIOUS ANIMALS			
Species	Total Daily Sleep Time (h)	Daily REM Time (h)	% REM
Echidna	9.0	?	?
Opossum	18.0	5.0	27.8
Hedgehog	10.0	3.5	35.0
Mole	8.5	2.0	23.5
Bat	19.0	3.0	15.8
Baboon	9.5	1.0	10.5
Humans	8.0	2.0	25.0
Armadillo	17.0	3.0	17.6
Rabbit	8.0	1.0	12.5
Hamster	14.0	3.0	21.4
Rat	13.0	2.5	19.2
Squirrel	14.0	3.0	21.4
Guinea pig	9.5	1.0	10.5
Dolphin	10.0	?	?
Seal	6.0	1.5	25.0
Cat	12.5	3.0	24.0
Dog	10.0	3.0	30.0
Horse	3.0	0.5	16.7
Giraffe	2.0	0.5	25.0

Total daily sleep time includes daily REM time. Values are rounded to the half hour and exclude prolonged drowsiness. Some values are averages for two or more members of the same genus. Question marks indicate reported absence of REM sleep.
Source: Kryger et al., 1994

as an adaptive response that promoted safety by keeping early mammals out of danger. Clearly, it was to our ancestors' advantage to be safely asleep at night rather than walking around, easy prey for night stalkers.

However, the immobilization theory does not adequately explain the function of sleep in light of our situation today. We are now as unlikely to be eaten by a tiger during the night as during the day. If sleep was purely an adaptive response, why hasn't it been eliminated, or at least decreased among humans during the evolution of our species? Clearly, sleep must serve another purpose as well.

An alternative theory maintains that inactivity during periods following food gathering is a good way to conserve energy. The **energy conservation theory** is supported by the

observation that sleep time and metabolic rate display a similar ontogenic (developmental) pattern (Walker & Berger, 1980). Average daily sleep time decreases with age, as does metabolic rate. In addition, animals with a lower metabolic rate typically sleep less than those with a higher metabolic rate (however, there are numerous exceptions). Sleep can be viewed teleologically as both a way to eliminate unnecessary danger and a way to conserve energy.

If we follow the development of sleep over time, evolutionary changes can be inferred. As I mentioned, sleep is found in all vertebrates, yet only warmblooded vertebrates exhibit REM sleep. The similarities among mammalian and avian (bird) sleep patterns have led researchers to speculate that these patterns evolved *in conjunction with endothermy*

Box 13–2

Sleep Deprivation Experiments

One of the most interesting questions in the study of sleep is, simply enough, "Why do we sleep?" One way to help ascertain the function of sleep is to study the effects of its deprivation (a subject with which many of you have experience). Researchers have put extensive effort into studying the effects of sleep deprivation, in both human and nonhuman subjects.

William C. Dement, a pioneer in sleep research, conducted the first controlled sleep deprivation experiments in 1960. Dement was interested in studying the effects of a specific type of deprivation, REM sleep deprivation (a term which he used as a synonym for "dream deprivation," a correlation which is now known to be only partly correct). His original experimental design, which continues to be employed today, comprises alternations between REM sleep deprivation (determined by EEG and EMG monitoring), normal sleep, and NREM sleep deprivation. The NREM sleep deprivation serves as a control to ensure that experimental results are due to REM sleep deprivation and not total sleep deprivation. Typically the subject spends a few nights in each stage of deprivation.

The experimental results showed an interesting phenomenon. As REM sleep deprivation continued, the subject displayed an increase in attempts to reach the REM sleep stage. When the subject was finally allowed to sleep normally, he or she experienced an increase in the number of episodes of REM sleep in the sleep cycle as well as an increased proportion of REM sleep versus NREM sleep. This phenomenon is now known as **REM rebound**. REM rebound was not observed during the control condition, indicating the response was due solely to a lack of REM sleep (Dement, 1960; Dement & Fisher, 1963).

Other results of REM sleep deprivation are ambiguous. Some studies have indicated anxiety, irritability, inability to concentrate, and increase in appetite, whereas other studies do not corroborate these findings. Overall, the experiments on human subjects indicate a need for REM sleep (confirmed by REM rebound), but there is disagreement on the consequences of not satisfying the need.

Other studies have attempted to determine the effects of total sleep deprivation on human subjects. However, prolonged sleep deprivation is difficult to achieve because after a certain amount of deprivation, subjects exhibit brief periods of sleep (ten to thirty seconds) during which they still appear wakeful and active (your professors will never know if you catch a few winks!) It is possible to deprive subjects long enough to observe some effects of deprivation; however, as with the REM sleep deprivation experiments, the results are ambiguous. Some effects observed following about 36 hours of deprivation included changes in subsequent sleep structure; disruption of metabolism, thermoregulation, and the immune system; severe mood changes; and impairment of psychological performance (cognition, memory, and learning). Attention to these psychological effects in particular has resulted in a push for more reasonable working hours for medical residents, to reduce the potential dangers to their patients. Interestingly, only about 30 percent of the total lost sleep time is recovered in subsequent nights, with most of the time consisting of Stages 3 and 4. One man once remained awake for 260 hours, after which he slept for 14 hours and 40 minutes and awoke feeling entirely refreshed (Thorpy & Yager, 1991).

The importance of Stages 3 and 4 sleep is demonstrated in experiments in which subjects reduce their total

(warmbloodedness), which is also found only in birds and mammals. The relationship between sleep and body temperature will be discussed in greater detail in the following section. However, substantial differences in sleep patterns exist even among warmblooded species. In some species, fascinating sleep patterns can be found that seem to have evolved in response to evolutionary changes. For example, the bottlenose dolphin, common porpoise, fur seal, and manatee all have

sleep patterns in which the two cerebral hemispheres take turns sleeping! Apparently, this unihemispheric form of sleeping allows one hemisphere to remain awake and alert during the other hemisphere's "sleep" to keep the animal from drowning. In addition, researchers have reported that these species exhibit very little or no REM sleep (Mukhametov, 1984).

While the study of the evolution of sleep provides some insight into function, it again leaves many questions unan-

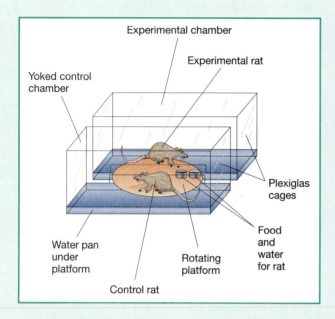

Experimental chamber

Experimental rat

Yoked control chamber

Plexiglas cages

Food and water for rat

Water pan under platform

Rotating platform

Control rat

water! So, current experiments have sought to eliminate these confounds by setting up elaborate controls. One experiment by Rechtschaffen et al. (1989) paired yoked rats on a separated turntable surrounded by water (see figure). The turntable was activated each time the experimental rat entered REM sleep, forcing it to awaken. The control rat was subject to the same conditions with the exception that it could sleep while the experimental rat was naturally awake. Thus, both total and REM sleep time were reduced significantly in the experimental rat, while the other rat acted as a generally sleep-deprived control. As the experiment progressed, the experimental, REM-deprived rats showed weight loss (attributed to increased catabolism), poor appearance, skin lesions, loss of balance, and a decrease in EEG amplitude (indicating decreased brain activity). In addition, a number of these rats died. Necropsies (autopsy on animals) showed the experimental rats had larger adrenals and more stomach ulcers, indicating they suffered a higher degree of stress than the control rats. A number of additional internal problems were found, though not all experimental rats suffered the same problems. The yoked control rats did not show the same effects. While it was clear that REM sleep deprivation had an adverse effect on the animals, the researchers could not determine a specific histological or biochemical cause of death.

Interestingly, there was a high correlation between REM sleep deprivation and survival time in the experiment. This correlation was not found between total sleep deprivation and survival time, indicating that (in rats at least) REM sleep is important to survival (Rechtschaffen et al., 1989). Obviously, similar experiments are not possible in humans for ethical reasons, so it is necessary to generalize and extrapolate from animal experiments such as these.

sleep time. These studies have found that Stage 2 sleep and the REM period decrease while Stages 3 and 4 sleep remain constant (Horne & Wilkinson, 1985). This apparent importance of deep sleep will be discussed when we examine theories of sleep.

Past experiments on sleep deprivation in animals other than humans have been plagued by poor design and confounding results. One design put rats on a rounded hill surrounded by water. When the rats entered REM sleep, their muscles relaxed and they fell into the water, giving them a rousing waking. The subsequent deaths of many of the rats were attributed to a lack of REM sleep rather than the more probable cause: the stress of continually falling into the

swered. The theories presented in the following section address the problem of sleep from a more biological standpoint, describing what sleep does for and to the body itself.

Restoration or Elimination?

Another prevalent theory concerning the purpose of sleep speculates that sleep serves as a period of restoration for the body, allowing metabolism and protein synthesis to

occur. Evidence for those processes in the waking state is argument against the restorative theory. This differs from the energy conservation theory in that it posits an *active role for body healing and development* in sleep, rather than simple prevention of energy loss. The **restorative theory** of sleep dates back to Aristotle, who believed sleep was necessary to preserve the "primary organ," which he believed to be the heart. Though his conceptions of the mechanisms were incorrect, Aristotle's insight into the function of sleep was keen.

In support of the restorative theory, researchers have found that tissue synthesis is higher during sleep than waking (Adam & Oswald, 1977). In addition, about 80 percent of the total daily secretion of growth hormone occurs during slow wave sleep (Born, Muth, & Fehm, 1988; Mendelson, 1987). Shapiro et al. (1984) found that catabolism, as expressed by body oxygen consumption, is lowered during sleep. As mentioned earlier in the chapter, sleep deprivation leads to an increase in slow wave sleep, as do periods of starvation (MacFayden, Oswald & Lewis, 1973). It has also been found that children in their developmental years and athletes have higher proportions of slow wave sleep than the general population. These findings indicate that slow wave sleep does indeed serve a restorative purpose.

While NREM sleep is implicated in bodily restoration, researchers hypothesize that REM sleep is important in brain restitution. Increased brain protein synthesis during REM sleep supports the theory that REM sleep is important in CNS restitution (Drucker-Colin, 1979).

The fact that REM sleep is found only in endotherms suggests a possible relationship between REM sleep and thermoregulation. In their experiments on sleep deprivation in rats, Rechtschaffen et al. (1989) found that body temperature decreased as deprivation time increased (refer to Box 13–2). This finding also supports the theory that REM sleep plays some role in thermoregulation.

Alternatively, sleep can be regarded as a mechanism for ridding the body of unwanted waste material (a discounted notion) or excessive sensory input (a current hypothesis). This **elimination theory**, suggested by Crick and Mitchison (1983), asserts that REM sleep is a mechanism for *reverse learning* of inappropriate behavior patterns that have been acquired during the preceding period of wakefulness. They postulate that an overabundance of daily experience and sensory input leads to an overload of neuronal networks. During REM sleep, the theory holds, stimulation of the forebrain weakens the synaptic strength of extraneous connections, thus "unlearning" activity patterns. Although this theory explains the need for REM sleep, it does not address the need for other aspects of the sleep pattern, such as slow wave sleep.

In short, both the restoration theory and the elimination theory give insight into the question of the function of sleep, but neither gives a definitive or conclusive answer.

Jouvet's Theory of Sleep

Another theory on the function of sleep was proposed by Jouvet in 1978. In what is termed the **genetic programming hypothesis**, Jouvet proposed that REM sleep is needed to modify innate behavior patterns by facilitating transcription of genetic material. According to Jouvet, in more advanced animals who rely heavily on learning, this modification is needed to prevent innate behavior from getting lost as experiences accumulate. Therefore, REM deprivation should lead to an inability to modify certain behavior patterns, resulting in behavioral similarities (more stereotypical behavior) among REM-deprived subjects.

Jouvet's theory has been corroborated by a number of findings. REM deprivation has been shown to increase stereotypical, drive-related behavior such as aggression and locomotive behavior in rodents (Hicks & Adams, 1976; Hicks et al., 1979) and increased sexual interest in humans (Zarcone, De La Pena, & Dement, 1960).

The best evidence in support of this hypothesis comes from Sastre and Jouvet's (1979) observations. By making bilateral lesions in the subcoerulear nucleus, in the lower part of the pons, Jouvet was able to suppress the muscle atonia characteristic of REM sleep in cats. After this surgery, the animals frequently engaged in stereotypical drive-related behaviors, such as stalking, grooming, flight, and fighting, during REM sleep. It was as if the cats were "acting out" their dreams. Based on the actions of the cats, it was concluded that innate behavior patterns were present during REM sleep, presumably so that they could be modified in light of recent learning.

Psychological Theories of Dreams

Other major theories on the function of sleep propose that sleep serves a psychological as well as a physiological purpose. Since dreams often have an emotional quality, at the forefront of most of these theories is the study of dreams and their meanings.

One of the most well-known and influential theories on dreams was put forth by Sigmund Freud. Freud believed that dreams were the expression of subconscious elements of the psyche. He termed the actual dream experiences the **manifest content**, and the underlying psychological association the **latent content**. The complicated process by which latent content is transformed into manifest content (the actual dream) is referred to as the **dreamwork**. According to Freud, dreams serve the purpose of expressing otherwise hidden desires and urges. He believed that consciously elucidating the meanings of dreams allows an individual to better understand his or her psyche.

Carl Jung (1974) also believed dreams are purposeful, though his theories differed from those of Freud. He believed dreams give hints and messages about the dreamer's life and future. This theory stemmed from his belief that dreams express themes from the *collective unconscious*, a state composed of instincts from the most primitive levels of the mind. Jung asserted these primitive instincts presented themselves to the dreamer in the form of *archetypes,* symbolic entities more cultural in nature than Freud's manifest content.

Other researchers have suggested that dreams serve a problem-solving purpose. In a unique attempt to collect problem-solving dreams, Schatzman (1983) gave subjects specific scientific, arithmetic, or artistic problems to solve in their dreams. Several of the subjects reported solving the problems in their dreams, but Schatzman had no reliable way of making sure the subjects did not think about the problems while awake. Consider your own experience. Have you ever woken up with the solution to a problem that was troubling you when you fell asleep?

One of the most exciting new theories, supported by some experimental evidence, suggests that sleep is needed to consolidate *complex learning* (not strictly associative or nonassociative) (Chapter 15) for items such as faces or conversations.

Now that we have examined a number of different theories of sleep, evolutionary, biological, and psychological, one thing should be clear. As of yet, no one definitive answer to the question "Why do we sleep?" has been found. Sleep appears to serve a wide variety of functions, and the debate over which is the most important is likely to continue well into the future.

Sleep Disorders

Sleep disorders, or apparent sleep disorders, are very common (almost "epidemic") in industrialized countries. However, experts agree that true **insomnia** is actually quite rare. Rather than lack of sleep per se, more of the complaints are found, upon examination, to be disturbances of sleep *patterns* brought on by any of a host of causes ranging from depression to drug or alcohol abuse to the stresses and strains of everyday life. Failure to appreciate this fact has led to a number of inappropriate treatments for "insomnia" when the underlying problem goes unrecognized and untreated (for example, see Box 13–3).

Insomnias

The term *insomnia* is generally used to describe the condition of anyone who suffers from inadequate or unrefreshing sleep. Obviously, there are a number of problems inherent in this loose definition. First, the amount of sleep needed differs for every individual. Some people get by fine on

three hours of sleep a night; others need twelve to feel refreshed. It is a person's perception of sleep *quality* rather than sleep *time* that should be used to evaluate sleep. Difficulties also arise in assessing quality of sleep. People often judge the quality of their sleep on how they feel during the day, although the two may be unrelated. Certainly there are many factors besides sleep quality that influence whether you have a "good day" or a "bad day." The misinterpretation of symptoms has led to a recent change in the classification of insomnia from a disorder in and of itself to a specific symptom that can be associated with a variety of medical and psychiatric disorders (Ohayon et al., 1997). It has been reported that up to 35 percent of the population experience some degree of insomnia, with half of that group describing it as a "serious" problem (National Institute of Mental Health, 1984). Figure 13–10 shows some of the factors involved in developing insomnia.

Major complaints of insomniacs include difficulty falling asleep, frequent awakenings, short sleep time, and unre-

Figure 13–10   *Development and Treatment of Insomnia.* Any stressful event can cause transient insomnia, and many people experience it at some time during their lives. More serious is when psychological or physiological factors aggravate this insomnia, promoting anxiety and the self-fulfilling idea that one will not be able to sleep, leading to chronic insomnia. Treatments can include medications, but because insomnia is often a symptom of a larger problem, eliminating the root cause (the stressor) is generally the most successful solution.

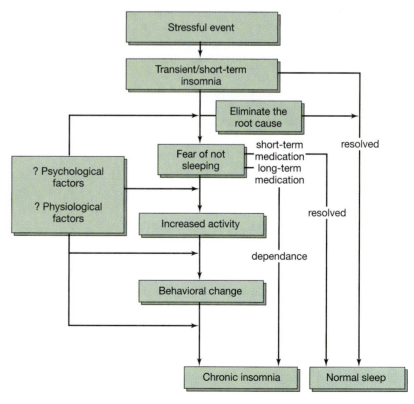

Box 13–3

"Sleeping Medications" and the Elderly

Though people of all ages experience problems in the sleep-wake cycle, complaints are found most often among the elderly. As with most behaviors, the sleep pattern changes with age. In general, slow wave sleep decreases with age, the circadian sleep-wake rhythm weakens, sleep becomes more disrupted, sleep efficiency declines, and there is an increased likelihood of problems associated with sleep, such as insomnia and sleep apnea (see figure). The combination of these factors has led to the widespread use of sleeping medications, or **hypnotics**, among the elderly. Studies have found that, on average, 10 to 15 percent of the elderly use prescribed hypnotics, and women more often than men.

During the first half of the twentieth century, the most commonly used hypnotics were the *barbituates*. However, unwanted side effects led to their replacement by the *benzodiazepines*, currently the most frequently used hypnotics. The benzodiazepines exert their effect by modulating GABA transmission.

Though use of hypnotics can be beneficial for short-term, symptomatic control, long-term use often exacerbates the problem, causing drug dependency and drug-related symptoms, especially among the elderly. Ideally, sleeping medication should exert its effects only during sleep. However, *residual drug effects,* in which the sedative effects of the drug persist throughout the day, are common. These residual effects, which can be additive (traces of some hypnotics can be found the following night) are worse in the elderly due to a reduced metabolism. The accumulation of these drugs often leads to impaired mental performance, which can be mistaken for senility.

Another ill effect of long-term hypnotic use is referred to as **rebound insomnia** (not to be confused with REM rebound), which is severe insomnia that follows the withdrawal of the medication. In order to treat the rebound insomnia, many patients turn to other types of sleeping medication, exacerbating the problem.

In addition, patients often experience REM rebound following drug withdrawal. This is due to the fact that many hypnotics alter the sleep cycle, suppressing both REM and Stage 4 sleep. Vivid dreaming and nightmares often accompany the REM rebound, causing sleep to be fragmented and unrestful.

Another problem with sleeping medications, especially among the elderly, is *misdiagnosis*. As we discussed earlier, insomnia is often the symptom of a larger problem, physical or psychological. In the elderly, a common cause of insomnia is depression. Once diagnosed with "insom-

freshing sleep. In addition, many people also report daytime effects of insomnia such as fatigue, irritability, depression, anxiety, mood changes, and inability to concentrate. In such cases, it is difficult to separate the cause from the effect, since it is possible that a particular patient's insomnia is caused by a root disorder that also causes the daytime symptoms. For example, a person suffering from depression is likely to experience both insomnia and daytime fatigue. If care is not taken in diagnosis, the daytime symptoms might be attributed to insomnia and the true psychiatric problem might be overlooked.

Clearly, the accurate assessment of insomnia is crucial to determining treatment. To this end, a careful classification system has been devised in which insomnia is divided into different groups depending on its cause.

The first type is insomnia associated with *behavioral* or *psychophysiological causes*. Patients with psychophysiological insomnia have trouble falling asleep because of a preoccupation with falling asleep. Many of you have probably experienced this at some time. You lie in bed thinking, "I've got to fall asleep, I've got to fall asleep." Of course, as you've learned, this does nothing to aid the sleep process; it isn't until you think about something else that sleep finally occurs. This type of insomnia is caused by learned associations that prevent sleep by causing undue stress.

Behavioral insomnias include practices that have a negative effect on the sleep pattern, such as smoking, ingestion of excessive caffeine (see Figure 13–9), daytime napping, irregular sleep patterns, and vigorous exercise before bedtime. These insomnias also include a number of problems associ-

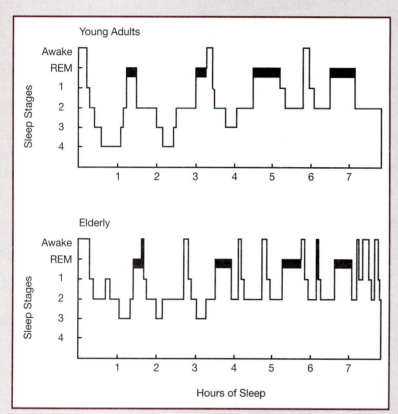

Young Adults

Elderly

Hours of Sleep

aid" solution, allowing the real problem to go unnoticed and untreated.

A final potential problem with the use of sleeping medications is their use in institutions for the elderly. Hypnotics are used by the elderly much more in institutions than in the general population. This fact has led some researchers to hypothesize that institutions use hypnotics as an easy form of behavioral control. It has been suggested that sleeping medications are used to suit the needs of the institution rather than the needs of the individuals housed there. Dr. William C. Dement, a leading figure in the study of sleep, described the use of hypnotic drugs in these institutions for the elderly as "an abomination" (Dement, Miles, & Carskadon, 1982). The idea that the elderly are easily "taken care of" with the prescription of a hypnotic drug raises serious questions about the morality of such institutions and those who support them.

Though sleeping medications can have beneficial short-term effects (Nowell et al., 1997), the severity of their potential problems requires the exercise of caution. The widespread use of hypnotics among the elderly today indicates that these problems need to be more carefully explained and considered.

nia," the patient begins to rely on the sleeping medications, which, due to residual effects, may only exacerbate the depression. The symptomatic treatment is a "band-

ated with insomnia in children, such as refusing to go to bed at the appropriate time.

Particularly important to diagnose correctly are the second type, those insomnias associated with *psychiatric disorders,* such as depression, bipolar disorder, anxiety disorders, and alcoholism (Chapter 18). Treatment of the specific psychiatric disorder is crucial to resolution of the sleep complaint.

Neurological disorders such as Parkinson's disease and epilepsy cause a third type of insomnia, characterized by an inability to maintain sleep once it has been achieved. A rare disorder of the central nervous system that displays this type of severe insomnia is **fatal familial insomnia**. In this deadly disorder, it is believed that the presence of an abnormal protein in the brain causes the CNS to degenerate, culminating

in coma and death. There is no known treatment (Lugaresi et al., 1986).

Insomnia may also be caused by *environmental* factors, such as light, noise, temperature, or altitude. Particular sleep disturbances such as sleep terrors, nightmares, and night sweats, as well as the sleep apneas, which will be discussed later in this section, may also lead to insomnia. Other causes that will also be discussed in greater detail later are disorders of rhythmicity and, ironically enough, the use of sleeping medications.

The treatment of insomnia varies according to the cause. Most patients deal with insomnia without professional help. However, inability to obtain rest is a serious problem and outside help is sometimes appropriate. A large number of treatments are available, ranging from books describing forms of self-help to counseling to medication. Because insomnia is usually the symptom of a larger problem, the most effective treatment is accurate diagnosis and treatment of the primary problem.

Disorders of Rhythmicity

Another category of disorders associated with sleep and biological rhythms are loosely classified as *disorders of rhythmicity*. One such disorder is **seasonal affective disorder (SAD)**. SAD is characterized by an onset of depression at a particular time of year, specifically mid to late fall and continuing into winter as the nights grow longer (Young et al., 1997). It is believed to be caused by a delayed circadian rhythm at this time of year, related to decreased light exposure. SAD is diagnosed if patients report depression, overeating, carbohydrate craving, oversleeping, decreased sex drive, and loss of concentration for at least two consecutive winters. These patients are usually fine during the remainder of the year, and depression abates as the days grow longer. The major form of treatment for SAD is light therapy. This treatment involves exposure to light of more than 2,000 lux for two or more hours in the morning. This measure is roughly equivalent to staring at a 60-watt light bulb from one meter away, although there are certainly more interesting ways to go about it. Depending on the time of day, exposure of this magnitude can reset the circadian rhythms and suppress melatonin secretion (Lewy et al., 1980; Minors, Waterhouse, Wirz-Justice, 1991). The light therapy in the morning presumably induces corrective phase shifts in the patient's circadian rhythm. However, afternoon and evening therapy have also been reported to be beneficial. As of yet, no clear mechanism for the therapeutic effect of light therapy has been found, but the technique has been found useful, especially in the northern latitudes where winter nights are longest.

In a number of disorders of rhythmicity, the circadian rhythm is altered, either by environmental time cues or through a defect in the internal pacemaker. One such disorder is **delayed sleep phase syndrome**, in which the individual has a very late sleep onset (3 to 6 A.M.) and a late arousal time (11 A.M. to 2 P.M.). Studies of this disorder have shown that the circadian rhythm of body temperature is shifted so that the low point occurs about four hours later than usual. In many cases, this disorder is caused by environmental cues, such as an adolescent's tendency to stay up late. However, it can also be caused by an abnormality in the circadian pacemaker in the suprachiasmatic nucleus. Treatment for this disorder usually involves chronotherapy, an interesting technique in which bedtime is delayed even further by increasing increments each night. Eventually, this method has the patient going to bed twenty hours later than the previous abnormal bedtime, which works out to be the same time of day

as if he or she had gone to bed four hours earlier, and the conventional twenty-four-hour day is thus reestablished. This method of going to bed later rather than earlier is used because the body seems to be able to delay its sleep schedule more easily than it can advance it.

Another example of the difficulty in correcting a transient disturbance in circadian rhythms is one with which you are probably already familiar, **jet lag** (Waterhouse, Reilly, & Atkinson (1997). This term refers to the symptoms experienced after one has passed rapidly through time zones. These symptoms include fatigue, insomnia, and gastrointestinal problems. The severity of the symptoms depends on the number of time zones crossed, direction of travel, and individual adaptation time. Studies (and personal experiences) have shown that jet lag is worse when traveling eastward, when adaptation requires an earlier bedtime and arousal time. In this case it again seems that the body has a harder time adapting to earlier bedtimes than later. Typically, resynchronization occurs at a rate of one and a half hours per day following a westbound flight, but only one hour per day following an eastbound flight. So, if you fly from New York to California (a three-hour time difference), you will need two days to adjust to the time change; but if you fly from California to New York, the adjustment will take three days. In order to minimize jet lag, you should prepare for the time change in advance, gradually shifting sleep and eating times. Recently, a popular but untested therapy for jet lag involving melatonin supplements has been proposed. The author's advice corresponds with that of the National Institute on Aging (1997): Consumers should be hesitant to take diet supplements that have not been examined scientifically for potential health hazards.

The last disorder of rhythmicity we will examine is **shiftwork disorder**, a transient disorder that affects people who work unusual hours. Symptoms include disturbed sleep patterns, fatigue, high injury rates, gastritis, and ulcers. Problems vary among individuals, occurring most frequently in workers who rotate shifts and those who work the night shift but attempt to return to a normal schedule on their days off. Unlike jet lag, in this disorder environmental cues remain opposed to the sleep-wake cycle, making adaptation more difficult. Because light is the primary zeitgeber, it may be impossible to ever fully adapt to a schedule in opposition to light cues. Obviously, there is much concern in the work force regarding this problem, and research on possible solutions continues (Arendt et al., 1997).

Other Disorders

One of the most striking neurological disorders involving sleep is **narcolepsy** (*narku* = numbness and *lepsis* = seizure). Narcolepsy is characterized by *sleep attacks* that occur uncontrollably and often at inappropriate times. These brief sleep episodes can occur anytime during the day and can range in duration from only five minutes up to an hour. One symptom of narcolepsy is *sleep paralysis,* the inability to move just prior to sleep and upon awakening. Muscle paralysis is normal during REM sleep (REM muscle atonia) but occurs at inappropriate times in narcoleptics. In addition to this sleep paralysis, narcoleptics will also often experience dreaming, like that of REM sleep, while awake and immobile! These often terrifying experiences are termed **hypnagogic hallucinations** (*hypnos* = sleep and *agogos* = leading).

An interesting feature of narcolepsy is a phenomenon called *cataplexy* (*kata* = down and *plexis* = stroke). Cataplexy is a sudden loss of muscle tone usually elicited in response to an emotional or physical stimulus. Laughter, anger, surprise, or sudden physical strain can trigger an attack. During a cataplexic attack, the jaw sags, arms drop, and knees unlock, often resulting in complete collapse. Like sleep paralysis, cataplexy is a normal feature of REM sleep that has intruded into the waking state (Pollmacher, Mullingston, & Lauer, 1997).

From the symptoms, it seems reasonable to suggest that narcolepsy is caused by inappropriate activation of the neural mechanisms that control REM sleep (Garcia-Rill, 1997). Indeed, the symptoms can be successfully treated with *tricyclic antidepressants,* such as imipramine, indicating their cause is an abnormality in transmitter function.

Another interesting disorder of REM sleep is **REM sleep behavior disorder,** or REM sleep without muscle atonia. Whereas normal people are immobile during REM sleep, people with this disorder are able to act out their dreams, an often dangerous experience! This disorder can develop as a result of withdrawal from alcohol or other drugs.

Characterized by cessation of breathing during sleep, **sleep apnea** is divided into two types: *central sleep apnea syndrome* and *obstructive sleep apnea syndrome* (Kushida et al., 1997). Usually, sleep apnea is caused by a combination of the two. Central sleep apnea refers to a loss of respiratory effort, which results in a cessation of air flow for ten seconds or

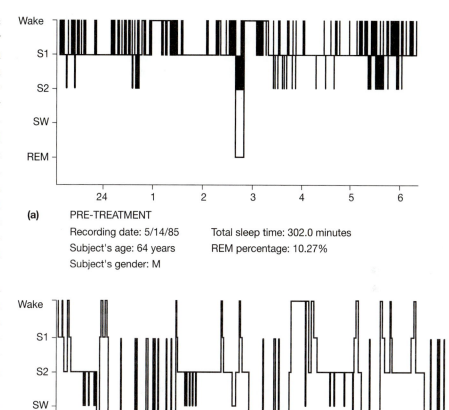

(a) PRE-TREATMENT
Recording date: 5/14/85   Total sleep time: 302.0 minutes
Subject's age: 64 years   REM percentage: 10.27%
Subject's gender: M

(b) POST-TREATMENT
Recording date: 6/3/85   Total sleep time: 432.50 minutes
Subject's age: 64 years   REM percentage: 38.61%
Subject's gender: M

Figure 13–11 *Obstructive Sleep Apnea.* (a) Prior to treatment, a patient with obstructive sleep apnea shows continual awakenings and an absence of slow wave sleep. (b) After treatment this same patient spends much more time in REM and slow wave sleep, sleeps longer, and awakens less often. (Adapted from Nino-Murcia et al., 1988)

more in adults. Patients will awake several times during the night, gasping for breath. This type of apnea is commonly seen in people with disorders that affect respiratory control, such as lesions of the spinal cord or brainstem.

Obstructive sleep apnea is due to upper-airway obstructions, which include a narrow nasal airway, enlarged tonsils, tongue tissues, or an enlarged soft palate. One feature of this syndrome is *snoring,* caused by a partial obstruction of the airway. When the obstruction becomes more complete, the person awakens choking for breath, leading to severe sleep disruption. In Figure 13–11a, you can see that this patient with obstructive sleep apnea syndrome awakens frequently and spends very little time in slow wave and REM sleep. In Figure 13–12b, after treatment, the patient sleeps longer, awakens much less frequently, and spends more time in both slow wave and REM sleep.

Both types of apnea, but particularly obstructive sleep apnea, are exacerbated by obesity. Obesity causes a narrowing of the airway, increased pressure on the chest, and impairment of diaphragm function due to large abdominal size.

Another terrifying syndrome currently under intense study is **sudden infant death syndrome (SIDS).** SIDS is used to describe the as yet unexplained condition that causes otherwise healthy infants to die suddenly in their sleep (Spiers & Guntheroth, 1997). SIDS is often confused with sleep apnea in children. The relationship between sleep apnea and incidence of SIDS is unclear, partly due to difficulty in identification. However, it appears that the incidence of SIDS is slightly greater in infants recovering from respiratory problems than in normal infants, implicating a disruption of respiration as a factor in SIDS. In addition, there appear to be a number of predisposing factors including low birth weight, premature birth, maternal smoking during pregnancy, twins or multiple births, and hereditary factors (having a sibling who died of SIDS). Also, infants born to mothers addicted to cocaine or heroin are at greater risk. Much progress in reducing SIDS deaths seems to have come from the educational campaign to encourage new parents to put infants to sleep on their backs.

Though no one problem has been identified that sufficiently explains the cause of death, autopsies frequently reveal a number of similar findings. Hemorrhages in the lungs, pericardium (tissue surrounding the heart), and thymus (gland in the upper chest involved in the immune system) indicate that the victims may have suffered from upper respiratory tract obstructions (Beckwith, 1973). A number of studies have found that a combination of infectious agents and **hypoxemia,** a low blood-oxygen level, causes symptoms similar to those found in SIDS autopsies (Guntheroth et al., 1980). Abnormalities have been found in the brainstem as well, indicating problems within the central nervous system potentially leading to **hypoxia,** a reduction of oxygen to the tissues below the level necessary for cellular metabolism. The relationships among these various findings is still unclear, but expanding technology is affording researchers better opportunities to study the mechanisms underlying this deadly syndrome.

Some authorities believe that the most prevalent sleep disorder is one that is caused by sleeping medications themselves. **Drug dependency insomnia** is a consequence of long term use of barbiturate or benzodiazapine sleeping medications, which can produce addiction and dependency just as other drugs can (Chapter 17). Many studies have shown that the addiction process may be quite rapid, in such a manner that the consumer requires greater doses to fall asleep shortly after medication begins and experiences very disturbed sleep if medication is stopped, even after only a few days of consumption.

SUMMARY

The sleep-wake cycle exhibited by animals and humans is one example of an endogenous circadian rhythm, regulated by external environmental cues known as zeitgebers. Various studies have shown that the internal pacemaker responsible for controlling circadian rhythms is located in the suprachiasmatic nucleus of the hypothalamus.

The sleep pattern of humans is divided into two major categories, non-REM and REM sleep. These divisions are identified by various physiological measures such as the EEG, EMG, and EOG. NREM sleep is further divided into four sleep stages, each with distinguishing physiological features. The latter two stages, Stages 3 and 4, are known collectively as slow wave sleep. The second major division, REM sleep, is characterized by three major features: a desynchronized EEG, loss of muscle tone, and periodic bursts of rapid eye movements.

Studies have found a variety of different neural and humoral factors involved in the regulation of sleep and waking.

The "sleep-inducing" factors include serotonin, muramyl peptides, delta sleep–inducing peptides, and adenosine. Factors that promote wakefulness include acetylcholine, norepinephrine, dopamine, and histamine. The exact mechanisms by which these substances function are still under study, as are the neural mechanisms underlying the sleep and dreaming process.

A number of theories have been proposed to explain the function of sleep. Various aspects of the sleep cycle can be explained through examination of evolutionary roots, while other aspects become clear when the biology of sleep is examined. Jouvet proposes sleep is a mechanism for genetic re-programming following learning. Psychological theories also offer explanations for the sleep process, specifically why we dream.

As with most behaviors, there are a number of problems associated with sleep. One of the most common sleep disorders, insomnia, can be caused by a variety of different problems, and careful diagnosis is needed. Other disorders of sleep range from harmless, transient jet lag to the fatal sudden infant death syndrome. Most sleep disorders are still under study, and advancing technology is giving researchers better opportunities to elucidate the causes of these problems and provide treatment. Some sleep disorders, such as snoring and sleep apnea, may be related to disorders of metabolism, a subject we shall explore in Chapter 14.

REVIEW QUESTIONS

1. Why is the suprachiasmatic nucleus important?
2. What is REM sleep?
3. How are EEG records made?
4. Why is it believed that there is a reticular inactivating system?
5. What is the best cure for insomnia?
6. List the theories of why sleep is needed.
7. List the theories of why dreaming is needed.
8. List the major sleep disorders.

THOUGHT QUESTIONS

1. Everybody dreams and hence there are abundant theories to explain the incidence of dreaming from the perspective of the welfare of the organism. Sleep terrors are also very common, especially among children. Teleologically, why do they exist?

2. What does a cat dream about when it twitches its paws and moves its mouth? Is there any way to determine if you are right?

3. Most areas of neuroscience have benefited from the use of *simple systems* (eutelous nervous systems). What would a simple system for the study of sleep look like?

KEY CONCEPTS

acetylcholine (ACh) (p. 312)
activation-synthesis theory (p. 316)
adenosine (p. 312)
ascending reticular activating system (ARAS) (p. 314)
cataplexy (p. 313)
circadian rhythm (p. 305)
delayed sleep phase syndrome (p. 324)
delta sleep–inducing peptide (DSIP) (p. 312)
dopamine (DA) (p. 314)
dreamwork (p. 320)
drowsy state (p. 308)
drug dependency insomnia (p. 326)
electromyogram (EMG) (p. 308)

electroencephalogram (EEG) (p. 308)
elimination theory (p. 320)
energy conservation theory (p. 317)
fatal familial insomnia (p. 323)
genetic programming hypothesis (p. 320)
histamine (p. 315)
hypnagogic hallucinations (p. 325)
hypnotics (p. 322)
hypoxemia (p. 326)
hypoxia (p. 326)
immobilization theory (p. 317)
insomnia (p. 321)
jet lag (p. 324)
K complexes (p. 309)
latent content (p. 320)

locus coeruleus (p. 313)
manifest content (p. 320)
melatonin (p. 307)
muramyl peptide (MP) (p. 311)
muscle atonia (p. 310)
narcolepsy (p. 324)
non-REM (NREM) sleep (p. 307)
norepinephrine (NE) (p. 313)
pineal gland (p. 307)
PGO spike (p. 310)
raphé nuclei (p. 311)
rapid eye movements (p. 310)
rebound insomnia (p. 322)
REM rebound (p. 318)
REM sleep (p. 308)
REM sleep behavior disorder (p. 325)
restorative theory (p. 319)
restless legs syndrome (p. 315)

retinohypothalamic tract (p. 306)
seasonal affective disorder (SAD) (p. 324)
serotonin (p. 311)
shift-work disorder (p. 324)
sleep apnea (p. 325)
sleep-inducing factors (p. 311)
sleep peptides (p. 311)
sleep spindle (p. 309)
sleep terrors (p. 309)
slow wave sleep (p. 308)
somnambulism (p. 309)
Stage 1 sleep (p. 308)
Stage 2 sleep (p. 308)
sudden infant death syndrome (SIDS) (p. 326)
suprachiasmatic nucleus (SCN) (p. 306)
zeitgeber (p. 306)

Is it only the mouth and belly that are injured by hunger and thirst? Men's minds are also injured by them.

Mencius (372–289 B.C.)

14

Eating, Drinking, and Homeostasis

In order for the brain to carry out its various electrical and chemical operations, and thereby affect behavior, basic energy requirements must be met in a relatively stable environment. The focus of this chapter is to examine more thoroughly the specific metabolic needs of the brain and the ways in which these obligations are met and maintained under normal conditions.

Brain Metabolism

The brain is metabolically the most active of all the organs; consequently its demands for oxygen and glucose are continuous and profuse. Even a brief interruption in the flow of blood containing these nutrients can have devastating effects on brain function, as its supply of these substances is critical for normal function. The maintenance of homeostasis (a primary function of brain activity, see Box 5–4) is dependent on regulation of these two constituents. Table 14–1 shows what portion of critical body resources are used by the brain. Studies investigating substrates and waste produced by brain metabolism make use of the fact that substances taken up by brain tissue from the blood are higher in concentration in the arterial inflow than in the venous outflow, and the converse is true for substances released by brain tissue. Despite much investigation of neural substrates and products, the only consistently *positive* **arteriovenous differences** (a lower substance level in venous outflow than arterial inflow) that have been found during normal functioning have been for glucose and oxygen. Reliable *negative* arteriovenous differences (a higher substance level in venous outflow than arterial inflow) have been shown only for carbon dioxide.

Blood-Brain Barrier and Glucose Utilization

The brain is separated in many ways from the blood circulation. This isolation is necessary to insure that the brain cells are maintained in a stable, well-regulated chemical environment. Neurons require a bath of consistent ionic composition and are much less tolerant of changes than are other cells. Therefore, substances that circulate in the blood in fluctuating concentrations are excluded from the brain, which helps

Table 14–1	THE PORTION OF CRITICAL BODY RESOURCES UTILIZED BY THE BRAIN
Brain: Percent of Total Body	
Weight	2%–3%
Cardiac Output	15%
Oxygen Consumption	20%
Blood Glucose Consumption	25%

At each interface where brain cells come into contact with blood there are **tight junctions**, which are formed when a cell's surface closely contacts the adjacent cells, leaving no spaces between them. Tight junctions contrast with the *gap junctions* found in most capillaries in the periphery. Gap junctions, formed by contact between adjacent capillary lining cells, allow bloodborne chemicals to diffuse out of a capillary into the extracellular environment as do pores, paracellular gaps and continuous basement membranes (Figure 14–1). The tight junction arrangement in the central nervous system prevents movement of nonlipid soluble substances across the barrier. Selective carriers and ion pumps are situated on the interface cells to transport electrolytes and essential nutrients. Glucose crosses the BBB by such a carrier mechanism. The regulation of glucose uptake across the BBB is governed by a constant (Michaelis constant, K_m, see Appendix). With a concentration below the K_m of the central nervous system,

to prevent wide fluctuations in electrolytes surrounding brain tissue. The most extensive interface between the brain and the systemic circulation occurs at the **blood-brain barrier (BBB)**.

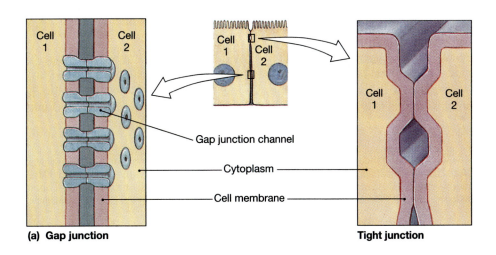

(a) Gap junction   **Tight junction**

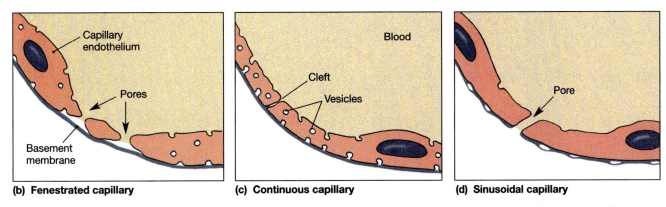

(b) Fenestrated capillary   **(c) Continuous capillary**   **(d) Sinusoidal capillary**

Figure 14–1 *Junctions Located in the Body.* Tight junctions are located at every interface where brain cells come in contact with blood. These junctions prevent non-lipid soluble materials from crossing the BBB. In contrast to these tight junctions located in the CNS, gap junctions are scattered throughout the periphery. These allow chemicals located in the blood to diffuse into the extracellular environment. There are also larger pores in blood vessels that allow nutrients and metabolites to pass. (a) Gap junctions and tight junctions; (b) fenestrated capillaries; (c) continuous capillaries; (d) sinusoidal capillaries.

small changes in the level of glucose in arterial blood cause significant changes in the amount transported across the BBB. When concentrations of glucose in the blood are low, it is more actively transported across the BBB by the carrier mechanism. However, arterial blood concentrations of glucose at or above the K_m of the CNS saturate the carrier molecules, and only a limited amount of glucose enters the brain by diffusion. Thus, glucose levels in brain vary directly with blood glucose concentrations although, because of limitations of the transport mechanism, brain glucose is always lower than blood glucose. Beyond the BBB, brain cells take up glucose much more avidly: Glucose can be taken up into nerve terminals by carrier processes that have an affinity for glucose thirty times higher than that of the BBB carrier mechanism.

Once in the cells, glucose enters the glycolytic pathways where it is converted to pyruvate and then metabolized through the Krebs cycle (Chapter 2). Brain glucose is metabolized to produce energy for cellular work or converted to amino acids and lipids. Glucose is transported into the cell, where it undergoes **glycolysis**. The specifics of this process were discussed in Chapter 2. The general steps in glycolysis, as it takes place in the brain, are shown in Figure 14–2, which also indicates the specific uses the brain has for the energy generated from glucose breakdown. In the absence of glucose, the brain uses amino acids and fatty acids, ultimately

metabolizing essential nutrients and membranes, which results in permanent cell damage. During starvation, ketone bodies are metabolized in place of glucose. Glycogen stores are also used by the brain for energy. Although present in relatively low concentration in brain, glycogen is a unique energy reserve that requires no energy for its locally controlled metabolism (contrast with the creation of glucose from *liver* glycogen, Chapter 6). The accepted role of glycogen is that of a carbohydrate reserve that is utilized when glucose levels fall. However, glycogen appears to be rapidly and continually synthesized and degraded in brain tissue (19 μmol/kg/min), which implies that, even under steady-state conditions, local carbohydrate reserves are important for brain function. Glucocorticoid hormones that penetrate the BBB increase glycogen turnover, suggesting that this energy supply may be particularly useful in accommodating increased demands during times of stress. Glucocorticoids also feedback onto peptide-secreting cells in the hypothalamus and pituitary to regulate the levels of these hormones in the fight-or-flight response (Figure 14–3 and Box 6–2).

Oxygen Requirements

The brain has been likened to an "oxygen furnace." The rate of oxygen consumption by an entire brain of average weight (1,400 g) is approximately 49 ml O_2/min. The enormity of this

Figure 14–2 *Metabolism of Glucose in the Brain.* Glycolysis in the brain cells converts glucose into pyruvate. In aerobic respiration, the Krebs cycle forms NADH for conversion of ADP to ATP in the respiratory chain. Glutamate can be stored or converted into GABA or glutamine. The action of the sodium/potassium ATPase pump is maintained by ATP. Water enters cells down osmotic and hydrostatic gradients.

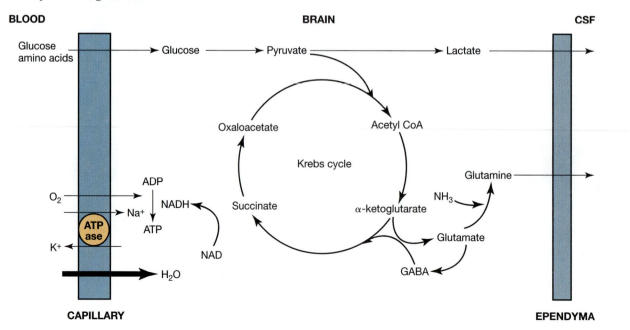

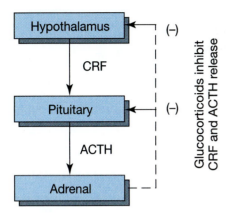

Figure 14–3 *Glucocorticoid Feedback in the Hypothalamic Pituitary Axis.* Glucocorticoids that penetrate the BBB feed back onto peptide-secreting cells in the hypothalamus and pituitary, thereby regulating the release of hormones from endocrine systems. This figure illustrates factors controlling the release of hormones from the anterior pituitary and the use of negative feedback inhibition in influencing further hormonal release.

rate can be better appreciated when it is compared with the metabolic rate of the body as a whole. For instance the average person weighs about 70 kg and consumes approximately 250 ml O_2/min. Therefore, the brain, which represents only about 2 percent of total body weight, accounts for an astounding 20 percent of total oxygen consumption. In children this fraction is even more staggering in that as much as 50 percent of the body's oxygen is consumed by the brain during periods in the first decade of life (see Table 14–1).

Circulation Requirements

Cerebral blood flow must be able to accommodate the brain's insatiable appetite for oxygen outlined previously. For the whole brain the rate of blood flow is about 15 percent of total cardiac output. This enormous demand for blood continues unabated: Even during sleep there is only a relatively small decrease in cerebral metabolic rate, and this decrease may vanish during REM sleep. As is the case with much of the brain's activity, this rate of flow must be maintained within inflexible limits. For instance, a 50 percent decrease in cerebral blood flow is sufficient to cause loss of consciousness in normal, healthy adults.

Glucose Requirements

The normal brain is restricted almost exclusively to glucose as the substrate for its energy. Twenty-five percent of the glucose in the blood is used to service the needs of the brain. Glucose is also a major carbon source for a wide variety of simple and complex molecules. Most other tissues are more flexible with respect to their energy sources, and although they are capable of utilizing glucose, they do not exploit it as a primary metabolite. For example, heart, kidney, and even liver (the carbohydrate storehouse) predominantly derive their energy from fatty acids. The testis is the only other tissue that has been found to rely so exclusively on carbohydrate for energy.

Blood Flow

Because circulation to the brain is so critical, the uninterrupted supply of glucose and oxygen through the blood is insured by various homeostatic mechanisms. In addition to maintaining a constant level of total blood flow to the brain, these mechanisms make continuous adjustments that satisfy metabolic needs of specific nuclei and structures. The compensatory adjustments associated with this maintenance must be sensitive to the highly restricted constraints of brain metabolism. How is the complex task of blood flow regulation accomplished?

Perfusion Pressure and Autoregulation

Blood flow is a dynamic property of brain function that is intimately tied to brain activity. As activity in a particular brain region increases, its metabolic demands (energy use) also rise. To meet these higher needs, there is a local increase in cerebral blood flow. Blood flow is also regulated throughout the entire brain. This is important because the arterial blood pressure can vary widely, and proper blood supply in the brain is dependent upon local fine-tuning. The **perfusion pressure** of the blood supply to the brain is equal to the difference between the arterial blood pressure and the cerebral venous pressure. The cerebral venous pressure is usually the same as the pressure of the CSF. Arterial blood pressure in the body can vary within a relatively wide range (40 to 200 mg of mercury) without affecting cerebral blood flow. The cerebral arterioles (small arteries) constrict when blood pressure increases and dilate when blood pressure is lowered. The process by which cerebral vessels alter their diameter to maintain a constant blood flow in spite of alterations in perfusion pressure is called **autoregulation**.

How is the diameter of the cerebral arterioles altered? Two general hypotheses have been developed that attempt to account for these adaptations:

1. *Metabolic hypothesis* accounts for vasodilation (expansion of vessels) in response to hypotension (low blood pressure). A decrease in blood pressure results in a transient reduction in flow. This decreased blood flow culminates in a buildup of metabolites, which causes vasodilation. Proposed signals for this feedback are hydrogen ions (or acidity), potassium ions, or adenosine.

Table 14–2	EFFECT OF NEUROTRANSMITTERS ON THE CEREBRAL CIRCULATION			
Neurotransmitter	Direct cerebrovascular effects	Effects on cerebral oxygen or glucose metabolism		Net alteration in cerebral blood flow
		Global	Local	
Acetylcholine	Dilation	No change	Increase (predominantly)	Increase
Dopamine	Dilation	Increase	Increase (predominantly)	Increase
Noradrenaline	Constriction	Increase	—	Increase
Serotonin	Dilation/Constriction	Reduction	Reduction	Reduction
Histamine	Dilation	No effect	—	Increase
GABA	Dilation	Reduction	Reduction	Reduction
VIP	Dilation	Increase	Increase	Increase
Substance P	Dilation	—	—	Increase

GABA - γ-aminobutyric acid; VIP = vasoactive intestival polypeptide.

2. *Myogenic hypothesis* accounts for vasoconstriction (constriction of vessels) in response to hypertension (high blood pressure). An intrinsic property of vascular smooth muscle causes it to contract in response to a rise in pressure. This is also known as the **Bayliss effect.**

A third hypothesis, called the neurogenic hypothesis, postulates that changes in blood vessel diameter are under sympathetic or parasympathetic control. However, autoregulation is preserved when regulation of these inputs is blocked by severing the nerves connecting the blood vessels to the sympathetic and parasympathetic systems. Interfering with these nerves can alter the autoregulatory response, but not prevent it, indicating that autonomic inputs may modulate but not mediate the adjustments made in response to changes in blood pressure.

Input to the autoregulatory mechanisms can arise from diverse sources. Venous pressure, CSF pressure, and pressure related specifically to CO_2 levels can all effect autoregulation. For instance, you could hyperventilate (absorb more O_2 and expel more CO_2 than normal) until you felt dizzy, which could eventually lead to a loss of consciousness. This is partly due to vasoconstriction in response to decreases in blood CO_2 concentration. In contrast, changes in arterial O_2 levels have little effect on cerebral blood flow. Only very low or very high levels of O_2 will produce autoregulatory effects. Cerebral arterioles are, however, sensitive to changes in pH of surrounding extracellular fluid (metabolite concentration, which in turn is influenced by CO_2 levels). There are limits to the ability of the vessels to autoregulate. For example, at very high blood pressure, there is forced dilation of the cerebral vessels, and a condition known as hypertensive encephalopathy results. On the other hand, during extreme hypotension (low blood pressure), signs of cerebral hypoxia become evident. Neurotransmitters are also known to have effects on cerebral blood flow (Table 14–2). Some of the effects are indirect, resulting from the direct changes the transmitters produce on metabolism. For instance, norepinephrine and dopamine (by stimulating metabolism) and serotonin (5-HT) and GABA (by decreasing cell metabolism) indirectly affect blood flow. Other transmitters, such as peptides, are capable of acting directly on arterioles as vasoconstrictors (e.g., vasopressin) or vasodilators (e.g., Substance P).

Blood Supply and Anoxia

Several major arteries supply blood to the brains of most mammals (Figure 14–4). Internal **carotid arteries** merge with the **basilar artery** (formed by junction of two *vertebral arteries*) and give rise to the **circle of Willis.** This elegant design insures that blood will continue to be supplied throughout the brain even if blood flow from one of the major arteries is cut off through an event such as a stroke or physical trauma.

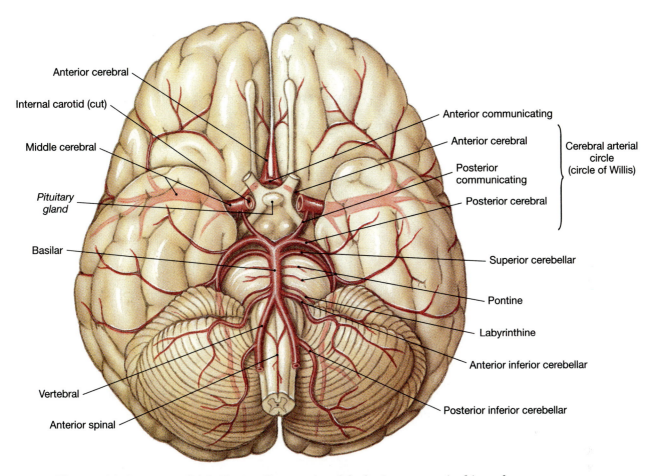

Figure 14–4 *Arteries of the Brain.* The arteries of the brain are organized in such an intricate manner so that if blood supply from one of the major arteries is severed, the brain will continue receiving blood. The major arteries that supply blood to the brain are the internal carotid arteries and the basilar artery.

In medical crises, such as cardiac arrest in which blood flow is stopped, damage to the brain occurs earliest and is most decisive in determining the degree of recovery. Consciousness is lost seconds after oxygen delivery stops, although residual oxygen in the lungs and circulating blood can retard the onset of brain damage during **anoxia** (no blood O_2) or **asphyxia** (low blood O_2). Circulation failure to the brain results in nerve cell death within five minutes. During such an interruption of blood flow, a complex series of changes is triggered: Lactate builds up inside the cell, which lowers brain pH; the modest energy charge stored as ATP and phosphocreatine is depleted; GABA secretion begins to increase; and free fatty acid levels rise, exposing cells to energy depletion. Ionic changes also occur along with amino acid alterations; extracellular potassium increases, the amino acid excitatory neurotransmitters glutamate and aspartate are released, and calcium enters and overstimulates cells already depleted of energy. The calcium entry also initiates

degradative processes that result in membrane breakdown (Figure 14–5). The absence of glucose is equally destructive, but the time course to irreversible damage from hypoglycemia (low blood sugar) is longer because other substrates such as ketone bodies can be used in place of glucose for a short time.

Energy Use

In addition to oxygen, the exclusive and highly positive arteriovenous difference for glucose indicates that the net energy made available to the brain is ultimately derived from the oxidation of this sugar. This is the situation under normal circumstances; as noted earlier, other substrates (such as ketone bodies and local glycogen stores) may be used in extreme circumstances. Why does the brain need so much energy? The high requirement of nervous tissue is probably related to energy demands for transmitter synthesis, packaging, secretion, uptake, and sequestration; for

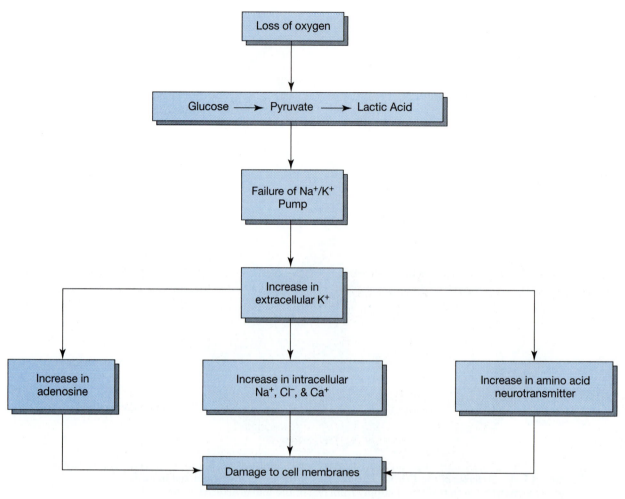

Figure 14–5 *Effects of Circulation Failure on the Brain.* If blood flow to the brain is interrupted, a complex series of changes occurs, which cause nerve cell death within five minutes. The loss of oxygen causes lactate to build up within the cells. This toxic buildup leads to the failure of the sodium/potassium pump, which in turn causes an increase in extracellular potassium. This leads to an increase in intracellular calcium, which overstimulates the nerve cells and further depletes them of energy, while also leading to membrane breakdown. Consequently, nerve cell death occurs.

ion pumping to maintain ionic gradients; for intracellular transport; and for synthesis of complex lipids and macromolecules in both neuronal and glial cells. But by far the vast majority of energy is utilized in maintaining ionic gradients: It is estimated that 25 to 50 percent of brain energy utilization is related to Na, K-ATPase activity (Box 14–1). Na, K-ATPase functions in the Na$^+$–K$^+$ exchange pump which, as you saw in Chapter 3, is essential for maintaining ion gradients.

Cooling Mechanisms

The very high rate of metabolism in the brain results in the production of large amounts of heat. Mammalian brains are dependent upon stable temperatures for normal function. For example, in humans a rise in body temperature from 98.6° to 107° F can result in convulsions, hallucinations, permanent neural damage, and death. Various homeostatic mechanisms have evolved to insure that the temperature of the brain will remain low enough for normal activity. In all mammals, cool arterial blood serves to dissipate excess brain heat. Carnivores and some hoofed mammals such as camels, cows, and goats have developed a special organ for heat dissipation. The *rete mirabile* ("wonderful net"), a tangle of small arteries in the cavernous sinus (a reservoir of venous blood at the base of the brain), works as a heat exchanger. In animals that do not sweat, this system, which brings blood

Box 14–1

How Bright Is the Light Bulb?

The brain does not do mechanical work, like that of cardiac or skeletal muscle, or osmotic work, as the kidney does in concentrating urine. Instead, nervous tissue is continuously active in producing electrical activity mainly through synaptic excitation, inhibition, and action potential conduction. The electrical energy is ultimately derived from chemical processes, and the majority of the brain's energy consumption is used for maintaining ionic gradients to sustain and restore the membrane potentials after excitation and inhibition have occurred. You may have heard the argument that humans are undeveloped organisms because we "only use 20 percent of our brain." It was certainly not an electrophysiologist who originated this rumor! If brain cells are not active (maintaining this electrical gradient is an active process), they die. Therefore, according to some measures at least, your brain is working at 100 percent of its capacity all the time. What you do with all of that energy is up to you!

A colloquial view equates concentrated mental effort (thinking) with mental work (energy consumption). It has been suggested that complex problem solving in areas like mathematics involves a high demand for mental activity. However, there appears to be no increased energy utilization by the brain during such processes. Total cerebral blood flow and oxygen consumption remain unchanged during the exertion of mental effort. It is possible that the areas that participate in the processes of mental effort or reasoning may represent too small a fraction of the brain for changes in their functional and metabolic activities to be reflected in the energy metabolism of the brain as a whole.

On the other hand, correlations between cerebral metabolic rate and mental activity have been obtained in humans in a variety of pathological states involving brain damage (not comparable to mental effort in normal people). Regardless of the cause of the disorder, graded reductions in cerebral oxygen consumption are accompanied by parallel graded reductions in the degree of mental activity, all the way to extreme cases such as coma.

Oxygen is utilized in the brain almost entirely for the oxidation of carbohydrates. The energy equivalent of the total cerebral metabolic rate is approximately 0.25 kcal/min. This energy is used mostly for the ATP-consuming sodium/potassium pump (see Chapter 3). Thus, if it is assumed that the bulk of brain energy is utilized for the synthesis of high-energy phosphate bonds, that the efficiency of the energy conservation is approximately 20 percent, and that the free energy of hydrolysis of the terminal phosphate of ATP is approximately 7 kcal/mol, then the energy expenditure can be estimated to support the steady turnover of close to 7 mmol of ATP per minute in the entire human brain. On average, half the terminal phosphate groups of ATP turn over in approximately three seconds; in certain regions, turnover is probably considerably faster. We are all familiar with the cartoon character who gets an idea, represented as a light bulb above the head. Well, in spite of the fact that the brain is using more blood and oxygen than other organs, this energy consumption is modest in physical terms. If a light bulb did represent our brain energy usage it would burn all the time, whether we had an idea or not, and would be rated at about 25 watts, duller than the bulbs found in the cheapest motels.

cooled through evaporation in the muzzle to the labyrinthine carotid net, enables the brain to stay cool with a minimum of water expenditure.

In humans, an entirely different system protects the brain from overheating. Two alternate pathways for blood coming from the face and scalp provide opportunities for heat to be conserved or given off. Blood can return directly through the external jugular vein or by a more circuitous path (Figure 14–6). In this second pathway through an arterial structure

called the *carotid rete* in the sinuses, cooled blood is shunted from the skin surface through the braincase (inside of the skull) and helps to cool the brain. With increases in body temperature, a person's face will flush as arteries dilate, cooling blood through sweat evaporation (an effect also seen in blushing upon emotional stimuli). This cooler blood enters meningeal veins and sinuses of the dura mater via emissary veins. From these sites it flows in surface veins, removing heat from the brain so that by the time the blood leaves the

Figure 14–6 *Major Veins of the Head and Neck.* The temperature of the blood flowing through the brain is regulated as the blood flows through the brain and scalp. Blood can successfully be cooled by evaporation as it flows close to the surface of the face, thus cooling the brain.

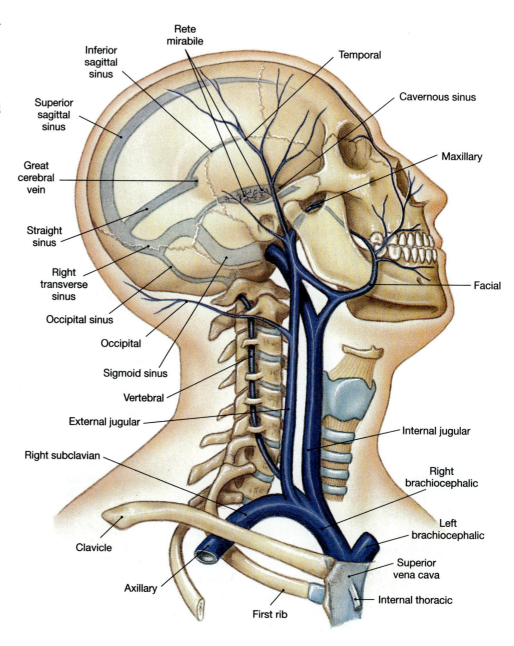

skull in the internal jugular vein, it is warmer than the arterial blood supply.

Techniques for Studying Brain Activity

How do we go about studying brain metabolism? In vitro studies have limited use in examining potential rather than actual performance, because the techniques involved are likely to grossly alter metabolic activity as they rely on an interruption in the structural and functional integrity of the network. Valid identification of normally used substrates and products of cerebral energy metabolism, as well as reliable estimations of their rates of utilization and production, can only be obtained in the intact organism. The simplest way to study the metabolism of the CNS in vivo is to correlate spontaneous or experimentally produced alterations in the chemical composition of the blood, CSF, or both with changes in cerebral physiological functions or gross CNS-mediated behavior. Such methods first demonstrated the need for glucose as a substrate for cerebral energy metabolism since glucose deprivation induced unconsciousness. Hypoglycemia produced by insulin or other means was shown to alter cerebral function in ways that could only be restored to normal by the administration of glucose.

The availability of better analytical chemical techniques makes it possible to measure specific metabolites and enzyme activities in brain tissue at selected times during or after exposure of the animal to an experimental condition. These methods have enabled the estimation of rates of flux through the various steps of known metabolic pathways as well as the identification of control points in the pathways where regulation may be exerted. For example, specific glucose metabolites can be examined with radioactive tracers. This method requires that the animal be sacrificed and the tissue analyzed before any changes occur. One difficulty with this method is that post-mortem changes are extremely rapid and cannot always be prevented even when the tissue is analyzed immediately.

Another technique involves administering radioactive precursors and sometime later removing the brain and isolating and evaluating the products of the radioactive precursor. This method is particularly effective in studies of neurotransmitter synthesis and metabolism, lipid metabolism, protein synthesis, and distribution of glucose carbon through various pathways. For instance, Sokoloff et al. (1977) developed a method to follow the transport of glucose across the BBB into the brain and its incorporation into the metabolic cycle (Figure 14–7). The basis of the method is that a nonnatural analog of glucose, 2-deoxyglucose (2-DG), is transported in the same way as glucose across the blood-brain barrier. However, once within the cell it cannot be metabolized as well as glucose. Quantitative autoradiography (measurement of the use or binding of a substance in a brain region) is done with a radioactive form of 2-DG, 2-deoxy-D-^{14}C-glucose (^{14}C-DG). The ^{14}C-labeled compound is injected, and after thirty to forty five minutes have elapsed to allow uptake of all the substrate, the brain is removed, and sections are autoradiographed on X-ray film. The autoradiograms are pictorial representations of the relative rates of glucose utilization in all the structural components of the brain. With knowledge of the final concentration of the isotope in the various sections of the brain and the original level of the isotope in the blood, an estimate of cerebral metabolic rate for glucose can be obtained. We will make use of such metabolic measurements when we discuss human neurobiology in Chapter 16. For now, let's see what these methods have taught us about control of body energy by the brain.

Eating

Eating, or feeding, is the process of absorbing the energy necessary to sustain life through the medium of food (energy whose ultimate source is the sun.) The desire to begin eating is controlled by a person's appetite, whereas the motivational state that terminates eating is satiety.

As I am sure you know from personal experience, eating behavior involves many variables. External influences such as time of day, odorific cues, and other environmental factors contribute to eating behavior, as do internal influences, such as hunger. Neuroscientists interested in feeding have attempted to understand what the CNS is monitoring when hunger occurs and what brain or endocrine responses result from this input. Many theorists investigate ingestive behavior in terms of energy homeostasis. For instance, when the sympathetic nervous system is active, energy is being used, and when the parasympathetic system is active, energy is being stored. This information appears to be coupled to neural activity that induces changes in eating behavior. Researchers have found that spontaneous eating is inversely correlated with sympathetic activity. The signals for these changes involve neuroanatomical, neurochemical, and neurophysiological mechanisms.

Homeostasis

Over a hundred years ago Claude Bernard observed that an organism's metabolism was dependent upon the stability of body water, oxygen, temperature, and energy reserves and that "their equilibrium is the result of compensation established as continually and as exactly as if by a very sensitive balance" (1856) Fifty years later, Walter Cannon (1929) first used the term **homeostasis** to describe the maintenance of stability of the internal environment with regard to these and other variables. We have seen how critical constant levels of oxygen and glucose are to the function of the brain. In general, homeostasis is maintained through mechanisms that *evaluate, compare,* and *adjust* particular aspects of function. For all physiological systems there is some optimal level of activity called a **set point**. Mechanisms are in place that continuously monitor the operation of the system and compare it to this optimal level. Observations confirm that body weight is under homeostatic control. For instance, if people or laboratory an-

Figure 14–7 *Autoradiography of 2-Deoxyglucose.* Injection of a radioactive precursor of glucose enables the examination of the path glucose follows when crossing the BBB and the manner in which it is incorporated into the metabolic cycle. See Figure 13–1 for an experimental application of this technique.

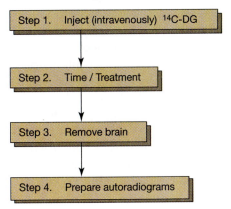

imals either increase or decrease their food intake, there is a concomitant increase or decrease (respectively) in the rate of metabolism. In one study, adult rats were randomly assigned to one of three groups: (a) *chow controls*—those receiving free access to "rat-chow," (b) *obese controls*—free access to a high-fat diet, and (c) *obese cycling*—free access to high-fat diet until obese, then forced to diet, then resumed free access for two cycles of loss and regain. The "dieting" rats lost weight at only half the rate of the chow controls and regained it three times as fast as the controls during the second cycle. By the end of the experiment, obese cycling rats were maintaining the same body weight as the chow controls while consuming significantly less food (Brownell et al., 1986). (In this way dieting by simply eating less can be seen as counterproductive! Dieting, coupled with efforts to increase metabolism, such as exercise, is more likely to be effective.) As we discuss the "appetites" of the brain more specifically, further examples of homeostasis will become evident.

In order to supply adequate amounts of glucose to the brain, the blood itself must be sufficiently furnished with this sugar. The amount of glucose available for energy utilization is an example of a physiological state that is regulated through complex homeostatic mechanisms. Neural output controlling ingestion is modulated by a variety of inputs involving set points in both central and peripheral activity. In order to examine specific mechanisms implicated in feeding behavior, it is first helpful to understand some of the basics of energy metabolism.

Ultimately, fuel for brain work comes from the food we eat, but there are several important steps that must take place after a meal before nutrients are available to the brain. During the **absorptive phase** of digestion, when food is present in the digestive tract, the level of glucose in the blood begins to rise. This is due to the fact that this is the metabolic phase during which the body is operating on the energy from a recently consumed meal and is storing the excess as body fat, glycogen, and proteins. As the increase in glucose levels is detected by the brain, changes in the activity of the autonomic nervous system are induced (a decrease in sympathetic, and increase in parasympathetic activity), which stimulate the pancreas to secrete the hormone **insulin**. This enables the glucose to be taken by cells and used as an immediate energy source. Extra glucose goes first to fill carbohydrate stores as glycogen and finally into storage as fat (Figure 14–8).

Glucose is converted to **glycogen** in the presence of insulin. Glycogen is a complex carbohydrate that is stored in the cells of the liver and also (in very limited amounts) in the brain and muscles to be used during bursts of activity. As glucose levels begin to decline following the absorptive phase, changes occur that are indicative of the **fasting phase**, during

which energy is extracted from fat and glycogen stores. The pancreas stops secreting insulin and begins secreting **glucagon**. Glucagon is another peptide hormone. It converts glycogen back into glucose and also promotes the breakdown of fat into free fatty acids. During the fasting phase, the brain is supplied with glucose from glycogen stores located in the liver, while the rest of the body gets its energy elsewhere.

The reason for the difference in the main source of energy between nervous tissue and other tissue has to do with the relative abilities of cells to absorb glucose. One of the unique features of CNS tissue is its ability to utilize glucose in the absence of insulin. In order to use glucose, cells other than nervous tissue require insulin to alter the permeability of cell membranes and make them receptive to the flow of glucose. Since insulin is only present during the absorptive phase, other cells of the body must get their energy from other sources when food is not in the digestive tract. This energy source is from fat stores.

Role of Glucose in Eating Behavior

The **glucostatic theory** proposes that it is the level of blood glucose that controls eating behavior. Blood glucose levels are monitored by receptors in the hypothalamus that trigger the initiation or cessation of eating. Given the dependence of the brain on glucose, this idea seems both attractive and simplistic at first glance. Unfortunately, it does not explain a number of phenomena, such as increased appetite in diabetics. The most prevalent form of diabetes, *diabetes mellitus,* is characterized by an insulin deficiency. This leads to abnormally high levels of blood glucose, which according to the glucostatic theory should preclude any motivation to eat. This is not the case. In fact diabetics are often prone to **hyperphagia**, which is an abnormal increase in appetite. This theory has since been revised and, while still largely accepted, now focuses on glucose levels in the cells, not in the blood.

Investigations into the role of glucose in the control of appetite and satiety have shown that food-deprived animals given glucose injections into the hepatic portal vein (which leads to the liver) will not eat. In contrast, glucose injections in the jugular vein (which leads to the brain) do not affect the animals' hunger, and they eat as expected. From these findings researchers have concluded that cells in the liver monitor glucose levels and provide this information to the brain (Russek, 1971). This information from the liver is carried via the vagus nerve to the **lateral hypothalamus (LH)**, one area of the hypothalamus associated with hunger (Figure 14–9). Despite the fact that injecting glucose into the hepatic portal vein of the liver terminates hunger, if the vagal input to the liver is severed, eating still occurs. This indicates that liver signals are not the only initiators of eating.

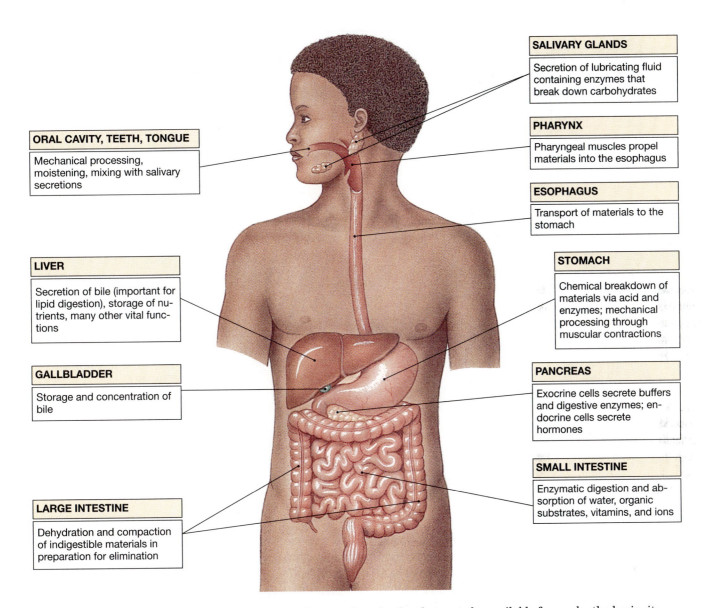

ORAL CAVITY, TEETH, TONGUE

Mechanical processing, moistening, mixing with salivary secretions

LIVER

Secretion of bile (important for lipid digestion), storage of nutrients, many other vital functions

GALLBLADDER

Storage and concentration of bile

LARGE INTESTINE

Dehydration and compaction of indigestible materials in preparation for elimination

SALIVARY GLANDS

Secretion of lubricating fluid containing enzymes that break down carbohydrates

PHARYNX

Pharyngeal muscles propel materials into the esophagus

ESOPHAGUS

Transport of materials to the stomach

STOMACH

Chemical breakdown of materials via acid and enzymes; mechanical processing through muscular contractions

PANCREAS

Exocrine cells secrete buffers and digestive enzymes; endocrine cells secrete hormones

SMALL INTESTINE

Enzymatic digestion and absorption of water, organic substrates, vitamins, and ions

Figure 14–8 *Components of the Digestive System.* In order for glucose to be available for use by the brain, it first must be consumed in the form of food. Glucose levels in the blood begin to rise when food is present in the digestive tract. This increase in glucose levels is detected by the body, which stimulates the pancreas to secrete insulin.

The lateral hypothalamus also contains receptors capable of measuring blood glucose levels directly, which seem to act cooperatively with glucose receptors located in the liver. Experimenters have found that injections of glucose into the hepatic portal vein affect the receptors in the lateral hypothalamus (Shimizu et al., 1983). Therefore, current theory holds that these overlapping systems monitor levels of glucose and can either independently or cooperatively affect behavior. Glucose utilization is not the only event that receptors in these areas can measure. Administrations of

mannose, fructose, and ketone bodies also result in a decrease of food intake, indicating that the relevant chemoreceptors detect metabolic utilization of various fuels, not just glucose. Since fructose cannot cross the BBB, this data also establishes a role for peripheral mechanisms in the detection of sugar levels.

How is the lateral hypothalamus affected by this input? Initially researchers thought that stimulation of the lateral hypothalamus made animals hungry, but closer scrutiny determined that although animals ate more, their responses

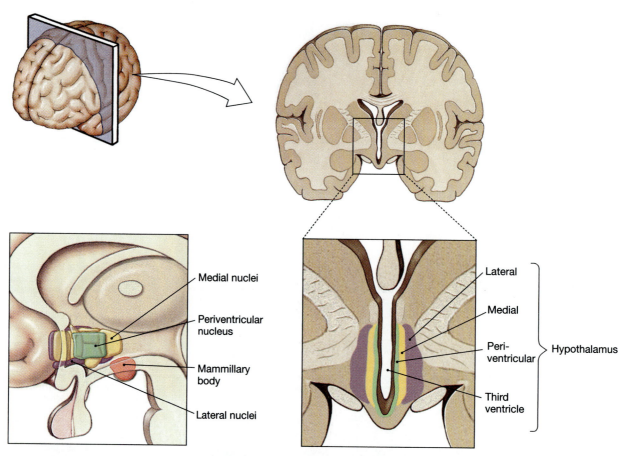

Figure 14–9 *Zones of the Hypothalamus.* The lateral area of the hypothalamus is associated with hunger.

were not congruent with an increase in hunger. For instance, animals stimulated in the lateral hypothalamus appear particularly focused on *sensory* qualities of food and will self-stimulate this area in order to acquire the smell or sight of food even in the absence of food. Why would rats find stimulation rewarding if it made them hungry and they could not satisfy that drive? One possibility is that stimulation of the lateral hypothalamus results in a pleasurable sensory experience. Berridge and Valenstein (1991) investigated this possibility by observing taste reactions during electrical stimulation of the lateral hypothalamus. Their findings did not support this hypothesis. Rats' reactions following lateral hypothalamus stimulation were more indicative of an aversive, rather than a pleasurable experience. They suggest that electrical stimulation of the lateral hypothalamus potentiates the value of external stimuli in such a way that these stimuli acquire enhanced incentive value in reward systems (see Chapter 11).

Role of Lipids in Eating Behavior

We mentioned that excess glucose is first stored in carbohydrate form as glycogen and, once those stores are "full," is then converted to fat. Fats are stored in adipose tissue as **triglycerides**, composed of one glycerol molecule and three fatty acids (Figure 14–10). During the fasting phase an increase in sympathetic activity to adipose tissue, the pancreas, and the adrenal medulla results in the breakdown of triglycerides. The fatty acids are then directly metabolized by all cells, except the brain, which is further supplied with glucose from the conversion of glycerol in the liver.

The **lipostatic theory**, which is not directly incompatible with the glucostatic theory, suggests that eating behavior is regulated by mechanisms that act to maintain an ideal (set point) weight. Since weight is largely a reflection of the amount of body fat a person has, this theory attempts to explain eating on the basis of fat stores in adipose tissue. Researchers have shown that food intake is also affected by the metabolism of fatty acids. When glucose sources are reduced, the result is an increased dependence on fat sources and vice versa. When carbohydrate depletion is coupled with an inability to utilize fats (produced by the chemical *methyl palmoxitrate,* which prevents their metabolism) an increase in food intake results, indicating that, in the absence of carbo-

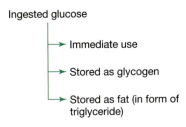

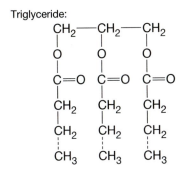

Figure 14–10 *Utilization of Glucose.* Glucose enters the body once carbohydrates are ingested. Excess glucose is then stored in carbohydrate form as glycogen. Once these stores are full, the remaining glucose is stored in the form of fat. Fat is stored in adipose tissues as triglycerides. In order to be metabolized by cells, triglycerides must first be broken down into fatty acids. This is done by the pancreas and adrenal medulla.

hydrates, alterations in fatty acid metabolism are sufficient to stimulate eating, and lending support to the idea of lipostatic regulation of eating behavior.

Hypothalamic Circuits

Historically, eating behavior was understood in terms of activity in two nuclei of the hypothalamus. The lateral hypothalamus has been called the hunger center since all mammals respond to stimulation of the lateral hypothalamus by eating. Stimulation of an adjacent area, the **ventromedial hypothalamus (VMH)**, produces a decrease in food intake. Researchers speculated that these areas worked alternately to yield increases and decreases in food intake, and studies seemed to support this contention (Figure 14–11). Lesions in the lateral hypothalamus result in an enhanced breakdown of fat stores by the release of glucagon from the pancreas, it stimulates the digestion of triglycerides in the body's fat tissue creating free fatty acids, and consequently provides an increase in free fatty acids in the blood. This mechanism underlies the profound decrease in eating observed with lateral hypothalamus lesions and further supports the contention that fat levels are homeostatically regulated when the lateral hypothalamus is intact (see Figure 14–11). Other effects of lateral hypothalamus lesions on eating are not as clear-cut.

For instance, the prolonged period of aphagia (the complete cessation of eating) seen after lateral hypothalamus lesions appears to ensue from destruction of dopaminergic neurons ascending through the lateral hypothalamus; this results in a decrease in overall cerebral arousal, which inhibits all voluntary behaviors, not just feeding.

Lesions of the VMH also result in dramatic weight change, although the mechanisms for this are not as clearly delineated. Teitelbaum (1955) noted two stages in the changes in body size after VMH lesions. In the initial *dynamic phase*, animals eat incessantly, sometimes tripling their body weight. The resulting obesity is maintained during the *static phase*, when weight gain is not so dramatic. Observations of the truly dramatic changes in weight led to assumptions that animals with lesions in the VMH could never be sated. This does not appear to be the case. Teitelbaum conducted experiments in which rats were induced to eat more (and gain even more weight) after entering the static phase. When these animals were again allowed to regulate their own intake freely, they returned to the weight they were after the initial, dynamic change in weight. He observed that the animal's behavior seemed to reflect a new, higher set point for weight, and hypothesized that the activity of the VMH is modulated by body weight to control eating.

More recent investigations have shed light on some of the mechanisms involved in these changes. Duggan and Booth (1986) hypothesize that a decrease in satiety resulting from a speedup in gastric emptying causes VMH obesity. Indeed, vagotomy (which abolishes the autonomic input to the stomach and causes gastric emptying to cease) has sometimes been shown to reverse obesity in VMH-lesioned subjects. Other studies suggest that this obesity is at least partly the re-

Figure 14–11 *Summary of Effects from Lateral Hypothalamic Lesions.* These ablations decrease eating.

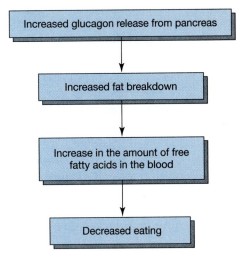

sult of changes in metabolism. For instance, lesioned animals that are pair-fed with unlesioned controls (yoked to receive the same amount of food), or restricted to their preoperative caloric intake, often display abnormal weight gain. VMH lesions result in hyperinsulinemia (elevated release and plasma levels of insulin), which retards the breakdown of fat, augments fat storage, and makes organisms chronically hungry (see King & Frohman, 1982, for a detailed discussion). Increased levels of insulin have been noted as early as twenty minutes after VMH lesions (Berthoud & Jeanrenaud, 1979), and animals often begin eating large meals before they are even fully recovered from the anesthesia (Becker & Kissileff, 1974).

Researchers have been investigating the relationship between the VMH and adipose thermogenesis (heat production by adipose fat tissue) in recent years (Amir, 1990; Amir & De Blasio, 1991). There are two classes of adipose tissue: brown adipose tissue and white adipose tissue. White adipose tissue makes up our long-term energy stores, while brown adipose tissue serves a special function in heat production. Brown adipose cells are mitochondrial-rich and produce *nonshivering thermogenesis* when fuel is broken down. (It is the high density of mitochondria that gives the tissue its brown appearance. These mitochondria generate heat instead of ATP.) The cells are stimulated by the hypothalamus (including the VMH, paraventricular nucleus, posterior, suprachiasmatic, preoptic, and supraoptic nuclei) to become active after feeding and produce a rise in temperature. They also function in the production of heat during cold by adjusting the efficiency of energy utilization in response to levels of body fat. Thermogenesis is regulated by the sympathetic nervous system. One cause of obesity appears to implicate a decreased ability of brown adipose cells to produce heat. VMH-lesioned animals demonstrate an impairment in the expression of nonshivering thermogenesis. Amir and De Blasio found that this effect was stimulated by NE and blocked by insulin administration in the VMH.

The precise etiology of the behavioral and physiological disturbances in VMH-lesioned animals has remained elusive despite half a century of research. In summary, lesions of the VMH have been shown to produce changes in eating behavior, gastric emptying, insulin secretion, fat mobilization, and thermogenesis (Figure 14–12). It seems likely that the obesity shown in these animals is a result of combinations of these and possibly other effects that will become more clear as research in this area continues. Moreover, the shift from satiety to hunger is no longer thought to result from some ubiquitous metabolic or nutritional deficit, but as a consequence of the widespread changes that result as organisms

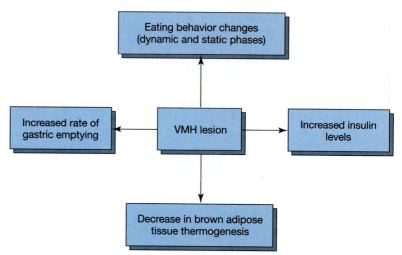

Figure 14–12   *Summary of Effects from Ventromedial Hypothalamic Lesions.* These ablations cause eating behavior to change.

enter the fasting phase from the absorptive phase. It is the decrease in available energy that occurs when metabolism shifts from glucose to free fatty acids that signals hunger and results in eating behavior (Stricker & Verbalis, 1990).

Role of Monoamines and Peptide Hormones in Feeding

In addition to those already discussed, many other substances are known to affect eating behavior. Of these, the monoamines norepinephrine (NE), serotonin (5-HT), and dopamine (DA) have been shown to play critical roles. NE inhibits the activity of certain satiety-producing cells. Researchers studied these effects in rats given access to sweetened milk after injecting either saline or NE in the paraventricular nucleus (PVN). Rats injected with NE ingested over three times as much as those injected with saline (Matthews et al., 1986). On the other hand, 5-HT appears to be implicated in producing satiety; it is released from the lateral hypothalamus following food ingestion and if microinjected into the hypothalamus can produce a satiety effect. DA in the LH has also been shown to suppress food intake, and dopamine agonists such as amphetamine and cocaine are known **anorectics** (appetite suppressants). The mechanisms underlying these actions are still being worked out but appear to result from dopamine's activity on limbic structures.

Peptide hormones also serve to modulate food intake. **Neuropeptide Y (NPY)** appears to induce physiological changes that increase food appetite by interacting with another peptide (*galanin*) and corticosterone (see Box 14–2). Dynorphin, an endorphin (see Chapter 11), also appears to increase the tendency to eat by increasing feeding reward. Investigations indicate that intracerebroventricular administration of hypo-thalamic *growth hormone–releasing factor* stimulates food intake in both food-deprived and nondeprived rats, suggesting that this hormone may also be involved in modulating feeding behavior (Vaccarino & Hayward, 1988). Other peptides such as *bombesin* and *neurotensin* contribute to satiety. For instance, neurotensin injected into the PVN produces a decrease in food intake. Cholecystokinin (CCK) has also been implicated in the production of satiety (see Box 14–3).

Eating Disorders

Obesity

Eating disorders are very prevalent in our society and pose serious health problems. According to recent surveys of U.S. adults, about 30 percent are significantly overweight, 12 percent being grossly so (Brownell & Rodin, 1994). The incidence of eating disorders is continuing to rise. Each of the behavioral disorders (obesity, anorexia, and bulimia) arise through complex interactions of sociocultural, psychological, and biological factors; current research addresses influences from all of these areas. For the purposes of this review, the focus will be on the biological influences on behavior that are caused by these disorders.

The underlying mechanisms of obesity are probably as varied externally and internally as the mediators of eating behavior discussed so far. One theory proposes that some people are prone to high levels of insulin, which also promotes the buildup of fat. Food is stored as fat rather than utilized, which reduces the amount of available energy. To compensate for this relative "deprivation" of energy, organisms seek more food. In other words, some people may not be fat because they eat too much, but eat too much because they are fat. Thus obesity, while commonly classified as an eating disorder, could in this context be considered a metabolic disorder.

The discussion of hypothalamic influences on eating and satiety might lead us to hypothesize that overweight people have different homeostatic responses for these behaviors (Figure 14–13). Animal research and common sense suggest that either a decreased sensitivity in the VMH or hyperresponsivity following LH input would result in weight gain. Some of the changes in metabolism in obese subjects are surely due to weight cycling resulting from dieting. With each cycle of restricted food intake (dieting) followed by periods of nondieting, weight was lost more slowly and gained more rapidly.

Another cause of obesity may involve alterations in the levels of opioid peptides produced within the body. Elevated levels of endorphins have been found in genetically obese rats (Margules et al., 1978) and have stimulated food intake when injected into the VMH of sated rats (Grandison & Guidotti, 1977). Further, the opioid antagonist naloxone has been

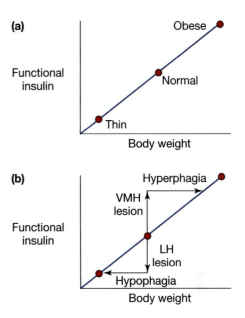

Figure 14–13 *Some Biological Underpinnings for Obesity.* (a) Diagrammatic relationship between functional insulin and body weight: Increased insulin levels promote the buildup of fat, thus food is stored as fat, which decreases the amount of available energy, thus causing the need to ingest more food. (b) Diagrammatic relationship between functional insulin and body weight following lesions of the VMH and the ventrolateral hypothalamic nuclei.

shown to decrease food intake in deprived rats, to abolish the overeating of genetically obese rats (Holtzman, 1974), and to lead to weight loss when administered in humans (Hollister et al., 1981).

Anorexia Nervosa

Anorexia nervosa is a condition characterized by severe self-starvation accompanied by other psychological disturbances and affecting 1 to 2 percent of the population, more prevalently among women (Musnam & Smolak, 1997). In addition to dramatic weight loss (25 percent of original body weight) by self-starvation, self-induced **emesis** (vomiting), excessive exercise, or abuse of laxatives, patients generally exhibit an intense fear of becoming fat and a distortion of perceived body size. Anorexia nervosa is currently most common in teenage females, although about one in ten cases is male. The effects of the disease are grave: 10 percent of anorexic patients never recover and die from medical complications due to chronic malnutrition.

Anorexia is frequently accompanied by amenorrhea (cessation of menstruation) in females, and in males there can be a loss of sexual potency. Because of these disturbances in sexual function, along with alterations in water regulation and temperature control, many of the biological theories focus on

Box 14–2

A Role for Insulin in the Brain

Until relatively recently is was thought that insulin was unable to cross the BBB and therefore did not affect the CNS. However, in the late 1970s insulin and insulin receptors were found to be present in neural tissue. In the past few years, a growing body of evidence has pointed to the idea that brain insulin comes from the periphery and crosses the BBB with the aid of a specialized transport system. The search is on to find a function for this hormone in the brain! Much of current investigation focuses on insulin's supposed role in energy metabolism.

As humans (and other mammals) evolved, their energy (food) supplies were alternately abundant and scarce. This variation in the availability of food necessitated the evolution of homeostatic mechanisms to maintain energy stores (fat) to carry people through the periods of scarcity. As we have seen, the CNS plays an important role in maintaining energy stores in adipose tissue, through changes in metabolic activity. Experiments in which animals are over- or underfed support the hypothesis that fat stores are regulated by homeostatic mechanisms that affect food intake and energy use. This is partly why it is so difficult to lose weight and keep it off by dieting. In fact, about 95 percent of dieters eventually return to their prediet weight. (You should be consoled: It is also difficult to gain weight since increases in caloric intake are met by altered feeding practices and enhanced energy expenditure through sympathetic activation.)

The existence of CNS controls for this regulation had been hypothesized as early as the 1930s, but an exact mechanism has remained elusive despite much research. In a paper by Schwartz, Figlewicz, Baskin, Woods, and Porte (1993) the hypothesis that insulin is such a signal to the CNS is reviewed. In addition, insulin uptake from plasma into the CSF has been documented following either a meal or intravenous administration of glucose. This appears to be secondary to insulin entry into the brain, which occurs via a specialized transport system across the BBB. The hypothalamus has a dense population of insulin receptors, and when very small quantities of insulin are injected there, food intake is reduced. Even better support for a physiological role in which CNS insulin suppresses food intake comes from studies using antibodies directed against insulin. When insulin antibodies are injected into the hypothalamus, increased food intake and weight gain results.

How does CNS insulin affect food intake? One theory centers around its interactions with neuropeptide Y (NPY). NPY is synthesized in the arcuate nucleus of the hypothalamus, which projects to other hypothalamic nuclei including the paraventricular nucleus. Centrally administered NPY increases feeding. Further, the production and release of NPY is controlled, at least in part, by the energy state of the animal. In rats, for instance, food deprivation results in an increase of NPY in these areas; the level of NPY returns to normal after the rats eat. Importantly, the presence of insulin is negatively correlated with the amount of hypothalamic messenger RNA encoding NPY; in other words, the more insulin present, the less NPY coded for by

alterations in hypothalamic function. One of the obvious difficulties in interpreting such research is recognizing whether the abnormalities that occur are the cause of starvation or its consequences. Interestingly, as many as 25 percent of female cases develop amenorrhea and display low levels of reproductive hormones prior to significant weight loss. Further, patients often do not resume menstruation once they return to their predisease weights. These two pieces of evidence suggest that alterations in hypothalamic activity may precede anorexia. High cortisol levels in anorexics, which are probably the result of a hypersecretion of CRH (corticotropin-releasing hormone) are also indicative of hypothalamic influences. There are also disturbances in thermoregulation, levels of thyroid and gonadotropin hormones, and vasopressin, but these alterations appear to be a result of weight loss rather than a cause. The fact that many patients with anorexia nervosa also fulfill diagnostic criteria for depression, and in some cases appear to respond to treatment with antidepressants, suggests a possible relationship between anorexia and affective disorders (see Chapter 18).

The involvement of monoamine neurotransmitters in anorexia has been investigated extensively. Leibowitz (1986)

the messenger RNA in the hypothalamus.

Schwartz et al. (1993) suggest that an insulin deficiency induced by fasting would cause an increase in NPY and therefore result in feeding. They found that intracerebroventricular administration of insulin during food deprivation prevented the fasting-induced increase of NPY in the paraventricular nucleus. The paraventricular nucleus has a role in activating thermogenesis by brown adipose tissue via sympathetic pathways. Insulin in the paraventricular nucleus promotes this thermogenesis, and NPY appears to play a role as well. Administration of NPY into the paraventricular nucleus suppresses sympathetic outflow to brown adipose tissue, and reduces thermogenesis in this manner.

In summary, this research suggests a model in which central insulin regulates energy homeostasis (see figure). Caloric deprivation is responsible for a decrease in circulating insulin and, thus, a decrease in CNS insulin levels.

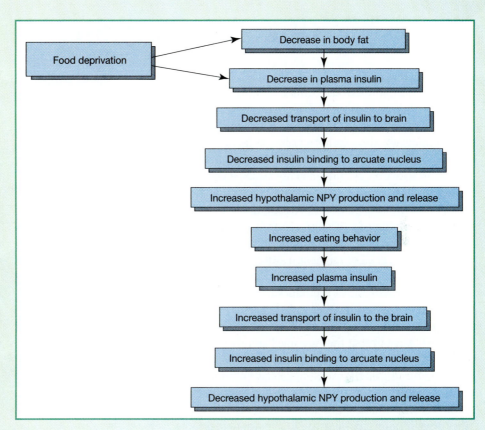

This results in enhanced expression and release of NPY from the paraventricular nucleus. This peptide stimulates food intake, and may also suppress sympathetic activity (and brown adipose tissue thermogenesis). With food ingestion, insulin is again present, NPY effects are diminished, and energy consumption increases.

has shown that norepinephrine injected into the hypothalamus stimulates animals to eat. Norepinephrine metabolites (products of norepinephrine breakdown) have been found to be low in anorexic patients and were found to remain below controls after recovery from anorexia (Kaye et al., 1984).

Bernstein and Borson (1986) suggested a novel explanation for the self-starvation in anorexic patients by noting the similarities between conditioned food aversions and appetite loss in anorexia. In addition, they noted that when rats were made anorexic they also developed specific aversions to a single available diet and suggest that in some disorders, inges-

tion of food produces discomfort, which may act as a signal for the development of taste aversions. For instance, one well-documented form of anorexia develops in patients undergoing treatment for cancer. These treatments often result in nausea, which is readily associated with recent food ingestion (even when patients "know" that treatment is making them feel ill), and a specific dislike for those foods develops. It has been found that roughly 50 percent of chemotherapy patients develop unstable aversions to new and unfamiliar foods. (Some doctors even warn their patients not to eat their favorite foods just before treatment, as the effects of this sort

Box 14–3

CCK: A Satiety Signal?

Wouldn't it be great if we could take a pill to turn off hunger! Besides any personal enthusiasm you might have for such a drug, pharmaceutical companies in the interest of marketing diet aids would be very excited. In the 1950s amphetamine was thought to be such a drug. Before people became aware of the negative side effects it produced (including addiction, seizures, and psychosis) it was widely prescribed. In spite of such negative results, the desirability of having an appetite suppressant for use in weight control has continued to prompt research into this area.

In the 1970s evidence accumulated suggesting that cholecystokinin, or CCK, might be a satiety hormone (i.e., the body's own signal to stop eating). For instance, administration of systemic CCK produced a decrease in food intake, without affecting other ingestive behaviors such as water intake. Further, after CCK administration, rats "appeared" sated in that they groomed and then went to sleep, just as rats do following a meal. Many thought that the key to turning off the eating signal had been found. As it turned out, closer investigation revealed that these observations were indistinguishable from the effects of another drug, lithium chloride (which is known to make rats sick), or from simply interrupting a feeding period by removing the rats' access to food. Deutsch and Hardy (1977) proposed that CCK might disrupt food intake by producing nausea, and many studies seemed to bear this out. For instance, CCK, like lithium chloride, produces **conditioned taste aversion**. Conditioned taste aversion was first described by Garcia and Koelling in 1966 (see figure). They showed that when animals eat a novel food before being made to feel gastrointestinal distress (through drug treatment or radiation) they will subsequently avoid that food. This dislike apparently occurs because the food becomes associated with the discomfort induced by the treatment. If injections of either CCK or lithium chloride are paired

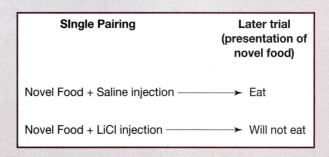

Single Pairing	Later trial (presentation of novel food)
Novel Food + Saline injection ⟶	Eat
Novel Food + LiCl injection ⟶	Will not eat

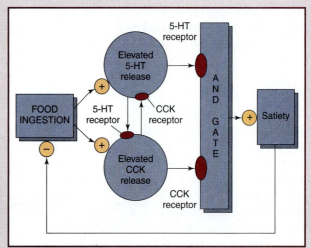

with the ingestion of a novel food, animals will subsequently avoid that food. Administration of CCK or lithium chloride also stimulate oxytocin secretion and a decrease in gastric emptying, which are also known to result from gastrointestinal distress. In humans, effects of CCK administration range from abdominal cramps to nausea and emesis (induced vomiting).

However, CCK has also produced satiety without evidence of nausea. For instance, Figlewicz et al. (1992) found

of learning are probable and persistent, even when concerning foods that the patient is familiar with.) Long-lasting discomfort could engender aversion to a broad range of foods and thereby lead to a global reduction in food intake.

Patients with anorexia nervosa report a high frequency of symptoms like early satiety, gastric discomfort, and spontaneous vomiting of meals. It has not yet been established whether these are consequences of starvation or physiological characteristics of people who later develop anorexia. Even if these symptoms were secondary to starvation, they could provide a basis for aversion learning that would worsen and prolong the anorexia, in part accounting for the dif-

that intracerebroventricular (ICV) injections of CCK caused a decrease in meal size. They suggest that ICV administration of CCK results in a peripheral release of CCK, perhaps via the vagus, and that this endogenous CCK is responsible for inhibiting food intake. In fact, plasma CCK levels are increased following injection of small quantities. Another group has suggested that CCK suppresses feeding by lessening the palatability of food, not by promoting satiety, discomfort, or illness. They note that CCK decreases meal size but does not delay meal onset after brief food deprivation (Ettinger, Thompson & Staddon, 1986). The fact that CCK alters taste preferences without affecting water intake seems to support this contention. It seems that CCK can have varied effects depending upon route of administration, dose, and the specific experimental procedure. Experimenters have noted the value of separating the satiety, palatability, and debilitating effects of CCK.

Recent studies have investigated the effects produced by CCK at different receptors. There are two known CCK receptor types, CCK_A and CCK_B receptors, which were originally described by Moran et al. in 1986, who suggested that CCK_A receptors were found in the gastrointestinal and pancreatic organs and that CCK_B receptors were located in the brain. Experiments using drugs that block these receptors also allow for the identification of effects produced by endogenous CCK (the brain's own peptide). For instance, exogenous (peptide administered as a drug) CCK's effects on food intake are blocked by devazepide (a CCK_A receptor antagonist) but not by L–365, 260 (a CCK_B receptor antagonist) Further, endogenous CCK induces satiety through action at the CCK_A receptor (Dourish et al, 1989; Smith, Tyrka, & Gibbs, 1991), while the neurally mediated behavioral changes indicative of satiety are blocked by CCK_B receptor antagonists. Thus it appears that CCK is acting both peripherally and centrally via different receptor types to produce satiety. The completeness of the evidence for CCK action led researchers to believe that they had found the single agent that controlled satiety.

To make this simple, elegant explanation of satiety production slightly more complex (you should have known!), serotonin (5-HT) receptor antagonists were subsequently found to increase food consumption both centrally and peripherally, and these effects appear to interact with CCK effects. Stallone, Nicolaidis, & Gibbs (1989) found that 5-HT antagonists decreased the reduction in food intake produced by CCK, suggesting that exogenous CCK brings about an increase in brain 5-HT release, which functions to enhance satiety. Conversely, others found that enhanced 5-HT activity may increase endogenous CCK activity resulting in decreased food consumption (Cooper, Dourish, & Barber, 1990). A model of satiety involving these interactions has recently been proposed by Cooper & Dourish (1990) that suggests that both 5-HT and CCK actions function to achieve normal within-meal satiety. The individual effects of each of these endogenous messengers are facilitated by activity of the other; together they cooperate to produce the behavioral changes associated with satiety (see figure).

We can conclude that, although CCK may play a role in satiety, CCK is not the satiety hormone. Current understanding in the field has revealed that our first inclinations were "just too good to be true" and that further investigation will be necessary to understand the role that CCK and other substances play in eating behavior. Lately a new compound, **leptin**, has been associated with obesity in mice (Harris et al., 1998). However, in a manner that parallels the other chapters in the story of the search for a perfect diet remedy, leptin has also failed to live up to its promise as the basis for a chemically enhanced diet technique.

ficulty in treatment, as well as for the high percentage of patients who relapse.

Bulimia

Bulimia has not been investigated for as long as anorexia although recent statistics suggest its incidence to be somewhere between 1 percent and 5 percent among young women in the United States. It is characterized by recurrent compulsive episodes of binge eating (rapid consumption of large quantities of food), a fearful preoccupation with becoming fat, and a practice of behaviors aimed at counteracting the fattening effects of food such as induced vomiting or laxative abuse. Despite these actions, bulimics tend to maintain their normal body weight, with very few fluctuations. Bulimics, like anorexics, are prone to menstrual abnormalities; as many as one-third of normal-weight bulimics display highly erratic menstrual cycles. Also, as with anorexics, these abnormalities are likely to involve hypothalamic irregularities that predate evidence of the pathology. In addition, bulimia does involve several other hazardous consequences, including the fact that repeated use of emetics to induce vomiting can cause poisoning and lead to heart failure. Furthermore, repeated purging can upset the electrolytic balance, affecting heart rhythms and injuring the kidneys, stomach, and esophagus, and even cause a person's teeth to rot.

Monoamines are again hypothesized to be involved. The protein-rich, carbohydrate-poor diet often consumed by dieters is thought to inhibit 5-HT synthesis, which in turn decreases feelings of satiety and induces carbohydrate cravings. This may exacerbate the starve-binge cycle and subsequent counteractive measures experienced by bulimics. Many of the findings concerning the gonadotropins, thyroid hormones, and NE in anorexics are also substantiated in bulimics. Several antidepressants including phenelzine, imipramine, and amitriptyline have shown promising results in treating bulimia. Naltrexone was also found to produce significant decreases in binge episodes in bulimic patients (Jonas & Gold, 1986).

Drinking

When water is consumed by drinking or by eating foods with a high water content (like watermelon), the first event that occurs within the body is a signal that is sent to the brain indicating that thirst has been satisfied. This signal takes a few minutes to reach the brain following the consumption of water. Then the process of water absorption into the blood from the gut occurs over a period ranging from ten to forty minutes. The absorbed water is then distributed throughout the four fluid-filled compartments of the body. The smallest of these portions goes to the cerebrospinal fluid, while the largest amount of this fluid is located within the cells. The remaining fluid is located within the blood and the spaces between cells. The distribution of water among these compartments is delicately regulated by physiological control mechanisms within the body.

Although you could survive for months without eating (by obtaining energy from stored fats), there is no such store for water. In fact, when considering the hierarchy of physiological drives that govern behavior, water is a more basic need than food. Thirst, the desire for water, induces drinking, or the behavior of seeking and consuming water. Only severe pain or oxygen deprivation are more successful at motivating behavior than thirst. Water is necessary in order to help maintain

the chemical balance between cells and their environment. Ion concentrations need to be kept relatively stable in order for all cells to function properly. You have already seen that these concentrations are critical for neural cells to be able to conduct electrical and chemical information. The ionic equilibrium is dependent upon water because of **osmolarity**, the concentration of solutes in a solution (Chapter 3). In fact, the homeostatic mechanisms responsible for maintaining concentration of solutes in the extracellular fluid are so proficient that levels rarely become elevated or reduced by more than 2 percent.

Water is lost through evaporation at the skin surface and mucosal surfaces of the respiratory system, as well as through urination and defecation. Most mammals (including humans) consume more water than is necessary and excrete the excess. Sodium, potassium, and magnesium are also usually obtained in greater amounts than required. For instance, sodium balance can be maintained under normal conditions (in the absence of profuse perspiration) on an intake of less than 17 mmol of salt per day; most people in western cultures consume more than 100 mmol of salt a day. In the sections that follow we will explore the mechanisms for salt and water consumption and excretion.

Thirst

There are two places in the body that water can be found: within cells and outside cells. If there is a water deficit in the extracellular environment, the ionic concentration outside the cell will be higher than the concentration inside the cell (intracellular). This will result in diffusion, as water from inside the cell is pushed (through osmotic force) outside. Alternatively, you could increase the ionic concentration outside the cells without decreasing the amount of water. For instance if you have ever gargled with saltwater to treat a sore throat, or eaten an anchovy pizza, the same results are obtained. The increased concentration of salt ions in the extracellular fluid causes water to diffuse into the extracellular spaces from inside the cells. Anytime there is a water deficit inside the cells a phenomenon called **osmotic thirst** occurs (Figure 14–14a).

It is also possible to lose salt from the extracellular environment. This can happen through perspiration or urination. A low concentration of salt outside the cells forces water to diffuse into the cells, creating a shortage of water outside cells. This produces a different kind of thirst called **volemic thirst** (Figure 14–14b). Volemic thirst can also be produced directly in cases where the entire volume of extracellular fluid, not just the salt level, decreases through blood loss, diarrhea, or vomiting. Both salt and fluid are lost in these instances, and both must be replaced. It is impossible to slake osmotic thirst,

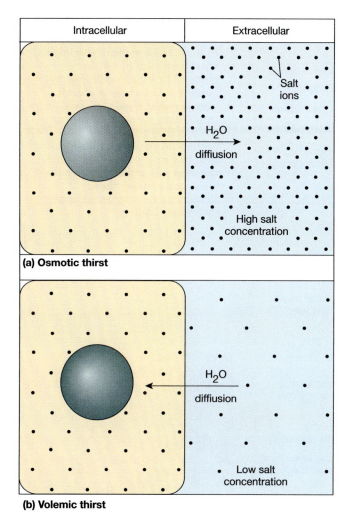

(a) Osmotic thirst

Intracellular | Extracellular

Salt ions

H₂O diffiusion

High salt concentration

(b) Volemic thirst

H₂O diffiusion

Low salt concentration

Figure 14–14 *Thirst.* (a) Osmotic thirst: Loss of intracellular fluid caused by increased concentration of salt ions in the extracellular fluid is detected by osmoreceptors in the hypothalamus. (b) Volemic thirst: A low concentration of salt outside the cells causes water to diffuse into the cells, creating a water shortage in the extracellular environment.

even in extreme cases such as shipwreck, by drinking sea water. Ingesting such high amounts of excess salt temporarily alleviates volemic thirst, but as water exits the cells to ease the high extracellular concentration of salt, a very demanding osmotic thirst is produced. You can probably now understand why Coleridge's *Ancient Mariner* lamented, "Water, water, everywhere,/Nor any drop to drink."

In order to compensate for these seemingly opposed thirsts, both water and salt levels must be regulated. Water deficits are detected by specialized receptors. **Osmoreceptors** are biological devices specialized in detecting changes in osmolarity and located in cells of the **preoptic nucleus** of the

hypothalamus. Lesioning this area results in an inability to respond to osmotic thirst. Further, injections of small quantities of salt solution in this area (but not in others), produces drinking. Volemic thirst is detected by **baroreceptors** (volume receptors) in the atria of the heart and the kidneys that monitor changes in blood volume reflective of deficits in extracellular fluid. All of these receptor types can be thought of in general terms as responsive to changes in fluid pressure. Osmoreceptors, for instance, are thought to become active when they shrink as a result of their own dehydration. Baroreceptors are also sensitive to pressure changes in the blood. Their positions in the heart, kidney, and vena cava (which is a major vein to the heart) are ideally located to respond to changes in blood pressure. You may have heard that people with high blood pressure should avoid salt in their diets. Eating food with a lot of salt results in osmotic thirst as fluid from inside the cells moves into the extracellular space to counteract the difference in osmolarity. This increase in the amount of extracellular fluid results in an increase in blood pressure. If this increase is prolonged among "salt sensitive" people, the risk of heart damage and strokes is highly increased. However, most people regulate this process and have less need to control dietary salt intake. Salt movement out of the blood is a function of the kidneys, the organ in which urine is formed. The role the kidneys play in maintaining tolerable salt and water levels will be discussed in the next section.

Kidney

The kidney contains a specialized structure called the **nephron** that is modulated by hormones to secrete or absorb water or salt (Figure 14–15). Each nephron is made up of a closed bulb, called **Bowman's capsule**, and a long coiled tubule. Fluid is filtered from the nephrons through the **glomerulus** (a group of tiny capillaries), and excess fluid and minerals are excreted to the **ureter**. From there the fluid is transferred to the **bladder** where it is stored and subsequently released through the **urethra**, or urinary tract.

Exchange of substances occurs between blood capillaries and nephrons. Blood enters the kidney through the **renal artery**, a short vessel coming directly from the aorta. The renal artery branches into arterioles that each penetrate into the cuplike depression of a single Bowman's capsule. Within each of these capsules, the arteriole forms a glomerulus of even tinier vessels that eventually reconvene to form the **renal vein**. Filtration from the blood occurs in the glomerulus, and selective reabsorption of water and desirable solutes (e.g., glucose, amino acids, and salt) takes place in the **convoluted tubules**. Thus, the fully functioning kidney removes salt and water from the blood and restores the amount of salt and water that the blood requires to maintain proper tonicity. Also, the kid-

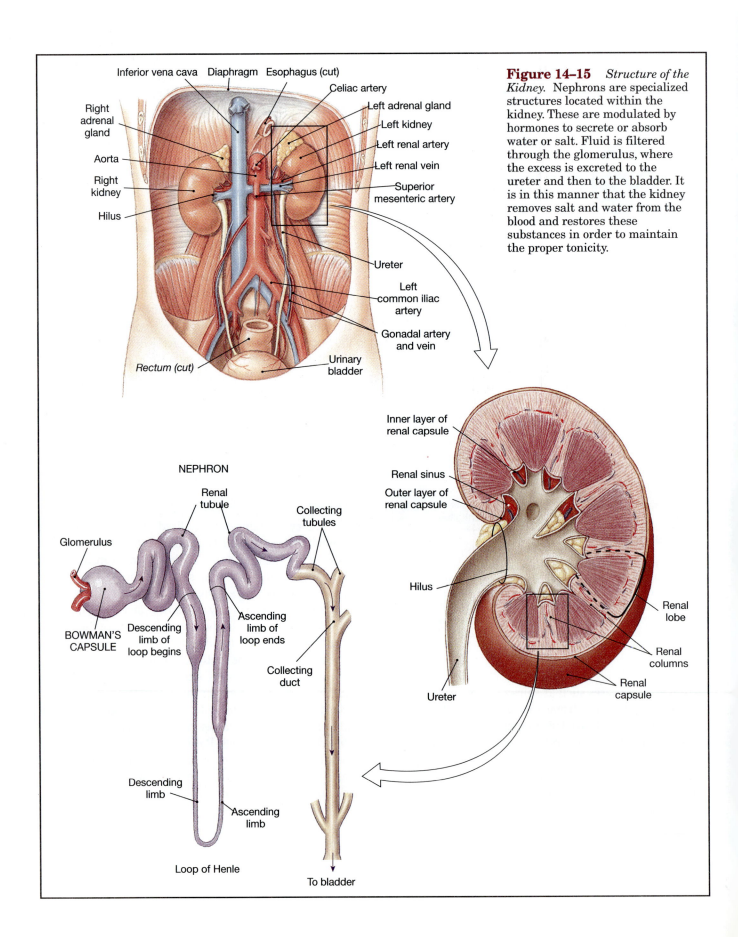

Inferior vena cava Diaphragm Esophagus (cut)

Celiac artery

Right adrenal gland

Left adrenal gland

Left kidney

Left renal artery

Aorta

Left renal vein

Right kidney

Superior mesenteric artery

Hilus

Ureter

Left common iliac artery

Gonadal artery and vein

Rectum (cut)

Urinary bladder

Figure 14–15 *Structure of the Kidney.* Nephrons are specialized structures located within the kidney. These are modulated by hormones to secrete or absorb water or salt. Fluid is filtered through the glomerulus, where the excess is excreted to the ureter and then to the bladder. It is in this manner that the kidney removes salt and water from the blood and restores these substances in order to maintain the proper tonicity.

Inner layer of renal capsule

Renal sinus

Outer layer of renal capsule

Hilus

Renal lobe

Renal columns

Renal capsule

Ureter

NEPHRON

Renal tubule

Collecting tubules

Glomerulus

Ascending limb of loop ends

BOWMAN'S CAPSULE

Descending limb of loop begins

Collecting duct

Descending limb

Ascending limb

Loop of Henle

To bladder

ney is the body's main means of excreting nitrogenous waste, primarily in the form of urea.

Hormonal Modulation: Aldosterone, Vasopressin, and Angiotensin

Aldosterone is a steroid hormone secreted by the cortex of the adrenal gland that causes the kidneys to retain sodium. **Vasopressin** (also known as *antidiuretic hormone,* or **ADH**) causes water conservation by the kidneys, or a decrease in the amount of water in the urine. ADH is a peptide hormone that is made in the hypothalamus (supraoptic and paraventricular nuclei) and released by the posterior pituitary. Interestingly, vasopressin is secreted, and the kidneys begin conserving water, *before* we are stimulated to feel thirsty. Because water conservation is the first response, we evolved so as *not* to have to change our behavior (and get up from studying this chapter and begin securing water) immediately following an increase in plasma osmolarity, leaving us free from worrying about the location of the nearest water fountain or soda machine until our internal homeostatic mechanisms can no longer deal with the deficit. In *diabetes insipidus,* a de-

ficiency of vasopressin causes an excessive loss of water through urination. People with this condition are perpetually thirsty.

During volemic thirst, when both salt and water stores are depleted, cells in the kidney respond to the decrease in blood flow and secrete the enzyme **renin**. Once in the blood, renin catalyzes the conversion of the blood plasma protein **angiotensinogen** into **angiotensin I**. Angiotensin I is further converted into **angiotensin II** by lung enzymes. Angiotensin II, an active hormone, produces many effects: It stimulates the release of aldosterone from the adrenal gland (conserves sodium in the kidney), causes the pituitary to release vasopressin (conserves water in the kidney), and finally, initiates both a water and salt appetite (Figure 14–16).

Although various aspects of angiotensin II's role in fluid regulation and drinking remain controversial and unclear, it is widely accepted that its effects are mediated at least in part through stimulation of receptor sites located within the circumventricular organs of the brain that contain angiotensin II receptors. One of these brain areas is the **subfornical organ (SFO)**, which is located immediately beneath the fornix. Lesions in this structure abolish drinking in response to an-

Figure 14–16 *Summary of the Renin-Angiotensin Cascade.* Renin is one signal that regulates blood salt and water balance.

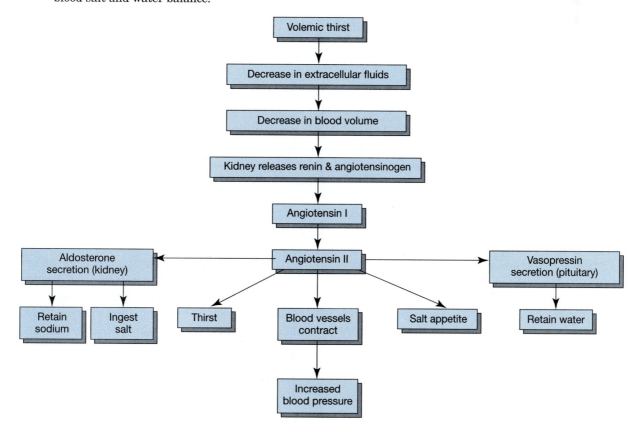

Figure 14–17 *Proposed Role for Neural Angiotensin in Salt and Water Balance.* Angiotensin may control drinking behavior.

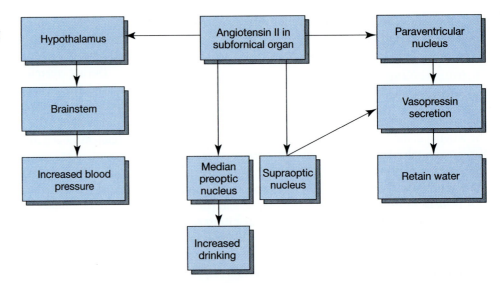

giotensin II in the blood; small amounts of angiotensin II applied directly to this area result in drinking behavior. Exciting the cells in the SFO with angiotensin II produces the behavioral, endocrine (hormonal), and autonomic (visceral) changes described earlier. Connections from the SFO to the **median preoptic nucleus** of the hypothalamus induce drinking, and angiotensin II may mediate this interaction. Lesions in the median preoptic nucleus abolish drinking in response to plasma angiotensin, and so does the application of *saralasin* (an angiotensin II antagonist) in this area. The SFO also projects to the supraoptic and paraventricular nuclei and results in vasopressin secretion from the pituitary. The SFO also projects to the hypothalamus, which in turn connects to brainstem nuclei that influence blood pressure (Figure 14–17).

Angiotensin works in combination with aldosterone to produce a salt appetite. Salt-deprived animals will discontinue displaying an appetite for salt when the **zona incerta** of the ventral thalamus is bathed in salt solution. Further, electrical stimulation in this area induces a salt craving. SFO is a primary site of action for the dipsogenic (increase in drinking behavior; *dipso* = to drink, *genic* = to create) activity of bloodborne angiotensin II, whereas angiotensin II in CSF appears to initiate dipsogenic activity principally at the **organum vasculosum of the lamina terminalis (OVLT)** and hypothalamic median preoptic area(Figure 14–18). Czech and Stein (1992) were interested in studying angiotensin II's role in drinking by measuring cerebral blood flow (as an indicator of neuronal activity) in response to a ventricular injection of angiotensin II. They found that many brain areas were affected by angiotensin. Some areas showed an alteration of cerebral blood flow that was reversed by ingestion of a small

amount of water. These areas, all involved in drinking behavior, included: hypothalamic nuclei (e.g., supraoptic nucleus), zona incerta, limbic structures (e.g., medial septum), cortical areas (e.g., piriform cortex) and motor structures (e.g., globus pallidus). Many of these areas affected by peptide hormones are specialized structures in the brain that send neurites outside of the BBB. These "windows in the brain" are necessary for the hormones to affect central processes because large, hydrophilic molecules like peptides are unable to cross the BBB.

Aldosterone was found to stimulate a salt appetite through actions in the **medial amygdala**; lesions to the medial amygdala prevent the effects of aldosterone. Aldosterone in combination with brain angiotensin can program an increased salt appetite for life. (Epstein, 1991) Thus, salt deprivation (that releases aldosterone) and angiotensin have the ability to "teach" salt cravings. Once salt levels are within homeostatic range, the liver appears to detect this balance, signals the brain (via the vagus nerve), and the appetite for salt is decreased. Aldosterone, being a steroid hormone (see Chapter 12), crosses the BBB directly; but angiotensin, being a peptide, is unable to cross the BBB and hence is produced by the brain itself.

Thus, theory holds that in response to alterations in osmolarity signifying thirst, osmoreceptors and volemic receptors initiate changes that encourage the reabsorption of water from the kidneys and the initiation of drinking behavior. These changes restore the balance of salt and water, and we are no longer thirsty. There is one big problem with this theory. The restoration of osmolarity is not simultaneous with drinking. Following ingestion, water must be absorbed from the small intestine into the blood, and then delivered to the

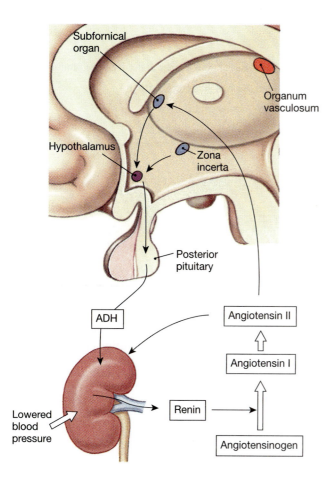

Figure 14–18 *Communication from the Kidney to the Brain.* Under conditions of lowered blood volume or pressure, the kidney secretes renin into the bloodstream. Renin in the blood promotes the synthesis of the peptide angiotensin II, which excites the neurons in the subfornical organ. The subfornical neurons stimulate the hypothalamus, causing an increase in vasopressin (ADH) production, increasing water retention and causing a feeling of thirst.

various compartments (intra- and extracellular). This process takes some time (about forty five minutes), but we do not continue drinking until homeostasis is restored (think about what would happen if you drank water continuously for forty five minutes). Somehow, before the effects of water intake are experienced by the tissues in need, our thirst is slaked. What is the signal that causes a cessation of drinking even before physical requirements are satisfied? Apparently the cells in the supraoptic and paraventricular nuclei respond to the presence of water in the mouth, esophagus, stomach, and eventually small intestine without having to experience this water directly. These nuclei in turn inhibit vasopressin release and cause a decrease in the motivation to drink. The liver is also responsive to the presence of water, and inhibits vasopressin secretion as well as informing the brain (via the vagus nerve) to inhibit drinking.

SUMMARY

Continuous and sufficient levels of oxygen and glucose are necessary to maintain normal brain function. The brain is metabolically very active, and its needs are reflected in high energy consumption relative to other parts of the body. Cerebral blood flow, responsible for providing these substrates, is highly regulated. Once glucose reaches the cells of the brain, it is broken down to provide energy for neural function. Homeostatic mechanisms are also important for regulating the energy sources to be used in brain (and other) metabolism.

Historically, eating behavior was thought to be controlled by interacting centers in the hypothalamus, namely the VMH and LH. This view turned out to be overly simplistic and has

since been modified many times. Our understanding currently includes active roles for these and other brain areas in concert with numerous neurotransmitter and hormonal systems as well as signals from the periphery. The direction of energy flow (into or out of storage) as well as activity in the autonomic nervous system are thought to be some of the peripheral signals contributing to this balance. Salt and water balance are also highly regulated. Osmotic balance is maintained through the activity of specialized receptors that detect changes in fluid levels both inside and outside of cells. These changes induce hormonal signals that result in changes in behavior, salt retention and excretion, and water absorption or excretion.

REVIEW QUESTIONS

1. How does the body store energy?

2. In what form does the body use energy?

3. What organ uses the most energy?

4. What does the brain need most of it's energy to do?

5. Contrast the actions of insulin and glucagon.

6. List the theories of how hunger and satiety are produced.

7. What brain mechanisms control thirst?

8. What hormones control thirst?

9. Why are "windows in the brain" needed?

THOUGHT QUESTIONS

1. Teleologically, why do people become overweight? Given your answer, do you think it will ever be possible to design a diet drug without side effects?

2. Trade in salt was one of the first forms of ancient commerce. What do you think the reasons were for this fact?

KEY CONCEPTS

absorptive phase (p. 338)
ADH (p. 351)
aldosterone (p. 351)
angiotensin I (p. 351)
angiotensin II (p. 351)
angiotensinogen (p. 351)
anorectics (p. 342)
anorexia nervosa (p. 343)
anoxia (p. 333)
arteriovenous differences (p. 328)
asphyxia (p. 333)
autoregulation (p. 321)
baroreceptors (p. 349)
basilar artery (p. 332)
Bayliss effect (p. 332)
bladder (p. 349)

blood-brain barrier (BBB) (p. 329)
Bowman's capsule (p. 349)
bulimia (p. 347)
carotid arteries (p. 332)
cholecystokinin (p. 342)
circle of Willis (p. 332)
conditioned taste aversion (p. 346)
convoluted tubules (p. 349)
emesis (p. 343)
fasting phase (p. 338)
glomerulus (p. 349)
glucagon (p. 338)
glucostatic theory (p. 338)
glycogen (p. 338)
glycolysis (p. 330)

homeostasis (p. 337)
hyperphagia (p. 338)
insulin (p. 338)
lateral hypothalamus (LH) (p. 338)
leptin (p. 347)
lipostatic theory (p. 340)
medial amygdala (p. 352)
median preoptic nucleus (p. 352)
nephron (p. 349)
neuropeptide Y (NPY) (p. 342)
organum vasculosum of the lamina terminalis (OVLT) (p. 352)
osmolarity (p. 348)
osmoreceptors (p. 349)

osmotic thirst (p. 348)
perfusion pressure (p. 331)
preoptic nucleus (p. 349)
renal artery (p. 349)
renal vein (p. 349)
renin (p. 351)
set point (p. 337)
subfornical organ (SFO) (p. 351)
tight junctions (p. 329)
triglycerides (p. 340)
ureter (p. 349)
urethra (p. 349)
vasopressin (ADH) (p. 351)
ventromedial hypothalamus (VMH) (p. 341)
volemic thirst (p. 348)
zona incerta (p. 352)

I would have you imagine, then, that there exists in the mind of a man a block of wax, which is of different sizes in different men; harder, moister, and having more or less of purity in one than another, and in some of an intermediate quality . . . Let us say that this tablet is a gift of Memory, the mother of the Muses; and that when we wish to remember anything which we have seen, or heard, or thought in our own minds, we hold the wax to the perceptions and thoughts, and in that material receive the impression of them as from the seal of a ring; and that we remember and know what is imprinted as long as the image lasts; but when the image is effaced, or cannot be taken, then, we forget and do not know.

Plato (c. 428–348 B.C.) *from* Dialogues, Theaetetus, *191*

15

Development and Learning

From its initial developmental beginnings to the last stages of life, the brain has an enormous capacity for reorganization and regeneration referred to as neuronal plasticity. This plasticity, including cell migration, cell proliferation, dendritic proliferation, axonal elongation, and synapse formation, provides a means for the brain to establish and reorganize its connections according to genetic instruction and environmental demands, whether they be during early development, following damage, or to accommodate learning and memory processes. This allows for the survival of the organism through adaptation to a changing world.

In this chapter we will explore the fundamental cellular mechanisms involved in the different varieties of learning. But first we must discover how the brain is put together in the first place, how the block of wax is assembled and molded to accommodate learning throughout life.

Development of the Nervous System

At some point along the way in your study of the nervous system you have probably wondered how such an incredibly complex system is put together. How are all of these neurons generated from a single-celled embryo? How do neurons know what type they are? How do the neurons know their place in the vast regions of the system? How do such specific connections form? How much neuronal plasticity is maintained throughout the life span of an organism? All of these questions and many more have been addressed experimentally since the late 1800s, providing many answers but at the same time raising more complex questions about the establishment and maintenance of the nervous system. Developmental neurobiology is one of the most active areas of study in nervous systems because an understanding of the mechanisms involved in laying down the system will lead to an understanding of the factors underlying its normal function and those that are responsible for things that go wrong. Perhaps with this knowledge we will someday understand what is necessary to correct defective brain systems or will even be able to enhance some aspects of the normal system.

In the following section we will explore **neurogenesis**, how neurons are born (*neuro* = nerve, *genesis* = birth); how they migrate to their correct position; how they differentiate and de-

355

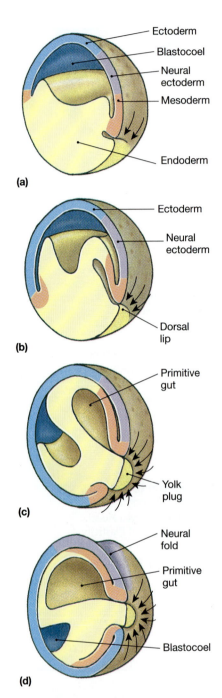

(a)
- Ectoderm
- Blastocoel
- Neural ectoderm
- Mesoderm
- Endoderm

(b)
- Ectoderm
- Neural ectoderm
- Dorsal lip

(c)
- Primitive gut
- Yolk plug

(d)
- Neural fold
- Primitive gut
- Blastocoel

Figure 15–1   *Gastrulation—Formation of Ectoderm, Mesoderm, and Endoderm.* A surface view of an amphibian embryo in the process of gastrulation where the outermost blastomeres form an invagination that leads to the rise of three germ layers: the ectoderm, mesoderm, and endoderm.

velop their individual morphology, excitability, and connectivity; and the degree to which plasticity is maintained by many components of the system long after initial development has ceased. Neuronal development is governed by two main factors: genetics and environment. As you will see, en-

vironmental influences provide the bulk of information necessary for development of a functional nervous system.

Neurogenesis

Embryonic Development and Induction

The development of the nervous system begins early on in the human embryo. After only two weeks following fertilization the first components of what will be the future nervous system begin to form. The first step in embryonic development involves the fertilized egg dividing into many cells called **blastomeres** around a central cavity called the **blastocoel**. This structure is called the **blastocyst**. During the next step, **gastrulation**, the blastomeres begin to move and reorganize, forming an invagination that results in three different tissue layers: the **ectoderm** or outer layer, the **mesoderm** or middle layer, and the **endoderm** or inner layer, collectively termed the **germ tissue layers** (Figure 15–1). The cells of the ectoderm give rise to the nervous system and skin; the mesoderm develops into muscle, skeleton, connective tissue, and cardiovascular and urogenital systems; and the endoderm forms the gut and other internal organs.

In the early 1920s, Spemann and Mangold (1924) discovered that the dorsal lip of the blastopore possessed unique organizing capabilities. They transplanted this portion of the salamander gastrula into other undifferentiated embryos and found that it *induced* well-formed parts of a second embryo, particularly the early structures of the nervous system. (*Induction* is the process of prompting a nearby tissue to differentiate). Other transplanted areas of the gastrula were incorporated into the host tissue and did not have this organizing capability. These early studies exemplify the importance of surrounding tissue in developmental regulation.

During the next developmental stage, **neurulation**, a groove forms along the anterior-posterior axis of the ectoderm. Ectodermal cells on either side of this **neural groove** thicken and form the **neural plate**, which lies on the dorsal surface or top of the embryo, with the groove lying in the middle of the folds. The folds of the plate meet, covering the groove, and fuse together forming the **neural tube** (Figure 15–2), which will give rise to the brain and spinal cord of the central nervous system. During the neural tube formation, some cells break away from the neural plate and end up just

Figure 15–2   *Neural Tube Formation.* The processes of neurulation begin with the neural plate. When the plate sinks, the neural folds will gradually meet and they will create the neural tube. The cells that break away from the neural plate and end up outside near the dorsal surface of the neural tube become neural crest cells, which will be components of the peripheral nervous system.

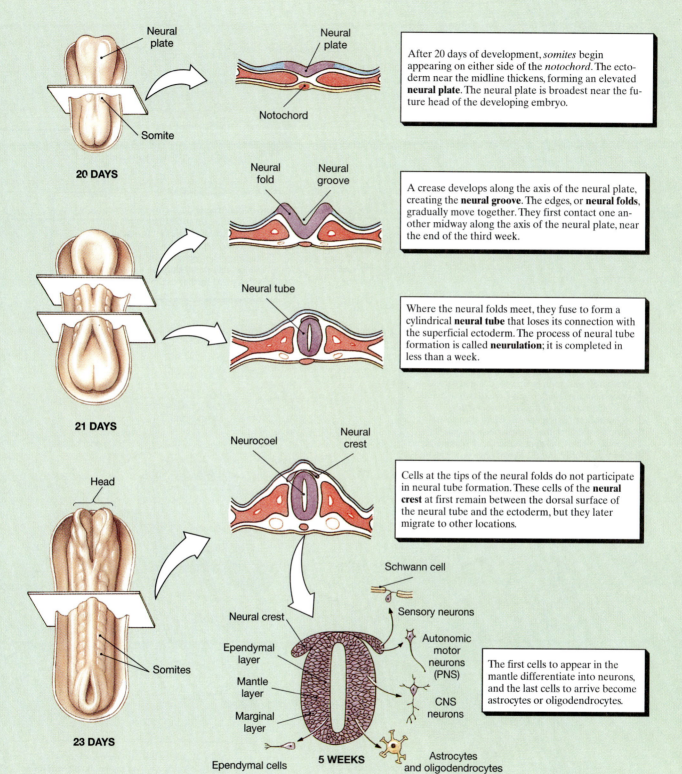

20 DAYS

Neural plate

Somite

Neural plate

Neural plate

Notochord

After 20 days of development, *somites* begin appearing on either side of the *notochord*. The ectoderm near the midline thickens, forming an elevated **neural plate**. The neural plate is broadest near the future head of the developing embryo.

21 DAYS

Neural fold

Neural groove

A crease develops along the axis of the neural plate, creating the **neural groove**. The edges, or **neural folds**, gradually move together. They first contact one another midway along the axis of the neural plate, near the end of the third week.

Neural tube

Where the neural folds meet, they fuse to form a cylindrical **neural tube** that loses its connection with the superficial ectoderm. The process of neural tube formation is called **neurulation**; it is completed in less than a week.

23 DAYS

Head

Somites

Neurocoel

Neural crest

Cells at the tips of the neural folds do not participate in neural tube formation. These cells of the **neural crest** at first remain between the dorsal surface of the neural tube and the ectoderm, but they later migrate to other locations.

Schwann cell

Sensory neurons

Autonomic motor neurons (PNS)

CNS neurons

Astrocytes and oligodendrocytes

Ependymal cells

5 WEEKS

Neural crest

Ependymal layer

Mantle layer

Marginal layer

The first cells to appear in the mantle differentiate into neurons, and the last cells to arrive become astrocytes or oligodendrocytes.

The neural tube increases in thickness as its epithelial lining undergoes repeated mitoses. By the middle of the fifth developmental week, there are three distinct layers. The **ependymal layer** lines the enclosed cavity, or **neurocoel**. The ependymal cells continue their mitotic activities, and daughter cells create the surrounding **mantle layer**. Axons from developing neurons form a superficial **marginal layer**.

Figure 15–3 *Human Brain Development.* The three initial structures that will eventually give rise to the brain are the prosencephalon, mesencephalon, and rhombencephalon. The prosencephalon forms the telencephalon and diencephalon, while the rhombencephalon divides in to the metencephalon and myelencephalon. The developing mesencephalon will produce the cerebral aqueduct and surrounding tissue.

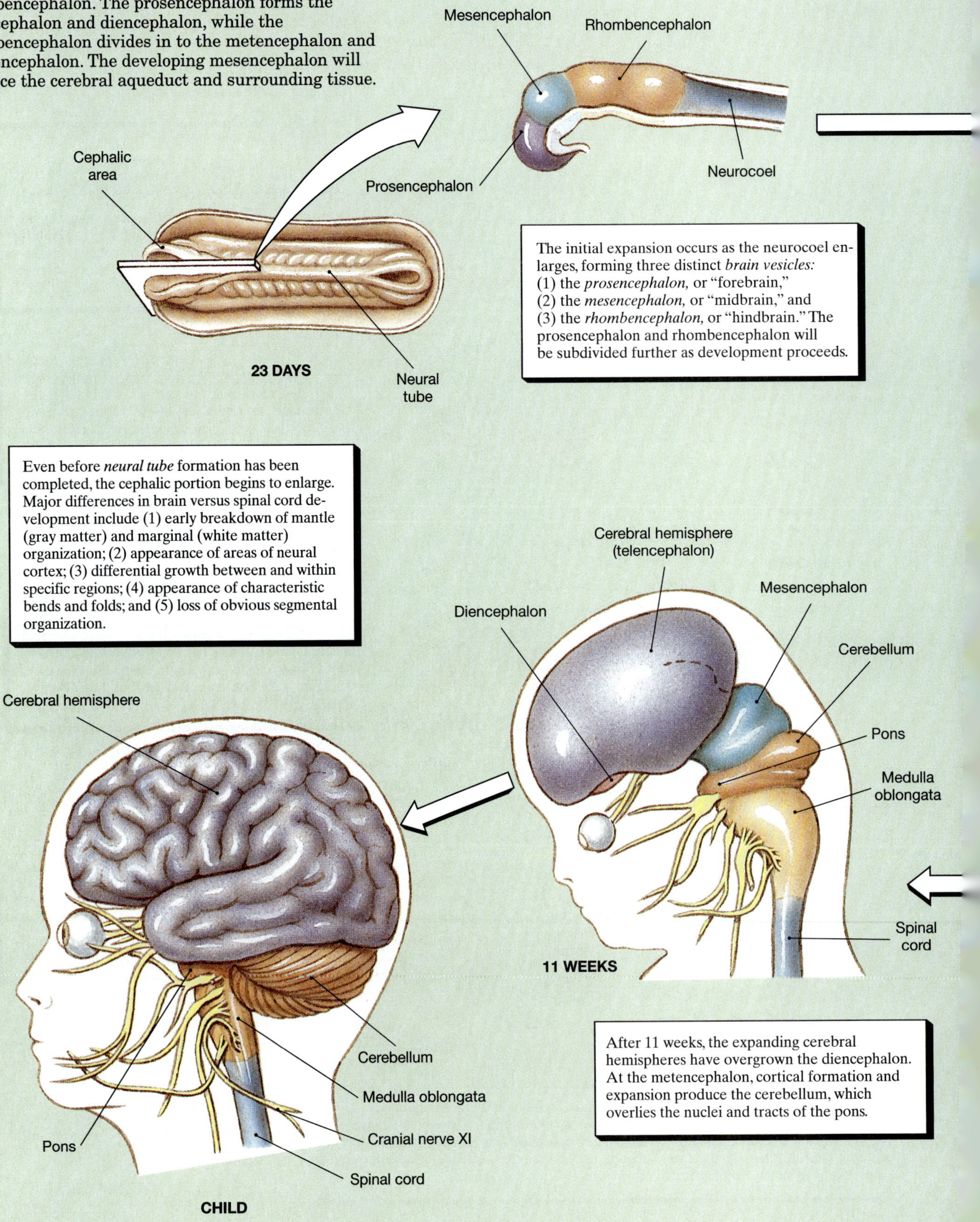

Mesencephalon

Rhombencephalon

Prosencephalon

Neurocoel

Cephalic area

23 DAYS

Neural tube

The initial expansion occurs as the neurocoel enlarges, forming three distinct *brain vesicles:*
(1) the *prosencephalon,* or "forebrain,"
(2) the *mesencephalon,* or "midbrain," and
(3) the *rhombencephalon,* or "hindbrain." The prosencephalon and rhombencephalon will be subdivided further as development proceeds.

Even before *neural tube* formation has been completed, the cephalic portion begins to enlarge. Major differences in brain versus spinal cord development include (1) early breakdown of mantle (gray matter) and marginal (white matter) organization; (2) appearance of areas of neural cortex; (3) differential growth between and within specific regions; (4) appearance of characteristic bends and folds; and (5) loss of obvious segmental organization.

Cerebral hemisphere (telencephalon)

Mesencephalon

Diencephalon

Cerebellum

Pons

Medulla oblongata

Spinal cord

11 WEEKS

Cerebral hemisphere

Cerebellum

Medulla oblongata

Cranial nerve XI

Pons

Spinal cord

CHILD

After 11 weeks, the expanding cerebral hemispheres have overgrown the diencephalon. At the metencephalon, cortical formation and expansion produce the cerebellum, which overlies the nuclei and tracts of the pons.

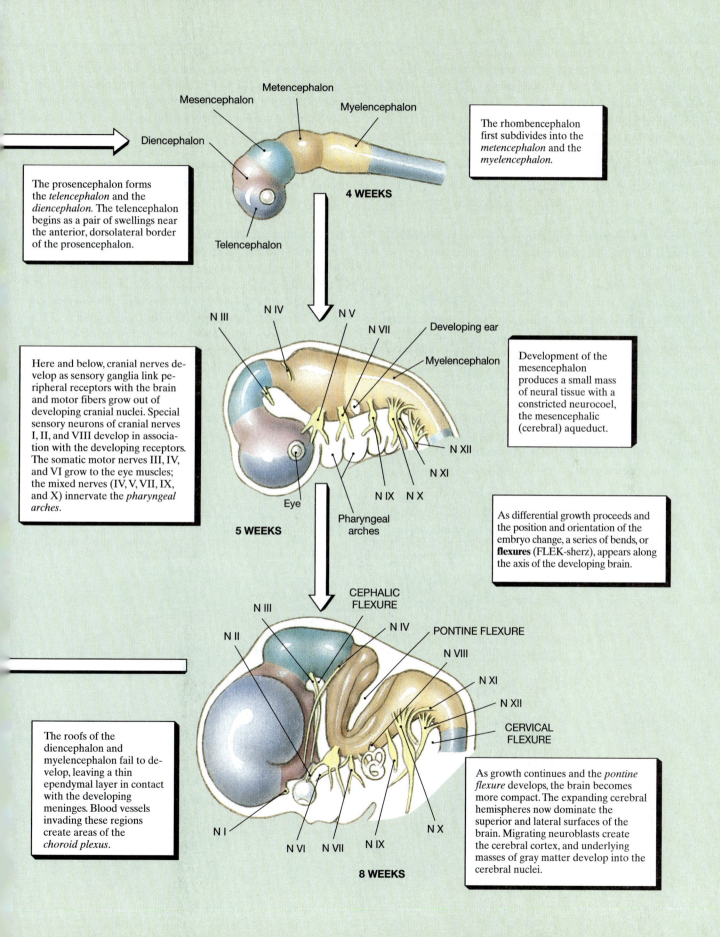

The prosencephalon forms the *telencephalon* and the *diencephalon*. The telencephalon begins as a pair of swellings near the anterior, dorsolateral border of the prosencephalon.

The rhombencephalon first subdivides into the *metencephalon* and the *myelencephalon*.

Mesencephalon

Metencephalon

Myelencephalon

Diencephalon

Telencephalon

4 WEEKS

Here and below, cranial nerves develop as sensory ganglia link peripheral receptors with the brain and motor fibers grow out of developing cranial nuclei. Special sensory neurons of cranial nerves I, II, and VIII develop in association with the developing receptors. The somatic motor nerves III, IV, and VI grow to the eye muscles; the mixed nerves (IV, V, VII, IX, and X) innervate the *pharyngeal arches*.

Development of the mesencephalon produces a small mass of neural tissue with a constricted neurocoel, the mesencephalic (cerebral) aqueduct.

N III   N IV   N V

N VII

Developing ear

Myelencephalon

N XII

N XI

N IX   N X

Eye

Pharyngeal arches

5 WEEKS

As differential growth proceeds and the position and orientation of the embryo change, a series of bends, or **flexures** (FLEK-sherz), appears along the axis of the developing brain.

The roofs of the diencephalon and myelencephalon fail to develop, leaving a thin ependymal layer in contact with the developing meninges. Blood vessels invading these regions create areas of the *choroid plexus*.

CEPHALIC FLEXURE

N III

N II

N IV   PONTINE FLEXURE

N VIII

N XI

N XII

CERVICAL FLEXURE

N I

N VI   N VII   N IX

N X

As growth continues and the *pontine flexure* develops, the brain becomes more compact. The expanding cerebral hemispheres now dominate the superior and lateral surfaces of the brain. Migrating neuroblasts create the cerebral cortex, and underlying masses of gray matter develop into the cerebral nuclei.

8 WEEKS

outside but next to the dorsal surface of the neural tube. These cells form the **neural crest** which gives rise to spinal and autonomic ganglia and glial cell components of the peripheral nervous system as well as to other types of nonneural tissue.

Just under the neural tube some mesodermal cells will have developed into the **notochord**, which will eventually become part of the nonneural portions of the spinal cord such as supporting tissue, and the **somites**, on each side of the notochord, which will become vertebrae of the spinal cord, skeletal muscle, and dermis. It makes sense that these nonneural structures develop at the same time and in close proximity to the spinal cord since the nonneural components of the spinal cord will surround and protect the spinal cord itself.

Cell Proliferation

At this point in embryonic development, cell proliferation along the neural tube results in distinct specializations along the rostral-caudal axis, giving rise to specific brain divisions. Three swellings or bulges at the most rostral end are called the **prosencephelon** or the forebrain vesicle, followed by the midbrain vesicle or **mesencephelon**, and then the **rhombencephelon** or hindbrain vesicle. These three structures eventually become the cerebral hemispheres, the midbrain, and the brainstem, respectively (Figure 15–3 on previous page). The neural tube has a central lumen, like the hole in the middle of a donut. The inner surface of the tube that sits closest to the

lumen is called the **ventricular layer** since this wall will form the ventricles of the brain. The outer surface of the tube is called the **marginal layer** (Fig, 15–4). Cell proliferation, or **mitosis** (defined in Chapter 12), involves a series of steps: A neural cell ready to divide originates in the ventricular zone, moves up the outer surface of the tube to the marginal zone (perhaps to acquire information concerning its future disposition), returns to the ventricular zone, replicates its DNA information, divides, and then once again returns to the marginal zone and migrates away to form the layers of the central nervous system (Cowan, 1978; Sauer, 1935). Both future neurons and nonneuronal glial cells result from this process.

During the time when cells are replicating their DNA and dividing (which only happens at this point in time for most neurons) it is possible to inject radioactively labeled DNA precursors into a cell which are incorporated into the dividing cells of the embryo after injection, thus labeling them at the moment they are "born." With this method, called **autoradiography**, it is possible to follow the progression of each cell along its migratory pathway to its final destination within the brain (Figure 15–5). Pasko Rakic (1974) used this method to determine how cortical layers are formed and found that the cells with the earliest birthdays formed the bottom layer (layer VI) of the cortex (line A in Figure 15–5); those born later migrated across these cells to form each additional layer on up to layer I (lines F and G in Figure 15–5). This is described as

Figure 15–4 *Neural Tube Cell Proliferation.* Cell proliferation in the lumen of the neural tube involves several steps: A neural cell divides in the ventricular zone, moves up to the marginal zone (possibly to acquire disposition information), returns to the ventricular zone where it replicates its DNA information and divides again, and then returns to the marginal zone to begin forming the layers of the central nervous system. (Sauer, 1935)

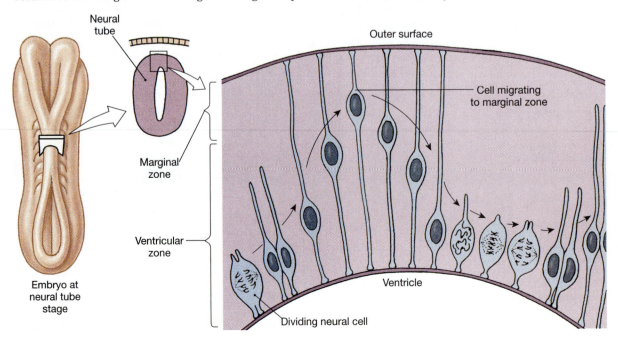

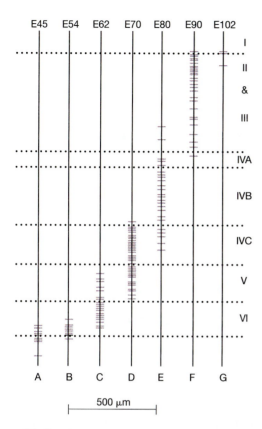

Figure 15–5 *Cortical Cell Migration.* Rakic determined which cells were in the different cortical layers by injecting radioactively labeled DNA precursors into fetuses to follow cells in the migratory pathways. Horizontal markers on each vertical line indicate the positions of the neurons, the numbers at the top of the lines indicate the days of gestation. The roman numerals represent the different cortical layers. Rakic found that those neurons born first made up the bottom of the cortex (VI, line A) and those born later migrated over the previous cells to form additional layers (I and II, lines F and G). (Rakic, 1974)

an inside-out pattern, and a great deal of research has addressed the question of why the cortex might form this way. It has been suggested that as cells migrate to their final destination they receive important information about their precise final location within the structure and the type of cell they will differentiate into from the other cells that they come into contact with. You can imagine that genetic predisposition may set limitations (e.g., a neuronal precursor cell cannot become a liver cell), but environmental influences contribute to the final identity of a neuron.

Neuronal Migration

After a cell has completed mitosis (never dividing again) it is called a neuronal precursor or a **neuroblast** because many of the characteristics of a mature neuron, such as the shape of its cell body, its dendritic and axonal branches, and its neuro-

transmitter, have not yet developed and only come about once the cell finds its appropriate place in the brain. Again, this should tell you something about the importance of environmental influences on neuronal disposition. Some cells must migrate many millimeters to reach their destinations. How do developing neurons know where to migrate and when to stop?

Like the amoeba, migrating neuroblasts extend parts of themselves in one direction, which pulls the rest of the cell along a particular route. These membrane extensions are called **lamellipodia** and exhibit a ruffling motion as they move along some surface. Some migrating neuroblasts initially follow long fibers of **radial glial cells** that form a scaffolding in the developing nervous system; presumably the scaffolding is constructed exclusively for this purpose, since in most cases radial glial scaffolding disappears after migration of the neuroblasts is complete (Figure 15–6). This occurs particularly in cortical areas where radial migration across a layered structure (from the bottom to top layer) is important. Migrating neuroblasts remain constantly apposed to these fibers compared with other processes they may encounter, suggesting the physical direction of migrating neuroblasts by radial glial processes (Hatten, 1990; Rakic, 1972). The necessity of radial glial scaffolding for directing neuronal migration and the importance of properly guided neuronal migration to the ultimate organization in some systems is aptly demonstrated by genetic mutants in which appropriate radial glial scaffolding is disrupted. In a certain type of mouse, named *weaver* due to its uncoordinated weaving motions, radial glial scaffolding is disordered in the cerebellum, and granule cells (Chapter 10) do not migrate to their appropriate destinations within this structure, resulting in severe motor impairment (Rakic & Sidman, 1973). Evidence suggests that the interactions between migrating neuroblasts and radial glia are critical for both normal organization of the scaffolding and normal migration along the scaffolding (Galileo et al., 1992; Hatten, Liem, & Mason, 1986). **Cell surface molecules** (molecules embedded in the cell membrane) are likely important for these types of adhesive interactions (Edmondson et al., 1988) as well as for interactions between migrating neuroblasts that do not use radial glial guidance and their substrates (the substances the cells contact as they migrate). Neural crest cells migrating to form the peripheral nervous system pass through long stretches of embryonic *mesenchyme* (embryonic connective tissue) and are thought to be guided by cues in this environment. These cues are **extracellular matrix molecules** such as *fibronectin* and *laminin*. Interaction between cell surface molecules on migrating neural crest cells generally classified as **integrins** (a family of glycoproteins) and molecules in the local environment are important for determining migratory patterns, destinations, and final neuronal characteristics. Blocking the action of either integrins on the neural crest cells or

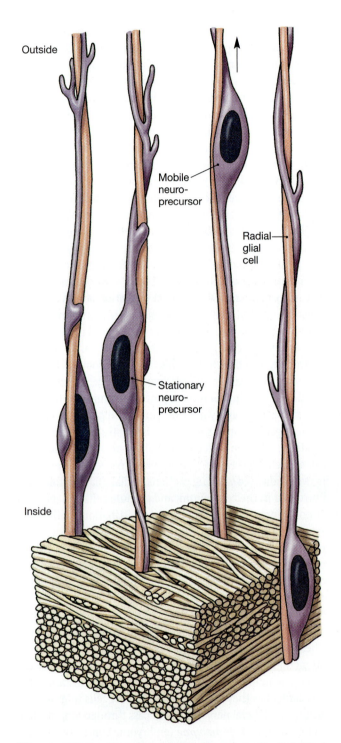

Outside

Mobile
neuro-
precursor

Radial
glial
cell

Stationary
neuro-
precursor

Inside

Figure 15–6 *Neuroblast Migrating along Radial Glial Scaffolding.* The cortical region has long fibers of radial glial cells that allow neuroblasts to migrate to levels of higher organization. The deepest cortical region is represented at the bottom of the diagram while more superficial layers are represented at the top of this diagram. (Rakic, 1972)

fibronectin or laminin in the extracellular matrix with antibodies hinders neural crest cell migration (Bronner-Fraser, 1985, 1986). **Neural cell adhesion molecules (NCAMs)**, surface proteins with trophic influence, play significant roles during many developmental stages and continue to play a role in adult forms of plasticity (for review, see Jessell, 1988).

Neuronal Differentiation

What happens when a neuroblast reaches its final destination and how does it know when it is there? A multitude of environmental factors influence neuronal maturation and differentiation. Some of these include neighbor interactions, environmental molecular cues, and electrical activity from surrounding neurons. In some species, the environment plays no role at all, with cell lineage completely controlling the type of neuron a neuroblast will become; in such cases all progeny from a single precursor cell will migrate to a similar location and become the same type of cell. For example, the nematode worm *Caenorhabditis elegans* develops its nervous system through a stereotyped developmental program dependent on invariant cell lineages. Environmental interactions play little or no role; deleting or adding neighboring cells does not affect the development of any particular cell in this system. In this case genetic programs activated differentially in each cell are the sole determinants of differentiation and the ultimate map of the nervous system. Can you imagine why this might be disadvantageous in more complex systems? The main drawback is the lack of flexibility. All information about cell fate must be coded for within the genes of such a creature without input from environmental changes. This eliminates the possibility of environmentally induced changes that may have adaptive advantages. It also reduces the likelihood of recovery from any type of environmental insult (such as drought or flood) or genetic error, since each cell has a predetermined job and cannot easily take over the job of a damaged neighbor. See the section "Command Neurons and Motor Tapes," Chapter 10, for examples of how *identified cells* acquire unique roles in behavior.

Neuronal Fate Determination

In most species, neuronal fate is guided by genetic information, environmental interactions, and cell-cell interactions. For example, in the vertebrate retina, a single precursor can give rise to any one of the varied cell types there (Wetts & Fraser, 1988). With the advent of new techniques for labeling cell lineages (such as retroviral markers passed on to all daughter cells), the dogma of cortical development such that all progeny of a precursor will be restricted to one functional subdivision and even one radial unit has been questioned. Walsh and Cepko (1992) have shown that clonally related neurons are widely dispersed across cortical regions and cell fate is determined much later than originally thought. This suggests that the cortex is initially functionally equivalent, that is, containing cells that may adopt a wide range of roles in adulthood, and is later molded into functional areas by cell-cell interactions. This allows for flexibility in cortical development and likely underlies the extensive cortical evolution of primates.

Other types of experiments show clearly that environment can determine and even change the predisposition of neurons. For example, when tissue samples from different cortical areas are switched, the neurons take on the characteristics of those in the new location. O'Leary and Stanfield (1989) transplanted late fetal neurons from the visual cortical area to the motor cortical area in a newborn host rodent (Figure 15–7). The transplanted visual cortical neurons differentiated and established connections (both afferent and efferent) appropriate for their new locations. Presumably this would yield a normal contribution to behavior in the adult. This also happens when motor cortex is transplanted to visual cortical areas, and when visual cortex is transplanted to the somatosensory cortical regions. In the latter case, even morphological features develop within the transplanted tissue that are characteristic of its new location. Barrel fields, which represent whisker organization in somatosensory cortex, can

be seen within the visual cortex transplant, suggesting a functional reorganization of the transplanted tissue appropriate for its new location (Schlaggar & O'Leary, 1991).

Neural crest cells have been shown to have similar pluripotent nature, which is gradually refined through interactions along the cells' migratory pathways. Uncommitted precursor cells take one of several pathways, each ending in differentiation into a distinct part of the peripheral nervous system. Neural crest cells transplanted from one pathway to another acquire the characteristics of cells in the pathway they end up in regardless of their original position (Le Douarin, 1986). Further studies by Le Douarin and Dupin (1993) found that they could establish the fate map of a neural crest cell along the neuraxis prior to the onset of the migration and that the tissue environment in which the crest cells migrated was important in determining their fate. This strongly suggests that environmental interactions control the fate of neural crest cells.

Determination of Neurotransmitter Phenotype

Determination of neurotransmitter phenotype is also dependent on environmental cues. Recall that **phenotype** is the word used to describe the function and structure of a mature cell. This has been most clearly demonstrated in the periph-

Figure 15–7   *Pluripotent Nature of Developing Neocortex.* Visual cortical neurons from late fetuses were transplanted into the motor cortical area of newborn rats. The dye Fast Blue was injected into the pyramidal tract to show that the cells now sent axons to the cord just as cells originally in the motor cortex would. (O'Leary et al., 1989)

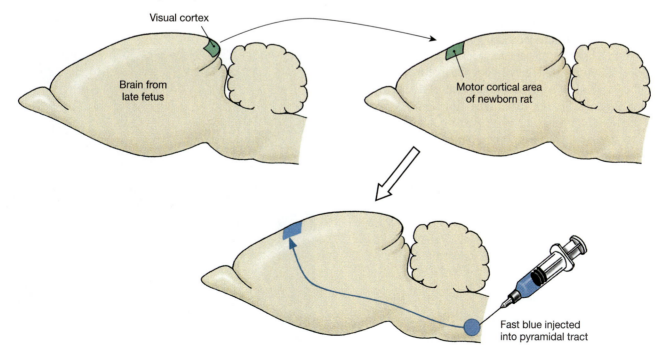

eral nervous system. Sympathetic neurons in the autonomic nervous system originally all have noradrenergic properties. Some of these neurons innervate sweat glands and at this point change their original noradrenergic (using norepinephrine) characteristics to cholinergic (using acetylcholine). How does this dramatic change in transmitter phenotype come about?

Schotzinger and Landis have examined this issue and shown that, at least within this neuronal population, the transmitter is flexible and can be changed very late in development depending on the type of target these cells innervate (Landis, 1990; Schotzinger and Landis, 1988). The researchers took rats and transplanted foot pads, which contain sweat glands, into hairy skin areas, which do not contain sweat glands. They found that axons from the noradrenergic neurons that would normally innervate these hairy skin areas change their transmitter phenotype to cholinergic when they encounter transplanted sweat gland. This implies that target information can be a critical factor in determining final neuronal characteristics. The factor responsible for such changes is still being sought. Recently, it has been discovered that the switch from noradrenergic to cholinergic can be reproduced in culture when the neonatal sympathetic neurons are treated with members of the cytokine family of molecules; however, the exact chemical has still not be found (Landis, 1996).

Development of Electrical Properties

Like physical and chemical properties, electrical properties of neurons emerge during differentiation and appear to change over the course of development. The early development of excitability of amphibian spinal neurons is characterized by a change from a long-lasting Ca^{++}-dependent action potential to a brief Na^+-dependent impulse (Spitzer & Lamborghini, 1976). The differentiation of the mature action potential is dependent on the development of a specific K^+ current (Ribera & Spitzer, 1989). What function do you suppose the initial Ca^{++} signal serves? Perhaps, along with the many molecular signals from the other cells and from the environment, these Ca^{++} signals also participate in guiding the differentiation of neighboring neurons. Some recent evidence supporting a developmental role for ionic conductance in post-mitotic cells is the finding that calcium channel activity, which is associated with neurotransmitter release in the adult, directs migration of cerebellar cells before their contacts are established (Komuro & Rakic, 1992).

Axon Development and Growth Cone Guidance

Once a migrating neuron arrives at its destination, and in some cases even before, its characteristic arrangement of dendrites and axon collaterals must take shape. Again, environmental cues and intercellular interactions are critical for accurate process outgrowth and specificity of both efferent (incoming) and afferent (outgoing) connectivity. Each neuron develops a dendritic arbor (Chapter 2) that will support incoming afferent input specific for that cell. This arbor is dependent on the position of the cell in the brain and, in the case of layered structures, the layer in which it sits. The neuron must also extend its axon, sometimes for very long distances, to find the target cells it must communicate with. Such **pathfinding** and **target recognition** are critical during axonal elongation for establishing appropriate contacts within the nervous system.

The tip of the newly extended axon is called the **growth cone**; it looks like a flattened hand, with extended **filopodia** for fingers (Figure 15–8). The cytoplasm of the growth cone contains the filamentous protein machinery important for cell motility. Growth cones have receptors that allow them to respond to molecular factors in the environment and, through second messenger systems, affect their motility. Growth cone morphology and dynamics appears to depend on the growth cone's location along its migratory route. When following some physical component along the path, the growth cone's shape is simple and constricted, but when interpretation of

Figure 15–8 *Growth Cone Movement.* The flattened tip of the axon is known as the growth cone. When it is activated at choice points, it loses its restricted shape and generates more filopodia while becoming more elongated. Filopodia work their way through extracellular material by following signals to their targets. In this specimen, the microtubules are labeled green and the actin filaments are labeled red.

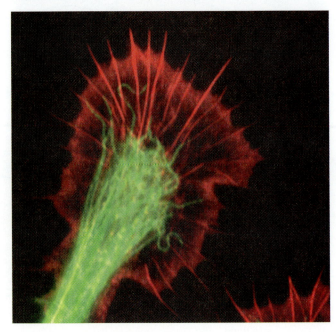

chemical signals is required, particularly at choice points, the growth cone's morphology becomes more complex with many filopodia actively extended, apparently sampling the chemical cues in the environment. Ramón y Cajal (1955) was the first to describe growth cones and thought they might act like "battering rams," working their way through the extracellular matrix by following signals to their targets.

Tropic Factors and Other Guides

There are many **tropic factors** that provide directional cues for axons either through attractive and adhesive interactions or by repulsive cues. Other factors, confusingly called **trophic factors**, support process growth but don't provide directional information. **Nerve growth factor (NGF)**, a protein, is an exception since it does both and as you might guess is one of the most critical factors for the survival of some neurons (Box 15–1). Examples of **chemoaffinity** (the role of peptides, hormones, and NCAMs in guiding development) and cell-cell interactions responsible for axonal guidance are many and varied (see Figure 15–8 and Shirasaki, Katsumata, & Murakami, 1998). The floor plate, a midline structure in mammalian brains, attracts commissural axons and guides them across the midline (Tessier-Lavigne et al., 1988). In the grasshopper's nervous system, **guidepost cells** direct sensory axons to change directions at specific points along the axonal trajectory (Taghert et al., 1982). Even other axons can serve as scaffolding to guide later-arriving axons to their appropriate destinations (Goodman et al., 1984). Removing these beacons causes growth cones to wander in inappropriate directions. There are other tropic factors that provide guidance for dendrites. The transient subplate zone attracts dendrites to increase the growth and maturation of the subplate neurons (Mrzljak et al., 1992).

Repulsive cues also play a role in growth cone guidance. Central nervous system growth cones and peripheral nervous system growth cones collapse and retract when they come into contact with one another (Kapfhammer & Raper, 1987), which may prevent inappropriate overlap between the two systems. Myelin formed by oligodendrocytes in the central nervous system causes collapse of growth cones that contact it (Schwab & Caroni, 1988), thus preventing contact onto these axons once myelination has begun. CNS myelin contains cell surface glycoproteins responsible for this repulsion and likely prevents regeneration in this system. Peripheral nervous system myelin produced by Schwann cells does not contain cell surface glycoproteins and therefore has regenerative capabilities. Substrate-bound repulsive molecules, attached to connective tissue, can also be found in many systems. If the force of repulsive cues, in oligodendrocytes for example, could be overcome, then an exciting prospect for treatment of spinal cord injury could result.

Adhesion Molecules

Adhesion molecules are cell surface glycoproteins that mediate attractive cell-cell and cell-matrix interactions (for review, see Jessell, 1988). These molecules belong to one of three families categorized by similarities in structure. Each family has members that are specific to neurons as well as those that are found on nonneuronal cells. The neural cell adhesion molecule (NCAM, one of the NCAMs mentioned earlier) is a member of the immunoglobulin superfamily and is the most ubiquitous of those neuronal adhesion molecules that mediate cell-cell interactions. Edelman (1986) found that disrupting these molecules with antibodies causes chaos in the developing nervous system. In other words, synapses require NCAM to form in an orderly manner. NCAM has several forms that appear differentially during development and maturation. Interestingly, the form most abundant in actively developing nervous systems is also expressed at high levels in brain areas (such as the hippocampus) that support plasticity in adulthood. This suggests that developmental plasticity and the plasticity retained in adulthood may share common mechanisms. In the second group, members in the cadherin family such as **N-cadherin** also mediate cell-cell interactions, but unlike NCAM their adhesive properties require extracellular Ca^{++} for stabilization. The third family, the integrins, mediate adhesion between neurons and extracellular matrix molecules such as fibronectin and laminin. All of these glycoproteins serve as general guides in the nervous system since they are expressed on the surface of most neurons, but there are likely more specific adhesive molecules yet to be discovered. Recent research has pointed to nonprotein adhesion molecules (such as *glycosaminoglycans*) as important in development (Litwack et al., 1998).

Molecular Gradients

Molecular gradients are regions in which molecules are more concentrated at one end. Once growth cones reach their target area, they follow molecular gradients to locate their precise position within that area. This phenomenon has been studied in systems that must maintain a certain topography, such as the retinotectal system (Figure 15–9) for the retinotopic map (Chapter 9). Ganglion cells in the dorsal area of the retina seek contact with cells in the ventral tectum. Ventral retinal ganglion cells contact neurons in the dorsal tectum. The initial precision of this projection is directed by molecular gradients and repulsive cues. Researchers developed an in vitro membrane composed of alternating stripes of anterior and posterior tectum. Retinal ganglion cell axons from the temporal retina extend only along the anterior tectal stripes (Figure 15–10). Walter, Henke-Fahle, & Bonhoeffer (1987) found that this occurs due to a high concentration

Box 15–1

Levi-Montalcini and Nerve Growth Factor

In the late 1940s, Viktor Hamburger and his student Elmer Bueker were interested in the role of target tissue in attracting and sustaining developing sensory neurons in the peripheral nervous system. Bueker (1948) transplanted tumor tissue along the spinal column in chick embryos and found that sensory axons grew toward and contacted the tumor tissue and that the dorsal root ganglion near the tumor was enlarged. Rita Levi-Montalcini along with Hamburger systematically studied this phenomenon, which led to the discovery of one of the most significant trophic factors in the nervous system.

Levi-Montalcini developed an in vitro assay culturing tumors along with implanted chick sensory ganglia (see figure comparing the stimulated culture on the right with the unstimulated one on the left). Factors from the tumor induced extensive neurite outgrowth from the sensory ganglion (Levi-Montalcini, Meyer, & Hamburger, 1954). The next step involved characterizing this factor. Was the active component of the factor a nucleic acid or a protein? Cohen and Levi-Montalcini (1956) eliminated the nucleic acids as a candidate by treating the tumor with snake venom, a source of phosphodiesterase that destroys nu-

cleic acids, but to their surprise they found snake venom alone stimulates fiber outgrowth even more than the tumor extract. This serendipitous observation indicated that the factor was a protein found in both tumor extract and snake venom; they later isolated and named it nerve growth factor (NGF). The salivary gland in mammals is the analogue to the snake venom gland; the salivary gland in male rats also contains NGF. This has been an abundant source of the factor, facilitating the investigation of the effects of NGF in the nervous system.

NGF affects many but not all cell types in the nervous system. It clearly plays a role in directing process outgrowth and stabilizing contacts of the sympathetic and sensory ganglia. Sympathetic target tissues contain high levels of NGF proportional to its innervation by autonomic axons (Korsching & Thoenen, 1983), and antibodies to NGF eliminate the sympathetic ganglia when administered during their development (Levi-Montalcini, 1972). In the mammalian brain, NGF plays a role in supporting cholinergic neurons in the basal forebrain; loss of this support causes these cells to die. This is the cholinergic population lost in Alzheimer's disease; one future treatment will likely in-

of a repulsive molecule on the posterior stripes rather than an attractive molecule on the anterior stripes. Dorsoventral gradients of adhesive molecules have also been found that direct growth cones along this tectal plane (Trisler, Schneider, & Nirenberg, 1981), possibly using an interplay between attractive and repulsive forces.

Synaptogenesis

Synaptogenesis is the process of synapse formation once the growth cones have met their targets. Pre- and postsynaptic specializations must form in order for synaptic stabilization and functional signaling between neurons to be achieved. This rather protracted process (lasting three to four weeks in the rat) begins when axon reaches its final target cell. Signals from both the axon and the target cell are important in

this process. If this contact is not established, the neuron sending the axon may die. Since central nervous synapses are difficult to access, synaptogenesis has been studied most thoroughly at the neuromuscular junction outside the CNS (Figure 15–11). The principles that apply here are likely to also apply within the CNS.

The first event of synaptogenesis involves the motor neuron growth cone extending to its muscle target. Even at early stages, growth cone releases acetylcholine (ACh) in small amounts and developing muscle cells respond to this release. Spontaneous miniature end plate potentials can be recorded in the earliest stages of contact well before the development of any specializations. At the site of initial contact, nicotinic ACh receptors on the postsynaptic membrane migrate from their original dispersed positions and aggregate at the synap-

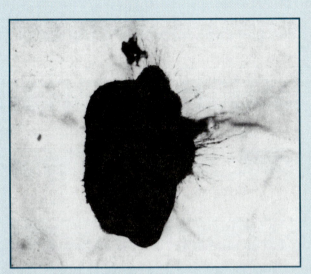

Source: Purves & Lichtman, 1980

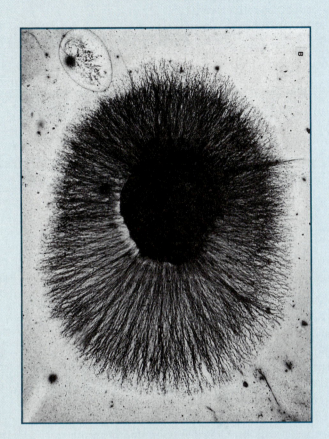

clude increasing the amount of NGF in these regions in an attempt to rescue these cells, but many cells in the CNS do not respond to NGF, limiting the value of the approach.

Although NGF does not support neuron survival in all regions of the CNS, other factors have been identified that work elsewhere in place of NGF. Some of these include *brain derived neurotrophic factor (BDNF)*, which promotes motor neuron survival, and *ciliary neurotrophic factor (CNTF)*, which is released following muscle injury to promote regeneration. The search continues for neurotrophic factors having both general and specific effects in developing and mature nervous systems, since the possibilities for clinical application in treating neurodegenerative diseases are immense.

tic site. Many thousands more are newly synthesized at this site, generating a concentration of receptors several thousand times higher than in other regions of the muscle membrane. ACh release does not induce receptor aggregation; another molecule called **agrin** released from the axon induces both receptor and acetylcholinesterase aggregation (McMahan & Wallace, 1989). Extrajunctional receptors (e.g., AChR outside of the end plate region) disappear due to suppression by the increased electrical activity of the muscle cell following contact with the presynaptic element (Lomo & Rosenthal, 1972).

The **basal lamina** is the extracellular matrix that sits between the pre- and postsynaptic sites and contains many molecules that contribute to maintenance of the synapse and differentiation of the axon terminal. The presynaptic terminal develops specializations important for efficient signaling, such as high densities of Ca^{++} channels, an active zone, and clustering of synaptic vesicles. If the motor axon is damaged, it will regenerate, contact its original synaptic site, and develop axonal specializations even in the absence of the muscle cell. Components of the basal lamina are thought to direct this process (McMahan & Wallace, 1989).

Activity-Dependent Fine-Tuning of the Nervous System

During development many more neurons and axons are generated than are needed in the mature nervous system. These "extras" must eventually be eliminated, and this is accomplished through competitive interactions. Many axons reach their target, but only a limited number form functional con-

Figure 15–9 *The Retinotectal Projection.* The path of the retinotectal projection begins when ganglion cells in the retina seek to make contact with cells in the tectum.

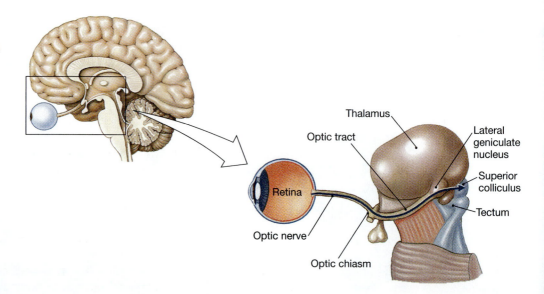

tacts. Axons must compete for targets as well as access to trophic factors (such as NGF) that maintain synaptic contacts. This mechanism is thought to occur where concurrent activity between the pre- and postsynaptic neuron is critical for strengthening that synapse, thus giving it the edge it needs to survive.

At the neuromuscular junction of the somatic nervous system, each muscle cell is initially contacted by axons from several motor neurons. Synapse elimination results in the innervation of each muscle cell by only one axon terminal. This also occurs in the neuromuscular contact in the autonomic nervous system (Purves & Lichtman, 1980). Activity-dependent competitive interactions play a major role in this process (Thompson, Kuffler, & Jansen, 1979).

Although the initial retinotectal map is established through chemoaffinity mechanisms, refinement of these maps requires activity. Axonal aboration is sculpted through synchronous firing of adjacent retinal ganglion cells. Those contacts with the tectum target cells originating from cells in other retinal areas are not active at the same time as those from the active subpopulation of retinal ganglion cells; those inactive tectal contacts are eliminated. Blocking action potentials with TTX or synchronizing all ganglion cell activity with strobe lights prevents the refinement of retinotectal projections (Fawcett & O'Leary, 1985; Schmidt & Eisele, 1985; for review, see Shatz, 1990).

Activity-dependent afferent segregation in the developing visual cortex serves as a model for studying the mecha-

Figure 15–10 *Molecular Gradients in Target Tissue.* The retinotectal projection is mediated by molecular gradients and repulsive cues. Retinal ganglion cells extend only along anterior tectal stripes because there is a high concentration of a repulsive molecule on the posterior stripes. Left panel: strips of repulsive molecule. Right panel: axon migration between strips.

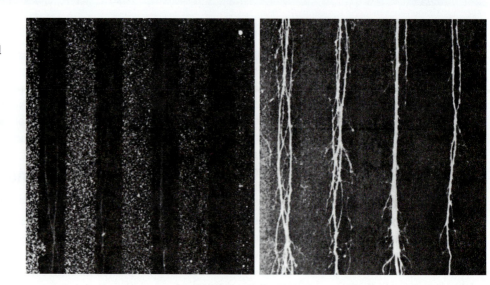

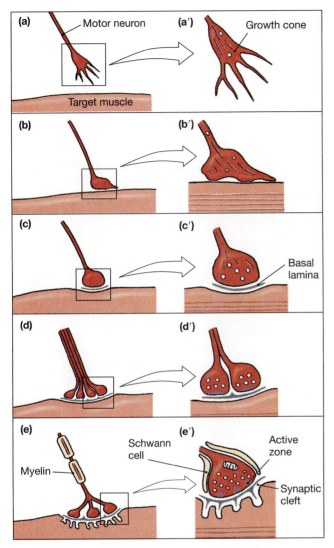

Figure 15–11 *Synapse Formation of the Neuro-muscular Junction.* Areas (a) through (e) are shown at higher magnifications in (a') through (e'). The motor neuron growth cone approaches the muscle target (a) and proceeds to make contact (b). The basal lamina appear after differentiation of the presynaptic terminal (c). As the basal lamina are being generated, the terminal is generating Ca⁺⁺ channels, an active zone, and a clustering of synaptic vesicles. Many axons will converge on the synaptic site (d). All axons will be eliminated except for one which will be encapsulated by a Schwann cell (e). (Hall & Sanes, 1993)

nisms underlying synaptic modification (Box 15–2), which may bridge the gap between developmental neurobiology and learning and memory. A great deal of evidence suggests that the synaptic strengthening and synapse elimination during development parallels these types of events associated with learning and long-term potentiation (which will be discussed in the following section). NMDA receptors, cor-

related activity, and specificity appear to be important in plasticity.

Learning Theory

Learning is the process whereby experience changes behavior, presumably through some change in the nervous system, a process called **neural plasticity**. Learning cannot be measured directly; it is inferred from observed behavioral changes of an organism following events occurring in its environment, or from performance on exams given by sadistic professors! The events or stimuli that induce behavioral changes must be relevant or adaptive to that organism for learning to occur. It would not be practical for animals to attend and respond to all external stimuli; most irrelevant events are filtered (Chapter 9). Therefore, attentiveness or arousal is an important component necessary for learning to occur. When you are drowsy and tired in an early morning class due to a late night on the town, it is more difficult to attend to and learn about what is being taught. (If you are sleeping it is impossible—scientifically, those tapes that you play while you sleep cannot work, although they my give you more confidence.) As you can imagine, attentiveness, motivation, and state of mind are more important in more complex forms of learning than in simpler forms.

There are several levels or types of learning. **Complex learning** includes those forms of learning that cannot easily be classified by simple definitions or categories. Simpler forms of learning include **reflexive learning** (any change in synaptic efficacy over time), which may occur in the peripheral nervous system rather than the central nervous system. Other simpler types of learning such as nonassociative learning and simple associative learning, which will be discussed in the next sections, occur in the central nervous system and can be observed in both invertebrates and vertebrates. Regardless of the level, alterations in physiological, morphological, and biochemical properties result in observable changes in behavior. The goal of many neuroscientists is to understand the different mechanisms underlying behavioral changes during learning.

Nonassociative Learning: Habituation and Sensitization

Nonassociative learning simply means that no association is formed between two events or stimuli. This type of learning includes habituation and sensitization, which can be observed at the level of the spinal cord in vertebrates as well as in simple invertebrate nervous systems.

Habituation is measured behaviorally as progressively weaker responses to a repeated stimulus. In other words, the organism learns to ignore stimuli or events that are of no

The Visual System as a Model for Development and Plasticity

Activity-dependent reorganization and modification of the nervous system occurs at high levels during development but continues, albeit at lower levels, throughout the life span of an organism. In the visual system, patterns of activity generated by retinal ganglion cells are critical for producing a functional and correctly wired visual system at higher brain levels. Activity patterns are typically produced by stimuli in the visual world but can also be generated by spontaneous activity. What happens when activity patterns are perturbed? Many studies have shown that accurate functional organization of the thalamic and cortical visual area is dependent on correctly patterned afferent activity.

In mammalian visual systems, inputs from each eye remain segregated at the thalamic level; alternating layers of the thalamus are formed representing afferents from the left and right eyes. This segregation is also maintained in primary visual cortex and is represented by ocular dominance columns. At the cortical level, ocular dominance columns are formed through competitive interactions between inputs originating from each eye to layer IV. Convergence of information from the two eyes occurs in cortical layers above and below layer IV (left figure).

When one eye is sutured closed during a critical period after birth (right figure), this segregation does not occur. When the eye is opened at a later time, cells in primary visual cortex do not respond to stimulus presented to this eye, but only to stimulus presented to the eye that remained open (Hubel & Weisel, 1970). Ocular dominance columns representing the closed eye shrink and are taken over by

---

consequence. You have already read about a form of habituation in Chapter 9 as adaptation of sensory systems to the stimulus of wearing clothes or sitting down. This adaptation allows the organism to filter out unimportant events so that it may attend to more important things, such as an approaching predator or the impending doom of a comprehensive final exam.

Sensitization is measured as an increased response to repeated weak stimuli after the organism has been aroused by a noxious or intense stimuli, such as a painful pinch, or a loud sound, such as a gunshot. You have probably experienced this following a frightening experience, such as being narrowly missed by a speeding car as you ride your bicycle along the roadway. As you continue down the road you are

more acutely aware of every passing car. Sensitization overrides habituation so the organism can attend to and quickly respond to a threat to its survival.

Associative Learning

Associative learning is more of interest to learning theorists since it involves "making a connection" between previously unrelated processes. Associating or linking events or stimuli is the basis for many types of learning at all levels. As you hear about the different aspects of the brain, the associations you make between all of these parts are important in understanding the brain as a system. This would be considered complex learning since higher cognitive processes are involved, but associative learning can occur at lower levels as well. Clas-

input from the opened eye (Hubel, Weisel, & LeVay, 1977). This demonstrates that sensory deprivation resulting in loss of activity and therefore loss of competitive capabilities of an afferent system can alter structural and functional properties of primary cortical areas.

What is the basis for these competitive interactions? Adjacent retinal cells tend to fire together or are synchronously active, whereas those farther apart are asynchronous. Axons from synchronously active inputs cooperate to depolarize target cells and stabilize their synaptic contacts and therefore have a competitive advantage. Competition between inputs from the two eyes, each of which has a different activity pattern, results in the functional seg-

regation of ocular dominance columns. Blocking neural activity in both eyes prevents formation of ocular dominance columns due to lack of interactions, but when they are stimulated asynchronously, competing activity is reestablished and ocular dominance columns do form (Stryker & Harris, 1986; Stryker & Strickland, 1984). These studies demonstrate the importance of patterned activity in visual system development.

Plasticity in the visual system appears to be governed by mechanisms similar to those proposed to underlie plasticity associated with learning and memory processes (see section on Hebb's postulate, this chapter). Concurrent activity between the pre- and postsynaptic elements is necessary for synapse stability. If presynaptic activity is eliminated in one axon then that axon loses its ability to maintain its contact. Blocking postsynaptic receptors thought to be involved in enhancement of synaptic efficacy (such as NMDA receptors, see Figure 15–25) also disrupts the normal activity-dependent segregation of inputs in this system (Bear et al., 1990). Evidence from studies of plasticity in both the developing visual system and systems involved in learning processes suggests that these changes may share common cellular mechanisms. Plasticity in adulthood may be in a continuum of developmental plasticity. Study of both developing and adult organisms will contribute to a better understanding of their differences and similarities and may lead to a cure for developmental abnormalities in brain function (e.g., Down's syndrome) presently intractable to treatment because understanding is incomplete.

sical conditioning and operant conditioning are two examples of simpler forms of associative learning and can be demonstrated in many species, from snails to humans.

Classical conditioning was first demonstrated by the Russian physiologist Ivan Pavlov (1906). His discovery was serendipitous; he was originally studying the digestive system in dogs when he observed the behavioral consequences of his experimental procedure. His procedure involved attaching a dog to a harness every day before the food arrived. Soon, the dogs began to respond to the presence of the harness in a way that indicated they anticipated being fed. He then turned this research interest to studying this association and transfer of representation that occurs in the psyche and is manifested in behavior.

Classical conditioning involves the development of an association between a relevant or **unconditional stimulus** (US), which by itself leads to an **unconditional response** (UCR), and a **conditioned stimulus** (CS) that does not initially produce such a response, such as a tone or a light. For example, if you taste your favorite food (the unconditional stimulus) you will begin to salivate (unconditional response). If you see the sign of a restaurant (conditioned stimulus) shortly before you taste the food, and if this occurs on several different occasions, you will form an association between the food and the sign. The sign alone will be sufficient to induce salivation and anticipation of eating that food. This reaction to the sign alone is called the **conditional response** (CR). It is usually quite similar to the unconditional response but may be a bit weaker.

Figure 15–12 *Gambling and Operant Conditioning.* Operant conditioning involves an association between a stimulus and a response. When people are rewarded for pulling the lever on a slot machine, they repeat the process. Learning research has shown that *variable reinforcement,* such as that provided by a slot machine that pays off only occasionally, is even more effective than constant reinforcement in maintaining the conditioned behavior.

A strong association is established between the food and the sign without your conscious awareness that it has occurred, so this association can also be referred to as reflexive conditioning. The time between the appearance of the two stimuli is important. The sign must precede the food by no more than a brief period of time or no association will be made between the conditioned and unconditioned stimuli. This association must occur several times; once is not enough. These simple learned associations allow animals to predict relationships between events in their environment. Conditional responses can be extinguished if the CS appears alone on several occasions. This unlearning or disassociation is critical; since the tone no longer predicts the occurrence of food, it would not be adaptive for an animal to continue to behave as though it does.

Operant conditioning also involves associations, not between two stimuli but rather between a behavior and an event in the environment (Figure 15–12). The psychologist Edward Thorndike (1898) initially described this type of learning as trial-and-error learning. For example, if a rat is placed in a box with a lever which, when depressed, dispenses food, the rat will learn that pressing the lever (the behavior) produces the food (the event). At first, the rat will wander around the box exhibiting various types of rat behavior (grooming, rearing, sniffing, etc.) but will eventually come to explore the lever, press it, and find food. After repeated occurrences of this incident, the rat will come to associate the activity of lever pressing (but not rearing or sniffing) with the dispensed food and will press the lever when it is hungry. This learned association

between behavior and environmental events was the basis for the popularized learning philosophies developed by the psychologist B. F. Skinner (1938) and used in creating behavior-management schemes for schoolchildren and wage-workers. This type of learning allows the animal to predict outcomes of its own specific behaviors and to control its environment through acting out those behaviors.

Another form of simple learning that is a special model of classical conditioning and operant conditioning is **food aversion** (initially tested experimentally by Garcia, Ervin, & Koelling, 1966; see Chapter 14). This type of learning requires only one occurrence to change behavior. Another difference is that the stimulus and its consequences can be separated in time by many hours. Perhaps you have experienced this type of single-trial learning if you have ever eaten bad food that made you sick some hours later or have become sick several hours after a meal for reasons unrelated to food. Subsequent exposure to that particular food, whether it is bad or not, will cause you to avoid it, since the association between the food and the illness has been established. This powerful form of learning is an adaptive mechanism that ensures the survival of animals by causing them to steer clear of foods that are poisonous or unwholesome.

Many of the types of learning mentioned here have been investigated at the nervous system level. Specific biophysical and biochemical changes have been clearly demonstrated to correlate with the behavioral changes associated with learning (some of these are discussed later). Intense research investigating these cellular mechanisms is based on the assumption that they are conserved across species as well as across systems within a species and that understanding them at the level of simple reflexes or in simple invertebrate systems will help us to understand complex forms of learning in more sophisticated systems such as mammalian brains.

Complex Learning

Complex learning includes many types of defined learning as well as some that are less well defined, from plasticity in instinctive behavior (Box 15–3) to higher cognitive processes. Learned associations between stimuli or events are part of complex learning but not the whole story; unlike associative learning, more complex forms of learning are not so obviously stimulus-directed and are called complex because the association cannot be readily identified. An important requirement of complex learning is that the behavior be maintained in the absence of reinforcement. One example of this is **imprinting**, also a form of classical conditioning. Some animals form a strong attachment to the first significant stimulus they are exposed to just after birth. This stimulus is usually the mother who provides care, nourishment, and protection to her young. You can appreciate that this type of

Box 15–3

Learning of Bird Song: A Novel Neural Mechanism

The dogma that states "no new neurons are born anytime after initial neurogenesis early in development" has been challenged by extensive study of the neural mechanisms underlying song learning in passerine birds (for review, see Konishi, 1989). Birds such as finches and canaries learn how to sing their particular songs by listening to adult birds sing while they are young and practicing this learned song template when they reach reproductive age (Marler, 1981). Young birds match their own song to the learned template and eventually perfect their production of the song of their species. If they are deprived of this experience early on (by rearing in isolation or by deafening), they are unable to produce the refined song needed for mating, territorial protection, and other types of intraspecies communication. The song they produce is distorted and the necessary complexity never develops.

Male birds typically produce song and therefore this behavior is an example of sexual dimorphism (Chapter 12). Male brains are organized by hormones very early in development, which lays the groundwork for the plasticity necessary in specific brain regions involved in song production later in life. Females treated with androgens during this critical period will produce song later on in adulthood (with

continued hormonal treatment) as if they were male birds. The dimorphic nuclei increase in size when the hormone levels are high during the mating season, correlating with increased song production during this time. These size changes are not as apparent in females that do not sing, and song nuclei in females are significantly smaller than in males (Nottebohm, 1981; Nottebohm & Arnold, 1976).

Neuroanatomical studies of these seasonal brain changes in adult songbirds have revealed that the size increase is due in part to dendritic growth but more surprisingly it is also due to actual mitotic generation of new neurons in the song nuclei circuitry (Patton & Nottebohm, 1984). This is the most dramatic example to date of anatomical changes and reorganization that accompany behavioral learning in adult vertebrates. This type of hormonally regulated plasticity is rarely observed in mammalian brains and is probably not a major mechanism underlying neural plasticity in general. Nonetheless, it is an interesting way to produce substantial neuroanatomical changes very quickly during a particular time period, resulting in major functional alterations manifested at the behavioral level that are necessary for the songbird's survival and reproductive success.

bonding or imprinting is yet another adaptive mechanism crucial to the young animals' survival. This type of learning has been studied extensively in avian species, the most popular example being Konrad Lorenz's ducklings (Lorenz, 1970; Figure 15–13). Lorenz, an ethologist, substituted himself for the mother duck, which caused the newly hatched ducklings to imprint onto him, following Lorenz wherever he wandered as they would their own mother. Other researchers have

Figure 15–13 *Imprinting in Birds.* Imprinting, in which newborns identify the first moving object they see as their mother, is a form of complex learning. Konrad Lorenz (shown with adopted ducklings) was the first to describe this form of learning.

Figure 15–14 *Children Imitating Adults.* Imitative learning is also a form of complex learning.

found that chicks will even imprint onto inanimate objects such as a rotating disc. This type of learning occurs only within a limited time frame or **critical period** after birth and demonstrates an important link between characteristics of learning and development.

Other forms of learning include imitative or **observational learning** and latent learning. Imitative learning can best be observed in humans and includes skill and language acquisition (Figure 15–14). It is unclear whether or not this type of learning occurs in other animals, and the basis for this type of learning is unknown. Latent learning involves incorporating nonspecific information about an environment that appears to facilitate later learning of specific things in that same environment. For example, if a rat is placed in a maze without reward at the goal sites and allowed to explore this new environment for a short period of time, that "experienced" rat will later learn to solve the maze and reach the goal more quickly than a "naive" rat that has never seen the maze. It is unclear what is being learned that facilitates maze performance later on, but it may be that the rats have simply learned that there is nothing to fear in this environment.

Finally, **spatial learning** is important for both humans and other animals to successfully navigate through the environment they live in to find food, mates, and a safe haven. Foraging animals, particularly, depend on spatial learning to find and remember the location of rich food sources and to remember if a food source has been depleted in a certain area so time and energy are not wasted returning to that area again and again. People depend on spatial learning to find their way around sometimes extremely complex environments, like big cities, and to locate the grocery store when they are hungry, the university when it's class time, and home when they want to relax. Spatial learning involves forming complex associations between many stimuli such as objects in the environment, specific landmarks, and even the position of the sun or magnetic fields (in some animals such as insects and migrating birds), unlike latent learning which involves just being in the specific environment. Try to think of the many instances during your day when spatial learning may come into play.

Simple System Models for Plasticity

Mammalian brains are composed of millions of neurons and, in turn, these neurons form millions of synapses with one another. Although neuroanatomical studies have provided a great deal of information about the structure of the nervous system, the detailed connectivity within each brain region and among the different regions is enormously complex; such complexity makes it difficult to study the effect on behavior of changes at the single-cell level. A great deal of progress has been made, and it is now possible to record gross extracellular changes of cells within a specific brain area in freely behaving animals as they perform tasks such as maze learning. Yet to truly understand the mechanisms involved in learning, a more detailed and specific cellular approach is required. It is not enough to say "a cell in area X changes its firing rate when the rat reaches the goal at the end of a maze, so this cell might be involved in learning the goal location." There are many alternative explanations for gross electrophysiological changes that have nothing to do with learning. To begin to understand the relationship between brain and behavioral modifications, we must start with a complete understanding of stereotyped learned behavior and the modifications in a completely mapped nervous system or subsystem that accompany the behavior.

The Virtue of Simple Systems

Invertebrates have far fewer neurons, and therefore fewer connections, than vertebrates. In some animals these neurons are very large and can be seen without the aid of a microscope, can be readily identified since they appear in the same location between individuals, and are easily accessible for study in immobilized creatures still capable of performing some behaviors. Parts of the nervous system of one particular invertebrate, *Aplysia californica*, a marine snail, have been extensively mapped and many of its neurons have been identified. Extensive study of modifications within this nervous system in response to several types of simple learning ("Command Neurons and Motor Tapes," Chapter 10) has supplied a great deal of fundamental information about possible neural mechanisms underlying learned behavior. Other invertebrate systems not as completely understood have also contributed to this understanding.

Aplysia and *Hermissenda*

Eric Kandel et al. (1976) have developed *Aplysia* as a model preparation (an easy example of something too intricate to be studied elsewhere) for neural plasticity that accompanies simple forms of learning. In this preparation it is possible to simultaneously record discrete electrophysiological events and correlate them with behavioral modifications that indicate the occurrence of habituation, sensitization, and classical conditioning (Bao, Kandel, & Hawkins, 1998). *Aplysia* has several body parts such as a head, tail, foot, and a central area that includes the gill, which draws oxygen from sea water, and an attached mantle and siphon that covers and protects the gill (Figure 15–15). These parts are interconnected through its nervous system composed of principal and interneuron populations that utilize various neurotransmitters. Any stimulus touching the mantle or siphon activates a reflex that withdraws the gill toward the body (aptly named the **gill-withdrawal reflex**, see Figure 15–15). Repetitive weak stimuli to this area, such as the brushing of passing seaweed or a light touch from a water jet in the laboratory, results in a gradual weakening of the gill-withdrawal response (habituation, Figure 15–16a, top). The magnitude of the response can be measured by comparing the dimensions of the protruding gill before and after the stimulus as well as measuring the length of time the gill remains withdrawn. Applying a strong stimulus such as a shock to the mantle complex where stimuli have habituated restores the original total withdrawal of the gill, replacing the habituated response with a strong response to repetitive weak stimulation (**dishabituation**, Figure 15–16, bottom). In addition to habituation, sensitization of the gill-withdrawal reflex can be induced by a strong shock to the head or tail, which results in an enhanced reflex response to subsequent weak stimuli to the mantle (Figure 15–17).

Sensory neurons from the mantle and siphon monosynaptically contact the motor neurons that are responsible for gill-withdrawal and are the principal components of the gill-

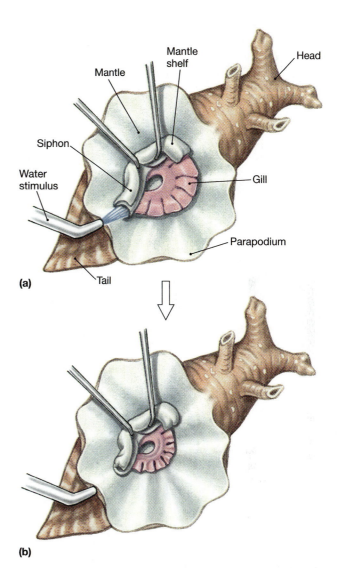

Figure 15–15   Aplysia's *Anatomy and Gill-Withdrawal Reflex.* Since the gill-withdrawal reflex is masked by the parapodia and mantle of *Aplysia*, they must be pulled back to view the reflex. The gill-withdrawal reflex includes the siphon and the mantle shelf. Part (a) shows the relaxed position of the gill. Part (b) shows the response to a weak stimulus presented to the siphon.

withdrawal reflex pathway (Figure 15–16b). Electrophysiological activity can be measured at the sensory, or presynaptic, neuron and the motor, or postsynaptic, neuron simultaneously during the development of habituation in this pathway. What sorts of changes at the level of the neuron do you think occur during the development of habituation? Would the presynaptic cell fire more or fewer times with each repeated weak stimulus? What about postsynaptic cell activity? By isolating each cellular component of the pathway and testing for the development of habituation, it was found that the

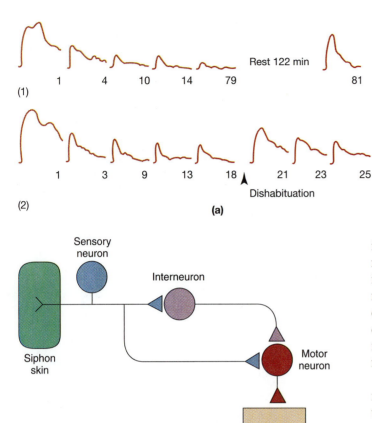

Figure 15–16 *Habituation of Gill-Withdrawal Reflex in Aplysia.* (a) The top part of the figure depicts repeated weak stimuli to the gill which will result in a gradual weakening of the response (habituation). The bottom of the figure shows what occurs when a strong stimulus is applied to restore the original response (dishabituation). (b) The gill-withdrawal reflex pathway includes sensory neurons from the siphon synapsing onto interneurons and motor neurons.

change occurs at the synapse between the pre- and postsynaptic cell. The stimulated sensory neuron fires the same action potential each time, but as habituation develops, each action potential releases less and less neurotransmitter from the presynaptic terminal, which decreases the response of the postsynaptic cell. Therefore, the changes responsible for habituation are considered to be presynaptic changes (Byrne, 1982; Castellucci et al., 1970; Kupfermann et al., 1970).

How was this determined? A statistical method called quantal analysis (Chapter 5) enabled the researchers to come to this conclusion (Castellucci & Kandel, 1974). Each action potential causes secretion from a certain number of tiny vesicles filled with neurotransmitter. The postsynaptic response to the transmitter in each vesicle is called a quantum (Chapter 5). The release of these vesicles is dependent on the influx

of Ca^{++} ions into the activated neuron (recall the dynamics of ionic membrane currents during an action potential from Chapter 4). Each quantum causes a certain amount of change in the postsynaptic potential when the transmitter binds to its receptor on the postsynaptic membrane surface. The release of many quanta will result in a large change in the postsynaptic potential; the release of fewer quanta will produce a proportionately smaller change. Alternatively, synaptic changes can occur on the postsynaptic side. For example, a change in receptor sensitivity will produce a change in the postsynaptic potential even if the number of quanta released from the presynaptic terminal remains constant. Quantal analysis helps to determine if the changes are presynaptic (fewer quanta or amount of neurotransmitter released) or postsynaptic (a change in receptor sensitivity). In the case of habituation of the gill-withdrawal reflex, quantal analysis determined that the decreased motor response is a result of less transmitter being released from the presynaptic terminal (Figure 15–16b).

Is the mechanism of sensitization similar to the mechanism of habituation? An increase rather than a decrease in transmitter release occurs in sensitization, and thus the change is still presynaptic (Carew, Castellucci, & Kandel, 1971; Castellucci & Kandel, 1976; Kandel et al., 1976). Also, sensitization involves a few more neurons (Figure 15–17a). These are interneurons that converge onto the monosynaptic reflex pathway and modify the release of transmitter from the presynaptic sensory neuron.

A good deal of evidence has been gathered regarding the molecular and cellular modifications leading to sensitization (Klein & Kandel, 1980; Siegelbaum, Camrado, & Kandel, 1982). Interneurons converging onto the sensory neuron of this reflex pathway release the neurotransmitter serotonin (5-HT). When serotonin binds to its receptors on the sensory neuron a second-messenger cascade is initiated. The receptor interacts with a G protein, which activates another membrane-bound protein, *adenylate cyclase* (Chapter 6). Adenylate cyclase in turn stimulates an increase of *cyclic AMP* concentration within the neuron, which activates cyclic AMP–dependent *protein kinases*. These protein kinases phosphorylate or modify the structure of the K^+ channels, which results in a decrease of K^+ efflux. This prolongs the action potential (since repolarization is dependent on K^+ movement across the membrane) and lengthens the time that the Ca^{++} channels are open, thus allowing more Ca^{++} into the cell. As mentioned earlier, neurotransmitter release is dependent on Ca^{++} influx since each vesicle needs several Ca^{++} ions to initiate the release of its contents. The more Ca^{++} moving into the neuron, the more quanta are released; the result of this

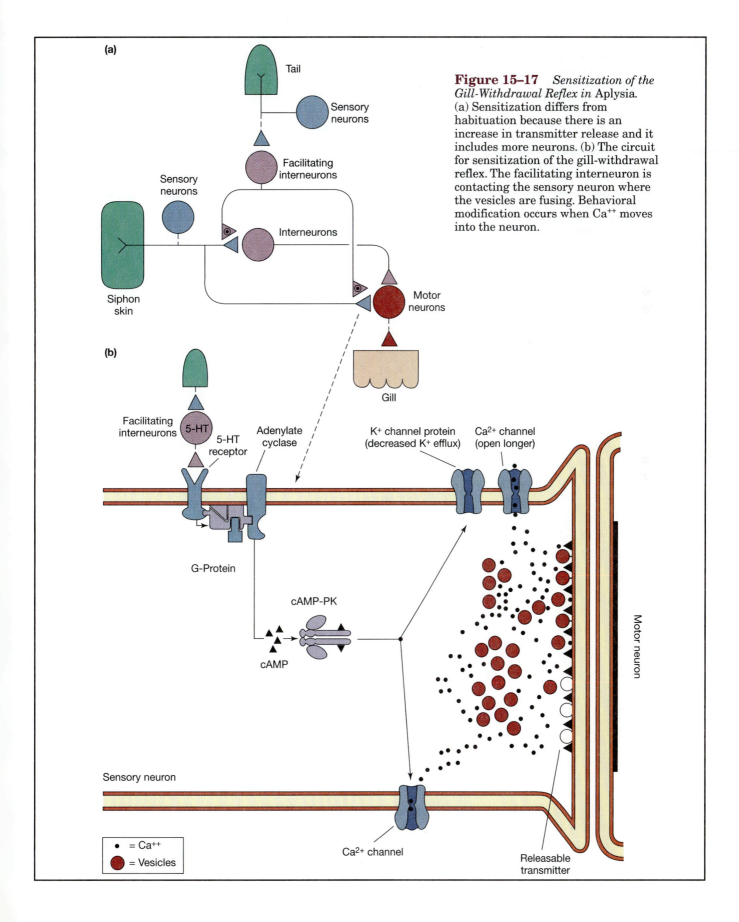

Figure 15–17 *Sensitization of the Gill-Withdrawal Reflex in* Aplysia. (a) Sensitization differs from habituation because there is an increase in transmitter release and it includes more neurons. (b) The circuit for sensitization of the gill-withdrawal reflex. The facilitating interneuron is contacting the sensory neuron where the vesicles are fusing. Behavioral modification occurs when Ca^{++} moves into the neuron.

Figure 15–18 *Classical Conditioning in* Aplysia. (a) Circuit showing convergence of facilitating interneurons onto the synapse to be strengthened (CS⁺) and the synapse used for control (CS⁻). (b) The tail stimulated (US) with the mantle stimulus (CS⁺) but not the siphon stimulus (CS⁻). (c) Recordings in sensory cells show that their action potentials don't change with conditioning stimuli (compare "pre" to "post"). However, the synaptic response in the motor neuron is enhanced with paired stimuli (CS⁺) but not unpaired stimuli (CS⁻). (Adapted from Hawkins et al., 1983)

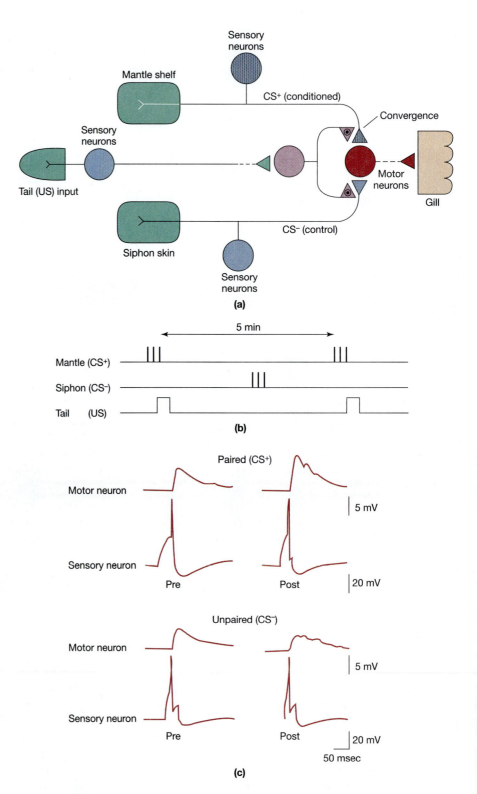

long cascade of events is synaptic plasticity, a change in the properties of a single neuron resulting in the behavioral modification of sensitization (Figure 15–17b).

Carew, Hawkins, and Kandel (1983) have furthered our knowledge of the neural basis of learning through classical conditioning studies in *Aplysia* (Figure 15–18). Using the same gill-withdrawal reflex system described earlier, they paired a weak stimulus to the mantle (the conditioned stimulus) with a strong shock to the tail (the unconditioned stimulus). After several trials the weak shock to the mantle produced the same increased withdrawal of the gill as the strong shock to the tail. Again, the temporal component of the occurrence of the conditioned and unconditioned stimulus was critical. If the time between the weak mantle shock and the strong tail shock was greater than one second, the association between these two stimuli did not occur (i.e., the weak mantle shock did not produce the increased gill-withdrawal reflex). The molecular basis for this type of learning is similar to that described earlier for sensitization (though the new paradigm is *associative* instead of *nonassociative*) (Kandel et al., 1983). The sensory neuron from the tail contacts the facilitating interneurons, which in turn synapse with the presynaptic terminal of the mantle sensory neuron. The synapse is thus modified after repeated pairings of these two stimuli; with the additional input of the interneurons from the tail, a weak stimulus to the mantle results in increased withdrawal of the gill. As you can see, although the players in the circuits may be different, the underlying cellular mechanisms can be quite similar for different types of learning. It is likely that this concept extends to mammalian systems as well.

Hermissenda, another snail-like marine invertebrate, provides a similarly simple nervous system in which to investigate learning at the cellular level. Crow and Alkon (1978; Crow, 1988) have studied changes in this animal's nervous system at the primary sensory level (rather than the sensory motor level as in *Aplysia*) following classical conditioning. Typical *Hermissenda* behavior includes positive phototaxis (it crawls toward a light source); this behavior can be suppressed if a light (conditioned stimulus) is paired with rotation (unconditioned stimulus) of a circular platform that it sits on. When *Hermissenda* perceives light, its foot elongates and it moves toward the light. When the platform it sits on is rotated, its foot shortens. This is the motor response modified by the CS-US pairing: The light is associated with rotation, and after conditioning, light alone will result in foot shortening (conditioned response) and therefore suppression of movement toward the light.

What are the cellular mechanisms involved? *Hermissenda* has eyes that contain two types of photoreceptor cells that are mutually inhibitory. Type A cells, when activated, lead to positive phototaxis; type B cells inhibit type A. With the development of conditioning, type B cell K^+ currents are prolonged (similar biochemical mechanisms may apply as described for sensitization in *Aplysia*), which increases their response (Acosta-Urquidi, Alkon, & Newry, 1984; Crow &

Alkon, 1980; Crow & Forrester, 1986). Thus, type A cells are more strongly inhibited resulting in a decreased movement toward light. *Hermissenda's* system and the cellular mechanisms involved in learning have not been worked out as thoroughly as those in *Aplysia*, but these types of studies still contribute some knowledge about learning at different levels of the nervous system.

Other Simple Systems

Another way to study the biological basis of behavior is through the use of genetic mutants that exhibit abnormal learning behavior. The fruit fly, *Drosophila melanogaster*, has been used extensively by researchers to understand the biology of genetics and a great deal is known about the genetic machinery of this insect. Several mutations induced by chemical mutagens have resulted in flies that exhibit behavioral deficits in associative learning without sensory or motor impairments (Aceves-Pina et al., 1983; Quinn, Harris, & Benzer, 1974; Tully, 1987). The limitation of this model system is the inaccessibility of *Drosophila's* tiny nervous system, which precludes the identification and biophysical investigation of the neural pathways involved in learning.

The learning paradigm typically involves the association of a particular odor (CS) with shock (US) or some variation of this, resulting in classical conditioning. Normal flies learn this association easily and escape the shock applied to a grid when the associated odor appears. Flies impaired in this learning ability are appropriately named *dunce, rutabaga, turnip, amnesiac*, and so on, each exhibiting specific deficits in acquisition or retention of the association and each having a particular genetic mutation affecting a distinct aspect of monoamine (serotonin) or cyclic AMP cascade pathways (Chapter 6, Dudai, 1985, 1988). These particular mutations affect both nonassociative and associative forms of learning (Duerr & Quinn, 1982), suggesting that, at least, similar mechanisms are involved in different types of learning.

As you recall from the earlier discussion of both nonassociative and associative learning in *Aplysia* and *Hermissenda*, both monoamines, specifically serotonin, and second-messenger cascades involving cyclic AMP are critical cellular events underlying these forms of learning. These findings in *Drosophila* provide additional support for the hypothesis that common cellular mechanisms underlie various forms of learning in different species as well as lending insight into the kinds of cellular events involved in learning in vertebrates.

Vertebrate Models for Plasticity

Many different approaches have been developed to study changes that occur at the nervous system level during learning events in vertebrates. Some of these include brain lesions, isolated brain preparations in vitro, neuromuscular junction studies, and recording in awake animals. Early studies focused on identifying the locus or brain area specifically involved in learning and storing memories via ablation of various brain regions. Others focused on identifying changes in the peripheral system that exhibit simpler forms of learning, such as the neuromuscular junction. Results from lesion studies implicated certain brain areas as being involved in learning, and these areas are the focus of electrophysiological studies conducted in awake animals. Reduced preparations taken from these areas and kept intact in a special chamber can be studied for their cellular and biochemical properties (e.g., brain slices maintained in vitro). Information from all of these types of research has provided a better understanding of how the vertebrate brain processes and stores information. Because of the complexity of the vertebrate brain, at this point in time it is still impossible to obtain the same level of information about cellular mechanisms underlying learning in vertebrates as has been accomplished for *Aplysia*.

What vertebrate areas are important for learning and memory? How is information encoded, processed, stored, and retrieved? Which cellular mechanisms are involved in these processes? Answers to these questions are actively being sought. Several criteria must be met in order to establish a biological basis of learning: [1] There must be loss of learning or memory following removal of a brain area suspected to be involved in learning processes. [2] Electrophysiological changes in that region must correspond to learning events and not solely to motor or sensory activity. [3] The time course of cellular change must correspond to that of learning and memory. [4] Inhibition of identified cellular processes must also prevent or disrupt learning and memory functions.

The Search for the Engram

The physiological psychologist Karl Lashley (1929, 1950) spent most of his scientific career attempting to locate the neural **engram**, specific brain regions involved in learning and information storage or actual physical sites of newly generated connections formed during associative learning. Lashley evaluated maze learning in rats following either knife cuts or ablation of small areas of cerebral cortex. He found that it did not matter which cortical area was damaged but that the amount of cortical damage was important in maze learning: A rat with only a slight lesion could still navigate the maze, but rats with greater lesions performed more poorly, indicating that a single memory might be represented in more than one location in the brain. His assumption that maze learning was governed exclusively by cortical areas was in error, as you will see later in this chapter, but the idea that one memory could have multiple representations in the brain

originated from his work (see the discussion of aggregate field theory versus cellular connectionism in Chapter 1).

From the earlier discussion of localized neural circuits in *Aplysia* that undergo discrete changes during learning, you already know that in invertebrates there are specific areas and connections that are involved in different types of learning. In Chapter 8 you read about different functions subserved by various cortical regions such as primary visual cortex. In addition, many subcortical regions have been identified that are important for various forms of learning. In hindsight, Lashley's paradigms designed to locate the engram were not really appropriate for this purpose although this was not realized at the time. Highly localized and less destructive ablation techniques are still used to identify memory pathways; some are even reversible, using cold temperatures or drugs that temporarily block neural transmission (like novocaine does so you do not feel the dentists' drill). Even so, results from ablation experiments can only tell you what happens to a behavior in the absence of a structure but not how that structure participates in learning and memory processes (e.g., is it the site of plasticity or simply a relay in the network?).

Hebb's Postulate

Donald Hebb (1949), a student of Lashley's, believed that changes in specific neural connections did underlie learning, and he developed a scheme which modeled those changes. His model has been the driving force for neurophysiologists looking for a neural memory mechanism. This model, known as Hebb's postulate, states that a synapse is strengthened by concurrent activity between the pre- and postsynaptic cell. Only then can changes occur that maintain the encoded bits of information. This theme of activity dependency recurs in development, learning, and any form of synaptic plasticity where persistent changes must take place in order to produce a functional change.

Many ideas about the biological basis of learning and memory that are considered guiding principles today originated with Hebb. For example, he theorized that each memory was represented by a distributed network of neurons he called the **cell assembly**, connected by strengthened synapses resulting from concurrent activation. Since each neuron has connections with many others, each one could participate in many memory representations through these divergent connections. This early connectionistic view has grown into the explosive field of neural modeling, or the use of computers to mimic learning in living systems.

Enriched Environments

While studying maze learning in rats, Hebb discovered that environmental stimulation produced rats that were much better learners than rats living in the typical small cage with

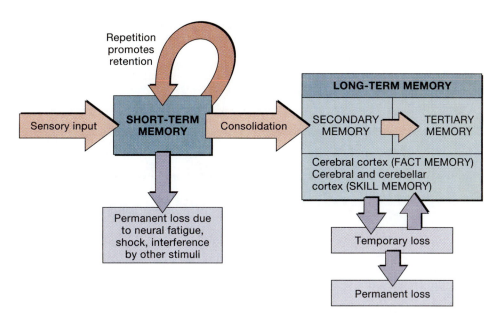

Figure 15–19 *Memory Storage.* The steps needed for short-term memory and long-term memory and the process of consolidation to transfer short-term memory into long-term memory.

just food and water and maybe another rat for stimulation. He had taken a group of rats home for his children to play with for a time, which would be returned to the lab at a later date for maze testing. He found that these rats learned the complex mazes much faster than rats that lived under laboratory conditions; he concluded that their **enriched environment** contributed to their increased learning ability. This discovery led to neuroanatomical investigation of brain changes that accompany enriched environmental living. Amazingly, a number of dramatic and consistent changes were discovered. Enriched rats had heavier brains, a thicker cortex, increased number and complexity of dendritic branches, and more dendritic spines, all suggesting increased connections between neurons, which could underlie their exceptional learning ability (Bennett et al., 1964; Globus et al., 1973; Greenough & Volkmar, 1973). This scientific evidence was used to bolster support for Head Start programs providing enriched environments for underprivileged preschool children.

Discrete Stages of Learning

Hebb was instrumental in emphasizing the distinction between **short-term memory** lasting minutes to hours and **long-term memory** lasting days to months (Figure 15–19). His dual trace hypothesis of memory suggested that short-term memory involves establishing a neural circuit that encodes an event through concurrent activity, and long-term memory comes about through repetition of activation of this neural trace, or *reverberatory activity*, which leads to persistent cellular changes, thus stabilizing the neural representation. So yes, it would pay to read this chapter more than once before the exam! This process of transforming short memories into long-lasting ones is called **consolidation**. Other distinct stages

of learning and memory processes include the **acquisition** or actual learning (your reading of this page) and **retrieval** of consolidated or stored information (quick—what is the definition of short-term memory?). You have probably experienced the fragility of short-term memory when initially trying to remember a phone number that you have just learned. If you are interrupted prior to dialing the number, it is unlikely that you will remember it. Your best friend's phone number, which you have repeated to yourself and dialed many times, is a well-established memory that is less prone to disruption and has undergone the long-term memory processes needed to stabilize a learned event.

The Functional Organization of Memory

Brenda Milner, a student of Hebb's interested in the neuropsychology of amnesia in people, studied the effects of temporal lobe removal on memory processes. At that time (1940s and 1950s), one treatment for intractable and uncontrollable epilepsy was bilateral removal of brain regions in the temporal lobe, since this area is highly susceptible to epileptic activity. The brain structures typically removed included the hippocampus, amygdala, and surrounding retrohippocampal cortical regions (Figure 15–20). One patient who received this treatment, referred to by the initials H. M., was intensely studied by Milner and was found to have severely impaired memory abilities following his surgery (Milner, 1972; Scoville & Milner, 1957). H. M. could clearly recall memories of events occurring prior to the surgery, and therefore his existing long-term memory remained intact, but he could not recall events occurring after the surgery. This impairment of short-term memory and consolidation processes, also called **anterograde amnesia**, since the subject cannot remember events subse-

Figure 15–20 *Surgery for Epilepsy.* These are the areas destroyed in surgery that is performed for intractable epilepsy.

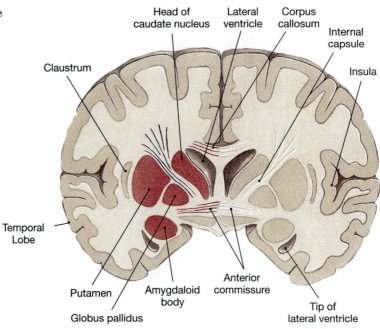

quent to the brain damage or surgery, leaves H. M. incapable of remembering who he has spoken to, who he has met, where he placed things, where he lives, everything with a spatial or temporal associative component. This particular type of memory is called **declarative memory** ("knowing that") and involves establishing complex associations between what is already in memory and incoming information and developing relational representations between them, such as knowing facts (e.g., where he is at a particular moment). Interestingly, H. M. is not impaired in another type of memory, **procedural memory** ("knowing how"), which involves establishing a simple relationship between one stimulus and one response without reference to other stored memory items. This includes skill learning such as mirror reading or even solving a puzzle that requires specific learned motor responses. It should be noted that there is emerging evidence indicating that damage to the basal ganglia (as in Parkinson's or Huntington's disease) impairs procedural memory. The difference in impairment suggests that those structures removed from H. M.'s brain carry out general declarative memory processes and specific short-term memory consolidation, whereas other intact structures are involved with establishing procedural memory.

Vertebrate Model Systems

The Hippocampus

Milner's findings led to intensive study of the effects of hippocampal removal on learning and memory processes in many animal species, with the goal of developing an animal model in which to study at least some forms of memory in mammalian brains. The volumes of data generated from these studies support the current extensive use of the hippocampus as a model system in which to study learning and memory processes at the behavioral, biophysical, anatomical, biochemical, and molecular levels.

The **hippocampus** is a bilateral C-shaped structure that lies under the cortical mantle (Figure 15–21) and is considered *archicortex* ("old" cortex) since its principal components have only three layers (compared with six layers in the neocortex). Information from the environment is processed by primary and associational cortical areas and then sent to the *entorhinal cortex*, the gateway to the hippocampus proper. In the simplest terms, the *entorhinal cortex* sends a massive projection (the *perforant pathway*) to the first stage in the trisynaptic circuit of the hippocampus proper, the *dentate gyrus*. Principal neurons, called granule cells, of the dentate gyrus project to cells of the next stage, *area CA_3* (CA stands for *cornis ammonis*, or "Ammon's Horn," a reference to classical mythology). CA_3 pyramidal cells contact the last processing stage of the hippocampus proper, *area CA_1*, by the way of the *Schaeffer collateral fiber pathway*. From here, hippocampally processed information leaves through the *subiculum*, the primary output structure. The subiculum sends this information to several subcortical and cortical areas, as well as back to the entorhinal cortex, which feeds this processed information back to cortical areas from which it came. This simple view of hippocampal trisynaptic circuitry (granule to CA_3 to CA_1; see Anderson, Bliss, & Skrede, 1971) seems a perfect model system exemplifying Hebb's proposed cell assem-

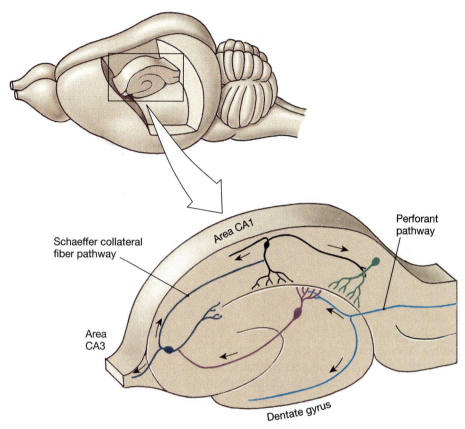

Figure 15–21   *The Hippocampus.* Hippocampal formation in a rat where the overlying cortical surface has been removed. (Amaral & Witter, 1989)

bly where information could reverberate, undergo changes necessary for long-term memory, and be sent to various other brain regions for storage. Another major output pathway from the hippocampus is the fornix (the large bundle of axons leaving the hippocampus), which circles around the thalamus before terminating in the hypothalamus. More recent anatomical studies have shown that hippocampal circuitry is not as straightforward as once thought (Amaral & Witter, 1989); there are many intrinsic connections among all hippocampal areas, commissural connections (from left cortex to right or vice versa), and input from many subcortical areas. More sophisticated approaches are needed to understand how all of these interactions within this system together mediate learning and memory.

As you can see from Fig 15–21, the hippocampus at its lowest level of organization appears to be arranged in discrete lamellae (layers) along its axis. Cutting out and removing a "slice" from anywhere along this axis leaves you with a piece of the hippocampus with its trisynaptic circuit intact. This characteristic of hippocampal anatomy has led to the development of the in vitro slice preparation. Hippocampal slices are removed and kept functioning in a chamber supplied with

vital nutrients, ions, and oxygen. This limited preparation allows for direct study of cellular processes (electrophysiological and biochemical) that may be involved in information processing in this structure, and a great deal of information has been gathered from its use.

One of the most consistently intriguing features of plasticity in the hippocampus is the phenomenon displayed by dendritic spines of granule cells when synaptic activation occurs. These actually change their morphology by alterations in the cytoskeleton when the synapse is activated repeatedly. The physical change in geometry is mediated by intracellular actin-like filaments and hence is similar to the movement of muscle fibers (Fifkova & Morales, 1997). This result has inspired a great deal of theorizing about the cerebral mechanisms for learning and memory.

Curiously, the opposite effect occurs within the hippocampus upon stressful stimuli; dendrites atrophy and plasma levels of stress hormones such as corticosterone rise. The elevated hormone levels may actually cause the atrophy and other chronic changes, such as alterations in the immune system, that are associated with stress (Galea et al., 1997; McEwen et al., 1997).

An interesting physiological property of the hippocampus is long-lasting increase in synaptic strength following brief, high-frequency stimulation of afferent fibers, first reported by Bliss and Lomo (1973). This type of plasticity is referred to as **long-term potentiation** (LTP; Douglas & Goddard, 1975, see next section). LTP can be induced in several hippocampal areas (Anderson et al., 1977; Buzsaki, 1980) as well as in many other brain regions in behaving animals (Lee, 1983; Racine, Milgram, & Hafner, 1983) and then studied. However, most of the biophysical information concerning LTP has come from in vitro and anesthetized preparations. LTP has been proposed as a process that underlies memory storage, yet its natural occurrence in the brain has not been observed.

Like H. M.'s experience, hippocampal lesions in many species result in memory impairments for certain types of learning whereas others are spared. Specifically, spatial learning abilities in rats are dramatically impaired following hippocampal lesions when the demands of the task require complex associations between environmental cues and the location of the animal as it moves through the maze. Cue learning, where the goal location is identified by an obvious cue, is not impaired (for an extensive review, see O'Keefe and Nadel, 1978; Jarrard, 1986). Studies in monkeys have demonstrated that lesions to certain hippocampal areas, particularly the retrohippocampal areas including the entorhinal cortex, produce severe memory impairments in tasks that have a significant temporal component, such as the delayed nonmatching to sample task typically used to test primate memory (Zola-Morgan, Squire, & Amaral, 1989). Monkeys with lesions like H. M.'s develop similar memory impairment and sparing and serve as an animal model of human amnesia. Clearly, the hippocampus is a valuable model for studying learning and memory mechanisms but it is not the only crucial area. As we shall see in the following section, many other areas, including frontal cortical areas and the cerebellum, are important for various types of memory and learning processes.

Long-Term Potentiation (LTP)

In 1973, Bliss and Lomo, studying the biophysical properties of the hippocampus, discovered the phenomena of long-term potentiation. Their experiment involved recording EPSPs (excitatory postsynaptic potentials, Chapter 5) in the dentate gyrus from a stimulating electrode placed in the hippocampal perforant fiber pathway, which activated many axons simultaneously; they evaluated the changes in the evoked potential in response to weak test pulses. They found a dramatic increase in the amplitude of both the action potential and EPSP that lasted for up to ten hours in some cases (Figure 15–22), and they explained these changes as an increase in efficiency of synaptic transmission at the perforant path–dentate synapse. Since this activity-dependent change was long lasting, they hypothesized that it may be a biological mechanism underlying information storage, but cautioned that this synchronous, repetitive activation of thousands of axons may not really occur in life where axons probably fire asynchronously. Nonetheless, a great number of laboratories began intensive studies to unravel the underlying mechanisms of this synthetic phenomenon and its relationship to learning in animals.

Many synapses display changes in efficacy with repetitive activation. Almost certainly, many of these changes have little or nothing to do with learning. The neuromuscular junction is not commonly conceived as a locus for learning in the animal but experiences both decreases in efficacy with repetitive activation (exhaustion and transmitter depletion) and increases (post-tetanic potentiation thought to arise because of calcium accumulation in the endplate with numerous incoming action potentials). These phenomena appear in different preparations depending on the stimulus parameters and since they do not last as long as LTP in the hippocampus

probably do not model memory mechanisms very well. The fact that there is such a wide variety of mechanisms for synaptic plasticity has caused investigators to wonder if perhaps LTP is just an epiphenomenon of physiological changes observed in any system with non-physiological stimuli. Nevertheless, LTP compels interest in the theoretician because no other central change displays extinction and improvement with repeated presentations of the stimulus in a manner so similar to learning as produced behaviorally. Since LTP is found in the hippocampus (among other brain regions) and the hippocampus has been associated with memory storage independently, the phenomenon of hippoacampal LTP continues to attract interest.

The appeal of this phenomenon as a memory mechanism candidate is clear if you consider what sorts of synaptic changes would be necessary for strengthening and stabilizing connections between neurons in a circuit that represents a memory. Some of these include concurrent activation between the pre- and postsynaptic neuron (recall Hebb's postulate) and quickly initiated and enduring changes in synaptic efficacy. In addition, LTP should occur in candidate memory storage areas (i.e., hippocampus) and be induced with stimuli that mimic endogenous patterns of activity. Many of these issues have been addressed experimentally, but at this point in time the most important issue—the natural occurrence of LTP during learning—has not. For recent reviews of the LTP field see Baudry and Davis, 1991; Brown, et al., 1988; Madison, Malenka, & Nicoll, 1991.

LTP has been studied most extensively at hippocampal synapses in both intact animals and with in vitro preparations (Figure 15–22). Certain properties such as cooperativity, associativity and specificity are displayed by LTP (Figure 15–23). In other words, weak and strong inputs can cooperate to produce LTP and are associated when simultaneous. The strong input can potentiate by itself (specificity), but the weak one requires the strong input to potentate. Convergence of simultaneous activity from multiple inputs depolarizes the postsynaptic cell sufficiently to activate the N-methyl-D-asparate (NMDA) receptor (a glutamate receptor subtype), resulting in increased Ca^{++} influx (Figure 15–24). Ca^{++}, acting as a second messenger, stimulates protein kinase activity, which triggers persistent postsynaptic changes. These changes may also activate a retrograde messenger that travels to the presynaptic cell, activating kinases there, which establish persistent increases in transmitter release. There is increasing evidence that this retrograde messenger is nitric oxide, a gas in pure form (Izumi et al., 1998) but other candidates exist (see below). Both pre- and postsynaptic cellular changes underlie initiation and maintenance of LTP. Ca^{++} influx at the postsynaptic site is a critical factor. Treatments

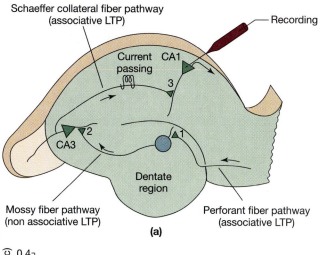

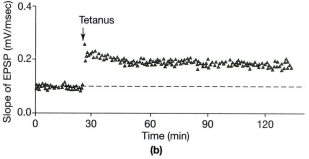

Figure 15–22 *LTP in Hippocampal Pathways.* (a) The pathways in the hippocampus that are capable of LTP: the perforant fiber pathway, the mossy fiber pathway, and the Schaeffer collateral fiber pathway. The arrows denote the direction of the impulse flow and the synapses undergoing plasticity are labelled 1, 2, and 3. (b) Association between stimuli produces LTP in synapse 3, as made evident by a faster-rising EPSP. (Kandel et al., 1991)

that eliminate Ca^{++} prevent LTP from occurring (Lynch et al., 1983) and addition of Ca^{++} alone produces LTP (Malenka et al., 1988). Blocking Ca^{++} influx through the NMDA channel with NMDA antagonists such as APV blocks LTP, suggesting that the critical component for initiation is opening of the NMDA channel resulting in a postsynaptic Ca^{++} increase (Collingridge, Kelly, & McLennan, 1983). This high level of postsynaptic Ca^{++} activates two kinases: Ca^{++}/calmodulin kinase and protein kinase C, which results in persistent enhancement of synaptic transmission (Malinow, Madison, & Tsien, 1988; Malinow et al., 1989).

Along with physiological and biochemical changes, postsynaptic anatomical changes have been detected following LTP. Changes in the shape of the postsynaptic membrane have been found that would result in lowered membrane resistance and an enhanced postsynaptic response (Fifkova & Anderson, 1981; van Harreveld & Fifkova, 1975; Lledo et al.,

1998). Increases in synapse density following LTP, indicating formation of new synapses, have also been described (Chang & Greenough, 1984; Lee et al., 1980).

Recently, there has been a great deal of interest in finding the "retrograde messenger" that delivers information about postsynaptic changes to the presynaptic terminal to stimulate changes at that site for maintenance of LTP (see Figure 15–24). Presynaptic changes such as increased transmitter release have been found either by measuring the amount of neurotransmitter released following LTP induction (Bliss et al., 1986) or through methods analyzing the postsynaptic response to transmitter release (Bekkers & Stevens, 1990). How might a retrograde messenger work? Perhaps a retrograde messenger diffuses out of the postsynaptic cell, travels to and enters the presynaptic cell membrane, activating kinases that enhance transmitter release and initiate LTP. Some candidates include arachidonic acid (Lynch, Errington, & Bliss, 1989, Williams et al., 1989), nitric oxide (O'Dell et al., 1991; Schuman & Madison, 1991), and perhaps even carbon monoxide (Verma et al., 1993).

How does LTP relate to learning and memory? Davis, Butcher, & Morris (1992) have tested the effects of NMDA antagonists on LTP and spatial memory in rats (which is dependent on the hippocampus). They found that the NMDA antagonist AP5 blocks LTP and spatial learning simultaneously. Rats with a certain level of AP5 in their hippocampi could not perform the spatial tasks, and LTP could not be induced in these animals. This lends some support to the hypothesis that LTP is a mechanism of memory. Unfortunately, LTP cannot be detected in the brain without applying strong artificial stimulation and therefore cannot be studied directly in relation to behavioral changes associated with learning. This is one hurdle that needs to be crossed before LTP can conclusively be considered the neurobiological basis of memory.

LTP has been demonstrated in all hippocampal regions as well as in neocortical areas, brainstem and thalamic nuclei, and autonomic ganglia in a wide range of species (Tyler & DiScenna, 1987). There may be various forms of LTP since differences in induction parameters, time course, and neurotransmitter mechanisms exist between regions. Nonetheless, a recent report describes similar characteristics of cortical LTP in rats and cats and CA1 hippocampal LTP in rats, suggesting that common principles govern plasticity in these areas (Kirkwood et al., 1993).

It is unknown whether similar cellular mechanisms underlie the various forms of LTP, but if so perhaps LTP is simply a common characteristic of all synapses. Since LTP is found in structures that have not been directly associated with memory (e.g., the optic tectum of goldfish), it is more

Figure 15–23 *Properties of LTP.* (a) The weak afferents will not potentiate when stimulated alone. (b) Association between simultaneous activation of weak and strong afferents produces potentiation of both. (c) The strong afferents can potentiate by themselves. Thus, the strong afferents can potentiate the weak synapses, indicating that the mechanism for LTP must be postsynaptic. (Kandel et al., 1991)

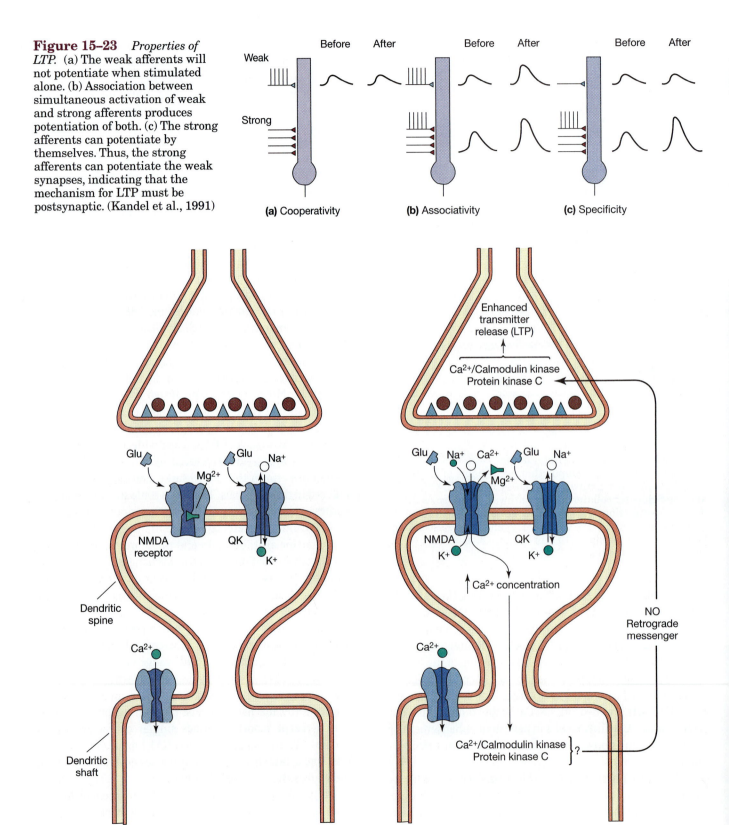

Figure 15–24 *Induction of LTP.* (a) The postsynaptic cell is depolarized by activation of the NMDA receptor in the dendritic spine; (b) Increase of intracellular Ca^{++} allows the dendritic spine to trigger Ca^{++}-dependent kinases, which in turn induce LTP. The retrograde messenger may be nitric oxide.

likely that the phenomenon is a general physiological characteristic of synapses. Still, the scientific community anxiously awaits each new development in the field of LTP research, partly because more promising models for learning are not yet available.

The Cerebellum and Nictitating Membrane Response

Thompson and colleagues have developed a method to record and trace physiological changes accompanying a classically conditioned **nictitating membrane response** in the intact brain of anesthetized rabbits (Thompson, 1983; Thompson et al., 1976). The nictitating membrane lies under the eyelid and lowers to cover and protect the eye. A puff of air to the eye elicits this reflexive response. When the air puff (US) is paired with a tone (CS), the CS alone will elicit the response (CR). Unfortunately, people do not have nictitating membranes so the applicability to humans is uncertain.

Initial studies recorded changes in hippocampal activity during the development of this learned association; once learned, the tone alone would elicit increased hippocampal activity prior to the response (Berger & Thompson, 1978). Further studies found that hippocampal lesions did not impair the acquisition or the retention of this learned response (Mauk & Thompson, 1987; Solomon & Moore, 1975). This prompted the investigators to look elsewhere for the locus of neural change underlying this type of reflexive associative learning. The **cerebellum** (Figure 15–25), which controls many motor responses (see Box 10–2), was targeted. Physiological changes in activity accompanying the learning of this response were recorded and were compared to subjects with lesions of a particular cerebellar area, the **dentate-interpositus nucleus**. In the lesioned subjects, both acquisition and retention of this conditioned response were abolished (Krupa, Thompson, & Thompson, 1993; Lavond, McCormick, & Thompson, 1984; Yeo, Hardiman, & Glickstein, 1985).

The Vestibulo-ocular Reflex

Visual acuity depends on the stability of the eyes with respect to the surroundings, since images moving across the retina must be focused and processed accurately. Head movements would impede this process if not for a reflex, called the vestibulo-ocular reflex (VOR), that generates compensatory smooth eye movements that are equal and opposite to the head movement. The VOR undergoes motor learning through changes in the strength of synapses in parts of the pathway mediating it. Neural pathways from the vestibular system to the eyes are modulated by cerebellar input for adaptation to changing visual conditions.

Miles and Lisberger (1981; Lisberger, 1988) studied plasticity of the VOR in monkeys wearing magnifying lenses, thus

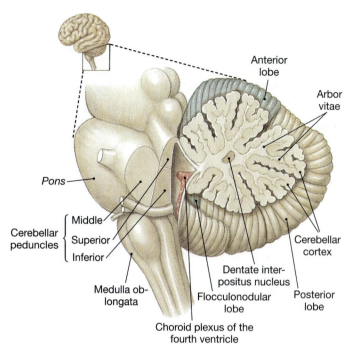

Figure 15–25 *The Cerebellum.* A cross-sectional view of the cerebellum and its components.

changing their view of the visual environment (Figure 15–26). By measuring the change in the ratio of head to eye movement, they found that the VOR changed to compensate for the magnified view of the world. With 2X magnification, the world is perceived to move at twice the rate during head rotation and the VOR must double the velocity of the compensatory eye movements in order to keep images on the retina stable. The VOR is tested in the light and the change due to image magnification continues to occur when it is tested in darkness. This motor learning is a gradual process and appears to be regulated by input from a cerebellar nucleus called the flocculus, although this is not the main site of the enhanced synaptic efficacy. The actual site of motor learning in this system is still being sought.

The studies discussed throughout this chapter emphasize the importance of clearly identifying the brain area or circuit involved with a particular form of learning through multiple techniques. Correlative physiological changes alone do not necessarily mean that an area is the site of plasticity underlying the behavioral change, but merely that it may be a player in the complex interactions among many brain regions during any type of behavior. Since the cerebellum is involved in regulating and modifying motor responses, it may be the site where processes underlying procedural or skill learning occur. Yet, it can be noted that the memory for a process can occur someplace other than where the control over that process occurs.

Figure 15–26: *The Vestibulo-ocular Reflex.* Miles and Lisberger's studies (1981) on plasticity of the VOR in monkeys found that the VOR changed to compensate for the monkey's magnified view. The lower diagram indicates that the VOR's input can be modified in the brainstem and cerebellum before commands are sent to the motor neurons. (Lisberger, 1988)

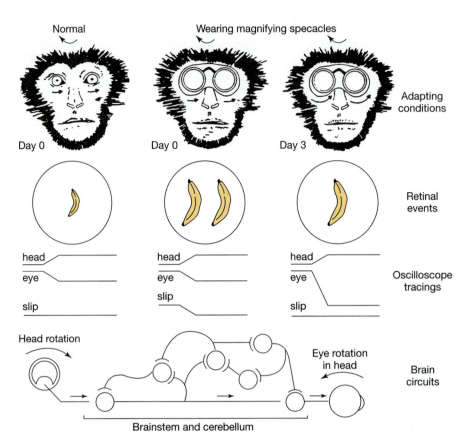

SUMMARY

Nervous system plasticity and flexibility originate during the first stages of embryonic development and are maintained in an ordered succession throughout the life span of an organism. Early developmental events shape the complex structure of the nervous system. Neurogenesis produces immature precursor neurons, which migrate to their correct locations following environmental cues. Differentiation of mature neuronal characteristics is also guided by environmental cues and interactions with other cells. Each neuron has its own individual morphology, neurotransmitter, biophysical properties, and connectivity. Once a neuron finds its place in the brain, it extends its axonal growth cone toward its target guided by adhesive molecules along its path and molecular gradients at the target site. Synapse formation and synapse stabilization are dependent on molecular cues as well as activity-dependent competition for trophic factors. Refinement of synaptic connections and remodeling is mainly activity-dependent and occurs during the later stages of development and adulthood. It is this refinement and remodeling that likely supports learning and memory processes.

Learning can be classified as nonassociative or associative, simple or complex, but at any level changes in neuronal biochemical or biophysical properties result in observable changes in behavior. These modifications can be measured directly in invertebrate nervous systems during simple forms of learning, and the mechanisms involved are thought to be similar for more complex learning in mammalian brains. Damage to specific brain regions produces learning and memory deficits in many species, including humans. One such region, the hippocampus, provides a model for the study of mechanisms that may underlie learning and memory processes. Candidate sites of learning in the nervous system are identified by combining lesion, electrophysiological, and behavioral studies. Changes in synaptic strength can be physiologically measured in mammalian pathways involved in learning processes. LTP governed by Hebbian mechanisms may be one form of synaptic modification for memory storage. The neural basis of learning and memory is still being sought and is a fascinating area of research. Someday we will be able to pinpoint the mechanism that causes you to remember exactly where you left your car keys after searching for them for an hour.

REVIEW QUESTIONS

1. Cite an example of associative learning and of nonassociative learning.

2. What is complex learning?

3. Describe habituation and sensitization in *Aplysia* and provide the mechanism for each.

4. What is the relationship between the hippocampus and learning?

5. Describe Hebb's postulate and provide a molecular mechanism.

6. What is chemoaffinity?

7. What is induction?

8. List the criteria for experimental identification of a learning mechanism in the brain.

9. How does surgical closure of one eye alter the structure of the visual system?

10. What mechanisms of development are also involved in learning?

THOUGHT QUESTIONS

1. Attention deficit disorder (ADD) is a developmental abnormality in which the affected individual cannot segregate significant from insignificant stimuli. Review the material on trophic factors (Chapter 2) and synapse elimination and activity-dependent fine-tuning of the nervous system (this chapter) and provide a cellular theory of the origin of this condition.

2. Given your theory of ADD, (question 1) propose a proper treatment for the disorder.

KEY CONCEPTS

acquisition (p. 381)
adhesion molecules (p. 365)
agrin (p. 367)
anterograde amnesia (p. 381)
associative learning (p. 370)
autoradiography (p. 360)
basal lamina (p. 367)
blastocoel (p. 356)
blastomeres (p. 356)
blastocyst (p. 356)
cell assembly (p. 380)
cell surface molecules (p. 361)
cerebellum (p. 387)
chemoaffinity (p. 365)
classical conditioning (p. 370)
complex learning (p. 369)
conditioned response (p. 371)
conditioned stimulus (p. 371)
consolidation (p. 381)
critical period (p. 374)
declarative memory (p. 382)

dentate-interpositus nucleus (p. 387)
dishabituation (p. 375)
ectoderm (p. 356)
endoderm (p. 356)
engram (p. 380)
enriched environment (p. 381)
extracellular matrix molecules (p. 361)
filopodia (p. 364)
food aversion (p. 372)
gastrulation (p. 356)
germ tissue layers (p. 356)
gill-withdrawal reflex (p. 375)
growth cone (p. 364)
guidepost cells (p. 365)
habituation (p. 369)
hippocampus (p. 382)
imprinting (p. 373)
integrins (p. 361)
lamellipodia (p. 361)
latent learning (p. 374)

long-term memory (p. 381)
long-term potentiation (p. 383)
marginal layer (p. 360)
mesencephalon (p. 360)
mesoderm (p. 386)
N-cadherin (p. 365)
nerve growth factor (NGF) (p. 365)
neural cell adhesion molecules (NCAMs) (p. 362)
neural crest (p. 356)
neural groove (p. 356)
neural plasticity (p. 369)
neural plate (p. 356)
neural tube (p. 356)
neuroblast (p. 361)
neurogenesis (p. 355)
neurulation (p. 356)
nictitating membrane response (p. 387)
nonassociative learning (p. 369)
notochord (p. 360)

observational learning (p. 374)
operant conditioning (p. 372)
pathfinding (p. 364)
phenotype (p. 363)
procedural memory (p. 382)
prosencephalon (p. 360)
radial glial cells (p. 361)
reflexive learning (p. 369)
repulsive cues (p. 365)
retrieval (p. 381)
rhombencephalon (p. 360)
sensitization (p. 370)
short-term memory (p. 381)
spatial learning (p. 379)
somites (p. 360)
target recognition (p. 364)
trophic factors (p. 365)
tropic factors (p. 365)
unconditioned response (p. 371)
unconditioned stimulus (p. 371)
ventricular layer (p. 360)

We find ourselves entering a realm of fascination and paradox, all of which centers on the ambiguity of the "concrete." In particular, as physicians, as therapists, as teachers, as scientists we are invited, indeed compelled, towards an exploration of the concrete. . . . The concrete can open doors, and it can close them too. It can constitute the portal to sensibility, imagination, depth. Or it can confine the possessor (or the obsessed) to meaningless particulars. . . . The concrete, equally, may become a vehicle of mystery . . . fully as much as any abstract conception.

Oliver Sacks The Man Who Mistook His Wife for a Hat, *1985*

Language and Higher Cognitive Function

"Higher cognitive function" is a pretentious phrase used by neuroscientists when they mean "thinking." We are quite certain that people think (remember the discussion of Descartes in Chapter 1?) and thus much of our understanding of higher cognitive function comes from the study of people. Language, in particular, is primarily if not exclusively a human attribute and in our society is the most common means whereby thoughts are expressed. Therefore, much research on higher cognitive function is also research on the neuroscience of language. The definition of language as "speech; the expression of ideas by words or written symbols; communication between animals" includes other species from the animal kingdom besides ourselves, however higher cognitive function is best understood in humans. Nevertheless we have more evidence that nonhuman animals think than we have of animal language. Therefore some animal models can also provide us insight into higher cognitive function.

Much of what we know about higher cognitive functions, including language, comes from studying individuals who lack some of these functions. In most of us, language and thought, feeling and movement, the abstract and the concrete are in each case inextricably associated. Only when one element is missing (thought without language, movement without feeling, or the concrete without the abstract) can we examine the remaining trait unobscured, as it were, by normal function and come to a greater understanding and appreciation of its importance.

In this chapter we will explore aspects of consciousness that are close to the internal experience that each of us regards as uniquely ours, the "core self." As the distinguished neurologist Oliver Sacks points out, this core self is very tightly associated with concrete experiences that we share with other people: language, implements, and values. We will review those concrete experiences we share with other animals and in the process learn more about what it means to be human.

Human Neurobiology

Scientific investigation of the human nervous system has both advantages and disadvantages over the study of other organisms. In physiological studies people have an advantage over nonhuman subjects because they can describe to the experimenter what they are experiencing, using common language. In anatomical studies, this advantage is preserved through a verbal record that can be made of a person's experiences prior to death and autopsy. Finally, humans are more cooperative than experimental animals, enduring procedures that experimental animals would not willingly accept (such as instruction to "stay very still" while in the CAT scanner) once the importance and necessity has been explained.

Theoretical Limits and Practical Problems

An example of the value of human neurobiology can be found in the search for the **command neuron**. Recall from Chapter 10 that there is a hypothetical structure at the apex of descending motor commands that makes the decision to act. In theory, the command neuron also dwells at the apex of converging sensory input since the decision to act depends on environmental circumstances. Studies of invertebrate behavior, which is driven largely by instinct, have found a few examples of single cells that satisfy the criteria for a command neuron (in that their activity is both *sufficient* and *necessary* for a behavior to come about). However, for more complex organisms and for behaviors more elaborate than, say, an escape reflex, the search for the command cell has been very difficult.

Dualists are very interested in the command cell because, in addition to integrating sensory input and organizing motor output the command cell must be the repository for *free will*, or the avenue whereby spontaneous activity that is not determined by preexisting conditions is generated. Animals can be *trained* to respond to a cue; it is not clear that this response is completely voluntary in the human sense. Thus, research on free will must be conducted on people to ensure that the behavior is voluntary or volitional.

Elegant studies of volitional behavior have been conducted by neuroscientists in collaboration with neurosurgeons. Such studies are possible because the brain has no free nerve endings (Chapter 11) and hence does not experience pain when probed by a scalpel or electrode. Furthermore, anesthesia to the point of unconsciousness actually poses a threat to the patient's welfare, since this total, or "global," anesthesia can interfere with breathing. Finally, since the patient can actually assist the neurosurgeon in some procedures (see "Neurosurgery on Awake Individuals" and "Penfield's Observations," this chapter), the technique of surgery on a conscious patient (sedated of course and with local anesthetic around the wound margins) is the favored method for some neurosurgery and much general surgery (Figure 16–1).

While recording from sensory or motor cortex progressively more remote from primary cortex (i.e., in association

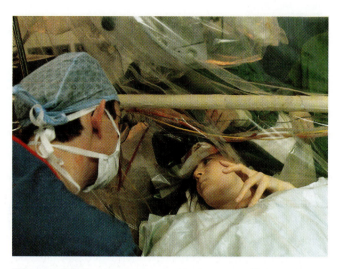

Figure 16–1 *Neurosurgery Performed on a Conscious Patient.* Several modern surgeries are now performed on patients who are fully conscious.

cortex), it is possible to acquire evidence of thought progressively farther from action in time (and presumably progressively closer to the voluntary decision at the origin of the impulse to act). Studies by Benjamin Libet (1985, 1987, 1989) investigated this phenomena by measuring the time between the report of a conscious decision to act and the onset of cerebral activity. The results are impressive: Cortical activity significantly preceded the report of "wanting" to act by at least several hundred milliseconds, that is, the freely voluntary movement began subconsciously. Furthermore, Libet has postulated that stimuli we normally cannot sense consciously can nevertheless evoke considerable neuronal activity. These apparent endowments show unique potential in the area of understanding human thought and the extensive networks that we still must uncover about the mind and its capabilities.

Thus it can be appreciated that human neurobiology offers potential that no animal studies could readily provide. Add to the theoretical limits on animal studies the unique feature that people, as far as we know, are the only organisms capable of self-reflection and we have another reason, albeit controversial, to look to human research for the most promising new developments in neuroscience (Box 16–1).

Nevertheless, it must be observed that human studies have intrinsic limitations as well. Obviously, intrusive brain studies are not possible with human subjects and we must rely on trauma or cerebrovascular accidents that may have damaged areas other than those of interest in order to access experimental parameters. Carefully controlled studies are usually possible with people, but they lack the variability and the same extent of control that can be achieved with animal

Box 16–1

The Importance of Introspection

Psychology, of which neuroscience is a "biological relative," came about in part because of a lack of trust in the potential for reflection, philosophy, or religion to provide reliable truths about the nature of internal experience. Experimentalists like Thorndike, Watson, and later Skinner emphasized only what was observable, namely behavior. Their impetus enabled the description of the kinetics and stimulus requirements for learning and memory and placed constraints on the potential neural bases for these processes but did not shed much light on the biological mechanisms of learning.

While introspection may have had heuristic value in propelling the advance of neuroscience at the molecular, cellular, and systems levels, this value was rarely made explicit in scholarly papers or even in conversation among practitioners. The approach taken to problems was still inherently reductionistic and cumulative, embracing the hope that general truths would emerge from the particulars.

A startling development in neuroscience in recent years is the growing feeling—first a vague hunch, then a general angst, and finally a conviction openly expressed by some—that neither behaviorism or reductionism alone, nor the two in combination, would be adequate to attack the problem of consciousness. Consciousness too often does not achieve overt expression, making behavioristic analysis impossible, and appears to be organized on the basis of aggregate field theory, making reductionistic analysis difficult. These investigators have attempted to generate theoretical insights leading to testable hypotheses about consciousness based on reflection and comparison with complex systems other than the mind and the brain.

The interested reader will find a spirited defense of this new introspection in Roger Sperry's Nobel Prize acceptance speech, which included a commentary on the split-brain work, providing insight into the mind/body problem (1982).

Progress on Mind-Brain Problem

In closing, it remains to mention briefly that one of the more important direct results of the split-brain work is a revised concept of the nature of consciousness and its fundamental relation to brain processing. . . . The key development is a switch from prior noncausal, parallelist views to a new causal or "interactionist" interpretation that ascribes to inner experience an integral causal control role in brain function and behavior. In effect, and without resorting to dualism, the mental forces of the conscious mind are restored to the brain of objective science from which they had long been excluded on materialist-behaviorist principles.

The spreading acceptance of the revised causal view and the reasoning involved carry important implications for science and for scientific views of man and nature. Cognitive introspective psychology and related cognitive science can no longer be ignored experimentally, or written off as "a science of epiphenomena" or as something that must in principle reduce eventually to neurophysiology. The event of inner experience, as emergent properties of brain processes, become themselves explanatory causal constructs in their own right, interacting at their own level with their own laws and dynamics. The whole world of inner experience (the world of the humanities), long rejected by twentieth-century scientific materialism, thus becomes recognized and included within the domain of science.

Basic revisions in concepts of causality are involved, in which the whole, besides being "different from and greater than the sum of the parts," also causally determines the fate of the parts without interfering with the physical or chemical laws of the subentities at their own level. It follows that physical science no longer perceives the world to be reducible to quantum mechanics or to any other unifying ultra element or field force. The qualitative, holistic properties at all different levels become causally real in their own form and have to be included in the causal account. Quantum theory in these terms no longer replaces or subsumes classical mechanics but rather just supplements or complements.

The results add up to a fundamental change in what science has stood for throughout the materialist-behaviorist era. . . . The former scope of science, its limitations, world perspectives, views of human nature, and its societal role as an intellectual, cultural, and moral force all undergo profound change. Where there used to be conflict and an irreconcilable chasm between the scientific and the traditional humanistic views of man and the world . . . , we now perceive a continuum. A unifying new interpretative framework emerges . . . with far-reaching impact not only for science but for those ultimate value-belief guidelines by which mankind has tried to live and find meaning.

and in vitro studies. Furthermore, it is not ethically possible to eliminate every variable except for the experimental one from both experimental and control subjects. Put plainly, animals can be bred, housed, and treated in every way identical to one another until the essential measurement is made, but what two groups of people would submit to this uniformity?

Results from Communication in and with Other Species

Perhaps the best approach to the understanding of higher function, and consciousness, given the limitations described earlier, would involve collaboration between species. Before this thought is dismissed as hopelessly naive, consider some steps that have already been taken in this direction. Apart from the human studies already described, the best understanding of volitional behavior at a high level of association motor cortex has been acquired by studying monkeys. The monkeys in these experiments learn a practical purpose (as opposed to the scientific purpose) from the experimenters and readily approach the experimental apparatus to engage in trials of motor learning ability. Single unit records are made from primary motor cortex; as expected, cells of the primary motor cortex are activated in anticipation of limb movement. In adjacent association cortex, units fire even earlier than those of primary motor cortex in anticipation of movement, and the firing can be modified as the monkey becomes more adept at a task. For example, the monkey may be required to solve a problem of imagery, in which an object must be rotated mentally in order to solve the problem. The response properties of the cells of the association cortex change as the image is rotated (Evarts, Wise, & Bousfield, 1985; Georgeopoulos et al., 1989). Such experiments get close to the mental apparatus involved in thinking and problem solving, central functions that undoubtedly work the same in people as in monkeys (See Chapter 10).

Better known are the experiments conducted over the years by anthropologists and linguists (experts in the study of human speech including its sounds, history, nature, and structure) in which apes are taught symbolic logic and even the elements of language. Most celebrated of these is Washoe, a chimpanzee that acquired the ability to form simple requests using symbols (Gardner & Gardner, 1978). Much controversy exists in the field of animal language, however, since animals have very sophisticated, but non-human speech and problem-solving skills. An example that is well-known to language researchers as a caution against overinterpretation comes from a circus horse named "Clever Hans." The horse was a popular side show because of his claimed ability to make mathematical calculations (addition mostly) and indicate the answers by tapping a hoof for

Figure 16–2 *Animal Communication.* Some researchers believe that chimpanzees and other animals are capable of symbolic thought and language. Indeed, recent research has identified an enlargement in the left hemisphere of apes that may be a precursor of our speech center.

the correct number of times. However, scientific examination proved that Hans could only perform this feat in the visual presence of a trainer. The calculations requested by a *hidden* trainer evoked no response or incorrect responses. After further study, it was found that Clever Hans was responding to subconscious cues in the trainer's expression, which turned from worried to proud and satisfied as the correct answer was approached. While Clever Hans's ability to read such nonverbal cues was indeed remarkable, he did not demonstrate an understanding of language. Current study of language aptitude in animals by no means suffers from the same methodological problems as the case of Clever Hans (Figure 16–2). Nevertheless, the growing field of acquired language in nonhuman species and the long-standing investigation of animal communication in the wild remain fraught with disputes among investigators and confusion regarding the meaning of the results. It seems that the best lesson to be learned from animal communication is that true language is unique to our species.

Results from Diagnostic Neurology

After the time of Broca (Chapter 1) and Brown-Sequard (Chapter 7), **diagnostic neurology**, the deduction of the location of central nervous system damage based on behavioral signs, was developed into a fine science. Asking the question "Where is the lesion?" generations of medical students learned specific behavioral expressions of each type of brain damage. While this was done in the name of patient welfare, in fact there was little the neurologist could do for the brain-damaged patients; perhaps the greatest contribution of diagnostic neurology was to advance knowledge of the normal localization of function by accidental experiment. The systematic pairing of symptoms with brain regions did not occur evenly. Some parts of the brain, such as the basal ganglia and areas surrounding the internal capsule, are especially prone to vascular damage and hence neurology acquired a wealth of information regarding their functions. Other parts of the brain, such as medulla, pons, midbrain, and thalamus, remained obscure to neurology since damage to these regions was usually lethal, leaving no record of behavioral deficit. By a cruel paradox of nature, much of our knowledge about the functions of brain, like some neocortex that does not often suffer vascular accident, comes from warfare that generated a plentitude of head injuries distributed widely throughout the brain. The diagnostic neurology of the time of the Civil War, and of World War I, remains to this day the most complete set of descriptions of the behavioral deficits resulting from certain head injuries.

Whereas diagnostic neurology aimed to help patients by deducing the extent and area of the central damage by behavioral signs alone, noninvasive imaging techniques such as **magnetic resonance imaging (MRI)** can visualize the extent of central damage directly, without the need for extensive neurological exam. Because of such advances the field of neuroscience will now grow more from the experimental use of such new imaging technologies than from the behavioral study of brain-damaged individuals. (These techniques will be discussed shortly).

The following sections outline the classical neurological deficits and their central correlates: aphasia (inability to communicate), apraxia (inability to move), agnosia, (inability to understand), alexia (inability to read), and dyslexia (the difficulty in reading displayed often as a learning disorder).

Aphasias

It is estimated that language evolved no earlier than about 100,000 years ago. Yet the vast majority of the human nervous system achieved its current state millions of years ago. How can we resolve this discrepancy in time? The answer may lie in use of preexisting structures for new purposes. We have seen how gene duplication gave rise to numerous homologous hormones in Chapter 12. It seems likely that symbolic language likewise developed from elaborate, but nonsymbolic, communication schemes. Goodall's studies of chimpanzees in the wild reveal the intricacy of communication in this species, which could not have been much different from our hominid ancestors 100,000 years ago (Goodall, 1986; Figure 16–3). Indeed, the example of Clever Hans cited earlier reveals how common nonlinguistic communication is among mammals. Now researchers are beginning to close in on the neur-

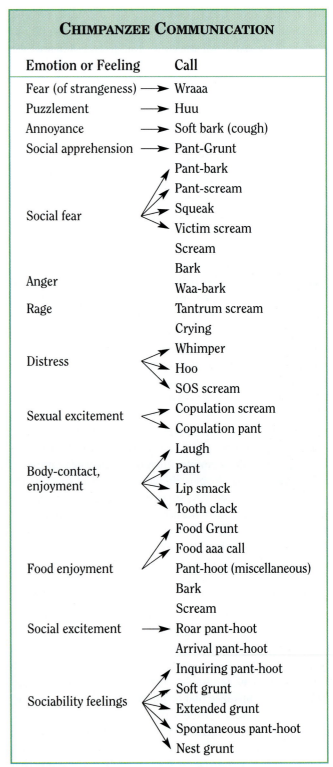

CHIMPANZEE COMMUNICATION	
Emotion or Feeling	**Call**
Fear (of strangeness) ⟶	Wraaa
Puzzlement ⟶	Huu
Annoyance ⟶	Soft bark (cough)
Social apprehension ⟶	Pant-Grunt
Social fear	Pant-bark
	Pant-scream
	Squeak
	Victim scream
Anger	Scream
	Bark
	Waa-bark
Rage	Tantrum scream
Distress	Crying
	Whimper
	Hoo
	SOS scream
Sexual excitement	Copulation scream
	Copulation pant
Body-contact, enjoyment	Laugh
	Pant
	Lip smack
	Tooth clack
Food enjoyment	Food Grunt
	Food aaa call
	Pant-hoot (miscellaneous)
	Bark
	Scream
Social excitement ⟶	Roar pant-hoot
	Arrival pant-hoot
Sociability feelings	Inquiring pant-hoot
	Soft grunt
	Extended grunt
	Spontaneous pant-hoot
	Nest grunt

Source: Goodall (1986).

Figure 16–3 *Chimpanzee Communication of Emotion and Feeling.* Standardized chimpanzee calls denoting specific emotions and feelings.

al mechanisms for language using studies of aphasia (Blumenstein, 1997).

Broca's aphasia is a disorder that predominantly affects the production of speech with little deficit in spoken or written language comprehension. Damage has occurred in "Broca's area" (motor association cortex in frontal lobe), and the result is lethargic, labored speech, difficulty in using appropriate grammatical constructions (such as conjunctions, prepositions, articles, and verb agreement), mispronunciations, and characteristic trouble with finding the correct word to use (or anomia, *a* = without, *nomia* = name). Interestingly, the words produced are usually meaningful and appropriate. Indeed, the words that patients are able to sputter out are often *only* meaningful words, being descriptive and specific in nature. Individuals with Broca's are aware of the errors they are making and do try to correct themselves. Finally, Broca's aphasia is characterized by poor recognition of word order. Although patients can understand the vocabulary of sentences, they may not be able to distinguish the subject from the object. For example, "the dog chases the mail carrier" may not be differentiated from "the mail carrier chases the dog." Sentences that are quite obvious, such as "the artist paints with acrylics" do not present as many comprehensional problems (Kolb & Whishaw, 1996).

Wernicke's aphasia is characterized by a substantial deficit in comprehension but retention of speech fluency, resulting from damage to the left posterior region of the temporal lobe. Few descriptive and content words are used, but there are no pauses in between words, and articulating sentences is not a strain. Contrary to Broca's aphasia, an individual with Wernicke's aphasia is not aware of any deficit in understanding what others are saying nor of the incomprehensible speech he or she is producing. However, the person is still able to follow proper conversation conduct such as taking turns in speaking, pausing to hear an answer to a question, and reacting to facial expressions of the other speaker. When presented with a variety of objects to name, the individual will produce nonsense words with articulate confidence: Presented a quarter, one patient said, "minkt"; shown a comb, he said "sahk." When shown the objects a second time, patients will give different nonsense words than before, and occasionally they may name an object correctly (Kolb & Whishaw, 1996).

There is recent evidence, based on fossil records of hominid skulls, that growth in regions of the left hemisphere corresponding to Broca's area and Wernicke's area occurred at about the time in prehistory that symbolic language evolved (Galaburda et al., 1978). This confirms the theory of

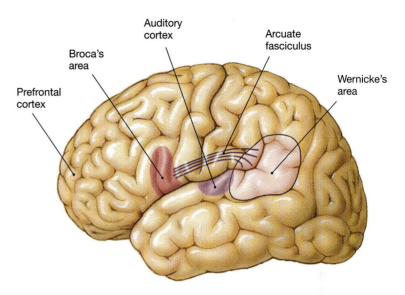

Figure 16–4   *The Speech Circuit.* The distinctive areas of Broca and Wernicke contribute to an extensive language circuit involved in speech production and interpretation. Auditory cortex on the lateral left side of the brain converges on Wernicke's area in the temporal lobe and relays information to Broca's area in the lateral frontal lobe.

Broca and Wernicke in many respects; there is a speech circuit (Figure 16–4) between auditory cortex on the left side, passing to Wernicke's area in association temporal cortex, and thence to Broca's area in the left frontal lobe via the arcuate fasciculus. Broca's area lies adjacent to primary motor cortex for the organs of articulation in speech.

Lesions of the left brain can produce total or **global aphasia** (*a* = without, *phasia* = speech), in which there is neither comprehension of the spoken word nor production of speech. Lesions on the right side rarely have this effect. However, Benson (1986) has performed extensive studies on patients with right hemisphere lesions and has discovered that, while language may be intact in its elemental form, right hemisphere patients exhibit poverty of speech, especially in **prosody** (the rhythm, inflection, and especially, the timbre and melody of speech). In Benson's subjects, evidence arose that the right hemisphere contributed substantially to every feature of language except for **syntax** (the ordering of words into meaningful statements). Curiously, it is syntax in particular that seems to define the difference between symbolic human language and nonhuman communication; while much of nonhuman communication is rich in prosody, it lacks syntax, or the ability to put words together in a logical order (see Figure 16–3).

Table 16–1 lists a number of different aphasias that have been described, including Broca's and Wernicke's. The main point that the student can gather from these data is that language can be *fragmented*, leaving most function intact and

Table 16–1	APHASIC SYNDROMES	
Syndrome	Speech Production	Language Errors
Fluent Aphasias Wernicke (sensory)	Fluent speech, without articulary disorders	Neologism and/or anomias, or paraphasias, poor comprehension & repetition
Transcortical (isolation syndrome)	Fluent speech, without articulary disorders, good repetition	Verbal paraphasias & anomias; poor comprehension
Conduction	Fluent, sometimes halting speech, but without articulary disorders	Phonemic paraphasia and neologisms, phonemic groping; poor repetition; fairly good comprehension
Anomic	Fluent speech, without articulary disorders	Anomia and occasional paraphasias
Nonfluent Aphasias Broca, severe	Laborious articulation	Speechless with recurring utterances or syndrome of phonetic disintegration; poor repetition
Broca, mild	Slight but obvious articulatory disorders	Phonemic paraphasia with anomia; agrammatism; dysprosody
Transcortical Motor	Marked tendency to reduction and inertia, without articulary disorders; good repetition	Uncompleted sentences and anomias; naming better than spontaneous speech
Global	Laborious articulation	Speechlessness with recurring utterances; poor comprehension; poor repetition
"Pure" Aphasias Alexia without agraphia	Normal	Poor reading
Agraphia	Normal	Poor writing
Word Deafness	Normal	Poor comprehension; poor repetition

Neologism: a new word or phrase of the patient's own making.
Paraphasia: substituting one word for another, jumbling words and sentences unintelligibly.
Phoneme: smallest unit of sound which controls meaning.
Dysprosody: poor variation in stress, pitch, and rhythm of speech to convey meaning.

Source: Kolb & Whishaw (1996).

with very specific deficits displayed. This supports an argument that the higher cortical function for language must, to some degree, obey the laws of cellular connectionism (Chapter 1).

Apraxias

Apraxia (*a* = without, *praxia* = movement) is more than the inability to move (which can result from muscle weakness, lower motor neuron disease, upper motor neuron disease, or damage to motor cortex). Pure apraxia is inability to make movement with *cognitive intent* and is due to more diffuse damage to premotor structures (Karaken et al., 1998). Examples are ideomotor apraxia and constructional apraxia. Lesions in the left parietal cortex (which is a premotor area and on the same side as language) result in **ideomotor apraxia** in which patients are unable to perform a simple motor movement when asked to, such as waving "hello," but can in fact

move their hands reflexively. The extensive involvement of physical movement in human communication is apparent in persons with ideomotor apraxia because although the lesion is only in one area, the effects are bilateral.

Constructional apraxia involves an inability to solve spatial puzzles or draw diagrams. This results again from parietal lobe lesions (on either side) and illustrates how even communication by drawing entails more brain structures than just the language structures of the frontal and temporal lobes.

Agnosias

The parietal lobes are the source of neural structures that lie very close to the actual point of convergence between somatosensory input and the initiation of motor output (Chapter 10). The **posterior parietal zone** (Figure 16–5), most

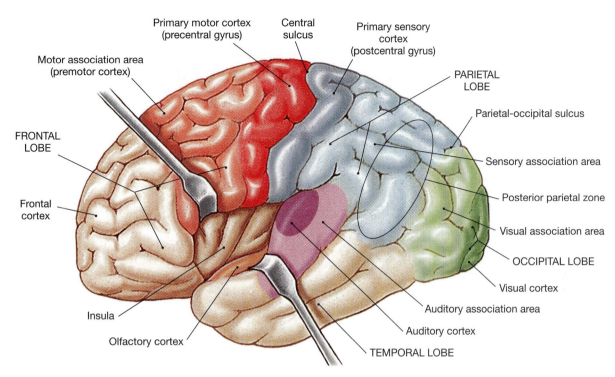

Figure 16–5 *Topographical Map of the Cerebral Cortex.* Anatomical landmarks on the cerebral cortex. Notice the area of the posterior parietal zone.

remote from primary somatosensory cortex in the postcentral gyrus, is a region which, if damaged, creates an array of inabilities that collectively are called **agnosias** (*a* = without, *gnosia* = to know). Organization of a map of the outside world ("these things are to my left, these things are to my right") is a posterior parietal function. Without it, a patient seems unaware of the very concept of left and right. The principle of decussation holds (though to a lesser degree than for primary sensory or motor cortical function), so it is possible for a patient with damage to one side of the posterior parietal zone to deny the existence of *one-half of the outside world*. In one famous clinical history, an individual with spatial agnosia went about his daily life turning always to the right, the left half of the world not existing for him (Sacks, 1985). Other patients with agnosia may have normal vision and movement but inability to recognize objects, places or people (Milner, 1997).

A person with a poorly formed or absent map of the body's relation to the outside world may display, on the side opposite to the parietal lobe lesion, **optic ataxia**, or the inability to locate or grasp objects. Patients with optic ataxia are able to move and see normally, but spatial relations have lost their meaning and manipulation must be accomplished by trial and error.

Depending on the extent, and side, of parietal damage, a person may display agnosia of a very particular kind; he or she may deny the existence of a specific body part or place in

the world. Brief descriptions of these patients are provided in Box 16–2 and later, in Box 16–4.

Alexias

Somewhere between language structures in all people and visual structures in literate people must lie neural circuitry that enables comprehension and generation of written language. There is probably more than one site in the brain responsible for this since lesion data produce few examples of pure **alexia** (writing without reading) and **agraphia** (reading without writing) (but see Beversdorf et al., 1997).

Often seen in conjunction with prosopagnosia (see Box 16–2), alexia results particularly from damage to the left occipital lobes (association regions adjacent to primary visual cortex). Alexia and verbal agnosia for objects presented visually can also result from **disconnection syndromes**, in which the pertinent brain regions in the occipital and parietal lobes are intact but connections between them are severed. Pure disconnection agnosia is rare but has been explored using experimental animals.

Dyslexia

Difficulty in reading is more common than alexia and is not associated with structural damage of a substantial nature though failure to develop asymmetry in the planum temporale has been associated with reading problems (Gauger, Lom-

Box 16–2

Prosopagnosia and "Blindsight"

If the left hemisphere (parietal, occipital, temporal, and frontal lobes) seems particularly devoted to linguistic function, the right side has its own equally rich and important role, one that is still becoming fully appreciated.

The complexity of language can be estimated by the number of words in the average vocabulary, which varies from a few thousand words to over 60,000, depending on the language. Now, for contrast, imagine the number of faces a person can recognize in a lifetime. As one estimate, I'll take my experience as a college professor. I take pride in recognizing each of my students on sight and by name. I meet approximately 100 new students each semester, and so after ten years I have learned to recognize 2,000 students on sight. Add to this the faces I have come to recognize outside of class (I estimate this to be about the same) and the faces I have learned to recognize in media such as TV and movies, and multiply by decades of life, and it becomes apparent that I have learned as many faces as an average language contains words. When it is considered that this learning of faces continues for a lifetime, while most language learning happens early in life, then the astounding requirements of the neural circuitry for face recognitions becomes apparent.

It should come as no surprise, then, that the brain has intricate machinery for facial recognition equal in mass and complexity to that for verbal recognition (considering, of course, that the linguistic concepts of prosody, grammar, and syntax have their facial equivalents of expression, place specificity, and group context). When this machinery is damaged, as when a stroke, tumor, or injury is encountered on the *right* side of the posterior and occipital lobes, a distortion of the world occurs that is as pro-

found as when language is disrupted. Called **prosopagnosia** (prosa-PA-nose-ee-ah), a deficit of being unable to recognize faces (including one's own!), the disorder is one of the most fascinating, yet least investigated and described, of the agnosias.

Severe prosopagnosia (usually due to bilateral damage) can extend to the very concept of face (see Sack's *The Man Who Mistook His Wife for a Hat* in the Further Readings section). Lesser degrees can include every face but the patient's, or every commonly recognized face (such as famous people's), but not strange or upside-down faces. Patients with prosopagnosia are not always aware that they have a deficit, since the memory of faces is stored in the same brain region as the recognition machinery. The patient no longer sees, recognizes, remembers, or even comprehends the existence of faces.

There are some syndromes that separate abilities more distinctly, however. **Blindsight** is a phenomenon that occurs when the occipital pole of the brain is damaged around the primary visual cortex in the calcarine fissure and is characterized by subconscious vision (reporting that something "seemed" to be there and being able to discriminate between objects) without conscious knowledge of an object or stimulus (a subjective impression that one has really never "seen" the object).

If the damage is only to a circumscribed area, a separation occurs in the stream of information from primary to association cortex. One avenue, the **dorsal stream**, guides movements and aspects of visual memory. Another pathway, the **ventral stream**, organizes conscious recognition of objects. When the ventral stream is disrupted and the dorsal stream left intact, the patient cannot acknowl-

bardino, & Leonard, 1997). **Dyslexia** (*dys* = bad, difficult; *lexis* = word, phrase) is impaired reading ability reflected by a competency level below that expected on the basis of the individual's level of intelligence and is more often categorized as a learning disability. The disability is not caused by visual problems, and individuals have normal object and picture recognition abilities. As such, theorists believe that it is more likely to be due to maturational lag, environmental deprivation, a defect in the **lateralization** (unequal representation of unique

psychological functions) between the hemispheres, or abnormalities in visual and language area connectivity.

About four times more frequent in male children than females, dyslexia was at first thought to have a genetic explanation. There are intriguing suggestions that biochemical differences may account for learning disabilities, as researchers learned that they could reliably identify disabled students based on chemical analysis of hair samples (Pihl & Parkes, 1977). Neurologists Geschwind and Galaburda (1985)

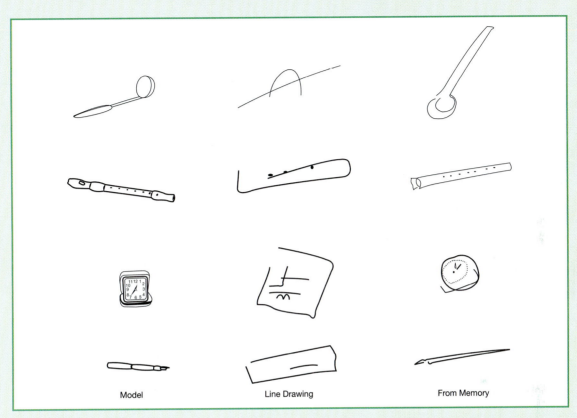

Model   Line Drawing   From Memory

Source: Kolb & Wishaw (1996)

edge stimuli in the visual field contralateral to the lesion. However, the dorsal stream has still referred information about these stimuli to memory!

The figure shows a series of objects (left column) presented to the "blind" portion of such an individual's visual field. The middle row are drawings made by the patient as she attempted to copy the object using visual cues. Then, after the object was removed, the patient was asked to draw the object from memory (right column). Because conscious recognition of objects (the ventral stream) was affected, the drawings done while using the model as a guide are poorer than those done from memory (the dorsal stream visual memory being unaffected).

Thus, even though the process of "seeing" seems to us a unified (some would say "gestalt") experience, studies in neuropsychology reveal that it is in fact a multivariate experience, one that can be fragmented into separate neural, and conscious, entities.

have examined brains of dyslexics post-mortem and have found cytological abnormalities in the left hemisphere (Figure 16–6).

There is a proposal that there may be cultural dimensions to dyslexia. Languages with photographic structure may be organized more bilaterally (i.e., there will be more right-hemisphere involvement) than phonogrammic languages (languages that use letters). However, systematic examination has failed to document such differences using a number of techniques (Rapport, Tan, & Whitaker, 1983). Dyslexia should not be taken as a single condition. Rather it is many, a fact that confounds the choice of theories for its origin. A particularly interesting form is **deep dyslexia**, a form restricted to semantic errors. People with this condition differ from other dyslexics since they can read some words and all letters perfectly well, but they have difficulty with words that are abstract or that indicate an action or function (such as verbs). In **phonological dyslexia**, reading as a whole is intact,

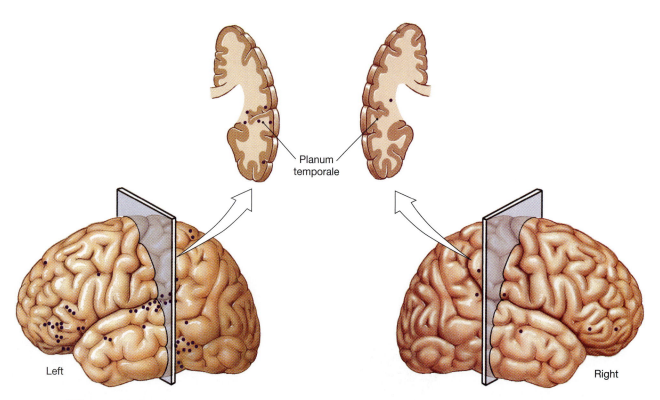

Figure 16–6 *Cytological Abnormalities Indicative of Dyslexia.* A depiction of an individual with dyslexia: The dots refer to areas of cellular abnormalities. The inset shows the planum temporale. Notice the asymetrical involvement of cortical areas. (Adapted from Geschwind & Galaburda, 1985)

but the individual is unable to repeat or pronounce nonsense syllables. These are just two of the many specific, reported varieties of dyslexia. Not surprisingly then, development of simple and aggressive treatments for the conditions are not expected in the near future. Fortunately, this is not distressing to many individuals with dyslexia as they have adapted their reading *abilities* to meet societal expectations and have flourished in technical and academic environments. Indeed, some conditions in dyslexia afford individuals the ability to make unique connections within communication that unaffected individuals cannot readily perceive.

Of late, studies and researchors have come to suggest that dyslexia is over-diagnosed. Some recent studies have purported to find a biological, even genetic link to explain the condition, but others have failed to replicate these results (see editorial, *Scientific American*, August 1995; pg. 14).

Deficiencies in lateralization of function, or some similar developmental process, seems more likely to play a role in the etiology of dyslexia, an issue we shall explore in Box 16–3.

Much research into language has centered around sex differences in ability and understanding. Recently, Harasty et al. (1997) reported that females have proportionally larger Wernike and Broca regions compared with males. Shaywitz et al. (1995) used letter recognition, rhyme, and semantic tasks to measure brain activation in right-handed males and females. The researchers found these phonological tasks predominantly elicited activity in the left inferior frontal gyrus region in males, but in females more diffuse, bilateral inferior frontal gyrus regions were activated, proposing further differences in the functional organization of the brain for language.

The Concept of Latent Circuits and Latent Function

As we learned in Chapter 2, mitosis of central nervous system neurons stops before adulthood and no new connections form after myelination is complete in adolescence. Considering this fact, it is remarkable how much function can be recovered after brain damage. Head injury resulting in coma of six hours or longer is fatal almost half the time, but among those that survive many will eventually reacquire much function that was lost. Figure 16–7 shows some representative data for aphasias. Depending on the type, substantial recovery can be expected in five years in each case but the most severe ("global") aphasia.

Box 16–3

Lateralization of Function

The segregation of function between the hemispheres is called the "lateralization of function." Though the most readily interpretable hemispheric differences in function are to be found in patients who have had the corpus callosum severed (Chapter 1), there is evidence for some lateralization of function in intact brains as well. **Heschl's gyrus** (right side larger) and the **planum temporale** (left side larger) are examples of asymmetry between the hemispheres (see figure). In addition, anatomical studies over the years have found a number of other differences. The right side is heavier than the left and has a larger medial geniculate nucleus and a wider frontal lobe. The left side contains more gray matter than the right, and several regions are larger, including the cingulate gyrus, the lateral posterior nucleus of the thalamus, and the inferior parietal lobe (Kolb & Whishaw, 1996).

To prevent accidental damage to speech structures during neurosurgery, Wada, Clarke, and Hamm (1975) developed an interesting probe into lateralization of function in intact brains. In the **sodium amytal test**, or "Wada test," anesthetic is injected into the carotid artery on one side alone before surgery, and a neurological exam is performed to test language capacity. The test showed that anesthesia of the left hemisphere produced aphasia in 96 percent of right-handed people (together with contralateral apraxia, of course, since decussation occurs in motor systems). However, only 70 percent of left-handed people displayed aphasia after left-hemisphere anesthesia. Thus, some 30 percent of left-handers have either right-brain language function or bilateral language function. In addition to sparing some language function from the surgeon's knife, this procedure provided confirmation that language is lateralized in intact as well as split brains.

Response latency tests, in which information is presented to only one side of the brain, such as aural tests in which sounds are presented to only the left or right auditory field, have developed some reproducible differences. Some studies have shown that music is preferentially processed in the right hemisphere, as opposed to

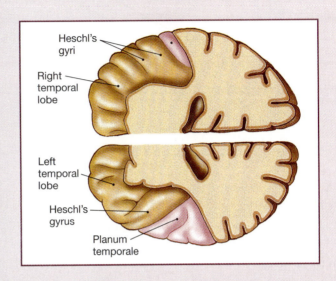

most other sounds, such as language, in which the left dominates (Kimura, 1973). A study of Braille reading suggests that spatial features of language may be processed differently by the hemispheres; Braille seems to be interpreted more rapidly by the left hand, again predicting right hemisphere involvement (Rudel, Denckla, & Spalten, 1974).

However, laterality studies are subject to methodological criticism. Often the results are not comparable between different tests of the same function, and even a single subject can appear to shift laterality by practicing the test. One critic has suggested that the laterality effects might be explained by the brain unconsciously scanning from one visual field to another during a test, producing an apparent left side advantage without real hemispheric specialization (Efron, 1990).

It may very well be the case that both hemispheres share most functions, but that one dominates transiently, depending on behavioral circumstances. In this manner, the mind might employ two parallel mechanisms to arrive at the best thought between them in a manner one author has compared to a two-house legislature (Jaynes, 1976).

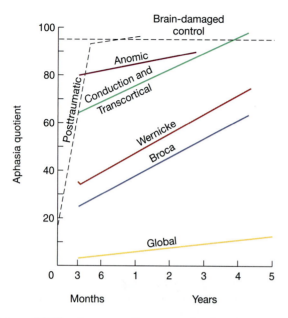

Figure 16–7 *Language Recovery after Stroke.* Comparative recovery relating to initial language deficit and improvement. Each line signifies a patient. The dashed line represents a post-trauma patient. (Kolb & Whishaw, 1996)

How is this possible if no new connections are forming? Let's return to our consideration of transmitter function and recall that most synapses in the brain are inhibitory. At a particular moment in time, this inhibition holds in abeyance all possible behaviors but the one actually displayed (in other words, the vast majority of possible excitatory outputs of cortex are suppressed). One model of cortical function would even suggest that one hemisphere inhibits the other in those cases where hemispheric dominance is expressed (Jaynes, 1976). If this inhibition is chronic, the residual capacity of the other hemisphere, or of another brain region within a hemisphere, to fill in when needed may be called a **latent function** of cortex, a function suppressed normally but exhibited in unusual cases such as those involving brain damage.

Also, recall that supernumerary synapses form in development, and most neural systems display **synapse elimination** (Chapter 15) during maturation. This elimination should not be thought of as diminishing neural capacity. Rather, normal acquisition of skill and coordination probably involves this segregation and withdrawal of synaptic contacts. Data are lacking in the case of brain damage in adulthood, but myelination in adults does not appear to pose the same barrier to synapse elimination that it does to synapse formation in the adult brain. One explanation for the remarkable recovery sometimes seen with brain damage is that a trophic response (Chapter 15) occurs in which

synapse elimination or *disinhibition* unmasks latent circuits.

Emotion

Our understanding of the neurological basis of emotion lags far behind that of most other neocortical functions despite the overwhelming significance emotion has on our "humanness." It is difficult to interview patients about emotion. Sometimes people cannot even find words to describe how they feel. To discuss emotion we must examine each component: the physiological, the behavioral, and the cognitive. *However*, it should be noted that any study of emotion should be critically approached and looked at with an open mind for several reasons. Emotion entails a number of structures at several levels of the brain and many of these structures are **subcortical** (Whalen et al., 1998). Damage to these structures often affects the brainstem areas necessary for vital function, thus few patients are available for neuropsychological analysis. Furthermore, many studies use animals assuming that responses to stimuli can be equated to a human emotion or feeling.

Physiological constituents of emotion include the central and autonomic system and neurohormonal and visceral activity. For example, there are alterations in heart rate, blood flow, and blood pressure; increase in perspiration (sweaty palms); the release of serotonin and epinephrine; and digestive system manifestations ("butterflies," inhibited digestion, dry mouth). Interestingly, these distinct changes *can* be differentiated between specific emotions, such as rage and fear, even though *both* activate the sympathetic division of the autonomic nervous system. Behaviors are other indications of particular emotional states: Facial expression is the obvious one, as well as tone of voice, loquaciousness, posture, and a combination of physiology and behavior—crying. Finally, the cognitive aspect of emotion is a personal self-inferred state that encompasses "feelings" we report, such as envy or gratitude, and other cognitive features including hope, ideas, memories, aspirations, and so on. These components will sum to our "emotion." Although this uniquely personal experience is interpreted by each one of us in our own way and the physiological, behavioral, and cognitive reactions vary in magnitude in each of us, there *is* accord among different cultures as to matching emotional states with particular facial expressions.

The extensive diversity of characterizing emotion seen here leads us to believe that emotion is a multiple-structure system. Furthermore, it would seem that there are several levels of organization. The initial sensory information—the visual, auditory, olfactory, or tactile stimuli—is received and processed through the cortex and then routed to the appropriate associative cortex. From there a higher-level system involving the processing of other elemental initial information may arise, such as formulating and matching with other stimuli. Finally, subjective feelings and intuition (most likely species-specific) may be processed, resulting in a cumulative summation of several systems manifested in an emotion (Kolb & Whishaw, 1996).

It has been proposed that the **limbic system**, specifically the frontal cortex, the inferior temporal cortex, the paralimbic cortex, and the amygdala, is primarily responsible for the expression of emotion. Through the use of clinical studies, researchers have been able to piece together the prime areas involved in emotion location. Because of the calming effect seen in chimpanzees after frontal lobotomies, some neuropsychiatrists ventured that the procedure could be useful for individuals with severe mental illness. The surgeries involved severing the fibers connecting the frontal limbic structures as well as ablation of the frontal association areas and cutting fiber tracts connecting the thalamus with the prefrontal cortex. Although the patients showed signs of reduced anxiety, there was some development of epilepsy, personality changes, and slight degeneration of intellectual abilities. Later studies of frontal cortical lesions of primates resulted in reduced social interactions, poor social conduct (loss of dominance and social skills), altered social behavior (females attacking a dominant male, for example), diminishing facial expression and body gestures, and diminished vocalizations. Studies of *human* patients with right-hemisphere lesions show that not only does their speech lack prosody (rhythm and expression), but they perform poorly on tests of humor and social nuance. Damage to the temporal lobes in particular (as in temporal lobe epilepsy) can produce emotional disturbances, especially of the form of humorless moralism, religiosity, and obsessiveness, leading some researchers to define a **temporal lobe personality** in people displaying these characteristics (as opposed to normal morality and religion). Patients with left frontal lobe lesions show decreased talking, whereas right frontal lobe lesions result in garrulousness. Frontal lobe lesions in either hemisphere reduce the number of facial expressions seen.

At another level, several researchers have shown "emotional" responses in animals merely by stimulation of a particular area of the thalamus and hypothalamus. Stimulation of distinctly different areas of the hypothalamus in the cat results in behavior seen in an attack-mode against another cat (hissing, baring teeth, piloerection) or hunting behavior towards a possible feast (crouching, pouncing, stealthlike attention). These affective responses led researchers to believe that the thalamus is responsible for the activation of cortical neurons in response to autonomic arousal.

Subcortical damage, particularly to a part of the limbic system including the amygdala, can produce a peculiar form of emotional blindness called, after its discoverers, the **Klüver-Bucy syndrome**. Monkeys with lesions in the amygdala and visual association areas of the temporal cortex show a loss of fear (dulling of emotion), hypersexuality, hyperorality (inappropriate objects are put in the mouth), and visual agnosias. In humans, the syndrome is exhibited as a result of neurological disorders (Trimble, Mendez, & Cummings, 1997). Like the primates, the patients are unusually placid and indifferent to objects and people. They must imitate others in order to perform most daily tasks, such as eating with a fork, and often do not remember people, objects, or spatial relationships well. Hyperorality is prominent and appetites are insatiable, even for nonfood items. Sexuality is also pronounced, and reports of homosexuality in originally heterosexual individuals have been documented.

Overall, more work remains to be done in the area of emotion than in almost any other field in higher-function research. Fortunately, as we learn more about the emotional life of experimental animals, we can hope to acquire insights into this aspect of the human condition as well.

Memory

Since Lashley's search for the engram (Chapter 1), scientists have sought a locale in the brain for specific memories. No single part of the brain, when damaged, yields deficits explicitly for memories alone, independent of other higher functions. However, several important results point to the **hippocampal formation** in the limbic system as an especially significant structure for certain events in the formation of memories. O'Keefe and Nadel (1978) used lesioning and recording of activity of the hippocampus to accumulate evidence that specific memories for places (i.e., spatial relations between the body and the outside world) were stored in this structure. Olton and Papas (1979) found that the hippocampus was necessary for "working" memory, the type of memory necessary to conduct a series of related behaviors (such as a conversation) over a short period of time. Mishkin and Appenzeller (1987) found that, in monkeys, hippocampal and amygdala damage produced deficits particularly in recognition memory, memory for things such as faces and objects. The amygdala has also been implicated for emotional memory. These disparate findings point to a new theory proposing that the hippocampus integrates sensory inputs from different modalities to form complex engrams (Sutherland & Rudy, 1989). More recently a distinction has been made between **implicit memory** (unconscious and unintentional, such as classical conditioning) and **explicit memory** (conscious recollection). Implicit memory may be a property of all neural systems, since all systems are capable of plasticity. Explicit memory may not really have a focus in the brain either, but some structures may be more involved than others. The amygdala is implicated as being responsible for emotional memory and the rhinal cortex in recording object-recognition. Studies in humans by Penfield and Roberts (1959) showed that stimulation of the temporal lobe elicited memories or auditory hallucination and recollections of past events. According to a theory of Mortimer Mishkin (Mishkin et al., 1997) explicit memory dwells on a *circuit* between the prefrontal cortex, portions of the thalamus and limbic system, and diffuse neurotransmitter projections from the hindbrain (Figure 16–8, 16–9, and 16–10).

The postulated complex connections in which memory appears to reside are further illustrated as we examine the different types of memory loss. **Infantile amnesia** is memory loss everyone "suffers" from. Some researchers believe that the memories are in fact there (they are just not retrievable), and thus there is a separate memory system for adults and infants (undoubtedly, Freud would have his own interpretation of this phenomenon). **Posttraumatic amnesia** results from injury. The severity of memory loss depends on the severity of the accident. Memory loss includes moments leading up to the accident as well as directly following the trauma, even if the individual is

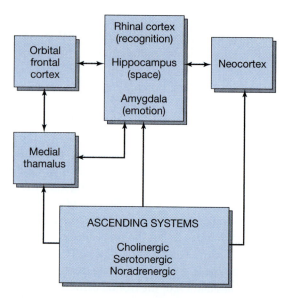

Figure 16–9 *Model for the Anatomy of Explicit Memory.* This figure shows the brain sites involved in and the proposed pathway to explain explicit memory. Notice the interconnectedness of this circuit; damage to any one area will result in deficiencies in explicit memory. (Adapted from Petri & Mishkin, 1994.)

Figure 16–8 *Limbic Structures and Memory.* Various limbic structures, especially the hippocampus, are thought to be involved with memory. More likely, since any behavior is the product of all brain regions working in concert, memory involves these structures acting in concert with many other neural systems.

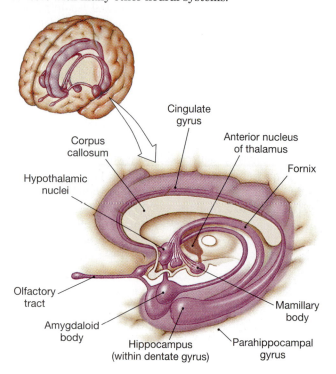

conscious and is able to report. The amnesia has been reported to come back after time. **Transient global amnesia** is correlated with the incidence of migraines, hypoglycemia, epilepsy, concussions, and brain embolisms and ischemia (in general, an interruption of blood flow to the brain has occurred). The results are significant anterograde amnesia (lasting moments to days) as well as retrograde amnesia. Memory loss can be permanent. There is also memory loss resulting from use of tranquilizers, alcohol, and electroconvulsive shock therapy, which has cumulative amnesiac effects over subsequent sessions (Kolb & Whishaw, 1996). Modern studies of amnesia using non-invasive imaging methods tend to indicate an organic cause for each (Venneri and Caffara, 1998).

Ironically, some of our best understanding of memory formation comes not from work with animals or with brain-damaged people, but from attempts to model learning and memory using computers. Such effort makes up a major component of *cognitive neuroscience*, one of the fastest growing sub-disciplines of the field (Gazzaniga, 1994; O'Reilly et al., 1998).

Organic Brain Syndromes

Some forms of brain damage arise from discrete lesions due to tumors, vascular accidents such as strokes, ischemic attacks, aneurysms, or head trauma. These yield the relatively specific deficits described above. Other forms of brain damage

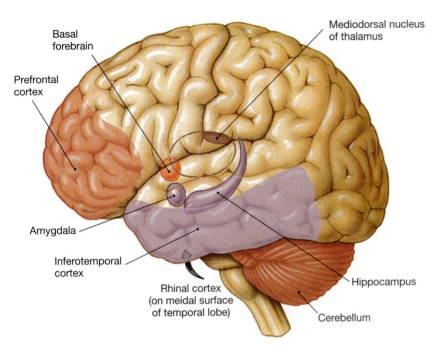

Basal forebrain

Prefrontal cortex

Mediodorsal nucleus of thalamus

Amygdala

Inferotemporal cortex

Rhinal cortex (on meidal surface of temporal lobe)

Hippocampus

Cerebellum

Figure 16–10 *Brain Structures Contributing to Memory.* The areas and specific structures that contribute to the formation and storage of memory. Notice the possibility of incurring damage to other higher cognitive functions as well as memory when these structures are injured.

arise from identifiable physical causes but have more general debilitating effects. These are called **organic brain syndromes**. There are so many of these that we will just consider a few, selected because of their prevalence or because they illustrate some particular point of neuroscientific interest.

Down Syndrome

There are several genetic anomalies that seem to have particular impact on the development of the nervous system. **Trisomies** are essentially accidents of meiosis in which an extra copy of one or more chromosomes arises, leaving each cell with two copies instead of the usual one. Trisomy of chromosome 21 produces **Down Syndrome**, (also called Trisomy 21, "trisomy" because a fusion of an abnormal complement of *two genes* with the normal one yields three copies in mitosis) and leads to the development of an abnormally small brain, gross abnormalities in the shape and size of the temporal lobes, and developmental disability that extends throughout life. Individuals with Down syndrome also exhibit physical manifestations including flattened skull and nose, folds of skin over the eyes, short stature, and thick tongue, as well as heart defects and chronic sinus problems (Figure 16–11). Mothers who conceive later in life (over age 35) have increased incidence of Down syndrome among their offspring (due to less reliable spontaneous abortion of fetuses with trisomies). Often a cytogenetic assay is performed on embryonic cells drawn from the amniotic fluid of expectant mothers in this age range to screen for this condition. Although individuals with Trisomy 21 statistically tend to have shorter life-expectancy rates, the range and severity of abnormalities and

mental deficiencies vary tremendously. Persons with Down are able to obtain higher education and hold full-time jobs with extensive responsibilities.

Phenylketonuria

The name **phenylketonuria** is derived from the clinical observation that some infants have abnormally high levels of the amino acid phenylalanine in the urine. It is the result of a recessive, autosomal gene that cannot program sufficient enzymatic activity for metabolizing phenylalanine. If left untreated, the accumulation of this amino acid in the blood leads to **microcephaly** (small head size) and mental retardation. However, infants are now commonly screened for this condition, which can be corrected by eliminating phenylalanine from the diet (check out your soda can for the warning label), and severe cases of the disease are becoming uncommon.

Cerebellar Ataxia

Repeated jarring blows to the head have a cumulative effect on CNS function. Particularly common among prize fighters with long careers, the catchall name for this type of brain injury is **pugilistic dementia**. The dementia can take several forms, depending on the individual, but the first brain region to be affected is often the cerebellum. This is because the cerebellum lies at the back of the skull; consequently, when the head is snapped back or hit repeatedly and relentlessly the cerebellum is crammed against the back of the skull and suffers much more mechanical impact than other brain regions. However, another major reason for the cerebellum to be especially susceptible to brain trauma lies in the fact that

Figure 16–11 *Individuals with Down Syndrome.* The physical characteristics and health complications that arise due to the inherited Trisomy 21 condition sometimes lowers the life span of these individuals.

it has an extremely high density of neurons and, as many of them are inhibitory in nature, they are tonically active and have higher metabolic requirements than other cells (review Purkinje cells in Chapter 10). Thus the first region to succumb to metabolic stress is often the cerebellum. Chronic cerebellar damage is irreversible and is known as **cerebellar ataxia** (one form of pugilistic dementia), since it is predominantly a disorder of movement. Acutely, some of the same symptoms are seen upon a single severe blow to the head, as when a fighter is said to be **"punch drunk,"** which is characterized by weakness in lower limbs, unsteady gait, hand tremors, speech disturbances, spastic muscles, and slow thought processes (Figure 16–12); but in that case the symptoms are reversible. Young fighters recover normal motor function after the fight is over, however this condition is also seen in seasoned fighters *after* retirement. The phrase "punch drunk" is illustrative of the metabolic sensitivity of the cerebellum since the same symptoms are also seen upon intoxication with alcohol.

Korsakoff's Disease

Long-term, or chronic, exposure to alcohol can also produce irreversible damage to the CNS. One of the most severe examples, seen only when alcoholic beverages are the sole source of calories for an extended period, is **Korsakoff's disease**. This is not really a direct effect of alcohol (which can alone produce permanent brain damage) but a nutritional deficiency due to lack of thiamine in the diet. This vitamin

shortage appears to damage parts of the limbic system involved in memory formation, particularly the **mammilary bodies** of the hypothalamus. Korsakoff's patients sometimes have near-total lack of short-term memory, yielding a behavioral state "frozen in time" at the onset of their alcoholism. A particularly poignant example of this is to be found in the "Lost Mariner," one of Oliver Sacks's tales in *The Man Who Mistook His Wife for a Hat*, about an individual who went on a drinking binge to celebrate the end of WWII and lived for decades hence as if he was still in his twenties and Truman was still president.

Spongiform Encephalopathies

One of a variety of disorders called **spongiform encephalopathies** because they render brain tissue perforated, or "spongelike," in histological appearance (Figure 16–13), **Creutzfeldt-Jakob disease** predominantly affects older adults. It is characterized by dementia, shocklike contractions and violent twitches, an inability to coordinate movements, and speech disturbances (due to muscle spasticity). The symptoms are progressive and the disease is terminal, usually within one year of onset. It is possibly mediated by a **slow virus** that produces pathology and nerve cell degeneration only many years after initial infection. Such viruses appear to be the most exotic of all life forms (if indeed they can be said to live at all) in that they are very simple chemically, resembling large molecules rather than entire organisms. For example scrapie, a spongiform encephalopathy in sheep, was found to be mediated by a simple virus lacking nucleic acid altogether and consisting only of protein (recall that a virus has a protein coat with its nucleic acid inside, enters the nucleus of a cell and takes over metabolic processes of the cell, replicating itself hundreds of times). The name **prions** was coined to describe these strange particles. A point of great importance and current research is the degree to which prions or other infectious agents are responsible for the other encephalopathies such as multiple sclerosis (an autoimmune disease in which the myelin sheaths gradually degenerate, nerve impulses slow and ultimately cease, and afflicted individuals lose control of their muscles) and amyotrophic lateral sclerosis (Lou Gehrig's disease). A particularly sinister prospect is to be found in **mad cow disease**, which some investigators believe infected British cattle fed scrapie-containing sheep offal and which may have been transferred to humans ingesting the beef (Chesbro, 1998).

Kuru is a spongiform encephalopathy occurring in people and is certain to be mediated by a prionlike particle. However, you need not fear infection from this source, for it has been shown by Casleton Gajdusek and his collaborators (Liberski & Gajdusek, D.C., 1997) that the kuru agent is only

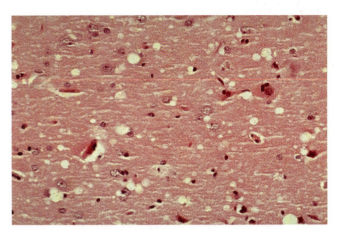

Figure 16–13 *Creutzfeldt-Jakob Disease.* The appearance of the "spongelike" tissue of Creutzfeldt-Jakob disease. This slide is taken from the occipital lobe.

transmitted by tribespeople in New Guinea who ritualistically consume the brains of relatives who have died of the disease. Since cannibalism is no longer practiced in New Guinea, the only known route of infection is gone and the natural form of kuru can be said to be eradicated. However, the slow virus remains of interest as a model for study of the other encephalopathies, such as those described earlier, that may be produced by an as yet unidentified prionlike agent. As a marginal note, I received my start in neuroscience by working on kuru virus at the National Institutes of Health as a college student. Much of the work at that time entailed an attempt to get kuru to infect an organism that would succumb rapidly to the disorder so that it could be studied, the incubation period in primates being ten to fifteen years and too long to design efficient experiments. Needless to say, the major hazard of the work was accidental infection, a prospect, I am happy to report, that has been eliminated by the considerable passage of time. The reader should not become alarmed by the foregoing discussion of slow viruses since the prospects for infection are very low. For example, as of the present writing the number of suspected human cases of mad cow disease is fewer than ten in the world.

Alzheimer's Disease

There is a disease process of uncertain etiology that is likely to affect a large proportion of us later in life. **Alzheimer's disease** is a progressive disorder of mid- to late life that is irreversible and incurable (Mattson, 1997). Alzheimer's disease is characterized by loss of memory, robbing the elderly of their most precious possession, even to the extent of causing loss of recognition of close family members. A survey of your class will reveal how widespread the condition is among the older members of a family. Its pathology reveals two cytological

Figure 16–12 *Punch Drunk Syndrome.* The damage that these fighters are inflicting on each other's cerebellums can be devastating to their coordination, speech, and cognitive processes.

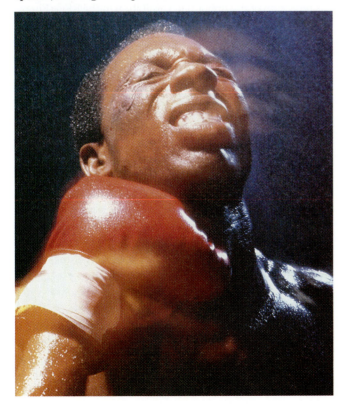

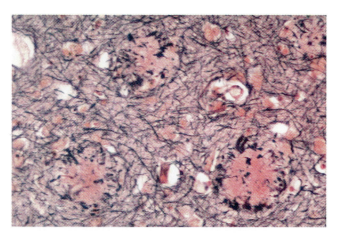

Figure 16–14   *Alzheimer's Disease: Plaques and Neurofibrillary Tangles*. Characteristic senile plaques and neurofibrillary tangles seen in a microphotograph of the hippocampal cortex in Alzheimer's disease using a silver stain.

signs, apparent only during autopsy: **plaques**, or lesions, containing an abnormal accumulation of a protein called ß-**amyloid**, and **neurofibrillary tangles**, or masses of apparently disorganized nerve fibers (Figure 16–14). At present it is unclear which pathological change, plaques or tangles, contributes most substantially or directly to the disease process. Therefore, both have been the object of intense scrutiny by researchers intent on finding a cause, and possibly a cure, for Alzheimer's disease. ß-amyloid is normally found in the brain as part of an integral membrane protein. As with many proteins, the ß-amyloid is first synthesized as a larger precursor that is then processed into the mature species (Figure 16–15a). In Alzheimer's disease, the processing appears disordered and the precursor may be cleaved in a different region than in normal brains (Figure 16–15b). Possibly, the abnormally cleaved protein cannot be cleared readily from the membrane, leading to accumulation in the plaques (Gandy & Greengard, 1992).

Some of the amyloid-containing plaques are shown in Figure 16–16 (Roses, 1994). They appear in the brains of people that carry an E_4 *allele* (abnormal gene version) for a **cholesterol-transporting protein** called apolipoprotein. Individuals carrying two genes for version allele E_4 are very likely to acquire Alzheimer's disease (Figure 16–17), whereas a single or double dose of allele E_3 (found in 78 percent of the population) in place of E_4 delays the appearance of the plaques. A small percentage of the population carries the E_2 allele, which actually appears to protect against Alzheimer's disease (Figure 16–17). Since all alleles carry some risk of Alzheimer's, a disturbing possibility is that the plaques are growing in all of us to some degree and merely not causing the behavioral signs

until growing to some pathological threshold. This possibility is borne out of post-mortem analysis of younger individuals who died of other causes. As shown in Table 16–2, there were more plaques in the brains of these automobile accident victims that held the E_4, or Alzheimer's allele, than in victims with other alleles (Nicoll, Roberts, & Graham, 1995).

The tangles have also been investigated extensively. Aluminum cation has been found to induce the tangles in laboratory animals, leading to the fear that aluminum in the diet (as from aluminum cans or antacid medicines) could be causing the disorder. To date, however, no strong evidence for aluminum accumulation in Alzheimer's victims has been obtained. We can only hope that continued research sheds more understanding on the etiology of Alzheimer's and leads to treatment and a cure.

Epilepsy

Recall from Chapter 1 the evidence that inhibition prevails over excitation in the brain. The normal function of cortex requires that most excitatory circuits are suppressed at any given moment, leaving only one or a few to give rise to behavior. Unfortunately, this is not always the case. Again as a result of metabolic insult, inhibitory circuits may drop out periodically, leaving unbounded excitation in the clinical condition known as **epilepsy**. Epilepsy may also be caused by abnormal potassium channel function (Stoffel & Jan, 1998). Epileptic seizures can be characterized by the behavioral result or by the reflection of the unbounded excitation in the EEG (Figure 16–18). The excitation is usually first manifest as a stiffening of the body in the **tonic phase**. Excitatory cells appear to have endogenous pacemaker or bursting properties (Chapter 4), so after the tonic phase there is a shaking phase, driven by synchronous bursting activity in cortex, known as the **clonic phase**. Seizures normally start in one part of cortex (the "focus") and spread elsewhere from there. If the focus is in association cortex, sometimes the patient reports an *aura* or premonition that a seizure is about to occur. Sometimes, as in *temporal lobe epilepsy* this aura may have an emotional or religious aspect. As the excitation spreads into motor cortex, the clonic phase spreads throughout the body, usually involving the extremities in a stereotypic order (called a Jacksonian March after its discoverer, Hughlings Jackson). If the spread is restricted, a small seizure is seen (sometimes called an "absence" seizure since the patient reports only a lapse in consciousness). Larger spread can produce *petit mal* seizures, involving part of the body, or *grand mal* seizures, which involve the entire body and may be life threatening. Fortunately, most epilepsy can be treated with drugs that enhance GABA-mediated inhibition in the brain, a vast improvement over the former treatment of cutting the corpus callosum to reduce the severity of the seizures.

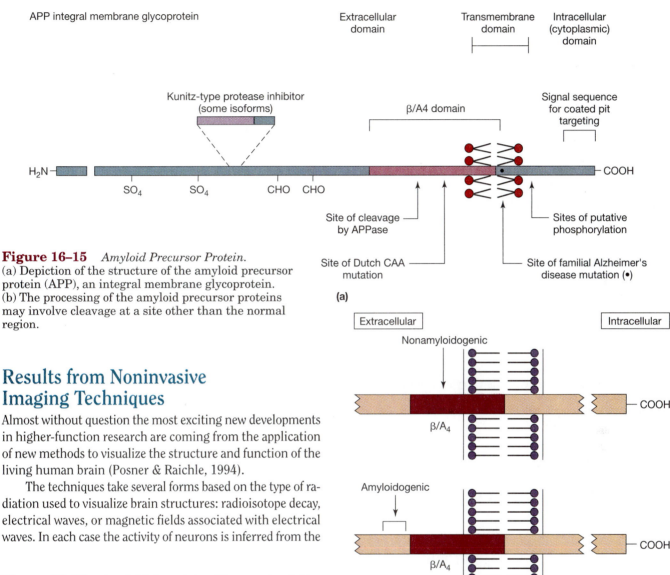

Figure 16–15 *Amyloid Precursor Protein.*
(a) Depiction of the structure of the amyloid precursor protein (APP), an integral membrane glycoprotein.
(b) The processing of the amyloid precursor proteins may involve cleavage at a site other than the normal region.

Results from Noninvasive Imaging Techniques

Almost without question the most exciting new developments in higher-function research are coming from the application of new methods to visualize the structure and function of the living human brain (Posner & Raichle, 1994).

The techniques take several forms based on the type of radiation used to visualize brain structures: radioisotope decay, electrical waves, or magnetic fields associated with electrical waves. In each case the activity of neurons is inferred from the

Figure 16–16 *Amyloid-Containing Plaques.* Amyloid-containing plaques in the brain of a person that carries the E_4 allele for apolipoprotein located on chromosome 19.

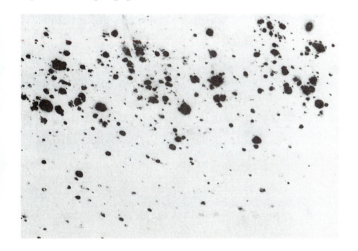

record, either directly in electromagnetic recording or indirectly as reflected in regional blood flow or metabolism.

Positron Emission Tomography (PET)

The theory behind **positron emission tomography (PET)** scanning, entails exposure of the brain, through the blood, to a positron-emitting nuclide. Such a tracer emits a positron (opposite of an electron) upon nuclear decay. As soon as a positron encounters an electron (which is not very far away), they annihilate each other with the emission of two gamma rays in opposite directions. Since photons pass

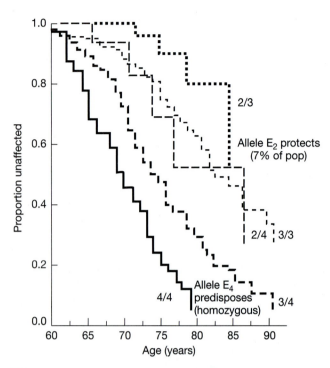

Figure 16–17 *Proportion of Unaffected Individuals and Allele Frequencies.* Individuals carrying the E_4 allele are more likely to develop Alzheimer's than individuals who carry at least one E_3 allele or those who have the E_2 allele.

through matter without much deflection, no damage is done to the brain and the source of the annihilation can be located outside the cranium with light-detecting diodes.

PET images are usually displayed by computer as slices, or slabs, through the living tissue. Figure 16–19 shows one such result, with changes in the image in this case reflecting increased blood flow in a particular region corresponding to increased electrical activity. Another is shown in Figure 16–20.

Magnetic Resonance Imaging (MRI)

Originally called nuclear magnetic resonance (NMR), the name of this method was changed to avoid odious associations with nuclear weapons. In fact, it is innocuous since no isotope is necessary to form the image, only the magnetic equivalent of the resonance normally found between chem-

ical bonds of a particular nature. Thus, magnetic resonance imaging (MRI) can be used to detect brain *water* (O-H resonance), methyl groups (C-H resonance) and so forth.

The images from MRI are striking in their clarity (Figures 16–21 and 16–22). Figure 16–21 shows a midsagittal view of the human brain, and it is apparent that enough detail exists to pinpoint the location and extent of any abnormality (vascular damage, tumor, etc.). Clinically, MRI presents a substitute for diagnostic neurology, since the question "Where is the lesion?" no longer need be answered based on the observation of behavioral deficit. This development has had great impact on medical practice, with some of the work of neurology now being done by neurosurgeons and neuroradiologists and some (for treatment of head injuries as well as diagnosis of brain injuries too small, subtle, or widespread to be visualized by MRI) going to specialists in the growing field of **neuropsychology.**

Computerized Axial Tomography (CAT)

Computerized axial tomography, the CAT scan, is a well-known imaging technique to visualize neurological disease or trauma. It involves a patient being "shelved" into a central hole that contains an X-ray tube and an X-ray detector that rotates around the skull, or the area of interest. Approximately twelve successive X-rays are taken around the entire perimeter. The differential absorption of X-rays by the various structures results in differentiated shades of gray depicting borders and regions. A computer records all the information of the structures and translates these images into a complex yet detailed transverse picture. Imaging en-

Table 16–2	E_4 ALLELE FREQUENCY IN HEAD INJURED PATIENTS*	
Proportion of head-injured patients with deposition of beta-amyloid		
	Proportion of head-injured patients with plaques	
apo E genotype	Ratio	%
2/2	0/2	0
2/3	0/7	0
3/3	5/41	12
2/4 (heterozygous E_4)	1/4	25
3/4 (heterozygous E_4)	11/30	37
4/4 (homozygous E_4)	6/6	100

Frequency of individuals expressing the E_4 allele and other alleles as observed in individuals with head injuries.

Source: Adapted from Nicoll et al., (1995)

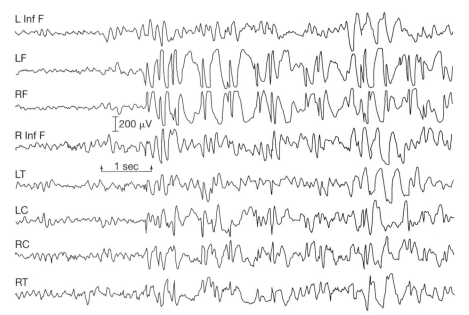

Figure 16–18   *Characteristics of Epileptic Seizures and Spells.* EEG record of a mentally retarded 4½-year-old boy with grand mal seizures, psychomotor seizures, and akinetic spells. There is a strong family history of epilepsy. The record shows spikes, polyspikes, and atypical spike and wave combinations mainly from the frontal region, which occur abruptly in a fairly normal background. Letters on left indicate positions of electrodes on skull. (Kolb & Whishaw, 1996)

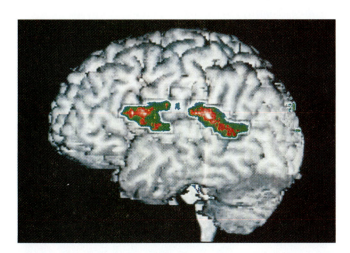

Figure 16–19   *Color Positron Emission Topography (PET).* Scan of the human brain showing areas involved in verbal short-term memory. Here, the left cerebral hemisphere is seen. Highlighted in green-red are two regions of high activity associated with Broca's area (at left) and the inferior parietal/superior temporal cortex (at right). These regions were activated when the subject was keeping in mind a string of letters for a few seconds. Active areas show increases in cerebral blood flow detected by PET and then superimposed on a three-dimensional MRI (magnetic resonance imaging) view of the brain.

hancement techniques and injected iodinated radiopaque substances sharpen the picture and increase resolution. There are advanced CAT scans that can create three-dimensional as well as moving images.

Cerebral Blood Flow Measurements

Before PET and MRI, it was possible to gain some impression of brain activity from differences in arterial and venous blood concentration. Anything absent in venous blood that was present in arterial blood must reflect something consumed by the brain (glucose and O_2 being examples). Likewise, anything present in venous blood but lacking in arterial blood reflects something produced by the brain (CO_2 for example, measured by gas chromatography). A/V blood differences are obviously not very precise in terms of the particular structure consuming the metabolite or generating the waste product, but they have been used to provide certain important insights into global brain function (that the brain is more active during sleep than wakefulness, for example; Chapter 13).

Electrical and Magnetic Records Across the Skull

We have already considered the electrical signal obtained by the minute part of the equivalent circuit that emanates from the skull (EEG records, Chapter 4). What has long been known but only recently applied to neurobiology is that each electrical event has a magnetic equivalent, recorded in the **magnetoencephalogram (MEG)**. MEG records can also provide precise localization of cortical events.

Use of all three new methods (PET, MRI, and MEG) has yielded useful data. It remains to be seen which of the techniques, or some as yet undescribed new method, will provide the most complete information about the functioning human brain.

To date, noninvasive imaging has provided our best evidence that higher cognitive function is organized by principles of cellular connectionism as opposed to aggregate field theory (Chapter 1). However, there is also strong support for aggregate field theory emerging from recordings from the surface of the brain. EEG records from an elaborate 64-channel multielectrode array sample the activity of thousands of neurons across a broad swath of cortex. Using this method it

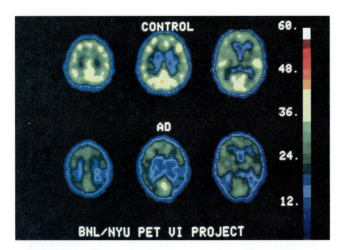

Figure 16–20 *Brain Function and Regional Blood Flow.* Cerebral metabolism is altered by Alzheimer's disease. PET scan shows metabolism in three sections through a normal human brain (top) and in a brain of a patient suffering from Alzheimer's disease (bottom). Yellow and green indicate higher levels of activity, blue indicates lower levels.

is possible to identify cortex that is *multi-modal* (e.g. that responds to both auditory and somatosensory stimuli). Most fascinating of all about these new data is the occurence of "gamma waves" (40 Hz oscillations) in such multi-modal cortex that seem to be associated with conscious awareness and may be the electrophysiological correlate of consciousness itself (McDonald et al., 1998).

Results from Brain Stimulation

The brain's lack of pain perception capacity (to direct activation) permits brain stimulation studies that complement the recording investigations cited at the beginning of the chapter. These provide provoking, but as yet inconclusive, information about the normal organization of cortex.

Neurosurgery on Awake Individuals

The stimulation studies are possible ethically because (1) global anesthesia is more dangerous, especially to a brain-damaged individual, than local anesthesia and (2) given the symptoms of brain damage due to, say, a vascular accident the surgeon can use the patient's report of the effects of brain stimulation as a guide for proximity to the damage. Such individuals are sedated, of course, but are still responsive to questions posed by the surgeon.

Penfield's Observations

The technique of using patient responses to guide an operation was pioneered by a Canadian neurosurgeon named Wilder Penfield (Chapter 10). Penfield would expose and

stimulate a large cortical surface (much smaller areas are exposed today). Marking the location of each site stimulated, he would then ask the patient to report his thoughts or experiences. Stimulation in primary visual cortex produced the illusion, as reported by the patient, of flashes of light in the visual field contralateral to the side stimulated. Stimulation of somatosensory cortex produced **paresthesia**, or a tingling sensation on the opposite side of the body (of course, no painful sensations were reported; Chapter 11). Stimulation of motor or premotor cortex elicited involuntary movements of the contralateral limbs and digits. Stimulation in temporal lobe, the site of a number of epileptic focuses, sometimes produced the illusion of sound or, interestingly, words or music if the stimulation was done in temporal association cortex.

Most interestingly, if the stimulus was applied in association cortex of a very high order (remote from primary, sensory, or motor cortical areas), the subjects would often report memories of a very elaborate yet specific nature. Sometimes the memories would be very poignant evocations of events in the person's childhood, or "multimedia" experiences in that sensory recall in several different modalities (sight, sound, smell, touch) were involved.

Figure 16–21 *Examples of MRI and CAT Scan Imaging.* Noninvasive imaging permits scientific investigation of conscious human brain function.

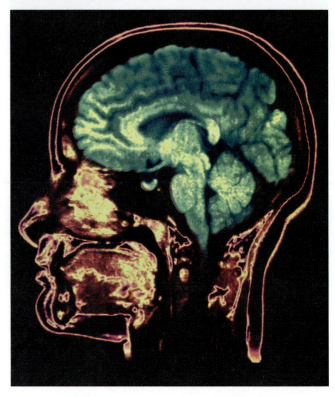

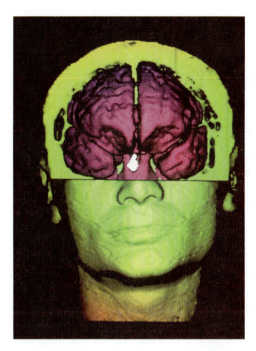

Figure 16–22 *MRI Image of the Human Brain.* The spectacular clarity that is seen with an MRI image allows a noninvasive approach to diagnose and treat head injuries.

An immense amount of scientific discussion followed Penfield's announcement of his discoveries. At one level of interpretation the results seem to be strong argument for **cellular connectionism**, the notion that brain regions are specialized by function (Chapter 1), since they would suggest that each site of stimulation contained the neural structures for the specific engram for the memory supplied by the patient. On the other hand, such data as Penfield's (which have been replicated by other neurosurgeons) could also support **aggregate field theory** (the idea that function is a property of a diffuse *network* of brain regions; Chapter 1) since, just like a hologram can be elicited by light striking any part of a holographic plate, perhaps punctate stimulation elicited a widespread pattern of activity in the brain and the widespread pattern itself constituted the engram. After all, every point of stimulation involves activation not only of the cell bodies in the area but also, by orthodromic (Chapters 2 and 4) activation, everything that region projects to, and everything the postsynaptic cells project to, and everything those followers project to, and on in this manner until, presumably, a large portion of the brain is affected. Furthermore, punctate stimuli would also affect everything projecting to the area (by antidromic activation; Chapters 2 and 4), and everything projecting through the area (such as axons going through on their way somewhere else).

The observations of Penfield and his followers remain one of the most widely observed but difficult to interpret set of findings in neuroscience. What is your position regarding their significance?

Consciousness and the Self

Of all higher functions, including language, **consciousness** (awareness of self and outside world) seems the hardest to localize in brain. If any central function appears to be organized according to aggregate field theory, it is consciousness. In looking for the threshold in brain damage where consciousness no longer exists, or in examining animal life to find the boundary between sentient beings and insensate creatures, we find no clear boundaries until we encounter **coma**, in humans, or the distinction between plants and animals. In other words, everywhere we look for consciousness in animals we find it to some degree. It has manifestation everywhere, in every brain region and in all organisms. What can neuropsychology possibly tell us about such a ubiquitous, yet ephemeral, phenomenon? A partial answer can be found in the fascinating accounts of the fragmented inner nature of individuals afflicted with very high order agnosias, such as agnosia of the passage of time or of the self.

Is It Possible to Be "Less of a Person?"

There is in the history of neurology an extensive record of a type of brain damage most students find hard to comprehend upon first encounter. Parts of the brain, when damaged, produce no simple sensory deficit or failure of comprehension, but agnosia of a different kind. Damage to the frontal lobes (as in the procedure of frontal lobotomy) results in a condition in which there is a deficit in planning and foresight (combined with general docility in *some* individuals). Damage to the temporal lobes (as for patient H. M. who had bilateral resection of the hippocampus to alleviate epilepsy) can produce inability to understand the passage of time, or form new memories, creating an "eternal present." Obviously, since consciousness involves the anticipation of the future and the memory of the past (the notion that "something is happening") damage in each of these areas can be said to have robbed the individual of some aspect of consciousness.

But is this all? Central to the notion of the self in a time continuum is the notion of "self" at all. Is it possible that the identity of the self is also a property of a particular brain region? Though the literature is incomplete (for how would you ask a patient whether a "self" exists, and how would he or she answer if it didn't?) some insights are to be found in cases when partial damage to the self occurs, as described in Box 16–4. It seems that if there is a higher function that obeys the principle of aggregate field theory, the sense of "self" would be that higher function.

Box 16–4

Unilateral Neglect

Oliver Sacks describes, in his essay "The Man Who Fell Out of Bed" (see *The Man Who Mistook His Wife for a Hat*), the case of a young man who awoke one morning to find a severed leg in bed with him. Reacting with horror, he threw the leg out of bed, only to find himself sitting on the floor next to the macabre object. Thoughts raced through his mind. How could this hideous body part have arrived in his bed? Who could have conceived of such a horrible act as to place it there? It was New Year's Eve, perhaps some drunken friend was playing a practical joke on him.

Upon discovery in this condition (of course with his functioning leg still attached to his body) the man was taken to the neurologist, who recognized in him the type of contralateral denial typical of a parietal lobe condition known as **unilateral neglect**. Patients with (unfortunately irreversible) lesions of this sort will disown parts of their body, neglecting to dress or take care of that side of the body and generally live a "half-life," even though sensory reflexes and motor tone are normal on the neglected side. The following narration is from Oliver Sacks's account of the experience with his patient.

"Look at it!" he cried, with revulsion on his face. "Have you ever seen such a creepy, horrible thing? I thought a cadaver was just dead. But this is uncanny! And somehow—it's ghastly—it seems stuck to me!" He seized it with both hands, with extraordinary violence, and tried to tear it off his body, and, failing, punched it in an access of rage.

"Easy!" I said. "Be calm! Take it easy! I wouldn't punch that leg like that."

"And why not?" he asked, irritably, belligerently.

"Because it's *your* leg," I answered. "Don't you know your own leg?"

He gazed at me with a look of compounded stupefaction, incredulity, terror and amusement, not unmixed with a jocular sort of suspicion, "Ah Doc!" he said. "You're fooling me! You're in cahoots with that nurse—you shouldn't kid patients like this!"

"I'm not kidding," I said. "That's your own leg."

He saw from my face that I was perfectly serious—and a look of utter terror came over him. "You say it's my leg, Doc? Wouldn't you say that a man should know his own leg?"

"Absolutely," I answered. "He *should* know his own leg. I can't imagine him *not* knowing his own leg. Maybe *you're* the one who's been kidding all along?"

"I swear to God, cross my heart, I haven't . . . . A man *should* know his own body, what's his and what's not—but this leg, this *thing*"—another shudder of distaste—"doesn't feel right, doesn't feel real—and it doesn't *look* part of me."

"What *does* it look like?" I asked in bewilderment, being, by this time, as bewildered as he was.

"What does it look like?" He repeated my words slowly. "I'll tell you what it looks like. It *looks like nothing on earth*. How can a thing like that belong to me? I don't know *where* a thing like that belongs . . . ." His voice trailed off. He looked terrified and shocked.

"Listen," I said. "I don't think you're well. Please allow us to return you to bed. But I want to ask you one final question. If this—this thing—is *not* your left leg" (he had called it a "counterfeit" at one point in our talk, and expressed his amazement that someone had gone to such lengths to "manufacture" a "facsimile") "then where *is* your own left leg?"

Once more he became pale—so pale that I thought he was going to faint. "I don't know," he said. "I have no idea. It's disappeared. It's gone. It's nowhere to be found . . . ."

Unknown to medical science, since it would be impossible to ask a patient if it had occurred, is complete bilateral neglect. In such a hypothetical case it might be presumed that consciousness, as well as the "self," were no longer present, leaving a sensing, acting, behaving body without a person inside (or with the person "elsewhere"), "the lights on and nobody home." Readers who are curious about the nature of consciousness and the self could begin their study of the subject by reading other accounts of unilateral neglect in the neurological literature.

SUMMARY

Human neurobiology provides insights into language, consciousness, and "the self" that are not available from animal studies. This is because the human species is the only one that can inform the experimenter of what is being experienced internally. Introspection, once rejected by science, provides one avenue for self-experimentation and experimentation on the self. Animals can learn to cooperate, and even communicate, in some experiments addressed at volition and consciousness. Studies of individuals with aphasia, apraxia, agnosia, alexia, and emotional deficits can yield insight into the functioning of the normal brain. Latent function in the brain, as suggested by aggregate field theory, may account for some recovery of function after brain damage. Positron emission tomography, magnetic resonance imaging, and magnetoencephalography complement lesion studies in localization of higher functions to specific regions of cortex and produce evidence that supports cellular connectionism. Stimulation of the brain in awake humans yields data suggestive of cellular connectionism as well as aggregate field theory. Consciousness is elusive in man and animals and comes closer than any other cerebral function to organization by the principles of aggregate field theory.

REVIEW QUESTIONS

1. Why is human neurobiology superior to research on animals for some purposes?

2. List the common behavioral deficits studied in diagnostic neurology.

3. What is noninvasive imaging and why is it important?

4. What are latent circuits and why are they important?

5. How do the observations of Wilder Penfield relate to the issue of aggregate field theory and cellular connectionism?

6. Where is consciousness located in the brain?

7. What is unilateral neglect?

8. What is hemispheric specialization?

THOUGHT QUESTIONS

1. In the 1970s, a college student in California was found to lack a corpus callosum entirely. He had majored in geography and maintained a "B" average. Comment on the role of the corpus callosum in college life.

2. Design an experiment to localize the specific brain region (ideally a single cell) whose activity arises from "free will."

KEY CONCEPTS

Dreams! Always dreams! And the more ambitious and delicate the soul, all the more impossible the dreams. Every man possesses his own dose of natural opium, ceaselessly secreted and renewed, and from birth to death how many hours can we reckon of positive pleasure, of successful and decided action? Shall we ever live in, be part of, that picture my imagination has painted, and that resembles you?

Charles Baudelaire
Paris Spleen, *1869*

17

Psychopharmacology

Baudelaire was a French poet of the mid-nineteenth century and an "opium-eater," one of a group of writers (then and now) who found literary inspiration in the effect of drugs on consciousness and feeling. His insight, *that drugs have effect because they mimic the action of natural brain chemicals*, is a profound one in the field of **psychopharmacology** or the science of drug action on mental processes. As is often the case, his insight was neglected outside of the artistic community until it was "rediscovered" by scientists almost a hundred years later in the course of neurobiological research into the mechanisms of drug action. In this chapter, we will examine how specific drugs produce their physiological and behavioral effects as well as factors that influence the intensity and duration of those effects. These factors that influence drug effects are collectively referred to as **pharmacokinetics** (literally "the movement of drugs" or the science of drug uptake and elimination). We will also discuss three phenomena associated with the use of many drugs: addiction, tolerance, and withdrawal.

Drugs can be classified into several categories based on the general type of effect produced. **Depressants** produce a general decrease of cognitive and behavioral processes (or a decrease in activity). We will examine three of the most commonly used depressants: **alcohol**, **barbiturates** (sedatives), and **benzodiazepines** (tranquilizers). Although the effects of marijuana (depressant or stimulant) are highly variable between individuals and social circumstances, **marijuana** is considered (along with alcohol) in the section "Central Nervous System Depressants." **Stimulants** produce a general increase in behavior and thought. The two most popular legal stimulants are **nicotine** and **caffeine**. Two common illegal stimulants are **amphetamine** and **cocaine**.

We will also examine two types of drugs that fall into neither of the above categories: hallucinogens and opiates. **Hallucinogens** are substances that alter an individual's perception of reality. **Opiates** are products of the opium poppy or synthetic derivatives that are frequently used medically to produce analgesia (Chapter 11), but they can also produce euphoria (a feeling of well-being) when used nonmedically.

Agonists and Antagonists

Chapter 5 summarized all aspects of normal synaptic transmission. Neurotransmitters are synthesized, released, and diffuse across the synaptic cleft to interact with receptors and induce changes in the postsynaptic cell. All of the drugs discussed in this chapter achieve their physiological effect either by influencing some aspect of synaptic transmission or by behaving as the endogenous transmitter would. Drugs can influence neurotransmitter synthesis, release, or re-uptake, or they can interact with the receptor in place of the endogenous transmitter. A drug that mimics or facilitates the action of the endogenous transmitter is called an **agonist** (from the Greek for "contestant") by psychopharmacologists (note the far more restricted definition of the term used in discussion of synaptic physiology, Chapter 5). A drug that prevents the normal activity of the endogenous transmitter is called an **antagonist**.

It is interesting to speculate on the reasons why various plants and other naturally occurring products would affect synaptic transmission in animals and humans. A reasonable possibility is that there is adaptive evolutionary value for the plant to do so. All of the drugs to be discussed have severely unpleasant, if not fatal, effects in high doses. A prehistoric animal or human that ingested a plant and got violently ill would certainly avoid that plant in the future. Even the smaller doses that are currently used for medicinal or recreational purposes would make an organism less fit to survive predation and would pose other risks. Therefore, it was probably an important evolutionary adaptation for plants to affect or mimic neurotransmission.

Pharmacokinetics

In order to exert its effects, a drug must go through three steps: administration, distribution, and elimination. First, a drug must be administered in some manner. After absorption into the bloodstream, the drug is distributed via the blood to various organs and tissues throughout the body. Finally, the drug must be eliminated from the body. We will examine each of these processes in turn.

Administration

Drugs are administered by one of several routes. In humans, the most common route of drug administration is *oral*. The major advantage to the oral route is convenience. However, the drug must be able to survive the harsh environment of the stomach long enough to reach the blood and be distributed throughout the body, which can be a potential problem. Another common route of administration is *intravenous* or directly into a vein (*IV*). The major advantage is speed, since the entire drug dose immediately enters the bloodstream

without having to be absorbed. Intravenous injections are therefore the most common mode of administration in clinical emergency situations. A significant potential risk is the speed with which an extremely high concentration of drug can be achieved, which creates the danger of overdose.

Other less frequently used routes include subcutaneous, or beneath the skin (*SC*); intramuscular, or into the muscle tissue (*IM*); and rectal administration. Drug concentrations in blood peak much more slowly via these routes than by IV administration because of the increased time it takes for the drug to be absorbed into the bloodstream. A route, used primarily in experimental studies with animals, is intraperitoneal, or injection into the gut cavity (*IP*). The risk of infection makes this a rare route for drug administration in humans. Lastly, drugs in gaseous form may be inhaled directly into the lungs. Inhaled drugs reach the bloodstream and thus the brain very quickly.

Distribution

Some drugs, such as ethyl alcohol (ethanol), are distributed equally throughout the body, due to their ability to diffuse across cell membranes. Most drugs are distributed unequally, primarily because of their inability to cross cell membranes. However, this impermeability is not a big problem for many drugs since numerous important synaptic processes occur extracellularly (e.g., receptor blockade, transmitter reuptake). Still, it's important to remember that, in order to produce an effect, drugs must act at the appropriate receptor or synapse and that most synapses of importance to psychopharmacology lie behind the hard-to-cross **blood-brain barrier** (Figure 17–1), which is an obstacle to penetrate for hydrophilic compounds described in Chapter 8.

Elimination

Most drugs are intended to have temporary action, and then return the body to its normal state after a period of time; hence, they must be eliminated from the body. The duration of action of a given drug is typically expressed by a concept called **half-life**. A drug's half-life is defined as the amount of time that it takes to eliminate 50 percent of the drug dose from the body. Obviously, the longer half-life that a drug has, the longer its physiological activity. It takes approximately six half-lives to reduce most drugs to ineffective concentrations. Most drugs are metabolized, or broken down, primarily by the liver, although some drugs are excreted unchanged. A drug is typically broken down into its component molecules, which are referred to, logically enough, as **metabolites**. Most metabolites have no physiological effect, although some exhibit activity that exceeds that of the parent compound in intensity and duration. For example, the antidepressant drug

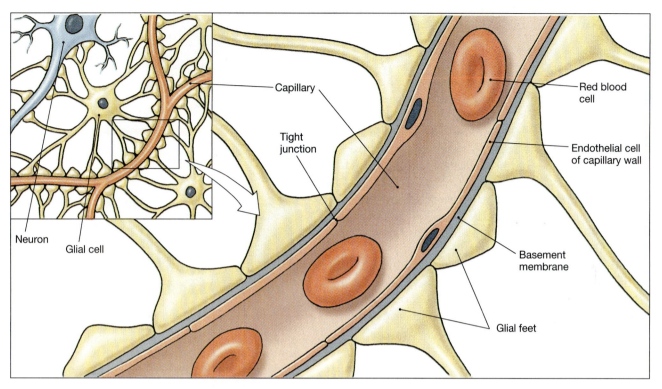

Figure 17–1 *The Blood-Brain Barrier.* In order for drugs to exert their effects on the brain, they must first cross the blood-brain barrier. The endothelial cells in the capillary walls are joined tightly together in the brain, and branches from astrocytes, or glial feet, surround the capillaries further strengthening this barrier. Thus, drugs must be able to pass through these tight junctions, or they must be able to diffuse through the hydrophobic barrier created by the astrocytes.

trimipramine, which has a half-life of 8 to 10 hours, is broken down to the active metabolite protriptyline with a half-life of 55 to 125 hours! Therefore, these active metabolites extend the duration of action of the parent compound (in the best of cases) or they produce undesirable independent actions ("side effects" in undesirable cases).

Addiction, Tolerance, and Withdrawal

With chronic use, tolerance, addiction, and withdrawal become issues with many drugs. **Tolerance** is the phenomenon in which more and more drug is required to produce a desired physiological effect. Tolerance often leads to **addiction**, which is loosely defined as the physiological and psychological need for a drug. If that drug is removed after tolerance has developed, **withdrawal** results, which is a time period marked by often painful physical and psychological symptoms. Interestingly, withdrawal from a drug is usually characterized by the *opposite* symptoms that the drug induces. For example, morphine use causes symptoms like euphoria and constipation, whereas morphine withdrawal is characterized by dysphoria and diarrhea.

An interesting explanation for these effects is the **opponent process theory**, which is derived from psychological literature. Solomon (1980) examined this theory in order to explain the tolerance, addiction, and withdrawal that occurs after prolonged use of many drugs. Opponent process theory argues from the general principle that we have emphasized throughout the text that the body constantly strives for homeostasis. A drug (or "A-process") produces physiological perturbations from homeostasis. The body immediately attempts to reduce those perturbations by initiating the opposite response (called the "B-process"). According to Solomon, the B-process gets stronger with continual exposure to the A-process; thus, the A-process logically gets weaker. Tolerance results from the body's attempt to maintain homeostasis by producing bigger and bigger B-processes.

Addiction is defined as the need to take a drug to avoid the presumably aversive B-process. When addiction exists and the drug (A-process) is removed, all that is left in withdrawal are the massive opposite effects of the drug (B-process). This potentially explains why the symptoms of withdrawal are opposite from the effects of the drug.

Central Nervous System Depressants

Alcohol and Marijuana

Alcohol and marijuana are perhaps the two most popular mood-elevating substances in the world. Most estimates show that about two-thirds of Americans of legal drinking age consume alcohol on a regular basis. Furthermore, it is estimated that millions of individuals suffer from drinking problems. Marijuana use, on the other hand, declined among high-school students throughout the country in the 1980s (Julien, 1992) but recent evidence indicates that use of this drug may once again be on the rise (Trinkoff & Storr, 1997). Both alcohol and marijuana lead to sedation and relaxation at moderate doses, but their similarities end there.

Ethyl alcohol, or ethanol, is a naturally occurring byproduct of the distillation and fermentation of sugar. Alcohol is ingested in beverage form with different beverages having different amounts of alcohol. Beer, a popular alcoholic drink perhaps familiar to some readers, typically contains 3 to 5 percent alcohol by volume. The alcohol content in wine averages about 10 to 20 percent alcohol by volume, whereas, whiskey, rum, and gin average about 40 to 50 percent alcohol by volume. The chemical structure of ethanol is shown in Figure 17–2.

After ingestion, alcohol passes through the stomach, where absorption is poor, and enters the small intestine, where absorption is rapid. A full stomach does indeed slow alcohol absorption into the bloodstream, which is consistent with much well-intentioned advice. Alcohol levels in the blood peak approximately thirty to sixty minutes after ingestion ends. Also, alcohol freely crosses cell membranes and thus travels freely throughout the body.

Alcohol is a CNS depressant, and the acute effects of an ethanol dose demonstrate its effect. Common behavioral effects from a dose of alcohol include visual impairment, lack of motor coordination, increased reaction time, euphoria, and release from inhibitions.

Following absorption, alcohol is metabolized in the liver largely by an enzyme called *alcohol dehydrogenase*, which produces the alcohol metabolite *acetaldehyde*. Much of the acetaldehyde can be used by the body as a nutrient. A fraction of the consumed alcohol is excreted by the lungs, which is the basis for the breath test that is used to assess blood alcohol levels in drunk driving cases. **Disulfiram** ("antabuse") in-

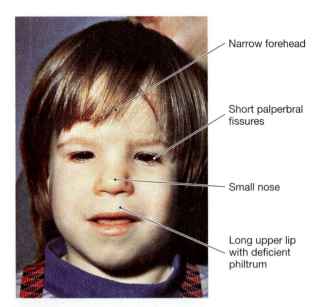

Figure 17–3 *Fetal Alcohol Syndrome.* Fetal alcohol syndrome is the result of women consuming alcohol during pregnancy, and it can have many severe effects on the child; among them are physical malformations such as those shown here.

terferes with the metabolism of alcohol, which causes acetaldehyde levels to rise to toxic amounts when alcohol is consumed. The results of toxicity are severe headaches and nausea that prevent the people from consuming alcohol after the drug is taken.

Both behavioral and biochemical tolerance to alcohol develop as a result of chronic ingestion, and a painful withdrawal syndrome occurs after alcohol consumption ceases. The withdrawal syndrome is characterized by nausea, anxiety, hallucinations, and sometimes convulsions. Moreover, chronic alcohol use is associated with numerous deleterious effects.

Prolonged alcohol use has also been associated with a syndrome known as **Korsakoff's disease**; this disease results in a debilitating memory loss that may be due to vitamin deficiencies (primarily vitamin B_1) that often occur as the result of the frequently poor diet of alcoholics (e.g., alcohol alone; recall Chapter 16). The mammillary bodies in the brain are preferentially affected by Korsakoff's disease. **Cirrhosis** is a weakening of the liver caused by excessive metabolism of ethanol, which arises from the accumulation of fat in the liver plus fibrous intrusion, nodule formation, distortion of liver architecture (due to liver damage from alcohol metabolites) leading to disruption of function. Cirrhosis, which is much more prevalent than Korsakoff's disease, is often seen in alcoholics, and it can be fatal. Finally, **fetal alcohol syndrome** (see Figure 17–3) often appears in children of mothers who drink during pregnancy and is characterized by low birth

Figure 17–2 *The Structure of Ethanol.* Alcohol is one of the most popular central nervous system depressants—its easy accessibility and social acceptance may have contributed to its popularity.

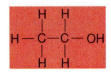

weight, low IQ, and arrested development (failure to grow to full size). Although the critical amount of ethanol is unknown, it appears that the more alcohol that is ingested the greater the likelihood of the syndrome developing. For this reason, physicians now routinely advise pregnant women to completely abstain from alcohol.

Marijuana is a product of the *cannabis sativa* plant. Its active ingredient, **THC** or delta–9-tetrahydrocannabinol (see Figure 17–4 for structure), produces a myriad of effects that are difficult to classify. At low to moderate doses, the effects are primarily sedative-hypnotic; at high doses, marijuana can produce euphoria and hallucinations. Most users are apparently seeking the sedative-hypnotic effects since more efficient means of experiencing hallucinations exist.

Marijuana's typical route of entry is through inhalation, via a cigarette or pipe, although it may also be eaten in the form of cookies or brownies. Absorption via inhalation is rapid, and the drug readily enters the CNS after absorption from the lungs into the blood. After ingestion, blood levels fall rapidly due to redistribution of the drug into the body fat. The half-life of this process is approximately thirty minutes, and it accounts for the subjective feeling of being "high" that lasts for several hours (or several half-lives; recall from the section on pharmacokinetics that it takes about six half-lives to eliminate a drug). The behavioral effects peak approximately two to three hours after ingestion. The next phase of elimination is much slower, with a half-life of thirty hours, although values as high as four days have been reported. As a result, the effects of marijuana persist much longer than the "high," and THC remains detectable in the body for days or weeks!

The primary effects of marijuana are subtle mood alterations and euphoria, but they can be accompanied by an increase in appetite and a distortion in the perception of time. Some side effects of marijuana use include increased hunger, paranoia, and apathy.

Lately, marijuana has been used for some therapeutic purposes such as relief from pain due to intraocular pressure

caused by glaucoma, and alleviation of nausea from both chemotherapy and AIDS medication (Bayer, 1997; O'Connell, 1997). In some jurisdictions, doctors in private practice are increasingly exploring the use of marijuana for medicinal purposes. In 1996, this trend led two states, Arizona and California, to legalize the therapeutic use of marijuana. The adverse health effects associated with chronic use appear to be less severe than with chronic alcohol use. The major health risk appears to be lung pathologies—as would be expected with any inhaled substance. Some data suggest that chronic marijuana use is associated with immunosuppression, which is also seen in chronic use of alcohol and other depressants such as barbiturates and benzodiazepines.

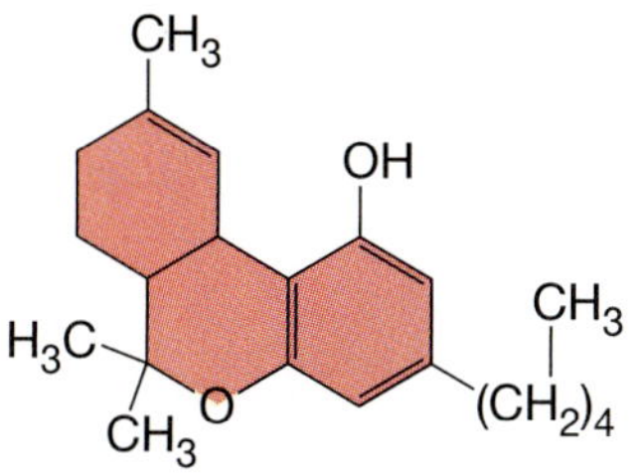

Many states have reduced legal penalties for possession of small amounts of marijuana. Research has shown that, while it is certainly not innocuous, marijuana is not the "killer weed" it was once considered to be.

Mechanism of Action: Membrane Theories

The mechanisms of action of alcohol and marijuana have been relatively unclear until recently. Traditionally, it was thought that they must act by disrupting neuronal membranes since no receptor for either drug had been found, but they clearly induced significant effects in the CNS. This "membrane fluidization" effect is certainly true for ethanol but is no longer accepted for marijuana since the recent discovery of a specific receptor for THC. Since ethanol readily dissolves in all cell membranes in the CNS, it presumably causes the neuronal membrane to become more flexible, which would reduce the efficiency of nerve impulses and disrupt the activity of membrane-bound proteins (receptors).

Mechanism of Action: Receptor Theories

Although there is no specific ethanol receptor, alcohol does influence the activity of both the GABA receptor and the n-methyl-d-aspartate (NMDA) receptor, a subtype of glutamate receptor (recall from Chapter 5 that GABA often produces synaptic inhibition and glutamate produces synaptic excitation). Alcohol does not even have its own binding site on these receptors but rather mediates ion flux through these two channels. In the case of GABA, alcohol acts similarly to benzodiazepines (discussed later in this chapter) by potentiating (or enhancing) normal GABA activity. This potentiation leads to increases in Cl⁻ flux into the cell, and thus it increases net inhibition.

Alcohol has the opposite effect at the NMDA receptor. The NMDA receptor is connected to a Ca^{++} channel, and it responds to glutamate. When glutamate binds, the channel opens and Ca^{++} is free to enter the cell. Glycine must be present for glutamate to open the channel. Ethanol prevents

Figure 17–4   *The Chemical Structure of THC.* Many people smoke marijuana for its mood-elevating effects, but—unlike alcohol—it is illegal and not easily accessible.

Marijuana
(Δτ—Tetrahydrocannabinol)

glycine from executing its normal role in enhancing glutamate activity. Therefore, less Ca^{++} enters the cell in the presence of ethanol. Alcohol thus achieves its ubiquitous inhibitory effects quite efficiently by potentiating the activity of a major inhibitory neurotransmitter candidate (GABA) and by impairing the activity of a major excitatory receptor (NMDA) in the brain.

In the past several years, researchers have isolated a specific cannabinoid receptor in rat brain (Devane et al., 1988). This receptor binds THC with high affinity, and it presumably mediates the behavioral effects of marijuana. The receptor is densely localized in the basal ganglia and cerebellum—two important components of the extrapyramidal motor system. These receptors are the apparent mechanism whereby marijuana influences motor activity. The cannabinoid receptor is also moderately dense in the cerebral cortex, particularly the frontal cortex. It is presumably this population of receptors that mediate euphoria, temporal distortions, and relaxing cognitive effects associated with marijuana use (Herkenham et al., 1991). Recently, the endogenous ligand for the cannabinoid receptor was identified and named anandamide (Devane et al., 1992). New techniques enable the visualization of the receptor in conscious human subjects (Gatley et al, 1988).

Sedatives and Tranquilizers

The pace and stress of modern life cause many individuals to seek drugs that decrease anxiety via global depression of CNS activity. Ethyl alcohol, barbiturates, and benzodiazepines all have been used to calm people suffering from anxiety. All of these compounds diminish self-awareness and anxiety in small doses, cause lethargy in larger doses, and lead to unconsciousness in very high doses. We have already discussed the effects of alcohol. In this section, we will consider the actions of barbiturates (sedatives) and benzodiazepines (tranquilizers). It is important to note that the actions of CNS depressants (barbiturates, benzodiazepines, and alcohol) tend to be supra-additive: In other words, the ingestion of two CNS depressants produce greater effects than if the drugs were taken alone. Therefore, it is quite dangerous and sometimes fatal to combine CNS depressants.

The barbiturates are a class of compounds that induce behavioral and cognitive depression. They are unusual among drugs since their source is wholly synthetic (i.e., they are not found naturally, as in a plant or animal). They are generally taken orally and then distributed throughout the body by the bloodstream. They differ in their length of action; for instance, phenobarbital, a long-acting barbiturate, has a half-life of 80 to 100 hours. Barbiturates produce their effect by acting as a GABA agonist. The characteristic barbiturate molecule is shown in Figure 17–5. A barbiturate binding site is located on

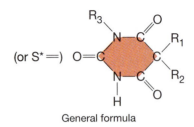

Figure 17–5   *Barbiturates*. The "R" in the chemical structure represents the portion of the chemical structure that varies among different barbiturates.

the GABA receptor complex (see Box 17–1), and GABA activity is facilitated when barbiturates bind. The barbiturates were originally used as antianxiety drugs before the synthesis of the benzodiazepines. Currently, barbiturates are used as sleep-aids and as anticonvulsants in some cases. In low doses, the behavioral effects of barbiturates may be indistinguishable from alcohol, with common outcomes being loss of inhibition and euphoria. The risks of barbiturate use are addiction and tolerance, and upon withdrawal, insomnia is often seen, which is a paradox since they are often taken to produce sleep (see Chapter 13).

The overwhelming majority of antianxiety drugs currently prescribed are from a class of compounds called the benzodiazepines (like barbiturates, they are wholly synthetic). In 1960, the first benzodiazepine, chlordiazepoxide (or **Librium**), was introduced. Later, Librium was essentially replaced by another less potent benzodiazepine called diazepam (or **Valium**); however, other benzodiazepines (such as Xanax) may have surpassed Valium's popularity in the last several years. The prototypic benzodiazepine structure is shown in Figure 17–6. The benzodiazepines are among the most widely prescribed drugs ever. In the mid–1970s, approximately 100 million prescriptions *per year* were written for benzodiazepines, primarily Valium.

Figure 17–6   *Benzodiazepines*. The "R" in the chemical structure represents the portion of the chemical structure that varies among different benzodiazepines.

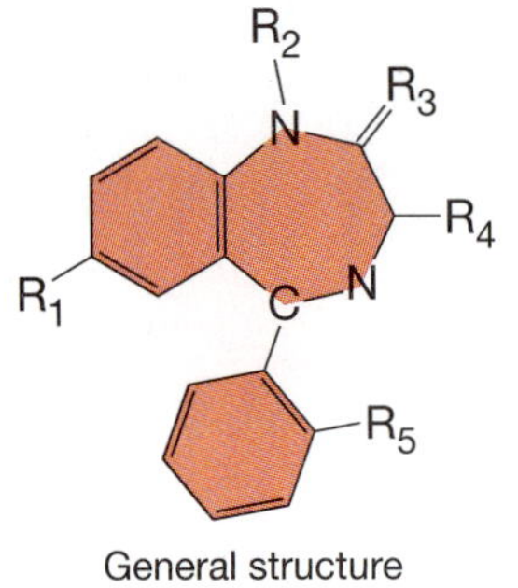

Box 17–1

The GABA Receptor Complex

GABA, as you should be aware by now, is the major inhibitory transmitter candidate in the brain. GABA is ubiquitous and is found in large quantities all over the brain. The GABA receptor surrounds a Cl^- channel; thus, the binding of GABA and GABA agonists to this receptor increases Cl^- influx into the cell. This results in a net synaptic inhibition via several mechanisms: In postsynaptic cells, it occurs by damping the membrane potential at E_{Cl}, and in presynaptic cells, it occurs by inhibiting transmitter release (see Box 5–3). GABA agonists produce effects consistent with inhibition, which are sedation, depression, and an anticonvulsant effect.

The GABA receptor is a complex protein molecule that is affected by numerous drugs, such as benzodiazepines and barbiturates. The receptor molecule is actually composed of three separate functional domains, or subunits (see figure). These domains are named the alpha, beta, and gamma subunits. Benzodiazepines bind to the alpha subunit and potentiate GABA activity as described. Antagonists for benzodiazepine receptor also exist. RO 157788, for example, will block the benzodiazepine-induced potentiation of GABA activity if administered concurrently with a benzodiazepine.

As mentioned in the text, benzodiazepine receptors also respond to inverse agonists, compounds that bind to the benzodiazepine receptor and produce the opposite effects of an agonist. A compound like FG 7142, for example, will bind to the benzodiazepine receptor and produce anxiety. Reasonably good evidence exists that the gamma subunit is where ethanol exerts its physiological effects. GABA itself binds to the beta subunit. Interestingly, barbiturates don't bind to a particular subunit, but rather they produce their effects by binding somewhere in the Cl^- channel itself. A GABA mimicker, like muscimol, will also increase Cl^- flux and thus increase net inhibition.

Substances that function as antagonists to the GABA receptor complex produce effects consistent with overex-

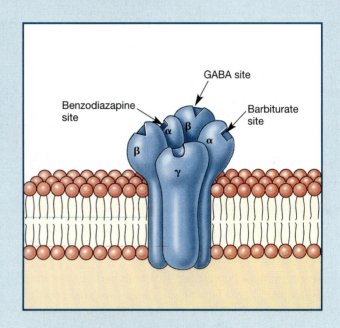

citation. Injections of picrotoxin, a product of an East Indian plant, are followed by seizures and convulsions because this antagonist prevents GABA binding. Experimental studies using picrotoxin further demonstrate the importance of GABA, and inhibition in general, for the effective functioning of the brain.

Brain inhibition does, in fact, have its politics. Benzodiazepines (tranquilizers) are among the most heavily prescribed drugs in the world. Statistically, the bulk of these prescriptions are made by male doctors to female patients. Feminist scholars have questioned the desirability of making women more "tranquil," even if it is at their own request. In developing your own opinion on this issue (and in the unfortunate prospect that you may one day feel the need for tranquilizing medication), carefully review what we have described in this case and in previous sections regarding the role of inhibition in the brain. The drugs, if used, will only produce more of it.

Although usage has declined, 1989 figures indicated that 65 million prescriptions were written for benzodiazepines annually (Julien, 1992).

Like barbiturates, benzodiazepines produce their physiological effect by facilitating GABA activity; likewise, they are consumed orally and circulated in the blood. Benzodiazepines are similar to barbiturates in that they both have binding sites on the GABA receptor. Although the benzodiazepines as a group are quite effective anxiety-reducers, or **anxiolytics** (*lytic* means "dissolve"), they are not without side effects. The two most commonly reported side effects are drowsiness and lethargy. More women than men receive prescriptions for Valium, perhaps for several reasons. First, women are more likely than men to seek medical attention for anxiety, and second, men are possibly more likely to self-medicate, primarily through the use of alcohol, in order to eliminate feelings of anxiety. Symptoms of tolerance, addiction, and withdrawal from benzodiazepine use are similar to those of barbiturates; in addition, benzodiazepines have a great hazard of overdose potential, especially if taken with alcohol. It is hoped that the reader does not need this book to be aware of the tragedy associated with mixing pills and alcohol, which is so vividly exemplified in popular culture by the untimely deaths of Marilyn Monroe, Elvis Presley, Jim Morrison, Janis Joplin, Jimi Hendrix, and John Belushi.

Mechanism of Action:
The Prospect of Natural Ligands

We have commented on the fact that both barbiturates and benzodiazepines have a binding site on the GABA receptor. It is commonly thought that if a receptor, or binding site, is capable of influencing physiology in the brain, then an endogenous substance that utilizes that receptor must exist (discussed later in the chapter). A tremendous amount of research has focused on the search for endogenous benzodiazepinelike substances.

Initially, an anxiolytic, similar to a benzodiazepine, was suspected to be the native compound. In the years after the discovery of the benzodiazepine receptor, many candidate molecules were examined and rejected. However, one candidate remain the most promising: **desmethyldiazepam**, a metabolite of many prescribed benzodiazepines. In the past several years, this compound has been isolated from both rodent and bovine brain. Diazepam (a benzodiazepine) has been isolated from cow cortex. Some neurotransmitters are synthesized with few metabolic steps from commonly ingested foods. Diazepam and its derivatives are present in many common foods, and it is therefore *conceivable* that benzodiazepines function as anxiolytic transmitters without modification (Sangameswaran et al., 1986).

The benzodiazepine receptor is apparently unique in that it responds to **inverse agonists**—substances that do not block transmitter activity like antagonists but instead bind to the receptor and produce an effect *opposite* to that of the agonist. At the benzodiazepine receptor, an inverse agonist would therefore be **anxiogenic** (*genic* means "producing"); and it would produce an increase in anxiety, fear, and heart rate and

cause sweating and discomfort. Fairly good evidence exists that a substance isolated from bovine cortex, called β-carboline–3-carboxylate (β-CCB), functions as an endogenous anxiogenic and binds strongly to benzodiazepine receptors. Interestingly, levels have been shown to increase in rat cortex following exposure to stress (Medina et al., 1987).

The research suggests that the endogenous ligand for the benzodiazepine receptor may actually be an anxiogenic and not an anxiolytic. The finding that levels of β-CCB increase in rat cortex after stress indicates the potential role that the endogenous anxiogenic plays in alerting the organism to an emergency situation. The next several years should prove very interesting in the search for the endogenous benzodiazepine receptor ligands and in understanding the role of adaptation to stress (Adamec, 1997).

Mechanism of Action:
Chloride Conductance and CNS Output

All of the CNS depressants we have discussed produce their effect at least partially by facilitating the action of GABA, the major inhibitory neurotransmitter candidate in the brain. The effect of GABA is to open chloride (Cl^-) channels. Cl^- that enters the cell produces a hyperpolarization, which makes the cell less likely to fire. The opening of Cl^- channels via GABA activity, or any mechanism, actually inhibits a cell in three separate ways.

First, chloride (being a negative ion) takes the cell further away from threshold when it enters the cell. Second, Cl^- flux will tend to stabilize or clamp the cell at E_{Cl}, which is typically near the resting membrane potential. Finally, an influx of Cl^- will increase membrane conductance and reduce, or shunt, the amplitude of the EPSP. So the overall effect of increasing chloride conductance is to increase inhibition through several mechanisms.

Central Nervous System Stimulants

Nicotine and Caffeine

You may be surprised to learn that when you smoke a cigarette or drink a cup of coffee, you are ingesting a psychoactive drug. Nicotine is the primary active ingredient in all tobacco products. Caffeine is found in many beverages and foods including coffee, tea, cola, and chocolate. Both nicotine and caffeine are powerful CNS stimulants, but they act through different mechanisms. They also differ markedly in their associations with various pathologies.

The primary method of ingestion of nicotine is inhalation through the use of cigarettes, cigars, and pipes, although comparable blood levels are reached from a dose of chewing tobacco. Absorption of nicotine through the lungs is almost as efficient as by i.v. administration. Nicotine is eliminated

Figure 17–7 *The Chemical Structure of Nicotine.* Nicotine is the addictive drug sought by tobacco users.

Nicotine

after being metabolized into an inactive compound with a half-life of two hours. Nicotine produces its effects by acting as an agonist at a particular subtype of acetylcholine receptor (aptly named the nicotinic receptor, Chapter 5). Nicotine is a powerful CNS stimulant that produces feelings of alertness. It also appears to increase irritability; and it suppresses appetite in most smokers, which may lead to weight loss. Nicotine also exerts side effects that include increases in blood pressure and heart rate. The chemical structure of nicotine is presented in Figure 17–7.

Nicotine usage is associated with numerous health risks. Although the incidence of smoking has declined in the past thirty years, it is still the leading cause of preventable, premature death in the world. Although dependence (addiction) and all of the pharmacological effects of tobacco are mediated by nicotine, all of the long-term toxicities are due to tars and multiple compounds released by the burning of a cigarette. The diseases most associated with prolonged tobacco use are cancers (primarily lung) and coronary heart disease. A 1988 Surgeon General's report confirmed that nicotine is an addictive drug, and it has corresponding tolerance and withdrawal symptoms. Nevertheless, though tobacco use among young people has declined from 30 percent to 20percent since the 1970s, those that still smoke are smoking more, rendering the use of tobacco a substantial health threat (Julien, 1992).

Over the last ten years, probable evidence has accumulated that exposure to "secondhand smoke," or smoke from other people's cigarettes, is associated with thousands of deaths per year. This knowledge has initiated a plethora of legislation prohibiting smoking in public places. These new restrictive laws, while publicly controversial, are justified by the effects of secondhand smoke, which include asthma and ear infections as well as potentially lethal harm.

Caffeine is probably the most widely used drug in the world. It has been estimated that 80 percent of adults consume at least three cups of coffee a day. As mentioned, caffeine is present in many common beverages and foods. A typical cup of coffee, for example contains approximately 100 mg of caffeine, and a twelve-ounce can of caffeinated soda contains 35 to 60 mg. Caffeine is absorbed rapidly through the lumen of the gut and reaches significant levels in the blood within thirty minutes. The central nervous system effects peak approximately two hours after ingestion. Caffeine has a half-life

of three to five hours, after which mild withdrawal symptoms may be noted. These symptoms are to be distinguished from the more severe withdrawal symptoms experienced after long-term caffeine use. The chemical structure of caffeine is shown in Figure 17–8.

The molecular action of caffeine was unknown for many years. Many of its central nervous system effects can be attributed to its ability to block **phosphodiesterase** and increase levels of **cAMP** (recall, from Chapter 6, that phosphodiesterase is the enzyme that breaks down cAMP). Evidence, obtained in the 1980s, indicates that caffeine is also an **adenosine** receptor antagonist. Adenosine plays a role in sedation and bronchospasm. Thus, blockade of adenosine receptors with caffeine produces the opposite behavioral effects: mental alertness and bronchodilation.

The primary effects of caffeine are an increase in alertness and a decrease in fatigue. These effects are evident after one to two cups of coffee (or some sodas) for the average person. Also, as many asthma suffers can attest, caffeine relaxes the bronchi, making breathing easier. Caffeine may have some undesirable side effects, the most well-known being nervousness and an exacerbation of hypertension in those susceptible to this disorder. However, these effects appear to be transient and mild, and they probably do not contribute significantly to the risk of heart disease.

While not innocuous, caffeine certainly has been associated with much less pathology than nicotine. At very high doses (greater than 1000 mg) caffeine has been occasionally reported to cause irritability, nervousness, muscle twitching, and insomnia. Some reports have suggested that caffeine can cause panic attacks in some vulnerable individuals, but the evidence is far from complete. Caffeine can be addictive, and tolerance may lead some people to drink too much in a given day. All in all, the health evidence is clear that for a quick midday pick-me-up, a cup of coffee is much better for you than a cigarette.

Amphetamine and Cocaine

We have already discussed both legal and illegal depressants, and we just discussed the legal stimulants. Now, we move to a discussion of the two most common *illegal* CNS stimulants: amphetamine and cocaine. These two drugs exert powerful

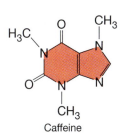

Figure 17–8 *The Chemical Structure of Caffeine.* Caffeine acts by increasing cAMP levels in the brain.

Caffeine

Figure 17–9 *Amphetamines.* A variety of different amphetamines exist with structures similar to this one.

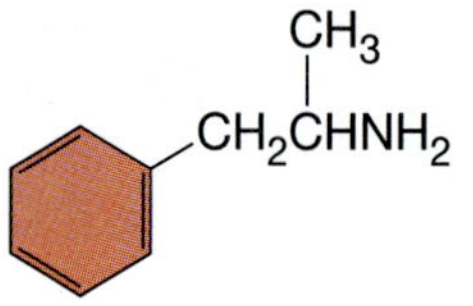

Amphetamine

effects through overlapping mechanisms, each involving dopamine neurotransmission. Both are associated with extreme abuse potential. Studies with primates and rats, for example, have shown that animals permitted to self-administer cocaine with no limitations will often overdose and die. Furthermore, chronic use of these two substances can lead to very serious health consequences.

Amphetamine is a synthetic compound with a chemical structure quite similar to the catecholamines (see Figure 17–9). It has a half-life of eighteen to twenty-four hours after oral administration, or absorption intranasally as a "cutting" agent for cocaine. Intravenous use is also common. After circulation in the blood, amphetamine is metabolized by the liver. Medical uses of amphetamine are rare. Sometimes, it is used in the treatment of narcolepsy, a disease characterized by lapsing into sleep at inopportune times (Chapter 13). Its appetite-suppressing effects are also used occasionally in the treatment of obesity. One derivative of amphetamine does, however, have some therapeutic use. Methylpheridate (**Ritalin**) is used successfully, but controversially, to treat attention deficit disorder (ADD) in children. This use of amphetamine to treat "hyperactivity" is possible because of a developmental paradox. Children respond to some stimulants in a manner opposite from adults (sedating instead of arousing). This paradox is compounded by two recent tendencies. First is the controversial attempt to diagnose ADD in adults. Some adults identified in this manner are still treated with Ritalin, even though it is no longer calming for them (it may, like a cup of coffee or a cigarette, help them "focus" their attention on a particular task). The second is a movement to disparage the entire concept of ADD, in children as well as adults. Some theorists believe, for example, that "ADD" is a normal response to abnormal stimuli such as too much candy, soda pop, or TV. Recall from Chapter 15 that most postsynaptic structures receive excessive synapses early in life and normal development causes synapses to *withdraw* (also, review "trophic factors" in Chapter 2). If this process is prolonged it is easy to see how certain children might have difficulty "paying attention."

The numerous physiological and cognitive effects of amphetamine include increases in blood pressure, motor activity, libido, and pain threshold. It results in decreases in bronchial muscle tone (a good thing for asthmatics), fatigue, and appetite. Amphetamine also produces a euphoric state that is presumably the goal of most users. High doses often result in a subjective feeling of paranoia. Prolonged usage often results in a state that is so similar to paranoid schizophrenia that mental health experts are sometimes unable to distinguish the two.

Addiction and tolerance occur often in i.v. users; but when amphetamine is prescribed (e.g., for weight loss), addiction occurs only occasionally. Withdrawal symptoms, as usual, produce the opposite effects that the drug produces: primarily a severe depression. Fatal overdoses are usually the result of a cerebral hemorrhage.

Cocaine is derived from a naturally occurring plant that is found in abundance in Bolivia, Colombia, and Peru. Cocaine's structure is shown in Figure 17–10. Although cocaine use is not legal for any purpose, current estimates show that 20 to 30 million Americans have tried it, several million use it regularly, and every day several thousand Americans try it for the first time.

Cocaine can be ingested nasally, and it is absorbed rapidly into the blood through the mucosal membranes that line the nasal passages. A powerful derivative of cocaine, "crack," can be smoked, which leads to rapid absorption into the blood. Crack is produced by extracting cocaine through a solvent. This preparation dramatically increases the concentration of cocaine in the mixture. The rapidity of action and concentration of crack combine to increase substantially the significant abuse potential that is already associated with cocaine use. Although crack is more expensive, it is also more effective, which creates a major social problem among users (addiction).

Cocaine is eventually metabolized by a specific esterase and is then eliminated from the body. One genetic variant of this esterase is not very efficient in metabolizing cocaine, which results in a much longer half-life than the usual fifteen to thirty minutes, and in rare instances, the variant enzyme combined with cocaine use could result in death. Readers may have heard of Len Bias, a star basketball player at the University of Maryland, who was drafted by the Boston Celtics. Bias apparently had the less efficient variant of this es-

Figure 17–10 *Cocaine.* Even though cocaine is an illegal drug, many people have tried it, and some people continue to use it on a regular basis.

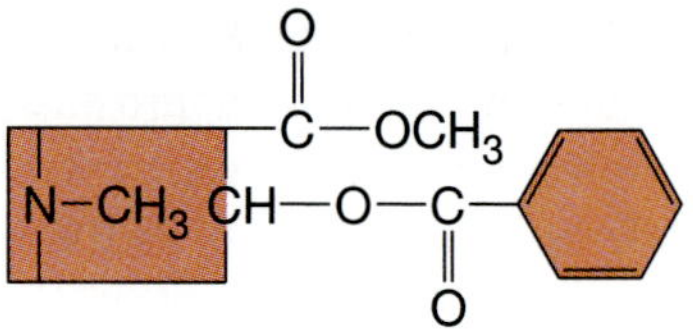

Cocaine

terase and died upon ingesting cocaine for the first time.

Cocaine induces many of the same effects as amphetamine. Cocaine ingestion is characterized by increased heart rate, blood pressure, and body temperature. It also produces a pronounced euphoria—again, the primary effect desired by most users. In high concentrations, cocaine also acts as a local anesthetic by blocking voltage-dependent Na⁺ channels.

Numerous health problems are associated with cocaine use. Acutely, cocaine may indirectly lead to cardiovascular or cerebrovascular accidents in weak blood vessels, due primarily to the significant increase in both heart rate and blood pressure. Chronically, those risks become more pronounced and tolerance develops. Thus, the individual requires more drug to achieve the euphoric effects, which further increases the cardiovascular risks. Tolerance to cocaine develops rapidly, and hence the user's habit grows quite expensive. Addiction seems to have both a physiological and a psychological dimension since periodic or "binge" use may create addiction just as continuous use does.

Mechanism of Action: Dopamine Autoreceptors

Cocaine and amphetamine seem to share a common mode of action on presynaptic receptors. Aminergic synapses, including dopaminergic synapses, have the common property of expressing receptors on the *presynaptic* membrane as well as the *postsynaptic* membrane. Such presynaptic receptors are not uncommon in other transmitter systems (found, for example, in GABAergic presynaptic inhibition, Chapter 5). However, S. Z. Langer (1997), has studied the aminergic system in detail, and has come to believe that the presynaptic receptors are different in nature from those found in other transmitter systems. For example, it appears that as dopamine is secreted it binds not only to receptors on the target cell but also to the receptors on the dopaminergic cell itself in the immediate vicinity of the site of release. While the postsynaptic receptors can be excitatory or inhibitory and may be of a variety of alpha- and beta-receptor subtypes, the receptors on the presynaptic membrane, called **autoreceptors** (Figure 17–11a), are often inhibitory and of the alpha-subtype. Thus, they have a homeostatic function; they shut down transmission once it has occurred.

It is sometimes difficult to distinguish drugs that affect the autoreceptors from those, like cocaine and amphetamine,

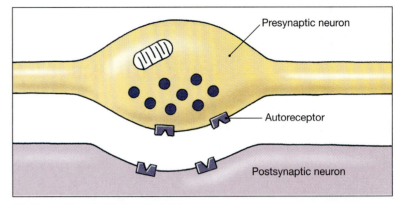

(a) Varicosity with "autoreceptors"

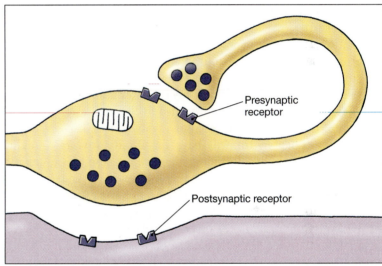

(b) Varicosity with "autapse"

Figure 17–11 *Autoreceptors and Autapses.* (a) Autoreceptors are located on the presynaptic neuron. They are thought to be involved in a negative feedback loop, which controls the amount of neurotransmitter released by the presynaptic neuron. Some drugs affect autoreceptors and disrupt the negative feedback loop. (b) Autapses involve receptors on the presynaptic neuron that are located in areas where the presynaptic neuron synapses with itself. Like autoreceptors, if autapses are affected by drugs, they cannot properly regulate neurotransmitter release.

that are thought to affect re-uptake mechanisms (discussed next). Further, as the aminergic nerve plexus (Chapter 6) lies in loose anatomical association with the postsynaptic sites and releases transmitter that diffuses to relatively distant sites of action, it is sometimes difficult to distinguish autoreceptor mechanisms from those that involve some more conventional self-association synapses, or **autapses** (Figure 17–11b). An autapse mechanism involves two synapses, whereas the autoreceptor mechanism involves only one. Confusion over microscopic sites of action is a major barrier to effective drug

Box 17–2

The Problem of Specificity

A popular misconception of drugs is that they are "magic bullets," substances that automatically travel to the right spot, do their assigned jobs, and then vanish. Unfortunately, this is nowhere near the case. Drugs, when administered, are very unselective about where they go in the body. Their travel around the body is restricted only by the ability to penetrate cell membranes and the blood-brain barrier.

Recall that a drug produces an effect because it acts at a specific receptor or multiple receptors. Even assuming that a given drug affects only one receptor system, a particular receptor typically mediates numerous effects. For example, a drug intended to elevate the action of dopamine at the receptor involved in schizophrenia (Chapter 18) will have an affinity for *all* dopamine receptors—including allosteric sites on synthesis enzymes, autoreceptors, re-uptake receptors, and breakdown enzymes—in addition to the postsynaptic receptor types (see figure). Another example is if you were to take an amphetamine, or one of its derivatives, to lose weight you would probably succeed (in the short term); however, you would also experience all of the other effects of amphetamine, such as increased libido, increased motor activity, sleep difficulties, and possibly addiction. All of these different effects result from the molecular actions of amphetamine at various receptor subtypes. As described in the text, these increase catecholamine (norepinephrine and dopamine) release, and block catecholamine re-uptake. Similarly, an anxiety-ridden person prescribed Valium will probably feel less anxious but will also feel lethargic and drowsy. Again, all of these different effects are due to the potentiation of GABAergic activity.

A drug is typically taken (either for medical or recreational purposes) for one or a few of its effects. We arbitrarily label all of the other effects of the drug as "side effects." The action of a drug cannot always be restricted so that it produces the desired effects without the undesirable effects. Therefore, much pharmacological research is dedicated to the problem of specificity. Consider the problems encountered in the pharmaceutical treatment of hypertension (high blood pressure). "Beta-blockers," such as **propranolol**, effectively lower blood pressure by preventing sympathetic norepinephrine from accelerating the heart. However, such drugs also penetrate the CNS and interfere with noradrenergic transmission there, producing undesirable psychological side effects such as nightmares or depression. Conversely, attempts to *increase* noradrenergic transmission in the central nervous system in order to alleviate depression often have the undesirable consequence of exacerbating hypertension, a condition often found in depressed patients (who tend to be elderly, Chapter 18). Such drugs that affect the heart have the common feature of being able to *stop* the heart at high enough doses. How ironic that the first medical therapy for depressed patients, who as we will see in Chapter 18 often have diagnostic feature of suicidal ideation, placed in their hands a convenient means for effecting their own demise!

Millions of dollars are spent on industrial research and development to seek an effective antidepressant with no overdose potential. One promising candidate was developed that had a sufficient affinity for the central receptors, so that it was able to alleviate depression, but had a *lack* of affinity for cardiac receptors, which made suicide an unlikely prospect. However, the researchers had ne-

design; overcoming this barrier is a very exciting area of current research in psychopharmacology (Box 17–2).

Mechanism of Action: Dopamine Re-uptake

Amphetamine and cocaine exert their effects by similar actions on the catecholamine synapses. The central catecholamines, norepinephrine and dopamine, are partially

inactivated in the synapse by a re-uptake mechanism, a protein that binds to the transmitter molecule and transports it back into the presynaptic cell. Both amphetamine and cocaine block this process from happening, thus amplifying the effect of each catecholamine molecule released. In addition, amphetamine causes more transmitter to be released, which extends the duration of amphetamine activity mak-

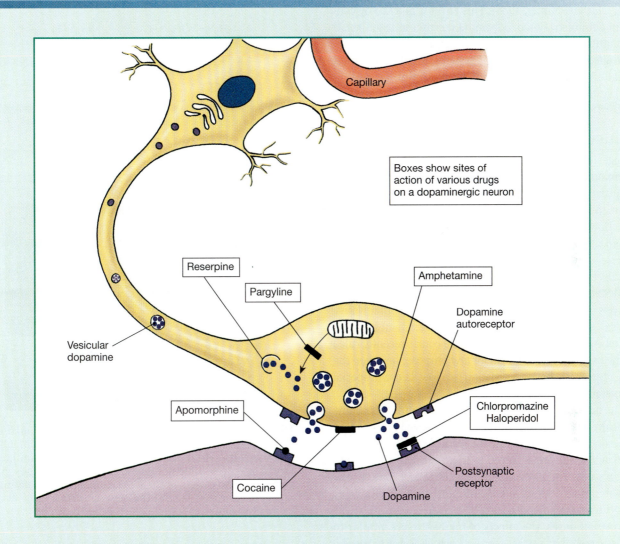

Boxes show sites of action of various drugs on a dopaminergic neuron

Capillary

Reserpine

Pargyline

Amphetamine

Dopamine autoreceptor

Vesicular dopamine

Apomorphine

Chlorpromazine Haloperidol

Cocaine

Dopamine

Postsynaptic receptor

glected yet a *third* population of receptors that could create side effects. *All* the viscera receive sympathetic innervation, not just the heart. Autonomic innervation of the penis produces erections, and the drug activated these receptors in about 10 percent of the men who took it. The consequence was **priapism** (constant erection), a condi-

tion which can be very painful and requires surgical correction—a lot to ask of an already depressed individual! Because of this story and others like it, the search for more effective and safe therapies for treating depression is ongoing. The latest developments in this area will be reviewed in Chapter 18.

ing it longer than that of cocaine. On the other hand, cocaine produces a much more intense euphoric effect than that of amphetamine. Although these drugs potentiate both norepinephrine and dopamine activity, it is accepted that dopamine potentiation (and not norepinephrine) mediates both the euphoric feelings and the abuse potential of these drugs.

Dopamine is thought to be the critical transmitter involved in areas of the brain associated with reward. Olds and Milner in a series of classic experiments in the 1950s set out to examine the influence of brain stimulation on maze running, but then serendipitously they found that a rat with an electrode implanted in areas rich in dopamine will perform a response (e.g., press a lever) thousands of times an hour in order to receive electrical stimulation (see discussion in Chapter 11, Olds and Milner, 1954). This effect is blocked by concurrent administration of dopamine receptor antagonists. It is thought that most stimuli, or drugs, that produce a euphoric effect act via dopaminergic systems. Interestingly, most clinical antidepressants also act on dopamine (as well as other) systems and are used to produce mood elevations (see Chapter 18).

Hallucinogens

As suggested by its name, the primary effect of our next class of compounds, the hallucinogens, is to induce sensory and perceptual alterations. It is a somewhat arbitrary distinction since many drugs will produce hallucinations in high enough doses. However, we will focus on those drugs whose primary effect in moderate doses is to induce hallucinations.

A frequently used hallucinogen is the peyote plant, a cactus indigenous to the deserts of Mexico and the southwestern United States. Its hallucinogenic properties have been used for centuries in the religious rites of the Aztecs and other Native American tribes. Although it is used as a sacrament in several Native American religions, the federal courts recently ruled that the use of peyote is illegal for any purpose; however, the U.S. Congress has begun legislation to allow its use in special circumstances.

The active ingredient in peyote is **mescaline**. Mescaline is typically ingested orally in the form of mescal buttons (the dried crown of the cactus), and is absorbed rapidly by the gut. Significant levels are achieved in the brain within thirty to sixty minutes. The physiological effects persist for approximately ten hours. Mescaline is not metabolized by the body and is thus excreted unchanged.

In small doses, the effects of mescaline are similar to what is observed in a stress response, which is due to mescaline's structural similarity to norepinephrine (Figure 17–12). These effects include an increase in heart rate and blood pressure, and pupillary dilation. These are not the effects desired by the vast majority of mescaline users. At higher doses, mescaline induces vivid visual hallucinations. Users report seeing brightly colored lights or geometric patterns and designs. Less frequently, users report seeing visions of animal or people. Neurotoxicity (neuron death) has been reported from the use of hallucinogens.

Other synthetic, mescalinelike hallucinogens have been produced. A dangerous and illegal example is MDMA (3,4-methylenedioxymethamphetamine), known popularly as ecstasy (like other hallucinogens, it is taken orally). Ecstasy induces effects similar to those of mescaline. However, studies using monkeys and rodents indicate that ecstasy destroys serotonin neurons, which would presumably perturb sleep, among other things (Insel et al., 1989). Thus, ecstasy may be

Figure 17–12 *Similarities between Norepinephrine and Mescaline.* The chemical structures of norepinephrine and mescaline (from the peyote plant) are very similar. Drugs often resemble neurotransmitters. Thus, they either potentiate the effects of the neurotransmitter by acting as an agonist, or they inhibit the neurotransmitter by acting as an antagonist.

an extremely dangerous way for humans to experience hallucinations. However, the hallucinogens seem to have little risk of addiction, tolerance, and withdrawal.

Probably the best known hallucinogenic compound is lysergic acid diethylamide, or **LSD**. LSD was first synthesized by Swiss chemist Albert Hoffman in 1938; he had been looking for possible drug therapies that could be derived from the fungus in ergoted (spoiled) grain, *Claviceps purpurea*. Hoffman inadvertently took the first LSD "trip" in 1943 after accidentally ingesting some of the substance. He reported feeling a bizarre constellation of effects including a dreamlike state similar to drunkenness and fantastic visual hallucinations. LSD remained essentially a laboratory curiosity for some time until it became popular in the mid–1960s partly as a consequence of recreational use by neuroscientists themselves, among them Dr. Timothy Leary. Usage has decreased substantially since that time.

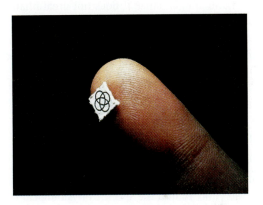

Figure 17–13 *Similarities among Serotonin, LSD, and Psilocybin.* Both LSD and psilocybin induce psychedelic effects; however, LSD is much more potent than psilocybin (a product of various kinds of mushrooms). Melatonin is another endogenous substance with structural similarity to serotonin and psilocybin.

LSD is also usually taken orally in the form of blots on paper or sugar cubes, and it has a rapid onset of action (thirty to sixty minutes) due to circulation in the blood. The half-life of LSD is approximately three hours and effects last from ten to twelve hours. LSD produces some mild physiological changes such as an increase in heart rate and blood pressure, and pupillary dilation. However, the primary effects are perceptual alterations, characterized by sensory distortions, disruptions of thought, and hallucinations. Less frequently reported effects are occasional psychotic episodes and **synesthesia**, a mixing of sensory modalities. Individuals experiencing this effect report "hearing colors" or "seeing odors."

Tolerance to LSD does develop, but it is typically not a practical issue since such minuscule amounts are needed to produce effects. Physical and psychological addictions to LSD apparently do not develop. Dangers associated with LSD use are restricted primarily to the possibility of a psychotic episode (severe break from reality) while under the influence of the drug, which can lead to suicide. Although the notion is popularly believed, there is no empirical evidence for "flashbacks," the idea of having a trip months to years after having ingested LSD.

Another relatively popular hallucinogenic compound is **psilocybin** ("magic mushrooms"), a product of various kinds of mushrooms common in the American Southwest. After being ingested orally, psilocybin is converted by the body to the active ingredient psilocin, which is approximately 200 times less powerful than LSD. Psilocybin, like LSD, produces distortions of thought and perception (compare the structures of LSD and psilocybin to serotonin, Figure 17–13). Its psychedelic effects have given it a rich history in folklore, but its mechanism of action and risks of addiction, tolerance, and withdrawal remain obscure—like for the other hallucinogens.

Phenylcyclohexyl piperadine (PCP), a synthetic drug popularly known as *angel dust*, is a difficult drug to classify. It was developed in 1963 as an analgesic and anesthetic. It was initially promising since it did not decrease heart rate or blood pressure, as many other anesthetics do. When ingested orally, PCP induces a trancelike state after it has entered the bloodstream and thus is known as a dissociative anesthetic. Its effects typically last from four to six hours. It was pulled from the market in 1965 because of complaints of irritability from patients, but flourished illegally on the street. PCP is not a true hallucinogen since it does not create hallucinations, but it does induce euphoria, distortions of body image, and a sense of "floating" through space. The dangers associated with use of PCP include extreme mood swings and psychotic behavior, sometimes leading to violence. Tolerance develops, and abrupt withdrawal is associated with fearfulness and trembling.

Mechanism of Action: Results of Neuropharmacology

A great deal of neuropharmacological research has been conducted in an effort to find the specific physiological mechanisms that mediate the effects of the various hallucinogens. Most of the research has focused on LSD since it was originally the most popular hallucinogen. Aghajanian and Haigler (1974) have performed electrophysiological studies to understand the cellular actions of LSD. The researchers recorded from single cells in the raphé nucleus, a major serotonergic nucleus. They found that LSD decreased electrical activity of the neurons in the raphé nucleus (Figure 17–14), and it produced less transmitter turnover as measured by the presence of serotonin metabolites. The explanation offered was that LSD is a serotonin agonist at inhibitory autoreceptors, thus resulting in a net depression of raphé activity. This theory has received recent confirmation (Marek & Aghajanian, 1996).

Clues to the mechanism of action of many hallucinogenic compounds are provided by their structural similarity to endogenous transmitters. As mentioned earlier, mescaline, the active component of the peyote plant, closely resembles the norepinephrine molecule (recall Figure 17–12). Furthermore, LSD has some structural relation to serotonin, which is why Aghajanian and Haigler chose to examine the raphé nucleus. Psilocin, the active element in psilocybin mushrooms, is even more structurally similar to serotonin (recall Figure 17–13). Examinations of the chemical structure of drugs often provide very valuable hints as to where these drugs are exerting their physiological effects.

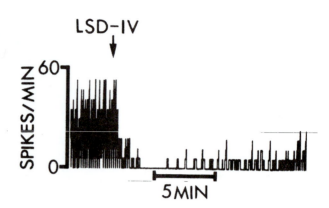

Figure 17–14 *LSD Action on the Raphé Nucleus.* An electrophysiological single cell recording from the raphé nucleus illustrates the effects that LSD has on the serotonergic neurons. The arrow indicates the point of intravenous administration of LSD in a laboratory rat. Following the administration of LSD, there is a period of inhibition in which the neurons are no longer firing action potentials. This inhibitory period suggests that LSD is affecting the normal transmission of serotonin. Aghajanian and Haigler postulate that LSD is a serotonin agonist affecting the autoreceptors. (Aghajanian & Haigler, 1974)

Opiates

An opiate is defined as any drug (natural or synthetic) that has properties similar to opium or its primary active compound, morphine. **Opium**, an extract of the opium poppy, has been used for centuries as a remedy for pain, diarrhea, and cough. **Morphine** and **codeine** are derivatives of opium that are legally available today with a physician's prescription; opium in its raw form is illegal.

Morphine is the more powerful of the two opium derivatives, and it is more frequently used and abused. Morphine was a very popular drug in the nineteenth century, and it was legal and quite accessible to the public. In fact, it could be purchased in any drugstore and was even available by mail order! By the end of the century, the abuse potential was apparent, so early in this century, federal law restricted morphine's use to medical purposes only. It is still a commonly used analgesic under medical supervision.

Morphine can be administered by various routes, although it is typically taken intravenously by those seeking the euphoric effects. It circulates through the blood and is then eliminated by the liver. Upon ingestion, morphine produces a myriad of effects including analgesia, euphoria, sedation, respiratory depression, cough suppression, and pupillary constriction. Side effects include nausea, vomiting, and occasional asthmalike symptoms due to its respiratory depressive effects. Morphine also has a potential for addiction and overdose, which is often a result of tolerance

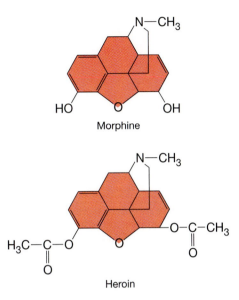

Morphine

Heroin

Figure 17–15 *The Opiates Morphine and Heroin.*
Opiates typically are derived from the opium poppy;
however, heroin is a synthetic derivative. Heroin has many
of the same effects as morphine, but it is more potent than
morphine, creating a greater potential risk for abuse. The
similarities in chemical structure of the two drugs account
for their similar effects.

and an attempt to overcome withdrawal symptoms. Morphine has serious a risk of abuse due to its powerful euphoric
effects.

A synthetic derivative of morphine, **heroin**, is approximately ten times more powerful than morphine; thus, it carries an even stronger abuse potential. The societal dangers
of heroin use have recently increased dramatically, largely
because South American sources have replaced Asian heroin
with drugs of much greater purity and potency. Overdoses,
even in college communities, are on the rise. The structures
of morphine and heroin are shown in Figure 17–15.

Mechanism of Action: Heterogeneity of Opiate Receptors

Opiates produce their effects via specific opiate receptors, first
described in the early 1970s (Pert & Snyder, 1973). It has subsequently been determined that there are several opiate receptor subtypes with different CNS distributions and
functions. The first subtype is the *mu* opiate receptor. This
subtype is heavily localized (or has high density) in the periaqueductal gray region (PAG), which is known to be an important structure for the production of analgesia (Chapter
11). It is the *mu* receptors that mediate many of the effects of
morphine. *Mu* receptors are further subdivided into *mu*–1
and *mu*–2 subtypes. It is the *mu*–1 receptor subtypes that

presumably mediate the analgesic and euphoric effects of
morphine, and it is the *mu*–2 receptors that are involved in
the respiratory depressive effects.

The other opiate receptor subtypes are the *kappa*, *sigma*,
and *delta* receptors. *Kappa* receptors are densely localized in
the spinal cord, and they are a major site of action for the endogenous opioid peptides (discussed later). They mediate
analgesia by blocking the pain information at its source in
the spinal cord. The *delta* receptors are less well characterized, but they are thought to be involved in alterations of affect and euphoria. Finally, the *sigma* receptors are present in
the limbic system, and they are involved in **dysphoria**, or feelings of discomfort (opposite of euphoria). In general, opiate
receptors are widely scattered throughout the brain, indicating that they are involved in other functions in addition to
pain modulation.

Mechanism of Action: Natural Opiate Agonists and Synthetic Opiate Antagonists

Once the opiate receptor was discovered in 1973, a frantic
search for endogenous ligands for this receptor was initiated. Two penta-peptides (peptides with five amino acids) were
found first, and they were named met-enkephalin and leu-
enkephalin. It was later determined that three separate types
of **endogenous opiates** (as they came to be known) actually
existed. The enkephalins represented only one of the three
families. Enkephalins bind to *mu* and *delta* receptors in the
PAG, and thus function in endogenous pain suppression. A
second molecule, β-endorphin, is derived from the pro-opiomelanocortin (POMC) molecule. It is coreleased from the
pituitary with adrenocorticotropic hormone (ACTH), and it
may have a role in stress responses. Finally, the third family is the dynorphins, which are also localized primarily in
the PAG and appear to serve a role as endogenous pain fa-
cilitators. The sequences of these endogenous opiates are
found in Figure 17–16.

Pharmaceutical antagonists have been developed to block
the opiate receptors. There is more medical interest in blocking analgesia than blocking the pain transmitters. Medical
interest in blocking the opiate receptor is high since this intervention can be used as emergency therapy for overdose of
narcotics (any drug derived from opium or with opiate-like activity), which can be fatal. These compounds, as would be expected, block the effects of morphine and endogenous opiates.
The two most common opiate antagonists are naloxone and
naltrexone. Naloxone binds preferentially to *mu* receptors,
but it will bind to all of the receptor subtypes in high enough
doses. Naloxone is a pure antagonist that simply blocks the actions of any opiates. Naltrexone works very similarly to naloxone but has a longer duration of action.

Name	Amino acid sequence
Leucine-enkephalin	*Tyr-Gly-Gly-Phe*-Leu-OH
Methionine-enkephalin	*Tyr-Gly-Gly-Phe*-Met-OH
β-Endorphin	*Tyr-Gly-Gly-Phe*-Met-Thr-Ser-Glu-Lys-Ser-Gln-Thr-Pro-Leu-Val-Thr-Leu-Phe-Lys-Asn-Ala-Ile-Val-Lys-Asn-Ala-His-Lys-Gly-Gln-OH
Dynorphin	*Tyr-Gly-Gly-Phe*-Leu-Arg-Arg-Ile-Arg-Pro-Lys-Leu-Lys-Trp-Asp-Asn-Gln-OH
α-Neoendorphin	*Tyr-Gly-Gly-Phe*-Leu-Arg-Lys-Tyr-Pro-Lys

Figure 17–16 *The Structures of Opioid Peptides.* After the opiate receptors were identified, scientists everywhere went on a hunt for the endogenous opiates, and what they found were the opioid peptides, which are created by the body and bind to the opiate receptors to mediate analgesia.

SUMMARY

Whether drugs are used for medical, recreational, or religious purposes, they act by either blocking the action of a native transmitter (antagonists) or mimicking its action (agonists). A drug's onset and duration of action depends on its pharmacokinetics; and much research involves the administration, distribution, and elimination of drugs, along with their metabolites within the body. Depending on a drug's pharmacokinetics, addiction, tolerance, and withdrawal symptoms may occur in addition to its primary effects.

Alcohol and marijuana, one legal and the other not, are nevertheless the most prevalent mood-altering drugs. While both seem to have direct effects on cell membranes, each also appears to act on a receptor protein in place of an endogenous agonist that has yet to be fully characterized. Benzodiazepines (tranquilizers) and barbiturates (sedatives) act on allosteric sites on the GABA receptor and increase chloride flux, which enhances brain inhibition.

Central nervous system stimulants include the widely used drugs caffeine and nicotine but also the dangerous "speedlike" drugs amphetamine and cocaine. These latter two appear to act on the brain by inhibiting the re-uptake and recycling of dopamine at its sites of release. Thus, these drugs have two effects, the first being a "high" because excess dopamine is available to bind to postsynaptic receptors and the second being a "crash" because endogenous dopamine stores have been depleted. The mechanism of action of hallucinogens is obscure, but it probably relates to their interactions with monoamine systems. Opiates act in place of endogenous opioid peptides, and they produce euphoria, tolerance, addiction, and withdrawal symptoms, which make them among the most dangerous drugs of abuse.

REVIEW QUESTIONS

1. Name the drugs that act on the GABA receptor complex.

2. What is the mechanism of action for benzodiazepines?

3. What clues to the action of hallucinogens are to be found in their structure?

4. How do opiates act on the brain?

5. How does caffeine act on the brain?

6. How does alcohol act on the brain?

7. How do the actions of cocaine and amphetamine compare?

8. Describe the theories of how addiction occurs.

THOUGHT QUESTIONS

1. If reward systems in the brain use a common dopaminergic mechanism (Chapter 11), why are some drugs more addictive than others?

2. If benzodiazepines, barbiturates, and alcohol all act allosterically on the GABA receptor to increase Cl⁻ flux, why don't they have identical subjective effects?

3. Ritalin, an amphetamine, is commonly prescribed for Attention Deficit Disorder (ADD). Say that synapse elimination is normally distributed throughout childhood, with some children experiencing segregation of synapses earlier than others, who form discrete synaptic connections later in life. Say further that "ADD" is no more than a variably diagnosed and poorly recognized refelction of this developmental lag in some children. What therapy would you propose for ADD? Comment on the use of Ritalin to treat this condition.

KEY CONCEPTS

addiction (p. 419)
adenosine (p. 425)
agonist (p. 418)
alcohol (p. 417)
amphetamine (p. 417)
antagonist (p. 418)
anxiogenic (p. 424)
anxiolytics (p. 424)
autapses (p. 427)
autoreceptors (p. 427)
barbiturates (p. 417)
benzodiazepines (p. 417)
β-CCB (p. 424)
blood-brain barrier (p. 418)

caffeine (p. 417)
cAMP (p. 425)
cirrhosis (p. 420)
cocaine (p. 417)
codeine (p. 432)
depressants (p. 417)
desmethyldiazepam (p. 424)
disulfiram (p. 420)
dysphoria (p. 433)
ecstasy (p. 430)
endogenous opiates (p. 433)
fetal alcohol syndrome (p. 420)
half-life (p. 418)
hallucinogens (p. 417)

heroin (p. 433)
inverse agonists (p. 424)
Korsakoff's disease (p. 430)
Librium (p. 422)
LSD (p. 430)
marijuana (p. 417)
mescaline (p. 430)
metabolites (p. 418)
morphine (p. 432)
nicotine (p. 417)
opiates (p. 417)
opium (p. 432)
opponent process theory (p. 419)

PCP (p. 432)
pharmacokinetics (p. 417)
phosphodiesterase (p. 425)
priapism (p. 429)
propranolol (p. 428)
psilocybin (p. 431)
psychopharmacology (p. 417)
Ritalin (p. 426)
stimulants (p. 417)
synesthesia (p. 431)
THC (p. 421)
tolerance (p. 419)
Valium (p. 422)
withdrawal (p. 419)

I am beginning to consider madness a disease like any other.

Vincent van Gogh
In a letter to his brother, Theo, *1889*

18

The Biology of Mental Illness

Between his celebrated amputation of an earlobe and his suicide, van Gogh was lucid enough to comment accurately upon his own condition as well as execute *The Starry Night* (Figure 18–1), a painting many have thought reflected his insanity. In fact, historians have found that the painting accurately reflects the position of the constellation Aries and the planet Venus on the night it was painted (Swerdlow, 1997). Van Gogh's genius, and perhaps his insanity, are reflected in other great works including *The Night Cafe* (Figure 18–2). The subject of psychiatry (the study and treatment of the mentally ill) seems to have an abundance of individuals, like van Gogh, whose behavior is clearly aberrant but who have other normal or even praiseworthy features. It is such cases on the "border" between normalcy and eccentricity that make the subject of psychiatry so fascinating to the neuroscientist.

Fyodor Dostoyevsky, himself suffering from temporal lobe epilepsy, often chose characters for his novels (*The Double, Crime and Punishment, The Brothers Karamazov*) whose behavior deviated from Russian norms of the time. Indeed, many of his characters would likely today be diagnosed as mentally ill. To justify his choice of subject matter, Dostoyevsky wrote the following preface to *The Brothers Karamazov*:

In beginning the life story of my hero, Alexey Fyodorovich Karamazov, I find myself in somewhat of a quandary. Namely, although I call Alexey Fyodorovich my hero, I myself know that he is by no means a great man, and hence I foresee such unavoidable questions as these: "What is so remarkable about your Alexey Fyodorovich, that you have chosen him as your hero? What has he accomplished? What is he known for, and by whom? Why should I, the reader, waste time learning the facts of his life?"

The last question is the most fateful, for to it I can only answer: "Perhaps you will see for yourself from the novel." Well, suppose you

Figure 18–1 The Starry Night *(June 1889).* Do you think van Gogh's painting was inspired or hindered by his madness? (Oil on canvas, 29 x 36¼" [73.7 x 92.1 cm]. The Museum of Modern Art, New York. Acquired through the Lillie P. Bliss Bequest. Photograph © 1999 The Museum of Modern Art, New York.)

Figure 18–2 The Night Cafe *(September 1888).* For van Gogh this painting expressed "the powers of darkness in a low public house—where one can ruin oneself, go mad or commit a crime." Some experts believe van Gogh's madness was caused by excessive drinking of absinthe, a liquor with toxic traces of the plant wormwood. Four months after completing this work van Gogh cut off part of his ear and gave it to a prostitute whom he loved.

read the novel, and fail to see, and so do not agree that my Alexey Fyodorovich is remarkable? I say this because unhappily I anticipate it. For me he is remarkable, but I doubt strongly whether I shall succeed in proving this to the reader. The fact is, if you please, that he is a protagonist, but a vague and undefined protagonist. And, in truth, in times such as ours it would be strange to require clarity of people. One thing, I dare say, is fairly certain: this man is odd, even eccentric. But oddness and eccentricity interfere rather than help, especially when everyone is trying to put the particulars together and to find some sort of common meaning in the general confusion. In most cases the eccentric is a particularity, a separate element. Isn't that so?

Now, if you do not agree with this last thesis, and answer, "It isn't so,"" or "It isn't always so," then I, if you please, might become encouraged about the significance of my hero, Alexey Fyodorovich. For not only is an eccentric "not always" a particularity and a separate element, but on the contrary, it happens sometimes that such a person, I dare say, carries within himself the very heart of the whole, and the rest of the men of his epoch have for some reason been temporarily torn from it, as if by a gust of wind. . . .

Incidental to providing an apology for devoting lengthy works of fiction to subjects outside normal experience, Dostoyevsky also gives us insight into the nature of his great art. Art succeeds, in part, by removing us from the mundane and everyday and causing us to examine life from a different per-

spective. From consideration of the abnormal, normal experience is enriched and life proceeds with greater insight than before.

A little bit of an understanding of mental illness can be dangerous, however. Students learning for the first time about various disorders are apt to find symptoms of mental disturbance in their friends, family members, and even in themselves. ("*Now* I understand by boyfriend. He's schizophrenic!")

My goal in this chapter is to present modern research in the areas of serious mental illness so that, as Dostoyevsky suggested, we can acquire enhanced understanding of the universal aspects of mental function, shared between those of us who are ill and those of us who are not. In doing so, I shall try to help you resist the temptation of self-diagnosis and excursion into amateur psychiatry. Remember, the overall occurrence of mental illness is low, so the chances are slim that you or the person sitting next to you is suffering from any of the disorders described here.

The Taxonomy of Mental Illness: The DSM IV

At one time it was believed that everyone was destined to be mentally ill as a result of normal senescence. **Senility** was thought to be the universal fate of the very old, a belief that could be sustained because many people died of other causes (heart attacks, infections, influenza, etc.) before reaching old age, disguising the fact that most elderly people maintain robust mental faculties throughout their life span. Today senility is known to be result of a collection of specific disease states, each present in only a fraction of the elderly, including **Alzheimer's disease** (progressive mental deterioration manifested by loss of memory, confusion, and disorientation, usually beginning in late middle life and leading to death in five to ten years) and **multi-infarct dementia** (steplike deterioration in intellectual function as a result of insufficient blood supply to cerebral hemispheres). As these diseases come about for different reasons, the use of the term *senility* to describe mental illness in the elderly is no longer accepted.

Nevertheless, the concept of senility left a lasting impression on the identification and treatment of the mentally ill (those with disorders of the mind or intellect) of all ages. In the nineteenth century and before, individuals suffering from a wide variety of ailments, from organic brain syndrome (Chapter 16) to psychosis, neurosis, and even criminal tendencies, were considered to have similar forms of dementia and were housed together in mental asylums. In 1896, Emil Kraepelin, a German physician, published a textbook purporting to discern differences among the insane in terms of disease processes. One set of patients appeared unusually young for the inmate population as a whole and seemed to have discrete symptoms that separated them from the rest. Kraepelin thought that these patients had an accelerated case of mental illness and called the disorder **dementia praecox**, or "premature senility." A contemporary of Kraepelin, a Swiss physician named Eugen Bleuler, corresponded with him extensively regarding the condition, adding extensive observations of the actual patients' behaviors, which had up to that point been neglected as an indicator of disease processes. Bleuler came to call the new disease **schizophrenia**. With the detailed behavioral observation of Kraepelin, Bleuler, Sigmund Freud, and others a new medical specialty, **psychiatry** (the medical specialty concerned with the diagnosis and treatment of mental disorders), was born from the neurology that preceded it.

The story of biological psychiatry since the time of Kraepelin and Bleuler is characterized by progressive refinement of diagnosis for a large number of mental illnesses and effective drug treatment for three of them. The proliferation (some would say explosion) in the number of diagnostic categories can be appreciated by consulting the **Diagnostic and Statistical Manual** for psychiatric disorders, now in its fourth revision (**DSM IV**). A vast array of discrete illnesses ranging from adjustment disorders to math phobias are included in the DSM IV. Critics of psychiatric diagnosis charge that the recent creation of so many illnesses threatens to make mental patients of us all. On the other hand, precise diagnosis is the key to effective treatment, and the addition of new categories

is a logical extension of the method of careful observation that led to the science of neurology and the understanding of the biological basis for the deficits seen upon brain damage (see Chapters 1 and 16). One of the goals of psychiatry is to find a biological basis for mental illness using careful analysis of behavior as a starting point.

Psychiatrists, and others who treat the mentally ill, often use language that implies a dualistic position in the mind/body problem (see Chapter 1). When confronted with a particular symptom, or even when discussing an entire diagnostic category, it is common to find the therapist asking "Is it *biological* in origin or *psychological* in origin?"

Psychiatric problems are almost invariably divided (explicitly or implicitly) into psychological complaints ("mind"), best treated with therapy, and brain disorders ("body"), best treated with drugs. Review Chapter 1 and evaluate how a determined monist might respond to the central question of psychiatry, "Is it biological or psychological?"

The mind/body problem is often confused with another, separate issue in psychiatry. Assuming that it is correct to classify psychiatric ailments as either biological or psychological, there is widespread disagreement over how many should be placed in each category. At one extreme are proponents of the **antipsychiatry** movement who believe virtually all psychiatric complaints are psychological in origin. R. D. Laing, Thomas Szasz, and others of this movement in the 1960s and 1970s held that even severe disturbances such as schizophrenia were due to social trauma ("normal responses to an abnormal society" in the words of one "antipsychiatrist"). Some adherents of this movement experimented with releasing seriously ill patients from mental hospitals and treating them with group therapy instead of drugs. The results of these experiments were sometimes disastrous; the benefits of drug therapy have become so apparent that it is hard to find a proponent of antipsychiatry in the medical community today (though it lives on in some alternative approaches to mental health).

At the opposite extreme is the belief that all psychiatric illnesses are biological in origin. Called the **medical model**, presumably because proponents of this belief would favor medication as part of therapy, this belief has led to experiments in the prescription of antidepressant drugs to a wide variety of people including some who are not depressed and even some who display no psychiatric abnormality at all.

Since you may pursue a career in mental health or be unfortunate enough to experience mental illness at some time in your life, discussions about the dichotomy in approaches to treatment and the mind/body problem are essential. Clear understanding of the dichotomy will allow you to be both a more careful practitioner and well-informed consumer of mental health services. First, recall that the logic of the mind/body problem compels adherence to one position or the other, monism and dualism are mutually exclusive. In contrast, debate regarding the medical model and antipsychiatry contains no such compulsion; it is logically consistent to adopt either extreme or any intermediate position. The debate over the medical model is independent of the mind/body problem; a person could be a perfect monist and believe in drug therapy, psychotherapy, or a combination of the two. Likewise, a firm and committed dualist could, with perfect logic, adhere to either the medical or antipsychiatry model. The overwhelming majority of practitioners take an intermediate stance, acknowledging the failures of past experiments with both extremes. Second, far from encompassing the mind/body problem, the debate over the medical model largely presumes that the issue has been resolved in favor of dualism. Too often lost in the discussion is the monistic possibility that drugs and psychotherapy may actually be treating the same thing, even to the extent of having the same neurochemical consequences.

Clear thinking about the mind/body problem, and how it relates to the medical model in psychiatry, too often eludes even specialists in the field. Your clear thinking on this subject will be of great value in understanding what is to follow. For example, effective drug therapy exists for three types of psychiatric disorders: schizophrenia, affective illness, and anxiety disorders. The actions of the drugs point toward certain biological substrates for the conditions and hence are suitable subjects for the biological approach found in the remainder of this chapter. Organization of the material in this biological orientation, however, does not constitute an endorsement by the author for either dualism or the use of the medical model in treating the conditions. The position you take is a very personal one, there is no right or wrong way to look at this issue.

Schizophrenia

Schizophrenia is a group of disorders, perhaps only loosely related, that have the common feature of at least a six-month period of disturbances of communication, perception, or thought processes. Affect (emotion) may be abnormal too, but it appears as a blunted or disengaged affect when it accompanies schizophrenia. Schizophrenia is almost certainly due to neurological (i.e., biological) disease in the brain (Ismail, Cantos-Grace, & McNeil, 1998).

From the outset, schizophrenia has been viewed as a thought disorder in which impaired perception was a more prominent feature than disturbance of affect (disorders of mood). Once erroneously associated with the existence of "multiple personalities," which is now known to be a symptom of other maladies such as *posttraumatic stress disorder*, schizophrenia appears to be more purely a disorder in the apprehension of reality (the way in which reality is perceived) than a disturbance of personality. Much current research is devoted to the cognitive structure that leads to the delusional beliefs developed by schizophrenics. One model posits that an inability to segregate relevant from irrelevant sensory stimuli combined with a similar deficit in filtering relevant and irrelevant memories produces the delusional state (Hemsley, 1993; Fig 18–3).

Figure 18–3 *Model of Cognitive Abnormalities and Symptoms of Schizophrenia.* This diagram shows some of the possible cognitive failures that allow perceptions to yield delusional beliefs in the schizophrenic mind.

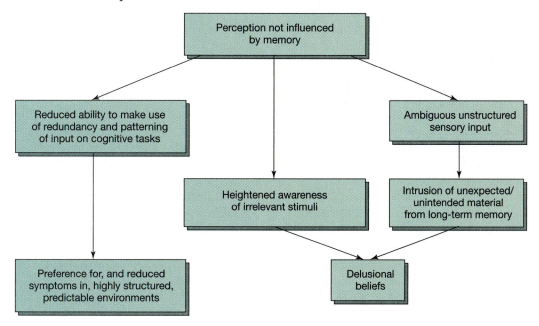

Figure 18–4 *The Work of an Artist with Schizophrenia.* What evidence, if any, do you see of a disturbed thought process in this artwork by an artist with schizophrenia?

Figure 18–4 represents artistic expression of a patient exhibiting delusional thinking due to schizophrenia.

Another model for the origin of the delusions is more purely sensory in nature. Schizophrenics sometimes experience hallucinations (hearing nonexistent voices, for example, is an earmark of the condition). Other sensory disturbances include **synesthesia**, or illusions that sensory experience arising from one modality actually arises from another. For example, a person may report hearing colors while seeing sounds. In either case the central distinction between schizophrenia and other serious mental illness is the **florid symptoms** of the disease, which reflect the presence of distinctive behaviors including disorganized thinking, paranoia, delusions of grandeur, and bizarre ideation (i.e., thoughts of being persecuted or having one's actions controlled by God). These florid symptoms are often preceded by residual or **negative symptoms**. These symptoms are reflected in the absence of normal and social behaviors such as neglect of personal hygiene, odd behavior and ideas, social isolation, withdrawal, and catatonia. Some other types of mental illness are characterized by the presence of abnormal *feelings* such as those found in the affective disorders of mood and anxiety (see "Affective Disorders" section, in this chapter). While a schizophrenic may be lucid enough, especially with proper medication, to feel badly *because* he or she has a mental illness, these feelings are a negative affect secondary to the disease process and should not be confused with the primary symptoms of schizophrenia.

A major problem in the design of effective treatment strategies as well as a barrier to understanding the causes of schizophrenia is that schizophrenics often exhibit **sponta-** neous remission and **spontaneous relapse**, meaning that they may get better (remission) or worse (relapse) without medical intervention. A major problem with understanding many mental disorders (such as affective illness, described later) is that the cyclical nature of schizophrenia makes design of an effective drug regimen difficult. As you read the sections that follow, try to think of what other problems of a technical or procedural nature might make a neuroscientific analysis of mental illness difficult.

Schizophrenia also differs from some of the other major psychiatric illnesses in that it appears to strike early in life, often during late adolescence or early adulthood but sometimes even in childhood (Bhatara, Gupta, & Fluggrud-Breckenridge, 1998). After onset, it appears to obey the "**Rule of Thirds**": One-third of the patients will spontaneously recover and never again need treatment; another third will exhibit spontaneous remission and relapse and can sometimes be managed with medication; and one-third will remain ill for life, requiring continuous medication and hospitalization. The Rule of Thirds also seems to apply to other poorly understood nonpsychiatric ailments, a fact that has led some specialists to believe that conditions that obey the Rule of Thirds are not single diseases but rather several that are lumped together because of imprecise diagnoses.

Neuroleptic Drugs

Figure 18–5 illustrates probably the greatest success story of biological psychiatry (the branch of psychiatry emphasizing pharmacologic, genetic, and molecular approaches to treatment and diagnosis of mental disorders). It shows the patient population in American mental institutions since the turn of the century, and there is a marked inflection around the year 1956 when an upward trend is reversed downwards. No agreement exists as to the reasons for the demographic change, but the sharp rise in the beginning of this century seems likely to be due to better diagnosis as a result of the work by Kraepelin and Bleuler. The decrease coincides with the widespread introduction in 1956 of the first drug for the treatment of schizophrenia, **chlorpromazine** (trade name Thorazine). Since the advent of chlorpromazine, and realization of its effectiveness, a large number of analogs (similar chemical structures) have been synthesized and used clinically. (Why do you think there are so many? See the answer in "So Many Choices.") Collectively, these drugs are called **neuroleptics** (Fig 18–6). When effective, neuroleptics can quickly and dramatically reduce the florid symptoms of schizophrenia, leaving the negative symptoms somewhat less affected. In normal people, neuroleptics have a sedating action, seeming to reduce the rewarding quality of stimuli (i.e., less pleasure will be derived from activities like social engagements, eating,

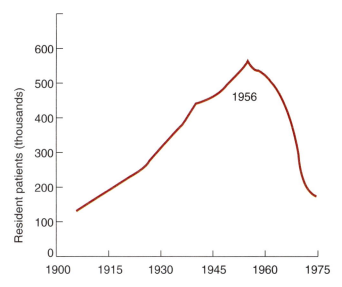

Figure 18–5 *The Greatest Success Story of Biological Psychiatry.* Patient populations in public mental health institutions from 1900 through 1975. Notice the reversal of the upward trend in 1956 when the first drugs for the treatment of schizophrenia became available.

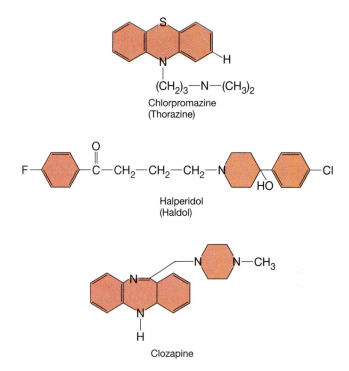

Figure 18–6 *The Chemical Structures of Three Neuroleptic Drugs.* The antipsychotic efficacy of these drugs is most likely related to the blockade of postsynaptic dopaminergic receptors in the mesocortical projection. However, other neurotransmitter systems may be involved. Adverse reactions include, but are not limited to, Parkinsonlike symptoms, dry mouth, blurred vision, constipation, and urinary retention.

and sex); in fact neuroleptics were first developed as sedatives for surgical patients.

Parallel with Dopamine Binding

A very remarkable feature of neuroleptic drugs is that they all appear to bind to brain dopamine receptors (recall that dopamine is a transmitter candidate) and act as antagonists once there. Further, another class of neuroleptics called atypical neuroleptics, including Clozapine, that bind to both dopamine and serotonin receptors has been developed. There appears to be a direct correlate between the clinical efficacy of these drugs and their affinity for dopamine receptors. This relationship strongly indicates that the underlying deficit in schizophrenia is an abnormality of the dopamine systems; there is too much dopaminergic transmission in some regions of the brain. This theory is called the **dopaminergic hypothesis.**

The dopaminergic hypothesis receives confirmation from a number of different sources. Figure 18–7 shows postmortem data in which tissue levels of dopamine and norepinephrine are compared in a normal brain and the brain of a schizophrenic subject. These data seem to provide evidence for a higher proportion of dopamine to norepinephrine levels in schizophrenics (Oke, Carver, & Adams, 1993).

Though not a complete explanation of the condition (since it doesn't explain why dopamine levels are too high), the dopaminergic hypothesis is central to drug treatment of and much research into schizophrenia. However, the development

of atypical neuroleptics, including Clozapine, may question the strength of the dopamine hypothesis as these effective drugs bind to both dopamine and serotonin receptors.

So Many Choices

Why are there so many neuroleptic drugs in use? Remember, the action of a transmitter is determined by the receptor expressed by the postsynaptic cell; the transmitter has no intrinsic action of its own. Recall also that there is more than one receptor type for most transmitters (often including excitatory as well as inhibitory receptors) and there are many different circuits in the brain that employ a given transmitter. There are at least *four* systems in the brain, and one in the periphery, that utilize dopamine. In sympathetic ganglia, the **small intensely fluorescent cells** (cells visible under fluorescent light after histological staining with fluorescent dyes) are dopaminergic; thus dopamine plays a role in autonomic function (recall that the sympathetic ganglia are involved in autonomic function). In the brain there are three dopaminergic projections: the **nigrostriatal projection** in which dopamine is involved in *extrapyramidal motor behavior* (Chapters 5 and 10), the **tuberoinfundibular projection**, in which dopamine regulates the release of pituitary peptides (Chapter 12), and the **mesolimbic system**, in which the release of dopamine creates rewarding feelings during reinforcement (Chapters 11 and 17). To these systems we can now add another projection that may gate or regulate the correct interpretation of sensory stimuli, the **mesocortical system**. This is very likely the system that is perturbed in schizophrenia and is the one targeted by effective neuroleptic drugs.

In order to be effective antagonists, the neuroleptic drugs must resemble the dopamine agonist structurally. Since by

Figure 18–7 *Comparison of Dopamine/Norepinephrine in Normal and Schizophrenic Subjects.* Notice the different dopamine/norepinephrine ratios in thalamic sections from a normal subject (left) and from a schizophrenic subject (right). Dark areas indicate more dopamine. (Oke, Carver & Adams, 1993)

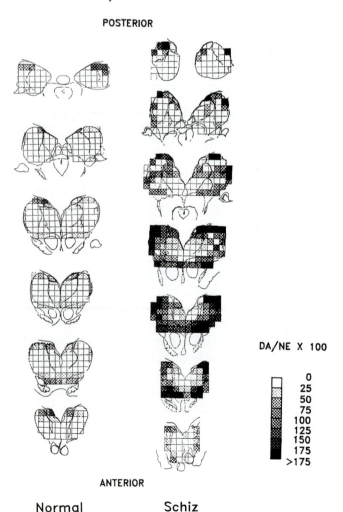

DOPAMINE/NOREPINEPHRINE

POSTERIOR

DA/NE X 100

```
       0
      25
      50
      75
     100
     125
     150
     175
    >175
```

ANTERIOR

Normal   Schiz

definition all dopamine receptors bind dopamine, neuroleptic drugs have overlapping affinity for each dopamine receptor type and every dopaminergic system. Thus, drugs that alleviate the florid symptoms of schizophrenia are also going to have other unwanted effects. The side effect of neuroleptics on the mesolimbic system is the opposite of dopamine; thus neuroleptic drugs do not create pleasurable or rewarding feelings. A major handicap in neuroleptic maintenance is patient refusal to continue medication.

The effect of neuroleptics in the nigrostriatal projection resembles the deficit seen upon dopamine depletion from the basal ganglia in Parkinson's disease. Tremors result that resemble Parkinson's symptoms, and a deficit in voluntary movement can lead to paralysis in severe cases. This disorder is called **tardive dyskinesia** and can be a severe problem when long-term neuroleptic administration is anticipated, as the effects persist even when use of the neuroleptic is discontinued. The disorder is an **iatrogenic** condition (meaning "a disease caused by the doctor;" from the Greek root *iatros* for healer and *genesis* for born) and is a prime example of the hazards of medication that we shall review at the end of this chapter.

Though all ligands for the dopamine receptors will have overlapping binding affinity, this is not to say that the affinity for each type will be the same. On the contrary, drug design (or nature's bounty) can create drugs that bind tightly, rapidly, or primarily to one receptor type and loosely, slowly, or slightly to other receptor types (look at the "concept of affinity" in the Appendix). In rare fortunate cases drugs act at only one of several receptors for a transmitter; these drugs are called **specific ligands**. More commonly drugs favor one receptor type over others; these are called **selective ligands**. The reason why so many neuroleptic drugs are available for clinical use is that pharmaceutical companies have searched diligently for a neuroleptic that will act only on the receptors involved in psychosis, lacking side effects and iatrogenic hazards. So far, no specific ligand has been discovered, but research has uncovered increasing numbers of selective ligands and we may hope for more progress toward a pure neuroleptic in the future.

Receptor Theories

So far we have discussed schizophrenia in terms of an excess of dopamine transmission. Dopaminergic transmission can be disordered at the receptor level in postsynaptic structures as well. The fact that long-term neuroleptic medication leads to permanent changes, like tardive dyskinesia, which endure even after drug withdrawal, illustrates that dopamine receptor number, and possibly receptor affinity, are regulated developmentally. **Down-regulation** is a response to excess agonist in which postsynaptic sensitivity decreases in response

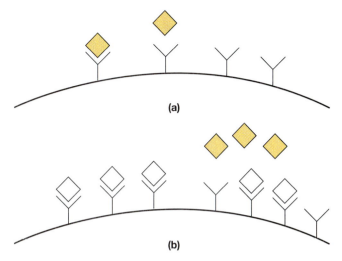

Figure 18–8 *Receptor Occupancy Elicits Receptor Synthesis.* (a) Partial occupancy by native agonist of receptor sites on a postsynaptic cell maintains a constant number of receptors. (b) During up-regulation high receptor occupancy by exogenous antagonist elicits the synthesis of more receptors.

to increased activation intensity. Similarly, **up-regulation** is an increase in postsynaptic sensitivity in response to chronic blockade with antagonist (Figure 18–8).

Difficulties in Diagnosis

A challenge to the proper diagnosis of schizophrenia is that fact that symptoms vary so widely among patients. This has led some investigators to propose that the disorder should be divided into two categories, Type I (characterized by florid symptoms) and Type II (characterized by negative symptoms). As shown in Table 18–1, Type I schizophrenia seems to be

characterized by an increase in dopamine receptors of the D_2 type and a concomitant increase in concentrations of VIP, a peptide cotransmitter (vasoactive intestinal peptide, Chapter 5). Type II, on the other hand, seems to be characterized better by cell loss in the temporal lobe and hippocampus (Crow, Taylor, & Tyrrell, 1986).

Adding to the difficulty associated with symptom heterogeneity is the fact that some symptoms (paranoia, delusions of grandeur) are shared with other mental disorders and may even occur as unusual events in "normal" experience. An intriguing example is synesthesia, the phenomenon of confounding sensory experience arising from one modality with that of another modality (e.g., "hearing colors" or "seeing sounds.") Synesthesia is sometimes encountered as a sign of schizophrenia but occasionally in other circumstances as well. For example, synesthesia has been an experience of several prominent visual artists and musicians, including some who have incorporated synesthetic phenomena into their work, such as the Russian composer Aleksandr Scriabin and British artist David Hockney. Also, synesthesia is sometimes produced by use of psychedelic drugs, an observation that led to one prominent hypothesis about the etiology of schizophrenia (Box 18–1). An excellent account of an individual who was synesthetic, but not schizophrenic, can be found in *The Mind of the Mnemonist*, by A.B. Luria (1968). This is an account of an individual who exploited his synesthesia to accomplish prodigious feats of memory, making a living as a sideshow performer with a carnival.

Genetic Factors and Structural Differences

The clinical observation that schizophrenia tends to run in families led to several well-known studies designed to test the hypothesis that the disorder was genetic in origin. Examin-

Table 18–1	PROPOSED DIVISION OF SCHIZOPHRENIA INTO TWO CATEGORIES BASED ON SYMPTOM VARIETY	
	Type I	**Type II**
Symptoms	positive	negative (esp. poverty of speech)
Response to neuroleptics	good	poor
Intellectual impairment	absent	present
Dyskinesia	absent	sometimes present
Underlying pathological changes	(a) D_2 receptors increased (b) VIP in amygdala increased	cell loss in temporal lobe including cells of parahippocampal gyrus and CCK and somatostain cells in hippocampus
Eponym	Bleuler	Pinel and Haslam

Source: Crow, T. J., Taylor, G. R., & Tyrrell, D. A. J. (1986)

Box 18–1

The Story of "Transmethylation"

The efficacy of the neuroleptic drugs, introduced in the 1950s, strongly suggested a neurochemical basis for schizophrenia that involved the monoamine transmitters. As reviewed later in this chapter, two enzymes are largely responsible for metabolizing the monoamines. One of them, **catecholamine-O-methyl transferase (COMT)**, as the name implies, adds a methyl group to oxygens on the ring structure of the catecholamines dopamine and norepinephrine. A similar methyltransferase adds methyl groups to the amine of serotonin in its metabolism. These metabolites include DMPEA for dopamine and DMT for serotonin (see figure). Normally these metabolites are cleared from the brain by the blood and either sequestered in the liver or excreted in the urine. However, some early studies suggested that higher than normal levels of DMPEA and DMT were found in the urine of schizophrenic patients.

This observation intrigued researchers because the methylated dopamine and serotonin resembled to a marked degree the psychedelic drugs mescaline and psilocybin (see figures here and in Chapter 17). Also shown in the figure is bufotenine, a constituent of toad skin, which has also been found to have psychedelic properties.

The striking similarity fueled investigation that led to a theory of the etiology of schizophrenia, the **transmethylation hypothesis**, that posited that perhaps methylated

Serotonin
(5-Hydroxytryptamine)

DMT
(N,N-Dimethyltryptamine)

Bufotenine
(5-Hydroxydimethyltryptamine)

Psilocybin

metabolites of dopamine, norepinephrine, or serotonin accumulated to an abnormal degree in the brains of schizophrenics and caused the florid symptoms in a manner suggestive of an extended or chronic "trip" on mescaline or psilocybin. Experimentation on human subjects showed that large doses of DMPEA and DMT could produce hallucinations, though the potency was less than for the non-endogenous drugs (more DMPEA and DMT was required to produce the hallucinations). Extensive tests on blood and autopsy specimens from schizophrenics failed to yield any reliable differences in DMPEA and DMT levels from those in other mental patients or from those in normal individuals. This last failure caused many scientists to reject the transmethylation hypothesis. However, the hypothesis remains an intriguing possibility and endures as an important piece of the schizophrenia puzzle. Since it is unethical to withhold effective medication from patients, autopsy specimens from schizophrenics who have *not* been treated with neuroleptics are rare. Hence it is not possible to tell whether neurochemical changes, or the lack thereof, are features of the disease process or the result of medication. This problem is not limited to the study of schizophrenia; it applies to other mental illnesses treated with drug therapy. Reflect on the ethical limitations of human research before reading the section on the hazards of medication.

ing data from genetically identical twins, adopted and reared apart, researchers found a modest but significant correlation between shared genes and a common disposition to develop schizophrenia. Environmental factors could not account for the correlation, the researchers claimed, because adoptive families of the twins were different. However, no mapping study could identify a single gene, or chromosome, that carried the defect; in addition, the correlation was too weak to predict definitively the onset of the disease. Rather, the results seemed to point to a genetic **predisposing factor**, itself unrelated to schizophrenia (but curiously seeming to covary significantly with artistic aptitude and interest), that might render individuals more susceptible to succumbing to schizophrenia.

The search for the schizophrenic "trigger" led researchers down a number of different avenues of inquiry. One path came from the observation derived from PET scans (Chapter 16) that seemed to indicate that the cerebral ventricles of schizophrenics were larger then for age-matched controls (Figure 18–9, "Level of Risk;" Cannon et al., 1993). This finding was not universally replicable for schizophrenics, however, and as for other symptoms, it appeared to characterize other patients as well, such as those who experienced difficult childbirth (Figure 18–9, "Delivery Complications" and "Type of Anesthetic"). Review the mechanism for noninvasive imaging techniques in Chapter 16 before evaluating the PET scan results. Do you think that schizophrenics would behave the same as normal controls in the PET scanner, given the symptoms associated with this disease?

A Viral Cause?

The intuition derived from previous work seemed to point toward an underlying cause, as yet unidentified, that itself was influenced by a variety of factors, including genetics, health of the mother, complications in delivery, and socioeconomic status. Most models postulated that this root cause, once identified, could explain the perturbations in dopaminergic transmission, structural changes in the brain, and so forth.

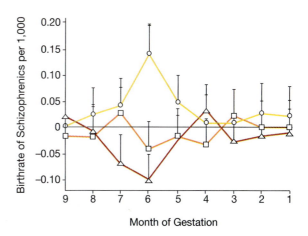

Figure 18–10   *Birthrate of Schizophrenics per 1,000 versus Months of Gestation.* The mean schizophrenia birthrate following three levels of exposure to influenza at each of the nine months of gestation. Orange indicates low influenza rate, red indicates medium influenza rate, and yellow indicates high influenza rate. (Barr et al., 1990)

While this central cause has yet to be identified, current research has produced a very promising possibility. Using careful statistical analysis in a country (Denmark) with exceptionally detailed medical records, it was discovered that the number of schizophrenic offspring born to mothers who had experienced influenza infection during the second trimester of pregnancy was disproportionately high (Barr, Mednick, & Munk-Jorgensen, 1990). Figure 18–10 illustrates a statistical summary of data showing an increase in the incidence of schizophrenic offspring peaking at around the sixth month of gestation in mothers that had experienced a lot of flu infection (yellow), a moderate amount of infection (red), and very little infection (orange).

Though these data require confirmation with additional study, the suggested **viral etiology** for schizophrenia is presently one of the most exciting areas of investigation in psychiatric research.

Affective Disorders

The other major psychosis, affective illness, complements schizophrenia in that apprehension of reality is intact but feelings about reality are disordered. You may be familiar with some of the categories of affective illness, which include manic and depressive episodes as well as dysthymia. A person with **affective illness** perceives sensory stimuli correctly, has orderly thought processes, and correctly places himself or herself in the scheme of everyday relationships. Delusions, such as they exist, are of an *egocentric variety*. A depressed individual may feel that he or she is cursed in some way, whereas a manic individual may believe the he or she is om-

Figure 18–9   *Data Supporting the Theory that Schizophrenics Have Larger Cerebral Ventricles.* Mean overall cerebrospinal fluid (CSF)–brain ratio (an indicator of ventricle size) by level of genetic risk for schizophrenia, delivery complications, and type of anesthetic at delivery. All three factors were significant. (Cannon et al., 1993)

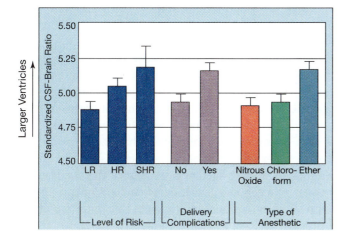

nipotent or immortal. These egocentric delusions can easily be confused with paranoia or delusions of grandeur in schizophrenia, and care must be taken by the practitioner not to confuse symptoms of one condition with symptoms of the other. To complicate matters, some schizophrenics become depressed *because* they are schizophrenic, again making proper diagnosis difficult. Also, there are a number of conditions such as **agoraphobia** (fear of public places), anorexia and bulimia (disorders of body image), and **paranoid (delusional) thought disorder** that have features of *both* schizophrenia *and* affective illness and present challenges to the clinician trying to design effective treatment strategies. Finally, there are specific *symptoms* of schizophrenia that can also characterize other conditions. For example, **catatonia** (complete withdrawal from social contact) is seen in severe depression as well as in schizophrenia. Without other indicators, confident diagnosis of either schizophrenia or depression is sometimes impossible in such a case.

However, compared to other psychiatric conditions such as **neuroses** (a disorder characterized primarily by anxiety with no disorganization of personality or distortion of reality) and **adjustment disorders** (disorders manifested in maladaptive reactions to psychological stress that cease when the stress ceases) in which there seems to be almost as many disease states as there are patients, schizophrenia and affective illness seem to be relatively discrete categories. Most practitioners believe that, with sufficient information, it is usually possible to separate the two. Though it is not supposed to happen (since accurate diagnosis ideally precedes treatment) it is unrealistic to deny that the ultimate diagnosis in ambiguous cases sometimes depends on response to medication: If the patient improves on administration of neuroleptics, then he or she must have been schizophrenic; if the patient improves on administration of antidepressants, then he or she must have been depressed.

Mania

The most dangerous aspect of affective illness, and the most representative of severe madness in the popular imagination is **mania**. Manic individuals experience accelerated thought processes, euphoria, exaggerated sexual or physical appetites, illusions of invincibility, and grandiose ambitions. During manic episodes people are likely to quit their jobs, leave their spouses, and take up some activity such as gambling or auto racing that leads them into disaster. The danger of mania, in addition to ruined lives, is primarily death by accident. People in the grip of mania seem unaware of ordinary dangers or are unconcerned by them. There is effective medication for mania, which was discovered by accident (Box 18–2); as you can imagine, the major problem with management of mania

is reluctance to take prescribed drugs, as the patient often denies the existence of a mental problem. Decisions regarding involuntary commitment to mental hospitals, always rife with civil liberties issues, often involve manic individuals held against their will by family or physicians for their own safety.

Unipolar and Bipolar Illness

Mania usually has one benefit; it doesn't last very long. Affective illness, like schizophrenia, spontaneously remits and relapses and to a striking degree appears to involve endogenous rhythms and cycles of various periodicity. Manic individuals usually experience **depression** after manic episodes, sometimes appearing to become depressed *because* of the damage done during mania. The symptoms of depression are the opposite of mania: In place of euphoria there are thoughts of suicide; in place of exaggerated sexual or physical appetites there is **anhedonia** (lack of pleasure in food, sex, or exercise); in place of accelerated thought there is **psychomotor retardation** (the patient's conversation seems like "a 45 rpm record played at 33 rpm").

In addition to diagnostic indicators of depression there are clinical signs that alert the practitioner to the presence of the disorder (much like auditory hallucinations are an "earmark" of schizophrenia). In conversation, the depressed patient states that he is *helpless* to prevent the bad things that have befallen him, his situation is *hopeless* with no possibility of improvement, and he is *worthless* because he has brought it all on himself because of his own character flaws. Complaints of sleep disturbances are very common in cases of depression, so much so that a clinician is instantly alert to the diagnosis when the sign is encountered. Depressed individuals are sometimes unaware that they are depressed and go to the doctor complaining of insomnia. The problem is usually not insomnia (see Chapter 13) but rather an abnormal distribution of sleep in which the depressed patient awakes too early in the morning, robbing him or herself of essential REM sleep. The most dangerous feature of depression, of course, is the potential for suicide. This hazard also complicates the clinician's attempts to treat the condition with drugs, as we shall see later.

Unipolar illness is characterized by periods of depression that alternate with normal emotional states. These periods can be very long, so that the individual seems always depressed, or they may cycle with periods of normalcy as in bipolar illness (described next). Statistically, unipolar illness is twice as common among women than men. This may be due to greater willingness among women to seek help, greater willingness among doctors to recognize the condition in women, or a genuine gender-based etiology for this form of depression. In contrast to schizophrenia, affective illness

Box 18–2

John Cade
and the Discovery of Lithium

In 1948, an Australian psychologist named John Cade was interested in sleep and dreaming (Cade, 1975). Recall from Chapter 13 that there are two theoretical models for sleep, one positing that sleep is an active process needed to restore some substance needed for wakefulness and the other suggesting that sleep is a passive process needed to eliminate some substance that accumulated during wakefulness. Cade decided to test the second theory. Asking himself "What accumulated in the waking state?" he settled on *urine* as a possibility. After all, we only drink when we are awake; perhaps some chemical waste is the signal used by the body to induce sleep.

Cade's first experiment was to inject urine into rabbits to see if he could get them to go to sleep. Though they didn't sleep after urine injections, Cade was encouraged by the fact that they did appear to slow down somewhat.

Cade then sought to identify the chemical constituent of urine that had the effect. *Urea* is the major nitrogenous waste product in urine, and Cade went to the local chemical storehouse looking for crystalline urea to try in his experiment. Not a chemist, he first selected *sodium urate*, a salt of urea, but found that he couldn't get the crystals to go into solution. He then went back to the storehouse looking for a different urea salt. He found a bottle of lithium urate and when he returned to the lab he found that he could get the salt into solution readily. Furthermore, the injection of lithium urate into rabbits profoundly sedated them, at first appearing to confirm his hypothesis.

John Cade realized shortly that the sedation produced by the injections was not the same as sleep. Moreover, it became apparent that the active ingredient was not the urea, but the counter ion, **lithium**. Cade went on to test lithium in other contexts, eventually showing that it alleviated the mania displayed by bipolar patients.

Lithium in the forms of tablets, capsules, or syrup remains today the most widely used treatment for mania. A metal in the same family as the monovalent cations

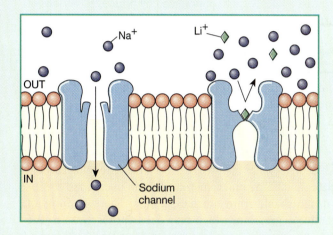

sodium and potassium, lithium is thought to act by entering the sodium channel and sticking there, attenuating sodium influx during all action potentials and EPSPs (see figure). Its global effects slow all neural activity, in such manner as to tranquilize manic individuals.

The story of the discovery of lithium is told here to illustrate two important points. One is the contingent and serendipitous nature of some scientific discovery. A portion (by no means all) of scientific advances arise from unlikely sources and odd investigations. A second purpose is to illustrate the relatively sparse theoretical security behind many drugs used in psychiatric practice. The unwitting consumer may, in some cases, be led to believe that technology has created a "magic bullet" perfectly designed to remedy his or her particular problem and only that problem. The reality in some cases may be haphazard in the sense that some drugs and therapies are used with almost no knowledge of their mechanism of action. This is a theme we shall return to when we consider electroconvulsive shock therapy (Box 18–3), the design of antidepressant drugs, and the hazards of medication.

tends to develop later in life, in middle age or among the elderly. The reason for this age distribution is unclear but may be related to the fact that people sleep less with advanced age (Chapter 13) and hence may be more likely to complain of insomnia and become available for diagnosis.

Bipolar illness (so called because of the oscillations between mania and depression) is far less common than unipolar illness and is characterized by a brief episode of mania, followed by depression, punctuated by prolonged periods of normal affect. On occasion, a single cycle is experienced; other bipolar patients cycle through the states with varying degrees of regularity and periodicity. Fortunately, the swing between the careless self-disregard of mania followed by the suicidal tendencies of depression is the least common type of affective illness.

A Diagnostic Continuum

A recent development is psychiatry involves the recognition that depression (as opposed to mania) has psychological correlates and behavioral symptoms that in many ways are indistinguishable from normal sadness. The symptoms of reactive depression, which may occur in response to the death of a spouse or the loss of a job, have long been recognized to be the same as those of unipolar illness. Once thought of as "psychological depression" (as opposed to unipolar illness, or "biological" depression), reactive depression is now seen as having the same biological components as unipolar illness. More recently, everyday sadness, of the kind experienced by all people independent of major life events, has also been incorporated into the continuum, which now extends all the way from normalcy to psychosis. This has led to the widespread use of antidepressant drugs and the confirming discovery that people in all categories will often feel better after taking them. Whether the positive advance made by understanding that all depression is biological will be followed by the equally important understanding that all depression is also psychological is an issue we will consider at the end of this chapter when we discuss the hazards of medication.

A Disorder of Circadian Rhythmicity?

Some people experience depression only at particular seasons. In northern climates, this season is often the winter when the days grow short and the nights grow long. Seasonal affective disorder (SAD), which is most commonly characterized by winter depression that includes morning hypersomnia, weight gain, increased appetite, and low energy, is the name that has been assigned to this condition. The recognition of the dependence of certain forms of affective illness on circadian cycles has reignited research into the periodic, or cyclical, nature of many forms of depression.

One promising avenue has involved treating SAD with strong artificial light to mimic the sun's rays early in the morning. Another has focused on melatonin, an indolamine related to serotonin secreted in circadian fashion by the pineal gland. Though dietary supplements of melatonin as a sleep aid and to improve mood are probably ineffective, for the reasons we have explored elsewhere in this book (Chapters 5, 6, and 13), the melatonin produced by the central nervous system, may very well play a role in affective illness. Certainly the oft-observed phenomenon that depressed people awake too early in the morning, or otherwise have diurnal fluctuations in symptoms and severity, fits in well with the understanding of SAD and its treatment in pointing to an internal pacemaker as the source of the perturbation in the various forms of affective illness.

The Design and Pursuit of Antidepressant Drugs

Let us return to the suggestion made earlier on how to converse with a dualist on the subject of mental illness. Those of you with a taste for practical jokes can do a very creditable impersonation of a psychiatrist at a party of doctors and health professionals: Mention any disorder that comes to mind and ask the seemingly unanswerable question, "Is it biological or psychological?" After the hemming and hawing and plethora of opinions that follow, ask thoughtfully, "Do you think _____ is involved?" (Insert the name of any monoamine transmitter candidate: serotonin, dopamine, norepinephrine, epinephrine, or histamine). Since behavior, both pathological and normal, is the product of the simultaneous action of every transmitter in the brain, you will be certain to have picked one that is, in some way, "involved" in the condition under discussion. Furthermore, you will impress your "colleagues" with your up-to-date knowledge about the disorder, since you can be certain that the substance is under current investigation somewhere.

In short, there is, a monoamine hypothesis to account for almost every disorder. Just as the dopamine hypothesis of depression is supported by the fact that schizophrenic symptoms can be created by dopamine agonists, the monoamine hypothesis is supported by the finding that a monoamine antagonist can cause depression. Based on the anatomical fact that the monoamine transmitters arise in the brainstem and project *diffusely* throughout the forebrain, it is easy to understand how theorists have envisioned compounds as having global effects that change neural function everywhere all at once and generally reorganize behavior. An abnormality in monoaminergic transmission probably does underlie most mental illness. But which monoamine transmitter? And what aspect of that transmitter's physiology and chemistry: synthesis, presynaptic action, postsynaptic effect, breakdown, re-uptake, receptor

Box 18–3

Ugo Cerletti and Electroconvulsive Shock

In 1938, an Italian physician named Ugo Cerletti was investigating the idea that criminals were genetically inferior to law-abiding citizens. This notion was in harmony with the social climate at the time, for Italy was dominated by fascist politics in the years before World War II. Cerletti's approach was to look for indicators of inferior heredity in the physiognomy of prisoners. Similar to *phrenology*, this approach postulated that mental characteristics would be apparent in the physical appearance of the face and skull.

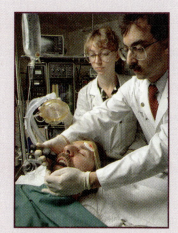

In the course of this investigation, Cerletti came across an individual who had remained silent for fifteen years. Today, we would recognize this condition as catatonia (characterized by stupor, negativism, or periods of physical rigidity), a possible symptom of either schizophrenia or mood disorders like depression. The fundamentals of "bioelectricity" (the idea that electrical currents played a part in muscular and neurophysiology) were under investigation elsewhere in the 1930s, so Cerletti was inspired to see if electrical current could have an effect on this individual. He attached leads to the wall socket and passed alternating current (50 Hz, 220V) across the skull of the inmate, and was gratified that the patient then uttered his first words in fifteen years. He said (in Italian), "Don't ever do that again." After lapsing back into silence, Cerletti applied the current several times more and discovered a longer-term change in the inmate's behavior. The subject began not only to speak but to engage in conversation, and this change in behav-

ior endured well after the stimulus sessions were stopped.

Thus was born the "science" of electroconvulsive therapy (ECT). ECT was, before the introduction of antidepressant drugs, the treatment of choice for severe depression. It remains today the major recourse in cases of depression that don't respond to drugs (Olfsun et al., 1998). Cursed at one time with an unsavory reputation (perhaps because of the circumstances of its origin or because patients have uncontrollable seizures upon ECT), the procedure has been somewhat refined in modern usage. This procedure is now used primarily to treat major depression in hospitalized patients. Further, ECT is now performed after complete sedation (to avoid seizures) and is often reported to have salutary effects on the patient's well-being. Likewise, it has lost some it its stigma (Thomas Eagleton, the Democratic senator from Missouri, was forced to step down as George McGovern's vice-presidential running mate in 1972 after it was revealed that he had received ECT early in adulthood) and joins drug therapy as an option for those suffering from affective illness. Still, the theoretical foundations of ECT remain no more secure than they were in Cerletti's time; it works, but we don't know why. One inconclusive theory suggests ECT affects the brain's biochemistry (Frankel, 1984). This theory proposes that the seizures produced by the electric shock release above-normal levels of gamma aminobutyric acid (GABA), which decreases activity in the overactive areas of the brain associated with depression.

---

density, enzyme synthesis? And what part of the brain is affected the most, since each transmitter has multiple roles in multiple circuits?

The search for answers to these questions occupies much of biological psychiatrists' time and an overwhelming amount of drug development research. The search for an effective an-

tidepressant therapy started in a serendipitous manner, much as it did for the treatment of mania. This history is the subject of Box 18–3. The story of drug therapies for depression begins with the monoamine hypothesis and the identification of enzymes responsible for regulating monoamine levels in the extracellular space. One of these, monoamine oxidase (MAO),

produces inactive metabolites of dopamine and norepinephrine and another, catecholamine-o-methyl transferase (COMT),
produces methylated compounds that may or may not be inactive (discussed in Box 18–1). An early pharmaceutical approach to depression presumed that, unlike schizophrenia,
the condition might be due to *too little* catecholamine in the
brain. Thus, **MAO inhibitors** were used to combat the illness.
The first used was *pargyline*, but current MAO inhibitors are
clorgyline and selegiline (Deprenyl). As with amphetamines,
which also increase extracellular catecholamine levels (Chapter 17), MAO inhibitors can reverse depressed behavior. However, reflection on the transmitter chemistry of the autonomic
nervous system (Chapter 6) will reveal a major problem with
their use. MAO is also responsible for terminating catecholamine action in the autonomic nervous system, including
the sympathetic innervation of the heart. Thus MAO inhibitors
will artificially accelerate heart rate, in addition to their desired
action on the CNS. Hypertension (high blood pressure) is a
disorder of midlife and old age (the same demographic segment at risk for depression); an accelerated heart rate can exacerbate hypertension. Pause to review the symptoms of
depression and see if you can discover another major problem with this type of antidepressant medication (the answer
is provided at the end of the next paragraph).

To circumvent the undesirable side effects of MAO inhibitors and to achieve a drug more selective for the central
receptor population involved in depression, a new set of drugs,
the **tricyclic antidepressants**, was developed and achieved use
in the 1950s and 1960s. Figure 18–11 shows the structures of
some of these drugs. Imipramine, desipramine, and amitriptyline are among the most prescribed of the tricyclics. Nothing
in the structures gives a direct hint about their mode of action (they resemble most closely the structure of *neuroleptic*
drugs; see Figure 18–6). Neurochemical investigation showed
that the tricyclics had a host of various effects, with the common theme of elevating extracellular monoamine concentrations. Though they have less cardiovascular side effects than
the MAO inhibitors, and hence are less dangerous for hypertensive patients to use, they still had sufficient autonomic action to be lethal if overdoses were consumed. Thus the first
step taken by a doctor prescribing an MAO inhibitor or tricyclic antidepressant to a depressed patient might be to place
in the patient's hands the means for his or her own dispatch!

As part of the ongoing effort to find antidepressants without undesirable side effects and without overdose potential,
pharmaceutical researchers developed drugs initially called
atypical antidepressants because they lacked the three-ring
structure of the tricyclic drugs. The most recent products of
this effort have come to be known as **selective serotonin re-
uptake inhibitors (SSRIs)** because they are thought to have

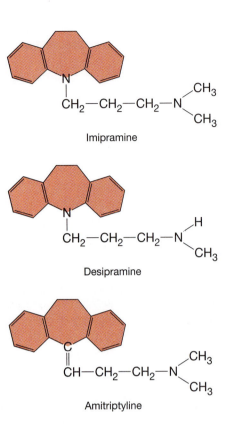

Figure 18–11   *Chemical Structures of Three Tricyclic
Antidepressant Drugs.* The antidepressant efficacies of
these drugs share a common theme of elevating
extracellular monoamine concentrations, though a host of
other neurochemical effects are observed. Adverse
reactions to these drugs include, among other things, fine
hand tremors, blurred vision, urinary retention, dry
mouth, and constipation.

particular effect on raising the extracellular concentration of
serotonin. The postulated neurochemical mechanism is almost certainly not directly related to the clinical effect, since
the effect on serotonin re-uptake is immediate but the therapeutic benefit (alleviation of depression) takes one to two
weeks to develop. This lapse between neurochemical kinetics
and clinical effect is a confound common to many antidepressants, including the tricyclics. The fact that this gap is
understandably not advertised to the public gives a false impression that the effect of the drugs is well understood by
medical science. The gap also increases the risks of the use of
antidepressants—picture a depressed patient having to take
a potentially lethal drug for one to two weeks before feeling
better! The structures of some newer antidepressants are
shown in Figure 18–12, which includes fluoxetine (Prozac),
sertraline (Zoloft) and paroxetine (Paxil).

Of these antidepressants, Prozac has clearly taken its
place in modern pop culture. For a flavor of the current con-

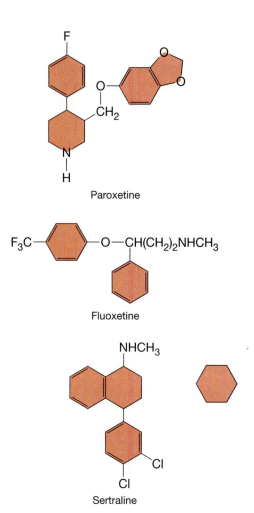

Paroxetine

Fluoxetine

Sertraline

Figure 18–12 *The Chemical Structures of Three Selective Serotonin Re-uptake Inhibitors (SSRIs).* The antidepressant efficacy of these drugs is claimed to be related to their ability to block the re-uptake of serotonin, thereby increasing the serotonin concentrations in the synaptic cleft. While this increase in concentration is almost immediate, the therapeutic benefits take one to two weeks to develop. The success rate of SSRIs is around 85 percent and the SSRIs are generally better tolerated than traditional antidepressants. Some adverse reactions include anxiety, agitation, sleep disturbance, slight tremors, headaches, and sexual dysfunction (e.g., delayed ejaculation and impotence).

troversy on this theme, consult the opposing viewpoints presented in *Listening to Prozac* and *Talking Back to Prozac* cited in the "References" section (and see Figure 18–13).

Anxiety Disorders

Anxiety disorders are characterized by a different type of anxiety than that felt by most of us. The disordered anxiety is a dread, fear, or generalized avoidance behavior that is not read-

"I'm always like this, and my family was wondering if you could prescribe a mild depressant."

Figure 18–13 *Prescription of Psychoactive Drugs Is Becoming More Common.* Do you think too many people turn to medication to alleviate emotional problems?

ily assignable to real danger and sometimes may not be associated with any stimulus at all.

Among the most heavily prescribed medications (again mostly to female patients) are **anxiolytics** (drugs for the treatment of anxiety or "tranquilizers," see Chapter 17). The structure of some common anxiolytics is shown in Figure 18–14. Most commonly used anxiolytics are in a chemical family called the **benzodiazepines**, and the common chemical names of these compounds thus often contains the suffix "-azepam" (as in *timazepam*, or *lorazepam*, and so forth.) As for the antidepressants, there are a wide array of benzodiazepine drugs available, the pharmaceutical industry being alert to the prospects of unwanted side effects. A major danger of tranquilizer use is addiction, so benzodiazepines have varying affinities, clearance rates (rate at which the drug is removed from the body through metabolic processes), and dose regimens so as to avert chemical dependence. Physicians are cautioned to be alert for signs of addiction when the drugs are used for an extended period of time. There is growing concern that the tranquilizers are overprescribed, often to addicted individuals who will seek medication from more than one doctor in order to maintain a constant supply.

The common mode of action of benzodiazepines is an allosteric ligand for the GABA receptor (Chapter 17), an action that increases the affinity, and hence the inhibitory potency, of this transmitter. Alcohol also appears to have an allosteric affinity for this receptor and it is probably for this reason that the tranquilizers and alcohol have a synergistic action, making them very dangerous when taken in combination.

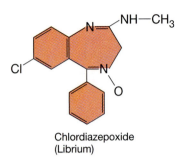

Chlordiazepoxide
(Librium)

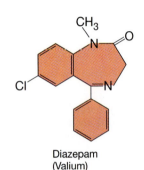

Diazepam
(Valium)

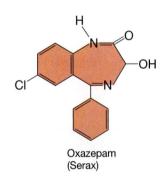

Oxazepam
(Serax)

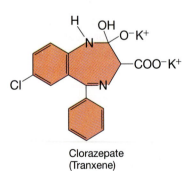

Clorazepate
(Tranxene)

Figure 18–14 *The Chemical Structures of Four Anxiolytics.* The antianxiety efficacy of these drugs is related to their ability to act as an allosteric ligand for the GABA receptor. Adverse reactions include drowsiness, dizziness, and disorientation. These effects rarely require discontinuation of the drug and are easily managed by dose reduction.

The Hazards of Medication

A person in serious need of psychotropic medication is not likely to be deterred from taking the drug by fear of its dangers. Many drugs are highly effective in alleviating the symptoms of schizophrenia, affective illness, or anxiety, and they are usually safe if used as prescribed under a doctor's supervision.

It is to the other person, not in serious need, that the remainder of this chapter is addressed. Maintenance on med-

ication presents numerous hazards, some known and listed below and others as yet undescribed, that should cause hesitation before one seeks the convenient and excessively available pharmacological solution to everyday problems.

To recap some of the issues discussed in this chapter, the following issues constitute potential drawbacks to the use of prescription psychotropic drugs:

1. Drugs and therapies in current use, such as lithium, ECT, and antidepressants, often lack theoretical foundation for their use. Their action is poorly understood and hence may entail undiscovered dangers.

2. Prescription drugs, like the tranquilizers, may be addictive and produce unwanted withdrawal effects.

3. Medication such as MAO inhibitors and tricyclics may exacerbate preexisting conditions or even pose an added threat of suicide.

4. Drugs taken in combination, such as tranquilizers and alcohol, may produce unintended overdose.

5. Long-term maintenance produces trophic consequences, such as tardive dyskinesia, that are in most cases poorly understood.

Finally, chemical dependency on prescription medication can have unintended and potentially disastrous social costs in terms of hospitalization and lost productivity as well as personal ramifications in terms of shattered lives, all of which should be considered before medication is started. Be as careful with what drugs you put in your mouth as you are with the food you eat and the water you drink.

Conclusion

The French essayist Montaigne (1533–1592) once wrote, "A man must be a little bit mad if he does not want to be even more stupid!" The careful reader of this chapter will understand the difference between "a little bit of madness" (experienced by many of us) and "a lot of madness" (requiring medication).

As for the "stupidity," any reader who has lasted this far in the book has pondered the nature of free will, has strove to master the physical basis for nervous system function, has tried to comprehend the chemical nature of the "lust for life" and the "tablet of memory," has endeavored to "know thyself" (as admonished by Socrates in Chapter 1), and therefore, in the opinion of the author, has reached the end of this course of study in no danger of dull or complacent self-neglect.

SUMMARY

The study and treatment of mental illness is a clinical specialty known as psychiatry, which has interest to the layperson for the light it sheds on normal behavior. Division of psychiatric populations into discrete categories began with the description of psychosis by Kraepelin and Bleuler and proceeded to differential diagnosis guided by the DSM IV. "Antipsychiatry" and the "medical model" constitute two extreme views of mental illness but do not relate directly to monistic or dualistic views of the mind.

Major illnesses that respond to medication provide the best hope for understanding biological cause. Schizophrenia is characterized by disorganized thinking, paranoia, delusions of grandeur, and bizarre ideation. It often responds to treatment with neuroleptic drugs. These appear to work by inhibiting the binding of dopamine; the neurochemical cause of the disease may be an excess of transmitter, an excess of receptor, or an abnormal accumulation of methylated metabolites. The ultimate cause may be related to genetic or structural predisposition or viral infection.

Mania and depression are characterized by delusions of affect and are treated variously by lithium, electroconvulsive shock therapy, light therapy, and antidepressant drugs. The proximate (immediate) cause may be a monoamine transmitter imbalance and the ultimate (original) cause may be related to a perturbation of endogenous rhythms. Several of the current treatments of affective illness are poorly understood and lack theoretical foundation.

Anxiety disorders (involving anxiety reactions in response to stress) are commonly treated with benzodiazepine tranquilizers. These act by binding to an allosteric site on the GABA receptor, as does alcohol.

There are several hazards associated with psychotropic medication that the educated consumer should consider before accepting prescription drugs, including anxiolytics, SSRIs (e.g., Prozac, Zoloft, and Paxil), and tricyclics (e.g., imipramine and desipramine).

REVIEW QUESTIONS

1. How do neuroleptics act on the brain?
2. What is tardive dyskinesia?
3. List the theories for the etiology of schizophrenia.
4. How does lithium act? What is it used for?
5. List the therapies for depression and cite their advantages and disadvantages.
6. What are the major hazards of antidepressant medication?
7. What drug treatment might be explored for anxiety disorder?
8. List some features of psychosis that differentiate between schizophrenia and affective illness.

THOUGHT QUESTIONS

1. Disease processes often arise from adaptive mechanisms gone awry. What adaptive properties does depression have? What about schizophrenia and panic disorder?
2. Consumers claim that alcohol and chocolate can be used to combat depression, but experts say that they may *cause* depression instead. Comment on this disparity in perception.

KEY CONCEPTS

adjustment disorders (p. 446)
affective illness (p. 445)
agoraphobia (p. 446)
Alzheimer's disease (p. 438)
anhedonia (p. 446)
antipsychiatry (p. 438)
anxiolytics (p. 451)
atypical antidepressants (p. 450)
bipolar illness (p. 448)
benzodiazepines (p. 451)
catatonia (p. 446)
catecholamine-o-methyl
    transferase (COMT) (p. 444)
chlorpromazine (p. 440)
dementia praecox (p. 438)
depression (p. 446)
Diagnostic and Statistical
    Manual IV (DSM IV) (p. 458)

dopaminergic hypothesis
    (p. 441)
down-regulation (p. 442)
electroconvulsive shock therapy
    (ECT) (p. 449)
florid symptoms (p. 440)
iatrogenic (p. 442)
lithium (p. 447)
mania (p. 446)
MAO inhibitors (p. 450)
medical model (p. 438)
melatonin (p. 448)
mesocortical system (p. 442)
mesolimbic system (p. 442)
monoamine hypothesis (p. 448)
multi-infarct dementia (p. 438)
negative symptoms (p. 440)
neuroleptics (p. 440)

neuroses (p. 446)
nigrostriatal projection (p. 441)
paranoid (delusional) thought
    disorder (p. 446)
physiognomy (p. 449)
pineal gland (p. 448)
predisposing factor (p. 445)
psychiatry (p. 438)
psychomotor retardation
    (p. 446)
reactive depression (p. 448)
"Rule of Thirds" (p. 440)
schizophrenia (p. 438)
seasonal affective disorder
    (SAD) (p. 448)
selective ligands (p. 442)
selective serotonin re-uptake
    inhibitors (SSRIs) (p. 450)

senility (p. 457)
small intensely fluorescent cells
    (p. 441)
specific ligands (p. 442)
spontaneous relapse (p. 440)
spontaneous remission (p. 440)
synesthesia (p. 440)
tardive dyskinesia (p. 442)
transmethylation hypothesis
    (p. 444)
tricyclic antidepressants
    (p. 450)
tuberoinfundibular projection
    (p. 442)
up-regulation (p. 443)
unipolar illness (p. 446)
viral etiology (p. 445)

APPENDIX

Further Topics in Biology and Chemistry

Methods of Chemical Identification

How did we learn to distinguish one polymer from another and come to know their chemical structures? The chemical constituents of biological materials can be separated from one another based on their molecular characteristics. Since this technique was first used to isolate *chlorophyll*, the chemical that makes plants green, and was visualized as a band of green color, the procedures are generically called chromatography (*chroma* = color). A simple form of chromatography, known as *gel filtration chromatography*, separates molecules based on their size or *molecular weight*. Agar beads (like gelatin) trap small molecules while larger ones pass through. Other forms of chromatography, such as *high-pressure liquid chromatography* (HPLC) separate different polymers, as well as small compounds such as neurotransmitters and their metabolites, based on their relative hydrophilicity and hydrophobicity.

How are the compounds detected once they are separated from one another? Polymers such as proteins and *peptides* (small proteins) are often detected by bioassay (a method for quantifying the effects on a biological system by its exposure to a substance), such as endocrine action for hormones and catalytic capacity for enzymes. Others are

Figure A1 *RIA.* Radioimmunoassay (RIA) is used to find a substance using a marked antibody. The antibody can be bound to labeled antigen, leaving unlabeled antigen free (bottom, left). Or it can be bound to unlabeled antigen, leaving labeled antigen free (bottom, right). Thus, the amount of free labeled antigen is a reflection of the presence of unlabeled antigen and can be used to measure unlabeled antigen in a sample where it's concentration is unknown.

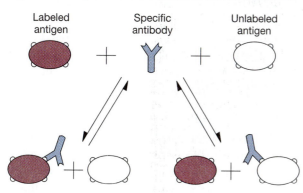

detected by a very sensitive procedure developed by Rosalyn Yalow and others, a breakthrough for which they received the Nobel Prize (Yalow, 1992). The method is called *radioimmunoassay* (RIA) because it employs *antibodies* made by the immune system to detect *antigen* (foreign substance) levels in a sample. Here's how it works. Rabbits are made immune to a substance of interest (say a particular hormone) by injecting the substance into the bloodstream. Then, the antibodies produced by the rabbit to fight off the foreign hormone are collected by lancing a vein in the ear and collecting a small amount of blood (most rabbits used in academic research are subjected to procedures no more painful than these). Then a measured quantity of the hormone is made radioactive. When the antibody (from the rabbit) and the antigen (the radioactive hormone) are incubated together they *precipitate* or clump together to form a radioactive solid, which is then measured for level of activity. When the level of radioactivity of the solid precipitate is known, additional samples containing unknown quantities of the hormone can be added. The nonradioactive hormone in the unknown will compete for antibody with the radioactive hormone and consequently the precipitate will be less radioactive. The precise amount of radioactivity that is lost is correlated with the concentration of hormone in the unknown and thus the amount of hormone in the unknown can be determined precisely. Other sensitive methods for detecting polymers are *immunocytochemistry* and *autoradiography*. These receive brief treatment in Chapter 11.

The Concept of Affinity

Central to neuroscience, and indeed to all biology, is the concept of affinity. Once it is grasped, diverse issues such as relative *potency* of drugs, the *speed* of the body's response to various stimuli, and the *actions* of transmitters, hormones, enzymes, and receptors can all be explained with relative ease.

Let us call all things that chemically bind to proteins *ligands* and give them the abbreviation "L." Ligands include all transmitters, drugs, hormones, and the substrates for enzymatic reactions. First let's consider a ligand that interacts with a membrane *receptor* (R) to form the bound complex "LR." We write the reaction as follows:

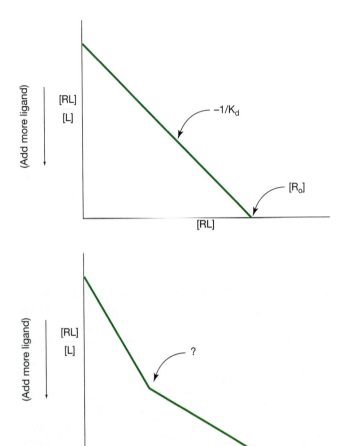

Figure A2   *The Concept of Affinity.* Affinity is the measure of how tightly and quickly two chemicals, for example a receptor and a ligand, bind together.

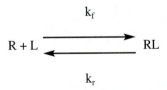

where k_f is the rate constant for the forward or binding reaction and k_r the rate constant for the reverse or unbinding reaction. The rate constant is a value that describes how quickly an individual ligand molecule binds to an individual receptor, but that is not the same as the velocity of the overall reaction (i.e., *how many* bindings or unbindings happen in a given period of time). Velocity depends on the *concentration* of the reactants, being high when reactant concentration is high and low when reactant concentration is low, for a given rate constant. Thus:

$$v_f = k_f [R] [L]$$

where v_f is the velocity and $[R]$ and $[L]$ are the *concentrations* of R and L, respectively.

Most biological reactions go in both directions to some degree and, if given sufficient time, a *balance* will be achieved between the two tendencies. This balance is called equilibrium. At equilibrium $v_f = v_r$ and

$$k_f [R] [L] = k_r [RL]$$

Though equilibrium is related to reaction rate (called *kinetics*), its value is independent of time since equilibrium is defined as that state achieved after all forces have had adequate time to reach a balance. To define this point of balance, we describe a new quantity, the *association constant*, or k_{ass}, which is *not* a rate constant and can be described without units of time.

$$k_{ass} = [RL]/[R] [L]$$

By convention, the same quantity is usually described as the reciprocal relation, the *dissociation constant*, k_{diss}, or k_d (which is $1/k_{ass}$) and

$$k_d = [R] [L]/[RL]$$

The k_d is very important and can be comprehended easily without reference to equations. *It is that concentration of ligand required to fill half the receptors at equilibrium.* Obviously, if a ligand binds tightly or quickly to the receptors, little of it will be required to fill half of the receptors, whereas if it binds loosely or slowly more will be required. It is, in other words, inversely related to affinity as follows: When affinity is high, k_d is low; and when affinity is low, k_d is high.

In chemical terms, k_d is a property of the *potency* of a drug or *efficacy* of a transmitter or hormone. In the whole body, however, potency and efficacy are related not just to the binding reaction but also to what happens after binding has occurred. Thus, some active receptors have greater effect on cells than others do. To describe potency at the cellular and organismic level, a *different* constant is required. I will call this k_D (capital letter to distinguish it from k_d, but this is not always the notation that is used, unfortunately). The k_D is defined as that concentration of drug needed to bring about half the maximum effect.

Determination of k_d with binding studies yields great molecular insight into ligand/receptor interactions but determination of k_D (with dose-response curves) often leaves unanswered questions regarding mechanism. Let's consider a surprising result available with binding studies to illustrate this point. (The math is included only to assure you of the security of the conclusion. It would take a hard-hearted instructor to ask you to commit it to memory or to reconstruct it on your own.)

If we define $[R_o]$ as the *total number of receptors*, bound and unbound, then

$$[R] = [R_o] - [RL]$$

Substituting into the equation (given earlier) that defines k_d, we obtain

$$k_d = \frac{([R_o] - [RL]) \, [L]}{[RL]}$$

Multiply both sides by $[RL]/[L]$,

$$k_d \, [RL]/[L] = [R_o] - [RL]$$

Finally, multiply both sides by $1/K_d$ and we obtain

$$[RL]/[L] = [R_o]/K_d - 1/K_d \, [RL]$$

This is called the Scatchard equation and it permits us to gather a great deal of information with just one set of experimental measurements. Let's say we could measure [RL]. In practice, this is done by making L radioactive, incubating the tissue containing R with the "hot" L (in known concentrations), washing away the unbound L, and measuring the amount of radioactivity remaining. Then, a plot of [RL]/[L] vs. [RL], a Scatchard plot, reveals several things of interest (see [a] in the figure). The *slope* can be used to calculate k_d and the horizontal intercept is the equivalent of R_o. In other words, with one set of measurements we have determined *both* the total number of receptors (also known as *Bmax*, for "maximum binding") *and* their affinity for the ligand. In practice, the Scatchard plot sometimes has a curved line in it (see [b] in the figure). Considerable confusion reigned in the scientific community over the meaning of "curvilinear" Scatchard plots when they were first seen. The actual meaning(s) turned out to be very profound for the development of modern biology. See if you can guess what a curvilinear Scatchard plot indicated before the answer is provided for you at the end of this section.

Two scientists labored in keen competition to be the first to evaluate the affinity and number of insulin receptors, since they thought the measurement could contribute to a cure for diabetes. Both simultaneously found curvilinear Scatchard plots and pondered the possible meaning of two apparent values for k_d. One decided that it must mean that there were two different *types* of insulin receptor, each with different affinity.

The other, more cautious, went back to the equations based on kinetics (shown at the beginning of this section) and decided to obtain a second, independent value for k_d using kinetic measurements. In this manner, it was found that a *single population of receptors* had two identical binding sites on each molecule. Occupancy of one site lowered affinity for the second, a molecular mechanism for *homeostasis* (see Box 5–4). This phenomenon is called negative cooperativity and is a feature of many receptor proteins including the insulin receptor and the acetylcholine receptor (Chapter 5). Though the first scientist was wrong about insulin receptors, he was close to the truth since many ligands have since been shown to have multiple receptor types for various functions (Chapter 5).

Einstein and Thermodynamics

In the later part of the nineteenth century and the early part of the twentieth, scientists experimented with "closed systems," or devices that allowed chemical reactions to occur in isolation from influences other than those intrinsic to the molecules involved. Of course, it is impossible to separate such a system completely from the rest of the universe, but careful control over pressure, volume, heat introduced, and heat radiated away permitted the scientists to take these unavoidable interactions with the environment into account.

It was first observed that energy and matter were interconvertible. In other words, energy could be obvious as *work* (e.g., heat release when a solid undergoes combustion) or less obvious as *stored* energy (as for an uncombusted, but potentially combustible, solid). Then it was established that the sum of stored and work energy was *constant* for closed systems. In other words, energy is neither created nor destroyed: When added to one process it must be subtracted from somewhere else. On a hot summer day, have you ever noticed the ice in your glass of water? The liquid becomes colder (loses heat) but at the same time, the ice begins to melt (gains heat). This frustrated some early chemists who were hoping (as some still do) for an inexhaustible source of cheap energy ("the perpetual motion machine"). Frustrations aside, the observation led to a very powerful statement about nature. With the additional assumption that the universe is a closed system, the findings found expression in the "First Law of Thermodynamics":

The energy of the universe is constant.

Another property of closed systems became apparent in the process of the experiments: The degree of order (or its opposite, chaos) within a system can be quantified precisely. In the presence of heat, all particles begin to move and this motion can be described as probabilistic or random. Any order that exists at the outset is unlikely to endure, just as a deck

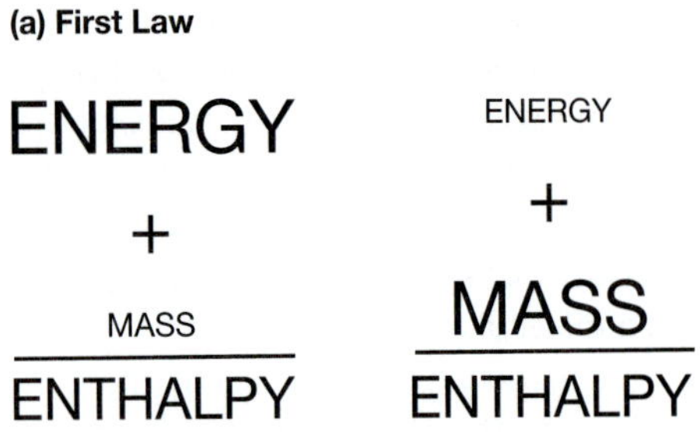

(a) First Law

ENERGY

+

$$\frac{MASS}{\text{ENTHALPY}}$$

ENERGY

+

$$\frac{\text{MASS}}{\text{ENTHALPY}}$$

(b) Second Law

EVERYTHING FALLS APART

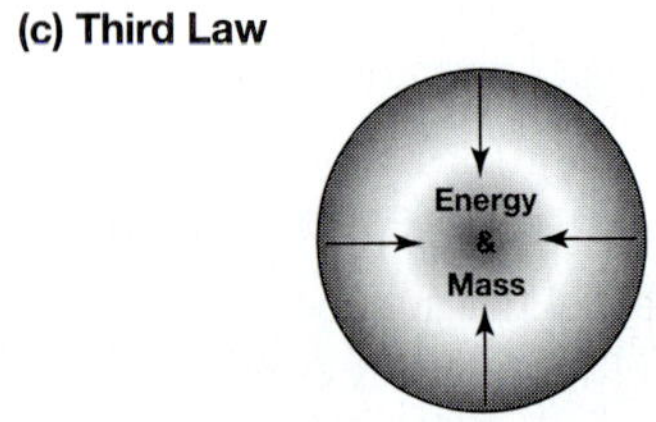

(c) Third Law

Figure A3   *The Laws of Thermodynamics.*
(a) Energy and mass can interconvert, but the combined total is always the same. (b) Entropy always increases. (c) Atomic structure and activity collapse at absolute zero.

of cards placed in order and separated by suit are unlikely to be as orderly after being shuffled. The measured degree of disorder, or chaos, of a system is called *entropy*. Again treating the universe as a closed system, the "Second Law of Thermodynamics" states:

The entropy of the universe is increasing.

Like the first, the second law is a very powerful statement about reality. Also like the first law, the second law can be confirmed in everyday life for systems very much smaller than the entire universe. Many of you may be saying, for example, "I know that the entropy of my checkbook is increasing every day!"

But there is hope for order in the universe, since (as in the earlier example) entropy requires heat to express itself. In the absolute absence of temperature, there is no motion and hence no entropy (so although we would be frozen to death, at least at absolute zero—the temperature at which molecular motion is hypothesized to cease—our checkbooks would be balanced!). This observation finds expression in the "Third Law of Thermodynamics":

Entropy is zero at the absolute zero of temperature.

For our present subject, the first law ("enthalpy" or the heat exchanged) is manifested by the electrostatic force on particles separated by the semipermeable membrane, and the second law is manifested in the diffusion force that counteracts the force of enthalpy. The third law finds expression in the idea that all organisms exist at some temperature far above absolute zero. Using this absolute or "Kelvin" scale (after its

creator, Lord Kelvin), we see that a squid living in the ocean is at an absolute temperature around 287° K and our bodies are around 310° K; this is a very small difference in absolute terms. Thus the temperature term in the Nernst equation does not need adjustment from species to species and the equilibrium potentials calculated in Chapter 3 can be assumed to be about the same everywhere.

So that you may appreciate the soundness of our understanding of the electrical signaling in the brain, it is wise to consider the reasons for the great confidence we have for the foundations of this signaling (i.e., the Nernst and Goldman equations see Chapter 3) which are based on the laws of thermodynamics. Like all conclusions in science, the laws of thermodynamics have an *empirical* foundation, which is to say they were arrived at by inductive reasoning (reasoning drawn from facts) and experimental observations. As such they do not have the power of deduced truth (conclusion reached by inferring), since another observation could always vitiate or invalidate the effect of the previous ones. We say, therefore, that scientific statements are "falsifiable" and that these statements become more secure (moving from "hypotheses" to "theories" and ultimately "laws") as they resist successive attempts at falsification. The laws of thermodynamics have resisted many attempts at falsification and hence are very secure indeed.

Albert Einstein, whose theory of relativity did so much to challenge Newtonian mechanics and our everyday notions of space and time, also had a great impact on our intellectual culture. Cultural relativism, or the notion that the observer's acquired assumptions and predilections actually determine the nature of reality, played a significant role in the development of some approaches to the understanding of human behavior (see the discussion of Sokal, 1996 in Box 1–2). However, our consideration of electrical signaling leaves very little room for relativistic explanation, since it is developed systematically from the laws of thermodynamics, which most scientists accept as unchallengeable. Einstein himself said that he could not imagine a universe that did not obey the laws and even his famous dictum $E = MC^2$ ("energy equals mass times a constant squared") itself is an expression of them. Thus, to the degree that scientific "certainty" can be bestowed on any theory, our theory regarding electrical signaling is "certain."

The Electrometer

The electrometer consists of two parts, the amplifier and oscilloscope. Although the internal workings of an amplifier are complex, function of the device is very simple. As the name implies the amplifier takes a very small signal (such as the action potential of a single cell in the brain) and amplifies it to make it more apparent. The symbol for the amplifier is shown in the figure together with a diagram of the other component of an electrometer, the oscilloscope.

The oscilloscope, which gives a record of voltage as it changes with time, consists of two parts. First is the "cathode ray tube," which, as the name suggests, is a vacuum tube with a strong negatively charged cathode. The cathode emits a ray of negatively charged electrons that leap through the vacuum ("like charges repel") toward the screen, which is positively charged. The ray is much like an arc of electricity or a lightning bolt, but its trajectory is very straight and focused tightly as a small dot of electrons colliding with the screen. The surface of the screen is made of a phosphorescent compound so that each electron gives off a burst of light and the dot glows brightly.

The second part is the "time base," which consists of two plates, one to the right of the electron beam and one to the left. The plates are hooked up to a voltage source that makes first one plate positive, then the other in an alternating or oscillating manner (hence "oscilloscope"). As a consequence the electron beam is drawn first to one plate, then the other, and the dot sweeps across the screen. The experimenter chooses how fast the oscilloscope will oscillate; the sweep may be slow, or so fast that the dot becomes a line of light going from left to right across the screen. Hence the horizontal axis of the oscilloscope face represents time, the scale being the choice of the operator.

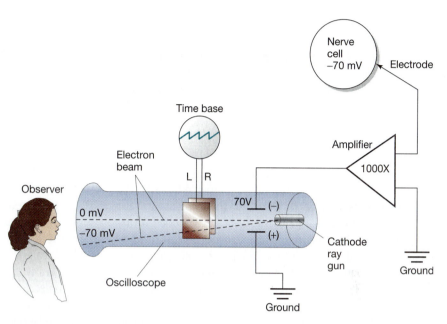

Figure A4   *The Electrometer.* The electrometer is actually an oscilloscope and an amplifier.

The amplified signal from the cell (neuron or muscle cell) is connected to another plate, this one above the beam, and the ground or reference is connected to a fourth plate below the beam. The oscilloscope receives the amplified negative potential from the inside of the cell on the upper plate and the beam of electrons is deflected downward (again, "like charges repel"). Again, the magnitude of the deflection depends on the value of the amplifier, which is at the choice of the experimenter. In this manner the electrometer (oscilloscope and amplifier) can represent transmembrane voltage changes so that the membrane potential, the action potential, and synaptic potentials can be observed.

Genetic Engineering

The new ability of molecular biology to isolate and identify messenger RNA biochemically has vastly increased our understanding of the function of single molecules of protein, such as membranous receptors and channels. It has also led to a revolution in biotechnology known as genetic engineering. If even a tiny bit of interesting RNA can be isolated it can be converted into DNA by an enzyme (reverse transcriptase) that reverses the transcription process. Then the DNA of interest can be transferred to a host cell (typically into a bacterium using a virus called a "phage vector," but more recently mammalian cells as well). The host cells can be encouraged to multiply, eventually producing enormous quantities of the particular DNA (and sometimes the RNA and protein). It is easier to determine the sequence of the DNA and RNA that codes for a particular protein than it is to sequence the protein itself, since only four bases make up genetic material and protein is made up of twenty amino acids. Large quantities of particular strands of DNA made available by genetic engineering can be sequenced and the protein sequence deduced from the genetic code. The sequences coding for the proteins of the potassium channel (see Figure 4–8) and the sodium channel (see Figure 4–6) were obtained in this way.

The great power of gene transfer and isolation techniques has led to a massive research project that approaches the science of the brain and body in a way very much different from the experiments we have considered up to now. Since the analytic power of molecular genetics exceeds that of other forms of experimental inquiry, why not begin by sequencing the entire genome and sorting out the function of individual gene products later? Being the dominant species on the planet (at least in terms of research funding) people chose *our* genome as the target of analysis, and the Human Genome Project was born. At last count the venture to sequence the entire human genome involved many countries, an estimated cost of $3 billion, and the work of hundreds of scientists and technicians over a period projected to be as long as twenty years. Dramatic advances have already emerged from the work on similar projects. The complete sequence has been obtained of the genomes of 141 viruses, 57 subcellular organelles such as mitochondria, 2 bacteria species and a eukaryote (the yeast *saccharomyces cerevisiae*). The work on the 3 billion base pairs of the human genome is still in its infancy, however. An accessible goal is to *map* (or locate) each gene in the genome, a project that is required before the sequence can be supplied. This is expected to be complete by the year 2005. In addition, individual human genes of interest have been sequenced and it appears possible that these collectively may account for as much as half the entire human genome (Schuler et al., 1996).

The project is endorsed and led by some of the most distinguished names in molecular biology including James Watson, the codiscoverer of DNA, and has the great merit of building on much that we have previously learned about the body using more primitive techniques. For example, homology (similar structure due to shared ancestry) in channel structure would allow us to deduce the function of a newly sequenced bit of DNA that had sequences in common with known channel genes (similarly for enzymes, receptors, and hormones, which together make up a large percentage of the expressed genome). With the use of computers it might well be possible to pluck from the entire sequence a list of *all chan-*

nels, all hormones, and *all receptors* that the human body contains.

The Human Genome Project has not met with universal approval, however. One major criticism involves the fact that the majority of the genetic material in the genome does not code for protein at all, but rather has some other function or perhaps no function at all. Why sequence all this "noise" in the human genome? Further, since many of the basic processes in our body are shared with simpler organisms, why not start with these (presumably shorter and cheaper) genomes? These criticisms have been partly answered by a refocus of the Human Genome Project on just those 100,000 or so genes that are thought to be expressed. Also, the complete sequence of the genomes of model organisms such as the nematode, fruit fly, and mouse are now under investigation as well and the genome map of some simple organisms is now known completely. Another early controversy involved the question of *whose* genome to sequence. What gender or race of human would be selected (at great expense) to be the type specimen of humanity? This concern has been partly deflected by the recent finding that the human genome is over 98 percent shared by all races of humanity, leaving the question of which specimen to use somewhat less urgent (as long as both the Y and the X chromosomes receive equal treatment!).

A more enduring problem with the project involves the method itself. Sequencing DNA is stultifying work, adding little to the intellectual stature of the many scientists expected to take part in the routine aspects of the project. Furthermore, even with increased automation, the project would largely proceed without explicit hypotheses, separating it clearly from the tradition of the scientific method (Chapter 1). Proponents counter that many great advances have also had this quality. The project has been likened to the epoch-making moon landings of the 1960s and 1970s, "big science" projects without which our civilization could not advance. Advocates of "small science" fear that the diversion of research money to the Human Genome Project might damage individual research grants. Why must we do something merely because we have the capacity to do it? As one distinguished geneticist said, "There is no question that sequencing the entire human genome would be a remarkable accomplishment. But on the other hand, translating Shakespeare into cuneiform would also be a remarkable accomplishment."

It seems almost everyone has an opinion regarding the importance of this venture, or its lack of significance. What's yours?

REFERENCES

CHAPTER 1

Eccles, J. (Ed.). (1982). *Mind and brain: the many faceted problems*. Washington, DC: Paragon House.

Gould, S. J. (1981). *The mismeasure of man*. New York: Norton.

LaMettrie, J. O. (1748). *L'homme machine*. Luzac: Leyden. (published anonymously).

Shelley, M., (1982). *Frankenstein*. Chicago: University of Chicago Press.

Sokal, A. (1996). *Transgressing the boundaries: Toward a transformative hermeneutics of quantum gravity*. Social Text 14 (#1 and 2).

Sherrington, C. (1947). *The integrative action of the nervous system*. New York: Cambridge University Press.

Sperry, R. W. (1980). Mind-brain interaction: Mentalism, yes; dualism, no. *Neuroscience*, 5, 195–206.

Sperry, R. W. (1982). Some effects of disconnecting the cerebral hemispheres. *Science*, 217, 1223–1226.

CHAPTER 2

Alberts, B., Bray, D., Lewis, J., Raff, M., Roberts, K., & Watson, J. (1994). *Molecular biology of the cell* (3rd ed.). New York: Garland.

Cech, T. R. (1989). Self-splicing and enzymatic activity of an intervening sequence RNA from tetrahymena. In T. Frängsmyr (Ed.), *Les Prix Nobel* 1989 (pp. 162–188). Stockholm: Almqvist & Wiksell. Reprinted in *Bioscience Reports*, 10, 240–261 (1990).

Hall, Z. (1992). *An introduction to molecular neurobiology*. Sanderland, MA: Sinauer Associates.

Lehninger, A. L. (1993). *Biochemistry*. New York: Worth.

Sperry, R. (1963). Chemoaffinity in the orderly growth of nerve fiber patterns and connections. *Proceedings of National Academy of Science (USA)*, 50, 703–710.

CHAPTER 3

Cech, T. R. (1989). Self-splicing and enzymatic activity of an intervening sequence RNA from tetrahymena. In T. Frängsmyr (Ed.), *Les Prix Nobel* 1989 (pp. 162–188). Stockholm: Almqvist & Wiksell. Reprinted in *Bioscience Reports*, 10, 240–261 (1990).

Hille, B. (1992). *Ionic channels of excitable membranes* (2nd ed.). Sunderland, MA: Sinauer Associates.

Hodgkin, A. L. (1976). Chance and design in electrophysiology: An informal account of certain experiments on nerves carried out between 1934 and 1952. *Journal of Physiology (London)*, 263, 1–21.

Nicholls, J. G., Martin, A. R., & Wallace, B. (1991). *From neuron to brain: A cellular approach to the function of the nervous system* (3rd ed.). Sunderland, MA: Sinauer Associates.

CHAPTER 4

Heuser, J. E., Resse, T. S., Dennis, M. J., Jan, Y., Jan, L., & Evans, L. (1979). Synaptic vesicle exocytosis captured by quick freezing and correlated with quantal transmitter release. *Journal of Cell Biology, 81*, 25–300.

Hodgkin, A. L. (1976). Chance and design in electrophysiology: An informal account of certain experiments on nerves carried out between 1934 and 1952. *Journal of Physiology (London)*, 263, 1–21.

Katz, B. (1966). *Nerve, muscle & synapse*. New York: McGraw-Hill.

Nicholls, J. G., Martin, A. R., & Wallace, B. (1991). *From neuron to brain: A cellular approach to the function of the nervous system* (3rd ed.). Sunderland, MA: Sinauer Associates.

CHAPTER 5

Branton, D., Arch, S., Smock, T., & Mayeri, R. (1978). Evidences for mediation of a neuronal interaction by a behaviorally active, peptide. *Proceedings of the National Academy Science* (USA), 75, 5732–5736.

Becq, Z. M. (1975). *Chemical transmission of nerve impulses: A historical sketch*. Oxford, UK: Pergaman Press.

Cooper, J., Bloom, F. E., & Roth. (1991). *The biochemical basis of neuropharmacology* (6th ed.). New York: Oxford University Press.

Dudel, J., & Kuffler, S. W. (1961). Presynaptic inhibition at the crayfish neuromuscular junction. *Journal Physiology*, 155, 543–562.

Hall, Z. (1992). *An introduction to molecular neurobiology*. Sunderland, MA: Sinauer Associates.

Heuser, J. E., Resse, T. S., Dennis, M. J., Jan, Y., Jan, L., & Evans, L. (1979). Synaptic vesicle exocytosis captured by quick freezing and correlated with quantal transmitter release. *Journal of Cell Biology, 81*, 25–300.

Jan, Y-N., Jan, L., & Kuffler, S. (1979). A peptide as a possible transmitter in the sympathetic ganglion of the frog. *Proceedings of the National Academy Science* (USA), 76, 1501–1506.

Llinás, R., & Sugimori, M. (1980). Electrophysiological properties of in vitro Purkinje cell dendrites in mammalian cerebellar slices. *Journal of Physiology*, 305, 197–213.

Olivera, B. M., Gray, W. R., Zeikas, R., McIntosh, J. M., Varga, J., Rivier, J., de Santos, R., & Cinz, L.T. (1985). Peptide neurotoxins from fish-haunting cone snails. *Science*, 230, 1338–1343.

Nicholls, J., Martin, A. R., & Wallace, B. (1991). *From neuron to brain* (3rd ed.). Sunderland, MA: Sinauer Associates.

Parkinson, J. (1817). *An essay on the shaking palsy*. London (Publisher unknown).

Siegel, G., Agranoff, B., Albers, R. W., & Molinoff, P. (1989). *Basic neurochemistry* (4th ed.). New York: Raven Press.

CHAPTER 6

Alberts, B., Bray, D., Lewis, J., Raff, M., Roberts, K., & Watson, J. (1994). *Molecular biology of the cell* (3rd ed.). New York: Garland.

Hall, Z. (1992). *Introduction to Molecular Neurobiology*. Sunderland, MA: Sinauer Associates.

CHAPTER 7

Carpenter, M. B. (1991). *Core text of neuroanatomy* (4th ed.). New York: Williams & Wilkins.

Horner, C. (1991). Editorial. *Neuroscience Newsletter* March/April, 1991.

Society for Neuroscience. *Handbook for the use of animals in research*. Washington, DC.

Vallbö, A. B. (1971). Muscle spindle response at the onset of isometric voluntary contractions in man: Time differences between fusimotor and skeletomotor effects. *Journal of Physiology*, 218, 405–431.

CHAPTER 8

Cooper, J., Bloom, F. & Roth, R. (1996). *The biochemical basis of neuropharmocolgy*. New York: Oxford University Press.

Gould, S. J. (1981) *The mismeasure of man*. New York: W. W. Norton.

Kandel, E. R., Schwartz, J. H., & Jessell ,T. M. (1991). *Principles of neural science* (3rd ed.). New York: Elsevier.

CHAPTER 9

Chiszar, D., Hobika, G., & Smith, H. M. (1993). Prairie rattlesnakes (*Crotalus viridis*) respond to rodent blood with chemosensory searching. *Brain, Behavior, and Evolution, 41*, 229–233.

DeValois, R. L., DeValois, K. K. (1980). Spatial Vision. *Annal Review of Psychology, 31*, 309–341.

Dowling, J. E.(1979). Information processing by local curcuits: The vertebrate retina as a model system. In F.O. Schmitt and F. G. Worden (Eds.) *The Neurosciences, Fourth Study Program*. Cambridge, MA: MIT Press.

Dowling, J. E. & Werblin, R. S. (1971). Synaptic organization of the vertebrate retina. *Vision Research, 31*, 1–15.

Gross, C. G. (1973). Visual functions of inferotemporal cortex. In R. Jung (Ed.), *Handbook of sensory physiology: Vol 7: Central processing of visual information*. Springer-Verlag.

Hubel, D. H., & Wiesel, T. N. (1959). Receptive fields of single neurones in the cat's striate cortex. *Journal of Physiology* (London) *148*, 574–591.

Hubel, D. H., & Wiesel, T. N. (1962). Receptive fields, binocular interaction and functional architecture in the cat's visual cortex. *Journal of Physiology* (London) *160*, 106–154.

Hubel, D. H., & Wiesel, T. N. (1979). Brain mechanisms of vision. *Scientific American, 241*, 150–162.

Kandel, E. R., Schwartz, J. H., & Jessell, T. M. (1991). *Principles of neural science* (3rd ed.). Norwalk, CT: Appleton & Lange.

Kuffler, S. (1953). Discharge patterns and functional organization of mammalian retina. *Journal of Neurophysiology, 16*, 37–68.

Sacks, O. (1985). *The man who mistook his wife for a hat and other clinical tales*. New York: Harper Collins.

Spear, P. (1993). Neural basis of visual deficits during aging. *Vision Research, 33*, 2589–2609.

Von Bekesy, G. et al. (1980) *Experiments in hearing*. E. G. Wever (editor and translator). New York: McGraw-Hill.

CHAPTER 10

Ayala, G. F., Dichter, M., Gumnit, R. J., Matsumoto, H., & Spencer, W. A. (1973). Genesis of epileptic interictal spikes: New knowledge of cortical feedback systems suggests a neurophysiological explanation of brief paroxysms. *Brain Research*, 52, 1–17.

Burke, J. R., Enghild, J. J., Martin, M. E., Jou, Y. S., Myers, R. M., Roses, A. D., Vance, J. M., & Strittmatter, W. J. (1996). Huntington and DRPLA proteins selectively interact with the enzyme GAPDH. *Nature Medicine, 2*, (3) 347–350.

Desai, C., Garriga, G., McIntire, S. L., & Horvitz, H. R. (1988). A genetic pathway for the development of the *Caenorhabditis elegans* HSN motor neurons. *Nature, 336,* (6200) 638–646.

Evarts, E. U., & Tanji, J. (1976). Reflex and intended responses in the motor cortex pyramidal tract neurons of the monkey. *Journal Neurophysiology,* 39, (5) 1069–1080.

Friesen, W. O. (1989). Neuronal control of leech swimming movements. In J. W. Jacklet (Ed.), *Neuronal and cellular oscillators,* (pp. 269–316). New York: Dekker.

Georgopoulos, A. P., Kalaska, J. F., Caminiti, R., & Massey, J. T. (1982). On the relations between the direction of two-dimensional arm movements and cell discharge in primate motor cortex. *Journal of Neuroscience, 2,* (11) 1527–1537.

Hernandez, T. D. & Naritoku, D.K. (1997). Seizures, epilepsy and functional recovery after traumatic brain injury: a reappraisal. *Neurology, 48,* (4) 803–806.

Kalchman, M. A., Koide, H. B., McCutcheon, K., Graham, R. K., Nichol, K., Nishiyama, K., Kazemi-Esfarjani, P., Lynn, F. C., Wellington, C., Metzler, M., Goldberg, Y. P., Kanazawa, I., Gietz, R. D., & Hayden, M. R. (1997). HIP1, a human homologue of S. cerevisiae Sla2p, interacts with membrane-associated huntington in the brain. *Nature Genetics, 16,* (1), 44–53.

Lisberger, S. G., Morris, E. J., & Tychsen, L. (1987). Visual motor processing and sensory-motor integration for smooth pursuit eye movements. *Annual Review of Neuroscience, 10,* 97–129.

Llinas, R., & Sotelo, C. (Eds.). (1992). *The cerebellum revisited.* New York: Springer-Verlag.

Lorenz, K. (1970). *Studies on animal and human behavior: Vols. I & II.* Cambridge, MA: Harvard University Press.

Mountcastle, V. (1978). An organizing principle for cerebral function: The unit module and the distributed system. In Edelman, G. & Mountcastle, V. *The Mindful Brain* (pp. 7–50). Cambridge, MA: MIT Press.

Nicoll, R. A., Malenka, R., & Rauer, J. (1990). Functional comparison of neurotransmitter receptor subtypes of the mammalian nervous system. *Physiology Research,* 70, 513–565.

Nieuwenhuys, T., Voogd, J., & van Huijzen, C. (1988). *The human central nervous system: A synopsis and atlas* (3rd ed.). Berlin, Germany: Springer.

Penfield, W. (1958). Functional localization of the temporal and deep sylvian areas. *Research Publication of the Association for Research on Nervous and Mental Diseases,* 36, 210–226.

Roland, P. E., Larsen, B., Lassen, N. A., & Skinhof, E. (1980). Supplementary motor area and other cortical areas in organization of voluntary movements in man. *Journal of Neurophysiology, 43,* 118–136.

Shinoda, Y., Yokota, J. I., & Futami, T. (1981). Divergent projection of individual corticospinal axons to motor neurons of multiple muscles in the monkey. *Neuroscience Letters,* 23, 7–12.

Siegfried, J., & Lippitz, B. (1994). Chronic electrical stimulation of the VL-VPL complex and of the pallidum in the treatment of movement disorders: Personal experience since 1982. *Stereotactic and Functional Neurosurgery,* 62(1–4), 71–75.

Sulston, J. E., & Horvitz, H. R. (1977). Post-embryonic cell lineages of the nematode, *Caenorhabditis elegans. Developmental Biology, 56,* 110–56.

Wine, J. J., & Krasne, T. B. (1982). The cellular organization of crayfish escape behavior. In D. C. Sandman & H. Atwood (Eds.), *The biology of crustacea: Vol. 4* (pp. 241–292.). New York: Academic Press.

CHAPTER 11

Akil, H., Mayer, D. J., & Liebeskind, J. C. (1976). Antagonism of stimulation-produced analgesia by naloxone, a narcotic antagonist *Science, 191,* 961–962.

M.S. Bear, B. W. Connors, & M. A. Paradiso (1996). Neuroscience: Exploring the brain. Baltimore, MD: Williams & Wilkie.

Belcher, G., Smock, T., & Fields, H. L. (1982). Effect of intrathecal ACTH on opiate analgesia in the rat. *Brain Research, 247,* 373–377.

Dyck, P. J. et al. (1975). *Peripheral neuropathy.* Philadelphia: W.B. Saunders Co.

Fibiger, H., LePiane, F., Zakubovic, A., & Phillips, A. (1987). The role of dopamine in intracranial self-stimulation of the ventral tegmental area. *Journal of Neuroscience* 7, 3888–3896.

Fields, H. L. (1981) An endorphin-mediated analgesia system: Experimental and clinical observations. In H. Martin and S. Reichlin (Eds.), *Neurosecretion and brain peptides.* New York: Raven Press.

Fields, H. L. (1987). *Pain.* New York: McGraw-Hill.

Fields, H. L., Emson, P., Leigh, B., Gilbert, R., & Iverson, L. L. (1980) Multiple opiate receptor sites on primary afferent fibers. *Nature,* 284, 351–353.

Fields, H. L., Malick, A., & Burstein, R. (1995). Dorsal horn projection targets of ON and OFF cells in the rostromedial medulla. *Journal of Neurophysiology, 74,* 1742–1759.

Hertzman, P. A., Blevins, W. C., Mayer, J., Greenfield, B., Ting, M., & Gleida, G. J. (1990). Association of the eosinophilia-myalgia syndrome with the ingestion of tryptophan. *New England Journal of Medicine, 322,* 869–874.

Hosobuchi, Y., Adams, J. E., & Linschitz, R. (1977). Pain relief by electrical stimulation of the central gray matter in humans and its reversal by naloxone. *Science, 197,* 183–186.

Hughes, J., Smith, L. W., & Kosterlitz, H. (1975). Identification of two related pentapeptides with brain opiate activity. *Nature, 258,* 577–579.

Jessell, T., & Iverson, L. L. (1977). Opiate analgesics inhibit Substance P prelease from rat trigeminal nucleus. *Nature, 268,* 549–551.

Konishi, S., & Otsuka, M. (1985). Blockade of slow excitatory postsynaptic potentials by Substance Pantagonists in guinea pig sympathetic ganglia. *Journal of Physiology, 361,* 115–130.

Levine, J., Gordon, N., & Fields, H. L. (1979). Naloxone dose-dependently produces analgesia and hyperalgesia in postoperative pain. *Nature, 278,* 740–741.

Melzack, R., & Wall, P. D. (1965). Pain mechanisms: A neurohistory. *Science, 150,* 971–979.

Mudge, A., Leeman, S., & Fischbach, G. (1979). Ehkephalin inhibits the release of Substance P from sensory neurons in culture and decreases action potential duration. *Proceedings of the National Academy of Sciences (USA), 76,* 526–576.

Nagy, J. I., Iverson, L., Goedert, N., Chapman, D., & Hunt, S. P. (1983). Dose-dependent effects of capsaicin on primary sensory neurons in the neonatal rat. *Journal of Neuroscience, 3,* 399–406.

Nicoll, R. A., Alger, B. E., & Jahr, C. E. (1980). Enkephalin blocks inhibitory pathways in the vertebrate CNS. *Nature, 287,* 22–25.

Olds, J., & Milner, B. (1954). Positive reinforcement produced by electrical stimulation of the septral area and other regions of the rat brain. *Journal of Comparative and Physiological Psychology, 47,* 419–427.

Peterson, C., Maier, S. F., & Seligman, M. E. P. (1993). *Learned helplessness.* New York: Oxford University Press.

Phillips, A. G., Blaha, C., & Fibiger, H. (1989). Neurochemical correlates of brain stimulation reward measured by *exvivo* and *invivo* analyses. *Neuroscience and Biobehavioral Reviews, 13,* 99–104.

Smock, T., & Fields, H. L. (1981). ACTH blocks opiate-induced analgesia in the rat. *Brain Research, 213,* 202–206.

Stellar, J. R., Kelley, A., & Corbett, D. (1983). Effects of peripheral and central hypothalamic self-stimulation: Evidence for both reward and motor deficits. *Pharmacology, Biochemistry and Behavior 18,* 433–442.

Strumwasser, F. (1974). Neuronal principles organizing periodic behaviors. In F. O. Schmidt & F. G. Worden (Eds.), *The neurosciences: Third study program* (pp. 459–478). Cambridge, MA: MIT Press.

Wiertelak, E. P., Maier, S. F., & Watkins, L. R. (1992). Learning to activate CCK anti-analgesia: Light cues abolish morphine analgesia. *Science, 256,* 330–333.

CHAPTER 12

Abel, G. G., Barlow, D. H., Blanchard, E.B., & Arnold, D. (1977). The components of rapists' sexual arousal. *Archives of General Psychiatry, 34,* 895–903.

Albeck, D., Paynter, K., Arnold, S., Colaprete, S., Knittle, S., Bradley, B., Okpaku, A., Green, J. C., Grampsas, S., & Smock, T. (1991). Peptidergic transmission in the brain: VI. Behavioral consequences of central activation. *Peptides, 12,* 413–418.

Albeck, D., Smock, T., McMechen, P., Purves, D., & Floyd, L. (1990). Peptidergic transmission in the brain: I. Vasopressin-like signal in the hippocampus. *Brain Research, 511,* 7–14.

Arch, S., Linstedt, A., Whitney, G., Teal, P., & Smock, T. (1986). Neuropeptide routing in the bag cells: Kinetic differences in the appearance of newly labeled peptides in transport and secretion. *Journal of Neuroscience, 6,* 1545–1552.

Arch, S., & Smock, T. (1977). Egg-laying behavior in *Aplysia californica. Behavioral Biology, 19,* 45–54.

Argiolas, A., Collu, M., Gessa, G., Melis, M., & Serra, G. (1988). The oxytocin antagonist d(ch$_3$)^3 tyr (me)-orn^8-vasotocin inhibits male copulatory performance in rats. *European Journal of Pharmacology, 149,* 389–392.

Bailey, J. M., & Pillard, R. C. (1991). A genetic study of male sexual orientation. *Archives of General Psychiatry, 48,* 1089–1096.

Bancroft, J. (1984). Hormones and human sexual behavior. *Journal of Sex and Marital Therapy, 10,* 3–21.

Barkley, M. S., & Goldman, B. D. (1977). A quantitative study of serum testosterone, sex accessory organ weight growth and the development of intermale aggression in the mouse. *Hormones and Behavior, 9,* 21–48.

Becker, J. B., Breedlove, S. M., & Crews, C. D. (Eds.). (1992). *Behavioral endcrinology.* Cambridge, MA: MIT Press.

Booth, A., Shelley, G., Mazur, A., Tharp, G., & Kittok, R. (1989). Testosterone and winning and losing in human competition. *Hormones and Behavior, 23,* 556–571.

Branton, W. D., Arch, S., Smock, T., & Mayeri, E. (1978). Evidence for mediation of a neuronal interaction by a behaviorally active peptide. *Proceedings of the National Academy of Sciences (USA), 75,* 5732–5736.

Breedlove, S. M. (1984). Steroid influences on the development and function of a neuromuscular system. *Progress in Brain Research, 61,* 147–170.

Buhrich, N., Bailey, J. M., & Martin, N. G. (1991). Sexual orientation, sexual identity, and sex-dimorphic behaviors in male twins. *Behavioral Genetics, 21*, 75–96.

Bult, A., van der Zee, E. A., Compaan, J. C., & Lyndi, C. B. (1992). Differences in the number of argnine vasopressin immunoreactive neurons exist in the suprachiasmatic nuclei of house mice selected for differences in nest building behavior. *Brain Research, 578*, 335–338.

Carlsen, E. A., Giwercman, A., Kerding, N., & Skakkebaek, N. E. (1992). Evidence for decreasing quality of semen during the past 50 years. *British Medical Journal, 305*, 609–613.

Carter, C. S., DeVries, A. C., & Getz, L. L. (1995). Physiological substrates of mammalian monogamy: The prairie vole model. *Neuroscience and Biobehavior Reviews, 19*, 303–314.

Cooper, A. J. (1986). Progestins in the treatment of male sex offenders: A review. *Canadian Journal of Psychiatry, 31*, 73–79.

DeVries, G. J., Buijs, R. M., Van Leeuwen, F. W., Caffe, A. R., & Swaab, D.F. (1985). The vasopressinergic innervation of the brain in normal and castrated rats. *Journal of Comparative Neurology, 233*, 236–254.

Dixson, A. F. (1980). Androgens and aggressive behavior in primates: A review. *Aggressive Behavior 6*, 37–67.

Edwards, D. A. (1969). Early androgen stimulation and aggressive behaviour in male and female mice. *Physiology and Behavior, 4*, 333–338.

Garritano, J., Martinez, J., Grossman, K., Intemann, P., Merritt, K., Pfoff, R., & Smock, T. (1996). The output of the hippocampus is inhibited during sexual behavior in the male rat. *Experimental Brain Research, 111*, 35–40.

Guillette, J. B. Gross, T. S., Masson, G. R., Matter, J. M., Percival, H. F., & Woodward, A. R. (1994). Developmental abnormalities of the gonad and abnormal sex hormone concentrations in juvenile alligators from contaminated and control lakes in Florida. *Environmental Health Perspectives, 102*, 680–688.

Gordon, G. G., Southren, A. L., Tochimoto, S., Olivo, J., Altman, K., Rand, J., & Lemberger, L. (1970). Effect of medroxyprogesterone acetate (Provera) on the metabolism and biological activity of testosterone. *Journal of Clinical Endocrinology and Metabolism, 30*, 449–456.

Gould, S. J. (1981). *The mismeasure of man*. New York: W. W. Norton.

Haug, M., Brain, P. F., & Kamis, A. B. (1986). A brief review comparing the effects of sex steroids on two forms of aggression in laboratory mice. *Neuroscience Biobehavior Review, 10*, 463–468.

Heim, N., & Hursch, C. J. (1979). Castration for sex offenders: Treatment or punishment? A review and critique of recent European literature. *Archives of Sexual Behavior, 8*, 281–304.

Imperato-McGinley, J., Guerrero, L., Gautier, T., & Peterson, R. E. (1974). Steroid 5-alpha reductase deficiency in man: An inherited form of male pseudohermaphroditism. *Science, 1*, 1213–1215.

Johnson, F., & Whalen, R. E. (1988). Testicular hormones reduce individual differences in the aggressive behavior of male mice: A theory of hormone action. *Neuroscience and Behavorial Review, 12*, 93–99.

Kelley, D. B. (1986). The genesis of male and female brains. *Annual Review of Neuroscience, 9*, 499–502.

Kinsey, W. et al. (1948) *Sexual behavior in the human male,* Philadelphia: W.B. Saunders Co.

Langevin, R., Paitich, D., Hucker, S., Newman, S., Ramsay, G., Pope, S., Geller, G., & Anderson, C. (1979). The effect of assertiveness training, Provera and sex of therapist in the treatment of genital exhibitionism. *Journal of Behavior Therapy and Experimental Psychiatry, 10*, 275–282.

LeVay, S. (1991). A difference in hypothalamic structure between heterosexual and homosexual men. *Science, 253*, 1034–1037.

Malamuth, N. M., Heim, M., & Feshbach, S. (1980). Sexual responsiveness of college students to rape depictions: Inhibitory and disinhibitory effects. *Journal of Personality and Social Psychology, 38*, 399–408.

Mazur, A., & Lamb, T. A. (1980). Testosterone, status, and mood in human males. *Hormones and Behavior, 14*, 236–246.

McClintock, M. K. (1971). Menstrual synchrony and suppression. *Nature, 229*, 244–245.

McClintock, M. K. (1978). Estrous synchrony and its mediation by airborne chemical communication (*Rattus norvegicus*). *Hormones and Behavior, 10*, 264–276.

McClintock, M. K. (1987). A functional approach to the behavioral endocrinology of rodents. In D. Crews (Ed.), *Psychobiology of reproductive behavior: An evolutionary perspective* (pp. 176–203). Englewood Cliffs, NJ: Prentice Hall.

McKinney, T. D., & Desjardins, C. (1973). Intermale stimuli and testicular function in adult and immature house mice. *Biology of Reproduction, 9*, 370–378.

Meyer, W. J., Walker, P. A., Emory, L. E., & Smith, E. R. (1985). Physical, metabolic, and hormonal effects on men of long-term therapy with medroxyprogesterone acetate. *Fertility and Sterility, 43*, 102–106.

Minerbo, G., Albeck, D., Goldberg, E., Lindberg, T., Nakari, M., Martinez, C., Garritano, J., & Smock, T. (1994). Activity of peptidergic neurons in the amygdala during sexual behavior in the male rat. *Experimental Brain Research, 97*, 444–450.

Money, J. (1961). Sex hormones and other variables in human eroticism. In W.C. Young (Ed.), *Sex and Internal Secretions* (pp. 1383–1400). Baltimore: Williams & Wilkins.

Money, J., & Bennett, R. G. (1981). Postadolescent paraphilic sex offenders: Antiandrogenic and counseling therapy follow-up. *International Journal of Mental Health, 10*, 122–133.

Moore, F. L. (1992). Evolutionary precedents for behavioral actions of oxytocin and vasopressin. *Annals of the New York Academy of Sciences, 652*, 156–165.

Moss, R. L., & McCann, S.M. (1973). Induction of mating behavior in rats by luteinizing hormone-releasing factor. *Science, 181*, 177–179.

Murphy, M. R., Seckl, J. R., Burton, S., Checkley, S. A., & Lightman, S. L. (1987). Changes in oxytocin and vasopressin secretion during sexual activity in men. *Journal of Clinical Endocrinology and Metabolism, 65*, 738–741.

Nakanishi et al. (1995). *Nucleotide sequence of precursor. Nature, 278*, 423–427.

Nelson, R. J. (1995). *An introduction to behavioral endocrinology*. Sunderland, MA: Sinauer Associates.

Pedersen, C. A., Ascher, J. A., Monroe, Y. L., & Prange, A. J. (1982). Oxytocin induces maternal behavior in virgin female rats. *Science, 216*, 648–649.

Pfaff, D. W., & Scwartz-Giblin, S. (1988). Cellular mechanisms of female reproductive behaviors. In E. Knobil & J. McNeill (Eds.), *The physiology of reproduction*, (pp. 1487–1568). New York: Raven Press.

Pope, H. G., & Katz, D. L. (1989). Homicide and near-homicide by anabolic steroid users. *Journal of Clinical Psychiatry, 51*, 28–31.

Raloff, B. (1994). That feminine touch. *Science News, 145*, 56–59.

Rosenblatt, J. S., Mayer, A. D., & Giordano, A. L. (1988). Hormonal basis for the onset of maternal behavior in the rat. *Psychoneuroendocrinology, 13*, 29–46.

Sapolsky, R. M., Krey, L. C. ,& McEwen, B. S. (1986). The neuroendocrinology of stress and aging: The glucocorticoid cascade hypothesis. *Endocrine Reviews, 7*, 284–301.

Sherwin, B. B., & Suranyi-Cadotte, B. E. (1990). Up-regulatory effect of estrogen on platelet ^{3}H-imipramine binding sites in surgically menopausal women. *Biological Psychiatry, 28*, 339–348.

Smock, T., Albeck, D., McMechen, P., & Purves, D. (1990). Peptidergic transmission in the brain: II. Mediation by a vasopressin-like peptide. (1990). *Brain Research, 511*, 15–20.

Smock, T., Albeck, D., & Stark, P., (1998). A peptidergic basis for sexual behavior. *Progress in brain research*. (In press).

Smock, T., Arnold, S., Albeck, D., Emerson, P., Garritano, J., Burrows, K., Derber, W., Sanson, C., Marrs, K., Weatherley, H., & Kruse, K. (1992). A peptidergic circuit for reproductive behavior. *Brain Research, 598*, 138–142.

Smock, T., & Fields, H. L. (1981). ACTH$_{(1-24)}$ blocks opiate-induced analgesia in the rat. *Brain Research, 212*, 202–206.

Stark, C. P., Alpern, H. P., Fuhrer, J., Trowbridge, M. G., Wimbish, H., & Smock, T. (1998). The medial amygdaloid nucleus modifies social behavior in male rats. *Physiology & Behavior, 63*, 253–259.

Tavris, C. (1992). *The mismeasure of woman*. New York: Simon & Schuster.

Tegelman, R., Carlström, K., & Pousette, A. (1988). Hormone levels in male ice hockey players during a 26-hour cup tournament. *International Journal of Andrology, 11*, 361–368.

Vermuelan, et al. (1972) Testosterone secretion and metabolism in male semescence. *Journal of Clinical Endocrinology and Metabolism, 34*, 730–735.

Wallen, K. (1990). Desire and ability: Hormones and the regulation of female sexual behavior. *Neuroscience Biobehavioral Review, 14*, 233–241.

Winslow, J. T., Hastings, N., Carter, C. S., Harbaugh, C. R., & Insel, T. R. (1993). A role for central vasopressin in pair-bonding in monogamous prairie voles. *Nature, 365*, 545–548.

Whitman, D. C., & Albers, H. E. (1995). Role of oxytoxin in the hypothalamic regulation of sexual receptivity in hamsters. *Brain Research, 686*, 73–79.

Yarbrough, W. G., Quarmby, V. E., Simental, J. A., Joseph, D. R., Sar, M., Lubahn, D. B., Olsen, K. L., French, F. S., & Wilson, E.M. (1990). A single base mutation in the androgen receptor gene causes insensitivity in the testicular feminized rat. *Journal of Biological Chemistry, 265*, 8893–8900.

Yen, S.S., & Jaffe, R.B. (1991). *Reproductive Endocrinology* (3rd ed.). Philadelphia: W.B. Saunders.

Young, E. A., Spencer, R. L., & McEwen, B. S. (1990). Changes at multiple levels of the hypothalamic-pituitary-adrenal axis following repeated electroconvulsive shock. *Psychoneuroendocrinology, 15*, 165–172.

CHAPTER 13

Ackermann, P., & Borbely, A. A. (1997). Low frequency (^{1}Hz) oscillations in the human sleep electroencephalogram. Journal of Neuroscience, 81(1), 213–222.

Adam, K., & Oswald, I. (1977) Sleep is for tissue restoration. *Journal of the Royal College of Physicians (London), 11*, 376–88.

Amzica, F., & Steriade, M. (1997). The k-complex: its slow (^{1}Hz) rhythmiticity and relation to delta waves. *Neurology, 49*(4), 959–959.

Arendt, J., Skene, D. J., Middleton, B., Lockley, S. W., & Deacon, S. (1997). Efficacy of metabolism in jet lag, shift work, and blindness. *Journal of Biological Rhythms, 12*(6), 604–617.

Arkin, A., Antrobus, J. & Ellman, S. (1978). *The mind in sleep: Psychology and psychophysiology.* Mahwah, NJ: L. Erlbaum Associates, Inc.

Beckwith, J. B. (1973). The sudden infant death syndrome. *Current Problems in Pediatrics, 3*, 3–35.

Berridge, C. W. (1998). Modulation of forebrain electroencephalographic activity and behavioral state by the locus coerciteus-noradrenergic system: Involvement of the medial septal area. *Advances in Pharmacology, 42*, 744–748.

Born, J., Muth, S., & Fehm, H. L. (1988). The significance of sleep onset and slow wave sleep for nocturnal release of growth hormone (GH) and cortisol. *Psychoneuroendocrinology, 13*, 233–243.

Braun, A. R., Balkin, T. J., Wessenten, N. J., Carson, R. E., Varga, M., Baldwin, P., Selbie, S., Belenky, G., & Herscovitch, P. (1997). Regional cerebral blood flow throughout the sleep-wake cycle: An H_2O PET study. *Brain, 120*(7), 1173–1197.

Biello, S. M., Golombek, D. A., & Harrington, M. E. (1997). Neuropeptide Y and glutamate block each other's phase shifts in the suprachiasmatic nucleus in vitro. *Neuroscience, 77*(4), 1049–1057.

Bremer, F. (1935). Quelque properties de l'activé électrique du cortex cerebral "isolé." [Researching the electrical activity of the isolated cerebral cortex]. *Compte Rendu Societé Biologic* (Paris), *118*, 1241.

Bult, A., Hiestand, L., Van der Zee, E. A., & Lynch, C. B. (1993). Circadian rhythms differ between selected mouse lines: A model to study the role of vasopressin neurons in the suprachiasmatic nuclei. *Brain Research Bulletin, 32*, 623–627.

Chedid, L. (1983). Immunopharmacology of muramyl peptides: New horizons. *Progress in Immunology, 5*, 1349–1358.

Coleman, G. J., & Francis, A. J. P. (1987). The effect of ambient temperature cycles upon circadian rhythms of the stripe-faced dunnart, *Sminthopsis macroura. Journal of Comparative Physiology A, 167*, 357–362.

Cooper, R. (Ed.). (1994). *Sleep* (p. 148). London: Chapman & Hall.

Crick, F., & Mitchison, G. (1983). The function of dream sleep. *Nature, 304*, 111–114.

Delashaw, J., Foutz, A., Guilleminault, C., & Dement, W. C. (1978). Cholinergic mechanisms and cataplexy in dogs. *Experimental Neurology, 66*, 745–757.

Dement, W. C. (1960). The effect of dream deprivation. *Science, 131*, 1705–1707.

Dement, W. C., Ferguson, J., Cohen, H., & Barchas, J. (1969). Non-chemical methods and data using a biochemical model: The REM quanta. In A. Mandrell & M. P. Mandrell (Eds.), *Psychochemical research in man: methods, strategy and theory,* (pp. 275–325). New York: Academic Press.

Dement, W. C., & Fisher, C. (1963). Experimental interference with the sleep cycle. *Canadian Psychiatric Association Journal, 8*, 400–405.

Dement, W. C. Miles, L. E., & Carskadon, M. A. (1982). "White paper" on sleep and aging. *Journal of the American Geriatrics Society, 30*(1), 25–50.

Drucker-Colin, R. (1979). Protein molecules and the regulation of REM sleep: Possible implications for function. In D. Wheatley (Ed.), *Psychopharmacology of sleep* (pp. 1–18). New York: Raven Press.

Garcia-Rill, E. (1997). Disorders of the reticular activating system. *Medical Hypotheses, 49*(5), 379–387.

Gessa, G. L., Porceddu, M. L., Collu, M. Mereu, G., Serra, M., Ongini, E., & Biggo, G. (1985). Sedation and sleep induced by high doses of apomorphine after blockade of D_1 receptors by SCH 23390. *European Journal Pharmacology, 109*, 269–274.

Gillin, J. C., Sutton, L., Ruiz, C., Darko, D., Golshoa, S., Risch, S. C., & Janowsky, D. (1991). The effects of scopolomine on sleep and mood in depressed patients with a history of alcoholism and a normal comparison group. *Biological Psychiatry, 30*, 157–169.

Guntheroth, W. G., Kawabori, I., Breazeale, D.G., Garlinghouse, L. E., & Van Hoosier, G. L. (1980). The role of respiratory infection in intrathoracic petechiae. *American Journal of Diseases of Childhood, 134*, 364–66.

Hau, M., & Gwinner, E. (1997). Adjustment of house sparrow circadian rhythms to a simultaenously applied light and food zeitgeber. *Physiology and Behavior, 62*, 973–981.

Hicks, R. A., & Adams, G. (1976). REM sleep deprivation and exploration in young rats. *Psychological Reports, 38*, 1154.

Hicks, R. A., Moore, J. D., Hayes, C., Phillips, N., & Hawkins, J. (1979). REM sleep deprivation increases aggression in the male rat. *Physiology and Behavior, 22*, 1097–1100.

Hobson, J. A., & McCarley, R., (1977). The brain as a dream state generator: An activation-synthesis hypothesis of the dream process. *American Journal of Psychiatry, 134*, 1335–1348.

Horne, J. A., & Wilkinson, S. (1985). Chronic sleep reduction: Daytime vigilance performance and EEG measures of sleepiness with particular reference to "practice" effects. *Psychophysiology, 22*, 69–78.

Horner, R. L., Sanford, L. D., Annis, D., Pack, A. I., & Morrison, A. R. (1997). Serotonin at the laterodorsal tegmental nucleus suppresses rapid eye-movement sleep in freely behaving rats, *Journal of Neuroscience, 17*(9), 7541–7552.

Imeri, L., Bianchi, S., & Mancia, M. (1997). Muramyl dipeptide and IL–1 effects on sleep and brain temperature after inhibition of serotonin synthesis. *American Journal of Physiology, 273*(5), R1663–R1668.

Jouvet, M. (1978). Does a genetic programming of the brain occur during paradoxical sleep? In P. A. Buser & A. Rougel-Beser (Eds.), *Cerebral correlates of conscious experience.* (pp. 245–261). Amsterdam: Elsevier.

Jouvet, M., Buda, C., Cespuglio, R., & Dubois, P. M. (1986). Hypnogenic effects of some hypothalamo-pituitary peptides. In W. E. Bunney, Jr., E. Costa, & S. G. Putkin (Eds.), *Clinical neuropharmocology: Vol. 9* (Suppl. 4, pp. 465–467). New York: Raven Press.

Jouvet, M., Vimont, P., & Delorme, F. (1965). Suppresion élective du sommeil paradoxal chez le chat par les inhibiteurs de la monoamine oxydase. [Suppression of paradoxical sleep in the cat by inhibitors of monamine oxidase]. *Compte Rendu Societé Biologie* (Paris), *159*, 1595–1599.

Jung, C. G. (1974). *Dreams* (R. F. C. Hull, Trans.), Princeton, NJ: Princeton University Press.

Koella, W. P., Feldstein, A., & Czicman, J. S. (1968). The effect of parachlorophenylalanine on the sleep of cats. *Electroencephalography and Clinical Neurophysiology, 25*, 481–90.

Kryger, M. H., Roth, T. & Dement, W.C. (1994). *Principle and practice of sleep medicine.* (2nd ed.) Philadelphia: W.B. Saunders Co.

Kushida, C. A., Guillemhault, C., Clerk, A. A., & Dement, W. C. (1997). Nasal obstruction and obstructive sleep apnea: A review. *Allergy and Asthma Proceedings, 18*(2), 69–71.

Lewy, A. J., Wehr, T. A., Goodwin, F. K., Newsome, D. A., & Markey, S. P. (1980). Light suppresses melatonin secretion in humans. *Science, 210*, 1276–1269.

Liu, C., Ding, J. M., Faiman, L. E., & Gillette, M. U. (1997). Coupling of muscarinic cholinergic receptors and cGMP in nocturnal regulation of the suprachiasmatic circadian clock. *Journal of Neuroscience, 17*(2), 659–666.

Liu, C., Weaver, D. R., Strogate, S. H., & Reppert, S. M. (1997). Cellular construction of a circardian clock: Period determination in the suprachrasmatic nuclei. *Cell, 91*(6), 855–860.

Lugaresi, E., Midori, R., Montagna, P., Basuzzi, A., Cotelli, P., Lugaresi, A., Tinuper, P., Zucconi, M., & Gambetti, P. (1986). Fatal familial insomnia and dysautonomia with selective degeneration of thalamic nuclei. *New England Journal of Medicine, 315*, 997–1003.

MacFayden, U. M., Oswald, I., & Lewis, S. A. (1973). Starvation and human slow-wave sleep. *Journal of Applied Physiology, 35*, 391–394.

McCarley et al. (1987). REM sleep dreams and the activation-synthesis hypothesis. *American Journal of Psychistry, 138*, 904–912.

Menaker, M., & Ralph, M. R. (1989). GABA regulation of circadian responses to light: I. Involvement of $GABA_A$-benzodiazapine and $GABA_B$ receptors. *Journal of Neuroscience, 9*, 2858–2865.

Menaker, M., Ralph, M. R., Foster, R. G., & Davis, F. C. (1990). Transplanted suprachiasmatic nucleus determines circadian period. *Science, 247*, 975–978.

Mendelson, W. B. (1987). Neuroendocrinology and sleep. In W. B. Mendelson, (ed.) *Human sleep: Research and clinical care* (pp. 129–179). New York: Plenum Medical Book.

Mereu, G. P., Scarnati, E., Pagletti, E., Pellegrini, B., Chessa, P., Di Chiara, G., & Gessa, G. L. (1979). Sleep induced by low doses of apomorphine in rats. *Electroencephalography and Clinical Neurophysiology, 46*, 214–219.

Minors, D. S., Waterhouse, J. M., & Wirz-Justice, A. (1991). A human phase-response curve to light. *Neuroscience Letters, 133*, 36–40.

Moore, R. Y., & Lenn, N. J. (1972). A retinohypothalamic projection in the rat. *Journal of Comparative Neurology, 146*, 1–14.

Moruzzi, G., & Magoun, H. W. (1949). Brainstem reticular formation and activation of the EEG. *Electroencephalography and Clinical Neurophysiology, 1*, 455.

Mukhametov, L. M. (1984). Sleep in marine mammals. *Experimental Brain Research, 8*, (Suppl.), 227–238.

National Institute of Mental Health, Consensus Development Conference. (1984). Drugs and insomnia: The use of medications to promote sleep. *Journal of the American Medical Association, 251*, 2410–2414.

National Institute on Aging. (1997). Pills, patches, and shots: Can hormones prevent aging? Washington, D.C.

Nino-Marcia, G., Bliwise, D., Keenan, S. & Feibusch, K. (1988). *Treatment of obstructive sleep apnea with CPAP and protriptyline.* Chest, 94(6), 1314–1315.

Nowell, P. D., Mazumdar, S., Buysse, D. J., Dew, M. A., Reynolds, C. F., & Kupfer, D. J. (1997). Benzodiazephines and zolpidem for chronic insomnia: A meta-analysis of treatment efficacy. *Journal of the American Medical Association, 278*(4), 2170–2177.

Ohayon, M. M., Caulet, M., Priest, R. G., & Guilleminault, G. (1997). DSM IV and ICSD–90 insomnia symptoms and sleep dissatisfaction. *British Journal of Psychiatry, 171*, 382–388.

Orr, E., & Quay, W. B. (1975). Hypothalamic 24-hour rhythms in histamine, histidine decarboxylase, and histamine-N-methyltransferase. *Endocrinology, 96*, 941–945.

Pappenheimer, J. R., Miller, T. B., & Goodrich, C. A. (1967). Sleep-promoting effects of cerebrospinal fluid from sleep-deprived goats. *Proceedings of the National Academy of Sciences (USA), 58*, 513–517.

Pollmacher, T., Mullington, J., & Lauer, C. J. (1997). REM sleep disinhibition at sleep onset: A comparison between narcolepsy and depression. *Biological Psychiatry, 42*(8), 713–720.

Rechtschaffen, A., Bergmann, B. M., Everson, C. A., Kushida, C. A., & Gilliland, M. A. (1989). Sleep deprivation in the rat: X. Integration and discussion of the findings. *Sleep, 12*, 68–87.

Sakai, K. (1980). Some anatomical and physiological properties of ponto-mesencephalic tegmental neurons with special reference to the PGO waves and postural atonia during paradoxical sleep in the cat. In J. A. Hobson & M. B. Brazier (Eds.), *The reticular formation revisited* (pp. 427–447). New York: Raven Press.

Sastre, J. P., & Jouvet, M. (1979). Le comportement onirique du chat. [The dreaming behavior of the cat]. *Physiology and Behavior, 22*, 979–989.

Schatzman, M. (1983). Solve your problems in your sleep. *New Scientist, 98*, 682–83.

Schenck, C. H., & Mahowald, M. W. (1996). Long-term nightly benzodiazepine treatment of injurious parasomnias and other disorders of disrupted nocturnal sleep in 170 adults. *American Journal of Medicine, 100*(3), 333–337.

Shapiro, C. M., Goll, C. C., Cohen, G. R., & Oswald, I. (1984). Heat production during sleep. *Journal of Applied Physiology, 56*, 671–677.

Shiromani, P., & McGinty, D. J. (1986). Pontine neuronal response to local cholinergic microinfusion: Relation to REM sleep. *Brain Research, 386*, 20–31.

Steriade, M. (1996). Arousal: reordering the reticular activating system. *Science, 272*(5259), 225–226.

Soyka, M., & Rothenhaeusler, H. B. (1997). Delta sleep-inducing peptide in opioid detoxification. *American Journal of Psychiatry, 154*(5), 714–715.

Spiers, P. S., & Guntheroth, W. G. (1997). The seasonal distribution of infant deaths by age: a comparison of sudden infant death syndrome and other causes of death. *Journal of Paediatrics and Child Health, 33*(5), 408–412.

Thorpy, M. J., & Yager, J. (1991). *The encyclopedia of sleep and sleep disorders* (pp. 127,201). New York: Facts on File.

Tosini, G., & Menaker, M. (1998). Multioscillatory circadian organization in a vertebrate, *Journal of Neuroscience, 18*(3), 1105–1114.

Turek, F., & Wee, B. (1989). Carbachol phase shifts the circadian rhythm of locomotor activity in the Djungarian hamster. *Brain Research, 505*, 209–214.

Vizuete, M. L., Traiffort, E., Bouthenet, M. L., Ruat, M., Souil, E., Tardivel-Lacombe, J., & Schwartz, J. C. (1997). Detailed mapping of the histamine receptors and its transcripts in guinea-pig brain. *Neuroscience, 80*(2), 321–343.

Vodelholzer, U., Homyak, M., Thiel, B., Huwig-Poppe, C., Kiemen, A., Konig, A., Backhaus, J., Reimann, D., Berger, M. & Hohagen, R. (1998). Impact of experimentally induced serotonin deficiency by tryphophan depletion on sleep EEG in healthy subjects. *Neuropsychopharmacology, 18*(2), 112–124.

Walker, J., & Berger, R. J. (1980). Sleep as an adaptation for energy conservation functionally related to hibernation and shallow torpor. *Progress in Brain Research, 53*, 255–278.

Waterhouse, J., Reilly, T., & Atkinson, G. (1997). Jet lag. *Lancet, 350*(9091), 1611–1616.

Webb, W. B. (1974). Sleep as an adaptive response. *Perception and Motor Skills, 38*, 1023–1027.

Wetter, T. C., & Pollmacher, T. (1997). Restless legs and periodic movements in sleep syndromes. *Journal of Neurology, 244*, S37–S35.

Young, M. A., Meaden, P. M., Fogg, L. R., Cheris, E. A., & Eastman, C. I. (1997). Which environmental variables are related to the onset of seasonal affective behavior? *Journal of Abnormal Psychology, 106*, 554–562.

Zarcone, V., De La Pena, A., & Dement, W. C. (1974). Heightened sexual interest and sleep disturbance. *Perception & Motor Skills, 39*, 1135–1141.

CHAPTER 14

Amir, S. (1990). Activation of brown adipose tissue thermogenesis by chemical stimulation of the posterior hypothalamus. *Brain Research, 534*, 303–308.

Amir, S., & De Blasio, E. (1991). Activation of brown adipose tissue thermogenesis by chemical stimulation of the hypothalamic supraoptic nucleus. *Brain Research, 563*, 349–352.

Becker, E. E., & Kissileff, H. R. (1974). Inhibitory controls of feeding by the ventromedial hypothalamus. *American Journal of Physiology, 226*, 383–396.

Bernard, C. (1856). *Leçons de physiologie experimentale appliquée à lamédrine praites au Collège de France.* [Results of practical experiments in applied physiology at the College of France.] Balliere, Paris.

Bernstein, I. L., & Borson, S. (1986). Learned food aversion: A component of anorexia syndromes. *Psychological Review, 93*, 462–472.

Berridge, K. C., & Valenstein, E. S. (1991). What psychological process mediates feeding evoked by electrical stimulation of the lateral hypothalamus? *Behavioral Neuroscience, 105*, 3–14.

Berthoud, H. R., & Jeanrenaud, B. (1979). Acute hyperinsulinemia and its reversal by vagotomy after lesions of the ventromedial hypothalamus in anesthetized rats. *Endocrinology, 105*, 146–151.

Brownell, K. D., Greenwood, M .R. C., Stellar, E., & Shrager, E. E. (1986). The effects of repeated cycles of weight loss and regain in rats. *Physiology & Behavior, 38*, 459–464.

Brownell, K. D., & Rodin, J. (1994). The dieting maelstrom: Is it possible and advisable to lose weight. *American Psychologist, 49*, 781–791.

Cannon, W. B. (1929). *Bodily changes in pain, hunger, fear and rage.* New York: Appleton.

Cooper, S. J., & Dourish, C .T. (1990). Multiple cholecystokinin (CCK) receptors and CCK-monoamine interactions are instrumental in the control of feeding. *Physiology & Behavior, 48*, 849–857.

Cooper, S. J., Dourish, C. T., & Barber, D. J. (1990). Reversal of the anorectic effect of (+)-Fenfluramine in the rat by the selective cholecystokinin receptor antagonist MK–329. *British Journal of Pharmacology, 99*, 65–70.

Czech, D. A., & Stein, E. A. (1992). Effect of drinking on angiotensin-II-induced shifts in regional cerebral blood flow in the rat. *Brain Research Bulletin, 28*, 529–535.

Deutsch, J. A., & Hardy, W. T. (1977). Cholecystokinin produces bait shyness in rats. *Nature, 266*, 196–198.

Dourish, C. T., Ruckert, A. C., Tattersall, F. D., & Iversen, S. D. (1989). Evidence that decreased feeding induced by systemic injection of cholecystokinin is mediated by CCK-A receptors. *European Journal of Pharmacology, 173*, 233–234.

Duggan, J. P., & Booth, D. A. (1986). Obesity, overeating, and rapid gastric emptying in rats with ventromedial hypothalamic lesions. *Science, 231*, 609–611.

Epstein, A. N. (1991). Neurohormonal control of salt intake in the rat. *Brain Research Bulletin, 27*, 315–320.

Ettinger, R. H., Thompson, S., & Staddon, J. E. R. (1986). Cholecystokinin, diet palatability, and feeding regulation in rats. *Physiology & Behavior, 36*, 801–809.

Figlewicz, D. P., Nadzan, A. M., Sipols, A. J., Green, P. K., Liddle, R. A., Porte, D. Jr., & Woods, S. C. (1992). Intraventricular CCK–8 reduces single meal size in the baboon by interaction with type-A receptors. *American Journal of Physiology, 263*, 863–867.

Garcia, J., & Koelling, R. A. (1966). Relation of cue to consequence in avoidance learning. *Psychonomic Science, 4*, 123–124.

Grandison, L., & Guidotti, L. (1977). Stimulation of food intake by muscimol and ß-endorphin. *Neuropharmacology, 16*, 533–536.

Harris, R. B., Zhou, J., Redmann, S. M., Smagin, G. N., Smith, S. R., Rodgers, E., & Zachwieja, J. J. (1998). A leptin dose-response study in obese (ob/ob) and lean (+/?) mice. *Endocrinology, 139*(1), 8–19.

Hollister, L. E., Johnson, K., Bookhabzer, D., & Gillespie, H. K. (1981). Adverse effects of naltrexone in subjects not dependent on opiates. *Drug & Alcohol Dependence, 8*, 37–41.

Holtzman, S. C. (1974). Behavioural effects of separate and combined administration of naloxone and d-amphetamine. *Journal of Pharmacology & Experimental Therapeutics, 189*, 51–60.

Jonas, J., & Gold, M. (1986). Naltrexone reverses bulimic symptoms. *Lancet, 1*, 807–810.

Kaye, W. H., Ebert, M. H., Gwirtsman, H. E., & Weiss, S. R. (1984). Differences in brain serotonergic metabolism between nonbulimic and bulimic patients with anorexia nervosa. *American Journal of Psychiatry, 141*, 1598–1601.

King, B. M., & Frohman, L. A. (1982). The role of vagally mediated hyperinsulinemia in hypothalamic obesity. *Neuroscience & Biobehavioral Reviews, 6*, 205–214.

Leibowitz, S. F. (1986). Brain monoamines and peptides: Role in the control of eating behavior. *Federation Proceedings, 45*, 1396–1403.

Matthews, J. W., Booth, D. A., & Stolerman, I. P. (1986). Intrahypothalamic noradrenaline injection in the rat enhances operant licking, but not lever pressing for milk reward. *Appetite, 7*(4), 355–364.

Margules, D. L., Moisset, B., Lewis, M. J., Shibuya, H., & Pert, C. B. (1978). ß-endorphin is associated with overeating in genetically obese mice (ob/ob) and rats (fa/fa). *Science, 202*, 988–991.

Moran, T., Robinson, P., Goldrich, M. S., & McHugh, P. (1986). Two brain cholecystokinin receptors: Implications for behavioral actions. *Brain Research, 362*, 175–179.

Musnam, S. K., & Smolak, L. (1997). Femininity, masculinity, and disordered eating in a meta-analytic review. *International Journal of Eating Disorders, 22*(3), 231–242.

Russek, M. (1971). Hepatic receptors and the neurophysiological mechanisms controlling feeding behavior. In S. Ehrenpreis (Ed.), *Neurosciences research* (Vol. 4). New York: Academic Pess.

Schwartz, M. W., Figlewicz, D. P., Baskin, D. G., Woods, S. C., & Porte, D. Jr. (1993). Insulin in the brain: A hormonal regulator of energy balance. *Endocrine Reviews, 13*, 387–414.

Shimizu, N., Oomura, Y., Novin, D., Grijalva, C., & Cooper, P. H. (1983). Functional correlations between lateral hypothalamic glucose-sensitive neurons and hepatic protal glucose-sensitive units in rat. *Brain Research, 265,* 49–54.

Smith, G. P., Tyrka, A., & Gibbs, J. (1991) Type-A CCK receptors mediate the inhibition of food intake and activity by CCK–8 in 9- to 12-day-old rat pups. *Pharmacology, Biochemistry & Behavior, 38,* 207–210.

Sokoloff, L., Reivich, M., Kennedy, C., Des Rosiers, M. H., Patlak, C. S., Pettigrew, K. D., Sakurada, O., & Shinohara, M. (1977). The [14C]deoxyglucose method for the measurement of local cerebral glucose utilization: Theory, procedure, and normal values in the conscious and anesthetized albino rat. *Journal of Neurochemistry, 29,* 897–916.

Stallone, D., Nicolaidis, S., & Gibbs, J. (1989). Cholecystokinin-induced anorexia depends on serotonergic function. *American Journal of Physiology, 256,* R1138–R1141.

Stricker, E. M., & Verbalis, J. G. (1990). Control of appetite and satiety: Insights from biologic and behavioral studies. *Nutrition Reviews, 48,* 49–56.

Teitelbaum, P. (1955). Sensory control of hypothalamic hyperphagia. *Journal of Comparative & Physiological Psychology, 48,* 156–163.

Vaccarino, F. J., & Hayward, M. (1988). Microinjections of growth hormone-releasing factor into the medial preoptic area/suprachiasmatic nucleus region of the hypothalamus stimulate food intake in rats. *Regulatory Peptides, 21,* 21–28.

CHAPTER 15

Aceves-Pina, E. O., Booker, R., Duerr, J. S., Livingston, M. S., Quinn, W. G., Smith, R. F., Sziber, P. P., Tempel, B. L., & Tully, T. P. (1983). Learning and memory in *Drosophila,* studied with mutants. *Cold Spring Harbor Symposium on Quantitative Biology, 48,* 831–840.

Acosta-Urquidi, J., Alkon, D. L., & Newry, J. T. (1984). Ca++ -dependent protein kinase injection in a photoreceptor mimics biophysical effects of associative learning. *Science, 224,* 1254–1275.

Amaral, D. G., & Witter, M. P. (1989). The three-dimensional organization of the hippocampal formation: A review of anatomical data. *Neuroscience, 31,* 571–591.

Anderson, P., Bliss, T. V. P., & Skrede, K. K. (1971). Lamellar organization of hippocampal excitatory pathways. *Experimental Brain Research, 13,* 222–238.

Anderson, P., Sundberg, S. H., Sveen, O., & Wigstrom, H. (1977). Specific long-lasting potentiation of synaptic transmission in hippocampal slices. *Nature, 266,* 736–737.

Bao, J. X., Kandel, E. R., & Hawkins, R. D. (1998). Involvement of presynaptic and postsynaptic mechanisms in a cellular analog of classical conditioning of *Aplysia* sensory-motor neuron synapses in isolated cell culture. *Journal of Neuroscience, 18*(1), 458–466.

Baudry, M., & Davis, J. (1991). *Long-term potentiation: A debate of current issues.* Cambridge, MA: MIT Press.

Bear, M. F., Kleinschmidt, A., Gu, Q., & Singer, W. (1990). Disruption of experience-dependent synaptic modifications in striate cortex by infusion of an NMDA receptor antagonist. *Journal of Neuroscience, 10,* 909–925.

Bekkers, J. M., & Stevens, C. F. (1990). Presynaptic mechanism for long-term potentiation in the hippocampus. *Nature, 346,* 724–729.

Bennett, E. L., Diamond, M. C., Krech, D., & Rosenzweig, M. R. (1964). Chemical and anatomical plasticity of brain. *Science, 146,* 610–619.

Berger, T. W., & Thompson, R. F. (1978). Neuronal plasticity in the limbic system during classical conditioning of the rabbit nictitating response: I. The hippocampus. *Brain Research, 145,* 323–346.

Bliss, T. V.P., Douglas, R. M., Errington, M. L., & Lynch, M. A. (1986). Correlation between long-term potentiation and release of endogenous amino acids from dentate gyrus of anesthetized rats. *Journal of Physiology, 377,* 391–408.

Bliss, T. V. P., & Lomo, T. (1973). Long-lasting potentiation of synaptic transmission in the dentate area of the anesthetized rabbit following stimulation of the perforant path. *Journal of Physiology, 232,* 331–356.

Bronner-Fraser, M. (1985). Alterations in neural crest migration by a monoclonal antibody that affects cell adhesion. *Journal of Cell Biology, 101,* 610–617.

Bronner-Fraser, M. (1986). An antibody to a receptor for fibronectin and laminin perturbs cranial neural crest development in vivo. *Developmental Neurobiology, 117,* 528–536.

Brown, T. H., Chapman, P. F., Kairiss, E. W. & Keenan, C. L. (1988). Long-term synaptic potentiation. *Science, 242,* 724–728.

Bueker, E. D. (1948). Implantation of tumors in the hind limb field of the embryonic chick and the developmental response of the lumbosacral nervous system. *Anatomical Record, 102,* 369–390.

Buzsaki, G. (1980). Long-term potentiation of the commissural path-CA$_1$ pyramidal cell synapse in the hippocampus of the freely moving rat. *Neuroscience Letters, 19,* 293–296.

Byrne, J. H. (1982). Analysis of the synaptic depression contributing to habituation of gill-withdrawal reflex in *Aplysia californica. Journal of Neurophysiology, 48,* 431–438.

Carew, T. J., Castellucci, V. F., & Kandel, E. R. (1971). An analysis of dishabituation and sensitization of the gill-withdrawal reflex in *Aplysia. International Journal of Neuroscience, 2,* 79–98.

Carew, T. J., Hawkins, R. D., & Kandel, E. R. (1983). Differential classical conditioning of a defensive withdrawal reflex in *Aplysia californica. Science, 219,* 397–400.

Castellucci, V. F., & Kandel, E. R. (1974). A quantal analysis of the synaptic depression underlying habituation of the gill-withdrawal reflex in *Aplysia. Proceedings of the National Academy of Science, 194,* 5004–5008.

Castelluci, V. F., & Kandel, E. R. (1976). Presynaptic facilitation as a mechanism for behavioral sensitization in *Aplysia. Science, 194,* 1176–1178.

Castellucci, V. F., Pinsker, H., Kupfermann, I., & Kandel, E. R. (1970). Neuronal mechanisms of habituation and dishabituation of the gill-withdrawal reflex in *Aplysia. Science, 167,* 1745–1748.

Chang, F. L., & Greenough, W. T. (1984). Transient and enduring morphological correlates of synaptic activity and efficacy change in the rat hippocampal slice. *Brain Research, 309,* 35–46.

Cohen, S., & Levi-Montalcini, R. (1956). A nerve growth stimulating factor isolated from snake venom. *Proceedings of the National Academy of Science, 42,* 571–574.

Collingridge, G. L., Kelly, S. J., & McLennan, H. (1983). The antagonism of amino acid-induced excitations of rat hippocampal CA$_1$ neurons in vitro. *Journal of Physiology, 334,* 19–31.

Cowan, W. M. (1978). Aspects of neural development. *International Review of Physiology, 17,* 149–191.

Crow, T. (1988). Cellular and molecular analysis of associative learning and memory in *Hermissenda. Trends in Neuroscience, 11,* 136–142.

Crow, T., & Alkon, D. L. (1978). Retention of an associative behavioral change in *Hermissenda. Science, 201,* 1239–1241.

Crow, T., & Alkon, D. L. (1980). Associative behavioral modification in *Hermissenda*: Cellular correlates. *Science, 209,* 412–414.

Crow, T., & Forrester, J. (1986). Light paired with serotonin mimics the effects of conditioning on phototactic behavior in *Hermissenda. Proceedings of the National Academy of Science, 83,* 7975–7978.

Davis, S., Butcher, S. P., & Morris, R. G. M. (1992). The NMDA receptor antagonist D–2-amino–5-phosphopentanoate (D-AP5) impairs spatial learning and LTP *in vivo* at intracerebral concentrations comparable to those that block LTP *in vitro. Journal of Neuroscience, 12,* 21–34.

Douglas, R. M., & Goddard, G. (1975). Long-term potentiation of the perforant-granule cell synapse in the rat hippocampus. *Brain Research, 86,* 205–215.

Dudai, Y. (1985). Genes, enzymes, and learning in *Drosophila. Trends in Neuroscience, 8,* 18–21.

Dudai, Y. (1988). Neurogenetic dissociation of learning and short-term memory in *Drosophila. Annual Review of Neuroscience, 11,* 537–563.

Duerr, J. S., & Quinn, W. G. (1982). Three *Drosophila* mutations that block associative learning also affect habituation and sensitization. *Proceedings from the National Academy of Science. 79,* 3646–3650.

Edelman, G. M. (1986). Cell adhesion molecules in the regulation of animal form and tissue pattern. *Annual Review of Cell Biology, 2,* 81–116.

Edmondson, J. C., Liem, R. K. H., Kuster, J. E., & Hatten, M. E. (1988). Astrotactin: A novel neuronal cell surface antigen that mediates neuron-astroglial interactions in cerebellar microcultures. *Journal of Cell Biology, 106,* 505–517.

Fawcett, J. W., & O'Leary, D. D. M. (1985). The role of electrical activity in the formation of topographic maps in the nervous system. *Trends in Neuroscience, 8,* 201–206.

Fifkova, E., & Anderson, C. L. (1981). Stimulation-induced changes in dimensions of stalks of dendritic spines in the dentate molecular layer. *Experimental Neurology, 74,* 621–627.

Fifkova, E., & Morales, M. (1992). Actin matrix of dendritic spines, synaptic plasticity, and long-term potentiation. *International Review of Cytology, 139,* 267–307.

Galea, L. A., McEwen, B. S., Tanapat, P., Deak, T., Spencer, R. L., & Dhabar, R. S. (1997). Sex differences in dendritic atrophy of CA$_3$ pyramidal neurons in response to chronic restraint stress. *Neuroscience, 81,* 689–697.

Galileo, D. S., Majors, J., Horwitz, A. F., & Sanes, J. R. (1992). Retrovirally introduced antisense integrin RNA inhibits neuroblast migration in vivo. *Neuron, 6,* 1117–1131.

Garcia, J., Ervin, F. R., & Koelling, R. A. (1966). Learning with prolonged delay of reinforcement. *Psychonomic Science, 5,* 121–122.

Globus, A., Rosenzweig, M. R., Bennett, E. L., & Diamond, M. C. (1973). Effects of differential experience on dendritic spine counts in rat cerebral cortex. *Journal of Comparative & Physiological Psychology, 82,* 175–181.

Goodman, C. S., Bastiani, M. J., Doe, C. Q., du Lac, S., Helfand, S. L., Kuwanda, J. Y., & Thomas, J. B. (1984). Cell recognition during neural development. *Science, 225,* 1271–1279

Greenough, W. T., & Volkmar, F. R. (1973). Pattern of dendritic branching in occipital cortex of rats reared in complex environments. *Experimental Neurology, 40,* 491–504.

Hall & Sanes, J. (1993). Synaptic structure and development: The neuromuscular junction. *Cell Supplement*, 99–121.

Hatten, G. E., Liem, R. K. H., & Mason, C. A. (1986). Weaver mouse cerebellar granule neurons fail to migrate on wild-type astroglial processes in vitro. *Journal of Neuroscience, 6*, 2675–2683.

Hatten, M. E. (1990). Riding the glial monorail: A common mechanism for glial-guided neuronal migration in different regions of the developing mammalian brain. *Trends in Neuroscience, 13*, 179–184.

Hawkins, R. D., Abrams, T. W., Carew, T. J., & Kandel, E. R. (1983). A cellular mechanism of classical conditioning in *Aplysia*: Activity-dependent amplification of presynaptic facilitation. *Science, 219*, 400–405.

Hebb, D. O. (1949). *The organization of behavior*. New York: Wiley.

Hubel, D. H., & Wiesel, T. N. (1970). The period of susceptibility to the physiological effects of unilateral eye closure in kittens. *Journal of Physiology, 206*, 419–436.

Hubel, D. H., Weisel, T.N., & LeVay, S. (1977). Plasticity of ocular dominance columns in the monkey striate cortex. *Philosophical Transactions of the Royal Society, London B, 278*, 377–409.

Izumi, Y., Katsuki, H., Benz., A. M., & Zorumski, C. F. (1998). Oxygen deprivation produces delayed inhibition of long-term potentiation by activation of NMDA receptors and nitric oxide synthase. *Journal of Cerebral Blood Flow and Metabolism, 18*(1), 97–108.

Jarrard, L. E. (1986). Selective hippocampal lesions and behavior: Implication for current research and theorizing. In R. L. Issaacson & K. H. Pribram (Eds.), *The hippocampus* (pp. 93–126). New York: Plenum Press.

Jessell, T. M. (1988). Adhesion molecules and the hierarchy of neural development. *Neuron, 1*, 3–13.

Kandel, E. R., Abrams, T., Bernier, L., Carew, T. J., Hawkins, R. D., & Schwartz, J. H. (1983). Classical conditioning and sensitization share aspects of the same molecular cascade in *Aplysia*. *Cold Spring Harbor Symposium on Quantitative Biology, 48*, 821–830.

Kandel, E. R., Brunelli, M., Byrne, J., & Castellucci, V. (1976). A common presynaptic locus for the synaptic changes underlying short-term habituation and sensitization of the gill-withdrawal reflex in *Aplysia*. *Cold Spring Harbor Symposium on Quantitative Biology, 60*, 465–482.

Kapfhammer, J.P., & Raper, J. A. (1987). Interactions between growth cones and neurites growing from different neural tissues in culture. *Journal of Neuroscience, 7*, 1595–1600.

Kirkwood, A., Dudek, S. M., Gold, J. T., Aizenman, C. D., & Bear, M. F. (1993). Common forms of synaptic plasticity in the hippocampus and neocortex in vitro. *Science, 260*, 1518–1521.

Klein, M., & Kandel, E. R. (1980). Mechanism of calcium current modulation underlying presynaptic facilitation and behavioral sensitization in *Aplysia*. *Proceedings of the National Academy of Science, 77*, 6912–6916.

Komuro, H., & Rakic, P. (1992). Selective role of N-type calcium channels in neuronal migration. *Science, 257*, 806–809.

Konishi, M. (1989). Birdsong for neurobiologists. *Neuron, 3*, 542–549.

Korsching, S., & Thoenen, H. (1983). Nerve growth factor in sympathetic ganglia and corresponding target organs of the rat: Correlation with density of sympathetic innervation. *Proceedings of the National Academy of Science, 80*, 3513–3516.

Krupa, D. J., Thompson, J. K., & Thompson, R. F. (1993). Localization of a memory trace in the mammalian brain. *Science, 260*, 989–991.

Kupfermann, I., Castellucci, V., Pinsker, H., & Kandel, E. R. (1970). Neuronal correlates of habituation and dishabituation of the gill-withdrawal reflex in *Aplysia*. *Science, 167*, 1743–1745.

Landis, S. C. (1990). Target regulation of neurotransmitter phenotype. *Trends in Neuroscience, 13*, 344–350.

Landis, S. C. (1996). The development of cholinergic sympathetic neurons: A role for neuropoietic cytokines. *Perspectives in Developmental Neurobiology, 1*, 53–63.

Lashley, K. S. (1929). *Brain mechanisms of intelligence: A quantitative study of injuries to the brain*. Chicago: Chicago University Press.

Lashley, K. S. (1950). In search of the engram. *Symposia of the Society for Experimental Biology, 4*, 454–482.

Lavond, D. G., McCormick, D. A., & Thompson, R. F. (1984). A nonrecoverable learning deficit. *Physiological Psychology, 12*, 103–110.

Le Douarin, N. M. (1986). Cell line segregation during peripheral nervous system ontogeny. *Science, 231*, 1515–1522.

Le Douarin, N. M., & Dupin, E. (1993). Cell lineage analysis in neural crest ontogeny. *Journal of Neurobiology, 2*, 146–161.

Lee, K. L. (1983). Sustained modification of neuronal activity in the hippocampus and neocortex. In W. Seifert (Ed.), *Neurobiology of the hippocampus* (pp. 265–272). New York: Academic Press.

Lee, K. S., Schottler, F., Oliver, M., & Lynch, G. (1980). Brief bursts of high-frequency stimulation produce two types of structural change in rat hippocampus. *Journal of Neurophysiology, 44*, 247–258.

Levi-Montalcini, R. (1972). The morphological effects of immunosympathectomy. In G. Steiner & E. Schonbaum (Eds.), *Immunosympathectomy* (pp. 55–78), Amsterdam: Elsevier.

Levi-Montalcini, R., Meyer, H., & Hamburger, V. (1954). In vitro experiments on the effects of mouse sarcomas 180 and 37 on the spinal and sympathetic ganglia of the chick embryo. *Cancer Research, 14*, 49–57.

Lisberger, S. G. (1988). The neural basis for motor learning in the vestibulo-ocular reflex in monkeys. *Trends in Neuroscience, 11*, 147–152.

Litwack, E. D., Ivans, J. K., Kumbuser, A., Paine-Saunders, S., Stipp, C. S., & Lander, A. D. (1998). Expression of the heparin sulfate proteoglycan glypican–1 in the developing rodent. *Developmental Dynamics, 211*(1), 72–87.

Lledo, P. M., Zhang, X., Sudhof, Z. C., Malenka, R. C., & Nicoll, R. A. (1998). Postsynaptic membrane fusion and long-term potentiation. *Science, 279*(5349), 399–403.

Lomo, T., & Rosenthal, J. (1972). Control of ACh sensitivity by muscle activity in the rat. *Journal of Physiology, 221*, 493–513.

Lorenz, D. Z. (1970). *Studies on animal and human behavior*. Cambridge, MA: Harvard University Press.

Lynch, M. A., Errington, M. L., & Bliss, T. V. P. (1989). Nordihydroguaiaretic acid blocks the synaptic component of long-term potentiation and the associated increases in release of glutamate and arachidonate: An *in vivo* study in the dentate gyrus of the rat. *Neuroscience, 30*, 693–701.

Madison, D. V., Malenka, R. C., & Nicoll, R. A. (1991). Mechanisms underlying long-term potentiation of synaptic transmission. *Annual Review of Neuroscience, 14*, 379–397.

Malenka, R. C., Kauer, J. A., Zucker, R. J., & Nicoll, R. A. (1988). Postsynaptic calcium is sufficient for potentiation of hippocampal synaptic transmission. *Science, 242*, 81–84.

Malinow, R., Madison, D. V., & Tsien, R. W. (1988). Persistent protein kinase activity underlies long-term potentiation. *Nature, 335*, 820–824.

Malinow, R., Schulman, H., Madison, D. V., & Tsien, R. W. (1989). Inhibition of postsynaptic PKC or CaMKII blocks induction but not expression of LTP. *Science, 245*, 862–866.

Marler, P. (1981). Birdsong: The acquisition of a learned motor skill. *Trends in Neuroscience, 4*, 88–94.

Mauk, M. D., & Thompson, R. F. (1987). Retention of classically conditioned eyelid responses following acute decerebration. *Brain Research, 403*, 89–95.

McEwen, B. S., Biron, C. A., Brunson, K. W., Bullock, K., Chambers, W. H., Dhabar, R. S., Goldfarb, R. H., Kitson, R. P., Miller, A. H., Spencer, R. L., & Weiss, J.M. (1997). The role of adrenalcorticoids as modulators of immune function in health and disease: Neural, endocrine and immune interactions. *Brain Research: Brain Research Reviews, 23*, 79–133.

McMahan, U. J., & Wallace, B. G. (1989). Molecules in basal lamina that direct the formation of synaptic specializations at neuromuscular junction. *Developmental Neuroscience, 11*, 227–247.

Miles, F. A., & Lisberger, S. G. (1981). Plasticity in the vestibulo-ocular reflex: A new hypothesis. *Annual Review of Neuroscience, 4*, 273–299.

Milner, B. (1972). Disorders of learning and memory after temporal lobe lesions in man. *Clinical Neurosurgery, 19*, 421–446.

Mrzljak, L., Uylings, H. B., Kostovic, I., & van Eden, C. G. (1992). Prenatal development of neurons in the human prefrontal cortex: II. A quantitative Golgi study. *Journal of Comparative Neurology, 4*, 485–496.

Nottebohm, F. (1981). A brain for all seasons: Cyclical anatomical changes in song control nuclei of the canary brain. *Science, 214*, 1368–1370.

Nottebohm, F., & Arnold, A. P. (1976). Sexual dimorphism in vocal control areas of the songbird brain. *Science, 194*, 211–213.

O'Dell, T. J., Hawkins, R. D., Kandel, E. R., & Arancio, O. (1991). Test of the roles of two diffusible substances in long-term potentiation: Evidence for nitric oxide as a possible early retrograde messenger. *Proceedings of the National of Academy of Science, 88*, 11285–11289.

O'Keefe, J., & Nadel, L. (1978). *The hippocampus as a cognitive map*. Oxford, England: Clarendon Press.

O'Leary, D. D. M., & Stanfield, B. B. (1989). Selective elimination of axons extended by developing cortical neurons is dependent on regional locale: Experiments utilizing fetal cortical transplant. *Journal of Neuroscience, 9*, 2230–2246.

Patton, J. A., & Nottebohm, F. N. (1984). Neurons generated in the adult brain are recruited into functional circuits. *Science, 225*, 1046–1048.

Pavlov, I. P. (1906). The scientific investigation of the psychological faculties of processes in the higher animals. *Science, 24*, 613–619.

Purves, D., & Lichtman, J. W. (1980) Elimination of synapses in the developing nervous system. *Science, 210*, 153–157.

Quinn, W. G., Harris, W. A., & Benzer, S. (1974). Conditioned behavior in *Drosophila melanogaster*. *Proceedings of the National Academy of Science, 71*, 708–712.

Racine, R. J., Milgram, N. W., & Hafner, S. (1983). Long-term potentiation phenomena in the rat limbic forebrain. *Brain Research, 260*, 217–231.

Rakic, P. (1972). Mode of cell migration to the superficial layers of fetal monkey neocortex. *Journal of Comparative Neurology, 145*, 61–84.

Rakic, P. (1974). Neurons in rhesus monkey visual cortex: Systemic relation between time of origin and eventual disposition. *Science, 183*, 425–427.

Rakic, P., & Sidman, R. L. (1973). Weaver mutant mouse cerebellum: Defective neuronal migration secondary to specific abnormality of Bergmann glia. *Proceeding of National Academy of Science, 70*, 240–244.

Ramón-y-Cajal, S. (1955). Histologie du Système Nerveaux. [Anatomy of the Nervous System.] II. Madrid: C.S.I.C.

Ribera, A. B., & Spitzer, N. C. (1989). A critical period of transcription required for differentiation of the action potential of spinal neurons. *Neuron, 2*, 1055–1062.

Sauer, F. C. (1935). Mitosis in the neural tube. *Journal of Comparative Neurology, 62*, 377–405.

Schlaggar, B. L., & O'Leary, D. D. M. (1991). Potential of visual cortex to develop an array of functional units unique to somatosensory cortex. *Science, 252*, 1556–1560.

Schmidt, J. T., & Eisele, L. E. (1985). Stroboscopic illumination and dark rearing block the sharpening of the regenerated retinotectal map in goldfish. *Neuroscience, 14*, 535–546.

Schotzinger, R. J., & Landis, S. C. (1988). Cholinergic phenotype developed by noradrenergic sympathetic neurons after innervation of a novel cholinergic target *in vivo*. *Nature, 335*, 637–639.

Schuman, E. M., & Madison, D. B. (1991). A requirement for the intercellular messenger nitric oxide in long-term potentiation. *Science, 254*, 1503–1506.

Schwab, M. E., & Caroni, P. (1988). Oligodendrocytes and CNS myelin are nonpermissive substrates for neurite growth and fibroblast spreading in vitro. *Journal of Neuroscience, 8*, 2381–2393.

Scoville, W. B., & Milner, B. (1957). Loss of recent memory after bilateral hippocampal lesions. *Journal of Neurology, Neurosurgery, & Psychiatry, 20*, 11–21.

Shatz, C. J. (1990). Impulse activity and the patterning of connections during CNS development. *Neuron, 5*, 745–756.

Shirasaki, R., Katsumata, R., & Murakami, F. (1998). Change in chemoattractant responsiveness of developing axons at an intermediate target. *Science, 279* (5347), 105–107.

Siegelbaum, S. A., Camrado, J. S., & Kandel, E. R. (1982). Serotonin and cyclic AMP close single K+ channels in *Aplysia* sensory neurons. *Nature, 299*, 413–417.

Skinner, B. F. (1938). *The behavior of organisms: An experimental analysis*. New York: Appleton-Century.

Solomon, P. R., & Moore, J. W. (1975). Latent inhibition and stimulus generalization for the classically conditioned nictitating membrane response in rabbits following dorsal hippocampal ablation. *Journal of Comparative Physiological Psychology, 89*, 1192–1203.

Spitzer, N. C., & Lamborghini, J. E. (1976). The development of the action potential mechanism of amphibian neurons isolated in cell culture. *Proceedings of the National Academy of Science, 73*, 1641–1645.

Stryker, M. P., & Harris, W. (1986). Binocular impulse blockade prevents the formation of ocular dominance columns in cat visual cortex. *Journal of Neuroscience, 6*, 2117–2133.

Stryker, M. P., & Strickland, S. L. (1984). Physiological segregation of ocular dominance columns on the pattern of afferent electrical activity. *Investigative Opthalmology & Visual Science, 25*, 278.

Taghert, P. H., Bastiani, M. J., Ho, R. K., & Goodman, C. S. (1982). Guidance of pioneer growth cones: Filopedial contacts and coupling revealed with an antibody to Lucifer Yellow. *Developmental Biology, 94*, 391–399.

Tessier-Lavigne, M., Placzek, M., Lumsden, A. G. S., Dodd, J., & Jessell, T. M. (1988). Chemotropic guidance of developing axons in the mammalian central nervous system. *Nature, 336*, 775–778.

Thompson, R. F. (1983). Neuronal substrates of simple associative learning: Classical conditioning. *Trends in Neuroscience, 6*, 270–275.

Thompson, R. F., Berger, T. W., Cegavske, C. F., Patterson, M. M., Roemer, R. A., Teyler, T. J., & Young, R. A. (1976). The search for the engram. *American Psychologist, 31*, 209–227.

Thompson, W. J., Kuffler, D. P., & Jansen, J. K. S. (1979). The effects of prolonged, reversible block of nerve impulses on the elimination of polyneuronal innervation of newborn rat skeletal muscle fibers. *Neuroscience, 4*, 271–281.

Thorndike, E. L. (1898). Animal intelligence: An experimental study of the associative processes in animals. *Psychological Review Series Monographs, 4* (Suppl. 2), 1–109.

Trisler, G. D., Schneider, M. D., & Nirenberg, M. (1981). A topographic gradient of molecules in retina can be used to identify neuron position. *Proceedings of the National Academy of Science, 78*, 2145–2149.

Tully, T. (1987). Drosophila learning and memory revisited. *Trends in Neuroscience, 10*, 330–335.

Tyler, T. J., & DiScenna, P. (1987). Long-term potentiation. *Annual Review of Neuroscience, 10*, 131–161.

van Harreveld, A., & Fifkova, E. (1975). Swelling of dendritic spines in the fascia dentata after stimulation of the perforant fibers as a mechanism of post-tetanic potentiation. *Experimental Neurology, 49*, 736–749.

Verma, A., Hirsch, D. J., Glatt, C. E., Ronnett, G. V., & Snyder, S. H. (1993). Carbon monoxide: A putative neural messenger. *Science, 259*, 381–384.

Walsh, C., & Cepko, C. L. (1992).Widespread dispersion of neuronal clones across functional regions of the cerebral cortex. *Science, 255*, 434–455.

Walter, J., Henke-Fahle, S., & Bonhoeffer, F. (1987). Avoidance of posterior tectal membranes by temporal retinal axons. *Development, 101*, 909–913.

Wetts, R., & Fraser, S. E. (1988). Multipotent precursors can give rise to all major cell types of the frog retina. *Science, 239*, 1142–1145.

Williams, J. H., Errington, M. L., Lynch, M. A., & Bliss, T. V. P. (1989). Arachidonic acid induces a long-term activity-dependent enhancement of synaptic transmission in the hippocampus. *Nature, 341*, 739–742.

Yeo, C. H., Hardiman, M. J., & Glickstein, M. (1985). Classical conditioning of the nictitating membrane response of the rabbit. I. Lesions of the cerebellar nuclei. *Experimental Brain Research, 60*, 87–98.

Zola-Morgan, S., Squire, L. R., & Amaral, D. G. (1989). Lesions of the amygdala that spare adjacent cortical regions do not impair memory or exacerbate the impairment following lesions of the hippocampal formation. *Journal of Neuroscience, 9*, 1922–1936.

CHAPTER 16

Benson, D. F. (1986). Aphasia and lateralization of language. *Cortex, 22*, 71–86.

Beversdorf, D. Q., Ratcliffe, N. R., Rhodes, C. H., & Reeves, A. G. (1997). Pure alexia: Clinical pathological evidence for a lateralized visual language association cortex. *Clinical Neuropathology, 16*(6), 328–331.

Blumenstein, S. E. (1997). A perspective on the neurobiology of language. *Brain and Language, 60*(3), 335–346.

Chesbro, B. (1998). BSE and prions: Uncertainties about the agent. *Science, 279*(5347), 42–43.

Editorial. (1993). Misreading dyslexia: Researchers debate causes and prevalence of disorder. *Scientific American*, (August), 14.

Efron, R. (1990). *The decline and fall of hemispheric specialization*. Hillsdale, NJ: Erlbaum.

Evarts, E. V., Wise, S. P., & Bousfield, D. (1985). *The motor system in neurobiology*. New York: Elsevier Biomedical Press.

Galaburda, A. M., Lethay, M., Kemper, T. L., & Geschwind, N. (1978). Right-left asymmetries of the brain. *Science, 199*(4331), 852–856.

Gandy, S., & Greengard, P. (1992). Amyloidogenesis in Alzheimer's disease: Some possible therapeutic opportunities. *Trends in Pharmacological Sciences, 13*, 108–113.

Gardner, R. A., & Gardner, B. T. (1978). Comparative psychology and language acquisition. *Annals of the New York Academy of Sciences, 309*, 37–76.

Gauger, L. M., Lombardino, L. J., & Leonard, C. M. (1997). Brain morphology in children with specific language impairment. *Journal of Speech, Language, and Hearing Research, 40*(6), 1272–1284.

Gazzaniga, M. (1994). *The cognitive neurosciences*. Cambridge, MA: MIT Press.

Georgopoulos, A. P., Lurito, J. T., Petrides, M., Schwartz, A. B., & Massey, J. T. (1989). Mental rotation of the neuronal population vector. *Science, 243*, 234–236.

Geschwind, N., & Galaburda, A. M. (1985). *Cerebral lateralization*. Cambridge, MA: MIT Press.

Goodall, J. (1986). *The chimpanzees of Gombe*. Cambridge, MA: The Belknap Press of Harvard University.

Harasty, J., Double, K. L., Halliday, G. M., Krill, J. J., & McRitchie, D. A. (1997). Language-associated cortical regions are proportionally larger in the female brain. *Archives of Neurology, 54*(2), 171–176.

Jaynes, J. (1976). *The origins of consciousness in the breakdown of the bicameral mind*. Boston: Houghton Mifflin.

Karaken, D. A., Unverzagt, G., Caldemeyer, K., Farlow, M. R., & Hutchins, G. D. (1998). Functional brain imaging in apraxia. *Archives of Neurology, 55* (1), 107–113.

Kimura, D. (1973). The asymmetry of the human brain. *Scientific American, 228*(3), 70–78.

Kimura D. (1992) . Sex differences in the brain. *Scientific American 267*(3), 118–125.

Kolb, B. & Whishaw, I. Q. (1996). *Fundamentals of human neuropsychology* (4th ed.). New York: Freeman.

Liberski, P. P., & Gajdusek, D. C. (1997). Kuru: Forty years later, a historical note. *Brain Pathology, 7*(1), 555–560.

Libet, B. (1985). Unconscious cerebral initiative and the role of conscious will in voluntary action. *Behavioral & Brain Sciences, 8*, 529–566.

Libet, B. (1987). Are the mental experiences of will and self-control significant for the performance of a voluntary act? *Behavioral & Brain Sciences, 10*, 783–786.

Libet, B. (1989). The timing of a subjective experience. *Behavioral & Brain Sciences, 12*, 183–185.

Macdonald, K. D., Fifkova, E., Jones, M. S. & Barth, D. S. (1998). Focal stimulation of the thalamic reticular nucleus induces local gamma waves in cortex. *Journal of Neurophysiology, 79*, 474–477.

Mattson, M. P. (1997). Advances fuel Alzheimer's conundrum. *Nature Genetics, 17*(3), 254–256.

Milner, A. D. (1997). Vision without knowledge. *Philosophical Transactions of the Royal Society of London: B Biological Sciences*, 352(1358), 1249–1256.

Mishkin, M., & Appenzeller, T. (1987). The anatomy of memory. *Scientific American*, 256(6), 80–89.

Mishkin, M., Suzuki, W. A., Gadran, D. G., & Vargha-Khadem, F. (1997). Hierarchical organization of cognitive memory. *Philosophical Transactions of the Royal Society of London B. Biological Sciences, 352*(1360), 1461–1467.

Nicoll, J. A. R., Roberts, G. W., & Graham, D. L. (1995). Apolipoprotein E⁴ allele is associated with deposition of amyloid ß-protein following head injury. *Nature Medicine, 1*(7), 135–137.

O'Keefe, J., & Nadel, L. (1978). *The hippocampus as a cognitive map*. Oxford, England: Oxford University Press.

Olton, D. S., & Papas, B. C. (1979). Spatial memory and hippocampal function. *Neuropsychologia, 17*, 669–682.

O'Reilly, R. C., Munkata, Y., & McClelland, J. L. (1998). *Explorations of computational neuroscience: Understanding the mind by simulating the brain*. Cambridge, MA: MIT Press. (in press).

Penfield, W., & Roberts, L. (1959). Speech and brain mechanisms. Princeton, NJ: Princeton University Press.

Petri, N., & Mishkin, M. (1994). Behaviorism, cognitivism, and the neuropsychology of memory. *American Scientist, 82*, 30–37.

Pihl, R. O., & Parkes, M. (1977). Hair element content in learning disabled children. *Science, 198*, 204–206.

Posner, M. I. & Raichle, M. E. (1994). *Images of mind*. New York: Freeman.

Rapport, R. L., Tan, C. T., & Whitaker, H. A. (1983). Language function and dysfunction among Chinese- and English-speaking polyglots: Cortical stimulation, Wada testing, and clinical studies. *Brain and Language, 18*, 342–360.

Roses, A. D. (1994). Apolipoprotein E affects the rate of Alzheimer's disease expression: ß-amyloid burden is a secondary consequence dependent of APOE genotype and duration of disease. *Journal of Neuropathology and Experimental Neurology, 53* (5), 429–437.

Rudel, R. G., Denckla, M. B., & Spalten, E. (1974). The functional asymmetry of Braille letter learning in normal sighted children. *Neurology, 24*, 733–738.

Sacks, O. (1985). *The man who mistook his wife for a hat and other clinical tales*. New York: Simon & Schuster.

Shaywitz, B. A., Shaywitz, S. E., Pugh, K. R., Constable, R. T., Skudlarski, P., Fulbright, R. K., Bronen, R. A., Shankweiler, D. P., & Katz, L. (1995). Sex differences in the functional organization of the brain for language. *Nature, 373* (6515), 607–609.

Sperry, R. (1982). Some effects of disconnecting the cerebral hemispheres. *Science, 217*, 1223–1226.

Stoffel, M., & Jan, L. Y. (1998). Epilepsy genes: Excitement traced to potassium channels. *Nature Genetics, 18*(1), 6–8.

Sutherland, R. J., & Rudy, J. W. (1989). Configural association theory: The role of the hippocampal formation in learning, memory, and amnesia. *Psychobiology, 17*, 129–144.

Trimble, M. R., Mendez, M. F., & Cummings, J. L. (1997). Neuropsychiatric symptoms from the temporolimbic lobes. *Journal of Neuropsychiatry and Clinical Neuroscience, 9*(3), 429–438.

Venneri, A., & Caffara, P. (1998). Transient autobiographic amnesia: EEG and single-photon emission CT evidence of an organic etiology. *Neurology, 50* (1), 186–191.

Wada, J. A., Clarke, R., & Hamm, A. (1975). Cerebral hemispheric asymmetry in humans: Cortical speech zones in 100 adult and 100 infant brains. *Archives of Neurology, 32*, 239–246.

Whalen, P. J., Rausch, S. L., Etcoff, N. L. McInerney, S. C., Lee, M. B., & Janke, M. A. (1998). Masked presentations of emotional facial expressions modulate amygdala activity without explicit knowledge. *Journal of Neuroscience, 18*(1), 411–418.

CHAPTER 17

Adamec, B. (1997). Transmitter systems involved in neural plasticity underlying increased anxiety and defense—implications for understanding anxiety following traumatic stress. *Neuroscience and Biobehavioral Reviews, 21*(6), 755–765.

Aghajanian, G. K., & Haigler, H. J. (1974). Mode of action of LSD on serotonergic neurons. In E. Costa, G. L. Gessa, & M. Sandler (Eds.), *Advances in biochemical pharmacology* (Vol. 10, pp. 167–178). New York: Raven Press.

Bayer, R. (1997). The medicinal uses of marijuana. *Annals of Internal Medicine, 127*(12), 1134.

Devane, W. A., Dysarz, F. A. I., Johnson, M. R., Melvin, L. S., & Howlett, A. C. (1988). Determination and characterization of a cannabinoid receptor in rat brain. *Molecular Pharmacology, 34*, 605–613.

Devane, W. A., Hanus, L., Breuer, A., Pertwee, R. G., Stevenson, L. A., Griffin, G., Gibson, D., Mandelbaum, A., Etinger, A., & Mechoulaum, R. (1992). Isolation and structure of a brain constituent that binds to the cannabinoid receptor. *Science, 258* (5090), 1946–1949.

Gatley, S. J., Lan, R., Voltkow, N. D., Pappas, N., King, P., Wong, C. T., Gifford, A. N., Pyatt, B., Dewey, S. L., & Makriyannis, A. (1998). Imaging the brain marijuana receptor: Development of a radioligand that binds to cannabinoid CB₁ receptors in vivo. *Journal of Neurochemistry, 70*(1), 417–423.

Herkenham, M., Lynn, A. B., Johnson, M. R., Melvin, L. S., deCosta, B. R., & Rice, K. C. (1991). Characterization and localization of cannabinoid receptors in rat brain: A quantitative in vitro autoradiographic study. *Journal of Neuroscience, 11*, 563–583.

Insel, T. R., Battaglia, G., Johannessen, J. N., Marra, S., & DeSouza, E. B. (1989). 3, 4-Methylenedioxymethamphetamine (ecstasy) selectively destroys brain serotonin terminals in rhesus monkeys. *Journal of Pharmacology & Experimental Therapeutics, 249*, 713–720.

Julien, R. M. (1992). *A primer of drug action*. New York: Freeman.

Langer, S. Z. (1997). 25 years since the discovery of presynaptic receptors: Present knowledge and future perspectives. *Trends in Pharmacological Sciences, 18*(3), 95–99.

Marek, G. J., & Aghajanian, G. K. (1996). LSD and the phenethylamine hallucinogen DOI are potent partial agonists at 5-HT₂ₐ receptors on interneurons in rat piriform cortex. *Journal of Pharmacology and Experimental Therapeutics, 278*(3), 1373–1382.

Medina, J. H., Pena, C., Novas, M. L., Paladini, A. C., & DeRobertis, E. (1987). Acute stress induces an increase in rat cerebral cortex levels of n-butyl-ß-carboline-3-carboxylate, an endogenous benzodiazepine binding inhibitor. *Neurochemistry International, 11*, 255–259.

O'Connell, T. J. (1997). The medicinal uses of marijuana. *Annals of Internal Medicine, 127*(12), 1134.

Olds, J., & Milner, B. (1954). Positive reinforcement produced by electrical stimulation of the septal area and other regions of the rat brain. *Journal of Comparative and Physiological Psychology, 47*, 419–427.

Pert, C. B., & Snyder, S. H. (1973). Opiate receptor: Demonstration in nervous tissue. *Science, 179*, 1011–1014.

Sangameswaran, C., Fales, H. M., Friedrich, P., & De-Blas, A. L. (1986). Purification of a benzodiazepine-like immunoreactivity in human brain. *Proceedings of the National Academy of Science, USA, 83*, 9236–9240.

Solomon, R. L. (1980). The opponent-process theory of acquired motivation: The cost of pleasure and the benefits of pain. *American Psychologist, 35*, 691–712.

Trinkoff, A.M., & Storr, C.L. (1997). Collecting substance-use data with an anonymous mailed survey. *Drug and Alcohol Dependence, 48*, 1–8.

CHAPTER 18

Barr, C. E., Mednick, S. A., & Munk-Jorgensen, P. (1990). Exposure to influenza epidemics during gestation and adult schizophrenia. *Archives of General Psychiatry, 47*, 869–874.

Bhatara, V. S., Gupta, S., & Flugsrud-Brekenridge, M. (1998). Childhood-onset schizophrenia. *Archives of General Psychiatry, 55*(1), 90–92.

Breggin, P. R., & Breggin, G. R. (1994). *Talking back to Prozac*. New York: St. Martin's Press.

Cade, J. R. (1975). Lithium—when, why and how? *Medical Journal of Australia, 1*(22), 684–686.

Cannon, T. D., Mednick, S. A., Parnas, J., Schulsinger, F., Praestholm, J., & Vestergaard, A. (1993). Developmental brain abnormalities in the offspring of schizophrenic mothers. I. Contributions of genetic and perinatal factors. *Archives of General Psychiatry, 50*(7), 551–564.

Crow, T. J., Taylor, G. R., & Tyrrell, D. A. J. (1986). Two syndromes in schizophrenia and the viral hypothesis. *Progress in Brain Research, 65*, 17–27.

Frankel, F. H. (1984). The use of electroconvulsive therapy in suicidal patients. *American Journal of Psychotherapy, 38*, 384–391.

Hemsley, D. R. (1993). Perception and cognition in schizophrenia. In R. L. Cromwell & C. R. Snyder (Eds.), *Schizophrenia: Origins, processes, treatment and outcome* (pp. 135–150). New York: Oxford University Press.

Ismail, B., Cantor-Graae, E., & McNeil, Z. F. (1998). Neurological abnormalities in schizophrenic patients and their siblings. *American Journal of Psychiatry*, 155(1), 84–89.

Kramer, D. (1993). *Listening to Prozac*. New York: Viking.

Luria, A.B. (1968). *The mind of the mnemonist*. New York: Basic Books.

Olfsun, M., Marcus, S., Sackheim, H. A., Thompson, J., & Pincus, H. A. (1998). Use of ECT for the inpatient treatment of recurrent major depressions. *American Journal of Psychiatry, 155*(1), 22–29.

Oke, A. F., Carver, L. A., & Adams, R. N. (1993). Dopamine-initiated disturbances of thalamic information processing in schizophrenia? In R. L. Cromwell & C. R. Snyder (Eds.), *Schizophrenia: Origins, processes, treatment and outcome* (pp. 31–47). New York: Oxford University Press.

Swerdlow, J. (1997). Vincent van Gogh: Lullaby of color. *National Geographic, 192,*(4), 101–129.

APPENDIX

Schuler, G. D., & 113 co-authors. (1996). A gene map of the human genome. *Science, 274,* 540–546.

Yalow, R. (1992). The Nobel lecture on immunology. (The Nobel Prize for Physiology and Medicine, 1977, awarded to Rosalyn S. Yalow.) *Scandinavian Journal of Immunology, 35* (1), 1–23.

FURTHER READINGS

CHAPTER 1

BOOKS

Behaviorism

Modgil, S. M., & Modgil, C. (Ed.). (1987). *B. F. Skinner: Consensus and controversy*. Philadelphia, Falmer Press.

Skinner, B. F.(1974). *About behaviorism*. New York: Random House.

Broca, Paul

Sagan, C. (1979). *Broca's brain: Reflections on the romance of science*. New York: Random House.

Schiller, F. (1992). *Paul Broca, founder of French anthropology, explorer of the brain*. New York: Oxford University Press.

Darwin, Charles/Evolution

Bell, P. R.(1959). *Darwin's biological work: Some aspects reconsidered*. Cambridge, England: Cambridge University Press.

Darwin, Charles (1987). Geology, transmutation of species, metaphysical enquiries. In P. H. Barret (Ed.), *Charles Darwin's notebooks, 1836–1844*, Ithaca, NY: Cornell University Press.

Poulton, E. B. (1896). *Charles Darwin and the theory of natural selection*. New York: Macmillian.

Ward, C. H. (1943). *Charles Darwin and the theory of evolution*. New York: New Home Library.

Da Vinci, Leonardo

Randall, J. H. (1961). *The School of Padua and the emergence of modern science*. Padua, Italy: Editrice Antenore.

Zammattio, C. (1980). *Leonardo the scientist*. New York: McGraw Hill.

Determinism/Free Will

Thomas, R. (1969). *Essays on the active powers of man*. Cambridge, MA: MIT Press, Cambridge.

Mind/Body Problem

Baker, G. P. (1996). *Descartes' dualism*. New York: Routledge.

Chalmers, D. J. (1996). *The conscious mind: In search of a fundamental theory*. New York: Oxford University Press.

Descartes, R. (1961). *Rules for the direction of the mind*. (L. Lafleur, trans.). Indianapolis, IN: Liberal Arts Press. (Original work published in 1637)

Foster, J. (1991). *The immaterial self: A defense of the cartesian dualist conception of mind*. New York: Routledge.

Leder, D. (1990). *The absent body*. Chicago: University of Chicago Press

Martin, C. (1991). *Mind, brain, behavior: The mind/body problem and the philosophy of psychology*. New York: Walter de Gruyter.

Smythies, J., & Beloff, J. (Ed.). (1989). *The case for dualism*. Charlottesville: University Press of Virginia.

Phrenology

Cooter, R. (1984). *The cultural meaning of popular science: Phrenology and the organization of consent in nineteenth century Britain*. New York: Cambridge University Press.

Leahey, T. H. (1984). *Psychology's occult double: Psychology and the problem of pseudoscience*. Chicago: Nelson-Hall.

Reductionism

Charles, D., & Lennon, K. (Ed.). (1992). *Reduction, explanation, and realism*. New York: Oxford University Press.

Dupre, J. (1993). *The disorder of things: Metaphysical foundations of the disunity of science*. Cambridge, MA: Harvard University Press.

Idinopulos, T. A., & Yonan E. A. (Ed.). (1994). *Religion and reductionism: Essays on Eliade, Segal, and the challenge of the social sciences for the study of religion*. New York: Brill.

Solipsism

Dore, C. (1989). *God, suffering and solipsism*. New York: St. Martin's Press.

Sperry, Roger

Erdmann, E. (1991). *Beyond a world divided: Human values in the brain-mind science of Roger Sperry*. New York: Random House.

Trevarthen, C. B. (1990). *Brain circuits and functions of the mind: Essays in honor of Roger W. Sperry*. New York: Cambridge University Press.

Teleology

Bogdan, R. J. (1994). *Grounds for cognition: How goal-guided behavior shapes the mind*. Hillsdale, NJ: Erlbaum.

Henerson, L. J. (1917). *The order of nature*. Cambridge, MA: Harvard University Press.

Kant, I. (1931). *Kant's critique of judgment*. (J. H. Bernard, Trans.). London: Macmillan. (Original worked published in 1788)

Templeton, J. M. (Ed.). (1994). *Evidence of purpose: Scientists discover the creator*. New York: Continuum.

CHAPTER 2

BOOKS

Axoplasmic Transport

Iqbal, Z. (1986). *Axoplasmic transport*. Boca Raton, FL: CRC Press.

Ochs, S. (1982). *Axoplasmic transport and its relation to other nerve functions*. New York: Wiley.

DNA

Watson, J. D. (1968). *The double helix: A personal account of the discovery of the structure of DNA*. New York: Atheneum.

Genes

Andreoli, T. E. (1987) *Membrane Physiology*. New York: Plenum Medical Book Co.

Benos, D. J. (1991). *Developmental biology of membrane transport systems*. San Diego, CA: Academic Press.

Claudio, T. (1990). *Protein-membrane interactions*. San Diego, CA: Academic Press.

Kotyk, A. (1988). *Biophysical chemistry of membrane functions*. New York: Wiley.

Papa, S., & Tager, J. M. (Ed.). (1995). *Biochemistry of cell membranes: A compendium of selected topics*. Boston: Birkhauser Verlag.

Restak, R. M. (1994). *Receptors*. New York: Bantam Books.

Rodriguez, R. L., & Chamberlin, M. J. (1982). *Promoters: Structure and function*. New York: Praeger.

Stein, W. D. (1990). *Channels, carriers, and pumps: An introduction to membrane transport*. San Diego, CA: Academic Press.

Weiss, T. F. (1996). *Cellular biophysics*. Cambridge, MA: MIT Press.

Yeagle, P. (1993). *The membranes of cells*. San Diego, CA: Academic Press.

Myelin

Martenson, R. E. (1992). *Myelin: Biology and chemistry*. Boca Raton, FL: CRC Press.

Neuronal Development and Repair

Cuello, A. C. (Ed.). (1993). *Neuronal cell death and repair*. New York: Elsvier.

Dale, P. (1994). *Neural activity and the growth of the brain*. New York: Cambridge University Press.

Motoy, K. (1995). *The synapse: Function, plasticity, and neurotrophism*. New York: Oxford University Press.

Shaw, C. A. (1996). *Receptor dynamics in neural development*. Boca Raton, FL: CRC Press.

See also Chapter 15.

Proteins

Agutter, P. S. (1991). *Between nucleus and cytoplasm*. New York: Chapman & Hall.

Avila, J. (1990). *Microtubule proteins.*, Boca Raton, FL: CRC Press.

Burgoyne, R. D. (1991). *The neuronal cytoskeleton*. New York: Wiley-Liss.

Iakushevich, L. V. (1996). *Methods of theoretical physics and their applications to biopolymer science*. Commack, NY: Nova Science Publishers.

Kreis, T., & Vale, R. (1993) *Guidebook to the cytoskeletal and motor proteins*. New York: Oxford University Press.

Kyte, J. (1995). *Mechanism in protein chemistry*. New York: Garland.

Parry, D. (1995). *Intermediate filament structure*. Austin, TX: Landes.

Steiner, R. F. (1991). *The physical chemistry of biopolymer solutions: Application of physical techniques to the study of proteins and nucleic acids*. Teaneck, NJ: World Scientific.

Transmitters

Bjorklund, T. H. (1984). *Classical transmitters in the CNS*. New York: Elsvier.

See also Chapters 4 and 5.

ARTICLES

Decussation

Sperry, R. (1982). Some effects of disconnecting the cerebral hemispheres. *Science, 217*(4566), 1223–1226.

Dendrites

Barinaga, M. (1995). Dendrites shed their dull image. *Science, 268*, 200–201.

DNA

Matsuoda, M., Nagawa, F., Akazaki, K., Kingsbury, L., Yoshida, K., Müller, U., Larue, D. T., Winer, J. A., & Sakano, H. (1991). Detection of somatic DNA recombination in the transgenic mouse brain. *Science, 254*, 81–86.

Golgi, Camillo

Altamura, A. C. (1996). Camillo Golgi (1843–1926). *American Journal of Psychiatry, 153*(4), 552.

Membrane Transport

Ayala, S. J. (1994). Transport and internal organization of membranes: Vesicles, membrane networks and GTP-binding proteins. *Journal of Cell Science, 107*(4), 753–763.

Bohl, E., Shuman, H. A., & Boos, W. (1995). Mathematical treatment of the kinetics of binding protein dependent transport systems reveals that both the substrate loaded and unloaded binding proteins interact with the membrane components. *Journal of Theoretical Biology, 172*(1), 83.

Campbell, J. L., & Schekman, R. (1996). The sorting of membrane proteins during the formation of ER-derived transport vesicles. *NATO ASI series. Series H, Cell Biology, 96,* 209.

Cid-Arregui, A., Parton, R. G., Simons, K., & Dotti, C. G. (1995). Nocodazole-dependent transport, and Brefeldin A–sensitive processing and sorting, of newly synthesized membrane proteins in cultured neurons. *Journal of Neuroscience, 15*(6), 4259.

Ossig, R., Laufer, W., Schmitt, H. D., & Gallwitz, D. (1995). Functionality and specific membrane localization of transport GTPases carrying C-terminal membrane anchors of synaptobrevin-like proteins. *EMBO Journal, 14*(15), 3645.

Verde, C., Pascale, M. C., Martire, G., Lotti, L. V., Torrisi, M. R., Helenius, A., & Bonatti, S. (1995). Effect of ATP depletion and DTT on the transport of membrane proteins from the endoplasmic reticulum and the intermediate compartment to the Golgi complex. *European Journal of Cell Biology, 67*(3), 267.

Neuron Development

Iversen, S. D., & Dunnett, S. B.(1989). Functional compensation afforded by grafts of foetal neurones. *Progression Neuro-Psychopharmacology & Biological Psychiatry, 13,* 453–567.

Neuron Doctrine

Dierig, S. (1994). Extending the neuron doctrine: Carl Ludwig Schleich (1859–1922) and his reflections on neuroglia at the inception of the neural-network concept in 1894. *Trends in Neuroscience, 17*(11), 449.

Shepherd, G. M., De Felipe, J., Jones, E. G., & Young J. Z. (1992). Foundations of the neuron doctrine. *Nature, 356,* 624.

Proteins

Rao, A., & Steward, O. (1991). Evidence that protein constituents of post-synaptic membrane specializations are locally synthesized: Analysis of proteins synthesized within synaptosomes. *Journal of Neuroscience, 11*(9), 2881–2895.

Ramón y Cajal, Santiago

DeFelipe, J., & Jones E. G. (1992) Santiago Ramón y Cajal and methods in neurohistology. *Trends in Neurosciences, 15*(7), 237.

Vesicles

Colombo, M. I., Mayorga, L. S., Casey, P. J., & Stahl, P. D. (1992). Evidence of a role for heterotrimeric GTP-binding proteins in endosome fusion. *Science, 255,* 1695–1700.

CHAPTER 3

BOOKS

Electric Circuits

Cook, N. S. (Ed.). (1990). *Potassium channels: Structure, classification, function, and therapeutic potential.* New York: Halsted Press.

DePont, J. (1992). *Molecular aspects of transport proteins.* New York: Elsevier.

Johnson, D. E. (1992). *Electric circuit analysis.* Englewood Cliffs, NJ: Prentice Hall.

Kinne, R. K. H. (1990). *Basic principles in transport.* New York: Karger.

See also Chapter 2.

Molecular Bonding

Fliszar, S. (1994). *Atoms, chemical bonds, and bond dissociation energies.* New York: Springer-Verlag.

March, N. H. (1993) *Chemical physics of free molecules.* New York: Plenum Press.

Winter, M. J. (1994) *Chemical bonding.* New York: Oxford University Press.

Zewail, A. (Ed.). (1992). *The chemical bond: Structure and dynamics.* Boston: Academic Press.

Sodium/Potassium Pump

Horisberger, J. D. (1994). *The Na/K-ATPase: Structure-function relationship.* Boca Raton, FL: CRC Press.

Thermodynamics

Craig, N. C. (1992). *Entropy analysis: An introduction to chemical thermodynamics.* New York: VCH Publishers.

Goldstein, M. (1993). *The refrigerator and the universe: Understanding the laws of energy.* Cambridge, MA: Harvard University Press.

Mackey, M. C. (1992). *Time's arrow: The origins of thermodynamic behavior.* New York: Springer-Verlag.

Nernst, W. (1907). *Experimental and theoretical applications of thermodynamics to chemistry.* New York: Scribner's.

ARTICLES

Ion Channels

Cohen, S. A., & Barachi, R. L. (1992). Voltage-dependent sodium channels. *International Review of Cytology, 137*(C), 55–104.

Coulter, K. L., Perier, F., Radeke, C. M., & Vandenberg, C. A. (1995). Identification and molecular localization of a pH-sensing domain for the inward rectifier and potassium channel HIR. *Neuron, 15*(5), 1157.

De Rycker, C., & Schoffeniels, E. (1990). Molecular aspects of human brain sodium channel. *Neuroscience, 38*(3), 809.

Ferrer-Montiel, A. V., & Montal, M. (1994). Structure-function relations in ligand-gated ion channel: Reconstitution in lipid bilayers and heterologous expression. *Methods, 6*(1), 60.

Landes, G. M., Curran, M. E., & Keating, M. T. (1995). Molecular characterization and refined genomic localization of three human potassium ion channel gates. *Cytogenetics and Cell Genetics, 70*(3–4), 280.

Min, L., Jan, Y. N., & Jan, L. Y. (1992). Specification of subunit assembly by the hydrophilic amino-terminal domain of the shaker potassium channel. *Science, 257,* 1225.

Pak, M. D., Covarrubias, M., Ratcliffe, A., & Salkoff, L. (1991). A mouse brain homolog of the *Drosophila Shab* K+ channel with conserved delayed-rectifier properties. *Journal of Neuroscience, 11*(3), 869–880.

Pongs, O. (1993). Receptor site for open channel blockers of shaker voltage-gated potassium channels: molecular approaches. *Journal of Receptor Research, 13*(1–4), 503–512.

Sato, C., & Matsumoto, G. (1993). A sodium channel model. *Annals of the New York Academy of Sciences, 707,* 330.

Schoenherr, R., & Heinemann, S. H. (1996). Molecular determinants for activation and inactivation of HERG, a human inward rectifier potassium channel. *Journal of Physiology, 493*(3), 635.

Shahjahan, M., Yamada, M., Nagaya, M., Kawai, M., & Nakazawa, A. (1993). Cloning and characterization of sodium channel cDNA from puffer fish. *Annals of the New York Academy of Sciences, 707,* 346.

Yao, X., Chang, A. Y., Boulpaep, E. L., Segal, A. S., & Desir, G. V. (1996) Molecular cloning of a glibenclamide-sensitive, voltage-gated potassium channel expressed in rabbit kidney. *Journal of Clinical Investigation, 97*(11), 2525.

Yellen, G., Jurman, M. E., Abramson, T., & MacKinnon, R. (1991). Mutations affecting internal TEA blockade identify the probable pore-forming region of a potassium channel. *Science, 251,* 939.

Membrane Potential

Berdan, R. C., Essaw, J. C., & Wang, R. (1993). Alterations in membrane potential after axotomy at different distances from the soma of an identified neuron and the effect of depolarization on neurite outgrowth and calcium channel expression. *Journal of Neurophysiology, 69*(1), 151.

Molecular Bonding

Sutcliffe, B. T. (1996). The development of the idea of a chemical bond. *International Journal of Quantum Chemistry, 58*(6), 645.

Nernst Equation

Aoki, K. (1991). Nernst equation complicated by electric random percolation at conducting polymer-coated electrodes. *Journal of Electroanalytical Chemistry and Interfacial Electrochemistry, 310*(1–2), 1–12.

Feiner, A. S. & McEvoy, A. J. (1994). The Nernst equation. *Journal of Chemical Education, 71*(6), 493.

Thermodynamics

Leff, H. S. (1996). Thermodynamic entropy: The spreading and sharing of energy. *American Journal of Physics, 64*(10), 1261.

CHAPTER 4

BOOKS

Action Potentials

Byrne, J. H. (1994). *An introduction to membrane transport and bioelectricity: Foundations of general physiology and electrochemical signaling.* New York: Raven Press.

Deutsch, S. (1993). *Understanding the nervous system: An engineering perspective.* New York: IEEE Press.

Douglas, J. 1992). *Nerve and muscle excitation.* Sunderland, MA: Sinauer Associates.

Calcium Channel

Bock, G. R., & Ackrill, K. (1995). *Calcium waves, gradients and oscillations.* Chichester, England: Wiley.

Foa, P. P., & Walsh, M. F. (1994). *Ion channels and ion pumps: Metabolic and endocrine relationships in biology and clinical medicine.* New York: Springer-Verlag.

Hurwitz, L., Partridge, L. D., & Leach, J. K. (1991). *Calcium channels: Their properties, functions, regulation and clinical relevance.* Boca Raton, FL: CRC Press.

Jeff, T. Allen, A., Noble, D., & Reuter, H. (Eds.). (1989). *Sodium-calcium exchange.* New York: Oxford University Press.

Kostiuk, P. G. (1992). *Calcium ions in nerve cell function.* New York: Oxford University Press.

Morad, M. (Ed.). (1988). *The calcium channel: Structure, function and implications.* New York: Springer-Verlag, 1988.

Venter, J. C., & Triggle, D. (Eds.). (1987). *Structure and physiology of the slow inward calcium channel.* New York: Liss.

Potassium Channel

Colatsky, T. J. (Ed.). (1988). Potassium channels: Basic function and therapeutic aspects. *Proceedings of the 29th annual A. N. Richards Symposium* [held at Valley Forge]. New York: Liss.

ARTICLES

Action Potentials

Hausser, M., Stuart, G., Racca, C., & Sakmann, B. (1995). Axonal initiation and active dendritic propagation of action potentials in substantia nigra neurons. *Neuron, 15*(3), 637.

Hollins, B., & Ikeda, S. R. (1996). Inward currents underlying action potentials in rat adrenal chromaffin cells. *Journal of Neurophysiology, 76*(2), 1195.

Inglis, J. T., Leeper, J. B., Burke, D., & Gandevia, S. C. (1996). Morphology of action potentials recorded from human nerves using microneurography. *Experimental Brain Research, 110*(2), 308.

Kiss, I., & Shizgal, P. (1989). Improved artifact rejection and isolation of compound action potentials by means

of digital subtraction. *Journal of Neuroscience, 30,* 219–229.

Larkum, M. E., Rioult, M. G., & Lusher, H.-R. (1996). Propagation of action potentials in the dendrites of neurons from rat spinal cord slice culture. *Journal of Neurophysiology, 75*(1), 154.

Mackenzie, P. J., Umemiya, M., & Murphy, T. H. (1996). Ca2+ imaging of CNS axons in culture indicates reliable coupling between single action potentials and distal functional release site. *Neuron, 16*(4), 783.

Pichon, Y. (1995). Pharmacological induction of rhythmical activity and plateau action potentials in unmyelinated axons. *Journal of Physiology, 89* (4–6), 171.

Pinault, D. (1995). Backpropagation of action potentials generated at ectopic axonal loci: Hypothesis that axon terminals integrate local environmental signals. *Brain Research, 21*(1), 42.

Tibbs, G. R., Dolly, J. O., & Nicholls, D. G. (1996). Evidence for the induction of repetitive action potentials in synaptosomes by K+ channel inhibitors: An analysis of plasma membrane ion fluxes. *Journal of Neurochemistry, 67*(1), 389.

Calcium Channels

Callewaert, G., Eilers, J., & Konnerth, A. (1996). Axonal calcium entry during fast "sodium" action potentials in rat cerebellar Purkinje neurons. *Journal of Physiology, 495*(3), 641.

Charles, A. C., & Hales, T. G. (1995). Mechanisms of spontaneous calcium oscillations and action potentials in immortalized hypothalamic (GT1–7) neurons. *Journal of Neurophysiology, 73*(1), 56.

Hiromu, Y. (1993). Diversity of calcium channel subtypes in presynaptic terminals of the chick ciliary ganglion. *Annals of the New York Academy of Sciences, 707,* 379.

Koike, T., Tanaka, S., & Takashima, A. (1993). L-type calcium channel regulates depolarization-induced survival of rat superior cervical ganglion cells in vitro. *Annals of the New York Academy of Sciences, 707,* 356–358.

Lancaster B., Nicoll, R. A., & Perkel, D. J. (1991). Calcium activates two types of potassium channels in rat hippocampal neurons in culture. *Journal of Neuroscience, 11*(1), 23–30.

Lueke, J. I., Dunlap, K., & Turner, T. J. (1993). Multiple calcium channel types control glutamatergic synaptic transmission in the hippocampus. *Neuron, 11*(5), 895–902.

Markram, H. Helm, P. J., & Sakmann, B. (1995). Dendritic calcium transients evoked by single back-propagating action potentials in rat neocortical pyramidal neurons. *Journal of Physiology, 485*(1), 1.

Niidome, T., & Mori, Y. (1993). Primary structure and tissue distribution of a novel calcium channel from rabbit brain. *Annals of the New York Academy of Sciences, 707,* 368.

Singer, D., Biel, M., Lotan, I., Flockerzi, V., Hofmann, F., & Dascal, N. (1991). The roles of the subunits in the function of the calcium channel. *Science, 253,* 1553–1556.

Human Genome Project

Gibbons, A. (1991). Genome patent fight erupts. *Science, 254,* 183–186.

Roberts, L. (1992). NIH gene patents, round two. *Science, 255,* 912–914.

Patch Clamping

Hamill, O. P., Huguenard, J. R., & Prince, D. A. (1991). Patch-clamp studies of voltage-gated currents in identified neurons of the rat cerebral cortex. *Cerebral Cortex, 1*(1), 48–61.

Potassium Conductance

Alkadhi, K. A., & Simples, J. E. (1991). Effects of inorganic potassium channel blockers on calcium require-

ment of transmission in a sympathetic ganglion. *Journal of the Autonomic Nervous System, 34*(2–3), 221.

Bezanilla, F., Perozo, E., Papazian, D. M., & Stephani, E. (1991). Molecular basis of gating charge immobilization in shaker potassium channel. *Science, 254,* 679–684.

Chung, J. M., & Spencer, A. N. (1996). Effect of dopamine on a voltage-gated potassium channel in a jellyfish motor neuron. *Journal of Biochemistry and Molecular Biology, 29*(2), 151.

Pape, H. C., Budde, T., Mager, R., & Kisvardy, Z. F. (1994). Prevention of Ca++-mediated action potentials in GABAergic local circuit neurons of rat thalamus by a transient K+ current. *Journal of Physiology, (London), 478,* 403–422.

Sodium Conductance

Callaway, J. C., & Ross, W. N. (1995). Frequency-dependent propagation of sodium action potentials in dendrites of hippocampal CA1 pyramidal neurons. *Journal of Neurophysiology, 74*(4), 1395.

Colling, S. B., & Wheal, H. V. (1994). Fast sodium action potentials are generated in the distal apical dendrites of rat hippocampal CA1 pyramidal cells. *Neuroscience Letters, 172*(1–2), 73.

West, J. W,. Numann, R., Murphy, B. J., Scheuer, T., & Catterall, W. A. (1991). A phosphorylation site in the Na+ channel required for modulation by protein kinase C. *Science, 254,* 866–868.

Chapter 5

BOOKS

Acetylcholine

Aquilonius, S., & Gillberg, P. (1990). *Cholinergic neurotransmission: Functional and clinical aspects.* New York: Elsevier.

Frotshcer, M., & Misgeld, U. (Eds.). (1989). *Central cholinergic synaptic transmission.* Boston: Birkauser Verlag.

Shafferman, A., & Velan, B. (1992). *Multidisciplinary approaches to cholinesterase functions.* New York: Plenum Press.

Skok, V. I. (1989). *Neuronal acetylcholine receptors.* New York: Consultants Bureau.

Stone, T. W. (Ed.). (1995). *CNS neurotransmitters and neuromodulators: Acetylcholine.* Salem, MA: CRC Press.

Wess, J. (1995). *Molecular mechanisms of muscarinic acetylcholine receptor function.* Austin, TX: R. G. Landes.

Adrenaline

Limbird, L. (Ed.). (1988). *The alpha–2 adrenergic receptors.* Clifton, NJ: Humana Press.

Stolk, J. M., U'Prichard, D. C., & Fuxe, K. (1988). *Epinephrine in the central nervous system.* New York: Oxford University Press.

Agonists and Antagonists

Barnard, E. A., & Costa, E. (Eds.). (1989). *Allosteric modulation of amino acid receptors: Therapeutic implications.* New York: Raven Press.

Bowery, N. G., Bittiger, H., & Olpe, H. R. (Eds.). (1990). *GABA^β receptors in mammalian function.* New York: Wiley.

Rodgers, R. J., & Cooper, S. J. (1991). *5-HT1A agonists, 5-HT3 antagonists and benzodiazepines: Their comparative behavioral pharmacology.* New York: Wiley.

Amino Acids as Transmitters

Baskys, A. (1994). *Metabotrophic glutamate receptors.* Austin, TX: R. G. Landes.

Krogsgaard-Larsen, P., & Hansen, J. J. (Eds.). (1992). *Excitatory amino acid receptors: Design of agonists and antagonists.* New York: E. Horwood.

Ottersen, O. P., & Storm-Mathisen, J. (Eds.). (1990). *Glycine neurotransmission.* New York: Wiley.

Palfreyman, M. G., Reynolds, I. J., & Skolnick, P. (Ed.). (1994)., CRC Press. *Direct and allasteric control of glutamate receptors.* Baco Raton: FL

Schwartz, J. C., & Haas, H. L. (Eds.). (1992). *The histamine receptor.* New York: Wiley-Liss.

Wheal, H. V., & Thomson, A. M. (1991). *Excitatory amino acids and synaptic transmission.* San Diego, CA: Academic Press.

Binding Sites

Roberts, S. M. (1989). Molecular recognition: Chemical and biochemical problems. *Proceedings of an International University of Exeter.* Cambridge, England: Royal Society of Chemistry.

Dopamine

Ashby, C. R. (1996). *The modulation of dopaminergic neurotransmission by other neurotransmitters.* Boca Raton, FL: CRC Press.

Fuxe, K. (Ed.). (1994). *Trophic regulation of the basal ganglia: Focus on dopamine neurons.* Tarrytown, NY: Pergamon.

Niznik, H. B. (Ed.). (1994). *Dopamine receptors and transporters: Pharmacology, structure, and function.* New York: Marcel Dekker.

Smeets, J. A. J. W., & Reiner, A. (Eds.). (1994). *Phylogeny and development of catecholamine systems in the CNS of vertebrates.* Cambridge, England: University of Cambridge Press.

Stone, T. W. (Ed.). (1996). *CNS neurotransmitters and neuromodulators: dopamine.* Salem, MA: CRC Press.

Waddington, J. L. (1993). *D1: D2 dopamine Receptor interactions: Neuroscience and psychopharmacologyj.* San Diego, CA: Academic Press.

GABA

Alkon, D. L. (1993). *Long-term transformation of an inhibitory into an excitatory GABAergic synaptic response.* Bethesda, MD: National Institute of Neurological and Communicative Disorders and Stroke.

Erdo, S. L. (Ed.). (1992). *GABA outside the CNS.* New York: Springer-Verlag.

Gap Junctions

Kanno, Y. (Ed.). (1995). *Intercellular communication through gap junctions.* New York: Elsevier.

Neuromuscular Junction

Kelly, A. M., & Blau, H. M. (Eds.). (1992). *Neuromuscular development and disease.* New York: Raven Press.

Vrbova, G. (1995). *Nerve-muscle interaction.* New York: Chapman & Hall.

Noradrenaline

Fillenz, M. (1990). *Noradrenergic neurons.* Cambridge, England: Cambridge University Press.

Heal, D. J., & Marsden, C. A. (Eds.). (1990). *The pharmacology of noradrenaline in the central nervous system.* New York: Oxford University Press.

Receptors

Giesen-Crouse, E. (Ed.). (1993). *Peripheral benzodiazepine receptors.* London: Academic Press.

Restak, R. M. (1994). *Receptors.* New York: Bantam Books.

Serotonin

Fozard, J. R., & Saxena, P. (Eds.). (1991). *Serotonin: Molecular biology, receptors, and functional effects.* Boston: Birkhauser Verlag.

Marsden, C. A., & Heal, D. J. (Ed.). (1992). *Central serotonin receptors and psychotrophic drugs.* Boston: Blackwell Scientific.

Stahl, S. M. (Ed.). (1992). *Serotonin 1A receptors in depression and anxiety.* New York: Raven Press.

Whitaker-Azmita, P. M., & Peroutka, S. J. (Eds.). (1990). *The neuropharmacology of serotonin*. New York: New York Academy of Sciences.

Substance P

Leeman, S. E., Krause, J. E., & Lembeck, F. (Eds.). (1991). *Substance P and related peptides*. New York: New York Academy of Sciences.

Synapse

Nicholls, D. G. (1994). *Proteins, transmitters, and synapses*. Oxford, England: Blackwell Scientific Publications.

Powis, D. A., & Bunn, S. J. (1995). *Neurotransmitter release and its modulation*. New York: Cambridge University Press.

Stone, T. W. (Ed.). (1991). *Aspects of synaptic transmission*. New York: Taylor & Francis.

Zimmermann, H. (1993). *Synaptic transmission: Cellular and molecular basis*. New York: Oxford University Press.

Vasopressin and Oxytocin

Ivell, R., & Russel, J. A. (Eds.). (1995). *Oxytocin: Cellular and molecular approaches in medicine and research*. New York: Plenum Press.

Pedersen, C. A. (Ed.). (1992). *Oxytocin in maternal, sexual, and social behaviors*. New York: New York Academy of Sciences.

ARTICLES

Acetylcholine

Eriksson, P., Ahlbom, J., & Fredriksson, A. (1992). Exposure to DDT during a defined period in neonatal life induces permanent changes in brain muscarinic receptors and behavior in adult mice. *Brain Research, 582*(2), 277–281.

Fabiani, M. E., Vlahos, R., & Story, D. F. (1996). Epithelium-dependent inhibition of cholinergic transmission in rat isolated trachea by potassium channel openers. *Pharmacological Research, 33*(4–5), 261.

Halvorsen, S. W., Schmid, H. A., McEachern, A. E., & Berg, D. K. (1991). Regulation of acetylcholine receptors on chick ciliary ganglion neurons by components from synaptic target tissue. *Journal of Neuroscience, 11*(7), 2177–2186.

Hasselmo, M. E., & Bower, J. M. (1992). Cholinergic suppression specific to intrinsic not afferent fiber synapses in rat piriform (olfactory) cortex. *Journal of Neurophysiology, 6*(5), 1222–1229.

Luetje, C. W., & Patrick, J. (1991). Both alpha- and beta-subunits contribute to the agonist sensitivity of neuronal nicotinic acetylcholine receptor. *Journal of Neuroscience, 11*(3), 837–845

Quirion, R., Wilson, A., Rowe, W., & Aubert, I. (1995). Facilitation of acetylcholine release and cognitive performance by an M-sub-2-muscarinic receptor antagonist in aged memory-impaired rats. *Journal of Neuroscience, 15*(2), 1455–1462.

Schulz, D. W., Loring, R. H., Aizenman, E., & Zigmond, R. E. (1991). Autoradiographic localization of putative nicotinic receptors in the rat brain using ^{125}I-neuronal bungarotoxin. *Journal of Neuroscience, 11*(1), 287–297.

Stanley, E. F., & Goping, G. (1991). Characterization of a calcium current in a vertebrate cholinergic presynaptic nerve terminal. *Journal of Neuroscience, 11*(4), 985–993.

Tan, H. S., & Collewijn, H. (1992). Muscarinic nature of cholinergic receptors in the cerebellar flocculus involved in the enhancement of the rabbit's optokinetic response. *Brain Research, 591*(2), 337–340.

Amino Acids as Transmitters

Bernath, S. (1992). Calcium-independent release of amino acid neurotransmitters: Fact or fiction? *Progress in Neurobiology, 38*, 57–91.

Carre, G. P., & C. W. Harley (1991). Population spike facilitation in the dentate gyrus following glutamate to the lateral supramammillary nucleus. *Brain Research, 568*, 307–310.

Giampaolo, M., Costa, E., Armstrong, D. M., & Vicini, S. (1991). Glutamate receptor subtypes mediate excitatory synaptic currents of dopamine neurons in midbrain slices. *Journal of Neuroscience, 11*(5), 1359–1366.

Jahr, C. E. (1992). High probability opening of NMDA receptor channels by L-glutamate. *Science, 255*, 470–472.

McCormick, D. A., & Williamson, A. (1991). Modulation of neuronal firing mode in cat and guinea pig LGN and by histamine: Possible cellular mechanisms of histaminergic control of arousal. *Journal of Neuroscience, 11*(10), 3188–3199.

Rainnie, D. G., & Shinnick-Gallagher, P. (1992). Trans-ACPD and L-APB presynaptically inhibit excitatory glutamatergic transmission in the basolateral amygdala (BLA). *Neuroscience Letters, 139*, 87–91.

Sah, P., Hestrin, S., & Nicoll, R. A. (1989). Tonic activation of NMDA receptors by ambient glutamate enhances excitation of neurons. *Science, 246*, 815.

Tabb, J. S., Kisk, P. E., Van Dyke, R., & Tetsufumi, U. (1992). Glutamate transport into synaptic vesicles: Roles of membrane potential, pH gradient, and intravesicular pH. *Journal of Biological Chemistry, 267* (22), 15412.

Yoon, K., & Rothman, S. M. (1991). Adenosine inhibits excitatory but not inhibitory synaptic transmission in the hippocampus. *Journal of Neuroscience, 11*(5), 1375–1380.

Autonomic Nervous System

Alevizos, A., Weiss, K., & Koester, J. (1989). SCP-containing R20 neurons modulate respiratory pumping in *Aplysia. Journal of Neuroscience, 9*(9), 3058–3071.

Cotransmitters

Church, P. J., & Lloyd, P. E. (1991). Expression of diverse neuropeptide cotransmitters by identified motorneurons in *Aplysia. Journal of Neuroscience, 11*(3), 618–625.

Dopamine

Hu, X.-T., & White, F. J. (1992). Repeated D1 dopamine receptor agonist administration prevents the development of both D1 and D2 striatal receptor supersensitivity following denervation. *Synapse, 10*, 206–216.

Lowenstein, P. R., Joyce, J. N., Coyle, J. T., & Marshall, J. F. (1990). Striosomal organization of cholinergic and dopaminergic uptake sites and cholinergic M1 receptors in the adult human stratum: A quantitative receptor autoradiographic study. *Brain Research, 510*, 122–126.

Mandel, R. J., Wilcox, R. E., & Randall, P. K. (1992). Behavioral quantification of striatal dopaminergic supersensitivity after bilateral 6-hydroydopamine lesions in the mouse. *Pharmacology, Biochemistry and Behavior, 41*, 343–347.

Zigmond, M. J., Abercrombie, E. D., Berger, T. W., Grace, A. A., & Stricker, E. M. (1990). Compensations after lesions of central dopaminergic neurons: Some clinical and basic implication. *Trends in Neuroscience, 13*(7), 290–296.

Escape Responses

Chichery, M. P., & Chichery, R. (1987). The anterior basal lobe and control of pre-capture in the cuttlefish (*sepia officinalis*). *Physiology and Behavior, 40*, 329–336.

Cleal, K. S., & Prete, F. R. (1996). The predatory strike of free ranging praying mantises, sphodromantis lineola (Burmeister): II. Strikes in the horizontal plane. *Brain, Behavior and Evolution, 48*(4), 191–204.

Eaton, R. C., Hofve, J. C., & Fetcho, J. R. (1995). Beating the competition: The reliability hypothesis for Mauthner axon size. *Brain, Behavior, and Evolution, 45*(4), 183–194.

Engel, J. E., & Wu, C.-F. (1996). Altered habituation of an identified escape circuit in Drosophila memory mutants. *Journal of Neuroscience, 16*(10), 3486–3499.

Faber, D. S., Korn, D., & Lin, J.-W. (1991). Role of medullary networks and postsynaptic membrane properties in regulating Mauthner cell responsiveness to sensory excitation. *Brain, Behavior, and Evolution, 37*(5), 286–297.

Foreman, M. B., & Eaton, R. C. (1993). The direction change concept for reticulospinal control of goldfish escape. *Journal of Neuroscience, 13*(10), 4101–4113.

Evoked Potential

Heginbotham, L. R., & Dunwiddie, T. V. (1991). Long-term increases in the evoked population spike in the CA1 region of rat hippocampus induced by beta-adrenergic receptor activation. *Journal of Neuroscience, 11*(8), 2519–2527.

McCarthy, G. Wood, C. C., & Allison, T. (1991). Cortical somatosensory evoked potentials: I. Recordings in the monkey macaca fascicularis. *Journal of Neurophysiology, 66*(1), 53–63.

Peng, Y., & Horn, J. P. (1991). Continuous repetitive stimuli are more effective than bursts for evoking LHRH release in bullfrog sympathetic ganglia. *Journal of Neuroscience, 11*(1), 85–95.

GABA/Benzodiazepine

Kellogg, C. K., Sullivan, A. T., Biran, D., & Ison, J. R. (1991). Modulation of noise-potentiated acoustic startle via the benzodiazepine-gamma-aminobutyric acid receptor complex. *Behavioral Neuroscience, 105*(5), 640–646.

Michelson, H. B., & Wong, R. K. S. (1991). Excitatory synaptic responses mediated by GABA_A receptors in the hippocampus. *Science, 253*, 1420–1423.

Primus, R. J., & Kellogg, C. K. (1991). Experience influences environmental modulation of function at the benzodiazepine/GABA receptor chloride channel complex. *Brain Research, 545*, 257–264.

Rown, G. A., & Lucki, I. (1992). Discriminative stimulus properties of the benzodiazepine receptor antagonist flumazenil. *Psychopharmacology, 107*, 103–112.

Stefanski, R., Palejko, W., Kostowski, W., & Plaznik, A. (1992). The comparison of benzodiazepine derivatives and serotonergic agonists and antagonists in two animal models of anxiety. *Neuropharmacology, 31*(12), 1257–1258.

Nitric Oxide

Snyder, S. H. (1992). Nitric oxide: First in a new class of neurotransmitters? *Science, 257*, 494–496.

Noradrenaline

West, W. L., Yeomans, D. C., & Proudfit, H. K. (1993). The function of noradrenergic neurons in mediating antinociception induced by electrical stimulation of the locus coeruleus in two different sources of Sprague-Dawley rats. *Brain Research, 626*(1–2), 127–135.

Serotonin

Dringenberg, H. C., & Vanderwolf, C. H. (1994). Transcallosal evoked potentials: Behavior-dependent modulation by muscarinic and serotonergic receptors. *Brain Research Bulletin, 34*(6), 555–562.

Minor, B. G., Wojciech, D., Post, C., Jonsson, G., & Archer, T. (1988). Noradrenergic and serotonergic involvement in brief shock-induced analgesia in rats. *Behavioral Neuroscience, 102*(6), 915–924.

Synapse

Alder, J., Lu, B., Valtorta, F., Greengard, P., & Poo, M. (1992). Calcium-dependent transmitter secretion reconstituted in *xenopus* oocytes: Requirement for synaptophysin. *Science, 257*, 657–661.

Alevizos, A., Weiss, K. R., & Koester, J. (1991). Synaptic actions of identified peptidergic cell R15 in *Aplysia*:

II. Contraction of pleuroabdominal connectives mediated by motor neuron L7. *Journal of Neuroscience, 11*(5), 1275–1281.

Betz, W. J., & Bewick, G. W. (1992). Optical analysis of synaptic vesicle recycling at the frog neuromuscular junction. *Science, 255*, 200–203.

Cohen, M. W., Jones, O. T., & Angelides, K. J. (1991). Distribution of Ca^{2+} channels on frog motor nerve terminals revealed by fluorescent omega-conotoxin. *Journal of Neuroscience, 11*(4), 103–1039.

Delaney, K., Tank, D. W., & Zucker, R. S. (1991). Presynaptic calcium and serotonin-mediated enhancement of transmitter release at crayfish neuromuscular junction. *Journal of Neuroscience, 11*(9), 2631–2643.

Gruol, D. H., Jacquin, T., & Yool, A. J. (1991). Single-channel K+ currents recorded from the somatic and dendritic regions of cerebellar Purkinje neurons in culture. *Journal of Neuroscience, 11*(4), 1002–1015.

Hall, D. H., and Russell, R. L. (1991). The posterior nervous system of the nematode *Caenorhabditis elegans*: Serial reconstruction of identified neurons and complete pattern of synaptic transmission. *Journal of Neuroscience, 11*(1),1–22.

Vasopressin and Oxytocin

Landgraf, R. (1992). Central release of vasopressin: Stimuli, dynamics, consequences. *Progress in Brain Research, 91*, 29–39.

Messenberg, G., & Simmons, W. H. (1987). Specific antagonists of the acute behavioral response to centrally administered vasopressin in mice. *Neuropharmacology, 26*(1), 79–83.

CHAPTER 6

BOOKS
Alpha-adrenergic Receptors

Fujiwara, M., Sugimoto, T., & Kogure, K. (Eds.). (1992). *Alpha-adrenoreceptors: Signal transduction, ionic channels, and effector organs*. Princeton. NJ: Excerpta Medica.

Ruffolo, R. R. (Ed.). (1991). *Alpha-adrenoreceptors: Molecular biology, biochemistry and pharmacology*. New York: Karger.

Angina Pectoris

Braunwald, E. (1994). *Unstable angina: Diagnosis and management [microform]*. Rockville, MD: U. S. Dept. of Health and Human Services.

Autonomic Nervous System

Burnstock, G., & Hoyle, C. H. V. (Eds.). (1992). *Autonomic neuroeffector mechanisms*. Philadelphia: Harwood Academic Publishers.

Karczar, A. G., Koketsu, K., & Nishi, S. (Eds.). (1986). *Autonomic and enteric ganglia*. New York: Plenum Press.

Korczyn, D. (Ed.). (1995). *Handbook of autonomic nervous system dysfunction*. New York: Dekker.

Loewy, A. D., & Spyer, K. M. (Eds.). (1990). *Central regulation of autonomic functions*. New York: Oxford University Press.

Nilsson, S., & Holmgren, S. (Eds.). (1994). *Comparative physiology and evolution of the autonomic nervous system*. Chur, Switzerland: Harwood Academic Publishers.

Autoreceptors

Dunwiddie, T. V., & Lovinger, D. M. (1993). *Presynaptic receptors in the mammalian brain*. Boston: Birkhauser.

Kalsner, S., & Westfall, T. C. (1990). *Presynaptic receptors and the question of autoregulation of neurotransmitter release*. New York: New York Academy of Sciences.

Beta-adrenergic Receptors

Perkins, J. P. (Ed.). (1991). *The beta-adrenergic receptors*. Clifton, NJ: Humana Press.

Teague, S. M., & Hordinsky, J. R. (1992). *Tolerance of beta blocked hypertensives during orthostatic and altitude stresses*. Springfield, VA: Available through the National Technical Information Service.

Endocrinology

Brook, G. D., & Marshall, N. J. (1996). *Essential endocrinology* (3rd ed.) Cambridge, MA: Blackwell Science.

Goodman, H. M. (1994). *Basic medical endocrinology* (2nd ed.) New York: Raven Press.

Hadley, M. E. (1992). *Endocrinology* (3rd ed.) Englewood Cliffs, NJ: Prentice Hall.

G Proteins

Iismaa, T. P., Biden, T. J., & Shine, J. (1995). *G protein–coupled receptors*. Austin, TX: Landes.

Peroutka, S. J. (Ed.). (1994)., *Handbook of receptors and channels: G protein–coupled receptors*. Boca Raton, FL: CRC Press.

Ruffolo, R. R., & Hollinger, M. A. (Eds.). (1995)., *G protein–coupled transmembrane signaling mechanisms*. Boca Raton, FL: CRC Press.

Peripheral Neurotransmitters

Bell, C. (Ed.). (1991). *Novel peripheral neurotransmitters*. New York: Pergamon Press.

Second Messengers

Bell, R. M., Exton, J. H., & Prescott, S. M. (Eds.). (1996). *Lipid second messengers*. New York: Plenum Press.

Boulton, A. A., Baker, G. B., & Taylor, C. W. (Eds.). (1992). *Intracellular messengers*. Totowa, NJ: Humana Press.

Municion, M., & Miras-Portugal, M. T. (Eds.). (1994). *Cell signal transduction, second messengers, and protein phosphorylation in health and disease*. New York: Plenum Press.

ARTICLES
Alpha-adrenergic Receptors

Pascual, J., del Arco, C., Gonzalez, A. M., & Pazos, A. (1992). Quantitative light microscopic autoradiographic localization of a sub–2-adrenoceptors in the human brain. *Brain Research, 585*(1–2), 116–127.

Malik, K. F., Morrell, J. I., & Feder, H. H. (1993). Effects of alpha–2-adrenergic drugs in the medial preoptic area and medial basal hypothalamus on lordosis in the guinea pig. *Brain Research, 628*(1–2), 26–30.

Surprenant, A., Horstman, D. A., Akbarali, H., & Limbird, L. E. (1992). A point mutation of the α2-adrenoceptor that blocks coupling to potassium but not calcium currents. *Science, 257*, 977–980.

Autoreceptors

Hjorth, S., & Auerbach, S. B. (1995). 5-HT-sub(1A) autoreceptors and the mode of action of selective serotonin reuptake inhibitors (SSRI). *Behavioral Brain Research, 73*(1–2), 281–283

Mott, D. D., Xie, C., Wilson, W. A., & Swartzwelder, H. S. (1993). GABA-sub(B) autoreceptors mediate activity-dependent disinhibition and enhance signal transmission in the dentate gyrus. *Journal of Neurophysiology, 69*(3), 674–691.

Tepper, J. M., & Groves, P. M. (1990). In vivo electrophysiology of central nervous system terminal autoreceptors. (Reprinted from *Presynaptic receptors and the question of autoregulation of neurotransmitter release*.) *Annals of the New York Academy of Sciences, 604*, 470–487.

G Proteins

Cohen-Armon, M., Hammel, I., Anis, Y., Homburg, S., & Dekel, N. (1996). Evidence for endogenous ADP-ribosylation of GTP-binding proteins in neuronal cell nucleus: Possible induction by membrane depolarization. *Journal of Biological Chemistry, 271*(42), 26200.

Kwatra, M. M., Lefkowitz, R. J., & Caron, M. G. (1994). Partially purified reconstituted G protein–coupled receptors as substrates of specific receptor kinases. *Methods, 6*(1), 11.

Lamb, T. D., & Pugh, E. N., Jr. (1992). G protein cascades: Gain and kinetics. *Trends in Neuroscience, 15*(8), 291–298.

Shiekhattar, R., & Aston-Jones, G. (1994). Activation of adenylate cyclase attenuates the hyperpolarization following single action potentials in brain noradrenergic neurons independently of protein kinase A. *Neuroscience, 62*(2), 523.

Second Messengers

Finch, E. A., Turner, T. J., & Goldin, S. M. (1991). Calcium as a coagonist of inositol 1,4,5-triphosphate-induced calcium release. *Science, 252*, 443–446.

Kasai, H., & Petersen, O. H. (1994). Spatial dynamics of second messengers: IP-sub-3- and cAMP as long-range and associative messengers. *Trends in Neuroscience, 17*(3), 95–101.

Nakanishi, S., Maeda, N., & Mikoshiba, K. (1991). Immunohistochemical localization of an inositol 1,4,5-triphosphate receptor, P^{400} in neural tissue: Studies in developing and adult mouse brain. *Journal of Neuroscience, 11*(7), 2075–2086.

Numann, R., Catterall, W. A., & Scheuer, T. (1991). Functional modulation of brain sodium channels by protein kinase C phosphorylation. *Science, 254*, 115–118.

Reinhart, R. H., Sungwon, C., Martin, B. L., Brautigan, D. L., & Levitan, I. B. (1991). Modulation of calcium-activated potassium channels from rat brain by protein kinase A and phosphatase 2A. *Journal of Neuroscience, 11*(6), 1627–1635.

CHAPTER 7

BOOKS
Electric Fish

Moller, P. (1995). *Electric fishes: History and behavior*. New York: Chapman & Hall.

Whittaker, V. P. (1992). *The cholinergic neuron and its target: The electromotorinnervation of the electric ray "torpedo" as a model*. Boston: Birkhauser.

Neuroanatomy

Butler, A. B. (1996). *Comparative vertebrate neuroanatomy: Evolution and adaptation*. New York: Wiley-Liss.

Filley, C. M. (1995). *Neurobehavioral anatomy*. Niwot, CO: University Press of Colorado.

Nauta, W. J. H. (1993). *Neuroanatomy: Selected papers of Walle J. H. Nauta*. Boston: Birkhauser.

Nolte, J. (1993). *The human brain: An introduction to its functional anatomy*. St Louis, MO: Mosby.

ARTICLES
Development

Cameron, W. E., Jodkowski, H. F., & Guthrie, R. D. (1991). Electrophysiological properties of developing phrenic motorneurons in the cat. *Journal of Neurophysiology, 65*(3), 671–679.

Houenou, L. J., McManaman, J. L., Prevette, D., & Oppenheim, R. W. (1991). Regulation of putative muscle-derived neurotrophic factors by muscle activity and innervation: *in vivo* and *in vitro* studies. *Journal of Neuroscience, 11*(9), 2829–2837.

Dorsal Horn

Koerber, H. R., Seymour, A. W., & Mendell, L. M. (1991). Tuning of spinal networks to frequency components of spike trains in individual afferents. *Journal of Neuroscience, 11*(10), 3178–3187.

Electric Fish

Rankin, C. H., & Moller, P. (1992). Temporal patterning of electric organs discharges in the African electric catfish. *Malapterurus electricus* (Gmelin). *Journal of Fish Biology, 40*, 49–58.

Locomotion

Noga, B. R., Kriellaars, D. J., & Jordan, L. M. (1991). The effect of selective brainstem or spinal cord lesions on treadmill locomotion evoked by stimulations of the mesencephalic or pontomedullary locomotor regions. *Journal of Neuroscience, 11*(6), 1691–1700.

Wetzel, M. C. (1990). Learning and rhythmic human EMG in ecological perspective. *Physiology and Behavior, 48*, 113–120.

Spinal Reflexes

Menelson, B., & Frank, E. (1991). Specific monosynaptic sensory-motor connections form in the absence of patterned neural activity and motorneuronal cell death. *Journal of Neuroscience, 11*(5), 1390–1403.

Sachs, B. D., & Bitran, D. (1990). Spinal block reveals roles for brain and spinal cord in the mediation of reflexive penile erections in rats. *Brain Research, 528*, 99–108.

Motor Pathways

Lee, M. T., & O'Donovan, M. J. (1991). Organization of hindlimb muscle afferent projections to lumbosacral motorneurons in the chick embryo. *Journal of Neuroscience, 11*(8), 2564–2573.

Spinal Nerves

Niijima, A., Jiang, Z.-Y., Daunton, N. G., & Fox, R. A. (1987). Effect of copper sulfate on the rate of afferent discharge in the gastric branch of the vagus nerve in the rat. *Neuroscience Letters, 80*, 71–74.

Nudo, R. J., & Masterton, R. B. (1989). Descending pathways to the spinal cord: II. Quantitative study in tectospinal tract in 23 mammals. *Journal of Comparative Neurology, 286*, 96–119.

CHAPTER 8

BOOKS

Blood-Brain Barrier

Pardridge, W. M. (1991). *Peptide drug delivery to the brain.* New York: Raven Press.

Segal, M. B. (ed.). (1992). *Barriers and fluids of the eye and brain.* Boca Raton, FL: CRC Press.

Bell's Palsy

Waxman, B. (1984). *Electrotherapy for treatment of facial nerve paralysis.* Rockville, MD: U. S. Dept. of Health and Human Services, Public Health Service.

Carpal Tunnel Syndrome

Butler, S. J. (1996). *Conquering carpal tunnel syndrome and other repetitive strain injuries: A self-care program.* Oakland, CA: New Harbinger Publications.

Cranial Nerves

Szekely, G. (1993). *The efferent system of cranial nerve nuclei: A comparative neuromorphological study.* Berlin, Germany: Springer-Verlag.

Hemiplegia

Bach-y-Rita, P. (1995). *Nonsynaptic diffusion neurotransmission and late brain reorganization.* New York: Demos.

Limbic System

Kalivas, P. W., & Barnes, C. D. (eds.). (1993). *Limbic motor system and neuropsychiatry.* Boca Raton, FL: CRC Press.

Neocortex

Young, M. P. (1995). *The analysis of cortical connectivity.* Austin, TX: R. G. Landes.

Phrenology

Cooter, R. (1984). *The cultural meaning of popular science: Phrenology and the organization of consent in nineteenth-century Britain.* Cambridge, MA: Cambridge University Press.

Leahey, T. H. (1983). *Psychology's occult doubles: Psychology and the problem of pseudoscience.* Chicago: Nelson-Hall.

Fowler, O. S. (1842). *Phrenology proved, illustrated, and applied.* New York: O. S. & L. N. Fowler.

Sizer, N. (1882). *Forty years in phrenology: Embracing recollections of history, anecdote, and experience.* New York: Fowler & Wells.

Stroke

Bevan, R. D., & Bevan, J. A. (1994). *The human brain circulation: Functional changes in disease.* Totowa, NJ: Humana Press.

Ventricles

Boulton, A. A., Baker, G. B., & Walz, W. (eds.). (1988). *The neuronal microenvironment.* Clifton, NJ: Humana Press.

Vestibulo-ocular Reflex

Peterka, R. J. (1991). *Relation between perception of vertical axis rotation and vestibulo-ocular reflex symmetry.* Portland, OR: Good Samaritan Hospital & Medical Center.

Sharpe, J. A., & Baraber, H. O. (eds.). (1993). *The vestibulo-ocular reflex and vertigo.* New York: Raven Press.

ARTICLES

Basal Ganglia

Gimenez-Amaya, J.-M., & Graybiel, A. M. (1991). Modular organization of projection neurons in the matrix compartment of the primate striatum. *Journal of Neuroscience, 11*(3), 779–791.

Snyder-Keller, A. M. (1991). Development of striatal compartmentalization following pre- or postnatal dopamine depletion. *Journal of Neuroscience, 11*(3), 10–21.

Blood-Brain Barrier

Beazley, L. D., & Tennant, M. (1992). A breakdown of the blood-brain barrier is associated with optic nerve regeneration in the frog. *Visual Neuroscience, 9*, 001–007.

Goldman, H., Berman, R. F., Gershon, S., Murphy, S., Morehead, M., & Altman, H. J. (1991). Cerebrovascular permeability and cognition in the aging rat. *Neurobiology of Aging, 13*, 57–62.

Brainstem Projections

Aston-Jones, G., Akaoka, H., Charlety, P., & Chouvet, G. (1991). Serotonin selectively attenuates glutamate-evoked activation of noradrenergic locus coeruleus neurons. *Journal of Neuroscience, 11*(3), 760–769.

Berridge, C. W., & Foote, S. L. (1991). Effects of locus coeruleus activation on electroencephalographic activity in neocortex and hippocampus. *Journal of Neuroscience, 11*(10), 3135–3145.

Neocortex

Garcia-Munoz, M., Young, S. J., & Groves, P. M. (1991). Terminal excitability of the corticostriatal pathway. I. Regulation by dopamine receptor stimulation. *Brain Research, 551*, 195–206.

Jacobs, K. M., & Donoghue, J. P. (1991). Reshaping the cortical motor map by unmasking latent intracortical connectins. *Science, 251*, 944–946.

LoTurco, J. J., Blanton, M. G., & Kriegstein, A. R. (1991). Initial expression and endogenous activation of NMDA channels in early neocortical development. *Journal of Neuroscience, 11*(3), 792–799.

Walsh, C., & Cepko, C. L. (1992). Widespread dispersion of neuronal clones across functional regins of the cerebral cortex. *Science, 255*, 434–440.

Webster, M. J., Ungerleider, L. G., & Bachevalier, J. (1991). Connections of inferior temporal areas TE and TEO with medial temporal-lobe structures in infant and adult monkeys. *Journal of Neuroscience, 11*(4), 1095–1116.

CHAPTER 9

BOOKS

Auditory System

Durrant, J. D. (1995). *Bases of hearing science.* Baltimore: Williams & Wilkins.

Fay, R. R., & Popper, A. N. (Eds.). (1994). *Comparative hearing: mammals.* New York: Springer-Verlag.

Kryter, K. D. (1994). *The handbook of hearing and the effects of noise: Physiology, psychology, and public health.* San Diego, CA: Academic Press.

Olfaction and Gustation

Doty, R. L. (Ed.). (1995). *Handbook of olfaction and gustation.* New York: Dekker.

Laing, D. G., Doty, R. L., & Beripohl, W. (Eds.). (1992). *The human sense of smell.* New York: Springer-Verlag.

Schab, F. R., & Crowder, R. G. (1995). *Memory for odors.* Mahwah, NJ: Erlbaum.

Somatosensory

Baumgarner, C. (1993). *Clinical electrophysiology of the somatosensory cortex: A combined study using electrocorticography, scalp-EEG, and magnetoencephalography.* Vienna: Springer-Verlag.

Vision

Daw, N. (1995). *Visual development.* New York: Plenum Press.

Hubel, D. H. (1995). *Eye, brain, and vision.* New York: Scientific American Library.

Tovee, M. J. (1996). *An introduction to the visual system.* Cambridge; MA: Cambridge University Press.

Wandell, B. A. (1995). *Foundations of vision.* Sunderland, MA: Sinauer.

Zeki, S. (1993). *A vision of the brain.* Oxford, England: Blackwell Scientific Publications.

ARTICLES

Acoustic Startle

Commissaris, R. L., Harrington, G. M., Baginski, T. J., & Altman, H. J. (1988). MR/Har and MNRA/Har Maudsley rat strains: Differences in acoustic startle habituation. *Behavior Genetics, 18*(6), 663–669.

Hammond, G. R., & Leitner, D. S. (1990). Augmentation of the rat's acoustic startle reflex by nonreflexogenic stimuli. *Behavioral Neuroscience, 104*(6), 841–848.

Parham K., & Willott, J. F. (1990). Effects of inferior colliculus lesions on the acoustic startle response. *Behavioral Neuroscience, 104–*(6), 831–840.

Adaptation

King, C., & Hall, W. G. (1990). Developmental change in unilateral olfactory habituation is mediated by anterior commissure maturation. *Behavioral Neuroscience, 104*(5), 796–807.

Miller, E. K., Gochin, P. M., & Gross, C. (1991). Habituation-like decrease in the responses of neurons in inferior temporal cortex of the macaque. *Visual Neuroscience, 7*, 357–362.

Agnosia

Humphrey, G. K., Goodale, M. A., & Gurnsey, R. (1991). Orientation discrimination in a visual form agnosic: Evidence from the McCollough Effect. *Psychological Science, 2*(5), 331–335.

Anosmia

Walker, J. C., Reynolds, J. H., Warren, W. W., & Sidman, J. D. (1990). Responses of normal and anosmic subjects to odorants. In B. G. Green, J. R. Mason & M. R. Kare, (eds.), *Chemical Senses: Vol. 2.* New York: Dekker.

Auditory System

Fuchs, P. A., & Murrow, B. W. (1992). Cholinergic inhibition of short (outer) hair cells of the chick's cochlea. *Journal of Neuroscience, 12*(3), 800–809.

Fujita, I., & Konishi, M. (1991). The role of GABAergic inhibition in processing of interaural time difference in the owl's auditory system. *Journal of Neuroscience, 11*(3), 722–739.

Glendenning, K. K., Masterton, R. B., Baker, B. N., & Wenthold, R. J. (1991). Acoustic chiasm III: Nature, distribution, and sources of afferents to the lateral superior olive in the cat. *Journal of Comparative Neurobiology, 310*, 377–400.

Hellman, W. S., & Hellman, R. P. (1990). Intensity discrimination as the driving force for loudness. Application to pure tones in quiet. *Journal of the Acoustical Society of America, 87*(3), 1255–1265.

Knudsen, E. I., Esterly, S. D., & du Lac, S. (1991). Stretched and upside-down maps of auditory space in the optic tectum of blind-reared owls: Acoustic basis and behavioral correlates. *Journal of Neuroscience, 11*(6), 1727–1747.

Rajan, R. (1990). Functions of the efferent pathways to the mammalian cochlea. In M. Rowe & L. Aitkin (Eds.), *Information processing in mammalian auditory and tactile system* (pp. 81–96). New York: Wiley-Liss.

Ruggero, M. A., & Rich, N. C. (1991). Furosemide alters organ of corti mechanics: Evidence for feedback of outer hair cells upon the basilar membrane. *Journal of Neuroscience, 11*(4), 1057–1067.

Simmons, A. M., Schwartz, J. J., & Ferragamo, M. (1992). Auditory nerve representation of a complex communication sound in backgrounds. *Journal of the Acoustical Society of America, 919*(5), 2831–2844.

Binocular Vision

Grasse, K. L., & Cynader, M. (1991). The accessory optic system in frontal-eyed animals. In A. Leventhal (Ed.), *Vision and visual dysfunction: Vol. 4*, (pp. 111–139). New York: Macmillian Press.

Moore, R. J., Spear, P. D., Kim, C. B. Y., & Xue, J.-T. (1992). Binocular processing in the cat's dorsal lateral geniculate nucleus: III. Spatial frequency, orientation, and direction sensitivity of nondominant-eye influences. *Experimental Brain Research, 89*, 588–598.

Depth Perception

Lepore, F., Samson, A., Paradis, M.-C., Ptito, M., & Guillemot, J.-P. (1992). Binocular interaction and disparity coding at the 17–18 border: Contribution of the corpus callosum. *Experimental Brain Research, 90*, 129–140.

Development of Sensory Systems

Boothe, R. G. (1990). Experimentally induced and naturally occurring monkey models of human amblyopia. In M. A. Berkley & W. C. Stebbins, (Eds.), *Comparative perception: Vol. I. Basic mechanisms* (pp. 461–486). Wiley.

Coleman, J., McDonald, A. J., Pinek, B., & Zrull, M. C. (1992). The inferior colliculus: Calbindin and parvalbumin immunosensitivity in neural grafts. *Experimental Neurobiology, 115*, 142–145.

Hagedorn, M., & Fernald, R. D. (1992). Retinal growth and cell addition during embryogenesis in the teleost, *Haplochromis burtoni. Journal of Comparative Neurology, 321*, 193–208.

Harmon, A. M. (1991). Generation and death of cells in the dorsal lateral geniculate nucleus and superior colliculus of the wallaby, *Setonix brachyurus* (quokka). *Journal of Comparative Neurology, 313*, 469–478.

Holtzman, D. A., & Halpern, M. (1990). Embryonic and neonatal development of the vomeronasal and olfactory systems in garter snakes (*Thamnophis spp.*). *Journal of Morphology. 203*(2), 123–140.

Neville, H. J. (1990). Intermodal competition and compensation in development. (Reprinted from *The development and neural bases of higher cognitive functions.*) *Annals of the New York Academy of Sciences, 608*, 71–91.

Northmore, D. P. M., & Celenza, M. A. (1992). Recovery of contrast sensitivity during optic nerve regeneration in fish. *Experimental Neurobiology, 115*, 69–72.

Tong, L., Kalil, R. E., & Spear, P. D. (1991). Development of the projections from the dorsal lateral geniculate nucleus to the lateral suprasylvian visual area of cortex in the cat. *Journal of Comparative Neurology, 314*, 526–533.

Gustation

Bice, P. J., & Kiefer, S. W. (1990). Taste reactivity in alcohol preferring and nonpreferring rats. *Alcoholism: Clinical and Experimental Research, 14*(5), 721–727.

Bigiani, A. R., & Roper, S. D. (1991). Mediation of responses to calcium in taste cells by modulation of a potassium conductance. *Science, 252*, 126–128.

Scott, T. R., & Plata-Salaman, C. R. (1991). Coding of taste quality. In T. V. Getchell (Ed.), *Smell and taste in health and disease* (pp. 345–368). New York: Raven Press.

Odor Avoidance

Sullivan, R. M., & Wilson, D. A. (1991). Neural correlates of conditioned odor avoidance in infant rats. *Behavioral Neuroscience, 105*(2), 307–312.

Olfaction

Cornwell-Jones, C. A., Decker, M. W., Gianulli, T., Wright, E. L., & McGaugh, J. L. (1990). Norepinephrine depletion reduces the effects of social and olfactory experience. *Brain Research Bulletin, 25*, 643–649.

Slotnick, B. M., & Risser, J. M. (1990). Odor memory and odor learning in rats with lesions of the lateral olfactory tract and mediodorsal thalamic nucleus. *Brain Research, 529*, 23–29.

Walker, J. C., Kurtz, D. B., Shore, F. M., Ogden, M. W., & Reynolds, J. H. (1990). Apparatus for the automated measurement of the responses of humans to odorants. *Chemical Senses, 15*(2), 165–177.

Photoreceptors

Hood, D. C., & Birch, D. G. (1992). A computational model of the amplitude and implicit time of the *b*-wave of the human ERG. *Visual Neuroscience, 8*, 107–126.

Sensory Deprivation and Recovery

Mitchell, D. E. (1991). The long-term effectiveness of different regimens of occlusion on recovery from early monocular deprivation in kittens. *Phil. Trans. R. Soc. Lond. B., 333*, 51–79.

Skavenski, A. A., & Heinen, S. J. (1991). Recovery of visual responses in foveal V1 neurons following bilateral lesions in adult monkey. *Experimental Brain Research, 83*, 670–674.

Somatosensory Systems

Brown, P. B., Gladfelter, W. E., Culberson, J. C., Covalt-Dunning, D., Sonty, R. V., Pubols, L. M., & Millecchia, R. J. (1991). Somatotopic organization of single primary afferent axon projections to cat spinal cord dorsal horn. *Journal of Neuroscience, 11*(1), 298–309.

De Ryck, M., Von Reempts, J., Duytschaever, H., Van Deuren, B., & Clincke, G. (1992). Neocortical localization of tactile/proprioceptive limb placing reactions in the rat. *Brain Research, 573*, 44–60.

Garraghty, P. E., Pons, T. P., & Kaas, J. H. (1990). Ablations of areas 3b (SI proper) and 3a of somatosensory cortex in Marmosets deactivate the second and parietal ventral somatosensory areas. *Somatosensory and Motor Research, 7*(2), 125–135.

Sound Localization

Heffner, R. S., & Heffner, H. E. (1992). Visual factors in sound localization in mammals. *Journal of Comparative Neurobiology, 317*, 219.

Stanford, T. R., Kuwada, S., & Batra, R. (1992). A comparison of the interaural time sensitivity of neurons in the inferior colliculus and thalamus of the unanesthetized rabbit. *Journal of Neuroscience, 12*(8), 3200–3216.

Vestibular System

Corcoran, M. L., Fox, R. A., & Daunton, N. G. (1990). The susceptibility of Rhesus monkeys to motion sickness. *Aviation, Space, and Environmental Medicine, 61*(9), 807–809.

Stoffregen, T. A., & Riccio, G. E. (1991). An ecological critique of the sensory conflict theory of motion sickness. *Ecological Psychology, 3*(3), 159–194.

Vision

Baizer, J. S., Underleider, L. G., & Desimone, R. (1991). Organization of visual inputs to the inferior temporal and posterior parietal cortex in macaques. *Journal of Neuroscience, 11*(1), 168–190.

Berkley, M. A. (1990). Behavioral determination of the spatial selectivity of contrast adaptation in cats: Some evidence for a common plan in the mammalian visual system. *Visual Neuroscience, 4*, 413–426.

Chalupa, L. M., & Dreher, B. (1991). High precision systems require high precision "blueprints": A new view regarding the formation of connections in the mammalian visual system. *Journal of Cognitive Neuroscience, 3*(3), 209–219.

Condo, G. J., & Casagrande, V. A. (1990). Organization of cytochrome oxidase staining in the visual cortex of nocturnal primates (*Galago crassicaudatus* and *Galago senegalensis*): I. Adult patterns. *Journal of Comparative Neurobiology, 293*, 632–645.

Cooper, R. M., Thurlow, G. A., & Jeeva, A. (1991). Effects of flashing-diffuse light on [2-^{14}C] deoxyglucose uptake in the visual system of the black-hooded rat. *Behavioral Brain Research, 46*, 63–70.

DeMarco, P. J., Jr., Bilotta, J., & Powers, M. K. (1991). DL–2-amino–4-phosphonobutyric acid does not eliminate "on" responses in the visual system of goldfish. *Proc. Natl. Acad. Sci. USA, 88*, 3787–3791.

Doyan, J., & Milner, B. (1991). Right temporal-lobe contribution to global visual processing. *Neuropsychologia, 29*(5), 343–360.

Dunlop, S. A., Humphrey, M. F., & Beazley, L. D. (1992). Displaced retinal ganglion cells in normal frogs and those with regenerated optic nerves. *Anatomy and Embryology, 185*(5), 431–438.

Ellard, C. G., Chapman, D. G., & Cameron, K. A. (1991). Calibration of retinal image size with distance in the Mongolian gerbil: Rapid adjustment of calibrations in different contexts. *Perception & Psychophysics, 40*(1), 38–42.

Erickson, M. A., Robinson, P., & Lisman, J. (1992). Deactivation of visual transduction without guanosine triphosphate hydrolysis by G protein. *Science, 257*, 1255–1258.

Gûntûrkûn, O. (1991). The functional organization of the avian visual system. In R. J., Andrew (Ed.), *Neural and Behavioral Plasticity* (pp. 92–105). New York: Oxford University Press.

Kosslyn, S. M., Flynn, R. A., Amsterdam, J. B., & Wang, G. (1990). Components of high-level vision: A cognitive neuroscience analysis and accounts of neurological syndromes. *Cognition, 34*, 203–277.

Löwel, S., & Singer, W. (1992). Selection of intrinsic horizontal connections in the visual cortex by correlated neuronal activity. *Science, 255*, 209–212.

Martinet, L., Serviëre, J., & Peytevin, J. (1992). Direct retinal projections of the "non-image forming" system to the hypothalamus, anterodorsal thalamus and basal telencephalon of mink (*Mustela vison*) brain. *Experimental Brain Research, 89*, 373–382.

Merigan, W. H., Katz, L. M., & Maunsell, J. H. R. (1991). The effects of parvocellular lateral geniculate lesions on the acuity and contrast sensitivity of macaque monkeys. *Journal of Neuroscience, 11*(4), 994–1001.

Mignard, M., & Malpeli, J. G. (1991). Paths of information flow through visual cortex. *Science, 251*, 1249–1251.

Schiller, P. H., Logothetis, N. K., & Charles, E. R. (1991). Parallel pathways in the visual system: Their role in perception at isoluminance. *Neuropsychologia. 29*(6), 433–441.

Siegel, R. M., & Read, H. L. (1993). Temporal processing in the visual brain. (Reprinted from *Temporal information processing in the nervous system: Spatial reference to dyslexia and dysphasia.*) Annals of the New York Academy of Sciences, *682*, 171–178.

Van Essen, D. C., Anderson, C. H., & Felleman, D. J.(1992). Information processing in the primate visual system: An integrated systems perspective. *Science, 255*, 419–423.

Weller, R. E., & Kaas, J. H. (1989). Parameters affecting the loss of ganglion cells of the retina following ablations of striate cortex in primates. *Visual Neuroscience, 3*, 327–349.

Zeki, S., Watson, D. G., Lueck, C. J., Friston, K. J., Kennard, C., & Frackowiak, R. S. J. (1991). A direct demonstration of functional specialization in human visual cortex. *Journal of Neuroscience, 11*(3), 641–649.

Zheng, D., LaMantia, A.-S., & Purves, D. (1991). Specialized vascularization of the primate visual cortex. *Journal of Neuroscience, 11*(8), 2622–2629.

Zimmerman, R. P., & Levine, M. W. (1991). Complicated substructure from simple circularly symmetric Gaussian processes within the centers of goldfish ganglion cell receptive fields. *Visual Neuroscience, 7*, 547–559.

Visual Acuity

Hodos, W., Macko, K. A., & Bessette, B. B. (1984). Near-field acuity changes after visual system lesions in pigeons: II. Telencephalon. *Behavioral Brain Research, 13*, 15–30.

Visuospatial

Adelstein, A., & Crowne, D. P. (1991). Visuospatial asymmetries and interocular transfer in the split-brain rat. *Behavioral Neuroscience, 105*(3), 459–469.

Mondor, T. A., & Bryden, M. P. (1992). On the relation between visual spatial attention and visual field asymmetries. *Quarterly Journal of Experimental Psychology. 44*(3), 529–555.

Oakley, M. T., & Eason, R. G. (1990). Subcortical gating in the human visual system during spatial selective attention. *International Journal of Psychophysiology, 9*, 105–120.

CHAPTER 10

BOOKS

Cerebellar Ataxia

Lechtenberg, R. (Ed.). (1993). *Handbook of cerebellar diseases*. New York: Dekker.

Frontal Lobe

Fuster, J. M. (1989). *The prefrontal cortex: Anatomy, physiology, and neurophysiology of the frontal lobe*. New York: Raven Press.

Passingham, R. E. (1993). *The frontal lobes and voluntary action*. Oxford, England: Oxford University Press.

Huntington's Disease

Wexler, A. (1995). *Mapping fate: A memoir of family, risk and genetic research*. New York: Random House.

Oculomotor System

Carpenter, R. H. S. (Ed.). (1991). *Eye movements*. Boca Raton, FL: CRC Press.

Parkinson's Disease

Hanin, I., Yoshida, M., & Fisher, A. (Eds.). (1995). *Alzheimer's and Parkinson's diseases: Recent developments*. New York: Plenum Press.

Olanow, C. W., Jenne, P., & Youdim, M. (Eds.). (1996). *Neurodegeneration and neuroprotection in Parkinson's disease*. London: Academic Press.

Schneider, J. S., & Gupta, M. (Eds.). (1993). *Current concepts in Parkinson's disease research*. Lewiston, NY: Hogrefe & Huber.

ARTICLES

Akinesia

Berridge, K. C., Fentress, J. C., & Treit, D. (1988). A triggered hyperkinesia induced in rats by lesions of the corpus striatum. *Experimental Neurobiology, 99*, 259–268.

Catalepsy

Gallegos, G., Salazar, L., Ortiz, M., Marquez, W., Davis, A., Sanchez, S., & Conner, D. (1990). Simple disturbance of the dam in the neonatal period can alter haloperidol-induced catalepsy in the adult offspring. *Behavioral and Neural Biology, 53*, 172–188.

Meyer, M. E., Cottrell, G. A., Van Hartesveldt, C. (1992). Dopamine D1 antagonist potentiates the durations of bar and cling catalepsy and the dorsal immobility response in rats. *Pharmacology, Biochemistry and Behavior, 41*, 507–510.

Coordination and Planning of Movements

Milliken, G. W., Ward, J. P., & Erickson, C. I. (1991). Interdependent digit control in foraging by the aye-aye (*Daubentonia madagascariensis*). *Folia Primatologica, 56*, 219–224.

Epilepsy and Seizures

Grace, G. M., Corcoran, M. E., & Skelton, R. W. (1990). Kindling with stimulation of the dentate gyrus: II. Effects on evoked field potentials. *Brain Research, 509*, 257–265.

Thomas, J. (1990). Gender difference insusceptibility to picrotoxin-induced seizures is seizure- and stimulation-dependent. *Brain Research Bulletin, 24*, 7–10.

Escape Behavior (Mauthner Cells)

Fetcho, J. R. (1992). Excitation of motor neurons by the Mauthner axon in goldfish: Complexities in a "simple" reticulospinal pathway. *Journal of Neurophysiology, 67*(6), 1574–1586.

Execution of Movements

Wolff, P. H., Michel, G. F., Ovrut, M., & Drake, C. (1990). Rate and timing precision of motor coordination in developmental dyslexia. *Developmental Psychology, 26*(3), 349–359.

Mossy Fiber

Golarai, G., Cavazos, J. E., & Sutula, T. P. (1992). Activation of the dentate gyrus pentylenetetrazol–evoked seizures induces mossy fiber synaptic reorganization. *Brain Research, 593*, 257–264.

Motor Cortex

Martin, J. H., & Ghez, C. (1991). Impairments in reaching during reversible inactivation of the distal forelimb representation of the motor cortex in the cat. *Neuroscience Letters, 133*, 61–64.

Motor Impairments

Fowler, S. C., & Mortell, C. (1992). Low doses of haloperidol interfere with rat tongue extensions during licking: A quantitative analysis. *Behavioral Neuroscience, 106*(2), 386–395.

MPTP

Weihmuler, F. B., Hadjiconstantinou, M., & Bruno, J. P. (1990). Dopamine receptors and sensorimotor behavior in MPTP-treated mice. *Behavioral Brain Research, 38*, 263–273.

Oculomotor System

Andersen, R. A., Bracewell, R. M., Barash, S., Gnadt, J. W., & Fogassi, L. (1990). Eye position effects on visual, memory, and saccade-related activity in areas LIP and 7a of Macaque. *Journal of Neuroscience, 10*(4), 1176–1196.

Borel, L., & Lacour, M. (1992). Functional coupling of the stabilizing eye and head reflexes during horizontal and vertical linear motion in the cat. *Experimental Brain Research, 91*, 191–206.

Glimcher, P. W., & Sparks, D. L. (1993). Effects of low-frequency stimulation of the superior colliculus on spontaneous and visually guided saccades. *Journal of Neurophysiology, 69*(3), 953–964.

Heinen, S. J., & Skavenski, A. A. (1992). Adaptation of saccades and fixation to bilateral foveal lesions in adult monkey. *Vision Research, 32*(4), 365–373.

Kowler, E. (1990). The role of visual and cogitive processes in the control of eye movement. *Eye movements and their role in visual and cognitive processes*. New York: Elsevier.

Munoz, D. P., Gutton, D., & Pélsson, D. (1991). Control of orientating gaze shifts by the tectoreticulospinal system in the head-free cat: III. Spatiotemporal characteristics of phasic motor discharge. *Journal of Neurophysiology, 66*(5), 1642–1666.

Terrence, R. S., & Sparks, D. L. (1994). Systematic errors for saccades to remembered targets: Evidence for a dissociation between saccade matrics and activity in the superior colliculus. *Vision Research, 34*(1), 93–106.

Parkinson's Disease

Hunat, E., Castro, R., Diaz-Palarea, M. D., & Rodriguez, M. (1988). Conditioning of the early behavioral response to apomorphine in the rotational model of Parkinson's disease. *European Journal of Psychology, 145*, 323–327.

Jicha, G. A., & Salamone, J. D. (1991). Vacuous jaw movements and feeding deficits in rats with ventrolateral striatal dopamine depletion: Possible relation to Parkinsonian symptoms. *Journal of Neuroscience, 11*(12), 3822–3829.

Strecker, R. E., Miao, R., & Loring, J. F. (1989). Survival and function of aggregate cultures of rat fetal dopamine neurons grafted in a rat model of Parkinson's disease. *Experimental Brain Research, 76*, 315–322.

Purposeful Movements

Amrhein, P. C., Stelmach, G. E., & Goggin, N. L. (1991). Age differences in the maintenance and reconstructing of movement preparation. *Psychology and Aging, 6*(3), 451–466.

West, M. O., Carelli, R. A., Pomerantz, M., Cohen, S. M., Gardner, J. P., Chapin, J. K., & Woodward, D. J. (1990). A region in the dorsolateral striatum of the rat exhibiting single-unit correlations with specific locomotor limb movements. *Journal of Neurophysiology, 64*(4), 1233–1246.

Tremors

Stratton, S. E., & Lorden, J. F. (1991). Effect of hamaline on cells of the inferior olive in the absence of tremor: Differential response of genetically dystonic and harmaline-tolerant rats. *Neuroscience, 41*(4), 543–549.

CHAPTER 11

BOOKS

Endogenous Opiates

Hammer, R. P. (Ed.). (1993). *The neurobiology of opiates*. Boca Raton, FL: CRC Press.

Nociception System

Belmonte, C., & Cervero, F. (Eds.). (1996). *Neurobiology of nociceptors*. Oxford, England: Oxford University Press.

Wood, J. N. (Ed.). (1993). *Capsaicin in the study of pain*. London: Academic Press.

ARTICLES

Appetitive Behavior

Berridge, K. C., & Cromwell, H. C. (1990). Motivational-sensorimotor interaction controls aphagia and exaggerated treading after striatopallidal lesions. *Behavioral Neuroscience, 104*(5), 778–795.

Blackburn, J. R., Pfaus, J. G., & Phillips, A. G. (1992). Dopamine functions in appetitive and defensive behaviours. *Progress in Neurobiolgy, 39*(3), 247–279.

Winn, P. (1991). Cholinergic stimulation of substantia nigra: Effects on feeding, drinking, and sexual behavior in the male rat. *Psychopharmacology, 104,* 208–214.

Wolgin, D. L., & Wade, J. V. (1990). Effect of lithium chloride-induced aversion on appetitive and consummatory behavior. *Behavioral Neuroscience, 104*(3), 438–440.

Development of Nociception

Hamm, R. J., & Knisely, J. S. (1988). Developmental aspects of nociception. *Brain Research and Bulletin, 21,* 933–946.

Endogenous Opiates

Dass, C., Kusmierz, J. J., & Desiderio, D. M. (1991). Mass spectrometric quantification of endogenous beta-endorphin. *Biological Mass Spectrometry, 20,* 130–138.

Olson, G. A., Olson, R. D., & Kastin, A. J. (1991). Endogenous opiates: 1990. *Peptides, 12,* 1407–1432.

Hyperalgesia and Hypoalgesia

Coderre, T. J., Vaccarino, A. L., & Melzack, R. (1990). Central nervous system plasticity in the tonic pain response to subcutaneous formalin injection. *Brain Research, 535,* 155–158.

Foo, H., & Westbrook, R. F. (1991). Effects of hypophysectomy and adrenalectomy on naloxone-induced analgesia. *Psychopharmacology, 103,* 177–182.

Helmstetter, F. J., & Landeira-Fernandez, J. (1990). Conditional hypoalgesia is attenuated by naltrexone applied to the periaqueductal gray. *Brain Research, 537,* 88–92.

Leitner, D. S. (1989). Multisensory deficits in rats produced by acute exposure to cold swim stress. *Behavioral Neuroscience, 103*(1), 151–157.

Rodgers, R. J., Lee, C., & Shepherd, J. K. (1992). Effects of diazepam on behavioural and antinociceptive responses to the elated plus-maze in male mice depend upon treatment regimen and prior maze experience. *Psychopharmacology, 106,* 102–110.

Thurston, C. L., Campbell, I. G., Culhane, E. S., Carstens, E., & Watkins, L. R. (1992). Characterization of intrathecal vasopressin-induced antinociception, scratching behavior, and motor suppression. *Peptides, 13,* 17–25.

Westbrook, R. F., Greeley, J. D., Nabke, C. P., & Swinbourne, A. L. (1991). Aversive conditioning in the rat: Effects of a benzodiazepine and of an opioid agonist and antagonist on conditioned hypoalgesia and fear. *Journal of Experimental Psychology, 17*(3), 219–230.

Nociception

McLaughlin, C. R., Lichtman, A. H., Fanselow, M. S., & Cramer, C. P. (1990). Tonic nociception in neonatal rats. *Pharmacology Biochemistry and Behavior, 36,* 859–862.

Pain Pathway

Rausell, E., Cusick, C. G., Taub, E., & Jones, E. G. (1992). Chronic deafferentiation in monkeys differentially affects nociceptive and nonnociceptive pathways distinguished by specific calcium-binding proteins and down-regulates gamma-aminobutyric acid type A receptors at thalamic levels. *Proceedings of the National Academy of Sciences (USA), 89,* 2751–2575.

Reward

Gallistel, C. R., Leon, M., Waraczynski, M., & Hanau, M. S. (1991). Effect of current on the maximum possible reward. *Behavioral Neuroscience, 105*(6), 901–912.

Self-Stimulation Studies

Bielajew, C., & Shizgal, P. (1986). Evidence implicating descending fibers in self-stimulation of the medial forebrain bundle. *Journal of Neuroscience, 6*(4), 919–929.

Cazala, P. (1990). Dose-dependent effects of morphine differentiate self-administration elicited from lateral hypothalamus and mesencephalic central gray area in mice. *Brain Research, 527,* 280–285.

Nicholls, D. S., & Thorn, B. E. (1990). Stimulation-produced analgesia and its cross-tolerance between dorsal and ventral PAG loci. *Pain, 41,* 347–352.

Stellar, J. R., Hall, F. S., & Waraczynski, M. (1991). The effects of excitotoxin lesions of the lateral hypothalamus on self-stimulation reward. *Brain Research, 541,* 29–40.

Stress-Induced Analgesia

Kinsley, C. H., Mann, P. E., & Bridges, R. S. (1988). Prenatal stress alters morphine- and stress-induced analgesia in male and female rats. *Pharmacology Biochemistry and Behavior, 30,* 123–128.

Marek, P., Yirmiya, R., Panocka, I., & Liebeskind, (1989). Genetic influences on brain stimulation-produced analgesia in mice: I. Correlation with stress-induced analgesia.

CHAPTER 12

BOOKS

Aggression

Archer, J. (Ed.). (1994). *Male violence.* London: Routledge.

Homosexuality

DeCecco, J. P., & Parker, D. A. (Ed.). (1995). *Sex, cells, and same-sex desire: The biology of sexual preference.* New York: Haworth Press.

Hamer, D. H. (1994). *The science of desire: The search for the gay gene and the biology of behavior.* New York: Simon & Schuster.

Murphy, T. (Ed.). (1994). *Gay ethics: Controversies in outing, civil rights, and sexual science.* New York: Haworth Press.

Pheromones

Kohl, J. V. (1995). *The scent of eros: Mysteries of odor in human sexuality.* New York: Continuum.

Sex Determination

Hunter, R. H. F. (1995). *Sex determination, differentiation, and intersexuality in placental mammals.* Cambridge, England: Cambridge University Press.

Solari, A. J. (1994). *Sex chromosomes and sex determination in vertebrates.* Boca Raton, FL: CRC Press.

Sexual Dimorphism

Ghesquiere, J., Martin, R. D., & Newcombe, F. (1985). *Human sexual dimorphism.* London: Taylor & Francis.

Steroids

Bohl, M., & Duax, W. L. (Ed.). (1992). *Molecular structure and biological activity of steroids.* Boca Raton, FL: CRC Press.

Parker, M. G. (Ed.). (1993). *Steroid hormone action.* Oxford, England: IRL Press.

Vasopressin and Oxytocin

Pedersen, C. A. (Ed.). (1992). *Oxytocin in maternal, sexual, and social behaviors.* New York: New York Academy of Sciences.

ARTICLES

Aggression

Adamec, R. E. (1991). The role of the temporal lobe in feline aggression and defense. *Psychological Record, 41,* 233–253.

Castration

Wee, B. E. F., Weaver, D. R., & Clemens, L. G.(1988). Hormonal restoration of masculine sexual behavior in long-term castrated B6D2F1 mice. *Physiology and Behavior, 42,* 77–82.

Courting

Keddy-Hector, A. C., Wilczynski, W., & Ryan, M. J. (1992). Call patterns and basilar papilla tuning in cricket frogs: II. Intrapopulation variation and allometry. *Brain, Behavior & Evolution, 39,* 238–246.

Estrus

Hampson, E. (1990). Variations in sex-related cognitive abilities across the menstrual cycle. *Brain & Cognition, 14,* 26–43.

Luine, V., & Hearns, M. (1990). Relationship of gonadal hormone administration, sex, reproductive status and age to monoamine oxidase activity within the hypothalamus. *Journal of Neuroendocrinology, 2*(4), 423–428.

Rose, J. D., & Bieber, S. L. (1984). Joint and separate effects of estrogen and progesterone on responses on midbrain neurons to lordosis-controlling somatic stimuli in the female golden Syrian hamster. *Journal of Neurophysiology, 51*(5), 40–54.

Wade, G. N., & Schneider, J. E. (1992). Metabolic fuels and reproduction in female mammals. *Neuroendocrinology, 16,* 235–272.

Maternal Behavior

Numan, M., & Numan, M. J. (1991). Preoptic-brainstem connections and maternal behavior in rats. *Behavioral Neuroscience, 5*(6), 13–29.

Oxytocin

Kow, L.-M., Johnson, A. E., Ogawa, S., & Pfaff, D. W. (1991). Electrophysiological actions of oxytocin on hypothalamic neurons in vitro: Neuropharmacological characterization and effects of ovarian steroids. *Neuroendocrinology, 54,* 526–535.

Primary Sex Characteristics

Halawani, M. E. E., Silsby, J. L. Youngren, O. M, & Phillips, R. E. (1991) Exogenous prolactin delays photo-induced sexual maturity and suppresses ovariectomy-induced luteinizing hormone secretion in the turkey (*Meleagris gallopavo*). *Biology of Reproduction, 44,* 420–424.

Receptivity

Blache, D., Fabre-Nys, C. J., & Venier, G. (1991). Ventromedial hypothalamus as a target for oestradiol action on proceptivity, receptivity and luteinizing hormone surge of the ewe. *Brain Research, 546,* 241–249.

Delville, Y., & Blaustein, J. D. (1991). A site for estradiol priming of progesterone-facilitated sexual receptivity in the ventrolateral hypothalamus of female guinea pigs. *Brain Research, 559,* 191–199.

Frye, C. A., Mermelstein, P. G., & DeBold, J. F. (1992). Evidence for a non-genomic action of progesterone on sexual receptivity in hamster ventral tegmental area but not hypothalamus. *Brain Research, 578,* 87–93.

Hnatzuk, O. C., Lisciotto, C. A., DonCarlos, L. L., Carter, C., and Morrell, J. L. (1994). Estrogen receptor immunoreactivity in specific brain areas of the prairie vole (*Microtus ochrogaster*) is altered by sexual receptivity and genetic sex. *Journal of Neuroendocrinology, 6,* 89–100.

Wilson, C. A., Thody, A. J., Hole, D. R., Grierson, J. P., & Celis, M. E. (1991). Interaction of estradiol, alpha-melanocyte-stimulating hormone, and dopamine in the regulation of sexual receptivity in the female rat. *Neuroendocrinology, 54,* 14–22.

Sexual Behavior

Ågmo, A., & Berenfeld, R. (1990). Reinforcing properties of ejaculation in the male rat: Role of opioids and dopamine. *Behavioral Neuroscience, 4*(1), 177–182.

Bazzett, T., Lumley, L., Bitran, D., Markowski, V., Warner, R., & Hull, E. (1992). Male rat copulation following 6-OHDA lesions of the medial preoptic area: Resistance to repeated administration and rapid behavioral recovery. *Brain Research, 580,* 164–170.

Dohanich, G. P., McMullan, D. M., Cada, D. A., & Mangum, K. (1991). Muscarinic receptor subtypes and sexual behavior in female rats. *Pharmacolgy Biochemistry & Behavior, 38*, 115–174.

Elliott, A. S., & Nunez, A. A. (1992). Photoperiod modulates the effects of steroids on sociosexual behaviors of hamsters. *Physiology & Behavior, 51*, 1189–1193.

Floody, O. R. (1989). Lateralized effects on hamster lordosis of unilateral hormonal and somatosensory stimuli. *Brain Research Bulletin, 22*, 745–749.

Jubilan, B. M. , & Nyby, J. G. (1992). The intrauterine position phenomenon and precopulatory behaviors of house mice. *Physiology & Behavior, 51*, 857–872.

Koskinen, I., Hendricks, S., Yells, D., Fitzpatrick, D., & Graber, B. (1991). Yohimbine and naloxone: Effects on male rat sexual behavior. *Physiology & Behavior, 50*, 589–593.

Pfaus, J. G., & Phillips, A. G. (1991). Role of dopamine in anticipatory and consummatory aspects of sexual behavior in the male rat. *Behavioral Neuroscience, 5*(5), 727–743.

Sexual Dimorphism

Grisham, W., Casto, J. M., Kashon, M. L., Ward, I. L., & Ward, O. B. (1992). Prenatal flutamide alters sexually dimorphic nuclei in the spinal cord of male rats. *Brain Research, 578*, 69–74.

Kerchner, M., & Ward, I. L. (1992). SDN-MPOA volume in male rats is decreased by prenatal stress, but is not related to ejaculatory behavior. *Brain Research, 581*, 244–251.

Kimura, D. (1992). Sex differences in the brain. *Scientific American, 267*, 118–125.

Kolb, B., & Stewart, J. (1991). Sex-related differences in dendritic branching of cells in the prefrontal cortex of rats. *Journal of Neuroendocrinology, 3*(1), 96–99.

Reid, S. N. M., & Juraska, J. (1992). Sex differences in the gross size of the rat neocortex. *Journal of Comparative Neurology, 321*, 442–447.

Whaling, C. S., Zucker, I., Wade, G. N., & Dark, J. (1990). Sexual dimorphism in brain weight of meadow voles: Role of gonadal hormones. *Developmental Brain Research, 53*, 270–275.

Sexual Identity

Grober, M. S., & Bass, A. H. (1991). Neuronal correlates of sex/role change in labrid fishes: LHRH-like immunoreactivity. *Brain, Behavior & Evolution, 38*, 302–312.

Jacobs, L. F., Gaulin, S. J. C., Sherry, D. F., & Hoffman, G. E. (1990). Evolution of spatial cognition: Sex-specific patterns of spatial behavior predict hippocampal size. *Proceedings of the National Academy of Sciences (USA), 87*, 6349–6352.

Landsman, R. (1991). Captivity affects behavioral physiology: Plasticity in signaling sexual identity. *Experientia, 47*, 31–38.

Songbirds

Brenowitz, E. A., & Arnold, A. P. (1990). The effects of systematic androgen treatment on androgen accumulation in song control regions of the adult female canary brain. *Journal of Neurobiology, 21*(6), 837–843.

Nordeen, E. J., & Nordeen, K. W. (1990). Neurogenesis and sensitive periods in avian song learning. *Trends in Neurosciences, 13*(1), 31–36.

Schlinger, B. A., & Arnold, A. P. (1991). Brain is the major site of estrogen synthesis in a male songbird. *Proceedings of the National Academy of Sciences (USA), 88*, 4191–4194.

Chapter 13

ARTICLES

Circadian Rhythms

Powers, M. K., & Barlow, R. B. (1985). Behavioral correlates of circadian rhythms in the *Limulus* visual system. *Biological Bulletin, 169*, 578–591.

Stanley, B. G., Schwartz, D. H., Hernandez, L., Leibowitz, S. F., & Hoebel, B. G. (1989). Patterns of extracellular 5-hydroxyindoleacetic acid (5-HIAA) in the paraventricular hypothalamus (PVN): Relation to circadian rhythm and deprivation-induced eating behavior. *Pharmacology Biochemistry & Behavior, 33*, 257–260.

REM

Arankowsky-Sandoval, G., Aquilar-Roblero, R., Próspero-García, O., & Drucker-Colín, R. (1987). Rapid eye movement (REM) sleep and ponto-geniculo-occipital (PGO) spike density are increased by somatic stimulation. *Brain Research, 400*, 155–158.

Merchant-Nancy, H., Vásquez, J., Aguilar-Roblero, R., & Drucker-Colín, R. (1992). c-*fos* proto-oncogene changes in relation to REM sleep duration. *Brain Research, 579*, 342–346.

Ramm, P., & Frost, B. J. (1986). Cerebral and local cerebral metabolism in the cat during slow wave and REM sleep. *Brain Research, 365*, 112–124.

Rhythmicity

Harrington, M. E., Eskes, G. A., Dickson, P., & Rusak, B. (1990). Lesions dorsal to the suprachiasmatic nuclei abolish split activity rhythms of hamsters. *Brain Research Bulletin, 24*, 593–597.

SAD and Seasonal cycles

Nelson, R. J. (1990). Mechanisms of seasonal cycles of behavior. *Annual Review of Psychology, 41*, 81–108.

Zucker, I. (1988). Seasonal affective disorders: Animal models *non fingo*. *Journal of Biological Rhythms, 3*(2),209–223.

Sleep Theories

Kryger, M. H., Roth, T., & Demant, W. C. (1989). *Principles and practices of sleep disorders in medicine.* New York: W. B. Saunders Co.

Stone, W. S., Altman, H. J., Berman, R. F., Caldwell, D. F., & Kilbey, M. M. (1989). Association of sleep parameters and memory in intact old rats and young rats with lesions in the nucleus basalis magnocellularis. *Behavioral Neuroscience, 103*(4), 755–764.

Chapter 14

ARTICLES

Arousal

Teyke, T., Weiss, K. R., & Kupfermann, I. (1991). Activity of identified cerebral neuron correlates with food-induced arousal in *Aplysia*. *Neuroscience Letters, 133*, 307–310.

Angiotensin

Czech, D. A., & Stein, E. A. (1992). Effect of drinking on angiotensin II–induced shifts in regional cerebral blood flow in the rat. *Brain Research Bulletin, 28*, 529–535.

Anorexia Nervosa

Davies, B. T., Wellman, P. J., & DiCarlo, B. (1992). Microinjection of the 1-agonist methoxamine into the paraventricular hypothalamus induces anorexia in rats. *Brain Research Bulletin, 28*, 633–635.

Kanarek, R. B., Glick, A. L., & Marks-Kaufman, R. (1991). Dietary influences on the acute effects of anorectic drugs. *Physiology & Behavior, 49*, 149–152.

Nishita, J. K., Ellinwood, E. H., Rockwell, K. W. J., Kuhn, C. M., Hoffman, G. W., McCall, W. V., & Manepalli, J. N. (1989). Abnormalities in the response of plasma arginine vasopressin during hypertonic saline infusion in patients with eating disorders. *Biological Psychiatry, 26*, 73–86.

Bulimia

Kirkham, T. C., & Cooper, S. J. (1991). Opioid peptides in relation to the treatment of obesity and bulimia. In S. R. Bloom and G. Burnstock (Eds.), *Peptides: A target for new drug development* (pp. 28–44). London: IBC Technical Services.

McCann, U. D., Rossiter, E. M., King, R. J., & Agras, W. S. (1991). Nonpurging bulimia: A distinct subtype of bulimia nervosa. *International Journal of Eating Disorders, 10*(6), 679–687.

CCK (in satiety)

Conover, K. L., Collins, S. M., & Weingarten, H. P. (1989). Pyloroplasty does not disrupt liquid phase gastric emptying or CCK-induced satiety. *Physiology & Behavior, 45*, 523–528.

Cooper, S. J., Dourish, C. T., & Clifton, P. G. (1992). CCK antagonists and CCK-monoamine interactions in the control of satiety. *Am J Clin Nutr, 55*, 291S–295S.

Conditioned Taste Aversion

Bermúdez-Rattoni, F. Fernández, J. Sánchez, M., Aguilar-Roblero, R., & Drucker-Colín, R. (1987). Fetal brain transplants induce recuperation of taste aversion learning. *Brain Research, 416*, 147–152.

Bernstein, I. L., & Borson, S. (1986). Learned food aversion: A component of anorexia syndromes. *Psychological Review, 93*(4), 462–472.

Breslin, P. A. S., Davidson, T. L., & Grill, H. J. (1990). Conditioned reversal of reactions to normally avoided tastes. *Physiology & Behavior, 47*, 535–538.

Spector, A. C., Norgen, R., & Grill, H. J. (1992). Parabrachial gustatory lesions impair taste aversion learning in rats. *Behavioral Neuroscience, 106*(1), 147–161.

Feeding

Baker, B. J., & Booth, D. A. (1990). Effects of *dl*-fenfluramine on dextrin and casein intakes influenced by textural preferences. *Behavioral Neuroscience, 104*(1), 153–159.

Berridge, K. C., & Valenstein, E. (1991). What psychological process mediates feeding evoked by electrical stimulation of the lateral hypthalmus? *Behavioral Neuroscience, 105*(1), 3–14.

Butera, P. C., Willard, D. M., & Raymond, S. A. (1992). Effects of PVN lesions on the responsiveness of female rats to estradiol. *Brain Research, 576*, 304–310.

Cropper, E. C., Kupfermann, I., & Weiss, K. R. (1990). Differential firing patterns of the peptide-containing cholinergic motor neurons B15 and B16 during feeding behavior in *Aplysia*. *Brain Research, 522*, 176–179.

Kulkosky, P. J. (1988). Bombesin and ceruletide-induced grooming and inhibition of ingestion in the rat. (Reprinted from *Neural mechanism and biological significance of grooming behavior.*) *Annals of the New York Academy of Sciences, 525*, 201–218.

Novin, D., O'Farrell, L., & Acevedo-Cruz, A. (1991). The metabolic bases for "paradoxical" and normal feeding. *Brain Research Bulletin, 27*, 435–438.

Stricker, E. M., & Verbalis, J. G. (1991). Caloric and noncaloric controls of food intake. *Brain Research Bulletin, 27*, 299–303.

Teyke, T., Weiss, K. R., & Kupfermann, I. (1990). Appetitive feeding behavior of *Aplysia*: Behavioral and neural analysis of directed head tuning. *Journal of Neuroscience, 10*(12), 3922–3934.

Vaccarino, F. J., Feifel, D., Rivier, J., & Vale, W. (1991). Antagonism of central growth hormone-releasing factor activity selectivity attenuates dark-onset feeding in rats. *Journal of Neuroscience, 11*(12), 3924–3927.

Feeding Mechanics

Westneat, M. W., & Hall, W. G. (1992). Ontogeny of feeding motor patterns in infant rats: An electromyographic analysis of suckling and chewing. *Behavioral Neuroscience, 100*, 539–554.

Feeding Neurotransmitters

Bakshi, V. P., & Kelley, A. E. (1993). Feeding induced by opioid stimulation of the ventral striatum: Role of opiate receptor subtypes. *Journal of Pharmacology & Experimental Therapeutics, 265*(3), 1253–1260.

Blundell, J. E. (1992). Serotonin and the biology of feeding. *Am J Clin Nutr, 55*, 155S–159S.

Clifton, P. G., Rusk, I. N., & Cooper, S. J. (1991). Effects of dopamine D1 and Dopamine D2 antagonists on the free feeding and drinking patterns of rats. *Behavioral Neuroscience, 105*(2), 272–281.

Hall, W. G. (1989). Neural systems for early independent ingestion: Regional metabolic changes during ingestive responding and dehydration. *Behavioral Neuroscience, 103*(2), 386–411.

Hsiao, S., & Fan, R. J. (1993). Additivity of taste-specific effects of sucrose and quinine: Microstructural analysis of ingestive behavior in rats. *Behavioral Neuroscience, 107*(2), 317–326.

Kow, L.-M., & Pfaff, D. W. (1989). Responses of hypothalamic paraventricular neurons in vitro to norepinephrine and other feeding-relevant agents. *Physiology & Behavior, 46*, 265–271.

Nobrega, J. N., & Coscina, D. V. (1990). Regional changes in brain 14C–2-deosyglucose uptake after feeding-inducing intrahypothalamic norepinephrine injections. *Brain Research Bulletin, 24*, 249–255.

Glucose Mobilization

Siviy, S. M., Kritikos, A., Atrens, D. M., & Shepherd, A. (1989). Effects of norepinephrine infused in the paraventricular hypothalamus on energy expenditure in the rat. *Brain Research, 487*, 79–88.

Homeostasis and Body Weight Set Point

Henderson, D., Fort, M. M., Rashotte, M. E., & Henderson, R.P. (1992). Ingestive behavior and body temperature of pigeons during long-term cold exposure. *Physiology & Behavior, 52*, 455–469.

Insulin

Amir, S., Schiavetto, A., & Pollock, R. (1990). Insulin co-injection suppresses the thermogenic response to glutamate microinjection into the VMH in rats. *Brain Research, 527*, 326–329.

Figlewicz, D. P., & Szot, P. (1991). Insulin stimulates membrane phospholipid metabolism by enhancing endogenous sub–1-adrenergic activity in the rat hippocampus. *Brain Research, 550*, 101–107.

King, B. M., & Frohman, L. A. (1982). The role of vagally mediated hyperinsulinemia, in hypothalamic obesity. *Neuroscience & Biobehavioral Reviews, 6*, 205–216.

Lateral Hypothamlaus

Clark, J. M., Clark, A. J. M., Bartle, A., & Winn, P. (1991). The regulation of feeding and drinking in rats with lesions of the lateral hypothalamus made by *N*-methyl-D-aspartate. *Neuroscience, 45*(3), 631–640.

Neuropeptide Y

Smialowski, A., Lewinska-Gastol, L., & Smialowska, M. (1992). The behavioural effects of neuropeptide Y (NPY) injection into the rat brain frontal cortex. *Neuropeptides, 21*, 153–156.

Stanley, B. G., Daniel, D. R., Chin, A. S., & Leibowitz, S. F. (1985). Paraventricular nucleus injections of peptide YY and neuropeptide Y preferentially enhance carbohydrate ingestion. *Peptides, 6*, 1205–1211.

Obesity

Hoebel, B. G., Rada, P., Mark, G. P., Parada, M., Puig De Parada, M., Pothos, E., & Hernandez, L. (1996). Hypothalamic control of accumbens dopamine: A system for feeding reinforcement. *Molecular & Genetic Aspects of Obesity, 5*, 263–280.

Meisel, R. L., Hays, T. C, Del Paine, S. N., & Luttrell, V. R. (1990). Induction of obesity by group housing in female Syrian hamsters. *Physiology & Behavior, 47*, 815–817.

Stenger, J., Fournier, T., & Bielajew, C. (1991). The effects of chronic ventromedial hypothalamic stimulation on weight gain in rats. *Physiology & Behavior, 50*, 1209–1213.

Wilson, L. M., Currie, P. J., & Gilson, T. L. (1991). Thermal preference behavior in preweaning genetically obese (*ob/ob*) and lean (+/?, +/+) mice. *Physiology & Behavior, 50*, 155–160.

Regulation

Kow, L.-M., & Pfaff, D. W. (1987). Neuropeptides TRH and cyclo(His-Pro) share neuromodulatory but not stimulatory action on hypothalamic neurons in vitro: Implication for the regulation of feeding. *Exp Brain Res, 67*, 93–99.

Satiety

Geiselman, P. J. (1987). Carbohydrates do not always produce satiety: An explanation of the appetite- and hunger-stimulating effects of hexoses. *Progress in Psychobiology & Physiological Psychology, 12*, 1–45.

Thirst

Clark, J. M., Clark, A. J. M., Warne, D., Rugg, E. L., Lightman, S. L., & Winn, P. (1991). Neuroendocrine and behavioral responses to hyperosmolarity in rats with lesions of the lateral hypothalamus made by *N*-methyl-D-aspartate. *Neuroscience, 45*, 625–629.

Contreras, R. J., & Smith, J. C. (1990). NaCl concentration alters temporal patterns of drinking and eating by rats. *Chemical Senses, 15*(3), 295–310.,

Ehrlich, K. J., & Fitts, D. A. (1990). Atrial natriuretic peptide in the subfornical organ reduces drinking induced by angiotensin or in response to water deprivation. *Behavioral Neuroscience, 104*(2), 365–372.

García-Hernández, F., Aguilar-Roblero, R., & Drucker-Colín, R. (1987). Transplantation of the feed occipital cortex to the third ventricle of SCN-lesioned rats induces a diurnal rhythm in drinking behavior. *Brain Research, 418*, 193–197.

Vasopressin

Murphy, H. M., & Wideman, C. H. (1992). Vasopressin, corticosterone levels, and gastric ulcers during food-restriction stress. *Peptides, 13*, 373–376.

CHAPTER 15

BOOKS

Nervous System Development

Cuello, A. C. (Ed.). (1993). *Neuronal cell death and repair.* New York: Elsevier.

Hall, Z. W. (1992). *An introduction to molecular neurobiology.* Sunderland, MA: Sinauer Associates.

Ibanez, C. F. (1995). *Life and death in the nervous system role of neurotrophic factors and their receptors.* Oxford, England: Pergamon.

Jacobson, M. (1978). *Developmental neurobiology.* New York: Plenum Press.

Kandel, E. R., Schwartz, J. H., & Jessell, T. M. (1991). *Principles of neural science* (3rd ed.). New York: Elsevier.

Martinez, J. L., Jr., & Kesner, R. P. (1991). *Learning and memory.* San Diego, CA: Academic Press.

Mayer, R. J., & Brown, I. R. (Ed.). (1994). *Heat shock proteins in the nervous system.* London: Academic Press.

Patterson, P. H., & Purves, D. (1982). *Readings in developmental neurobiology.* Cold Springs Harbor, NY: Cold Springs Harbor Laboratory.

Purves, D., & Lichtman, J. W. (1985). *Principles of neural development.* Sunderland, MA: Sinauer Associates.

Squire, L. R. (1987). *Memory and brain.* New York: Oxford University Press.

Squire, L. R., Weinberger, N. M., Lynch, G., & McGaugh, J. L. (1991). *Memory: Organization and locus of change.* New York: Oxford University Press.

Plasticity

Baudry, M., Thompson, R. F., & Davis, J. L. (Eds.). (1993). *Synaptic plasticity: Molecular, cellular, and functional aspects.* Cambridge, MA: MIT Press.

Byrne, J. H., & Berry, W. O. (1989). *Neural models of plasticity.* San Diego, CA: Academic Press.

Kolb, B. (1995). *Brain plasticity and behavior.* Mahwah, NJ: Erlbaum.

McGaugh, J. L., Bermudez-Rattoni, F., & Prado-Alcala, R. (1995). *Plasticity in the central nervous system: Learning and memory.* Mahwah, NJ: Erlbaum.

Voronin, L. L. (1993). *Synaptic modifications and memory: An electrophysiological analysis.* Berlin, Germany: Springer-Verlag.

ARTICLES

Amnesia

Dickson, C. T., & Vanderwolf, C. (1990). Animal models of human amnesia and dementia: Hippocampal and amygdala ablation compared with serotonergic and cholinergic blockade in the rat. *Behavioural Brain Research, 41*, 215–227.

Gaffan, D., & Gaffan, E. A. (1991). Amnesia in man following transection of the fornix. *Brain, 114*, 2611–2618.

Jaffard, R., Beracochea, D., & Yoon, C. (1991). The hippocampal-mamillary system: Anterograde and retrograde amnesia. *Hippocampus, 1*(3), 275–278.

Langlais, P. J., Mandel, R. J., & Mair, R. G. (1992). Diencephalic lesions, learning impairments, and intact retrograde memory following acute thiamine deficiency in the rat. *Behavioural Brain Research, 48*, 177–185.

Aplysia

Bergold, P.J., Beushausen, S. A., Sacktor, T. C., Cheley, S., Bayley, H., & Schwartz, J. H. (1992). A regulatory subunit of the cAMP-dependent protein kinase down-regulated in *Aplysia* sensory neurons during long-term sensitization. *Neuron, 8*, 387–397.

Hawkins, R. D., & Kandel, E. R. (1990). Hippocampal LTP and synaptic plasticity in *Aplysia*: Possible relationship of associative cellular mechanisms. *The Neurosciences, 2*, 391–401.

Mayford, M., Barzilai, A., Keller, F., Schacher, S., & Kandel, E. R. (1992). Modulation of an NCAM-related adhesion molecule with long-term synaptic plasticity in *Aplysia*. *Science, 256*, 638–644.

Small, S. A., Cohen, T. E., Kandel, E. R., & Hawkins, R. D. (1992). Identified FMRFamide-immunoreactive neuron LPL 16 in the left pleural ganglion of *Aplysia* produces presynaptic inhibition of siphon sensory neurons. *Journal of Neuroscience, 12*, 1616–1627.

Associative learning

Edeline, J.-M., & Weinberger, N. M. (1992). Associative returning in the thalamic source of input to the amygdala and auditory cortex: Receptive field plasticity in the medial division of the medial geniculate body. *Behavioral Neuroscience, 106*(1), 81–105.

Fowler, S. C., Skjoldager, P. D., Liao, R.-M., Chase, J. M., & Johnson, J. S. (1991). Distinguishing between haloperidol's and decamethonium's disruptive effects on operant behavior in rats: Use of measurements that complement response rate. *Journal of the Experimental Analysis of Behavior, 56*, 239–260.

Grau, J. W., Salinas, J. A., Illich, P. A., & Meagher, M. W. (1990). Associative learning and memory for an antinociceptive response in the spinalized rat. *Behavioral Neuroscience, 104*(3), 489–494.

Attention

Harley, C. (1991). Noradrenergic and locus coeruleus modulation of the perforant path-evoked potential in rat denate gyrus supports a role for the locus coeruleus in attentional and memorial processes. *Progress in Brain Research, 88*, 307–321.

Avoidance Learning

Archer, T., Soderberg, U., Ross, S. B., & Jonsson, G. (1984). Role of olfactory bulbectomy and DSP4 treatment in avoidance learning in the rat. *Behavioral Neuroscience, 98*(3), 496–505.

Mair, R. G., Otto, T. A., Knoth, R. L., Rabchenuk, S. A., & Langlais, P. J. (1991). Analysis of aversively conditioned learning and memory in rats recovered from pyrithiamine-induced thiamine deficiency. *Behavioral Neuroscience, 105*(3), 351–359.

Axon Development

Lewin, G. R., Ritter, A. M., & Mendell, L. M. (1992). On the role of nerve growth factor in the development of myelinated nociceptors. *Journal of Neuroscience, 12*(5), 1896–1905.

Brain Damage

Farah, M. J., McMullen, P. A., & Meyer, M. M. (1991). Can recognition of living things be selectively impaired? *Neuropsychologia, 29*(2), 185–193.

Feeney, D. M. (1991). Pharmacologic modulation of recovery after brain injury: A reconsideration of diaschisis. *Journal of Neurological Rehabilitation, 5*, 113–128.

McDaniel, W. F., Jones, P. D., & Weaver, T. L. (1991). Medial frontal lesions, postoperative treatment with an ACTH(4–9) analog, and acquisition of a winshift spatial strategy. *Behavioural Brain Research, 44*, 107–112.

Stackman, R. W., & Walsh, T. J. (1992). Chlordiazepoxide-induced working memory impairments: Site specificity and reversal by Flumazenil (RO15–1788). *Behavioral and Neural Biology, 57*, 233–243.

Brain Maturation

Cramer, C. P. (1988). Experience during suckling increases weight and volume of rat hippocampus. *Developmental Brain Research, 42*, 151–155.

Ramirez, J. J., Jhaveri, S., Hahm, J.-O., & Schneider, G. E. (1990). Maturation of projections from occipital cortex to the ventrolateral geniculate and superior colliculus in postnatal hamsters. *Developmental Brain Research, 55*, 1–9.

Robinson, S. R., & Smotherman, W. P. (1992). The amniotic sac as scaffolding: Prenatal ontogeny of an action pattern. *Developmental Pschobiology, 24*(7), 463–485.

Spears, N., Meyer, J. S., Whaling, C. S., Wade, G. N., Zucker, I., & Dark, J. (1990). Long day lengths enhance myelination of midbrain and hindbrain regions of developing meadow voles. *Developmental Brain Research, 55*, 103–108.

Classical Conditioning

Blazis, D. E., & Moore, J. W. (1991). Conditioned stimulus duration in classical trace conditioning: Test of a real-time neural network model. *Behavioural Brain Research, 43*, 73–78.

Cruikshank, S. J., Edeline, J. M., & Weinberger, N. M. (1992). Stimulaiton at a site of auditory-somatosensory convergence in the medial geniculate nucleus in an effective unconditioned stimulus for fear conditioiong. *Behavioral Neuroscience, 106*(3), 471–483.

Mazurski, E. J., & Beninger, R. J. (1991). Effects of selective drugs for dopaminergic D1 and D2 receptors on conditioned locomotion in rats. *Psychopharmacology, 105*, 107–112.

Sears, L. L., & Steinmetz, J. E. (1990). Acquisition of classically conditioned-related activity in the hippocampus is affected by lesions of the cerebellar interpositus nucleus. *Behavioral Neuroscience, 104*(5), 681–692.

Steinmetz, J. E., & Sengelaub, D. R. (1992). Possible conditioned stimulus pathway for classical eyelid conditioning in rabbits. *Behavioral & Neural Biology, 57*, 103–115.

Complex Learning

Altman, H. J., Normile, H. J., Galloway, M. P., Ramirex, A., & Azmitia, E. C. (1990). Enhanced spatial discrimination learning in rats following 5,7-DHT-induced serotonergic deafferentation of the hippocampus. *Brain Research, 518*, 61–66.

Bryden, M. P., George, J., & Inch, R. (1990). Sex differences and the role of figural complexity in determining the rate of mental rotation. *Perceptual & Motor Skills, 70*, 467–477.

Lassalle, J. M., Bulman-Fleming, B., & Wahlsten, D. (1991). Hybrid vigour and maternal environment in mice: II. Water escape learning, open-field activity and spatial memory. *Behavioural Processes, 23*, 35–45.

Taube, J. S., Kesslak, J. P., & Cotman, C. W. (1992). Lesions of the rat postsubiculum impair performance on spatial tasks. *Behavioral & Neural Biology, 57*, 131–143.

Watson, N. V., & Kimura, D. (1991). Nontrivial sex differences in throwing and intercepting: Relation to psychometrically defined spatial functions. *Person. Indiv. Diff., 12*(5), 375–385.

Habituation

Dworkin, B. R., & Dworkin, S. (1990). Learning of physiological responses: I. Habituation, sensitization, and classical conditioning. *Behavioral Neuroscience, 104*(2), 298–319.

Leaton, R. N., & Supple, W. F. (1991). Medial cerebellum and long-term habituation of acoustic startle in rats. *Behavioral Neuroscience, 105*(6), 804–816.

Rankin, C. H., & Broster, B. S. (1992). Factors affecting habituation and recovery from habituation in the nematode *Caenorhabditis elegans*. *Behavioral Neuroscience, 106*(2), 239–249.

Smotherman, W. P., & Robinson, S. R. (1992). Habituation in the rat fetus. *Quarterly Journal of Experimental Psychology, 44B*(3/4), 215–230.

Hermissenda

Lederhendler, I. I., Collin, C., & Alkon, D. L. (1990). Sequential changes of potassium currents in *Hermissenda* type B photoreceptor during early stages of classical conditioning. *Neuroscience Letters, 110*, 28–33.

Matzel, L. D., Schreurs, B. G., & Alkon, D. L. (1990). Pavlovian conditioning of distinct components of *Hermissenda's* responses to rotation. *Behavioral & Neural Biology, 54*, 131–145.

Matzel, L. D., Schreurs, B. G., Lederhendler, I., & Alkon, D. L. (1990). Acquisition of conditioned associations in *Hermissenda*: Additive effects of contiguity and the forward interstimulus interval. *Behavioral Neuroscience, 104*(4), 597–606.

Hippocampus

Eichenbaum, H., & Otto, T. (1992). The hippocampus—What does it do? *Behavioral & Neural Biology, 57*(2), 2–36.

Jucker, M., Kametani, H., Bresnahan, E. L., & Ingram, D. K. (1990). Parietal cortex lesions do not impair retention performance of rats in a 14-unit T-maze unless hippocampal damage is present. *Physiology & Behavior, 47*, 207–212.

Leaton, R. N., & Borszcz, G. S. (1990). Hippocampal lesions and temporally chained conditioned stimuli in a conditioned supression paradigm. *Psychobiology,18*(1), 81–88.

Mizumori, S. J. Y., Barnes, C. J., & McNaughton, B. L. (1990). Behavioral correlates of theta-on and theta-off cells recorded from hippocampal formation of mature young and aged rats. *Experimental Brain Research, 80*, 365–373.

Moyer, J. R., Deyo, R. A., & Disterhoft, J. F. (1990). Hippocampectomy disrupts trace eye-blink conditioning in rabbits. *Behavioral Neuroscience, 104*(2), 243–252.

Penick, S., & Solomon, P. R. (1991). Hippocampus, context, and conditioning. *Behavioral Neuroscience, 105*(5), 611–617.

Port, R. L., Sample, J. A., & Seybold, K. S. (1991). Partial hippocampal pyramidal cell loss alters behavior in rats: Implications for and animal model of schizophrenia. *Brain Research Bulletin, 26*(6), 993–996.

Schmajuk, N. A., & DiCarlo, J. J. (1991). A neural network approach to hippocampal function in classical conditioning. *Behavioral Neuroscience, 105*(1), 82–110.

Schmajuk, N. A., & DiCarlo, J. J. (1992). Stimulus configuration, classical conditioning, and hippocampal function. *Psychological Review, 99*(2), 268–305.

Thompson, L. T., Deyo, R. A., & Disterhoft, J. F. (1990). Nimodipine enhances spontaneous activity of hippocampal pyramidal neurons in aging rabbits at a dose that facilitates associative learning. *Brain Research, 535*, 119–130.

Thompson, L. T., Moskal, J. R., & Disterhoft, J. F. (1992). Hippocampus-dependent learning facilitated by a monoclonal antibody or D-cycloserine. *Nature, 359*, 638–641.

Wickens, J. R., & Abraham W. C. (1991). The involvement of L-type calcium channels in heterosynaptic long-term depression in the hippocampus. *Neuroscience Letters, 130*, 128–132.

Long-Term Memory

Anderson, M. J., Petros, T. V., Beckwith, B. E., Mitchell, W. W., & Fritz, S. (1991). Individual differences in the effect of time of day on long-term memory access. *American Journal of Psychology, 104*(2), 241–255.

Nadel, L. (1992). Multiple memory systems: What and why. *Journal of Cognitive Neuroscience, 4* (3), 179–188.

Long-Term Potentiation

Hargreaves, E. L., Cain, D. P., & Vanderwolf, C. H. (1990). Learning and behavioral long-term potentiation: Importance of controlling for motor activity. *Journal of Neuroscience, 10*(5), 1472–1478.

Jeffery, K. J., Abraham, W. C., Dragunow, M., & Mason, S. E. (1990). Induction of Fos-like immunoreactivity and the maintenance of long-term potentiation in the dentate gyrus of unanesthetized rats. *Molecular Brain Research, 8*, 267–274.

Laroche, S., Jay, T. M., & Thierry, A. (1990). Long-term potentiation in the prefrontal cortex following stimulation of the hippocampal CA1/subicular region. *Neuroscience Letters, 114*, 184–190.

Otto, T., Eichenbaum, H., Wiener, S. I., & Wible, C. G. (1991). Learning-related patterns of CA1 spike trains parallel stimulation parameters optimal for inducing hippocampal long-term potentiation. *Hippocampus, 1* (2), 181–192.

Robinson, G. B., & Reed, G. D. (1992). Effect of MK-801 on the induction and subsequent decay of long-term potentiation in the unanesthetized rabbit hippocampal denate gyrus. *Brain Research, 569*, 78–85.

Memory Retrieval

Devauges, V., & Sara, S. J. (1991). Memory retrieval enhancement by local coeruleus stimulation: Evidence for mediation by beta-receptors. *Behavioural Brain Research, 43*, 93–97.

Stone, W. S., Rudd, R. J., Ragozzine, M. E., & Gold, P. E. (1992). Glucose attenuation of deficits in memory retrieval in altered light: Dark cycles. *Psychobiology, 20*(1), 47–50.

Memory Storage

Ammassari-Teule, M., Pavone, F., Castellano, C., & McGaugh, J. L. (1991). Amygdala and dorsal hippocampus lesions block the effects of GABAergic drugs on memory storage. *Brain Research, 551*, 104–109.

Miller, E. K., Li, L., & Desimone, R. (1991). A neural mechanism for working and recognition memory in inferior temporal cortex. *Science, 254*, 1377–1379.

NMDA

Christie, B. R., & Abraham, W. C. (1992). MNDA-dependent heterosynaptic long-term depression in the dentate gyrus of anaesthetized rats. *Synapse, 10*, 1–6.

Robinson, G. B. (1991). Kindling-induced potentiation of excitatory and inhibitory inputs to hippocampal dentated granule cells: II. Effects of the NMDA antagonist MK–801. *Brain Research, 562*, 26–33.

Xie, X., Berger, T. W., & Barrionuevo, G. (1992). Isolated NMDA receptor-mediated synaptic responses express both LTP and LTD. *Journal of Neurophysiology, 67*(4), 1009–1013.

Neuronal Growth & Differentiation

Neve, R. L., Ivins, K. J., Benowitz, L. I., During, M. J., & Geller, A. I. (1992). Molecular analysis of the function of the neuronal growth-associated protein GAP–43 by genetic intervention. *Molecular Neurobiology, 5*, 131–141.

Neuronal Migration

Schwanzel-Fukuda M., Abraham, S., Crossin, K. L., Edelman, G. M., & Pfaff, D. W. (1992). Immunocytochemical demostration of neural cell adhesion molecule (NCAM) along the migration route of luteinizing hormone-releasing hormone (LHRH) neurons in mice. *Journal of Comparative Neurology, 321*, 1–18.

Nictitating Membrane Response

Kirkpatrick-Steger, K., Linden, S. V., & Gormezano, I. (1992). Effects of MDA upon differential serial compound conditioning and reflex modification of the rabbit's nictitave membrane response. *Pharmocology Biochemistry & Behavior, 41*, 333–342.

Nowak, A. J., & Gormezano, I. (1990). Electrical stimulation of brainstem nuclei: Elicitation, modification, and conditioning of the rabbit nictitating membrane response. *Behavioral Neuroscience, 104*(1), 4–10.

Richards, W. G., Ricciardi, T. N., & Moore, J. W. (1991). Activity of spinal trigeminal pars oralis and adjacent reticular formation units during differential conditioning of the rabbit nictitating membrane response. *Behavioural Brain Research, 44*, 195–204.

Steinmetz, J. E., Sears, L. L., Gabriel, M., Kubota, Y., Poremba, A., & Kang, E. (1991). Cerebellar interpositus nucleus lesions disrupt classical nictitating membrane conditioning but not discriminative avoidance learning in rabbits. *Behavioural Brain Research, 45*, 71–80.

Plasticity

Gabriel, M., Vogt, B. A., Kubota, Y., Poremba, A., & Kang, E. (1991). Training-stage related neuronal plasticity in limbic thalamus and cingulate cortex during learning: A possible key to mnemonic retrieval. *Behavioural Brain Research, 46*, 175–185.

Jones, T. A., & Schallert, T. (1992). Overgrowth and pruning of dendrites in adult rats recovering from neocortical damage. *Brain Research, 581*, 156–160.

Kupfermann I., Rosen, S., Teyke, T., Cropper, E. C., Miller, M., Vilim, F., & Weiss, K. R. (1989). Neurobiology of behavioral states in *Aplysia*: Non-associative forms of plasticity of feeding responses. In N. Elsner & W. Singer (Eds.)., *Proceedings of the 17th Göttingen Neurobiology Conference* (pp. 47–59). New York: Georg Thieme Verlag Stuttgart.

Shors, T. J., Foy, M. R., Levine, S. & Thompson, R. F. (1990). Unpredictable and uncontrollable stress impairs neuronal plasticity in the rat hippocampus. *Brain Research Bulletin, 24*, 663–667.

Protein Kinase C

Florez, J. C., Nelson, R. B., & Routtenberg, A. (1991). Contrasting patterns of protein phosphorylation in human normal and Alzheimer brain: Focus on protein kinase C and protein F1/GAP–43. *Experimental Neurology, 112*, 264–272.

Recovery

Poplawsky, A., & Isaacson, R. L. (1989). Brief ganglioside treatment produces delayed enhancement of functional recovery after medial septal lesions. *Brain Research, 495*, 396–400.

Spatial Memory

Luine, V., & Hearns, M. (1990). Spatial memory deficits in aged rats: Contributions of the cholinergic system assesseed by ChAT. *Brain Research, 523*, 321–324.

Santucci, A. C., Kanof, P. D., & Haroutunian, V. (1991). Fetal transplant-induced restoration of spatial memory in rats with lesions of the nucleus basalis of Meynert. *Journal of Neural Transplantation and Plasticity, 2*(1), 65–74.

Williams, C. L., Barnett, A. M., & Meck, W. H. (1990). Organizational effects of early gonadal secretions on sexual differentiation in spatial memory. *Behavioral Neuroscience, 104*(1), 84–97.

Taste Aversion

Chambers, K. C. (1990). A neural model for conditioned taste aversions. *Annual Review of Neuroscience, 13*, 373–385.

Horvitz, J. C., & Ettenberg, A. (1991). Conditioned incentive properties of a food-paired conditioned stimulus remain intact during dopamine receptor blockade. *Behavioral Neuroscience, 105*(4), 536–541.

Kiefer, S. W., & Orr, M. R. (1992). Taste avoidance, but not aversion, learning in rats lacking gustatory cortex. *Behavioral Neuroscience, 106*(1), 140–146.

Parker, L. A. (1991). Taste reactivity response elicited by reinforcing drugs: A dose-response analysis. *Behavioral Neuroscience, 105*(6), 955–964.

Risinger, F. O., & Cunningham, C. L. (1992). Genetic differences in ethanol-induced hyperglycemia and conditioned taste aversion. *Life Sciences, 50*(16), 113–118.

Tuning of Nervous System

Black, J. E., Isaacs, K. R., Anderson, B. J., & Alcantara, A. A. (1990). Learning causes synaptogenesis, whereas motor activity causes angiogenesis, in cerebellar cortex of adult rats. *Proc. Natl. Acad. Sci., 87*, 5568–5572.

Campbell, K. A. (1990). Plasticity in the propagation of hippocampal stimulation-induced activity: A [14-C]2-deoxyglucose mapping study. *Brain Research, 520*, 199–207.

Tamborski, A., Lucot, J. B., & Hennessy, M. B. (1990). Central dopamine turnover in guinea pig pups during separation from their mothers in a novel environment. *Behavioral Neuroscience, 104*(4), 607–611.

Songbirds

Brenowitz, E. A., Nalls, B., Wingfield, J. C., & Kroodsma, D. E. (1991). Seasonal changes in avian song nuclei without seasonal changes in song repertoire. *Journal of Neuroscience, 11*(5), 1367–1374.

Nordeen, K. W., & Nordeen, E. J.(1992). Auditory feedback is necessary for the maintenance of sterotyped song in adult zebra finches. *Behavioral and Neural Biology, 57*, 58–62.

Visual Input

Cahusac, P. M., Rolls, E. T., & Marriot, F. H. (1991). Potentiation of neuronal responses to natural visual input paired with postsynaptic activation in the hippocampus of the awake monkey. *Neuroscience Letters, 124*, 39–43.

Desimone, R. (1991). Face-selective cells in the temporal cortex of monkeys. *Journal of Cognitive Neuroscience, 3*(1), 1–8.

Farah, M. J., Monheit, M. A., & Wallace, M. A. (1991). Unconscious perception of "extinguished" visual stimuli: Reassessing the evidence. *Neuropsychologia, 29*(10), 949–958.

Withdrawal Reflex

Dowman, R. (1992). Possible startle response contamination of the spinal nociceptive withdrawal reflex. *Pain, 49*, 187–197.

CHAPTER 16

BOOKS

Adams, J. H., & Duchen, L. W. (Eds.). (1992). *Greenfield's neuropathology* (5th ed.). New York: Oxford University Press.

Dennett, D. C. (1991) *Consciousness explained*. Boston: Little, Brown.

Jaynes, J. (1976). *The origins of consciousness in the breakdown of the bicameral mind*. Boston: Houghton Mifflin.

Kolb, B., & Whishaw, I. Q. (1996) *Fundamentals of Neuropsychology* (4th ed.). New York: Freeman.

Pearlman, A. L., & Collins, R. C. (Eds.). (1990). *Neurobiology of disease*. New York: Oxford University Press.

Pincus, J. H., & Tucker, G. J. (1985). *Behavioral neurology* (3rd ed.). New York: Oxford University Press.

Sacks, O. (1985). *The man who mistook his wife for a hat*. New York: Harper Perennial.

Alexia

Gregg, N. (1995). *Written expression disorders*. Dordrecht, The Netherlands: Kluwer Academic Publishers.

Plaut, D. C. (1994). *Connectionist modeling in cognitive neuropsychology: A case study*. Hillsdale, NJ: Erlbaum.

Aphasia

Benson, F. D. (1996). *Aphasia: A clinical perspective*. New York: Oxford University Press.

Cohn, R. (1996). *Aphasia: A pathophysiological key to memory function and "volitional" naming*. Commack, New York: Nova Science Publishers.

Paradis, M. (1993). *Foundations of aphasia rehabilitation*. Oxford, England: Pergamon Press.

Cerebellar Ataxia

Triarhou, L. C. (1997). *Neural transplantation in cerebellar ataxia*. Austin, TX: Landes.

Coma

McCallagh, P. J. (1993). *Brain dead, brain absent, brain donors: Human subjects or human objects?* New York: Wiley.

Creutzfeldt Jakob Disease

Liberski, P. P. (Ed.). (1989). *Neuroaxonal dystrophy: An ultrastructural link between subacute spongiform virus encephalopathies and Alzheimer's disease*. Bethesda, MD: National Institute of Neurological and Communicative Disorder and Stroke.

Down Syndrome

Berg, J. M., Karlinsky, H., & Holland, A. J. (Eds.). (1993). *Alzheimer disease, Down's syndrome, and their relationship*. Oxford, England: Oxford University Press.

Emotions

Birbaumer, N., & Ohman, A. (Eds.). (1993). *The structure of emotion: Psychophysiological, cognitive and clinical aspects*. Seattle, WA: Hogrete & Huber.

Damasio, A. R. (1994). *Descartes' error: Emotion, reason, and the human brain*. New York: Putnam.

LeDoux, J. E. (1996). *The emotional brain: The mysterious underpinnings of emotional life*. New York: Simon & Schuster.

ARTICLES

Sperry, R. (1982). Some effects of disconnecting the cerebral hemispheres. *Science, 217*, 1223–1226.

Anosias

Bermejo, R., & Zeigler, H. P. (1989). Trigeminal deafferentation and prehension in the pigeon. *Behavioral Brain Research, 35*, 55–61.

Goodale, M. A., & Milner, A. D. (1992). Separate visual pathways for perception and action. *TINS, 15*(1), 20–25.

Jerger, R. (1990). Visuomotor feeding perturbations after lateral telencephalic lesions in pigeons. *Behavioural Brain Research, 40,* 73–80.

Aphasia

Basso, A., Farabola, M., Grassi, M. P., Laiacona, M., & Zanobio, M. E., (1990). Aphasia in left-handers., *Brain & Language, 38,* 233–252.

Basso, A., & Scarpa, M. T., (1990)., Traumatic aphasia in children and adults: A comparison of clinical features and evolution. *Cortex, 26,* 501–514.

Apraxia

Poizner, H., Mack, L., Verfaellie, M., Gonzalez Rothi, L. J., & Heilman, K. M. (1990). Three-dimensional computergraphic analysis of apraxia. *Brain, 113,* 85–101.

Attention

Posner, M. I., (1992). Attention as a cognitive and neural system. *American Psychological Society, 1*(1), 11–14.

Posner, M. I., & Driver, J., (1992)., The neurobiology of selective attention. *Current Opinion in Neurobiology, 2,* 165–169.

Dyslexia

Wolff, P. H., Michel, G. F., & Ovrut, M., (1990). Rate variables and automatized naming in developmental dyslexia. *Brain & Language, 39,* 556–575.

Emotion

Baum, A., Grunberg, N. E., & Singer, J. E., (1992). Biochemical measurements in the study of emotion. *American Psychological Society, 3*(1), 56–60.

Henke, P. G., Ray, A., & Sullivan, R. M., (1991). The amygdala: Emotions and gut functions. *Digestive Diseases & Sciences, 36*(11), 1633–1643.

Vanderwolf, C. H., Kelly, M. E., Kraemer, P., & Streather, A. (1988). Are emotion and motivation localized in the limbic system and nucleus accumbens? *Behavioural Brain Research, 27,* 45–58.

Zacharko, R. M., & Anisman, H., (1991)., Stressor-induced anhedonia in the mesocorticolimbic system. *Neuroscience & Biobehavioral Reviews, 15,* 391–405.

Epilepsy

Desiderio, D. M., Wyler, A. R., & Somes, G. (1992). Proenkephalin A neuropeptides in human epileptogenic tissue. *Journal of Epilepsy, 5,* 105–110.

Green, R. C., Blume, H. W., Kupferschmid, S. B., & Mesulam, M.-M. (1989). Alterations of hippocampal acetylcholinesterase in human temporal lobe epilepsy. *Annals of Neurology, 26*(3), 347–351.

Holmes, K. H., Bilkey, D. K., Laverty, R., & Goddard, G. V. (1990). The N-methyl-D-aspartate antagonists aminophosphonovalerate and carboxypiperazinephosphonate retard the development and expression of kindled seizures. *Brain Research, 506,* 227–235.

Lencz, T., McCarthy, G., Bronen, R. A., Scott, T. M., Inserni, J. A., Sass, K. J., Novelly, R. A., Kim, J. H., & Spencer, D. D. (1992). Quantitative magnetic resonance imaging in temporal lobe epilepsy: Relationship to neuropathology and neuropsychological function. *Annals of Neurology, 31*(6), 629–637.

Sloviter, R. S. (1991). Permanently altered hippocampal structure, excitability, and inhibition after experimental status epilepticus in the rat: The "dormant basket cell" hypothesis and its possible relevance to temporal lobe epilepsy. *Hippocampus, 1*(1), 41–66.

Sutula, T. P. (1991). Reactive changes in epilepsy: Cell death and axons sprouting induced by kindling. *Epilepsy Research, 62*–70.

Hypertension

Lawler, J. E., Sanders, B. J., Cox, R. H., & O'Connor, E. F. (1991). Baroflex function in chronically stressed borderline hypertensive rats. *Physiology & Behavior, 49,* 539–542.

Language Comprehension

Neville, H., Nicol, J. L., Barss, A., Forster, K. I., & Garrett, M. F. (1991). Synaptically based sentence processing classes: Evidence from event-related brain potentials. *Journal of Cognitive Neuroscience, 3*(2), 151–165.

Memory

Aigner, T. G., Mitchell, S. J., Aggleton, J. P., DeLong, M. R., Struble, R. G., Price, D. L., Wenk, G. L., Pettigrew, K. D., & Mishkin, M. (1991). Transient impairment of recognition memory following ibotenic-acid lesions of the basal forebrain in macaques. *Experimental Brain Research, 86,* 18–26.

Hasselmo, M. E., & Bower, J. M. (1993). Acetylcholine and memory. *TINS, Trends in Neuroscience, 16*(6), 218–222.

Holmes, P. V., & Drugan, R. C. (1991). Differential effects of anxiogenic central and peripheral benzodiazepine receptor ligands in tests of learning and memory. *Psychopharmacology, 104,* 249–254.

Malkova, L., Mishkin, M., & Bachevalier, J. (1995). Long-term effects of selective neonatal temporal lobe lesions on learning and memory in monkeys. *Behavioral Neuroscience, 109*(2), 212–226.

McAndrews, M. P., & Moscovitch, M. (1990). Transfer effects in implicit tests of memory. *Journal of Experimental Psychology, 16*(5), 772–788.

Moscovitch, M. (1992). Memory and working-with-memory: A component process model based on modules and central systems. *Journal of Cognitive Neuroscience, 4*(3), 257–267.

Pigott, S., & Milner, B. (1993). Memory for different aspects of complex visual scenes after unilateral temporal- or frontal-lobe resection. *Neuropsychologia, 31*(1), 1–15.

Sakuri, Y. (1990). Cells in the rat auditory system have sensory-delay correlates during the performance of an auditory working memory task. *Behavioral Neuroscience, 104*(6), 856–868.

Rigidity

Roberts, A. C., Robbins, T. W., Everitt, B. J., & Muir, J. L. (1992). A specific form of cognitive rigidity following excitotoxic lesions of the basal forebrain in marmosets. *Neuroscience, 47*(2), 251–264.

Speech

Werker, J. F., & Tees, R. C. (1992). The organization and reorganization of human speech perception. *Annual Review of Neuroscience, 15,* 377–402.

Stress

Anisman, H., & Zacharko, R. M. (1992). Resistance to stress: Multiple neurochemical, behavioral and genetic factors. *Journal of Psychopharmacology, 6*(1), 8–10.

Drugan, R. C., & Holmes, P. V. (1991). Central and peripheral benzodiazepine receptors: Involvement in an organism's response to physical and psychological stress. *Neuroscience & Biobehavioral Reviews, 15,* 277–298.

Pitman, D. L., Ottenweller, J. E., & Natelson, B. H. (1990). Effect of stressor intensity on habituation and sensitization of glucocorticoid responses in rats. *Behavioral Neuroscience, 104*(1), 28–36.

Zalcman, S., Irwin, J., & Anisman, H. (1991). Stressor induced alterations of natural killer cell activity and central catecholamines in mice. *Pharmacology, Biochemistry & Behavior, 39,* 361–366.

Visuospatial Attention

Muir, J. L., Robbins, T. W., & Everitt, B. J. (1992). Disruptive effects of muscimol infused into the basal forebrain on conditional discrimination and visual attention: Differential interactions with cholinergic mechanisms. *Psychopharmacology, 107,* 541–550.

Parasuraman, R., Greenwood, P. M., Haxby, J. V., & Grady, C. L. (1992). Visuospatial attention in dementia of the Alzheimer type. *Brain, 115,* 711–733.

Vocalization

Carden, S. E., & Hofer, M. A. (1990). The effects of opioid and benzodiazepine antagonists on dam-induced reductions in rat pup isolation distress. *Developmental Psychobiology, 23*(8), 797–808.

Hofer, M. A., & Shair, H. N. (1991). Independence of ultrasonic vocalization and thermogenic responses in infant rats. *Behavioral Neuroscience, 105*(1), 41–48.

Provine, R. R., & Yong, Y. L. (1991). Laughter: A stereotyped human vocalization. *Ethology, 89,* 115–124.

CHAPTER 17

BOOKS

Alcohol

Deitrich, R. A., & Erwin, G. (Eds.). (1996). *Pharmacological effects of ethanol on the nervous system.* Boca Raton, FL: CRC Press.

Grisolia, S., & Felipo, V. (1993). *Cirrhosis, hyperammonemia, and hepatic encephalopathy.* New York: Plenum Press.

Hunt, W. A., & Nixon, S. J. (Eds.). (1993). *Alcohol-induced brain damage.* Rockville, MD: The Institute.

Amphetamines

Ali, S. F., & Takahashi, Y. (Eds.). (1996). *Cellular and molecular mechanisms of drugs and abuse: Cocaine, iogaine, and substituted amphetamines.* New York: The New York Academy of Sciences.

Cocaine

Volkow, N. D., & Swann, A. C. (Eds.). (1990). *Cocaine in the brain.* New Brunswick, NJ: Rutgers University Press.

Marijuana

Lundqvist, T. (1995). *Cognitive dysfunctions in chronic cannabis users observed during treatment: An integrative approach.* Stockholm, Sweden: Almqvit & Wiksell.

Murphy, L., & Bartke, A. (Eds.). (1992). *Marijuana/cannabinoids: Neurobiology and neurophysiology.* Boca Raton, FL: CRC Press.

Maternal Drug Use

Miller, M. W. (Ed.). (1992). *Development of the central nervous system: Effects of alcohol and opiates.* New York: Wiley-Liss.

Zagon, I. S., & Slotkin, T. A. (Eds.). (1992). *Maternal substance abuse and the developing nervous system.* San Diego: Academic Press.

Nicotine

Adlkofer, F., & Thurau, K. (1991). *Effects of nicotine on biological systems.* Boston: Birkhauser.

Gold, M. S. (1995). *Tobacco.* New York: Plenum Medical Book.

Opiates

Cooper, R. J., & Cooper, S. J. (Eds.). (1988). *Endorphins, opiates, and behavioural processes.* Chichester, England: Wiley.

Psychopharmacology

Balfour, D. J. K. (1990). *Psychotropic drugs of abuse.* New York: Pergmon Press.

Baskys, A., & Remington, G. (Eds.). (1996). *Brain mechanisms and psychotropic drugs.* Boca Raton, FL: CRC Press.

Cooper, J. R., Bloom, F. E., & Roth, R. H. (1986). *The biochemical basis of neuropharmacology.* (5th ed.). New York: Oxford University Press.

Feldman, R. S., & Quenzer, C. F. (1995). *Fundamentals of neuropsychopharmacology.* (2nd ed.) Sunderland, MA: Sinauer Associates.

Fishbein, D. H. (1996). *The dynamics of drug abuse.* Boston: Allyn & Bacon.

Gillman, E. G., Rail, T. W., Nies, A. S., & Taylor, P. (Eds.). (1990). *Goodman and Gilman's the pharmacological basis of therapeutics* (8th ed.). New York: Pergamon Press.

Julien, R. M. (1992). *A primer of drug action* (6th ed.). New York: Freeman.

Watson, R. R. (Ed.). (1992). *Drugs of abuse and neurobiology*. Boca Raton, FL: CRC Press.

Ritalin

Ingersoll, B. D. (1993). *Attention deficit disorder and learning disabilities: Realities, myth, and controversial treatments*. New York: Doubleday.

Silver, L. B. (1992). *Attention-deficit hyperactivity disorder: A clinical guide to diagnosis and treatment*. Washington D. C., American Psychiatric Press.

Tolerance

Goudie, A. J., & Emmett-Oglesby, M. W. (1989). *Psychoactive drugs: Tolerance and sensitization*. Clifton, NJ: Humana Press.

Pratt, J. A. (1991). *The biological bases of drug tolerance and dependence*. London: Academic Press.

Withdrawal

Maldonado, R. (1996). *Neurobiological mechanisms of opiate withdrawal*. New York: Chapman & Hall.

Wesson, D. R. (1995). *Detoxification from alcohol and other drugs*. Rockville, MD: U. S. Department of Health and Human Services, Public Health Service.

ARTICLES

Alcohol

Barron, S., Kelly, S. J., & Riley, E. P. (1991). Neonatal alcohol exposure alters suckling behavior in neonatal rat pups. *Pharmacology Biochemistry & Behavior, 39,* 423–427.

Cunningham, C.L., Niehus, D.R., Malott, D. H., & Prather, L .K. (1992). Genetic differences in the rewarding and activating effects of morphine and ethanol. *Pschopharmacology, 187,* 385–393.

Kelley, S. J., Mahoney, J. C., Randich, A., & West, J. R. (1991). Indices of stress in rats: Effects of sex, perinatal alcohol and artificial rearing. *Physiology & Behavior, 49,* 751–756.

Kulkosky, P. J., Sanchez, M. R., & Marrinan, D. A., (1992). Bombesin reduces alcohol choice in nutritive expectancy and limited-access procedures., *Alcohol, 9,* 123–127.

Risinger, F. O., Dickinson, S. D., & Cunningham, C. L. (1992). Haloperidol reduces ethanol-induced motor activity stimulation but not conditioned place preference. *Psychopharmacology, 107,* 453–456.

Amphetamine

Basse-Tomusk, A., & Rebec, G. V. (1990). Corticostriatal and thalamic regulation of amphetamine-induced ascorbate release in the neostriatum. *Pharmacology Biochemistry & Behavior, 35,* 55–60.

Clarke, P. B. S., & Franklin, K. B. J. (1992). Infusions of 6-hydroxydopamine into the nucleus accumbens abolish the analgesic effect of amphetamine but not of morphine in the formalin test., *Brain Research, 580,* 106–110.

Haracz, J. L., Tschanz, J. T. Griffth, K. E., & Rebec, G. V. (1991). Bilateral cortical ablations attenuate amphetamine-induced excitations of neostriatal motor-related neurons in freely moving rats. *Neuroscience Letters, 134,* 127–130.

Jones, J. R., Caul, W. F., & Hill, J. O. (1992) The effects of amphetamine on body weight and energy expenditure., *Physiology & Behavior, 51,* 1–5.

Kelley, A. E., & Throne, L. C. (1992). NMDA receptors mediate the behavioral effects of amphetamine infused into the nucleus accumbens. *Brain Research Bulletin, 29,* 247–254.

Kirkby, R. D., & Kokkinidis, L. (1991). Amphetamine sensitization and amygdala kindling: Pharmacological evaluation of catecholaminergic and cholinergic mechanisms., *Brain Research Bulletin, 26,* 357–364.

O'Dell, S. J., Weihmuller, F. B., & Marshall, J. F. (1991). Multiple methamphetamine injections induce marked increases in extracellular striatal dopamine which correlate with subsequent neurotoxicity. *Brain Research, 564,* 256–260.

Pierce, R. C., & Rebec, G. V. (1992). Dopamine-, NMDA-, and sigma receptor antagonists exert differential effects on basal and amphetamine-induced changes in neostriatal ascorbate and DOPAC in awake, behaving rats. *Brain Research, 579,* 59–66.

Robinson, T. E., & Camp, D. M. (1990). Does amphetamine preferentially increase the extracellular concentration of dopamine in the mesolimbic system of freely moving rats? *Neuropsychopharmacology, 3*(3), 163–173.

Ryan, L. J., Linder, J. C., Martone, M. E., & Groves, P. M., (1990). Histological and ultrastructural evidence the D-amphetamine causes degeneration in neostriatum and frontal cortex of rats., *Brain Research, 518,* 67–77.

Sills, T. L., & Vaccarino, F. J. (1991). Facilitation and inhibition of feeding by a single dose of amphetamine: Relationship to baseline intake and accumbens cholecystokinin. *Psychopharmacology, 105,* 329–334.

Benzodiazepines

Andrews, J. S., & Stephens, D. N. (1991). Discriminative stimulus properties of the benzodiazepine receptor partial agonist beta–carbolines abecarnil and ZK–95962: A comparison with chlordiazepoxide. *Behavioral Pharmacology, 2,* 171–185.

Finlay, J. M., Damsma, G., & Fibiger, H. C. (1992). Benzodiazepine-induced decreases in extracellular concentrations of dopamine in the nucleus accumbens after acute and repeated administration. *Psychopharmacology, 106,* 202–208.

Caffeine

Guillet, R., & Kellogg, C. K. (1991). Neonatal caffeine exposure alters developmental sensitivity to adenosine receptor ligands. *Pharmacology Biochemistry and Behavior, 40,* 811–817.

Marrion, N. V., & Adams, P. R. (1992). Release of intracellular calcium and modulation of membrane currents by caffeine in bull-frog sympathetic neurones. *Journal of Physiology, 445,* 515–535.

Cocaine

Anday, E. K., Cohen, M. E., Kelley, N. E., & Leitner, D. S. (1989). Effect of in utero cocaine exposure on startle and its modification. *Developmental Pharmacology & Therapeutics, 12,* 137–145.

Gauvin, D. V., Criado, J. R., Moore, K. R., & Holloway, F. A. (1990). Potentiation of cocaine's discriminative effects by caffeine: A time-effect analysis. *Pharmacology Biochemistry & Behavior, 36,* 195–197.

Kehoe, P., & Boylan, C. J. (1992). Cocaine-induced effects on isolation stress in neonatal rats. *Behavioral Neuroscience, 106*(2), 374–379.

Kuhar, M. J., Ritz, M. C., & Boja, J. W. (1991). The dopamine hypothesis of the reinforcing properties of cocaine. *Trends in Neurosciences, 14*(7), 299–302.

Williams, H. P., Manderscheid, P. Z., Schwartz, M., & Frank, R. A. (1991). Cocaine's effects on rate of intracranial self-stimulation. *Pharmacology Biochemistry & Behavior, 40,* 273–277.

Witkin, J. F., Nichols, D. E., Terry, P., & Katz, J. L. (1991). Behavioral effects of selective dopaminergic compounds in rats discriminating cocaine injections. *Journal of Pharmacology & Experimental Therapeutics, 257*(2), 706–712.

Dopamine

Gruen, R. J., Deutch, A. Y., & Roth, R. H. (1990). Perinatal diazepam exposure: Alterations in exploratory behavior and mesolimbic dopamine turnover. *Pharmacology Biochemistry and Behavior, 36,* 169–175.

Hoffman, D. C., & Wise, R. A. (1992). Locomotor-activating effects of the D_2 agonist bromocriptine show environment-specific sensitization following repeated injections. *Psychopharmacology, 107,* 277–284.

Kalivas, P. W., & Stewart, J. (1991). Dopamine transmission in the initiation and expression of drug- and stress-induced sensitization of motor activity. *Brain Research Reviews, 16,* 223–244.

Weihmuller, F. B., O'Dell, S. J., Marshall, J. F. (1992). MK–801 protection against methamphetamine-induced striatal dopamine terminal injury is associated with attenuated dopamine overflow. *Synapse, 11,* 155–163.

Hallucinogens

Ellison, G. D. (1991). Animal models of hallucinations. *Neuromethods, 18,* 151–195.

Muscarine

Vanderwolf, C. H. (1991). Anti-muscarininc drug effects in a swim-to-platform test: dose-response relations. *Behavioural Brain Research, 44,* 217–219.

Nicotine

Acri, J. B., Grunberg, N. E., & Morse, D. E. (1991). Effects of nicotine on the acoustic startle reflex amplitude in rats. *Psychopharmacology, 104,* 244–248.

Opiates

Bakshi, V. P., & Kelley, A. E. (1993). Striatal regulation of mophine-induced hyperphagia: An anatomical mapping study. *Psychopharmacology, 111,* 207–214.

Barr, G. A., & Rossi, G. (1992). Conditioned place preference from ventral tegmental injection of morphine in neonatal rats. *Developmental Brain Research, 66,* 133–136.

Ben-Eliyahu, S., Marek, R., Vaccarino, A. L., Mogil, J. S., Sternberg, W. F., & Liebeskind, J. C. (1992). The NMDA receptor antagonist MK–801 prevents long-lasting nonassociative morphine tolerance in the rat. *Brain Research, 575,* 304–308.

Kinsley, C. H., & Bridges, R. S. (1990). Morphine treatment and reproductive condition alter olfactory preferences for pup and adult male odors in female rats. *Developmental Psychobiology, 23*(4), 331–347.

Lielbiech, I., Yirmiya, R., & Liebeskind, J. C., (1991). Intake of and preference for sweet solutions are attenuated in morphine-withdrawn rats. *Behavioral Neuroscience, 105*(6), 965–970.

Mitchell, J. B., & Stewart, J. (1990). Facilitation of sexual behaviors in the male rat in the presence of stimuli previously paired with systematic injections of morphine. *Pharmacology Biochemistry & Behavior, 35,* 367–372.

Neisewander, J. L., Pierce, R. C., & Bardo, M. T. (1990). Naloxone enhances the expression of morphine-induced conditioned place preference. *Psychopharmacology, 100,* 201–205.

Schnur, P. (1992). Conditioned morphine withdrawal in the hamster. *Psychopharmacology, 107,* 517–522.

Shaham, Y., Alvares, K., Nespor, S. M., & Grunberg, N. E. (1992). Effects of stress on oral morphine and fentanyl self-administration in rats. *Pharmacology Biochemistry & Behavior, 41,* 615–619.

Stewart, J., & Wise, R. A. (1992). Reinstatement of heroin self-administration habits: Morphine prompts and naltrexone discourages renewed responding after extinction. *Psychopharmacology, 108,* 79–84.

Tolerance

McLaughlin, C. R., Lichtman, A. H., Fanselow, M. S., & Cramer, C. P. (1989). Pro-Leu-Gly-NH2 serves as a conditioned stimulus in the acquisition of conditioned tolerance. *Behavioral Neuroscience, 103*(2), 447–451.

Wolgin, D. L., & Thompson, G. B. (1989). Contingent suppression of tolerance to the "anorexigenic" effect of haloperidol. *Behavioral Neuroscience, 103*(3), 673–677.

Withdrawal

Fanselow, M. S., & Cramer, C. P. (1988). The ontogeny of opiate tolerance and withdrawal in infant rats. *Pharmacology Biochemistry & Behavior, 31*, 431–438.

Gauvin, D. V., Youngblood, B. D., & Holloway, F. A. (1992). The discriminative stimulus properties of acute ethanol withdrawal (hangover) in rats. *Alchoholism: Clinical & Experimental Research, 16*(2), 336–341.

CHAPTER 18

BOOKS

Alzheimer's Disease

Heston, L. L. (Ed.). (1997). *Progress in Alzheimer's disease and similar conditions*. Washington, DC: American Psychiatric Press.

Morris, R. G. (Ed.). (1996). *The cognitive neuropsychology of Alzheimer-type dementia*. Oxford, England: Oxford University Press.

Parks, R. W., Zec, R. F., & Wilson, R. S. (1993). *Neuropsychology of Alzheimer's disease and other dementias*. New York: Oxford University Press.

Schwartz, M. F. (1990). *Modular deficits in Alzheimer-type dementia*. Cambridge, MA: MIT Press.

Anxiolytics and Antidepressants

File, S. F. (Ed.). (1991). *Psychopharmacology of anxiolytics and antidepressants*. New York: Pergamon Press.

Smith, M. C. (1991). *A social history of the minor tranquilizers: The quest for small comfort in the age of anxiety*. New York: Pharmaceutical Products Press.

Turkington, C. (1994). *Making the Prozac decision: Your guide to antidepressants*. Los Angeles: Lowell House.

Benzodiazepines

Giesen-Crouse, E. (Ed.). (1993). *Peripheral benzodiazepine receptors*. London: Academic Press.

Rodgers, R. J., & Cooper, S. J. (1991). *5-HT1A agonists, 5-HT3 antagonists and benzodiazepines: Their comparative behavioural pharmacology*. Chichester, England: Wiley.

Bipolar Disorder

Davies, K. E., & Tilghman, S. M. (Eds.). (1993). *Genome maps and neurological disorders*. Plainview, New York: Cold Spring Harbor Laboratory Press.

Hendrix, M. L. (1993). *Decade of the brain: Bipolar disorder*. Rockville, MD: US Department of Health and Human Services.

Mogens, S. (1993). *Lithium treatment of manic-depressive illness: A practical guide*. Basel, Switzerland: Karger.

Depression

Montgomery, S. A., & Corn, T. H. (Eds.). (1994). *Psychopharmacology of depression*. Oxford, England: Oxford University Press.

Schizophrenia

David, A. S., & Cutting, J. C. (Eds.). (1994). *The neuropsychology of schizophrenia*. Hove, England: Erlbaum.

Hirsch, S. R., & Weinberger, D. R. (Eds.). (1995). *Schizophrenia*. Oxford, England: Blackwell Science.

McKenna, P. J. (1994). *Schizophrenia: From mind to molecule*. Washington DC: American Psychiatric Press.

Winokur, G. (1996). *The natural history of mania, depression, and schizophrenia*. Washington DC: American Psychiatric Press.

Seasonal Affective Disorder

Rosenthal, N. E. (1993). *Winter blues: Seasonal affective disorder: What it is and how to overcome it*. New York: Guilford Press.

Wetterberg, L. (Ed.). (1993). *Light and biological rhythms in man*. Oxford, England: Oxford University Press.

Senility

Huppert, F. A., Brayne, C., & O'Connor, D. W. (Eds.). (1994). *Dementia and normal aging*. Cambridge, England: Cambridge University Press.

Meier-Ruge, W. (Ed.). (1993). *Dementing brain disease in old age*. Basel; Switzerland: Karger.

Nicholson, C. D. (Ed.). (1994). *Anti-dementia agents: Research and prospects for therapy*. London: Academic Press.

Synesthesia

Cytowic, R. E. (1993). *The man who tasted shapes: A bizarre medical mystery offers revolutionary insights into emotions, reasoning, and consciousness*. New York: Putnam.

Tardive Dyskinesia

Haag, H., & Hippius, H. (1992). *Tardive dyskinesia*. Seattle, WA: Hogrefe & Huber.

ARTICLES

Alzheimer's Disease

Feldman, J. I., Murphy, C., Davidson, T. M., Jalowayski, A. A., Galindo de Jaime, G. (1991). The rhinologic evaluation of Alzheimer's disease. *Laryngoscope, 101*(11), 1198–1202.

Pappas, B. A., Sunderland, T., Weingartner, H. M., Vitiello, B., Martinson, H., & Putnam, K. (1992). Alzheimer's disease and feeling-of-knowing for knowledge and episodic memory. *Journal of Gerontology, 47*(3), 159–164.

Rouleau, I., Salmon, D. P., Butters, N., Kennedy, C., & McGuire, K. (1992). Quantitative and qualitative analyses of clock drawings in Alzheimer's and Huntington's disease. *Brain and Cognition, 18*, 70–87.

Rupniak, N. M. J., Tye, S. J., Brazell, C., Heald, A., Iversen, S. D., & Pagella, P. G. (1992). Reversal of cognitive impairment by heptyl physostigmine, a long-lasting cholinesterase inhibitor, in primates. *Journal of the Neurological Sciences, 107*, 246–249.

Anxiolytics and Antidepressants

Archer, T., & Minor, B. (1989). Behavior of mother rats in conflict tests sensitive to antianxiety agents. *Behavioral Neuroscience, 103*, 193–201.

Treit, D., & Pesold, C. (1990). Septal lesions inhibit fear reactions in two animal models of anxiolytic drug action. *Physiology & Behavior, 47*, 365–371.

Benzodiazepines

Rodgers, R. J., & Waters, A. J. (1985). Benzodiazepines and their antagonists: A pharmacoethological analysis with particular reference to effects on "aggression." *Neuroscience & Biobehavioral Reviews, 9*, 21–35.

Bipolar Disorder

Kofman, O., & Belmaker, R. H. (1990). Intracerebroventricular *myo*-inositol antagonizes lithium-induced suppression of rearing in rats., *Brain Research, 534*, 345–347.

Laughlin, C. R., & Cramer, C. P. (1989). Acute administration of lithium carbonate interferes with suckling in neonatal rats. *Pharmacology Biochemistry & Behavior, 32*, 453–458.

Swann, A. C., Secunda, S. K., Koslow, S. H., Katz, M. M., Bowden, C. L., Mass, J. W., Davis, J. D., & Robins, E. (1991). Mania: Sympathoadrenal function and clinical state. *Psychiatry Research, 37*, 195–205.

Depression

Deptula, D., Manevitz, A., & Yozawitz, A. (1991). Asymmetry of recall in depression. *Journal of Clinical & Experimental Neuropsychology, 13*(6), 854–879.

Planznik, A., & Kostowski, W. (1991). The involvement of serotonin and noradrenaline in the psychopathological processes of stress and depression: Animal models and the effect of antidepressant drugs. *Polish Journal of Pharmacology and Pharmacy, 43*, 301–322.

Generalized Anxiety Disorder

Wu, J. C., Buchsbaum, M. S., Hershey, T. G., Hazlett, E., Sicotte, N., & Johnson, J. C. (1991). PET in generalized anxiety disorder. *Biological Psychiatry, 29*, 1181–1199.

Mental Retardation

Fox, R., & Gross, S., III. (1990). Mental retardation and perception of global motion. *Perception & Psychophysics, 48*(3), 252–258.

Obsessive-Compulsive Disorder

Cottraux, J., Mollard, E., Bouvard, M., Marks, I., Sluys, M., Nury, A. M., Douge, R., & Cialdella, P. (1990). A controlled study of fluvoxamine and exposure in obsessive-compulsive disorder. *International Clinical Psychopharmacology, 5*, 17–30.

Tien, A. Y., Pearlson, G. D., Machlin, S. R., Bylsma, F. W., & Hoehn-Saric, R. (1992). Oculomotor performance in obsessive-compulsive disorder. *American Journal of Psychiatry, 149*(5), 641–646.

Parkinson's Disease

Taylor, J. R., Elsworth, J. D., Roth, R. H., Sladek, J. R., Jr., Collier, T. J., & Redmond, D. E., Jr. (1991). Grafting of fetal substantia nigra to striatum reverses behavioral deficits induced by MPTP in primates: A comparison with other types of grafts as controls. *Experimental Brain Research, 85*, 335–348.

Schizophrenia

Barta, P. E., Pearlson, G. D., Powers, R. E., Richards, S. S., & Tune, L. E. (1990). Auditory hallucinations and smaller superior temporal gyral volume in schizophrenia. *American Journal of Psychiatry, 147*(11), 1457–1462.

Benson, K. L., Faull, K. F., & Zarcone., V. P., Jr. (1991). Evidence for the role of serotonin in the regulation of slow wave sleep in schizophrenia. *Sleep, 14*(2), 133–139.

Csernansky, J. G., King, R. J., Faustman, W. O., Moses, J. A., Poscher, M. E., & Faull, K. F. (1990). 5-HIAA in cerebrospinal fluid and deficit schizophrenic characteristics. *British Journal of Psychiatry, 156*, 501–507.

Faustman, W. O., Moses, J. A., Ringo, D. L., Newcomer, J. W. (1991). Left-handedness in male schizophrenic patients is associated with increased impairment on the Luria-Nebraska neuropsychological battery. *Biological Psychiatry, 30*, 326–334.

Grace, A. A. (1991). Phasic versus tonic dopamine release and the modulation of dopamine system responsivity: A hypothesis for the etiology of schizophrenia. *Neuroscience, 41*(1), 1–24.

Sumiyoshi, T., Stockmeier, C. A., Overholser, J. C., & Thompson, P. A. (1995). Dopamine D-sub-4 receptors and effects of guanine nucleotides on (-sup-3H) raclopride binding in postmortem caudate nucleus of subjects with schizophrenia or major depression. *Brain Research, 681*(1–2), 109–116.

Taller, A. M., Asher, D. M., Pomeroy, K. L., & Basil, E. (1996). Search for viral nucleic acid sequences in brain tissues of patients with schizophrenia using nested polymerase chain reaction. *Archives of General Psychiatry, 53*(1), 32–40.

Senility

Goldman, H., Berman, R. F., Gershon, S., Murphy, S. L., & Altman, H. J. (1987). Correlation of behavioral and cerebrovascular functions in the aging rat. *Neurobiology of Aging, 8*, 409–416.

Scheft, B. K., & Biederman, J. J. (1990). Emotional effects of self-generated behavior and the influence of resourcefulness and depressed mood. *Journal of Social & Clinical Psychology, 9*(3), 354–366.

Wassef, A., Smith, E. M., Rose, R. M., Gardner, R., Nguyen, H., & Meyer, W. J. (1990). Mononuclear leukocyte glucocorticoid receptor binding characteristic and down-regulation in major depression. *Psychoneuroendocrinology, 15*(1), 59–68.

Raz, N., Torres, I. J., Spencer, W. D., White, K., & Acker, J. D. (1992). Age related regional differences in cerebellar vermis observed in vivo. *Archives of Neurology, 49*, 412–416.

Sharp, P. E., Barnes, C. A., & McNaughton, B. L. (1987). Effects of aging on environmental modulation of hip-pocampal evoked responses. *Behavioral Neuroscience, 101*(2), 170–178.

Tardive Dyskinesia

Neisewander, J. L., Lucki, I., & McGonigle, P. (1991). Neurochemical changes associated with the persistence of spontaneous oral dyskinesia in rats following chronic reserpine treatment. *Brain Research, 558*, 27–35.

See, R. E., & Ellison, G. (1990). Intermittent and continuous haloperidol regimens produce different types of oral dyskinesias in rats. *Psychopharmacology, 100*, 404–412.

CREDITS

Photographs

All chapter opening photos: Comstock.

Chapter 1 Figure 1–2 Brian Warling, International Museum of Surgical Science; Figure 1–3 Aristotle (384–322 BCE), Greek philosopher, Marble head. Height 33 cm, MA 80. Louvre, Dept. des Antiquities Grecques/Romaines, Paris, France. © Photograph by Erich Lessing, Art Resource, NY; Figure 1–4 Frans Hals "Portrait of René Descartes" (1596–1650). Louvre, Paris, France. Giraudon, Art Resource, NY; Figure 1–5(a) PhotoDisc, Inc.; Figure 1–5(b) Fred McConnaughey, Photo Researchers, Inc.; Figure 1–5(c) K.H. Switak, Photo Researchers, Inc.; Figure 1–5(d) PhotoDisc, Inc.; Figure 1–7 National Library of Science; Figure in Box 1–1 Kjell B. Sandved, Photo Researchers, Inc.; Figure in Box 1–3 J. Levy, R.W. Sperry, & C. Trevarthen (courtesy of Norma Sperry).

Chapter 2 Figure 2–1 Manfred Kage, Peter Arnold, Inc.; Figure 2–3 Corbis-Bettman; Figure 2–4 Ed Reschke; Figure 2–12(b) Dr. Don Fawcett, Photo Researchers, Inc.; Figure 2–25 Biophoto Associates/Science Source, Photo Researchers, Inc.; Figure 2–26 (actin network) Dr. Robert Goldman; Figure 2–26 (microtubules) David M. Phillips/The Population Council/Science Source, Photo Researchers, Inc.; Figure 2–26 (neurofilaments) Dr. Don Fawcett/E. Mugnaini, Photo Researchers, Inc.; Figure 2–30(b) Courtesy of Dr. Steven M. Rothman (1988). *The Journal of Cell Biology, 107,* 1508; Figure 2–31 CNRI/Science Photo Library, Photo Researchers, Inc.; Figure in Box 2–1 Science Photo Library, Photo Researchers, Inc.

Chapter 3 Figure 3–3 Courtesy of Tom Fenchel, from *Ecology of Protozoa.*

Chapter 4 Figure 4–14(b), (c) Prof. John Heuser, Ph.D.; Figure in Box 4–3 Biophoto Associates, Photo Researchers, Inc.

Chapter 5 Figure 5–6 (left) Don Fawcett/Science Source, Photo Researchers, Inc.; (right) Oliver Meckes/Ottawa, Photo Researchers, Inc.; Figure 5–15(b) (top) Alfred Owczarzak, Biological Photo Service; (center) Science Photo Library, Custom Medical Stock Photo, Inc.; (bottom) Courtesy of Richard L. Rotundo, Ph.D., University of Miami School of Medicine; Figure 5–17 Eva Fifkova, M.D., Ph.D.; Figure 5–23(b) Scott Camazine, M. Marchaterre, Photo Researchers, Inc.; Figure in Box 5–1, p. 100 (left) Michael McCoy, Photo Researchers, Inc.; (right) Michael Marten/Science Photo Library, Photo Researchers, Inc.; p. 101 (left) © Tom McHugh, 1979. Steinhart Aquarium. Photo Researchers, Inc.; (right) Stuart Kenter Associates; Figure in Box 5–4 Daniel P. Perl, M.D. Mount Sinai School of Medicine.

Chapter 6 Figure 6–7 Dr. Virginia Pickel; Figure 6–10 Okapia, Photo Researchers, Inc.; Figure 6–15 Prof. Tim Smock; Figure in Box 6–1 M. Kowal, Custom Medical Stock Photo, Inc.

Chapter 7 Figure 7–3(c) Ralph T. Hutchings.

Chapter 8 Figure in Box 8–4 Brooks/Brown, Photo Researchers, Inc.

Chapter 9 Figure 9–4 Ward's Natural Science Establishment, Inc.; Figure 9–5 Prof. P. Motta, Dept. of Anatomy, University "La Sapienza," Rome/Science Photo Library, Photo Researchers, Inc.; Figure 9–13 El Greco, 1541–1614, "Vision of St. John" (Opening of Fifth Seal) ca. 1608. The Metropolitan Museum of Art, Rogers Fund, 1956. (56.48) Photograph © The Metropolitan Museum of Art; Figure 9–14(b) Ed Reschke, Peter Arnold, Inc.; Figure 9–14(d) Custom Medical Stock Photo, Inc.; Figure 9–25 D. H. Hubel, T.N. Wiesel, and M.P. Stryker, (1978). Anatomical demonstration of orientation columns in the Macaque monkey. *Journal of Comparative Neurology, 177,* 361–379. Reprinted by permission.

Chapter 10 Figure 10–5 Dr. Apostolos Georgopoulos; Figure 10–13 Gian Garriga; Figure 10–15 Gerard Lacz, Peter Arnold, Inc.; Figure in Box 10–2 L. O'Shaugnhessy, Leslie O'Shaugnhessy Studios.

Chapter 11 Figure 11–5 (bottom) J.L. Ochoa, P.J. Pyck, et al. (Eds.) (1975). *Peripheral Neuropathy* , 1st ed. Philadelphia: W.B. Saunders Co.; Figure 11–9(a) Patrick W. Mantyh; Figure 11–14 Courtesy of Prof. Allan Basbaum; Figure 11–18 Courtesy of Prof. Allan Basbaum; Figure in Box 11–1 John Dudak, Phototake NYC; Figure in Box 11–2 Stewart Hendry; Figure in Box 11–3 Dr. Howard Fields, radiographs courtesy of Prof. John E. Adams.

Chapter 12 Figure 12–12 Dr. M. Konishi; Figure 12–16 John Mitchell, Photo Researchers, Inc.; Figure in Box 12–1 Howard W. Jones, Jr., M.D.; Figure in Box 12–3 Photofest.

Chapter 13 Figure 13–1 W.J. Schwartz & H. Gainer (1977) Superchiasmatic nucleus: Use of 14-C labeled deoxyglucose uptake as a functional marker. *Science, 197,* 1089–1091; Figure 13–2 John Cancalosi, Peter Arnold, Inc.

Chapter 15 Figure 15–8 Courtesy of Christopher Cohan, Ph.D., Assoc. Prof., & E. Weinhofer; Figure 15–10 F. Bonhoeffer; Figure 15–12 Bonnie Kamin, PhotoEdit; Figure 15–13 Nina Leen, Stuart Kenter Associates; Figure 15–14 Andy Sacks, Tony Stone Images; Figures in Box 15–1 Courtesy of Dale Purves, M.D. From D. Purves and J. Lichtman (1980). Elimination of synapses in the developing nervous system. *Science, 210,* 153–157; Figures in Box 15–2 Courtesy of David H. Hubel, T. N. Wiesel, & S. LeVay (1977). Plasticity of ocular dominance columns in monkey striate cortex. *Philosophical Transactions of the Royal Society of London (Biol.), 278,* 377–409.

Chapter 16 Figure 16–1 James King-Holmes/Science Photo Library, Photo Researchers, Inc.; Figure 16–2 Susan Kuklin, Photo Researchers, Inc.; Figure 16–11 (left and right) Richard Hutchings, Photo Researchers, Inc.; Figure 16–12 Bill Robbins, Tony Stone Images; Figure 16–13 Ralph C. Eagle, Jr., M.D., Photo Researchers, Inc.; Figure 16–14 Martin Rotker, Phototake, NYC; Figure 16–16 Duke University Medical Center; Figure 16–19 Wellcome Dept. of Cognitive Neurology/Science Photo Library, Photo Researchers, Inc.; Figure 16–20 Dr. Mony De Leon, Peter Arnold, Inc.; Figure 16–21

Scott Camazine, Photo Researchers, Inc.; **Figure 16–22** GJLP/CNRI, Phototake NYC.

Chapter 17 **Figure 17–3** A. P.Streissguth, S. Landesman-Dwyer, J.C. Martin, & D.W. Smith (1980). Teratogenic effects of alcohol in humans and laboratory animals. *Science, 209*, 353–361; **Figure 17–12** (bottom) R. Konig/Jacana, Photo Researchers, Inc.; **Figure 17–13** (top) James Beveridge, Visuals Unlimited; **Figure 17–13** (bottom) Custom Medical Stock Photo, Inc.

Chapter 18 **Figure 18–1** Vincent Van Gogh, "Starry Night". (1889). Oil on canvas, 29 x 36 1/4" (73.7 x 92.1 cm). The Museum of Modern Art, New York. Acquired through the Lillie P. Bliss Bequest. Photograph © 1999 The Museum of Modern Art, New York; **Figure 18–2** Van Gogh, "Night Cafe". © Yale University Art Gallery, CT; **Figures 18–4, 18–7** Dr. Arvin F. Oke; **Figure in Box 18–3** W. & D. McIntyre, Photo Researchers, Inc.

Cartoons, Figures & Tables

Chapter 1 **Figure 1–8** Adapted from F. Martini (1998). *Fundamentals of Anatomy and Physiology*, 4th ed., p. 447. Upper Saddle River, NJ: Prentice Hall. © Prentice Hall. Reprinted with permission.

Chapter 2 **Figure 2–6** From F. Martini (1998). *Fundamentals of Anatomy and Physiology*, 4th ed., p. 372. Upper Saddle River, NJ: Prentice Hall. © Prentice Hall. Reprinted with permission; **Figure 2–8** Adapted from F. Martini (1998). *Fundamentals of Anatomy and Physiology*, 4th ed., p. 433. Upper Saddle River, NJ: Prentice Hall. © Prentice Hall. Reprinted with permission; **Figure 2–9** From F. Martini (1998). *Fundamentals of Anatomy and Physiology*, 4th ed., p. 37. Upper Saddle River, NJ: Prentice Hall. © Prentice Hall. Reprinted with permission; **Figure 2–10** Adapted from F. Martini (1998). *Fundamentals of Anatomy and Physiology*, 4th ed., p. 52. Upper Saddle River, NJ: Prentice Hall. © Prentice Hall. Reprinted with permission; **Figure 2–15** From F. Martini (1998). *Fundamentals of Anatomy and Physiology*, 4th ed., p. 94. Upper Saddle River, NJ: Prentice Hall. © Prentice Hall. Reprinted with permission; **Figure 2–18** From F. Martini (1998). *Fundamentals of Anatomy and Physiology*, 4th ed., p. 53. Upper Saddle River, NJ: Prentice Hall. © Prentice Hall. Reprinted with permission; **Figure 2–19** From F. Martini (1998). *Fundamentals of Anatomy and Physiology*, 4th ed., pp. 96–97. Upper Saddle River, NJ: Prentice Hall. © Prentice Hall. Reprinted with permission; **Figure 2–20(b)** From F. Martini (1998). *Fundamentals of Anatomy and Physiology*, 4th ed., p. 69. Upper Saddle River, NJ: Prentice Hall. © Prentice Hall. Reprinted with permission; **Figure 2–22** From F. Martini (1998). *Fundamentals of Anatomy and Physiology*, 4th ed., p. 923. Upper Saddle River, NJ: Prentice Hall. © Prentice Hall. Reprinted with permission; **Figure 2–23** From F. Martini (1998). *Fundamentals of Anatomy and Physiology*, 4th ed., p. 922. Upper Saddle River, NJ: Prentice Hall. © Prentice Hall. Reprinted with permission; **Figure 2–24** Adapted from F. Martini (1998). *Fundamentals of Anatomy and Physiology*, 4th ed., p. 59. Upper Saddle River, NJ: Prentice Hall. © Prentice Hall. Reprinted with permission; **Figure 2–27** Adapted from F. Martini (1998). *Fundamentals of Anatomy and Physiology*, 4th ed., p. 372. Upper Saddle River, NJ: Prentice Hall. ©

Prentice Hall. Reprinted with permission; **Figure 2–34** Adapted from by F. Martini (1998). *Fundamentals of Anatomy and Physiology*, 4th ed., p. 407. Upper Saddle River, NJ: Prentice Hall. © Prentice Hall. Reprinted with permission.

Chapter 3 **Figure 3–1(a)** Adapted from F. Martini (1998). *Fundamentals of Anatomy and Physiology*, 4th ed., p. 36. Upper Saddle River, NJ: Prentice Hall. © Prentice Hall. Reprinted with permission; **Figure 3–1(b)** Adapted from F. Martini (1998). *Fundamentals of Anatomy and Physiology*, 4th ed., p. 34. Upper Saddle River, NJ: Prentice Hall. © Prentice Hall. Reprinted with permission; **Figure 3–2** Adapted from F. Martini (1998). *Fundamentals of Anatomy and Physiology*, 4th ed., p. 42. Upper Saddle River, NJ: Prentice Hall. © Prentice Hall. Reprinted with permission; **Figure 3–5** From F. Martini (1998). *Fundamentals of Anatomy and Physiology*, 4th ed., p. 73. Upper Saddle River, NJ: Prentice Hall. © Prentice Hall. Reprinted with permission; **Figure 3–6** Adapted from F. Martini (1998). *Fundamentals of Anatomy and Physiology*, 4th ed., p. 82. Upper Saddle River, NJ: Prentice Hall. © Prentice Hall. Reprinted with permission; **Figure 3–9** Adapted from F. Martini (1998). *Fundamentals of Anatomy and Physiology*, 4th ed., p. 82. Upper Saddle River, NJ: Prentice Hall. © Prentice Hall. Reprinted with permission.

Chapter 4 **Figure 4–10** Adapted from F. Martini (1998). *Fundamentals of Anatomy and Physiology*, 4th ed., p. 395. Upper Saddle River, NJ: Prentice Hall. © Prentice Hall. Reprinted with permission; **Figure 4–13(a)** Adapted from by F. Martini (1998). *Fundamentals of Anatomy and Physiology*, 4th ed., p. 373. Upper Saddle River, NJ: Prentice Hall. © Prentice Hall. Reprinted with permission; **Figure 4–14(a)** Adapted from F. Martini (1998). *Fundamentals of Anatomy and Physiology*, 4th ed., p. 373. Upper Saddle River, NJ: Prentice Hall. © Prentice Hall. Reprinted with permission; **Figure in Box 4–3** Adapted from by F. Martini (1998). *Fundamentals of Anatomy and Physiology*, 4th ed., p. 381. Upper Saddle River, NJ: Prentice Hall. © Prentice Hall. Reprinted with permission.

Chapter 5 **Figure 5–3(a)** Adapted from F. Martini (1998). *Fundamentals of Anatomy and Physiology*, 4th ed., p. 404. Upper Saddle River, NJ: Prentice Hall. © Prentice Hall. Reprinted with permission; **Figure 5–4** From R. Llinás & M. Sugimori (1980). Electrophysiological properties of in vitro Purkinje cell dendrites in mammalian cerebellar slices. *Journal of Physiology, 305*, 197–213. Copyright 1980. Reprinted by permission of the Physiological Society; **Figure 5–9** Adapted from F. Martini (1998) *Fundamentals of Anatomy and Physiology*, 4th ed., p. 398. Upper Saddle River, NJ: Prentice Hall. © Prentice Hall. Reprinted with permission; **Figure 5 14** From F. Martini (1998). *Fundamentals of Anatomy and Physiology*, 4th ed., p. 399. Upper Saddle River, NJ: Prentice Hall. © Prentice Hall. Reprinted with permission.

Chapter 6 **Figure 6–1** From F. Martini (1998). *Fundamentals of Anatomy and Physiology*, 4th ed., p. 371. Upper Saddle River, NJ: Prentice Hall. © Prentice Hall. Reprinted with permission; **Figure 6–5** (left) From F. Martini (1998). *Fundamentals of Anatomy and Physiology*, 4th ed., p. 519. Upper Saddle River, NJ: Prentice Hall. © Prentice Hall. Reprinted with permission; **Figure 6–5(b)** From F. Martini (1998). *Fundamentals of Anatomy and Physiology*, 4th ed., p. 525. Upper Saddle River, NJ: Prentice Hall. © Prentice Hall.

Reprinted with permission; Figure 6–13 From F. Martini (1998). *Fundamentals of Anatomy and Physiology*, 4th ed., p. 531. Upper Saddle River, NJ: Prentice Hall. © Prentice Hall. Reprinted with permission; Figure 6–14 Adapted from F. Martini (1998). *Fundamentals of Anatomy and Physiology*, 4th ed., p. 495. Upper Saddle River, NJ: Prentice Hall. © Prentice Hall. Reprinted with permission.

Chapter 7   Quotation, p. 146 From C. Sherrington (1947). *The integrative action of the nervous system.* New York: Cambridge University Press; Figure 7–1 Adapted from F. Martini (1998). *Fundamentals of Anatomy and Physiology* , 4th ed., p. 21. Upper Saddle River, NJ: Prentice Hall. © Prentice Hall. Reprinted with permission; Figure 7–2(a) From F. Martini (1998). *Fundamentals of Anatomy and Physiology*, 4th ed., p. 218. Upper Saddle River, NJ: Prentice Hall. © Prentice Hall. Reprinted with permission; Figure 7–2(b) From F. Martini (1998) *Fundamentals of Anatomy and Physiology*, 4th ed., p. 418. Upper Saddle River, NJ: Prentice Hall. © Prentice Hall. Reprinted with permission; Figure 7–3(a), (b) From F. Martini (1998). *Fundamentals of Anatomy and Physiology*, 4th ed., p. 419. Upper Saddle River, NJ: Prentice Hall. © Prentice Hall. Reprinted with permission; Figure 7–4(a) From F. Martini (1998). *Fundamentals of Anatomy and Physiology*, 4th ed., p. 422. Upper Saddle River, NJ: Prentice Hall. © Prentice Hall. Reprinted with permission; Figure 7–4(b) From F. Martini (1998). *Fundamentals of Anatomy and Physiology*, 4th ed., p. 418. Upper Saddle River, NJ: Prentice Hall. © Prentice Hall. Reprinted with permission; Figure 7–5 From F. Martini (1998). *Fundamentals of Anatomy and Physiology*, 4th ed., p. 426. Upper Saddle River, NJ: Prentice Hall. © Prentice Hall. Reprinted with permission; Figure 7–7 Adapted from F. Martini (1998). *Fundamentals of Anatomy and Physiology*, 4th ed., pp. 462, 499. Upper Saddle River, NJ: Prentice Hall. © Prentice Hall. Reprinted with permission; Figure 7–8 Adapted from F. Martini (1998). *Fundamentals of Anatomy and Physiology*, 4th ed., p. 495. Upper Saddle River, NJ: Prentice Hall. © Prentice Hall. Reprinted with permission; Figure 7–10 Adapted from F. Martini (1998). *Fundamentals of Anatomy and Physiology*, 4th ed., p. 434. Upper Saddle River, NJ: Prentice Hall. © Prentice Hall. Reprinted with permission; Figure 7–11 Adapted from F. Martini (1998). *Fundamentals of Anatomy and Physiology*, 4th ed., p. 431. Upper Saddle River, NJ: Prentice Hall. © Prentice Hall. Reprinted with permission; Figures 7–12, 7–13, 7–14 Adapted from F. Martini (1998). *Fundamentals of Anatomy and Physiology*, 4th ed., p. 434. Upper Saddle River, NJ: Prentice Hall. © Prentice Hall. Reprinted with permission; Figures in Box 7–1(a), (b) Adapted from F. Martini (1998). *Fundamentals of Anatomy and Physiology*, 4th ed., p. 419. Upper Saddle River, NJ: Prentice Hall. © Prentice Hall. Reprinted with permission.

Chapter 8   Figure 8–1 Adapted from F. Martini (1998). *Fundamentals of Anatomy and Physiology*, 4th ed., p. 465. Upper Saddle River, NJ: Prentice Hall. © Prentice Hall. Reprinted with permission; Figures 8–3 Adapted from F. Martini (1998). *Fundamentals of Anatomy and Physiology*, 4th ed., p. 475. Upper Saddle River, NJ: Prentice Hall. © Prentice Hall. Reprinted with permission; Figure 8–4(a) Adapted from F. Martini (1998). *Fundamentals of Anatomy and Physiology*, 4th ed., p. 475. Upper Saddle River, NJ: Prentice Hall. © Prentice Hall. Reprinted with permission; Figure 8–5 From J. Cooper, F. Bloom, & R. Roth (1996). *The biochemical basis of neu-

ropharmocology*, 7th ed. New York: Oxford University Press. © 1970, 1974, 1978, 1982, 1986, 1991, 1996 by Oxford University Press. Used by Permission of Oxford University Press, Inc.; Figure 8–6 Adapted from F. Martini (1998). *Fundamentals of Anatomy and Physiology*, 4th ed., p. 463, 464. Upper Saddle River, NJ: Prentice Hall. © Prentice Hall. Reprinted with permission; Figure 8–7 Adapted from F. Martini (1998). *Fundamentals of Anatomy and Physiology*, 4th ed., p. 464. Upper Saddle River, NJ: Prentice Hall. © Prentice Hall. Reprinted with permission; Figure 8–9 Adapted from F. Martini (1998). *Fundamentals of Anatomy and Physiology*, 4th ed., p. 467. Upper Saddle River, NJ: Prentice Hall. © Prentice Hall. Reprinted with permission; Figure 8–10 Adapted from F. Martini (1998). *Fundamentals of Anatomy and Physiology*, 4th ed., p. 467. Upper Saddle River, NJ: Prentice Hall. © Prentice Hall. Reprinted with permission; Figure 8–12 Adapted from F. Martini (1998). *Fundamentals of Anatomy and Physiology*, 4th ed., p. 452. Upper Saddle River, NJ: Prentice Hall. © Prentice Hall. Reprinted with permission; Figure 8–13 Adapted from F. Martini (1998). *Fundamentals of Anatomy and Physiology*, 4th ed., p. 450. Upper Saddle River, NJ: Prentice Hall. © Prentice Hall. Reprinted with permission.

Chapter 9   Figure 9–2(a) From F. Martini (1998). *Fundamentals of Anatomy and Physiology*, 4th ed., p. 494. Upper Saddle River, NJ: Prentice Hall. © Prentice Hall. Reprinted with permission; Figure 9–2(b) From F. Martini (1998). *Fundamentals of Anatomy and Physiology*, 4th ed., p. 499. Upper Saddle River, NJ: Prentice Hall. © Prentice Hall. Reprinted with permission; Figure 9–3(a) Adapted from F. Martini (1998). *Fundamentals of Anatomy and Physiology*, 4th ed., p. 571. Upper Saddle River, NJ: Prentice Hall. © Prentice Hall. Reprinted with permission; Figure 9–3(b) From F. Martini (1998). *Fundamentals of Anatomy and Physiology*, 4th ed., p. 571. Upper Saddle River, NJ: Prentice Hall. © Prentice Hall. Reprinted with permission; Figure 9–3(c) From F. Martini (1998). *Fundamentals of Anatomy and Physiology*, 4th ed., p. 570. Upper Saddle River, NJ: Prentice Hall. © Prentice Hall. Reprinted with permission; Figure 9–4 From F. Martini (1998). *Fundamentals of Anatomy and Physiology*, 4th ed., p. 578. Upper Saddle River, NJ: Prentice Hall. © Prentice Hall. Reprinted with permission; Figure 9–6 From G. Von Bekesy et al. (1960). *Experiments in hearing.* New York: McGraw-Hill. © 1960 the McGraw-Hill Companies. Reprinted by permission of the McGraw-Hill Companies; Figure 9–8 From F. Martini (1998). *Fundamentals of Anatomy and Physiology*, 4th ed., p. 584. Upper Saddle River, NJ: Prentice Hall. © Prentice Hall. Reprinted with permission; Figure 9–9 From F. Martini (1998). *Fundamentals of Anatomy and Physiology*, 4th ed., p. 575. Upper Saddle River, NJ: Prentice Hall. © Prentice Hall. Reprinted with permission; Figure 9–10 From F. Martini (1998). *Fundamentals of Anatomy and Physiology*, 4th ed., p. 575. Upper Saddle River, NJ: Prentice Hall. © Prentice Hall. Reprinted with permission; Figure 9–11 From F. Martini (1998). *Fundamentals of Anatomy and Physiology*, 4th ed., p. 549. Upper Saddle River, NJ: Prentice Hall. © Prentice Hall. Reprinted with permission; Figure 9–12 From F. Martini (1998). *Fundamentals of Anatomy and Physiology*, 4th ed., p. 547. Upper Saddle River, NJ: Prentice Hall. © Prentice Hall. Reprinted with permission; Figure 9–14 From F. Martini (1998). *Fundamentals of Anatomy and Physiology*, 4th ed., p. 552. Upper Saddle River, NJ: Prentice Hall. © Prentice Hall. Reprinted with permission; Figure 9–15 From F. Martini (1998). *Fundamentals of Anatomy and Physiology*, 4th ed., p.

563. Upper Saddle River, NJ: Prentice Hall. © Prentice Hall. Reprinted with permission; **Figure 9–16** From F. Martini (1998). *Fundamentals of Anatomy and Physiology*, 4th ed., p. 568. Upper Saddle River, NJ: Prentice Hall. © Prentice Hall. Reprinted with permission; **Figure 9–19** From J.E. Dowling (1979). Information processing by local circuits: The vertebrate retina as a model system. In F.O. Schmitt & F.G. Worden (Eds.). *The neurosciences, fourth study program*. Cambridge, MA: MIT Press. © 1979. Reprinted by permission of MIT Press; **Figures 9–21, 9–22** Adapted from F. Martini (1998). *Fundamentals of Anatomy and Physiology*, 4th ed., p. 569. Upper Saddle River, NJ: Prentice Hall. © Prentice Hall. Reprinted with permission; **Figure 9–24** From D. H. Hubel & T.N. Weisel (1959). Receptive fields of single neurones in the cat's striate cortex. *Journal of Physiology* (London), *148*, 574–591. Reprinted by permission of the Physiological Society; **Figure 9–26** From E. Kandel et al. (1991). *Principles of neural science*, 3rd ed. © 1991. Appleton Lange. Reprinted by permission; **Figure 9–27** From D. H. Hubel & T.N. Weisel (1962). Receptive fields binocular interaction and functional architecture in the cat's visual cortex. *Journal of Physiology* (London), *160*, 106–154. Reprinted by permission of the Physiological Society; **Figure 9–28** From E. Kandel et al. (1991). *Principles of neural science.*, 3rd ed. © 1991 Appleton Lange. Reprinted by permission; **Figure in Box 9–1** Adapted from F. Martini (1998). *Fundamentals of Anatomy and Physiology*, 4th ed., pp. 494, 499. Upper Saddle River, NJ: Prentice Hall. © Prentice Hall. Reprinted with permission; **Figure in Box 9–3** Adapted from F. Martini (1998). *Fundamentals of Anatomy and Physiology*, 4th ed., p. 409. Upper Saddle River, NJ: Prentice Hall. © Prentice Hall. Reprinted with permission.

Chapter 10   **Figure 10–1** Adapted from F. Martini (1998). *Fundamentals of Anatomy and Physiology*, 4th ed., p. 449. Upper Saddle River, NJ: Prentice Hall. © Prentice Hall. Reprinted with permission; **Figure 10–4** From J. Shinoda, J.I. Yokota, & T. Fatami (1981). Divergent projection of individual cortieospinal axons to motorneurons of multiple muscles in the monkey. *Neuroscience Letters, 23*, 7–12. © 1981. Reprinted with permission from Elsevier Science; **Figure 10–5** From A.P. Georgopoulos, J.F. Kalaska, R. Caminiti, & J.T. Massey (1982). On the relations between the direction of two-dimensional arm movements and cell discharge in primate motor cortex. *Journal of Neuroscience, 2* (11), 1527–1537; **Figure 10–7** Adapted from F. Martini (1998). *Fundamentals of Anatomy and Physiology*, 4th ed., p. 472. Upper Saddle River, NJ: Prentice Hall. © Prentice Hall. Reprinted with permission; **Figure 10–8** Adapted from F. Martini (1998). *Fundamentals of Anatomy and Physiology*, 4th ed., p. 472. Upper Saddle River, NJ: Prentice Hall. © Prentice Hall. Reprinted with permission; **Figure 10–12** From B.F. Ayala, M. Dichter, R.J. Gumnit, H. Matsumoto, & W.A. Spencer (1973). Genesis of epileptic intercall spikes: New knowledge of cortical feedback systems suggests a neurophysical explanation of brief paroxysons. *Brain Research, 52*: 1–17. © 1973. Reprinted with kind permission of Elsevier Science - NL, Sara Burgerhartstraat 25, 1055 KV Amsterdam, The Netherlands; **Figure 10–14** Adapted from W.O. Friesen (1989). Neuronal control of leech swimming movements. In J.W. Jacklet (Ed.), *Neuronal and cellular oscillators*. Pp. 269–316. New York: Dekker. **Figure in Box 10–1** Adapted from F. Martini (1998). *Fundamentals of Anatomy and Physiology*, 4th ed., p. 458. Upper Saddle River, NJ: Prentice Hall. © Prentice Hall. Reprinted with permission.

Chapter 11   **Figure 11–1** Adapted from M. S. Bear, B. W. Connors, & M. A. Paradiso (1996). *Neuroscience: Exploring the brain*. Baltimore, MD: Williams & Wilkie. Copyright 1996. Reprinted by permission; **Figure 11–3** From H. Fibiger, F. LePiane, A. Zakubovic, & A. Phillips (1987). The role of dopamine in intracranial self-stimulation of the ventral tegmental area. *Journal of Neuroscience, 7*, 3888–3896; **Figure 11–5** From P.J. Dyck et al. (1975). *Peripheral neuropathy*. Philadelphia: W.B. Saunders. Copyright © 1975; **Table 11–2** From H.L. Fields (1981). An endorphin-mediated analgesia system: Experimental and clinical observations. In H. Martin and S. Reichlin (Eds.), *Neurosecretion and brain peptides*. New York: Lippincott-Raven Publishers. © 1981 Raven Press. Reprinted by permission of Lippincott-Raven Publishers.

Chapter 12   **Quotation, p. 278** T.S. Eliot (1930) "Sweeney Agonistes." *Bartlett's familiar quotations*. New York: Little Brown & Co.; **Figure 12–2** From N. Nakanishi et al. (1995). Nucleotide sequence of precursor. *Nature, 278*, 423–427. Reprinted with permission from *Nature*. © 1995. Macmillan Magazines, Ltd.; **Figure 12–3** Adapted from F. Martini (1998). *Fundamentals of Anatomy and Physiology*, 4th ed., pp. 602, 604. Upper Saddle River, NJ: Prentice Hall. © Prentice Hall. Reprinted with permission; **Figure 12–5** Adapted from F. Martini (1998). *Fundamentals of Anatomy and Physiology*, 4th ed., p. 605. Upper Saddle River, NJ: Prentice Hall. © Prentice Hall. Reprinted with permission; **Figure 12–10(a)** From Vermuelen et al. (1972). Testosterone secretion and metabolism in male semescence. *Journal of Clinical Endocrinology and Metabolism, 34*, 730–735. © 1972 The Endocrine Society. Reprinted by permission of the Endocrine Society; **Figure 12–10(b)**, **Figure 12–11** From W. Kinsey et al. (1948). *Sexual behavior in the human male*. Philadelphia: W.B. Saunders Co. © 1948. Reprinted by permission of W.B. Saunders Co.; **Figure 12–13** From R.J. Nelson (1995). *An introduction to behavioral endocrinology*. Sunderland, MA: Sinauer Associates; **Figure 12–14** From F. Martini (1998). *Fundamentals of Anatomy and Physiology*, 4th ed., p. 1071. Upper Saddle River, NJ: Prentice Hall. © Prentice Hall. Reprinted with permission; **Figure 12–15** From K. Wallen (1990). Desire and ability: Hormones and the regulation of female sexual behaviors. *Neuroscience and Behavioral Reviews, 14*, 233–241. © 1990. Reprinted with permission of Elsevier Science; **Figure 12–19** From *Experimental Brain Research, 1–97*, 477, figure #7. New York: Springer-Verlag, Inc. © Dr. David S. Albeck, Rockefeller University; **Figure in Box 12–2** From *Environmental Health Perspectives, 102*, 683. (public domain); **Table 12–1** From S.S. Yen & R.B. Jaffe (1991). *Reproductive endocrinology*, 3rd ed. Philadelphia: W.B. Saunders Co. © 1991. Reprinted by permission of W.B. Saunders Co.

Chapter 13   **Quotation, p. 305** Anais Nin (1950) *Bartlett's familiar quotations*. New York: Little Brown & Co.; **Figure 13–3** Adapted from F. Martini (1998). *Fundamentals of Anatomy and Physiology*, 4th ed., p. 467. Upper Saddle River, NJ: Prentice Hall. © Prentice Hall. Reprinted with permission; **Figure 13–4** From F. Martini (1998). *Fundamentals of Anatomy and Physiology*, 4th ed., p. 506. Upper Saddle River, NJ: Prentice Hall. © Prentice Hall. Reprinted with permission; **Figure 13–5** Adapted from F. Martini (1998). *Fundamentals of Anatomy and Physiology*, 4th ed., p. 504. Upper Saddle River, NJ: Prentice Hall. © Prentice Hall. Reprinted with permission; **Figure 13–6** From A. Arkin, J. Antrobus, & S. Ellman (1978). *The mind in* *sleep: Psychology and psychophysiology.* Mahwah, NJ: L. Erlbaum Associates, Inc. © 1978. Reprinted by permission of Lawrence Erlbaum Associates, Inc.; **Figure 13–9** From **R**. McCarley et al. (1981). REM sleep dreams and the activation-synthesis hypothesis. *American Journal of Psychiatry, 138*, 904–912. © 1981. Reprinted by permission of the American Psychiatric Association; **Figure 13–11** Data supplied by G. Nino-Murcia, Stanford University Sleep Disorder Center, Stanford, CA; **Figure in Box 13–1** Adapted from by F. Martini (1998). *Fundamentals of Anatomy and Physiology*, 4th ed., p. 507. Upper Saddle River, NJ: Prentice Hall. © Prentice Hall. Reprinted with permission; **Figure in Box 13–2, Table 13–2** From M.H. Kryger et al. (1989). *Principles and practices of sleep medicine*, 2nd ed. Philadelphia: W.B. Saunders Co. © 1989. Reprinted by permission of W.B. Saunders Co.

Chapter 14 **Figure 14–4** From F. Martini (1998). *Fundamentals of Anatomy and Physiology*, 4th ed., p. 745. Upper Saddle River, NJ: Prentice Hall. © Prentice Hall. Reprinted with permission; **Figure 14–6** From F. Martini (1998). *Fundamentals of Anatomy and Physiology*, 4th ed., p. 751. Upper Saddle River, NJ: Prentice Hall. © Prentice Hall. Reprinted with permission; **Figure 14–8** From F. Martini (1998). *Fundamentals of Anatomy and Physiology*, 4th ed., p. 863. Upper Saddle River, NJ: Prentice Hall. © Prentice Hall. Reprinted with permission; **Figure 14–15(a)** From F. Martini (1998). *Fundamentals of Anatomy and Physiology*, 4th ed., p. 963. Upper Saddle River, NJ: Prentice Hall. © Prentice Hall. Reprinted with permission; **Figure 14–15(b)** Adapted from F. Martini (1998). *Fundamentals of Anatomy and Physiology*, 4th ed., p. 964. Upper Saddle River, NJ: Prentice Hall. © Prentice Hall. Reprinted with permission; **Figure 14–15(c)** Adapted from F. Martini (1998). *Fundamentals of Anatomy and Physiology*, 4th ed., p. 965. Upper Saddle River, NJ: Prentice Hall. © Prentice Hall. Reprinted with permission.

Chapter 15 **Figure 15–2** From F. Martini (1998). *Fundamentals of Anatomy and Physiology*, 4th ed., p. 379. Upper Saddle River, NJ: Prentice Hall. © Prentice Hall. Reprinted with permission; **Figure 15–3** From F. Martini (1998). *Fundamentals of Anatomy and Physiology*, 4th ed., pp. 454, 455. Upper Saddle River, NJ: Prentice Hall. © Prentice Hall. Reprinted with permission; **Figure 15–4** From F.C. Sauer (1935). Mitosis in the neural tube. *Journal of Comparative Neurology, 62*: 377–405. © 1935. Reprinted by permission of John Wiley & Sons, Inc.; **Figure 15–5** From P. Rakic (1974). Neurons in rhesus monkey visual cortex: Systematic relation between time of origin and eventual disposition. *Science, 183*, 425– 427. © 1974. Reprinted by permission of the American Association for the Advancement of Science; **Figure 15–6** From P. Rakic (1972). Mode of cell migration to the superficial layers of fetal monkey neocortex. *Journal of Comparative Neurology, 145*, 61– 84. © 1972. Reprinted by permission of John Wiley & Sons, Inc.; **Figure 15–7** From D. O'Leary & B. Stanfield (1989). Selective elimination of axons extended by developing cortical neurons is dependent on regional locale: Experiments utilizing fetal cortical transplants. *Journal of Neuroscience, 9*, 2230–2246. Reprinted by permission; **Figure 15–11** From Hall & J. Sanes (1993). Synaptic structure and development: The neuromuscular junction. *Cell Supplement*, 99–121. Copyright 1993. Reprinted by permission of Joshua Sanes; **Figure 15–18** From R.D. Hawkins, T.W. Abrams, T.J. Carew, & E.R. Kandel (1983). A cellular mechanism of classical conditioning in *Aplysia* : Activity-de-

pendent amplification of presynaptic facilitation. *Science, 219*, 400–405; **Figure 15–20** From F. Martini (1998). *Fundamentals of Anatomy and Physiology*, 4th ed., p. 462. Upper Saddle River, NJ: Prentice Hall. © Prentice Hall. Reprinted with permission; **Figure 15–21** From D. Amaral & M. Witter (1989). The three-dimensional organization of the hippocampal formation: A review of anatomical data. *Neuroscience, 31*, 573 (figure 2). © 1989. Reprinted with the permission of Elsevier Science; **Figure 15–22, Figure 15–23** From E. Kandel et al. (1991). *Principles of Neural Science*, 3rd ed. © 1991. Reprinted by permission of Cell Press; **Figure 15–25** From F. Martini (1998). *Fundamentals of Anatomy and Physiology*, 4th ed., p. 472. Upper Saddle River, NJ: Prentice Hall. © Prentice Hall. Reprinted with permission; **Figure 15–26** From S.G. Lisberger (1988). The neural basis for motor learning in the vestibulo-ocular reflex in monkeys. *Trends in Neuroscience, 11*, 148 (box 1). © 1988. Reprinted with the permission of Elsevier Science; **Figure in Box 15–1** From D. Purves & J. Lichtman (1980). Elimination of synapses in the developing nervous system. *Science, 210*, 153–157.

Chapter 16 **Quotations on p. 390 and in Box 16–4** From O. Saks. (1985). *The man who mistook his wife for a hat and other clinical tales.* New York: Simon & Schuster. ©1970, 1981, 1983, 1984, 1985 by Oliver Saks. Reprinted with permission; **Figure 16–3** From J. Goodall (1986). *The chimpanzees of Gombe.* Cambridge, MA: Harvard University Press. Reprinted by permission of the publisher Harvard University Press, © 1986 by the President and Fellows of Harvard College; **Figures 16–4, 16–5** Adapted from F. Martini (1998). *Fundamentals of Anatomy and Physiology* , 4th ed., p. 458. Upper Saddle River, NJ: Prentice Hall. © Prentice Hall. Reprinted with permission; **Figure 16–7** From B. Kolb & I. Whishaw (1996). *Fundamentals of human neuropsychology.* (4th ed.). New York: W.H. Freeman and Co. ©1996 by W.H. Freeman and Co. Used with permission; **Figure 16–8** Adapted from F. Martini (1998). *Fundamentals of Anatomy and Physiology*, 4th ed., p. 464. Upper Saddle River, NJ: Prentice Hall. © Prentice Hall. Reprinted with permission; **Figure 16–9** From N. Petri & M. Mishkin (1994). Behaviorism, cognitivism, and the neuropsychology of memory. *American Scientist, 82*, 30–37. ©1994. Reprinted by permission; **Figure 16–18, Figure in Box 16–2, Table 16–1** From B. Kolb & I. Whishaw (1996). *Fundamentals of human neuropsychology.* (4th ed.). New York: W.H. Freeman and Co. ©1996 by W.H. Freeman and Co. Used with permission; **Table 16–2** From J.A.R. Nicoll et al. (1995). A polyprotein E4 allele is associated with deposition of analyzed Beta-protein following head injury. *Nature, 1(17)*, 135–137. Reprinted by permission of *Nature.* ©1995 Macmillan Magazines, Ltd.

Chapter 17 **Figure 17–14** Courtesy of Dr. G.K. Aghajanian. G.K. Aghanian & H.J. Haigler (1974). Mode of action of LSD on serotonergic neurons. In E. Costa, G.L. Gessa, & M. Sandler (Eds.), *Advances in biochemical pharmacology* (Vol. 10, pp. 167–178). New York: Raven Press.

Chapter 18 **Figure 18–7** From A.F. Oke, L.A. Carver, & R.N. Adams (1993). Dopamine-initiated disturbances of thalamic information processing in schizophrenia? In R.L. Cromwell & C.R. Snyder (Eds.), *Schizophrenia: Origins, processes, treatment and outcome.* Pp. 31–47. New York: Oxford University Press. Courtesy of Dr. Arvin F. Oke; **Figure 18–9** From T. Cannon et al. (1993). Developmental brain abnormalities in the offspring of schizophrenic mothers. I. Contri-

SUBJECT INDEX